Collins
GERMAN
DICTIONARY

ESSENTIAL EDITION

Published by Collins
An imprint of HarperCollins Publishers
Westerhill Road
Bishopbriggs
Glasgow G64 2QT

First Edition 2018

10 9 8 7 6 5 4 3 2

ISBN 978-0-00-827074-2

collinsdictionary.com

Typeset by
Davidson Publishing Solutions, Glasgow

Printed and bound by
CPI Group (UK) Ltd, Croydon, CR0 4YY

A catalogue record for this book is available from the British Library.

If you would like to comment on any aspect of this book, please contact us at the given address or online.
E-mail: dictionaries@harpercollins.co.uk
facebook.com/collinsdictionary
@collinsdict

Acknowledgements
We would like to thank those authors and publishers who kindly gave permission for copyright material to be used in the Collins Corpus. We would also like to thank Times Newspapers Ltd for providing valuable data.

INHALT

CONTENTS

EINFÜHRUNG

Wir freuen uns sehr, dass Sie sich zum Kauf eines Collins Wörterbuchs Deutsch entschlossen haben. Wir wünschen Ihnen viel Spaß beim Gebrauch in der Schule, zu Hause, im Urlaub und im Beruf.

Diese Einführung wird Ihnen einige nützliche Hinweise dazu geben, wie Sie am besten von Ihrem neuen Wörterbuch profitieren. Schließlich bietet Ihnen das Worterbuch nicht nur Stichwörter und Übersetzungen, sondern auch zahlreiche Zusatzinformationen in jedem einzelnen Eintrag. Mit Hilfe all dieser Informationen können Sie zum einen modernes Deutsch lesen und verstehen, zum anderen auch aktiv auf Deutsch kommunizieren.

Dieses Wörterbuch gibt Ihnen vor dem eigentlichen Wörterbuchtextteil selbst eine Liste aller verwendeten Abkürzungen sowie eine Übersicht zu Aussprache und Gebrauch phonetischer Umschrift. Darüber hinaus finden Sie noch eine Auflistung zu den regelmäßigen deutschen Substantivendungen sowie zu unregelmäßigen englischen und deutschen Verben.

WIE FINDE ICH WAS?

Die verschiedenen Schriftarten, Schriftgrößen, Symbole, Abkürzungen und Klammern helfen Ihnen dabei, sich innerhalb der Informationen, die das Wörterbuch bietet, zurechtzufinden. Die Konventionen, die diesem Wörterbuch zugrunde liegen, sowie auch der Gebrauch verschiedener Symbole werden im Folgenden näher erläutert.

STICHWÖRTER

Die Wörter, die Sie in Ihrem Wörterbuch nachschlagen, die Stichwörter, sind in alphabetischer Reihenfolge angeordnet. Sie sind **fett** gedruckt, sodass Sie sie schnell finden. Die Stichwörter, die rechts und links oben auf jeder Seite erscheinen, sind das jeweils erste Stichwort einer Seite, wenn es sich dabei um eine linke Seite handelt, bzw. das letzte Stichwort einer Seite, wenn es sich um eine rechte Seite handelt. Informationen zu Form und Gebrauch des jeweiligen Stichworts werden im Anschluss an die Lautschrift in Klammern angegeben. Normalerweise sind diese Angaben in abgekürzter Form und *kursiver Schrift* (z.B. (*fam*) für umgangssprachlich oder (*Comm*) als Sachgebietsangabe für Wirtschaft).

Wo es sich anbietet, werden zusammengehörige Wörter und Wortgruppen in einem Eintrag zusammengefasst (z.B. **gather**, **gathering**; **höflich**, **Höflichkeit**). Hierbei sind die Stichwörter innerhalb des Nests von der Schriftgröße etwas kleiner als das erste Stichwort. Geläufige Ausdrücke, in denen das Stichwort vorkommt, erscheinen ebenfalls **fett**, aber in einer anderen Schriftgröße. Die Tilde (~) steht hierbei für das Hauptstichwort am Anfang eines Eintrags. So steht beispielsweise im Eintrag ‚**Mitte**' der Ausdruck ‚**~ Juni**' für ‚**Mitte Juni**'.

PHONETISCHE UMSCHRIFT

Die Aussprache jedes Stichworts findet sich in phonetischer Umschrift in eckigen Klammern jeweils direkt hinter dem Stichwort selbst (z.B. **mountain** ['mauntɪn]). Eine Liste der Lautschriftzeichen mit Erklärungen finden Sie auf S. xi.

BEDEUTUNGEN

Die Übersetzung der Stichwörter ist in Normalschrift angegeben. Gibt es mehrere Bedeutungen oder Gebrauchsmöglichkeiten, so sind diese durch einen Strichpunkt voneinander zu unterscheiden. Sie finden oft weitere Angaben in Klammern vor den jeweiligen Übersetzungen. Diese zeigen Ihnen typische Kontexte auf, in denen das Stichwort verwendet werden kann (z.B. **breakup** (*of meeting, organisation*)), oder sie liefern Synonyme (z.B. **fit** (*suitable*)).

GRAMMATISCHE HINWEISE

Die Wortartangabe finden Sie als Abkürzung und in *kursiver Schrift* direkt hinter der Ausspracheinformation zum jeweiligen Stichwort (z.B. *vt*, *adj*, *n*).

Die Genusangaben zu deutschen Substantiven werden wie folgt angegeben: *m* für Maskulinum, f für Femininum und nt für Neutrum. Darüber hinaus finden Sie neben dem Stichwort in Klammern Genitiv- und Pluralform (**Abenteuer** (-*s*, -)).

Die Genusangabe zur deutschen Übersetzung findet sich ebenfalls in *kursiver Schrift* direkt hinter dem Hauptbestandteil der Übersetzung.

INTRODUCTION

We are delighted you have decided to buy this dictionary and hope you will enjoy and benefit from using it at school, at home, on holiday or at work.

This introduction gives you a few tips on how to get the most out of your dictionary – not simply from its comprehensive wordlist but also from the information provided in each entry. This will help you to read and understand modern German, as well as to communicate and express yourself in the language.

This dictionary begins by listing the abbreviations used in the text and illustrating the sounds shown by the phonetic symbols. Next you will find regular German noun endings and English irregular verbs followed by a section on German irregular verbs.

USING YOUR COLLINS DICTIONARY

A wealth of information is presented in the dictionary, using various typefaces, sizes of type, symbols, abbreviations and brackets. The conventions and symbols used are explained in the following sections.

HEADWORDS

The words you look up in the dictionary – 'headwords' – are listed alphabetically. They are printed in **bold** for rapid identification. The headwords appearing at the top of each page indicate the first (if it appears on a left-hand page) and last word (if it appears on a right-hand page) dealt with on the page in question.

Information about the usage or form of certain headwords is given in brackets after the phonetic spelling. This usually appears in abbreviated form and in italics (e.g. (*fam*), (*Comm*)).

Where appropriate, words related to headwords are grouped in the same entry (**gather**, **gathering**; **höflich**, **Höflichkeit**) in a slightly smaller bold type than the headword. Common expressions in which the headword appears are shown in a different size of bold roman type. The swung dash, **~**, represents the main headword at the start of each entry. For example, in the entry for '**Mitte**' the phrase '**~ Juni**' should be read '**Mitte Juni**'.

PHONETIC SPELLINGS

The phonetic spelling of each headword (indicating its pronunciation) is given in square brackets immediately after the headword (e.g. **mountain** ['mauntɪn]). A list of these spellings is given on page xi.

MEANINGS

Headword translations are given in ordinary type and, where more than one meaning or usage exists, they are separated by a semicolon. You will often find other words in italics in brackets before the translations. These offer suggested contexts in which the headword might appear (e.g. **breakup** (*of meeting, organisation*)) or provide synonyms (e.g. **fit** (*suitable*)).

GRAMMATICAL INFORMATION

Parts of speech are given in abbreviated form in italics after the phonetic spellings of headwords (e.g. *vt*, *adj*, *n*).

Genders of German nouns are indicated as follows: *m* for a masculine, *f* for a feminine, and *nt* for a neuter noun. Genitive and plural forms of nouns are also shown next to the headword (**Abenteuer** (-*s*, -)).

The gender of the German translation appears in *italics* immediately following the key element of the translation.

ABKÜRZUNGEN		ABBREVIATIONS
auch	*a.*	also
Abkürzung	*abk, abbr*	abbreviation
Akronym	*acr*	acronym
Adjektiv	*adj*	adjective
Adverb	*adv*	adverb
Landwirtschaft	*Agr*	agriculture
Akkusativ	*akk*	accusative
Akronym	*akr*	acronym
Anatomie	*Anat*	anatomy
Artikel	*art*	article
Bildende Künste	*Art*	fine arts
Astronomie, Astrologie	*Astr*	astronomy, astrology
Auto, Verkehr	*Auto*	automobiles, traffic
Luftfahrt	*Aviat*	aviation
Biologie	*Bio*	biology
Botanik	*Bot*	botany
britisch	*BRIT*	British
schweizerisch	*CH*	Swiss
Chemie	*Chem*	chemistry
Film	*Cine*	cinema
Wirtschaft	*Comm*	commerce
Konjunktion	*conj*	conjunction
Dativ	*dat*	dative
Eisenbahn	*Eisenb*	railways
Elektrizität	*Elek, Elec*	electricity
besonders	*esp*	especially
und so weiter	*etc*	et cetera
etwas	*etw*	something
Femininum	*f*	feminine
umgangssprachlich	*fam*	familiar, informal
übertragen	*fig*	figurative
Finanzen, Börse	*Fin*	finance
Fotografie	*Foto*	photography
Gastronomie	*Gastr*	cooking, gastronomy
Genitiv	*gen*	genitive
Geographie, Geologie	*Geo*	geography, geology
Geschichte	*Hist*	history
Imperativ	*imper*	imperative
Imperfekt	*imperf*	past tense
Informatik und Computer	*Inform*	computing
Interjektion, Ausruf	*interj*	interjection
unveränderlich	*inv*	invariable
unregelmäßig	*irr*	irregular
jemand, jemandem	*jd, jdm*	someone, somebody
jemanden, jemandes	*jdn, jds*	

Rechtsprechung	*Jur*	law
Konjunktion	*konj*	conjunction
Bildende Künste	*Kunst*	fine arts
Sprachwissenschaft, Grammatik	*Ling*	linguistics, grammar
Maskulinum	*m*	masculine
Mathematik	*Math*	mathematics
Medizin	*Med*	medicine
Meteorologie	*Met*	meteorology
Maskulinum und Femininum	*mf*	masculine and feminine
Militär	*Mil*	military
Musik	*Mus*	music
Substantiv	*n*	noun
Seefahrt	*Naut*	nautical, naval
Neutrum	*nt*	neuter
Zahlwort	*num*	numeral
oder	*o*	or
pejorativ, abwertend	*pej*	pejorative
Physik	*Phys*	physics
Plural	*pl*	plural
Politik	*Pol*	politics
Partizip Perfekt	*pp*	past participle
Präfix	*pref*	prefix
Präposition	*prep*	preposition
Pronomen	*pron*	pronoun
1. Vergangenheit	*pt*	past tense
Eisenbahn	*Rail*	railways
Religion	*Rel*	religion
siehe	*s.*	see
	sb	someone, somebody
schottisch	*Scot*	Scottish
Singular	*sing*	singular
Skisport	*Ski*	skiing
	sth	something
Technik	*Tech*	technology
Nachrichtentechnik	*Tel*	telecommunications
Theater	*Theat*	theatre
Fernsehen	*TV*	television
Typographie, Buchdruck	*Typo*	printing
unpersönlich	*unpers*	impersonal
(nord)amerikanisch	*US*	(North) American
Verb	*vb*	verb
Hilfsverb	*vb aux*	auxiliary verb
intransitives Verb	*vi*	intransitive verb
reflexives Verb	*vr*	reflexive verb
transitives Verb	*vt*	transitive verb
vulgär	*vulg*	vulgar
Zoologie	*Zool*	zoology
ungefähre Entsprechung	≈	cultural equivalent
abtrennbares Präfix	|	separable prefix

[ː] Längezeichen, length mark
['] Betonung, stress mark
[ɼ] Bindungs-R, 'r' pronounced before a vowel

alle Vokallaute sind nur ungefähre Entsprechungen
all vowel sounds are approximate only

VOKALE UND DIPHTHONGE

pl**a**nt, **a**rm, f**a**ther	[ɑː]	B**a**hn
fi**an**cé	[ɑ̃ː]	**En**semble
l**i**fe	[aɪ]	w**ei**t
h**ou**se	[au]	H**au**t
m**a**n, s**a**d	[æ]	
b**u**t, s**o**n	[ʌ]	B**u**tler
g**e**t, b**e**d	[e]	M**e**tall
n**a**me, l**a**me	[eɪ]	
ago, bett**er**	[ə]	bitt**e**
b**ir**d, h**er**	[ɜː]	
th**ere**, c**are**	[ɛə]	m**eh**r
it, w**i**sh	[ɪ]	B**i**schof
b**ee**, m**e**, b**ea**t, bel**ie**f	[iː]	v**ie**l
h**ere**	[ɪə]	B**ie**r
n**o**, l**ow**	[əʊ]	
n**o**t, l**o**ng	[ɒ]	P**o**st
l**aw**, **a**ll	[ɔː]	M**o**nd
b**oy**, **oi**l	[ɔɪ]	H**eu**
p**u**sh, l**oo**k	[ʊ]	P**u**lt
y**ou**, d**o**	[uː]	H**u**t
p**oo**r, s**u**re	[ʊə]	

KONSONANTEN

been, **b**lind	[b]	**B**all
do, ha**d**	[d]	**d**ann
jam, ob**j**ect	[dʒ]	
father, wol**f**	[f]	**F**ass
go, be**g**	[g]	**G**ast
house	[h]	**H**err
youth, Ind**i**an	[j]	**j**a
keep, mil**k**	[k]	**k**alt
lamp, oi**l**, i**ll**	[l]	**L**ast
man, a**m**	[m]	**M**ast
no, ma**nn**er	[n]	**N**uss

lo**ng**, si**ng**	[ŋ]	la**ng**
El Ni**ñ**o	[ɲ]	El Ni**ñ**o
paper, ha**pp**y	[p]	**P**akt
red, d**r**y	[r]	**r**ot
stand, **s**and, ye**s**	[s]	Ra**ss**e
ship, sta**ti**on	[ʃ]	**Sch**al
tell, fa**t**	[t]	**T**al
thank, dea**th**	[θ]	
this, fa**th**er	[ð]	
church, cat**ch**	[tʃ]	Ru**tsch**
voice, li**v**e	[v]	**w**as
water, **we**, **wh**ich	[w]	
lo**ch**	[x]	Ba**ch**
zeal, the**s**e, ga**z**e	[z]	Ha**s**e
plea**s**ure	[ʒ]	**G**enie

REGULAR GERMAN NOUN ENDINGS

nominative		*genitive*	*plural*	*nominative*		*genitive*	*plural*
-ade	*f*	-ade	-aden	-ist	*m*	-isten	-isten
-ant	*m*	-anten	-anten	-ium	*nt*	-iums	-ien
-anz	*f*	-anz	-anzen	-ius	*m*	-ius	-iusse
-ar	*m*	-ars	-are	-ive	*f*	-ive	-iven
-är	*m*	-ärs	-äre	-keit	*f*	-keit	-keiten
-at	*nt*	-at(e)s	-ate	-lein	*nt*	-leins	-lein
-atte	*f*	-atte	-atten	-ling	*m*	-lings	-linge
-chen	*nt*	-chens	-chen	-ment	*nt*	-ments	-mente
-ei	*f*	-ei	-eien	-mus	*m*	-mus	-men
-elle	*f*	-elle	-ellen	-nis	*f*	-nis	-nisse
-ent	*m*	-enten	-enten	-nis	*nt*	-nisses	-nisse
-enz	*f*	-enz	-enzen	-nom	*m*	-nomen	-nomen
-ette	*f*	-ette	-etten	-rich	*m*	-richs	-riche
-eur	*m*	-eurs	-eure	-schaft	*f*	-schaft	-schaften
-euse	*f*	-euse	-eusen	-sel	*nt*	-sels	-sel
-heit	*f*	-heit	-heiten	-tät	*f*	-tät	-täten
-ie	*f*	-ie	-ien	-tiv	*m, nt*	-tivs	-tive
-ik	*f*	-ik	-iken	-tor	*m*	-tors	-toren
-in	*f*	-in	-innen	-tum	*m, nt*	-tums	-tümer
-ine	*f*	-ine	-inen	-ung	*f*	-ung	-ungen
-ion	*f*	-ion	-ionen	-ur	*f*	-ur	-uren

Substantive, die mit einem geklammerten 'r' oder 's' enden (z.B. **Angestellte(r)** *mf*, **Beamte(r)** *m*, **Gute(s)** *nt*) werden wie Adjektive dekliniert:

Nouns listed with an 'r' or an 's' in brackets (eg **Angestellte(r)** *mf*, **Beamte(r)** *m*, **Gute(s)** *nt*) take the same endings as adjectives:

der Angestellte *m*
ein Angestellter *m*
der Beamte *m*
ein Beamter *m*
das Gute *nt*
ein Gutes *nt*

die Angestellte *f*
eine Angestellte *f*

die Angestellten *pl*
Angestellte *pl*
die Beamten *pl*
Beamte *pl*

UNREGELMÄSSIGE ENGLISCHE VERBEN

present	*past tense*	*past participle*
arise (arising)	arose	arisen
awake (awaking)	awoke	awoken
be (am, is, are; being)	was, were	been
bear	bore	born(e)
beat	beat	beaten
become (becoming)	became	become
begin (beginning)	began	begun
bend	bent	bent
bet (betting)	bet	bet
bid (bidding)	bid	bid
bind	bound	bound
bite (biting)	bit	bitten
bleed	bled	bled
blow	blew	blown
break	broke	broken
breed	bred	bred
bring	brought	brought
build	built	built
burn	burnt (*o* burned)	burnt (*o* burned)
burst	burst	burst
buy	bought	bought
can	could	(been able)
cast	cast	cast
catch	caught	caught
choose (choosing)	chose	chosen
cling	clung	clung
come (coming)	came	come
cost	cost	cost
creep	crept	crept
cut (cutting)	cut	cut
deal	dealt	dealt
dig (digging)	dug	dug
do (does)	did	done
draw	drew	drawn
dream	dreamed (*o* dreamt)	dreamed (*o* dreamt)
drink	drank	drunk
drive (driving)	drove	driven
eat	ate	eaten
fall	fell	fallen
feed	fed	fed
feel	felt	felt
fight	fought	fought
find	found	found
flee	fled	fled
fling	flung	flung
fly (flies)	flew	flown
forbid (forbidding)	forbade	forbidden
foresee	foresaw	foreseen
forget (forgetting)	forgot	forgotten
forgive (forgiving)	forgave	forgiven
freeze (freezing)	froze	frozen

present	past tense	past participle
get (getting)	got	got, (*US*) gotten
give (giving)	gave	given
go (goes)	went	gone
grind	ground	ground
grow	grew	grown
hang	hung (*o* hanged)	hung (*o* hanged)
have (has; having)	had	had
hear	heard	heard
hide (hiding)	hid	hidden
hit (hitting)	hit	hit
hold	held	held
hurt	hurt	hurt
keep	kept	kept
kneel	knelt (*o* kneeled)	knelt (*o* kneeled)
know	knew	known
lay	laid	laid
lead	led	led
lean	leant (*o* leaned)	leant (*o* leaned)
leap	leapt (*o* leaped)	leapt (*o* leaped)
learn	learnt (*o* learned)	learnt (*o* learned)
leave (leaving)	left	left
lend	lent	lent
let (letting)	let	let
lie (lying)	lay	lain
light	lit (*o* lighted)	lit (*o* lighted)
lose (losing)	lost	lost
make (making)	made	made
may	might	–
mean	meant	meant
meet	met	met
mow	mowed	mown (*o* mowed)
must	(had to)	(had to)
pay	paid	paid
put (putting)	put	put
quit (quitting)	quit (*o* quitted)	quit (*o* quitted)
read	read	read
rid (ridding)	rid	rid
ride (riding)	rode	ridden
ring	rang	rung
rise (rising)	rose	risen
run (running)	ran	run
saw	sawed	sawn
say	said	said
seek	sought	sought
see	saw	seen
sell	sold	sold
send	sent	sent
set (setting)	set	set
shake (shaking)	shook	shaken
shall	should	–
shine (shining)	shone	shone
shoot	shot	shot
show	showed	shown
shrink	shrank	shrunk
shut (shutting)	shut	shut
sing	sang	sung
sink	sank	sunk

present	*past tense*	*past participle*
sit (sitting)	sat	sat
sleep	slept	slept
slide (sliding)	slid	slid
sling	slung	slung
slit (slitting)	slit	slit
smell	smelt (*o* smelled)	smelt (*o* smelled)
sow	sowed	sown (*o* sowed)
speak	spoke	spoken
speed	sped (*o* speeded)	sped (*o* speeded)
spell	spelt (*o* spelled)	spelt (*o* spelled)
spend	spent	spent
spin (spinning)	spun	spun
spit (spitting)	spat	spat
split (splitting)	split	split
spoil	spoiled (*o* spoilt)	spoiled (*o* spoilt)
spread	spread	spread
spring	sprang	sprung
stand	stood	stood
steal	stole	stolen
stick	stuck	stuck
sting	stung	stung
stink	stank	stunk

present	*past tense*	*past participle*
strike (striking)	struck	struck
strive (striving)	strove	striven
swear	swore	sworn
sweep	swept	swept
swell	swelled	swollen (*o* swelled)
swim (swimming)	swam	swum
swing	swung	swung
take (taking)	took	taken
teach	taught	taught
tear	tore	torn
tell	told	told
think	thought	thought
throw	threw	thrown
thrust	thrust	thrust
wake (waking)	woke (*o* waked)	woken (*o* waked)
wear	wore	worn
weave (weaving)	wove (*o* weaved)	woven (*o* weaved)
weep	wept	wept
win (winning)	won	won
wind	wound	wound
write (writing)	wrote	written

IRREGULAR GERMAN VERBS

Infinitiv	*Präsens 2., 3. Singular*	*Präteritum*	*Partizip Perfekt*
backen	backst *o* bäckst, backt *o* bäckt	backte *o* buk	gebacken
befehlen	befiehlst, befiehlt	befahl	befohlen
beginnen	beginnst, beginnt	begann	begonnen
beißen	beißt, beißt	biss	gebissen
bergen	birgst, birgt	barg	geborgen
betrügen	betrügst, betrügt	betrog	betrogen
biegen	biegst, biegt	bog	gebogen
bieten	bietest, bietet	bot	geboten
binden	bindest, bindet	band	gebunden
bitten	bittest, bittet	bat	gebeten
blasen	bläst, bläst	blies	geblasen
bleiben	bleibst, bleibt	blieb	geblieben
braten	brätst, brät	briet	gebraten
brechen	brichst, bricht	brach	gebrochen
brennen	brennst, brennt	brannte	gebrannt
bringen	bringst, bringt	brachte	gebracht
denken	denkst, denkt	dachte	gedacht
dringen	dringst, dringt	drang	gedrungen
dürfen	darfst, darf	durfte	gedurft
erschrecken	erschrickst, erschrickt	erschrak	erschrocken
essen	isst, isst	aß	gegessen
fahren	fährst, fährt	fuhr	gefahren
fallen	fällst, fällt	fiel	gefallen
fangen	fängst, fängt	fing	gefangen
finden	findest, findet	fand	gefunden
fliegen	fliegst, fliegt	flog	geflogen
fließen	fließt, fließt	floss	geflossen
fressen	frisst, frisst	fraß	gefressen
frieren	frierst, friert	fror	gefroren
geben	gibst, gibt	gab	gegeben
gehen	gehst, geht	ging	gegangen
gelingen	–, gelingt	gelang	gelungen

Infinitiv	*Präsens 2., 3. Singular*	*Präteritum*	*Partizip Perfekt*
gelten	giltst, gilt	galt	gegolten
genießen	genießt, genießt	genoss	genossen
geschehen	–, geschieht	geschah	geschehen
gewinnen	gewinnst, gewinnt	gewann	gewonnen
gießen	gießt, gießt	goss	gegossen
gleichen	gleichst, gleicht	glich	geglichen
gleiten	gleitest, gleitet	glitt	geglitten
graben	gräbst, gräbt	grub	gegraben
greifen	greifst, greift	griff	gegriffen
haben	hast, hat	hatte	gehabt
halten	hältst, hält	hielt	gehalten
hängen	hängst, hängt	hing	gehangen
heben	hebst, hebt	hob	gehoben
heißen	heißt, heißt	hieß	geheißen
helfen	hilfst, hilft	half	geholfen
kennen	kennst, kennt	kannte	gekannt
klingen	klingst, klingt	klang	geklungen
kommen	kommst, kommt	kam	gekommen
können	kannst, kann	konnte	gekonnt
kriechen	kriechst, kriecht	kroch	gekrochen
laden	lädst, lädt	lud	geladen
lassen	lässt, lässt	ließ	gelassen
laufen	läufst, läuft	lief	gelaufen
leiden	leidest, leidet	litt	gelitten
leihen	leihst, leiht	lieh	geliehen
lesen	liest, liest	las	gelesen
liegen	liegst, liegt	lag	gelegen
lügen	lügst, lügt	log	gelogen
mahlen	mahlst, mahlt	mahlte	gemahlen
meiden	meidest, meidet	mied	gemieden
messen	misst, misst	maß	gemessen
mögen	magst, mag	mochte	gemocht
müssen	musst, muss	musste	gemusst
nehmen	nimmst, nimmt	nahm	genommen
nennen	nennst, nennt	nannte	genannt
pfeifen	pfeifst, pfeift	pfiff	gepfiffen

Infinitiv	*Präsens 2., 3. Singular*	*Präteritum*	*Partizip Perfekt*
raten	rätst, rät	riet	geraten
reiben	reibst, reibt	rieb	gerieben
reißen	reißt, reißt	riss	gerissen
reiten	reitest, reitet	ritt	geritten
rennen	rennst, rennt	rannte	gerannt
riechen	riechst, riecht	roch	gerochen
rufen	rufst, ruft	rief	gerufen
saufen	säufst, säuft	soff	gesoffen
saugen	saugst, saugt	sog *o* saugte	gesogen *o* gesaugt
schaffen	schaffst, schafft	schuf	geschaffen
scheiden	scheidest, scheidet	schied	geschieden
scheinen	scheinst, scheint	schien	geschienen
schieben	schiebst, schiebt	schob	geschoben
schießen	schießt, schießt	schoss	geschossen
schlafen	schläfst, schläft	schlief	geschlafen
schlagen	schlägst, schlägt	schlug	geschlagen
schleichen	schleichst, schleicht	schlich	geschlichen
schließen	schließt, schließt	schloss	geschlossen
schmeißen	schmeißt, schmeißt	schmiss	geschmissen
schmelzen	schmilzt, schmilzt	schmolz	geschmolzen
schneiden	schneidest, schneidet	schnitt	geschnitten
schreiben	schreibst, schreibt	schrieb	geschrieben
schreien	schreist, schreit	schrie	geschrien
schweigen	schweigst, schweigt	schwieg	geschwiegen
schwellen	schwillst, schwillt	schwoll	geschwollen
schwimmen	schwimmst, schwimmt	schwamm	geschwommen
schwören	schwörst, schwört	schwor	geschworen
sehen	siehst, sieht	sah	gesehen
sein	bist, ist	war	gewesen
senden	sendest, sendet	sandte	gesandt
singen	singst, singt	sang	gesungen
sinken	sinkst, sinkt	sank	gesunken
sitzen	sitzt, sitzt	saß	gesessen

Infinitiv	*Präsens 2., 3. Singular*	*Präteritum*	*Partizip Perfekt*
sollen	sollst, soll	sollte	gesollt
sprechen	sprichst, spricht	sprach	gesprochen
springen	springst, springt	sprang	gesprungen
stechen	stichst, sticht	stach	gestochen
stehen	stehst, steht	stand	gestanden
stehlen	stiehlst, stiehlt	stahl	gestohlen
steigen	steigst, steigt	stieg	gestiegen
sterben	stirbst, stirbt	starb	gestorben
stinken	stinkst, stinkt	stank	gestunken
stoßen	stößt, stößt	stieß	gestoßen
streichen	streichst, streicht	strich	gestrichen
streiten	streitest, streitet	stritt	gestritten
tragen	trägst, trägt	trug	getragen
treffen	triffst, trifft	traf	getroffen
treiben	treibst, treibt	trieb	getrieben
treten	trittst, tritt	trat	getreten
trinken	trinkst, trinkt	trank	getrunken
tun	tust, tut	tat	getan
verderben	verdirbst, verdirbt	verdarb	verdorben
vergessen	vergisst, vergisst	vergaß	vergessen
verlieren	verlierst, verliert	verlor	verloren
verschwinden	verschwindest, verschwindet	verschwand	verschwunden
verzeihen	verzeihst, verzeiht	verzieh	verziehen
wachsen	wächst, wächst	wuchs	gewachsen
wenden	wendest, wendet	wandte	gewandt
werben	wirbst, wirbt	warb	geworben
werden	wirst, wird	wurde	geworden
werfen	wirfst, wirft	warf	geworfen
wiegen	wiegst, wiegt	wog	gewogen
wissen	weißt, weiß	wusste	gewusst
wollen	willst, will	wollte	gewollt
ziehen	ziehst, zieht	zog	gezogen
zwingen	zwingst, zwingt	zwang	gezwungen

Deutsch – Englisch

German – English

A *abk* (= *Autobahn*) ≈ M (BRIT)
à *präp* (*bes Comm*) at
Aal (**-(e)s**, **-e**) *m* eel

SCHLÜSSELWORT

ab *präp +dat* from; **Kinder ab 12 Jahren** children from the age of 12; **ab morgen** from tomorrow; **ab sofort** as of now
▶ *adv* **1** off; **links ab** to the left; **der Knopf ist ab** the button has come off; **ab nach Hause!** off home with you!
2 (*zeitlich*): **von da ab** from then on; **von heute ab** from today, as of today
3 (*auf Fahrplänen*): **München ab 12.20** leaving Munich 12.20
4: **ab und zu** *od* **an** now and then *od* again

ab|bauen *vt* to dismantle; (*verringern*) to reduce
ab|beißen *unreg vt* to bite off
ab|bestellen *vt* to cancel
ab|biegen *unreg vi* to turn off; (*Straße*) to bend
Abbildung *f* illustration
ab|blasen *unreg vt* (*fig: umg*) to call off
ab|blenden *vi* to dip (BRIT) *od* dim (US) one's headlights
Abblendlicht *nt* dipped (BRIT) *od* dimmed (US) headlights *pl*
ab|brechen *unreg vt* to break off; (*Gebäude*) to pull down; (*aufhören*) to stop; (*Comput*) to abort
ab|bremsen *vi* to brake, to slow down
ab|bringen *unreg vt*: **jdn von etw ~** to dissuade sb from sth; **jdn vom Weg ~** to divert sb
ab|buchen *vt* to debit
ab|danken *vi* to resign
ab|drehen *vt* (*Gas*) to turn off; (*Licht*) to switch off ▶ *vi* (*Schiff*) to change course
Abend (**-s**, **-e**) *m* evening; **gegen ~** towards (the) evening; **zu ~ essen** to have dinner *od* supper; **heute ~** this evening
Abendbrot *nt* supper
Abendessen *nt* supper
Abendkasse *f* (*Theat*) box office
Abendkleid *nt* evening gown
Abendmahl *nt* Holy Communion
abends *adv* in the evening
Abenteuer (**-s**, **-**) *nt* adventure
Abenteuerurlaub *m* adventure holiday
aber *konj* but; (*jedoch*) however ▶ *adv*: **oder ~** or else; **das ist ~ schön** that's really nice
abergläubisch *adj* superstitious
ab|fahren *unreg vi* to leave, to depart
Abfahrt *f* departure; (*Autobahnabfahrt*) exit; (*Ski*) descent; (*Piste*) run
Abfahrtslauf *m* (*Ski*) downhill (event)
Abfahrtszeit *f* departure time
Abfall *m* waste; (*von Speisen etc*) rubbish (BRIT), garbage (US)
Abfalleimer *m* rubbish bin (BRIT), garbage can (US)
abfällig *adj* disparaging
ab|färben *vi* (*Wäsche*) to run; (*fig*) to rub off
ab|fertigen *vt* to prepare for dispatch; (*an Grenze*) to clear
ab|finden *unreg vt* to pay off ▶ *vr* to come to terms
Abfindung *f* (*von Gläubigern*) payment; (*Geld*) sum in settlement
ab|fliegen *unreg vi* to take off
Abflug *m* departure; (*Start*) take-off
Abflughalle *f* departure lounge
Abflugzeit *f* departure time
Abfluss *m* (*Öffnung*) outlet
Abflussrohr *nt* drainpipe; (*von sanitären Anlagen*) waste pipe
ab|fragen *vt* to test; (*Comput*) to call up
ab|führen *vt* to lead away; (*Gelder, Steuern*) to pay ▶ *vi* (*Med*) to have a laxative effect
Abführmittel *nt* laxative
Abgabe *f* handing in; (*von Ball*) pass; (*Steuer*) tax; (*einer Erklärung*) giving
abgabenfrei *adj* tax-free

abgabenpflichtig *adj* liable to tax
Abgas *nt* waste gas ■ **Abgase** *pl* exhaust fumes *pl*
Abgassonderuntersuchung *f* exhaust emission test
ab|geben *unreg vt* (*Gegenstand*) to hand *od* give in; (*Wärme*) to give off; (*Amt*) to hand over; (*Erklärung, Urteil*) to give; (*darstellen*) to make ▶ *vr*: **sich mit jdm/etw ~** to associate with sb/ bother with sth
ab|gehen *unreg vi* to go away, to leave; (*Post*) to go; (*Knopf etc*) to come off; (*abgezogen werden*) to be taken off; (*Straße*) to branch off; **etw geht jdm ab** (*fehlt*) sb lacks sth
abgelegen *adj* remote
abgemacht *adj* fixed; **~!** done!
abgeneigt *adj* averse; **ich wäre nicht ~, das zu tun** I wouldn't mind doing that
Abgeordnete(r) *f(m)* member of parliament
abgesehen *adj*: **es auf jdn/etw ~ haben** to be after sb/sth; **~ von ...** apart from ...
abgespannt *adj* tired out
abgestanden *adj* stale; (*Bier*) flat
abgestorben *adj* numb; (*Biol, Med*) dead
abgestumpft *adj* (*Person*) insensitive
abgetragen *adj* worn
ab|gewöhnen *vt*: **jdm/sich etw ~** to cure sb of sth/give sth up
ab|haken *vt* to tick off (Brit), to check off (*US*)
ab|halten *unreg vt* (*Versammlung*) to hold; **jdn von etw ~** (*fernhalten*) to keep sb away from sth; (*hindern*) to keep sb from sth
abhanden|kommen *vi* to get lost
Abhang *m* slope
ab|hängen *unreg vt* (*Bild*) to take down; (*Anhänger*) to uncouple; (*Verfolger*) to shake off; **von jdm/etw ~** to depend on sb/sth; **das hängt ganz davon ab** it all depends
abhängig *adj*: **~ (von)** dependent (on)
ab|hauen *unreg vt* to cut off ▶ *vi* (*umg*) to clear off *od* out; **hau ab!** beat it!
ab|heben *unreg vt* to lift (up); (*Geld*) to withdraw ▶ *vi* (*Flugzeug*) to take off; (*Rakete*) to lift off; (*Karten*) to cut
ab|holen *vt* to fetch, to collect; (*am Bahnhof etc*) to pick up, to meet
Abholmarkt *m* cash and carry
ab|horchen *vt* (*Med*) to listen to
ab|hören *vt* (*Vokabeln*) to test; (*Telefongespräch*) to tap; (*Tonband etc*) to listen to
Abitur (**-s**, **-e**) *nt German school-leaving examination*, ≈ A-levels *pl* (Brit)

Abitur

The **Abitur** is the German school-leaving examination which is taken at the age of 18 or 19 by pupils at a *Gymnasium*. It is taken in four subjects and is necessary for entry to university.

ab|kaufen *vt*: **jdm etw ~** to buy sth from sb; **das kauf ich dir nicht ab!** (*umg*) I don't believe you
ab|klingen *unreg vi* to die away
ab|kommen *unreg vi* to get away; **(vom Thema) ~** to get off the subject; **von der Straße/einem Plan ~** to leave the road/give up a plan
Abkommen (**-s**, **-**) *nt* agreement
ab|koppeln *vt* (*Anhänger*) to unhitch
ab|kratzen *vt* to scrape off ▶ *vi* (*umg*) to kick the bucket
ab|kühlen *vt* to cool down ▶ *vr* (*Mensch*) to cool down *od* off; (*Wetter*) to get cool
ab|kürzen *vt* to shorten; (*Wort*) to abbreviate; **den Weg ~** to take a shortcut
Abkürzung *f* abbreviation; (*Weg*) shortcut
ab|laden *unreg vt* to unload
Ablage *f* (*Aktenordnung*) filing; (*für Akten*) tray
Ablauf *m* (*Abfluss*) drain; (*von Ereignissen*) course; (*einer Frist, Zeit*) expiry (Brit), expiration (*US*)
ab|laufen *unreg vi* (*abfließen*) to drain away; (*Ereignisse*) to happen; (*Frist, Zeit, Pass*) to expire
ab|legen *vt* to put *od* lay down; (*Kleider*) to take off; (*Gewohnheit*) to get rid of; (*Prüfung*) to take, to sit (Brit); (*Schriftwechsel*) to file (away) ▶ *vi* (*Schiff*) to cast off
ab|lehnen *vt* to reject; (*missbilligen*) to disapprove of; (*Einladung*) to decline ▶ *vi* to decline
ab|lenken *vt* to distract ▶ *vi* to change the subject
Ablenkung *f* distraction

ab|lesen *unreg vt* to read
ab|liefern *vt* to deliver
ab|machen *vt* to take off; (*vereinbaren*) to agree
Abmachung *f* agreement
ab|melden *vt* (*Auto*) to take off the road ▶ *vr* to give notice of one's departure; (*im Hotel*) to check out
ab|messen *unreg vt* to measure
ab|nehmen *unreg vt* to take off, to remove; (*Führerschein*) to take away; (*Hörer*) to lift, to pick up ▶ *vi* to decrease; (*schlanker werden*) to lose weight; (*Tel*) to pick up the phone
Abneigung *f* aversion, dislike
ab|nutzen *vt* to wear out
Abonnement (**-s**, **-s** *od* **-e**) *nt* subscription
Abonnent(in) *m(f)* subscriber
abonnieren *vt* to subscribe to
ab|raten *unreg vi*: **jdm von etw ~** to advise sb against sth
ab|räumen *vt* to clear up *od* away; (*Tisch*) to clear
Abrechnung *f* settlement; (*Rechnung*) bill
ab|regen (*umg*) *vr* to calm *od* cool down
Abreise *f* departure
ab|reisen *vi* to leave
ab|reißen *unreg vt* (*Haus*) to tear down; (*Blatt*) to tear off ▶ *vi*: **den Kontakt nicht ~ lassen** to stay in touch
ab|runden *vt* to round off
abrupt *adj* abrupt
Abs. *abk* = **Absender**
ab|sagen *vt* to cancel, to call off; (*Einladung*) to turn down ▶ *vi* (*ablehnen*) to decline; **jdm ~** to tell sb that one can't come
Absatz *m* (*Comm*) sales *pl*; (*neuer Abschnitt*) paragraph; (*Schuhabsatz*) heel
ab|schaffen *vt* to abolish, to do away with
ab|schalten *vt*, *vi* (*lit*, *umg*) to switch off
ab|schätzen *vt* to estimate; (*Lage*) to assess
abscheulich *adj* abominable
ab|schicken *vt* to send off
ab|schieben *unreg vt* (*ausweisen*) to deport
Abschied (**-(e)s**, **-e**) *m* parting; **(von jdm) ~ nehmen** to say goodbye (to sb)
Abschiedsfeier *f* farewell party
Abschlagszahlung *f* interim payment
Abschleppdienst *m* (*Aut*) breakdown service (Brit), towing company (*US*)
ab|schleppen *vt* to (take in) tow
Abschleppseil *nt* towrope
ab|schließen *unreg vt* (*Tür*) to lock; (*beenden*) to conclude, to finish; (*Vertrag*, *Handel*) to conclude
Abschluss *m* (*Beendigung*) close, conclusion; (*von Vertrag*, *Handel*) conclusion
ab|schmecken *vt* (*kosten*) to taste; (*würzen*) to season
ab|schminken *vr* to remove one's make-up ▶ *vt* (*umg*): **sich** *dat* **etw ~** to get sth out of one's mind
ab|schnallen *vr* to unfasten one's seat belt
ab|schneiden *unreg vt* to cut off ▶ *vi* to do, to come off; **bei etw gut/ schlecht ~** (*umg*) to come off well/ badly in sth
Abschnitt *m* section; (*Kontrollabschnitt*) counterfoil (Brit), stub (*US*)
ab|schrauben *vt* to unscrew
ab|schrecken *vt* to deter, to put off
ab|schreiben *unreg vt* to copy; (*verloren geben*) to write off; (*Comm*) to deduct
abschüssig *adj* steep
ab|schwächen *vt* to lessen; (*Behauptung*, *Kritik*) to tone down
ab|schwellen *unreg vi* (*Geschwulst*) to go down; (*Lärm*) to die down
absehbar *adj* foreseeable; **in absehbarer Zeit** in the foreseeable future
ab|sehen *unreg vt* (*Ende*, *Folgen*) to foresee ▶ *vi*: **von etw ~** to refrain from sth
abseits *adv* out of the way ▶ *präp +gen* away from
Abseits *nt* (*Sport*) offside
Abseitsfalle *f* (*Sport*) offside trap
ab|senden *unreg vt* to send off
Absender *m* sender
ab|setzen *vt* (*niederstellen*) to put down; (*aussteigen lassen*) to drop (off); (*Comm*) to sell; (*Fin*) to deduct; (*streichen*) to drop ▶ *vr* (*sich entfernen*) to clear off; (*sich ablagern*) to be deposited
Absicht *f* intention; **mit ~** on purpose

absichtlich *adj* intentional, deliberate
absolut *adj* absolute
ab|specken (*umg*) *vi* to lose weight
ab|speichern *vt* (*Comput*) to save
ab|sperren *vt* to block *od* close off; (*Tür*) to lock
Absperrung *f* (*Vorgang*) blocking *od* closing off; (*Sperre*) barricade
ab|spielen *vt* (*CD etc*) to play ▸ *vr* to happen
ab|springen *unreg vi* to jump down/ off; (*sich distanzieren*) to back out
ab|spülen *vt* to rinse; **Geschirr ~** to wash up (BRIT), to do the dishes
Abstand *m* distance; (*zeitlich*) interval; **~ halten** (*Aut*) to keep one's distance
ab|stauben *vt, vi* to dust; (*umg: mitgehen lassen*) to help oneself to, to pinch
Abstecher (**-s**, **-**) *m* detour
ab|steigen *unreg vi* (*vom Rad etc*) to get off, to dismount; **in einem Gasthof ~** to put up at an inn
ab|stellen *vt* (*niederstellen*) to put down; (*Auto*) to park; (*ausschalten*) to turn *od* switch off; (*Missstand, Unsitte*) to stop
Abstellraum *m* storeroom
Abstieg (**-(e)s**, **-e**) *m* descent; (*Sport*) relegation
ab|stimmen *vi* to vote ▸ *vt*: **~ (auf** *+akk*) (*Interessen*) to match (with); (*Termine, Ziele*) to fit in (with) ▸ *vr* to agree
abstoßend *adj* repulsive
abstrakt *adj* abstract
ab|streiten *unreg vt* to deny
Abstrich *m* (*Med*) smear; **Abstriche machen** to lower one's sights
Absturz *m* fall; (*Aviat*) crash
ab|stürzen *vi* to fall; (*Aviat*) to crash
absurd *adj* absurd
Abszess (**-es**, **-sse**) *m* abscess
ab|tauen *vt, vi* to thaw; (*Kühlschrank*) to defrost
Abtei (**-**, **-en**) *f* abbey
Abteil (**-(e)s**, **-e**) *nt* compartment
Abteilung *f* (*in Firma, Kaufhaus*) department; (*in Krankenhaus, Jur*) section
ab|treiben *unreg vt* (*Kind*) to abort ▸ *vi* to be driven off course; (*Frau*) to have an abortion
Abtreibung *f* abortion
ab|trocknen *vt* to dry
ab|warten *vt* to wait for ▸ *vi* to wait
abwärts *adv* down
Abwasch (**-(e)s**) *m* washing-up
ab|waschen *unreg vt* (*Schmutz*) to wash off; (*Geschirr*) to wash (up)
Abwasser (**-s**, **-wässer**) *nt* sewage
ab|wechseln *vi, vr* to alternate; (*Personen*) to take turns
abwechselnd *adj* alternate
Abwechslung *f* change; (*Zerstreuung*) diversion
ab|weisen *unreg vt* to turn away; (*Antrag*) to turn down
abweisend *adj* (*Haltung*) cold
abwesend *adj* absent
Abwesenheit *f* absence
ab|wiegen *unreg vt* to weigh out
ab|wimmeln (*umg*) *vt* (*Person*) to get rid of
ab|wischen *vt* to wipe off *od* away; (*putzen*) to wipe
ab|zählen *vt* to count (up); **abgezähltes Fahrgeld** exact fare
Abzeichen *nt* badge
ab|zeichnen *vt* to draw, to copy; (*unterschreiben*) to initial ▸ *vr* to stand out; (*fig: bevorstehen*) to loom
ab|ziehen *unreg vt* to take off; (*Bett*) to strip; (*subtrahieren*) to take away, to subtract ▸ *vi* to go away
Abzug *m* (*von Truppen*) withdrawal; (*Betrag*) deduction; (*Rabatt*) discount; (*von Waffen*) trigger; (*Phot*) print
abzüglich *präp +gen* less
ab|zweigen *vi* to branch off ▸ *vt* to set aside
Abzweigung *f* junction
Accessoires *pl* accessories *pl*
ach *interj* oh; **~ so!** I see!
Achse (**-**, **-n**) *f* axis; (*Aut*) axle
Achsel (**-**, **-n**) *f* shoulder
Achsenbruch *m* (*Aut*) broken axle
acht *num* eight; **~ Tage** a week
Acht (**-**) *f* attention; **sich in ~ nehmen (vor** *+dat*) to be careful (of), to watch out (for); **etw außer ~ lassen** to disregard sth
achte(r, s) *adj* eighth
Achtel *nt* eighth
achten *vt* to respect ▸ *vi*: **~ (auf** *+akk*) to pay attention (to)
Achterbahn *f* roller coaster
acht|geben *unreg vi*: **~ (auf** *+akk*) to take care (of)
achthundert *num* eight hundred

achtmal *adv* eight times
Achtung *f* attention; (*Ehrfurcht*) respect ▸ *interj* look out!
achtzehn *num* eighteen
achtzig *num* eighty
Acker (**-s**, **Äcker**) *m* field
Adapter (**-s**, **-**) *m* adapter
addieren *vt* to add (up)
Adel (**-s**) *m* nobility
adelig *adj* noble
Ader (**-**, **-n**) *f* vein
ADHS (**-**) *nt abk* (= *Aufmerksamkeitsdefizit/ Hyperaktivitätsstörung*) ADHD (= *attention deficit hyperactivity disorder*)
Adjektiv (**-s**, **-e**) *nt* adjective
Adler (**-s**, **-**) *m* eagle
adoptieren *vt* to adopt
Adoption *f* adoption
Adoptiveltern *pl* adoptive parents *pl*
Adoptivkind *nt* adopted child
Adrenalin (**-s**) *nt* adrenalin
Adressbuch *nt* directory; (*privat*) address book
Adresse (**-**, **-n**) *f* (*auch Comput*) address
adressieren *vt*: **~ (an** *+akk***)** to address (to)
ADSL *nt abk* (= *Asymmetric Digital Subscriber Line*) ADSL
Advent (**-(e)s**, **-e**) *m* Advent
Adventskranz *m* Advent wreath
Adverb *nt* adverb
Aerobic (**-s**) *nt* aerobics *sing*
Affäre (**-**, **-n**) *f* affair
Affe (**-n**, **-n**) *m* monkey
Afghanistan (**-s**) *nt* Afghanistan
Afrika (**-s**) *nt* Africa
Afrikaner(in) (**-s**, **-**) *m(f)* African
afrikanisch *adj* African
After (**-s**, **-**) *m* anus
AG (**-**) *f abk* (= *Aktiengesellschaft*) ≈ plc (BRIT), ≈ corp., inc. (*US*)
Agent(in) *m(f)* agent
Agentur *f* agency
aggressiv *adj* aggressive
Ägypten (**-s**) *nt* Egypt
aha *interj* aha!
ähneln *vi +dat* to be like, to resemble ▸ *vr* to be alike *od* similar
ahnen *vt* to suspect; **du ahnst es nicht!** you have no idea!
ähnlich *adj +dat* similar (to); **das sieht ihm (ganz) ~!** (*umg*) that's just like him!
Ähnlichkeit *f* similarity
Ahnung *f* idea, suspicion; **keine ~!** no idea
ahnungslos *adj* unsuspecting
Ahorn (**-s**, **-e**) *m* maple
Aids (**-**) *nt* Aids
aidskrank *adj* suffering from Aids
Aidstest *m* Aids test
Airbag (**-s**, **-s**) *m* (*Aut*) airbag
Akademie *f* academy
Akademiker(in) (**-s**, **-**) *m(f)* university graduate
akklimatisieren *vr* to become acclimatized
Akkordeon (**-s**, **-s**) *nt* accordion
Akku (**-s**, **-s**) (*umg*) *m* battery
Akkusativ (**-s**, **-e**) *m* accusative (case)
Akne (**-**, **-n**) *f* acne
Akrobat(in) (**-en**, **-en**) *m(f)* acrobat
Akt (**-(e)s**, **-e**) *m* act; (*Kunst*) nude
Akte (**-**, **-n**) *f* file; **etw zu den Akten legen** (*lit, fig*) to file sth away
Aktenkoffer *m* attaché case
Aktie (**-**, **-n**) *f* share
Aktiengesellschaft *f* public limited company (BRIT), corporation (*US*)
Aktion *f* campaign; (*Polizeiaktion, Suchaktion*) action
Aktionär(in) (**-s**, **-e**) *m(f)* shareholder
aktiv *adj* active
aktivieren *vt* to activate
aktualisieren *vt* (*Comput*) to update
aktuell *adj* topical; (*Mode*) up-to-date
Akupunktur *f* acupuncture
Akustik *f* acoustics *pl*
akustisch *adj* acoustic
akut *adj* acute
AKW *nt abk* = **Atomkraftwerk**
Akzent (**-(e)s**, **-e**) *m* accent; (*Betonung*) stress
akzeptieren *vt* to accept
Alarm (**-(e)s**, **-e**) *m* alarm
Alarmanlage *f* alarm system
alarmieren *vt* to alarm; **die Polizei ~** to call the police
Albanien (**-s**) *nt* Albania
albern *adj* silly
Albtraum *m* nightmare
Album (**-s**, **Alben**) *nt* album
Algerien (**-s**) *nt* Algeria
Alibi (**-s**, **-s**) *nt* alibi
Alimente *pl* alimony *sing*
Alkohol (**-s**, **-e**) *m* alcohol
alkoholfrei *adj* non-alcoholic; **alkoholfreies Getränk** soft drink
Alkoholiker(in) (**-s**, **-**) *m(f)* alcoholic

alkoholisch *adj* alcoholic
Alkoholtest *m* Breathalyser®
All (**-s**) *nt* universe

SCHLÜSSELWORT

alle(r, s) *adj* **1** (*sämtliche*) all; **wir alle** all of us; **alle Kinder waren da** all the children were there; **alle Kinder mögen ...** all children like ...; **alle beide** both of us/them; **sie kamen alle** they all came; **alles Gute** all the best; **alles in allem** all in all
2 (*mit Zeit- oder Maßangaben*) every; **alle vier Jahre** every four years; **alle fünf Meter** every five metres
▶ *pron* everything; **alles was er sagt** everything he says, all that he says
▶ *adv* (*zu Ende, aufgebraucht*) finished; **die Milch ist alle** the milk's all gone, there's no milk left; **etw alle machen** to finish sth up

Allee (**-**, **-n**) *f* avenue
allein *adj*, *adv* alone; (*ohne Hilfe*) on one's own, by oneself; **nicht ~** (*nicht nur*) not only
alleinerziehend *adj* single-parent
Alleinerziehende(r) *f*(*m*) single parent
alleinstehend *adj* single
allerbeste(r, s) *adj* very best
allerdings *adv* (*zwar*) admittedly; (*gewiss*) certainly
Allergie *f* allergy
allergisch *adj* allergic; **auf etw** *akk* **~ reagieren** to be allergic to sth
allerhand (*umg*) *adj unver* all sorts of; **das ist doch ~!** that's a bit much!
Allerheiligen *nt* All Saints' Day
allerhöchste(r, s) *adj* very highest
allerhöchstens *adv* at the very most
allerlei *adj unver* all sorts of
allerletzte(r, s) *adj* very last
allerwenigste(r, s) *adj* very least
alles *pron* everything; *siehe auch* **alle**
Alleskleber (**-s**, **-**) *m* all-purpose adhesive
allgemein *adj* general; **im Allgemeinen** in general
alljährlich *adj* annual
allmählich *adj* gradual ▶ *adv* gradually
Allradantrieb *m* all-wheel drive
Alltag *m* everyday life
alltäglich *adj* daily; (*gewöhnlich*) commonplace
allzu *adv* all too
Allzweckreiniger (**-s**, **-**) *m* multi-purpose cleaner
Alpen *pl* Alps *pl*
Alphabet (**-(e)s**, **-e**) *nt* alphabet
alphabetisch *adj* alphabetical
Alptraum *m* = **Albtraum**

SCHLÜSSELWORT

als *konj* **1** (*zeitlich*) when; **damals als ...** (in the days) when ...; **gerade als ...** just as ...; (*gleichzeitig*) as
2 (*in der Eigenschaft*) an; **als Antwort** as an answer; **als Kind** as a child
3 (*bei Vergleichen*) than; **ich kam später als er** I came later than he (did) *od* later than him; **lieber ... als ...** rather ... than ...; **nichts als Ärger** nothing but trouble
4: **als ob/wenn** as if

also *konj* so; (*folglich*) therefore; **~ gut** *od* **schön!** okay then
alt *adj* old
Altar (**-(e)s**, **-äre**) *m* altar
Alter (**-s**, **-**) *nt* age; (*hohes*) old age; **er ist in deinem ~** he's your age; **im ~ von** at the age of
alternativ *adj* alternative
Alternative *f* alternative
Altersheim *nt* old people's home
Altglas *nt* used glass (*for recycling*)
Altglascontainer *m* bottle bank
altmodisch *adj* old-fashioned
Altpapier *nt* waste paper
Altstadt *f* old town
Alufolie *f* tinfoil
Aluminium (**-s**) *nt* aluminium (BRIT), aluminum (US)
Alzheimerkrankheit *f* Alzheimer's disease
am = **an dem**; **am 15. März** on March 15th; **am letzten Sonntag** last Sunday; **am Morgen/Abend** in the morning/evening; **am besten/schönsten** best/most beautiful
Amateur(in) *m*(*f*) amateur
ambulant *adj* outpatient
Ambulanz *f* (*Krankenwagen*) ambulance; (*in der Klinik*) outpatients' department
Ameise (**-**, **-n**) *f* ant

amen *interj* amen
Amerika (**-s**) *nt* America
Amerikaner(in) (**-s**, **-**) *m(f)* American
amerikanisch *adj* American
Ampel (**-**, **-n**) *f* traffic lights *pl*
Amsel (**-**, **-n**) *f* blackbird
Amt (**-(e)s**, **Ämter**) *nt* office; (*Posten*) post
amtlich *adj* official
amüsant *adj* amusing
amüsieren *vt* to amuse ▶ *vr* to enjoy o.s.

SCHLÜSSELWORT

an *präp +dat* **1** (*räumlich*: *wo?*) at; (*auf, bei*) on; (*nahe bei*) near; **an diesem Ort** at this place; **an der Wand** on the wall; **zu nahe an etw** too near to sth; **unten am Fluss** down by the river; **Köln liegt am Rhein** Cologne is on the Rhine
2 (*zeitlich*: *wann?*) on; **an diesem Tag** on this day; **an Ostern** at Easter
3: **arm an Fett** low in fat; **an etw sterben** to die of sth; **an (und für) sich** actually
▶ *präp +akk* **1** (*räumlich*: *wohin?*) to; **er ging ans Fenster** he went (over) to the window; **etw an die Wand hängen/schreiben** to hang/write sth on the wall
2 (*woran?*): **an etw denken** to think of sth
3 (*gerichtet an*) to; **ein Gruß/eine Frage an dich** greetings/a question to you
▶ *adv* **1** (*ungefähr*) about; **an die Hundert** about a hundred
2 (*auf Fahrplänen*): **Frankfurt an 18.30** arriving Frankfurt 18.30
3 (*ab*): **von dort/heute an** from there/today onwards
4 (*angeschaltet, angezogen*) on; **das Licht ist an** the light is on; **ohne etwas an** with nothing on; *siehe auch* **am**

anal *adj* anal
analog *adj* analogous; (*Comput*) analog
Analyse (**-**, **-n**) *f* analysis
analysieren *vt* to analyse (Brit), to analyze (US)
Ananas (**-**, **-** *od* **-se**) *f* pineapple
an|baggern *vt* (*umg*) to chat up (Brit), to come on to (US)
Anbau *m* (*Agr*) cultivation; (*Gebäude*) extension
an|bauen *vt* (*Agr*) to cultivate; (*Gebäudeteil*) to build on
an|behalten *unreg vt* to keep on
anbei *adv* enclosed (*form*); **~ schicken wir Ihnen ...** please find enclosed ...
an|beten *vt* to worship
an|bieten *unreg vt* to offer ▶ *vr* to volunteer
an|binden *unreg vt* to tie up
Anblick *m* sight
an|braten *unreg vt* to brown
an|brechen *unreg vt* to start; (*Vorräte*) to break into ▶ *vi* to start; (*Tag*) to break; (*Nacht*) to fall
an|brennen *unreg vi* to catch fire; (*Koch*) to burn
an|bringen *unreg vt* to bring; (*festmachen*) to fasten
Andacht (**-**, **-en**) *f* devotion; (*Gottesdienst*) prayers *pl*
an|dauern *vi* to last, to go on
andauernd *adj* continual
Andenken (**-s**, **-**) *nt* memory; (*Reiseandenken*) souvenir
andere(r, s) *adj* other; (*verschieden*) different; **am anderen Tage** the next day; **von etwas anderem sprechen** to talk about something else; **unter anderem** among other things
andererseits *adv* on the other hand
ändern *vt* to alter, to change ▶ *vr* to change
andernfalls *adv* otherwise
anders *adv*: **~ (als)** differently (from); **jemand/irgendwo ~** somebody/somewhere else; **~ aussehen/klingen** to look/sound different
andersherum *adv* the other way round
anderswo *adv* elsewhere
anderthalb *adj* one and a half
Änderung *f* alteration, change
an|deuten *vt* to indicate; (*Wink geben*) to hint at
Andorra (**-s**) *nt* Andorra
Andrang *m* crush; **es herrschte großer ~** there was a huge crowd
an|drohen *vt*: **jdm etw ~** to threaten sb with sth
aneinander *adv* at/on/to *etc* one another *od* each other; **sich ~ gewöhnen** to get used to each other

aneinander|geraten *vi* to clash
aneinander|legen *vt* to put together
an|erkennen *unreg vt* to recognize, to acknowledge; (*würdigen*) to appreciate
Anerkennung *f* recognition, acknowledgement; (*Würdigung*) appreciation
an|fahren *unreg vt* to deliver; (*fahren gegen*) to hit; (*umg*) to bawl at ▶ *vi* to drive up; (*losfahren*) to drive off
Anfall *m* (*Med*) attack
anfällig *adj* delicate; **~ für etw** prone to sth
Anfang (**-(e)s**, **-fänge**) *m* beginning, start; **zu ~** at the beginning; **~ fünfzig** in one's early fifties; **~ Mai/1994** at the beginning of May/1994
an|fangen *unreg vi* to begin, to start; **damit kann ich nichts ~** (*nützt mir nichts*) that's no good to me
Anfänger(in) (**-s**, **-**) *m(f)* beginner
anfangs *adv* at first
Anfangsbuchstabe *m* initial *od* first letter
an|fassen *vt* to handle; (*berühren*) to touch ▶ *vi* to lend a hand
Anflug *m* (*Aviat*) approach; (*Spur*) trace
an|fordern *vt* to demand
Anforderung *f* +*gen* demand (for); (*Comm*) requisition
Anfrage *f* inquiry
an|freunden *vr* to make friends
an|fühlen *vt*, *vr* to feel; **es fühlt sich gut an** it feels good
Anführungszeichen *pl* quotation marks *pl*
Angabe *f* statement; (*Tech*) specification; (*umg*: *Prahlerei*) boasting ■ **Angaben** *pl* (*Auskunft*) particulars *pl*
an|geben *unreg vt* to give; (*anzeigen*) to inform on; (*bestimmen*) to set ▶ *vi* (*umg*) to boast; (*Sport*) to serve
Angeber(in) (**-s**, **-**) (*umg*) *m(f)* show-off
angeblich *adj* alleged
angeboren *adj* +*dat* inborn
Angebot *nt* offer; (*Comm*): **~ (an** +*dat***)** supply (of); **~ und Nachfrage** supply and demand
angebracht *adj* appropriate
angebrannt *adv*: **das Fleisch schmeckt ~** the meat tastes burnt
angebunden *adj*: **kurz ~ sein** (*umg*) to be abrupt *od* curt
angeheitert *adj* tipsy
an|gehen *unreg vt* to concern ▶ *vi* (*Feuer*) to light; (*umg*: *beginnen*) to begin
angehend *adj* prospective
Angehörige(r) *f(m)* relative
Angeklagte(r) *f(m)* accused, defendant
Angel (**-**, **-n**) *f* fishing rod; (*Türangel*) hinge
Angelegenheit *f* affair, matter
Angelhaken *m* fish hook
angeln *vt* to catch ▶ *vi* to fish
Angeln (**-s**) *nt* angling, fishing
Angelrute *f* fishing rod
angemessen *adj* appropriate, suitable
angenehm *adj* pleasant; **~!** (*bei Vorstellung*) pleased to meet you
angenommen *pp von* **annehmen** ▶ *adj* assumed; **~, wir ...** assuming we ...
angesehen *pp von* **ansehen** ▶ *adj* respected
angesichts *präp* +*gen* in view of, considering
Angestellte(r) *f(m)* employee
angetan *adj*: **von jdm/etw ~ sein** to be taken with sb/sth
angewiesen *adj*: **auf jdn/etw ~ sein** to be dependent on sb/sth
an|gewöhnen *vt*: **jdm/sich etw ~** to accustom sb/become accustomed to sth
Angewohnheit *f* habit
Angina (**-**, **Anginen**) *f* tonsillitis
Angina Pectoris (**-**) *f* angina
Angler(in) (**-s**, **-**) *m(f)* angler
an|greifen *unreg vt* to attack; (*anfassen*) to touch; (*beschädigen*) to damage
Angriff *m* attack; **etw in ~ nehmen** to make a start on sth
Angst (**-**, **Ängste**) *f* fear; **~ haben (vor** +*dat***)** to be afraid *od* scared (of); **jdm ~ machen** to scare sb
ängstigen *vt* to frighten ▶ *vr*: **sich ~ (vor** +*dat od* **um)** to worry (o.s.) (about)
ängstlich *adj* nervous; (*besorgt*) worried
an|haben *unreg vt* to have on
an|halten *unreg vt* to stop ▶ *vi* to stop; (*andauern*) to persist
anhaltend *adj* persistent
Anhalter(in) (**-s**, **-**) *m(f)* hitch-hiker; **per ~ fahren** to hitch-hike

anhand *präp +gen* with; **~ eines Beispiels** by means of an example
an|hängen *unreg vt* to hang up; (*Wagen*) to couple up; (*Zusatz*) to add (on); **eine Datei an eine E-Mail ~** (*Comput*) to attach a file to an email
Anhänger (**-s**, **-**) *m* supporter; (*Aut*) trailer; (*am Koffer*) tag; (*Schmuck*) pendant
anhänglich *adj* devoted
Anhieb *m*: **auf ~** straight off
an|himmeln (*umg*) *vt* to idolize, to worship
an|hören *vt* to listen to ▶ *vr* to sound; **das hört sich gut an** that sounds good
Anis (**-es**, **-e**) *m* aniseed
Anker (**-s**, **-**) *m* anchor
ankern *vt*, *vi* to anchor
Ankerplatz *m* anchorage
Anklage *f* accusation; (*Jur*) charge
an|klagen *vt* to accuse
an|klicken *vt* (*Comput*) to click on
an|klopfen *vi* to knock
an|kommen *unreg vi* to arrive; (*Anklang finden*): **bei jdm (gut) ~** to go down well with sb ▶ *vi unpers*: **es kommt darauf an** it depends; (*wichtig sein*) that is what matters
an|kreuzen *vt* to mark with a cross
an|kündigen *vt* to announce
Ankunft (**-**, **-künfte**) *f* arrival
Ankunftszeit *f* time of arrival
Anlage *f* disposition; (*Begabung*) talent; (*Park*) gardens *pl*; (*Beilage*) enclosure; (*Tech*) plant; (*umg*: *Stereoanlage*) (stereo) system; (*Fin*) investment
Anlass (**-es**, **-lässe**) *m*: **~ (zu)** cause (for); (*Ereignis*) occasion; **aus ~** *+gen* on the occasion of
an|lassen *unreg vt* to leave on; (*Motor*) to start
Anlasser (**-s**, **-**) *m* (*Aut*) starter
anlässlich *präp +gen* on the occasion of
Anlauf *m* run-up
an|laufen *unreg vi* to begin; (*Film*) to be showing; (*Fenster*) to mist up; (*Metall*) to tarnish
an|legen *vt* to put; (*anziehen*) to put on; (*gestalten*) to lay out; (*Geld*) to invest ▶ *vi* to dock; (*Naut*) to berth; **es auf etw** *akk* **~** to be out for sth/to do sth; **sich mit jdm ~** (*umg*) to quarrel with sb
Anlegestelle *f* mooring
an|lehnen *vt* to lean; (*Tür*) to leave ajar; **(sich) an etw** *akk* **~** to lean on *od* against sth
an|leiern (*umg*) *vt* to get going
Anleitung *f* instructions *pl*
Anliegen (**-s**, **-**) *nt* matter; (*Wunsch*) wish
Anlieger (**-s**, **-**) *m* resident; **~ frei** no thoroughfare – residents only
an|lügen *unreg vt* to lie to
an|machen *vt* to attach; (*einschalten*) to switch on; (*Salat*) to dress; **jdn ~** (*umg*) to turn sb on; (*umg*: *ansprechen*) to chat sb up (Brit), to come on to sb (*US*); (*umg*: *beschimpfen*) to have a go at sb
Anmeldeformular *nt* registration form
an|melden *vt* to announce ▶ *vr* (*sich ankündigen*) to make an appointment; (*polizeilich, für Kurs etc*) to register
Anmeldeschluss *m* deadline for applications, registration deadline
Anmeldung *f* registration; (*Antrag*) application
an|nähen *vt* to sew on
annähernd *adj* approximate, rough ▶ *adv* approximately; **nicht ~ so viel** not nearly as much
Annahme (**-**, **-n**) *f* acceptance; (*Vermutung*) assumption
annehmbar *adj* acceptable
an|nehmen *unreg vt* to accept; (*Namen*) to take; (*Kind*) to adopt; (*vermuten*) to suppose, to assume
Annonce (**-**, **-n**) *f* advertisement
annullieren *vt* to annul
an|öden (*umg*) *vt* to bore stiff
anonym *adj* anonymous
Anorak (**-s**, **-s**) *m* anorak
an|packen *vt* to grasp; (*fig*) to tackle; **mit ~** to lend a hand
an|passen *vt* (*fig*) to adapt ▶ *vr* to adapt
Anpfiff *m* (*Sport*) (starting) whistle; (*Spielbeginn*) kick-off; (*umg*: *Tadel*) roasting
an|probieren *vt* to try on
Anrede *f* form of address
an|reden *vt* to address
an|regen *vt* to stimulate
Anregung *f* stimulation; (*Vorschlag*) suggestion
Anreise *f* journey there/here
an|reisen *vi* to arrive

Anreiz *m* incentive
an|richten *vt* to serve up; **Unheil ~** to make mischief
Anruf *m* call
Anrufbeantworter *m* (telephone) answering machine, answerphone
an|rufen *unreg vt* to call out to; (*Tel*) to ring up, to phone, to call
ans = **an das**
Ansage *f* announcement
an|sagen *vt* to announce; **angesagt sein** to be recommended; (*modisch sein*) to be the in thing
an|schaffen *vt* to buy
an|schauen *vt* to look at
Anschein *m* appearance; **allem ~ nach** to all appearances; **den ~ haben** to seem, to appear
anscheinend *adv* apparently
an|schieben *unreg vt* (*Fahrzeug*) to push
Anschlag *m* notice; (*Attentat*) attack
an|schlagen *unreg vt* to put up; (*beschädigen*) to chip ▶ *vi* (*wirken*) to have an effect; **an etw** *akk* **~** to hit against sth
an|schließen *unreg vt* to connect up; (*in Steckdose*) to plug in ▶ *vi*: **an etw** *akk* **~** (*zeitlich*) to follow sth ▶ *vr*: **sich jdm/etw ~** to join sb/sth
anschließend *adj* adjacent; (*zeitlich*) subsequent ▶ *adv* afterwards; **~ an** *+akk* following
Anschluss *m* (*Elek, Eisenb, Tel*) connection; (*von Wasser etc*) supply; **im ~ an** *+akk* following; **kein ~ unter dieser Nummer** number unobtainable
Anschlussflug *m* connecting flight
an|schnallen *vt* to buckle on ▶ *vr* to fasten one's seat belt
Anschrift *f* address
an|schwellen *unreg vi* to swell (up)
an|sehen *unreg vt* to look at; **jdm etw ~** to see sth (from sb's face); **jdn/etw als etw ~** to look on sb/sth as sth
an sein *siehe* **an**
an|setzen *vt* (*festlegen*) to fix; (*zubereiten*) to prepare ▶ *vi* (*anfangen*) to start, to begin; **zu etw ~** to prepare to do sth
Ansicht *f* (*Anblick*) sight; (*Meinung*) view, opinion; **zur ~** on approval; **meiner ~ nach** in my opinion
Ansichtskarte *f* picture postcard
ansonsten *adv* otherwise
an|spielen *vi*: **auf etw** *akk* **~** to refer *od* allude to sth
Anspielung *f*: **~ (auf** *+akk***)** allusion (to)
an|sprechen *unreg vt* to speak to; (*bitten, gefallen*) to appeal to ▶ *vi*: **~ auf** *+akk* (*Patient*) to respond (to)
ansprechend *adj* attractive
Ansprechpartner *m* contact
an|springen *unreg vi* (*Aut*) to start
Anspruch (**-s**, **-sprüche**) *m* (*Recht*): **~ (auf** *+akk***)** claim (to); **jdn/etw in ~ nehmen** to occupy sb/take up sth
anspruchslos *adj* undemanding
anspruchsvoll *adj* demanding
Anstalt (**-**, **-en**) *f* institution
Anstand *m* decency
anständig *adj* decent; (*umg*) proper; (*groß*) considerable
an|starren *vt* to stare at
anstatt *präp +gen* instead of
an|stecken *vt* to pin on; (*Med*) to infect ▶ *vr*: **ich habe mich bei ihm angesteckt** I caught it from him ▶ *vi* (*fig*) to be infectious
ansteckend *adj* infectious
Ansteckungsgefahr *f* danger of infection
an|stehen *unreg vi* to queue (up) (Brit), to line up (*US*); (*Verhandlungspunkt*) to be on the agenda
anstelle, an Stelle *präp +gen* in place of
an|stellen *vt* (*einschalten*) to turn on; (*Arbeit geben*) to employ; (*umg: machen*) to do ▶ *vr* to queue (up) (Brit), to line up (*US*); **was hast du wieder angestellt?** what have you been up to now?
Anstoß *m* impetus; (*Sport*) kick-off
an|stoßen *unreg vt* to push; (*mit Fuß*) to kick ▶ *vi* to knock, to bump; **~ auf** *+akk* to drink (a toast) to
anstößig *adj* offensive, indecent
an|strengen *vt* to strain ▶ *vr* to make an effort
anstrengend *adj* tiring
Antarktis (**-**) *f* Antarctic
Anteil (**-s**, **-e**) *m* share; (*Mitgefühl*) sympathy; **~ nehmen an** *+dat* to share in; (*sich interessieren*) to take an interest in
Antenne (**-**, **-n**) *f* aerial
Antibabypille *f* (contraceptive) pill
Antibiotikum (**-s**, **-ka**) *nt* antibiotic
antik *adj* antique

Antilope (-, **-n**) *f* antelope
Antiquariat (**-(e)s**, **-e**) *nt* secondhand bookshop
Antiquitäten *pl* antiques *pl*
Antiquitätenhändler(in) *m(f)* antique dealer
Antiviren- *adj* (*Comput*) antivirus
Antivirensoftware *f* antivirus software
an|törnen (*umg*) *vt* to turn on
Antrag (**-(e)s**, **-träge**) *m* proposal; (*Parl*) motion; (*Gesuch*) application; **einen ~ auf etw** *akk* **stellen** to make an application for sth
an|treffen *unreg vt* to meet
an|treiben *unreg vt* to drive on; (*Motor*) to drive; (*anschwemmen*) to wash up; **jdn zur Eile/Arbeit ~** to urge sb to hurry up/to work
an|treten *unreg vt* (*Amt*) to take up; (*Reise*) to start, to begin
Antrieb *m* (*lit, fig*) drive; **aus eigenem ~** of one's own accord
an|tun *unreg vt*: **jdm etw ~** to do sth to sb; **sich** *dat* **etwas ~** (*Selbstmord begehen*) to kill oneself
Antwort (-, **-en**) *f* answer, reply; **um ~ wird gebeten** RSVP
antworten *vi* to answer, to reply
an|vertrauen *vt*: **jdm etw ~** to entrust sb with sth
Anwalt (**-(e)s**, **-wälte**) *m* lawyer
Anwältin *f* lawyer
an|weisen *unreg vt* to instruct; (*zuteilen*) to assign
Anweisung *f* instruction; (*Postanweisung, Zahlungsanweisung*) money order
an|wenden *unreg vt* to use; (*Gesetz, Regel*) to apply
Anwender(in) (**-s**, **-**) *m(f)* user
Anwendung *f* use; (*auch Comput*) application
anwesend *adj* present
Anwesenheit *f* presence
an|widern *vt* to disgust
Anwohner(in) (**-s**, **-**) *m(f)* resident
Anzahl *f*: **~ (an** *+dat***)** number (of)
an|zahlen *vt*: **100 Euro ~** to pay 100 euros as a deposit
Anzahlung *f* deposit
Anzeichen *nt* sign
Anzeige (-, **-n**) *f* (*Werbung*) advertisement; (*Comput*) display; (*bei Polizei*) report
an|zeigen *vt* (*zu erkennen geben*) to show; (*bekannt geben*) to announce; (*bei Polizei*) to report
an|ziehen *unreg vt* to attract; (*Kleidung*) to put on; (*Schraube, Seil*) to pull tight ▶ *vr* to get dressed
anziehend *adj* attractive
Anzug *m* suit
anzüglich *adj* (*anstößig*) offensive
an|zünden *vt* to light
an|zweifeln *vt* to doubt
Aperitif (**-s**, **-s** *od* **-e**) *m* aperitif
Apfel (**-s**, **Äpfel**) *m* apple
Apfelmus *nt* apple purée
Apfelsaft *m* apple juice
Apfelsine (-, **-n**) *f* orange
Apfelwein *m* cider
Apostroph (**-s**, **-e**) *m* apostrophe
Apotheke (-, **-n**) *f* pharmacy, chemist's (shop) (BRIT)
Apotheker(in) (**-s**, **-**) *m(f)* pharmacist, (dispensing) chemist (BRIT)
App (**-s**) *f* app
Apparat (**-(e)s**, **-e**) *m* piece of apparatus; (*Fotoapparat*) camera; (*Telefon*) telephone; (*Rundf, TV*) set; **am ~** (*als Antwort*) speaking; **am ~ bleiben** to hold the line
Appartement (**-s**, **-s**) *nt* flat (BRIT), apartment (*bes US*)
Appetit (**-(e)s**, **-e**) *m* appetite; **guten ~!** enjoy your meal
appetitlich *adj* appetizing
Applaus (**-es**, **-e**) *m* applause
Aprikose (-, **-n**) *f* apricot
April (**-(s)**, **-e**) (*pl selten*) *m* April; *siehe auch* **September**
apropos *adv* by the way
Aquaplaning (**-(s)**) *nt* aquaplaning
Aquarell (**-s**, **-e**) *nt* watercolour (BRIT), watercolor (US)
Aquarium *nt* aquarium
Äquator (**-s**) *m* equator
Araber(in) (**-s**, **-**) *m(f)* Arab
arabisch *adj* Arab; (*Arabien betreffend*) Arabian; (*Sprache*): **auf A~** in Arabic
Arbeit (-, **-en**) *f* work; (*Stelle*) job; (*Erzeugnis*) piece of work
arbeiten *vi* to work
Arbeiter(in) (**-s**, **-**) *m(f)* worker; (*ungelernt*) labourer (BRIT), laborer (US)
Arbeitgeber (**-s**, **-**) *m* employer
Arbeitnehmer (**-s**, **-**) *m* employee
Arbeits- *in zW* labour (BRIT), labor (US)
Arbeitsagentur *f* job agency

Arbeitsamt *nt* employment exchange, Job Centre (BRIT)
Arbeitserlaubnis *f* work permit
arbeitslos *adj* unemployed
Arbeitslose(r) *f(m)* unemployed person; **die Arbeitslosen** *pl* the unemployed *pl*
Arbeitslosengeld *nt* unemployment benefit
Arbeitslosenhilfe *f* unemployment benefit
Arbeitslosigkeit *f* unemployment
Arbeitsplatz *m* place of work; (*Stelle*) job
Arbeitsspeicher *m* (*Comput*) main memory
Arbeitszeit *f* working hours *pl*
Arbeitszimmer *nt* study
Archäologe (**-n**, **-n**) *m* arch(a)eologist
Archäologin *f* arch(a)eologist
Architekt(in) (**-en**, **-en**) *m(f)* architect
Architektur *f* architecture
Archiv (**-s**, **-e**) *nt* archive
ARD *f abk* (= *Arbeitsgemeinschaft der öffentlich-rechtlichen Rundfunkanstalten der Bundesrepublik Deutschland*) *German broadcasting corporation*
arg *adj* bad, awful ▸ *adv* awfully, very
Argentinien (**-s**) *nt* Argentina, the Argentine
Ärger (**-s**) *m* (*Wut*) anger; (*Unannehmlichkeit*) trouble
ärgerlich *adj* (*zornig*) angry; (*lästig*) annoying
ärgern *vt* to annoy ▸ *vr* to get annoyed
Argument *nt* argument
Arktis (-) *f* Arctic
arm *adj* poor
Arm (**-(e)s**, **-e**) *m* arm; (*Flussarm*) branch
Armaturenbrett *nt* instrument panel; (*Aut*) dashboard
Armband *nt* bracelet
Armbanduhr *f* (wrist) watch
Armee (-, **-n**) *f* army
Ärmel (**-s**, -) *m* sleeve
Ärmelkanal *m* (English) Channel
Armut (-) *f* poverty
Aroma (**-s**, **Aromen**) *nt* aroma
arrogant *adj* arrogant
Arsch (**-es**, **Ärsche**) (!) *m* arse (BRIT), ass (*US*)
Arschloch (!) *nt* (*Mensch*) arsehole (BRIT !), asshole (*US* !)
Art (-, **-en**) *f* (*Weise*) way; (*Sorte*) kind, sort; (*Biol*) species; **auf diese ~ und Weise** in this way; **es ist nicht seine ~, das zu tun** it's not like him to do that; **Schnitzel nach ~ des Hauses** chef's special escalope
Arterie *f* artery
artig *adj* good, well-behaved
Artikel (**-s**, -) *m* article
Artischocke (-, **-n**) *f* artichoke
Artist(in) (**-en**, **-en**) *m(f)* (circus) performer
Arznei *f* medicine
Arzt (**-es**, **Ärzte**) *m* doctor
Arzthelfer(in) *m(f)* doctor's assistant
Ärztin *f* doctor
ärztlich *adj* medical
Asche (-, **-n**) *f* ash
Aschenbecher *m* ashtray
Aschermittwoch *m* Ash Wednesday
Asiat(in) (**-en**, **-en**) *m(f)* Asian
asiatisch *adj* Asian, Asiatic
Asien (**-s**) *nt* Asia
Aspekt (**-(e)s**, **-e**) *m* aspect
Asphalt (**-(e)s**, **-e**) *m* asphalt
Ass (**-es**, **-e**) *nt* ace
aß *vb siehe* **essen**
Assistent(in) (**-en**, **-en**) *m(f)* assistant
Ast (**-(e)s**, **Äste**) *m* branch
Asthma (**-s**) *nt* asthma
Astrologie *f* astrology
Astronaut(in) (**-en**, **-en**) *m(f)* astronaut
Astronomie *f* astronomy
Asyl (**-s**, **-e**) *nt* asylum; (*Heim*) home; (*Obdachlosenasyl*) shelter
Asylant(in) (**-en**, **-en**) *m(f)* asylum seeker
Atelier (**-s**, **-s**) *nt* studio
Atem (**-s**) *m* breath
atemberaubend *adj* breathtaking
Atembeschwerden *pl* breathing difficulties *pl*
atemlos *adj* breathless
Atempause *f* breather
Athen (**-s**) *nt* Athens
Äthiopien (**-s**) *nt* Ethiopia
Athlet(in) (**-en**, **-en**) *m(f)* athlete
Athletik *f* athletics *sing*
Atlantik (**-s**) *m* Atlantic
Atlas (- *od* **-ses**, **-se** *od* **Atlanten**) *m* atlas
atmen *vt, vi* to breathe
Atmung *f* respiration
Atom (**-s**, **-e**) *nt* atom
Atombombe *f* atom bomb
Atomkraftwerk *nt* nuclear power station

Atommüll *m* nuclear waste
Atomwaffen *pl* nuclear *od* atomic weapons *pl*
Attentat (**-(e)s**, **-e**) *nt*: **~ (auf** *+akk***)** (attempted) assassination (of)
Attest (**-(e)s**, **-e**) *nt* certificate
attraktiv *adj* attractive
Attrappe (**-**, **-n**) *f* dummy
ätzend *adj* (*umg*: *furchtbar*) dreadful, horrible; (: *toll*) magic
Aubergine (**-**, **-n**) *f* aubergine, eggplant (*US*)

SCHLÜSSELWORT

auch *adv* **1** (*ebenfalls*) also, too, as well; **das ist auch schön** that's nice too *od* as well; **er kommt — ich auch** he's coming — so am I, me too; **auch nicht** not … either; **ich auch nicht** nor I, me neither; **oder auch** or; **auch das noch!** not that as well!
2 (*selbst*, *sogar*) even; **auch wenn das Wetter schlecht ist** even if the weather is bad; **ohne auch nur zu fragen** without even asking
3 (*wirklich*) really; **du siehst müde aus — bin ich auch** you look tired — (so) I am; **so sieht es auch aus** (and) that's what it looks like
4 (*auch immer*): **wer auch** whoever; **was auch** whatever; **wie dem auch sei** be that as it may; **wie sehr er sich auch bemühte** however much he tried

audiovisuell *adj* audiovisual

SCHLÜSSELWORT

auf *präp +dat* (*wo?*) on; **auf dem Tisch** on the table; **auf der Reise** on the way; **auf der Post/dem Fest** at the post office/party; **auf der Straße** on the road; **auf dem Land/der ganzen Welt** in the country/the whole world
▶ *präp +akk* **1** (*wohin?*) on(to); **auf den Tisch** on(to) the table; **auf die Post gehen** to go to the post office; **auf das Land** into the country; **etw auf einen Zettel schreiben** to write sth on a piece of paper
2: **auf Deutsch** in German; **auf Lebenszeit** for my/his lifetime; **bis auf ihn** except for him; **auf einmal** at once; **auf seinen Vorschlag (hin)** at his suggestion
▶ *adv* **1** (*offen*) open; **auf sein** to be open; **das Fenster ist auf** the window is open
2 (*hinauf*) up; **auf und ab** up and down; **auf und davon** up and away; **auf!** (*los!*) come on!
3 (*aufgestanden*) up; **auf sein** to be up; **ist er schon auf?** is he up yet?
▶ *konj*: **auf dass** (so) that

auf|atmen *vi* to heave a sigh of relief
auf|bauen *vt* to erect, to build (up); (*gestalten*) to construct; (*gründen*): **~ (auf** *+dat***)** to found (on) ▶ *vr*: **sich vor jdm ~** to draw o.s. up to one's full height in front of sb; **sich eine Existenz ~** to make a life for oneself
auf|bewahren *vt* to keep
auf|bleiben *unreg vi* (*Laden*) to remain open; (*Person*) to stay up
auf|blenden *vt* (*Scheinwerfer*) to turn on full beam
auf|brechen *unreg vt* to break open ▶ *vi* to burst open; (*gehen*) to start, to set off
auf|drängen *vt*: **jdm etw ~** to force sth on sb ▶ *vr*: **sich jdm ~** to intrude on sb
aufdringlich *adj* pushy
aufeinander *adv* on top of one another; (*vertrauen*) each other
aufeinander|folgen *vi* to follow one another
aufeinander|prallen *vi* (*Autos etc*) to collide; (*Truppen*, *Meinungen*) to clash
Aufenthalt *m* stay; (*Eisenb*) stop
Aufenthaltserlaubnis *f*, **Aufenthaltsgenehmigung** *f* residence permit
Aufenthaltsraum *m* day room; (*in Betrieb*) recreation room
auf|essen *unreg vt* to eat up
auf|fahren *unreg vi* (*herankommen*) to draw up; (*wütend werden*) to flare up; **~ auf** *+akk* (*Auto*) to run *od* crash into
Auffahrt *f* (*Hausauffahrt*) drive; (*Autobahnauffahrt*) slip road (Brit), entrance ramp (*US*)
Auffahrunfall *m* pile-up
auf|fallen *unreg vi* to be noticeable; **jdm ~** to strike sb; **das fällt gar nicht auf** nobody will notice
auffallend *adj* striking
auffällig *adj* conspicuous, striking

auf|fangen *unreg vt* to catch; (*Aufprall etc*) to cushion
auf|fassen *vt* to understand
Auffassung *f* (*Meinung*) opinion; (*Auslegung*) view; (*auch:* **Auffassungsgabe**) grasp
auf|fordern *vt* (*befehlen*) to call upon; (*bitten*) to ask
auf|frischen *vt* to freshen up; (*Kenntnisse*) to brush up
auf|führen *vt* (*Theat*) to perform; (*in einem Verzeichnis*) to list ▶ *vr* (*sich benehmen*) to behave
Aufführung *f* (*Theat*) performance
Aufgabe (**-**, **-n**) *f* task; (*Sch*) exercise; (*Hausaufgabe*) homework
Aufgang *m* (*Treppe*) staircase
auf|geben *unreg vt* (*verzichten auf*) to give up; (*Paket*) to send, to post; (*Gepäck*) to register; (*Bestellung*) to give; (*Inserat*) to insert; (*Rätsel, Problem*) to set ▶ *vi* to give up
auf|gehen *unreg vi* (*Sonne, Teig*) to rise; (*sich öffnen*) to open; (*klar werden*) to become clear
aufgelegt *adj*: **gut/schlecht ~ sein** to be in a good/bad mood
aufgeregt *adj* excited
aufgeschlossen *adj* open, open-minded
aufgeschmissen (*umg*) *adj* in a fix
aufgrund, auf Grund *präp +gen*: **~ von** on the basis of; (*wegen*) because of
auf|haben *unreg vt* (*Hut etc*) to have on; (*Arbeit*) to have to do
auf|halten *unreg vt* (*Person*) to detain; (*Entwicklung*) to check; (*Tür, Hand*) to hold open; (*Augen*) to keep open ▶ *vr* (*wohnen*) to live; (*bleiben*) to stay
auf|hängen *unreg vt* to hang up
auf|heben *unreg vt* (*hochheben*) to raise, to lift; (*aufbewahren*) to keep
Aufheiterungen *pl* (*Met*) bright periods *pl*
auf|holen *vt* (*Zeit*) to make up ▶ *vi* to catch up
auf|hören *vi* to stop; **~, etw zu tun** to stop doing sth
auf|klären *vt* (*Geheimnis etc*) to clear up; (*Person*) to enlighten; (*sexuell*) to tell the facts of life to
Aufkleber (**-s**, **-**) *m* sticker
auf|kommen *unreg vi* (*Wind*) to come up; (*Zweifel, Gefühl*) to arise; (*Mode*) to start; **für den Schaden ~** to pay for the damage
auf|laden *unreg vt* to load; (*Handy etc*) to charge; (*Handykarte etc*) to top up
Auflage *f* edition; (*Zeitung*) circulation; (*Bedingung*) condition
auf|lassen *unreg* (*umg*) *vt* (*Hut, Brille*) to keep on; (*Tür*) to leave open
Auflauf *m* (*Koch*) pudding; (*Menschenauflauf*) crowd
auf|legen *vt* to put on; (*Hörer*) to put down ▶ *vi* (*Tel*) to hang up
auf|leuchten *vi* to light up
auf|lösen *vt* to dissolve; (*Konto*) to close; (*Firma*) to wind up
Auflösung *f* dissolving; (*von Rätsel*) solution; (*von Bildschirm*) resolution
auf|machen *vt* to open; (*Kleidung*) to undo ▶ *vr* to set out
aufmerksam *adj* attentive; **jdn auf etw** *akk* **~ machen** to point sth out to sb
Aufmerksamkeit *f* attention, attentiveness; (*Geschenk*) token (gift)
auf|muntern *vt* (*ermutigen*) to encourage; (*erheitern*) to cheer up
Aufnahme (**-**, **-n**) *f* (*Beginn*) beginning; (*in Verein etc*) admission; (*Phot*) shot; (*auf Tonband etc*) recording
Aufnahmeprüfung *f* entrance test
auf|nehmen *unreg vt* (*beginnen*) to take up; (*in Verein etc*) to admit; (*in Liste etc*) to include; (*begreifen*) to take in
auf|passen *vi* (*aufmerksam sein*) to pay attention; (*vorsichtig sein*) to take care; **auf jdn/etw ~** to look after *od* watch sb/sth
Aufprall (**-(e)s**, **-e**) *m* impact
auf|prallen *vi*: **auf etw** *akk* **~** to hit sth, to crash into sth
Aufpreis *m* extra charge
auf|pumpen *vt* to pump up
Aufputschmittel *nt* stimulant
auf|räumen *vt, vi* (*Dinge*) to clear away; (*Zimmer*) to tidy up
aufrecht *adj* (*lit, fig*) upright
auf|regen *vt* to excite; (*ärgerlich machen*) to irritate, to annoy ▶ *vr* to get excited
aufregend *adj* exciting
Aufregung *f* excitement
auf|reißen *unreg vt* (*Umschlag*) to tear open; (*Augen*) to open wide; (*Tür*) to throw open; (*umg: Mädchen*) to pick up

Aufruf *m* call

auf|rufen *unreg vt* (*Namen*) to call out; (*auffordern*): **jdn ~ (zu)** to call upon sb (for)

auf|runden *vt* (*Summe*) to round up

aufs = **auf das**

Aufsatz *m* essay

auf|schieben *unreg vt* (*verzögern*) to put off, to postpone

Aufschlag *m* (*Ärmelaufschlag*) cuff; (*Preisaufschlag*) surcharge; (*Tennis*) service

auf|schlagen *unreg vt* (*öffnen*) to open; (*verwunden*) to cut; (*Zelt, Lager*) to pitch, to erect ▸ *vi* (*aufprallen*) to hit; (*teurer werden*) to go up; (*Tennis*) to serve

auf|schließen *unreg vt* to open up ▸ *vi* (*aufrücken*) to close up

auf|schneiden *unreg vt* to cut open; (*Brot*) to cut up ▸ *vi* (*umg*) to brag

Aufschnitt *m* (slices of) cold meat

auf|schreiben *unreg vt* to write down

Aufschrift *f* inscription; (*Etikett*) label

Aufschub (**-(e)s**, **-schübe**) *m* delay, postponement

Aufsehen (**-s**) *nt* stir; **großes ~ erregen** to cause a sensation

Aufseher(in) (**-s**, **-**) *m(f)* guard; (*im Betrieb*) supervisor; (*Museumsaufseher*) attendant; (*Parkaufseher*) keeper

auf sein *siehe* **auf**

auf|setzen *vt* to put on; (*Dokument*) to draw up ▸ *vi* (*Flugzeug*) to touch down

Aufsicht *f* supervision; **die ~ haben** to be in charge; **bei einer Prüfung ~ führen** to invigilate (BRIT) *od* supervise an exam

auf|spannen *vt* (*Schirm*) to put up

auf|sperren *vt* (*Mund*) to open wide

auf|springen *unreg vi* (*hochspringen*) to jump up; (*sich öffnen*) to spring open; **~ auf** *+akk* to jump onto

auf|stehen *unreg vi* to get up; (*Tür*) to be open

auf|stellen *vt* (*aufrecht stellen*) to put up; (*aufreihen*) to line up; (*Programm etc*) to draw up; (*leisten*: *Rekord*) to set up

Aufstieg (**-(e)s**, **-e**) *m* (*auf Berg*) ascent; (*Fortschritt*) rise; (*beruflich, Sport*) promotion

Aufstrich *m* spread

auf|tanken *vi* to get petrol (BRIT) *od* gas (US) ▸ *vt* to refuel

auf|tauchen *vi* to turn up; (*aus Wasser etc*) to emerge; (*Zweifel*) to arise

auf|tauen *vi* to thaw; (*fig*) to relax

Auftrag (**-(e)s**, **-träge**) *m* order; (*Anweisung*) commission; (*Aufgabe*) mission; **im ~ von** on behalf of

auf|tragen *unreg vt* (*Essen*) to serve; (*Farbe*) to put on

auf|treten *unreg vi* to appear; (*sich verhalten*) to behave; (*fig*: *eintreten*) to occur

Auftritt *m* (*von Schauspieler*) entrance; (*lit, fig*: *Szene*) scene

auf|wachen *vi* to wake up

auf|wachsen *unreg vi* to grow up

Aufwand (**-(e)s**) *m* expenditure; (*Kosten*) expense

aufwändig *adj, adv* costly

auf|wärmen *vt* to warm up

aufwärts *adv* upwards; **es geht ~** things are looking up

auf|wecken *vt* to wake(n) up

aufwendig *adj, adv* costly

auf|wischen *vt* to wipe up

auf|zählen *vt* to count out

auf|zeichnen *vt* to sketch; (*schriftlich*) to jot down; (*auf Band*) to record

Aufzeichnung *f* (*schriftlich*) note; (*Tonbandaufzeichnung, Filmaufzeichnung*) recording

auf|ziehen *unreg vt* (*öffnen*) to pull open; (*Uhr*) to wind; (*Kinder*) to raise, to bring up; (*Tiere*) to rear; (*umg*: *necken*) to tease ▸ *vi* (*Gewitter, Wolken*) to gather

Aufzug *m* (*Fahrstuhl*) lift (BRIT), elevator (US); (*Kleidung*) get-up; (*Theat*) act

Auge (**-s**, **-n**) *nt* eye; **unter vier Augen** in private; **das kann leicht ins ~ gehen** (*fig*: *umg*) it might easily go wrong

Augenarzt *m* eye specialist

Augenärztin *f* eye specialist

Augenblick *m* moment; **im ~** at the moment

Augenbraue *f* eyebrow

Augenbrauenstift *m* eyebrow pencil

Augenoptiker(in) *m(f)* optician

Augentropfen *pl* eyedrops *pl*

Augenzeuge *m* eye witness

Augenzeugin *f* eye witness

August (**-(e)s** *od* **-**, **-e**) (*pl selten*) *m* August; *siehe auch* **September**

Auktion *f* auction

SCHLÜSSELWORT

aus *präp +dat* **1** (*räumlich*) out of
2 (*von ... her*) from; **er ist aus Berlin** he's from Berlin; **aus dem Fenster** out of the window
3 (*gemacht/hergestellt aus*) made of; **ein Herz aus Stein** a heart of stone
4 (*auf Ursache deutend*) out of; **aus Mitleid** out of sympathy; **aus Erfahrung** from experience; **aus Spaß** for fun
5: **aus ihr wird nie etwas** she'll never get anywhere
▶ *adv* **1** (*zu Ende*) finished, over; **aus sein** to be over; **aus und vorbei** over and done with
2 (*ausgeschaltet, ausgezogen*) off; **aus sein** to be out; **Licht aus!** lights out!
3 (*in Verbindung mit von*): **von Rom aus** from Rome; **vom Fenster aus** out of the window; **von sich aus** (*selbstständig*) of one's own accord; **von mir aus** as far as I'm concerned

Aus (-) *nt* (*Sport*) outfield; **ins ~ gehen** to go out
aus|atmen *vi* to breathe out
aus|bauen *vt* to extend; (*herausnehmen*) to take out, to remove
aus|bessern *vt* to mend, to repair
aus|bilden *vt* to educate; (*Lehrling, Soldat*) to instruct, to train; (*Fähigkeiten*) to develop
Ausbildung *f* education; (*von Lehrling, Soldat*) training, instruction; (*von Fähigkeiten*) development
Ausblick *m* (*lit, fig*) outlook, view
aus|brechen *unreg vi* to break out ▶ *vt* to break off; **in Tränen/Gelächter ~** to burst into tears/out laughing
aus|breiten *vt* to spread (out); (*Arme*) to stretch out ▶ *vr* to spread
Ausbruch *m* outbreak; (*von Vulkan*) eruption; (*Gefühlsausbruch*) outburst; (*von Gefangenen*) escape
aus|buhen *vt* to boo
Ausdauer *f* stamina; (*Beharrlichkeit*) perseverance
aus|dehnen *vt, vr* to stretch; (*Nebel, fig: Macht*) to extend
aus|denken *unreg vt*: **sich** *dat* **etw ~** to think sth up
Ausdruck (**-s, -drücke**) *m* expression; (*Comput*) hard copy
aus|drucken *vt* (*Text*) to print out
aus|drücken *vt* (*auch vr: formulieren, zeigen*) to express; (*Zigarette*) to put out; (*Zitrone*) to squeeze
ausdrücklich *adj* express, explicit ▶ *adv* expressly
auseinander *adv* (*getrennt*) apart; **weit ~** far apart
auseinander|gehen *unreg vi* (*Menschen*) to separate; (*Meinungen*) to differ; (*Gegenstand*) to fall apart
auseinander|halten *unreg vt* to tell apart
auseinander|setzen *unreg vt* to set forth, to explain ▶ *vr* (*sich befassen*) to concern o.s.; **sich mit jdm ~** (*sich streiten*) to argue with sb
Auseinandersetzung *f* argument
Ausfahrt *f* (*des Zuges etc*) leaving, departure; (*Autobahnausfahrt, Garagenausfahrt*) exit
aus|fallen *unreg vi* (*Zähne, Haare*) to fall *od* come out; (*nicht stattfinden*) to be cancelled; (*nicht funktionieren*) to break down; (*Resultat haben*) to turn out
ausfindig *adj*: **~ machen** to discover
aus|flippen (*umg*) *vi* to freak out
Ausflug *m* excursion, outing
Ausfluss *m* (*Med*) discharge
aus|fragen *vt* to interrogate, to question
Ausfuhr (**-, -en**) *f* export
aus|führen *vt* (*verwirklichen*) to carry out; (*Person*) to take out; (*Comm*) to export; (*erklären*) to give details of
ausführlich *adj* detailed ▶ *adv* in detail
aus|füllen *vt* to fill up; (*Fragebogen etc*) to fill in
Ausgabe *f* (*Geld*) expenditure; (*Buch*) edition; (*Nummer*) issue
Ausgang *m* way out, exit; (*Ende*) end; (*Ergebnis*) result; **kein ~** no exit
aus|geben *unreg vt* (*Geld*) to spend; (*austeilen*) to issue, to distribute ▶ *vr*: **sich für etw/jdn ~** to pass o.s. off as sth/sb
ausgebucht *adj* fully booked
ausgefallen *adj* (*ungewöhnlich*) exceptional
aus|gehen *unreg vi* (*auch Feuer, Ofen, Licht*) to go out; (*Benzin*) to run out; (*Haare, Zähne*) to fall *od* come out; (*Resultat haben*) to turn out; **mir ging**

das Benzin aus I ran out of petrol (BRIT) *od* gas (*US*); **wir können davon ~, dass ...** we can proceed from the assumption that ...
ausgelassen *adj* exuberant
ausgeleiert *adj* worn
ausgenommen *konj* except
ausgerechnet *adv* just, precisely; **~ du** you of all people; **~ heute** today of all days
ausgeschlossen *pp von* **ausschließen** ▶ *adj* (*unmöglich*) impossible, out of the question
ausgesprochen *adj* (*Faulheit, Lüge etc*) out-and-out; (*unverkennbar*) marked ▶ *adv* decidedly; **~ gut** really good
ausgezeichnet *adj* excellent
ausgiebig *adj* (*Gebrauch*) full, good; (*Essen*) generous, lavish
aus|gießen *unreg vt* (*aus einem Behälter*) to pour out; (*Behälter*) to empty
aus|gleichen *unreg vt* to balance (out) ▶ *vi* (*Sport*) to equalize
Ausguss *m* (*Spüle*) sink; (*Abfluss*) outlet
aus|halten *unreg vt* to bear, to stand ▶ *vi* to hold out; **das ist nicht zum A~** that is unbearable
aus|händigen *vt*: **jdm etw ~** to hand sth over to sb
Aushang *m* notice
Aushilfe *f* help; (*Person*) (temporary) worker
aus|kennen *unreg vr* to know a lot; (*an einem Ort*) to know one's way about
aus|kommen *unreg vi*: **mit jdm ~** to get on with sb; **mit etw ~** to get by with sth
Auskunft (**-**, **-künfte**) *f* information; (*nähere*) details *pl*; (*Stelle*) information office; (*Tel*) inquiries
aus|lachen *vt* to laugh at
aus|laden *unreg vt* to unload; (*umg: Gäste*) to cancel an invitation to
Auslage *f* shop window (display)
Auslagen *pl* outlay *sing*, expenditure *sing*
Ausland *nt* foreign countries *pl*; **im ~** abroad; **ins ~** abroad
Ausländer(in) (**-s**, **-**) *m*(*f*) foreigner
ausländerfeindlich *adj* hostile to foreigners, xenophobic
ausländisch *adj* foreign
Auslandsgespräch *nt* international call
Auslandsschutzbrief *m* international travel cover
aus|lassen *unreg vt* to leave out; (*Wort etc*) to omit ▶ *vr*: **sich über etw** *akk* **~** to speak one's mind about sth
aus|laufen *unreg vi* to run out; (*Behälter*) to leak; (*Naut*) to put out (to sea); (*langsam aufhören*) to run down
aus|legen *vt* (*Waren*) to lay out; (*Geld*) to lend; (*Text etc*) to interpret
aus|leihen *unreg vt* (*verleihen*) to lend; **sich** *dat* **etw ~** to borrow sth
aus|loggen *vi, vr* (*Comput*) to log out *od* off
aus|lösen *vt* (*Explosion, Schuss*) to set off; (*hervorrufen*) to cause
Auslöser (**-s**, **-**) *m* (*Phot*) release
aus|machen *vt* (*Licht, Radio*) to turn off; (*Feuer*) to put out; (*vereinbaren*) to agree; (*Anteil darstellen, betragen*) to represent; (*bedeuten*) to matter; **das macht ihm nichts aus** it doesn't matter to him; **macht es Ihnen etwas aus, wenn ...?** would you mind if ...?
Ausmaß *nt* dimension; (*fig*) scale
Ausnahme (**-**, **-n**) *f* exception
ausnahmsweise *adv* by way of exception, for once
aus|nutzen *vt* (*Zeit, Gelegenheit*) to use; (*Mensch, Gutmütigkeit*) to exploit
aus|packen *vt* to unpack
aus|probieren *vt* to try (out)
Auspuff (**-(e)s**, **-e**) *m* (*Tech*) exhaust
Auspuffrohr *nt* exhaust (pipe)
Auspufftopf *m* (*Aut*) silencer (BRIT), muffler (*US*)
aus|rauben *vt* to rob
aus|räumen *vt* (*Dinge*) to clear away; (*Schrank, Zimmer*) to empty; (*Bedenken*) to put aside
aus|rechnen *vt* to calculate
Ausrede *f* excuse
aus|reden *vi* to have one's say ▶ *vt*: **jdm etw ~** to talk sb out of sth
ausreichend *adj* sufficient, adequate; (*Sch*) adequate
Ausreise *f* departure; **bei der ~** when leaving the country
Ausreiseerlaubnis *f* exit visa
aus|reisen *vi* to leave the country
aus|reißen *unreg vt* to tear *od* pull out ▶ *vi* (*Riss bekommen*) to tear; (*umg*) to make off
aus|renken *vt* to dislocate
aus|richten *vt* (*Botschaft*) to deliver; (*Gruß*) to pass on; **etwas/nichts bei**

jdm ~ to get somewhere/nowhere with sb; **ich werde es ihm ~** I'll tell him
aus|rufen *unreg vt* to cry out; **jdn ~ (lassen)** (*über Lautsprecher etc*) to page sb
Ausrufezeichen *nt* exclamation mark
aus|ruhen *vt, vi, vr* to rest
Ausrüstung *f* equipment
aus|rutschen *vi* to slip
aus|schalten *vt* to switch off; (*fig*) to eliminate
Ausschau *f*: **~ halten (nach)** to look out (for), to watch (for)
aus|scheiden *unreg vt* (*Med*) to excrete ▶ *vi*: **~ (aus)** to leave; (*aus einem Amt*) to retire (from); (*Sport*) to be eliminated (from)
aus|schlafen *unreg vi, vr* to have a lie-in ▶ *vt* to sleep off
Ausschlag *m* (*Med*) rash; **den ~ geben** (*fig*) to tip the balance
aus|schlagen *unreg vt* to knock out; (*verweigern*) to decline ▶ *vi* (*Pferd*) to kick out
ausschlaggebend *adj* decisive
aus|schließen *unreg vt* to shut *od* lock out; (*fig*) to exclude
ausschließlich *adv* exclusively ▶ *präp +gen* excluding, exclusive of
Ausschnitt *m* (*Teil*) section; (*von Kleid*) neckline; (*Zeitungsausschnitt*) cutting (BRIT), clipping (US)
Ausschreitung *f* (*geh*) excess ■ **Ausschreitungen** *pl* riots *pl*
aus|schütten *vt* to pour out; (*Eimer*) to empty
aus|sehen *unreg vi* to look; **gut ~** to look good/well; **es sieht nach Regen aus** it looks like rain; **es sieht schlecht aus** things look bad
aus sein *siehe* **aus**
außen *adv* outside; (*nach außen*) outwards; **~ ist es rot** it's red (on the) outside
Außenbordmotor *m* outboard motor
Außenminister(in) *m(f)* foreign minister
Außenseite *f* outside
Außenseiter(in) **(-s, -)** *m(f)* outsider
Außenspiegel *m* (*Aut*) outside mirror
außer *präp +dat* (*räumlich*) out of; (*abgesehen von*) except ▶ *konj* (*ausgenommen*) except; **~ Gefahr sein** to be out of danger; **~ Betrieb** out of order; **~ sich** *dat* **sein/geraten** to be beside o.s.; **~ wenn** unless; **~ dass** except
außerdem *konj* besides
äußere(r, s) *adj* outer, external
außergewöhnlich *adj* unusual
außerhalb *präp +gen* outside
äußerlich *adj* external
äußern *vt* to utter, to express; (*zeigen*) to show ▶ *vr* to give one's opinion; (*sich zeigen*) to show itself
außerordentlich *adj* extraordinary
außerplanmäßig *adj* unscheduled
äußerst *adv* extremely
äußerste(r, s) *adj* utmost; (*räumlich*) farthest; (*Termin*) last possible
Äußerung *f* remark
aus|setzen *vt* (*Kind, Tier*) to abandon; (*Belohnung*) to offer ▶ *vi* (*aufhören*) to stop; (*Pause machen*) to have a break; **was haben Sie daran auszusetzen?** what's your objection to it?
Aussicht *f* view; (*in Zukunft*) prospect
aussichtslos *adj* hopeless
Aussichtsturm *m* observation tower
Aussiedler(in) **(-s, -)** *m(f)* (*Auswanderer*) emigrant
aus|spannen *vi* (*erholen*) to relax ▶ *vt* to spread *od* stretch out; **er hat ihm die Freundin ausgespannt** (*umg*) he's nicked his girlfriend
aus|sperren *vt* to lock out
Aussprache *f* pronunciation; (*Unterredung*) (frank) discussion
aus|sprechen *unreg vt* to pronounce; (*äußern*) to say, to express ▶ *vr*: **sich ~ (über** *+akk***)** to speak (about) ▶ *vi* (*zu Ende sprechen*) to finish speaking
aus|spülen *vt* to rinse
Ausstattung *f* (*Kleidung*) outfit; (*Aufmachung*) make-up; (*Einrichtung*) furnishing
aus|stehen *unreg vt* to stand, to endure ▶ *vi* (*noch nicht da sein*) to be outstanding; **ich kann ihn nicht ~** I can't stand him
aus|steigen *unreg vi* to get out; **aus der Gesellschaft ~** to drop out (of society)
Aussteiger(in) (*umg*) *m(f)* dropout
aus|stellen *vt* to exhibit, to display; (*umg: ausschalten*) to switch off; (*Rechnung etc*) to make out; (*Pass, Zeugnis*) to issue
Ausstellung *f* exhibition
aus|sterben *unreg vi* to die out

aus|strahlen *vt, vi* to radiate; (*Rundf*) to broadcast
Ausstrahlung *f* (*Rundf, TV*) broadcast; (*fig*) charisma
aus|strecken *vt, vr* to stretch out
aus|suchen *vt* to select
Austausch *m* exchange
aus|tauschen *vt* to exchange
aus|teilen *vt* to distribute, to give out
Auster (**-, -n**) *f* oyster
aus|tragen *unreg vt* (*Post*) to deliver; (*Wettkämpfe*) to hold
Australien (**-s**) *nt* Australia
Australier(in) (**-s, -**) *m(f)* Australian
australisch *adj* Australian
aus|trinken *unreg vt* (*Glas*) to drain; (*Getränk*) to drink up ▶ *vi* to finish one's drink
aus|trocknen *vt, vi* to dry up
aus|üben *vt* (*Beruf*) to practise (BRIT), to practice (*US*); (*Einfluss*) to exert
Ausverkauf *m* sale
ausverkauft *adj* (*Karten, Artikel*) sold out
Auswahl *f*: **eine ~ (an** *+dat***)** a selection (of), a choice (of)
aus|wählen *vt* to select, to choose
aus|wandern *vi* to emigrate
auswärtig *adj* (*nicht am/vom Ort*) out-of-town; (*ausländisch*) foreign
auswärts *adv* outside; **~ spielen** to play away
Auswärtsspiel *nt* away game
aus|wechseln *vt* to replace; (*Sport*) to substitute
Ausweg *m* way out
aus|weichen *unreg vi*: **jdm/etw ~** (*lit*) to move aside *od* make way for sb/sth; (*fig*) to sidestep sb/sth; **jdm/einer Begegnung ~** to avoid sb/a meeting
Ausweis (**-es, -e**) *m* identity card; (*Pass*) passport; (*Mitgliedsausweis, Bibliotheksausweis etc*) card
aus|weisen *unreg vt* to expel ▶ *vr* to prove one's identity
Ausweiskontrolle *f* identity check
Ausweispapiere *pl* identity papers *pl*
auswendig *adv* by heart; **~ lernen** to learn by heart
aus|wuchten *vt* (*Aut*) to balance
aus|zahlen *vt* (*Lohn, Summe*) to pay out; (*Arbeiter*) to pay off ▶ *vr* (*sich lohnen*) to pay
aus|zeichnen *vt* to honour (BRIT), to honor (*US*); (*Comm*) to price ▶ *vr* to distinguish o.s.
aus|ziehen *unreg vt* (*Kleidung*) to take off ▶ *vr* to undress ▶ *vi* (*aus Wohnung*) to move out
Auszubildende(r) *f(m)* trainee; (*als Handwerker*) apprentice
Auto (**-s, -s**) *nt* (motor-)car, automobile (*US*); **~ fahren** to drive
Autoatlas *m* road atlas
Autobahn *f* motorway (BRIT), expressway (*US*)
Autobahnauffahrt *f* motorway access road (BRIT), on-ramp (*US*)
Autobahnausfahrt *f* motorway exit (BRIT), off-ramp (*US*)
Autobahnkreuz *nt* motorway (BRIT) *od* expressway (*US*) intersection
Autobombe *f* car bomb
Autofähre *f* car ferry
Autofahrer(in) *m(f)* motorist, driver
Autofahrt *f* drive
Autogramm *nt* autograph
Automat (**-en, -en**) *m* machine
Automatik *f* (*Aut*) automatic transmission
automatisch *adj* automatic
Automechaniker(in) *m(f)* car mechanic
Autor (**-s, -en**) *m* author
Autoradio *nt* car radio
Autoreifen *m* car tyre (BRIT) *od* tire (*US*)
Autoreisezug *m* motorail train
Autorennen *nt* motor race; (*Sportart*) motor racing
Autorin *f* authoress
Autoschlüssel *m* car key
Autotelefon *nt* car phone
Autounfall *m* car *od* motor accident
Autoverleih *m*, **Autovermietung** *f* car hire (BRIT) *od* rental (*US*)
Axt (**-, Äxte**) *f* axe (BRIT), ax (*US*)
Azubi (**-s, -s**) (*umg*) *f(m) abk* = **Auszubildende**

B *f abk* = **Bundesstraße**
Baby (**-s**, **-s**) *nt* baby
Babynahrung *f* baby food
Babysitter (**-s**, **-**) *m* baby-sitter
Bach (**-(e)s**, **Bäche**) *m* stream
Backblech *nt* baking tray
Backbord (**-(e)s**, **-e**) *nt* (*Naut*) port
Backe (**-**, **-n**) *f* cheek
backen *unreg vt*, *vi* to bake
Backenzahn *m* molar
Bäcker(in) (**-s**, **-**) *m(f)* baker
Bäckerei *f* bakery; (*Bäckerladen*) baker's (shop)
Backofen *m* oven
Backpulver *nt* baking powder
Backstein *m* brick
Backwaren *pl* bread, cakes and pastries *pl*
Bad (**-(e)s**, **Bäder**) *nt* bath; (*Schwimmen*) swim; (*Ort*) spa; **ein ~ nehmen** to have *od* take a bath
Badeanzug *m* bathing suit
Badehose *f* bathing *od* swimming trunks *pl*
Badekappe *f* bathing cap
Bademantel *m* bath(ing) robe
Bademeister(in) *m(f)* swimming pool attendant
baden *vi* to bathe, to have a bath ▸ *vt* to bath
Baden-Württemberg *nt* Baden-Württemberg
Badeort *m* spa
Badesachen *pl* swimming things *pl*
Badetuch *nt* bath towel
Badewanne *f* bath(tub)
Badezimmer *nt* bathroom
baff *adj*: **~ sein** (*umg*) to be flabbergasted
Bagger (**-s**, **-**) *m* excavator; (*Naut*) dredger
Baggersee *m* (flooded) gravel pit
Bahamas *pl*: **die ~** the Bahamas *pl*
Bahn (**-**, **-en**) *f* railway (*BRIT*), railroad (*US*); (*Weg*) road, way; (*Spur*) lane; (*Rennbahn*) track; (*Astron*) orbit; (*Stoffbahn*) length; **mit der ~** by train *od* rail/tram
bahnbrechend *adj* pioneering
BahnCard® (**-**, **-s**) *f* rail card (*allowing 50% or 25% reduction on tickets*)
Bahnfahrt *f* railway (*BRIT*) *od* railroad (*US*) journey
Bahnhof *m* station; **auf dem ~** at the station
Bahnlinie *f* (railway (*BRIT*) *od* railroad (*US*)) line
Bahnsteig *m* platform
Bahnstrecke *f* railway (*BRIT*) *od* railroad (*US*) line
Bahnübergang *m* level (*BRIT*) *od* grade (*US*) crossing
Bakterien *pl* bacteria *pl*
bald *adv* (*zeitlich*) soon; (*beinahe*) almost; **bis ~!** see you soon
baldig *adj* early, speedy
Balkan *m*: **der ~** the Balkans *pl*
Balken (**-s**, **-**) *m* beam
Balkon (**-s**, **-s** *od* **-e**) *m* balcony
Ball (**-(e)s**, **Bälle**) *m* ball; (*Tanz*) dance, ball
Ballett (**-(e)s**, **-e**) *nt* ballet
Ballon (**-s**, **-s** *od* **-e**) *m* balloon
Ballspiel *nt* ball game
Ballungsgebiet *nt* conurbation
Baltikum (**-s**) *nt*: **das ~** the Baltic States *pl*
Bambus (**-ses**, **-se**) *m* bamboo
Bambussprossen *pl* bamboo shoots *pl*
banal *adj* banal
Banane (**-**, **-n**) *f* banana
band *etc vb siehe* **binden**
Band[1] (**-(e)s**, **Bände**) *m* (*Buchband*) volume
Band[2] (**-(e)s**, **Bänder**) *nt* (*Stoffband*) ribbon, tape; (*Fließband*) production line; (*Zielband*, *Tonband*) tape; (*Anat*) ligament; **etw auf ~ aufnehmen** to tape sth
Band[3] (**-**, **-s**) *f* band, group
Bandage (**-**, **-n**) *f* bandage
bandagieren *vt* to bandage
Bande (**-**, **-n**) *f* band; (*Straßenbande*) gang

Bandscheibe *f* (*Anat*) disc
Bandwurm *m* tapeworm
Bank[1] (**-**, **Bänke**) *f* (*Sitzbank*) bench
Bank[2] (**-**, **-en**) *f* (*Geldbank*) bank
Bankautomat *m* cash dispenser
Bankkarte *f* bank card
Bankkonto *nt* bank account
Bankleitzahl *f* bank code number
Banknote *f* banknote
Bankverbindung *f* (*Kontonummer etc*) banking *od* account details *pl*
bar *adj* +*gen*: **bares Geld** cash; **etw (in) ~ bezahlen** to pay sth (in) cash
Bar (**-**, **-s**) *f* bar
Bär (**-en**, **-en**) *m* bear
barfuß *adj* barefoot
barg *etc vb siehe* **bergen**
Bargeld *nt* cash
bargeldlos *adj* non-cash
Barkeeper (**-s**, **-**) *m* barman, bartender
Barometer (**-s**, **-**) *nt* barometer
barsch *adj* brusque
Barsch (**-(e)s**, **-e**) *m* perch
Barscheck *m* open *od* uncrossed cheque (Brit), open check (*US*)
Bart (**-(e)s**, **Bärte**) *m* beard
bärtig *adj* bearded
Barzahlung *f* cash payment
Basar (**-s**, **-e**) *m* bazaar
Baseballmütze *f* baseball cap
Basel (**-s**) *nt* Basle
Basilikum (**-s**) *nt* basil
Basis (**-**, **Basen**) *f* basis
Baskenland *nt* Basque region
Basketball *m* basketball
Bass (**-es**, **Bässe**) *m* bass
basta *interj*: **(und damit) ~!** (and) that's that!
basteln *vt* to make ▶ *vi* to do handicrafts
Bastler(in) (**-s**, **-**) *m(f)* do-it-yourselfer
bat *etc vb siehe* **bitten**
Batterie *f* battery
Bau (**-(e)s**) *m* (*Bauen*) building, construction; (*Aufbau*) structure; (*Baustelle*) building site; (*pl Baue*: *Tierbau*) hole, burrow; (*pl Bauten*: *Gebäude*) building
Bauarbeiten *pl* building *od* construction work *sing*; (*Straßenbau*) roadworks *pl* (Brit), roadwork *sing* (*US*)
Bauarbeiter(in) *m(f)* building worker
Bauch (**-(e)s**, **Bäuche**) *m* belly; (*Anat*) stomach
Bauchgefühl *nt*: **ein ~ haben** to have a gut reaction
Bauchnabel *m* navel
Bauchredner(in) *m(f)* ventriloquist
Bauchschmerzen *pl* stomachache *sing*
Bauchspeicheldrüse *f* pancreas
Bauchtanz *m* belly dancing
Bauchweh *nt* stomachache
bauen *vt* to build; (*Tech*) to construct
Bauer (**-n** *od* **-s**, **-n**) *m* farmer; (*Schach*) pawn
Bäuerin *f* farmer; (*Frau des Bauern*) farmer's wife
Bauernhof *m* farm
baufällig *adj* dilapidated
Baujahr *nt* year of construction; (*von Auto*) year of manufacture
Baum (**-(e)s**, **Bäume**) *m* tree
Baumarkt *m* DIY superstore
Baumwolle *f* cotton
Bauplatz *m* building site
Baustein *m* building stone; (*Spielzeug*) brick; (*fig*) element
Baustelle *f* building site; (*bei Straßenbau*) roadworks *pl* (Brit), roadwork (*US*)
Bauteil *nt* prefabricated part (of building)
Bauunternehmer(in) *m(f)* contractor, builder
Bauwerk *nt* building
Bayern *nt* Bavaria
beabsichtigen *vt* to intend
beachten *vt* to take note of; (*Vorschrift*) to obey; (*Vorfahrt*) to observe
beachtlich *adj* considerable
Beachvolleyball *nt* beach volleyball
Beamte(r) (**-n**, **-n**) *m* official; (*Staatsbeamte*) civil servant
Beamtin *f* official; (*Staatsbeamtin*) civil servant
beanspruchen *vt* to claim; (*Zeit, Platz*) to take up; **jdn ~** to take up sb's time
beanstanden *vt* to complain about
Beanstandung *f* complaint
beantragen *vt* to apply for
beantworten *vt* to answer
bearbeiten *vt* to work; (*Material*) to process; (*Thema*) to deal with; (*Chem*) to treat; (*Buch*) to revise; (*umg*: *beeinflussen wollen*) to work on
Bearbeitungsgebühr *f* handling charge
beatmen *vt*: **jdn künstlich ~** to give sb artificial respiration
beaufsichtigen *vt* to supervise
beauftragen *vt* to instruct; **jdn mit etw ~** to entrust sb with sth

Becher (**-s**, **-**) *m* mug; (*ohne Henkel*) tumbler; (*für Joghurt*) pot
Becken (**-s**, **-**) *nt* basin; (*Mus*) cymbal; (*Anat*) pelvis
bedanken *vr*: **sich (bei jdm) ~** to say thank you (to sb)
Bedarf (**-(e)s**) *m* need; (*Comm*) demand; **je nach ~** according to demand; **bei ~** if necessary
Bedarfshaltestelle *f* request stop
bedauerlich *adj* regrettable
bedauern *vt* to be sorry for; (*bemitleiden*) to pity
bedauernswert *adj* (*Zustände*) regrettable; (*Mensch*) unfortunate
bedeckt *adj* covered; (*Himmel*) overcast
bedenken *unreg vt* to consider
Bedenken (**-s**, **-**) *nt* (*Überlegen*) consideration; (*Zweifel*) doubt; (*Skrupel*) scruples *pl*
bedenklich *adj* doubtful; (*bedrohlich*) dangerous
bedeuten *vt* to mean; (*wichtig sein*) to be of importance
bedeutend *adj* important; (*beträchtlich*) considerable
Bedeutung *f* meaning; (*Wichtigkeit*) importance
bedienen *vt* to serve; (*Maschine*) to operate ▶ *vr* (*beim Essen*) to help o.s.
Bedienung *f* service; (*Kellner etc*) waiter/waitress; (*Zuschlag*) service (charge)
Bedienungsanleitung *f* operating instructions *pl*
Bedienungsfehler *m* operating error; **einen ~ machen** (*Comput*) to do something wrong
Bedingung *f* condition; **mit** *od* **unter der ~, dass ...** on condition that ...
bedrohen *vt* to threaten
Bedürfnis (**-ses**, **-se**) *nt* need; **das ~ nach etw haben** to need sth
Beefsteak (**-s**, **-s**) *nt* steak; **deutsches ~** hamburger
beeilen *vr* to hurry
beeindrucken *vt* to impress, to make an impression on
beeinflussen *vt* to influence
beeinträchtigen *vt* to affect adversely
beenden, beendigen *vt* to end, to finish
beerdigen *vt* to bury
Beerdigung *f* funeral, burial
Beere (**-**, **-n**) *f* berry; (*Traubenbeere*) grape
Beet (**-(e)s**, **-e**) *nt* (*Blumenbeet*) bed
befahl *etc vb siehe* **befehlen**
befahrbar *adj* passable; (*Naut*) navigable
befahren *unreg vt* (*Straße*) to use; (*Pass*) to drive over; (*Naut*) to navigate ▶ *adj*: **stark/wenig ~** busy/quiet
Befehl (**-(e)s**, **-e**) *m* command, order; (*Comput*) command
befehlen *unreg vt* to order ▶ *vi* to give orders; **jdm etw ~** to order sb to do sth
befestigen *vt* to fasten; **~ an** *+dat* to fasten to
befeuchten *vt* to moisten
befinden *unreg vr* to be
befohlen *pp von* **befehlen**
befolgen *vt* to follow
befördern *vt* (*senden*) to transport, to send; (*beruflich*) to promote
Beförderung *f* transport; (*beruflich*) promotion
Befragung *f* poll
befreundet *adj* friendly; **wir sind schon lange (miteinander) ~** we have been friends for a long time
befriedigen *vt* to satisfy
befriedigend *adj* satisfactory
Befriedigung *f* satisfaction
befristet *adj* limited
befruchten *vt* to fertilize; (*fig*) to stimulate
Befund (**-(e)s**, **-e**) *m* findings *pl*; (*Med*) diagnosis
befürchten *vt* to fear
befürworten *vt* to support
begabt *adj* gifted
Begabung *f* talent, gift
begann *etc vb siehe* **beginnen**
begegnen *vi*: **jdm ~** to meet sb
begehen *unreg vt* (*Straftat*) to commit; (*geh: feiern*) to celebrate
begehrt *adj* in demand; (*Junggeselle*) eligible
begeistern *vt* to fill with enthusiasm; (*inspirieren*) to inspire ▶ *vr*: **sich für etw ~** to get enthusiastic about sth
begeistert *adj* enthusiastic
Beginn (**-(e)s**) *m* beginning; **zu ~** at the beginning
beginnen *unreg vt, vi* to start, to begin
beglaubigen *vt* to certify
Beglaubigung *f* certification
begleiten *vt* to accompany
Begleiter(in) (**-s**, **-**) *m(f)* companion

Begleitperson *f* plus-one; **sie war ihre ~ auf der Party** she was her plus-one for the party
Begleitung *f* company; (*Mus*) accompaniment
beglückwünschen *vt*: **~ (zu)** to congratulate (on)
begonnen *pp von* **beginnen**
begraben *unreg vt* to bury
Begräbnis (**-ses**, **-se**) *nt* burial, funeral
begreifen *unreg vt* to understand
Begrenzung *f* boundary; (*fig*) restriction
Begriff (**-(e)s**, **-e**) *m* concept, idea; **im ~ sein, etw zu tun** to be about to do sth; **schwer von ~** (*umg*) slow on the uptake
begründen *vt* (*Gründe geben*) to justify
Begründung *f* justification
begrüßen *vt* to greet, to welcome
Begrüßung *f* greeting, welcome
behaart *adj* hairy
behalten *unreg vt* to keep; (*im Gedächtnis*) to remember
Behälter (**-s**, **-**) *m* container
behandeln *vt* to treat
Behandlung *f* treatment
behaupten *vt* to claim, to maintain ▶ *vr* to assert o.s.
Behauptung *f* claim, assertion
beheizen *vt* to heat
behelfen *unreg vr*: **sich mit etw ~** to make do with sth
beherbergen *vt* (*lit, fig*) to house
beherrschen *vt* (*Situation*) to control; (*Sprache, Gefühle*) to master ▶ *vr* to control o.s.
Beherrschung *f* (*von Situation*) control; **die ~ verlieren** to lose one's temper
behilflich *adj* helpful; **jdm ~ sein (bei)** to help sb (with)
behindern *vt* to hinder
Behinderte(r) *f(m)* person with a disability
behindertengerecht *adj* suitable for people with a disability
Behörde (**-**, **-n**) *f* authorities *pl*

SCHLÜSSELWORT

bei *präp +dat* **1** (*nahe bei*) near; (*zum Aufenthalt*) at, with; (*unter, zwischen*) among; **bei München** near Munich; **bei uns** at our place; **beim Friseur** at the hairdresser's; **bei seinen Eltern wohnen** to live with one's parents; **bei einer Firma arbeiten** to work for a firm; **etw bei sich haben** to have sth on one; **jdn bei sich haben** to have sb with one; **bei Goethe** in Goethe; **beim Militär** in the army
2 (*zeitlich*) at, on; (*während*) during; (*Zustand, Umstand*) in; **bei Nacht** at night; **bei Nebel** in fog; **bei Regen** if it rains; **bei solcher Hitze** in such heat; **bei meiner Ankunft** on my arrival; **bei der Arbeit** when I'm *etc* working; **beim Fahren** while driving

bei|behalten *unreg vt* to keep
bei|bringen *unreg vt*: **jdm etw ~** (*zu verstehen geben*) to make sb understand sth; (*lehren*) to teach sb sth
beide *pron, adj* both; **meine beiden Brüder** my two brothers, both my brothers; **wir ~** we two; **einer von beiden** one of the two; **alle(s) ~(s)** both (of them); **~ Mal** both times
beieinander *adv* together
Beifahrer(in) (**-s**, **-**) *m(f)* passenger
Beifahrerairbag *m* (*Aut*) passenger airbag
Beifahrersitz *m* passenger seat
Beifall (**-(e)s**) *m* applause
beige *adj* beige
Beigeschmack *m* aftertaste
Beil (**-(e)s**, **-e**) *nt* axe (Brit), ax (*US*)
Beilage *f* (*Buchbeilage etc*) supplement; (*Koch*) accompanying vegetables; (*getrennt serviert*) side dish
beiläufig *adj* casual ▶ *adv* casually
Beileid *nt* condolence, sympathy; **herzliches ~** deepest sympathy
beiliegend *adj* (*Comm*) enclosed
beim = **bei dem**
Bein (**-(e)s**, **-e**) *nt* leg
beinah, beinahe *adv* almost, nearly
beinhalten *vt* to contain
beisammen *adv* together
Beisammensein (**-s**) *nt* get-together
beiseite *adv* aside
beiseite|legen *vt* (*sparen*) to put by
Beispiel (**-(e)s**, **-e**) *nt* example; **sich** *dat* **an jdm ein ~ nehmen** to take sb as an example; **zum ~** for example
beißen *unreg vt, vi* to bite; (*stechen: Rauch, Säure*) to burn ▶ *vr* (*Farben*) to clash
Beitrag (**-(e)s**, **Beiträge**) *m* contribution; (*Zahlung*) subscription; (*Versicherungsbeitrag*) premium

bei|tragen *unreg vt, vi*: **~ (zu)** to contribute (to)
bekannt *adj* (well-)known; (*nicht fremd*) familiar; **~ geben** to announce publicly; **mit jdm ~ sein** to know sb; **jdn mit jdm ~ machen** to introduce sb to sb
Bekannte(r) *f(m)* friend; (*entfernter*) acquaintance
bekanntlich *adv* as is well known, as you know
Bekanntschaft *f* acquaintance
beklagen *vr* to complain
Bekleidung *f* clothing
bekommen *unreg vt* to get, to receive; (*Kind*) to have; (*Zug*) to catch, to get ▸ *vi*: **jdm ~** to agree with sb
beladen *unreg vt* to load
Belag (**-(e)s**, **Beläge**) *m* coating; (*Zahnbelag*) tartar; (*auf Zunge*) fur
belasten *vt* (*lit*) to burden; (*fig*: *bedrücken*) to trouble, to worry; (*Comm*: *Konto*) to debit; (*Jur*) to incriminate
belästigen *vt* to annoy, to pester; (*sexuell*) to harass
Belästigung *f* annoyance, pestering; **sexuelle ~** sexual harassment
belebt *adj* (*Straße*) crowded
Beleg (**-(e)s**, **-e**) *m* (*Comm*) receipt; (*Beweis*) proof
belegen *vt* (*Kuchen*, *Brot*) to spread; (*Platz*) to reserve, to book; (*Kurs*, *Vorlesung*) to register for; (*beweisen*) to prove
belegt *adj* (*Zunge*) furred; (*Zimmer*) occupied; **belegte Brote** open sandwiches
beleidigen *vt* to insult; (*kränken*) to offend
Beleidigung *f* insult; (*Jur*) slander; (: *schriftlich*) libel
beleuchten *vt* to light, to illuminate; (*fig*) to throw light on
Beleuchtung *f* lighting, illumination
Belgien (**-s**) *nt* Belgium
Belgier(in) (**-s**, **-**) *m(f)* Belgian
belgisch *adj* Belgian
belichten *vt* to expose
Belichtung *f* exposure
Belichtungsmesser *m* exposure meter
Belieben *nt*: **(ganz) nach ~** (just) as you wish
beliebig *adj* as you like; **~ viel** as much as you like; **ein beliebiges Thema** any subject you like *od* want
beliebt *adj* popular; **sich bei jdm ~ machen** to make o.s. popular with sb
beliefern *vt* to supply
bellen *vi* to bark
Belohnung *f* reward
Belüftung *f* ventilation
belügen *unreg vt* to lie to
bemerkbar *adj* noticeable; **sich ~ machen** (*Person*) to make *od* get o.s. noticed; (*Unruhe*) to become noticeable
bemerken *vt* (*wahrnehmen*) to notice; (*sagen*) to mention
bemerkenswert *adj* remarkable, noteworthy
Bemerkung *f* remark
bemitleiden *vt* to pity
bemühen *vr* to make an effort; **sich um eine Stelle ~** to try to get a job
Bemühung *f* effort
bemuttern *vt* to mother
benachbart *adj* neighbouring (BRIT), neighboring (*US*)
benachrichtigen *vt* to inform
Benachrichtigung *f* notification
benachteiligen *vt* to (put at a) disadvantage, to victimize
benehmen *unreg vr* to behave
Benehmen (**-s**) *nt* behaviour (BRIT), behavior (*US*)
beneiden *vt* to envy; **jdn um etw ~** to envy sb sth
Beneluxländer *pl* Benelux (countries *pl*)
benommen *adj* dazed
benötigen *vt* to need
benutzen *vt* to use
Benutzer(in) (**-s**, **-**) *m(f)* user
benutzerfreundlich *adj* user-friendly
Benutzerkonto *nt* (*Comput*) user account
Benutzername *m* (*Comput*) username
Benutzeroberfläche *f* (*Comput*) user/system interface
Benutzerunterstützung *f* (*Comput*) help desk
Benutzung *f* utilization, use
Benzin (**-s**, **-e**) *nt* (*Aut*) petrol (BRIT), gas(oline) (*US*)
Benzinkanister *m* petrol (BRIT) *od* gas (*US*) can

Benzintank *m* petrol (BRIT) *od* gas (*US*) tank
Benzinuhr *f* petrol (BRIT) *od* gas (*US*) gauge
beobachten *vt* to observe
Beobachtung *f* observation
bequem *adj* comfortable; (*Ausrede*) convenient; (*Person*) lazy; **machen Sie es sich ~** make yourself at home
Bequemlichkeit *f* comfort; (*Faulheit*) laziness
beraten *unreg vt* to advise; (*besprechen*) to discuss, to debate ▶ *vr* to consult
Beratung *f* advice; (*Besprechung*) consultation
berauben *vt* to rob
berechnen *vt* to calculate; (*Comm*) to charge
berechnend *adj* (*Mensch*) calculating
berechtigen *vt* to entitle; (*fig*) to justify
berechtigt *adj* justified
bereden *vt* (*besprechen*) to discuss
Bereich (**-(e)s**, **-e**) *m* area; (*Ressort, Gebiet*) sphere
bereisen *vt* to travel through
bereit *adj* ready; **zu etw ~ sein** to be ready for sth; **sich ~ erklären** to declare o.s. willing; **(sich) ~ machen** to prepare, to get ready
bereiten *vt* to prepare; (*Kummer, Freude*) to cause
bereit|legen *vt* to lay out
bereit|machen *vt, vr siehe* **bereit**
bereits *adv* already
Bereitschaft *f* readiness; **in ~ sein** to be on the alert *od* on stand-by
bereit|stehen *unreg vi* to be ready
bereuen *vt* to regret
Berg (**-(e)s**, **-e**) *m* mountain; (*kleiner*) hill
bergab *adv* downhill
bergauf *adv* uphill
Bergbahn *f* mountain railway (BRIT) *od* railroad (*US*)
bergen *unreg vt* (*retten*) to rescue; (*enthalten*) to contain
Bergführer(in) *m(f)* mountain guide
bergig *adj* mountainous
Bergschuh *m* walking boot
Bergsteigen *nt* mountaineering
Bergsteiger(in) *m(f)* mountaineer
Bergung *f* (*von Menschen*) rescue; (*von Material*) recovery
Bergwacht *f* mountain rescue service
Bergwerk *nt* mine
Bericht (**-(e)s**, **-e**) *m* report
berichten *vt, vi* to report
berichtigen *vt* to correct
Bernstein *m* amber
berüchtigt *adj* notorious, infamous
berücksichtigen *vt* to consider, to bear in mind
Beruf (**-(e)s**, **-e**) *m* occupation, profession; (*Gewerbe*) trade; **was sind Sie von ~?** what do you do for a living?
beruflich *adj* professional
Berufsausbildung *f* vocational *od* professional training
Berufsschule *f* vocational *od* trade school
berufstätig *adj* employed
Berufsverkehr *m* commuter traffic
beruhigen *vt* to calm ▶ *vr* (*Mensch*) to calm (o.s.) down; (*Situation*) to calm down
beruhigend *adj* reassuring
Beruhigungsmittel *nt* sedative
berühmt *adj* famous
berühren *vt* to touch; (*gefühlsmäßig bewegen*) to affect; (*flüchtig erwähnen*) to mention, to touch on ▶ *vr* to touch
besaufen *unreg* (*umg*) *vr* to get drunk *od* stoned
beschädigen *vt* to damage
beschäftigen *vt* to occupy; (*beruflich*) to employ ▶ *vr* to occupy *od* concern o.s.
beschäftigt *adj* busy, occupied
Beschäftigung *f* (*Beruf*) employment; (*Tätigkeit*) occupation; (*geistige Beschäftigung*) preoccupation
Bescheid (**-(e)s**, **-e**) *m* information; **~ wissen (über** *+akk***)** to be well-informed (about); **ich weiß ~** I know; **jdm ~ geben** *od* **sagen** to let sb know
bescheiden *unreg adj* modest
bescheinigen *vt* to certify; (*bestätigen*) to acknowledge
Bescheinigung *f* certificate; (*Quittung*) receipt
bescheißen *unreg* (*!*) *vt* to cheat
bescheuert (*umg*) *adj* stupid
beschimpfen *vt* to abuse
Beschiss (**-es**) (*umg*) *m*: **das ist ~** that is a cheat
beschissen *pp von* **bescheißen** ▶ *adj* (*!*) bloody awful, lousy
beschlagnahmen *vt* to confiscate
Beschleunigung *f* acceleration

beschließen *unreg vt* to decide on; (*beenden*) to end, to close
Beschluss (**-es**, **Beschlüsse**) *m* decision
beschränken *vt* to limit, to restrict (auf +*akk* to) ▸ *vr*: **sich ~ auf** +*akk* to limit *od* restrict o.s. to
Beschränkung *f* limitation
beschreiben *unreg vt* to describe; (*Papier*) to write on
Beschreibung *f* description
beschuldigen *vt* to accuse
Beschuldigung *f* accusation
beschummeln (*umg*) *vt*, *vi* to cheat
beschützen *vt*: **~ (vor** +*dat***)** to protect (from)
Beschwerde (**-**, **-n**) *f* complaint ▪ **Beschwerden** *pl* (*Leiden*) trouble
beschweren *vt* to weight down; (*fig*) to burden ▸ *vr* to complain
beschwipst *adj* tipsy
beseitigen *vt* to remove
Beseitigung *f* removal
Besen (**-s**, **-**) *m* broom
besetzen *vt* (*Haus, Land*) to occupy; (*Platz*) to take, to fill; (*Posten*) to fill; (*Rolle*) to cast
besetzt *adj* full; (*Tel*) engaged, busy; (*Platz*) taken; (*WC*) engaged
Besetztzeichen *nt* engaged tone (BRIT), busy signal (*US*)
besichtigen *vt* to visit, to look at
besiegen *vt* to defeat
Besitz (**-es**) *m* possession; (*Eigentum*) property
besitzen *unreg vt* to own; (*Eigenschaft*) to have
Besitzer(in) (**-s**, **-**) *m(f)* owner
besoffen (*umg*) *adj* sozzled
besondere(r, s) *adj* special; (*eigen*) particular; (*eigentümlich*) peculiar; **nichts Besonderes** nothing special
Besonderheit *f* peculiarity
besonders *adv* especially, particularly; (*getrennt*) separately
besorgen *vt* (*kaufen*) to purchase; (*erledigen: Geschäfte*) to deal with
besprechen *unreg vt* to discuss
Besprechung *f* meeting, discussion
besser *adj* better; **es geht ihm ~** he feels better; **~ gesagt** or rather
bessern *vt* to improve ▸ *vr* to improve; (*Mensch*) to reform
Besserung *f* improvement; **gute ~!** get well soon!

beständig *adj* (*ausdauernd*) constant (*auch fig*); (*Wetter*) settled
Bestandteil *m* part, component
bestätigen *vt* to confirm; (*anerkennen*) to acknowledge
Bestätigung *f* confirmation; (*Anerkennung*) acknowledgement
beste(r, s) *adj* best; **sie singt am besten** she sings best; **so ist es am besten** it's best that way; **am besten gehst du gleich** you'd better go at once
bestechen *unreg vt* to bribe
Bestechung *f* bribery
Besteck (**-(e)s**, **-e**) *nt* cutlery
bestehen *unreg vi* to exist; (*andauern*) to last ▸ *vt* (*Probe, Prüfung*) to pass; (*Kampf*) to win; **~ auf** +*dat* to insist on; **~ aus** to consist of
bestehlen *unreg vt* to rob
bestellen *vt* to order; (*kommen lassen*) to arrange to see; (*Grüße, Auftrag*) to pass on
Bestellnummer *f* order number
Bestellung *f* (*Comm*) order; (*Bestellen*) ordering
bestens *adv* very well
bestimmen *vt* (*Regeln*) to lay down; (*Tag, Ort*) to fix; (*ausersehen*) to mean; (*ernennen*) to appoint
bestimmt *adj* (*entschlossen*) firm; (*gewiss*) certain, definite ▸ *adv* definitely, for sure
Bestimmung *f* (*Verordnung*) regulation; (*Verwendungszweck*) purpose
Best.-Nr. *abk* = **Bestellnummer**
bestrafen *vt* to punish
bestrahlen *vt* to shine on; (*Med*) to treat with X-rays
bestreiten *unreg vt* (*abstreiten*) to dispute
Bestseller (**-s**, **-**) *m* best-seller
bestürzt *adj* dismayed
Besuch (**-(e)s**, **-e**) *m* visit; (*Person*) visitor; **~ haben** to have visitors
besuchen *vt* to visit; (*Sch etc*) to attend
Besucher(in) (**-s**, **-**) *m(f)* visitor
Besuchszeit *f* visiting hours *pl*
betäuben *vt* (*Med*) to anaesthetize (BRIT), to anesthetize (*US*)
Betäubung *f*: **örtliche ~** local anaesthetic (BRIT) *od* anesthetic (*US*)
Betäubungsmittel *nt* anaesthetic (BRIT), anesthetic (*US*)

Bete (**-**, **-n**) *f*: **Rote ~** beetroot (*Brit*), beet (*US*)
beteiligen *vr*: **sich (an etw** *dat***) ~** to take part (in sth), to participate (in sth) ▸ *vt*: **jdn (an etw** *dat***) ~** to give sb a share *od* interest (in sth)
Beteiligung *f* participation; (*Anteil*) share; (*Besucherzahl*) attendance
beten *vi* to pray
Beton (**-s**, **-s**) *m* concrete
betonen *vt* to stress
Betonung *f* stress, emphasis
Betracht *m*: **in ~ kommen** to be concerned *od* relevant; **nicht in ~ kommen** to be out of the question; **etw in ~ ziehen** to consider sth
betrachten *vt* to look at; (*fig*) to consider
beträchtlich *adj* considerable ▸ *adv* considerably
Betrag (**-(e)s**, **Beträge**) *m* amount, sum
betragen *unreg vt* to amount to ▸ *vr* to behave
betreffen *unreg vt* to concern, to affect; **was mich betrifft** as for me
betreffend *adj* relevant, in question
betreten *unreg vt* to enter; (*Bühne etc*) to step onto; **„B~ verboten"** "keep off/out"
betreuen *vt* to look after
Betreuer(in) (**-s**, **-**) *m(f)* carer; (*Kinderbetreuer*) child-minder
Betrieb (**-(e)s**, **-e**) *m* (*Firma*) firm; (*Anlage*) plant; (*Tätigkeit*) operation; (*Treiben*) bustle; **außer ~ sein** to be out of order; **in ~ sein** to be in operation
betriebsbereit *adj* operational
Betriebsrat *m* workers' council
Betriebssystem *nt* (*Comput*) operating system
betrinken *unreg vr* to get drunk
betroffen *pp von* **betreffen** ▸ *adj* (*bestürzt*) amazed, perplexed; **von etw ~ werden** *od* **sein** to be affected by sth
Betrug (**-(e)s**) *m* deception; (*Jur*) fraud
betrügen *unreg vt* to cheat; (*Jur*) to defraud; (*Ehepartner*) to be unfaithful to
Betrüger(in) (**-s**, **-**) *m(f)* cheat
betrunken *adj* drunk
Bett (**-(e)s**, **-en**) *nt* bed; **ins** *od* **zu ~ gehen** to go to bed
Bettbezug *m* duvet cover
Bettdecke *f* blanket
betteln *vi* to beg
Bettlaken *nt* sheet
Bettler(in) (**-s**, **-**) *m(f)* beggar
Betttuch *nt* sheet
Bettwäsche *f*, **Bettzeug** *nt* bedclothes *pl*, bedding
beugen *vt* to bend ▸ *vr +dat* (*sich fügen*) to bow (to)
Beule (**-**, **-n**) *f* bump
beunruhigen *vt* to disturb, to alarm ▸ *vr* to become worried
beurteilen *vt* to judge
Beute (**-**) *f* booty, loot; (*von Raubtieren etc*) prey
Beutel (**-s**, **-**) *m* bag
Bevölkerung *f* population
bevollmächtigen *vt* to authorize
bevor *konj* before
bevor|stehen *unreg vi* (*Schwierigkeiten*) to lie ahead; (*Gefahr*) to be imminent; **(jdm) ~** to be in store (for sb)
bevorstehend *adj* imminent
bevorzugen *vt untr* to prefer
bewachen *vt* to watch, to guard
bewegen *vt*, *vr* to move; **jdn zu etw ~** to induce sb to do sth
Bewegung *f* movement, motion; (*innere*) emotion; (*körperlich*) exercise
Bewegungsmelder (**-s**, **-**) *m* sensor (*which reacts to movement*)
Beweis (**-es**, **-e**) *m* proof; (*Zeichen*) sign
beweisen *unreg vt* to prove; (*zeigen*) to show
bewerben *unreg vr*: **sich ~ (um)** to apply (for)
Bewerbung *f* application
bewilligen *vt* to grant, to allow
bewirken *vt* to cause, to bring about
bewohnen *vt* to live in
Bewohner(in) (**-s**, **-**) *m(f)* inhabitant; (*von Haus*) resident
bewölkt *adj* cloudy, overcast
Bewölkung *f* clouds *pl*
bewundern *vt* to admire
bewundernswert *adj* admirable
bewusst *adj* conscious; (*absichtlich*) deliberate; **sich** *dat* **einer Sache** *gen* **~ sein** to be aware of sth
bewusstlos *adj* unconscious
Bewusstlosigkeit *f* unconsciousness
Bewusstsein *nt* consciousness; **bei ~** conscious
bezahlen *vt* to pay (for); **es macht sich bezahlt** it will pay
Bezahlschranke *f* (*Comput*) paywall

Bezahlung *f* payment
bezeichnen *vt* (*kennzeichnen*) to mark; (*nennen*) to call; (*beschreiben*) to describe
Bezeichnung *f* (*Zeichen*) mark, sign; (*Ausdruck*) term
beziehen *unreg vt* (*mit Überzug*) to cover; (*Haus, Position*) to move into; (*erhalten*) to receive; (*Zeitung*) to subscribe to, to take ▶ *vr*: **sich ~ auf** *+akk* to refer to
Beziehung *f* (*Verbindung*) connection; (*Verhältnis*) relationship; (*Hinsicht*) respect; **Beziehungen haben** (*vorteilhaft*) to have connections *od* contacts
beziehungsweise *adv* or; (*genauer gesagt*) or rather
Bezirk (**-(e)s**, **-e**) *m* district
Bezug (**-(e)s**, **Bezüge**) *m* (*Hülle*) covering; **in ~ auf** *+akk* with reference to; **mit** *od* **unter ~ auf** *+akk* regarding
bezüglich *präp +gen* concerning
bezweifeln *vt* to doubt
BH (**-s**, **-(s)**) *m abk* (= *Büstenhalter*) bra
Bhf. *abk* = **Bahnhof**
Biathlon (**-s**, **-s**) *m od nt* biathlon
Bibel (**-**, **-n**) *f* Bible
Biber (**-s**, **-**) *m* beaver
Bibliothek (**-**, **-en**) *f* (*auch Comput*) library
biegen *unreg vt*, *vr* to bend ▶ *vi* to turn
Biegung *f* bend
Biene (**-**, **-n**) *f* bee
Bier (**-(e)s**, **-e**) *nt* beer; **zwei ~, bitte!** two beers, please
Biergarten *m* beer garden
Bierzelt *nt* beer tent
bieten *unreg vt* to offer; (*bei Versteigerung*) to bid ▶ *vr* (*Gelegenheit*): **sich jdm ~** to present itself to sb; **sich** *dat* **etw ~ lassen** to put up with sth
Bikini (**-s**, **-s**) *m* bikini
Bild (**-(e)s**, **-er**) *nt* picture; (*Foto*) photo; (*fig*) image
bilden *vt* to form; (*erziehen*) to educate; (*ausmachen*) to constitute ▶ *vr* to arise; (*erziehen*) to educate o.s.
Bilderbuch *nt* picture book
Bildhauer *m* sculptor
Bildschirm *m* (*TV*, *Comput*) screen
Bildschirmschoner (**-s**, **-**) *m* (*Comput*) screen saver
Bildung *f* formation; (*Wissen, Benehmen*) education
Bildungsurlaub *m* educational holiday
Billard (**-s**, **-e**) *nt* billiards *sing*
billig *adj* cheap; (*gerecht*) fair
Billigflieger *m* budget *od* low-cost airline
Billigflug *m* cheap flight
Binde (**-**, **-n**) *f* bandage; (*Armbinde*) band; (*Med*) sanitary towel (Brit) *od* napkin (US)
Bindehautentzündung *f* conjunctivitis
binden *unreg vt* to bind, to tie
Bindestrich *m* hyphen
Bindfaden *m* string
Bindung *f* bond, tie; (*Ski*) binding
Biodiesel (**-s**, **-**) *m* biodiesel
Biokraftstoff *m* biofuel
Bioladen *m* health food shop (Brit) *od* store (US)
Biologie *f* biology
biologisch *adj* biological; (*Anbau*) organic
Biomüll *m* organic waste
bipolar *adj* bipolar
Birke (**-**, **-n**) *f* birch
Birne (**-**, **-n**) *f* pear; (*Elek*) (light) bulb

SCHLÜSSELWORT

bis *präp +akk*, *adv* **1** (*zeitlich*) till, until
2 (*bis spätestens*) by; **Sie haben bis Dienstag Zeit** you have until *od* till Tuesday; **bis Dienstag muss es fertig sein** it must be ready by Tuesday; **bis auf Weiteres** until further notice; **bis in die Nacht** into the night; **bis bald!/gleich!** see you later/soon
3 (*räumlich*) (up) to; **ich fahre bis Köln** I'm going as far as Cologne; **bis an unser Grundstück** (right *od* up) to our plot; **bis hierher** this far
4 (*bei Zahlen, Angaben*) up to; **bis zu** up to
5: **bis auf etw** *akk* (*außer*) except sth; (*einschließlich*) including sth
▶ *konj* **1** (*mit Zahlen*) to; **10 bis 20** 10 to 20
2 (*zeitlich*) till, until; **bis es dunkel wird** till *od* until it gets dark; **von ... bis ...** from ... to ...

Bischof (**-s**, **Bischöfe**) *m* bishop
bisher *adv* till now, hitherto
Biskuit (**-(e)s**, **-s** *od* **-e**) *m od nt* biscuit
biss *etc vb siehe* **beißen**
Biss (**-es**, **-e**) *m* bite

bisschen *adj*: **ein ~** a bit of ▶ *adv*: **ein ~** a bit; **kein ~** not at all
bissig *adj* (*Hund*) snappy; (*gefährlich*) vicious; (*Bemerkung*) cutting
Bit (**-(s)**, **-(s)**) *nt* (*Comput*) bit
bitte *interj* please; (*als Antwort auf Dank*) you're welcome; **wie ~?** (I beg your) pardon?
Bitte (**-**, **-n**) *f* request
bitten *unreg vt* to ask; **~ um** to ask for
bitter *adj* bitter
Blähungen *pl* (*Med*) wind *sing*
blamieren *vr* to make a fool of o.s., to disgrace o.s. ▶ *vt* to let down, to disgrace
Blankoscheck *m* blank cheque (*Brit*) *od* check (*US*)
Blase (**-**, **-n**) *f* bubble; (*Med*) blister; (*Anat*) bladder
blasen *unreg vt, vi* to blow
Blasenentzündung *f* cystitis
blass *adj* pale
Blatt (**-(e)s**, **Blätter**) *nt* leaf; (*von Papier*) sheet
blättern *vi*: **in etw** *dat* **~** to leaf through sth
Blätterteig *m* flaky *od* puff pastry
blau *adj* blue; (*umg*) drunk, stoned; (*Koch*) boiled; (*Auge*) black; **blauer Fleck** bruise
Blaubeere *f* bilberry
Blaulicht *nt* flashing blue light
blau|machen (*umg*) *vi* to skive off work
Blech (**-(e)s**, **-e**) *nt* tin, sheet metal; (*Backblech*) baking tray
Blechschaden *m* (*Aut*) damage to bodywork
Blei (**-(e)s**, **-e**) *nt* lead
bleiben *unreg vi* to stay; **das bleibt unter uns** (*fig*) that's (just) between ourselves; **etw ~ lassen** (*unterlassen*) to give sth a miss
bleich *adj* pale
bleichen *vt* to bleach
bleifrei *adj* (*Benzin*) unleaded
bleihaltig *adj* (*Benzin*) leaded
Bleistift *m* pencil
Blende (**-**, **-n**) *f* (*Phot*) aperture
Blick (**-(e)s**, **-e**) *m* (*kurz*) glance; (*Anschauen*) look; (*Aussicht*) view; **Liebe auf den ersten ~** love at first sight; **mit einem ~** at a glance
blicken *vi* to look; **sich ~ lassen** to put in an appearance
blieb *etc vb siehe* **bleiben**
blies *etc vb siehe* **blasen**
blind *adj* blind; (*Glas etc*) dull
Blinddarm *m* appendix
Blinddarmentzündung *f* appendicitis
Blindenhund *m* guide dog
Blindenschrift *f* braille
blinken *vi* to twinkle, to sparkle; (*Licht*) to flash, to signal; (*Aut*) to indicate
Blinker (**-s**, **-**) *m* (*Aut*) indicator
blinzeln *vi* to blink, to wink
Blitz (**-es**, **-e**) *m* (flash of) lightning; (*Phot*) flash
blitzen *vi*: **es blitzt** (*Met*) there's a flash of lightning
Blitzlicht *nt* flashlight
Block (**-(e)s**, **Blöcke**) *m* (*lit, fig*) block; (*von Papier*) pad
Blockflöte *f* recorder
Blockhaus *nt* log cabin
blockieren *vt* to block ▶ *vi* (*Räder*) to jam
Blockschrift *f* block letters *pl*
blöd *adj* stupid
blödeln (*umg*) *vi* to fool around
Blog (**-s**, **-s**) *m od nt* (*Comput*) blog
bloggen *vi* to blog
Blogosphäre (**-**, **-n**) *f* blogosphere
blond *adj* blond; (*Frau*) blonde

SCHLÜSSELWORT

bloß *adj* **1** (*unbedeckt*) bare; (*nackt*) naked; **mit der bloßen Hand** with one's bare hand; **mit bloßem Auge** with the naked eye
2 (*alleinig*: *nur*) mere; **der bloße Gedanke** the very thought; **bloßer Neid** sheer envy
▶ *adv* only, merely; **lass das bloß!** just don't do that!; **wie ist das bloß passiert?** how on earth did that happen?

blühen *vi* to bloom; (*fig*) to flourish
Blume (**-**, **-n**) *f* flower; (*von Wein*) bouquet
Blumenbeet *nt* flower bed
Blumengeschäft *nt* flower shop, florist's
Blumenkohl *m* cauliflower
Blumenstrauß *m* bunch of flowers
Blumentopf *m* flowerpot

Bluse (-, **-n**) *f* blouse
Blut (-**(e)s**) *nt* blood
Blutbild *nt* blood count
Blutdruck *m* blood pressure
Blüte (-, **-n**) *f* blossom; (*fig*) prime
bluten *vi* to bleed
Blütenstaub *m* pollen
Bluter (**-s**, -) *m* (*Med*) haemophiliac (BRIT), hemophiliac (*US*)
Bluterguss *m* haemorrhage (BRIT), hemorrhage (*US*); (*auf Haut*) bruise
Blutgruppe *f* blood group
blutig *adj* bloody
Blutkonserve *f* unit *od* pint of stored blood
Blutprobe *f* blood sample
Bluttransfusion *f* blood transfusion
Blutung *f* bleeding
Blutvergiftung *f* blood poisoning
Blutwurst *f* black pudding
BLZ *abk* = **Bankleitzahl**
Bock (-**(e)s**, **Böcke**) *m* buck, ram; (*Gestell*) trestle; (*Sport*) buck; **~ haben, etw zu tun** (*umg*: *Lust*) to fancy doing sth
Boden (**-s**, **Böden**) *m* ground; (*Fußboden*) floor; (*Meeresboden, Fassboden*) bottom; (*Speicher*) attic
Bodenpersonal *nt* (*Aviat*) ground staff
Bodenschätze *pl* mineral wealth *sing*
Bodensee *m*: **der ~** Lake Constance
bog *etc vb siehe* **biegen**
Bogen (**-s**, -) *m* (*Biegung*) curve; (*Archit*) arch; (*Waffe, Mus*) bow; (*Papier*) sheet
Bohne (-, **-n**) *f* bean
Bohnenkaffee *m* real coffee
Bohnensprosse *f* bean sprout
bohren *vt* to drill
Bohrer (**-s**, -) *m* drill
Boiler (**-s**, -) *m* water heater
Boje (-, **-n**) *f* buoy
Bolivien *nt* Bolivia
Bombe (-, **-n**) *f* bomb
Bon (**-s**, **-s**) *m* voucher; (*Kassenzettel*) receipt
Bonbon (**-s**, **-s**) *nt* sweet (BRIT), candy (*US*)
Bonus (- *od* **-ses**, **-se** *od* **Boni**) *m* bonus
Boot (-**(e)s**, **-e**) *nt* boat
Bord (-**(e)s**, **-e**) *m* (*Aviat, Naut*) board; **an ~** on board; **an ~ gehen** (*Schiff*) to go on board; (*Flugzeug*) to board
Bordell (**-s**, **-e**) *nt* brothel
Bordstein *m* kerb(stone) (BRIT), curb(stone) (*US*)
borgen *vt* to borrow; **jdm etw ~** to lend sb sth; **sich** *dat* **etw ~** to borrow sth
Börse (-, **-n**) *f* stock exchange; (*Geldbörse*) purse
Börsengang *m* (*Fin*) flotation; **seit dem ~ dieser Firma** since this company was floated
bös *adj* = **böse**
bösartig *adj* malicious; (*Med*) malignant
Böschung *f* slope; (*Uferböschung etc*) embankment
böse *adj* bad, evil; (*zornig*) angry; **bist du mir ~?** are you angry with me?
boshaft *adj* malicious
Bosnien (**-s**) *nt* Bosnia
Bosnien-Herzegowina (**-s**) *nt* Bosnia-Herzegovina
böswillig *adj* malicious
bot *etc vb siehe* **bieten**
botanisch *adj* botanical; **botanischer Garten** botanical gardens *pl*
Botschaft *f* message; (*Pol*) embassy
Botschafter(in) (**-s**, -) *m(f)* ambassador
Bouillon (-, **-s**) *f* consommé
Boutique (-, **-n**) *f* boutique
Bowle (-, **-n**) *f* punch
Box *f* (*Behälter*) box; (*Lautsprecherbox*) speaker
boxen *vi* to box
Boxer(in) (**-s**, -) *m(f)* boxer
Boxkampf *m* boxing match
Boykott (-**(e)s**, **-s**) *m* boycott
brach *etc vb siehe* **brechen**
brachte *etc vb siehe* **bringen**
Branchenverzeichnis *nt* trade directory
Brand (-**(e)s**, **Brände**) *m* fire
Brandenburg (**-s**) *nt* Brandenburg
Brandsalbe *f* ointment for burns
Brandung *f* surf
Brandwunde *f* burn
brannte *etc vb siehe* **brennen**
Brasilien *nt* Brazil
braten *unreg vt* to roast; (*in Pfanne*) to fry
Braten (**-s**, -) *m* roast, joint
Brathähnchen *nt* roast chicken
Bratkartoffeln *pl* fried/roast potatoes *pl*
Bratpfanne *f* frying pan
Bratspieß *m* spit
Bratwurst *f* grilled sausage
Brauch (-**(e)s**, **Bräuche**) *m* custom

brauchen *vt* (*bedürfen*) to need; (*müssen*) to have to; (*verwenden*) to use; **wie lange braucht man, um ...?** how long does it take to ...?; **das braucht seine Zeit** it takes time; **du brauchst es nur zu sagen** you only need to say
brauen *vt* to brew
Brauerei *f* brewery
braun *adj* brown; (*von Sonne*) tanned
Bräune (-, **-n**) *f* brownness; (*Sonnenbräune*) tan
Brause (-, **-n**) *f* shower; (*Getränk*) lemonade
Braut (-, **Bräute**) *f* bride
Bräutigam (**-s**, **-e**) *m* bridegroom
brav *adj* (*artig*) good
bravo *interj* well done
BRD (-) *f abk* (= *Bundesrepublik Deutschland*) FRG

BRD

BRD (*Bundesrepublik Deutschland*) is the official name for the Federal Republic of Germany, and was the name given to the former West Germany as opposed to East Germany (the *DDR*). It comprises 16 *Länder* (see *Land*); the 11 that were part of the former West Germany were joined by the 5 new *Länder* of the former East Germany when the two countries reunited on 3 October 1990.

brechen *unreg vt, vi* to break; (*speien*) to vomit
Brechreiz *m* nausea
Brei (**-(e)s**, **-e**) *m* (*Masse*) pulp; (*Koch*) gruel; (*Haferbrei*) porridge (BRIT), oatmeal (*US*); (*für Kinder, Kranke*) mash
breit *adj* broad; (*bei Maßangabe*) wide
Breite (-, **-n**) *f* breadth; (*bei Maßangabe*) width; (*Geog*) latitude
Breitengrad *m* degree of latitude
Bremen (**-s**) *nt* Bremen
Bremsbelag *m* brake lining
Bremse (-, **-n**) *f* brake; (*Zool*) horsefly
bremsen *vi* to brake ▸ *vt* (*Auto*) to brake; (*fig*) to slow down
Bremsflüssigkeit *f* brake fluid
Bremslicht *nt* brake light
Bremspedal *nt* brake pedal
Bremsspur *f* tyre (BRIT) *od* tire (*US*) marks *pl*
Bremsweg *m* braking distance
brennen *unreg vi* to burn, to be on fire; **es brennt!** fire!
Brennnessel *f* nettle
Brennspiritus *m* methylated spirits *pl*
Brennstab *m* fuel rod
Brennstoff *m* liquid fuel
Brett (**-(e)s**, **-er**) *nt* board, plank; (*Bord*) shelf; (*Spielbrett*) board ■ **Bretter** *pl* (*Ski*) skis *pl*; **Schwarzes ~** notice board
Brettspiel *nt* board game
Brezel (-, **-n**) *f* pretzel
Brief (**-(e)s**, **-e**) *m* letter
Brieffreund(in) *m(f)* penfriend, pen-pal
Briefkasten *m* letter box; (*Comput*) mailbox
Briefmarke *f* postage stamp
Briefpapier *nt* notepaper
Brieftasche *f* wallet
Briefträger(in) *m(f)* postman, postwoman
Briefumschlag *m* envelope
briet *etc vb siehe* **braten**
Brille (-, **-n**) *f* spectacles *pl*; (*Schutzbrille*) goggles *pl*
bringen *unreg vt* to bring; (*mitnehmen, begleiten*) to take; (*Theat, Film*) to show; (*Rundf, TV*) to broadcast; **jdn dazu ~, etw zu tun** to make sb do sth; **jdn nach Hause ~** to take sb home; **jdn auf eine Idee ~** to give sb an idea
Brise (-, **-n**) *f* breeze
Brite (**-n**, **-n**) *m* Briton, Britisher (*US*); **die Briten** the British
Britin *f* Briton, Britisher (*US*)
britisch *adj* British
Brocken (**-s**, -) *m* piece, bit; (*Felsbrocken*) lump of rock
Brokkoli *pl* broccoli
Brombeere *f* blackberry
Bronchitis (-, **-tiden**) *f* bronchitis
Bronze (-, **-n**) *f* bronze
Brosche (-, **-n**) *f* brooch
Brot (**-(e)s**, **-e**) *nt* bread; (*Brotlaib*) loaf; **das ist ein hartes ~** (*fig*) that's a hard way to earn one's living
Brötchen *nt* roll
Brotzeit (SÜDD) *f* (*Pause*) ≈ tea break
browsen *vi* (*Comput*) to browse
Browser (**-s**, -) *m* (*Comput*) browser
Bruch (**-(e)s**, **Brüche**) *m* breakage; (*zerbrochene Stelle*) break; (*Med: Eingeweidebruch*) rupture, hernia; (*Beinbruch etc*) fracture; (*Math*) fraction

brüchig *adj* brittle
Brücke (-, **-n**) *f* bridge
Bruder (**-s**, **Brüder**) *m* brother
Brühe (-, **-n**) *f* broth, stock; (*pej*) muck
Brühwürfel *m* stock cube (BRIT), bouillon cube (*US*)
brüllen *vi* to bellow, to roar
brummen *vi* (*Bär, Mensch etc*) to growl; (*Insekt, Radio*) to buzz; (*Motor*) to roar ▸ *vt* to growl
brünett *adj* brunette
Brunnen (**-s**, **-**) *m* fountain; (*tief*) well; (*natürlich*) spring
Brust (-, **Brüste**) *f* breast; (*Männerbrust*) chest
Brustschwimmen *nt* breast-stroke
Brustwarze *f* nipple
brutal *adj* brutal
brutto *adv* gross
Bube (**-n**, **-n**) *m* (*Schurke*) rogue; (*Karten*) jack
Buch (**-(e)s**, **Bücher**) *nt* book
Buche (-, **-n**) *f* beech tree
buchen *vt* to book; (*Betrag*) to enter
Bücherei *f* library
Buchfink *m* chaffinch
Buchhalter(in) (**-s**, **-**) *m(f)* accountant
Buchhandlung *f* bookshop
Büchse (-, **-n**) *f* tin, can
Buchstabe (**-ns**, **-n**) *m* letter (of the alphabet)
buchstabieren *vt* to spell
Bucht (-, **-en**) *f* bay
Buchung *f* booking; (*Comm*) entry
Buckel (**-s**, **-**) *m* hump
bücken *vr* to bend; **sich nach etw ~** to bend down *od* stoop to pick sth up
Buddhismus (**-**) *m* Buddhism
Bude (-, **-n**) *f* booth, stall; (*umg*) digs *pl* (BRIT) *od* place (*US*)
Büfett (**-s**, **-s**) *nt* sideboard; **kaltes ~** cold buffet
Büffel (**-s**, **-**) *m* buffalo
Bügel (**-s**, **-**) *m* (*Kleiderbügel*) hanger; (*Steigbügel*) stirrup; (*Brillenbügel*) arm
Bügelbrett *nt* ironing board
Bügeleisen *nt* iron
Bügelfalte *f* crease
bügelfrei *adj* non-iron
bügeln *vt, vi* to iron
Bühne (-, **-n**) *f* stage
Bühnenbild *nt* set
Bulgare (**-n**, **-n**) *m* Bulgarian
Bulgarien (**-s**) *nt* Bulgaria
bulgarisch *adj* Bulgarian; (*Sprache*): **auf B~** in Bulgarian
Bulimie *f* (*Med*) bulimia
Bulle (**-n**, **-n**) *m* bull ▪ **die Bullen** *pl* (*pej, umg*) the fuzz *sing*, the cops
Bummel (**-s**, **-**) *m* stroll
bummeln *vi* to stroll; (*trödeln*) to dawdle; (*faulenzen*) to loaf around
Bummelzug *m* slow train
bumsen *vi* (*umg: koitieren*) to bonk, to have it off (BRIT)
Bund[1] (**-(e)s**, **Bünde**) *m* (*Freundschaftsbund etc*) bond; (*Organisation*) union; (*Pol*) confederacy; (*Hosenbund, Rockbund*) waistband
Bund[2] (**-(e)s**, **-e**) *nt* bunch; (*Strohbund*) bundle
Bundes- *in zW* Federal
Bundesfreiwilligendienst *m see note*

BUNDESFREIWILLIGENDIENST

Since compulsory military service was abolished in 2011, the **Bundesfreiwilligendienst** (national voluntary service) has largely replaced the former *Zivildienst* (community service for those opting out of military service) and the *Freiwilliges Soziales Jahr* and *Freiwilliges Ökologisches Jahr* (voluntary social year and voluntary ecological year). Volunteers must sign up for a period of 6–12 months and are then given the opportunity to work in a non-profit organisation. They receive a small payment for their work.

Bundeskanzler(in) *m(f)* Federal Chancellor
Bundesland *nt* state, Land
Bundesliga *f* (*Sport*) national league
Bundespräsident(in) *m(f)* President
Bundesrat *m* (*in Deutschland*) Upper House (of the German Parliament); (*in der Schweiz*) Council of Ministers
Bundesregierung *f* Federal Government
Bundesrepublik *f* Federal Republic; **~ Deutschland** Federal Republic of Germany
Bundesstraße *f* Federal Highway, main road

Bundestag *m* Lower House (of the German Parliament)
Bundeswehr *f* German Armed Forces *pl*

BUNDESWEHR

The **Bundeswehr** is the name for the German armed forces. In peacetime the Defence Minister is the head of the Bundeswehr, but in wartime, the *Bundeskanzler* takes over. The *Bundeswehr* comes under the jurisdiction of NATO.

Bündnis (**-ses**, **-se**) *nt* alliance
bunt *adj* coloured (BRIT), colored (*US*); (*gemischt*) mixed
Buntstift *m* coloured (BRIT) *od* colored (*US*) pencil, crayon
Burg (-, **-en**) *f* castle
Bürger(in) (**-s**, -) *m(f)* citizen
bürgerlich *adj* (*Rechte*) civil; (*Klasse*) middle-class; (*pej*) bourgeois
Bürgermeister(in) *m(f)* mayor
Bürgersteig *m* pavement (BRIT), sidewalk (*US*)
Büro (**-s**, **-s**) *nt* office
Büroklammer *f* paper clip
Bürokratie *f* bureaucracy
Bursche (**-n**, **-n**) *m* lad
Bürste (-, **-n**) *f* brush
bürsten *vt* to brush
Bus (**-ses**, **-se**) *m* bus
Busbahnhof *m* bus station
Busch (**-(e)s**, **Büsche**) *m* bush, shrub
Busen (**-s**, -) *m* bosom
Bushaltestelle *f* bus stop
Buslinie *f* bus route
Bußgeld *nt* fine
Büstenhalter *m* bra
Butter (-) *f* butter
Butterbrot *nt* (piece of) bread and butter
Buttermilch *f* buttermilk
b. w. *abk* (= *bitte wenden*) pto
Byte (**-s**, **-s**) *nt* (*Comput*) byte
bzw. *abk* = **beziehungsweise**

ca. *abk* (= *circa*) approx.
Café (**-s**, **-s**) *nt* café
Cafeteria (-, **-s**) *f* cafeteria
campen *vi* to camp
Camping (**-s**) *nt* camping
Campingbus *m* camper
Campingplatz *m* camp(ing) site
CD *f abk* (= *Compact Disc*) CD
CD-Brenner *m* CD burner
CD-ROM (-, **-s**) *f* CD-ROM
Cello (**-s**, **-s** *od* **Celli**) *nt* cello
Celsius *m* Celsius
Cent (**-(s)**, **-(s)**) *m* cent
Chamäleon (**-s**, **-s**) *nt* chameleon
Champagner (**-s**, -) *m* champagne
Champignon (**-s**, **-s**) *m* button mushroom
Chance (-, **-n**) *f* chance
Chaos (-) *nt* chaos
Chaot(in) (**-en**, **-en**) *m(f)* (*umg*) disorganized person, scatterbrain
chaotisch *adj* chaotic
Charakter (**-s**, **-e**) *m* character
charakteristisch *adj*: **~ (für)** characteristic (of), typical (of)
charmant *adj* charming
Charterflug *m* charter flight
chartern *vt* to charter
Chat (**-s**, **-s**) *m* (*Comput*) chat
chatten *vi* (*Comput*) to chat
checken *vt* (*überprüfen*) to check; (*umg*: *verstehen*) to get
Chef(in) (**-s**, **-s**) *m(f)* head; (*umg*) boss
Chefarzt *m* senior consultant
Chefärztin *f* senior consultant
Chemie (-) *f* chemistry

chemisch *adj* chemical; **chemische Reinigung** dry cleaning
Chemotherapie *f* chemotherapy
chic *adj unver* stylish, chic
Chiffre (-, **-n**) *f* (*Geheimzeichen*) cipher; (*in Zeitung*) box number
Chile (**-s**) *nt* Chile
Chili (**-s**, **-s**) *m* chilli
China (**-s**) *nt* China
Chinakohl *m* Chinese leaves *pl*
Chinese (**-n**, **-n**) *m* Chinaman, Chinese
Chinesin *f* Chinese woman
chinesisch *adj* Chinese
Chipkarte *f* smart card
Chips *pl* crisps *pl* (BRIT), chips *pl* (*US*)
Chirurg(in) (**-en**, **-en**) *m(f)* surgeon
Chlor (**-s**) *nt* chlorine
Cholera (-) *f* cholera
Cholesterin (**-s**) *nt* cholesterol
Chor (**-(e)s**, **Chöre**) *m* choir; (*Musikstück, Theat*) chorus
Choreografie *f* choreography
Christ (**-en**, **-en**) *m* Christian
Christbaum *m* Christmas tree
Christkind *nt* ≈ Father Christmas; (*Jesus*) baby Jesus
christlich *adj* Christian
Chrom (**-s**) *nt* chrome; (*Chem*) chromium
chronisch *adj* chronic
chronologisch *adj* chronological
Chrysantheme (-, **-n**) *f* chrysanthemum
circa *adv* (round) about
City (-, **-s**) *f* city centre (BRIT); **in der ~** in the city centre (BRIT), downtown (*US*)
clever *adj* clever
Clique (-, **-n**) *f* set, crowd
Cloud Computing *nt* Cloud Computing
Clown (**-s**, **-s**) *m* clown
Club (**-s**, **-s**) *m* club
CO_2-neutral *adj* carbon neutral
Cocktail (**-s**, **-s**) *m* cocktail
Cola (**-(s)**, **-s**) *nt od f* Coke®
Comicheft *nt* comic
Computer (**-s**, **-**) *m* computer
computergesteuert *adj* computer-controlled
Computergrafik *f* computer graphics *pl*
Computerspiel *nt* computer game
Computervirus *m* computer virus
Container (**-s**, **-**) *m* container
Cookie (**-s**, **-s**) *nt* (*Comput*) cookie
cool (*umg*) *adj* cool
Cord (**-(e)s**, **-e** *od* **-s**) *m* corduroy
Couch (-, **-es** *od* **-en**) *f* couch
Coupé (**-s**, **-s**) *nt* (*Aut*) coupé
Coupon (**-s**, **-s**) *m* coupon
Cousin (**-s**, **-s**) *m* cousin
Cousine (-, **-n**) *f* cousin
Crack (-) *nt* (*Droge*) crack
Creme (-, **-s**) *f* (*lit, fig*) cream; (*Koch*) mousse
Curry (**-s**) *m od nt* curry powder; (*indisches Gericht*) curry
Currywurst *f* curried sausage
Cursor (**-s**) *m* (*Comput*) cursor
Cyberangriff *m* cyberattack
Cybermobbing (**-s**, **-**) *nt* cyberbullying

SCHLÜSSELWORT

da *adv* **1** (*örtlich*) there; (*hier*) here; **da draußen** out there; **da sein** to be there; **da bin ich** here I am; **da, wo** where; **ist noch Milch da?** is there any milk left?
2 (*zeitlich*) then; (*folglich*) so
3: **da haben wir Glück gehabt** we were lucky there; **da kann man nichts machen** nothing can be done about it
▶ *konj* (*weil*) as, since

dabei *adv* (*räumlich*) close to it; (*zeitlich*) during this; (*obwohl, doch*) but, however; **~ sein** (*anwesend*) to be present; (*beteiligt*) to be involved; **ich bin ~!** count me in!; **es bleibt ~** that's settled; **er war gerade ~ zu gehen** he was just leaving; **ich finde gar nichts ~** I don't see any harm in it
Dach (**-(e)s**, **Dächer**) *nt* roof
Dachboden *m* attic, loft
Dachgepäckträger *m* (*Aut*) roof rack
Dachrinne *f* gutter
Dachs (**-es**, **-e**) *m* badger
dachte *etc vb siehe* **denken**
Dackel (**-s**, **-**) *m* dachshund
dadurch *adv* (*räumlich*) through it; (*durch diesen Umstand*) in that way; (*deshalb*) because of that, for that reason ▶ *konj*: **~, dass** because
dafür *adv* for it; (*anstatt*) instead; **er ist bekannt ~** he is well-known for that; **~ bin ich ja hier** that's what I'm here for; **er kann nichts ~ (, dass ...)** he can't help it (that ...)
dagegen *adv* against it; (*im Vergleich damit*) in comparison with it; (*bei Tausch*) for it; **ich habe nichts ~** I don't mind
daheim *adv* at home; **bei uns ~** back home
daher *adv* (*räumlich*) from there; (*Ursache*) from that ▶ *konj* (*deshalb*) that's why
dahin *adv* (*räumlich*) there; (*zeitlich*) then; (*vergangen*) gone; **bis ~** (*zeitlich*) till then; (*örtlich*) up to there; **ist es noch weit bis ~?** is there still far to go?
dahinter *adv* behind it
dahinterkommen *vi* to find out
Dahlie (**-**, **-n**) *f* dahlia
damals *adv* at that time, then
Dame (**-**, **-n**) *f* lady; (*Schach*, *Karten*) queen; (*Spiel*) draughts (Brit), checkers (*US*)
Damenbinde *f* sanitary towel (Brit) *od* napkin (*US*)
damit *adv* with it; (*begründend*) by that ▶ *konj* in order that *od* to; **was meint er ~?** what does he mean by that?; **genug ~!** that's enough!
Damm (**-(e)s**, **Dämme**) *m* dyke (Brit), dike (*US*); (*Staudamm*) dam; (*Hafendamm*) mole; (*Bahndamm*, *Straßendamm*) embankment
Dämmerung *f* twilight; (*Morgendämmerung*) dawn; (*Abenddämmerung*) dusk
Dampf (**-(e)s**, **Dämpfe**) *m* steam; (*Dunst*) vapour (Brit), vapor (*US*)
dampfen *vt* to vape ▶ *vi* to vape; (*Zug*) to puff
dämpfen *vt* (*Koch*) to steam; (*fig*) to dampen
Dampfer (**-s**, **-**) *m* steamer
Dampfkochtopf *m* pressure cooker
danach *adv* after that; (*zeitlich*) afterwards; (*gemäß*) accordingly; **mir war nicht ~ (zumute)** I didn't feel like it; **er sieht ~ aus** he looks it
Däne (**-n**, **-n**) *m* Dane
daneben *adv* beside it; (*im Vergleich*) in comparison
Dänemark (**-s**) *nt* Denmark
Dänin *f* Dane, Danish woman *od* girl
dänisch *adj* Danish
dank *präp* (*+dat od gen*) thanks to
Dank (**-(e)s**) *m* thanks *pl*; **vielen** *od* **schönen ~** many thanks; **jdm ~ sagen** to thank sb

dankbar *adj* grateful; (*Aufgabe*) rewarding
danke *interj* thank you, thanks; **~ schön (***od* **sehr)** thank you very much
danken *vi +dat* to thank; **nichts zu ~!** don't mention it
dann *adv* then; **~ eben nicht** well, in that case (there's no more to be said)
daran *adv* on it; (*stoßen*) against it; **es liegt ~, dass …** the cause of it is that …
darauf *adv* (*räumlich*) on it; (*zielgerichtet*) towards it; (*danach*) afterwards; **~ folgend** following; **es kommt ganz ~ an, ob …** it depends whether …; **am Tag ~** the next day
darauffolgend *adj* (*Tag, Jahr*) next, following
daraus *adv* from it; **was ist ~ geworden?** what became of it?
darin *adv* in (there), in it; **der Unterschied liegt ~, dass …** the difference is that …
Darlehen, Darlehn (**-s**, **-**) *nt* loan
Darm (**-(e)s**, **Därme**) *m* intestine; (*Wurstdarm*) skin
Darmgrippe *f* gastric influenza
dar|stellen *vt* to represent; (*Theat*) to act; (*beschreiben*) to describe
Darsteller(in) (**-s**, **-**) *m(f)* actor, actress
Darstellung *f* portrayal, depiction
darüber *adv* (*räumlich*) over/above it; (*fahren*) over it; (*mehr*) more; (*währenddessen*) meanwhile; (*sprechen, streiten*) about it
darum *konj* that's why; **es geht ~, dass …** the thing is that …
darunter *adv* (*räumlich*) under it; (*dazwischen*) among them; (*weniger*) less; **was verstehen Sie ~?** what do you understand by that?
darunterfallen *vi* to be included
das *pron* that ▶ *def art* the; **~ heißt** that is; *siehe auch* **der**
da sein *unreg vi siehe* **da**
dasjenige *pron siehe* **derjenige**
dass *konj* that
dasselbe *nt pron* the same
Datei *f* (*Comput*) file
Dateimanager *m* file manager
Daten *pl* (*Comput*) data; (*Angaben*) data *pl*
Datenaustausch *m* (*Comput*) file sharing
Datenbank *f* database
Datenmissbrauch *m* misuse of data
Datenschutz *m* data protection
Datenträger *m* data carrier
Datenverarbeitung *f* data processing
datieren *vt* to date
Dativ (**-s**, **-e**) *m* dative
Dattel (**-**, **-n**) *f* date
Datum (**-s**, **Daten**) *nt* date
Dauer (**-**, **-n**) *f* duration; (*gewisse Zeitspanne*) length; **auf die ~** in the long run
Dauerauftrag *m* standing order
dauerhaft *adj* lasting, durable
Dauerkarte *f* season ticket
dauern *vi* to last; **es hat sehr lang gedauert, bis er …** it took him a long time to …; **wie lange dauert es denn noch?** how much longer will it be?
dauernd *adj* constant ▶ *adv* always, constantly; **er lachte ~** he kept laughing
Dauerwelle *f* perm, permanent wave
Daumen (**-s**, **-**) *m* thumb
Daunendecke *f* down duvet
davon *adv* of it; (*räumlich*) away; (*weg von*) away from it; (*Grund*) because of it; (*mit Passiv*) by it; **das kommt ~!** that's what you get; **~ sprechen/wissen** to talk/know of *od* about it; **was habe ich ~?** what's the point?; **~ betroffen werden** to be affected by it
davon|laufen *unreg vi* to run away
davor *adv* (*räumlich*) in front of it; (*zeitlich*) before (that); **~ warnen** to warn about it
dazu *adv* (*legen, stellen*) by it; (*essen*) with it; **und ~ noch** and in addition; **~ fähig sein** to be capable of it
dazu|gehören *vi* to belong to it
dazu|kommen *unreg vi*: **kommt noch etwas dazu?** will there be anything else?
dazwischen *adv* in between; (*zusammen mit*) among them; **der Unterschied ~** the difference between them
dazwischen|kommen *unreg vi*: **es ist etwas dazwischengekommen** something (has) cropped up
DDR (**-**) *f abk* (*früher*: = *Deutsche Demokratische Republik*) GDR
Dealer(in) (**-s**, **-**) (*umg*) *m(f)* pusher

Deck (**-(e)s**, **-s** *od* **-e**) *nt* deck; **an ~ gehen** to go on deck
Decke (**-**, **-n**) *f* cover; (*Bettdecke*) blanket; (*Tischdecke*) tablecloth; (*Zimmerdecke*) ceiling
Deckel (**-s**, **-**) *m* lid
decken *vt* to cover; (*Tisch*) to lay, to set ▸ *vr*: **sich ~** (*Interessen*) to coincide; (*Aussagen*) to correspond
Decoder *m* (*TV*) decoder
defekt *adj* faulty
Defekt (**-(e)s**, **-e**) *m* fault, defect
definieren *vt* to define
Definition *f* definition
deftig *adj* (*Preise*) steep; **ein deftiges Essen** a good solid meal
dehnbar *adj* elastic
dehnen *vt*, *vr* to stretch
Deich (**-(e)s**, **-e**) *m* dyke (BRIT), dike (*US*)
dein *pron* your
deine(r, s) *poss pron* yours
deiner *gen von* **du** ▸ *pron* of you
deinetwegen *adv* (*für dich*) for your sake; (*wegen dir*) on your account
deinstallieren *vt* (*Programm*) to uninstall
Dekolleté, Dekolletee (**-s**, **-s**) *nt* low neckline
Dekoration *f* decoration; (*in Laden*) window dressing
dekorativ *adj* decorative
dekorieren *vt* to decorate; (*Schaufenster*) to dress
Delfin (**-s**, **-e**) *m* dolphin
delikat *adj* (*zart, heikel*) delicate; (*köstlich*) delicious
Delikatesse (**-**, **-n**) *f* delicacy
Delle (**-**, **-n**) (*umg*) *f* dent
Delphin (**-s**, **-e**) *m* = **Delfin**
dem *art dat von* **der**; **das**; **wie ~ auch sei** be that as it may
demnächst *adv* shortly
Demo (**-s**, **-s**) (*umg*) *f* demo
Demokratie *f* democracy
demokratisch *adj* democratic
demolieren *vt* to demolish
Demonstration *f* demonstration
demonstrieren *vt*, *vi* to demonstrate
den *art akk von* **der**
Denglisch (**-**) *nt* Denglisch
denkbar *adj* conceivable ▸ *adv*: **~ einfach** extremely simple
denken *unreg vi* to think ▸ *vt*: **für jdn/etw gedacht sein** to be intended *od* meant for sb/sth ▸ *vr* (*vorstellen*): **das kann ich mir ~** I can imagine; **ich denke schon** I think so; **an jdn/etw ~** to think of sb/sth
Denkmal (**-s**, **Denkmäler**) *nt* monument
Denkmalschutz *m*: **etw unter ~ stellen** to classify sth as a historical monument
denn *konj* for; (*konzessiv*): **es sei ~, (dass)** unless ▸ *adv* then; (*nach Komparativ*) than
dennoch *konj* nevertheless
Deo (**-s**, **-s**), **Deodorant** (**-s**, **-s**) *nt* deodorant
Deoroller *m* roll-on deodorant
Deospray *nt od m* deodorant spray
Deponie *f* dump, disposal site
Depression *f* depression
deprimieren *vt* to depress
deprimiert *adj* depressed

 **SCHLÜSSELWORT**

der (*f* **die**, *nt* **das**, *pl* **die**, *gen* **des**, **der**, **des**, *pl* **der**, *dat* **dem**, **der**, **dem**, *pl* **den**, *akk* **den**, **die**, **das**, *pl* **die**) *def art* the; **der Rhein** the Rhine; **der Klaus** (*umg*) Klaus; **die Frau** (*im Allgemeinen*) women; **der Tod/das Leben** death/life; **der Fuß des Berges** the foot of the hill; **gib es der Frau** give it to the woman; **er hat sich** *dat* **die Hand verletzt** he has hurt his hand
▸ *rel pron* **1** (*bei Menschen*) who, that
2 (*bei Tieren, Sachen*) which, that; **der Mann, den ich gesehen habe** the man who *od* whom *od* that I saw
▸ *demon pron* he/she/it; (*jener, dieser*) that; (*pl*) those; **der/die war es** it was him/her; **der mit der Brille** the one with the glasses; **ich will den (da)** I want that one

derart *adv* (*Art und Weise*) in such a way; (*vor adj*) so
derartig *adj* such, this sort of
deren *rel pron* (*gen sing von* **die**) whose; (*von Sachen*) of which; (*gen pl von* **der**, **die**, **das**) whose, of whom
dergleichen *pron* such; (*substantivisch*): **er tat nichts ~** he did nothing of the kind; **und ~ (mehr)** and suchlike
derjenige *pron* he/she/it; (*rel*) the one (who); (*von Sachen*) that (which)

dermaßen *adv* to such an extent, so
derselbe *m pron* the same
deshalb *adv, konj* therefore, that's why
Design (**-s**, **-s**) *nt* design
Desinfektionsmittel *nt* disinfectant
desinfizieren *vt* to disinfect
Desktop (-, **-(s)**) *m* (*Comput*) desktop
dessen *pron gen von* **der**; **das**
Dessert (**-s**, **-s**) *nt* dessert
desto *adv* all *od* so much the; **~ besser** all the better
deswegen *konj* therefore
Detail (**-s**, **-s**) *nt* detail
Detektiv(in) (**-s**, **-e**) *m(f)* detective
deutlich *adj* clear; (*Unterschied*) distinct
deutsch *adj* German; **auf D~** in German
Deutsche(r) *f(m)*: **er ist Deutscher** he is (a) German
Deutschland *nt* Germany
Devise (-, **-n**) *f* motto, device ■ **Devisen** *pl* (*Fin*) foreign currency *od* exchange
Dezember (**-(s)**, -) *m* December; *siehe auch* **September**
dezent *adj* discreet
Dia (**-s**, **-s**) *nt* slide
Diabetes (-, -) *m* (*Med*) diabetes
Diabetiker(in) (**-s**, -) *m(f)* diabetic
Diagnose (-, **-n**) *f* diagnosis
diagonal *adj* diagonal
Dialekt (**-(e)s**, **-e**) *m* dialect
Dialog (**-(e)s**, **-e**) *m* dialogue
Diamant *m* diamond
Diaprojektor *m* slide projector
Diät (-) *f* diet ■ **Diäten** *pl* (*Pol*) allowance *sing*; **(nach einer) ~ leben** to be on a special diet
Diavortrag *m* slide show
dich *akk von* **du** ▶ *pron* you ▶ *refl pron* yourself
dicht *adj* dense; (*Nebel*) thick; (*Gewebe*) close; (*undurchlässig*) (water)tight ▶ *adv*: **~ an/bei** close to; **~ bevölkert** densely *od* heavily populated
Dichter(in) (**-s**, -) *m(f)* poet; (*Autor*) writer
Dichtung *f* (*Tech*) washer; (*Aut*) gasket; (*Gedichte*) poetry; (*Prosa*) (piece of) writing
dick *adj* thick; (*fett*) fat
Dickdarm *m* (*Anat*) colon
Dickkopf *m* mule
Dickmilch *f* soured milk
die *def art* the; *siehe auch* **der**
Dieb(in) (**-(e)s**, **-e**) *m(f)* thief
Diebstahl *m* theft
diejenige *pron siehe* **derjenige**
Diele (-, **-n**) *f* (*Flur*) hall
Dienst (**-(e)s**, **-e**) *m* service; **außer ~** retired; **~ haben** to be on duty
Dienstag *m* Tuesday; **am ~** on Tuesday; **~ in acht Tagen** *od* **in einer Woche** a week on Tuesday, Tuesday week; **~ vor einer Woche** *od* **acht Tagen** a week (ago) last Tuesday
dienstags *adv* on Tuesdays
diensthabend *adj* (*Arzt, Offizier*) on duty
Dienstleistung *f* service
dienstlich *adj* official; (*Angelegenheiten*) business *attrib*
Dienstreise *f* business trip
Dienststelle *f* office
Dienstwagen *m* (*von Beamten*) official car
Dienstzeit *f* office hours *pl*; (*Mil*) period of service
diesbezüglich *adj* (*Frage*) on this matter
diese(r, s) *pron* this (one)
Diesel (**-s**) *m* (*Kraftstoff*) diesel fuel
dieselbe *f pron* the same
Dieselöl *nt* diesel oil
diesig *adj* (*Wetter*) misty, hazy
diesmal *adv* this time
Dietrich (**-s**, **-e**) *m* picklock
Differenz *f* difference
digital *adj* digital
Digitalanzeige *f* digital display
Digitalfernsehen *nt* digital TV
Digitalkamera *f* digital camera
Diktat (**-(e)s**, **-e**) *nt* dictation
Diktatur *f* dictatorship
DIN *f abk* (*= Deutsches Institut für Normung*) *German Institute for Standardization*; **~ A4** A4
Ding (**-(e)s**, **-e**) *nt* thing; **so wie die Dinge liegen, nach Lage der Dinge** as things are
Dingsbums (-) (*umg*) *nt* thingummybob (Brit)
Dinosaurier *m* dinosaur
Diphtherie *f* diphtheria
Diplom (**-(e)s**, **-e**) *nt* diploma
Diplomat(in) (**-en**, **-en**) *m(f)* diplomat
dir *dat von* **du** ▶ *pron* (to) you

direkt *adj* direct
Direktflug *m* direct flight
Direktor(in) *m(f)* director; (*von Schule*) principal, head (teacher) (Brit)
Direktübertragung *f* live broadcast
Dirigent(in) *m(f)* conductor
dirigieren *vt* to direct; (*Mus*) to conduct
Diskette *f* disk, diskette
Diskettenlaufwerk *nt* disk drive
Disko (-, **-s**) *f* disco
Diskothek (-, **-en**) *f* disco(theque)
diskret *adj* discreet
diskriminieren *vt* to discriminate against
Diskussion *f* discussion
diskutieren *vt*, *vi* to discuss
disqualifizieren *vt* to disqualify
Distanz *f* distance
Distel (-, **-n**) *f* thistle
Disziplin (-, **-en**) *f* discipline
divers *adj* various
dividieren *vt*: **~ (durch)** to divide (by)

SCHLÜSSELWORT

doch *adv* **1** (*dennoch*) after all; (*sowieso*) anyway; **er kam doch noch** he came after all; **du weißt es ja doch besser** you know more about it (than I do) anyway; **und doch, ...** and yet ...
2 (*als bejahende Antwort*) yes I do/it does *etc*; **das ist nicht wahr — doch!** that's not true — yes it is!
3 (*auffordernd*): **komm doch** do come; **lass ihn doch** just leave him; **nicht doch!** oh no!
4: **sie ist doch noch so jung** but she's still so young; **Sie wissen doch, wie das ist** you know how it is(, don't you?); **wenn doch** if only
▶ *konj* **1** (*aber*) but
2 (*trotzdem*) all the same; **und doch hat er es getan** but still he did it

Doktor (**-s**, **-en**) *m* doctor
Dokument *nt* document
Dokumentarfilm *m* documentary (film)
dokumentieren *vt* to document
Dolch (**-(e)s**, **-e**) *m* dagger
dolmetschen *vt*, *vi* to interpret
Dolmetscher(in) (**-s**, **-**) *m(f)* interpreter
Dolomiten *pl* (*Geog*): **die ~** the Dolomites *pl*
Dom (**-(e)s**, **-e**) *m* cathedral
Domäne (-, **-n**) *f* (*fig*) domain, province
Dominikanische Republik *f* Dominican Republic
Donau *f*: **die ~** the Danube
Döner (**-s**, **-**), **Döner Kebab** (**-(s)**, **-s**) *m* doner kebab
Dongle *m* (*Comput*) dongle
Donner (**-s**, **-**) *m* thunder
donnern *vi unpers* to thunder
Donnerstag *m* Thursday; *siehe auch* **Dienstag**
donnerstags *adv* (on) Thursdays
doof (*umg*) *adj* stupid
dopen *vt* to dope
Doping (**-s**) *nt* doping
Dopingkontrolle *f* (*Sport*) dope check
Doppel (**-s**, **-**) *nt* duplicate; (*Sport*) doubles
Doppelbett *nt* double bed
doppelklicken *vi* to double-click
Doppelpunkt *m* colon
Doppelstecker *m* two-way adaptor
doppelt *adj* double; **in doppelter Ausführung** in duplicate
Doppelzimmer *nt* double room
Dorf (**-(e)s**, **Dörfer**) *nt* village
Dorn (**-(e)s**, **-en**) *m* (*Bot*) thorn
Dörrobst *nt* dried fruit
dort *adv* there; **~ drüben** over there
dorther *adv* from there
Dose (-, **-n**) *f* box; (*Blechdose*) tin, can
dösen (*umg*) *vi* to doze
Dosenbier *nt* canned beer
Dosenöffner *m* tin (Brit) *od* can opener
Dotter (**-s**, **-**) *m* egg yolk
downloaden *vti* (*Comput*) to download
Downsyndrom *nt no pl* (*Med*) Down's Syndrome
Dozent(in) (**-en**, **-en**) *m(f)*: **~ (für)** lecturer (in), professor (of) (US)
Dr. *abk* = **Doktor**
Drache (**-n**, **-n**) *m* dragon
Drachen (**-s**, **-**) *m* kite
Drachenfliegen *nt* (*Sport*) hang-gliding
Draht (**-(e)s**, **Drähte**) *m* wire
drahtlos *adj* wireless
Drahtseilbahn *f* cable railway
Drama (**-s**, **Dramen**) *nt* drama
dramatisch *adj* dramatic

dran (*umg*) *adv* (*an der Reihe*): **jetzt bist du ~** it's your turn now; **früh/spät ~ sein** to be early/late
drang *etc vb siehe* **dringen**
Drang (**-(e)s**, **Dränge**) *m* (*Trieb*) urge; (*Druck*) pressure; **~ nach** urge *od* yearning for
drängeln *vt*, *vi* to push
drängen *vt* (*schieben*) to push; (*antreiben*) to urge ▶ *vi* (*eilig sein*) to be urgent; (*Zeit*) to press; **auf etw** *akk* **~** to press for sth
dran|kommen (*umg*) *unreg vi* (*an die Reihe kommen*) to have one's turn
drauf (*umg*) *adv*: **gut/schlecht ~ sein** to be in a good/bad mood
Draufgänger(in) (**-s**, **-**) *m*(*f*) daredevil
draußen *adv* outside
Dreck (**-(e)s**) *m* mud, dirt
dreckig *adj* dirty, filthy
drehen *vt* to turn; (*Zigaretten*) to roll; (*Film*) to shoot ▶ *vi* to turn, to rotate ▶ *vr* to turn; (*handeln von*): **sich um etw ~** to be about sth
Drehtür *f* revolving door
Drehzahlmesser *m* rev(olution) counter
drei *num* three; **~ viertel** three quarters
Dreieck *nt* triangle
dreieckig *adj* triangular
dreifach *adj* triple ▶ *adv* three times
dreihundert *num* three hundred
dreimal *adv* three times
Dreirad *nt* tricycle
dreißig *num* thirty
Dreiviertelstunde *f* three-quarters of an hour
dreizehn *num* thirteen
dressieren *vt* to train
Dressur *f* training
drin (*umg*) *adv*: **bis jetzt ist noch alles ~** everything is still quite open
dringen *unreg vi* (*Wasser, Licht, Kälte*): **~ (durch/in** *+akk***)** to penetrate (through/into); **auf etw** *akk* **~** to insist on sth
dringend *adj* urgent
drinnen *adv* inside, indoors
dritt *adv*: **wir kommen zu ~** three of us are coming together
dritte(r, s) *adj* third; **die D~ Welt** Third World; **3. Juni** 3(rd) June; (*gesprochen*) the third of June; **am 3. Juni** on 3(rd) June, on June 3(rd); (*gesprochen*) on the third of June; **München, den 3. Juni** Munich, June 3(rd)
Drittel (**-s**, **-**) *nt* third
drittens *adv* thirdly
Droge (**-**, **-n**) *f* drug
drogenabhängig *adj* addicted to drugs
Drogenentzug (**-(e)s**) *m* detox (*umg*), detoxification; (*from drugs*) withdrawal
Drogerie *f* chemist's shop (Brit), drugstore (*US*)

DROGERIE

A **Drogerie** is a type of supermarket selling cleaning products, cosmetics, perfumes and toiletries, as well as medication not requiring a prescription. There are several chains of *Drogerie* throughout Germany and Austria.

Drogeriemarkt *m* discount chemist's (Brit) *od* drugstore (*US*)
drohen *vi*: **(jdm) ~** to threaten (sb)
dröhnen *vi* (*Motor*) to roar; (*Stimme, Musik*) to ring, to resound
Drohung *f* threat
Drossel (**-**, **-n**) *f* thrush
drüben *adv* over there, on the other side
drüber (*umg*) *adv* = **darüber**
Druck (**-(e)s**, **-e**) *m* (*Zwang, Phys*) pressure; (*Typ: Vorgang*) printing; (*: Produkt*) print; (*fig: Belastung*) burden, weight
Druckbuchstabe *m* block letter; **in Druckbuchstaben schreiben** to print
drucken *vt*, *vi* (*Typ, Comput*) to print
drücken *vt* (*Knopf, Hand*) to press; (*fig: Preise*) to keep down ▶ *vi* to press; (*zu eng sein*) to pinch ▶ *vr*: **sich vor etw** *dat* **~** to get out of (doing) sth
drückend *adj* oppressive
Drucker (**-s**, **-**) *m* printer
Druckknopf *m* press stud (Brit), snap fastener
Drucksache *f* printed matter
Druckschrift *f* block letters *pl*
drunten *adv* down there
Drüse (**-**, **-n**) *f* gland
Dschungel (**-s**, **-**) *m* jungle
du *pron* you; **mit jdm per du sein** to be on familiar terms with sb

Duale Ausbildung *f see note*

DUALE AUSBILDUNG

Duale Ausbildung (dual apprenticeship) refers to a type of training that combines academic study with practical work and in which the apprentice gets to benefit both from learning the theory of the subject at a technical college and from on-the-job training. This is very popular in Germany where it is a highly regarded training system.

Dübel (**-s**, **-**) *m* plug; (*Holzdübel*) dowel
ducken *vt* (*Kopf*) to duck ▶ *vr* to duck
Dudelsack *m* bagpipes *pl*
Duett (**-(e)s**, **-e**) *nt* duet
Duft (**-(e)s**, **Düfte**) *m* scent
duften *vi* to be fragrant; **es duftet nach ...** it smells of ...
dulden *vt* to tolerate
dumm *adj* stupid
Dummheit *f* stupidity; (*Tat*) blunder, stupid mistake
Dummkopf *m* blockhead
dumpf *adj* (*Ton*) hollow, dull; (*Erinnerung, Schmerz*) vague
Düne (**-**, **-n**) *f* dune
Dünger (**-s**, **-**) *m* fertilizer
dunkel *adj* dark; (*Stimme*) deep; (*Ahnung*) vague; (*rätselhaft*) obscure; (*verdächtig*) dubious; **im Dunkeln tappen** (*fig*) to grope in the dark
Dunkelheit *f* darkness
dünn *adj* thin
Dunst (**-es**, **Dünste**) *m* vapour (BRIT), vapor (US); (*Wetter*) haze
dünsten *vt* to steam
Dur (**-**, **-**) *nt* (*Mus*) major

durch *präp +akk* **1** (*hindurch*) through; **durch den Urwald** through the jungle; **durch die ganze Welt reisen** to travel all over the world
2 (*mittels*) through, by (means of); (*aufgrund*) due to, owing to; **Tod durch Herzschlag/den Strang** death from a heart attack/by hanging; **durch die Post** by post; **durch seine Bemühungen** through his efforts
▶ *adj* **1** (*hindurch*) through; **die ganze Nacht durch** all through the night; **den Sommer durch** during the summer; **8 Uhr durch** past 8 o'clock; **durch und durch** completely
2 (*Koch: umg: durchgebraten*) done; **(gut) durch** well-done

durchaus *adv* completely; **~ nicht** not at all
Durchblick *m* view; **den ~ haben** (*fig: umg*) to know what's what
durch|blicken *vi* to look through; (*umg: verstehen*): **(bei etw) ~** to understand (sth); **etw ~ lassen** (*fig*) to hint at sth
Durchblutung *f* circulation (of blood)
durch|brennen *unreg vi* (*Draht, Sicherung*) to burn through; (*umg*) to run away
durchdacht *adj* well thought-out
durch|drehen *vt* (*Fleisch*) to mince ▶ *vi* (*umg*) to crack up
durcheinander *adv* in a mess; (*verwirrt*) confused
Durcheinander (**-s**) *nt* (*Verwirrung*) confusion; (*Unordnung*) mess
durcheinander|bringen *vt* to mess up; (*verwirren*) to confuse
durcheinander|reden *vi* to talk at the same time
durcheinander|trinken *vi* to mix one's drinks
Durchfahrt *f* transit; (*Verkehr*) thoroughfare; **~ verboten!** no through road
Durchfall *m* (*Med*) diarrhoea (BRIT), diarrhea (US)
durch|fallen *unreg vi* to fall through; (*in Prüfung*) to fail
durch|fragen *vr* to find one's way by asking
durch|führen *vt* to carry out
Durchgang *m* passage(way); (*Sport*) round; (*bei Wahl*) ballot
Durchgangsverkehr *m* through traffic
durchgefroren *adj* (*Mensch*) frozen stiff
durch|gehen *unreg vi* to go through; (*ausreißen: Pferd*) to break loose; (*Mensch*) to run away
durchgehend *adj* (*Zug*) through; (*Öffnungszeiten*) continuous

durch|halten *unreg vi* to last out ▶ *vt* to keep up
durch|kommen *unreg vi* to get through; (*überleben*) to pull through
durch|lassen *unreg vt* (*Person*) to let through; (*Wasser*) to let in
durch|lesen *unreg vt* to read through
durchleuchten *vt untr* to X-ray
durch|machen *vt* to go through; **die Nacht ~** to make a night of it
Durchmesser (**-s**, **-**) *m* diameter
Durchreise *f* transit; **auf der ~** passing through; (*Güter*) in transit
Durchreisevisum *nt* transit visa
durchs = **durch das**
Durchsage *f* intercom *od* radio announcement
durch|schauen *vt*, *vi* (*lit*) to look *od* see through
durch|schlagen *unreg vr* to get by
durch|schneiden *unreg vt* to cut through
Durchschnitt *m* (*Mittelwert*) average; **im ~** on average
durchschnittlich *adj* average ▶ *adv* on average
Durchschnittsgeschwindigkeit *f* average speed
durch|setzen *vt* to enforce ▶ *vr* (*Erfolg haben*) to succeed; (*sich behaupten*) to get one's way
durchsichtig *adj* transparent
durch|stellen *vt* (*Tel*) to put through
durch|streichen *unreg vt* to cross out
durchsuchen *vt untr* to search
Durchsuchung *f* search
durchwachsen *adj* (*Speck*) streaky; (*fig: mittelmäßig*) so-so
Durchwahl *f* (*Tel*) direct dialling; (*bei Firma*) extension
durch|ziehen *unreg vi* to pass through; **eine Sache ~** to finish off sth
Durchzug *m* (*Luft*) draught (BRIT), draft (*US*); (*von Truppen, Vögeln*) passage

 **SCHLÜSSELWORT**

dürfen *unreg vi* **1** (*Erlaubnis haben*) to be allowed to; **ich darf das** I'm allowed to (do that); **darf ich?** may I?; **darf ich ins Kino?** can *od* may I go to the cinema?; **es darf geraucht werden** you may smoke
2 (*in Verneinungen*): **er darf das nicht** he's not allowed to (do that); **das darf nicht geschehen** that must not happen; **da darf sie sich nicht wundern** that shouldn't surprise her
3 (*in Höflichkeitsformeln*): **darf ich Sie bitten, das zu tun?** may *od* could I ask you to do that?; **was darf es sein?** what can I get for you?
4 (*können*): **das dürfen Sie mir glauben** you can believe me
5 (*Möglichkeit*): **das dürfte genug sein** that should be enough; **es dürfte Ihnen bekannt sein, dass ...** as you will probably know ...

dürftig *adj* (*ärmlich*) poor; (*unzulänglich*) inadequate
dürr *adj* dried-up; (*Land*) arid; (*mager*) skinny
Durst (**-(e)s**) *m* thirst; **~ haben** to be thirsty
durstig *adj* thirsty
Dusche (**-**, **-n**) *f* shower
duschen *vi*, *vr* to have a shower
Duschgel *nt* shower gel
Düse (**-**, **-n**) *f* nozzle; (*Flugzeugdüse*) jet
Düsenflugzeug *nt* jet (plane)
Dussel (**-s**, **-**) (*umg*) *m* twit, berk
düster *adj* dark; (*Gedanken, Zukunft*) gloomy
Dutzend (**-s**, **-e**) *nt* dozen
duzen *vt to address with the familiar "du" form* ▶ *vr to address each other with the familiar "du" form*
DVD (**-**, **-s**) *f abk* (= *Digital Versatile Disc*) DVD
dynamisch *adj* dynamic
Dynamo (**-s**, **-s**) *m* dynamo
D-Zug *m* through train

Ebbe (-, **-n**) *f* low tide
eben *adj* level; (*glatt*) smooth ▶ *adv* just; (*bestätigend*) exactly
Ebene (-, **-n**) *f* plain; (*fig*) level
ebenfalls *adv* likewise
ebenso *adv* just as; **~ gut** just as well; **~ viel** just as much
Eber (**-s**, **-**) *m* boar
E-Book (**-s**, **-s**) *nt* e-book
E-Book-Reader *m* e-reader
Echo (**-s**, **-s**) *nt* echo
echt *adj* genuine; **ich hab ~ keine Zeit** (*umg*) I really don't have any time
Ecke (-, **-n**) *f* corner; (*Math*) angle; **gleich um die ~** just around the corner
eckig *adj* angular
Eckzahn *m* eye tooth
Ecstasy *nt* (*Droge*) ecstasy
edel *adj* noble
Edelstein *m* precious stone
EDV (-) *f abk* (= *elektronische Datenverarbeitung*) EDP
Efeu (**-s**) *m* ivy
Effekt (**-(e)s**, **-e**) *m* effect
egal *adj* all the same; **das ist mir ganz ~** it's all the same to me
egoistisch *adj* selfish, egoistic
ehe *konj* before
Ehe (-, **-n**) *f* marriage
Ehefrau *f* wife
Eheleute *pl* married couple *pl*
ehemalig *adj* former
ehemals *adv* formerly
Ehemann *m* married man; (*Partner*) husband
Ehepaar *nt* married couple
eher *adv* (*früher*) sooner; (*lieber*) rather, sooner; (*mehr*) more
Ehering *m* wedding ring
eheste(r, s) *adj* (*früheste*) first, earliest; **am ehesten** (*am wahrscheinlichsten*) most probably
Ehre (-, **-n**) *f* honour (BRIT), honor (US)
ehren *vt* to honour (BRIT), to honor (US)
ehrenamtlich *adj* honorary
Ehrengast *m* guest of honour (BRIT) *od* honor (US)
Ehrenwort *nt* word of honour (BRIT) *od* honor (US); **ich gebe dir mein ~** I give you my word
ehrgeizig *adj* ambitious
ehrlich *adj* honest
Ei (**-(e)s**, **-er**) *nt* egg
Eiche (-, **-n**) *f* oak (tree)
Eichel (-, **-n**) *f* acorn
Eichhörnchen *nt* squirrel
Eid (**-(e)s**, **-e**) *m* oath
Eidechse (-, **-n**) *f* lizard
Eierbecher *m* egg cup
Eierstock *m* ovary
Eieruhr *f* egg timer
Eifersucht *f* jealousy
eifersüchtig *adj*: **~ (auf** *+akk***)** jealous (of)
Eigelb (**-(e)s**, **-e** *od* **-**) *nt* egg yolk
eigen *adj* own; (*eigenartig*) peculiar
eigenartig *adj* peculiar
Eigenschaft *f* quality; (*Chem*, *Phys*) property; (*Merkmal*) characteristic
eigentlich *adj* actual, real ▶ *adv* actually, really; **was willst du ~ hier?** what do you want here anyway?
Eigentum *nt* property
Eigentümer(in) (**-s**, **-**) *m(f)* owner
Eigentumswohnung *f* freehold flat
eignen *vr* to be suited
Eilbrief *m* express letter
Eile (-) *f* haste
eilen *vi* (*Mensch*) to hurry; (*dringend sein*) to be urgent
eilig *adj* hurried; (*dringlich*) urgent; **es ~ haben** to be in a hurry
Eimer (**-s**, **-**) *m* bucket
ein(e) *num* one ▶ *indef art* a, an ▶ *adv*: **nicht ~ noch aus wissen** not to know what to do; **E~/Aus** (*an Geräten*) on/off
einander *pron* one another, each other
ein|arbeiten *vr*: **sich (in etw** *akk***) ~** to familiarize o.s. (with sth)
ein|atmen *vt*, *vi* to breathe in

Einbahnstraße *f* one-way street
ein|bauen *vt* to build in; (*Motor*) to install, to fit
Einbauküche *f* (fully-)fitted kitchen
ein|biegen *unreg vi* to turn
ein|bilden *vr*: **sich** *dat* **etw ~** to imagine sth
ein|brechen *unreg vi* (*einstürzen*) to fall in; (*Einbruch verüben*) to break in
Einbrecher(in) (**-s**, **-**) *m(f)* burglar
ein|bringen *unreg vt* to bring in; (*Geld, Vorteil*) to yield; (*mitbringen*) to contribute
Einbruch *m* (*Hauseinbruch*) break-in, burglary; **bei ~ der Nacht** at nightfall
Einbürgerung *f* naturalization
ein|checken *vt, vi* to check in
ein|cremen *vt* to put cream on
eindeutig *adj* unequivocal
ein|dringen *unreg vi*: **~ (in** *+akk***)** to force one's way in(to); (*in Haus*) to break in(to); (*Gas, Wasser*) to penetrate
Eindruck *m* impression
eine(r, s) *pron* one; (*jemand*) someone; **es kam eines zum anderen** it was (just) one thing after another
eineiig *adj* (*Zwillinge*) identical
eineinhalb *num* one and a half
einerseits *adv* on the one hand
einfach *adj* simple; (*nicht mehrfach*) single ▸ *adv* simply
Einfahrt *f* (*Vorgang*) driving in; (*von Zug*) pulling in; (*Min*) descent; (*Ort*) entrance
Einfall *m* (*Idee*) idea
ein|fallen *unreg vi* (*einstürzen*) to fall in, to collapse; (*Licht*) to fall; **sich** *dat* **etwas ~ lassen** to have a good idea; **was fällt Ihnen ein!** what do you think you're doing?
Einfamilienhaus *nt* detached house
einfarbig *adj* all one colour (Brit) *od* color (US); (*Stoff etc*) self-coloured (Brit), self-colored (US)
Einfluss *m* influence
ein|frieren *unreg vi* to freeze (in) ▸ *vt* to freeze
ein|fügen *vt* to fit in; (*zusätzlich*) to add; (*Comput*) to insert
Einfuhr (**-**) *f* import
ein|führen *vt* to introduce; (*Ware*) to import
Einführung *f* introduction
Eingabe *f* (*Dateneingabe*) input
Eingang *m* entrance
Eingangshalle *f* entrance hall
ein|geben *unreg vt* (*Daten etc*) to enter
eingebildet *adj* imaginary; (*eitel*) conceited
Eingeborene(r) *f(m)* native
ein|gehen *unreg vi* to be received; (*Tier, Pflanze*) to die; (*schrumpfen*) to shrink ▸ *vt* (*abmachen*) to enter into; (*Wette*) to make; **auf etw** *akk* **~** to go into sth; **auf jdn ~** to respond to sb
ein|gewöhnen *vr*: **sich ~ (in** *+dat***)** to settle down (in)
ein|gießen *unreg vt* to pour (out)
ein|greifen *unreg vi* to intervene
Eingriff *m* intervention; (*Operation*) operation
ein|halten *unreg vt* (*Regel*) to keep
einheimisch *adj* native
Einheimische(r) *f(m)* local
Einheit *f* unity; (*Maß, Mil*) unit
einheitlich *adj* uniform
ein|holen *vt* (*Vorsprung aufholen*) to catch up with; (*Verspätung*) to make up; (*Rat, Erlaubnis*) to ask
Einhorn *nt* unicorn
einhundert *num* one hundred
einig *adj* (*vereint*) united; **sich** *dat* **~ sein** to be in agreement
einige(r, s) *adj, pron* some ▸ *pl* some; (*mehrere*) several; **vor einigen Tagen** a few days ago; **dazu ist noch einiges zu sagen** there are still one or two things to say about that; **~ Mal** a few times
einigen *vr*: **sich (auf etw** *akk***) ~** to agree (on sth)
einigermaßen *adv* somewhat; (*leidlich*) reasonably
einiges *pron siehe* **einige**
Einkauf *m* purchase
ein|kaufen *vt* to buy ▸ *vi* to shop; **~ gehen** to go shopping
Einkaufsbummel *m*: **einen ~ machen** to go on a shopping spree
Einkaufstasche *f*, **Einkaufstüte** *f* shopping bag
Einkaufswagen *m* trolley (Brit), cart (US)
Einkaufszentrum *nt* shopping centre (Brit) *od* mall (US)
ein|klemmen *vt* to jam
Einkommen (**-s**, **-**) *nt* income
ein|laden *unreg vt* (*Person*) to invite; (*Gegenstände*) to load; **jdn ins Kino ~** to take sb to the cinema

Einladung *f* invitation
Einlass (-es, Einlässe) *m* admission; **jdm ~ gewähren** to admit sb
ein|lassen *unreg vr*: **sich mit jdm/auf etw** *akk* **~** to get involved with sb/sth
ein|leben *vr* to settle down
ein|legen *vt* (*einfügen*) to insert; (*Koch*) to pickle; (*Pause*) to have
ein|leiten *vt* to introduce, to start; (*Geburt*) to induce
Einleitung *f* introduction; (*von Geburt*) induction
ein|leuchten *vi*: **(jdm) ~** to be clear *od* evident (to sb)
einleuchtend *adj* clear
ein|loggen *vi* (*Comput*) to log on *od* in
ein|lösen *vt* (*Scheck*) to cash; (*Schuldschein, Pfand*) to redeem; (*Versprechen*) to keep
einmal *adv* once; (*erstens*) first of all, firstly; (*später*) one day; **noch ~** once more; **nicht ~** not even; **auf ~** all at once
einmalig *adj* unique; (*einmal geschehend*) single; (*prima*) fantastic
ein|mischen *vr*: **sich (in etw** *+akk***) ~** to interfere (with sth)
Einnahme (-, -n) *f* (*Geld*) takings *pl*; (*von Medizin*) taking
ein|nehmen *unreg vt* to take; (*Stellung, Raum*) to take up; **~ für/gegen** to persuade in favour of/against
ein|ordnen *vt* to arrange, to fit in ▸ *vr* to adapt; (*Aut*) to get in(to) lane
ein|packen *vt* to pack (up)
ein|parken *vt, vi* to park
ein|planen *vt* to plan for
ein|prägen *vt*: **sich** *dat* **etw ~** to memorize sth
ein|räumen *vt* (*ordnend*) to put away; (*zugestehen*) to admit
ein|reden *vt*: **jdm/sich etw ~** to talk sb/o.s. into believing sth
ein|reiben *unreg vt* to rub in
ein|reichen *vt* to hand in; (*Antrag*) to submit
Einreise *f* entry
Einreisebestimmungen *pl* entry regulations *pl*
Einreiseerlaubnis *f* entry permit
ein|reisen *vi*: **in ein Land ~** to enter a country
Einreisevisum *nt* entry visa
ein|renken *vt* (*Gelenk, Knie*) to put back in place
ein|richten *vt* (*Haus*) to furnish; (*schaffen*) to establish, to set up; (*arrangieren*) to arrange ▸ *vr* (*in Haus*) to furnish one's house; **sich ~ (auf** *+akk***)** (*sich vorbereiten*) to prepare o.s. (for); (*sich anpassen*) to adapt (to)
Einrichtung *f* (*Wohnungseinrichtung*) furnishings *pl*; (*öffentliche Anstalt*) organization; (*Dienste*) service
eins *num* one
Eins (-, -en) *f* one
einsam *adj* lonely
ein|sammeln *vt* to collect
Einsatz *m* (*Teil*) insert; (*Verwendung*) use; (*Spieleinsatz*) stake; (*Risiko*) risk; (*Mus*) entry
ein|schalten *vt* (*Elek*) to switch on
ein|schätzen *vt* to estimate, to assess
ein|schenken *vt* to pour out
ein|schiffen *vr* to embark
ein|schlafen *unreg vi* to fall asleep
ein|schlagen *unreg vt* (*Fenster*) to smash; (*Zähne, Schädel*) to smash in; (*Weg, Richtung*) to take ▸ *vi* to hit; (*Blitz*) to strike; (*Anklang finden*) to succeed; **auf jdn ~** to hit sb
ein|schließen *unreg vt* (*Person*) to lock in; (*Gegenstand*) to lock away; (*umgeben*) to surround; (*fig*) to include
einschließlich *adv* inclusive ▸ *präp +gen* inclusive of, including
ein|schränken *vt* to limit, to restrict; (*Kosten*) to cut down ▸ *vr* to cut down (on expenditure)
ein|schreiben *unreg vr* to register; (*Univ*) to enrol
Einschreiben *nt* registered (Brit) *od* certified (*US*) letter
ein|schüchtern *vt* to intimidate
ein|sehen *unreg vt* (*prüfen*) to inspect; (*Fehler etc*) to recognize; (*verstehen*) to see
einseitig *adj* one-sided
ein|senden *unreg vt* to send in
ein|setzen *vt* to put (in); (*in Amt*) to appoint; (*Geld*) to stake; (*verwenden*) to use ▸ *vi* (*beginnen*) to set in; (*Mus*) to enter, to come in ▸ *vr* to work hard; **sich für jdn/etw ~** to support sb/sth
Einsicht *f* insight; **zu der ~ kommen, dass ...** to come to the conclusion that ...
ein|sperren *vt* to lock up
ein|spielen *vt* (*Geld*) to bring in
ein|springen *unreg vi* (*aushelfen*) to stand in

Einspruch *m* objection
einspurig *adj* single-lane
Einstand *m* (*Tennis*) deuce
ein|stecken *vt* to insert; (*Elek: Stecker*) to plug in; (*Geld*) to pocket; (*mitnehmen*) to take; (*hinnehmen*) to swallow
ein|steigen *unreg vi* to get in *od* on; (*sich beteiligen*) to come in; **~!** (*Eisenb etc*) all aboard!
ein|stellen *vt* (*in Firma*) to employ, to take on; (*aufhören*) to stop; (*Geräte*) to adjust; (*Kamera etc*) to focus; (*Sender, Radio*) to tune in to; (*unterstellen*) to put ▸ *vr*: **sich auf jdn/etw ~** to adapt to sb/prepare o.s. for sth
Einstellung *f* (*von Gerät*) adjustment, setting; (*von Kamera etc*) focusing; (*von Arbeiter etc*) appointment; (*Haltung*) attitude
ein|stürzen *vi* to collapse
eintägig *adj* one-day
ein|tauschen *vt* to exchange
eintausend *num* one thousand
ein|teilen *vt* (*in Teile*) to divide (up)
eintönig *adj* monotonous
Eintopf *m* stew
ein|tragen *unreg vt* (*in Buch*) to enter ▸ *vr* to put one's name down
ein|treffen *unreg vi* to happen; (*ankommen*) to arrive
ein|treten *unreg vi* (*hineingehen*) to enter; (*sich ereignen*) to occur; **für jdn/etw ~** to stand up for sb/sth
Eintritt *m* entrance; **~ frei** admission free
Eintrittskarte *f* (admission) ticket
Eintrittspreis *m* admission charge
einverstanden *interj* agreed ▸ *adj*: **~ sein** to agree
Einwanderer *m* immigrant
ein|wandern *vi* to immigrate
einwandfrei *adj* perfect; **etw ~ beweisen** to prove sth beyond doubt
Einwegflasche *f* non-returnable bottle
ein|weichen *vt* to soak
ein|weihen *vt* (*Brücke*) to open; (*Gebäude*) to inaugurate; (*Person*): **in etw** *akk* **~** to initiate in sth
ein|werfen *unreg vt* to throw in; (*Brief*) to post; (*Geld*) to put in, to insert; (*Fenster*) to smash
ein|wickeln *vt* to wrap up; (*fig: umg*) to outsmart
Einwohner(in) (**-s**, **-**) *m(f)* inhabitant
Einwohnermeldeamt *nt* registration office
Einwurf *m* (*Öffnung*) slot; (*Sport*) throw-in
Einzahl *f* singular
ein|zahlen *vt* to pay in
Einzel (**-s**, **-**) *nt* (*Tennis*) singles *pl*
Einzelbett *nt* single bed
Einzelgänger(in) *m(f)* loner
Einzelhandel *m* retail trade
Einzelkind *nt* only child
einzeln *adj* single ▸ *adv* singly; **~ angeben** to specify; **der/die Einzelne** the individual; **etw im Einzelnen besprechen** to discuss sth in detail; **~ aufführen** to list separately *od* individually; **bitte ~ eintreten** please come in one (person) at a time
Einzelzimmer *nt* single room
ein|ziehen *unreg vt* (*Kopf*) to duck ▸ *vi* to move in
einzig *adj* only; (*ohnegleichen*) unique ▸ *adv*: **~ und allein** solely; **das Einzige** the only thing; **der/die Einzige** the only one; **kein einziges Mal** not once; **kein Einziger** nobody, not a single person
einzigartig *adj* unique
Eis (**-es**, **-**) *nt* ice; (*Speiseeis*) ice cream
Eisbahn *f* ice *od* skating rink
Eisbär *m* polar bear
Eisbecher *m* sundae
Eisberg *m* iceberg
Eisbergsalat *m* iceberg lettuce
Eiscafé *nt* ice-cream parlour (*Brit*) *od* parlor (*US*)
Eisen (**-s**, **-**) *nt* iron; **zum alten ~ gehören** (*fig*) to be on the scrap heap
Eisenbahn *f* railway, railroad (*US*)
eisern *adj* iron
eisgekühlt *adj* chilled
Eishockey *nt* ice hockey
Eiskaffee *m* iced coffee
eiskalt *adj* icy cold
Eiskunstlauf *m* figure skating
Eisschrank *m* fridge, icebox (*US*)
Eiswürfel *m* ice cube
Eiszapfen *m* icicle
eitel *adj* vain
Eiter (**-s**) *m* pus
Eiweiß (**-es**, **-e**) *nt* white of an egg; (*Chem*) protein

ekelhaft, ekelig *adj* nauseating, disgusting
ekeln *vt* to disgust ▶ *vr*: **sich vor etw** *dat* **~** to be disgusted at sth
EKG (-) *nt abk* (= *Elektrokardiogramm*) ECG
Ekzem (**-s**, **-e**) *nt* (*Med*) eczema
elastisch *adj* elastic
Elch (**-(e)s**, **-e**) *m* elk
Elefant *m* elephant
elegant *adj* elegant
Elektriker(in) (**-s**, **-**) *m(f)* electrician
elektrisch *adj* electric
Elektrizität *f* electricity
Elektroauto *nt* electric car
Elektrogerät *nt* electrical appliance
Elektroherd *m* electric cooker
Elektromotor *m* electric motor
Elektronik *f* electronics *sing*
elektronisch *adj* electronic
Elektrorasierer (**-s**, **-**) *m* electric razor
Element (**-s**, **-e**) *nt* element
elend *adj* miserable
Elend (**-(e)s**) *nt* misery
elf *num* eleven
Elf (**-**, **en**) *f* (*Sport*) eleven
Elfenbein *nt* ivory
Elfmeter *m* (*Sport*) penalty (kick)
Elster (**-**, **-n**) *f* magpie
Eltern *pl* parents *pl*
Elterngeld *nt* ≈ child benefit
Elternschaft *f* parenthood
Elternteil *m* parent
E-Mail (**-**, **-s**) *f* email
E-Mail-Adresse *f* Email address
e-mailen *vt* to email
emotional *adj* emotional
empfahl *etc vb siehe* **empfehlen**
empfand *etc vb siehe* **empfinden**
Empfang (**-(e)s**, **Empfänge**) *m* reception; (*Erhalten*) receipt; **in ~ nehmen** to receive
empfangen *unreg vt* to receive
Empfänger(in) (**-s**, **-**) *m(f)* receiver; (*Comm*) addressee
Empfängnisverhütung *f* contraception
empfehlen *unreg vt* to recommend
Empfehlung *f* recommendation
empfinden *unreg vt* to feel
empfindlich *adj* sensitive; (*Stelle*) sore; (*reizbar*) touchy
empfing *etc vb siehe* **empfangen**
empfohlen *pp von* **empfehlen**
empfunden *pp von* **empfinden**
empört *adj*: **~ (über** *+akk***)** indignant (at), outraged (at)
Ende (**-s**, **-n**) *nt* end; **am ~** at the end; (*schließlich*) in the end; **~ Dezember** at the end of December; **zu ~ sein** to be finished
enden *vi* to end
endgültig *adj* final, definite
Endivie *f* endive
endlich *adv* finally; **~!** at last!
Endspiel *nt* final(s)
Endstation *f* terminus
Endung *f* ending
Energie *f* energy
Energiebedarf *m* energy requirement
Energiegetränk *nt* energy drink
Energieverbrauch *m* energy consumption
Energiewende *f see note*

ENERGIEWENDE

Energiewende is the term for the German government's policy of gradually giving up fossil fuels and nuclear power, with the aim of having 35% renewable energies by 2020. It also involves energy savings, particularly of electricity, which is expected to be 80% renewable by 2050.

energisch *adj* energetic
eng *adj* narrow; (*Kleidung*) tight; limited; (*Freundschaft, Verhältnis*) close
engagieren *vt* to engage ▶ *vr* to commit o.s.
Engel (**-s**, **-**) *m* angel
England *nt* England
Engländer (**-s**, **-**) *m* Englishman; (*Junge*) English boy ▪ **die Engländer** *pl* the English, the Britishers (*US*)
Engländerin *f* Englishwoman; (*Mädchen*) English girl
englisch *adj* English; (*Sprache*): **auf E~** in English
Enkel (**-s**, **-**) *m* grandson
Enkelin *f* granddaughter
enorm *adj* enormous; (*umg*: *herrlich, kolossal*) tremendous
Entbindung *f* (*Med*) delivery
entdecken *vt* to discover; **jdm etw ~** to disclose sth to sb
Entdeckung *f* discovery
Ente (**-**, **-n**) *f* duck

entfernen *vt* to remove ▶ *vr* to go away
entfernt *adj* distant; **weit davon ~ sein, etw zu tun** to be far from doing sth
Entfernung *f* distance
entfreunden *vt* (*Internet*) to unfriend
entführen *vt* to kidnap
Entführer(in) (**-s**, **-**) *m(f)* kidnapper (BRIT), kidnaper (*US*)
Entführung *f* kidnapping (BRIT), kidnaping (*US*)
entgegen *präp +dat* contrary to, against ▶ *adv* towards
entgegengesetzt *adj* opposite; (*widersprechend*) opposed
entgegen|kommen *unreg vi +dat* to come towards; (*fig*): **jdm ~** to accommodate sb
entgegenkommend *adj* obliging
entgegnen *vt* to reply
entgehen *unreg vi*: **jdm ~** to escape sb's notice; **sich** *dat* **etw ~ lassen** to miss sth
entgiften *vi* to detox (*umg*), to detoxify
Entgiftung *f* detox (*umg*), detoxification
entgleisen *vi* (*Eisenb*) to be derailed; (*fig*: *Person*) to misbehave
enthalten *unreg vt* to contain ▶ *vr +gen*: **sich (der Stimme) ~** to abstain
entkommen *unreg vi* to escape
entkorken *vt* to uncork
entlang *präp* (*+akk od dat*) along ▶ *adv* along; **~ dem Fluss, den Fluss ~** along the river
entlang|gehen *unreg vi* to walk along
entlassen *unreg vt* to discharge; (*Arbeiter*) to dismiss
entlasten *vt* (*Arbeit abnehmen*) to take some of the load off
entmutigen *vt* to discourage
entnehmen *unreg vt +dat* to take from
entradikalisieren *vt* to deradicalize
entschädigen *vt* to compensate
Entschädigung *f* compensation
entscheiden *unreg vt, vi, vr* to decide; **darüber habe ich nicht zu ~** that is not for me to decide; **sich für jdn/etw ~** to decide in favour of sb/sth
entscheidend *adj* decisive; (*Stimme*) casting; **das Entscheidende** the decisive *od* deciding factor
Entscheidung *f* decision
entschließen *unreg vr* to decide
Entschluss *m* decision
entschuldigen *vt* to excuse ▶ *vr* to apologize ▶ *vi*: **~ Sie (bitte)!** excuse me; (*Verzeihung*) sorry
Entschuldigung *f* apology; (*Grund*) excuse; **jdn um ~ bitten** to apologize to sb; **~!** excuse me; (*Verzeihung*) sorry
entsetzlich *adj* dreadful, appalling
entsorgen *vt*: **eine Stadt ~** to dispose of a town's refuse and sewage
entspannen *vt, vr* (*Körper*) to relax; (*Pol*: *Lage*) to ease
Entspannung *f* relaxation
entsprechen *unreg vi +dat* to correspond to; (*Anforderungen, Wünschen*) to meet, to comply with
entsprechend *adj* appropriate ▶ *adv* accordingly ▶ *präp +dat*: **er wird seiner Leistung ~ bezahlt** he is paid according to output
entstehen *unreg vi*: **~ (aus** *od* **durch)** to arise (from)
enttäuschen *vt* to disappoint
Enttäuschung *f* disappointment
entweder *konj* either; **~ ... oder ...** either ... or ...
entwerfen *unreg vt* (*Modell*) to design; (*Vortrag, Gesetz etc*) to draft
entwerten *vt* to devalue; (*stempeln*) to cancel
Entwerter (**-s**, **-**) *m* (ticket-)cancelling (BRIT) *od* canceling (*US*) machine
entwickeln *vt* (*auch Phot*) to develop; (*Mut, Energie*) to show, to display ▶ *vr* to develop
Entwicklung *f* development; (*Phot*) developing
Entwicklungshelfer(in) *m(f)* VSO worker (BRIT), Peace Corps worker (*US*)
Entwicklungsland *nt* developing country
Entwurf *m* outline, design; (*Vertragsentwurf, Konzept*) draft
entzückend *adj* delightful, charming
Entzug (**-(e)s**) *m* withdrawal
Entzugserscheinung *f* withdrawal symptom
entzünden *vr* to catch fire; (*Med*) to become inflamed
Entzündung *f* (*Med*) inflammation
Epidemie *f* epidemic
Epilepsie *f* epilepsy
er *pron* he; (*Sache*) it
Erbe[1] (**-n**, **-n**) *m* heir
Erbe[2] (**-s**) *nt* inheritance; (*fig*) heritage

erben *vt* to inherit
Erbin *f* heiress
erblich *adj* hereditary
erblicken *vt* to catch sight of
erbrechen *unreg vt, vr* to vomit
Erbschaft *f* inheritance
Erbse (**-**, **-n**) *f* pea
Erdapfel (ÖSTERR) *m* potato
Erdbeben *nt* earthquake
Erdbeere *f* strawberry
Erde (**-**, **-n**) *f* earth; **zu ebener ~** at ground level
Erdgas *nt* natural gas
Erdgeschoss *nt* ground floor (BRIT), first floor (*US*)
Erdkunde *f* geography
Erdnuss *f* peanut
Erdöl *nt* (mineral) oil
Erdrutsch *m* landslide
Erdteil *m* continent
E-Reader *m* e-reader
ereignen *vr* to happen
Ereignis (**-ses**, **-se**) *nt* event
erfahren *unreg vt* to learn, to find out; (*erleben*) to experience ▶ *adj* experienced
Erfahrung *f* experience
erfinden *unreg vt* to invent
erfinderisch *adj* inventive
Erfindung *f* invention
Erfolg (**-(e)s**, **-e**) *m* success; (*Folge*) result; **~ versprechend** promising; **viel ~!** good luck!
erfolglos *adj* unsuccessful
erfolgreich *adj* successful
erforderlich *adj* necessary
erforschen *vt* to explore; (*Problem*) to investigate
erfreulich *adj* pleasing, gratifying
erfreulicherweise *adv* happily, luckily
erfrieren *unreg vi* to freeze (to death); (*Pflanzen*) to be killed by frost
Erfrischung *f* refreshment
erfüllen *vt* (*Raum etc*) to fill; (*fig: Bitte etc*) to fulfil (BRIT), to fulfill (*US*) ▶ *vr* to come true
ergänzen *vt* to complete ▶ *vr* to complement one another
Ergänzung *f* completion; (*Zusatz*) supplement
ergeben *unreg vt* (*Betrag*) to come to; (*zum Ergebnis haben*) to result in ▶ *vr* to surrender; (*folgen*) to result ▶ *adj* devoted; (*demütig*) humble
Ergebnis (**-ses**, **-se**) *nt* result
ergreifen *unreg vt* to seize; (*Beruf*) to take up; (*Maßnahmen*) to resort to; (*rühren*) to move
erhalten *unreg vt* to receive; (*bewahren*) to preserve; **gut ~** in good condition
erhältlich *adj* available
erheblich *adj* considerable
erhitzen *vt* to heat
erhöhen *vt* to raise; (*verstärken*) to increase
erholen *vr* to recover; (*entspannen*) to have a rest
erholsam *adj* restful
Erholung *f* recovery; (*Entspannung*) relaxation, rest
erinnern *vt*: **~ (an** *+akk***)** to remind (of) ▶ *vr*: **sich (an etw** *akk***) ~** to remember (sth)
Erinnerung *f* memory; (*Andenken*) souvenir; (*Mahnung*) reminder
erkälten *vr* to catch cold
erkältet *adj*: **~ sein** to have a cold
Erkältung *f* cold
erkennen *unreg vt* to recognize; (*sehen, verstehen*) to see; **jdm zu ~ geben, dass …** to give sb to understand that …
erkenntlich *adj*: **sich ~ zeigen** to show one's appreciation
Erker (**-s**, **-**) *m* bay
erklären *vt* to explain; (*Rücktritt*) to announce
Erklärung *f* explanation; (*Aussage*) declaration
erkundigen *vr*: **sich ~ (nach)** to inquire (about)
erlauben *vt* to allow, to permit ▶ *vr*: **sich** *dat* **etw ~** to permit o.s. sth; **jdm etw ~** to allow *od* permit sb (to do) sth; **~ Sie?** may I?; **was ~ Sie sich (eigentlich)!** how dare you!
Erlaubnis (**-**, **-se**) *f* permission
Erläuterung *f* explanation
erleben *vt* to experience; (*Zeit*) to live through; (*miterleben*) to witness; (*noch miterleben*) to live to see
Erlebnis (**-ses**, **-se**) *nt* experience
erledigen *vt* to deal with; (*ruinieren*) to finish
erledigt (*umg*) *adj* (*erschöpft*) shattered; (*ruiniert*) finished
erleichtert *adj* relieved
Erlös (**-es**, **-e**) *m* proceeds *pl*
ermahnen *vt* to admonish

Ermäßigung *f* reduction
ermitteln *vt* to determine; (*Täter*) to trace ▶ *vi*: **gegen jdn ~** to investigate sb
ermöglichen *vt +dat* to make possible (for)
ermorden *vt* to murder
ermüdend *adj* tiring
ermutigen *vt* to encourage
ernähren *vt* to feed; (*Familie*) to support ▶ *vr* to support o.s.; **sich ~ von** to live on
Ernährung *f* nourishment; (*Med*) nutrition
erneuern *vt* to renew; (*restaurieren*) to restore; (*renovieren*) to renovate
ernst *adj* serious ▶ *adv*: **~ gemeint** meant in earnest
Ernst (-es) *m* seriousness; **das ist mein ~** I'm quite serious; **im ~** in earnest
ernsthaft *adj* serious
Ernte (-, -n) *f* harvest
Erntedankfest *nt* harvest festival (BRIT), Thanksgiving (Day) (US)
ernten *vt* to harvest; (*Lob etc*) to earn
erobern *vt* to conquer
eröffnen *vt* to open
Eröffnung *f* opening
erogen *adj* erogenous
erotisch *adj* erotic
erpressen *vt* (*Geld etc*) to extort; (*jdn*) to blackmail
Erpressung *f* blackmail; (*von Geld*) extortion
erraten *unreg vt* to guess
erregen *vt* to excite; (*sexuell*) to arouse; (*ärgern*) to infuriate; (*hervorrufen*) to arouse ▶ *vr* to get excited *od* worked up
Erreger (-s, -) *m* causative agent
erreichbar *adj* accessible, within reach
erreichen *vt* to reach; (*Zug*) to catch
Ersatz (-es) *m* substitute; (*Schadenersatz*) compensation
Ersatzreifen *m* (*Aut*) spare tyre (BRIT) *od* tire (US)
Ersatzteil *nt* spare (part)
erscheinen *unreg vi* to appear
erschöpft *adj* exhausted
Erschöpfung *f* exhaustion
erschrecken[1] *vt* to startle, to frighten
erschrecken[2] *unreg vi* to be frightened *od* startled
erschreckend *adj* alarming
erschrocken *adj* frightened
erschwinglich *adj* affordable
ersetzen *vt* to replace; **jdm Unkosten** *etc* **~** to pay sb's expenses *etc*

 **SCHLÜSSELWORT**

erst *adv* **1** first; **mach erst (ein)mal die Arbeit fertig** finish your work first; **wenn du das erst (ein)mal hinter dir hast** once you've got that behind you
2 (*nicht früher als, nur*) only; (*nicht bis*) not till; **erst gestern** only yesterday; **erst morgen** not until tomorrow; **erst als** only when, not until; **wir fahren erst später** we're not going until later; **er ist (gerade) erst angekommen** he's only just arrived
3: **wäre er doch erst zurück!** if only he were back!

erstatten *vt* (*Unkosten*) to refund; **Anzeige gegen jdn ~** to report sb; **Bericht ~** to make a report
erstaunlich *adj* astonishing
erstbeste(r, s) *adj* first that comes along
erste(r, s) *adj* first; **das ~ Mal** the first time
erstens *adv* firstly, in the first place
ersticken *vi* (*Mensch*) to suffocate; **in Arbeit ~** to be snowed under with work
erstklassig *adj* first-class
erstmals *adv* for the first time
erstrecken *vr* to extend, to stretch
ertappen *vt* to catch
erteilen *vt* to give
Ertrag (-(e)s, Erträge) *m* yield; (*Gewinn*) proceeds *pl*
ertragen *unreg vt* to bear, to stand
erträglich *adj* tolerable, bearable
ertrinken *unreg vi* to drown
erwachsen *adj* grown-up
Erwachsene(r) *f(m)* adult
erwähnen *vt* to mention
erwarten *vt* to expect; (*warten auf*) to wait for; **etw kaum ~ können** to hardly be able to wait for sth
erwerbstätig *adj* (gainfully) employed
erwidern *vt* to reply; (*vergelten*) to return
erwischen (*umg*) *vt* to catch
erwünscht *adj* desired

Erz (**-es**, **-e**) *nt* ore
erzählen *vt*, *vi* to tell
Erzählung *f* story, tale
erzeugen *vt* to produce; (*Strom*) to generate
Erzeugnis (**-ses**, **-se**) *nt* product
erziehen *unreg vt* to bring up; (*bilden*) to educate, to train
Erzieher(in) (**-s**, **-**) *m(f)* educator; (*in Kindergarten*) nursery school teacher
Erziehung *f* bringing up; (*Bildung*) education
es *nom*, *akk pron* it; (*Baby*, *Tier*) he/she
Esel (**-s**, **-**) *m* donkey
essbar *adj* edible
essen *unreg vt*, *vi* to eat; **~ gehen** to eat out
Essen (**-s**, **-**) *nt* (*Mahlzeit*) meal; (*Nahrung*) food
Essig (**-s**, **-e**) *m* vinegar
Esslöffel *m* tablespoon
Esszimmer *nt* dining room
Estland *nt* Estonia
Etage (**-**, **-n**) *f* floor, storey (BRIT), story (US)
Etagenbett *nt* bunk bed
Etappe (**-**, **-n**) *f* stage
ethnisch *adj* ethnic
Etikett (**-(e)s**, **-e**) *nt* label
etliche(r, s) *pron pl* some, quite a few; **etliches** quite a lot
etwa *adv* (*ungefähr*) about; (*vielleicht*) perhaps; (*beispielsweise*) for instance
etwas *pron* something; (*fragend*, *verneinend*) anything; (*ein wenig*) a little ▶ *adv* a little
EU (**-**) *f abk* (= *Europäische Union*) EU
EU-Befürworter(in) *m(f)* Europhile
euch *pron* (*akk von ihr*) you; (*dat von ihr*) (to/for) you ▶ *refl pron* yourselves
euer *pron gen von* **ihr** ▶ *adj* your
EU-Gegner(in) *m(f)* Europhobe
EU-kritisch *adj* Eurosceptic
Eule (**-**, **-n**) *f* owl
eure(r, s) *pron* yours
euretwegen *adv* (*für euch*) for your sakes; (*wegen euch*) on your account
Euro (**-**, **-s**) *m* (*Fin*) euro
Eurocent *m* euro cent
Europa (**-s**) *nt* Europe
Europäer(in) (**-s**, **-**) *m(f)* European
europäisch *adj* European; **Europäische Union** European Union
Europameister *m* European champion
Europaparlament *nt* European Parliament
Euroschein, Euro-Schein *m* euro note; **wie sieht der Zweihunderteuroschein aus?** what does the two hundred euro note look like?
Euter (**-s**, **-**) *nt* udder
evangelisch *adj* Protestant
eventuell *adj* possible ▶ *adv* possibly, perhaps
ewig *adj* eternal ▶ *adv*: **ich habe Sie ~ lange nicht gesehen** (*umg*) I haven't seen you for ages
Ewigkeit *f* eternity
Ex *mf* ex
exakt *adj* exact
Examen (**-s**, **-** *od* **Examina**) *nt* examination
Exemplar (**-s**, **-e**) *nt* specimen; (*Buchexemplar*) copy
Exil (**-s**, **-e**) *nt* exile
Existenz *f* existence; (*Unterhalt*) livelihood, living
existieren *vi* to exist
exklusiv *adj* exclusive
exklusive *präp +gen* exclusive of, not including ▶ *adv* exclusive of, excluding
exotisch *adj* exotic
Experte (**-n**, **-n**) *m* expert, specialist
Expertin *f* expert, specialist
explodieren *vi* to explode
Explosion *f* explosion
Export (**-(e)s**, **-e**) *m* export
exportieren *vt* to export
extra *adj unver* (*umg*: *gesondert*) separate; (*besondere*) extra ▶ *adv* (*gesondert*) separately; (*speziell*) specially; (*absichtlich*) on purpose
Extra (**-s**, **-s**) *nt* extra
extrem *adj* extreme
E-Zigarette *f* e-cigarette

fabelhaft *adj* fabulous, marvellous (BRIT), marvelous (*US*)
Fabrik *f* factory
Facebook® *nt* Facebook®
Fach (**-(e)s**, **Fächer**) *nt* compartment; (*Sachgebiet*) subject
Facharzt *m* (medical) specialist
Fachärztin *f* (medical) specialist
Fachausdruck *m* technical term
Fächer (**-s**, **-**) *m* fan
Fachfrau *f* expert
Fachmann (**-(e)s**, **Fachleute**) *m* expert
Fachwerkhaus *nt* half-timbered house
Fackel (**-**, **-n**) *f* torch
fad, fade *adj* (*langweilig*) dull; (*Essen*) tasteless
Faden (**-s**, **Fäden**) *m* thread
fähig *adj*: **~ (zu** *od* *+gen***)** capable (of)
Fähigkeit *f* ability
Fahndung *f* search
Fahne (**-**, **-n**) *f* flag
Fahrausweis *m* ticket
Fahrbahn *f* carriageway (BRIT), roadway
Fähre (**-**, **-n**) *f* ferry
fahren *unreg vt* to drive; (*Rad*) to ride; (*befördern*) to drive, to take ▶ *vi* (*sich bewegen*) to go; (*Schiff*) to sail; (*abfahren*) to leave; **mit dem Auto/Zug ~** to go *od* travel by car/train; **links/rechts ~** to drive on the left/right
Fahrer(in) (**-s**, **-**) *m(f)* driver
Fahrerflucht *f* hit-and-run driving
Fahrgast *m* passenger
Fahrgeld *nt* fare
Fahrkarte *f* ticket
Fahrkartenautomat *m* ticket machine
Fahrkartenschalter *m* ticket office
fahrlässig *adj* negligent
Fahrlehrer(in) *m(f)* driving instructor
Fahrplan *m* timetable
fahrplanmäßig *adj* (*Eisenb*) scheduled
Fahrpreis *m* fare
Fahrrad *nt* bicycle
Fahrradweg *m* cycle path
Fahrschein *m* ticket
Fahrscheinautomat *m* ticket machine
Fahrschule *f* driving school
Fahrschüler(in) *m(f)* learner (driver)
Fahrspur *f* lane
Fahrstreifen *m* lane
Fahrstuhl *m* lift (BRIT), elevator (*US*)
Fahrt (**-**, **-en**) *f* journey; (*kurz*) trip; (*Aut*) drive; **gute ~!** safe journey!
Fahrtkosten *pl* travelling expenses *pl*
Fahrtrichtung *f* course, direction
fahrtüchtig *adj* fit to drive; (*Fahrzeug*) roadworthy
Fahrzeug *nt* vehicle
Fahrzeughalter(in) (**-s**, **-**) *m(f)* owner of a vehicle
Fahrzeugpapiere *pl* vehicle documents *pl*
fair *adj* fair
Fakultät *f* faculty
Falke (**-n**, **-n**) *m* falcon
Fall (**-(e)s**, **Fälle**) *m* (*Sturz*) fall; (*Sachverhalt, Jur, Gram*) case; **auf jeden ~, auf alle Fälle** in any case; (*bestimmt*) definitely; **gesetzt den ~** assuming (that); **das mache ich auf keinen ~** there's no way I'm going to do that
Falle (**-**, **-n**) *f* trap
fallen *unreg vi* to fall; **etw ~ lassen** to drop sth
fällig *adj* due
falls *adv* in case, if
Fallschirm *m* parachute
Fallschirmspringer(in) *m(f)* parachutist
falsch *adj* false; (*unrichtig*) wrong ▶ *adv*
fälschen *vt* to forge
Falschfahrer(in) *m(f)* *person driving the wrong way on the motorway*
Falschgeld *nt* counterfeit money

Fälschung *f* forgery

Faltblatt *nt* leaflet

Falte (**-, -n**) *f* (*Knick*) fold, crease; (*Hautfalte*) wrinkle; (*Rockfalte*) pleat

falten *vt* to fold

faltig *adj* (*Haut*) wrinkled; (*Rock usw*) creased

Familie *f* family

Familienname *m* surname

Familienstand *m* marital status

Fan *m* fan

fand *etc vb siehe* **finden**

fangen *unreg vt* to catch ▶ *vr* (*Mensch*: *nicht fallen*) to steady o.s.; (*fig*) to compose o.s.

Fanmeile *f* fan zone

Fantasie *f* imagination

fantastisch *adj* fantastic

Farbdrucker *m* colour printer

Farbe (**-, -n**) *f* colour (BRIT), color (US); (*zum Malen etc*) paint; (*Stofffarbe*) dye

färben *vt* to colour (BRIT), to color (US); (*Stoff, Haar*) to dye

Farbfernsehen *nt* colour (BRIT) *od* color (US) television

Farbfilm *m* colour (BRIT) *od* color (US) film

farbig *adj* coloured (BRIT), colored (US)

farblos *adj* colourless (BRIT), colorless (US)

Farbstoff *m* dye; (*Lebensmittelfarbstoff*) (artificial) colouring (BRIT) *od* coloring (US)

Farn (**-(e)s, -e**) *m* fern

Fasan (**-(e)s, -e(n)**) *m* pheasant

Fasching (**-s, -e** *od* **-s**) *m* carnival

Faschismus *m* fascism

Faser (**-, -n**) *f* fibre

Fass (**-es, Fässer**) *nt* vat, barrel; (*für Öl*) drum

fassen *vt* (*ergreifen*) to grasp; (*inhaltlich*) to hold; (*Entschluss etc*) to take; (*verstehen*) to understand ▶ *vr* to calm down; **nicht zu ~** unbelievable

Fassung *f* (*Umrahmung*) mounting; (*Lampenfassung*) socket; (*Wortlaut*) version; (*Beherrschung*) composure; **jdn aus der ~ bringen** to upset sb; **völlig außer ~ geraten** to lose all self-control

fast *adv* almost, nearly

fasten *vi* to fast

Fastenzeit *f* Lent

Fastnacht *f* Shrovetide carnival

fatal *adj* fatal; (*peinlich*) embarrassing

faul *adj* rotten; (*Person*) lazy; (*Ausreden*) lame

faulen *vi* to rot

faulenzen *vi* to idle

Faulheit *f* laziness

faulig *adj* putrid

Faust (**-, Fäuste**) *f* fist

Fausthandschuh *m* mitten

Fax (**-, -e**) *nt* fax

faxen *vt* to fax

FCKW (**-s, -s**) *m abk* (= *Fluorchlorkohlenwasserstoff*) CFC

Februar (**-(s), -e**) (*pl selten*) *m* February; *siehe auch* **September**

Feder (**-, -n**) *f* feather; (*Schreibfeder*) pen nib; (*Tech*) spring

Federball *m* shuttlecock

Federung *f* suspension

Fee (**-, -n**) *f* fairy

fegen *vt* to sweep

fehl *adj*: **~ am Platz** *od* **Ort** out of place

fehlen *vi* (*abwesend sein*) to be absent; **etw fehlt jdm** sb lacks sth; **du fehlst mir** I miss you; **was fehlt ihm?** what's wrong with him?; **wo fehlt es?** what's up? (*umg*)

Fehler (**-s, -**) *m* mistake, error; (*Mangel, Schwäche*) fault

Fehlerbeseitigung *f* (*Comput*) debugging

Fehlermeldung *f* (*Comput*) error message

Fehlzündung *f* (*Aut*) misfire

Feier (**-, -n**) *f* celebration

Feierabend *m end of the working day*; **~ haben** to finish work; **nach ~** after work

feierlich *adj* solemn

feiern *vt, vi* to celebrate

Feiertag *m* holiday

feig, feige *adj* cowardly

Feige (**-, -n**) *f* fig

Feigling *m* coward

Feile (**-, -n**) *f* file

fein *adj* fine; (*vornehm*) refined; **~!** great!

Feind(in) (**-(e)s, -e**) *m(f)* enemy

feindlich *adj* hostile

Feinkost (**-**) *f* delicacies *pl*

Feinschmecker(in) (**-s, -**) *m(f)* gourmet

Feinstaub *m* particulate matter

Feinwaschmittel *nt* mild(-action) detergent

Feld (**-(e)s, -er**) *nt* field; (*Schach*) square; (*Sport*) pitch

Feldsalat *m* lamb's lettuce
Feldweg *m* path
Felge (**-**, **-n**) *f* (wheel) rim
Fell (**-(e)s**, **-e**) *nt* fur; (*von Schaf*) fleece
Fels (**-en**, **-en**) *m*, **Felsen** (**-s**, **-**) *m* rock; (*Klippe*) cliff
felsig *adj* rocky
feminin *adj* feminine
Fenchel (**-s**) *m* fennel
Fenster (**-s**, **-**) *nt* window
Fensterbrett *nt* windowsill
Fensterladen *m* shutter
Fensterplatz *m* window seat
Fensterscheibe *f* windowpane
Ferien *pl* holidays *pl*, vacation (*US*); **~ haben** to be on holiday
Ferienhaus *nt* holiday home
Ferienkurs *m* holiday course
Ferienlager *nt* holiday camp (BRIT), vacation camp (*US*); (*für Kinder im Sommer*) summer camp
Ferienwohnung *f* holiday flat (BRIT), vacation apartment (*US*)
Ferkel (**-s**, **-**) *nt* piglet
fern *adj*, *adv* far-off, distant; **~ von hier** a long way (away) from here
Fernbedienung *f* remote control
Ferne (**-**, **-n**) *f* distance
ferner *adj*, *adv* further; (*weiterhin*) in future
Fernflug *m* long-distance flight
Ferngespräch *nt* long-distance call (BRIT), toll call (*US*)
ferngesteuert *adj* remote-controlled
Fernglas *nt* binoculars *pl*
Fernlicht *nt* (*Aut*): **mit ~ fahren** to drive on full beam
Fernsehapparat *m* television (set)
fern|sehen *unreg vi* to watch television
Fernsehen (**-s**) *nt* television; **im ~** on television
Fernseher (**-s**, **-**) *m* television (set)
Fernsehprogramm *nt* (*Sendung*) programme (BRIT), program (*US*); (*Fernsehzeitschrift*) (television) programme (BRIT) *od* program (*US*) guide
Fernstraße *f* major road
Fernverkehr *m* long-distance traffic
Ferse (**-**, **-n**) *f* heel
fertig *adj* (*bereit*) ready; (*beendet*) finished; (*gebrauchsfertig*) ready-made; **mit jdm/etw ~ werden** to cope with sb/sth; **~ bringen** *od* **machen** (*beenden*) to finish; **sich ~ machen** to get ready; **~ essen/lesen** to finish eating/reading
Fertiggericht *nt* ready-to-serve mea
fertig|machen (*umg*) *vt* (*Person*) to finish; (*körperlich*) to exhaust; (*moralisch*) to get down; *siehe auch* **fertig**
fest *adj* firm; (*Nahrung*) solid; (*Gehalt*) regular; (*Gewebe, Schuhe*) strong, sturdy ▶ *adv* (*schlafen*) soundly
Fest (**-(e)s**, **-e**) *nt* (*Feier*) celebration; (*Party*) party; **man soll die Feste feiern wie sie fallen** (*Sprichwort*) mak hay while the sun shines
fest|binden *unreg vt* to tie, to fasten
fest|halten *unreg vt* to seize, to hold fast; (*Ereignis*) to record ▶ *vr*: **sich ~ (a** **+*dat*)** to hold on (to)
Festland *nt* mainland
fest|legen *vt* to fix ▶ *vr* to commit o.s.
festlich *adj* festive
fest|machen *vt* to fasten; (*Termin etc*) to fix
fest|nehmen *unreg vt* to arrest
Festnetz *nt* (*Tel*) landline
Festplatte *f* (*Comput*) hard disk
fest|setzen *vt* to fix
fest|stehen *unreg vi* to be certain
fest|stellen *vt* to establish; (*sagen*) to remark
Festung *f* fortress
Festzelt *nt* marquee
Fete (**-**, **-n**) *f* party
fett *adj* fat; (*Essen etc*) greasy; **~ gedruckt** bold-type
Fett (**-(e)s**, **-e**) *nt* fat, grease
fettarm *adj* low fat
fettig *adj* greasy, fatty
feucht *adj* damp; (*Luft*) humid
Feuchtigkeit *f* dampness; (*von Luft*) humidity
Feuchtigkeitscreme *f* moisturizer
Feuchttuch *nt* wipe
Feuer (**-s**, **-**) *nt* fire; **haben Sie ~?** have you got a light?
Feueralarm *m* fire alarm
feuerfest *adj* fireproof
Feuerlöscher (**-s**, **-**) *m* fire extinguisher
Feuermelder (**-s**, **-**) *m* fire alarm
Feuertreppe *f* fire escape
Feuerwehr *f* fire brigade
Feuerwehrfrau *f* firefighter
Feuerwehrmann *m* firefighter

Feuerwerk *nt* fireworks *pl*
Feuerzeug *nt* (cigarette) lighter
Fichte (**-**, **-n**) *f* spruce
ficken (*!*) *vt*, *vi* to fuck (*!*)
Fieber (**-s**, **-**) *nt* fever, temperature; (*Krankheit*) fever; **~ haben** to have a temperature
Fieberthermometer *nt* thermometer
fiel *etc vb siehe* **fallen**
fies (*umg*) *adj* nasty
Figur (**-**, **-en**) *f* figure; (*Schachfigur*) chess piece
Filet (**-s**, **-s**) *nt* (*Koch*) fillet; (*Rinderfilet*) fillet steak
Filiale (**-**, **-n**) *f* (*Comm*) branch
Film (**-(e)s**, **-e**) *m* film, movie (*bes US*)
filmen *vt*, *vi* to film
Filter (**-s**, **-**) *m* filter
Filterkaffee *m* filter *od* drip (*US*) coffee
filtern *vt* to filter
Filterpapier *nt* filter paper
Filz (**-es**, **-e**) *m* felt
Finale (**-s**, **-(s)**) *nt* (*Sport*) final(s *pl*)
Finanzamt *nt* ≈ Inland Revenue Office (Brit), ≈ Internal Revenue Office (*US*)
finanziell *adj* financial ▶ *adv* financially
finanzieren *vt* to finance
finden *unreg vt* to find; (*meinen*) to think ▶ *vr* to be (found); **ich finde es gut/schlecht** I like/don't like it
fing *etc vb siehe* **fangen**
Finger (**-s**, **-**) *m* finger
Fingerabdruck *m* fingerprint
Fingerhandschuh *m* glove
Fingernagel *m* fingernail
Fink (**-en**, **-en**) *m* finch
Finne (**-n**, **-n**) *m* Finn
finnisch *adj* Finnish; (*Sprache*): **auf F~** in Finnish
Finnland *nt* Finland
finster *adj* dark; (*verdächtig*) dubious; (*verdrossen*) grim; (*Gedanke*) dark
Finsternis (**-**) *f* darkness, gloom
Firma (**-**, **-men**) *f* firm
Fisch (**-(e)s**, **-e**) *m* fish ■ **Fische** *pl* (*Astrol*) Pisces *sing*; **das sind kleine Fische** (*fig*: *umg*) that's child's play
fischen *vt*, *vi* to fish
Fischer (**-s**, **-**) *m* fisherman
Fischstäbchen *nt* fish finger (Brit), fish stick (*US*)
fit *adj* fit
Fitness *nt* fitness
Fitnesscenter (**-s**, **-**) *nt* fitness centre
Fitnesstrainer(in) *m(f)* fitness trainer, personal trainer
fix *adj* (*flink*) quick; **~ und fertig** finished; (*erschöpft*) done in
fixen (*umg*) *vi* (*Drogen spritzen*) to fix
Fixer(in) (*umg*) *m(f)* junkie (*umg*)
FKK *abk* = **Freikörperkultur**
flach *adj* flat; (*Gefäß*) shallow
Flachbildschirm *m* flat screen
Fläche (**-**, **-n**) *f* area; (*Oberfläche*) surface
Flagge (**-**, **-n**) *f* flag
Flamme (**-**, **-n**) *f* flame
Flanell (**-s**, **-e**) *m* flannel
Flasche (**-**, **-n**) *f* bottle; (*umg*: *Versager*) wash-out
Flaschenbier *nt* bottled beer
Flaschenöffner *m* bottle opener
Flaschenpfand *nt* deposit
flatterhaft *adj* fickle
flattern *vi* to flutter
flauschig *adj* fluffy
Flausen *pl* silly ideas *pl*
Flaute (**-**, **-n**) *f* calm; (*Comm*) recession
Flechte (**-**, **-n**) *f* (*Med*) dry scab; (*Bot*) lichen
flechten *unreg vt* to plait; (*Kranz*) to twine
Fleck (**-(e)s**, **-e**) *m* (*Schmutzfleck*) stain; (*Farbfleck*) patch
Flecken *m* = **Fleck**
fleckig *adj* marked; (*schmutzig*) stained
Fledermaus *f* bat
Fleisch (**-(e)s**) *nt* flesh; (*Essen*) meat
Fleischbrühe *f* meat stock
Fleischer(in) (**-s**, **-**) *m(f)* butcher
Fleischerei *f* butcher's (shop)
Fleischtomate *f* beef tomato
fleißig *adj* diligent, industrious
flennen (*umg*) *vi* to cry, to blubber
flexibel *adj* flexible
flexibilisieren *vt* to make more flexible; **die Arbeitszeit ~** to make working hours more flexible
flicken *vt* to mend
Flieder (**-s**, **-**) *m* lilac
Fliege (**-**, **-n**) *f* fly; (*Schlips*) bow tie
fliegen *unreg vt*, *vi* to fly
Fliese (**-**, **-n**) *f* tile
Fließband *nt* assembly *od* production line
fließen *unreg vi* to flow
fließend *adj* (*Rede*, *Deutsch*) fluent; (*Übergang*) smooth; **fließendes Wasser** running water

flirten *vi* to flirt
Flitterwochen *pl* honeymoon *sing*
flocht *etc vb siehe* **flechten**
Flocke (-, **-n**) *f* flake
flog *etc vb siehe* **fliegen**
Floh (**-(e)s**, **Flöhe**) *m* flea
Flohmarkt *m* flea market
Floskel (-, **-n**) *f* set phrase
floss *etc vb siehe* **fließen**
Floß (**-es**, **Flöße**) *nt* raft
Flosse (-, **-n**) *f* fin; (*Taucherflosse*) flipper
Flöte (-, **-n**) *f* flute; (*Blockflöte*) recorder
flott *adj* lively; (*elegant*) smart; (*Naut*) afloat
Fluch (**-(e)s**, **Flüche**) *m* curse
fluchen *vi* to curse, to swear
Flucht (-, **-en**) *f* flight
flüchten *vi* to flee
flüchtig *adj*: **jdn ~ kennen** to have met sb briefly
Flüchtling *m* refugee
Flug (**-(e)s**, **Flüge**) *m* flight
Flugbegleiter(in) *m(f)* (*Aviat*) flight attendant
Flugblatt *nt* pamphlet
Flügel (**-s**, **-**) *m* wing; (*Mus*) grand piano
Fluggast *m* airline passenger
Fluggesellschaft *f* airline (company)
Flughafen *m* airport
Flugkarte *f* airline ticket
Fluglotse *m* air traffic *od* flight controller
Flugmodus *m* airplane mode, flight mode
Flugplan *m* flight schedule
Flugplatz *m* airport; (*klein*) airfield
Flugschein *m* (*von Pilot*) pilot's licence (Brit) *od* license (*US*)
Flugschreiber *m* flight recorder
Flugsteig *m* gate
Flugstrecke *f* air route
Flugticket *nt* plane ticket
Flugverkehr *m* air traffic
Flugzeug (**-(e)s**, **-e**) *nt* plane
Flugzeugentführung *f* hijacking of a plane
Flunder (-, **-n**) *f* flounder
Fluor (**-s**) *nt* fluorine
Flur (**-(e)s**, **-e**) *m* hall
Fluss (**-es**, **Flüsse**) *m* river; (*Fließen*) flow
flüssig *adj* liquid
Flüssigkeit *f* liquid
flüstern *vt*, *vi* to whisper

Flut (-, **-en**) *f* (*lit*, *fig*) flood; (*Gezeiten*) high tide
Flutlicht *nt* floodlight
Fohlen (**-s**, **-**) *nt* foal
Föhn (**-(e)s**, **-e**) *m* foehn, *warm dry alpine wind*; (*Haartrockner*) hairdryer
föhnen *vt* to blow-dry
Folge (-, **-n**) *f* series, sequence; (*Fortsetzung*) instalment (Brit), installment (*US*); (*TV*, *Rundf*) episode; (*Auswirkung*) result; **etw zur ~ haben** to result in sth; **Folgen haben** to have consequences
folgen *vi +dat* to follow ▶ *vi* (*gehorchen*) to obey; **jdm ~ können** (*fig*) to follow *od* understand sb
folgend *adj* following
folgendermaßen *adv* as follows, in the following way
folglich *adv* consequently
Folie (-, **-n**) *f* foil
Fön® (**-(e)s**, **-e**) *m* hairdryer
fönen *vt siehe* **föhnen**
fordern *vt* to demand
fördern *vt* to promote; (*unterstützen*) to help
Forderung *f* demand
Forelle *f* trout
Form (-, **-en**) *f* shape; (*Gestaltung*) form; (*Gussform*) mould; (*Backform*) baking tin; **in ~ sein** to be in good form *od* shape
Formalität *f* formality
Format (**-(e)s**, **-e**) *nt* format
formatieren *vt* (*Text*, *Diskette*) to format
Formblatt *nt* form
formen *vt* to form, to shape
förmlich *adj* formal; (*umg*) real
formlos *adj* informal
Formular (**-s**, **-e**) *nt* form
formulieren *vt* to formulate
forschen *vi* to search; (*wissenschaftlich*) to (do) research
Forscher (**-s**, **-**) *m* research scientist
Forschung *f* research
Förster (**-s**, **-**) *m* forester; (*für Wild*) gamekeeper
fort *adv* away; (*verschwunden*) gone
fort|bewegen *vt*, *vr* to move away
Fortbildung *f* further education
fort|fahren *unreg vi* to depart; (*fortsetzen*) to continue
fort|gehen *unreg vi* to go away
fortgeschritten *adj* advanced

ortpflanzung *f* reproduction
ortschritt *m* advance; **Fortschritte machen** to make progress
ɔrtschrittlich *adj* progressive
ɔrt|setzen *vt* to continue
ortsetzung *f* continuation; (*folgender Teil*) instalment (BRIT), installment (*US*); **~ folgt** to be continued
oto (-s, -s) *nt* photo(graph)
otobuch *nt* photo book
otograf(in) (-en, -en) *m(f)* photographer
otografie *f* photography; (*Bild*) photograph
ɔtografieren *vt* to photograph ▶ *vi* to take photographs
otohandy *nt* camera phone
otokopie *f* photocopy
ɔtokopieren *vt* to photocopy
oul (-s, -s) *nt* foul
oyer (-s, -s) *nt* foyer
r. *abk* (= *Frau*) Mrs, Ms
racht (-, -en) *f* freight; (*Naut*) cargo; (*Preis*) carriage
rachter (-s, -) *m* freighter
rack (-(e)s, Fräcke) *m* tails *pl*
racking *nt* fracking
rage (-, -n) *f* question; **das ist gar keine ~, das steht außer ~** there's no question about it
ragebogen *m* questionnaire
ragen *vt, vi* to ask
ragezeichen *nt* question mark
ragwürdig *adj* dubious
ranken[1] *nt* Franconia
ranken[2] (-, -) *m*: **(Schweizer) ~** (Swiss) Franc
rankieren *vt* to stamp, to frank
rankreich (-s) *nt* France
ranzose (-n, -n) *m* Frenchman; (*Junge*) French boy
ranzösin *f* Frenchwoman; (*Mädchen*) French girl
ranzösisch *adj* French; (*Sprache*): **auf F~** in French
raß *etc vb siehe* **fressen**
rau (-, -en) *f* woman; (*Ehefrau*) wife; (*Anrede*) Mrs, Ms
rauenarzt *m* gynaecologist (BRIT), gynecologist (*US*)
rauenbewegung *f* feminist movement
rauenfeindlich *adj* misogynous
rauenhaus *nt* women's refuge

Fräulein *nt* (*pej*: *Hist*) young lady; (*Anrede*) Miss
frech *adj* cheeky
Frechheit *f* cheek
frei *adj* free; (*Stelle*) vacant; (*Mitarbeiter*) freelance; **„Zimmer ~"** "vacancies"; **im Freien** in the open air
Freibad *nt* open-air swimming pool
freiberuflich *adj* self-employed
freigebig *adj* generous
Freiheit *f* freedom
Freikarte *f* free ticket
Freikörperkultur *f* nudism
frei|lassen *unreg vt* to (set) free
freilich *adv*: **ja ~!** yes of course
Freilichtbühne *f* open-air theatre
frei|machen *vr*: **sich ~** (*beim Arzt*) to take one's clothes off
frei|nehmen *vt*: **sich** *dat* **einen Tag ~** to take a day off
Freisprechanlage *f* (*im Auto*) hands-free (car kit)
Freistoß *m* free kick
Freitag *m* Friday; *siehe auch* **Dienstag**
freitags *adv* on Fridays
freiwillig *adj* voluntary
Freizeichen *nt* (*Tel*) ringing tone
Freizeit *f* spare *od* free time
Freizeitpark *m* leisure park
fremd *adj* (*unvertraut*) strange; (*ausländisch*) foreign; (*nicht eigen*) someone else's
Fremde(r) *f(m)* stranger; (*Ausländer*) foreigner
Fremdenführer(in) *m(f)* (tourist) guide
Fremdenverkehr *m* tourism
Fremdenverkehrsamt *nt* tourist information office
Fremdenzimmer *nt* guest room
Fremdsprache *f* foreign language
Fremdwort *nt* foreign word
Frequenz *f* (*Rundf*) frequency
fressen *unreg vt, vi* to eat
Freude (-, -n) *f* joy, delight
freuen *vt unpers* to make happy *od* pleased ▶ *vr* to be glad *od* happy; **sich auf etw** *akk* **~** to look forward to sth; **sich über etw** *akk* **~** to be pleased about sth
Freund (-(e)s, -e) *m* friend; (*Liebhaber*) boyfriend
Freundin *f* friend; (*Liebhaberin*) girlfriend
freundlich *adj* kind, friendly

freundlicherweise *adv* kindly
Freundlichkeit *f* friendliness, kindness
Freundschaft *f* friendship
Frieden (**-s**, **-**) *m* peace
Friedhof *m* cemetery
friedlich *adj* peaceful
frieren *unreg vi* to freeze ▶ *vt unpers* to freeze; **ich friere, es friert mich** I am freezing
Frikadelle *f* meatball
frisch *adj* fresh; (*lebhaft*) lively; **~ gestrichen!** wet paint!; **sich ~ machen** to freshen (o.s.) up
Frischhaltefolie *f* clingfilm
Frischkäse *m* cream cheese
Friseur *m* hairdresser
frisieren *vt* (*Haar*) to do ▶ *vr* to do one's hair
Frist (**-**, **-en**) *f* period; (*Termin*) deadline; **eine ~ einhalten/verstreichen lassen** to meet a deadline/let a deadline pass
fristgerecht *adj* within the period stipulated
fristlos *adj* (*Entlassung*) instant
Frisur *f* hairdo, hairstyle
frittieren *vt* to deep fry
Frl. *abk* (*pej*: *Hist*: = *Fräulein*) Miss
froh *adj* happy; **ich bin ~, dass ...** I'm glad that ...
fröhlich *adj* merry, happy
Fronleichnam (**-(e)s**) *m* Corpus Christi
frontal *adj* frontal
fror *etc vb siehe* **frieren**
Frosch (**-(e)s**, **Frösche**) *m* frog
Frost (**-(e)s**, **Fröste**) *m* frost
Frostschutzmittel *nt* anti-freeze
Frottee, Frotté (**-(s)**, **-s**) *nt od m* towelling
Frucht (**-**, **Früchte**) *f* (*lit*, *fig*) fruit; (*Getreide*) corn
Fruchteis *nt* fruit-flavoured ice-cream
Fruchtsaft *m* fruit juice
früh *adj*, *adv* early; **heute ~** this morning
früher *adj* earlier; (*ehemalig*) former ▶ *adv* formerly
frühestens *adv* at the earliest
Frühjahr *nt* spring
Frühling *m* spring
Frühlingsrolle *f* spring roll
Frühstück *nt* breakfast
frühstücken *vi* to (have) breakfast
frühzeitig *adj* early
Frust (**-(e)s**) (*umg*) *m* frustration
frustrieren *vt* to frustrate

Fuchs (**-es**, **Füchse**) *m* fox
fühlen *vt*, *vi*, *vr* to feel
fuhr *etc vb siehe* **fahren**
führen *vt* to lead; (*Geschäft*) to run; (*Name*) to bear; (*Buch*) to keep ▶ *vi* to lead ▶ *vr* to behave
Führerschein *m* driving licence (BRIT), driver's license (*US*)
Führung *f* leadership; (*eines Unternehmens*) management; (*Mil*) command; (*Museumsführung*) conducted tour
füllen *vt* to fill; (*Koch*) to stuff ▶ *vr* to fill (up)
Füller (**-s**, **-**) *m* fountain pen
Füllung *f* filling
Fund (**-(e)s**, **-e**) *m* find
Fundbüro *nt* lost property office, lost and found (*US*)
Fundsachen *pl* lost property *sing*
fünf *num* five
fünfhundert *num* five hundred
fünfte(r, s) *adj* fifth
Fünftel (**-s**, **-**) *nt* fifth
fünfzehn *num* fifteen
fünfzig *num* fifty
Funk (**-s**) *m* radio
Funke (**-ns**, **-n**) *m* spark
funkeln *vi* to sparkle
Funkgerät *nt* radio set
Funktaxi *nt* radio taxi
Funktion *f* function
funktionieren *vi* to work, to function
Funktionskleidung *f* technical clothing
Funktionstaste *f* (*Comput*) function key
für *präp +akk* for; **was ~ ein ...?** what kind *od* sort of ...?; **Tag ~ Tag** day after day
Furcht (**-**) *f* fear
furchtbar *adj* terrible
fürchten *vt* to be afraid of, to fear ▶ *vr* **sich ~ (vor** *+dat***)** to be afraid (of)
fürchterlich *adj* awful
füreinander *adv* for each other
fürs = **für das**
Fürst (**-en**, **-en**) *m* prince
Fürstentum *nt* principality
fürstlich *adj* princely
Furunkel (**-s**, **-**) *nt od m* boil
furzen (*!*) *vi* to fart (*!*)
Fuß (**-es**, **Füße**) *m* foot; (*von Glas, Säule etc*) base; (*von Möbel*) leg; **zu ~** on foot; **zu ~ gehen** to walk

ußball *m* football
ußballmannschaft *f* football (BRIT) *od* soccer team
ußballplatz *m* football (BRIT) *od* soccer pitch
ußballspiel *nt* football (BRIT) *od* soccer match
ußballspieler(in) *m(f)* footballer (BRIT), soccer player (*US*)
ußboden *m* floor
ußgänger(in) (**-s**, **-**) *m(f)* pedestrian
ußgängerüberweg *m* pedestrian crossing (BRIT), crosswalk (*US*)
ußgängerzone *f* pedestrian precinct
ußpilz *m* (*Med*) athlete's foot
ußtritt *m* kick
ußweg *m* footpath
utter (**-s**, **-**) *nt* fodder; (*Stoff*) lining
ittern *vt* to feed; (*Kleidung*) to line
utur (**-s**, **-e**) *nt* future

G9 (**-**) *nt* (*Sch*) *school system lasting 13 years and leading to the Abitur school-leaving exams*
gab *etc vb siehe* **geben**
Gabe (**-**, **-n**) *f* gift
Gabel (**-**, **-n**) *f* fork
Gabelung *f* fork
Gage (**-**, **-n**) *f* fee
gähnen *vi* to yawn
Galerie *f* gallery
Galle (**-**, **-n**) *f* gall; (*Organ*) gall bladder
Galopp (**-s**, **-s** *od* **-e**) *m* gallop
galoppieren *vi* to gallop
galt *etc vb siehe* **gelten**
Gamer(in) (**-s**, **-**) *m(f)* (*Comput*) gamer
Gameshow *f* game show
gammeln (*umg*) *vi* to loaf about
Gammler(in) (**-s**, **-**) *m(f)* dropout
gang *adj*: **~ und gäbe** usual, normal
Gang (**-(e)s**, **Gänge**) *m* walk; (*Essensgang, Ablauf*) course; (*Flur etc*) corridor; (*Durchgang*) passage; (*Aut, Tech*) gear; (*Theat, Aviat*) aisle; **den ersten ~ einlegen** to engage first (gear); **in ~ bringen** to start up; (*fig*) to get off the ground
Gangschaltung *f* gears *pl*
Gangway *f* (*Naut*) gangway; (*Aviat*) steps *pl*
Gans (**-**, **Gänse**) *f* goose
Gänseblümchen *nt* daisy
Gänsehaut *f* goose pimples *pl*
ganz *adj* whole; (*vollständig*) complete ▶ *adv* quite; (*völlig*) completely; **~ Europa** all Europe; **sein ganzes Geld** all his money; **das mag ich**

~ **besonders gern(e)** I'm particularly fond of that; ~ **und gar nicht** not at all
ganztägig *adj* all-day *attrib*
ganztags *adv* (*arbeiten*) full time
Ganztagsschule *f* all-day school
Ganztagsstelle *f* full-time job
gar *adj* cooked, done ▸ *adv* quite; ~ **nicht/nichts/keiner** not/nothing/ nobody at all; ~ **nicht schlecht** not bad at all
Garage (-, **-n**) *f* garage
Garantie *f* guarantee
garantieren *vt* to guarantee
Garderobe (-, **-n**) *f* wardrobe; (*Abgabe*) cloakroom (BRIT), checkroom (*US*)
Gardine (-, **-n**) *f* curtain
Garn (**-(e)s**, **-e**) *nt* thread
Garnele (-, **-n**) *f* shrimp
garnieren *vt* to decorate; (*Speisen*) to garnish
Garten (**-s**, **Gärten**) *m* garden
Gärtner(in) (**-s**, **-**) *m(f)* gardener
Gärtnerei *f* nursery; (*Gemüsegärtnerei*) market garden (BRIT), truck farm (*US*)
Gas (**-es**, **-e**) *nt* gas; ~ **geben** (*Aut*) to accelerate
Gasflasche *f* gas canister
Gasheizung *f* gas heating
Gasherd *m* gas cooker
Gaskocher *m* gas cooker
Gaspedal *nt* accelerator, gas pedal (*US*)
Gasse (-, **-n**) *f* alley
Gast (**-es**, **Gäste**) *m* guest; **bei jdm zu** ~ **sein** to be sb's guest(s)
Gastarbeiter(in) *m(f)* (*old*) foreign worker
Gästebett *nt* spare bed
Gästebuch *nt* visitors' book
Gästezimmer *nt* guest room
gastfreundlich *adj* hospitable
Gastfreundschaft *f* hospitality
Gastgeber(in) (**-s**, **-**) *m(f)* host(ess)
Gasthaus *nt* hotel, inn
Gastland *nt* host country
Gastronomie *f* (*form: Gaststättengewerbe*) catering trade
Gastspiel *nt* (*Sport*) away game
Gaststätte *f* restaurant; (*Trinklokal*) pub
Gastwirt *m* innkeeper
GAU *m abk* (= *größter anzunehmender Unfall*) MCA, maximum credible accident
Gaumen (**-s**, **-**) *m* palate
Gaze (-, **-n**) *f* gauze
geb. *abk* = **geboren**
Gebäck (**-(e)s**, **-e**) *nt* (*Kekse*) biscuits *pl* (BRIT), cookies *pl* (*US*)
gebacken *pp von* **backen**
gebären *unreg vt* to give birth to
Gebärmutter *f* womb
Gebäude (**-s**, **-**) *nt* building
geben *unreg vt, vi* to give; (*Karten*) to deal ▸ *vt unpers*: **es gibt** there is/are; (*zukünftig*) there will be ▸ *vr* (*sich verhalten*) to behave, to act; **das gibt's doch nicht!** that's impossible!; **das wird sich schon** ~ that'll soon sort itself out
Gebet (**-(e)s**, **-e**) *nt* prayer
gebeten *pp von* **bitten**
Gebiet (**-(e)s**, **-e**) *nt* area; (*Hoheitsgebiet*) territory; (*fig*) field
gebildet *adj* educated
Gebirge (**-s**, **-**) *nt* mountains *pl*
gebirgig *adj* mountainous
Gebiss (**-es**, **-e**) *nt* teeth *pl*; (*künstlich*) dentures *pl*
gebissen *pp von* **beißen**
Gebläse (**-s**, **-**) *nt* fan, blower
geblasen *pp von* **blasen**
geblieben *pp von* **bleiben**
gebogen *pp von* **biegen**
geboren *pp von* **gebären** ▸ *adj* born; **Andrea Jordan, geborene Christian** Andrea Jordan, née Christian
geborgen *pp von* **bergen** ▸ *adj* secure, safe
geboten *pp von* **bieten**
gebracht *pp von* **bringen**
gebrannt *pp von* **brennen**
gebraten *pp von* **braten**
gebrauchen *vt* to use
Gebrauchsanweisung *f* directions *pl* for use
gebrauchsfertig *adj* ready for use
gebraucht *adj* used, second-hand
Gebrauchtwagen *m* second-hand *or* used car
gebrochen *pp von* **brechen**
Gebühr (-, **-en**) *f* charge; (*Maut*) toll; (*Honorar*) fee
Gebühreneinheit *f* (*Tel*) tariff unit
gebührenfrei *adj* free of charge
gebührenpflichtig *adj* subject to charges; **gebührenpflichtige Straße** toll road
gebunden *pp von* **binden**
Geburt (-, **-en**) *f* birth

ebürtig *adj*: **gebürtige Schweizerin** Swiss-born woman
eburtsdatum *nt* date of birth
eburtsjahr *nt* year of birth
eburtsort *m* birthplace
eburtstag *m* birthday; **herzlichen Glückwunsch zum ~!** happy birthday!
eburtsurkunde *f* birth certificate
ebüsch (**-(e)s**, **-e**) *nt* bushes *pl*
edacht *pp von* **denken**
edächtnis (**-ses**, **-se**) *nt* memory
edanke (**-ns**, **-n**) *m* thought; **sich über etw** *akk* **Gedanken machen** to think about sth
edankenstrich *m* dash
edeck (**-(e)s**, **-e**) *nt* cover(ing); (*Menü*) set meal
edenkstätte *f* memorial
edicht (**-(e)s**, **-e**) *nt* poem
edränge (**-s**) *nt* crush, crowd
edrungen *pp von* **dringen**
eduld (**-**) *f* patience
eduldig *adj* patient
edurft *pp von* **dürfen**
eehrt *adj*: **Sehr geehrter Herr Young** Dear Mr Young
eeignet *adj* suitable
efahr (**-**, **-en**) *f* danger; **auf eigene ~** at one's own risk; **außer ~** out of danger
efährden *vt* to endanger
efahren *pp von* **fahren**
efährlich *adj* dangerous
efälle (**-s**, **-**) *nt* (*von Land, Straße*) slope; (*Neigungsgrad*) gradient
efallen *pp von* **fallen**; **gefallen** ▶ *vi* (*unreg*): **jdm ~** to please sb; **er/es gefällt mir** I like him/it; **sich** *dat* **etw ~ lassen** to put up with sth
efallen (**-s**, **-**) *m* favour; **jdm einen ~ tun** to do sb a favour
efälligst (*umg*) *adv* kindly; **sei ~ still!** will you kindly keep your mouth shut!
efangen *pp von* **fangen**
efängnis (**-ses**, **-se**) *nt* prison
efäß (**-es**, **-e**) *nt* vessel (*auch Anat*), container
efasst *adj* composed, calm; **auf etw** *akk* **~ sein** to be prepared *od* ready for sth
eflochten *pp von* **flechten**
eflogen *pp von* **fliegen**
eflossen *pp von* **fließen**
eflügel (**-s**) *nt* poultry
efragt *adj* in demand

gefressen *pp von* **fressen**
gefrieren *unreg vi* to freeze
Gefrierfach *nt* freezer compartment
Gefrierschrank *m* (upright) freezer
Gefriertruhe *f* deep-freeze
gefroren *pp von* **frieren**; **gefrieren**
Gefühl (**-(e)s**, **-e**) *nt* feeling
gefunden *pp von* **finden**
gegangen *pp von* **gehen**
gegeben *pp von* **geben**
gegebenenfalls *adv* if need be

SCHLÜSSELWORT

gegen *präp +akk* **1** against; **nichts gegen jdn haben** to have nothing against sb; **X gegen Y** (*Sport, Jur*) X versus Y; **ein Mittel gegen Schnupfen** something for colds
2 (*in Richtung auf*) towards; **gegen Osten** to(wards) the east; **gegen Abend** towards evening; **gegen einen Baum fahren** to drive into a tree
3 (*ungefähr*) round about; **gegen 3 Uhr** around 3 o'clock
4 (*gegenüber*) towards; **gerecht gegen alle** fair to all
5 (*im Austausch für*) for; **gegen bar** for cash; **gegen Quittung** against a receipt
6 (*verglichen mit*) compared with

Gegend (**-**, **-en**) *f* area
gegeneinander *adv* against one another
Gegenfahrbahn *f* opposite carriageway
Gegenmittel *nt*: **~ (gegen)** (*Med*) antidote (to)
Gegensatz (**-es**, **Gegensätze**) *m* contrast; **im ~ zu** in contrast to
gegensätzlich *adj* contrary; (*widersprüchlich*) contradictory
gegenseitig *adj* mutual ▶ *adv*: **sich ~ helfen** to help each other
Gegenstand *m* object
Gegenteil *nt* opposite; **im ~** on the contrary
gegenteilig *adj* opposite, contrary
gegenüber *präp +dat* opposite; (*zu*) to(wards); (*angesichts*) in the face of ▶ *adv* opposite
gegenüber|stehen *unreg vi +dat* to face; (*Problem*) to be faced with

gegenüber|stellen *vt* to confront; (*fig*) to contrast
Gegenverkehr *m* oncoming traffic
Gegenwart *f* present
Gegenwind *m* headwind
gegessen *pp von* **essen**
geglichen *pp von* **gleichen**
geglitten *pp von* **gleiten**
Gegner(in) (**-s**, **-**) *m(f)* opponent
gegolten *pp von* **gelten**
gegossen *pp von* **gießen**
gegraben *pp von* **graben**
gegriffen *pp von* **greifen**
gehabt *pp von* **haben**
Gehackte(s) *nt* mince(d meat) (BRIT), ground meat (*US*)
Gehalt[1] (**-(e)s**, **-e**) *m* content
Gehalt[2] (**-(e)s**, **Gehälter**) *nt* salary
gehalten *pp von* **halten**
gehangen *pp von* **hängen**
gehässig *adj* spiteful, nasty
gehbehindert *adj* disabled
geheim *adj* secret; **~ halten** to keep secret
Geheimnis (**-ses**, **-se**) *nt* secret; (*rätselhaftes Geheimnis*) mystery
geheimnisvoll *adj* mysterious
Geheimnummer *f* (*von Kreditkarte*) PIN number
geheißen *pp von* **heißen**
gehen *unreg vi* (*auch Auto, Uhr*) to go; (*zu Fuß gehen*) to walk; (*funktionieren*) to work; **~ nach** (*Fenster*) to face; **wie geht es dir?** how are you *od* things?; **mir/ihm geht es gut** I'm/he's (doing) fine; **geht das?** is that possible?; **gehts noch?** can you manage?; **es geht** not too bad, O.K.; **das geht nicht** that's not on; **es geht um etw** it's about sth
Gehirn (**-(e)s**, **-e**) *nt* brain
Gehirnerschütterung *f* concussion
gehoben *pp von* **heben**
geholfen *pp von* **helfen**
Gehör (**-(e)s**) *nt* hearing
gehorchen *vi +dat* to obey
gehören *vi* to belong ▶ *vr unpers* to be right *od* proper; **das gehört sich nicht** it's not done; **wem gehört das Buch?** whose book is this?
gehörlos *adj* deaf
gehorsam *adj* obedient
Gehsteig *m*, **Gehweg** *m* pavement (BRIT), sidewalk (*US*)
Geier (**-s**, **-**) *m* vulture
Geige (**-**, **-n**) *f* violin
geil *adj* randy (BRIT), horny (*US*); (*umg: gut*) fantastic
Geisel (**-**, **-n**) *f* hostage
Geist (**-(e)s**, **-er**) *m* spirit; (*Gespenst*) ghost; (*Verstand*) mind
Geisterfahrer(in) (*umg*) *m(f)* ghost-driver (*US*), *person driving in the wrong direction*
geizig *adj* miserly, mean
gekannt *pp von* **kennen**
geklungen *pp von* **klingen**
geknickt *adj* (*fig*) dejected
gekniffen *pp von* **kneifen**
gekommen *pp von* **kommen**
gekonnt *pp von* **können** ▶ *adj* skilful (BRIT), skillful (*US*)
gekrochen *pp von* **kriechen**
Gel (**-s**, **-e**) *nt* gel
Gelächter (**-s**, **-**) *nt* laughter
geladen *pp von* **laden** ▶ *adj* loaded; (*Elek*) live; (*fig*) furious
gelähmt *adj* paralysed
Gelände (**-s**, **-**) *nt* land, terrain; (*von Fabrik, Sportgelände*) grounds *pl*; (*Baugelände*) site
Geländer (**-s**, **-**) *nt* railing; (*Treppengeländer*) banister(s)
Geländewagen *m* off-road vehicle, four-by-four
gelang *etc vb siehe* **gelingen**
gelassen *pp von* **lassen** ▶ *adj* calm; (*gefasst*) composed
Gelatine *f* gelatine
gelaufen *pp von* **laufen**
gelaunt *adj*: **schlecht/gut ~** in a bad/good mood
gelb *adj* yellow; (*Ampellicht*) amber (BRIT), yellow (*US*)
gelblich *adj* yellowish
Gelbsucht *f* jaundice
Geld (**-(e)s**, **-er**) *nt* money
Geldautomat *m* cash dispenser
Geldbeutel *m* purse
Geldbörse *f* purse
Geldbuße *f* fine
Geldschein *m* banknote
Geldstrafe *f* fine
Geldstück *nt* coin
Geldwechsel *m* exchange (of money); **„~"** "bureau de change"
Gelee (**-s**, **-s**) *nt od m* jelly
gelegen *pp von* **liegen** ▶ *adj* situated; (*passend*) convenient; **etw kommt jdm ~** sth is convenient for sb

elegenheit *f* opportunity; (*Anlass*) occasion

elegentlich *adj* occasional ▶ *adv* occasionally; (*bei Gelegenheit*) some time (or other)

elenk (**-(e)s**, **-e**) *nt* joint

elernt *adj* skilled

elesen *pp von* **lesen**

eliehen *pp von* **leihen**

elingen *unreg vi* to succeed; **es ist mir gelungen, etw zu tun** I succeeded in doing sth

elitten *pp von* **leiden**

elogen *pp von* **lügen**

elten *unreg vt* (*wert sein*) to be worth ▶ *vi* (*gültig sein*) to be valid; (*erlaubt sein*) to be allowed; **jdm viel/wenig ~** to mean a lot/not mean much to sb; **jdm ~** (*gemünzt sein auf*) to be meant for *od* aimed at sb; **etw ~ lassen** to accept sth; **als** *od* **für etw ~** to be considered to be sth

elungen *pp von* **gelingen**

emahlen *pp von* **mahlen**

emälde (**-s**, **-**) *nt* picture, painting

emäß *präp +dat* in accordance with ▶ *adj +dat* appropriate to

emein *adj* common; (*niederträchtig*) mean

emeinde (**-**, **-n**) *f* district; (*Bewohner*) community; (*Pfarrgemeinde*) parish; (*Kirchengemeinde*) congregation

emeinsam *adj* joint, common (*auch Math*) ▶ *adv* together; **etw ~ haben** to have sth in common

emeinschaft *f* community; **~ Unabhängiger Staaten** Commonwealth of Independent States

emessen *pp von* **messen**

emieden *pp von* **meiden**

emischt *adj* mixed

emocht *pp von* **mögen**

emüse (**-s**, **-**) *nt* vegetables *pl*

emüsehändler(in) *m(f)* greengrocer (Brit), vegetable dealer (US)

emusst *pp von* **müssen**

emustert *adj* patterned

emütlich *adj* comfortable, cosy; (*Person*) good-natured

enannt *pp von* **nennen**

enau *adj* exact, precise ▶ *adv* exactly, precisely ■ **Genaueres** *pl* further details *pl*; **etw ~ nehmen** to take sth seriously; **~ genommen** strictly speaking; **etw ~ wissen** to know sth for certain

genauso *adv* exactly the same (way); **~ gut/viel/viele Leute** just as well/much/many people (wie as)

genehmigen *vt* to approve; **sich** *dat* **etw ~** to indulge in sth

Genehmigung *f* approval

Generalkonsulat *nt* consulate general

Generation *f* generation

Genf (**-s**) *nt* Geneva

genial *adj* brilliant

Genick (**-(e)s**, **-e**) *nt* (back of the) neck

Genie (**-s**, **-s**) *nt* genius

genieren *vr* to be embarrassed

genießen *unreg vt* to enjoy

Genitiv *m* genitive

genmanipuliert *adj* genetically modified

Genom (**-s**, **-e**) *nt* genome

genommen *pp von* **nehmen**

genoss *etc vb siehe* **genießen**

genossen *pp von* **genießen**

Gentechnik *f* genetic engineering

Gentherapie *f* gene therapy

genug *adv* enough

genügen *vi* to be enough; **jdm ~** to be enough for sb

Genuss (**-es**, **Genüsse**) *m* pleasure; (*Zusichnehmen*) consumption

geöffnet *adj* open

Geografie *f* geography

Geologie *f* geology

Georgien (**-s**) *nt* Georgia

Gepäck (**-(e)s**) *nt* luggage (Brit)

Gepäckabfertigung *f* luggage (Brit) *od* baggage desk/office

Gepäckablage *f* luggage (Brit) *od* baggage rack

Gepäckannahme *f* (*Bahnhof*) luggage (Brit) *od* baggage office; (*Flughafen*) luggage (Brit) *od* baggage check-in

Gepäckaufbewahrung *f* left-luggage office (Brit), baggage check (US)

Gepäckausgabe *f* (*Bahnhof*) luggage (Brit) *od* baggage office; (*Flughafen*) baggage reclaim

Gepäckkontrolle *f* luggage (Brit) *od* baggage check

Gepäckstück *nt* piece of luggage (Brit) *od* baggage

Gepäckträger *m* porter; (*Fahrrad*) carrier

Gepäckwagen *m* luggage van (Brit), baggage car (US)

gepfiffen *pp von* **pfeifen**

gepflegt *adj* well-groomed; (*Park etc*) well looked after
gequollen *pp von* **quellen**

SCHLÜSSELWORT

gerade *adj* straight; (*aufrecht*) upright; **eine gerade Zahl** an even number
▶ *adv* **1** (*genau*) just, exactly; (*: speziell*) especially; **gerade deshalb** that's just *od* exactly why; **das ist es ja gerade!** that's just it; **gerade du** you especially; **warum gerade ich?** why me (of all people)?; **jetzt gerade nicht!** not now!; **gerade neben** right next to
2 (*eben, soeben*) just; **er wollte gerade aufstehen** he was just about to get up; **gerade erst** only just; **gerade noch** (only) just

geradeaus *adv* straight ahead
gerannt *pp von* **rennen**
Gerät (**-(e)s**, **-e**) *nt* device; (*Apparat*) gadget; (*Werkzeug*) tool; (*Zubehör*) equipment *no pl*
geraten *unreg pp von* **raten**; **geraten** ▶ *vi* (*gedeihen*) to thrive; (*gelingen*): **(jdm) ~** to turn out well (for sb); **gut/schlecht ~** to turn out well/badly; **an jdn ~** to come across sb
geräumig *adj* roomy
Geräusch (**-(e)s**, **-e**) *nt* sound; (*unangenehm*) noise
gerecht *adj* just, fair; **jdm/etw ~ werden** to do justice to sb/sth
gereizt *adj* irritable
Gericht (**-(e)s**, **-e**) *nt* court; (*Essen*) dish
gerieben *pp von* **reiben**
gering *adj* slight; (*niedrig*) low; (*Zeit*) short
geringfügig *adj* slight
gerissen *pp von* **reißen**
geritten *pp von* **reiten**
gern *adv* willingly, gladly; **etw ~ tun** to like doing sth; **~ geschehen!** you're welcome!
gerochen *pp von* **riechen**
Gerste (**-**, **-n**) *f* barley
Gerstenkorn *nt* (*im Auge*) stye
Geruch (**-(e)s**, **Gerüche**) *m* smell
Gerücht (**-(e)s**, **-e**) *nt* rumour (Brit), rumor (*US*)
gerufen *pp von* **rufen**
Gerümpel (**-s**) *nt* junk
gerungen *pp von* **ringen**
Gerüst (**-(e)s**, **-e**) *nt* (*Baugerüst*) scaffold(ing); (*fig*) framework
gesalzen *pp von* **salzen**
gesamt *adj* whole, entire; (*Kosten*) total; (*Werke*) complete
Gesamtschule *f* ≈ comprehensive school
gesandt *pp von* **senden²**
Gesäß (**-es**, **-e**) *nt* bottom
geschaffen *pp von* **schaffen²**
Geschäft (**-(e)s**, **-e**) *nt* business; (*Laden*) shop; (*Geschäftsabschluss*) dea
geschäftlich *adj* commercial ▶ *adv* o business
Geschäftsfrau *f* businesswoman
Geschäftsführer(in) *m(f)* manager; (*von Klub*) secretary
Geschäftsleitung *f* management
Geschäftsmann (**-(e)s**, **-leute**) *m* businessman
Geschäftsreise *f* business trip
geschehen *unreg vi* to happen
Geschenk (**-(e)s**, **-e**) *nt* present, gift
Geschenkgutschein *m* gift voucher
Geschenkpapier *nt* gift-wrapping paper, giftwrap
Geschichte (**-**, **-n**) *f* story; (*Sache*) affair; (*Historie*) history
geschickt *adj* skilful (Brit), skillful (US
geschieden *pp von* **scheiden** ▶ *adj* divorced
geschienen *pp von* **scheinen**
Geschirr (**-(e)s**, **-e**) *nt* crockery; (*Küchengeschirr*) pots and pans *pl*; (*Pferdegeschirr*) harness
Geschirrspülmaschine *f* dishwashe
Geschirrspülmittel *nt* washing-up liquid (Brit), dishwashing liquid (*US*)
Geschirrtuch *nt* tea towel (Brit), dishtowel (*US*)
geschissen *pp von* **scheißen**
geschlafen *pp von* **schlafen**
geschlagen *pp von* **schlagen**
Geschlecht (**-(e)s**, **-er**) *nt* sex; (*Gram*) gender
Geschlechtskrankheit *f* sexually-transmitted disease
Geschlechtsverkehr *m* sexual intercourse
geschlichen *pp von* **schleichen**
geschliffen *pp von* **schleifen²**
geschlossen *pp von* **schließen** ▶ *adj* closed
Geschmack (**-(e)s**, **Geschmäcke**) *m* taste

geschmacklos *adj* tasteless; (*fig*) in bad taste

geschmackvoll *adj* tasteful

geschmissen *pp von* **schmeißen**

geschmolzen *pp von* **schmelzen**

geschnitten *pp von* **schneiden**

geschoben *pp von* **schieben**

Geschoss (**-es**, **-e**) *nt* (*Stockwerk*) floor

geschossen *pp von* **schießen**

Geschrei (**-s**) *nt* cries *pl*; (*fig*) fuss

geschrieben *pp von* **schreiben**

geschützt *adj* protected

Geschwätz (**-es**) *nt* chatter; (*Klatsch*) gossip

geschwätzig *adj* talkative

geschweige *adv*: **~ (denn)** let alone

geschwiegen *pp von* **schweigen**

Geschwindigkeit *f* speed, velocity

Geschwindigkeitsbegrenzung *f* speed limit

Geschwister *pl* brothers and sisters *pl*

geschwollen *adj* pompous

geschwommen *pp von* **schwimmen**

geschworen *pp von* **schwören**

Geschwulst (**-**, **Geschwülste**) *f* growth

Geschwür (**-(e)s**, **-e**) *nt* ulcer

gesehen *pp von* **sehen**

gesellig *adj* sociable

Gesellschaft *f* society; (*Begleitung, Comm*) company; (*Abendgesellschaft etc*) party

gesessen *pp von* **sitzen**

Gesetz (**-es**, **-e**) *nt* law

gesetzlich *adj* legal

gesetzwidrig *adj* illegal

Gesicht (**-(e)s**, **-er**) *nt* face

Gesichtscreme *f* face cream

Gesichtswasser *nt* face lotion

gesoffen *pp von* **saufen**

gesogen *pp von* **saugen**

gespannt *adj* tense; (*begierig*) eager; **ich bin ~, ob** I wonder if *od* whether; **auf etw/jdn ~ sein** to look forward to sth/to meeting sb

Gespenst (**-(e)s**, **-er**) *nt* ghost

gesponnen *pp von* **spinnen**

Gespräch (**-(e)s**, **-e**) *nt* conversation; (*Diskussion*) discussion; (*Anruf*) call

gesprochen *pp von* **sprechen**

gesprungen *pp von* **springen**

Gestalt (**-**, **-en**) *f* form, shape; (*Person*) figure

gestanden *pp von* **stehen**; **gestehen**

Gestank (**-(e)s**) *m* stench

gestatten *vt* to permit, to allow; **~ Sie?** may I?

Geste (**-**, **-n**) *f* gesture

gestehen *unreg vt* to confess

gestern *adv* yesterday; **~ Abend/Morgen** yesterday evening/morning

gestiegen *pp von* **steigen**

gestochen *pp von* **stechen**

gestohlen *pp von* **stehlen**

gestorben *pp von* **sterben**

gestört *adj* disturbed; (*Rundfunkempfang*) poor

gestoßen *pp von* **stoßen**

gestreift *adj* striped

gestrichen *pp von* **streichen**

gestritten *pp von* **streiten**

gestunken *pp von* **stinken**

gesund *adj* healthy; **wieder ~ werden** to get better

Gesundheit *f* health; **~!** bless you!

gesundheitsschädlich *adj* unhealthy

gesungen *pp von* **singen**

gesunken *pp von* **sinken**

getan *pp von* **tun**

getragen *pp von* **tragen**

Getränk (**-(e)s**, **-e**) *nt* drink

Getränkeautomat *m* drinks machine *od* dispenser

Getränkekarte *f* (*in Café*) list of beverages; (*in Restaurant*) wine list

Getreide (**-s**, **-**) *nt* cereal, grain

getrennt *adj* separate; **~ leben** to live apart; **~ zahlen** to pay separately

getreten *pp von* **treten**

Getriebe (**-s**, **-**) *nt* (*Aut*) gearbox

getrieben *pp von* **treiben**

getroffen *pp von* **treffen**

getrunken *pp von* **trinken**

Getue (**-s**) *nt* fuss

geübt *adj* experienced

gewachsen *pp von* **wachsen²** ▶ *adj*: **jdm/etw ~ sein** to be sb's equal/equal to sth

Gewähr (**-**) *f* guarantee; **keine ~ übernehmen für** to accept no responsibility for

Gewalt (**-**, **-en**) *f* power; (*große Kraft*) force; (*Gewalttaten*) violence; **mit aller ~** with all one's might

gewaltig *adj* tremendous; (*Irrtum*) huge

gewandt *pp von* **wenden** ▶ *adj* deft, skilful (BRIT), skillful (US)

gewann *etc vb siehe* **gewinnen**

gewaschen *pp von* **waschen**

Gewebe (**-s**, **-**) *nt* (*Stoff*) fabric; (*Biol*) tissue
Gewehr (**-(e)s**, **-e**) *nt* (*Flinte*) rifle; (*Schrotbüchse*) shotgun
Geweih (**-(e)s**, **-e**) *nt* antlers *pl*
Gewerbe (**-s**, **-**) *nt* trade
Gewerbegebiet *nt* industrial estate (BRIT) *od* park (US)
gewerblich *adj* industrial
Gewerkschaft *f* trade *od* labor (US) union
gewesen *pp von* **sein**
Gewicht (**-(e)s**, **-e**) *nt* weight; (*fig*) importance
gewiesen *pp von* **weisen**
Gewinn (**-(e)s**, **-e**) *m* profit; (*bei Spiel*) winnings *pl*
gewinnen *unreg vt* to win; (*erwerben*) to gain; (*Kohle, Öl*) to extract ▶ *vi* to win; (*profitieren*) to gain
Gewinner(in) (**-s**, **-**) *m(f)* winner
gewiss *adj* certain ▶ *adv* certainly
Gewissen (**-s**, **-**) *nt* conscience; **ein gutes/schlechtes ~ haben** to have a clear/bad conscience
Gewitter (**-s**, **-**) *nt* thunderstorm
gewittern *vi unpers*: **es gewittert** there's a thunderstorm
gewogen *pp von* **wiegen** ▶ *adj +dat* well-disposed (towards)
gewöhnen *vt*: **jdn an etw** *akk* **~** to accustom sb to sth ▶ *vr*: **sich an etw** *akk* **~** to get used *od* accustomed to sth
Gewohnheit *f* habit; (*Brauch*) custom
gewöhnlich *adj* usual; (*durchschnittlich*) ordinary; (*pej*) common; **wie ~** as usual
gewohnt *adj* usual; **etw ~ sein** to be used to sth
gewonnen *pp von* **gewinnen**
geworben *pp von* **werben**
geworden *pp von* **werden**
geworfen *pp von* **werfen**
Gewürz (**-es**, **-e**) *nt* spice
Gewürznelke *f* clove
gewusst *pp von* **wissen**
Gezeiten *pl* tides *pl*
gezogen *pp von* **ziehen**
gezwungen *pp von* **zwingen**
Gibraltar (**-s**) *nt* Gibraltar
Gicht (**-**) *f* gout
Giebel (**-s**, **-**) *m* gable
gierig *adj* greedy
gießen *unreg vt* to pour; (*Blumen*) to water; (*Metall*) to cast
Gießkanne *f* watering can
Gift (**-(e)s**, **-e**) *nt* poison
giftig *adj* poisonous
Gigabyte *nt* (*Comput*) gigabyte
ging *etc vb siehe* **gehen**
Gipfel (**-s**, **-**) *m* summit, peak; (*fig*) height
Gips (**-es**, **-e**) *m* plaster
Gipsbein (*umg*) *nt* leg in plaster
Gipsverband *m* plaster (cast)
Giraffe (**-**, **-n**) *f* giraffe
Girokonto *nt* current account (BRIT), checking account (US)
Gitarre (**-**, **-n**) *f* guitar
Gitter (**-s**, **-**) *nt* bars *pl*
glänzen *vi* to shine (*auch fig*)
glänzend *adj* shining; (*fig*) brilliant
Glas (**-es**, **Gläser**) *nt* glass; **zwei ~ Wein** two glasses of wine
Glaser (**-s**, **-**) *m* glazier
Glasscheibe *f* pane
Glassplitter *m* splinter of glass
Glasur *f* glaze; (*Koch*) icing
glatt *adj* smooth; (*rutschig*) slippery; (*Lüge*) downright
Glatteis *nt* (black) ice
Glätteisen *nt* hair straighteners *pl*
Glatze (**-**, **-n**) *f* bald head
glauben *vt, vi* to believe; (*meinen*) to think; **jdm ~** to believe sb
gleich *adj* equal; (*identisch*) (the) same identical ▶ *adv* equally; (*sofort*) straight away; (*bald*) in a minute; **es ist mir ~** it's all the same to me; **sie sind ~ groß** they are the same size; **~ nach/an** right after/at
gleichberechtigt *adj* with equal rights
Gleichberechtigung *f* equal rights *pl*
gleichen *unreg vi*: **jdm/etw ~** to be like sb/sth ▶ *vr* to be alike
gleichfalls *adv* likewise; **danke ~!** the same to you
gleichgeschlechtlich *adj* homosexual, same-sex *attrib*
gleichgültig *adj* indifferent
gleichmäßig *adj* even, equal
gleichzeitig *adj* simultaneous
Gleis (**-es**, **-e**) *nt* track, rails *pl*; (*am Bahnhof*) platform (BRIT), track (US)
gleiten *unreg vi* to glide; (*rutschen*) to slide
Gletscher (**-s**, **-**) *m* glacier
Gletscherspalte *f* crevasse
glich *etc vb siehe* **gleichen**

Glied (**-(e)s**, **-er**) *nt* (*Arm, Bein*) limb; (*Penis*) penis

Gliedmaßen *pl* limbs *pl*

glitschig (*umg*) *adj* slippery

glitt *etc vb siehe* **gleiten**

glitzern *vi* to glitter; (*Stern*) to twinkle

Glocke (**-**, **-n**) *f* bell

Glockenspiel *nt* chime(s)

Glotze (**-**, **-n**) (*umg*) *f* TV set

glotzen (*umg*) *vi* to stare

Glück (**-(e)s**) *nt* luck; (*Freude*) happiness; **~ haben** to be lucky; **viel ~** good luck; **zum ~** fortunately

glücklich *adj* fortunate; (*froh*) happy

glücklicherweise *adv* fortunately

Glückwunsch *m*: **~ (zu)** congratulations *pl* (on)

Glühbirne *f* light bulb

glühen *vi* to glow

Glühwein *m* mulled wine

GmbH (**-**, **-s**) *f abk* (= *Gesellschaft mit beschränkter Haftung*) ≈ Ltd. (Brit), plc (Brit), Inc. (US)

Gold (**-(e)s**) *nt* gold

golden *adj* golden

Goldfisch *m* goldfish

Goldmedaille *f* gold medal

Golf (**-(e)s**, **-e**) *m* gulf; **der (Persische) ~** the Gulf

Golfplatz *m* golf course

Golfschläger *m* golf club

Gondel (**-**, **-n**) *f* gondola; (*von Seilbahn*) cable car

gönnen *vt*: **jdm etw ~** not to begrudge sb sth; **sich** *dat* **etw ~** to allow o.s. sth

googeln *vt* to google

Google® *nt* Google®

goss *etc vb siehe* **gießen**

Gott (**-es**, **Götter**) *m* god; (*als Name*) God

Gottesdienst *m* service

Göttin *f* goddess

Grab (**-(e)s**, **Gräber**) *nt* grave

graben *unreg vt* to dig

Graben (**-s**, **Gräben**) *m* ditch

Grabstein *m* gravestone

Grad (**-(e)s**, **-e**) *m* degree; **bis zu einem gewissen ~** up to a certain extent

Graf (**-en**, **-en**) *m* count, earl (Brit)

Grafik (**-**, **-en**) *f* (*Illustration*) diagram; (*Comput, Tech*) graphics

Grafikkarte *f* (*Comput*) graphics card

Grafikprogramm *nt* (*Comput*) graphics software

Gräfin *f* countess

Gramm (**-s**, **-e**) *nt* gram(me)

Grammatik *f* grammar

Graphik = **Grafik**

Gras (**-es**, **Gräser**) *nt* grass

grässlich *adj* horrible

Gräte (**-**, **-n**) *f* fish-bone

gratis *adj, adv* free (of charge)

gratulieren *vi*: **jdm (zu etw) ~** to congratulate sb (on sth); **(ich) gratuliere!** congratulations!

grau *adj* grey (Brit), gray (US)

grauhaarig *adj* grey-haired (Brit), gray-haired (US)

grausam *adj* cruel

gravierend *adj* grave

greifen *unreg vt* to seize ▶ *vi* (*nicht rutschen, einrasten*) to grip; **zu etw ~** (*fig*) to turn to sth

grell *adj* harsh

Grenze (**-**, **-n**) *f* border; (*zwischen Grundstücken, fig*) boundary; (*Staatsgrenze*) frontier; (*Schranke*) limit

grenzen *vi*: **~ an** *+akk* to border on

Grenzübergang *m* frontier crossing

Grieche (**-n**, **-n**) *m* Greek

Griechenland *nt* Greece

Griechin *f* Greek

griechisch *adj* Greek; (*Sprache*): **auf G~** in Greek

griesgrämig *adj* grumpy

Grieß (**-es**, **-e**) *m* (*Koch*) semolina

griff *etc vb siehe* **greifen**

Griff (**-(e)s**, **-e**) *m* grip; (*Vorrichtung*) handle

griffbereit *adj* handy

Grill (**-s**, **-s**) *m* grill

Grille (**-**, **-n**) *f* cricket

grillen *vt* to grill

grinsen *vi* to grin; (*höhnisch*) to smirk

Grippe (**-**, **-n**) *f* flu

grob *adj* coarse; (*Fehler, Verstoß*) gross; (*brutal, derb*) rough

Grönland (**-s**) *nt* Greenland

groß *adj* big, large; (*hoch*) tall; (*Freude, Werk*) great ▶ *adv* greatly; **im Großen und Ganzen** on the whole; **die Großen** (*Erwachsene*) the grown-ups

großartig *adj* great, splendid

Großbritannien (**-s**) *nt* (Great) Britain

Großbuchstabe *m* capital (letter)

Größe (**-**, **-n**) *f* size; (*Länge*) height; (*fig*) greatness

Großeltern *pl* grandparents *pl*

Großhandel *m* wholesale trade

Großmarkt *m* hypermarket

Großmutter *f* grandmother

Großraum *m*: **der ~ München** Greater Munich
groß|schreiben *unreg vt*: **ein Wort ~** to write a word with a capital; **großgeschrieben werden** (*umg*) to be stressed
Großstadt *f* city
Großvater *m* grandfather
großzügig *adj* generous; (*Planung*) on a large scale
Grotte (-, **-n**) *f* grotto
grub *etc vb siehe* **graben**
Grübchen *nt* dimple
Grube (-, **-n**) *f* pit
Gruft (-, **Grüfte**) *f* vault
grün *adj* green; (*Pol*): **die Grünen** the Greens; **grüner Salat** lettuce; **grüne Bohnen** French beans
Grünanlage *f* park
Grund (**-(e)s**, **Gründe**) *m* ground; (*von See, Gefäß*) bottom; (*fig*) reason; **aus gesundheitlichen** *etc* **Gründen** for health *etc* reasons
gründen *vt* to found
Gründer(in) (**-s**, **-**) *m(f)* founder
Grundgebühr *f* basic charge
Grundgesetz *nt* constitution
gründlich *adj* thorough
Gründonnerstag *m* Maundy Thursday
grundsätzlich *adj* fundamental ▸ *adv* fundamentally; (*prinzipiell*) on principle
Grundschule *f* primary (BRIT) *od* elementary school
Grundstück *nt* plot (of land); (*Anwesen*) estate
Grundwasser *nt* ground water
Grüne (**-n**) *nt*: **im Grünen** in the open air; **ins ~ fahren** to go to the country
Grüne(r) *f(m)* (*Pol*) Ecologist, Green
■ **die Grünen** *pl* (*als Partei*) the Greens
Grüner Punkt *see note*

GRÜNER PUNKT

The **Grüner Punkt** is a green spot symbol used on packaging to indicate that the packaging should not be thrown into the normal household refuse but kept separate for recycling. In Germany, recycling is financed by licences bought by manufacturers, the cost of which is often passed on to the consumer.

Gruppe (-, **-n**) *f* group
Gruselfilm *m* horror film
Gruß (**-es**, **Grüße**) *m* greeting; **viele Grüße** best wishes; **Grüße an** *+akk* regards to; **mit freundlichen Grüßen** (*als Briefformel*) Yours sincerely
grüßen *vt* to greet; **jdn von jdm ~** to give sb sb's regards; **jdn ~ lassen** to send sb one's regards
gucken *vi* to look
Gulasch (**-(e)s**, **-e**) *nt* goulash
gültig *adj* valid
Gummi (**-s**, **-s**) *nt od m* rubber
Gummiband *nt* rubber *od* elastic band
Gummibärchen *nt* jelly baby
Gummistiefel *m* rubber boot, wellington (boot) (BRIT)
günstig *adj* favourable (BRIT), favorable (*US*); (*Angebot, Preis etc*) good
gurgeln *vi* to gurgle; (*im Rachen*) to gargle
Gurke (-, **-n**) *f* cucumber; **saure ~** gherkin
Gurt (**-(e)s**, **-e**) *m* belt
Gürtel (**-s**, **-**) *m* belt; (*Geog*) zone
Gürtelrose *f* shingles *sing od pl*
GUS *f abk* (= *Gemeinschaft Unabhängiger Staaten*) CIS

SCHLÜSSELWORT

gut *adj* good; **alles Gute** all the best; **also gut** all right then
▸ *adv* well; **gut gehen** to work, to come off; **es geht jdm gut** sb's doing fine; **gut gemeint** well meant; **gut, aber ...** OK, but ...; **(na) gut, ich komme** all right, I'll come; **gut drei Stunden** a good three hours; **das kann gut sein** that may well be; **lass es gut sein** that'll do

Gutachten (**-s**, **-**) *nt* report
Gutachter(in) (**-s**, **-**) *m(f)* expert
gutartig *adj* (*Med*) benign
Güter *pl* goods *pl*
Güterbahnhof *m* goods station
Güterzug *m* goods train (BRIT), freight train (*US*)
gutgläubig *adj* trusting
Guthaben (**-s**) *nt* credit
gutmütig *adj* good-natured
Gutschein *m* voucher
Gutschrift *f* credit
GV-Lebensmittel *pl* (= *gentechnisch veränderte Lebensmittel*) GM foods

GVO *m abk* (*Agr:* = *gentechnisch veränderter Organismus*) GMO
GV-Pflanze *f* (= *gentechnisch veränderte Pflanze*) GM crop
Gymnasium *nt* ≈ grammar school (*BRIT*), high school (*US*)
Gymnastik *f* exercises *pl*, keep-fit; **~ machen** to do keep-fit (exercises)/ gymnastics
Gynäkologe (**-n**, **-n**) *m*, **Gynäkologin** *f* gynaecologist (*BRIT*), gynecologist (*US*)

Haar (**-(e)s**, **-e**) *nt* hair; **um ein ~** nearly
Haarbürste *f* hairbrush
Haarfestiger (**-s**, **-**) *m* setting lotion
Haarglätter *m* hair straighteners *pl*
haarig *adj* hairy; (*fig*) nasty
Haarschnitt *m* haircut
Haarspange *f* hair slide
Haartrockner (**-s**, **-**) *m* hairdryer
Haarwaschmittel *nt* shampoo
haben *unreg vt*, *Hilfsverb* to have; **Hunger/Angst ~** to be hungry/afraid; **Ferien ~** to be on holiday; **was hast du denn?** what's the matter (with you)?
Haben (**-s**, **-**) *nt* (*Comm*) credit
Habicht (**-(e)s**, **-e**) *m* hawk
Hacke (**-**, **-n**) *f* hoe; (*Ferse*) heel
hacken *vt* to hack, to chop; (*Erde*) to hoe
Hacker(in) (**-s**, **-**) *m(f)* (*Comput*) hacker
Hackfleisch *nt* mince, minced meat, ground meat (*US*)
Hafen (**-s**, **Häfen**) *m* harbour, harbor (*US*), port
Hafenstadt *f* port
Hafer (**-s**, **-**) *m* oats *pl*
Haferflocken *pl* rolled oats *pl* (*BRIT*), oatmeal (*US*)
Haft (**-**) *f* custody
haftbar *adj* liable, responsible
haften *vi* to stick; **~ für** to be liable *od* responsible for
Haftnotiz *f* Post-it®
Haftpflichtversicherung *f* third party insurance
Haftung *f* liability
Hagebutte (**-**, **-n**) *f* rose hip
Hagel (**-s**) *m* hail

hageln *vi unpers* to hail
Hahn (**-(e)s**, **Hähne**) *m* cock; (*Wasserhahn*) tap, faucet (*US*)
Hähnchen *nt* cockerel; (*Koch*) chicken
Hai (**-(e)s**, **-e**), **Haifisch** *m* shark
häkeln *vt* to crochet
Häkelnadel *f* crochet hook
Haken (**-s**, **-**) *m* hook; (*fig*) catch
halb *adj* half; **~ eins** half past twelve; **~ offen** half-open; **ein halbes Dutzend** half a dozen
Halbfettmilch *f* semi-skimmed milk
Halbfinale *nt* semi-final
halbieren *vt* to halve
Halbinsel *f* peninsula
Halbjahr *nt* half-year
halbjährlich *adj* half-yearly
Halbmond *m* half-moon; (*fig*) crescent
Halbpension *f* half-board (Brit), European plan (*US*)
halbseitig *adj*: **~ gelähmt** paralyzed on one side
halbtags *adv*: **~ arbeiten** to work part-time
halbwegs *adv* (*leidlich*) reasonably
Halbzeit *f* (*Sport*) half; (*Pause*) half-time
half *etc vb siehe* **helfen**
Hälfte (**-**, **-n**) *f* half
Halle (**-**, **-n**) *f* hall
Hallenbad *nt* indoor swimming pool
hallo *interj* hello
Hals (**-es**, **Hälse**) *m* neck; (*Kehle*) throat
Halsband *nt* (*Hundehalsband*) collar
Halskette *f* necklace
Hals-Nasen-Ohren-Arzt *m* ear, nose and throat specialist
Halsschmerzen *pl* sore throat *sing*
Halstuch *nt* scarf
Halt (**-(e)s**, **-e**) *m* stop; (*fester Halt*) hold; (*innerer Halt*) stability; **~!** stop!
haltbar *adj* durable; (*Lebensmittel*) non-perishable
Haltbarkeitsdatum *nt* best-before date
halten *unreg vt* to keep; (*festhalten*) to hold ▸ *vi* to hold; (*frisch bleiben*) to keep; (*stoppen*) to stop ▸ *vr* (*frisch bleiben*) to keep; (*sich behaupten*) to hold out; **~ für** to regard as; **~ von** to think of; **zu jdm ~** to stand *od* stick by sb
Haltestelle *f* stop
Halteverbot *nt*: **hier ist ~** you cannot stop here
Haltung *f* posture; (*fig*) attitude; (*Selbstbeherrschung*) composure; **~ bewahren** to keep one's composure
Hamburg (**-s**) *nt* Hamburg
Hamburger (**-s**, **-**) *m* (*Koch*) hamburger
Hammelfleisch *nt* mutton
Hammer (**-s**, **Hämmer**) *m* hammer; **das ist ein ~!** (*umg*: *unerhört*) that's absurd!
Hämorrhoiden, Hämorriden *pl* piles *pl*, haemorrhoids *pl* (Brit), hemorrhoids *pl* (*US*)
Hamster (**-s**, **-**) *m* hamster
Hand (**-**, **Hände**) *f* hand; **jdm die ~ geben** to shake hands with sb; **jdn bei der ~ nehmen** to take sb by the hand; **zu Händen von jdm** for the attention of sb
Handarbeit *f* manual work; (*Nadelarbeit*) needlework
Handball *m* handball
Handbremse *f* handbrake
Handbuch *nt* handbook, manual
Händedruck *m* handshake
Handel (**-s**) *m* trade; (*Geschäft*) transaction
handeln *vi* to trade; (*tätig werden*) to act ▸ *vr unpers*: **sich ~ um** to be about
Handelskammer *f* chamber of commerce
Handelsschule *f* business school
Handfeger (**-s**, **-**) *m* brush
Handfläche *f* palm *od* flat (of one's hand)
Handgelenk *nt* wrist
Handgepäck *nt* hand baggage *od* luggage
Händler(in) (**-s**, **-**) *m(f)* trader, dealer
handlich *adj* handy
Handlung *f* action; (*Tat*) act; (*in Buch*) plot; (*Geschäft*) shop
Handschelle *f* handcuff
Handschrift *f* handwriting; (*Text*) manuscript
Handschuh *m* glove
Handschuhfach *nt* (*Aut*) glove compartment
Handtasche *f* handbag (Brit), pocket book (*US*), purse (*US*)
Handtuch *nt* towel
Handwerk *nt* trade; (*Kunsthandwerk*) craft
Handwerker (**-s**, **-**) *m* workman
Handy (**-s**, **-s**) *nt* (*Tel*) mobile (phone) (Brit), cellphone (*US*)

handysüchtig *adj* addicted to use of one's mobile phone, nomophobic
Hanf (**-(e)s**) *m* hemp
Hang (**-(e)s**, **Hänge**) *m* inclination; (*Abhang*) slope
Hängebrücke *f* suspension bridge
Hängematte *f* hammock
hängen *unreg vi* to hang ▸ *vt*: **~ (an** *+akk***)** to hang (on(to)); **~ bleiben** to be caught; (*fig*) to remain, to stick
Hantel (**-**, **-n**) *f* (*Sport*) dumb-bell
Hardware (**-**, **-s**) *f* hardware
Harfe (**-**, **-n**) *f* harp
harmlos *adj* harmless
harmonisch *adj* harmonious
Harn (**-(e)s**, **-e**) *m* urine
Harnblase *f* bladder
Harpune (**-**, **-n**) *f* harpoon
hart *adj* hard; (*fig*) harsh; **~ bleiben** to stand firm; **~ gekocht** hard-boiled
hartnäckig *adj* stubborn
Hartz IV *f see note*

HARTZ IV

Hartz IV is one of the 'Hartz reforms' of the labour market that came into force between 2003 and 2005 in the time of Gerhard Schröder's government. The *Hartz IV* reform merged unemployment benefit and social security benefit into one single welfare package for all long-term unemployed.

Haschee (**-s**, **-s**) *nt* hash
Haschisch (**-**) *nt* hashish
Hase (**-n**, **-n**) *m* hare
Haselnuss *f* hazelnut
Hasenscharte *f* harelip
Hashtag (**-s**, **-s**) *m* (*auf Twitter*) hashtag
Hass (**-es**) *m* hate, hatred; **einen ~ (auf jdn) haben** (*umg*) to be really mad (with sb)
hassen *vt* to hate
hässlich *adj* ugly; (*gemein*) nasty
Hast (**-**) *f* haste
hastig *adj* hasty
hatte *etc vb siehe* **haben**
Haube (**-**, **-n**) *f* hood; (*Mütze*) cap; (*Aut*) bonnet (BRIT), hood (*US*)
Hauch (**-(e)s**, **-e**) *m* breath; (*Lufthauch*) breeze; (*fig*) trace
hauchdünn *adj* (*Scheiben*) wafer-thin
hauen *unreg vt* to hew, to cut; (*umg*) to thrash
Haufen (**-s**, **-**) *m* heap; **ein ~ (Bücher)** (*umg*) loads *od* a lot (of books)
häufig *adj* frequent ▸ *adv* frequently
Hauptbahnhof *m* central station
Hauptdarsteller(in) *m(f)* leading actor, leading actress
Haupteingang *m* main entrance
Hauptgericht *nt* main course
Hauptgeschäftszeit *f* peak (shopping) period
Hauptgewinn *m* first prize
Häuptling *m* chief(tain)
Hauptquartier *nt* headquarters *pl*
Hauptrolle *f* leading part
Hauptsache *f* main thing
hauptsächlich *adv* chiefly
Hauptsaison *f* peak *od* high season
Hauptsatz *m* main clause
Hauptschule *f* ≈ secondary modern (school) (BRIT), junior high (school) (*US*)
Hauptstadt *f* capital
Hauptstraße *f* main street
Hauptverkehrszeit *f* rush hour
Haus (**-es**, **Häuser**) *nt* house; **nach Hause** home; **zu Hause** at home
Hausarbeit *f* housework
Hausaufgabe *f* (*Sch*) homework
Hausbesitzer *m* house-owner
Hausbesuch *m* home visit
Hausflur *m* hall
Hausfrau *f* housewife
hausgemacht *adj* home-made
Haushalt *m* household; (*Pol*) budget
Hausherr *m* host; (*Vermieter*) landlord
häuslich *adj* domestic
Hausmann (**-(e)s**, **-männer**) *m* househusband
Hausmeister *m* caretaker, janitor
Hausnummer *f* house number
Hausordnung *f* house rules *pl*
Hausschlüssel *m* front-door key
Hausschuh *m* slipper
Haustier *nt* domestic animal
Haustür *f* front door
Haut (**-**, **Häute**) *f* skin; (*Tierhaut*) hide
Hautarzt *m* skin specialist, dermatologist
Hautärztin *f* skin specialist, dermatologist
Hautcreme *f* skin cream
Hautfarbe *f* complexion
Hbf. *abk* = **Hauptbahnhof**
Hebamme *f* midwife

Hebel (**-s**, **-**) *m* lever
heben *unreg vt* to raise, to lift
Hecht (**-(e)s**, **-e**) *m* pike
Heck (**-(e)s**, **-e**) *nt* stern; (*von Auto*) rear
Hecke (**-**, **-n**) *f* hedge
Heckklappe *f* tailgate
Heckscheibe *f* rear window
Hefe (**-**, **-n**) *f* yeast
Heft (**-(e)s**, **-e**) *nt* exercise book; (*Zeitschrift*) number
heftig *adj* fierce, violent
Heftklammer *f* staple
Heftpflaster *nt* sticking plaster
Heide (**-**, **-n**) *f* heath, moor
Heidekraut *nt* heather
Heidelbeere *f* bilberry
heidnisch *adj* pagan
heikel *adj* awkward; (*wählerisch*) fussy
heil *adj* in one piece, intact; **mit heiler Haut davonkommen** to escape unscathed
heilbar *adj* curable
Heilbutt (**-s**, **-e**) *m* halibut
heilen *vt* to cure ▶ *vi* to heal
heilig *adj* holy
Heiligabend *m* Christmas Eve
Heilige(r) *f*(*m*) saint
Heilmittel *nt* remedy
Heilpraktiker(in) (**-s**, **-**) *m*(*f*) non-medical practitioner
heim *adv* home
Heim (**-(e)s**, **-e**) *nt* home
Heimat (**-**, **-en**) *f* home (town/country *etc*)
Heimatland *nt* homeland
heim|fahren *unreg vi* to drive *od* go home
Heimfahrt *f* journey home
heimisch *adj* (*gebürtig*) native
heim|kommen *unreg vi* to come home
heimlich *adj* secret
Heimreise *f* journey home
Heimspiel *nt* home game
Heimweg *m* way home
Heimweh *nt* homesickness; **~ haben** to be homesick
Heimwerker(in) *m*(*f*) DIY enthusiast
Heirat (**-**, **-en**) *f* marriage
heiraten *vt*, *vi* to marry
Heiratsantrag *m* proposal (of marriage)
heiser *adj* hoarse
heiß *adj* hot; (*Diskussion, Kampf*) heated; **mir ist ~** I'm hot
heißen *unreg vi* to be called; (*bedeuten*) to mean ▶ *vi unpers*: **es heißt hier ...** it says here ...; **es heißt, dass ...** they say that ...; **wie ~ Sie?** what's your name?; **das heißt** that is
heiter *adj* cheerful; (*Wetter*) bright
heizen *vt* to heat
Heizkissen *m* (*Med*) heated pad
Heizkörper *m* radiator
Heizöl *nt* fuel oil
Heizpilz *m* patio heater
Heizung *f* heating
Hektar (**-s**, **-e**) *nt od m* hectare
Hektik *f* (*von Leben etc*) hectic pace
hektisch *adj* hectic
Held (**-en**, **-en**) *m* hero
Heldin *f* heroine
helfen *unreg vi* to help; (*nützen*) to be of use ▶ *vb unpers*: **es hilft nichts, du musst ...** it's no use, you'll have to ...; **sich** *dat* **zu ~ wissen** to be resourceful
Helfer(in) (**-s**, **-**) *m*(*f*) helper, assistant
hell *adj* clear; (*Licht, Himmel*) bright; (*Farbe*) light
hellblau *adj* light blue
hellblond *adj* ash-blond
Hellseher(in) *m*(*f*) clairvoyant
Helm (**-(e)s**, **-e**) *m* helmet
Hemd (**-(e)s**, **-en**) *nt* shirt; (*Unterhemd*) vest
hemmen *vt* to check; **gehemmt sein** to be inhibited
Hemmung *f* (*Psych*) inhibition; (*Bedenken*) scruple
Henkel (**-s**, **-**) *m* handle
Henne (**-**, **-n**) *f* hen
Hepatitis (**-**, **Hepatitiden**) *f* hepatitis

 **SCHLÜSSELWORT**

her *adv* **1** (*Richtung*): **komm her zu mir** come here (to me); **von England her** from England; **von weit her** from a long way away; **her damit!** hand it over!; **wo bist du her?** where do you come from?; **wo hat er das her?** where did he get that from?
2 (*Blickpunkt*): **von der Form her** as far as the form is concerned
3 (*zeitlich*): **das ist 5 Jahre her** that was 5 years ago; **ich kenne ihn von früher her** I know him from before

herab *adv* down
herablassend *adj* condescending

herab|sehen *unreg vi*: **~ (auf** *+akk***)** to look down (on)
herab|setzen *vt* to reduce; (*fig*) to disparage
heran *adv*: **näher ~!** come closer!
heran|kommen *unreg vi*: **(an jdn/etw) ~** to approach (sb/sth), to come near ((to) sb/sth)
heran|wachsen *unreg vi* to grow up
herauf *adv* up
herauf|beschwören *unreg vt* to evoke
herauf|ziehen *unreg vt* to draw *od* pull up ▶ *vi* to approach; (*Sturm*) to gather
heraus *adv* out
heraus|bekommen *unreg vt* to get out; (*fig*) to find *od* figure out; (*Wechselgeld*) to get back
heraus|bringen *unreg vt* to bring out
heraus|finden *unreg vt* to find out
heraus|fordern *vt* to challenge
Herausforderung *f* challenge
heraus|geben *unreg vt* (*Geld*) to give back; (*Buch*) to edit; (*veröffentlichen*) to publish ▶ *vi* (*Wechselgeld geben*): **können Sie (mir) ~?** can you give me change?
heraus|holen *vt*: **~ (aus)** to get out (of)
heraus|kommen *unreg vi* to come out; **dabei kommt nichts heraus** nothing will come of it
heraus|stellen *vr*: **sich ~ (als)** to turn out (to be)
heraus|ziehen *unreg vt* to pull out
Herbergseltern *pl* (youth hostel) wardens *pl*
Herbst (-(e)s, -e) *m* autumn, fall (*US*)
Herd (-(e)s, -e) *m* cooker
Herde (-, -n) *f* herd; (*Schafherde*) flock
herein *adv* in (here); **~!** come in!
herein|fallen *unreg vi*: **~ auf** *+akk* to fall for
herein|legen *vt*: **jdn ~** to take sb in
Herfahrt *f* journey here
Hergang *m* course of events
Hering (-s, -e) *m* herring
her|kommen *unreg vi* to come; **komm mal her!** come here!
Heroin (-s) *nt* heroin
Herpes (-) *m* (*Med*) herpes
Herr (-(e)n, -en) *m* (*Mann*) gentleman; (*adliger, Rel*) Lord; (*vor Namen*) Mr; **mein ~!** sir!; **meine Herren!** gentlemen!; **Lieber ~ A, Sehr geehrter ~ A** (*in Brief*) Dear Mr A
herrenlos *adj* ownerless
her|richten *vt* to prepare
herrlich *adj* marvellous (*Brit*), marvelous (*US*), splendid
Herrschaft *f* power, rule; **meine Herrschaften!** ladies and gentlemen!
herrschen *vi* to rule; (*bestehen*) to be
her|stellen *vt* to make, to manufacture
Hersteller (-s, -) *m* manufacturer
Herstellung *f* manufacture
herüber *adv* over (here)
herum *adv* (a)round; **um etw ~** around sth
herum|fahren *unreg vi* (*mit Auto*) to drive around
herum|führen *vt* to show around
herum|kommen *unreg* (*umg*) *vi*: **um etw ~** to get out of sth; **er ist viel herumgekommen** he has been around a lot
herum|kriegen *vt* to bring *od* talk round
herum|treiben *unreg vi, vr* to drift about
herunter *adv* downward(s)
heruntergekommen *adj* run-down
herunter|handeln *vt* (*Preis*) to beat down
herunter|holen *vt* to bring down
herunter|kommen *unreg vi* to come down
herunterladbar *adj* (*Comput*) downloadable
herunter|laden *unreg vt* (*Comput*) to download
hervor *adv* out
hervor|bringen *unreg vt* to produce; (*Wort*) to utter
hervor|heben *unreg vt* to stress
hervorragend *adj* excellent
hervor|rufen *unreg vt* to cause, to give rise to
Herz (-ens, -en) *nt* heart; (*Karten*) hearts *pl*; **mit ganzem Herzen** wholeheartedly; **sich** *dat* **etw zu Herzen nehmen** to take sth to heart
Herzanfall *m* heart attack
Herzbeschwerden *pl* heart trouble *sing*
Herzfehler *m* heart defect
herzhaft *adj* hearty
Herzinfarkt *m* heart attack
Herzklopfen *nt* palpitations *pl*
herzkrank *adj* suffering from a heart condition

herzlich *adj* cordial; **herzlichen Glückwunsch** congratulations *pl*
Herzog (**-(e)s**, **Herzöge**) *m* duke
Herzogin *f* duchess
Herzschlag *m* heartbeat; (*Med*) heart attack
Herzschrittmacher *m* pacemaker
Hessen (**-s**) *nt* Hesse
heterosexuell *adj* heterosexual
Hetze *f* (*Eile*) rush
hetzen *vt* to hunt ▸ *vi* (*eilen*) to rush
Heu (**-(e)s**) *nt* hay
heuer *adv* this year
heulen *vi* to howl; (*weinen*) to cry
Heuschnupfen *m* hay fever
Heuschrecke *f* grasshopper; (*in heißen Ländern*) locust
heute *adv* today; **~ Abend/früh** this evening/morning; **~ Morgen** this morning; **~ in einer Woche** a week today
heutig *adj* today's; **unser heutiges Schreiben** (*Comm*) our letter of today('s date)
heutzutage *adv* nowadays
Hexe (**-**, **-n**) *f* witch
Hexenschuss *m* lumbago
hielt *etc vb siehe* **halten**
hier *adv* here; **er ist von ~** he's a local (man)
hier|bleiben *unreg vi* to stay here
hierher *adv* here; **~ gehören** to belong here; (*fig: relevant sein*) to be relevant
hier|lassen *unreg vt* to leave here
hiermit *adv* hereby
hierzulande *adv* in this country
hiesig *adj* of this place, local
hieß *etc vb siehe* **heißen**
Hi-Fi-Anlage *f* hi-fi set *od* system
Hilfe (**-**, **-n**) *f* help; (*für Notleidende*) aid; **Erste ~** first aid; **~!** help!
hilflos *adj* helpless
hilfsbereit *adj* ready to help
Hilfsmittel *nt* aid
Himbeere (**-**, **-n**) *f* raspberry
Himmel (**-s**, **-**) *m* sky; (*Rel*) heaven
Himmelfahrt *f* Ascension
Himmelsrichtung *f* direction
himmlisch *adj* heavenly

SCHLÜSSELWORT

hin *adv* **1** (*Richtung*): **hin und zurück** there and back; **hin und her** to and fro; **bis zur Mauer hin** up to the wall; **wo ist er hin?** where has he gone?; **Geld hin, Geld her** money or no money
2 (*auf ... hin*): **auf meine Bitte hin** at my request; **auf seinen Rat hin** on the basis of his advice
3: **mein Glück ist hin** my happiness has gone

hinab *adv* down
hinab|gehen *unreg vi* to go down
hinauf *adv* up
hinauf|steigen *unreg vi* to climb
hinaus *adv* out
hinaus|gehen *unreg vi* to go out; **~ über** *+akk* to exceed
hinaus|laufen *unreg vi* to run out; **~ auf** *+akk* to come to, to amount to
hinaus|schieben *unreg vt* to put off, to postpone
hinaus|werfen *unreg vt* to throw out
hinaus|zögern *vt* to delay ▸ *vr* to be delayed
Hinblick *m*: **in** *od* **im ~ auf** *+akk* in view of
hindern *vt* to hinder; **jdn an etw** *dat* **~** to prevent sb from doing sth
Hindernis (**-ses**, **-se**) *nt* obstacle
Hinduismus *m* Hinduism
hindurch *adv* through; (*quer durch*) across; (*zeitlich*) over
hinein *adv* in
hinein|gehen *unreg vi* to go in; **~ in** *+akk* to go into, to enter
hinein|passen *vi* to fit in; **~ in** *+akk* to fit into
hin|fahren *unreg vi* to go; (*mit Auto*) to drive ▸ *vt* to take
Hinfahrt *f* journey there
hin|fallen *unreg vi* to fall down
Hinflug *m* outward flight
hing *etc vb siehe* **hängen**
hin|gehen *unreg vi* to go; (*Zeit*) to pass
hin|halten *unreg vt* to hold out; (*warten lassen*) to put off, to stall
hinken *vi* to limp; (*Vergleich*) to be unconvincing
hin|legen *vt* to put down ▸ *vr* to lie down
hin|nehmen *unreg vt* (*fig*) to put up with, to take
Hinreise *f* journey out
hin|setzen *vr* to sit down
hinsichtlich *präp +gen* with regard to
hin|stellen *vt* to put (down) ▸ *vr* to place o.s.

hinten *adv* behind; (*rückwärtig*) at the back
hinter *präp* (*+dat od akk*) behind; (: *nach*) after; **~ jdm her sein** to be after sb; **etw ~ sich** *dat* **haben** to have got through sth
Hinterachse *f* rear axle
Hinterbein *nt* hind leg
Hinterbliebene(r) *f*(*m*) surviving relative
hintere(r, s) *adj* rear, back
hintereinander *adv* one after the other; **zwei Tage ~** two days running
Hintereingang *m* rear entrance
Hintergedanke *m* ulterior motive
hintergehen *unreg vt untr* to deceive
Hintergrund *m* background
hintergrundbeleuchtet *adj* backlit
hinterher *adv* afterwards
Hinterkopf *m* back of one's head
hinterlassen *unreg vt untr* to leave
hinterlegen *vt untr* to deposit
Hintern (**-s**, **-**) (*umg*) *m* bottom, backside
Hinterradantrieb *m* (*Aut*) rear-wheel drive
Hinterteil *nt* behind
Hintertür *f* back door
hinüber *adv* across, over
hinüber|gehen *unreg vi* to go over *od* across
hinunter *adv* down
hinunter|schlucken *vt* (*lit, fig*) to swallow
Hinweg *m* journey out
hinweg|setzen *vr*: **sich ~ über** *+akk* to disregard
Hinweis (**-es**, **-e**) *m* (*Andeutung*) hint; (*Anweisung*) instruction; (*Verweis*) reference
hin|weisen *unreg vi*: **darauf ~, dass ...** to point out that ...
hinzu *adv* in addition
hinzu|fügen *vt* to add
hinzu|kommen *unreg vi*: **es kommt noch hinzu, dass ...** there is also the fact that ...
Hirn (**-(e)s**, **-e**) *nt* brain(s)
Hirnhautentzündung *f* (*Med*) meningitis
hirnverbrannt *adj* (*umg*) harebrained
Hirsch (**-(e)s**, **-e**) *m* stag
Hirse (**-**, **-n**) *f* millet
historisch *adj* historical
Hit (**-s**, **-s**) (*umg*) *m* (*Mus, fig, Internet*) hit
Hitze (**-**) *f* heat
hitzebeständig *adj* heat-resistant
Hitzewelle *f* heat wave
hitzig *adj* hot-tempered; (*Debatte*) heated
Hitzschlag *m* heatstroke
HIV-negativ *adj* HIV-negative
HIV-positiv *adj* HIV-positive
H-Milch *f* long-life milk, UHT milk
hob *etc vb siehe* **heben**
Hobby (**-s**, **-s**) *nt* hobby
Hobel (**-s**, **-**) *m* plane
hoch (*attrib* **hohe(r, s)**) *adj* high ▶ *adv*: **~ achten** to respect; **~ begabt** = **hochbegabt**; **das ist mir zu ~** (*umg*) that's above my head; **4 ~ 5** 4 to the power of 5
Hoch (**-s**, **-s**) *nt* (*Ruf*) cheer; (*Met*: *fig*) high
hochachtungsvoll *adv* yours faithfully
hochbegabt *adj* extremely gifted
Hochbetrieb *m*: **~ haben** to be at one's *od* its busiest
Hochdeutsch *nt* High German
Hochgebirge *nt* high mountains *pl*
Hochgeschwindigkeitszug *m* high-speed train
Hochhaus *nt* multi-storey building
hoch|heben *unreg vt* to lift (up)
hoch|laden *unreg vt* (*Comput*) to upload
Hochsaison *f* high season
Hochschule *f* college; (*Universität*) university
Hochschulreife *f*: **er hat (die) ~** ≈ he's got his A-levels (BRIT), he's graduated from high school (*US*)
hochschwanger *adj* heavily pregnant
Hochsommer *m* middle of summer
Hochspannung *f* high tension; (*Elek*) high voltage
Hochsprung *m* high jump
höchst *adv* highly, extremely
höchste(r, s) *adj* highest; (*äußerste*) extreme
höchstens *adv* at the most
Höchstform *f* (*Sport*) top form
Höchstgeschwindigkeit *f* maximum speed
höchstwahrscheinlich *adv* most probably
Hochwasser *nt* high water; (*Überschwemmung*) floods *pl*
hochwertig *adj* high-class
Hochzeit (**-**, **-en**) *f* wedding

Hochzeitsreise *f* honeymoon
Hochzeitstag *m* wedding day; (*Jahrestag*) wedding anniversary
hocken *vi*, *vr* to squat, to crouch
Hocker (**-s**, **-**) *m* stool
Hockey (**-s**) *nt* hockey
Hoden (**-s**, **-**) *m* testicle
Hof (**-(e)s**, **Höfe**) *m* (*Hinterhof*) yard; (*Bauernhof*) farm; (*Königshof*) court
hoffen *vi*: **~ (auf** *+akk***)** to hope (for)
hoffentlich *adv* hopefully
Hoffnung *f* hope
hoffnungslos *adj* hopeless
höflich *adj* polite
Höflichkeit *f* politeness
hohe(r, s) *adj siehe* **hoch**
Höhe (**-**, **-n**) *f* height; (*Anhöhe*) hill; **ein Scheck in ~ von ...** a cheque (BRIT) *od* check (US) for the amount of ...
Höhepunkt *m* climax; (*des Lebens*) high point
höher *adj*, *adv* higher
hohl *adj* hollow
Höhle (**-**, **-n**) *f* cave
holen *vt* to get, to fetch; (*Atem*) to take; **jdn/etw ~ lassen** to send for sb/sth; **sich** *dat* **eine Erkältung ~** to catch a cold
Holland (**-s**) *nt* Holland
Holländer (**-s**, **-**) *m* Dutchman
Holländerin *f* Dutchwoman, Dutch girl
holländisch *adj* Dutch
Hölle (**-**, **-n**) *f* hell
Hologramm (**-s**, **-e**) *nt* hologram
holperig *adj* bumpy
Holunder (**-s**, **-**) *m* elder
Holz (**-es**, **Hölzer**) *nt* wood
hölzern *adj* wooden
holzig *adj* woody
Holzkohle *f* charcoal
Homepage *nt* (*Comput*) home page
homosexuell *adj* homosexual
Honig (**-s**, **-e**) *m* honey
Honigmelone *f* honeydew melon
Honorar (**-s**, **-e**) *nt* fee
Hopfen (**-s**, **-**) *m* hops *pl*
hoppla *interj* whoops
Hörbuch *nt* audio book
horchen *vi* to listen; (*pej*) to eavesdrop
hören *vt*, *vi* to hear; **auf jdn/etw ~** to listen to sb/sth; **ich lasse von mir ~** I'll be in touch
Hörer (**-s**, **-**) *m* (*Rundf*) listener; (*Telefonhörer*) receiver
Hörgerät *nt* hearing aid
Horizont (**-(e)s**, **-e**) *m* horizon; **das geht über meinen ~** that is beyond me
Hormon (**-s**, **-e**) *nt* hormone
Hornhaut *f* hard skin; (*des Auges*) cornea
Hornisse (**-**, **-n**) *f* hornet
Horoskop (**-s**, **-e**) *nt* horoscope
Hörsaal *m* lecture room
Hörweite *f*: **in/außer ~** within/out of hearing *od* earshot
Hose (**-**, **-n**) *f* trousers *pl*, pants *pl* (*US*)
Hosenanzug *m* trouser suit, pantsuit (*US*)
Hosentasche *f* trouser pocket
Hosenträger *pl* braces *pl* (BRIT), suspenders *pl* (*US*)
Hotel (**-s**, **-s**) *nt* hotel
Hotelkette *f* hotel chain
Hotelzimmer *nt* hotel room
Hotspot *m* (wireless) hotspot
Hubraum *m* (*Aut*) cubic capacity
hübsch *adj* pretty, nice
Hubschrauber (**-s**, **-**) *m* helicopter
Huf (**-(e)s**, **-e**) *m* hoof
Hufeisen *nt* horseshoe
Hüfte (**-**, **-n**) *f* hip
Hügel (**-s**, **-**) *m* hill
hügelig *adj* hilly
Huhn (**-(e)s**, **Hühner**) *nt* hen; (*Koch*) chicken
Hühnchen *nt* young chicken
Hühnerauge *nt* corn
Hühnerbrühe *f* chicken broth
Hülle (**-**, **-n**) *f* cover(ing); (*Zellophanhülle*) wrapping
Hummel (**-**, **-n**) *f* bumblebee
Hummer (**-s**, **-**) *m* lobster
Humor (**-s**, **-e**) *m* humour (BRIT), humor (US); **~ haben** to have a sense of humo(u)r
humorlos *adj* humourless
humorvoll *adj* humorous
humpeln *vi* to hobble
Hund (**-(e)s**, **-e**) *m* dog
hundert *num* hundred
Hundertjahrfeier *f* centenary
hundertprozentig *adj*, *adv* one hundred per cent
hundertste(r, s) *adj* hundredth
Hündin *f* bitch
Hunger (**-s**) *m* hunger; **~ haben** to be hungry
hungern *vi* to starve
Hupe (**-**, **-n**) *f* horn

hupen *vi* to sound one's horn
Hüpfburg *f* bouncy castle®
hüpfen *vi* to hop, to jump
Hürde (-, **-n**) *f* hurdle
Hure (-, **-n**) *f* whore (*pej*)
hurra *interj* hooray
husten *vi* to cough
Husten (**-s**) *m* cough
Hustenbonbon *m od nt* cough drop
Hustensaft *m* cough mixture
Hut (**-(e)s**, **Hüte**) *m* hat
hüten *vt* to guard ▶ *vr* to watch out; **sich ~ zu** to take care not to; **sich ~ vor** *+dat* to beware of
Hütte (-, **-n**) *f* hut
Hüttenkäse *m* cottage cheese
Hyäne (-, **-n**) *f* hyena
Hybridauto *nt* hybrid car
Hydrant *m* hydrant
hygienisch *adj* hygienic
Hyperlink (**-s**, **-s**) *m* hyperlink
Hypnose (-, **-n**) *f* hypnosis
Hypnotiseur(in) *m(f)* hypnotist
hypnotisieren *vt* to hypnotize
Hypothek (-, **-en**) *f* mortgage
hysterisch *adj* hysterical; **einen hysterischen Anfall bekommen** (*fig*) to have hysterics

i

i. A. *abk* (= *im Auftrag*) p.p.
IC (-) *m abk* = **Intercityzug**
ICE *m abk* (= *Intercityexpresszug*) *German high-speed train*
ich *pron* I; **~ bins!** it's me!
ideal *adj* ideal
Idee (-, **-n**) *f* idea
identifizieren *vt* to identify
identisch *adj* identical
Identitätsdiebstahl *m* identity theft
Idiot (**-en**, **-en**) *m* idiot
idiotisch *adj* idiotic
Idol (**-s**, **-e**) *nt* idol
idyllisch *adj* idyllic
Igel (**-s**, **-**) *m* hedgehog
ignorieren *vt* to ignore
ihm *pron dat von* **er**; **es** (to) him, (to) it
ihn *pron akk von* **er** him; (*bei Tieren, Dingen*) it
ihnen *pron dat pl von* **sie** (to) them; (*nach Präpositionen*) them
Ihnen *pron dat von* **Sie** (to) you; (*nach Präpositionen*) you

SCHLÜSSELWORT

ihr *pron* **1** (*nom pl*) you; **ihr seid es** it's you
2 (*dat von sie*) (to) her; (*: bei Tieren, Dingen*) (to) it; **gib es ihr** give it to her; **er steht neben ihr** he is standing beside her
▶ *poss pron* **1** (*sing*) her; (*: bei Tieren, Dingen*) its; **ihr Mann** her husband
2 (*pl*) their; **die Bäume und ihre Blätter** the trees and their leaves

Ihr *poss pron* your

ihre(r, s) *poss pron* hers; (*eines Tieres*) its; (*von mehreren*) theirs; **sie taten das I~** (*geh*) they did their bit
Ihre(r, s) *poss pron* yours
ihretwegen *adv* (*für sie*) for her/its/their sake; (*wegen ihr, ihnen*) on her/its/their account
Ikone (-, **-n**) *f* icon
illegal *adj* illegal
Illusion *f* illusion; **sich** *dat* **Illusionen machen** to delude o.s.
illusorisch *adj* illusory
Illustration *f* illustration
Illustrierte (**-n**, **-n**) *f* picture magazine
im *präp* = **in dem**; **im Bett** in bed; **im Fernsehen** on TV; **im Radio** on the radio; **etw im Liegen/Stehen tun** do sth lying down/standing up
Imam (**-s**, **-e**) *m* imam
Imbiss (**-es**, **-e**) *m* snack
immer *adv* always; **~ wieder** again and again; **~ noch** still; **~ noch nicht** still not; **für ~** forever; **~ wenn ich ...** every time I ...; **~ schöner** more and more beautiful; **~ trauriger** sadder and sadder; **was/wer (auch) ~** whatever/whoever
immerhin *adv* all the same
immerzu *adv* all the time
Immigrant(in) *m(f)* immigrant
Immobilien *pl* real property (BRIT), real estate (*US*)
Immobilienhändler(in), **Immobilienmakler(in)** *m(f)* estate agent (BRIT), realtor (*US*)
immun *adj* immune
Immunschwäche *f* immunodeficiency
Immunsystem *nt* immune system
impfen *vt* to vaccinate
Impfpass *m* vaccination card
Impfstoff *m* vaccine
Impfung *f* vaccination
imponieren *vi +dat* to impress
Import (**-(e)s**, **-e**) *m* import
importieren *vt* to import
impotent *adj* impotent
imstande, im Stande *adj*: **~ sein** to be in a position; (*fähig*) to be able

SCHLÜSSELWORT

in *präp +akk* **1** (*räumlich: wohin*) in, into; **in die Stadt** into town; **in die Schule gehen** to go to school
2 (*zeitlich*): **bis ins 20. Jahrhundert** into *od* up to the 20th century
▸ *präp +dat* **1** (*räumlich: wo*) in; **in der Stadt** in town; **in der Schule sein** to be at school
2 (*zeitlich: wann*): **in diesem Jahr** this year; (*in jenem Jahr*) in that year; **heute in zwei Wochen** two weeks today

inbegriffen *adv* included
indem *konj*: **~ man etw macht** (*dadurch*) by doing sth
Inder(in) (**-s**, **-**) *m(f)* Indian
Indianer(in) (**-s**, **-**) *m(f)* American Indian, Native American
indianisch *adj* American Indian, Native American
Indien (**-s**) *nt* India
indirekt *adj* indirect
indisch *adj* Indian
indiskret *adj* indiscreet
individuell *adj* individual; **etw ~ anpassen** to customize sth
Indonesien (**-s**) *nt* Indonesia
Industrie *f* industry
Industriegebiet *nt* industrial area
industriell *adj* industrial
ineinander *adv* in(to) one another *od* each other
Infarkt (**-(e)s**, **-e**) *m* coronary (thrombosis)
Infektion *f* infection
Infektionskrankheit *f* infectious disease
infizieren *vt* to infect ▸ *vr*: **sich (bei jdm) ~** to be infected (by sb)
Info (**-s**, **-s**) (*umg*) *nt* (information) leaflet
infolge *präp +gen* as a result of, owing to
infolgedessen *adv* consequently
Informatik *f* information studies *pl*
Informatiker(in) (**-s**, **-**) *m(f)* computer scientist
Information *f* information *no pl*
informieren *vt*: **~ (über** *+akk***)** to inform (about) ▸ *vr*: **sich ~ (über** *+akk***)** to find out (about)
infrage, in Frage *adv*: **etw ~ stellen** to question sth
Infrastruktur *f* infrastructure
Infusion *f* infusion
Ingenieur *m* engineer
Ingwer (**-s**) *m* ginger
Inhaber(in) (**-s**, **-**) *m(f)* owner; (*Hausinhaber*) occupier; (*Lizenzinhaber*) licensee, holder; (*Fin*) bearer

Inhalt (**-(e)s**, **-e**) *m* contents *pl*; (*eines Buchs etc*) content; (*Math*: *Flächen*) area
Inhaltsangabe *f* summary
Inhaltsverzeichnis *nt* table of contents
Initiative *f* initiative; **die ~ ergreifen** to take the initiative
Injektion *f* injection
inklusive *präp +gen* inclusive of ▸ *adv* inclusive
inkonsequent *adj* inconsistent
Inland (**-(e)s**) *nt* (*Geog*) inland
Inlandflug *m* domestic flight
innen *adv* inside
Innenarchitekt(in) *m(f)* interior designer
Innenminister(in) *m(f)* minister of the interior, Home Secretary (Brit)
Innenspiegel *m* rearview mirror
Innenstadt *f* town *od* city centre (Brit) *od* center (*US*)
innere(r, s) *adj* inner; (*im Körper, inländisch*) internal
Innere(s) *nt* inside; (*Mitte*) centre (Brit), center (*US*); (*fig*) heart
Innereien *pl* innards *pl*
innerhalb *präp +gen*, *adv* within; (*räumlich*) inside
innerlich *adj* internal; (*geistig*) inward
innerste(r, s) *adj* innermost
Innovation *f* innovation
innovativ *adj* innovative
inoffiziell *adj* unofficial
ins = **in das**
Insasse (**-n**, **-n**) *m*, **Insassin** *f* (*einer Anstalt*) inmate; (*Aut*) passenger
insbesondere *adv* (e)specially
Inschrift *f* inscription
Insekt (**-(e)s**, **-en**) *nt* insect
Insel (**-**, **-n**) *f* island
Inserat (**-(e)s**, **-e**) *nt* advertisement
insgesamt *adv* altogether, all in all
insofern *adv* in this respect ▸ *konj* if; (*deshalb*) (and) so; **~ als** in so far as
Installateur *m* plumber; (*Elektroinstallateur*) electrician
installieren *vt* to install (*auch fig, Comput*)
Instinkt (**-(e)s**, **-e**) *m* instinct
Institut (**-(e)s**, **-e**) *nt* institute
Institution *f* institution
Instrument *nt* instrument
Insulin (**-s**) *nt* insulin
Inszenierung *f* production
intakt *adj* intact
intellektuell *adj* intellectual
intelligent *adj* intelligent
Intelligenz *f* intelligence
intensiv *adj* intensive
Intensivkurs *m* crash course
Intensivstation *f* intensive care unit
interaktiv *adj* (*Comput*) interactive
Intercityzug *m* inter-city train
interessant *adj* interesting
Interesse (**-s**, **-n**) *nt* interest; **~ haben an** *+dat* to be interested in
interessieren *vt*: **jdn (für etw** *od* **an etw** *dat*) **~** to interest sb (in sth) ▸ *vr*: **sich ~ für** to be interested in
Internat (**-(e)s**, **-e**) *nt* boarding school
international *adj* international
Internet (**-s**) *nt* internet; **im ~** on the internet; **im ~ surfen** to surf the net; **ins ~ stellen** to post on the internet
Internetangriff *m* cyber attack
Internetanschluss *m* internet connection
Internetauktion *f* internet auction
Internetcafé *nt* internet café
Internethandel *m* e-commerce
Internetseite *f* web page
Internetsicherheit *f* cybersecurity
Internetzugang *m* internet access
interpretieren *vt* to interpret
Interpunktion *f* punctuation
Interview (**-s**, **-s**) *nt* interview
interviewen *vt* to interview
intim *adj* intimate
intolerant *adj* intolerant
investieren *vt* to invest
inwiefern *adv* how far, to what extent
inwieweit *adv* to what extent
inzwischen *adv* meanwhile
iPad®, **I-Pad** *nt* iPad®
iPhone®, **I-Phone** *nt* iPhone®
Irak (**-s**) *m*: **(der) ~** Iraq
Iran (**-s**) *m*: **(der) ~** Iran
Ire (**-n**, **-n**) *m* Irishman
irgend *adv* at all; **wenn ~ möglich** if at all possible
irgendein(e, s) *adj* some, any
irgendetwas *pron* something; (*fragend, verneinend*) anything
irgendjemand *pron* somebody; (*fragend, verneinend*) anybody
irgendwann *adv* sometime
irgendwas (*umg*) *pron* something (or other); (*fragend, verneinend*) anything
irgendwie *adv* somehow

irgendwo *adv* somewhere (BRIT), someplace (US); (*fragend, verneinend, bedingend*) anywhere (BRIT), any place (US)
Irin *f* Irishwoman
irisch *adj* Irish; **Irische See** Irish Sea
Irland (**-s**) *nt* Ireland
ironisch *adj* ironic(al)
irre *adj* crazy, mad; **~ gut** (*umg*) way out (*umg*)
Irre(r) *f*(*m*) lunatic
irreführen *vt* to mislead
irremachen *vt* to confuse
irren *vi* to be mistaken; (*umherirren*) to wander ▶ *vr* to be mistaken
irrsinnig *adj* mad, crazy
Irrtum (**-s**, **-tümer**) *m* mistake, error
irrtümlich *adj* mistaken
ISBN *f abk* (= *Internationale Standardbuchnummer*) ISBN
Ischias (**-**) *m od nt* sciatica
Islam (**-s**) *m* Islam
islamisch *adj* Islamic
Island (**-s**) *nt* Iceland
Isländer(in) (**-s**, **-**) *m*(*f*) Icelander
isländisch *adj* Icelandic; (*Sprache*): **auf I~** in Icelandic
Isolierband *nt* insulating tape
isolieren *vt* to isolate; (*Elek*) to insulate
Israel (**-s**) *nt* Israel
Israeli[1] (**-(s)**, **-s**) *m* Israeli
Israeli[2] (**-**, **-(s)**) *f* Israeli
israelisch *adj* Israeli
Italien (**-s**) *nt* Italy
Italiener(in) (**-s**, **-**) *m*(*f*) Italian
italienisch *adj* Italian; (*Sprache*): **auf I~** in Italian

SCHLÜSSELWORT

ja *adv* **1** yes; **haben Sie das gesehen? — ja** did you see it? — yes(, I did); **ich glaube ja** (yes) I think so
2 (*fragend*) really; **ich habe gekündigt — ja?** I've quit — have you?; **du kommst, ja?** you're coming, aren't you?
3: **sei ja vorsichtig** do be careful; **Sie wissen ja, dass ...** as you know, ...; **tu das ja nicht!** don't do that!; **ich habe es ja gewusst** I just knew it; **ja, also ...** well you see ...

Jacht (**-**, **-en**) *f* yacht
Jacke (**-**, **-n**) *f* jacket; (*Wolljacke*) cardigan
Jackett (**-s**, **-s** *od* **-e**) *nt* jacket
Jagd (**-**, **-en**) *f* hunt; (*Jagen*) hunting
jagen *vi* to hunt ▶ *vt* to hunt; (*verfolgen*) to chase
Jäger (**-s**, **-**) *m* hunter
Jahr (**-(e)s**, **-e**) *nt* year; **die Sechzigerjahre** *od* **sechziger Jahre** the sixties *pl*; **mit dreißig Jahren** at the age of thirty
Jahrestag *m* anniversary
Jahreszahl *f* date, year
Jahreszeit *f* season
Jahrgang *m* age group; (*von Wein*) vintage; **er ist ~ 1950** he was born in 1950
Jahrhundert *nt* century
jährlich *adj*, *adv* yearly
Jahrmarkt *m* fair

Jahrtausend *nt* millennium
Jahrzehnt *nt* decade
jähzornig *adj* hot-tempered
Jalousie *f* venetian blind
Jamaika (**-s**) *nt* Jamaica
jämmerlich *adj* pathetic
jammern *vi* to wail
Januar (**-s**, **-e**) *m* January; *siehe auch* **September**
Japan (**-s**) *nt* Japan
Japaner(in) (**-s**, **-**) *m(f)* Japanese
japanisch *adj* Japanese; (*Sprache*): **auf J~** in Japanese
jaulen *vi* to howl
jawohl *adv* yes (of course)
Jazz (**-**) *m* jazz

SCHLÜSSELWORT

je *adv* **1** (*jemals*) ever; **hast du so was je gesehen?** did you ever see anything like it?
2 (*jeweils*) every, each; **sie zahlten je 15 Euro** they paid 15 euros each
▸ *konj* **1**: **je nach** depending on; **je nachdem** it depends; **je nachdem, ob …** depending on whether …
2: **je eher, desto** *od* **umso besser** the sooner the better

Jeans *pl* jeans *pl*
jede(r, s) *adj* (*einzeln*) each; (*von zweien*) either; (*jede von allen*) every ▸ *indef pron* (*einzeln*) each (one); (*jede(r) von allen*) everyone, everybody; **jeder Zweite** every other (one); **jedes Mal** every time, each time
jedenfalls *adv* in any case
jederzeit *adv* at any time
jedoch *adv* however
jemals *adv* ever
jemand *indef pron* somebody; (*bei Fragen, bedingenden Sätzen, Negation*) anyone, anybody
Jemen (**-s**) *m* Yemen
jene(r, s) *adj* that; (*pl*) those ▸ *pron* that one; (*pl*) those
jenseits *adv* on the other side ▸ *präp +gen* on the other side of, beyond
jetzig *adj* present
jetzt *adv* now; **~ gleich** right now; **bis ~** so far, up to now; **von ~ an** from now on
jeweils *adv*: **zu ~ 10 Euro** at 10 euros each
Job (**-s**, **-s**) (*umg*) *m* job
jobben (*umg*) *vi* to work, to have a job
Jod (**-(e)s**) *nt* iodine
joggen *vi* to jog
Jogging (**-s**) *nt* jogging
Jogginganzug *m* jogging suit, tracksuit
Johannisbeere *f*: **Rote ~** redcurrant; **Schwarze ~** blackcurrant
Joint (**-s**, **-s**) (*umg*) *m* joint
jonglieren *vi* to juggle
Jordanien (**-s**) *nt* Jordan
Journalist(in) *m(f)* journalist
jubeln *vi* to rejoice
Jubiläum (**-s**, **Jubiläen**) *nt* jubilee; (*Jahrestag*) anniversary
jucken *vi* to itch ▸ *vt*: **es juckt mich am Arm** my arm is itching; **das juckt mich doch nicht** (*umg*) I don't care
Juckreiz *m* itch
Jude (**-n**, **-n**) *m* Jew
Jüdin *f* Jew
jüdisch *adj* Jewish
Judo (**-(s)**) *nt* judo
Jugend (**-**) *f* youth
jugendfrei *adj* suitable for young people; (*Film*) U(-certificate), G (*US*)
Jugendherberge *f* youth hostel
jugendlich *adj* youthful
Jugendliche(r) *f(m)* young person
Jugendstil *m* (*Kunst*) Art Nouveau
Jugendzentrum *nt* youth centre (BRIT) *od* center (*US*)
Juli (**-(s)**, **-s**) (*pl selten*) *m* July; *siehe auch* **September**
jung *adj* young
Junge (**-n**, **-n**) *m* boy, lad ▸ *nt* young animal; (*pl*) young *pl*
Jungfrau *f* virgin; (*Astrol*) Virgo
Junggeselle *m* bachelor
Junggesellin *f* single woman
Juni (**-(s)**, **-s**) *m* June; *siehe auch* **September**
Jura *no art* (*Univ*) law
Jurist(in) *m(f)* lawyer
juristisch *adj* legal
Jurte *f* yurt
Justiz (**-**) *f* justice
Justizminister(in) *m(f)* minister of justice
Juwel (**-s**, **-en**) *m od nt* jewel
Juwelier(in) (**-s**, **-e**) *m(f)* jeweller (BRIT), jeweler (*US*)

Kabel (**-s**, **-**) *nt* (*Elek*) wire; (*stark*) cable
Kabelfernsehen *nt* cable television
Kabeljau (**-s**, **-e** *od* **-s**) *m* cod
kabellos *adj* wireless
Kabine *f* cabin; (*Zelle*) cubicle
Kachel (**-**, **-n**) *f* tile
Kachelofen *m* tiled stove
Käfer (**-s**, **-**) *m* beetle
Kaff (**-s**, **-s**) (*umg*) *nt* dump, hole
Kaffee (**-s**, **-s**) *m* coffee; **zwei ~, bitte!** two coffees, please
Kaffeekanne *f* coffeepot
Kaffeekapsel *f* coffee pod, coffee capsule
Kaffeeklatsch *m chat over coffee and cakes*, coffee klatsch (US)
Kaffeelöffel *m* coffee spoon
Kaffeemaschine *f* coffee maker
Kaffeepause *f* coffee break
Kaffeetasse *f* coffee cup
Käfig (**-s**, **-e**) *m* cage
kahl *adj* (*Mensch*, *Kopf*) bald; (*Baum*, *Wand*) bare
Kahn (**-(e)s**, **Kähne**) *m* boat, barge
Kai (**-s**, **-e** *od* **-s**) *m* quay
Kaiser (**-s**, **-**) *m* emperor
Kaiserin *f* empress
Kaiserschnitt *m* (*Med*) Caesarean (BRIT) *od* Cesarean (US) (section)
Kajak (**-s**, **-s**) *m od nt* kayak
Kajüte (**-**, **-n**) *f* cabin
Kakao (**-s**, **-s**) *m* cocoa
Kakerlake (**-**, **-n**) *f* cockroach
Kaktee (**-**, **-n**) *f* cactus
Kalb (**-(e)s**, **Kälber**) *nt* calf
Kalbfleisch *nt* veal
Kalender (**-s**, **-**) *m* calendar; (*Taschenkalender*) diary
Kalk (**-(e)s**, **-e**) *m* lime; (*Biol*) calcium
Kalorie (**-**, **-n**) *f* calorie
kalorienarm *adj* low-calorie
kalt *adj* cold; **mir ist (es) ~** I am cold
kaltblütig *adj* cold-blooded
Kälte (**-**) *f* coldness; (*Wetter*) cold
kam *etc vb siehe* **kommen**
Kambodscha *nt* Cambodia
Kamel (**-(e)s**, **-e**) *nt* camel
Kamera (**-**, **-s**) *f* camera
Kamerad(in) (**-en**, **-en**) *m(f)* comrade, friend
Kamerahandy *nt* camera phone
Kamille (**-**, **-n**) *f* camomile
Kamillentee *m* camomile tea
Kamin (**-s**, **-e**) *m* (*außen*) chimney; (*innen*) fireside; (*Feuerstelle*) fireplace
Kamm (**-(e)s**, **Kämme**) *m* comb; (*Bergkamm*) ridge; (*Hahnenkamm*) crest
kämmen *vt* to comb
Kammermusik *f* chamber music
Kampf (**-(e)s**, **Kämpfe**) *m* fight, battle; (*Wettbewerb*) contest; (*fig: Anstrengung*) struggle
kämpfen *vi* to fight
Kampfsport *m* martial art
Kanada (**-s**) *nt* Canada
Kanadier(in) (**-s**, **-**) *m(f)* Canadian
kanadisch *adj* Canadian
Kanal (**-s**, **Kanäle**) *m* (*Fluss*) canal; (*Rinne*) channel; (*für Abfluss*) drain; **der ~** (*auch:* **der Ärmelkanal**) the (English) Channel
Kanalinseln *pl* Channel Islands *pl*
Kanalisation *f* sewage system
Kanaltunnel *m* Channel Tunnel
Kanarienvogel *m* canary
Kandidat(in) (**-en**, **-en**) *m(f)* candidate
Känguru (**-s**, **-s**) *nt* kangaroo
Kaninchen *nt* rabbit
Kanister (**-s**, **-**) *m* can
Kännchen *nt* pot
Kanne (**-**, **-n**) *f* (*Krug*) jug; (*Kaffeekanne*) pot; (*Milchkanne*) churn; (*Gießkanne*) watering can
kannte *etc vb siehe* **kennen**
Kante (**-**, **-n**) *f* edge
Kantine *f* canteen
Kanton (**-s**, **-e**) *m* canton
Kanu (**-s**, **-s**) *nt* canoe
Kanzler(in) (**-s**, **-**) *m(f)* chancellor
Kap (**-s**, **-s**) *nt* cape

Kapazität *f* capacity; (*Fachmann*) authority
Kapelle *f* (*Gebäude*) chapel; (*Mus*) band
Kaper (-, -n) *f* caper
kapieren (*umg*) *vt, vi* to understand
Kapital (-s, -e *od* -ien) *nt* capital
Kapitän (-s, -e) *m* captain
Kapitel (-s, -) *nt* chapter
Kappe (-, -n) *f* cap
Kapsel (-, -n) *f* capsule
kaputt (*umg*) *adj* broken; (*Person*) exhausted
kaputt|gehen *unreg vi* to break; (*Schuhe*) to fall apart; (*Firma*) to go bust; (*Stoff*) to wear out
kaputt|machen *vt* to break; (*Mensch*) to wear out
Kapuze (-, -n) *f* hood
Karaffe (-, -n) *f* carafe; (*geschliffen*) decanter
Karamell (-s) *m* caramel
Karat (-(e)s, -e) *nt* carat
Karate (-s) *nt* karate
Kardinal (-s, **Kardinäle**) *m* cardinal
Karfreitag *m* Good Friday
kariert *adj* (*Stoff*) checked (BRIT), checkered (*US*); (*Papier*) squared
Karies (-) *f* caries
Karikatur *f* caricature
Karneval (-s, -e *od* -s) *m* carnival

KARNEVAL

Karneval is still a very popular tradition in many parts of Germany. People get together to sing, dance, eat, drink and generally make merry before Lent begins. *Rosenmontag*, the day before Shrove Tuesday, is the most important day of *Karneval* in the Rhineland. Most schools and businesses close on *Rosenmontag* to allow people to enjoy the parades and take part in the celebrations. In South Germany *Karneval* is called *Fasching*.

Kärnten (-s) *nt* Carinthia
Karo (-s, -s) *nt* square; (*Karten*) diamonds
Karosserie *f* (*Aut*) body(work)
Karotte (-, -n) *f* carrot
Karpfen (-s, -) *m* carp
Karriere (-, -n) *f* career
Karte (-, -n) *f* card; (*Landkarte*) map; (*Speisekarte*) menu; (*Eintrittskarte, Fahrkarte*) ticket; **Karten spielen** to play cards
Kartei *f* card index
Karteikarte *f* index card
Kartenprüfnummer *f* card security code, card verification number
Kartenspiel *nt* card game
Kartentelefon *nt* cardphone
Kartenvorverkauf *m* advance sale of tickets
Kartoffel (-, -n) *f* potato
Kartoffelbrei *m* mashed potatoes *pl*
Kartoffelchips *pl* potato crisps *pl* (BRIT), potato chips *pl* (*US*)
Kartoffelpuffer *m* potato cake (*made from grated potatoes*)
Kartoffelpüree *nt* mashed potatoes *pl*
Kartoffelsalat *m* potato salad
Karton (-s, -s) *m* cardboard; (*Schachtel*) cardboard box
Karussell (-s, -s) *nt* roundabout (BRIT), merry-go-round
Kaschmir (-s) *nt* (*Stoff*) Kashmir
Käse (-s, -) *m* cheese
Käsekuchen *m* cheesecake
Kasino (-s, -s) *nt* (*Spielkasino*) casino
Kaskoversicherung *f* (*Aut: Vollkaskoversicherung*) fully comprehensive insurance
Kasperletheater, Kasperltheater *nt* Punch and Judy (show)
Kasse (-, -n) *f* (*Geldkasten*) cashbox; (*in Geschäft*) till, cash register; (*Kinokasse, Theaterkasse etc*) box office; (*Krankenkasse*) health insurance; (*Sparkasse*) savings bank
Kassenbon *m* receipt
Kassenzettel *m* sales slip
Kassette *f* small box; (*Tonband, Phot*) cassette
Kassettenrekorder (-s, -) *m* cassette recorder
kassieren *vt* (*Gelder etc*) to collect; (*umg: wegnehmen*) to take (away) ▶ *vi*: **darf ich ~?** would you like to pay now?
Kassierer(in) (-s, -) *m(f)* cashier
Kastanie *f* chestnut
Kasten (-s, **Kästen**) *m* box (*auch Sport*), case
Kat (-, -s) *m abk* (*Aut*) = **Katalysator**
Katalog (-(e)s, -e) *m* catalogue (BRIT), catalog (*US*)

Katalysator *m* (*lit, fig*) catalyst; (*Aut*) catalytic converter
Katar *nt* Qatar
Katastrophe (**-, -n**) *f* catastrophe, disaster
Kategorie *f* category
Kater (**-s, -**) *m* tomcat; (*umg*) hangover
Kathedrale (**-, -n**) *f* cathedral
Katholik(in) (**-en, -en**) *m(f)* Catholic
katholisch *adj* Catholic
Katze (**-, -n**) *f* cat
Kauderwelsch (**-(s)**) *nt* jargon; (*umg*) double Dutch (*BRIT*)
kauen *vt, vi* to chew
Kauf (**-(e)s, Käufe**) *m* purchase; (*Kaufen*) buying; **ein guter ~** a bargain; **etw in ~ nehmen** to put up with sth
kaufen *vt* to buy
Käufer(in) (**-s, -**) *m(f)* buyer
Kauffrau *f* businesswoman
Kaufhaus *nt* department store
Kaufmann (**-(e)s, -leute**) *m* businessman; (*Einzelhandelskaufmann*) shopkeeper
Kaufpreis *m* purchase price
Kaufvertrag *m* bill of sale
Kaugummi *m* chewing gum
Kaulquappe (**-, -n**) *f* tadpole
kaum *adv* hardly, scarcely
Kaution *f* deposit; (*Jur*) bail
Kaviar *m* caviar
KB *nt abk* (= *Kilobyte*) KB, kbyte
Kegel (**-s, -**) *m* skittle; (*Math*) cone
Kegelbahn *f* bowling alley
kegeln *vi* to play skittles
Kehle (**-, -n**) *f* throat
Kehlkopf *m* larynx
Kehre (**-, -n**) *f* bend
kehren *vt, vi* (*mit Besen*) to sweep
Keilriemen *m* (*Aut*) fan belt
kein, keine *pron* none ▶ *adj* no, not any; **keine schlechte Idee** not a bad idea
keine(r, s) *indef pron* no one, nobody; (*von Gegenstand*) none; **keiner von ihnen** none of them
keinesfalls *adv* on no account
Keks (**-es, -e**) *m od nt* biscuit (*BRIT*), cookie (*US*)
Keller (**-s, -**) *m* cellar; (*Geschoss*) basement
Kellner(in) (**-s, -**) *m(f)* waiter, waitress
Kenia (**-s**) *nt* Kenya
kennen *unreg vt* to know; **~ Sie sich schon?** do you know each other (already)?; **kennst du mich noch?** do you remember me?
kennen|lernen *vt* to get to know ▶ *vr* to get to know each other; (*zum ersten Mal*) to meet
Kenntnis (**-, -se**) *f* knowledge *no pl*
Kennwort *nt* password
Kennzeichen *nt* mark; **(amtliches/polizeiliches) ~** (*Aut*) number plate (*BRIT*), license plate (*US*)
Kerl (**-s, -e**) (*umg*) *m* chap, bloke (*BRIT*), guy
Kern (**-(e)s, -e**) *m* (*Obstkern*) pip, stone; (*Nusskern*) kernel; (*Atomkern*) nucleus; (*fig*) heart, core
Kernenergie *f* nuclear energy
Kernkraft *f* nuclear power
Kernkraftwerk *nt* nuclear power station
Kerze (**-, -n**) *f* candle; (*Zündkerze*) plug
Ketchup, Ketschup (**-(s), -s**) *m od nt* ketchup
Kette (**-, -n**) *f* chain; (*Halskette*) necklace
keuchen *vi* to pant
Keuchhusten *m* whooping cough
Keule (**-, -n**) *f* club; (*Koch*) leg
Kfz (**-(s), -(s)**) *f abk* = **Kraftfahrzeug**
KG (**-, -s**) *f abk* = **Kommanditgesellschaft**
Kichererbse *f* chick pea
kichern *vi* to giggle
kidnappen *vt* to kidnap
Kiefer[1] (**-s, -**) *m* jaw
Kiefer[2] (**-, -n**) *f* pine
Kieme (**-, -n**) *f* gill
Kies (**-es, -e**) *m* gravel
Kiesel (**-s, -**) *m* pebble
kiffen (*umg*) *vt* to smoke pot *od* grass
Kilo (**-s, -(s)**) *nt* kilo
Kilobyte *nt* (*Comput*) kilobyte
Kilogramm *nt* kilogram
Kilometer *m* kilometre (*BRIT*), kilometer (*US*)
Kilometerstand *m* ≈ mileage
Kilometerzähler *m* ≈ mileometer
Kilowatt *nt* kilowatt
Kind (**-(e)s, -er**) *nt* child; **sie bekommt ein ~** she's having a baby
Kinderarzt *m* paediatrician (*BRIT*), pediatrician (*US*)
Kinderärztin *f* paediatrician (*BRIT*), pediatrician (*US*)
Kinderbetreuung *f* childcare
Kinderbett *nt* cot (*BRIT*), crib (*US*)

Kindergarten *m* nursery school
Kindergärtner(in) *m(f)* nursery-school teacher
Kindergeld *nt* child benefit (BRIT)
Kinderkrankheit *f* childhood illness
Kinderkrippe *f* crèche (BRIT), daycare center (*US*)
Kinderlähmung *f* polio(myelitis)
Kindermädchen *nt* nursemaid
kindersicher *adj* childproof
Kindersicherung *f* childproof safety catch; (*an Flasche*) childproof cap
Kindertagesstätte *f* day-nursery
Kinderteller *m* children's dish
Kinderwagen *m* pram (BRIT), baby carriage (*US*)
Kinderzimmer *nt* child's/children's room
Kindheit *f* childhood
kindisch *adj* childish
Kindle® *m* Kindle®
kindlich *adj* childlike
Kinn (**-(e)s**, **-e**) *nt* chin
Kino (**-s**, **-s**) *nt* cinema (BRIT), movies (*US*)
Kiosk (**-(e)s**, **-e**) *m* kiosk
Kippe (**-**, **-n**) *f* (*umg*) cigarette end
kippen *vi* to topple over ▶ *vt* to tilt
Kirche (**-**, **-n**) *f* church
Kirchturm *m* church tower, steeple
Kirchweih *f* fair
Kirmes (**-**, **-sen**) *f* (*Dialekt*) fair
Kirsche (**-**, **-n**) *f* cherry
Kirschtomate *f* cherry tomato
Kissen (**-s**, **-**) *nt* cushion; (*Kopfkissen*) pillow
Kissenbezug *m* pillow case
Kiste (**-**, **-n**) *f* box; (*Truhe*) chest
kitschig *adj* trashy
kitzelig *adj* (*lit, fig*) ticklish
kitzeln *vt*, *vi* to tickle
Kiwi (**-**, **-s**) *f* (*Frucht*) kiwi fruit
Klage (**-**, **-n**) *f* complaint; (*Jur*) action
klagen *vi* (*sich beschweren*) to complain
kläglich *adj* wretched
Klammer (**-**, **-n**) *f* (*in Text*) bracket; (*Büroklammer*) clip; (*Wäscheklammer*) peg (BRIT), pin (*US*); (*Zahnklammer*) brace
Klammeraffe *m* (*umg*) at-sign, @
klammern *vr*: **sich ~ an** +*akk* to cling to
klang *etc vb siehe* **klingen**
Klang (**-(e)s**, **Klänge**) *m* sound
Klappbett *nt* folding bed
klappen *vi unpers* to work; **hat es mit den Karten/dem Job geklappt?** did you get the tickets/job O.K.?
klappern *vi* to clatter, to rattle
Klapperschlange *f* rattlesnake
Klappstuhl *m* folding chair
klar *adj* clear; **sich** *dat* **im Klaren sein über** +*akk* to be clear about; **alles ~?** everything okay?
klären *vt* (*Flüssigkeit*) to purify; (*Probleme*) to clarify ▶ *vr* to clear (itself) up
Klarinette *f* clarinet
klar|kommen *unreg* (*umg*) *vi*: **mit jdm/etw ~** to be able to cope with sb/sth
klar|machen *vt*: **jdm etw ~** to make sth clear to sb
klar|stellen *vt* to clarify
Klärung *f* (*von Problem*) clarification
klasse (*umg*) *adj* smashing
Klasse (**-**, **-n**) *f* class; (*Sch*) form
Klassenarbeit *f* test
Klassenlehrer(in) *m(f)* class teacher
Klassenzimmer *nt* classroom
Klassik *f* (*Zeit*) classical period; (*Stil*) classicism
Klatsch (**-(e)s**, **-e**) *m* (*Gerede*) gossip
klatschen *vi* (*tratschen*) to gossip; (*Beifall spenden*) to applaud, to clap
klatschnass *adj* soaking wet
Klaue (**-**, **-n**) *f* claw; (*umg*: *Schrift*) scrawl
klauen *vt* (*umg*) to pinch
Klavier (**-s**, **-e**) *nt* piano
Klebeband *nt* adhesive tape
kleben *vt*, *vi*: **~ (an** +*akk***)** to stick (to)
klebrig *adj* sticky
Klebstoff *m* glue
Klebstreifen *m* adhesive tape
Klecks (**-es**, **-e**) *m* blot, stain
Klee (**-s**) *m* clover
Kleid (**-(e)s**, **-er**) *nt* (*Frauenkleid*) dress ■ **Kleider** *pl* clothes *pl*
Kleiderbügel *m* coat hanger
Kleiderschrank *m* wardrobe
Kleidung *f* clothing
klein *adj* little, small; **von ~ an** *od* **auf** (*von Kindheit an*) from childhood; **~ schneiden** to chop up
Kleinanzeige *f* small ad (BRIT), want ad (*US*)
Kleinbus *m* minibus
Kleingeld *nt* small change
Kleinigkeit *f* trifle; **eine ~ essen** to have a bite to eat
Kleinkind *nt* infant
klein|schreiben *unreg vt*: **ein Wort ~** to write a word with a small initial letter

Kleinstadt *f* small town
Kleister (**-s**, **-**) *m* paste
Klempner(in) (**-s**, **-**) *m(f)* plumber
klettern *vi* to climb
Klettverschluss *m* Velcro® fastener
klicken *vi* to click
Klient(in) *m(f)* client
Klima (**-s**, **-s** *od* **-te**) *nt* climate
Klimaanlage *f* air conditioning
Klimakompensation (**-**, **-en**) *f* carbon offset
klimatisiert *adj* air-conditioned
Klimawandel *m* climate change
Klinge (**-**, **-n**) *f* blade
Klingel (**-**, **-n**) *f* bell
klingeln *vi* to ring
klingen *unreg vi* to sound
Klinik *f* clinic
Klinke (**-**, **-n**) *f* handle
Klippe (**-**, **-n**) *f* cliff; (*im Meer*) reef; (*fig*) hurdle
Klischee (**-s**, **-s**) *nt* (*fig*) cliché
Klo (**-s**, **-s**) (*umg*) *nt* loo (BRIT), john (*US*)
Klopapier (*umg*) *nt* toilet paper
klopfen *vi* to knock; (*Herz*) to thump ▶ *vt* to beat
Kloß (**-es**, **Klöße**) *m* (*im Hals*) lump; (*Koch*) dumpling
Kloster (**-s**, **Klöster**) *nt* (*Männerkloster*) monastery; (*Frauenkloster*) convent
Klub (**-s**, **-s**) *m* club
klug *adj* clever
knabbern *vt*, *vi* to nibble
Knäckebrot *nt* crispbread
knacken *vi* to crack
Knall (**-(e)s**, **-e**) *m* bang
knallen *vi* to bang
knapp *adj* tight; (*Geld*) scarce; (*Mehrheit, Sieg*) narrow; (*Sprache*) concise; **~ zwei Stunden** just under two hours
Knauf (**-(e)s**, **Knäufe**) *m* knob
kneifen *unreg vt* to pinch ▶ *vi* to pinch; (*sich drücken*) to back out
Kneifzange *f* pincers *pl*
Kneipe (**-**, **-n**) (*umg*) *f* pub (BRIT), bar, saloon (*US*)
Knete (*umg*) *f* (*Geld*) dough
kneten *vt* to knead; (*Wachs*) to mould (BRIT), to mold (*US*)
knicken *vt*, *vi* (*brechen*) to break; (*Papier*) to fold; **geknickt sein** to be downcast
Knie (**-s**, **-**) *nt* knee; **in die ~ gehen** to kneel
Kniebeuge (**-**, **-n**) *f* knee bend
Kniegelenk *nt* knee joint
Kniekehle *f* back of the knee
knien *vi* to kneel
Kniescheibe *f* kneecap
Kniestrumpf *m* knee-length sock
kniff *etc vb siehe* **kneifen**
knipsen *vt* (*Fahrkarte*) to punch; (*Phot*) to snap ▶ *vi* (*Phot*) to take snaps/a snap
knirschen *vi* to crunch; **mit den Zähnen ~** to grind one's teeth
knitterfrei *adj* non-crease
knittern *vi* to crease
Knoblauch (**-(e)s**) *m* garlic
Knoblauchbrot *nt* garlic bread
Knoblauchzehe *f* clove of garlic
Knöchel (**-s**, **-**) *m* knuckle; (*Fußknöchel*) ankle
Knochen (**-s**, **-**) *m* bone
Knochenbruch *m* fracture
Knochenmark *nt* bone marrow
Knödel (**-s**, **-**) *m* dumpling
Knopf (**-(e)s**, **Knöpfe**) *m* button
Knopfdruck *m*: **auf ~** at the touch of a button
Knopfloch *nt* buttonhole
Knospe (**-**, **-n**) *f* bud
knoten *vt* to knot
Knoten (**-s**, **-**) *m* knot; (*Med*) lump
knurren *vi* (*Hund*) to growl; (*Magen*) to rumble; (*Mensch*) to mutter
knusprig *adj* crisp; (*Keks*) crunchy
knutschen (*umg*) *vi*, *vr* to snog
k. o. *adj* (*Sport*) knocked out; (*fig: umg*) whacked
Koalition *f* coalition
Koch (**-(e)s**, **Köche**) *m* cook
Kochbuch *nt* cookery book, cookbook
kochen *vi* to cook; (*Wasser*) to boil ▶ *vt* (*Essen*) to cook; (*Kaffee, Tee*) to make
Köchin *f* cook
Kochlöffel *m* kitchen spoon
Kochnische *f* kitchenette
Kochplatte *f* hotplate
Kochrezept *nt* recipe
Kochtopf *m* saucepan
Kode (**-s**, **-s**) *m* code
Köder (**-s**, **-**) *m* bait, lure
Koffein (**-s**) *nt* caffeine
koffeinfrei *adj* decaffeinated
Koffer (**-s**, **-**) *m* suitcase
Kofferraum *m* (*Aut*) boot (BRIT), trunk (*US*)
Kognak (**-s**, **-s**) *m* brandy
Kohl (**-(e)s**, **-e**) *m* cabbage

Kohle (-, **-n**) *f* coal; (*Holzkohle*) charcoal; (*Chem*) carbon; (*umg*: *Geld*): **die Kohlen stimmen** the money's right
Kohlehydrat (**-(e)s**, **-e**) *nt* carbohydrate, (*umg*) carb
Kohlendioxid (**-(e)s**, **-e**) *nt* carbon dioxide
Kohlenhydrat (**-(e)s**, **-e**) *nt* = **Kohlehydrat**
Kohlensäure *f* carbon dioxide; **ein Getränk ohne ~** a non-fizzy *od* still drink
Koje (-, **-n**) *f* cabin; (*Bett*) bunk
Kokain (**-s**) *nt* cocaine
Kokosnuss *f* coconut
Kolben (**-s**, **-**) *m* (*Tech*) piston; (*Maiskolben*) cob
Kolik *f* colic
Kollaps (**-es**, **-e**) *m* collapse
Kollege (**-n**, **-n**) *m* colleague
Kollegin *f* colleague
Köln (**-s**) *nt* Cologne
Kölnischwasser *nt* eau de Cologne
Kolonne (-, **-n**) *f* convoy
Kolumbien (**-s**) *nt* Columbia
Koma (**-s**, **-s** *od* **-ta**) *nt* (*Med*) coma
Kombi (**-s**, **-s**) *m* (*Aut*) estate (car) (Brit), station wagon (*US*)
Kombination *f* combination; (*Vermutung*) conjecture; (*Hemdhose*) combinations *pl*; (*Aviat*) flying suit
kombinieren *vt* to combine ▶ *vi* to deduce; (*vermuten*) to guess
Kombizange *f* (pair of) pliers
Komfort (**-s**) *m* luxury; (*von Möbel etc*) comfort
Komiker (**-s**, **-**) *m* comedian
komisch *adj* funny
Komma (**-s**, **-s** *od* **-ta**) *nt* comma
Kommanditgesellschaft *f* limited partnership
kommen *unreg vi* to come; (*näher kommen*) to approach; (*passieren*) to happen; (*gelangen, geraten*) to get; (*Blumen, Zähne, Tränen etc*) to appear; (*in die Schule, ins Gefängnis etc*) to go; **~ lassen** to send for; **zu sich ~** to come round *od* to; **zu etw ~** (*bekommen*) to acquire sth; (*Zeit dazu finden*) to get round to sth; **wer kommt zuerst?** who's first?
kommend *adj* coming; **(am) kommenden Montag** next Monday
Kommentar *m* commentary; **kein ~** no comment
Kommilitone (**-n**, **-n**) *m*, **Kommilitonin** *f* fellow student
Kommissar(in) *m(f)* police inspector
Kommode (-, **-n**) *f* (chest of) drawers
Kommunikation *f* communication
Kommunion *f* communion
Kommunismus *m* communism
Komödie *f* comedy
kompakt *adj* compact
Kompass (**-es**, **-e**) *m* compass
kompatibel *adj* (*auch Comput*) compatible
kompetent *adj* competent
komplett *adj* complete
Kompliment *nt* compliment
Komplize (**-n**, **-n**) *m* accomplice
kompliziert *adj* complicated
Komponist(in) *m(f)* composer
Kompost (**-(e)s**, **-e**) *m* compost
Komposthaufen *m* compost heap
Kompott (**-(e)s**, **-e**) *nt* stewed fruit
Kompresse (-, **-n**) *f* compress
Kompromiss (**-es**, **-e**) *m* compromise
Kondensmilch *f* condensed milk
Kondition *f* condition, shape; (*Durchhaltevermögen*) stamina
Konditorei *f* cake shop; (*mit Café*) café
Kondom (**-s**, **-e**) *m od nt* condom
Konfektionsgröße *f* clothes size
Konferenz *f* conference
Konfession *f* religion; (*christlich*) denomination
Konfetti (**-(s)**) *nt* confetti
Konfirmation *f* (*Eccl*) confirmation
Konfitüre (-, **-n**) *f* jam
Konflikt (**-(e)s**, **-e**) *m* conflict
konfrontieren *vt* to confront
Kongo (**-(s)**) *m* Congo
Kongress (**-es**, **-e**) *m* congress
König (**-(e)s**, **-e**) *m* king
Königin *f* queen
königlich *adj* royal
Königreich *nt* kingdom
Konkurrenz *f* competition

 **SCHLÜSSELWORT**

können (*pt* **konnte**, *pp* **gekonnt**, *als Hilfsverb* **können**) *vt*, *vi* **1** to be able to; **ich kann es machen** I can do it, I am able to do it; **ich kann es nicht machen** I can't do it, I'm not able to do it; **ich kann nicht ...** I can't ..., I cannot ...; **ich kann nicht mehr** I can't go on

2 (*wissen, beherrschen*) to know; **können Sie Deutsch?** can you speak German?; **er kann gut Englisch** he speaks English well; **sie kann keine Mathematik** she can't do mathematics
3 (*dürfen*) to be allowed to; **kann ich gehen?** can I go?; **könnte ich ...?** could I ...?; **kann ich mit?** (*umg*) can I come with you?
4 (*möglich sein*): **Sie könnten recht haben** you may be right; **das kann sein** that's possible; **kann sein** maybe

konsequent *adj* consistent
Konsequenz *f* consistency; **die Konsequenzen tragen** to take the consequences
konservativ *adj* conservative
Konserve (**-**, **-n**) *f* tinned (Brit) *od* canned food
Konservenbüchse *f*, **Konservendose** *f* tin (Brit), can
konservieren *vt* to preserve
Konservierungsmittel *nt* preservative
Konsonant *m* consonant
Konsul(in) (**-s**, **-n**) *m(f)* consul
Konsulat (**-(e)s**, **-e**) *nt* consulate
Kontakt (**-(e)s**, **-e**) *m* contact
kontaktarm *adj* unsociable
kontaktfreudig *adj* sociable
Kontaktlinsen *pl* contact lenses *pl*
Kontinent *m* continent
Konto (**-s**, **Konten**) *nt* account
Kontoauszug *m* statement (of account)
Kontoinhaber(in) *m(f)* account holder
Kontonummer *f* account number
Kontostand *m* bank balance
Kontrabass *m* double bass
Kontrast (**-(e)s**, **-e**) *m* contrast
Kontrolle (**-**, **-n**) *f* control, supervision; (*Passkontrolle*) passport control
kontrollieren *vt* to control; (*nachprüfen*) to check
Konzentration *f* concentration
Konzentrationslager *nt* concentration camp
konzentrieren *vt, vr* to concentrate
Konzept (**-(e)s**, **-e**) *nt* rough draft; **jdn aus dem ~ bringen** to confuse sb
Konzern (**-s**, **-e**) *m* combine
Konzert (**-(e)s**, **-e**) *nt* concert; (*Stück*) concerto
Konzertsaal *m* concert hall
koordinieren *vt* to coordinate
Kopf (**-(e)s**, **Köpfe**) *m* head; **pro ~** per person *od* head; **sich** *dat* **über etw** *akk* **den ~ zerbrechen** to rack one's brains over sth
Kopfhörer *m* headphone
Kopfkissen *nt* pillow
Kopfsalat *m* lettuce
Kopfschmerzen *pl* headache *sing*
Kopfstütze *f* headrest
Kopftuch *nt* headscarf
kopfüber *adv* head-first
Kopie *f* copy
kopieren *vt* to copy
Kopierer (**-s**, **-**) *m* (photo)copier
Kopilot(in) *m(f)* co-pilot
Koralle (**-**, **-n**) *f* coral
Koran (**-s**) *m* (*Rel*) Koran
Korb (**-(e)s**, **Körbe**) *m* basket; **jdm einen ~ geben** (*fig*) to turn sb down
Kord (**-(e)s**, **-e** *od* **-s**) *m* = **Cord**
Kordel (**-**, **-n**) *f* cord
Kork (**-(e)s**, **-e**) *m* cork
Korken (**-s**, **-**) *m* cork
Korkenzieher (**-s**, **-**) *m* corkscrew
Korn (**-(e)s**, **Körner**) *nt* grain
Kornblume *f* cornflower
Körper (**-s**, **-**) *m* body
Körperbau *m* build
Körpergeruch *m* body odour (Brit) *od* odor (*US*)
Körpergröße *f* height
körperlich *adj* physical
Körperteil *m* part of the body
Körperverletzung *f* (*Jur*): **schwere ~** grievous bodily harm
korrekt *adj* correct
Korrespondent(in) *m(f)* correspondent
Korrespondenz *f* correspondence
korrigieren *vt* to correct
Kosmetik *f* cosmetics *pl*
Kosmetikkoffer *m* vanity case
Kost (**-**) *f* (*Nahrung*) food; (*Verpflegung*) board
kostbar *adj* precious; (*teuer*) costly, expensive
kosten *vt* to cost; (*versuchen*) to taste ▸ *vi* to taste
Kosten *pl* cost(s); (*Ausgaben*) expenses *pl*; **auf ~ von** at the expense of
kostenlos *adj* free (of charge)
Kostenvoranschlag *m* (costs) estimate

köstlich *adj* (*Essen*) delicious; (*Einfall*) delightful; **sich ~ amüsieren** to have a marvellous time
Kostprobe *f* taste; (*fig*) sample
kostspielig *adj* expensive
Kostüm (**-s**, **-e**) *nt* costume; (*Damenkostüm*) suit
Kot (**-(e)s**) *m* excrement
Kotelett (**-(e)s**, **-e** *od* **-s**) *nt* cutlet, chop
Koteletten *pl* sideboards *pl* (BRIT), sideburns *pl* (US)
Kotflügel *m* (*Aut*) wing
kotzen (*!*) *vi* to puke (*!*), to throw up
Krabbe (**-**, **-n**) *f* shrimp
krabbeln *vi* to crawl
Krach (**-(e)s**, **-s** *od* **-e**) *m* crash; (*andauernd*) noise; (*umg*: *Streit*) quarrel
Kraft (**-**, **Kräfte**) *f* strength; (*von Stimme*, *fig*) power, force; (*Arbeitskraft*) worker; **in ~ treten** to come into effect
Kraftausdruck *m* swearword
Kraftfahrzeug *nt* motor vehicle
Kraftfahrzeugbrief *m* (*Aut*) logbook (BRIT), motor-vehicle registration certificate (US)
Kraftfahrzeugschein *m* (*Aut*) car licence (BRIT) *od* license (US)
Kraftfahrzeugsteuer *f* ≈ road tax
kräftig *adj* strong; (*Suppe*, *Essen*) nourishing
Kraftstoff *m* fuel
Kraftwerk *nt* power station
Kragen (**-s**, **-**) *m* collar
Krähe (**-**, **-n**) *f* crow
Kralle (**-**, **-n**) *f* claw
Kram (**-(e)s**) *m* stuff
Krampf (**-(e)s**, **Krämpfe**) *m* cramp; (*zuckend*) spasm
Krampfader *f* varicose vein
Kran (**-(e)s**, **Kräne**) *m* crane
Kranich (**-s**, **-e**) *m* (*Zool*) crane
krank *adj* ill, sick
kränken *vt* to hurt
Krankengymnastik *f* physiotherapy
Krankenhaus *nt* hospital
Krankenkasse *f* health insurance
Krankenpfleger *m* male nurse
Krankenschein *m* medical insurance certificate
Krankenschwester *f* nurse
Krankenversicherung *f* health insurance
Krankenwagen *m* ambulance
Krankheit *f* illness; (*chronisch*) disease
Kränkung *f* insult
Kranz (**-es**, **Kränze**) *m* wreath
krass *adj* crass; (*Unterschied*) extreme
kratzen *vt*, *vi* to scratch
Kratzer (**-s**, **-**) *m* scratch
kraulen *vi* (*schwimmen*) to do the crawl ▸ *vt* (*streicheln*) to tickle
Kraut (**-(e)s**, **Kräuter**) *nt* plant; (*Gewürz*) herb; (*Gemüse*) cabbage
Kräuterbutter *f* herb butter
Kräutertee *m* herb tea
Krautsalat *m* coleslaw
Krawatte (**-**, **-n**) *f* tie
kreativ *adj* creative
Krebs (**-es**, **-e**) *m* crab; (*Med*) cancer; (*Astrol*) Cancer
Kredit (**-(e)s**, **-e**) *m* credit; (*Darlehen*) loan
Kreditkarte *f* credit card
Kreide (**-**, **-n**) *f* chalk
Kreis (**-es**, **-e**) *m* circle; (*Stadtkreis etc*) district
kreischen *vi* to shriek, to screech
Kreisel (**-s**, **-**) *m* top; (*Verkehrskreisel*) roundabout (BRIT), traffic circle (US)
Kreislauf *m* (*Med*) circulation; (*fig*: *der Natur etc*) cycle
Kreislaufstörungen *pl* circulation trouble *sing*
Kreisverkehr *m* roundabout (BRIT), traffic circle (US)
Kresse (**-**, **-n**) *f* cress
Kreuz (**-es**, **-e**) *nt* cross; (*Anat*) small of the back; (*Karten*) clubs
kreuzen *vt* to cross ▸ *vr* to cross ▸ *vi* (*Naut*) to cruise
Kreuzfahrt *f* cruise
Kreuzgang *m* cloisters *pl*
Kreuzotter *f* adder
Kreuzschmerzen *pl* backache *sing*
Kreuzung *f* (*Verkehrskreuzung*) crossing, junction; (*Züchtung*) cross
Kreuzworträtsel *nt* crossword puzzle
kriechen *unreg vi* to crawl, to creep; (*pej*) to crawl
Kriechspur *f* crawler lane (BRIT)
Krieg (**-(e)s**, **-e**) *m* war
kriegen (*umg*) *vt* to get; (*erwischen*) to catch
Krimi (**-s**, **-s**) (*umg*) *m* thriller
Kriminalität *f* criminality
Kriminalpolizei *f* ≈ Criminal Investigation Department (BRIT), ≈ Federal Bureau of Investigation (US)

Kriminalroman *m* detective story
kriminell *adj* criminal
Krippe (-, **-n**) *f* manger, crib; (*Kinderkrippe*) crèche
Krise (-, **-n**) *f* crisis
Kristall[1] (**-s**, **-e**) *m* crystal
Kristall[2] (**-s**) *nt* (*Glas*) crystal
Kritik *f* criticism; (*Zeitungskritik*) review
Kritiker(in) (**-s**, -) *m(f)* critic
kritisch *adj* critical
kritzeln *vt*, *vi* to scribble, to scrawl
Kroate (**-n**, **-n**) *m* Croat
Kroatien (**-s**) *nt* Croatia
Kroatin *f* Croat
kroatisch *adj* Croatian; (*Sprache*): **auf K~** in Croatian
kroch *etc vb siehe* **kriechen**
Krokodil (**-s**, **-e**) *nt* crocodile
Krokus (-, - *od* **-se**) *m* crocus
Krone (-, **-n**) *f* crown
Kronleuchter *m* chandelier
Kropf (**-(e)s**, **Kröpfe**) *m* (*Med*) goitre (BRIT), goiter (*US*); (*von Vogel*) crop
Kröte (-, **-n**) *f* toad
Krücke (-, **-n**) *f* crutch
Krug (**-(e)s**, **Krüge**) *m* jug; (*Bierkrug*) mug
Krümel (**-s**, -) *m* crumb
krumm *adj* crooked
Krüppel (**-s**, -) *m* cripple (*pej*)
Kruste (-, **-n**) *f* crust
Kruzifix (**-es**, **-e**) *nt* crucifix
Kuba (**-s**) *nt* Cuba
Kübel (**-s**, -) *m* tub; (*Eimer*) pail
Kubikmeter *m* cubic metre (BRIT) *od* meter (*US*)
Küche (-, **-n**) *f* kitchen; (*Kochen*) cooking
Kuchen (**-s**, -) *m* cake
Kuchengabel *f* pastry fork
Küchenmaschine *f* food processor
Küchenpapier *nt* kitchen roll
Küchenschrank *m* kitchen cabinet
Kuckuck (**-s**, **-e**) *m* cuckoo
Kugel (-, **-n**) *f* ball; (*Math*) sphere; (*Mil*) bullet
Kugellager *nt* ball bearing
Kugelschreiber *m* ball-point (pen), Biro®
Kugelstoßen (**-s**) *nt* shot put
Kuh (-, **Kühe**) *f* cow
kühl *adj* (*lit*, *fig*) cool
kühlen *vt* to cool
Kühler (**-s**, -) *m* (*Aut*) radiator
Kühlerhaube *f* (*Aut*) bonnet (BRIT), hood (*US*)
Kühlschrank *m* refrigerator
Kühltasche *f* cool bag
Kühltruhe *f* freezer
Kühlwasser *nt* coolant
Kuhstall *m* cow-shed
Küken (**-s**, -) *nt* chicken
Kuli (**-s**, **-s**) *m* (*umg*: *Kugelschreiber*) Biro®
Kulisse (-, **-n**) *f* scene
Kult (**-(e)s**, **-e**) *m* worship, cult
Kultur *f* culture; (*Lebensform*) civilization
Kulturbeutel *m* toilet bag (BRIT)
kulturell *adj* cultural
Kümmel (**-s**, -) *m* caraway seed
Kummer (**-s**) *m* grief, sorrow
kümmern *vr*: **sich um jdn ~** to look after sb ▶ *vt* to concern; **sich um etw ~** to see to sth; **das kümmert mich nicht** that doesn't worry me
Kumpel (**-s**, -) (*umg*) *m* mate
Kunde (**-n**, **-n**) *m* customer
Kundendienst *m* after-sales service
kündigen *vi* to give in one's notice ▶ *vt* to cancel; **jdm ~** to give sb his notice; **zum 1. April ~** to give one's notice for April 1st; (*Mieter*) to give notice for April 1st; **(jdm) die Stellung ~** to give (sb) notice
Kündigung *f* notice
Kündigungsfrist *f* period of notice
Kundin *f* customer
Kundschaft *f* customers *pl*
künftig *adj* future
Kunst (-, **Künste**) *f* (*auch Sch*) art; (*Können*) skill
Kunstgewerbe *nt* arts and crafts *pl*
Künstler(in) (**-s**, -) *m(f)* artist
künstlerisch *adj* artistic
künstlich *adj* artificial
Kunststoff *m* synthetic material
Kunststück *nt* trick
Kunstwerk *nt* work of art
Kupfer (**-s**, -) *nt* copper
Kuppel (-, **-n**) *f* dome
kuppeln *vi* (*Aut*) to operate *od* use the clutch
Kupplung *f* (*auch Tech*) coupling; (*Aut etc*) clutch
Kur (-, **-en**) *f* (course of) treatment; (*im Kurort*) (health) cure
Kür (-, **-en**) *f* (*Sport*) free exercises *pl*
Kurbel (-, **-n**) *f* crank, winder
Kürbis (**-ses**, **-se**) *m* pumpkin
kurieren *vt* to cure

Kurort *m* health resort
Kurs (**-es**, **-e**) *m* course; (*Fin*) rate
kursiv *adv* in italics
Kurswagen *m* (*Eisenb*) through carriage
Kurve (**-**, **-n**) *f* curve; (*Straßenkurve*) bend
kurvenreich *adj*: **„kurvenreiche Strecke"** "bends"
kurz *adj* short; **~ und gut** in short; **~ gefasst** concise; **darf ich mal ~ stören?** could I just interrupt for a moment?
kurzärmelig *adj* short-sleeved
kürzen *vt* to cut short; (*in der Länge*) to shorten; (*Gehalt*) to reduce
kurzerhand *adv* on the spot
kurzfristig *adj* short-term
Kurzgeschichte *f* short story
kürzlich *adv* lately, recently
Kurzschluss *m* (*Elek*) short circuit
kurzsichtig *adj* short-sighted
Kurzurlaub *m* short holiday (BRIT), short vacation (*US*)
Kurzwelle *f* short wave
Kusine *f* cousin
Kuss (**-es**, **Küsse**) *m* kiss
küssen *vt*, *vr* to kiss
Küste (**-**, **-n**) *f* coast, shore
Küstenwache *f* coastguard (station)
Kutsche (**-**, **-n**) *f* coach, carriage
Kuvert (**-s**, **-e** *od* **-s**) *nt* envelope
Kuwait (**-s**) *nt* Kuwait
KZ (**-s**, **-s**) *nt abk* = **Konzentrationslager**

l

Labor (**-s**, **-e** *od* **-s**) *nt* lab
Labyrinth (**-s**, **-e**) *nt* labyrinth
Lache (**-**, **-n**) *f* (*Wasser*) pool, puddle
lächeln *vi* to smile
Lächeln (**-s**) *nt* smile
lachen *vi* to laugh
lächerlich *adj* ridiculous
Lachs (**-es**, **-e**) *m* salmon
Lack (**-(e)s**, **-e**) *m* lacquer, varnish; (*von Auto*) paint
lackieren *vt* to varnish; (*Auto*) to spray
Ladegerät *nt* (battery) charger
laden *unreg vt* (*Lasten*, *Comput*) to load; (*Handy etc*) to charge; (*einladen*) to invite
Laden (**-s**, **Läden**) *m* shop; (*Fensterladen*) shutter
Ladendieb(in) *m(f)* shoplifter
Ladendiebstahl *m* shoplifting
Ladenschluss *m* closing time
Ladung *f* (*Last*) load; (*Naut*, *Aviat*) cargo; (*Jur*) summons
lag *etc vb siehe* **liegen**
Lage (**-**, **-n**) *f* position, situation; (*Schicht*) layer; **in der ~ sein** to be in a position
Lager (**-s**, **-**) *nt* camp; (*Comm*) warehouse; (*Tech*) bearing
Lagerfeuer *nt* camp fire
lagern *vi* (*Dinge*) to be stored; (*Menschen*) to camp ▶ *vt* to store
Lagune (**-**, **-n**) *f* lagoon
lahm *adj* lame; (*umg*: *langsam*, *langweilig*) dull
lähmen, lahmlegen *vt* to paralyse (BRIT), to paralyze (*US*)
Lähmung *f* paralysis

Laib (**-s**, **-e**) *m* loaf
Laie (**-n**, **-n**) *m* layman
Laken (**-s**, **-**) *nt* sheet
Lakritze (**-**, **-n**) *f* liquorice
Lamm (**-(e)s**, **Lämmer**) *nt* lamb
Lampe (**-**, **-n**) *f* lamp
Lampenfieber *nt* stage fright
Lampenschirm *m* lampshade
Lampion (**-s**, **-s**) *m* Chinese lantern
Land (**-(e)s**, **Länder**) *nt* land; (*Nation, nicht Stadt*) country; (*Bundesland*) state; **auf dem ~(e)** in the country

LAND

The Federal Republic of Germany is divided into 16 **Länder**, namely Baden-Württemberg, Bayern, Berlin, Brandenburg, Bremen, Hamburg, Hessen, Mecklenburg-Vorpommern, Niedersachsen, Nordrhein-Westfalen, Rheinland-Pfalz, Saarland, Sachsen, Sachsen-Anhalt, Schleswig-Holstein and Thüringen. Each *Land* has its own parliament and constitution.

Landebahn *f* runway
landen *vt*, *vi* to land
Länderspiel *nt* international (match)
Landesgrenze *f* (national) frontier
Landesinnere(s) *nt* inland region
landesüblich *adj* customary
Landeswährung *f* national currency
landesweit *adj* countrywide
Landhaus *nt* country house
Landkarte *f* map
Landkreis *m* administrative region
ländlich *adj* rural
Landschaft *f* countryside; (*Kunst*) landscape
Landstraße *f* country road
Landung *f* landing
Landungsbrücke *f* jetty, pier
Landwirt(in) *m(f)* farmer
Landwirtschaft *f* agriculture
landwirtschaftlich *adj* agricultural
lang *adj* long; (*umg: Mensch*) tall ▶ *adv*: **~ anhaltender Beifall** prolonged applause; **den ganzen Tag ~** all day long; **die Straße ~** along the street
lange *adv* for a long time; (*dauern, brauchen*) a long time; **ich bleibe nicht ~** I won't stay long
Länge (**-**, **-n**) *f* length; (*Geog*) longitude
langen *vi* (*ausreichen*) to do, to suffice; (*fassen*): **~ nach** to reach for; **es langt mir** I've had enough
Langeweile *f* boredom
langfristig *adj* long-term ▶ *adv* in the long term
Langlauf *m* (*Ski*) cross-country skiing
längs *präp* (*+gen od dat*) along ▶ *adv* lengthways
langsam *adj* slow
Langschläfer *m* late riser
längst *adv*: **das ist ~ fertig** that was finished a long time ago
Langstreckenflug *m* long-haul flight
Languste (**-**, **-n**) *f* crayfish, crawfish (*US*)
langweilen *vt untr* to bore ▶ *vr untr* to be *od* get bored
langweilig *adj* boring
Langwelle *f* long wave
Laos (**-**) *nt* Laos
Lappen (**-s**, **-**) *m* cloth, rag
läppisch *adj* silly; (*Summe*) ridiculous
Laptop (**-s**, **-s**) *m* laptop
Lärche (**-**, **-n**) *f* larch
Lärm (**-(e)s**) *m* noise
las *etc vb siehe* **lesen**
Lasche (**-**, **-n**) *f* flap; (*Schuhlasche*) tongue
Laser (**-s**, **-**) *m* laser
Laserdrucker *m* laser printer

SCHLÜSSELWORT

lassen (*pt* **ließ**, *pp* **gelassen** *od als Hilfsverb* **lassen**) *vt* **1** (*unterlassen*) to stop; (*: momentan*) to leave; **lass das (sein)!** don't (do it)!; (*hör auf*) stop it!; **lass mich!** leave me alone!; **lassen wir das!** let's leave it; **er kann das Trinken nicht lassen** he can't stop drinking
2 (*zurücklassen*) to leave; **etw lassen, wie es ist** to leave sth (just) as it is
3 (*erlauben*) to let, to allow; **jdn ins Haus lassen** to let sb into the house
▶ *vi*: **lass mal, ich mache das schon** leave it, I'll do it
▶ *Hilfsverb* **1** (*veranlassen*): **etw machen lassen** to have *od* get sth done; **sich** *dat* **etw schicken lassen** to have sth sent (to one)
2 (*zulassen*): **jdn etw wissen lassen** to let sb know sth; **das Licht brennen lassen** to leave the light on
3: **lass uns gehen** let's go
▶ *vr*: **das lässt sich machen** that can be done

lässig *adj* casual
Last (**-**, **-en**) *f* load; (*Traglast*) burden; (*Naut, Aviat*) cargo
Laster (**-s**, **-**) *nt* vice ▸ *m* (*umg*) lorry (BRIT), truck
lästern *vt, vi* (*Gott*) to blaspheme; (*schlecht sprechen*) to mock; **über jdn/etw ~** to make nasty remarks about sb/sth
lästig *adj* troublesome, tiresome
Lastkraftwagen *m* heavy goods vehicle
Lastwagen *m* lorry (BRIT), truck
Latein (**-s**) *nt* Latin
Laterne (**-**, **-n**) *f* lantern; (*Straßenlaterne*) lamp, light
Latte (**-**, **-n**) *f* lath; crossbar; (*Sport*) goalpost
Latz (**-es**, **Lätze**) *m* bib
Lätzchen *nt* bib
Latzhose *f* dungarees *pl*
lau *adj* (*Nacht*) balmy; (*Wasser*) lukewarm
Laub (**-(e)s**) *nt* foliage
Laubfrosch *m* tree frog
Laubsäge *f* fretsaw
Lauch (**-(e)s**, **-e**) *m* leek
Lauf (**-(e)s**, **Läufe**) *m* run; (*Wettlauf*) race; (*Entwicklung, Astron*) course; (*Gewehrlauf*) barrel
Laufbahn *f* career
laufen *unreg vi* to run; (*umg: gehen*) to walk; (*funktionieren*) to work; (*gezeigt werden: Film, Stück*) to be on ▸ *vt* to run; **ihm läuft die Nase** he's got a runny nose
laufend *adj* running; (*Monat, Ausgaben*) current; **auf dem Laufenden sein/halten** to be/keep up to date
Läufer (**-s**, **-**) *m* (*Teppich*) rug; (*Sport*) runner; (*Schach*) bishop
Läuferin *f* (*Sport*) runner
Laufmasche *f* run, ladder (BRIT)
Laufwerk *nt* (*Comput*) drive
Laune (**-**, **-n**) *f* mood, humour (BRIT), humor (*US*); (*schlechte Laune*) temper
launisch *adj* moody
Laus (**-**, **Läuse**) *f* louse
lauschen *vi* to listen; (*heimlich*) to eavesdrop
laut *adj* loud ▸ *adv* loudly; (*lesen*) aloud ▸ *präp* (*+gen od dat*) according to
läuten *vt, vi* to ring
lauter *adv* (*nur*) nothing but
Lautsprecher *m* loudspeaker
Lautstärke *f* (*Rundf*) volume
lauwarm *adj* lukewarm
Lava (**-**, **Laven**) *f* lava
Lavendel (**-s**, **-**) *m* lavender
Lawine *f* avalanche
leasen *vt* to lease
Leasing (**-s**, **-s**) *nt* (*Comm*) leasing
leben *vt, vi* to live
Leben (**-s**, **-**) *nt* life
lebend *adj* living
lebendig *adj* living, alive; (*lebhaft*) lively
lebensgefährlich *adj* dangerous; (*Krankheit, Verletzung*) critical
Lebensgefährte *m*, **Lebensgefährtin** *f* partner
Lebenshaltungskosten *pl* cost of living *sing*
lebenslänglich *adj* for life; **~ bekommen** to get life
Lebenslauf *m* curriculum vitae (BRIT), CV (BRIT), resumé (*US*)
Lebensmittel *pl* food *sing*
Lebensmittelgeschäft *nt* grocer's
Lebensmittelvergiftung *f* food poisoning
Lebensretter *m* lifesaver
Lebensstandard *m* standard of living
Lebensunterhalt *m* livelihood
Lebensversicherung *f* life insurance
Lebenszeichen *nt* sign of life
Leber (**-**, **-n**) *f* liver
Leberfleck *m* mole
Leberpastete *f* liver pâté
Lebewesen *nt* creature
lebhaft *adj* lively, vivacious
Lebkuchen *m* gingerbread
leblos *adj* lifeless
Leck (**-(e)s**, **-e**) *nt* leak
lecken[1] *vi* (*Loch haben*) to leak
lecken[2] *vt, vi* (*schlecken*) to lick
lecker *adj* delicious, tasty
Leder (**-s**, **-**) *nt* leather
ledig *adj* single
leer *adj* empty
leeren *vt* to empty ▸ *vr* to (become) empty
Leerlauf *m* (*Aut*) neutral
Leertaste *f* space-bar
Leerung *f* emptying; (*Post*) collection
legal *adj* legal, lawful
legen *vt* to put, to place; (*Ei*) to lay ▸ *vr* to lie down; (*fig*) to subside
Legende (**-**, **-n**) *f* legend
leger *adj* casual

Lehm (**-(e)s**, **-e**) *m* loam
Lehne (**-**, **-n**) *f* arm; (*Rückenlehne*) back
lehnen *vt*, *vr* to lean
Lehnstuhl *m* armchair
Lehrbuch *nt* textbook
Lehre (**-**, **-n**) *f* teaching; (*beruflich*) apprenticeship; (*moralisch*) lesson
lehren *vt* to teach
Lehrer(in) (**-s**, **-**) *m(f)* teacher
Lehrgang *m* course
Lehrling *m* apprentice
lehrreich *adj* instructive
Leib (**-(e)s**, **-er**) *m* body
Leibgericht *nt* favourite (BRIT) *od* favorite (US) meal
Leiche (**-**, **-n**) *f* corpse
Leichenhalle *f* mortuary
Leichenwagen *m* hearse
leicht *adj* light; (*einfach*) easy ▶ *adv*: **es sich** *dat* **~ machen** to make things easy for o.s.; (*nicht gewissenhaft sein*) to take the easy way out; **~ verletzt** slightly injured
Leichtathletik *f* athletics *sing*
leicht|fallen *unreg vi*: **jdm ~** to be easy for sb
leichtsinnig *adj* careless
leid *adj*: **etw ~ haben** *od* **sein** to be tired of sth; *siehe auch* **leidtun**
Leid (**-(e)s**) *nt* grief, sorrow
leiden *unreg vt* to suffer; **jdn/etw nicht ~ können** not to be able to stand sb/sth ▶ *vi* to suffer
Leiden (**-s**, **-**) *nt* suffering; (*Krankheit*) complaint
Leidenschaft *f* passion
leidenschaftlich *adj* passionate
leider *adv* unfortunately; **ja, ~** yes, I'm afraid so; **~ nicht** I'm afraid not
leid|tun *unreg vi*: **es tut mir/ihm leid** I am/he is sorry; **er/das tut mir leid** I am sorry for him/about it
leihen *unreg vt* to lend; **sich** *dat* **etw ~** to borrow sth
Leihgebühr *f* hire charge
Leihmutterschaft *f* surrogacy, surrogate motherhood
Leihwagen *m* hired car (BRIT), rental car (US)
Leim (**-(e)s**, **-e**) *m* glue
Leine (**-**, **-n**) *f* cord; (*für Wäsche*) line; (*Hundeleine*) leash, lead
Leinen (**-s**, **-**) *nt* linen
Leintuch *nt* linen cloth; (*Bettuch*) sheet
Leinwand *f* (*Kunst*) canvas; (*Film*) screen
leise *adj* quiet; (*sanft*) soft
Leiste (**-**, **-n**) *f* ledge; (*Zierleiste*) strip; (*Anat*) groin
leisten *vt* (*Arbeit*) to do; (*Gesellschaft*) to keep; (*vollbringen*) to achieve; **sich** *dat* **etw ~** to allow o.s. sth; (*sich gönnen*) to treat o.s. to sth; **sich** *dat* **etw ~ können** to be able to afford sth
Leistenbruch *m* (*Med*) hernia
Leistung *f* performance; (*gute*) achievement
Leitartikel *m* leader
leiten *vt* to lead; (*Firma*) to manage; (*in eine Richtung*) to direct; (*Elek*) to conduct
Leiter[1] (**-s**, **-**) *m* leader, head
Leiter[2] (**-**, **-n**) *f* ladder
Leiterin *f* leader, head
Leitplanke *f* crash barrier
Leitung *f* (*Führung*) direction; (*von Firma*) management; (*Wasserleitung*) pipe; (*Kabel*) cable; (*Tel*) line; **eine lange ~ haben** to be slow on the uptake
Leitungswasser *nt* tap water
Lektion *f* lesson
Lektüre (**-**, **-n**) *f* (*Lesen*) reading; (*Lesestoff*) reading matter
Lende (**-**, **-n**) *f* loin
lenken *vt* to steer; **~ auf** *+akk* (*Blick, Aufmerksamkeit*) to direct at
Lenker *m* (*von Fahrrad, Motorrad*) handlebars *pl*
Lenkrad *nt* steering wheel
Lenkstange *f* handlebars *pl*
Leopard (**-en**, **-en**) *m* leopard
Lepra (**-**) *f* leprosy
Lerche (**-**, **-n**) *f* lark
lernen *vt*, *vi* to learn
Lernplattform *f* VLE (= *virtual learning environment*)
lesbisch *adj* lesbian
Lesebuch *nt* reader
lesen *unreg vt* to read; (*ernten*) to pick ▶ *vi* to read
Leser(in) (**-s**, **-**) *m(f)* reader
Leserbrief *m* reader's letter
leserlich *adj* legible
Lesezeichen *nt* bookmark
Lettland (**-s**) *nt* Latvia
letzte(r, s) *adj* last; (*neueste*) latest; **zum letzten Mal** for the last time; **in letzter Zeit** recently

letztens *adv* lately
letztere(r, s) *adj* the latter
Leuchte (-, **-n**) *f* lamp, light
leuchten *vi* to shine, to gleam
Leuchter (**-s**, -) *m* candlestick
Leuchtfarbe *f* fluorescent colour (BRIT) *od* color (*US*)
Leuchtreklame *f* neon sign
Leuchtturm *m* lighthouse
leugnen *vt, vi* to deny
Leukämie *f* leukaemia (BRIT), leukemia (*US*)
Leute *pl* people *pl*
Lexikon (**-s**, **Lexiken** *od* **Lexika**) *nt* encyclopaedia (BRIT), encyclopedia (*US*); (*Wörterbuch*) dictionary
Libanon (**-s**) *m*: **der ~** the Lebanon
Libelle (-, **-n**) *f* dragonfly
liberal *adj* liberal
Libyen (**-s**) *nt* Libya
Licht (**-(e)s**, **-er**) *nt* light
Lichtblick *m* cheering prospect
lichtempfindlich *adj* sensitive to light
Lichthupe *f*: **die ~ betätigen** to flash one's lights
Lichtjahr *nt* light year
Lichtmaschine *f* dynamo
Lichtschalter *m* light switch
Lichtschutzfaktor *m* sun protection factor, SPF
Lichtung *f* clearing
Lichtverschmutzung *f* light pollution
Lid (**-(e)s**, **-er**) *nt* eyelid
Lidschatten *m* eyeshadow
lieb *adj* dear; **Liebe Anna, lieber Klaus! ...** Dear Anna and Klaus, ...; **am liebsten lese ich Kriminalromane** best of all I like detective novels
Liebe (-, **-n**) *f* love
lieben *vt* to love
liebenswürdig *adj* kind
lieber *adv* rather; **ich gehe ~ nicht** I'd rather not go; **ich trinke ~ Wein als Bier** I prefer wine to beer
Liebesbrief *m* love letter
Liebeskummer *m*: **~ haben** to be lovesick
Liebespaar *nt* lovers *pl*
liebevoll *adj* loving
Liebhaber(in) (**-s**, -) *m(f)* lover
lieblich *adj* lovely; (*Duft, Wein*) sweet
Liebling *m* darling
Lieblings- *in zW* favourite (BRIT), favorite (*US*)
liebste(r, s) *adj* favourite
Liechtenstein (**-s**) *nt* Liechtenstein
Lied (**-(e)s**, **-er**) *nt* song; (*Eccl*) hymn
lief *etc vb siehe* **laufen**
Lieferant *m* supplier
lieferbar *adj* available
liefern *vt* to deliver; (*versorgen mit*) to supply
Lieferschein *m* delivery note
Lieferung *f* delivery
Lieferwagen *m* (delivery) van, panel truck (*US*)
Liege (-, **-n**) *f* bed; (*Campingliege*) camp bed (BRIT), cot (*US*)
liegen *unreg vi* to lie; (*sich befinden*) to be (situated); **mir liegt nichts/viel daran** it doesn't matter to me/it matters a lot to me; **woran liegt es?** what's the cause?; **~ bleiben** (*Person*) to stay in bed; (*nicht aufstehen*) to stay lying down; (*Ding*) to be left (behind); **~ lassen** (*vergessen*) to leave behind
Liegestuhl *m* deck chair
Liegestütz *m* (*Sport*) press-up (BRIT), push-up (*US*)
Liegewagen *m* (*Eisenb*) couchette car
lieh *etc vb siehe* **leihen**
ließ *etc vb siehe* **lassen**
Lift (**-(e)s**, **-e** *od* **-s**) *m* lift
Liga (-, **Ligen**) *f* (*Sport*) league
light *adj* (*Cola*) diet; (*fettarm*) low-fat; (*kalorienarm*) low-calorie; (*Zigaretten*) mild
Likör (**-s**, **-e**) *m* liqueur
lila *adj unver* purple
Lilie *f* lily
Limonade (-, **-n**) *f* lemonade
Limousine (-, **-n**) *f* saloon (car) (BRIT), sedan (*US*); (*umg*) limo
Linde (-, **-n**) *f* lime tree
lindern *vt* to alleviate, to soothe
Lineal (**-s**, **-e**) *nt* ruler
Linie *f* line
Linienflug *m* scheduled flight
linieren, liniieren *vt* to line
Link (**-s**, **-s**) *m* (*Comput*) link
linke(r, s) *adj* left
Linke (-, **-n**) *f* left side; (*linke Hand*) left hand; (*Pol*) left
links *adv* to the left; **~ von mir** on *od* to my left
Linkshänder(in) (**-s**, -) *m(f)* left-handed person
Linksverkehr *m* driving on the left

Linse (-, **-n**) *f* lentil; (*optisch*) lens
Lippe (-, **-n**) *f* lip
Lippenstift *m* lipstick
lispeln *vi* to lisp
List (-, **-en**) *f* cunning; (*Plan*) trick
Liste (-, **-n**) *f* list
Litauen (**-s**) *nt* Lithuania
Liter (**-s**, **-**) *m od nt* litre (BRIT), liter (*US*)
literarisch *adj* literary
Literatur *f* literature
Litschi (-, **-s**) *f* lychee, litchi
litt *etc vb siehe* **leiden**
live *adj, adv* (*Rundf, TV*) live
Lizenz *f* licence (BRIT), license (*US*)
Lkw, LKW (**-(s)**, **-(s)**) *m abk* = **Lastkraftwagen**
Lkw-Maut, LKW-Maut *f* toll for trucks
Lob (**-(e)s**) *nt* praise
loben *vt* to praise
Loch (**-(e)s**, **Löcher**) *nt* hole
lochen *vt* to punch holes in
Locher (**-s**, **-**) *m* punch
Locke (-, **-n**) *f* curl
locken *vt* to entice; (*Haare*) to curl
Lockenwickler (**-s**, **-**) *m* curler
locker *adj* loose; (*Haltung*) relaxed; (*Person*) easy-going
lockern *vt* to loosen ▶ *vr* (*Atmosphäre*) to get more relaxed
lockig *adj* curly
Löffel (**-s**, **-**) *m* spoon
log *etc vb siehe* **lügen**
Loge (-, **-n**) *f* (*Theat*) box
logisch *adj* logical
Lohn (**-(e)s**, **Löhne**) *m* reward; (*Arbeitslohn*) pay, wages *pl*
lohnen *vr unpers* to be worth it
Lohnerhöhung *f* wage increase, pay rise
Lohnsteuer *f* income tax
Lokal (**-(e)s**, **-e**) *nt* pub(lic house) (BRIT), bar
Lokomotive (-, **-n**) *f* locomotive
London (**-s**) *nt* London
Lorbeer (**-s**, **-en**) *m* laurel
Lorbeerblatt *nt* (*Koch*) bay leaf
los *adj* loose ▶ *adv*: **~!** go on!; **etw ~ sein** to be rid of sth; **was ist ~?** what's the matter?; **dort ist nichts/ viel ~** there's nothing/a lot going on there
Los (**-es**, **-e**) *nt* (*Schicksal*) lot, fate; (*in Lotterie*) lottery ticket
los|binden *unreg vt* to untie
löschen *vt* (*Feuer, Licht*) to put out, to extinguish; (*Durst*) to quench; (*Tonband*) to erase; (*Comput*) to delete
Löschtaste *f* (*Comput*) delete key
lose *adj* loose
Lösegeld *nt* ransom
losen *vi* to draw lots
lösen *vt* to loosen; (*Rätsel etc*) to solve; (*Chem*) to dissolve; (*Fahrkarte*) to buy ▶ *vr* (*aufgehen*) to come loose; (*Zucker etc*) to dissolve; (*Problem, Schwierigkeit*) to (re)solve itself
los|fahren *unreg vi* to leave
los|gehen *unreg vi* to set out; (*anfangen*) to start
los|lassen *unreg vt* (*Seil etc*) to let go of
löslich *adj* soluble
Lösung *f* (*eines Rätsels, Chem*) solution
los|werden *unreg vt* to get rid of
Lotterie *f* lottery
Lotto (**-s**, **-s**) *nt* ≈ National Lottery
Löwe (**-n**, **-n**) *m* lion; (*Astrol*) Leo
Löwenzahn *m* dandelion
Luchs (**-es**, **-e**) *m* lynx
Lücke (-, **-n**) *f* gap
Lückenbüßer (**-s**, **-**) *m* stopgap
lud *etc vb siehe* **laden**
Luft (-, **Lüfte**) *f* air; (*Atem*) breath
Luftballon *m* balloon
Luftblase *f* air bubble
luftdicht *adj* airtight
Luftdruck *m* atmospheric pressure
lüften *vt* to air; (*Geheimnis*) to reveal
Luftfahrt *f* aviation
Luftfeuchtigkeit *f* humidity
Luftfracht *f* air cargo
Luftkissenboot *nt*, **Luftkissenfahrzeug** *nt* hovercraft
Luftlinie *f*: **in der ~** as the crow flies
Luftmatratze *f* air mattress
Luftpirat *m* hijacker
Luftpost *f* airmail
Luftpumpe *f* (bicycle) pump
Luftröhre *f* (*Anat*) windpipe
Lüftung *f* ventilation
Luftveränderung *f* change of air
Luftverschmutzung *f* air pollution
Luftwaffe *f* air force
Luftzug *m* draught (BRIT), draft (*US*)
Lüge (-, **-n**) *f* lie
lügen *unreg vi* to lie
Lügner(in) (**-s**, **-**) *m(f)* liar
Luke (-, **-n**) *f* hatch
Lumpen (**-s**, **-**) *m* rag
Lunge (-, **-n**) *f* lung

Lungenentzündung *f* pneumonia
Lupe (**-**, **-n**) *f* magnifying glass; **unter die ~ nehmen** (*fig*) to scrutinize
Lust (**-**, **Lüste**) *f* joy, delight; (*Neigung*) desire; **~ haben zu** *od* **auf etw** *akk*/ **etw zu tun** to feel like sth/doing sth
lustig *adj* (*komisch*) amusing, funny; (*fröhlich*) cheerful
lutschen *vt, vi* to suck; **am Daumen ~** to suck one's thumb
Lutscher (**-s**, **-**) *m* lollipop
Luxemburg (**-s**) *nt* Luxembourg
luxuriös *adj* luxurious
Luxus (-) *m* luxury
Lymphknoten *m* lymph(atic) gland
Lyrik *f* lyric poetry

machbar *adj* feasible

SCHLÜSSELWORT

machen *vt* **1** to do; **was machst du da?** what are you doing there?; **das ist nicht zu machen** that can't be done
2 : **das Radio leiser machen** to turn the radio down; **aus Holz gemacht** made of wood; **Schluss machen** to finish (off)
3 (*verursachen: bewirken*) to make; **jdm Angst machen** to make sb afraid; **das macht die Kälte** it's the cold that does that
4 (*ausmachen*) to matter; **das macht nichts** that doesn't matter; **die Kälte macht mir nichts** I don't mind the cold
5 (*kosten, ergeben*) to be; **3 und 5 macht 8** 3 and 5 is *od* are 8; **was** *od* **wie viel macht das?** how much does that come to?
6: **was macht die Arbeit?** how's the work going?; **was macht dein Bruder?** how is your brother doing?; **das Auto machen lassen** to have the car done; **machs gut!** take care!; (*viel Glück*) good luck!
▸ *vi*: **mach schnell!** hurry up!; **mach schon!** come on!; **das macht müde** it makes you tired; **in etw** *dat* **machen** to be *od* deal in sth
▸ *vr* to come along (nicely); **sich an etw** *akk* **machen** to set about sth; **sich verständlich machen** to make o.s. understood; **sich** *dat* **viel aus jdm/etw machen** to like sb/sth

Macho (*umg*) *adj* macho
Macht (-, **Mächte**) *f* power
mächtig *adj* powerful; (*umg*: *ungeheuer*) enormous
machtlos *adj* powerless
Mädchen *nt* girl
Mädchenname *m* maiden name
Made (-, **-n**) *f* maggot
Magazin (**-s**, **-e**) *nt* magazine
Magen (**-s**, **-** *od* **Mägen**) *m* stomach
Magenband (**-(e)s**, **-bänder**) *nt* gastric band
Magenbeschwerden *pl* stomach trouble *sing*
Magengeschwür *nt* stomach ulcer
Magenschmerzen *pl* stomach-ache *sing*
mager *adj* lean; (*dünn*) thin; (*Käse, Joghurt*) low-fat
Magermilch *f* skimmed milk
Magersucht *f* (*Med*) anorexia
magersüchtig *adj* anorexic
magisch *adj* magical
Magnet (**-s** *od* **-en**, **-en**) *m* magnet
mähen *vt*, *vi* to mow
mahlen *unreg vt* to grind
Mahlzeit *f* meal ▶ *interj* enjoy your meal!
Mähne (-, **-n**) *f* mane
mahnen *vt* to remind; (*warnend*) to warn
Mahngebühr *f* reminder fee
Mahnung *f* warning; (*Mahnbrief*) reminder
Mai (**-(e)s**, **-e**) (*pl selten*) *m* May; *siehe auch* **September**
Maiglöckchen *nt* lily of the valley
Maikäfer *m* cockchafer
Mail (-, **-s**) *f* (*Comput*) email
mailen *vi*, *vt* to email
Mais (**-es**, **-e**) *m* maize, corn (*US*)
Maiskolben *m* corncob
Majestät *f* majesty
Majonäse (-, **-n**) *f* mayonnaise
Majoran (**-s**, **-e**) *m* marjoram
makaber *adj* macabre
Make-up (**-s**, **-s**) *nt* make-up
Makler(in) (**-s**, **-**) *m(f)* broker; (*Grundstücksmakler*) estate agent (Brit), realtor (*US*)
Makrele (-, **-n**) *f* mackerel
Makrone (-, **-n**) *f* macaroon
mal *adv* times
Mal (**-(e)s**, **-e**) *nt* (*Markierung*) mark; (*Zeitpunkt*) time; **das erste ~** the first time; **jedes ~** every time; **ein paar ~** a few times
Malaysia (**-s**) *nt* Malaysia
Malediven *pl*: **die ~** the Maldive Islands
malen *vt*, *vi* to paint
Maler(in) (**-s**, **-**) *m(f)* painter
Malerei *f* painting
malerisch *adj* picturesque
Mallorca (**-s**) *nt* Majorca
mal|nehmen *unreg vt*, *vi* to multiply
Malta (**-s**) *nt* Malta
Malware *f* (*Comput*) malware
Malz (**-es**) *nt* malt
Mama (-, **-s**) (*umg*) *f* mum(my) (Brit), mom(my) (*US*)
man *pron* one, you, people *pl*; **wie schreibt ~ das?** how do you spell that?
managen *vt* to manage
Manager(in) (**-s**, **-**) *m(f)* manager
manche(r, s) *adj* many a; (*pl*) a number of ▶ *pron* some
manchmal *adv* sometimes
Mandant(in) *m(f)* (*Jur*) client
Mandarine *f* mandarin, tangerine
Mandel (-, **-n**) *f* almond; (*Anat*) tonsil
Mandelentzündung *f* tonsillitis
Manege (-, **-n**) *f* ring
Mangel (**-s**, **Mängel**) *m* lack; (*Knappheit*) shortage; (*Fehler*) defect, fault; **~ an** *+dat* shortage of
mangelhaft *adj* poor; (*fehlerhaft*) faulty; (*Schulnote*) unsatisfactory
Manieren *pl* manners *pl*
Maniküre (-, **-n**) *f* manicure
manipulieren *vt* to manipulate
Manko (**-s**, **-s**) *nt* deficiency
Mann (**-(e)s**, **Männer**) *m* man; (*Ehemann*) husband
Männchen *nt* (*Tier*) male
männlich *adj* (*Biol*) male; (*fig*, *Gram*) masculine
Mannschaft *f* (*Sport*, *fig*) team; (*Naut*, *Aviat*) crew
Mansarde (-, **-n**) *f* attic
Manschettenknopf *m* cufflink
Mantel (**-s**, **Mäntel**) *m* coat; (*Tech*) casing, jacket
Mappe (-, **-n**) *f* briefcase; (*Aktenmappe*) folder
Märchen *nt* fairy tale
Marder (**-s**, **-**) *m* marten
Margarine *f* margarine
Marienkäfer *m* ladybird
Marihuana (**-s**) *nt* marijuana

Marinade (-, **-n**) *f* (*Koch*) marinade
Marine *f* navy
marinieren *vt* to marinate
Marionette *f* puppet
Mark (**-(e)s**) *nt* (*Knochenmark*) marrow
Marke (-, **-n**) *f* mark; (*Warensorte*) brand; (*Fabrikat*) make; (*Rabattmarke, Briefmarke*) stamp; (*Essen(s)marke*) luncheon voucher; (*aus Metall etc*) disc
Markenartikel *m* proprietary article
Markenzeichen *nt* trademark
markieren *vt* to mark
Markierung *f* marking
Markise (-, **-n**) *f* awning
Markt (**-(e)s, Märkte**) *m* market; **auf den ~ bringen** to launch
Markthalle *f* covered market
Marktlücke *f* gap in the market
Marktplatz *m* market place
Marktwirtschaft *f* market economy
Marmelade (-, **-n**) *f* jam
Marmor (**-s, -e**) *m* marble
Marmorkuchen *m* marble cake
Marokko (**-s**) *nt* Morocco
Marone (-, **-n**) *f* chestnut
Marsch (**-(e)s, Märsche**) *m* march
Märtyrer(in) (**-s, -**) *m(f)* martyr
März (**-(es), -e**) (*pl selten*) *m* March; *siehe auch* **September**
Marzipan (**-s, -e**) *nt* marzipan
Maschine *f* machine; (*Motor*) engine
maschinell *adj* machine(-), mechanical
Maschinenbau *m* mechanical engineering
Masern *pl* (*Med*) measles *sing*
Maske (-, **-n**) *f* mask
Maskenball *m* fancy-dress ball
maskieren *vr* to disguise o.s.; (*verkleiden*) to dress up
Maskottchen *nt* (lucky) mascot
maß *etc vb siehe* **messen**
Maß[1] (**-es, -e**) *nt* measure; (*Mäßigung*) moderation; (*Grad*) degree, extent; **in besonderem Maße** especially; **das ~ ist voll** (*fig*) that's enough (of that)
Maß[2] (-, **-(e)**) *f* litre (BRIT) *od* liter (US) of beer
Massage (-, **-n**) *f* massage
Masse (-, **-n**) *f* mass; **eine ganze ~** (*umg*) a great deal
Massendaten *pl* (*Comput*) mass data
massenhaft *adj* masses of
Massenmedien *pl* mass media *pl*
Massenproduktion *f* mass production
Masseur *m* masseur
Masseurin *f* masseuse
maßgeschneidert *adj* (*Anzug*) made-to-measure
massieren *vt* to massage
mäßig *adj* moderate
massiv *adj* solid; (*fig*) massive
maßlos *adj* extreme
Maßnahme (-, **-n**) *f* measure, step
Maßstab *m* rule, measure; (*fig*) standard; (*Geog*) scale
Mast (**-(e)s, -e(n)**) *m* mast; (*Elek*) pylon
Material (**-s, -ien**) *nt* material; (*Arbeitsmaterial*) materials *pl*
materialistisch *adj* materialistic
Materie *f* matter
materiell *adj* material
Mathe (-) *f* (*Sch: umg*) maths (BRIT), math (US)
Mathematik *f* mathematics *sing*
Mathematiker(in) (**-s, -**) *m(f)* mathematician
Matratze (-, **-n**) *f* mattress
Matrose (**-n, -n**) *m* sailor
Matsch (**-(e)s**) *m* mud; (*Schneematsch*) slush
matschig *adj* muddy; (*Schnee*) slushy
matt *adj* weak; (*glanzlos*) dull; (*Phot*) matt; (*Schach*) mate
Matte (-, **-n**) *f* mat
Matura (-) (ÖSTERR, SCHWEIZ) *f* *Austrian school-leaving examination*, ≈ A-levels (BRIT), ≈ High School Diploma (US)
Mauer (-, **-n**) *f* wall
Maul (**-(e)s, Mäuler**) *nt* mouth; **halts ~!** (*umg*) shut your face! (!)
Maulesel *m* mule
Maulkorb *m* muzzle
Maul- und Klauenseuche *f* (*Tiere*) foot-and-mouth disease
Maulwurf *m* mole
Maurer(in) (**-s, -**) *m(f)* bricklayer
Maus (-, **Mäuse**) *f* (*auch Comput*) mouse
Mausefalle *f* mousetrap
Mausklick *nt* (*Comput*) (mouse) click
Maustaste *f* mouse key *od* button
Maut (-, **-en**) *f* toll
maximal *adj* maximum
Mayonnaise (-, **-n**) *f* mayonnaise
Mazedonien (**-s**) *nt* Macedonia

Mechanik *f* mechanics *sing*; (*Getriebe*) mechanics *pl*
Mechaniker(in) (**-s**, **-**) *m(f)* mechanic
mechanisch *adj* mechanical
Mechanismus *m* mechanism
meckern *vi* to bleat; (*umg*) to moan
Mecklenburg-Vorpommern (**-s**) *nt* (state of) Mecklenburg-Vorpommern
Medaille (-, **-n**) *f* medal
Medien *pl* media *pl*
Medikament *nt* medicine
Meditation *f* meditation
meditieren *vi* to meditate
Medizin (-, **-en**) *f* medicine
medizinisch *adj* medical
Meer (**-(e)s**, **-e**) *nt* sea; **am ~(e)** by the sea
Meerenge *f* straits *pl*
Meeresfrüchte *pl* seafood
Meeresspiegel *m* sea level
Meerrettich *m* horseradish
Meerschweinchen *nt* guinea pig
Meerwasser *nt* sea water
Megabyte *nt* megabyte
Mehl (**-(e)s**, **-e**) *nt* flour
mehr *adv* more; **nie ~** never again; **es war niemand ~ da** there was no one left
mehrdeutig *adj* ambiguous
mehrere *indef pron* several; **mehreres** several things
mehrfach *adj* multiple; (*wiederholt*) repeated
Mehrfamilienhaus *nt* block of flats (Brit), apartment block (Schweiz)
Mehrgenerationenhaus *nt* *state-run centre that provides support and activities for people of different generations*
Mehrheit *f* majority
mehrmals *adv* repeatedly
mehrsprachig *adj* multilingual
Mehrwegflasche *f* returnable bottle
Mehrwertsteuer *f* value added tax, VAT
Mehrzahl *f* majority; (*Gram*) plural
meiden *unreg vt* to avoid
Meile (-, **-n**) *f* mile
mein *pron* my
meine(r, s) *poss pron* mine
meinen *vt* to think; (*sagen*) to say; (*sagen wollen*) to mean ▸ *vi* to think
meinetwegen *adv* (*für mich*) for my sake; (*wegen mir*) on my account; (*von mir aus*) as far as I'm concerned
Meinung *f* opinion; **meiner ~ nach** in my opinion
Meinungsumfrage *f* opinion poll
Meinungsverschiedenheit *f* difference of opinion
Meise (-, **-n**) *f* tit(mouse); **eine ~ haben** (*umg*) to be crackers
Meißel (**-s**, **-**) *m* chisel
meist *adv* mostly
meiste(r, s) *pron* most; **die meisten Leute** most people; **die ~ Zeit** most of the time; **am meisten** (the) most
meistens *adv* mostly
Meister (**-s**, **-**) *m* master; (*Sport*) champion
Meisterin *f* (*auf einem Gebiet*) master, expert; (*Sport*) (woman) champion
Meisterschaft *f* (*Sport*) championship
Meisterwerk *nt* masterpiece
melden *vt* to report ▸ *vr* to report; (*Sch*) to put one's hand up; (*freiwillig*) to volunteer; (*auf etw, am Telefon*) to answer
Meldung *f* announcement; (*Bericht*) report; (*Comput*) message
Melodie *f* melody, tune
Melone (-, **-n**) *f* melon
Memoiren *pl* memoirs *pl*
Menge (-, **-n**) *f* quantity; (*Menschenmenge*) crowd; (*große Anzahl*) lot (of)
Mengenrabatt *m* bulk discount
Mensa (-, **-s** *od* **Mensen**) *f* (*Univ*) refectory (Brit), commons (US)
Mensch (**-en**, **-en**) *m* human being, man; (*Person*) person; **kein ~** nobody
Menschenmenge *f* crowd (of people)
Menschenrechte *pl* human rights *pl*
Menschenverstand *m*: **gesunder ~** common sense
Menschheit *f* humanity, mankind
menschlich *adj* human; (*human*) humane
Menstruation *f* menstruation
Mentalität *f* mentality
Menü (**-s**, **-s**) *nt* (*auch Comput*) menu
Menüleiste *f* (*Comput*) menu bar
Merkblatt *nt* instruction sheet *od* leaflet
merken *vt* to notice; **sich** *dat* **etw ~** to remember sth
Merkmal *nt* sign, characteristic
merkwürdig *adj* odd
Messbecher *m* measuring cup
Messe (-, **-n**) *f* fair; (*Eccl*) mass
Messegelände *nt* exhibition centre (Brit) *od* center (US)

messen *unreg vt* to measure ▶ *vr* to compete
Messer (**-s**, **-**) *nt* knife
Messgerät *nt* measuring device, gauge
Messing (**-s**) *nt* brass
Metall (**-s**, **-e**) *nt* metal
Meteorologe (**-n**, **-n**) *m* meteorologist
Meter (**-s**, **-**) *m od nt* metre (BRIT), meter (*US*)
Metermaß *nt* tape measure
Methode (**-**, **-n**) *f* method
Metzger(in) (**-s**, **-**) *m(f)* butcher
Metzgerei *f* butcher's (shop)
Mexiko (**-s**) *nt* Mexico
MEZ *abk* (= *mitteleuropäische Zeit*) C.E.T.
mich *akk von* **ich** ▶ *pron* me; (*reflexiv*) myself
mied *etc vb siehe* **meiden**
Miene (**-**, **-n**) *f* look, expression
mies (*umg*) *adj* lousy
Mietauto *nt* hired car (BRIT), rental car (*US*)
Miete (**-**, **-n**) *f* rent
mieten *vt* to rent; (*Auto*) to hire (BRIT), to rent
Mieter(in) (**-s**, **-**) *m(f)* tenant
Mietshaus *nt* tenement, block of flats (BRIT) *od* apartments (*US*)
Mietvertrag *m* tenancy agreement
Mietwagen *m* = **Mietauto**
Migräne (**-**, **-n**) *f* migraine
Mikroblog *nt* microblog
Mikrofon (**-s**, **e**) *nt* microphone
Mikrowelle *f* microwave
Milch (**-**) *f* milk
Milchglas *nt* frosted glass
Milchkaffee *m* white coffee
Milchpulver *nt* powdered milk
Milchreis *m* rice pudding
Milchstraße *f* Milky Way
mild *adj* mild; (*Richter*) lenient; (*freundlich*) kind
Militär (**-s**) *nt* military, army
Milliarde (**-**, **-n**) *f* billion
Millimeter *m* millimetre (BRIT), millimeter (*US*)
Million (**-**, **-en**) *f* million
Millionär(in) (**-s**, **-e**) *m(f)* millionaire
Milz (**-**, **-en**) *f* spleen
Mimik *f* facial expression(s)
Minderheit *f* minority
minderjährig *adj* minor
minderwertig *adj* inferior
Minderwertigkeitskomplex *m* inferiority complex
mindeste(r, s) *adj* least
mindestens *adv* at least
Mindesthaltbarkeitsdatum *nt* best-before date, sell-by date (BRIT)
Mine (**-**, **-n**) *f* mine; (*Bleistiftmine*) lead; (*Kugelschreibermine*) refill
Mineralwasser *nt* mineral water
Minigolf *nt* miniature golf
minimal *adj* minimal
Minimum (**-s**, **Minima**) *nt* minimum
Minirock *m* miniskirt
Minister(in) (**-s**, **-**) *m(f)* (*Pol*) minister
Ministerium *nt* ministry
Ministerpräsident(in) *m(f)* prime minister
minus *adv* minus
Minus (**-**, **-**) *nt* deficit
Minute (**-**, **-n**) *f* minute
Mio. *abk* (= *Million(en)*) m
mir *dat von* **ich** ▶ *pron* (to) me; **ein Freund von ~** a friend of mine
Mirabelle *f* mirabelle, *small yellow plum*
mischen *vt* to mix; (*Karten*) to shuffle
Mischmasch (*umg*) *m* hotchpotch
Mischung *f* mixture
missachten *vt untr* to disregard
Missbrauch *m* abuse; (*falscher Gebrauch*) misuse
missbrauchen *vt untr* to abuse; (*falsch gebrauchen*) to misuse
Misserfolg *m* failure
Missgeschick *nt* misfortune
misshandeln *vt untr* to ill-treat
Mission *f* mission
misslingen *unreg vi untr* to fail
misstrauen *vi untr* to mistrust
Misstrauen (**-s**) *nt*: **~ (gegenüber)** distrust (of), suspicion (of)
misstrauisch *adj* distrustful, suspicious
Missverständnis *nt* misunderstanding
missverstehen *unreg vt untr* to misunderstand
Mist (**-(e)s**) *m* dung; (*umg*) rubbish
Mistel (**-**, **-n**) *f* mistletoe
mit *präp +dat* with; (*mittels*) by; **~ der Bahn** by train; **wie wärs ~ einem Bier?** (*umg*) how about a beer?; **~ 10 Jahren** at the age of 10; **wollen Sie ~?** do you want to come along?
Mitarbeiter(in) *m(f)* (*an Projekt*) collaborator; (*Kollege*) colleague; (*Angestellter*) member of staff

mit|bekommen *unreg vt* (*umg: hören*) to hear; (*verstehen*) to get
Mitbewohner(in) *m(f)* (*in Wohnung*) flatmate (Brit), roommate (*US*)
mit|bringen *unreg vt* to bring along
Mitbringsel (**-s**, **-**) *nt* small present
miteinander *adv* together, with one another
mit|erleben *vt* to see, to witness
Mitesser (**-s**, **-**) *m* blackhead
Mitfahrgelegenheit *f* lift
mit|geben *unreg vt* to give
Mitgefühl *nt* sympathy
mit|gehen *unreg vi* to go *od* come along
mitgenommen *adj* done in, in a bad way
Mitglied *nt* member
mithilfe *präp +gen*: **~ von** with the help of
mit|kommen *unreg vi* to come along; (*verstehen*) to follow
Mitleid *nt* sympathy; (*Erbarmen*) compassion
mit|machen *vt* to take part in
mit|nehmen *unreg vt* to take along *od* away; (*anstrengen*) to wear out, to exhaust
mit|schreiben *unreg vt* to write *od* take down ▶ *vi* to take notes
Mitschüler(in) *m(f)* schoolmate
mit|spielen *vi* to join in, to take part; (*in Mannschaft*) to play
Mittag (**-(e)s**, **-e**) *m* midday, noon, lunchtime; **morgen ~** tomorrow at lunchtime *od* noon; **(zu) ~ essen** to have lunch
Mittagessen *nt* lunch
mittags *adv* at lunchtime *od* noon
Mittagspause *f* lunch break
Mitte (**-**, **-n**) *f* middle; **sie ist ~ zwanzig** she's in her mid-twenties
mit|teilen *vt*: **jdm etw ~** to inform sb of sth
Mitteilung *f* communication
Mittel (**-s**, **-**) *nt* means; (*Methode*) method; (*Med*) medicine
Mittelalter *nt* Middle Ages *pl*
mittelalterlich *adj* medieval
Mittelamerika *nt* Central America (and the Caribbean)
Mitteleuropa *nt* Central Europe
Mittelfeld *nt* midfield
Mittelfinger *m* middle finger
mittelmäßig *adj* mediocre
Mittelmeer *nt* Mediterranean (Sea)
Mittelpunkt *m* centre (Brit), center (*US*); **im ~ stehen** to be centre-stage
mittels *präp +gen* by means of
Mittelstreifen *m* central reservation (Brit), median strip (*US*)
Mittelstürmer *m* centre forward
Mittelwelle *f* (*Rundf*) medium wave
mitten *adv* in the middle; **~ auf der Straße/in der Nacht** in the middle of the street/night
Mitternacht *f* midnight
mittlere(r, s) *adj* middle; (*durchschnittlich*) average
mittlerweile *adv* meanwhile
Mittwoch (**-(e)s**, **-e**) *m* Wednesday; *siehe auch* **Dienstag**
mittwochs *adv* on Wednesdays
Mixer (**-s**, **-**) *m* (*Küchenmixer*) blender
mobben *vt* to bully (at work)
Mobbing (**-s**) *nt* workplace bullying
Möbel (**-s**, **-**) *nt* (piece of) furniture
Möbelwagen *m* furniture *od* removal van (Brit), moving van (*US*)
mobil *adj* mobile
Mobilfunkmast (**-(e)s**, **-e(n)**) *m* (*Tel*) mobile phone mast (Brit), cell tower (*US*)
Mobilfunknetz *nt* cellular network
Mobiltelefon *nt* (*Tel*) mobile phone
möblieren *vt* to furnish
mochte *etc vb siehe* **mögen**
Mode (**-**, **-n**) *f* fashion
Modell (**-s**, **-e**) *nt* model
Modem (**-s**, **-s**) *nt* (*Comput*) modem
Modenschau *f* fashion show
Moderator(in) *m(f)* presenter
modern *adj* modern; (*modisch*) fashionable
Modeschmuck *m* fashion jewellery (Brit) *od* jewelry (*US*)
modisch *adj* fashionable
Modus (**-**, **Modi**) *m* way; (*Comput*) mode
Mofa (**-s**, **-s**) *nt* small moped
mogeln (*umg*) *vi* to cheat

SCHLÜSSELWORT

mögen (*pt* **mochte**, *pp* **gemocht**, *als Hilfsverb* **mögen**) *vt*, *vi* to like; **magst du/mögen Sie ihn?** do you like him?; **ich möchte ...** I would like ..., I'd like ...; **er möchte in die Stadt** he'd like to go into town; **ich möchte**

nicht, dass du ... I wouldn't like you to ...; **ich mag nicht mehr** I've had enough
▶ *Hilfsverb* to like to; (*wollen*) to want; **möchtest du etwas essen?** would you like something to eat?; **sie mag nicht bleiben** she doesn't want to stay; **das mag wohl sein** that may very well be; **was mag das heißen?** what might that mean?; **Sie möchten zu Hause anrufen** could you please call home?

nöglich *adj* possible
nöglicherweise *adv* possibly
Aöglichkeit *f* possibility
nöglichst *adv* as ... as possible
Aohn (**-(e)s**, **-e**) *m* (*Mohnblume*) poppy; (*Mohnsamen*) poppy seed
Aöhre (**-**, **-n**) *f* carrot
Aokka (**-s**) *m* mocha
Aoldawien (**-s**) *nt* Moldavia
Aolkerei *f* dairy
Aoll (**-**, **-**) *nt* (*Mus*) minor (key)
nollig *adj* cosy; (*dicklich*) plump
Aoment (**-(e)s**, **-e**) *m* moment; **im ~** at the moment; **~ mal!** just a minute!
nomentan *adj* momentary ▶ *adv* at the moment
Aonaco (**-s**) *nt* Monaco
Aonarchie *f* monarchy
Aonat (**-(e)s**, **-e**) *m* month; **sie ist im sechsten ~ (schwanger)** she's five months pregnant
nonatlich *adj* monthly
Aonatskarte *f* monthly ticket
Aönch (**-(e)s**, **-e**) *m* monk
Aond (**-(e)s**, **-e**) *m* moon
Aondfinsternis *f* eclipse of the moon
Aongolei *f*: **die ~** Mongolia
Aonitor *m* monitor
nonoton *adj* monotonous
Aonsun (**-s**, **-e**) *m* monsoon
Aontag (**-(e)s**, **-e**) *m* Monday; *siehe auch* **Dienstag**
nontags *adv* on Mondays
Aontenegro (**-s**) *nt* Montenegro
Aonteur(in) *m(f)* fitter
nontieren *vt* to assemble, to set up
Aonument *nt* monument
Aoor (**-(e)s**, **-e**) *nt* moor
Aoos (**-es**, **-e**) *nt* moss
Aoped (**-s**, **-s**) *nt* moped
Aoral (**-**, **-en**) *f* (*einer Geschichte*) moral
noralisch *adj* moral
Mord (**-(e)s**, **-e**) *m* murder
Mörder (**-s**, **-**) *m* murderer
Mörderin *f* murderess
morgen *adv* tomorrow; **~ früh** tomorrow morning
Morgen (**-s**, **-**) *m* morning; **am ~** in the morning
Morgenmantel *m* dressing gown
morgens *adv* in the morning
Morphium *nt* morphine
morsch *adj* rotten
Mosaik (**-s**, **-en** *od* **-e**) *nt* mosaic
Mosambik (**-s**) *nt* Mozambique
Moschee (**-**, **-n**) *f* mosque
Moskau (**-s**) *nt* Moscow
Moskito (**-s**, **-s**) *m* mosquito
Moslem (**-s**, **-s**) *m* Muslim
Most (**-(e)s**, **-e**) *m* (unfermented) fruit juice; (*Apfelwein*) cider
Motel (**-s**, **-s**) *nt* motel
motivieren *vt* to motivate
Motor (**-s**, **-en**) *m* engine; (*bes Elek*) motor
Motorboot *nt* motorboat
Motorenöl *nt* engine oil
Motorhaube *f* (*Aut*) bonnet (BRIT), hood (*US*)
Motorrad *nt* motorcycle
Motorradfahrer(in) *m(f)* motorcyclist
Motorroller *m* motor scooter
Motorschaden *m* engine trouble *od* failure
Motte (**-**, **-n**) *f* moth
Motto (**-s**, **-s**) *nt* motto
Mountainbike *nt* mountain bike
Möwe (**-**, **-n**) *f* seagull
Mrd. *abk* = **Milliarde**
MRT *f abk* (= *Magnetresonanztomographie*) MRI (= *magnetic resonance imaging*)
MS *abk* (= *multiple Sklerose*) MS
Mücke (**-**, **-n**) *f* midge
Mückenstich *m* midge *od* gnat bite
müde *adj* tired
muffig *adj* (*Luft*) musty
Mühe (**-**, **-n**) *f* trouble, pains *pl*; **sich** *dat* **~ geben** to go to a lot of trouble
muhen *vi* to moo
Mühle (**-**, **-n**) *f* mill; (*Kaffeemühle*) grinder
Müll (**-(e)s**) *m* rubbish, garbage (*US*)
Müllabfuhr *f* refuse *od* garbage (*US*) collection
Mullbinde *f* gauze bandage

Müllcontainer *m* waste container
Mülldeponie *f* rubbish (BRIT) *od* garbage (*US*) dump
Mülleimer *m* rubbish bin (BRIT), garbage can (*US*)
Mülltonne *f* dustbin (BRIT), trashcan (*US*)
Mülltrennung *f sorting and collecting household waste according to type of material*
Müllverbrennungsanlage *f* incinerating plant
Müllwagen *m* dustcart (BRIT), garbage truck (*US*)
multikulturell *adj* multicultural
multiple Sklerose *f* multiple sclerosis
multiplizieren *vt* to multiply
Mumie *f* mummy
Mumps (-) *m od f* mumps *sing*
München *nt* Munich
Mund (**-(e)s**, **Münder**) *m* mouth; **halt den ~!** shut up
Mundart *f* dialect
münden *vi*: **in etw** *akk* **~** to flow into sth
Mundgeruch *m* bad breath
Mundharmonika *f* mouth organ
mündlich *adj* oral
Mundwasser *nt* mouthwash
Munition *f* ammunition
Münster (**-s**, **-**) *nt* minster
munter *adj* lively
Münzautomat *m* slot machine
Münze (-, **-n**) *f* coin
Münzwechsler *m* change machine
murmeln *vt*, *vi* to murmur, to mutter
Murmeltier *nt* marmot
mürrisch *adj* sullen
Mus (**-es**, **-e**) *nt* purée
Muschel (-, **-n**) *f* mussel; (*Muschelschale*) shell
Museum (**-s**, **Museen**) *nt* museum
Musik *f* music
musikalisch *adj* musical
Musiker(in) (**-s**, **-**) *m(f)* musician
Musikinstrument *nt* musical instrument
musizieren *vi* to make music
Muskat (**-(e)s**, **-e**) *m* nutmeg
Muskel (**-s**, **-n**) *m* muscle
Muskelkater *m*: **einen ~ haben** to be stiff
Muskelzerrung *f* pulled muscle
muskulös *adj* muscular
Müsli (**-s**, **-**) *nt* muesli
Muslim (**-s**, **-s**) *m*, **Muslimin** *f* Muslim
Muss (**-**) *nt* necessity, must

 **SCHLÜSSELWORT**

müssen (*pt* **musste**, *pp* **gemusst**, *als Hilfsverb* **müssen**) *vi* **1** (*Zwang*) must (*nur im Präsens*), to have to; **ich muss es tun** I must do it, I have to do it; **ich musste es tun** I had to do it; **er muss es nicht tun** he doesn't have to do it; **muss ich?** must I?, do I have to?; **wann müsst ihr zur Schule?** when do you have to go to school?; **er hat gehen müssen** he (has) had to go; **muss das sein?** is that really necessary?; **ich muss mal** (*umg*) I need to go to the loo (BRIT) *od* bathroom (*US*)
2 (*sollen*): **das musst du nicht tun!** you oughtn't to *od* shouldn't do that; **Sie hätten ihn fragen müssen** you should have asked him
3: **es muss geregnet haben** it must have rained; **es muss nicht wahr sein** it needn't be true

Muster (**-s**, **-**) *nt* model; (*Dessin*) pattern; (*Probe*) sample
mustern *vt* (*Mil*) to examine; (*Truppen*) to inspect
Mut *m* courage; **jdm ~ machen** to encourage sb
mutig *adj* courageous
Mutter[1] (-, **Mütter**) *f* mother
Mutter[2] (-, **-n**) *f* (*Schraubenmutter*) nut
Muttersprache *f* native language
Muttertag *m* Mother's Day
Mutti (-, **-s**) (*umg*) *f* mum(my) (BRIT), mom(my) (*US*)
mutwillig *adj* deliberate
Mütze (-, **-n**) *f* cap

abk (= *Norden*) N

a *interj* well; **na also!** (well,) there you are (then)!; **na und?** so what?

abel (**-s**, **-**) *m* navel

SCHLÜSSELWORT

ach *präp* +*dat* **1** (*örtlich*) to; **nach Berlin** to Berlin; **nach links/rechts** (to the) left/right; **nach oben/hinten** up/back

2 (*zeitlich*) after; **einer nach dem anderen** one after the other; **nach Ihnen!** after you!; **zehn (Minuten) nach drei** ten (minutes) past *od* after (*US*) three

3 (*gemäß*) according to; **nach dem Gesetz** according to the law; **dem Namen nach** judging by his/her name; **nach allem, was ich weiß** as far as I know

▶ *adv*: **ihm nach!** after him!; **nach und nach** gradually, little by little; **nach wie vor** still

ach|ahmen *vt* to imitate

achbar(in) (**-s**, **-n**) *m(f)* neighbour (Brit), neighbor (*US*)

achbarschaft *f* neighbourhood (Brit), neighborhood (*US*)

ach|bestellen *vt* to order again

achdem *konj* after; (*weil*) since; **je ~ (ob)** it depends (whether)

ach|denken *unreg vi*: **über etw** *akk* **~** to think about sth

achdenklich *adj* thoughtful

acheinander *adv* one after the other

Nachfolger(in) (**-s**, **-**) *m(f)* successor

nach|forschen *vt*, *vi* to investigate

Nachfrage *f* inquiry; (*Comm*) demand

nach|fragen *vi* to inquire

nach|geben *unreg vi* to give way, to yield

Nachgebühr *f* surcharge; (*Post*) excess postage

nach|gehen *unreg vi* +*dat* to follow; (*erforschen*) to inquire (into); (*Uhr*) to be slow

nachher *adv* afterwards; **bis ~** see you later!

Nachhilfe *f* (*auch*: **Nachhilfeunterricht**) extra (private) tuition

nach|holen *vt* to catch up with; (*Versäumtes*) to make up for

nach|kommen *unreg vi* to follow; (*einer Verpflichtung*) to fulfil

nach|lassen *unreg vt* (*Summe*) to take off ▶ *vi* to decrease, to ease off; (*schlechter werden*) to deteriorate

nachlässig *adj* negligent, careless

nach|laufen *unreg vi*: **jdm ~** to run after *od* chase sb

nach|lösen *vi* to pay on the train/ when one gets off; (*zur Weiterfahrt*) to pay the extra

nach|machen *vt* to imitate, to copy; (*fälschen*) to counterfeit

Nachmittag *m* afternoon; **am ~** in the afternoon; **gestern/heute ~** yesterday/this afternoon

nachmittags *adv* in the afternoon

Nachnahme (**-**, **-n**) *f* cash on delivery (Brit), collect on delivery (*US*); **per ~** C.O.D.

Nachname *m* surname

nach|prüfen *vt* to check

nach|rechnen *vt* to check

Nachricht (**-**, **-en**) *f* (piece of) news *sing*; (*Mitteilung*) message

Nachrichten *pl* news *sing*

Nachsaison *f* off season

nach|schicken *vt* to forward

nach|schlagen *unreg vt* to look up

nach|sehen *unreg vt* (*prüfen*) to check

Nachspeise *f* dessert

nächstbeste(r, s) *adj*: **der ~ Zug/Job** the first train/job that comes along

nächste(r, s) *adj* next; (*nächstgelegen*) nearest

Nacht (**-**, **Nächte**) *f* night; **in der ~** at night; **in der ~ auf Dienstag** during Monday night

Nachtdienst *m* night duty
Nachteil *m* disadvantage
Nachthemd *nt* (*Damennachthemd*) nightdress (BRIT), nightgown; (*Herrennachthemd*) nightshirt
Nachtigall (**-**, **-en**) *f* nightingale
Nachtisch *m* dessert
Nachtklub *m* night club
Nachtleben *nt* night life
nach|tragen *unreg vt*: **jdm etw ~** to carry sth after sb; (*fig*) to hold sth against sb
nachträglich *adj* later, subsequent; (*zusätzlich*) additional ▶ *adv* later, subsequently; (*zusätzlich*) additionally
nachts *adv* by night
Nachtschicht *f* night shift
Nachttarif *m* off-peak tariff
Nachttisch *m* bedside table
Nachtzug *m* night train
Nachweis (**-es**, **-e**) *m* proof
Nachwirkung *f* aftereffect
nach|zahlen *vt*, *vi* to pay extra
nach|zählen *vt* to count again
Nacken (**-s**, **-**) *m* nape of the neck
nackt *adj* naked; (*Tatsachen*) plain, bare
Nadel (**-**, **-n**) *f* needle; (*Stecknadel*) pin
Nagel (**-s**, **Nägel**) *m* nail
Nagelbürste *f* nailbrush
Nagelfeile *f* nailfile
Nagellack *m* nail varnish (BRIT) *od* polish
Nagellackentferner (**-s**, **-**) *m* nail polish remover
Nagelschere *f* nail scissors *pl*
nah *adj* = **nahe**
nahe *adj* (*räumlich*) near(by); (*Verwandte*) near, close; (*Freunde*) close; (*zeitlich*) near; **~ liegend** obvious; **die nähere Umgebung** the immediate area
Nähe (**-**) *f* (*Umgebung*) vicinity; **in der ~** close by; **aus der ~** from close to
nahe|gehen *unreg vi* (*fig*): **jdm ~** to grieve sb
nahe|legen *vt* (*fig*): **jdm etw ~** to suggest sth to sb
nahe|liegen *unreg vi* (*fig*) to be obvious
nähen *vt*, *vi* to sew
Nähere(s) *nt* details *pl*
nähern *vr* to approach
nahezu *adv* nearly
nahm *etc vb siehe* **nehmen**
Nähmaschine *f* sewing machine
nahrhaft *adj* nourishing
Nahrung *f* food
Nahrungsmittel *nt* food(stuff)
Naht (**-**, **Nähte**) *f* seam; (*Med*) suture; (*Tech*) join
Nahverkehr *m* local traffic
Nahverkehrszug *m* local train
Nähzeug *nt* sewing kit
naiv *adj* naïve
Name (**-ns**, **-n**) *m* name
nämlich *adv* that is to say, namely; (*denn*) since
nannte *etc vb siehe* **nennen**
Napf (**-(e)s**, **Näpfe**) *m* bowl, dish
Narbe (**-**, **-n**) *f* scar
Narkose (**-**, **-n**) *f* anaesthetic (BRIT), anesthetic (*US*)
Narzisse (**-**, **-n**) *f* narcissus
naschen *vt* to nibble ▶ *vi*: **~ von** *od* **an** *+dat* to nibble at
Nase (**-**, **-n**) *f* nose
Nasenbluten (**-s**) *nt* nosebleed
Nasenloch *nt* nostril
Nasentropfen *pl* nose drops *pl*
Nashorn *nt* rhinoceros
nass *adj* wet
Nässe (**-**) *f* wetness
nässen *vt* to wet
Nation *f* nation
national *adj* national
Nationalfeiertag *m* national holiday
Nationalhymne *f* national anthem
Nationalität *f* nationality
Nationalmannschaft *f* national team
Nationalspieler(in) *m(f)* international (player)
NATO, Nato (**-**) *f abk*: **die ~** NATO
Natur *f* nature
natürlich *adj* natural ▶ *adv* naturally; (*selbstverständlich*) of course
naturrein *adj* natural, pure
Naturschutz *m*: **unter ~ stehen** to be legally protected
Naturschutzgebiet *nt* nature reserve (BRIT), national park (*US*)
Naturwissenschaft *f* natural science
Naturwissenschaftler *m* scientist
Navi (**-s**, **-s**) *m* (= *Navigationsgerät*, *Navigationssystem*) GPS, sat nav (BRIT)
Navigationssystem *nt* (*Aut*) navigation system
n. Chr. *abk* (= *nach Christus*) A.D.
Nebel (**-s**, **-**) *m* fog, mist

ebelig *adj* foggy, misty
ebelscheinwerfer *m* fog-lamp
ebelschlussleuchte *f* (*Aut*) rear og-light
eben *präp +akk* next to ▶ *präp +dat* next to; (*außer*) apart from, besides
ebenan *adv* next door
ebenbei *adv* at the same time; *außerdem*) additionally; (*beiläufig*) ncidentally
ebeneinander *adv* side by side
ebeneingang *m* side entrance
ebenfach *nt* subsidiary subject
ebenher *adv* (*zusätzlich*) besides; *gleichzeitig*) at the same time; *daneben*) alongside
ebenkosten *pl* extra charges *pl*, extras *pl*
ebensache *f* side issue
ebensächlich *adj* minor
ebensaison *f* low season
ebenstraße *f* side street
eblig *adj* = **nebelig**
ecken *vt* to tease
effe (**-n**, **-n**) *m* nephew
egativ *adj* negative
egativ (**-s**, **-e**) *nt* (*Phot*) negative
ehmen *unreg vt*, *vi* to take; **etw zu sich ~** to take sth; **sich ernst ~** to take o.s. seriously; **wie mans nimmt** depending on your point of view
eidisch *adj* envious
eigen *vi*: **zu etw ~** to tend towards sth
eigung *f* (*des Geländes*) slope; *Tendenz*) inclination; (*Vorliebe*) liking
ein *adv* no
ektarine *f* nectarine
elke (**-**, **-n**) *f* carnation; (*Gewürznelke*) clove
ennen *unreg vt* to name; (*mit Namen*) to call
eonazi *m* Neonazi
epal (**-s**) *nt* Nepal
erv (**-s**, **-en**) *m* nerve; **jdm auf die Nerven gehen** to get on sb's nerves
erven (*umg*) *vt*: **jdn ~** to get on sb's nerves
ervenzusammenbruch *m* nervous breakdown
ervös *adj* nervous
est (**-(e)s**, **-er**) *nt* nest; (*umg*: *Ort*) dump
ett *adj* nice; **sei so ~ und räum auf!** would you mind clearing up?
netto *adv* net
Netz (**-es**, **-e**) *nt* net; (*Einkaufsnetz*) string bag; (*System*: *Comput*) network; (*Stromnetz*) mains *sing od pl*
Netzanschluss *m* mains connection
Netzbetreiber *m* (*Comput*) internet provider
Netzkarte *f* season ticket
netzunabhängig *adj* off-grid
Netzwerk *nt* (*Comput*) network
Netzwerken *nt* (social) networking
neu *adj* new; (*Sprache, Geschichte*) modern; **was gibts Neues?** (*umg*) what's the latest?
Neubau (**-(e)s**, **-ten**) *m* new building
neuerdings *adv* (*kürzlich*) (since) recently
Neuerung *f* innovation, new departure
Neugier *f* curiosity
neugierig *adj* curious
Neuheit *f* novelty
Neuigkeit *f* news *sing*
Neujahr *nt* New Year
Neujahrstag *m* New Year's Day
neulich *adv* recently, the other day
Neumond *m* new moon
neun *num* nine
neunzehn *num* nineteen
neunzig *num* ninety
neureich *adj* nouveau riche
Neurologe *m*, **Neurologin** *f* neurologist
Neurose (**-**, **-n**) *f* neurosis
neurotisch *adj* neurotic
Neuseeland *nt* New Zealand
neutral *adj* neutral
neuwertig *adj* as new
Nicaragua (**-s**) *nt* Nicaragua

SCHLÜSSELWORT

nicht *adv* **1** (*Verneinung*) not; **er ist es nicht** it's not him, it isn't him; **er raucht nicht** (*gerade*) he isn't smoking; (*gewöhnlich*) he doesn't smoke; **ich kann das nicht — ich auch nicht** I can't do it — neither *od* nor can I; **es regnet nicht mehr** it's not raining any more; **nicht mehr als** no more than
2 (*Bitte, Verbot*): **nicht!** don't!, no!; **nicht berühren!** do not touch!; **nicht doch!** don't!
3 (*rhetorisch*): **du bist müde, nicht (wahr)?** you're tired, aren't you?;

das ist schön, nicht (wahr)? it's nice, isn't it?
4: **was du nicht sagst!** the things you say!

Nichte (**-**, **-n**) *f* niece
Nichtraucher *m* nonsmoker
nichts *pron* nothing; **für ~ und wieder ~** for nothing at all; **ich habe ~ gesagt** I didn't say anything
Nichtschwimmer (**-s**, **-**) *m* nonswimmer
nichtssagend *adj* meaningless
Nick (**-s**) *m* username
nicken *vi* to nod
Nickerchen *nt* nap
Nickname (**-ns**, **-n**) *m* username
nie *adv* never; **~ wieder** *od* **mehr** never again; **fast ~** hardly ever
nieder *adj* low; (*gering*) inferior ▶ *adv* down
niedergeschlagen *adj* depressed, dejected
Niederlage *f* defeat
Niederlande *pl*: **die ~** the Netherlands *pl*
Niederländer(in) (**-s**, **-**) *m(f)* Dutchman, Dutchwoman
niederländisch *adj* Dutch
Niederlassung *f* (*Comm*) branch
Niederösterreich *nt* Lower Austria
Niedersachsen *nt* Lower Saxony
Niederschlag *m* (*Chem*) precipitate; (*Met*) rainfall
niedlich *adj* sweet, cute
niedrig *adj* low
niemals *adv* never
niemand *pron* nobody, no-one; **ich habe niemanden gesehen** I haven't seen anyone
Niere (**-**, **-n**) *f* kidney
Nierenentzündung *f* kidney infection
nieseln *vi* to drizzle
Nieselregen *m* drizzle
niesen *vi* to sneeze
Niete (**-**, **-n**) *f* (*Tech*) rivet; (*Los*) blank; (*Reinfall*) flop; (*Mensch*) failure
Nigeria (**-s**) *nt* Nigeria
Nikotin (**-s**) *nt* nicotine
Nilpferd *nt* hippopotamus
nippen *vt*, *vi* to sip
nirgends *adv* nowhere
Nische (**-**, **-n**) *f* niche
Niveau (**-s**, **-s**) *nt* level

nobel *adj* (*großzügig*) generous; (*elegant*) posh (*umg*)
Nobelpreis *m* Nobel prize

 **SCHLÜSSELWORT**

noch *adv* **1** (*weiterhin*) still; **noch nicht** not yet; **noch nie** never (yet); **noch immer** *od* **immer noch** still; **bleiben Sie doch noch** stay a bit longer
2 (*in Zukunft*) still, yet; **das kann noch passieren** that might still happen; **er wird noch kommen** he'll come (yet)
3 (*nicht später als*): **noch vor einer Woche** only a week ago; **noch am selben Tag** the very same day; **noch im 19. Jahrhundert** as late as the 19th century; **noch heute** today
4 (*zusätzlich*): **wer war noch da?** who else was there?; **noch (ein)mal** once more, again; **noch dreimal** three more times; **noch einer** another one
5 (*bei Vergleichen*): **noch größer** even bigger; **das ist noch besser** that's better still; **und wenn es noch so schwer ist** however hard it is
6: **Geld noch und noch** heaps (and heaps) of money; **sie hat noch und noch versucht, …** she tried again and again to …
▶ *konj*: **weder A noch B** neither A nor B

nochmal, nochmals *adv* once more, again
Nominativ (**-s**, **-e**) *m* nominative
Nonne (**-**, **-n**) *f* nun
Nord (**-s**) *m* north
Nordamerika *nt* North America
Norddeutschland *nt* North(ern) Germany
Norden *m* north
Nordeuropa *nt* Northern Europe
Nordirland *nt* Northern Ireland
nordisch *adj* northern; (*Völker, Sprache*) Nordic
Nordkorea *nt* North Korea
nördlich *adj* northerly, northern
Nordpol *m* North Pole
Nordrhein-Westfalen (**-s**) *nt* North Rhine-Westphalia
Nordsee *f* North Sea
nordwärts *adv* northwards
nörgeln *vi* to grumble
Norm (**-**, **-en**) *f* norm; (*Größenvorschrift*) standard (specification)

ormal *adj* normal; **bist du noch ~?** (*umg*) have you gone mad?
ormalbenzin *nt* regular (petrol (BRIT) *od* gas (*US*))
ormalerweise *adv* normally
ormen *vt* to standardize
orwegen (-s) *nt* Norway
orweger(in) (-s, -) *m(f)* Norwegian
orwegisch *adj* Norwegian
ot (-, Nöte) *f* need; (*Armut*) poverty; (*Mangel*) want; (*Mühe*) trouble; (*Zwang*) necessity; **zur ~** if necessary; (*gerade noch*) just about
otar(in) (-s, -e) *m(f)* notary
otariell *adj*: **~ beglaubigt** attested by a notary
otarzt *m* emergency doctor
otaufnahme *f* A&E, casualty (BRIT), emergency room (*US*)
otausgang *m* emergency exit, fire exit
otbremse *f* emergency brake
otdienst *m*: **~ haben** (*Apotheke*) to be open 24 hours; (*Arzt*) to be on call
otdürftig *adj* scanty; (*behelfsmäßig*) makeshift
ote (-, -n) *f* note; (*Sch*) mark (BRIT), grade (*US*) ■ **Noten** *pl* (*Mus*) music *sing*
otfall *m* (case of) emergency
otfalls *adv* if need be
otieren *vt* to note
ötig *adj* necessary ▶ *adv*: **etw ~ haben** to need sth
otiz (-, -en) *f* note; (*Zeitungsnotiz*) item
otizblock *m* notepad
otizbuch *nt* notebook
otlage *f* crisis
otlanden *vi* to make a forced *od* emergency landing
otlandung *f* forced *od* emergency landing
otruf *m* emergency call
otrufsäule *f* emergency telephone
otwendig *adj* necessary
ovember (-(s), -) *m* November; *siehe auch* **September**
r. *abk* (= *Nummer*) no.
u *m*: **im Nu** in an instant
üchtern *adj* sober; (*Magen*) empty
udel (-, -n) *f* noodle ■ **Nudeln** *pl* pasta *sing*
ull *num* zero; **~ Fehler** no mistakes; **~ Uhr** midnight
ull (-, -en) *f* nought, zero; (*pej*: *Mensch*) dead loss
Nullerjahre *pl* 2000s, noughties (BRIT)
Nulltarif *m*: **zum ~** free of charge
Nummer (-, -n) *f* number
nummerieren *vt* to number
Nummernschild *nt* (*Aut*) number *od* license (*US*) plate
nun *adv* now ▶ *interj* well; **es ist ~ mal so** that's the way it is
nur *adv* just, only; **nicht ~ …, sondern auch …** not only … but also …; **alle, ~ ich nicht** everyone but me
Nürnberg (-s) *nt* Nuremberg
Nuss (-, Nüsse) *f* nut
Nussknacker (-s, -) *m* nutcracker
Nutte (-, -n) *f* tart (BRIT), hooker (*US*)
nutz *adj* = **nütze**
nütze *adj*: **zu nichts ~ sein** to be useless
nutzen *vi* to be of use ▶ *vt*: **(zu etw) ~** to use (for sth); **was nutzt es?** what use is it?
Nutzen (-s) *m* usefulness; (*Gewinn*) profit
nützlich *adj* useful
Nylon (-s) *nt* nylon

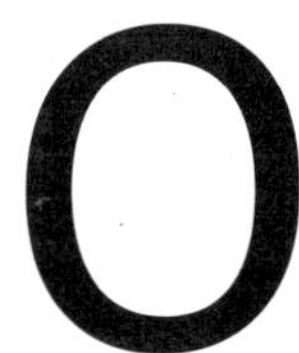

O *abk* (= *Osten*) E
Oase (**-**, **-n**) *f* oasis
ob *konj* if, whether; **(so) tun als ob** (*umg*) to pretend; **und ob!** you bet!
obdachlos *adj* homeless
oben *adv* above; (*in Haus*) upstairs; (*am oberen Ende*) at the top; **~ erwähnt**, **~ genannt** above-mentioned; **nach ~** up; **von ~** down; **siehe ~** see above
Ober (**-s**, **-**) *m* waiter
obere(r, s) *adj* upper
Oberfläche *f* surface
oberflächlich *adj* superficial
Obergeschoss *nt* upper storey *od* story (*US*)
oberhalb *präp +gen* above
Oberhemd *nt* shirt
Oberkörper *m* upper part of body
Oberlippe *f* upper lip
Oberösterreich *nt* Upper Austria
Oberschenkel *m* thigh
oberste(r, s) *adj* very top, topmost
Oberteil *nt* top
obig *adj* above
Objekt (**-(e)s**, **-e**) *nt* object
objektiv *adj* objective
Objektiv (**-s**, **-e**) *nt* lens
obligatorisch *adj* compulsory, obligatory
Oboe (**-**, **-n**) *f* oboe
Observatorium *nt* observatory
Obst (**-(e)s**) *nt* fruit
Obstkuchen *m* fruit tart
Obstsalat *m* fruit salad
obszön *adj* obscene
obwohl *konj* although
Ochse (**-n**, **-n**) *m* ox
Ochsenschwanzsuppe *f* oxtail sou
öd *adj* = **öde**
öde *adj* (*Land*) waste, barren; (*fig*) dull
oder *konj* or; **du kommst doch, ~?** you're coming, aren't you?
Ofen (**-s**, **Öfen**) *m* oven; (*Heizofen*) heater; (*Kohleofen*) stove; (*Herd*) cooker, stove
offen *adj* open; (*aufrichtig*) frank; (*Stelle*) vacant; **~ gesagt** to be hones
offenbar *adj* obvious
offensichtlich *adj* evident, obvious
öffentlich *adj* public
Öffentlichkeit *f* (*Leute*) public; (*einer Versammlung etc*) public nature
offiziell *adj* official
öffnen *vt*, *vr* to open
Öffner (**-s**, **-**) *m* opener
Öffnung *f* opening
Öffnungszeiten *pl* opening times *pl*
oft *adv* often
öfter *adv* more often *od* frequently
öfters *adv* often, frequently
ohne *präp +akk*, *konj* without; **~ Weiteres** without a second though (*sofort*) immediately
Ohnmacht *f* faint; (*fig*) impotence; **i ~ fallen** to faint
ohnmächtig *adj* unconscious; **sie ist ~** she has fainted
Ohr (**-(e)s**, **-en**) *nt* ear; (*Gehör*) hearing
Öhr (**-(e)s**, **-e**) *nt* eye
Ohrenarzt *m* ear specialist
Ohrenschmerzen *pl* earache *sing*
Ohrfeige *f* slap on the face
Ohrläppchen *nt* ear lobe
Ohrringe *pl* earrings *pl*
Ökoladen *m* wholefood shop
ökologisch *adj* ecological
ökonomisch *adj* economical
Ökosteuer *f* green tax
Ökostrom *m* green electricity
Ökosystem *nt* ecosystem
Oktanzahl *f* octane rating
Oktober (**-(s)**, **-**) *m* October; *siehe auc* **September**
Öl (**-(e)s**, **-e**) *nt* oil
Ölbaum *m* olive tree
ölen *vt* to oil; (*Tech*) to lubricate
Ölfarbe *f* oil paint
Ölgemälde *nt* oil painting
Ölheizung *f* oil-fired central heating
ölig *adj* oily
oliv *adj* olive-green

Olive (**-**, **-n**) *f* olive
Olivenöl *nt* olive oil
Ölmessstab *m* dipstick
Ölpest *f* oil pollution
Ölsardine *f* sardine
Ölstandanzeiger *m* (*Aut*) oil level indicator
Ölteppich *m* oil slick
Ölwechsel *m* oil change
Olympiade (**-**, **-n**) *f* Olympic Games® *pl*
olympisch *adj* Olympic®
Oma (**-**, **-s**) (*umg*) *f* granny
Omelett (**-(e)s**, **-s**) *nt* omelette (BRIT), omelet (*US*)
Omnibus *m* (omni)bus
onanieren *vi* to masturbate
Onkel (**-s**, **-**) *m* uncle
online *adj* (*Comput*) on-line
Onlinedienst *m* (*Comput*) on-line service
OP *m abk* = **Operationssaal**
Opa (**-s**, **-s**) (*umg*) *m* grandpa
Oper (**-**, **-n**) *f* opera; (*Opernhaus*) opera house
Operation *f* operation
Operationssaal *m* operating theatre (BRIT) *od* theater (*US*)
Operette *f* operetta
operieren *vt*, *vi* to operate; **sich ~ lassen** to have an operation
Opernhaus *nt* opera house
Opernsänger(in) *m(f)* opera singer
Opfer (**-s**, **-**) *nt* sacrifice; (*Mensch*) victim
Opium (**-s**) *nt* opium
Opposition *f* opposition
Optiker(in) (**-s**, **-**) *m(f)* optician
optimal *adj* optimal, optimum
optimistisch *adj* optimistic
orange *adj* orange
Orange (**-**, **-n**) *f* orange
Orangenmarmelade *f* marmalade
Orangensaft *m* orange juice
Orchester (**-s**, **-**) *nt* orchestra
Orchidee (**-**, **-n**) *f* orchid
Orden (**-s**, **-**) *m* (*Eccl*) order; (*Mil*) decoration
ordentlich *adj* (*anständig*) respectable; (*geordnet*) tidy, neat; (*umg*: *annehmbar*) not bad; (: *tüchtig*) proper
ordinär *adj* common, vulgar
ordnen *vt* to order, to put in order
Ordner (**-s**, **-**) *m* steward; (*Comm*) file
Ordnung *f* order; (*Geordnetsein*) tidiness; **geht in ~** (*umg*) that's all right *od* OK (*umg*)

Organ (**-s**, **-e**) *nt* organ; (*Stimme*) voice
Organisation *f* organization
organisieren *vt* to organize; (*umg*: *beschaffen*) to acquire ▶ *vr* to organize
Organismus *m* organism
Orgasmus *m* orgasm
Orgel (**-**, **-n**) *f* organ
Orgie *f* orgy
orientalisch *adj* oriental
orientieren *vr* to find one's way
Orientierung *f* orientation
Orientierungssinn *m* sense of direction
original *adj* original; **~ Meißener Porzellan** genuine Meissen porcelain
Original (**-s**, **-e**) *nt* original
originell *adj* original; (*komisch*) witty
Orkan (**-(e)s**, **-e**) *m* hurricane
Ort (**-(e)s**, **-e**) *m* place; **an ~ und Stelle** on the spot
Orthopäde (**-n**, **-n**) *m* orthopaedic (BRIT) *od* orthopedic (*US*) specialist, orthopaedist (BRIT), orthopedist (*US*)
örtlich *adj* local
Ortschaft *f* village, small town
Ortsgespräch *nt* local (phone) call
Ortstarif *m* local rate
Ortszeit *f* local time
Ossi *n see note*

> **OSSI**
>
> **Ossi** is a colloquial and rather derogatory word used to describe a German from the former *DDR*.

Ostdeutschland *nt* (*Pol*: *früher*) East Germany; (*Geog*) Eastern Germany
Osten (**-s**) *m* east
Osterei *nt* Easter egg
Osterglocke *f* daffodil
Osterhase *m* Easter bunny
Ostermontag *m* Easter Monday
Ostern (**-s**, **-**) *nt* Easter; **frohe** *od* **fröhliche ~!** Happy Easter!; **zu ~** at Easter
Österreich (**-s**) *nt* Austria
Österreicher(in) (**-s**, **-**) *m(f)* Austrian
österreichisch *adj* Austrian
Ostersonntag *m* Easter Day *od* Sunday
Osteuropa *nt* East(ern) Europe
östlich *adj* eastern, easterly
Ostsee *f* Baltic Sea

Ostwind *m* east wind
Otter (**-s**, **-**) *m* otter
outen *vt* to out
oval *adj* oval
Ozean (**-s**, **-e**) *m* ocean
Ozon (**-s**) *nt* ozone
Ozonloch *nt* hole in the ozone layer
Ozonschicht *f* ozone layer
Ozonwerte *pl* ozone levels *pl*

paar *adj unver*: **ein ~** a few; **ein ~ Mal** a few times; **ein ~ Äpfel** some apples
Paar (**-(e)s**, **-e**) *nt* pair; (*Liebespaar*) couple
pachten *vt* to lease
Päckchen *nt* small package; (*Zigaretten*) packet; (*Postpäckchen*) small parcel
packen *vt*, *vi* (*auch Comput*) to pack; (*fassen*) to grasp, to seize; (*umg*: *schaffen*) to manage; (*fig*: *fesseln*) to grip
Packpapier *nt* brown paper
Packung *f* packet
Packungsbeilage *f* package insert, patient information leaflet
Pädagoge (**-n**, **-n**) *m* educationalist
pädagogisch *adj* educational; **pädagogische Hochschule** college of education
Paddel (**-s**, **-**) *nt* paddle
Paddelboot *nt* canoe
paddeln *vi* to paddle
Paket (**-(e)s**, **-e**) *nt* packet; (*Postpaket*) parcel
Paketkarte *f* dispatch note
Pakistan (**-s**) *nt* Pakistan
Palast (**-es**, **Paläste**) *m* palace
Palästina (**-s**) *nt* Palestine
Palästinenser(in) (**-s**, **-**) *m*(*f*) Palestinian
Palette *f* palette; (*fig*) range; (*Ladepalette*) pallet
Palme (**-**, **-n**) *f* palm (tree)
Palmsonntag *m* Palm Sunday
Pampelmuse (**-**, **-n**) *f* grapefruit
pampig (*umg*) *adj* (*frech*) fresh

Pandemie *f* pandemic
panieren *vt* (*Koch*) to coat with egg and breadcrumbs
Panik *f* panic
Panne (-, **-n**) *f* (*Aut etc*) breakdown; (*Missgeschick*) slip
Pannendienst *m* breakdown service
Pantomime (-, **-n**) *f* mime
Panzer (**-s**, -) *m* (*Platte*) armour (BRIT) *od* armor (*US*) plate; (*Fahrzeug*) tank
Papa (**-s**, **-s**) (*umg*) *m* dad(dy), pa
Papagei (**-s**, **-en**) *m* parrot
Papier (**-s**, **-e**) *nt* paper ■ **Papiere** *pl* (identity) papers *pl*; (*Urkunden*) documents *pl*
Papiergeld *nt* paper money
Papierkorb *m* wastepaper basket; (*Comput*) recycle bin
Pappbecher *m* paper cup
Pappe *f* cardboard
Pappkarton *m* cardboard box
Pappteller *m* paper plate
Paprika (**-s**, **-s**) *m* (*Gewürz*) paprika; (*Paprikaschote*) pepper
Papst (**-(e)s**, **Päpste**) *m* pope
Paradies (**-es**, **-e**) *nt* paradise
parallel *adj* parallel
paralympisch *adj* Paralympic
Paranuss *f* Brazil nut
Parasit (**-en**, **-en**) *m* parasite
parat *adj* ready
Pärchen *nt* couple
Parfüm (**-s**, **-s** *od* **-e**) *nt* perfume
Parfümerie *f* perfumery
parfümieren *vt* to scent, to perfume
Pariser (**-s**, -) *m* (*umg: Kondom*) condom, rubber (*US*)
Park (**-s**, **-s**) *m* park
Park-and-Ride *nt* park and ride
Parkbank *f* park bench
parken *vt*, *vi* to park
Parkett (**-(e)s**, **-e**) *nt* parquet (floor); (*Theat*) stalls *pl* (BRIT), orchestra (*US*)
Parkhaus *nt* multistorey car park
Parklücke *f* parking space
Parkplatz *m* car park, parking lot (*US*); (*Parklücke*) parking place
Parkscheibe *f* parking disc
Parkuhr *f* parking meter
Parkverbot *nt* parking ban
Parlament *nt* parliament
Partei *f* party
Parterre (**-s**, **-s**) *nt* ground floor (BRIT), first floor (*US*); (*Theat*) stalls *pl* (BRIT), orchestra (*US*)
Partie *f* part; (*Spiel*) game; (*Mann, Frau*) catch; **mit von der ~ sein** to join in
Partitur *f* (*Mus*) score
Partizip (**-s**, **-ien**) *nt* participle
Partner(in) (**-s**, -) *m(f)* partner
Partnerschaft *f* partnership; **eingetragene ~** civil partnership
Partnerstadt *f* twin town (BRIT)
Party (-, **-s**) *f* party
Pass (**-es**, **Pässe**) *m* pass; (*Ausweis*) passport
passabel *adj* reasonable
Passagier (**-s**, **-e**) *m* passenger
Passamt *nt* passport office
Passant(in) *m(f)* passer-by
Passbild *nt* passport photo(graph)
passen *vi* to fit; (*auf Frage, Karten*) to pass; **~ zu** (*Farbe etc*) to go with; **Sonntag passt uns nicht** Sunday is no good for us; **das könnte dir so ~!** (*umg*) you'd like that, wouldn't you?
passend *adj* suitable; (*zusammenpassend*) matching; (*angebracht*) fitting; (*Zeit*) convenient; **haben Sie es ~?** (*Geld*) have you got the right money?
passieren *vi* to happen
passiv *adj* passive
Passkontrolle *f* passport control
Passwort *nt* password
Paste (-, **-n**) *f* paste
Pastellfarbe *f* pastel colour (BRIT) *od* color (*US*)
Pastete (-, **-n**) *f* pie; (*Pastetchen*) vol-au-vent
Pastor *m* minister; (*anglikanisch*) vicar
Pate (**-n**, **-n**) *m* godfather
Patenkind *nt* godchild
Patient(in) *m(f)* patient
Patientenverfügung *f* living will
Patin *f* godmother
Patrone (-, **-n**) *f* cartridge
patsch *interj* splash!
patschnass *adj* soaking wet
pauschal *adj* (*Kosten*) inclusive; (*Urteil*) sweeping
Pauschale (-, **-n**) *f* flat rate
Pauschalpreis *m* flat rate; (*für Hotel, Reise*) all-inclusive price
Pauschalreise *f* package tour
Pause (-, **-n**) *f* break; (*Theat*) interval; (*das Innehalten*) pause
Pavian (**-s**, **-e**) *m* baboon
Pay-TV *nt* pay-per-view television, pay TV

Pazifik (**-s**) *m* Pacific
PC *m abk* (= *Personal Computer*) PC
Pech (**-s**, **-e**) *nt* (*fig*) bad luck; **~ haben** to be unlucky; **~ gehabt!** tough! (*umg*)
Pedal (**-s**, **-e**) *nt* pedal
Pediküre (**-**, **-n**) *f* (*Fußpflege*) pedicure
peinlich *adj* (*unangenehm*) embarrassing, awkward; (*genau*) painstaking; **in seinem Zimmer herrschte peinliche Ordnung** his room was meticulously tidy; **er vermied es peinlichst, davon zu sprechen** he was at pains not to talk about it; **es war mir sehr ~** I was totally embarrassed
Peitsche (**-**, **-n**) *f* whip
Pelikan (**-s**, **-e**) *m* pelican
Pellkartoffeln *pl* jacket potatoes *pl*
Pelz (**-es**, **-e**) *m* fur
pendeln *vi* (*Zug, Fähre etc*) to shuttle; (*Mensch*) to commute
Pendelverkehr *m* shuttle service; (*Berufsverkehr*) commuter traffic
Pendler(in) (**-s**, **-**) *m(f)* commuter
penetrant *adj* sharp; (*Person*) pushing
Penis (**-**, **-se**) *m* penis
Pension *f* (*Geld*) pension; (*Ruhestand*) retirement; (*für Gäste*) guesthouse
pensioniert *adj* retired
Pensionsgast *m* boarder, paying guest
Peperoni (**-**, **-**) *f* chilli
per *präp +akk* by, per; (*pro*) per; (*bis*) by
perfekt *adj* perfect
Pergamentpapier *nt* greaseproof paper (Brit), wax(ed) paper (*US*)
Periode (**-**, **-n**) *f* period
Perle (**-**, **-n**) *f* (*lit, fig*) pearl
perplex *adj* dumbfounded
Person (**-**, **-en**) *f* person
Personal (**-s**) *nt* personnel; (*Bedienung*) servants *pl*
Personalausweis *m* identity card
Personalien *pl* particulars *pl*
Personenschaden *m* injury to persons
Personenwaage *f* scales *pl*
Personenzug *m* passenger train
persönlich *adj* personal ▶ *adv* personally; (*erscheinen*) in person; (*auf Briefen*) private (and confidential)
Persönlichkeit *f* personality
Peru (**-s**) *nt* Peru
Perücke (**-**, **-n**) *f* wig
pervers *adj* perverse
pessimistisch *adj* pessimistic
Pest (**-**) *f* plague
Petersilie *f* parsley
Petroleum (**-s**) *nt* paraffin (Brit), kerosene (*US*)
Pfad (**-(e)s**, **-e**) *m* path
Pfadfinder *m* Boy Scout
Pfadfinderin *f* Girl Guide
Pfahl (**-(e)s**, **Pfähle**) *m* post, stake
Pfand (**-(e)s**, **Pfänder**) *nt* security; (*Flaschenpfand*) deposit; (*im Spiel*) forfeit
Pfandflasche *f* returnable bottle
Pfanne (**-**, **-n**) *f* (frying) pan
Pfannkuchen *m* pancake
Pfarrei *f* parish
Pfarrer (**-s**, **-**) *m* priest
Pfau (**-(e)s**, **-en**) *m* peacock
Pfeffer (**-s**, **-**) *m* pepper
Pfefferkuchen *m* gingerbread
Pfefferminze *f* peppermint (plant)
Pfeffermühle *f* pepper mill
pfeffern *vt* to pepper
Pfeife (**-**, **-n**) *f* whistle; (*Tabakpfeife, Orgelpfeife*) pipe
pfeifen *unreg vt, vi* to whistle
Pfeil (**-(e)s**, **-e**) *m* arrow
Pfeiltaste *f* (*Comput*) arrow key
Pferd (**-(e)s**, **-e**) *nt* horse
Pferdeschwanz *m* (*Frisur*) ponytail
Pferdestall *m* stable
Pferdestärke *f* horsepower
pfiff *etc vb siehe* **pfeifen**
Pfifferling *m* chanterelle
Pfingsten (**-**, **-**) *nt* Whitsun
Pfingstsonntag *m* Whit Sunday, Pentecost (*Rel*)
Pfirsich (**-s**, **-e**) *m* peach
Pflanze (**-**, **-n**) *f* plant
pflanzen *vt* to plant
Pflanzenfett *nt* vegetable fat
Pflaster (**-s**, **-**) *nt* plaster; (*Straßenpflaster*) pavement (Brit), sidewalk (*US*)
Pflaume (**-**, **-n**) *f* plum
Pflege (**-**, **-n**) *f* care; (*Krankenpflege*) nursing
pflegebedürftig *adj* needing care
pflegeleicht *adj* easy-care
pflegen *vt* to look after; (*Kranke*) to nurse; (*Beziehungen*) to foster
Pflegeversicherung *f* geriatric care insurance
Pflicht (**-**, **-en**) *f* duty; (*Sport*) compulsory section; **Rechte und Pflichten** rights and responsibilities

pflichtbewusst *adj* conscientious
Pflichtfach *nt* (*Sch*) compulsory subject
Pflichtversicherung *f* compulsory insurance
pflücken *vt* to pick
Pforte (-, **-n**) *f* gate
Pförtner (**-s**, **-**) *m* porter, doorman
Pförtnerin *f* porter
Pfosten (**-s**, **-**) *m* post
Pfote (-, **-n**) *f* paw
pfui *interj* ugh!
Pfund (**-(e)s**, **-e**) *nt* (*Fin*) pound
pfuschen *vi* to bungle
Pfütze (-, **-n**) *f* puddle
Phantasie = **Fantasie**
phantastisch *adj* = **fantastisch**
Phase (-, **-n**) *f* phase
Philippinen *pl* Philippines *pl*
Philosophie *f* philosophy
Photo = **Foto**
Photoshop® *nt* Photoshop®
pH-Wert *m* pH value
Physik *f* physics *sing*
physisch *adj* physical
Pianist(in) *m(f)* pianist
Pickel (**-s**, **-**) *m* pimple; (*Werkzeug*) pickaxe; (*Bergpickel*) ice axe
Picknick (**-s**, **-e** *od* **-s**) *nt* picnic; **~ machen** to have a picnic
piepsen *vi* to chirp
piercen *vt*: **sich die Nase ~ lassen** to have one's nose pierced
Piercing (**-s**) *nt* (body) piercing
Pik (**-s**, **-s**) *nt* (*Karten*) spades
pikant *adj* spicy
Pilger(in) (**-s**, **-**) *m(f)* pilgrim
Pilgerfahrt *f* pilgrimage
Pille (-, **-n**) *f* pill
Pilot(in) (**-en**, **-en**) *m(f)* pilot
Pils (-, **-**) *nt* Pilsner (lager)
Pilz (**-es**, **-e**) *m* (*essbar*) mushroom; (*giftig*) toadstool; (*Med*) fungus
pingelig (*umg*) *adj* fussy
Pinguin (**-s**, **-e**) *m* penguin
Pinie *f* pine
pinkeln (*umg*) *vi* to pee
Pinsel (**-s**, **-**) *m* paintbrush
Pinzette *f* tweezers *pl*
Pistazie (-, **-n**) *f* pistachio
Piste (-, **-n**) *f* (*Ski*) piste; (*Aviat*) runway
Pistole (-, **-n**) *f* pistol
Pixel (**-s**) *nt* (*Comput*) pixel
Pizza (-, **-s**) *f* pizza
Plakat (**-(e)s**, **-e**) *nt* poster
Plakette (-, **-n**) *f* (*Abzeichen*) badge
Plan (**-(e)s**, **Pläne**) *m* plan; (*Karte*) map
planen *vt* to plan
Planet (**-en**, **-en**) *m* planet
planmäßig *adj* (*Eisenb*) scheduled
planschen *vi* to splash
plantschen *vi* to splash
Planung *f* planning
Plastik¹ *f* sculpture
Plastik² (**-s**) *nt* (*Kunststoff*) plastic
Plastikfolie *f* plastic film
Plastiktüte *f* plastic bag
Platin (**-s**) *nt* platinum
platsch *interj* splash!
platt *adj* flat; (*umg: überrascht*) flabbergasted; (*fig: geistlos*) flat, boring
Platte (-, **-n**) *f* (*Speisenplatte, Phot, Tech*) plate; (*Steinplatte*) flag; (*Schallplatte*) record
Plattenspieler *m* record player
Plattform *f* platform
Plattfuß *m* flat foot; (*Reifen*) flat tyre (*Brit*) *od* tire (*US*)
Platz (**-es**, **Plätze**) *m* place; (*Sitzplatz*) seat; (*Raum*) space, room; (*in Stadt*) square; (*Sportplatz*) playing field; **~ nehmen** to take a seat
Platzanweiser (**-s**, **-**) *m* usher
Platzanweiserin *f* usherette
Plätzchen *nt* spot; (*Gebäck*) biscuit
platzen *vi* to burst; (*Bombe*) to explode
Platzkarte *f* seat reservation
Platzverweis *m* sending-off
Platzwunde *f* cut
plaudern *vi* to chat, to talk
pleite (*umg*) *adj* broke
Pleite (-, **-n**) *f* bankruptcy; (*umg: Reinfall*) flop
Plombe (-, **-n**) *f* lead seal; (*Zahnplombe*) filling
plombieren *vt* (*Zahn*) to fill
plötzlich *adj* sudden ▶ *adv* suddenly
plump *adj* clumsy; (*Hände*) coarse; (*Körper*) shapeless
Plural (**-s**, **-e**) *m* plural
plus *adv* plus
Plus (-, **-**) *nt* plus; (*Fin*) profit; (*Vorteil*) advantage
Plüsch (**-(e)s**, **-e**) *m* plush
PLZ *abk* = **Postleitzahl**
Po (**-s**, **-s**) (*umg*) *m* bum (*Brit*), fanny (*US*)
Pocken *pl* smallpox *sing*
Podcast (**-s**, **-s**) *m* podcast
poetisch *adj* poetic
Pointe (-, **-n**) *f* punch line

Pokal (**-s**, **-e**) *m* goblet; (*Sport*) cup
pökeln *vt* to pickle
Pol (**-s**, **-e**) *m* pole
Pole (**-n**, **-n**) *m* Pole
Polen (**-s**) *nt* Poland
Police (-, **-n**) *f* insurance policy
polieren *vt* to polish
Polin *f* Pole, Polish woman
Politik *f* politics *sing*; (*eine bestimmte*) policy
Politiker(in) (**-s**, -) *m(f)* politician
politisch *adj* political
Politur *f* polish
Polizei *f* police
Polizeibeamte(r) *m* police officer
polizeilich *adj* police *attrib*
Polizeirevier *nt* police station
Polizeistunde *f* closing time
Polizeiwache *f* police station
Polizist(in) (**-en**, **-en**) *m(f)* police officer
Pollen (**-s**, -) *m* pollen
Pollenflug *m* pollen count
polnisch *adj* Polish
Polohemd *nt* polo shirt
Polster (**-s**, -) *nt* cushion; (*Polsterung*) upholstery; (*in Kleidung*) padding; (*fig: Geld*) reserves *pl*
polstern *vt* (*Möbel*) to upholster; (*Kleidung*) to pad
Polterabend *m party on the eve of a wedding*
poltern *vi* (*Krach machen*) to crash; (*schimpfen*) to rant
Polyester (**-s**, -) *m* polyester
Pommes frites, Pommes (*umg*) *pl* chips *pl* (BRIT), (French) fries *pl* (US)
Pony (**-s**, **-s**) *m* (*Frisur*) fringe (BRIT), bangs *pl* (US) ▶ *nt* (*Pferd*) pony
Popmusik *f* pop music
populär *adj* popular
Pop-up, Popup *nt* (*Comput*, *Wirts*) pop-up
Pore (-, **-n**) *f* pore
Pornografie *f* pornography
Porree (**-s**, **-s**) *m* leek
Portemonnaie (**-s**, **-s**) *nt* purse
Portier (**-s**, **-s**) *m* porter; (*Pförtner*) porter
Portion *f* portion, helping
Porto (**-s**, **-s** *od* **Porti**) *nt* postage
Portugal (**-s**) *nt* Portugal
Portugiese (**-n**, **-n**) *m* Portuguese
Portugiesin *f* Portuguese
portugiesisch *adj* Portuguese
Portwein *m* port
Porzellan (**-s**, **-e**) *nt* china
Posaune (-, **-n**) *f* trombone
Position *f* position
positiv *adj* positive
Post (-, **-en**) *f* post (office); (*Briefe*) post, mail
Postamt *nt* post office
Postanweisung *f* postal order (BRIT), money order
Postausgang *m* (*Internet*) outbox
Postbote *m* postman (BRIT), mailman (US)
Postbotin *f* postwoman (BRIT), mailwoman (US)
Posteingang *m* (*Internet*) inbox
posten *vt* (*auf Forum*, *Blog*) to post
Posten (**-s**, -) *m* post, position; (*Comm*) item; (*auf Liste*) entry
Poster (**-s**, **-(s)**) *nt* poster
Postfach *nt* post office box
Postkarte *f* postcard
postlagernd *adv* poste restante
Postleitzahl *f* postcode (BRIT), zip code (US)
postmodern *adj* postmodern
Postsparkasse *f* post office savings bank
Poststempel *m* postmark
Potenz *f* power; (*eines Mannes*) potency
prächtig *adj* splendid
prahlen *vi* to boast, to brag
Praktikant(in) *m(f)* trainee
Praktikum (**-s**, **Praktika** *od* **Praktiken**) *nt* practical training
praktisch *adj* practical; **praktischer Arzt** general practitioner
Praline *f* chocolate
Prämie *f* premium; (*Belohnung*) award
Präparat (**-(e)s**, **-e**) *nt* (*Biol*) preparation; (*Med*) medicine
Präservativ (**-s**, **-e**) *nt* condom
Präsident(in) *m(f)* president
Praxis (-, **Praxen**) *f* practice; (*Behandlungsraum*) surgery; (*von Anwalt*) office
Praxisgebühr *f surgery surcharge*
präzise *adj* precise
predigen *vt*, *vi* to preach
Predigt (-, **-en**) *f* sermon
Preis (**-es**, **-e**) *m* price; (*Siegespreis*) prize
Preisausschreiben *nt* competition
Preiselbeere *f* cranberry

preisgünstig *adj* inexpensive
Preislage *f* price range
Preisliste *f* price list
Preisschild *nt* price tag
Preisträger *m* prizewinner
preiswert *adj* inexpensive
Prellung *f* bruise
Premiere (-, **-n**) *f* premiere
Premierminister(in) *m(f)* prime minister, premier
Prepaidhandy *nt* prepaid mobile (BRIT), prepaid cell phone (*US*)
Presse (-, **-n**) *f* press
pressen *vt* to press
prickeln *vi* to tingle
Priester (**-s**, -) *m* priest
Primel (-, **-n**) *f* primrose
primitiv *adj* primitive
Prinz (**-en**, **-en**) *m* prince
Prinzessin *f* princess
Prinzip (**-s**, **-ien**) *nt* principle; **aus ~** on principle; **im ~** in principle
Priorität *f* priority
privat *adj* private
Privatfernsehen *nt* commercial television
privatisieren *vt* to privatize
pro *präp +akk* per; **~ Stück** each
Pro (-) *nt* pro
Probe (-, **-n**) *f* test; (*Teststück*) sample; (*Theat*) rehearsal
Probefahrt *f* test drive
Probezeit *f* probation period
probieren *vt* to try; (*Wein, Speise*) to taste, to sample ▶ *vi* to try; (*Wein, Speise*) to taste
Problem (**-s**, **-e**) *nt* problem
Produkt (**-(e)s**, **-e**) *nt* product
Produktion *f* production
produzieren *vt* to produce
Professor(in) *m(f)* professor
Profi (**-s**, **-s**) *m abk* pro
Profil (**-s**, **-e**) *nt* profile; (*von Reifen, Schuhsohle*) tread
Profit (**-(e)s**, **-e**) *m* profit
profitieren *vi*: **~ (von)** to profit (from)
Prognose (-, **-n**) *f* prediction, prognosis
Programm (**-s**, **-e**) *nt* programme (BRIT), program (*US*); (*Comput*) program; (*TV: Sender*) channel
programmieren *vt* (*Comput*) to program
Programmierer(in) (**-s**, -) *m(f)* programmer
Programmkino *nt* arts *od* repertory (*US*) cinema
Projekt (**-(e)s**, **-e**) *nt* project
Projektor *m* projector
Promenade (-, **-n**) *f* promenade
Promille (**-(s)**, -) (*umg*) *nt* alcohol level
Promillegrenze *f* legal (alcohol) limit
prominent *adj* prominent
Prominenz *f* VIPs *pl*
Propeller (**-s**, -) *m* propeller
prosit *interj* cheers!
Prospekt (**-(e)s**, **-e**) *m* leaflet, brochure
prost *interj* cheers!
Prostituierte (**-n**, **-n**) *f* prostitute
Protest (**-(e)s**, **-e**) *m* protest
Protestant(in) *m(f)* Protestant
protestantisch *adj* Protestant
protestieren *vi* to protest
Prothese (-, **-n**) *f* artificial limb; (*Zahnprothese*) dentures *pl*
Protokoll (**-s**, **-e**) *nt* (*von Sitzung*) minutes *pl*; (*diplomatisch*) protocol; (*Polizeiprotokoll*) statement
protzen *vi* to show off
protzig *adj* ostentatious
Proviant (**-s**, **-e**) *m* provisions *pl*
Provinz (-, **-en**) *f* province
Provision *f* (*Comm*) commission
provisorisch *adj* provisional
Provisorium (**-s**, **-ien**) *nt* provisional arrangement
provozieren *vt* to provoke
Prozent (**-(e)s**, **-e**) *nt* per cent
Prozess (**-es**, **-e**) *m* trial, case; (*Vorgang*) process
prozessieren *vi*: **~ (mit)** to go to law (with *od* against)
Prozession *f* procession
prüde *adj* prudish
prüfen *vt* to test; (*nachprüfen*) to check
Prüfung *f* (*Sch, Univ*) examination, exam; (*Überprüfung*) checking; **eine ~ machen** to take *od* sit (BRIT) an exam(ination)
Prügelei *f* fight
prügeln *vt* to beat ▶ *vr* to fight
PS *abk* (= *Pferdestärke*) hp; (= *Postskript(um)*) PS
pseudo- *in zW* pseudo
Pseudonym (**-s**, **-e**) *nt* pseudonym
Psychiater (**-s**, -) *m* psychiatrist
psychisch *adj* psychological
Psychoanalyse *f* psychoanalysis
Psychologe (**-n**, **-n**) *m* psychologist

Psychologie *f* psychology
Psychotherapie *f* psychotherapy
Pubertät *f* puberty
Publikum (**-s**) *nt* audience; (*Sport*) crowd
Pudding (**-s**, **-e** *od* **-s**) *m* blancmange
Pudel (**-s**, **-**) *m* poodle
Puder (**-s**, **-**) *m* powder
Puderzucker *m* icing sugar (BRIT), confectioner's sugar (*US*)
Puerto Rico (**-s**) *nt* Puerto Rico
Pulli (**-s**, **-s**) (*umg*) *m* sweater, jumper (BRIT)
Puls (**-es**, **-e**) *m* pulse
Pulver (**-s**, **-**) *nt* powder
Pulverkaffee *m* instant coffee
Pulverschnee *m* powdery snow
pummelig *adj* chubby
Pumpe (**-**, **-n**) *f* pump
pumpen *vt* to pump; (*umg*) to lend; (*: entleihen*) to borrow
Punkt (**-(e)s**, **-e**) *m* point; (*bei Muster*) dot; (*Satzzeichen*) full stop, period (*bes US*); **~ 12 Uhr** at 12 o'clock on the dot
pünktlich *adj* punctual
Pünktlichkeit *f* punctuality
Punsch (**-(e)s**, **-e**) *m* (hot) punch
Pupille (**-**, **-n**) *f* pupil
Puppe (**-**, **-n**) *f* doll
pur *adj* pure; (*völlig*) sheer; (*Whisky*) neat
Püree (**-s**, **-s**) *nt* purée; (*Kartoffelpüree*) mashed potatoes *pl*
Puste (**-**) (*umg*) *f* puff
Pustel (**-**, **-n**) *f* pustule
pusten (*umg*) *vi* to puff
Pute (**-**, **-n**) *f* turkey hen
Putsch (**-(e)s**, **-e**) *m* putsch
Putz (**-es**) *m* (*Mörtel*) plaster
putzen *vt* to clean; (*Nase*) to wipe, to blow; **sich** *dat* **die Zähne ~** to brush one's teeth
Putzfrau *f* cleaner
Putzlappen *m* cloth
Putzmann *m* cleaner
Puzzle (**-s**, **-s**) *nt* jigsaw (puzzle)
Pyjama (**-s**, **-s**) *m* pyjamas *pl* (BRIT), pajamas *pl* (*US*)
Pyramide (**-**, **-n**) *f* pyramid
Python (**-s**, **-s**) *m* python

q

Quadrat (**-(e)s**, **-e**) *nt* square
quadratisch *adj* square
Quadratmeter *m* square metre (BRIT) *od* meter (*US*)
quaken *vi* to croak; (*Ente*) to quack
Qual (**-**, **-en**) *f* pain, agony; (*seelisch*) anguish
quälen *vt* to torment ▶ *vr* (*sich abmühen*) to struggle; (*geistig*) to torment o.s.
Quälerei *f* torture, torment
qualifizieren *vt* to qualify; (*einstufen*) to label ▶ *vr* to qualify
Qualität *f* quality
Qualle (**-**, **-n**) *f* jellyfish
Qualm (**-(e)s**) *m* thick smoke
qualmen *vt, vi* to smoke
Quantität *f* quantity
Quarantäne (**-**, **-n**) *f* quarantine
Quark (**-s**) *m* quark; (*umg*) rubbish
Quartett (**-(e)s**, **-e**) *nt* (*Mus*) quartet; (*Karten*) ≈ happy families
Quartier (**-s**, **-e**) *nt* accommodation (BRIT), accommodations *pl* (*US*)
quasi *adv* virtually
Quatsch (**-es**) (*umg*) *m* rubbish
quatschen *vi* to chat
Quecksilber *nt* mercury
Quelle (**-**, **-n**) *f* spring; (*eines Flusses, Comput*) source
quellen *vi* (*hervorquellen*) to pour *od* gush forth
quer *adv* crossways, diagonally; (*rechtwinklig*) at right angles; **~ auf dem Bett** across the bed
querfeldein *adv* across country
Querflöte *f* flute

Querschnitt *m* cross section
querschnittsgelähmt *adj* paraplegic
Querstraße *f* intersecting road
quetschen *vt* to squash, to crush; (*Med*) to bruise
Quetschung *f* bruise
Queue (**-s**, **-s**) *nt* (*Billiard*) cue
quietschen *vi* to squeak; (*Bremsen*) to screech
quitt *adj* quits, even
Quitte (-, **-n**) *f* quince
Quittung *f* receipt
Quiz (-, -) *nt* quiz
Quote (-, **-n**) *f* proportion; (*Rate*) rate

Rabatt (**-(e)s**, **-e**) *m* discount
Rabe (**-n**, **-n**) *m* raven
Rache (**-**) *f* revenge, vengeance
Rachen (**-s**, **-**) *m* throat
rächen *vt* to avenge ▶ *vr* to take (one's) revenge
Rad (**-(e)s**, **Räder**) *nt* wheel; (*Fahrrad*) bike; **~ fahren** to cycle
Radar (**-s**) *m od nt* radar
Radarfalle *f* speed trap
Radarkontrolle *f* radar-controlled speed check
radeln *vi* to cycle
Radfahrer(in) *m(f)* cyclist
Radfahrweg *m* cycle track *od* path
radieren *vt* to rub out, to erase
Radiergummi *m* rubber (BRIT), eraser (*bes US*)
Radierung *f* etching
Radieschen *nt* radish
radikal *adj* radical
Radio (**-s**, **-s**) *nt* radio; **im ~** on the radio
radioaktiv *adj* radioactive
Radiosender *m* radio station
Radiowecker *m* radio alarm (clock)
Radkappe *f* (*Aut*) hub cap
Radler(in) (**-s**, **-**) *m(f)* cyclist
Radrennen *nt* cycle race; (*Sportart*) cycle racing
Radweg *m* cycle track *od* path
raffiniert *adj* crafty, cunning; (*Zucker*) refined
Rahm (**-s**) *m* cream
rahmen *vt* to frame
Rahmen (**-s**, **-**) *m* frame(work)
Rakete (-, **-n**) *f* rocket
rammen *vt* to ram

Rampe (-, **-n**) *f* ramp
ramponieren (*umg*) *vt* to damage
Ramsch (**-(e)s**, **-e**) *m* junk
ran (*umg*) *adv* = **heran**
Rand (**-(e)s**, **Ränder**) *m* edge; (*von Brille, Tasse etc*) rim; (*auf Papier*) margin; (*Schmutzrand, unter Augen*) ring; (*fig*) verge, brink
randalieren *vi* to (go on the) rampage
Randalierer(in) (**-s**, **-**) *m(f)* hooligan
Randstreifen *m* (*der Autobahn*) hard shoulder (Brit), shoulder (*US*)
rang *etc vb siehe* **ringen**
Rang (**-(e)s**, **Ränge**) *m* rank; (*Stand*) standing; (*Theat*) circle
rannte *etc vb siehe* **rennen**
ranzig *adj* rancid
Rap (**-(s)**, **-s**) *m* (*Mus*) rap
rappen *vi* (*Mus*) to rap
Rapper(in) (**-s**, **-**) *m(f)* (*Mus*) rapper
rar *adj* rare
rasant *adj* quick, rapid
rasch *adj* quick
rascheln *vi* to rustle
rasen *vi* to rave; (*sich schnell bewegen*) to race
Rasen (**-s**, **-**) *m* lawn
rasend *adj* furious
Rasenmäher (**-s**, **-**) *m* lawnmower
Rasierapparat *m* shaver
Rasiercreme *f* shaving cream
rasieren *vt*, *vr* to shave
Rasierklinge *f* razor blade
Rasiermesser *nt* razor
Rasierpinsel *m* shaving brush
Rasse (-, **-n**) *f* race; (*Tierrasse*) breed
Rassismus (**-**) *m* racism
Rassist(in) *m(f)* racist
rassistisch *adj* racist
Rast (-, **-en**) *f* rest
rasten *vi* to rest
Rastplatz *m* (*Aut*) lay-by (Brit), turnout (*US*)
Raststätte *f* service area
Rasur *f* shave
Rat (**-(e)s**, **-schläge**) *m* (piece of) advice; **um ~ fragen** to ask for advice
Rate (-, **-n**) *f* instalment (Brit), installment (*US*); **auf Raten kaufen** to buy on hire purchase (Brit) *od* on the installment plan (*US*)
raten *unreg vt*, *vi* to guess; (*empfehlen*): **jdm ~** to advise sb
Rathaus *nt* town hall
Ration *f* ration
ratlos *adj* at a loss, helpless
ratsam *adj* advisable
Rätsel (**-s**, **-**) *nt* puzzle; (*Worträtsel*) riddle; **vor einem ~ stehen** to be baffled
rätselhaft *adj* mysterious
Ratte (-, **-n**) *f* rat
rau *adj* rough, coarse; (*Wetter*) harsh
Raub (**-(e)s**) *m* robbery; (*Beute*) loot, booty
rauben *vt* to rob
Räuber (**-s**, **-**) *m* robber
Raubfisch *m* predatory fish
Raubkopie *f* pirate copy
Raubmord *m* robbery with murder
Raubtier *nt* predator
Raubüberfall *m* robbery with violence
Raubvogel *m* bird of prey
Rauch (**-(e)s**) *m* smoke
rauchen *vt*, *vi* to smoke
Raucher(in) (**-s**, **-**) *m(f)* smoker
räuchern *vt* to smoke
rauchig *adj* smoky
rauf (*umg*) *adv* = **herauf**
rauh *siehe* **rau**
Raum (**-(e)s**, **Räume**) *m* space; (*Zimmer, Platz*) room; (*Gebiet*) area
räumen *vt* to clear; (*Wohnung, Platz*) to vacate; (*wegbringen*) to shift, to move; (*in Schrank etc*) to put away
Raumfähre *f* space shuttle
Raumfahrt *f* space travel
Raumschiff *nt* spaceship
Raumstation *f* space station
Räumungsverkauf *m* clearance sale
Raupe (-, **-n**) *f* caterpillar
Raureif *m* hoarfrost
raus (*umg*) *adv* = **heraus**; **hinaus**
Rausch (**-(e)**, **Räusche**) *m* intoxication; **einen ~ haben** to be drunk
rauschen *vi* (*Wasser*) to rush; (*Baum*) to rustle; (*Radio etc*) to hiss
Rauschgift *nt* drug
Rauschgiftsüchtige(r) *f(m)* drug addict
raus|fliegen *unreg* (*umg*) *vi* to be chucked out
räuspern *vr* to clear one's throat
Razzia (-, **Razzien**) *f* raid
reagieren *vi*: **~ (auf** +*akk***)** to react (to)
Reaktion *f* reaction
real *adj* real
realistisch *adj* realistic

Realität *f* reality; **erweiterte ~** augmented reality
Realityshow *f* (*TV*) reality show
Realschule *f* ≈ middle school (*Brit*), junior high school (*US*)
Rebe (**-**, **-n**) *f* vine
rebellieren *vi* to rebel
Rebhuhn *nt* partridge
rechnen *vt*, *vi* to calculate ▶ *vr* to pay off; **~ mit** to reckon with; **~ auf** +*akk* to count on
Rechner (**-s**, **-**) *m* calculator; (*Comput*) computer
Rechnung *f* calculation(s); (*Comm*) bill (*Brit*), check (*US*); **auf eigene ~** on one's own account
recht *adj* right ▶ *adv* (*vor Adjektiv*) really, quite; **das ist mir ~** that suits me; **es geschieht ihm ~** it serves him right; **~ haben** to be right; **jdm ~ geben** to agree with sb
Recht (**-(e)s**, **-e**) *nt* right; (*Jur*) law
rechte(r, s) *adj* right; (*Pol*) right-wing
Rechte *f* right (hand); (*Pol*) Right
Rechte(s) *nt* right thing; **etwas/ nichts Rechtes** something/nothing proper
Rechteck (**-(e)s**, **-e**) *nt* rectangle
rechteckig *adj* rectangular
rechtfertigen *vt untr* to justify ▶ *vr untr* to justify o.s.
rechtlich *adj* legal
rechtmäßig *adj* legal, lawful
rechts *adv* on *od* to the right; **~ von** to the right of
Rechtsanwalt *m*, **Rechtsanwältin** *f* lawyer
Rechtschreibung *f* spelling
Rechtshänder(in) (**-s**, **-**) *m(f)* right-handed person
rechtsradikal *adj* (*Pol*) extreme right-wing
Rechtsverkehr *m* driving on the right
rechtswidrig *adj* illegal
rechtwinklig *adj* right-angled
rechtzeitig *adj* timely ▶ *adv* in time
recycelbar *adj* recyclable
recyceln *vt* to recycle
Recycling (**-s**) *nt* recycling
Recyclingpapier *nt* recycled paper
Redakteur(in) *m(f)* editor
Redaktion *f* editing; (*Leute*) editorial staff; (*Büro*) editorial office(s *pl*)
Rede (**-**, **-n**) *f* speech; (*Gespräch*) talk; **eine ~ halten** to make a speech
reden *vi* to talk, to speak ▶ *vt* to say; (*Unsinn etc*) to talk
Redewendung *f* idiom
Redner(in) (**-s**, **-**) *m(f)* speaker
reduzieren *vt* to reduce
Referat (**-(e)s**, **-e**) *nt* paper; **ein ~ halten (über** +*akk*) to give a paper (on)
reflektieren *vt*, *vi* to reflect
Reform (**-**, **-en**) *f* reform
Reformhaus *nt* health food shop
reformieren *vt* to reform
Regal (**-s**, **-e**) *nt* (book)shelves *pl*
Regel (**-**, **-n**) *f* rule; (*Med*) period
regelmäßig *adj* regular
regeln *vt* to regulate, to control; (*Angelegenheit*) to settle ▶ *vr*: **sich von selbst ~** to take care of itself
Regelung *f* regulation
Regen (**-s**, **-**) *m* rain
Regenbogen *m* rainbow
Regenbogenfamilie *f family with same-sex parents*
Regenmantel *m* raincoat
Regenschauer *m* shower (of rain)
Regenschirm *m* umbrella
Regenwald *m* (*Geog*) rain forest
Regenwurm *m* earthworm
Regie *f* (*Film etc*) direction
regieren *vt*, *vi* to govern, to rule
Regierung *f* government; (*Monarchie*) reign
Region *f* region
Regisseur(in) *m(f)* director
registrieren *vt* to register; (*umg: zur Kenntnis nehmen*) to note
regnen *vi unpers* to rain
regnerisch *adj* rainy
regulär *adj* regular
regulieren *vt* to regulate
Reh (**-(e)s**, **-e**) *nt* deer
Reibe (**-**, **-n**) *f* grater
reiben *unreg vt* to rub; (*Koch*) to grate
reibungslos *adj* smooth
reich *adj* rich
Reich (**-(e)s**, **-e**) *nt* empire; (*von König*) kingdom
reichen *vi* to reach; (*genügen*) to be enough *od* sufficient ▶ *vt* to hold out; (*geben*) to pass, to hand; (*anbieten*) to offer
reichhaltig *adj* ample, rich
reichlich *adj* ample; **~ Zeit** plenty of time
Reichtum (**-s**, **-tümer**) *m* wealth
reif *adj* ripe; (*Mensch, Urteil*) mature

Reif[1] (**-(e)s**) *m* hoarfrost
Reif[2] (**-(e)s**, **-e**) *m* (*Ring*) ring
reifen *vi* to mature; (*Obst*) to ripen
Reifen (**-s**, **-**) *m* ring, hoop; (*Fahrzeugreifen*) tyre (BRIT), tire (US)
Reifendruck *m* tyre (BRIT) *od* tire (US) pressure
Reifenpanne *f* puncture
Reihe (**-**, **-n**) *f* row; (*von Tagen etc, umg: Anzahl*) series *sing*; **der ~ nach** one after the other; **er ist an der ~** it's his turn
Reihenfolge *f* sequence
Reihenhaus *nt* terraced (BRIT) *od* row (US) house
Reiher (**-s**, **-**) *m* heron
rein[1] (*umg*) *adv* = **herein**; **hinein**
rein[2] *adj* pure; (*sauber*) clean
Reinfall (*umg*) *m* let-down
rein|fallen *vi*: **auf jdn/etw ~** to be taken in by sb/sth
reinigen *vt* to clean
Reinigung *f* cleaning; (*Geschäft*) cleaner's
Reinigungsmittel *nt* cleansing agent
Reis (**-es**, **-e**) *m* rice
Reise (**-**, **-n**) *f* journey; (*Schiffsreise*) voyage
Reiseapotheke *f* first-aid kit
Reisebüro *nt* travel agency
Reiseführer *m* guide(book); (*Mensch*) (travel) guide
Reisegepäck *nt* luggage
Reisegesellschaft *f* party of travellers (BRIT) *od* travelers (US)
Reisegruppe *f* tourist party; (*mit Reisebus*) coach party
Reiseleiter *m* courier
reisen *vi* to travel; **~ nach** to go to
Reisende(r) *f(m)* traveller (BRIT), traveler (US)
Reisepass *m* passport
Reiseroute *f* itinerary
Reisescheck *m* traveller's cheque (BRIT), traveler's check (US)
Reisetasche *f* travelling (BRIT) *od* traveling (US) bag *od* case
Reiseveranstalter *m* tour operator
Reiseverkehr *m* tourist *od* holiday traffic
Reiseversicherung *f* travel insurance
Reiseziel *nt* destination
reißen *unreg vt*, *vi* to tear; (*ziehen*) to pull, to drag; **etw an sich ~** to snatch sth up; (*fig*) to take sth over; **sich um etw ~** to scramble for sth; **wenn alle Stricke ~** (*fig: umg*) if the worst comes to the worst; **einen Witz ~** to crack a joke
Reißnagel *m* drawing pin (BRIT), thumbtack (US)
Reißverschluss *m* zip (fastener) (BRIT), zipper (US)
Reißzwecke *f* = **Reißnagel**
reiten *unreg vt*, *vi* to ride
Reiter (**-s**, **-**) *m* rider
Reithose *f* riding breeches *pl*
Reitstiefel *m* riding boot
Reiz (**-es**, **-e**) *m* stimulus; (*angenehm*) charm; (*Verlockung*) attraction
reizen *vt* to stimulate; (*unangenehm*) to irritate; (*verlocken*) to appeal to, to attract
reizend *adj* charming
Reizgas *nt* tear gas
Reklamation *f* complaint
Reklame (**-**, **-n**) *f* advertising; (*Anzeige*) advertisement
reklamieren *vi* to complain ▶ *vt* to complain about
Rekord (**-(e)s**, **-e**) *m* record
relativ *adj* relative ▶ *adv* relatively
relaxen *vi* to relax, to chill out
Religion *f* religion
religiös *adj* religious
Remoulade (**-**, **-n**) *f* remoulade
Renaissance (**-**, **-n**) *f* (*Hist*) Renaissance; (*fig*) revival
Rennbahn *f* racecourse; (*Aut*) racetrack
rennen *unreg vt*, *vi* to run
Rennen (**-s**, **-**) *nt* running; (*Wettbewerb*) race
Rennfahrer(in) *m(f)* racing driver (BRIT), race car driver (US)
Rennrad *nt* racing cycle
Rennwagen *m* racing car (BRIT), race car (US)
renommiert *adj*: **~ (wegen)** renowned (for), famous (for)
renovieren *vt* to renovate
Renovierung *f* renovation
rentabel *adj* profitable
Rente (**-**, **-n**) *f* pension
Rentenversicherung *f* pension scheme
Rentier *nt* reindeer
rentieren *vi*, *vr* to pay, to be profitable
Rentner(in) (**-s**, **-**) *m(f)* pensioner

Reparatur *f* repair
Reparaturwerkstatt *f* repair shop; (*Aut*) garage
reparieren *vt* to repair
Reportage (-, -**n**) *f* report
Reporter(in) (-**s**, -) *m(f)* reporter
Reptil (-**s**, -**ien**) *nt* reptile
Republik *f* republic
Reservat (-**(e)s**, -**e**) *nt* reservation
Reserve (-, -**n**) *f* reserve
Reserverad *nt* (*Aut*) spare wheel
reservieren *vt* to reserve
resignieren *vi* to resign
Respekt (-**(e)s**) *m* respect
respektieren *vt* to respect
Rest (-**(e)s**, -**e**) *m* remainder, rest; (*Überrest*) remains *pl*
Restaurant (-**s**, -**s**) *nt* restaurant
restaurieren *vt* to restore
Restbetrag *m* remainder
restlich *adj* remaining
restlos *adj* complete
Restmüll *m* non-recyclable waste
Resultat (-**(e)s**, -**e**) *nt* result
retten *vt* to save, to rescue
Rettich (-**s**, -**e**) *m* radish
Rettung *f* rescue; (*Hilfe*) help
Rettungsboot *nt* lifeboat
Rettungshubschrauber *m* rescue helicopter
Rettungsring *m* lifebelt, life preserver (*US*)
Rettungswagen *m* ambulance
retweeten *vt* (*auf Twitter*) to retweet
Reue (-) *f* remorse; (*Bedauern*) regret
reuen *vt*: **es reut ihn** he regrets it
revanchieren *vr* (*sich rächen*) to get one's own back, to have one's revenge; (*erwidern*) to return the compliment
Revolution *f* revolution
Rezept (-**(e)s**, -**e**) *nt* (*Koch*) recipe; (*Med*) prescription
Rezeption *f* (*von Hotel*) reception
rezeptpflichtig *adj* available only on prescription
R-Gespräch *nt* (*Tel*) reverse charge call (BRIT), collect call (*US*)
Rhabarber (-**s**) *m* rhubarb
Rhein (-**(e)s**) *m* Rhine
Rheinland-Pfalz *nt* Rhineland-Palatinate
Rheuma (-**s**) *nt* rheumatism
Rhythmus *m* rhythm
richten *vt* to direct; (*Waffe*) to aim; (*einstellen*) to adjust; (*instand setzen*) to repair; (*zurechtmachen*) to prepare ▶ *vr*: **sich ~ nach** to go by; **~ an** +*akk* to direct at; (*Briefe etc*) to address to
Richter(in) (-**s**, -) *m(f)* judge
Richtgeschwindigkeit *f* recommended speed
richtig *adj* right, correct; (*echt*) proper ▶ *adv* (*umg*: *sehr*) really
richtig|stellen *vt* to correct
Richtlinie *f* guideline
Richtung *f* direction; (*Tendenz*) tendency
Richtungstaste *f* arrow key
rieb *etc vb siehe* **reiben**
riechen *unreg vt*, *vi* to smell; **an etw** *dat* **~** to smell sth; **es riecht nach Gas** there's a smell of gas
rief *etc vb siehe* **rufen**
Riegel (-**s**, -) *m* bolt, bar
Riemen (-**s**, -) *m* strap; (*Gürtel*, *Tech*) belt
Riese (-**n**, -**n**) *m* giant
riesengroß *adj* gigantic, huge
Riesenrad *nt* big *od* Ferris wheel
riesig *adj* enormous, huge
riet *etc vb siehe* **raten**
Riff (-**(e)s**, -**e**) *nt* reef
Rind (-**(e)s**, -**er**) *nt* cow; (*Bulle*) bull; (*Koch*) beef ■ **Rinder** *pl* cattle *pl*
Rinde (-, -**n**) *f* rind; (*Baumrinde*) bark; (*Brotrinde*) crust
Rinderbraten *m* roast beef
Rinderwahn *m* mad cow disease
Rindfleisch *nt* beef
Ring (-**(e)s**, -**e**) *m* ring
Ringbuch *nt* ring binder
ringen *unreg vi* to wrestle
Ringer (-**s**, -) *m* wrestler
Ringfinger *m* ring finger
Ringkampf *m* wrestling bout
ringsherum *adv* round about
Rippe (-, -**n**) *f* rib
Rippenfellentzündung *f* pleurisy
Risiko (-**s**, -**s** *od* **Risiken**) *nt* risk
riskant *adj* risky
riskieren *vt* to risk
riss *etc vb siehe* **reißen**
Riss (-**es**, -**e**) *m* tear; (*in Mauer*, *Tasse etc*) crack
rissig *adj* cracked; (*Haut*) scratched
ritt *etc vb siehe* **reiten**
Ritter (-**s**, -) *m* knight
Rivale (-**n**, -**n**) *m*, **Rivalin** *f* rival
Rizinusöl *nt* castor oil
Robbe (-, -**n**) *f* seal
Roboter (-**s**, -) *m* robot

robust *adj* robust
roch *etc vb siehe* **riechen**
Rock (**-(e)s**, **Röcke**) *m* skirt
Rockmusik *f* rock music
Rodelbahn *f* toboggan run
rodeln *vi* to toboggan
Roggen (**-s**, **-**) *m* rye
Roggenbrot *nt* rye bread
roh *adj* raw; (*Mensch*) coarse, crude
Rohkost *f* raw fruit and vegetables *pl*
Rohr (**-(e)s**, **-e**) *nt* pipe; (*Bot*) cane; (*Schilf*) reed
Röhre (**-**, **-n**) *f* tube, pipe; (*Rundf etc*) valve; (*Backröhre*) oven
Rohrzucker *m* cane sugar
Rohstoff *m* raw material
Rokoko (**-s**) *nt* rococo
Rollator *m* (*Med*) walker, rollator
Rollbrett *nt* skateboard
Rolle (**-**, **-n**) *f* roll; (*Theat*, *Soziologie*) role
rollen *vt* to roll
Roller (**-s**, **-**) *m* scooter
Rollladen *m* shutter
Rollschuh *m* roller skate
Rollstuhl *m* wheelchair
Rolltreppe *f* escalator
Roman (**-s**, **-e**) *m* novel
Romantik *f* romanticism
romantisch *adj* romantic
römisch-katholisch *adj* Roman Catholic
röntgen *vt* to X-ray
Röntgenaufnahme *f* X-ray
Röntgenstrahlen *pl* X-rays *pl*
rosa *adj unver* pink
Rose (**-**, **-n**) *f* rose
Rosé (**-s**, **-s**) *m* rosé
Rosenkohl *m* Brussels sprouts *pl*
rosig *adj* rosy
Rosine *f* raisin
Rosmarin (**-s**) *m* rosemary
Rosskastanie *f* horse chestnut
Rost (**-(e)s**, **-e**) *m* rust; (*Gitter*) grill, gridiron
Rostbratwurst *f* grilled *od* barbecued sausage
rosten *vi* to rust
rösten *vt* to roast; (*Brot*) to toast
rostfrei *adj* (*Stahl*) stainless
rostig *adj* rusty
Rostschutz *m* rustproofing
rot *adj* red; **das Rote Kreuz** the Red Cross
Röteln *pl* German measles *sing*
röten *vt*, *vr* to redden
rothaarig *adj* red-haired
rotieren *vi* to rotate
Rotkehlchen *nt* robin
Rotkohl *m* red cabbage
Rotwein *m* red wine
Rouge (**-s**, **-s**) *nt* rouge
Route (**-**, **-n**) *f* route
Router *m* router
Routine *f* experience; (*Gewohnheit*) routine
RSI-Syndrom *nt abk* (= *Repetitive-Strain-Injury-Syndrom*) RSI (= *repetitive strain injury*)
rubbeln (*umg*) *vt*, *vi* to rub
Rübe (**-**, **-n**) *f* turnip; **Gelbe ~** carrot; **Rote ~** beetroot (Brit), beet (*US*)
rücken *vt*, *vi* to move
Rücken (**-s**, **-**) *m* back
Rückenlehne *f* back (of chair)
Rückenmark *nt* spinal cord
Rückenschmerzen *pl* backache *sing*
Rückenschwimmen *nt* backstroke
Rückenwind *m* following wind
Rückerstattung *f* refund
Rückfahrkarte *f* return ticket (Brit), round-trip ticket (*US*)
Rückfahrt *f* return journey
Rückfall *m* relapse
Rückflug *m* return flight
Rückgabe *f* return
rückgängig *adj*: **etw ~ machen** to cancel sth
Rückgrat *nt* spine, backbone
Rückkehr (**-**, **-en**) *f* return
Rücklicht *nt* rear light
Rückreise *f* return journey
Rucksack *m* rucksack
Rückschritt *m* retrogression
Rückseite *f* back; (*hinterer Teil*) rear; **siehe ~** see over(leaf)
Rücksicht *f* consideration; **~ nehmen auf** *+akk* to show consideration for
rücksichtslos *adj* inconsiderate; (*Fahren*) reckless; (*unbarmherzig*) ruthless
rücksichtsvoll *adj* considerate
Rücksitz *m* back seat
Rückspiegel *m* (*Aut*) rear-view mirror
Rückstand *m* arrears *pl*; **im ~ sein mit** (*Arbeit*, *Miete*) to be behind with
Rücktaste *f* backspace key
Rückvergütung *f* (*Comm*) refund
rückwärts *adv* backward(s), back
Rückwärtsgang *m* (*Aut*) reverse gear
Rückweg *m* return journey, way back

Rückzahlung *f* repayment
Ruder (-s, -) *nt* oar; (*Steuer*) rudder
Ruderboot *nt* rowing boat
rudern *vt, vi* to row
Ruf (-(e)s, -e) *m* call, cry; (*Ansehen*) reputation
rufen *unreg vt, vi* to call; (*ausrufen*) to cry
Rufnummer *f* (tele)phone number
Ruhe (-) *f* rest; (*Ungestörtheit*) peace, quiet; (*Gelassenheit, Stille*) calm; (*Schweigen*) silence; **lass mich in ~!** leave me alone
ruhen *vi* to rest
Ruhestand *m* retirement
Ruhestörung *f* breach of the peace
Ruhetag *m* closing day
ruhig *adj* quiet; (*bewegungslos*) still; (*Hand*) steady; (*gelassen, friedlich*) calm
Ruhm (-(e)s) *m* fame, glory
Rührei *nt* scrambled egg
rühren *vt* to move, to stir (*auch Koch*) ▸ *vr* to move
rührend *adj* touching, moving
Rührung *f* emotion
Ruine (-, -n) *f* ruin
ruinieren *vt* to ruin
rülpsen *vi* to burp, to belch
rum (*umg*) *adv* = **herum**
Rum (-s, -s) *m* rum
Rumänien (-s) *nt* Romania
Rummel (-s) (*umg*) *m* (*Trubel*) hustle and bustle; (*Jahrmarkt*) fair; (*Medienrummel*) hype
Rummelplatz *m* fairground
rumoren *vi* to make a noise
Rumpf (-(e)s, Rümpfe) *m* trunk; (*Aviat*) fuselage; (*Naut*) hull
rümpfen *vt* (*Nase*) to turn up
rund *adj* round ▸ *adv* (*etwa*) around; **~ um etw** round sth
Runde (-, -n) *f* round; (*in Rennen*) lap
Rundfahrt *f* (round) trip
Rundfunk (-(e)s) *m* broadcasting; (*Rundfunkanstalt*) broadcasting corporation; **im ~** on the radio
Rundgang *m* (*von Wachmann*) rounds *pl*; (*zur Besichtigung*): **~ (durch)** tour (of)
rundlich *adj* plump
Rundmail *f* group email
Rundreise *f* round trip
runter (*umg*) *adv* = **herunter**; **hinunter**
runzelig *adj* wrinkled
runzeln *vt* to wrinkle; **die Stirn ~** to frown
ruppig *adj* rough, gruff
Rüsche (-, -n) *f* frill
Ruß (-es) *m* soot
Russe (-n, -n) *m* Russian
Rüssel (-s, -) *m* snout; (*Elefantenrüssel*) trunk
Russin *f* Russian
russisch *adj* Russian
Russland (-s) *nt* Russia
Rüstung *f* (*Mil*) arming; (*Ritterrüstung*) armour (Brit), armor (US); (*Waffen etc*) armaments *pl*
Rutsch (-(e)s, -e) *m*: **guten ~!** (*umg*) have a good New Year!
Rutschbahn *f* slide
rutschen *vi* to slide; (*ausrutschen*) to slip
rutschig *adj* slippery
rütteln *vt, vi* to shake

S

s *abk* (= *Sekunde*) sec.; (= *siehe*) see
S *abk* (= *Süden*) S; (= *Seite*) p
Saal (**-(e)s**, **Säle**) *m* hall; (*für Sitzungen etc*) room
Saarland (**-s**) *nt* Saarland
sabotieren *vt* to sabotage
Sache (-, **-n**) *f* thing; (*Angelegenheit*) affair, business; (*Frage*) matter; **bei der ~ bleiben** to keep to the point
sachkundig *adj* (well-)informed
Sachlage *f* situation
sachlich *adj* matter-of-fact; (*Kritik etc*) objective; (*Irrtum, Angabe*) factual
sächlich *adj* neuter
Sachschaden *m* material damage
Sachsen (**-s**) *nt* Saxony
Sachsen-Anhalt (**-s**) *nt* Saxony Anhalt
sacht, sachte *adv* softly, gently
Sachverständige(r) *f(m)* expert
Sack (**-(e)s**, **Säcke**) *m* sack; (*umg!: Kerl, Bursche*) bastard (*!*)
Sackgasse *f* cul-de-sac, dead-end street (*US*)
Safe (**-s**, **-s**) *m od nt* safe
Saft (**-(e)s**, **Säfte**) *m* juice
saftig *adj* juicy
Sage (-, **-n**) *f* saga
Säge (-, **-n**) *f* saw
Sägemehl *nt* sawdust
sagen *vt, vi*: **(jdm etw) ~** to say (sth to sb), to tell (sb sth)
sägen *vt, vi* to saw
sagenhaft *adj* legendary; (*umg*) great, smashing
sah *etc vb siehe* **sehen**
Sahne (-) *f* cream
Saison (-, **-s**) *f* season
Saite (-, **-n**) *f* string
Sakko (**-s**, **-s**) *m od nt* jacket
Salami (-, **-s**) *f* salami
Salat (**-(e)s**, **-e**) *m* salad; (*Kopfsalat*) lettuce
Salatsoße *f* salad dressing
Salbe (-, **-n**) *f* ointment
Salbei (**-s**) *m* sage
salopp *adj* (*Kleidung*) casual; (*Sprache*) slangy
Salto (**-s**, **-s** *od* **Salti**) *m* somersault
Salz (**-es**, **-e**) *nt* salt
salzarm *adj* (*Koch*) low-salt
salzen *unreg vt* to salt
salzig *adj* salty
Salzkartoffeln *pl* boiled potatoes *pl*
Salzstange *f* pretzel stick
Salzstreuer *m* salt cellar
Salzwasser *nt* salt water
Samen (**-s**, **-**) *m* seed; (*Anat*) sperm
sammeln *vt* to collect
Sammler(in) (**-s**, **-**) *m(f)* collector
Sammlung *f* collection; (*Konzentration*) composure
Samstag *m* Saturday; *siehe auch* **Dienstag**
samstags *adv* (on) Saturdays
samt *präp +dat* (along) with, together with
Samt (**-(e)s**, **-e**) *m* velvet
Sanatorium *nt* sanatorium (*Brit*), sanitarium (*US*)
Sand (**-(e)s**, **-e**) *m* sand
Sandale (-, **-n**) *f* sandal
sandig *adj* sandy
Sandkasten *m* sandpit
Sandpapier *nt* sandpaper
Sandstrand *m* sandy beach
sandte *etc vb siehe* **senden[1]**
sanft *adj* soft, gentle
sang *etc vb siehe* **singen**
Sänger(in) (**-s**, **-**) *m(f)* singer
sanieren *vt* to redevelop; (*Betrieb*) to make financially sound
sanitär *adj* sanitary; **sanitäre Anlagen** sanitation *sing*
Sanitäter (**-s**, **-**) *m* first-aid attendant; (*in Krankenwagen*) ambulance man
sank *etc vb siehe* **sinken**
Saphir (**-s**, **-e**) *m* sapphire
Sardelle *f* anchovy
Sardine *f* sardine
Sarg (**-(e)s**, **Särge**) *m* coffin
saß *etc vb siehe* **sitzen**

Satellit (**-en**, **-en**) *m* satellite
Satellitenfernsehen *nt* satellite television
Satellitenschüssel *f* satellite dish
Satire (**-**, **-n**) *f*: **~ (auf** *+akk***)** satire (on)
satt *adj* full; (*Farbe*) rich, deep; **jdn/etw ~ sein** to be fed up with sb/sth; **sich ~ essen** to eat one's fill; **~ machen** to be filling
Sattel (**-s**, **Sättel**) *m* saddle
satt|haben *unreg vt*: **jdn/etw ~** to be fed up with sb/sth
Satz (**-es**, **Sätze**) *m* (*Gram*) sentence; (*Mus*) movement; (*Tennis*) set; (*Kaffeesatz*) grounds *pl*; (*Comm*) rate; (*Sprung*) jump
Satzzeichen *nt* punctuation mark
Sau (**-**, **Säue**) *f* sow; (*umg*) dirty pig
sauber *adj* clean; (*umg: ironisch*) fine; **~ machen** to clean
Sauberkeit *f* cleanness; (*einer Person*) cleanliness
säubern *vt* to clean
saublöd (*umg*) *adj* bloody (Brit *!*) *od* damn (*!*) stupid
Sauce (**-**, **-n**) *f* = **Soße**
Saudi-Arabien (**-s**) *nt* Saudi Arabia
sauer *adj* sour; (*Chem*) acid; (*umg*) cross; **saurer Regen** acid rain
Sauerkirsche *f* sour cherry
Sauerkraut (**-(e)s**) *nt* sauerkraut
säuerlich *adj* sourish
Sauermilch *f* sour milk
Sauerstoff *m* oxygen
saufen *unreg* (*umg*) *vt*, *vi* to drink, to booze
saugen *unreg vt*, *vi* to suck
Sauger (**-s**, **-**) *m* (*auf Flasche*) teat
Säugetier *nt* mammal
Säugling *m* infant, baby
Säule (**-**, **-n**) *f* column, pillar
Saum (**-(e)s**, **Säume**) *m* hem; (*Naht*) seam
Sauna (**-**, **-s**) *f* sauna
Säure (**-**, **-n**) *f* acid
sausen *vi* (*umg: eilen*) to rush; (*Ohren*) to buzz
Saustall (*umg*) *m* pigsty
Sauwetter (*umg*) *nt* bloody (Brit *!*) *od* damn (*!*) awful weather
S-Bahn *f abk* (= *Schnellbahn*) *high-speed suburban railway or railroad* (*US*)
scannen *vt* to scan
Scanner (**-s**, **-**) *m* scanner
schäbig *adj* shabby
Schach (**-s**, **-s**) *nt* chess; (*Stellung*) check
Schachbrett *nt* chessboard
Schachfigur *f* chessman
schachmatt *adj* checkmate
Schacht (**-(e)s**, **Schächte**) *m* shaft
Schachtel (**-**, **-n**) *f* box
schade *interj* (what a) pity *od* shame
Schädel (**-s**, **-**) *m* skull
Schädelbruch *m* fractured skull
schaden *vi +dat* to hurt; **einer Sache ~** to damage sth; **das schadet nichts** it won't do any harm
Schaden (**-s**, **Schäden**) *m* damage; (*Verletzung*) injury; (*Nachteil*) disadvantage; **jdm ~ zufügen** to harm sb
Schadenersatz *m* compensation, damages *pl*
schadhaft *adj* faulty, damaged
schädigen *vt* to damage; (*Person*) to do harm to, to harm
schädlich *adj*: **~ (für)** harmful (to)
Schadprogramm *nt* (*Comput*) malware
Schadstoff (**-(e)s**, **-e**) *m* pollutant
schadstoffarm *adj* low in pollutants
Schaf (**-(e)s**, **-e**) *nt* sheep
Schafbock *m* ram
Schäfer (**-s**, **-**) *m* shepherd
Schäferhund *m* Alsatian (dog) (Brit), German shepherd (dog) (*US*)
Schäferin *f* shepherdess
schaffen[1] *unreg vt* to create; (*Platz*) to make
schaffen[2] *vt* (*erreichen*) to manage, to do; (*erledigen*) to finish; (*Prüfung*) to pass; (*transportieren*) to take; **jdm (schwer) zu ~ machen** to cause sb (a lot of) trouble
Schaffner(in) (**-s**, **-**) *m(f)* (*Busschaffner*) conductor, conductress; (*Eisenb*) guard (Brit), conductor (*US*)
Schafskäse *m* sheep's *od* ewe's milk cheese
schal *adj* (*Getränk*) flat
Schal (**-s**, **-s** *od* **-e**) *m* scarf
Schälchen *nt* bowl
Schale (**-**, **-n**) *f* skin; (*abgeschält*) peel; (*Nussschale, Muschelschale, Eierschale*) shell; (*Geschirr*) dish, bowl
schälen *vt* to peel; (*Nuss*) to shell ▶ *vr* to peel
Schall (**-(e)s**, **-e**) *m* sound

Schalldämpfer *m* (*Aut*) silencer (BRIT), muffler (*US*)
Schallplatte *f* record
schalten *vt* to switch ▶ *vi* (*Aut*) to change (gear); (*umg: begreifen*) to catch on
Schalter (**-s**, **-**) *m* counter; (*an Gerät*) switch
Schaltfläche *f* (*Comput*) button
Schalthebel *m* (*Aut*) gear lever (BRIT), gearshift (*US*)
Schaltjahr *nt* leap year
Schaltknüppel *m* (*Aut*) gear lever (BRIT), gearshift (*US*)
Schaltung *f* (*Aut*) gear change
Scham (**-**) *f* shame; (*Schamgefühl*) modesty
schämen *vr* to be ashamed
Schande (**-**) *f* disgrace
Schanze (**-**, **-n**) *f* ski jump
Schar (**-**, **-en**) *f* (*Vögel*) flock; (*Menge*) crowd; **in Scharen** in droves
scharf *adj* sharp; (*Essen*) hot; **auf etw** *akk* **~ sein** (*umg*) to be keen on sth
Schärfe (**-**, **-n**) *f* sharpness; (*Strenge*) rigour (BRIT), rigor (*US*); (*an Kamera, Fernsehen*) focus
Scharlach (**-s**, **-e**) *m* scarlet; (*Krankheit*) scarlet fever
Scharnier (**-s**, **-e**) *nt* hinge
Schaschlik (**-s**, **-s**) *m od nt* (shish) kebab
Schatten (**-s**, **-**) *m* shadow
schattig *adj* shady
Schatz (**-es**, **Schätze**) *m* treasure; (*Person*) darling
schätzen *vt* (*abschätzen*) to estimate; (*Gegenstand*) to value; (*würdigen*) to value, to esteem; (*vermuten*) to reckon
Schätzung *f* estimate; (*das Schätzen*) estimation; (*Würdigung*) valuation
schätzungsweise *adv* (*ungefähr*) approximately
Schau (**-**) *f* show; (*Ausstellung*) exhibition
schauen *vi* to look
Schauer (**-s**, **-**) *m* (*Regenschauer*) shower; (*Schreck*) shudder
Schaufel (**-**, **-n**) *f* shovel; (*Kehrichtschaufel*) dustpan
schaufeln *vt* to shovel
Schaufenster *nt* shop window
Schaufensterbummel *m* window-shopping (expedition)
Schaukel (**-**, **-n**) *f* swing
schaukeln *vi* to swing, to rock
Schaulustige(r) *f(m)* onlooker
Schaum (**-(e)s**, **Schäume**) *m* foam; (*Seifenschaum*) lather; (*von Getränken*) froth
Schaumbad *nt* bubble bath
schäumen *vi* to foam
Schaumgummi *m* foam (rubber)
Schaumwein *m* sparkling wine
Schauplatz *m* scene
Schauspiel *nt* spectacle; (*Theat*) play
Schauspieler(in) *m(f)* actor, actress
Scheck (**-s**, **-s**) *m* cheque (BRIT), check (*US*)
Scheckkarte *f* cheque (BRIT) *od* check (*US*) card
Scheibe (**-**, **-n**) *f* disc (BRIT), disk (*US*); (*Brot etc*) slice; (*Glasscheibe*) pane
Scheibenbremse *f* (*Aut*) disc brake
Scheibenwaschanlage *f* (*Aut*) windscreen (BRIT) *od* windshield (*US*) washers *pl*
Scheibenwischer *m* (*Aut*) windscreen (BRIT) *od* windshield (*US*) wiper
Scheich (**-s**, **-e** *od* **-s**) *m* sheik(h)
Scheide (**-**, **-n**) *f* (*Anat*) vagina
scheiden *unreg vt* to separate; (*Ehe*) to dissolve; **sich ~ lassen** to get a divorce
Scheidung *f* divorce
Schein (**-(e)s**, **-e**) *m* light; (*Anschein*) appearance; (*Geldschein*) (bank)note
scheinbar *adj* apparent
scheinen *unreg vi* to shine; (*Anschein haben*) to seem
Scheinwerfer (**-s**, **-**) *m* floodlight; (*Theat*) spotlight; (*Aut*) headlight
Scheiß- (*umg!*) *in zW* bloody (BRIT!), damn(ed) (!)
Scheiße (**-**) (*umg!*) *f* shit (!)
scheißegal (*umg!*) *adj*: **das ist mir doch ~!** I don't give a shit (!)
scheißen *unreg* (*umg!*) *vi* to shit (!)
Scheitel (**-s**, **-**) *m* (*Haar*) parting (BRIT), part (*US*)
scheitern *vi* to fail
Schellfisch *m* haddock
Schema (**-s**, **-s** *od* **-ta**) *nt* scheme, plan; (*Darstellung*) schema
Schenkel (**-s**, **-**) *m* thigh
schenken *vt* to give; **sich** *dat* **etw ~** (*umg*) to skip sth
Scherbe (**-**, **-n**) *f* broken piece, fragment
Schere (**-**, **-n**) *f* scissors *pl*; (*groß*) shears *pl*; **eine ~** a pair of scissors

Scherz (**-es**, **-e**) *m* joke
scheu *adj* shy
scheuen *vr*: **sich ~ vor** *+dat* to be afraid of, to shrink from ▶ *vt* to shun ▶ *vi* (*Pferd*) to shy
scheuern *vt* to scrub; **jdm eine ~** (*umg*) to clout sb one
Scheune (**-**, **-n**) *f* barn
scheußlich *adj* dreadful
Schi *m* = **Ski**
Schicht (**-**, **-en**) *f* layer; (*Klasse*) class; (*in Fabrik etc*) shift
schick *adj* = **chic**
schicken *vt* to send ▶ *vr*: **sich ~ (in** *+akk*) to resign o.s. (to)
Schicksal (**-s**, **-e**) *nt* fate
Schiebedach *nt* (*Aut*) sunroof
schieben *unreg vt* to push; **die Schuld auf jdn ~** to put the blame on (to) sb
Schiebetür *f* sliding door
schied *etc vb siehe* **scheiden**
Schiedsrichter *m* referee, umpire; (*Schlichter*) arbitrator
schief *adj* crooked; (*Blick*) wry ▶ *adv* crookedly
schief|gehen *unreg* (*umg*) *vi* to go wrong
schielen *vi* to squint
schien *etc vb siehe* **scheinen**
Schienbein *nt* shinbone
Schiene *f* rail; (*Med*) splint
schier *adj* pure; (*fig*) sheer ▶ *adv* nearly, almost
schießen *unreg vi* to shoot ▶ *vt* to shoot; (*Ball*) to kick; (*Tor*) to score
Schiff (**-(e)s**, **-e**) *nt* ship, vessel; (*Kirchenschiff*) nave
Schifffahrt *f* shipping
schikanieren *vt* to harass; (*Mitschüler*) to bully
Schild[1] (**-(e)s**, **-e**) *m* shield
Schild[2] (**-(e)s**, **-er**) *nt* sign
Schilddrüse *f* thyroid gland
schildern *vt* to describe
Schildkröte *f* tortoise; (*Wasserschildkröte*) turtle
Schimmel (**-s**, **-**) *m* mould (BRIT), mold (US); (*Pferd*) white horse
schimmeln *vi* to go mouldy (BRIT) *od* moldy (US)
schimpfen *vi* (*sich beklagen*) to grumble; **mit jdm ~** to tell sb off
Schimpfwort *nt* term of abuse
Schinken (**-s**, **-**) *m* ham
Schirm (**-(e)s**, **-e**) *m* (*Regenschirm*) umbrella; (*Sonnenschirm*) parasol, sunshade
schiss *etc vb siehe* **scheißen**
Schlacht (**-**, **-en**) *f* battle
schlachten *vt* to slaughter
Schlachter (**-s**, **-**) *m* butcher
Schlaf (**-(e)s**) *m* sleep
Schlafanzug *m* pyjamas *pl* (BRIT), pajamas *pl* (US)
Schläfe (**-**, **-n**) *f* (*Anat*) temple
schlafen *unreg vi* to sleep; **~ gehen** to go to bed
schlaff *adj* slack; (*energielos*) limp; (*erschöpft*) exhausted
Schlafgelegenheit *f* place to sleep
Schlaflosigkeit *f* sleeplessness
Schlafmittel *nt* sleeping drug
schläfrig *adj* sleepy
Schlafsaal *m* dormitory
Schlafsack *m* sleeping bag
Schlaftablette *f* sleeping pill
Schlafwagen *m* sleeping car, sleeper
Schlafzimmer *nt* bedroom
Schlag (**-(e)s**, **Schläge**) *m* blow; (*Pulsschlag*, *Herzschlag*) beat; (*Elek*) shock; (*umg*: *Portion*) helping; (: *Art*) kind, type
Schlagader *f* artery
Schlaganfall *m* stroke
schlagartig *adj* sudden
schlagen *unreg vt* to hit; (*wiederholt schlagen*, *besiegen*) to beat; (*Sahne*) to whip ▶ *vi* to strike; (*Herz*) to beat ▶ *vr* to fight
Schläger (**-s**, **-**) *m* brawler; (*Sport*) bat; (*Tennis etc*) racket; (*Golf*) club; (*Hockeyschläger*) hockey stick
Schlägerei *f* fight, punch-up
schlagfertig *adj* quick-witted
Schlagloch *nt* pothole
Schlagobers (**-**, **-**) (ÖSTERR) *nt*, **Schlagsahne** *f* whipped cream
Schlagzeile *f* headline
Schlagzeug *nt* drums *pl*; (*in Orchester*) percussion
Schlamm (**-(e)s**, **-e**) *m* mud
schlampig (*umg*) *adj* sloppy
Schlange (**-**, **-n**) *f* snake; (*Menschenschlange*) queue (BRIT), line (US); **~ stehen** to (form a) queue (BRIT), to stand in line (US)
Schlangenlinie *f* wavy line
schlank *adj* slim
schlapp *adj* limp; (*locker*) slack

Schlappe (-, **-n**) (*umg*) *f* setback
schlau *adj* crafty, cunning
Schlauch (**-(e)s**, **Schläuche**) *m* hose; (*in Reifen*) inner tube
Schlauchboot *nt* rubber dinghy
schlecht *adj* bad ▶ *adv*: **es geht ihm ~** he's having a hard time; (*gesundheitlich*) he's not feeling well; (*finanziell*) he's pretty hard up
schlecht|machen *vt* to run down, to denigrate
schleichen *unreg vi* to creep
Schleier (**-s**, **-**) *m* veil
Schleife (-, **-n**) *f* (*auch Comput*) loop; (*Band*) bow
schleifen[1] *vt* (*ziehen, schleppen*) to drag
schleifen[2] *unreg vt* (*schärfen*) to grind; (*Edelstein*) to cut
Schleim (**-(e)s**, **-e**) *m* slime; (*Med*) mucus
Schleimhaut *f* mucous membrane
schlendern *vi* to stroll
schleppen *vt* to drag; (*Auto, Schiff*) to tow; (*tragen*) to lug
Schleswig-Holstein (**-s**) *nt* Schleswig-Holstein
Schleuder (-, **-n**) *f* catapult; (*Wäscheschleuder*) spin-dryer
schleudern *vt* to hurl; (*Wäsche*) to spin-dry ▶ *vi* (*Aut*) to skid
Schleudersitz *m* (*Aviat*) ejector seat
schlich *etc vb siehe* **schleichen**
schlicht *adj* simple, plain
schlichten *vt* (*beilegen*) to settle
schlief *etc vb siehe* **schlafen**
schließen *unreg vt* to close, to shut; (*beenden*) to close; (*Freundschaft, Bündnis, Ehe*) to enter into; (*folgern*): **~ (aus)** to infer (from) ▶ *vi, vr* to close, to shut
Schließfach *nt* locker
schließlich *adv* finally; (*schließlich doch*) after all
schliff *etc vb siehe* **schleifen**[2]
schlimm *adj* bad
schlimmer *adj* worse
schlimmste(r, s) *adj* worst
schlimmstenfalls *adv* at (the) worst
Schlinge (-, **-n**) *f* loop; (*Med*) sling
Schlips (**-es**, **-e**) *m* tie, necktie (*US*); **sich auf den ~ getreten fühlen** (*fig: umg*) to feel offended
Schlitten (**-s**, **-**) *m* sledge, sled; (*Pferdeschlitten*) sleigh
Schlittenfahren (**-s**) *nt* tobogganing
Schlittschuh *m* skate; **~ laufen** to skate
Schlitz (**-es**, **-e**) *m* slit; (*für Münze*) slot; (*Hosenschlitz*) flies *pl*
schloss *vb siehe* **schließen**
Schloss (**-es**, **-Schlösser**) *nt* lock; (*Bau*) castle
Schlosser (**-s**, **-**) *m* (*Autoschlosser*) fitter; (*für Schlüssel etc*) locksmith
Schlucht (-, **-en**) *f* gorge, ravine
schluchzen *vi* to sob
Schluck (**-(e)s**, **-e**) *m* swallow
Schluckauf (**-s**) *m* hiccups *pl*
schlucken *vi* to swallow
schludern (*umg*) *vi* to do slipshod work
schlug *etc vb siehe* **schlagen**
Schlüpfer (**-s**, **-**) *m* panties *pl*
schlürfen *vt, vi* to slurp
Schluss (**-es**, **-Schlüsse**) *m* end; (*Schlussfolgerung*) conclusion; **am ~** at the end; **~ machen mit** to finish with
Schlüssel (**-s**, **-**) *m* (*lit, fig*) key
Schlüsselbein *nt* collarbone
Schlüsselbund *m* bunch of keys
Schlüsselloch *nt* keyhole
Schlussfolgerung *f* conclusion
Schlusslicht *nt* rear light (Brit), taillight (*US*); (*fig*) tail ender
Schlussverkauf *m* clearance sale
schmächtig *adj* slight
schmal *adj* narrow; (*Person, Buch etc*) slender, slim; (*karg*) meagre (Brit), meager (*US*)
Schmalz (**-es**, **-e**) *nt* dripping; (*Schweineschmalz*) lard; (*fig*) sentiment, schmaltz
schmatzen *vi* to eat noisily
schmecken *vt, vi* to taste; **es schmeckt ihm** he likes it; **es sich ~ lassen** to tuck in
Schmeichelei *f* flattery
schmeichelhaft *adj* flattering
schmeicheln *vi*: **jdm ~** to flatter sb
schmeißen *unreg* (*umg*) *vt* to throw, to chuck
schmelzen *unreg vt* to melt; (*Erz*) to smelt ▶ *vi* to melt
Schmelzkäse *m* cheese spread
Schmerz (**-es**, **-en**) *m* pain; (*Trauer*) grief *no pl*; **Schmerzen haben** to be in pain
schmerzen *vt, vi* to hurt
Schmerzensgeld *nt* compensation
schmerzhaft *adj* painful

schmerzlos *adj* painless
Schmerzmittel *nt* painkiller
schmerzstillend *adj* pain-killing, analgesic
Schmerztablette *f* pain-killing tablet
Schmetterling *m* butterfly
Schmied (**-(e)s**, **-e**) *m* blacksmith
schmieden *vt* to forge; (*Pläne*) to devise
schmieren *vt* to smear; (*ölen*) to lubricate, to grease; (*bestechen*) to bribe ▶ *vi* (*schreiben*) to scrawl
Schmiergeld *nt* bribe
schmierig *adj* greasy
Schmierseife *f* soft soap
Schminke (**-**, **-n**) *f* make-up
schminken *vt*, *vr* to make up
schmiss *etc vb siehe* **schmeißen**
schmollen *vi* to sulk
schmollend *adj* sulky
schmolz *etc vb siehe* **schmelzen**
Schmuck (**-(e)s**, **-e**) *m* jewellery (BRIT), jewelry (*US*); (*Verzierung*) decoration
schmücken *vt* to decorate
schmuggeln *vt*, *vi* to smuggle
schmunzeln *vi* to smile benignly
schmusen (*umg*) *vi* to cuddle
Schmutz (**-es**) *m* dirt; (*fig*) filth
schmutzig *adj* dirty
Schnabel (**-s**, **Schnäbel**) *m* beak, bill; (*Ausguss*) spout
Schnake (**-**, **-n**) *f* (*Stechmücke*) gnat
Schnalle (**-**, **-n**) *f* buckle; (*an Handtasche, Buch*) clasp
Schnäppchen (*umg*) *nt* bargain
schnappen *vt* to catch ▶ *vi* to snap
Schnappschuss *m* (*Phot*) snapshot
Schnaps (**-es**, **Schnäpse**) *m* schnapps
schnarchen *vi* to snore
schnaufen *vi* to puff, to pant
Schnauzbart *m* moustache (BRIT), mustache (*US*)
Schnauze (**-**, **-n**) *f* snout, muzzle; (*Ausguss*) spout; (*umg*) gob
schnäuzen *vr* to blow one's nose
Schnecke (**-**, **-n**) *f* snail
Schneckenhaus *nt* snail's shell
Schnee (**-s**) *m* snow
Schneeball *m* snowball
Schneeflocke *f* snowflake
Schneegestöber *nt* snowstorm
Schneeglöckchen *nt* snowdrop
Schneegrenze *f* snowline
Schneekette *f* (*Aut*) snow chain
Schneemann *m* snowman
Schneepflug *m* snowplough (BRIT), snowplow (*US*)
Schneeregen *m* sleet
Schneeschmelze *f* thaw
Schneetreiben *nt* driving snow
Schneewehe *f* snowdrift
Schneide (**-**, **-n**) *f* edge; (*Klinge*) blade
schneiden *unreg vt* to cut ▶ *vr* to cut o.s.
Schneider (**-s**, **-**) *m* tailor
Schneiderin *f* dressmaker
Schneidezahn *m* incisor
schneien *vi* to snow
schnell *adj* quick, fast ▶ *adv* quick(ly), fast; **mach ~!** hurry up
Schnellhefter *m* loose-leaf binder
Schnellimbiss *m* snack bar
Schnellkochtopf *m* (*Dampfkochtopf*) pressure cooker
Schnellreinigung *f* express cleaner's
Schnellstraße *f* expressway
Schnellzug *m* fast *od* express train
schneuzen *vr siehe* **schnäuzen**
schnitt *etc vb siehe* **schneiden**
Schnitt (**-(e)s**, **-e**) *m* cut(ting); (*Schnittpunkt*) intersection; (*Querschnitt*) (cross) section; (*Durchschnitt*) average
Schnitte (**-**, **-n**) *f* slice; (*belegt*) sandwich
Schnittlauch *m* chive
Schnittmuster *nt* pattern
Schnittstelle *f* (*Comput*) interface
Schnittwunde *f* cut
Schnitzel (**-s**, **-**) *nt* scrap; (*Koch*) escalope
schnitzen *vt* to carve
Schnorchel (**-s**, **-**) *m* snorkel
schnorcheln *vi* to go snorkelling
schnüffeln *vi* to sniff
Schnuller (**-s**, **-**) *m* dummy (BRIT), pacifier (*US*)
Schnulze (**-**, **-n**) (*umg*) *f* schmaltzy film/book/song
Schnupfen (**-s**, **-**) *m* cold
schnuppern *vi* to sniff
Schnur (**-**, **Schnüre**) *f* string; (*Kordel*) cord; (*Elek*) flex
schnurlos *adj* (*Telefon*) cordless
Schnurrbart *m* moustache (BRIT), mustache (*US*)
schnurren *vi* to purr
Schnürsenkel *m* shoelace
schob *etc vb siehe* **schieben**

Schock (**-(e)s**, **-e**) *m* shock; **unter ~ stehen** to be in (a state of) shock
schockieren *vt* to shock
Schokolade (**-**, **-n**) *f* chocolate
Schokoriegel *m* chocolate bar
Scholle (**-**, **-n**) *f* (*Eisscholle*) ice floe; (*Fisch*) plaice

 SCHLÜSSELWORT

schon *adv* **1** (*bereits*) already; **er ist schon da** he's there/here already, he's already there/here; **ist er schon da?** is he there/here yet?; **warst du schon einmal dort?** have you ever been there?; **ich war schon einmal dort** I've been there before; **das war schon immer so** that has always been the case; **schon oft** often; **hast du schon gehört?** have you heard?; **wie schon so oft** as so often (before)
2 (*bestimmt*) all right; **du wirst schon sehen** you'll see (all right); **das wird schon noch gut gehen** that should turn out OK (in the end)
3 (*bloß*) just; **allein schon das Gefühl ...** just the very feeling ...; **schon der Gedanke** the mere *od* very thought; **wenn ich das schon höre** I only have to hear that
4 (*einschränkend*): **ja schon, aber ...** yes (well), but ...
5: **das ist schon möglich** that's quite possible; **schon gut** OK; **du weißt schon** you know; **komm schon** come on

schön *adj* beautiful; (*Mann*) handsome; (*nett*) nice; **schöne Grüße** best wishes
schonen *vt* to look after ▶ *vr* to take it easy
Schönheit *f* beauty
Schonkost (**-**) *f* light diet
schöpfen *vt* to scoop; (*Suppe*) to ladle
Schöpfkelle *f* ladle
Schöpfung *f* creation
Schoppen (**-s**, **-**) *m* (*Glas Wein*) glass of wine
Schorf (**-(e)s**, **-e**) *m* scab
Schorle (**-**, **-n**) *f* spritzer
Schornstein *m* chimney
Schornsteinfeger (**-s**, **-**) *m* chimney sweep
schoss *vb siehe* **schießen**
Schoß (**-es**, **-Schöße**) *m* lap
Schotte (**-n**, **-n**) *m* Scot, Scotsman
Schottin *f* Scot, Scotswoman
schottisch *adj* Scottish, Scots
Schottland (**-s**) *nt* Scotland
schräg *adj* slanting; (*schief, geneigt*) sloping; (*nicht gerade od parallel*) oblique
Schrank (**-(e)s**, **Schränke**) *m* cupboard (Brit), closet (US); (*Kleiderschrank*) wardrobe
Schranke (**-**, **-n**) *f* barrier
Schrankwand *f* wall unit
Schraube (**-**, **-n**) *f* screw
schrauben *vt* to screw
Schraubendreher (**-s**, **-**) *m* screwdriver
Schraubenschlüssel *m* spanner (Brit), wrench (US)
Schraubenzieher (**-s**, **-**) *m* screwdriver
Schraubverschluss *m* screw top, screw cap
Schreck (**-(e)s**, **-e**) *m* fright
schreckhaft *adj* jumpy
schrecklich *adj* terrible, dreadful
Schrei (**-(e)s**, **-e**) *m* scream; (*Ruf*) shout
Schreibblock *m* writing pad
schreiben *unreg vt* to write; (*buchstabieren*) to spell ▶ *vi* to write ▶ *vr*: **wie schreibt sich das?** how is that spelt?
Schreiben (**-s**, **-**) *nt* letter
Schreibfehler *m* spelling mistake
Schreibtisch *m* desk
Schreibwaren *pl* stationery *sing*
schreien *unreg vt, vi* to scream; (*rufen*) to shout
Schreiner (**-s**, **-**) *m* joiner
Schreinerei *f* joiner's workshop
schrie *etc vb siehe* **schreien**
schrieb *etc vb siehe* **schreiben**
Schrift (**-**, **-en**) *f* writing; (*Handschrift*) handwriting; (*Schriftart*) script; (*Typ*) typeface
schriftlich *adj* written ▶ *adv* in writing
Schriftsteller(in) (**-s**, **-**) *m(f)* writer
Schritt (**-(e)s**, **-e**) *m* step; **Schritte gegen etw unternehmen** to take steps against sth
Schrittmacher *m* pacemaker
Schrott (**-(e)s**, **-e**) *m* scrap metal; (*fig*) rubbish
schrubben *vt* to scrub

Schrubber (**-s**, **-**) *m* scrubbing brush
schrumpfen *vi* to shrink
Schubkarren *m* wheelbarrow
Schublade *f* drawer
schubsen (*umg*) *vt*, *vi* to shove, to push
schüchtern *adj* shy
schuf *etc vb siehe* **schaffen¹**
Schuh (**-(e)s**, **-e**) *m* shoe
Schuhcreme *f* shoe polish
Schuhgröße *f* shoe size
Schuhlöffel *m* shoehorn
schuld *adj*: **~ sein (an** *+dat***)** to be to blame (for); **er ist ~** it's his fault
Schuld (**-**, **-en**) *f* guilt; (*Fin*) debt; (*Verschulden*) fault; **~ haben (an** *+dat***)** to be to blame (for); **jdm (die) ~ geben, jdm die ~ zuschieben** to blame sb; **Schulden haben** to be in debt; **Schulden machen** to run up debts
schulden *vt* to owe
schuldig *adj* guilty; (*gebührend*) due; **jdm etw ~ sein** *od* **bleiben** to owe sb sth
Schule (**-**, **-n**) *f* school; **auf** *od* **in der ~** at school; **in die ~ kommen/gehen** to start school/go to school
Schüler(in) (**-s**, **-**) *m(f)* pupil
Schulferien *pl* school holidays *pl* (Brit) *od* vacation *sing* (*US*)
schulfrei *adj*: **die Kinder haben morgen ~** the children don't have to go to school tomorrow
Schulfreund(in) *m(f)* schoolmate
Schuljahr *nt* school year
Schulleiter(in) *m(f)* headteacher (*bes* Brit), principal
Schulter (**-**, **-n**) *f* shoulder
Schulterblatt *nt* shoulder blade
Schulung *f* training; (*Veranstaltung*) training course
schummeln (*umg*) *vi*: **(bei etw) ~** to cheat (at sth)
Schuppe (**-**, **-n**) *f* scale ■ **Schuppen** *pl* (*Haarschuppen*) dandruff
schuppen *vt* to scale ▶ *vr* to peel
Schuppen (**-s**, **-**) *m* shed
Schürze (**-**, **-n**) *f* apron
Schuss (**-es**, **-Schüsse**) *m* shot; (*Spritzer*: *von Wein*, *Essig etc*) dash
Schüssel (**-**, **-n**) *f* bowl
Schuster (**-s**, **-**) *m* shoemaker
Schutt (**-(e)s**) *m* rubble
Schüttelfrost *m* shivering
schütteln *vt* to shake ▶ *vr* to shake o.s.
schütten *vt* to pour; (*Zucker*, *Kies etc*) to tip ▶ *vi unpers* to pour (down)
Schutz (**-es**) *m* protection; (*Unterschlupf*) shelter; **jdn in ~ nehmen** to stand up for sb
Schutzblech *nt* mudguard
Schutzbrief *m* (international) travel cover
Schutzbrille *f* goggles *pl*
Schütze (**-n**, **-n**) *m* (*Scharfschütze*, *Sportschütze*) marksman; (*Astrol*) Sagittarius
schützen *vt* to protect
Schutzimpfung *f* immunization
schwach *adj* weak
Schwäche (**-**, **-n**) *f* weakness
Schwachstelle *f* weak point
Schwachstrom *m* weak current
Schwager (**-s**, **Schwäger**) *m* brother-in-law
Schwägerin *f* sister-in-law
Schwalbe (**-**, **-n**) *f* swallow
schwamm *vb siehe* **schwimmen**
Schwamm (**-(e)s**, **Schwämme**) *m* sponge; **~ drüber!** (*umg*) (let's) forget it!
Schwan (**-(e)s**, **Schwäne**) *m* swan
schwanger *adj* pregnant
Schwangerschaft *f* pregnancy
Schwangerschaftsabbruch *m* abortion
schwanken *vi* to sway; (*taumeln*) to stagger; (*Preise*, *Zahlen*) to fluctuate; (*zögern*) to hesitate
Schwanz (**-es**, **Schwänze**) *m* tail; (*umg!*: *Penis*) prick (*!*)
Schwarm (**-(e)s**, **Schwärme**) *m* swarm; (*umg*) heart-throb
schwärmen *vi* to swarm; **~ für** to be mad *od* wild about
schwarz *adj* black
Schwarzarbeit *f* illicit work
Schwarzbrot *nt* black bread
schwarz|fahren *unreg vi* to travel without paying; (*ohne Führerschein*) to drive without a licence (Brit) *od* license (*US*)
Schwarzfahrer(in) *m(f)* (*Bus etc*) fare dodger (*umg*)
Schwarzmarkt *m* black market
schwarz|sehen *vi unreg* (*umg*) to see the gloomy side of things
Schwarzwald *m* Black Forest

schwatzen *vi* to chatter
Schwätzer(in) (**-s**, **-**) *m(f)* chatterbox; (*Schwafler*) gasbag (*umg*); (*Klatschbase*) gossip
Schwebebahn *f* overhead railway (*Brit*) *od* railroad (*US*)
schweben *vi* to float; (*hoch*) to soar
Schwede (**-n**, **-n**) *m* Swede
Schweden (**-s**) *nt* Sweden
Schwedin *f* Swede
schwedisch *adj* Swedish
Schwefel (**-s**) *m* sulphur (*Brit*), sulfur (*US*)
schweigen *unreg vi* to be silent; (*still sein*) to keep quiet
Schweigen (**-s**) *nt* silence
Schweigepflicht *f* pledge of secrecy; (*von Anwalt etc*) requirement of confidentiality
Schwein (**-(e)s**, **-e**) *nt* pig; (*fig: umg*) (good) luck; (*gemeiner Mensch*) swine
Schweinebraten *m* roast pork
Schweinefleisch *nt* pork
Schweinegrippe *f* swine flu
Schweinerei *f* mess; (*Gemeinheit*) dirty trick
Schweiß (**-es**) *m* sweat
schweißen *vt, vi* to weld
Schweiz *f*: **die ~** Switzerland
Schweizer (**-s**, **-**) *m* Swiss ▶ *adj attrib* Swiss
Schweizerdeutsch *nt* Swiss German
schweizerisch *adj* Swiss
Schwelle (**-**, **-n**) *f* (*auch fig*) threshold
schwellen *unreg vi* to swell
Schwellung *f* swelling
schwer *adj* heavy; (*schwierig*) difficult, hard; (*schlimm*) serious, bad ▶ *adv* (*sehr*) very (much); (*verletzt etc*) seriously, badly
Schwerbehinderte(r) *f(m)* person with a severe disability
schwer|fallen *unreg vi*: **jdm ~** to be difficult for sb
schwerhörig *adj* hard of hearing
Schwert (**-(e)s**, **-er**) *nt* sword
Schwertlilie *f* iris
Schwester (**-**, **-n**) *f* sister; (*Med*) nurse
schwieg *etc vb siehe* **schweigen**
Schwiegereltern *pl* parents-in-law *pl*
Schwiegermutter *f* mother-in-law
Schwiegersohn *m* son-in-law
Schwiegertochter *f* daughter-in-law
Schwiegervater *m* father-in-law
schwierig *adj* difficult, hard
Schwierigkeit *f* difficulty; **in Schwierigkeiten kommen** to get into trouble
Schwimmbad *nt* swimming baths *pl*
Schwimmbecken *nt* swimming pool
schwimmen *unreg vi* to swim; (*treiben, nicht sinken*) to float; (*fig: unsicher sein*) to be all at sea
Schwimmer (**-s**, **-**) *m* swimmer
Schwimmflosse *f* flipper
Schwimmweste *f* life jacket
Schwindel (**-s**) *m* dizziness; (*Betrug*) swindle
schwindelfrei *adj* free from giddiness; **nicht ~ sein** to suffer from vertigo
schwindlig *adj* dizzy; **mir ist ~** I feel dizzy
Schwips (**-es**, **-e**) *m*: **einen ~ haben** to be tipsy
schwitzen *vi* to sweat
schwoll *etc vb siehe* **schwellen**
schwören *unreg vt, vi* to swear
schwul (*umg*) *adj* gay
schwül *adj* sultry, close
Schwung (**-(e)s**, **Schwünge**) *m* swing; (*Triebkraft*) momentum; (*fig: Energie*) energy; (*umg: Menge*) batch; **in ~ sein** (*fig*) to be in full swing
Schwur (**-(e)s**, **Schwüre**) *m* oath
Screenshot *m* (*Comput*) screenshot
scrollen *vi* (*Comput*) to scroll
sechs *num* six
sechshundert *num* six hundred
sechste(r, s) *adj* sixth
Sechstel (**-s**, **-**) *nt* sixth
sechzehn *num* sixteen
sechzig *num* sixty
See[1] (**-**, **-n**) *f* sea; **an der ~** by the sea
See[2] (**-s**, **-n**) *m* lake
Seegang *m* (motion of the) sea
Seehund *m* seal
Seeigel *m* sea urchin
seekrank *adj* seasick
Seele (**-**, **-n**) *f* soul
Seeleute *pl* seamen *pl*
seelisch *adj* mental; (*Belastung*) emotional
Seemann (**-(e)s**, **-leute**) *m* seaman, sailor
Seemeile *f* nautical mile
Seenot *f*: **in ~** (*Schiff etc*) in distress
Seepferd *nt*, **Seepferdchen** *nt* sea horse
Seerose *f* waterlily

Seestern *m* starfish
Seezunge *f* sole
Segel (**-s**, **-**) *nt* sail
Segelboot *nt* yacht
Segelfliegen (**-s**) *nt* gliding
Segelflugzeug *nt* glider
segeln *vt*, *vi* to sail
Segelschiff *nt* sailing vessel
sehen *unreg vt*, *vi* to see; (*in bestimmte Richtung*) to look; (*Fernsehsendung*) to watch; **sieht man das?** does it show?; **so gesehen** looked at in this way; **kann ich das mal ~?** can I have a look at it?; **mal ~!** we'll see!
Sehenswürdigkeiten *pl* sights *pl* (of a town)
Sehne (**-**, **-n**) *f* sinew; (*an Bogen*) string
sehnen *vr*: **sich ~ nach** to long *od* yearn for
Sehnenscheidenentzündung *f* (*Med*) tendinitis
Sehnsucht *f* longing
sehnsüchtig *adj* longing
sehr *adv* (*vor adj*, *adv*) very; (*mit Verben*) a lot, (very) much; **zu ~** too much
seicht *adj* shallow
Seide (**-**, **-n**) *f* silk
Seife (**-**, **-n**) *f* soap
Seifenoper *f* soap (opera)
Seifenschale *f* soap dish
Seil (**-(e)s**, **-e**) *nt* rope; (*Kabel*) cable
Seilbahn *f* cable railway

SCHLÜSSELWORT

sein (*pt* **war**, *pp* **gewesen**) *vi* **1** to be; **ich bin** I am; **du bist** you are; **er/sie/es ist** he/she/it is; **wir sind/ihr seid/sie sind** we/you/they are; **wir waren** we were; **wir sind gewesen** we have been
2: **seien Sie nicht böse** don't be angry; **sei so gut und ...** be so kind as to ...; **das wäre gut** that would *od* that'd be a good thing; **wenn ich Sie wäre** if I were *od* was you; **das wärs** that's all, that's it; **morgen bin ich in Rom** tomorrow I'll *od* I will *od* I shall be in Rome; **waren Sie mal in Rom?** have you ever been to Rome?
3: **wie ist das zu verstehen?** how is that to be understood?; **er ist nicht zu ersetzen** he cannot be replaced; **mit ihr ist nicht zu reden** you can't talk to her
4: **mir ist kalt** I'm cold; **was ist?** what's the matter?, what is it?; **ist was?** is something the matter?; **es sei denn(, dass ...)** unless ...; **wie dem auch sei** be that as it may; **wie wäre es mit ...?** how *od* what about ...?; **lass das sein!** stop that!
▶ *poss pron* his; (*bei Dingen*) its

seine(r, s) *poss pron* his; (*bei Tieren, Dingen*) its
seiner *gen von* **er**; **es** ▶ *pron* of him; (*bei Tieren, Dingen*) of it
seinetwegen *adv* (*für ihn*) for his sake; (*wegen ihm*) on his account; (*von ihm aus*) as far as he is concerned
seit *präp +dat* since; (*Zeitdauer*) for ▶ *konj* since; **er ist ~ einer Woche hier** he has been here for a week; **~ Langem** for a long time
seitdem *adv*, *konj* since
Seite (**-**, **-n**) *f* side; (*Buchseite*) page
Seitenairbag *m* (*Aut*) side-impact airbag
Seitensprung *m* affair
Seitenstechen *nt*: **~ haben/bekommen** to have/get a stitch
Seitenstraße *f* side road
Seitenstreifen *m* hard shoulder (BRIT), shoulder (US)
Seitenwind *m* crosswind
seither *adv*, *konj* since (then)
seitlich *adj* side *attrib*
Sekretär *m* secretary
Sekretariat (**-(e)s**, **-e**) *nt* secretary's office
Sekt (**-(e)s**, **-e**) *m* sparkling wine
Sekte (**-**, **-n**) *f* sect
Sekunde (**-**, **-n**) *f* second
Sekundenkleber *m* superglue
Sekundenschnelle *f*: **in ~** in a matter of seconds

SCHLÜSSELWORT

selbst *pron* **1**: **ich/er/wir selbst** I myself/he himself/we ourselves; **sie ist die Tugend selbst** she's virtue itself; **er braut sein Bier selbst** he brews his own beer; **wie gehts? — gut, und selbst?** how are things? — fine, and yourself?
2 (*ohne Hilfe*) alone, on my/his/one's *etc* own; **von selbst** by itself; **er kam**

von selbst he came of his own accord; **selbst gemacht** home-made ▶ *adv* even; **selbst wenn** even if; **selbst Gott** even God (himself)

selbständig *etc adj* = **selbstständig** *usw*
Selbstauslöser *m* (*Phot*) delayed-action shutter release
Selbstbedienung *f* self-service
Selbstbefriedigung *f* masturbation
Selbstbeherrschung *f* self-control
selbstbewusst *adj* self-confident
selbstklebend *adj* self-adhesive
Selbstmord *m* suicide
Selbstmordattentat *nt* suicide bombing
Selbstmordattentäter(in) *m(f)* suicide bomber
selbstsicher *adj* self-assured
selbstständig *adj* independent; (*arbeitend*) self-employed
selbstverständlich *adj* obvious ▶ *adv* naturally; **ich halte das für ~** I take that for granted
Selbstvertrauen *nt* self-confidence
Selfie *nt* selfie
Sellerie (**-s**, **-(s)** *od* **-**, **-n**) *m od f* celery
selten *adj* rare ▶ *adv* seldom, rarely
seltsam *adj* strange
Semester (**-s**, **-**) *nt* semester
Semikolon (**-s**, **-s**) *nt* semicolon
Seminar (**-s**, **-e**) *nt* seminar
Semmel (**-**, **-n**) *f* roll
Semmelbrösel, Semmelbröseln *pl* breadcrumbs *pl*
Senat (**-(e)s**, **-e**) *m* senate
senden[1] *unreg vt* to send
senden[2] *vt*, *vi* (*Rundf*, *TV*) to transmit, to broadcast
Sender (**-s**, **-**) *m* station; (*Anlage*) transmitter
Sendung *f* (*Rundf*, *TV*) transmission; (*Programm*) programme (BRIT), program (*US*)
Senf (**-(e)s**, **-e**) *m* mustard
Senior (**-s**, **-en**) *m* senior citizen
Seniorenpass *m* senior citizen's travel pass (BRIT)
senken *vt* to lower ▶ *vr* to sink
senkrecht *adj* vertical
Sensation *f* sensation
sensibel *adj* sensitive
sentimental *adj* sentimental
separat *adj* separate
September (**-(s)**, **-**) *m* September; **im ~** in September; **im Monat ~** in the month of September; **in diesem ~** this September; **Anfang/Ende/Mitte ~** at the beginning/end/in the middle of September
Serbien (**-s**) *nt* Serbia
Serie *f* series
seriös *adj* serious; (*anständig*) respectable
Serpentine *f* hairpin (bend)
Serum (**-s**, **Seren**) *nt* serum
Service[1] (**-(s)**, **-**) *nt* (*Geschirr*) service
Service[2] (**-**, **-s**) *m* (*Comm*, *Sport*) service
servieren *vt*, *vi* to serve
Serviette *f* napkin, serviette
Servolenkung *f* power steering
Sesam (**-s**, **-s**) *m* sesame
Sessel (**-s**, **-**) *m* armchair
Sessellift *m* chairlift
Set (**-s**, **-s**) *nt od m* set; (*Deckchen*) tablemat
setzen *vt* to put; (*Baum etc*) to plant; (*Segel*, *Typ*) to set ▶ *vr* (*Platz nehmen*) to sit down; (*Kaffee*, *Tee*) to settle; **sich zu jdm ~** to sit with sb
Seuche (**-**, **-n**) *f* epidemic
seufzen *vt*, *vi* to sigh
Sex (**-(es)**) *m* sex
Sexualität *f* sexuality
sexuell *adj* sexual
Seychellen *pl* Seychelles *pl*
Sfr, sFr. *abk* (= *Schweizer Franken*) sfr
Shampoo (**-s**, **-s**) *nt* shampoo
Shorts *pl* shorts *pl*

SCHLÜSSELWORT

sich *pron* **1** (*akk*): **er/sie/es ... sich** he/she/it ... himself/herself/itself; **sie** *pl*/**man ... sich** they/one ... themselves/oneself; **Sie ... sich** you ... yourself/yourselves *pl*; **sich wiederholen** to repeat oneself/itself
2 (*dat*): **er/sie/es ... sich** he/she/it ... to himself/herself/itself; **sie** *pl*/**man ... sich** they/one ... to themselves/oneself; **Sie ... sich** you ... to yourself/yourselves *pl*; **sie hat sich einen Pullover gekauft** she bought herself a jumper; **sich die Haare waschen** to wash one's hair
3 (*mit Präposition*): **haben Sie Ihren Ausweis bei sich?** do you have your pass on you?; **er hat nichts bei sich**

he's got nothing on him; **sie bleiben gern unter sich** they keep themselves to themselves
4 (*einander*) each other, one another; **sie bekämpfen sich** they fight each other *od* one another
5: **dieses Auto fährt sich gut** this car drives well; **hier sitzt es sich gut** it's good to sit here

sicher *adj* safe; (*gewiss*) certain; (*zuverlässig*) reliable; (*selbstsicher*) confident
Sicherheit *f* safety; (*auch Fin*) security; (*Gewissheit*) certainty; (*Selbstsicherheit*) confidence
Sicherheitsabstand *m* safe distance
Sicherheitsgurt *m* seat belt
sicherheitshalber *adv* to be on the safe side
Sicherheitsnadel *f* safety pin
Sicherheitsvorkehrung *f* safety precaution
sicherlich *adv* certainly, surely
sichern *vt* to secure; (*schützen*) to protect; (*Comput: Daten*) to back up
Sicherung *f* (*Sichern*) securing; (*Vorrichtung*) safety device; (*an Waffen*) safety catch; (*Elek*) fuse; **da ist (bei) ihm die ~ durchgebrannt** (*fig: umg*) he blew a fuse
Sicht (-) *f* sight; (*Aussicht*) view
sichtbar *adj* visible
sichtlich *adj* evident, obvious
Sichtverhältnisse *pl* visibility *sing*
Sichtweite *f*: **außer ~** out of sight
sie *pron* (*sing: nom*) she; (*: akk*) her; (*pl: nom*) they; (*: akk*) them
Sie *nom, akk pron* you
Sieb (**-(e)s**, **-e**) *nt* sieve; (*Koch*) strainer
sieben *num* seven
siebenhundert *num* seven hundred
siebte(r, s) *adj* seventh
Siebtel (**-s**, **-**) *nt* seventh
siebzehn *num* seventeen
siebzig *num* seventy
Siedlung *f* (*Häusersiedlung*) housing estate (Brit) *od* development (US)
Sieg (**-(e)s**, **-e**) *m* victory
siegen *vi* (*Sport*) to win
Sieger(in) (**-s**, **-**) *m(f)* (*Sport etc*) winner
Siegerehrung *f* (*Sport*) presentation ceremony
siehe *Imperativ* see
siezen *vt* to address as "Sie"
Signal (**-s**, **-e**) *nt* signal
Silbe (**-**, **-n**) *f* syllable
Silber (**-s**) *nt* silver
Silberhochzeit *f* silver wedding
Silbermedaille *f* silver medal
Silikon (**-s**, **-e**) *nt* silicone
Silvester (**-s**, **-**) *m od nt* New Year's Eve, Hogmanay (Scot)

SILVESTER

Silvester is the German name for New Year's Eve. Although not an official holiday, most businesses close early and shops shut at midday. Most Germans celebrate in the evening and at midnight they let off fireworks and rockets; the revelry usually lasts until the early hours of the morning.

Simbabwe (**-s**) *nt* Zimbabwe
SIM-Karte *f* SIM card
simpel *adj* simple
simsen (*umg*) *vt, vi* to text
simultan *adj* simultaneous
Sinfonie *f* symphony
Singapur (**-s**) *nt* Singapore
singen *unreg vt, vi* to sing
Single[1] (**-s**, **-s**) *m* (*Alleinlebender*) single person
Single[2] (**-**, **-s**) *f* (*Mus*) single
Singular *m* singular
sinken *unreg vi* to sink; (*Preise etc*) to fall, to go down
Sinn (**-(e)s**, **-e**) *m* mind; (*Wahrnehmungssinn*) sense; (*Bedeutung*) sense, meaning; **~ machen** to make sense; **das hat keinen ~** there is no point in that
sinnlich *adj* sensual, sensuous; (*Wahrnehmung*) sensory
sinnlos *adj* senseless; (*zwecklos*) pointless; (*bedeutungslos*) meaningless
sinnvoll *adj* meaningful; (*vernünftig*) sensible
Sirup (**-s**, **-e**) *m* syrup
Sitte (**-**, **-n**) *f* custom
Situation *f* situation
Sitz (**-es**, **-e**) *m* seat
sitzen *unreg vi* to sit; (*Bemerkung, Schlag*) to strike home; (*Gelerntes*) to have sunk in; **~ bleiben** (*Sch*) to have to repeat a year

Sitzgelegenheit *f* seats *pl*
Sitzplatz *m* seat
Sitzung *f* meeting
Sizilien (**-s**) *nt* Sicily
Skandal (**-s**, **-e**) *m* scandal
Skandinavien (**-s**) *nt* Scandinavia
Skateboard (**-s**, **-s**) *nt* skateboard
skateboarden *vi* to skateboard
Skelett (**-(e)s**, **-e**) *nt* skeleton
skeptisch *adj* sceptical (BRIT), skeptical (US)
Ski (**-s**, **-er**) *m* ski; **~ laufen** *od* **fahren** to ski
Skiläufer *m* skier
Skilehrer(in) *m(f)* ski instructor
Skilift *m* ski lift
Skipiste *f* ski run
Skispringen *nt* ski jumping
Skistiefel *m* ski boot
Skistock *m* ski pole
Skizze (**-**, **-n**) *f* sketch
Skonto (**-s**, **-s**) *nt od m* discount
Skorpion (**-s**, **-e**) *m* scorpion; (*Astrol*) Scorpio
Skulptur *f* sculpture
Slalom (**-s**, **-s**) *m* slalom
Slip (**-s**, **-s**) *m* (pair of) briefs *pl*
Slowakei *f* Slovakia
slowakisch *adj* Slovakian
Slowenien (**-s**) *nt* Slovenia
slowenisch *adj* Slovenian
Smartphone *nt* smartphone
Smoking (**-s**, **-s**) *m* dinner jacket (BRIT), tuxedo (US)
SMS (**-**, **-**) *f abk* (= *Short Message Service*) text message; **jdm eine ~ schicken** to send sb a text
Snowboard (**-s**, **-s**) *nt* snowboard
snowboarden *vi* to snowboard

SCHLÜSSELWORT

so *adv* **1** (*so sehr*) so; **so groß/schön** *etc* so big/nice *etc*; **so groß/schön wie ...** as big/nice as ...; **das hat ihn so geärgert, dass ...** that annoyed him so much that ...; **so viel (wie)** as much as; **rede nicht so viel** don't talk so much; **so weit sein** to be ready; **so weit wie** *od* **als möglich** as far as possible; **ich bin so weit zufrieden** by and large I'm quite satisfied; **so wenig (wie)** no more (than); **so einer wie ich** somebody like me; **na so was!** well I never!
2 (*auf diese Weise*) like this; **und so weiter** and so on; **... oder so was** ... or something like that; **das ist gut so** that's fine
3 (*umg: umsonst*): **ich habe es so bekommen** I got it for nothing
▸ *konj*: **so wie es jetzt ist** as things are at the moment
▸ *interj*: **so?** really?; **so, das wärs** right, that's it then

s. o. *abk* (= *siehe oben*) see above
sobald *konj* as soon as
Social Media *pl* social media
Socke (**-**, **-n**) *f* sock
Sodbrennen (**-s**) *nt* heartburn
Sofa (**-s**, **-s**) *nt* sofa
sofern *konj* if, provided (that)
soff *etc vb siehe* **saufen**
sofort *adv* immediately, at once
Sofortnachricht *f* instant message
Softeis (**-es**) *nt* soft ice-cream
Software (**-**, **-s**) *f* software
sog *etc vb siehe* **saugen**
sogar *adv* even
sogenannt *adj attrib* so-called
Sohle (**-**, **-n**) *f* sole
Sohn (**-(e)s**, **Söhne**) *m* son
Soja (**-**, **Sojen**) *f* soya
Sojasprossen *pl* bean sprouts *pl*
solang, solange *konj* as *od* so long as
Solarium *nt* solarium
solche(r, s) *adj* such; **ein solcher Mensch** such a person
Soldat (**-en**, **-en**) *m* soldier
solid, solide *adj* solid; (*Leben, Person*) respectable
solidarisch *adj* in *od* with solidarity; **sich ~ erklären** to declare one's solidarity
Soll (**-(s)**, **-(s)**) *nt* (*Fin*) debit (side); (*Arbeitsmenge*) quota, target

SCHLÜSSELWORT

sollen (*pt* **sollte**, *pp* **gesollt**, *als Hilfsverb* **sollen**) *Hilfsverb* **1** (*Pflicht, Befehl*) be supposed to; **du hättest nicht gehen sollen** you shouldn't have gone, you oughtn't to have gone; **soll ich?** shall I?; **soll ich dir helfen?** shall I help you?; **sag ihm, er soll warten** tell him he's to wait; **was soll ich machen?** what should I do?
2 (*Vermutung*): **sie soll verheiratet**

sein she's said to be married; **was soll das heißen?** what's that supposed to mean?; **man sollte glauben, dass ...** you would think that ...; **sollte das passieren, ...** if that should happen ... ▸ *vt, vi*: **was soll das?** what's all this about *od* in aid of?; **das sollst du nicht** you shouldn't do that; **was solls?** what the hell!

Solo (**-s**, **-s** *od* **Soli**) *nt* solo
Sommer (**-s**, **-**) *m* summer
Sommerferien *pl* summer holidays *pl* (Brit) *od* vacation *sing* (US)
sommerlich *adj* summer *attrib*; (*sommerartig*) summery
Sommerreifen *m* normal tyre (Brit) *od* tire (US)
Sommersprossen *pl* freckles *pl*
Sommerzeit *f* summertime
Sonderangebot *nt* special offer
sonderbar *adj* strange, odd
Sondermarke *f* special issue (stamp)
Sondermüll *m* dangerous waste
sondern *konj* but; **nicht nur ..., ~ auch** not only ..., but also
Sonderpreis *m* special price
Sonderschule *f* special school
Sonderzug *m* special train
Sonnabend *m* Saturday; *siehe auch* **Dienstag**
Sonne (**-**, **-n**) *f* sun
sonnen *vr* to sun o.s.
Sonnenaufgang *m* sunrise
Sonnenblume *f* sunflower
Sonnenbrand *m* sunburn
Sonnenbrille *f* sunglasses *pl*
Sonnencreme *f* suntan lotion
Sonnenmilch *f* suntan lotion
Sonnenöl *nt* suntan oil
Sonnenschein *m* sunshine
Sonnenschirm *m* sunshade
Sonnenstich *m* sunstroke
Sonnenuhr *f* sundial
Sonnenuntergang *m* sunset
sonnig *adj* sunny
Sonntag *m* Sunday; *siehe auch* **Dienstag**
sonntags *adv* (on) Sundays
sonst *adv* otherwise; (*mit pron, in Fragen*) else; (*gewöhnlich*) usually, normally ▸ *konj* otherwise; **~ noch etwas?** anything else?; **~ nichts** nothing else
sooft *konj* whenever
Sopran (**-s**, **-e**) *m* soprano (voice)
Sorge (**-**, **-n**) *f* care, worry
sorgen *vi*: **für jdn ~** to look after sb ▸ *vr*: **sich ~ (um)** to worry (about); **für etw ~** to take care of *od* see to sth
sorgfältig *adj* careful
sortieren *vt* to sort (out)
Sortiment *nt* assortment
sosehr *konj* as much as
Soße (**-**, **-n**) *f* sauce; (*Bratensoße*) gravy
Souvenir (**-s**, **-s**) *nt* souvenir
soviel *konj* as far as
soweit *konj* as far as
sowie *konj* (*sobald*) as soon as; (*ebenso*) as well as
sowohl *konj*: **~ ... als** *od* **wie auch ...** both ... and ...
sozial *adj* social; **sozialer Wohnungsbau** public-sector housing (programme); **soziales Netzwerk** social networking site; **soziale Medien** social media
Sozialhilfe *f* welfare (aid)
Sozialismus *m* socialism
Sozialkunde *f* social studies *sing*
Sozialversicherung *f* national insurance (Brit), social security (US)
Sozialwohnung *f* ≈ council flat (Brit), state-subsidized apartment (US)
Soziologie *f* sociology
sozusagen *adv* so to speak
Spachtel (**-s**, **-**) *m* spatula
Spaghetti, Spagetti *pl* spaghetti *sing*
Spalte (**-**, **-n**) *f* crack; (*Gletscherspalte*) crevasse; (*in Text*) column
spalten *vt, vr* to split
Spam (**-s**, **-s**) *nt* (*Comput*) spam
Spange (**-**, **-n**) *f* clasp; (*Haarspange*) hair slide
Spanien (**-s**) *nt* Spain
Spanier(in) (**-s**, **-**) *m(f)* Spaniard
spanisch *adj* Spanish
spann *vb siehe* **spinnen**
spannen *vt* (*straffen*) to tighten; (*befestigen*) to brace ▸ *vi* to be tight
spannend *adj* exciting, gripping
Spannung *f* tension; (*Elek*) voltage; (*fig*) suspense
Sparbuch *nt* savings book
sparen *vt, vi* to save
Spargel (**-s**, **-**) *m* asparagus
Sparkasse *f* savings bank
Sparkonto *nt* savings account

spärlich *adj* meagre (BRIT), meager (US); (*Bekleidung*) scanty
sparsam *adj* economical
Sparschwein *nt* piggy bank
Spaß (**-es**, **Späße**) *m* joke; (*Freude*) fun; **jdm ~ machen** to be fun (for sb); **viel ~!** have fun!
spät *adj*, *adv* late
Spaten (**-s**, **-**) *m* spade
später *adj*, *adv* later
spätestens *adv* at the latest
Spatz (**-en**, **-en**) *m* sparrow
spazieren *vi* (*Hilfsverb sein*) to stroll; **~ gehen** to go for a walk
Spaziergang *m* walk
Specht (**-(e)s**, **-e**) *m* woodpecker
Speck (**-(e)s**, **-e**) *m* bacon
Spedition *f* (*Umzugsfirma*) removal (BRIT) *od* moving (US) firm
Speiche (**-**, **-n**) *f* spoke
Speichel (**-s**) *m* saliva
Speicher (**-s**, **-**) *m* storehouse; (*Dachspeicher*) attic; (*Comput*) memory
Speicherkarte *f* memory card
speichern *vt* (*auch Comput*) to store; (*sichern*) to save
Speise (**-**, **-n**) *f* food; (*Gericht*) dish
Speisekarte *f* menu
Speiseröhre *f* (*Anat*) gullet, oesophagus (BRIT), esophagus (US)
Speisesaal *m* dining room
Speisewagen *m* dining car
Spende (**-**, **-n**) *f* donation
spenden *vt* to donate, to give
spendieren *vt*: **jdm etw ~** to treat sb to sth
Sperre (**-**, **-n**) *f* barrier; (*Verbot*) ban; (*Polizeisperre*) roadblock
sperren *vt* to block; (*Sport*) to suspend; (*verbieten*) to ban
Sperrstunde *f* closing time
Spesen *pl* expenses *pl*
spezialisieren *vr* to specialize
Spezialist(in) *m(f)*: **~ (für)** specialist (in)
Spezialität *f* speciality (BRIT), specialty (US)
speziell *adj* special ▶ *adv* especially
Spiegel (**-s**, **-**) *m* mirror
Spiegelei *nt* fried egg
Spiegelreflexkamera *f* reflex camera
Spiel (**-(e)s**, **-e**) *nt* game; (*Tätigkeit*) play(ing); (*Karten*) pack (BRIT), deck (US); (*Tech*) (free) play
Spielautomat *m* gambling machine; (*zum Geldgewinnen*) slot machine
spielen *vt*, *vi* to play; (*um Geld*) to gamble; (*Theat*) to perform, to act
spielend *adv* easily
Spieler(in) (**-s**, **-**) *m(f)* player; (*um Geld*) gambler
Spielfeld *nt* field
Spielfilm *m* feature film
Spielkasino *nt* casino
Spielkonsole *f* games console
Spielplatz *m* playground
Spielraum *m* room to manoeuvre (BRIT) *od* maneuver (US)
Spielregel *f* (*lit*, *fig*) rule of the game
Spielsachen *pl* toys *pl*
Spielzeug *nt* toy; (*Spielsachen*) toys *pl*
Spieß (**-es**, **-e**) *m* spear; (*Bratspieß*) spit
Spießer (**-s**, **-**) *m* bourgeois
Spikes *pl* (*Sport*) spikes *pl*; (*Aut*) studs *pl*
Spinat (**-(e)s**, **-e**) *m* spinach
Spinne (**-**, **-n**) *f* spider
spinnen *unreg vt* to spin ▶ *vi* (*umg*) to talk rubbish; (*verrückt*) to be crazy *od* mad; **du spinnst!** you must be mad
Spinnwebe *f* cobweb
Spion (**-s**, **-e**) *m* spy
Spionagesoftware *f* (*Comput*) spyware
spionieren *vi* to spy
Spirale (**-**, **-n**) *f* spiral; (*Med*) coil
Spirituosen *pl* spirits *pl*
Spiritus (**-**, **-se**) *m* (methylated) spirits *pl*
spitz *adj* pointed; (*Winkel*) acute; (*fig*: *Zunge*) sharp
Spitze (**-**, **-n**) *f* point, tip; (*Bemerkung*) taunt; (*erster Platz*) lead; (*Gewebe*) lace
Spitzer (**-s**, **-**) *m* sharpener
Spitzname *m* nickname
sponsern *vt* to sponsor
Sponsor (**-s**, **-en**) *m* sponsor
spontan *adj* spontaneous
Sport (**-(e)s**, **-e**) *m* sport; **treiben Sie ~?** do you do any sport?
Sportgetränk *nt* sports drink
Sporthalle *f* sports hall
Sportlehrer(in) *m(f)* games *od* PE teacher
Sportler(in) (**-s**, **-**) *m(f)* sportsman, sportswoman
sportlich *adj* sporting; (*Mensch*) sporty
Sportplatz *m* playing *od* sports field
Sportverein *m* sports club

Sportwagen *m* sports car
sprach *vb siehe* **sprechen**
Sprache (-, -**n**) *f* language
Sprachenschule *f* language school
Sprachführer *m* phrase book
Sprachkenntnisse *pl*: **mit englischen Sprachkenntnissen** with a knowledge of English
Sprachkurs *m* language course
Sprachsteuerung *f* voice control
sprang *vb siehe* **springen**
Spray (-**s**, -**s**) *m od nt* spray
Sprechanlage *f* intercom
sprechen *unreg vi* to speak, to talk ▶ *vt* to say; (*Sprache*) to speak; (*Person*) to speak to; **mit jdm ~** to speak *od* talk to sb
Sprecher(in) (-**s**, -) *m(f)* speaker; (*Rundf, TV*) announcer
Sprechstunde *f* consultation (hour); (*von Arzt*) (doctor's) surgery (Brit)
Sprechzimmer *nt* consulting room
Sprengstoff *m* explosive(s *pl*)
Sprichwort *nt* proverb
Springbrunnen *m* fountain
springen *unreg vi* to jump; (*Glas*) to crack; (*mit Kopfsprung*) to dive
Sprit (-**(e)s**, -**e**) (*umg*) *m* petrol (Brit), gas(oline) (US)
Spritze (-, -**n**) *f* syringe; (*Injektion*) injection; (*an Schlauch*) nozzle
spritzen *vt* to spray; (*Med*) to inject ▶ *vi* to splash; (*Med*) to give injections
Spruch (-**(e)s**, **Sprüche**) *m* saying
Sprudel (-**s**, -) *m* mineral water; (*süß*) lemonade
sprudeln *vi* to bubble
Sprühdose *f* aerosol (can)
sprühen *vi* to spray; (*fig*) to sparkle ▶ *vt* to spray
Sprühregen *m* drizzle
Sprung (-**(e)s**, **Sprünge**) *m* jump; (*Riss*) crack
Sprungbrett *nt* springboard
Sprungschanze *f* ski jump
Sprungturm *m* diving platform
Spucke (-) *f* spit
spucken *vt, vi* to spit
Spucktüte *f* sickbag
spuken *vi* to haunt; **hier spukt es** this place is haunted
Spülbecken *nt* sink
Spule (-, -**n**) *f* spool; (*Elek*) coil
Spüle (-, -**n**) *f* (kitchen) sink
spülen *vt* to rinse; (*Geschirr*) to wash; (*Toilette*) to flush ▶ *vi* to rinse; (*Geschirr*) to do the dishes
Spülmaschine *f* dishwasher
Spülmittel *nt* washing-up liquid (Brit), dishwashing liquid
Spülung *f* (*Wasserspülung*) flush
Spur (-, -**en**) *f* trace; (*Fußspur, Radspur, Tonbandspur*) track; (*Fährte*) trail; (*Fahrspur*) lane
spüren *vt* to feel
Spürhund *m* tracker dog
Spyware *f* (*Comput*) spyware
Squash (-) *nt* (*Sport*) squash
Staat (-**(e)s**, -**en**) *m* state
staatlich *adj* state *attrib*; (*staatseigen*) state-run
Staatsangehörigkeit *f* nationality
Staatsanwalt *m* public prosecutor
Staatsbürger *m* citizen
Staatsbürgerschaft *f* nationality; **doppelte ~** dual nationality
Staatsexamen *nt* (*Univ*) degree
Stab (-**(e)s**, **Stäbe**) *m* rod; (*Gitterstab*) bar
Stäbchen *nt* (*Essstäbchen*) chopstick
Stabhochsprung *m* pole vault
stabil *adj* stable; (*Möbel*) sturdy
stach *etc vb siehe* **stechen**
Stachel (-**s**, -**n**) *m* spike; (*von Tier*) spine; (*von Insekten*) sting
Stachelbeere *f* gooseberry
Stacheldraht *m* barbed wire
stachelig *adj* prickly
Stadion (-**s**, **Stadien**) *nt* stadium
Stadt (-, **Städte**) *f* town; (*Großstadt*) city
städtisch *adj* municipal
Stadtmauer *f* city wall(s *pl*)
Stadtmitte *f* town/city centre (Brit) *od* center (US)
Stadtplan *m* street map
Stadtrand *m* outskirts *pl*
Stadtrundfahrt *f* city tour
Stadtteil *m* district, part of town
Stadtviertel *m* district *od* part of a town
Stadtzentrum *nt* town/city centre (Brit) *od* center (US)
stahl *etc vb siehe* **stehlen**
Stahl (-**(e)s**, **Stähle**) *m* steel
Stall (-**(e)s**, **Ställe**) *m* stable; (*Kaninchenstall*) hutch; (*Schweinestall*) sty; (*Hühnerstall*) henhouse

Stamm (**-(e)s**, **Stämme**) *m* (*Baumstamm*) trunk; (*Menschenstamm*) tribe
stammen *vi*: **~ von** *od* **aus** to come from
Stammgast *m* regular (customer)
Stammkunde *m*, **Stammkundin** *f* regular (customer)
Stammtisch *m table reserved for the regulars*
stampfen *vi* to stamp; (*stapfen*) to tramp ▸ *vt* (*mit Stampfer*) to mash
stand *vb siehe* **stehen**
Stand (**-(e)s**, **Stände**) *m* (*Wasserstand, Benzinstand etc*) level; (*Stehen*) standing position; (*Zustand*) state; (*Spielstand*) score; (*Messestand etc*) stand; (*Klasse*) class
Ständer (**-s**, **-**) *m* stand
Standesamt *nt* registry office (Brit), city/county clerk's office (*US*)
ständig *adj* permanent; (*ununterbrochen*) constant, continual
Standlicht *nt* sidelights *pl* (Brit), parking lights *pl* (*US*)
Standort *m* location
Standpunkt *m* standpoint
Standspur *f* (*Aut*) hard shoulder (Brit), shoulder (*US*)
Stange (**-**, **-n**) *f* stick; (*Stab*) pole; (*Querstange*) bar; (*Zigaretten*) carton
Stangenbohne *f* runner bean
Stangenbrot *nt* French bread; (*Laib*) French stick (loaf)
stank *vb siehe* **stinken**
Stapel (**-s**, **-**) *m* pile
Star[1] (**-(e)s**, **-e**) *m* starling; **grauer/grüner ~** (*Med*) cataract/glaucoma
Star[2] (**-s**, **-s**) *m* (*Filmstar etc*) star
starb *vb siehe* **sterben**
stark *adj* strong; (*heftig, groß*) heavy; (*Maßangabe*) thick
Stärke (**-**, **-n**) *f* strength (*auch fig*); (*bei Maßangaben*) thickness; (*Wäschestärke, Koch*) starch
stärken *vt* to strengthen; (*Wäsche*) to starch
Starkstrom *m* high-voltage current
Stärkung *f* strengthening; (*Essen*) refreshment
starr *adj* stiff; (*unnachgiebig*) rigid; (*Blick*) staring
starren *vi* to stare
Start (**-(e)s**, **-e**) *m* start; (*Aviat*) takeoff
Startautomatik *f* (*Aut*) automatic choke
Startbahn *f* runway
starten *vi* to start; (*Aviat*) to take off ▸ *vt* to start
Starthilfekabel *nt* jump leads *pl* (Brit), jumper cables *pl* (*US*)
Station *f* station; (*Krankenstation*) hospital ward; (*Haltestelle*) stop
stationär *adj* stationary; (*Med*) in-patient *attrib*
Statistik *f* statistics *sing*
Stativ (**-s**, **-e**) *nt* tripod
statt *konj* instead of ▸ *präp* (*+dat od gen*) instead of
statt|finden *unreg vi* to take place
Statue (**-**, **-n**) *f* statue
Stau (**-(e)s**, **-e**) *m* blockage; (*Verkehrsstau*) (traffic) jam
Staub (**-(e)s**) *m* dust; **~ wischen** to dust
staubig *adj* dusty
staubsaugen (*pp* **staubgesaugt**) *vi untr* to vacuum
Staubsauger *m* vacuum cleaner
Staubtuch *nt* duster
Staudamm *m* dam
staunen *vi* to be astonished
Stausee *m* reservoir
Stauung *f* (*von Wasser*) damming-up; (*von Blut, Verkehr*) congestion
Std. *abk* (*= Stunde*) h.
Steak (**-s**, **-s**) *nt* steak
stechen *unreg vt* (*mit Nadel etc*) to prick; (*mit Messer*) to stab; (*mit Finger*) to poke; (*Biene etc*) to sting; (*Mücke*) to bite ▸ *vi* (*Sonne*) to beat down
Stechen (**-s**, **-**) *nt* (*Schmerz*) sharp pain
Stechmücke *f* gnat
Steckdose *f* (wall) socket
stecken *vt* to put; (*Nadel*) to stick; (*beim Nähen*) to pin ▸ *vi* (*auch unreg*) to be; (*festsitzen*) to be stuck; (*Nadeln*) to stick; **der Schlüssel steckt** the key is in the lock
Stecker (**-s**, **-**) *m* (*Elek*) plug
Steckrübe *f* swede, turnip
Steg (**-(e)s**, **-e**) *m* small bridge
stehen *unreg vi* to stand; (*sich befinden*) to be; (*in Zeitung*) to say; (*angehalten haben*) to have stopped ▸ *vi unpers*: **es steht schlecht um …** things are bad for …; **jdm ~** to suit sb; **~ bleiben** (*Uhr*) to stop; **~ lassen** to leave
stehlen *unreg vt* to steal
Stehplatz *m*: **ein ~ kostet 15 Euro** a standing ticket costs 15 euros

steif *adj* stiff
steigen *unreg vi* to rise; (*klettern*) to climb ▶ *vt*: **~ in** *+akk*/**auf** *+akk* to get in/on
steigern *vt* to raise ▶ *vr* to increase
Steigung *f* incline, gradient
steil *adj* steep
Steilhang *m* steep slope
Stein (**-(e)s**, **-e**) *m* stone
Steinbock *m* (*Astrol*) Capricorn
steinig *adj* stony
Steinschlag *m*: **„Achtung ~"** "danger – falling rocks"
Stelle (**-**, **-n**) *f* place; (*Arbeit*) post, job; (*Amt*) office; **ich an deiner ~** if I were you; **auf der ~** (*fig: sofort*) on the spot
stellen *vt* to put; (*Uhr etc*) to set; (*zur Verfügung stellen*) to supply ▶ *vr* (*bei Polizei*) to give o.s. up; (*vorgeben*) to pretend (to be)
Stellenangebot *nt* job offer; **„Stellenangebote"** "vacancies"
stellenweise *adv* in places
Stellenwert *m* (*fig*) status; **einen hohen ~ haben** to play an important role
Stellung *f* position; **~ nehmen zu** to comment on
Stellvertreter *m* representative; (*von Amts wegen*) deputy
Stempel (**-s**, **-**) *m* stamp
stempeln *vt* to stamp; (*Briefmarke*) to cancel
sterben *unreg vi* to die
Stereoanlage *f* stereo unit
steril *adj* sterile
sterilisieren *vt* to sterilize
Stern (**-(e)s**, **-e**) *m* star
Sternbild *nt* constellation
Sternschnuppe (**-**, **-n**) *f* falling star
Sternwarte *f* observatory
Sternzeichen *nt* (*Astrol*) sign of the zodiac
stets *adv* always
Steuer[1] (**-s**, **-**) *nt* (*Aut*) steering wheel
Steuer[2] (**-**, **-n**) *f* tax
Steuerberater(in) *m(f)* tax consultant
Steuerbord *nt* starboard
Steuererklärung *f* tax return
Steuerflucht *f* tax exile
Steuerflüchtling *m* tax exile
steuerfrei *adj* tax-free
Steuerknüppel *m* control column; (*Aviat, Comput*) joystick
steuern *vt* to steer; (*Flugzeug*) to pilot; (*Entwicklung, Tonstärke*) to control ▶ *vi* to steer
steuerpflichtig *adj* taxable
Steuerung *f* steering (*auch Aut*); (*von Flugzeug*) piloting; (*von Entwicklung*) control; (*Vorrichtung*) controls *pl*
Stich (**-(e)s**, **-e**) *m* (*Insektenstich*) sting; (*Messerstich*) stab; (*beim Nähen*) stitch; (*Färbung*) tinge; (*Karten*) trick; (*Kunst*) engraving
sticken *vt*, *vi* to embroider
Stickerei *f* embroidery
stickig *adj* stuffy, close
Stiefel (**-s**, **-**) *m* boot
Stiefmutter *f* stepmother
Stiefmütterchen *nt* pansy
Stiefvater *m* stepfather
stieg *vb siehe* **steigen**
Stiege (**-**, **-n**) *f* staircase
Stiel (**-(e)s**, **-e**) *m* handle; (*Bot*) stalk
Stier (**-(e)s**, **-e**) *m* bull; (*Astrol*) Taurus
Stierkampf *m* bullfight
stieß *vb siehe* **stoßen**
Stift (**-(e)s**, **-e**) *m* peg; (*Nagel*) tack; (*Buntstift*) crayon; (*Bleistift*) pencil
Stil (**-(e)s**, **-e**) *m* style
still *adj* quiet; (*unbewegt*) still
stillen *vt* (*Säugling*) to breast-feed
still|halten *unreg vi* to keep still
still|stehen *unreg vi* to stand still
Stimme (**-**, **-n**) *f* voice; (*Wahlstimme*) vote
stimmen *vi* to be right; **stimmt so!** (*beim Bezahlen*) keep the change
Stimmung *f* mood; (*Atmosphäre*) atmosphere
stinken *unreg vi* to stink
Stipendium *nt* grant; (*als Auszeichnung*) scholarship
Stirn (**-**, **-en**) *f* forehead
Stirnhöhle *f* sinus
Stock[1] (**-(e)s**, **Stöcke**) *m* stick; (*Bot*) stock
Stock[2] (**-(e)s**, **-** *od* **-werke**) *m* storey (BRIT), story (US)
Stockwerk *nt* storey (BRIT), story (US)
Stoff (**-(e)s**, **-e**) *m* (*Gewebe*) material; (*Materie*) matter; (*von Buch etc*) subject (matter); (*umg: Rauschgift*) dope
stöhnen *vi* to groan
stolpern *vi* to stumble, to trip
stolz *adj* proud
stoppen *vt* to stop; (*mit Uhr*) to time ▶ *vi* to stop

Stoppschild *nt* stop sign
Stoppuhr *f* stopwatch
Stöpsel (**-s**, **-**) *m* plug; (*für Flaschen*) stopper
Storch (**-(e)s**, **Störche**) *m* stork
stören *vt* to disturb; (*behindern*, *Rundf*) to interfere with; **stört es Sie, wenn ich rauche?** do you mind if I smoke?
stornieren *vt* (*Comm*) to cancel
Störung *f* disturbance; (*Tech*) fault
Stoß (**-es**, **Stöße**) *m* (*Schub*) push; (*Schlag*) blow; (*mit Fuß*) kick; (*Haufen*) pile
Stoßdämpfer *m* shock absorber
stoßen *unreg vt* (*mit Druck*) to shove, to push; (*mit Schlag*) to knock; (*mit Fuß*) to kick; (*anstoßen*) to bump; (*zerkleinern*) to pulverize ▶ *vr* to get a knock; **sich ~ an** *+dat* (*fig*) to take exception to
Stoßstange *f* (*Aut*) bumper
stottern *vt*, *vi* to stutter
Str. *abk* (= *Straße*) St.
Strafe (**-**, **-n**) *f* punishment; (*Jur*) penalty; (*Gefängnisstrafe*) sentence; (*Geldstrafe*) fine
strafen *vt*, *vi* to punish
Straftat *f* punishable act
Strafzettel (*umg*) *m* ticket
Strahl (**-(e)s**, **-en**) *m* ray, beam; (*Wasserstrahl*) jet
strahlen *vi* to radiate; (*fig*) to beam
Strähne (**-**, **-n**) *f* strand
Strand (**-(e)s**, **Strände**) *m* beach; **am ~** on the beach
Strandkorb *m* beach chair
strapazieren *vt* (*Material*) to be hard on; (*jdn*) to be a strain on
Straße (**-**, **-n**) *f* road; (*in Stadt*, *Dorf*) street
Straßenbahn *f* tram (Brit), streetcar (*US*)
Straßencafé *nt* pavement café (Brit), sidewalk café (*US*)
Straßenglätte *f* slippery road surface
Straßenkarte *f* road map
Straßenrand *m* roadside
Straßensperre *f* roadblock
Strategie *f* strategy
Strauch (**-(e)s**, **Sträucher**) *m* bush, shrub
Strauchtomate *f* vine-ripened tomato
Strauß[1] (**-es**, **Sträuße**) *m* (*Blumenstrauß*) bouquet
Strauß[2] (**-es**, **-e**) *m* ostrich
Strecke (**-**, **-n**) *f* stretch; (*Entfernung*) distance; (*Eisenb*, *Math*) line
strecken *vt* to stretch ▶ *vr* to stretch (o.s.)
streckenweise *adv* in parts
Streich (**-(e)s**, **-e**) *m* trick, prank
streicheln *vt* to stroke
streichen *unreg vt* (*berühren*) to stroke; (*auftragen*) to spread; (*durchstreichen*) to delete; (*nicht genehmigen*) to cancel
Streichholz *nt* match
Streichholzschachtel *f* matchbox
Streichkäse *m* cheese spread
Streifen (**-s**, **-**) *m* (*Linie*) stripe; (*Stück*) strip; (*Film*) film
Streifenwagen *m* patrol car
Streik (**-(e)s**, **-s**) *m* strike
streiken *vi* to strike
Streit (**-(e)s**, **-e**) *m* argument
streiten *unreg vi*, *vr* to argue
streng *adj* severe; (*Lehrer*, *Maßnahme*) strict; (*Geruch etc*) sharp
Stress (**-es**, **-e**) *m* stress
stressen *vt* to put under stress
stressig *adj* stressful
streuen *vt* to scatter ▶ *vi* (*mit Streupulver*) to grit; (*mit Salz*) to put down salt
Streufahrzeug *nt* gritter (Brit), sander
strich *vb siehe* **streichen**
Strich (**-(e)s**, **-e**) *m* (*Linie*) line
Strichcode *m* bar code (Brit), universal product code (*US*)
Strichkode *m* = **Strichcode**
Strichpunkt *m* semicolon
Strick (**-(e)s**, **-e**) *m* rope
stricken *vt*, *vi* to knit
Strickjacke *f* cardigan
Stricknadel *f* knitting needle
Stripper(in) (**-s**, **-**) *m(f)* stripper
stritt *vb siehe* **streiten**
Stroh (**-(e)s**) *nt* straw
Strohdach *nt* thatched roof
Strohhalm *m* (drinking) straw
Strom (**-(e)s**, **Ströme**) *m* river; (*fig*) stream; (*Elek*) current
Stromanschluss *m*: **~ haben** to be connected to the electricity mains
Stromausfall *m* power failure
strömen *vi* to stream, to pour
Strömung *f* current
Stromverbrauch *m* power consumption

Stromzähler *m* electricity meter
Strophe (-, **-n**) *f* verse
Strudel (**-s**, -) *m* whirlpool; (*Koch*) strudel
Struktur *f* structure
Strumpf (**-(e)s**, **Strümpfe**) *m* stocking
Strumpfhose *f* (pair of) tights *pl* (BRIT) *od* pantyhose *pl* (*US*)
Stück (**-(e)s**, **-e**) *nt* piece; (*etwas*) bit; (*Theat*) play; **am ~** in one piece
Student(in) *m(f)* student
Studentenausweis *m* student card
Studentenwohnheim *nt* hall of residence (BRIT), dormitory (*US*)
Studienfahrt *f* study trip
Studienplatz *m* university place
studieren *vt*, *vi* to study
Studium *nt* studies *pl*
Stufe (-, **-n**) *f* step; (*Entwicklungsstufe*) stage
Stuhl (**-(e)s**, **Stühle**) *m* chair
stumm *adj* silent; (*Med*) with a speech impairment
stumpf *adj* blunt; (*teilnahmslos, glanzlos*) dull
stumpfsinnig *adj* dull
Stunde (-, **-n**) *f* hour; (*Sch*) lesson
Stundenkilometer *pl* kilometres (BRIT) *od* kilometers (*US*) per hour
stundenlang *adj* for hours
Stundenlohn *m* hourly wage
Stundenplan *m* timetable
stündlich *adj* hourly
stur *adj* stubborn; **ein sturer Bock** (*umg*) a pig-headed fellow
Sturm (**-(e)s**, **Stürme**) *m* storm
stürmen *vi* (*Wind*) to blow hard; (*rennen*) to storm
Stürmer (**-s**, -) *m* (*Sport*) forward
stürmisch *adj* stormy; (*fig*) tempestuous; (*Liebhaber*) passionate; (*Beifall*) tumultuous
Sturmwarnung *f* gale warning
Sturz (**-es**, **Stürze**) *m* fall; (*Pol*) overthrow
stürzen *vt* (*werfen*) to hurl; (*Pol*) to overthrow; (*umkehren*) to overturn ▶ *vi* to fall; (*rennen*) to dash
Sturzhelm *m* crash helmet
Stute (-, **-n**) *f* mare
Stütze (-, **-n**) *f* support; (*Hilfe*) help
stützen *vt* to support; (*Ellbogen etc*) to prop up
stutzig *adj* perplexed, puzzled; (*misstrauisch*) suspicious
Styropor® (**-s**) *nt* (expanded) polystyrene
subjektiv *adj* subjective
Substanz *f* substance
subtrahieren *vt* to subtract
Subvention *f* subsidy
subventionieren *vt* to subsidize
Suche (-, **-n**) *f* search
suchen *vt* to look for ▶ *vi* to seek, to search; **~ und ersetzen** (*Comput*) search and replace
Suchmaschine *f* (*Comput*) search engine
Sucht (-, **Süchte**) *f* mania; (*Med*) addiction
süchtig *adj* addicted
Süchtige(r) *f(m)* addict
Süd (**-(e)s**) *m* south
Südafrika *nt* South Africa
Südamerika *nt* South America
Süddeutschland *nt* South(ern) Germany
Süden (**-s**) *m* south
Südeuropa *nt* Southern Europe
Südkorea *nt* South Korea
südlich *adj* southern
Südpol *m* South Pole
südwärts *adv* southwards
Sülze (-, **-n**) *f* (*Aspik*) aspic
Summe (-, **-n**) *f* sum; (*Gesamtsumme*) total
summen *vi* to buzz ▶ *vt* (*Lied*) to hum
Sumpf (**-(e)s**, **Sümpfe**) *m* swamp, marsh
sumpfig *adj* marshy
Sünde (-, **-n**) *f* sin
super (*umg*) *adj* super
Super (**-s**) *nt* (*Benzin*) four-star (petrol) (BRIT), premium (*US*)
Supermarkt *m* supermarket
Suppe (-, **-n**) *f* soup
Suppengrün *nt herbs and vegetables for making soup*
Suppenteller *m* soup plate
Surfbrett *nt* surfboard
surfen *vi* to surf
Surfer(in) *m(f)* surfer
Surrealismus *m* surrealism
süß *adj* sweet
süßen *vt* to sweeten
Süßigkeit: **Süßigkeiten** *pl* sweets (BRIT), candy (*US*)
süßsauer *adj* sweet-and-sour
Süßspeise *f* pudding, sweet (BRIT)
Süßstoff *m* sweetener

Süßwasser *nt* fresh water
Sylvester (**-s**, **-**) *nt* = **Silvester**
Symbol (**-s**, **-e**) *nt* symbol
Symbolleiste *f* (*Comput*) toolbar
Symmetrie *f* symmetry
symmetrisch *adj* symmetrical
sympathisch *adj* likeable; **er ist mir ~** I like him
Symphonie *f* symphony
Symptom (**-s**, **-e**) *nt* symptom
Synagoge (**-**, **-n**) *f* synagogue
synthetisch *adj* synthetic
Syrien (**-s**) *nt* Syria
System (**-s**, **-e**) *nt* system
systematisch *adj* systematic
Systemsteuerung *f* (*Comput*) control panel
Szene (**-**, **-n**) *f* scene

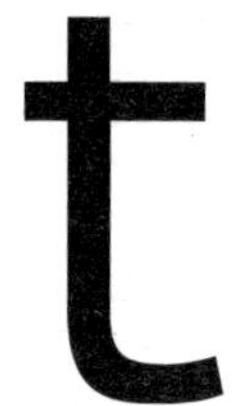

Tabak (**-s**, **-e**) *m* tobacco
Tabakladen *m* tobacconist's (BRIT), tobacco store (*US*)
Tabelle (**-**, **-n**) *f* table
Tablet *nt* (*Comput*) tablet
Tablett (**-(e)s**, **-s** *od* **-e**) *nt* tray
Tablette (**-**, **-n**) *f* tablet, pill
Tabulator *m* tabulator, tab (*umg*)
Tafel (**-**, **-n**) *f* (*festlicher Speisetisch, Math*) table; (*Anschlagtafel*) board; (*Wandtafel*) blackboard; (*Schiefertafel*) slate; (*Gedenktafel*) plaque; (*Schokoladentafel etc*) bar
Tafelwasser *nt* table water
Tafelwein *m* table wine
Tag (**-(e)s**, **-e**) *m* day; (*Tageslicht*) daylight; **am ~** during the day; **eines Tages** one day; **guten ~!** good morning/afternoon!
Tagebuch *nt* diary
tagelang *adv* for days
Tagesanbruch *m* dawn
Tagesausflug *m* day trip
Tagescreme *f* day cream
Tagesdecke *f* bedspread
Tageskarte *f* (*Eintrittskarte*) day ticket; (*Speisekarte*) menu of the day
Tageslicht *nt* daylight
Tagesmutter *f* child minder
Tagesordnung *f* agenda
Tageszeitung *f* daily (paper)
täglich *adj*, *adv* daily
tagsüber *adv* during the day
Tagung *f* conference
Taille (**-**, **-n**) *f* waist
Taiwan (**-s**) *nt* Taiwan
Takt (**-(e)s**, **-e**) *m* tact; (*Mus*) time

Taktik *f* tactics *pl*
taktlos *adj* tactless
taktvoll *adj* tactful
Tal (**-(e)s**, **Täler**) *nt* valley
Talent (**-(e)s**, **-e**) *nt* talent
talentiert *adj* talented
Tampon (**-s**, **-s**) *m* tampon
Tang (**-(e)s**, **-e**) *m* seaweed
Tank (**-s**, **-s**) *m* tank
tanken *vi* to fill up (with petrol (Brit) *od* gas (*US*)); (*Aviat*) to (re)fuel
Tanker (**-s**, **-**) *m* tanker
Tankstelle *f* petrol (Brit) *od* gas (*US*) station
Tankwart *m* petrol pump (Brit) *od* gas station (*US*) attendant
Tanne (**-**, **-n**) *f* fir
Tannenzapfen *m* fir cone
Tansania (**-s**) *nt* Tanzania
Tante (**-**, **-n**) *f* aunt
Tante-Emma-Laden (*umg*) *m* corner shop
Tanz (**-es**, **Tänze**) *m* dance
tanzen *vt*, *vi* to dance
Tänzer(in) (**-s**, **-**) *m(f)* dancer
Tanzfläche *f* dance floor
Tapete (**-**, **-n**) *f* wallpaper
tapezieren *vt* to (wall)paper
Tarantel (**-**, **-n**) *f* tarantula
Tarif (**-s**, **-e**) *m* tariff, (scale of) fares/charges; **nach/über/unter ~ bezahlen** to pay according to/above/below the (union) rate(s)
Tasche (**-**, **-n**) *f* bag; (*Hosentasche*) pocket; (*Handtasche*) handbag
Taschenbuch *nt* paperback
Taschendieb *m* pickpocket
Taschengeld *nt* pocket money
Taschenlampe *f* (electric) torch, flashlight (*US*)
Taschenmesser *nt* penknife
Taschenrechner *m* pocket calculator
Taschentuch *nt* handkerchief
Tasse (**-**, **-n**) *f* cup
Tastatur *f* keyboard
Taste (**-**, **-n**) *f* button; (*von Klavier, Computer*) key
Tastenfeld *nt* keyboard
tat *etc vb siehe* **tun**
Tat (**-**, **-en**) *f* action
Täter(in) (**-s**, **-**) *m(f)* culprit
tätig *adj* active; **in einer Firma ~ sein** to work for a firm
Tätigkeit *f* activity; (*Beruf*) occupation
tätowieren *vt* to tattoo
Tätowierung *f* tattoo
Tatsache *f* fact
tatsächlich *adj* actual ▸ *adv* really
Tau[1] (**-(e)s**, **-e**) *nt* rope
Tau[2] (**-(e)s**) *m* dew
taub *adj* deaf
Taube (**-**, **-n**) *f* (*Zool*) pigeon; (*fig*) dove
taubstumm *adj* with a speech and hearing impairment
tauchen *vt* to dip ▸ *vi* to dive; (*Naut*) to submerge
Taucher (**-s**, **-**) *m* diver
Taucheranzug *m* diving suit
Tauchsieder (**-s**, **-**) *m* portable immersion heater
tauen *vi unpers*: **es taut** it's thawing
Taufe (**-**, **-n**) *f* baptism
taufen *vt* to baptize; (*nennen*) to christen
taugen *vi*: **~ für** to do *od* be good for; **nicht ~** to be no good *od* useless
Tausch (**-(e)s**, **-e**) *m* exchange
tauschen *vt* to exchange, to swap
täuschen *vt* to deceive ▸ *vi* to be deceptive ▸ *vr* to be wrong
täuschend *adj* deceptive
Täuschung *f* deception; (*optisch*) illusion
tausend *num* a *od* one thousand
Tausendstel (**-s**, **-**) *nt* (*Bruchteil*) thousandth
Taxi (**-(s)**, **-(s)**) *nt* taxi
Taxifahrer(in) *m(f)* taxi driver
Taxistand *m* taxi rank (Brit) *od* stand (*US*)
Teamarbeit *f* teamwork
Technik *f* technology; (*Methode, Kunstfertigkeit*) technique
Techniker(in) (**-s -**) *m(f)* technician
technisch *adj* technical
Teebeutel *m* tea bag
Teekanne *f* teapot
Teelöffel *m* teaspoon
Teer (**-(e)s**, **-e**) *m* tar
Teesieb *nt* tea strainer
Teetasse *f* teacup
Teich (**-(e)s**, **-e**) *m* pond
Teig (**-(e)s**, **-e**) *m* dough
Teigwaren *pl* pasta *sing*
Teil (**-(e)s**, **-e**) *m od nt* part; (*Anteil*) share ▸ *nt* part; (*Bestandteil*) component; **zum ~** partly
teilen *vt* to divide; (*mit jdm*) to share ▸ *vr* to divide

Teilkaskoversicherung *f* third party, fire and theft insurance
Teilnahme (**-**, **-n**) *f* participation
teil|nehmen *unreg vi*: **an etw** *dat* **~** to take part in sth
Teilnehmer(in) (**-s**, **-**) *m(f)* participant
teils *adv* partly
teilweise *adv* partially, in part
Teilzeitarbeit *f* part-time job *od* work
Teint (**-s**, **-s**) *m* complexion
Telefon (**-s**, **-e**) *nt* (tele)phone
Telefonanruf *m* phone call
Telefonbuch *nt* phone directory
Telefongespräch *nt* phone call
telefonieren *vi* to phone; **mit jdm ~** to speak to sb on the phone
telefonisch *adj* phone; (*Benachrichtigung*) by phone
Telefonkarte *f* phone card
Telefonnummer *f* phone number
Telefonrechnung *f* phone bill
Telefonverbindung *f* phone connection
Telefonzelle *f* phone box (Brit) *od* booth (*US*), callbox (Brit)
Telefonzentrale *f* telephone exchange
Telegramm (**-s**, **-e**) *nt* telegram
Teleobjektiv *nt* telephoto lens
Teleskop (**-s**, **-e**) *nt* telescope
Teller (**-s**, **-**) *m* plate
Tempel (**-s**, **-**) *m* temple
Temperament *nt* temperament; (*Schwung*) vitality
temperamentvoll *adj* lively
Temperatur *f* temperature; **erhöhte ~ haben** to have a temperature
Tempo (**-s**, **-s**) *nt* speed
Tempolimit *nt* speed limit
Tendenz *f* tendency; (*Absicht*) intention
Tennis (**-**) *nt* tennis
Tennisplatz *m* tennis court
Tennisschläger *m* tennis racket
Tennisspieler *m* tennis player
Tenor (**-s**, **Tenöre**) *m* tenor
Teppich (**-s**, **-e**) *m* carpet
Teppichboden *m* wall-to-wall carpeting
Termin (**-s**, **-e**) *m* (*Zeitpunkt*) date; (*Frist*) deadline; (*Arzttermin etc*) appointment
Terminkalender *m* diary
Terpentin (**-s**, **-e**) *nt* turpentine, turps *sing*
Terrasse (**-**, **-n**) *f* terrace
Terror (**-s**) *m* terror
Terroranschlag *m* terrorist attack
terrorisieren *vt* to terrorize
Terrorismus *m* terrorism
Terrorismusbekämpfung *f* counterterrorism
Terrorist(in) *m(f)* terrorist
Test (**-s**, **-s**) *m* test
Testament *nt* will; **Altes/Neues ~** Old/New Testament
testen *vt* to test
Tetanus (**-**) *m* tetanus
Tetanusimpfung *f* (anti-)tetanus injection
teuer *adj* dear, expensive
Teufel (**-s**, **-**) *m* devil
Teufelskreis *m* vicious circle
Text (**-(e)s**, **-e**) *m* text; (*Liedertext*) words *pl*; (: *von Schlager*) lyrics *pl*
Textverarbeitung *f* word processing
Thailand (**-s**) *nt* Thailand
Theater (**-s**, **-**) *nt* theatre (Brit), theater (*US*); (*umg*) fuss
Theaterkasse *f* box office
Theaterstück *nt* (stage) play
Theke (**-**, **-n**) *f* (*Schanktisch*) bar; (*Ladentisch*) counter
Thema (**-s**, **Themen** *od* **-ta**) *nt* topic, subject
Themse *f*: **die ~** the Thames
Theologie *f* theology
theoretisch *adj* theoretical; **~ gesehen** in theory
Theorie *f* theory
Therapeut (**-en**, **-en**) *m* therapist
Therapie *f* therapy
Thermalbad *nt* thermal bath; (*Badeort*) thermal spa
Thermometer (**-s**, **-**) *nt* thermometer
Thermosflasche® *f* Thermos® flask
Thermostat (**-(e)s** *od* **-en**, **-e(n)**) *m* thermostat
These (**-**, **-n**) *f* thesis
Thron (**-(e)s**, **-e**) *m* throne
Thunfisch *m* tuna (fish)
Thüringen (**-s**) *nt* Thuringia
Thymian (**-s**, **-e**) *m* thyme
Tick (**-(e)s**, **-s**) *m* tic; (*Eigenart*) quirk; (*Fimmel*) craze
ticken *vi* to tick; **nicht richtig ~** (*umg*) to be off one's rocker
Ticket (**-s**, **-s**) *nt* ticket
tief *adj* deep; (*Ausschnitt, Ton*) low

Tief (**-s**, **-s**) *nt* (*Met*) low; (*seelisch*) depression
Tiefdruck *m* (*Met*) low pressure
Tiefe (-, **-n**) *f* depth
Tiefgarage *f* underground car park (BRIT) *od* parking lot (*US*)
tiefgekühlt *adj* frozen
Tiefkühlfach *nt* freezer compartment
Tiefkühlkost *f* frozen food
Tiefkühlschrank *m* = **Tiefkühltruhe**
Tiefkühltruhe *f* freezer, deep freeze (*US*)
Tiefpunkt *m* low point
Tier (**-(e)s**, **-e**) *nt* animal
Tierarzt *m*, **Tierärztin** *f* vet(erinary surgeon) (BRIT), veterinarian (*US*)
Tiergarten *m* zoo
Tierhandlung *f* pet shop (BRIT) *od* store (*US*)
tierisch *adj* animal *attrib*; **~ ernst** deadly serious; **ich hatte ~ Angst** I was dead scared
Tierpark *m* zoo
Tierquälerei *f* cruelty to animals
Tierschützer(in) (**-s**, **-**) *m(f)* animal rights campaigner
Tierversuch *m* animal experiment
Tiger (**-s**, **-**) *m* tiger
Tinnitus *m* (*Med*) tinnitus
Tinte (-, **-n**) *f* ink
Tintenfisch *m* cuttlefish; (*achtarmig*) octopus
Tintenstrahldrucker *m* ink-jet printer
Tipp (**-s**, **-s**) *m* (*Sport*, *Börse*) tip
tippen *vi* to tap; (*umg*: *schreiben*) to type ▶ *vt* to type; **auf jdn ~** (*umg*: *raten*) to tip sb
Tirol (**-s**) *nt* the Tyrol
Tisch (**-(e)s**, **-e**) *m* table
Tischdecke *f* tablecloth
Tischlerei *f* joiner's workshop; (*Arbeit*) joinery
Tischtennis *nt* table tennis
Titel (**-s**, **-**) *m* title
Titelbild *nt* cover (picture)
Toast (**-(e)s**, **-s** *od* **-e**) *m* toast
toasten *vt* to toast
Toaster (**-s**, **-**) *m* toaster
Tochter (-, **Töchter**) *f* daughter
Tod (**-(e)s**, **-e**) *m* death
Todesopfer *nt* casualty
Todesstrafe *f* death penalty
todkrank *adj* dangerously ill
tödlich *adj* fatal; (*Gift*) deadly, lethal
todmüde *adj* dead tired
todsicher (*umg*) *adj* absolutely *od* dead certain
Tofu (**-(s)**) *m* tofu
Toilette *f* toilet, lavatory (BRIT), restroom (*US*)
Toilettenpapier *nt* toilet paper
toi, toi, toi (*umg*) *interj* good luck
tolerant *adj* tolerant
toll *adj* mad; (*Treiben*) wild; (*umg*) terrific
Tollkirsche *f* deadly nightshade
Tollwut *f* rabies
Tomate (-, **-n**) *f* tomato
Tomatenmark (**-(e)s**) *nt* tomato purée
Tombola (-, **-s** *od* **Tombolen**) *f* tombola
Ton[1] (**-(e)s**, **-e**) *m* (*Erde*) clay
Ton[2] (**-(e)s**, **Töne**) *m* (*Laut*) sound; (*Mus*) note; (*Redeweise*) tone; (*Farbton*, *Nuance*) shade
Tonband *nt* tape
Tonbandgerät *nt* tape recorder
tönen *vi* to sound ▶ *vt* to shade; (*Haare*) to tint
Toner (**-s**, **-**) *m* toner
Tonerkassette *f* toner cartridge
Tonne (-, **-n**) *f* barrel; (*Maß*) ton
Topf (**-(e)s**, **Töpfe**) *m* pot
Töpfer(in) (**-s**, **-**) *m(f)* potter
Töpferei *f* pottery
Tor (**-(e)s**, **-e**) *nt* gate; (*Sport*) goal
Torhüter (**-s**, **-**) *m* goalkeeper
torkeln *vi* to stagger
Torschütze *m*, **Torschützin** *f* (goal) scorer
Torte (-, **-n**) *f* cake; (*Obsttorte*) flan
Torwart (**-(e)s**, **-e**) *m* goalkeeper
tot *adj* dead; **der tote Winkel** the blind spot
total *adj* total
Totalschaden *m* (*Aut*) complete write-off
Tote(r) *f(m)* dead person
töten *vt*, *vi* to kill
Totenkopf *m* skull
tot|lachen (*umg*) *vr* to laugh one's head off
Toto (**-s**, **-s**) *m od nt* ≈ pools *pl*
tot|schlagen *unreg vt* (*lit*, *fig*) to kill
Touchscreen *m* (*Tech*) touch screen
Tour (-, **-en**) *f* tour, trip
Tourismus *m* tourism
Tourist(in) *m(f)* tourist

Touristenklasse *f* tourist class
touristisch *adj* tourist *attrib*
Tournee (**-**, **-s** *od* **-n**) *f* (*Theat etc*) tour
traben *vi* to trot
Tracht (**-**, **-en**) *f* (*Kleidung*) costume, dress
Tradition *f* tradition
traditionell *adj* traditional
traf *etc vb siehe* **treffen**
Tragbahre *f* stretcher
tragbar *adj* portable
träge *adj* sluggish, slow
tragen *unreg vt* to carry; (*Kleidung, Brille*) to wear; (*Namen, Früchte*) to bear
Träger (**-s**, **-**) *m* carrier; (*an Kleidung*) (shoulder) strap; (*Holzträger, Betonträger*) (supporting) beam; (*Stahlträger, Eisenträger*) girder
Tragfläche *f* (*Aviat*) wing
Tragflügelboot *nt* hydrofoil
tragisch *adj* tragic
Tragödie *f* tragedy
Trainer(in) (**-s**, **-**) *m(f)* (*Sport*) trainer, coach
trainieren *vt* to train; (*Übung*) to practise (Brit), to practice (*US*) ▸ *vi* to train
Training (**-s**, **-s**) *nt* training
Trainingsanzug *m* track suit
Traktor *m* tractor
trampen *vi* to hitchhike
Tramper(in) (**-s**, **-**) *m(f)* hitchhiker
Träne (**-**, **-n**) *f* tear
tränen *vi* to water
Tränengas *nt* tear gas
trank *etc vb siehe* **trinken**
Transfusion *f* transfusion
Transitverkehr *m* transit traffic
Transplantation *f* transplantation; (*Hauttransplantation*) graft(ing)
Transport (**-(e)s**, **-e**) *m* transport
transportieren *vt* to transport
Transportmittel *nt* means *sing* of transport
Transportunternehmen *nt* carrier
Transvestit (**-en**, **-en**) *m* transvestite
trat *etc vb siehe* **treten**
Traube (**-**, **-n**) *f* grape; (*ganze Frucht*) bunch (of grapes)
Traubenzucker *m* glucose
trauen *vi +dat* to trust ▸ *vr* to dare ▸ *vt* to marry; **jdm/etw ~** to trust sb/sth
Trauer (**-**) *f* sorrow; (*für Verstorbenen*) mourning
Traum (**-(e)s**, **Träume**) *m* dream
träumen *vt, vi* to dream
traumhaft *adj* dreamlike; (*fig*) wonderful
traurig *adj* sad
Trauschein *m* marriage certificate
Trauung *f* wedding ceremony
Trauzeuge *m* witness (to a marriage)
treffen *unreg vt* to hit; (*Bemerkung*) to hurt; (*begegnen*) to meet; (*Entscheidung etc*) to make; (*Maßnahmen*) to take ▸ *vi* to hit
Treffen (**-s**, **-**) *nt* meeting
Treffer (**-s**, **-**) *m* (*Tor*) goal
Treffpunkt *m* meeting place
treiben *unreg vt* to drive; (*Sport*) to do ▸ *vi* (*Schiff etc*) to drift; (*Pflanzen*) to sprout; (*Medikamente*) to be diuretic
Treiber (**-s**, **-**) *m* (*Comput*) driver
Treibhaus *nt* greenhouse
Treibstoff *m* fuel
trendig *adj* trendy
trendy (*umg*) *adj* = **trendig**
trennen *vt* to separate; (*teilen*) to divide ▸ *vr* to separate; **sich ~ von** to part with
Trennung *f* separation
Treppe (**-**, **-n**) *f* stairs *pl*; (*im Freien*) steps *pl*
Treppengeländer *nt* banister
Treppenhaus *nt* staircase
Tresen (**-s**, **-**) *m* (*Theke*) bar; (*Ladentisch*) counter
Tresor (**-s**, **-e**) *m* safe
Tretboot *nt* pedal boat
treten *unreg vi* to step ▸ *vt* to kick; (*niedertreten*) to tread; **in Verbindung ~** to get in contact
treu *adj* faithful; (*Kunde, Fan*) loyal
Treue (**-**) *f* faithfulness; (*von Kunde, Fan*) loyalty
Triathlon (**-s**, **-s**) *nt* triathlon
Tribüne (**-**, **-n**) *f* grandstand; (*Rednertribüne*) platform
Trick (**-s**, **-e** *od* **-s**) *m* trick
Trickfilm *m* cartoon
trieb *etc vb siehe* **treiben**
Trieb (**-(e)s**, **-e**) *m* urge, drive; (*Neigung*) inclination; (*Bot*) shoot
Triebwerk *nt* engine
Trikot (**-s**, **-s**) *nt* vest; (*Sport*) shirt
trinkbar *adj* drinkable
trinken *unreg vt, vi* to drink
Trinkgeld *nt* tip
Trinkhalm *m* (drinking) straw
Trinkwasser *nt* drinking water

Trio (**-s**, **-s**) *nt* trio
Tripper (**-s**, **-**) *m* gonorrhoea (*Brit*), gonorrhea (*US*)
Tritt (**-(e)s**, **-e**) *m* step; (*Fußtritt*) kick
Trittbrett *nt* (*Aut*) running board
Triumph (**-(e)s**, **-e**) *m* triumph
triumphieren *vi* to triumph
trivial *adj* trivial
trocken *adj* dry
Trockenhaube *f* hair-dryer
Trockenheit *f* dryness
trocken|legen *vt* (*Kind*) to put a clean nappy (*Brit*) *od* diaper (*US*) on
trocknen *vt*, *vi* to dry
Trockner (**-s**, **-**) *m* dryer
Trödel (**-s**) (*umg*) *m* junk
Trödelmarkt *m* flea market
trödeln (*umg*) *vi* to dawdle
Trommel (**-**, **-n**) *f* drum
Trommelfell *nt* eardrum
trommeln *vt*, *vi* to drum
Trompete (**-**, **-n**) *f* trumpet
Tropen *pl* tropics *pl*
Tropf (**-(e)s**) (*umg*) *m* (*Med*: *Infusion*) drip (*umg*); **am ~ hängen** to be on a drip
tröpfeln *vi* to drip
tropfen *vt*, *vi* to drip
Tropfen (**-s**, **-**) *m* drop
tropfenweise *adv* in drops
tropfnass *adj* dripping wet
Tropfsteinhöhle *f* stalactite cave
tropisch *adj* tropical
Trost (**-es**) *m* consolation, comfort
trösten *vt* to console, to comfort
trostlos *adj* bleak; (*Verhältnisse*) wretched
Trostpreis *m* consolation prize
Trottoir (**-s**, **-s** *od* **-e**) *nt* pavement (*Brit*), sidewalk (*US*)
trotz *präp* (*+gen od dat*) in spite of
Trotz (**-es**) *m* pig-headedness; **jdm zum ~** in defiance of sb
trotzdem *adv* nevertheless ▶ *konj* although
trotzig *adj* defiant
trüb *adj* dull; (*Flüssigkeit*, *Glas*) cloudy; (*fig*) gloomy
Trüffel (**-**, **-n**) *f* truffle
trug *etc vb siehe* **tragen**
trügerisch *adj* deceptive
Truhe (**-**, **-n**) *f* chest
Trümmer *pl* wreckage *sing*; (*Bautrümmer*) ruins *pl*
Trumpf (**-(e)s**, **Trümpfe**) *m* trump
Trunkenheit *f* intoxication; **~ am Steuer** drink-driving
Truthahn *m* turkey
Tscheche (**-n**, **-n**) *m*, **Tschechin** *f* Czech
Tschechien (**-s**) *nt* Czech Republic
tschechisch *adj* Czech; **die Tschechische Republik** the Czech Republic
tschüs (*umg*) *interj* cheerio (*Brit*), so long (*US*)
T-Shirt (**-s**, **-s**) *nt* T-shirt
Tube (**-**, **-n**) *f* tube
Tuberkulose (**-**, **-n**) *f* tuberculosis
Tuch (**-(e)s**, **Tücher**) *nt* cloth; (*Halstuch*) scarf; (*Kopftuch*) (head)scarf
tüchtig *adj* efficient; (*fähig*) capable; (*umg*: *kräftig*) good
Tugend (**-**, **-en**) *f* virtue
tugendhaft *adj* virtuous
Tulpe (**-**, **-n**) *f* tulip
Tumor (**-s**, **-e**) *m* tumour (*Brit*), tumor (*US*)
tun *unreg vt* (*machen*) to do; (*legen*) to put ▶ *vi* to act ▶ *vr*: **es tut sich etwas/viel** something/a lot is happening; **jdm etw ~** to do sth to sb; **etw tut es auch** sth will do; **so ~, als ob** to act as if
Tunesien (**-s**) *nt* Tunisia
Tunfisch *m* = **Thunfisch**
Tunnel (**-s**, **-s** *od* **-**) *m* tunnel
Tunte (**-**, **-n**) (*pej*, *umg*) *f* fairy (*pej*)
tupfen *vt* to dab; (*mit Farbe*) to dot
Tupfen (**-s**, **-**) *m* dot
Tür (**-**, **-en**) *f* door; **an die ~ gehen** to answer the door
Türke (**-n**, **-n**) *m* Turk
Türkei *f*: **die ~** Turkey
Türkin *f* Turk
Türkis (**-es**, **-e**) *m* turquoise
türkisch *adj* Turkish
Turm (**-(e)s**, **Türme**) *m* tower; (*Kirchturm*) steeple; (*Sprungturm*) diving platform; (*Schach*) castle, rook
turnen *vi* to do gymnastic exercises
Turnen (**-s**) *nt* gymnastics *sing*; (*Sch*) physical education, PE
Turner(in) (**-s**, **-**) *m(f)* gymnast
Turnhalle *f* gym(nasium)
Turnhose *f* gym shorts *pl*
Turnier (**-s**, **-e**) *nt* tournament
Turnschuh *m* gym shoe
tuscheln *vt*, *vi* to whisper

Tussi (**-**, **-s**) (*umg*) *f* bird (BRIT), chick (*US*)
Tüte (**-**, **-n**) *f* bag
Tutorial *nt* tutorial
twittern *vi* (*auf Twitter*) to tweet
Typ (**-s**, **-en**) *m* type; (*Mann*) guy, bloke
Typhus (**-**) *m* typhoid (fever)
typisch *adj*: **~ (für)** typical (of)

u. *abk* = **und**
u. a. *abk* (= *und andere(s)*) and others; (= *unter anderem*) amongst other things
u. A. w. g. *abk* (= *um Antwort wird gebeten*) R.S.V.P.
U-Bahn *f abk* (= *Untergrundbahn*) underground (BRIT), subway (*US*)
übel *adj* bad; **jdm ist ~** sb feels sick; **jdm eine Bemerkung** *etc* **~ nehmen** to be offended at sb's remark *etc*
Übelkeit *f* nausea
üben *vt*, *vi*, *vr* to practise (BRIT), to practice (*US*)

 **SCHLÜSSELWORT**

über *präp +dat* **1** (*räumlich*) over, above; **zwei Grad über null** two degrees above zero
2 (*zeitlich*) over; **über der Arbeit einschlafen** to fall asleep over one's work
▶ *präp +akk* **1** (*räumlich*) over; (*hoch über*) above; (*quer über*) across
2 (*zeitlich*) over; **über Weihnachten** over Christmas; **über kurz oder lang** sooner or later
3 (*mit Zahlen*): **Kinder über 12 Jahren** children over *od* above 12 years of age; **ein Scheck über 200 Euro** a cheque for 200 euros
4 (*auf dem Wege*) via; **nach Köln über Aachen** to Cologne via Aachen; **ich habe es über die Auskunft erfahren** I found out from information
5 (*betreffend*) about; **ein Buch über ...**

a book about *od* on ...; **über jdn/etw lachen** to laugh about *od* at sb/sth **6**: **Macht über jdn haben** to have power over sb; **sie liebt ihn über alles** she loves him more than anything ▸ *adv* over; **über und über** over and over; **den ganzen Tag/die ganze Zeit über** all day long/all the time; **jdm in etw** *dat* **über sein** to be superior to sb in sth

überall *adv* everywhere
überanstrengen *vr untr* to overexert o.s.
überbacken *unreg vt untr* to put in the oven/under the grill
überbelichten *vt untr* (*Phot*) to overexpose
überbieten *unreg vt untr* to outbid; (*übertreffen*) to surpass; (*Rekord*) to break
Überbleibsel (**-s**, **-**) *nt* residue
Überblick *m* view; (*fig*: *Darstellung*) survey, overview; (*Fähigkeit*): **~ (über** *+akk*) grasp (of)
überbuchen *vt* to overbook
überdurchschnittlich *adj* above-average
übereinander *adv* one upon the other; (*sprechen*) about each other
überein|stimmen *vi* to agree
überempfindlich *adj* hypersensitive
überfahren *unreg vt untr* (*Aut*) to run over
Überfahrt *f* crossing
Überfall *m* (*Banküberfall*, *Mil*) raid; (*auf jdn*) assault
überfallen *unreg vt untr* to attack; (*Bank*) to raid
überfällig *adj* overdue
überfliegen *unreg vt untr* to fly over; (*Buch*) to skim through
Überfluss *m*: **~ (an** *+dat*) (super) abundance (of), excess (of)
überflüssig *adj* superfluous
überfordern *vt untr* to demand too much of; (*Kräfte etc*) to overtax
Überführung *f* (*Brücke*) bridge, overpass
überfüllt *adj* overcrowded
Übergabe *f* handing over
Übergang *m* crossing; (*Wandel*, *Überleitung*) transition
Übergangslösung *f* provisional solution, stopgap
übergeben *unreg vt untr* to hand over ▸ *vr untr* to be sick
Übergepäck *nt* excess baggage
Übergewicht *nt* excess weight
übergewichtig *adj* overweight
überglücklich *adj* overjoyed
Übergröße *f* oversize
überhaupt *adv* at all; (*im Allgemeinen*) in general; (*besonders*) especially; **wer sind Sie ~?** who do you think you are?
überheblich *adj* arrogant
überholen *vt untr* to overtake; (*Tech*) to overhaul
Überholspur *f* overtaking lane
überholt *adj* out-of-date
Überholverbot *nt* overtaking (BRIT) *od* passing ban
überhören *vt untr* to not hear; (*absichtlich*) to ignore
überladen *unreg vt untr* to overload ▸ *adj* (*fig*) cluttered
überlassen *unreg vt untr*: **jdm etw ~** to leave sth to sb
über|laufen *unreg vi* (*Flüssigkeit*) to flow over
überleben *vt untr* to survive
Überlebende(r) *f*(*m*) survivor
überlegen *vt untr* to consider ▸ *adj* superior; **ich habe es mir anders** *od* **noch einmal überlegt** I've changed my mind
Überlegung *f* consideration
überm = **über dem**
übermäßig *adj* excessive
übermorgen *adv* the day after tomorrow
übernächste(r, s) *adj*: **~ Woche** the week after next
übernachten *vi untr*: **(bei jdm) ~** to spend the night (at sb's place)
übernächtigt *adj* sleepy, tired
Übernachtung *f*: **~ mit Frühstück** bed and breakfast
übernehmen *unreg vt untr* to take on; (*Amt*, *Geschäft*) to take over ▸ *vr untr* to take on too much
überprüfen *vt untr* to check
Überprüfung *f* examination
überqueren *vt untr* to cross
überraschen *vt untr* to surprise
Überraschung *f* surprise
überreden *vt untr* to persuade; **jdn zu etw ~** to talk sb into sth
überreichen *vt untr* to hand over
übers = **über das**

überschätzen *vt untr, vr untr* to overestimate
überschlagen *unreg vt untr* (*berechnen*) to estimate ▶ *vr untr* to somersault; (*Stimme*) to crack
überschneiden *unreg vr untr* (*Linien*) to intersect; (*Termine*) to clash
Überschrift *f* heading
Überschwemmung *f* flood
Übersee *f*: **nach/in ~** overseas
übersehen *unreg vt untr* to look (out) over; (*nicht beachten*) to overlook
übersetzen *vt untr, vi untr* to translate
Übersetzer(in) (**-s**, **-**) *m(f)* translator
Übersetzung *f* translation
Übersicht *f* overall view; (*Darstellung*) survey
übersichtlich *adj* clear
überstehen *unreg vt untr* to get over; (*Winter etc*) to get through
Überstunden *pl* overtime *sing*
überstürzt *adj* (over)hasty
übertragbar *adj* transferable; (*Med*) infectious
übertragen *unreg vt untr* to transfer; (*Rundf*) to broadcast; (*Krankheit*) to transmit ▶ *vr untr* to spread ▶ *adj* figurative
Übertragung *f* (*Rundf*) broadcast; (*von Krankheit, Daten*) transmission
übertreffen *unreg vt untr* to surpass
übertreiben *unreg vt untr* to exaggerate; **man kann es auch ~** you can overdo things
Übertreibung *f* exaggeration
übertrieben *adj* exaggerated, excessive
überwachen *vt untr* to supervise; (*Verdächtigen*) to keep under surveillance
Überwachungskamera (**-**, **-s**) *f* CCTV camera
überweisen *unreg vt untr* to transfer; (*Patienten*) to refer
Überweisung *f* transfer; (*von Patient*) referral
überwiegend *adj* predominant
überwinden *unreg vt untr* to overcome ▶ *vr untr*: **sich ~, etw zu tun** to make an effort to do sth, to bring o.s. to do sth
überzeugen *vt untr* to convince
Überzeugung *f* conviction
überziehen[1] *unreg vt* to put on
überziehen[2] *unreg vt untr* to cover; (*Konto*) to overdraw; **ein Bett frisch ~** to change the sheets (on a bed)
üblich *adj* usual
übrig *adj* remaining; **die Übrigen** the others; **das Übrige** the rest; **im Übrigen** besides; **~ bleiben** to be left (over)
übrigens *adv* besides; (*nebenbei bemerkt*) by the way
übrig|haben *unreg vi*: **für jdn etwas ~** (*umg*) to be fond of sb
Übung *f* practice; (*Turnübung, Aufgabe etc*) exercise
Ufer (**-s**, **-**) *nt* bank; (*Meeresufer*) shore
UFO, Ufo (**-(s)**, **-s**) *nt abk* (*= unbekanntes Flugobjekt*) UFO
Uhr (**-**, **-en**) *f* clock; (*Armbanduhr*) watch; **wie viel ~ ist es?** what time is it?; **1 ~** 1 o'clock
Uhrzeigersinn *m*: **im ~** clockwise; **entgegen dem ~** anticlockwise (BRIT) counterclockwise (US)
Uhrzeit *f* time (of day)
Ukraine *f* Ukraine
UKW *abk* (*= Ultrakurzwelle*) VHF
Ulme (**-**, **-n**) *f* elm
Ultrakurzwelle *f* very high frequency

SCHLÜSSELWORT

um *präp +akk* **1** (*um herum*) (a)round; **um Weihnachten** around Christmas; **er schlug um sich** he hit about him
2 (*mit Zeitangabe*) at; **um acht (Uhr)** at eight (o'clock)
3 (*mit Größenangabe*) by; **etw um 4 cm kürzen** to shorten sth by 4 cm; **um 10% teurer** 10% more expensive; **um vieles besser** better by far; *siehe* **umso**
4: **der Kampf um den Titel** the battle for the title; **um Geld spielen** to play for money; **Stunde um Stunde** hour after hour; **Auge um Auge** an eye for an eye
▶ *präp +gen*: **um ... willen** for the sake of ...; **um Gottes willen** for goodness *od* (*stärker*) God's sake
▶ *konj*: **um ... zu** (in order) to ...; **zu klug, um zu ...** too clever to ...; *siehe auch* **umso**
▶ *adv* **1** (*ungefähr*) about; **um (die) 30 Leute** about *od* around 30 people
2 (*vorbei*): **die zwei Stunden sind um** the two hours are up

umarmen *vt untr* to embrace

Umbau (-(e)s, -e *od* **-ten)** *m* reconstruction, alteration(s *pl*)

um|bauen *vt* to rebuild, to reconstruct

um|blättern *vt* to turn over

um|bringen *unreg vt* to kill

um|buchen *vi* to change one's reservation *od* flight *etc*

um|drehen *vt* to turn (round) ▶ *vr* to turn (round)

Umdrehung *f* turn; (*Phys*) revolution

um|fahren *unreg vt* to run over

um|fallen *unreg vi* to fall down *od* over

Umfang *m* extent; (*von Buch*) size; (*Reichweite*) range; (*Math*) circumference

umfangreich *adj* extensive

Umfeld *nt* environment

Umfrage *f* poll

Umgang *m* company; (*mit jdm*) dealings *pl*

umgänglich *adj* sociable

Umgangssprache *f* colloquial language

Umgebung *f* surroundings *pl*; (*Milieu*) environment; (*Personen*) people in one's circle

um|gehen[1] *unreg vi* to go (a)round; **mit jdm/etw ~ können** to know how to handle sb/sth

umgehen[2] *unreg vt untr* (*Gesetz, Vorschrift etc*) to circumvent; (*vermeiden*) to avoid

Umgehungsstraße *f* bypass

umgekehrt *adj* reverse(d); (*gegenteilig*) opposite ▶ *adv* the other way around; **und ~** and vice versa

um|hören *vr* to ask around

um|kehren *vi* to turn back ▶ *vt* to reverse; (*Tasche etc*) to turn inside out

um|kippen *vt* to tip over ▶ *vi* to overturn; (*umg*: *ohnmächtig werden*) to keel over; (*fig*: *Meinung ändern*) to change one's mind

Umkleidekabine *f* changing cubicle (BRIT), dressing room (US)

Umkleideraum *m* changing room

Umkreis *m* neighbourhood (BRIT), neighborhood (US); **im ~ von** within a radius of

um|leiten *vt* to divert

Umleitung *f* diversion

um|rechnen *vt* to convert

Umrechnung *f* conversion

Umrechnungskurs *m* rate of exchange

Umriss *m* outline

um|rühren *vt, vi* to stir

ums = **um das**

Umsatz *m* turnover

um|schalten *vi*: **~ (auf** *+akk***)** to change over (to)

Umschlag *m* cover; (*Buchumschlag*) jacket; (*Med*) compress; (*Briefumschlag*) envelope

um|sehen *unreg vr* to look around *od* about; **sich ~ (nach)** to look out (for)

umso *konj*: **~ besser/schlimmer** so much the better/worse; **~ mehr, als …** all the more considering …

umsonst *adv* in vain; (*gratis*) for nothing

Umstand *m* circumstance

▪ **Umstände** *pl* (*fig*: *Schwierigkeiten*) fuss *sing*; **in anderen Umständen sein** to be pregnant; **Umstände machen** to go to a lot of trouble; **den Umständen entsprechend** much as one would expect (under the circumstances); **unter Umständen** possibly

umständlich *adj* (*Methode*) complicated; (*Ausdrucksweise, Erklärung*) long-winded; (*ungeschickt*) ponderous

um|steigen *unreg vi* (*Eisenb*) to change

um|stellen *vt* (*an anderen Ort*) to change round; (*Tech*) to convert ▶ *vr*: **sich ~ (auf** *+akk***)** to adapt o.s. (to)

Umstellung *f* change; (*Umgewöhnung*) adjustment; (*Tech*) conversion

Umtausch *m* exchange

um|tauschen *vt* to exchange

Umweg *m* detour

Umwelt *f* environment

Umweltbelastung *f* environmental pollution

umweltbewusst *adj* environmentally aware

umweltfreundlich *adj* environment-friendly; **umweltfreundliche Technologie** clean technology

umweltschädlich *adj* harmful to the environment

Umweltschutz *m* environmental protection

Umweltschützer (-s, -) *m* environmentalist

Umweltsteuer *f* green tax
Umweltverschmutzung *f* pollution (of the environment)
umweltverträglich *adj* not harmful to the environment
um|werfen *unreg vt* to overturn; (*fig*) to upset
um|ziehen *unreg vt, vr* to change ▸ *vi* to move
Umzug *m* procession; (*Wohnungsumzug*) move
unabhängig *adj* independent
unabsichtlich *adj* unintentional
unangenehm *adj* unpleasant
Unannehmlichkeit *f* inconvenience ■ **Unannehmlichkeiten** *pl* trouble *sing*
unanständig *adj* indecent
unappetitlich *adj* unsavoury (BRIT), unsavory (*US*)
unbeabsichtigt *adj* unintentional
unbedeutend *adj* insignificant, unimportant; (*Fehler*) slight
unbedingt *adj* unconditional ▸ *adv* absolutely
unbefriedigend *adj* unsatisfactory
unbegrenzt *adj* unlimited
unbekannt *adj* unknown
unbeliebt *adj* unpopular
unbemerkt *adj* unnoticed
unbequem *adj* (*Stuhl*) uncomfortable; (*Regelung*) inconvenient
unbeständig *adj* (*Mensch*) inconstant; (*Wetter*) unsettled; (*Lage*) unstable
unbestimmt *adj* indefinite
unbeteiligt *adj* unconcerned; (*uninteressiert*) indifferent
unbewacht *adj* unguarded
unbewusst *adj* unconscious
unbezahlt *adj* unpaid
unbrauchbar *adj* useless
und *konj* and; **~ so weiter** and so on; **na ~?** so what?
undankbar *adj* ungrateful; (*Aufgabe*) thankless
undenkbar *adj* inconceivable
undeutlich *adj* indistinct
undicht *adj* leaky
uneben *adj* uneven
unecht *adj* (*Schmuck etc*) fake
unehelich *adj* illegitimate
unendlich *adj* infinite ▸ *adv* endlessly
unentbehrlich *adj* indispensable
unentgeltlich *adj* free (of charge)
unentschieden *adj* undecided; **~ enden** (*Sport*) to end in a draw
unerfreulich *adj* unpleasant
unerhört *adj* unheard-of; (*unverschämt*) outrageous
unerlässlich *adj* indispensable
unerträglich *adj* unbearable
unerwartet *adj* unexpected
unerwünscht *adj* undesirable, unwelcome
unfähig *adj* incompetent; **zu etw ~ sein** to be incapable of sth
unfair *adj* unfair
Unfall *m* accident
Unfallflucht *f* hit-and-run (driving)
Unfallstation *f* emergency ward
Unfallstelle *f* scene of the accident
Unfallversicherung *f* accident insurance
unfreundlich *adj* unfriendly
Ungarn (**-s**) *nt* Hungary
Ungeduld *f* impatience
ungeduldig *adj* impatient
ungeeignet *adj* unsuitable
ungefähr *adj* approximate ▸ *adv* approximately; **so ~** more or less; **~ 10 Kilometer** about 10 kilometres
ungefährlich *adj* not dangerous, harmless
ungeheuer *adj* huge ▸ *adv* (*umg*) enormously
Ungeheuer (**-s, -**) *nt* monster
ungehorsam *adj* disobedient
ungelegen *adj* inconvenient
ungemütlich *adj* uncomfortable; (*Person*) disagreeable
ungenießbar *adj* inedible; (*nicht zu trinken*) undrinkable
ungenügend *adj* insufficient; (*Sch*) unsatisfactory
ungepflegt *adj* (*Garten etc*) untended; (*Person*) unkempt; (*Hände*) neglected
ungerade *adj* odd
ungerecht *adj* unjust
ungerechtfertigt *adj* unjustified
Ungerechtigkeit *f* unfairness, injustice
ungern *adv* unwillingly, reluctantly
ungeschickt *adj* clumsy
ungeschminkt *adj* without make-up
ungesund *adj* unhealthy
ungewiss *adj* uncertain
ungewöhnlich *adj* unusual
Ungeziefer (**-s**) *nt* vermin *pl*
ungezogen *adj* rude
ungezwungen *adj* natural
unglaublich *adj* incredible

Unglück *nt* misfortune; (*Pech*) bad luck; (*Unglücksfall*) disaster; (*Verkehrsunglück*) accident
unglücklich *adj* unhappy; (*erfolglos*) unlucky; (*unerfreulich*) unfortunate
unglücklicherweise *adv* unfortunately
ungültig *adj* invalid
ungünstig *adj* inconvenient
unheilbar *adj* incurable; **~ krank** terminally ill
unheimlich *adj* weird ▸ *adv* (*umg*) tremendously
unhöflich *adj* impolite
uni *adj* self-coloured (BRIT), self-colored (US)
Uni (-, **-s**) (*umg*) *f* university
Uniform (-, **-en**) *f* uniform
Universität *f* university
Unkenntnis *f* ignorance
unklar *adj* unclear
Unkosten *pl* expense(s *pl*)
Unkraut *nt* weeds *pl*; (*einzelne Pflanze*) weed
unlogisch *adj* illogical
unmissverständlich *adj* unmistakable
unmittelbar *adj* immediate
unmöbliert *adj* unfurnished
unmöglich *adj* impossible
unnahbar *adj* unapproachable
unnötig *adj* unnecessary
UNO *f abk* (= *United Nations Organization*): **die ~** the UN
unordentlich *adj* untidy
Unordnung *f* disorder
unpassend *adj* inappropriate; (*Zeit*) inopportune
unpersönlich *adj* impersonal
unpraktisch *adj* impractical, unpractical
unrecht *adj* wrong; **~ haben** to be wrong
Unrecht *nt* wrong; **zu ~** wrongly; **im ~ sein** to be wrong
unregelmäßig *adj* irregular
unreif *adj* unripe
unruhig *adj* restless; (*Schlaf*) fitful
uns *pron akk, dat von* **wir** us; (*reflexiv*) ourselves
unscharf *adj* (*Bild etc*) out of focus, blurred
unscheinbar *adj* insignificant; (*Aussehen, Haus etc*) unprepossessing
unschlüssig *adj* undecided
unschuldig *adj* innocent
unser *poss pron* our ▸ *pron gen von* **wir** of us
unsere(r, s) *poss pron* ours
unseriös *adj* untrustworthy
unsicher *adj* uncertain; (*Mensch*) insecure
Unsinn *m* nonsense
unsterblich *adj* immortal
unsympathisch *adj* unpleasant; **er ist mir ~** I don't like him
unten *adv* below; (*im Haus*) downstairs; (*an der Treppe etc*) at the bottom; **nach ~** down

SCHLÜSSELWORT

unter *präp +dat* **1** (*räumlich, mit Zahlen*) under; (*drunter*) underneath, below; **Mädchen unter 18 Jahren** girls under *od* less than 18 (years of age)
2 (*zwischen*) among(st); **sie waren unter sich** they were by themselves; **einer unter ihnen** one of them; **unter anderem** among other things
▸ *präp +akk* under, below

Unterarm *m* forearm
Unterbesetzung *f* understaffing
Unterbewusstsein *nt* subconscious
unterbrechen *unreg vt untr* to interrupt
Unterbrechung *f* interruption
unterdrücken *vt untr* to suppress; (*Leute*) to oppress
untere(r, s) *adj* lower
untereinander *adv* (*gegenseitig*) each other; (*miteinander*) among themselves *etc*
Unterführung *f* underpass
unter|gehen *unreg vi* to go down; (*Sonne*) to set; (*Volk*) to perish; (*Welt*) to come to an end; (*im Lärm*) to be drowned
Untergeschoss *nt* basement
Untergewicht *nt*: **(10 Kilo) ~ haben** to be (10 kilos) underweight
Untergrund *m* foundation; (*Pol*) underground
Untergrundbahn *f* underground (BRIT), subway (US)
unterhalb *präp +gen* below ▸ *adv* below; **~ von** below
Unterhalt *m* maintenance
unterhalten *unreg vt untr* to maintain; (*belustigen*) to entertain ▸ *vr untr* to talk; (*sich belustigen*) to enjoy o.s.

Unterhaltung *f* (*Belustigung*) entertainment; (*Gespräch*) talk
Unterhemd *nt* vest (BRIT), undershirt (*US*)
Unterhose *f* underpants *pl*
unterirdisch *adj* underground
Unterkiefer *m* lower jaw
Unterkunft (-, **-künfte**) *f* accommodation (BRIT), accommodations *pl* (*US*)
Unterlage *f* (*Beleg*) document; (*Schreibunterlage etc*) pad
unterlassen *unreg vt untr* (*versäumen*) to fail to do; (*sich enthalten*) to refrain from
unterlegen *adj* inferior; (*besiegt*) defeated
Unterleib *m* abdomen
Unterlippe *f* bottom *od* lower lip
Untermiete *f*: **bei jdm zur ~ wohnen** to rent a room from sb
Untermieter(in) *m(f)* lodger
unternehmen *unreg vt untr* to do; (*durchführen*) to undertake; (*Versuch, Reise*) to make
Unternehmen (**-s**, **-**) *nt* undertaking; (*Firma*) business
Unternehmensberater *m* management consultant
Unternehmer(in) (**-s**, **-**) *m(f)* entrepreneur
Unterricht (**-(e)s**) *m* lessons *pl*
unterrichten *vt untr* (*Sch*) to teach
unterschätzen *vt untr* to underestimate
unterscheiden *unreg vt untr* to distinguish ▸ *vr untr* to differ
Unterschenkel *m* lower leg
Unterschied (**-(e)s**, **-e**) *m* difference; **im ~ zu** as distinct from
unterschiedlich *adj* differing
unterschreiben *unreg vt untr* to sign
Unterschrift *f* signature
Untersetzer *m* tablemat; (*für Gläser*) coaster
unterste(r, s) *adj* lowest, bottom
unterstellen[1] *vt untr* to subordinate; (*fig*) to impute
unter|stellen[2] *vr* to take shelter
unterstreichen *unreg vt untr* (*lit, fig*) to underline
unterstützen *vt untr* to support
Unterstützung *f* support
untersuchen *vt untr* (*Med*) to examine; (*Polizei*) to investigate
Untersuchung *f* examination; (*polizeilich*) investigation
Untertasse *f* saucer
Unterteil *nt od m* lower part, bottom
Untertitel *m* subtitle
Unterwäsche *f* underwear
unterwegs *adv* on the way
unterzeichnen *vt untr* to sign
untreu *adj* unfaithful
untröstlich *adj* inconsolable
unüberlegt *adj* ill-considered ▸ *adv* without thinking
unverantwortlich *adj* irresponsible; (*unentschuldbar*) inexcusable
unverbindlich *adj* not binding; (*Antwort*) noncommittal ▸ *adv* (*Comm*) without obligation
unverbleit *adj* unleaded
unverheiratet *adj* unmarried
unvermeidlich *adj* unavoidable
unvernünftig *adj* foolish
unverschämt *adj* impudent
unverständlich *adj* unintelligible
unverträglich *adj* quarrelsome; (*Essen*) indigestible
unverwüstlich *adj* indestructible; (*Mensch*) irrepressible
unverzeihlich *adj* unpardonable
unverzüglich *adj* immediate
unvollständig *adj* incomplete
unvorsichtig *adj* careless
unwahrscheinlich *adj* improbable, unlikely ▸ *adv* (*umg*) incredibly
Unwetter *nt* thunderstorm
unwichtig *adj* unimportant
unwiderstehlich *adj* irresistible
unwillkürlich *adj* involuntary ▸ *adv* instinctively; (*lachen*) involuntarily
unwohl *adj* unwell, ill
unzählig *adj* innumerable, countless
unzerbrechlich *adj* unbreakable
unzertrennlich *adj* inseparable
unzufrieden *adj* dissatisfied
unzugänglich *adj* inaccessible
unzumutbar *adj* unreasonable
unzusammenhängend *adj* disconnected; (*Äußerung*) incoherent
unzutreffend *adj* incorrect
unzuverlässig *adj* unreliable
üppig *adj* (*Essen*) lavish; (*Vegetation*) lush
uralt *adj* ancient, very old
Uran (**-s**) *nt* uranium
Uraufführung *f* premiere
Urenkel(in) *m(f)* great-grandchild

Urgroßmutter *f* great-grandmother
Urgroßvater *m* great-grandfather
Urheber (**-s**, **-**) *m* originator; (*Autor*) author
Urin (**-s**, **-e**) *m* urine
Urkunde *f* document
Urlaub (**-(e)s**, **-e**) *m* holiday(s *pl*) (BRIT), vacation (*US*); **in ~ fahren** to go on holiday (BRIT) *od* vacation (*US*)
Urlauber (**-s**, **-**) *m* holiday-maker (BRIT), vacationer (*US*)
Urlaubsort *m* holiday (BRIT) *od* vacation (*US*) resort
urlaubsreif *adj* in need of a holiday (BRIT) *od* vacation (*US*)
Urne (**-**, **-n**) *f* urn
Ursache *f* cause; **keine ~!** (*auf Dank*) don't mention it, you're welcome; (*auf Entschuldigung*) that's all right
Ursprung *m* origin; (*von Fluss*) source
ursprünglich *adj* original ▶ *adv* originally
Ursprungsland *nt* (*Comm*) country of origin
Urteil (**-s**, **-e**) *nt* opinion; (*Jur*) sentence
urteilen *vi* to judge
Uruguay (**-s**) *nt* Uruguay
Urwald *m* jungle
USA *pl abk*: **die ~** the USA *sing*
USB-Anschluss *m* USB port
USB-Stick *m* (*Comput*) flash drive
USBV *f abk* (= *unkonventionelle Spreng- und Brandvorrichtung*) IED
usw. *abk* (= *und so weiter*) etc.
Utensilien *pl* utensils *pl*

V

Vagina (**-**, **Vaginen**) *f* vagina
Vandalismus *m* vandalism
Vanille (**-**) *f* vanilla
variieren *vt*, *vi* to vary
Vase (**-**, **-n**) *f* vase
Vater (**-s**, **Väter**) *m* father
väterlich *adj* fatherly
Vaterschaft *f* paternity
Vatertag *m* Father's Day
Vaterunser (**-s**, **-**) *nt* Lord's Prayer
V-Ausschnitt *m* V-neck
v. Chr. *abk* (= *vor Christus*) B.C.
vegan *adj* vegan
Veganer(in) (**-s**, **-**) *m(f)* vegan
Vegetarier(in) (**-s**, **-**) *m(f)* vegetarian
vegetarisch *adj* vegetarian
Veilchen *nt* violet
Vene (**-**, **-n**) *f* vein
Venedig (**-s**) *nt* Venice
Venezuela (**-s**) *nt* Venezuela
Ventil (**-s**, **-e**) *nt* valve
Ventilator *m* ventilator
verabreden *vt* to arrange ▶ *vr* to arrange to meet; **sich (mit jdm) ~** to arrange to meet (sb)
Verabredung *f* arrangement; (*Treffen*) appointment
verabschieden *vt* (*Gäste*) to say goodbye to; (*Gesetz*) to pass ▶ *vr*: **sich ~ (von)** to take one's leave (of)
verachten *vt* to despise
verächtlich *adj* contemptuous; (*verachtenswert*) contemptible
Verachtung *f* contempt
verallgemeinern *vt* to generalize
Veranda (**-**, **Veranden**) *f* veranda
veränderlich *adj* changeable

verändern *vt, vr* to change
Veränderung *f* change
veranlassen *vt* to cause
veranstalten *vt* to organize
Veranstalter(in) (**-s**, **-**) *m(f)* organizer
Veranstaltung *f* event
verantworten *vt* to accept responsibility for ▶ *vr* to justify o.s.
verantwortlich *adj* responsible
Verantwortung *f* responsibility
verärgern *vt* to annoy
verarschen (*umg!*) *vt*: **jdn ~** to take the mickey out of sb
Verb (**-s**, **-en**) *nt* verb
Verband (**-(e)s**, **Verbände**) *m* (*Med*) bandage; (*Bund*) association
Verbandkasten, Verbandskasten *m* medicine chest, first-aid box
Verbandzeug *nt* bandage, dressing material
verbergen *unreg vt, vr*: **(sich) ~ (vor** *+dat*) to hide (from)
verbessern *vt* to improve; (*berichtigen*) to correct ▶ *vr* to improve; (*sich korrigieren*) to correct o.s.
Verbesserung *f* improvement; (*Korrektur*) correction
verbiegen *unreg vi* to bend
verbieten *unreg vt* to forbid; **jdm etw ~** to forbid sb to do sth
verbinden *unreg vt* to connect; (*kombinieren*) to combine; (*Med*) to bandage ▶ *vr* to combine (*auch Chem*)
verbindlich *adj* binding; (*freundlich*) obliging
Verbindung *f* connection
verbleit *adj* leaded
verblüffen *vt* to amaze
verblühen *vi* to fade
verborgen *adj* hidden
Verbot (**-(e)s**, **-e**) *nt* ban
verboten *adj* forbidden; **Rauchen ~!** no smoking
Verbrauch (**-(e)s**) *m* consumption
verbrauchen *vt* to use up
Verbraucher(in) (**-s**, **-**) *m(f)* consumer
Verbrechen (**-s**, **-**) *nt* crime
Verbrecher(in) (**-s**, **-**) *m(f)* criminal
verbreiten *vt* to spread ▶ *vr* to spread
verbrennen *unreg vt* to burn
Verbrennung *f* burning; (*in Motor*) combustion
verbringen *unreg vt* to spend
verbunden *adj* connected; **ich/er** *etc* **war falsch ~** (*Tel*) it was a wrong number
Verdacht (**-(e)s**) *m* suspicion
verdächtig *adj* suspicious
verdächtigen *vt* to suspect
verdammt (*umg*) *adj, adv*: **~ noch mal!** bloody hell (*!*), damn (*!*)
verdanken *vt*: **jdm etw ~** to owe sb sth
verdarb *etc vb siehe* **verderben**
verdauen *vt* (*lit, fig*) to digest
verdaulich *adj* digestible; **das ist schwer ~** that is hard to digest
Verdauung *f* digestion
Verdeck (**-(e)s**, **-e**) *nt* (*Aut*) soft top
verderben *unreg vt* to spoil; (*schädigen*) to ruin; (*moralisch*) to corrupt ▶ *vi* (*Essen*) to rot; (*Mensch*) to go to the bad; **es mit jdm ~** to get into sb's bad books
verdienen *vt* to earn; (*moralisch*) to deserve
Verdienst (**-(e)s**, **-e**) *m* earnings *pl* ▶ *nt* merit; (*Leistung*): **~ (um)** service (to)
verdoppeln *vt* to double
verdorben *pp von* **verderben** ▶ *adj* spoilt; (*geschädigt*) ruined; (*moralisch*) corrupt
verdrehen *vt* to twist; (*Augen*) to roll; **jdm den Kopf ~** (*fig*) to turn sb's head
verdünnen *vt* to dilute
verdunsten *vi* to evaporate
verdursten *vi* to die of thirst
verehren *vt* to venerate, to worship (*auch Rel*)
Verehrer(in) (**-s**, **-**) *m(f)* admirer
Verein (**-(e)s**, **-e**) *m* club, association
vereinbar *adj* compatible
vereinbaren *vt* to agree upon
Vereinbarung *f* agreement
vereinigen *vt, vr* to unite
Vereinigtes Königreich *nt* United Kingdom
Vereinigte Staaten *pl* United States
Vereinigung *f* union; (*Verein*) association
Vereinte Nationen *pl* United Nations
vereisen *vi* to freeze, to ice over ▶ *vt* (*Med*) to freeze
vererben *vt* to bequeath; (*Biol*) to transmit ▶ *vr* to be hereditary
vererblich *adj* hereditary
verfahren *unreg vi* to act ▶ *vr* to get lost
Verfahren (**-s**, **-**) *nt* procedure; (*Tech*) process; (*Jur*) proceedings *pl*
verfallen *unreg vi* to decline; (*Haus*) to be falling down; (*Fin*) to lapse ▶ *adj* (*Pass*) expired; **~ in** *+akk* to lapse into

Verfallsdatum *nt* expiry date; (*der Haltbarkeit*) best-before date
verfärben *vr* to change colour (BRIT) *od* color (*US*)
Verfasser(in) (**-s**, **-**) *m(f)* author, writer
Verfassung *f* constitution (*auch Pol*); (*körperlich*) state of health
verfaulen *vi* to rot
verfehlen *vt* to miss
verfeinern *vt* to refine
Verfilmung *f* film (version)
verfluchen *vt* to curse
verfolgen *vt* to pursue; (*grausam, bes Pol*) to persecute
verfügbar *adj* available
verfügen *vi*: **~ über** *+akk* to have at one's disposal
Verfügung *f* order; **zur ~** at one's disposal; **jdm zur ~ stehen** to be available to sb
verführen *vt* to tempt; (*sexuell*) to seduce
verführerisch *adj* seductive
vergangen *adj* past; **vergangene Woche** last week
Vergangenheit *f* past
Vergaser (**-s**, **-**) *m* (*Aut*) carburettor (BRIT), carburetor (*US*)
vergaß *etc vb siehe* **vergessen**
vergeben *unreg vt* to forgive; (*weggeben*) to give away; (*Auftrag, Preis*) to award; (*Studienplätze, Stellen*) to allocate
vergebens *adv* in vain
vergeblich *adv* in vain ▶ *adj* vain, futile
vergehen *unreg vi* to pass by *od* away ▶ *vr*: **sich an jdm ~** to (sexually) assault sb
Vergehen (**-s**, **-**) *nt* offence (BRIT), offense (*US*)
Vergeltung *f* retaliation
vergessen *unreg vt* to forget
vergesslich *adj* forgetful
vergeuden *vt* to squander, to waste
vergewaltigen *vt* to rape
Vergewaltigung *f* rape
vergewissern *vr* to make sure
vergiften *vt* to poison
Vergiftung *f* poisoning
Vergissmeinnicht (**-(e)s**, **-e**) *nt* forget-me-not
Vergleich (**-(e)s**, **-e**) *m* comparison; (*Jur*) settlement; **im ~ mit** *od* **zu** compared with *od* to
vergleichen *unreg vt* to compare
Vergnügen (**-s**, **-**) *nt* pleasure; **viel ~!** enjoy yourself!
vergnügt *adj* cheerful
Vergnügungspark *m* amusement park
vergolden *vt* to gild
vergriffen *adj* (*Buch*) out of print; (*Ware*) out of stock
vergrößern *vt* to enlarge; (*mengenmäßig*) to increase; (*Lupe*) to magnify
Vergrößerung *f* enlargement; (*von Menge*) increase; (*mit Lupe*) magnification
Vergrößerungsglas *nt* magnifying glass
verh. *abk* = **verheiratet**
verhaften *vt* to arrest
verhalten *unreg vr* (*Sache*) to be; (*sich benehmen*) to behave
Verhalten (**-s**) *nt* behaviour (BRIT), behavior (*US*); **selbstverletzendes ~** self-harm
Verhältnis (**-ses**, **-se**) *nt* relationship; (*Math*) ratio ■ **Verhältnisse** *pl* (*Umstände*) conditions *pl*
verhältnismäßig *adj* relative ▶ *adv* relatively
verhandeln *vi* to negotiate; **über etw** *akk* **~** to negotiate sth *od* about sth
Verhandlung *f* negotiation
verheimlichen *vt*: **(jdm) etw ~** to keep sth secret (from sb)
verheiratet *adj* married
verhindern *vt* to prevent; **verhindert sein** to be unable to make it
Verhör (**-(e)s**, **-e**) *nt* interrogation; (*gerichtlich*) (cross-)examination
verhören *vt* to interrogate; (*vor Gericht*) to (cross-)examine ▶ *vr* to mishear
verhungern *vi* to starve
verhüten *vt* to prevent
Verhütung *f* prevention
Verhütungsmittel *nt* contraceptive
verirren *vr* to get lost
Verkauf *m* sale
verkaufen *vt*, *vi* to sell; **„zu ~"** "for sale"
Verkäufer(in) (**-s**, **-**) *m(f)* seller; (*im Außendienst*) salesman, saleswoman; (*in Laden*) shop assistant (BRIT), sales clerk (*US*)
verkäuflich *adj* saleable

Verkehr (**-s**, **-e**) *m* traffic; (*Umgang, bes sexuell*) intercourse; (*Umlauf*) circulation
verkehren *vi* (*Fahrzeug*) to run; **~ mit** to associate with
Verkehrsampel *f* traffic lights *pl*
Verkehrsamt *nt* tourist (information) office
Verkehrsinsel *f* traffic island
Verkehrsmittel *nt*: **öffentliche/ private ~** public/private transport *sing*
Verkehrsschild *nt* road sign
Verkehrsunfall *m* traffic accident
Verkehrszeichen *nt* road sign
verkehrt *adj* wrong; (*umgekehrt*) the wrong way round
verklagen *vt* to take to court
verkleiden *vt* to disguise; (*kostümieren*) to dress up ▶ *vr* to disguise o.s.; (*sich kostümieren*) to dress up
Verkleidung *f* disguise
verkleinern *vt* to make smaller, to reduce in size
verkneifen (*umg*) *vt*: **sich** *dat* **etw ~** to stop o.s. from doing sth; **ich konnte mir das Lachen nicht ~** I couldn't help laughing
verkommen *unreg vi* to deteriorate; (*Mensch*) to go downhill ▶ *adj* (*moralisch*) depraved
verkraften *vt* to cope with
verkühlen *vr* to get a chill
verkürzen *vt* to shorten
Verlag (**-(e)s**, **-e**) *m* publishing firm
verlangen *vt* to demand; (*wollen*) to want; (*Preis*) to ask; (*Qualifikation*) to require; (*erwarten von*) to ask of; (*fragen nach*) to ask for ▶ *vi*: **~ nach** to ask for; **Sie werden am Telefon verlangt** you are wanted on the phone; **~ Sie Herrn X** ask for Mr X
verlängern *vt* to extend; (*Pass, Abonnement etc*) to renew
Verlängerung *f* extension; (*Sport*) extra time; (*von Pass, Erlaubnis*) renewal
Verlängerungsschnur *f* extension cable
verlassen *unreg vt* to leave ▶ *vr*: **sich ~ auf** *+akk* to depend on ▶ *adj* desolate; (*Mensch*) abandoned
verlässlich *adj* reliable
Verlauf *m* course
verlaufen *unreg vi* (*zeitlich*) to pass; (*Farben*) to run ▶ *vr* to get lost; (*Menschenmenge*) to disperse
verlegen *vt* to move; (*verlieren*) to mislay; (*Buch*) to publish ▶ *adj* embarrassed
Verlegenheit *f* embarrassment; (*Situation*) difficulty
Verleih (**-(e)s**, **-e**) *m* (*Firma*) hire service
verleihen *unreg vt*: **etw (an jdn) ~** to lend sth (to sb); (*gegen Gebühr*) to rent sth (out) (to sb); (*Preis, Medaille*) to award sth (to sb)
verleiten *vt*: **~ zu** to tempt into
verlernen *vt* to forget
verletzen *vt* (*lit, fig*) to injure, to hurt
Verletzte(r) *f(m)* injured person
Verletzung *f* injury; (*Verstoß*) violation
verlieben *vr*: **sich ~ (in** *+akk***)** to fall in love (with)
verliebt *adj* in love
verlieren *unreg vt, vi* to lose
verloben *vr*: **sich ~ (mit)** to get engaged (to)
Verlobte(r) *f(m)*: **mein Verlobter** my fiancé; **meine ~** my fiancée
Verlobung *f* engagement
verlor *etc vb siehe* **verlieren**
verloren *pp von* **verlieren** ▶ *adj* lost; (*Eier*) poached; **~ gehen** to get lost
verlosen *vt* to raffle (off)
Verlosung *f* raffle
Verlust (**-(e)s**, **-e**) *m* loss
vermehren *vt, vr* to multiply; (*Menge*) to increase
vermeiden *unreg vt* to avoid
vermeintlich *adj* supposed
vermieten *vt* to let (BRIT), to rent (out); (*Auto, Fahrrad*) to hire out, to rent
Vermieter(in) (**-s**, **-**) *m(f)* landlord, landlady
vermischen *vt, vr* to mix
vermissen *vt* to miss; **vermisst sein, als vermisst gemeldet sein** to be reported missing
Vermittlung *f* (*Stellenvermittlung*) agency; (*Schlichtung*) mediation
Vermögen (**-s**, **-**) *nt* wealth; **ein ~ kosten** to cost a fortune
vermuten *vt* to suppose; (*argwöhnen*) to suspect
vermutlich *adj* presumed ▶ *adv* probably
Vermutung *f* supposition; (*Argwohn*) suspicion
vernachlässigen *vt* to neglect

vernetzt *adj* networked
vernichten *vt* to destroy
vernichtend *adj* (*fig*) crushing; (*Blick*) withering; (*Kritik*) scathing
Vernunft (-) *f* reason; **~ annehmen** to see reason
vernünftig *adj* sensible, reasonable
veröffentlichen *vt* to publish
verordnen *vt* (*Med*) to prescribe
Verordnung *f* order; (*Med*) prescription
verpachten *vt* to lease (out)
verpacken *vt* to pack; (*einwickeln*) to wrap
Verpackung *f* packaging
verpassen *vt* to miss
verpflegen *vt* to feed
Verpflegung *f* catering; (*Kost*) food; (*in Hotel*) board
verpflichten *vt* to oblige; (*anstellen*) to engage ▶ *vr*: **sich zu etw ~** to commit o.s. to doing sth
verprügeln *vt* to beat up
verraten *unreg vt* to betray; (*Geheimnis*) to divulge ▶ *vr* to give o.s. away
verrechnen *vt*: **~ mit** to set off against ▶ *vr* to miscalculate
verregnet *adj* rainy
verreisen *vi* to go away (on a journey); **er ist geschäftlich verreist** he's away on business
verrenken *vt* to contort; (*Med*) to dislocate; **sich** *dat* **den Knöchel ~** to sprain one's ankle
verringern *vt* to reduce
verrückt *adj* crazy, mad
versagen *vi* to fail
Versagen (**-s**) *nt* failure
Versager (**-s**, **-**) *m* failure
versalzen *vt* to put too much salt in
versammeln *vt*, *vr* to assemble, to gather
Versammlung *f* meeting
Versand (**-(e)s**) *m* dispatch; (*Versandabteilung*) dispatch department
Versandhaus *nt* mail-order firm
versäumen *vt* to miss; (*Pflicht*) to neglect; **es ~, etw zu tun** to fail to do sth
verschätzen *vr* to miscalculate
verschenken *vt* to give away
verschicken *vt* to send off
verschieben *unreg vt* to shift; (*Termin*) to postpone
verschieden *adj* different; (*mehrere*) various
Verschiedene(r, s) *pron* (*Menschen*) various people; (*Dinge*) various things *pl*
verschlafen *unreg vt* to sleep through; (*fig*: *versäumen*) to miss ▶ *vi*, *vr* to oversleep
verschlechtern *vr* to deteriorate, to get worse
Verschlechterung *f* deterioration
Verschleiß (**-es**, **-e**) *m* wear and tear
verschließbar *adj* lockable
verschließen *unreg vt* to lock
verschlimmern *vt* to make worse ▶ *vr* to get worse
verschlossen *adj* locked; (*fig*) reserved
verschlucken *vt* to swallow ▶ *vr* to choke
Verschluss *m* lock; (*von Kleid etc*) fastener; (*Phot*) shutter; (*Stöpsel*) plug
verschmutzen *vt* to soil; (*Umwelt*) to pollute
verschnaufen (*umg*) *vi*, *vr* to have a breather
verschneit *adj* covered in snow
verschnupft (*umg*) *adj*: **~ sein** to have a cold; (*beleidigt*) to be peeved (*umg*)
verschonen *vt*: **jdn mit etw ~** to spare sb sth
verschreiben *unreg vt* (*Med*) to prescribe
verschreibungspflichtig *adj* available only on prescription
verschwand *etc vb siehe* **verschwinden**
verschweigen *unreg vt* to keep secret; **jdm etw ~** to keep sth from sb
verschwenden *vt* to squander
Verschwendung *f* waste
verschwiegen *adj* discreet; (*Ort*) secluded
verschwinden *unreg vi* to disappear, to vanish; **verschwinde!** clear off! (*umg*)
verschwunden *pp von* **verschwinden**
Versehen (**-s**, **-**) *nt* oversight; **aus ~** by mistake
versehentlich *adv* by mistake
versenden *unreg vt* to send
versessen *adj*: **~ auf** +*akk* mad about
versetzen *vt* to transfer; (*verpfänden*) to pawn; (*umg*: *vergeblich warten lassen*) to stand up ▶ *vr*: **sich in jdn** *od* **in jds Lage ~** to put o.s. in sb's place

verseuchen *vt* to contaminate
versichern *vt* to insure; (*bestätigen*) to assure
Versicherung *f* insurance
Versicherungspolice *f* insurance policy
versilbert *adj* silver-plated
versinken *unreg vi* to sink
Version *f* version
versöhnen *vt* to reconcile ▸ *vr* to become reconciled
versorgen *vt* to provide, to supply; (*Familie etc*) to look after ▸ *vr* to look after o.s.
Versorgung *f* provision; (*Unterhalt*) maintenance; (*Altersversorgung etc*) benefit
verspäten *vr* to be late
verspätet *adj* late
Verspätung *f* delay; **~ haben** to be late
versprechen *unreg vt* to promise ▸ *vr* (*etwas Nichtgemeintes sagen*) to make a slip of the tongue
Verstand *m* mind; (*Fähigkeit zu denken*) reason; **den ~ verlieren** to go out of one's mind
verständigen *vt* to inform ▸ *vr* to communicate; (*sich einigen*) to come to an understanding
Verständigung *f* communication
verständlich *adj* understandable
Verständnis (**-ses**, **-se**) *nt* understanding; **für etw kein ~ haben** to have no understanding of *od* sympathy for sth
verständnisvoll *adj* understanding
verstauchen *vt* to sprain
Versteck (**-(e)s**, **-e**) *nt* hiding (place)
verstecken *vt*, *vr* to hide
verstehen *unreg vt*, *vi* to understand ▸ *vr* (*auskommen*) to get on
Versteigerung *f* auction
verstellbar *adj* adjustable
verstellen *vt* to move; (*Uhr*) to adjust; (*versperren*) to block; (*fig*) to disguise ▸ *vr* to pretend, to put on an act
verstopfen *vt* to block; (*Med*) to constipate
Verstopfung *f* obstruction; (*Med*) constipation
Verstoß *m*: **~ (gegen)** infringement (of), violation (of)
Versuch (**-(e)s**, **-e**) *m* attempt; (*Chem etc*) experiment
versuchen *vt* to try
vertauschen *vt* to exchange; (*versehentlich*) to mix up
verteidigen *vt* to defend
Verteidiger(in) (**-s**, **-**) *m(f)* defender; (*Anwalt*) defence (BRIT) *od* defense (*US*) lawyer
Verteidigung *f* defence (BRIT), defense (*US*)
verteilen *vt* to distribute
Vertrag (**-(e)s**, **Verträge**) *m* contract; (*Pol*) treaty
vertragen *unreg vt* to tolerate, to stand ▸ *vr* to get along; (*sich aussöhnen*) to become reconciled
verträglich *adj* good-natured; (*Speisen*) easily digested
vertrauen *vi*: **jdm ~** to trust sb
Vertrauen (**-s**) *nt* confidence; **~ zu jdm fassen** to gain confidence in sb
vertraulich *adj* (*geheim*) confidential
vertraut *adj* familiar; **sich mit dem Gedanken ~ machen, dass …** to get used to the idea that …
vertreten *unreg vt* to represent; (*Ansicht*) to hold
Vertreter(in) (**-s**, **-**) *m(f)* representative
Vertrieb (**-(e)s**, **-e**) *m* marketing; (*Abteilung*) sales department
vertrocknen *vi* to dry up
vertun *unreg vr* (*umg*) to make a mistake
vertuschen *vt* to hush *od* cover up
verunglücken *vi* to have an accident; **tödlich ~** to be killed in an accident
verunsichern *vt* to rattle (*fig*)
verursachen *vt* to cause
verurteilen *vt* to condemn
vervielfältigen *vt* to duplicate, to copy
verwählen *vr* (*Tel*) to dial the wrong number
verwalten *vt* to manage; (*Behörde*) to administer
Verwalter(in) (**-s**, **-**) *m(f)* administrator; (*Vermögensverwalter*) trustee
Verwaltung *f* management; (*behördlich*) administration
verwandt *adj*: **~ (mit)** related (to)
Verwandte(r) *f(m)* relative, relation
Verwandtschaft *f* relationship; (*Menschen*) relations *pl*
verwarnen *vt* to caution

verwechseln *vt*: **~ mit** to confuse with
verweigern *vt*: **jdm etw ~** to refuse sb sth
verwenden *unreg vt* to use; (*Mühe, Zeit, Arbeit*) to spend
Verwendung *f* use
verwirklichen *vt* to realize
verwirren *vt* to confuse
Verwirrung *f* confusion
verwitwet *adj* widowed
verwöhnen *vt* to spoil
verwunderlich *adj* surprising
Verwunderung *f* astonishment
verwüsten *vt* to devastate
verzählen *vr* to miscount
verzehren *vt* to consume
Verzeichnis (**-ses**, **-se**) *nt* list, catalogue (BRIT), catalog (*US*); (*in Buch*) index; (*Comput*) directory
verzeihen *unreg vt, vi* to forgive; **jdm etw ~** to forgive sb (for) sth; **~ Sie!** excuse me!
Verzeihung *f*: **~!** sorry!; **~, ...** (*vor Frage etc*) excuse me, ...; **(jdn) um ~ bitten** to apologize (to sb)
verzichten *vi*: **~ auf** *+akk* to forgo, to give up
verziehen *unreg vt* (*Kind*) to spoil ▶ *vr* to go out of shape; (*Gesicht*) to contort; (*verschwinden*) to disappear; **das Gesicht ~** to pull a face
verzieren *vt* to decorate
verzögern *vt* to delay ▶ *vr* to be delayed
Verzögerung *f* delay
verzweifeln *vi* to despair
verzweifelt *adj* desperate
Verzweiflung *f* despair
Vetter (**-s**, **-n**) *m* cousin
vgl. *abk* (= *vergleiche*) cf
Vibrator *m* vibrator
vibrieren *vi* to vibrate
Video (**-s**, **-s**) *nt* video
Videokamera *f* video camera
Videorekorder *m* video recorder
Videospiel *nt* video game
Vieh (**-(e)s**) *nt* cattle *pl*
viel *adj* a lot of, much ▶ *adv* a lot, much; **sehr ~** a great deal; **ziemlich ~** quite a lot; **noch (ein)mal so ~ (Zeit** *etc***)** as much (time *etc*) again; **einer zu ~** one too many; **viele Leute** a lot of people, many people; **~ zu wenig** much too little; **~ beschäftigt** very busy; **er geht ~ ins Kino** he goes a lot to the cinema; **~ besser** much better; **~ teurer** much more expensive; **~ zu ~** far too much; **in vielem** in many respects
vielleicht *adv* perhaps
vielmal, vielmals *adv* many times; **danke vielmals** many thanks
vielmehr *adv* rather
vielseitig *adj* (*Interessen*) varied; (*Mensch, Gerät*) versatile
vier *num* four; **auf allen vieren** on all fours
Viereck (**-(e)s**, **-e**) *nt* four-sided figure; (*Quadrat*) square
viereckig *adj* four-sided; (*quadratisch*) square
vierhundert *num* four hundred
viert *adj*: **wir gingen zu ~** four of us went
vierte(r, s) *adj* fourth
Viertel (**-s**, **-**) *nt* quarter; (*Stadtviertel*) district; **~ vor/nach drei** a quarter to/past three
Viertelfinale *nt* quarter-finals *pl*
vierteljährlich *adj* quarterly
Viertelstunde *f* quarter of an hour
vierzehn *num* fourteen; **in ~ Tagen** in a fortnight (BRIT), in two weeks (*US*)
vierzehntägig *adj* fortnightly
vierzehnte(r, s) *adj* fourteenth
vierzig *num* forty
Vietnam (**-s**) *nt* Vietnam
Villa (**-**, **Villen**) *f* villa
violett *adj* violet
Violine (**-**, **-n**) *f* violin
viral *adj* (*Comput*) viral
Virus (**-**, **Viren**) *m od nt* (*auch Comput*) virus
Visitenkarte *f* visiting card
Visum (**-s**, **Visa** *od* **Visen**) *nt* visa
Vitamin (**-s**, **-e**) *nt* vitamin
Vitrine (**-**, **-n**) *f* (*Schrank*) glass cabinet; (*Schaukasten*) showcase, display case
Vogel (**-s**, **Vögel**) *m* bird
Voicemail *f* (*Tel*) voice mail
Vokal (**-s**, **-e**) *m* vowel
Volk (**-(e)s**, **Völker**) *nt* people; (*Nation*) nation
Volksfest *nt* popular festival; (*Jahrmarkt*) fair
Volkshochschule *f* adult education centre (BRIT) *od* center (*US*)
Volkslied *nt* folk song
volkstümlich *adj* popular

voll *adj* full; **~ und ganz** completely
Vollbart *m* full beard
Vollbremsung *f* emergency stop
vollends *adv* completely
Volleyball (-(e)s) *m* volleyball
Vollgas *nt*: **mit ~** at full throttle; **~ geben** to step on it
völlig *adj* complete ▸ *adv* completely
volljährig *adj* of age
Vollkaskoversicherung *f* fully comprehensive insurance
vollkommen *adj* perfect; (*völlig*) complete ▸ *adv* completely
Vollkornbrot *nt* wholemeal (Brit) *od* whole-wheat (*US*) bread
voll|machen *vt* to fill (up)
Vollmacht *f* authority, power of attorney
Vollmilch *f* full-cream milk
Vollmond *m* full moon
Vollnarkose *f* general anaesthetic (Brit) *od* anesthetic (*US*)
Vollpension *f* full board
vollständig *adj* complete
voll|tanken *vt, vi* to fill up
Volltreffer *m* (*lit, fig*) bull's-eye
Vollwertkost *f* wholefoods *pl*
vollzählig *adj* complete
Volt (- *od* **-(e)s, -**) *nt* volt
Volumen (-s, - *od* **Volumina)** *nt* volume
vom = **von dem**

SCHLÜSSELWORT

von *präp +dat* **1** (*Ausgangspunkt*) from; **von ... bis** from ... to; **von morgens bis abends** from morning till night; **von ... nach ...** from ... to ...; **von ... an** from ...; **von ... aus** from ...; **von dort aus** from there; **etw von sich aus tun** to do sth of one's own accord; **von mir aus** (*umg*) if you like, I don't mind; **von wo/wann ...?** where/when ... from?
2 (*Ursache, im Passiv*) by; **ein Gedicht von Schiller** a poem by Schiller; **von etw müde** tired from sth
3 (*als Genitiv*) of; **ein Freund von mir** a friend of mine; **nett von dir** nice of you; **jeweils zwei von zehn** two out of every ten
4 (*über*) about; **er erzählte vom Urlaub** he talked about his holiday
5: **von wegen!** (*umg*) no way!

voneinander *adv* from each other

SCHLÜSSELWORT

vor *präp +dat* **1** (*räumlich*) in front of
2 (*zeitlich, Reihenfolge*) before; **ich war vor ihm da** I was there before him; **vor zwei Tagen** two days ago; **5 (Minuten) vor 4** 5 (minutes) to 4; **vor Kurzem** a little while ago
3 (*Ursache*) with; **vor Wut/Liebe** with rage/love; **vor Hunger sterben** to die of hunger; **vor lauter Arbeit** because of work
4: **vor allem, vor allen Dingen** above all
▸ *präp +akk* (*räumlich*) in front of
▸ *adv*: **vor und zurück** backwards and forwards

voran|gehen *unreg vi* to go ahead; **einer Sache** *dat* **~** to precede sth
voran|kommen *unreg vi* to make progress
voraus *adv* ahead; **im V~** in advance
Voraussage *f* prediction
voraus|sagen *vt* to predict
voraus|sehen *unreg vt* to foresee
voraus|setzen *vt* to assume; **vorausgesetzt, dass ...** provided that ...
Voraussetzung *f* requirement, prerequisite; **unter der ~, dass ...** on condition that ...
voraussichtlich *adv* probably
Vorbehalt *m* reservation
vor|behalten *unreg vt*: **sich/jdm etw ~** to reserve sth (for o.s.)/for sb
vorbei *adv* by, past; **aus und ~** over and done with
vorbei|bringen *unreg* (*umg*) *vt* to drop off
vorbei|gehen *unreg vi* to pass by, to go past
vorbei|kommen *unreg vi*: **bei jdm ~** to drop *od* call in on sb
vorbei|reden *vi*: **an etw** *dat* **~** to talk around sth
vor|bereiten *vt* to prepare
Vorbereitung *f* preparation
vor|bestellen *vt* to book (in advance)
Vorbestellung *f* advance booking
vor|beugen *vi +dat* to prevent
vorbeugend *adj* preventive
Vorbeugung *f* prevention

Vorbild *nt* model
vorbildlich *adj* model, ideal
Vorderachse *f* front axle
vordere(r, s) *adj* front
Vordergrund *m* foreground
Vorderseite *f* front (side)
Vordersitz *m* front seat
Vordruck *m* form
voreilig *adj* hasty, rash; **voreilige Schlüsse ziehen** to jump to conclusions
voreingenommen *adj* bias(s)ed
vor|enthalten *unreg vt*: **jdm etw ~** to withhold sth from sb
vorerst *adv* for the moment *od* present
vor|fahren *unreg vi* to drive (on) ahead; (*vors Haus etc*) to drive up
Vorfahrt *f* (*Aut*) right of way; **„~ (be) achten"** "give way" (BRIT), "yield" (US)
Vorfahrtsschild *nt* "give way" (BRIT) *od* "yield" (*US*) sign
Vorfahrtsstraße *f* major road
Vorfall *m* incident
vor|führen *vt* to show; (*Theaterstück, Kunststücke*): **(jdm) etw ~** to perform sth (to *od* in front of sb)
Vorgänger(in) (**-s**, **-**) *m(f)* predecessor
vor|gehen *unreg vi* (*voraus*) to go (on) ahead; (*nach vorn*) to go forward; (*handeln*) to act, to proceed; (*Uhr*) to be fast; (*Vorrang haben*) to take precedence; (*passieren*) to go on
Vorgehen (**-s**) *nt* action
Vorgesetzte(r) *f(m)* superior
vorgestern *adv* the day before yesterday
vor|haben *unreg vt* to intend; **hast du schon was vor?** have you got anything on?
vor|halten *unreg vt* to hold *od* put up; **jdm etw ~** to reproach sb for sth
Vorhand *f* forehand
vorhanden *adj* existing; (*erhältlich*) available
Vorhang *m* curtain
Vorhaut *f* (*Anat*) foreskin
vorher *adv* before(hand); **zwei Tage ~** two days before
Vorhersage *f* forecast
vorher|sehen *unreg vt* to foresee
vorhin *adv* not long ago, just now
vorinstalliert *adj* preinstalled
vor|kommen *unreg vi* to come forward; (*geschehen, sich finden*) to occur; (*scheinen*) to seem (to be); **sich** *dat* **dumm** *etc* **~** to feel stupid *etc*
Vorlage *f* model
vor|lassen *unreg vt* to admit; (*vorgehen lassen*) to allow to go in front
vorläufig *adj* temporary
vor|lesen *unreg vt* to read (out)
Vorlesung *f* (*Univ*) lecture
vorletzte(r, s) *adj* last but one
Vorliebe *f* preference
vor|machen *vt*: **jdm etw ~** to show sb how to do sth; **jdm etw ~** (*fig*) to fool sb
vor|merken *vt* to book; (*notieren*) to make note of
Vormittag *m* morning; **am ~** in the morning
vormittags *adv* in the morning, before noon
vorn *adv* in front; **von ~ anfangen** to start at the beginning; **nach ~** to the front; **er betrügt sie von ~ bis hinten** he deceives her right, left and centre
Vorname *m* first *od* Christian name
vornehm *adj* distinguished; (*Manieren etc*) refined; (*Kleid*) elegant
vor|nehmen *unreg vt*: **sich** *dat* **etw ~** to start on sth; (*beschließen*) to decide to do sth
vornherein *adv*: **von ~** from the start
Vorort *m* suburb
vorrangig *adj* primary
Vorrat *m* stock, supply
vorrätig *adj* in stock
Vorrecht *nt* privilege
Vorruhestand *m* early retirement
Vorsaison *f* early season
Vorsatz *m* intention; (*Jur*) intent
vorsätzlich *adj* intentional; (*Jur*) premeditated
Vorschau *f* (*Rundf*, *TV*) (programme (BRIT) *od* program (*US*)) preview; (*Film*) trailer
Vorschlag *m* suggestion, proposal
vor|schlagen *unreg vt* to suggest, to propose
vor|schreiben *unreg vt* (*befehlen*) to specify; **ich lasse mir nichts ~** I won't be dictated to
Vorschrift *f* regulation(s *pl*), rule(s *pl*); (*Anweisungen*) instruction(s *pl*)
vorschriftsmäßig *adv* as per regulations/instructions
Vorschule *f* nursery school

Vorsicht *f* caution, care; **~!** look out!; (*auf Schildern*) caution!; **~ Stufe!** mind the step!
vorsichtig *adj* careful
vorsichtshalber *adv* just in case
Vorsorge *f* precaution(s *pl*)
Vorsorgeprinzip *nt* precautionary principle
Vorsorgeuntersuchung *f* medical check-up
vorsorglich *adv* as a precaution
Vorspann *m* (*Film, TV*) opening credits *pl*
Vorspeise *f* starter
Vorsprung *m* projection; (*fig*) advantage, start
vor|stellen *vt* to put forward; (*vor etw*) to put in front; (*bekannt machen*) to introduce; **sich** *dat* **etw ~** to imagine sth
Vorstellung *f* (*Bekanntmachen*) introduction; (*Theat etc*) performance; (*Gedanke*) idea
Vorstellungsgespräch *nt* interview
vor|täuschen *vt* to feign
Vorteil (**-s**, **-e**) *m*: **~ (gegenüber)** advantage (over); **die Vor- und Nachteile** the pros and cons
vorteilhaft *adj* advantageous
Vortrag (**-(e)s**, **Vorträge**) *m* talk, lecture; **einen ~ halten** to give a lecture *od* talk
vorüber *adv* past, over
vorüber|gehen *unreg vi* to pass (by)
vorübergehend *adj* temporary ▶ *adv* temporarily, for the time being
Vorurteil *nt* prejudice
Vorverkauf *m* advance booking
vor|verlegen *vt* (*Termin*) to bring forward
Vorwahl *f* (*Tel*) dialling (BRIT) *od* area (*US*) code
Vorwand (**-(e)s**, **Vorwände**) *m* pretext
vorwärts *adv* forward
vorwärts|gehen *unreg vi* to progress
vorweg *adv* in advance
vorweg|nehmen *unreg vt* to anticipate
vor|werfen *unreg vt*: **jdm etw ~** to accuse sb of sth
vorwiegend *adv* predominantly
Vorwort (**-(e)s**, **-e**) *nt* preface
Vorwurf (**-(e)s**, **Vorwürfe**) *m* reproach; **jdm/sich Vorwürfe machen** to reproach sb/o.s.
vorwurfsvoll *adj* reproachful
vor|zeigen *vt* to show
vorzeitig *adj* premature
vor|ziehen *unreg vt* (*lieber haben*) to prefer
Vorzug *m* preference; (*gute Eigenschaft*) merit; (*Vorteil*) advantage
vorzüglich *adj* excellent
vulgär *adj* vulgar
Vulkan (**-s**, **-e**) *m* volcano
Vulkanausbruch *m* volcanic eruption

W. *abk* (= *West(en)*) W
Waage (**-**, **-n**) *f* scales *pl*; (*Astrol*) Libra
waagerecht *adj* horizontal
wach *adj* awake; **~ werden** to wake up
Wache (**-**, **-n**) *f* guard
Wachs (**-es**, **-e**) *nt* wax
wachsen[1] *unreg vi* to grow
wachsen[2] *vt* (*Skier*) to wax
Wachstum (**-s**) *nt* growth
Wachtel (**-**, **-n**) *f* quail
Wächter (**-s**, **-**) *m* guard; (*Museumswächter, Parkplatzwächter*) attendant
wackelig *adj* shaky, wobbly
Wackelkontakt *m* loose connection
wackeln *vi* (*Stuhl*) to be wobbly; (*Zahn, Schraube*) to be loose; **mit den Hüften/dem Schwanz ~** to wiggle one's hips/wag its tail
Wade (**-**, **-n**) *f* (*Anat*) calf
Waffe (**-**, **-n**) *f* weapon
Waffel (**-**, **-n**) *f* waffle; (*Eiswaffel*) wafer
wagen *vt* to risk; **es ~, etw zu tun** to dare to do sth
Wagen (**-s**, **-**) *m* vehicle; (*Auto*) car; (*Eisenb*) car, carriage (BRIT)
Wagenheber (**-s**, **-**) *m* jack
Wahl (**-**, **-en**) *f* choice; (*Pol*) election
wählen *vt* to choose; (*Pol*) to elect, to vote for; (*Tel*) to dial ▶ *vi* to choose; (*Pol*) to vote; (*Tel*) to dial
Wähler(in) (**-s**, **-**) *m(f)* voter
wählerisch *adj* choosy
Wahlkampf *m* election campaign
wahllos *adv* at random
Wahnsinn *m* madness
wahnsinnig *adj* insane, mad ▶ *adv* (*umg*) incredibly
wahr *adj* true; **das darf doch nicht ~ sein!** I don't believe it; **nicht ~?** that's right, isn't it?
während *präp +gen* during ▶ *konj* while
währenddessen *adv* meanwhile
Wahrheit *f* truth
wahr|nehmen *unreg vt* to perceive
Wahrsager *m* fortune-teller
wahrscheinlich *adj* probable ▶ *adv* probably
Wahrscheinlichkeit *f* probability
Währung *f* currency
Wahrzeichen *nt* symbol
Waise (**-**, **-n**) *f* orphan
Wal (**-(e)s**, **-e**) *m* whale
Wald (**-(e)s**, **Wälder**) *m* wood(s *pl*); (*groß*) forest
Waldbrand *m* forest fire
Waldsterben *nt loss of trees due to pollution*
Wales *nt* Wales
Waliser(in) (**-s**, **-**) *m(f)* Welshman, Welshwoman
walisisch *adj* Welsh
Wall (**-(e)s**, **Wälle**) *m* embankment
Wallfahrt *f* pilgrimage
Walnuss *f* walnut
Walross *nt* walrus
wälzen *vt* to roll (over); (*Bücher*) to hunt through; (*Probleme*) to deliberate on ▶ *vr* to wallow; (*vor Schmerzen*) to roll about; (*im Bett*) to toss and turn
Walzer (**-s**, **-**) *m* waltz
Wand (**-**, **Wände**) *f* wall; (*Trennwand*) partition; (*Felswand*) (rock) face
Wandel (**-s**) *m* change
wandeln *vt, vr* to change
Wanderer (**-s**, **-**) *m*, **Wanderin** *f* hiker
Wanderkarte *f* hiker's map
wandern *vi* to hike; (*Blick*) to wander; (*Gedanken*) to stray
Wanderung *f* hike
Wanderweg *m* trail, (foot)path
Wandmalerei *f* mural painting
Wandschrank *m* cupboard
wandte *etc vb siehe* **wenden**
Wange (**-**, **-n**) *f* cheek
wann *adv* when; **seit ~ bist/hast du ...?** how long have you been/have you had ...?
Wanne (**-**, **-n**) *f* tub
Wappen (**-s**, **-**) *nt* coat of arms

war *etc vb siehe* **sein**
warb *etc vb siehe* **werben**
Ware (**-**, **-n**) *f* ware ■ **Waren** *pl* goods *pl*
Warenhaus *nt* department store
Warenprobe *f* sample
Warenzeichen *nt* trademark
warf *etc vb siehe* **werfen**
warm *adj* warm; (*Essen*) hot; **mir ist ~** I'm warm; **~ laufen** (*Aut*) to warm up; *siehe auch* **warmhalten**
Wärme (**-**, **-n**) *f* warmth
wärmen *vt*, *vr* to warm (up), to heat (up) ▶ *vi* (*Kleidung*, *Sonne*) to be warm
Wärmflasche *f* hot-water bottle
warm|halten *unreg vt*: **sich** *dat* **jdn ~** (*fig*) to keep in with sb
Warnblinkanlage *f* (*Aut*) hazard warning lights *pl*
Warndreieck *nt* warning triangle
warnen *vt* to warn
Warnung *f* warning
Warnweste *f* hi-vis vest, reflective vest
warten *vi* to wait ▶ *vt* (*Auto*, *Maschine*) to service; **~ auf** +*akk* to wait for
Wärter(in) (**-s**, **-**) *m*(*f*) attendant
Wartesaal *m* (*Eisenb*) waiting room
Wartung *f* (*von Auto*, *Maschine*) servicing
warum *adv* why
Warze (**-**, **-n**) *f* wart
was *pron* what; (*umg*: *etwas*) something; **das, ~ ...** that which ...; **~ für ...?** what sort *od* kind of ...?; **alles, ~ er hat** everything he's got
Waschanlage *f* (*für Autos*) car wash
waschbar *adj* washable
Waschbecken *nt* washbasin
Wäsche (**-**, **-n**) *f* washing; (*Bettwäsche*) linen; (*Unterwäsche*) underwear; **in der ~** in the wash
Wäscheklammer *f* clothes peg (Brit), clothespin (US)
Wäscheleine *f* washing line (Brit), clothes line (US)
waschen *unreg vt*, *vi* to wash ▶ *vr* to (have a) wash; **sich** *dat* **die Hände ~** to wash one's hands; **~ und legen** (*Haare*) to shampoo and set
Wäscherei *f* laundry
Wäschetrockner *m* tumble-drier
Waschlappen *m* face cloth *od* flannel (Brit), washcloth (US); (*umg*) softy
Waschmaschine *f* washing machine
Waschmittel *nt* detergent
Waschsalon *m* Launderette® (Brit), Laundromat® (US)
Waschstraße *f* car wash
Wasser (**-s**, **-** *od* **Wässer**) *nt no pl* water
wasserdicht *adj* watertight; (*Stoff*, *Uhr*) waterproof
Wasserfall *m* waterfall
Wasserfarbe *f* watercolour (Brit), watercolor (US)
Wasserhahn *m* tap, faucet (US)
wässerig *adj* watery
Wasserkessel *m* kettle
Wasserleitung *f* water pipe
wasserlöslich *adj* water-soluble
Wassermann *m* (*Astrol*) Aquarius
Wassermelone *f* water melon
wasserscheu *adj* afraid of water
Wasserski *nt* water-skiing
Wasserspiegel *m* surface of the water; (*Wasserstand*) water level
Wassersport *m* water sports *pl*
Wasserverbrauch *m* water consumption
Wasserverschmutzung *f* water pollution
Wasserwaage *f* spirit level
Wasserwerk *nt* waterworks
waten *vi* to wade
Watt[1] (**-(e)s**, **-en**) *nt* (*Geog*) mud flats *pl*
Watt[2] (**-s**, **-**) *nt* (*Elek*) watt
Watte (**-**, **-n**) *f* cotton wool (Brit), absorbent cotton (US)
Wattestäbchen *nt* cotton(-wool) swab
WC (**-s**, **-s**) *nt abk* (= *Wasserklosett*) WC
Web *nt* (*Comput*): **das ~** the Web
Webadresse *f* (*Comput*) web address
Webinar *nt* (*Comput*) webinar
Webmail *nt* (*Comput*) webmail
Webseite *f* Web page
Wechsel (**-s**, **-**) *m* change
Wechselgeld *nt* change
wechselhaft *adj* (*Wetter*) variable
Wechseljahre *pl* menopause
Wechselkurs *m* rate of exchange
wechseln *vt* to change; (*Blicke*) to exchange ▶ *vi* to change
Wechselstrom *m* alternating current
Wechselstube *f* bureau de change
wecken *vt* to wake (up)
Wecker (**-s**, **-**) *m* alarm clock
Weckruf *m* (*Tel*) alarm call
wedeln *vi* (*mit Schwanz*) to wag; (*Ski*) to wedel
weder *konj* neither; **~ ... noch ...** neither ... nor ...

weg *adv* away; (*los, ab*) off; **er war schon ~** he had already left; **Finger ~!** hands off!
Weg (**-(e)s**, **-e**) *m* way; (*Pfad*) path; (*Route*) route; **sich auf den ~ machen** to be on one's way; **jdm aus dem ~ gehen** to keep out of sb's way
wegbereitend *adj* cutting-edge
weg|bleiben *unreg vi* to stay away
wegen *präp* (*+dat od gen*) because of
weg|fahren *unreg vi* to drive away; (*abfahren*) to leave
Wegfahrsperre *f* (*Aut*): **(elektronische) ~** (electronic) immobilizer
weg|gehen *unreg vi* to go away
weg|kommen *unreg vi*: **(bei etw) gut/schlecht ~** (*umg*) to come off well/badly (with sth)
weg|lassen *unreg vt* to leave out
weg|laufen *unreg vi* to run away *od* off
weg|legen *vt* to put aside
weg|machen (*umg*) *vt* to get rid of
weg|müssen *unreg* (*umg*) *vi* to have to go
weg|nehmen *unreg vt* to take away
weg|räumen *vt* to clear away
weg|schmeißen *unreg vt* to throw away
weg|tun *unreg vt* to put away
Wegweiser (**-s**, **-**) *m* signpost
weg|werfen *unreg vt* to throw away
weg|ziehen *unreg vi* to move away
weh *adj* sore
wehen *vt*, *vi* to blow; (*Fahnen*) to flutter
Wehen *pl* (*Med*) contractions *pl*
Wehrdienst *m see note*

WEHRDIENST

Wehrdienst refers to military service, which was compulsory until 2011. All men over the age of 18 were conscripted and those declared fit for service had to spend nine months in the *Bundeswehr* (armed forces). Conscientious objectors were allowed to opt out of military service and could instead spend the period carrying out *Zivildienst* (community service).

wehren *vr* to defend o.s.
weh|tun *unreg vt*: **jdm/sich ~** to hurt sb/o.s.
Weibchen *nt* (*Zool*) female
weiblich *adj* feminine; (*Biol*) female
weich *adj* soft; (*Ei*) soft-boiled
Weichkäse *m* soft cheese
weichlich *adj* soft
Weichspüler (**-s**, **-**) *m* fabric conditioner
Weide (**-**, **-n**) *f* (*Baum*) willow; (*Gras*) pasture
weigern *vr* to refuse
Weigerung *f* refusal
Weiher (**-s**, **-**) *m* pond
Weihnachten (**-**) *nt* Christmas
Weihnachtsabend *m* Christmas Eve
Weihnachtsbaum *m* Christmas tree
Weihnachtsferien *pl* Christmas holidays *pl* (BRIT), Christmas vacation *sing* (US)
Weihnachtsgeld *nt* Christmas bonus
Weihnachtsgeschenk *nt* Christmas present
Weihnachtslied *nt* Christmas carol
Weihnachtsmann *m* Father Christmas (BRIT), Santa Claus
Weihnachtsmarkt *m* Christmas market

WEIHNACHTSMARKT

The **Weihnachtsmarkt** is a market held in most large towns in German-speaking countries in the weeks prior to Christmas. People visit it to buy presents, toys and Christmas decorations, and to enjoy the festive atmosphere. Food and drink associated with the Christmas festivities can also be eaten and drunk there, for example, gingerbread and mulled wine.

Weihnachtstag *m*: **(erster) ~** Christmas day; **zweiter ~** Boxing Day (BRIT)
weil *konj* because
Weile (**-**) *f* while, short time
Wein (**-(e)s**, **-e**) *m* wine; (*Pflanze*) vine
Weinbeere *f* grape
Weinberg *m* vineyard
Weinbergschnecke *f* snail
Weinbrand *m* brandy
weinen *vt*, *vi* to cry
Weinglas *nt* wine glass
Weinkarte *f* wine list
Weinlese *f* vintage
Weinprobe *f* wine tasting

Weintraube *f* grape
weise *adj* wise
Weise (-, **-n**) *f* manner, way; **auf diese ~** in this way
weisen *unreg vt* to show
Weisheit *f* wisdom
Weisheitszahn *m* wisdom tooth
weiß *adj* white
Weißbrot *nt* white bread
Weißkohl *m* (white) cabbage
Weißwein *m* white wine
weit *adj* wide; (*Begriff*) broad; (*Reise, Wurf*) long ▸ *adv* far; **~ verbreitet** widespread; **wie ~ ist es ...?** how far is it ...?; **das geht zu ~** that's going too far; **~ gefehlt!** far from it!; **von Weitem** from a long way off
weiter *adj* wider; (*zusätzlich*) further ▸ *adv* further; **immer ~** on and on; (*Anweisung*) keep on (going); **und so ~** and so on; **~ nichts/niemand** nothing/nobody else
weiter|arbeiten *vi* to go on working
Weiterbildung *f* further education
weiter|empfehlen *unreg vt* to recommend (to others)
weiter|erzählen *vt* to pass on
weiter|gehen *unreg vi* to go on
weiterhin *adv*: **etw ~ tun** to go on doing sth
weiter|machen *vt, vi* to continue
weiter|reisen *vi* to continue one's journey
weitertwittern *vi* (*auf Twitter*) to retweet
weitgehend *adj* considerable ▸ *adv* largely
weitsichtig *adj* (*lit*) long-sighted (Brit), far-sighted (*US*); (*fig*) far-sighted
Weitsprung *m* long jump
Weitwinkelobjektiv *nt* (*Phot*) wide-angle lens
Weizen (**-s**, **-**) *m* wheat
Weizenbier *nt light, fizzy wheat beer*

SCHLÜSSELWORT

welche(r, s) *interrog pron* which; **welcher von beiden?** which (one) of the two?; **welchen hast du genommen?** which (one) did you take?; **welche Freude!** what joy! ▸ *indef pron* some; (*in Fragen*) any; **ich habe welche** I have some; **haben Sie welche?** do you have any?
▸ *rel pron* (*bei Menschen*) who; (*bei Sachen*) which, that; **welche(r, s) auch immer** whoever/whichever/whatever

welk *adj* withered
welken *vi* to wither
Welle (-, **-n**) *f* wave
Wellengang *m*: **starker ~** heavy sea(s) *od* swell
Wellenlänge *f* (*lit, fig*) wavelength
Wellensittich *m* budgerigar
Welpe (**-n**, **-n**) *m* pup
Welt (-, **-en**) *f* world; **auf der ~** in the world; **auf die ~ kommen** to be born
Weltall *nt* universe
Weltkrieg *m* world war
Weltmacht *f* world power
Weltmeister *m* world champion
Weltmeisterschaft *f* world *od* world's (*US*) championship; (*Fussball etc*) World Cup
Weltraum *m* space
Weltreise *f* trip round the world
Weltrekord *m* world record
Weltstadt *f* metropolis
weltweit *adj* world-wide
wem *dat von* **wer** ▸ *pron* to whom
wen *akk von* **wer** ▸ *pron* whom
Wende (-, **-n**) *f* turn; (*Veränderung*) change; **die ~** (*Pol*) (the) reunification (of Germany)
Wendekreis *m* (*Aut*) turning circle
Wendeltreppe *f* spiral staircase
wenden *unreg vt, vi, vr* to turn; **bitte ~!** please turn over; **sich an jdn ~** to go/come to sb
wenig *adj, adv* little; **ein ~** a little; **er hat zu ~ Geld** he doesn't have enough money
wenige *pl* few *pl*; **in wenigen Tagen** in (just) a few days
wenigste(r, s) *adj* least
wenigstens *adv* at least
wenn *konj* if; (*zeitlich*) when; **~ auch ...** even if ...; **~ ich doch ...** if only I ...
wennschon *adv*: **na ~!** so what?
wer *pron* who; **~ von euch?** which (one) of you?
Werbefernsehen *nt* commercial television
Werbegeschenk *nt* promotional gift
werben *unreg vt* to win; (*Mitglied*) to recruit ▸ *vi* to advertise

Werbespot *m* commercial
Werbung *f* advertising

SCHLÜSSELWORT

werden (*pt* **wurde**, *pp* **geworden** *od bei Passiv* **worden**) *vi* to become; **was ist aus ihm/aus der Sache geworden?** what became of him/it?; **es ist nichts/gut geworden** it came to nothing/turned out well; **es wird Nacht/Tag** it's getting dark/light; **mir wird kalt** I'm getting cold; **mir wird schlecht** I feel ill; **Erster werden** to come *od* be first; **das muss anders werden** that will have to change; **rot/zu Eis werden** to turn red/to ice; **was willst du (mal) werden?** what do you want to be?; **die Fotos sind gut geworden** the photos turned out well
▶ *Hilfsverb* **1** (*bei Futur*): **er wird es tun** he will *od* he'll do it; **er wird das nicht tun** he will not *od* he won't do it; **es wird gleich regnen** it's going to rain any moment
2 (*bei Konjunktiv*): **ich würde ...** I would ...; **er würde gern ...** he would *od* he'd like to ...; **ich würde lieber ...** I would *od* I'd rather ...
3 (*bei Vermutung*): **sie wird in der Küche sein** she will be in the kitchen
4 (*bei Passiv*): **gebraucht werden** to be used; **er ist erschossen worden** he has *od* he's been shot; **mir wurde gesagt, dass ...** I was told that ...

werfen *unreg vt* to throw
Werft (-, **-en**) *f* shipyard
Werk (**-(e)s**, **-e**) *nt* work; (*Fabrik, Mechanismus*) works *pl*
Werkstatt (-, **-stätten**) *f* workshop; (*Aut*) garage
Werktag *m* working day
werktags *adv* on working days
Werkzeug *nt* tool
Werkzeugkasten *m* toolbox
wert *adj* worth; **das ist nichts/viel ~** it's not worth anything/it's worth a lot
Wert (**-(e)s**, **-e**) *m* worth; (*Fin*) value; **~ legen auf** *+akk* to attach importance to; **es hat doch keinen ~** it's useless
Wertangabe *f* declaration of value
Wertgegenstand *m* article of value
wertlos *adj* worthless
Wertstoff *m* recyclable waste
wertvoll *adj* valuable
Wesen (**-s**, **-**) *nt* being; (*Natur, Character*) nature
wesentlich *adj* significant; (*beträchtlich*) considerable; **im Wesentlichen** essentially
weshalb *adv* why
Wespe (-, **-n**) *f* wasp
wessen *gen von* **wer** ▶ *pron* whose
Wessi *m see note*

WESSI

A **Wessi** is a colloquial and often derogatory word used to describe a German from the former West Germany.

Westdeutschland *nt* (*Pol: früher*) West Germany; (*Geog*) Western Germany
Weste (-, **-n**) *f* waistcoat, vest (*US*)
Westen (**-s**) *m* west
Westeuropa *nt* Western Europe
westlich *adj* western
weswegen *adv* why
Wettbewerb *m* competition
Wettbüro *nt* betting office
Wette (-, **-n**) *f* bet; **eine ~ abschließen** to make a bet
wetten *vt, vi* to bet; **ich wette mit dir um 50 Euro** I'll bet you 50 euros
Wetter (**-s**, **-**) *nt* weather
Wetterbericht *m* weather report
Wetterkarte *f* weather chart
Wetterlage *f* (weather) situation
Wettervorhersage *f* weather forecast
Wettkampf *m* contest
Wettlauf *m* race
Wettrennen *nt* race
WG *abk* = **Wohngemeinschaft**
Whirlpool® (**-s**, **-s**) *m* jacuzzi®
Whisky (**-s**, **-s**) *m* whisky (BRIT), whiskey (*US*, IRELAND)
wichtig *adj* important
wickeln *vt* to wind; (*Kind*) to change; **jdn/etw in etw** *akk* **~** to wrap sb/sth in sth
Wickeltisch *m* baby's changing table
Widder (**-s**, **-**) *m* ram; (*Astrol*) Aries
wider *präp +akk* against
widerlich *adj* disgusting
widerrufen *unreg vt untr* to retract; (*Anordnung*) to revoke

widersprechen *unreg vi untr*: **jdm ~** to contradict sb
Widerspruch *m* contradiction
Widerstand *m* resistance
widerstandsfähig *adj* resistant
widerwärtig *adj* nasty, horrid
widerwillig *adj* unwilling, reluctant
widmen *vt* to dedicate ▶ *vr* to devote o.s.
Widmung *f* dedication

 **SCHLÜSSELWORT**

wie *adv* how; **wie groß/schnell?** how big/fast?; **wie viel** how much; **wie viele Menschen** how many people; **wie wärs?** how about it?; **wie ist er?** what's he like?; **wie gut du das kannst!** you're very good at it; **wie bitte?** pardon? (*Brit*), pardon me? (*US*); (*entrüstet*) I beg your pardon!; **und wie!** and how!; **wie weit** to what extent
▶ *konj* **1** (*bei Vergleichen*): **so schön wie ...** as beautiful as ...; **wie ich schon sagte** as I said; **wie du** like you; **singen wie ein ...** to sing like a ...; **wie (zum Beispiel)** such as (for example)
2 (*zeitlich*): **wie er das hörte, ging er** when he heard that he left; **er hörte, wie der Regen fiel** he heard the rain falling

wieder *adv* again; **~ da sein** to be back (again); **~ ein(e) ...** another ...; **da sieht man mal ~ ...** it just shows ...
wieder|bekommen *unreg vt* to get back
wiederbeschreibbar *adj* (*CD, DVD*) rewritable
wiederholen *vt untr* to repeat
Wiederholung *f* repetition
Wiederhören *nt*: **auf ~** (*Tel*) goodbye
wieder|sehen *unreg vt* to see again; **auf W~** goodbye
Wiedervereinigung *f* reunification
Wiege (**-, -n**) *f* cradle
wiegen *unreg vt, vi* to weigh
Wien (**-s**) *nt* Vienna
wies *etc vb siehe* **weisen**
Wiese (**-, -n**) *f* meadow
Wiesel (**-s, -**) *nt* weasel
wieso *adv* why
wievielmal *adv* how often
wievielte(r, s) *adj*: **zum wievielten Mal?** how many times?; **den Wievielten haben wir?** what's the date?
wieweit *adv* to what extent
Wi-Fi *nt* Wi-Fi
Wiki *nt* (*Internet*) wiki
wild *adj* wild
Wild (**-(e)s**) *nt* game
wildfremd (*umg*) *adj*: **ein wildfremder Mensch** a complete *od* total stranger
Wildleder *nt* suede
Wildpark *m* game park
Wildschwein *nt* (wild) boar
Wille (**-ns, -n**) *m* will
willen *präp +gen*: **um ... ~** for the sake of ...
willkommen *adj* welcome; **jdn ~ heißen** to welcome sb
Wimper (**-, -n**) *f* eyelash
Wimperntusche *f* mascara
Wind (**-(e)s, -e**) *m* wind
Windel (**-, -n**) *f* nappy (*Brit*), diaper (*US*)
windig *adj* windy; (*fig*) dubious
Windjacke *f* windcheater
Windmühle *f* windmill
Windpark *m* wind farm
Windpocken *pl* chickenpox *sing*
Windschutzscheibe *f* (*Aut*) windscreen (*Brit*), windshield (*US*)
Windstärke *f* wind force
Windsurfen *nt* windsurfing
Winkel (**-s, -**) *m* (*Math*) angle; (*Gerät*) set square; (*in Raum*) corner
winken *vt, vi* to wave
Winter (**-s, -**) *m* winter
winterlich *adj* wintry
Winterreifen *m* winter tyre (*Brit*) *od* tire (*US*)
Winterschlussverkauf *m* winter sale
Wintersport *m* winter sports *pl*
winzig *adj* tiny
wir *pron* we; **~ alle** all of us, we all; **~ nicht** not us
Wirbel (**-s, -**) *m* whirl; (*Trubel*) hurly-burly; (*Aufsehen*) fuss; (*Anat*) vertebra
Wirbelsäule *f* spine
wirken *vi* to have an effect; (*erfolgreich sein*) to work; (*scheinen*) to seem
wirklich *adj* real
Wirklichkeit *f* reality
wirksam *adj* effective
Wirkung *f* effect
wirr *adj* confused

Wirrwarr (**-s**) *m* disorder, chaos
Wirsing, Wirsingkohl (**-s**) *m* savoy cabbage
Wirt (**-(e)s**, **-e**) *m* landlord
Wirtin *f* landlady
Wirtschaft *f* (*Gaststätte*) pub; (*eines Landes*) economy
wirtschaftlich *adj* economical; (*Pol*) economic
Wirtschaftslehre *f* business studies, economics
Wirtshaus *nt* inn
wischen *vt* to wipe
Wischer (**-s**, **-**) *m* (*Aut*) wiper
wissen *unreg vt*, *vi* to know; **woher weißt du das?** how do you know?
Wissen (**-s**) *nt* knowledge
Wissenschaft *f* science
Wissenschaftler(in) (**-s**, **-**) *m(f)* scientist; (*Geisteswissenschaftler*) academic
wissenschaftlich *adj* scientific
Witwe (**-**, **-n**) *f* widow
Witwer (**-s**, **-**) *m* widower
Witz (**-es**, **-e**) *m* joke; **mach keine Witze!** you're kidding!
witzig *adj* funny
W-LAN *m abk* (*Comput*: = *Wireless Local Area Network*) WLAN
wo *adv* where ▶ *konj* (*wenn*) if; **im Augenblick, wo ...** the moment (that) ...; **die Zeit, wo ...** the time when ...
woanders *adv* elsewhere
wobei *adv* (*rel*) ... in/by/with which; (*interrog*) how; **~ mir gerade einfällt ...** which reminds me ...
Woche (**-**, **-n**) *f* week; **einmal die ~** once a week
Wochenende *nt* weekend
Wochenendhaus *nt* weekend house
Wochenkarte *f* weekly ticket
wochenlang *adv* for weeks
Wochenmarkt *m* weekly market
Wochentag *m* weekday
wöchentlich *adj*, *adv* weekly
Wodka (**-s**, **-s**) *m* vodka
wodurch *adv* (*rel*) through which; (*interrog*) what ... through
wofür *adv* (*rel*) for which; (*interrog*) what ... for
wog *etc vb siehe* **wiegen**
woher *adv* where ... from
wohin *adv* where ... to; **~ man auch schaut** wherever you look

SCHLÜSSELWORT

wohl *adv* **1** well; (*behaglich*) at ease, comfortable; **bei dem Gedanken ist mir nicht wohl** I'm not very happy at the thought; **wohl oder übel** whether one likes it or not
2 (*gewiss*) certainly
3 (*vielleicht*) perhaps; **sie ist wohl zu Hause** she's probably at home; **das ist doch wohl nicht dein Ernst!** surely you're not serious!; **das mag wohl sein** that may well be; **ob das wohl stimmt?** I wonder if that's true; **er weiß das sehr wohl** he knows that perfectly well

Wohl (**-(e)s**) *nt* welfare; **zum ~!** cheers!
wohlbehalten *adj* safe and sound
wohl|fühlen *vr* (*zufrieden*) to feel happy; (*gesundheitlich*) to feel well
Wohlstand *m* prosperity
wohl|tun *unreg vi*: **jdm ~** to do sb good
Wohlwollen (**-s**) *nt* good will
Wohnanlage *f* housing complex; (BRIT) housing estate; **bewachte ~** gated community
Wohnblock (**-s**, **-s**) *m* block of flats (BRIT), apartment house (*US*)
wohnen *vi* to live
Wohngemeinschaft *f* people sharing a flat (BRIT) *od* apartment (*US*)
wohnhaft *adj* resident
Wohnmobil *nt* motor caravan (BRIT), motor home (*US*)
Wohnort *m* domicile
Wohnsitz *m* place of residence
Wohnung *f* flat (BRIT), apartment (*US*)
Wohnwagen *m* caravan (BRIT), trailer (*US*)
Wohnzimmer *nt* living room
Wolf (**-(e)s**, **Wölfe**) *m* wolf; (*Tech*) shredder; (*Fleischwolf*) mincer (BRIT), grinder (*US*)
Wolke (**-**, **-n**) *f* cloud
Wolkenkratzer *m* skyscraper
wolkenlos *adj* cloudless
wolkig *adj* cloudy
Wolle (**-**, **-n**) *f* wool

SCHLÜSSELWORT

wollen (*pt* **wollte**, *pp* **gewollt** *od als Hilfsverb* **wollen**) *vt*, *vi* to want; **ich will nach Hause** I want to go home;

er will nicht he doesn't want to; **sie wollte das nicht** she didn't want it; **wenn du willst** if you like; **ich will, dass du mir zuhörst** I want you to listen to me
▶ *Hilfsverb*: **er will ein Haus kaufen** he wants to buy a house; **ich wollte, ich wäre ...** I wish I were ...; **etw gerade tun wollen** to be just about to *od* going to do sth

womit *adv* what ... with; **~ kann ich dienen?** what can I do for you?
womöglich *adv* probably, I suppose
woran *adv*: **~ denkst du?** what are you thinking of?; **~ liegt das?** what's the reason for it?
worauf *adv* (*zeitlich*) whereupon; **~ wartest du?** what are you waiting for?
woraus *adv*: **~ ist das gemacht?** what is it made of?
Wort (**-(e)s**, **Wörter** *od* **-e**) *nt* word; **jdn beim ~ nehmen** to take sb at his word; **mit anderen Worten** in other words
Wörterbuch *nt* dictionary
wörtlich *adj* literal
worüber *adv*: **~ redet sie?** what is she talking about?
worum *adv*: **~ handelt es sich?** what's it about?
worunter *adv*: **~ leidet er?** what is he suffering from?
wovon *adv* (*rel*) from which; **~ redest du?** what are you talking about?
wozu *adv* (*rel*) to/for which; (*interrog*) what ... for/to; (*warum*) why; **~ soll das gut sein?** what's the point of that?
Wrack (**-(e)s**, **-s**) *nt* wreck
Wucher (**-s**) *m* profiteering
wuchs *etc vb siehe* **wachsen**[1]
wühlen *vi* to scrabble; (*Tier*) to root; (*Maulwurf*) to burrow
Wühltisch *m* bargain counter
wund *adj* sore
Wunde (**-**, **-n**) *f* wound
Wunder (**-s**, **-**) *nt* miracle; **es ist kein ~** it's no wonder
wunderbar *adj* wonderful, marvellous (BRIT), marvelous (*US*)
Wunderkerze *f* sparkler
wundern *vt* to surprise ▶ *vr*: **sich ~ über** *+akk* to be surprised at
wunderschön *adj* beautiful
wundervoll *adj* wonderful
Wundstarrkrampf *m* tetanus
Wunsch (**-(e)s**, **Wünsche**) *m* wish
wünschen *vt* to wish; **sich** *dat* **etw ~** to want sth
wünschenswert *adj* desirable
wurde *etc vb siehe* **werden**
Wurf (**-(e)s**, **Würfe**) *m* throw; (*Junge*) litter
Würfel (**-s**, **-**) *m* dice; (*Math*) cube
würfeln *vi* to throw (the dice); (*Würfel spielen*) to play dice ▶ *vt* (*Zahl*) to throw; (*Koch*) to dice
Würfelzucker *m* lump sugar
Wurm (**-(e)s**, **Würmer**) *m* worm
Wurst (**-**, **Würste**) *f* sausage; **das ist mir ~** (*umg*) I don't care
Würstchen *nt* frankfurter
Würze (**-**, **-n**) *f* seasoning
Wurzel (**-**, **-n**) *f* root
würzen *vt* to season; (*würzig machen*) to spice
würzig *adj* spicy
wusch *etc vb siehe* **waschen**
wusste *etc vb siehe* **wissen**
wüst *adj* untidy, messy; (*ausschweifend*) wild; (*öde*) waste; (*umg*: *heftig*) terrible
Wüste (**-**, **-n**) *f* desert
Wut (**-**) *f* rage, fury; **eine ~ (auf jdn/etw) haben** to be furious (with sb/sth)
wütend *adj* furious, enraged

x

X-Beine *pl* knock-knees *pl*
x-beliebig *adj* any (... whatever); **ein x-beliebiges Buch** any book (you like)
x-mal *adv* umpteen times

y

Yoga (**-(s)**) *m od nt* yoga

Z

zackig *adj* jagged; (*umg: Tempo*) brisk
zaghaft *adj* timid
zäh *adj* tough; (*Flüssigkeit*) thick
Zahl (**-**, **-en**) *f* number
zahlbar *adj* payable
zahlen *vt*, *vi* to pay; **~ bitte!** the bill *od* check (*US*) please!
zählen *vt* to count ▶ *vi*: **~ auf** *+akk* to count on; **~ zu** to be numbered among
Zahlenschloss *nt* combination lock
Zähler (**-s**, **-**) *m* (*Tech*) meter
zahlreich *adj* numerous
Zahlung *f* payment
Zahlungsanweisung *f* transfer order
zahm *adj* tame
zähmen *vt* to tame
Zahn (**-(e)s**, **Zähne**) *m* tooth
Zahnarzt *m*, **Zahnärztin** *f* dentist
Zahnbürste *f* toothbrush
Zahncreme *f* toothpaste
Zahnersatz *m* denture
Zahnfleisch *nt* gums *pl*
Zahnpasta *f*, **Zahnpaste** *f* toothpaste
Zahnradbahn *f* rack railway (BRIT) *od* railroad (*US*)
Zahnschmerzen *pl* toothache *sing*
Zahnseide *f* dental floss
Zahnspange *f* brace
Zahnstocher (**-s**, **-**) *m* toothpick
Zange (**-**, **-n**) *f* pliers *pl*; (*Zuckerzange etc*) tongs *pl*; (*Beißzange, Zool*) pincers *pl*; (*Med*) forceps *pl*
zanken *vi*, *vr* to quarrel
Zäpfchen *nt* (*Anat*) uvula; (*Med*) suppository
zapfen *vt* to tap
Zapfsäule *f* petrol (BRIT) *od* gas (*US*) pump
zappeln *vi* to wriggle; (*unruhig*) to fidget
zart *adj* (*weich, leise*) soft; (*Braten etc*) tender; (*empfindlich*) delicate
zartbitter *adj* (*Schokolade*) plain (BRIT), bittersweet (*US*)
zärtlich *adj* tender, affectionate
Zärtlichkeit *f* tenderness
■ **Zärtlichkeiten** *pl* caresses *pl*
Zauber (**-s**, **-**) *m* magic; (*Zauberbann*) spell
Zauberei *f* magic
Zauberer (**-s**, **-**) *m* magician; (*Zauberkünstler*) conjurer
zauberhaft *adj* magical, enchanting
Zauberin *f* magician; (*Zauberkünstlerin*) conjurer
Zauberkünstler *m* conjurer
Zaubermittel *nt* magical cure
zaubern *vi* to conjure, to do magic
Zauberspruch *m* (magic) spell
Zaun (**-(e)s**, **Zäune**) *m* fence
z. B. *abk* (*= zum Beispiel*) e.g.
ZDF *nt* (*= Zweites Deutsches Fernsehen*) *German television channel*
Zebra (**-s**, **-s**) *nt* zebra
Zebrastreifen *m* pedestrian crossing (BRIT), crosswalk (*US*)
Zecke (**-**, **-n**) *f* tick
Zehe (**-**, **-n**) *f* toe; (*Knoblauchzehe*) clove
Zehenspitze *f*: **auf Zehenspitzen** on tiptoe
zehn *num* ten
Zehnkampf *m* (*Sport*) decathlon
zehnte(r, s) *adj* tenth
Zehntel (**-s**, **-**) *nt* tenth (part)
Zeichen (**-s**, **-**) *nt* sign; (*Comput*) character
Zeichenblock *m* sketch pad
Zeichenerklärung *f* key
Zeichensetzung *f* punctuation
Zeichentrickfilm *m* (animated) cartoon
zeichnen *vi* to draw
Zeichnung *f* drawing
Zeigefinger *m* index finger
zeigen *vt* to show ▶ *vi* to point ▶ *vr* to show o.s.; **~ auf** *+akk* to point to; **es wird sich ~** time will tell; **es zeigte sich, dass ...** it turned out that ...
Zeiger (**-s**, **-**) *m* pointer; (*Uhrzeiger*) hand

Zeile (-, **-n**) *f* line
Zeit (-, **-en**) *f* time; **sich** *dat* **~ lassen** to take one's time; **von ~ zu ~** from time to time; **in letzter ~** recently
Zeitansage *f* (*Tel*) speaking clock
Zeitarbeit *f* temporary work
zeitgenössisch *adj* contemporary
zeitig *adj*, *adv* early
Zeitkarte *f* season ticket
zeitlich *adj* temporal; (*Reihenfolge*) chronological ▶ *adv*: **das kann sie ~ nicht einrichten** she can't find (the) time for that
Zeitlupe *f* slow motion
zeitnah *adj* prompt; (*aktuell*) contemporary ▶ *adv* promptly
Zeitplan *m* schedule
Zeitpunkt *m* point in time
Zeitraum *m* period
Zeitschrift *f* magazine
Zeitung *f* newspaper
Zeitungsanzeige *f* newspaper advertisement
Zeitverschiebung *f* time lag
Zeitvertreib *m* pastime; **zum ~** to pass the time
zeitweise *adv* for a time
Zeitzone *f* time zone
Zelle (-, **-n**) *f* cell
Zellophan (**-s**) *nt* cellophane
Zelt (**-(e)s**, **-e**) *nt* tent
zelten *vi* to camp
Zeltplatz *m* camp site
Zement (**-(e)s**, **-e**) *m* cement
Zentimeter *m od nt* centimetre (BRIT), centimeter (*US*)
Zentner (**-s**, **-**) *m* hundredweight
zentral *adj* central
Zentrale (-, **-n**) *f* central office; (*Tel*) exchange
Zentralheizung *f* central heating
Zentralverriegelung *f* (*Aut*) central locking
Zentrum (**-s**, **Zentren**) *nt* centre (BRIT), center (*US*)
zerbrechen *unreg vt*, *vi* to break
zerbrechlich *adj* fragile
Zeremonie *f* ceremony
zergehen *unreg vi* to melt
zerkleinern *vt* to reduce to small pieces
zerlegen *vt* to take to pieces; (*Fleisch*) to carve
zerquetschen *vt* to squash
zerreißen *unreg vt* to tear to pieces ▶ *vi* to tear
zerren *vt* to drag ▶ *vi*: **~ (an** *+dat***)** to tug (at)
Zerrung *f*: **eine ~** a pulled ligament/muscle
zerschlagen *unreg vt* to smash ▶ *vr* to fall through
zerschneiden *unreg vt* to cut up
zerstören *vt* to destroy
Zerstörung *f* destruction
zerstreuen *vt* to disperse, to scatter; (*Zweifel etc*) to dispel ▶ *vr* (*Menge*) to disperse
zerstreut *adj* scattered; (*Mensch*) absent-minded
zerteilen *vt* to divide into parts
Zertifikat (**-(e)s**, **-e**) *nt* certificate
Zettel (**-s**, **-**) *m* piece *od* slip of paper; (*Notizzettel*) note
Zeug (**-(e)s**, **-e**) (*umg*) *nt* stuff; (*Ausrüstung*) gear; **dummes ~** (stupid) nonsense
Zeuge (**-n**, **-n**) *m* witness
Zeugnis (**-ses**, **-se**) *nt* certificate; (*Sch*) report; (*Referenz*) reference
z. H., z. Hd. *abk* (= *zu Händen*) attn.
zickig (*umg*) *adj* touchy, bitchy
Zickzack (**-(e)s**, **-e**) *m* zigzag
Ziege (-, **-n**) *f* goat
Ziegel (**-s**, **-**) *m* brick; (*Dachziegel*) tile
Ziegenkäse *m* goat's cheese
Ziegenpeter *m* (*umg*) mumps *sing*
ziehen *unreg vt* to draw; (*zerren*) to pull; (*Schach etc*) to move; (*züchten*) to rear ▶ *vi* to draw; (*umziehen, wandern*) to move; (*Rauch, Wolke etc*) to drift; (*reißen*) to pull ▶ *vb unpers*: **es zieht** there is a draught (BRIT) *od* draft (*US*) ▶ *vr* (*Gummi*) to stretch; (*Gespräche*) to be drawn out; **den Tee ~ lassen** to let the tea stand
Ziehschwester (-, **-n**) *f* foster sister
Ziel (**-(e)s**, **-e**) *nt* (*einer Reise*) destination; (*Sport*) finish; (*Absicht*) goal, aim
zielen *vi*: **~ (auf** *+akk***)** to aim (at)
Zielgruppe *f* target group
ziellos *adj* aimless
Zielscheibe *f* target
ziemlich *adj attrib* (*Anzahl*) fair ▶ *adv* quite; **eine ziemliche Anstrengung** quite an effort; **~ lange** quite a long time
zierlich *adj* dainty
Ziffer (-, **-n**) *f* figure; **römische/arabische Ziffern** roman/arabic numerals

Zifferblatt *nt* dial, (clock *od* watch) face
zig (*umg*) *adj* umpteen
Zigarette *f* cigarette
Zigarettenautomat *m* cigarette machine
Zigarettenschachtel *f* cigarette packet *od* pack (*US*)
Zigarillo (**-s**, **-s**) *nt od m* cigarillo
Zigarre (-, **-n**) *f* cigar
Zigeuner(in) (**-s**, **-**) *m(f)* gipsy
Zimmer (**-s**, **-**) *nt* room
Zimmerlautstärke *f* reasonable volume
Zimmermädchen *nt* chambermaid
Zimmermann (**-(e)s**, **-leute**) *m* carpenter
Zimmerpflanze *f* indoor plant
Zimmervermittlung *f* accommodation (BRIT) *od* accommodations (*US*) service
Zimt (**-(e)s**, **-e**) *m* cinnamon
Zimtstange *f* cinnamon stick
Zink (**-(e)s**) *nt* zinc
Zinn (**-(e)s**) *nt* (*Element*) tin; (*in Zinnwaren*) pewter
Zipfel (**-s**, **-**) *m* corner; (*von Land*) tip; (*Hemdzipfel*) tail; (*Wurstzipfel*) end
Zipfelmütze *f* pointed cap
zirka *adv* about, approximately
Zirkel (**-s**, **-**) *m* (*Math*) pair of compasses
Zirkus (-, **-se**) *m* circus
zischen *vi* to hiss
Zitat (**-(e)s**, **-e**) *nt* quotation
zitieren *vt* to quote
Zitronat (**-(e)s**, **-e**) *nt* candied lemon peel
Zitrone (-, **-n**) *f* lemon
Zitronenlimonade *f* lemonade
Zitronensaft *m* lemon juice
zittern *vi* to tremble; **vor jdm ~** to be terrified of sb
zivil *adj* civilian; (*Preis*) moderate
Zivil (**-s**) *nt* plain clothes *pl*; (*Mil*) civilian clothing
Zivildienst *m* (*früher*) *alternative service (for conscientious objectors)*
zocken *vi* (*umg*) to gamble
Zoff (**-s**) *m* (*umg*) trouble
zog *etc vb siehe* **ziehen**
zögern *vi* to hesitate
Zoll (**-(e)s**, **Zölle**) *m* customs *pl*; (*Abgabe*) duty
Zollabfertigung *f* customs clearance
Zollamt *nt* customs office
Zollbeamte(r) *m* customs official
Zollerklärung *f* customs declaration
zollfrei *adj* duty-free
Zollkontrolle *f* customs (check)
zollpflichtig *adj* liable to duty
Zone (-, **-n**) *f* zone
Zoo (**-s**, **-s**) *m* zoo
Zoom (**-s**, **-s**) *nt* zoom shot; (*Objektiv*) zoom lens
Zopf (**-(e)s**, **Zöpfe**) *m* plait, pigtail
Zorn (**-(e)s**) *m* anger
zornig *adj* angry

 **SCHLÜSSELWORT**

zu *präp +dat* **1** (*örtlich*) to; **zum Bahnhof/Arzt gehen** to go to the station/doctor; **zur Schule/Kirche gehen** to go to school/church; **sollen wir zu Euch gehen?** shall we go to your place?; **sie sah zu ihm hin** she looked towards him; **zum Fenster herein** through the window; **zu meiner Linken** to *od* on my left
2 (*zeitlich*) at; **zu Ostern** at Easter; **bis zum 1. Mai** until May 1st; (*nicht später als*) by May 1st; **zu meiner Zeit** in my time
3 (*Zusatz*) with; **Wein zum Essen trinken** to drink wine with one's meal; **sich zu jdm setzen** to sit down beside sb; **setz dich doch zu uns** (come and) sit with us; **Anmerkungen zu etw** notes on sth
4 (*Zweck*) for; **Wasser zum Waschen** water for washing; **Papier zum Schreiben** paper to write on; **etw zum Geburtstag bekommen** to get sth for one's birthday
5 (*Veränderung*) into; **zu etw werden** to turn into sth; **jdn zu etw machen** to make sb (into) sth; **zu Asche verbrennen** to burn to ashes
6 (*mit Zahlen*): **3 zu 2** (*Sport*) 3-2; **das Stück zu 5 Euro** at 5 euros each; **zum ersten Mal** for the first time
7: **zu meiner Freude** *etc* to my joy *etc*; **zum Glück** luckily; **zu Fuß** on foot; **es ist zum Weinen** it's enough to make you cry
▶ *konj* to; **etw zu essen** sth to eat; **um besser sehen zu können** in order to see better; **ohne es zu wissen**

without knowing it; **noch zu bezahlende Rechnungen** outstanding bills
▶ *adv* **1** (*allzu*) too; **zu sehr** too much; **zu viel** too much; **zu wenig** too little; (*zu wenige*) too few
2 (*örtlich*) toward(s); **er kam auf mich zu** he came towards *od* up to me
3 (*geschlossen*) shut, closed; **die Geschäfte haben zu** the shops are closed; **auf/zu** (*Wasserhahn etc*) on/off
4 (*umg: los*): **nur zu!** just keep at it!; **mach zu!** hurry up!

zuallererst *adv* first of all
zuallerletzt *adv* last of all
Zubehör (**-(e)s**, **-e**) *nt* accessories *pl*
zu|bereiten *vt* to prepare
zu|binden *unreg vt* to tie up
Zucchini *pl* courgettes *pl* (Brit), zucchini(s) *pl* (*US*)
züchten *vt* (*Tiere*) to breed; (*Pflanzen*) to cultivate, to grow
zucken *vi* to jerk, to twitch; (*Strahl etc*) to flicker; **mit den Schultern ~** to shrug (one's shoulders)
Zucker (**-s**, **-**) *m* sugar; (*Med*) diabetes
Zuckerdose *f* sugar bowl
zuckerkrank *adj* diabetic
Zuckerrohr *nt* sugar cane
Zuckerrübe *f* sugar beet
Zuckerwatte *f* candy floss (Brit), cotton candy (*US*)
zu|decken *vt* to cover (up)
zu|drehen *vt* to turn off
zueinander *adv* to one other; (*in Verbverbindung*) together
zuerst *adv* first; (*zu Anfang*) at first; **~ einmal** first of all
Zufahrt *f* access; (*Einfahrt*) drive(way)
Zufahrtsstraße *f* access road; (*von Autobahn etc*) slip road (Brit), entrance ramp (*US*)
Zufall *m* chance; (*Ereignis*) coincidence; **durch ~** by accident; **so ein ~!** what a coincidence!
zufällig *adj* chance ▶ *adv* by chance; (*in Frage*) by any chance
zufrieden *adj* content(ed); (*befriedigt*) satisfied
zufrieden|geben *unreg vr*: **sich mit etw ~** to be satisfied with sth
Zufriedenheit *f* contentedness; (*Befriedigtsein*) satisfaction
zufrieden|stellen *vt* to satisfy
zu|fügen *vt* to add; (*Leid etc*): **jdm etw ~** to cause sb sth
Zug (**-(e)s**, **Züge**) *m* (*Eisenbahnzug*) train; (*Luftzug*) draught (Brit), draft (*US*); (*Ziehen*) pull(ing); (*Gesichtszug*) feature; (*Schach etc*) move; (*Charakterzug*) trait; (*an Zigarette*) puff, pull, drag; (*Schluck*) gulp
Zugabe *f* extra; (*in Konzert etc*) encore
Zugabteil *nt* train compartment
Zugang *m* entrance; (*Zutritt, fig*) access
Zugbegleiter *m* (*Eisenb*) guard (Brit), conductor (*US*)
zu|geben *unreg vt* (*zugestehen*) to admit; **zugegeben ...** granted ...
zu|gehen *unreg vi* (*schließen*) to shut
▶ *vi unpers* (*sich ereignen*) to happen; **auf jdn/etw ~** to walk towards sb/sth; **dem Ende ~** to be finishing; **es ging lustig zu** we/they had a lot of fun; **dort geht es streng zu** it's strict there
Zügel (**-s**, **-**) *m* rein
Zugführer *m* (*Eisenb*) chief guard (Brit) *od* conductor (*US*)
zugig *adj* draughty (Brit), drafty (*US*)
zügig *adj* speedy
zugleich *adv* (*zur gleichen Zeit*) at the same time; (*ebenso*) both
Zugluft *f* draught (Brit), draft (*US*)
zu|greifen *unreg vi* to seize *od* grab it/them; (*beim Essen*) to help o.s.; **~ auf** *+akk* (*Comput*) to access
zugrunde, zu Grunde *adv*: **~ gehen** to collapse; (*Mensch*) to perish
zugunsten, zu Gunsten *präp +gen od dat* in favour (Brit) *od* favor (*US*) of
Zugverbindung *f* train connection
zu|halten *unreg vt* to hold shut; **sich** *dat* **die Nase ~** to hold one's nose
Zuhause (**-s**) *nt* home
zu|hören *vi* to listen
Zuhörer (**-s**, **-**) *m* listener
zu|kleben *vt* to paste up
zu|kommen *unreg vi* to come up; **auf jdn ~** to come up to sb; **jdm etw ~ lassen** to give sb sth; **die Dinge auf sich** *akk* **~ lassen** to take things as they come
Zukunft (**-**, *no pl*) *f* future
zukünftig *adj* future ▶ *adv* in future

zu|lassen *unreg vt* (*hereinlassen*) to admit; (*erlauben*) to permit; (*Auto*) to license; (*umg*: *nicht öffnen*) to keep shut
zulässig *adj* permissible, permitted
zuletzt *adv* finally, at last
zuliebe *adv*: **jdm ~** (in order) to please sb
zum = **zu dem**; **~ dritten Mal** for the third time; **~ Scherz** as a joke; **~ Trinken** for drinking
zu|machen *vt* to shut; (*Kleidung*) to do up ▸ *vi* to shut
zumindest *adv* at least
zu|muten *vt*: **(jdm) etw ~** to expect *od* ask sth (of sb); **sich** *dat* **zu viel ~** to take on too much
zunächst *adv* first of all; **~ einmal** to start with
Zunahme (**-**, **-n**) *f* increase
Zuname *m* surname
zünden *vi* (*Feuer*) to ignite; (*Motor*) to fire ▸ *vt* to ignite; (*Rakete*) to fire
Zündkabel *nt* (*Aut*) plug lead
Zündkerze *f* (*Aut*) spark(ing) plug
Zündschlüssel *m* ignition key
Zündung *f* ignition
zu|nehmen *unreg vi* to increase; (*Mensch*) to put on weight
Zunge *f* tongue
Zungenkuss *m* French kiss
zunichte|machen *vt* to ruin
zunutze *adv*: **sich** *dat* **etw ~ machen** to make use of sth
zur = **zu der**
zurecht|finden *unreg vr* to find one's way (about)
zurecht|kommen *unreg vi* (*schaffen*) to cope
zurecht|machen *vt* to prepare ▸ *vr* to get ready
Zürich (**-s**) *nt* Zurich
zurück *adv* back
zurück|bekommen *unreg vt* to get back
zurück|bringen *unreg vt* to bring back
zurück|erstatten *vt* to refund
zurück|fahren *unreg vi* to travel back
zurück|geben *unreg vt* to give back; (*antworten*) to retort with
zurück|gehen *unreg vi* to go back; (*zeitlich*): **~ (auf** *+akk***)** to date back (to)
zurück|halten *unreg vt* to hold back; (*hindern*) to prevent ▸ *vr* to hold back
zurückhaltend *adj* reserved
zurück|holen *vt* to fetch back
zurück|kommen *unreg vi* to come back; **auf etw** *akk* **~** to return to sth
zurück|lassen *unreg vt* to leave behind
zurück|legen *vt* to put back; (*Geld*) to put by; (*reservieren*) to keep back; (*Strecke*) to cover
zurück|nehmen *unreg vt* to take back
zurück|rufen *unreg vt, vi* to call back
zurück|stellen *vt* to put back
zurück|treten *unreg vi* to step back; (*vom Amt*) to retire
zurück|zahlen *vt* to pay back
zurzeit *adv* at the moment
Zusage *f* promise; (*Annahme*) consent
zu|sagen *vt* to promise ▸ *vi* to accept; **jdm ~** (*gefallen*) to appeal to *od* please sb
zusammen *adv* together
Zusammenarbeit *f* cooperation
zusammen|arbeiten *vi* to cooperate
zusammen|brechen *unreg vi* to collapse; (*Mensch*) to break down
Zusammenbruch *m* collapse
zusammen|fassen *vt* to summarize; (*vereinigen*) to unite
zusammenfassend *adj* summarizing ▸ *adv* to summarize
Zusammenfassung *f* summary
zusammen|gehören *vi* to belong together
zusammen|halten *unreg vi* (*Freunde, fig*) to stick together
Zusammenhang *m* connection; **im/aus dem ~** in/out of context
zusammen|hängen *unreg vi* to be connected *od* linked
zusammenhängend *adj* coherent
zusammenhanglos, zusammenhangslos *adj* incoherent
zusammen|klappen *vt* (*Messer etc*) to fold
zusammen|knüllen *vt* to crumple up
zusammen|kommen *unreg vi* to meet; (*sich ereignen*) to occur at once *od* together
zusammen|legen *vt* (*falten*) to fold; (*Termine, Feste*) to combine ▸ *vi* (*Geld sammeln*) to club together
zusammen|nehmen *unreg vt* to summon up ▸ *vr* to pull o.s. together; **alles zusammengenommen** all in all
zusammen|passen *vi* to go well together

Zusammensein (**-s**) *nt* get-together
zusammen|setzen *vt* to put together ▶ *vr*: **sich ~ aus** to consist of
Zusammensetzung *f* composition
Zusammenstoß *m* collision
zusammen|stoßen *unreg vi* to collide
zusammen|zählen *vt* to add up
zusammen|ziehen *unreg vi* (*in Wohnung etc*) to move in together
Zusatz *m* addition
zusätzlich *adj* additional ▶ *adv* in addition
Zusatzprogramm *nt* (*Comput*) plug-in
zu|schauen *vi* to watch
Zuschauer(in) (**-s**, **-**) *m*(*f*) spectator ■ **Zuschauer** *pl* (*Theat*) audience *sing*
zu|schicken *vt*: **jdm etw ~** to send *od* forward sth to sb
Zuschlag *m* extra charge; (*Eisenb*) supplement
zuschlagpflichtig *adj* subject to an extra charge; (*Eisenb*) subject to a supplement
zu|schließen *unreg vt* to lock (up)
zu|sehen *unreg vi* to watch; (*dafür sorgen*) to take care
zu|sichern *vt*: **jdm etw ~** to assure sb of sth
Zustand *m* state, condition; **Zustände bekommen** *od* **kriegen** (*umg*) to have a fit
zustande, zu Stande *adv*: **~ bringen** to bring about; **~ kommen** to come about
zuständig *adj* competent, responsible
Zustellung *f* delivery
zu|stimmen *vi* to agree
Zustimmung *f* agreement; (*Einwilligung*) consent
zu|stoßen *unreg vi* (*fig*): **jdm ~** to happen to sb
Zutaten *pl* ingredients *pl*
zu|trauen *vt*: **jdm etw ~** to credit sb with sth; **jdm viel ~** to think a lot of sb; **jdm wenig ~** not to think much of sb
Zutrauen (**-s**) *nt*: **~ (zu)** trust (in)
zutraulich *adj* trusting; (*Tier*) friendly
zu|treffen *unreg vi* to be correct; (*gelten*) to apply
Zutritt *m* access; (*Einlass*) admittance; **kein ~, ~ verboten** no admittance
zuverlässig *adj* reliable
Zuverlässigkeit *f* reliability
Zuversicht (**-**) *f* confidence
zuversichtlich *adj* confident
zuvor *adv* before, previously; (*zunächst*) first
zuvor|kommen *unreg vi +dat* to anticipate; **jdm ~** to beat sb to it
zuvorkommend *adj* obliging
Zuwachs (**-es**) *m* increase, growth
zuwider *adv*: **etw ist jdm ~** sb loathes sth; **es ist mir ~** I hate *od* detest it
zu|winken *vi*: **jdm ~** to wave to sb
zuzüglich *präp +gen* plus
zwang *etc vb siehe* **zwingen**
Zwang (**-(e)s**, **Zwänge**) *m* compulsion; (*Gewalt*) coercion
zwängen *vt*, *vr* to squeeze
zwanglos *adj* informal
zwanzig *num* twenty
zwanzigste(r, s) *adj* twentieth
zwar *adv* to be sure; **das ist ~ ..., aber ...** that may be ... but ...; **und ~** in fact, actually
Zweck (**-(e)s**, **-e**) *m* purpose
zwecklos *adj* pointless
zwei *num* two
Zweibettzimmer *nt* twin-bedded room
zweideutig *adj* ambiguous; (*unanständig*) suggestive
zweifach *adj* double
Zweifel (**-s**, **-**) *m* doubt
zweifellos *adj* doubtless
zweifeln *vi*: **(an etw** *dat***) ~** to doubt (sth)
Zweifelsfall *m*: **im ~** in case of doubt
Zweig (**-(e)s**, **-e**) *m* branch
Zweigstelle *f* branch (office)
zweihundert *num* two hundred
zweimal *adv* twice
zweisprachig *adj* bilingual
zweispurig *adj* (*Aut*) two-lane
zweit *adv*: **wir sind zu ~** there are two of us
zweite(r, s) *adj* second
zweitens *adv* secondly
zweitgrößte(r, s) *adj* second largest
Zweitschlüssel *m* duplicate key
Zwerchfell *nt* diaphragm
Zwerg(in) (**-(e)s**, **-e**) *m*(*f*) dwarf (*pej*)
Zwetsche *f*, **Zwetschge** (**-**, **-n**) *f* plum
zwicken *vt* to pinch
Zwieback (**-(e)s**, **-e** *od* **-bäcke**) *m* rusk
Zwiebel (**-**, **-n**) *f* onion; (*Blumenzwiebel*) bulb

Zwilling (**-s**, **-e**) *m* twin ■ **Zwillinge** *pl* (*Astrol*) Gemini
zwingen *unreg vt* to force
zwinkern *vi* to blink; (*absichtlich*) to wink
zwischen *präp* (*+akk od dat*) between
Zwischenablage *f* (*Comput*) clipboard
zwischendurch *adv* in between
Zwischenfall *m* incident
Zwischenlandung *f* (*Aviat*) stopover
zwischenmenschlich *adj* interpersonal
Zwischenraum *m* space
Zwischensumme *f* subtotal
Zwischenzeit *f*: **in der ~** in the interim, meanwhile
zwitschern *vt*, *vi* to twitter, to chirp
zwölf *num* twelve
Zylinder (**-s**, **-**) *m* cylinder; (*Hut*) top hat
zynisch *adj* cynical
Zypern (**-s**) *nt* Cyprus
Zyste (**-**, **-n**) *f* cyst

German Grammar

1 Articles

1.1 The definite article

All German nouns are either masculine, feminine or neuter and are either singular or plural. The word you choose for *the* depends on whether the noun it is used with is masculine, feminine or neuter, singular or plural and on the case of the noun.

The forms of the definite article in each case are as follows:

Case	Masculine Singular	Feminine Singular	Neuter Singular	All Genders Plural
Nominative	**der**	**die**	**das**	**die**
Accusative	**den**	**die**	**das**	**die**
Genitive	**des**	**der**	**des**	**der**
Dative	**dem**	**der**	**dem**	**den**

The definite article is used with words like *prices*, *life* and *time* that describe qualities, ideas or experiences.

Das Leben ist schön. *Life is wonderful.*

In German, you have to use the definite article in front of masculine and feminine countries and districts, but you don't need it for neuter ones.

Die Schweiz ist auch schön. *Switzerland is also beautiful.*
Deutschland ist sehr schön. *Germany is very beautiful.*

The definite article is used with months of the year, except after the prepositions **seit**, **nach** and **vor**.

Der Dezember war ziemlich kalt. *December was quite cold.*

In certain common expressions, the definite article is used.

in die Stadt fahren *to go into town*
mit dem Zug/Bus/Auto *by train/bus/car*

After certain prepositions, the definite article can be shortened.

an dem → am **zu dem → zum**
in dem → im **zu der → zur**

Other words follow the same patterns as the definite article, for example: **aller**, **beide**, **dieser**, **einiger**, **jeder**, **jener**, **mancher**, **solcher**, **welcher**.

1.2 The indefinite article

In German, the word you choose for *a* depends on the gender of the noun, whether it is singular or plural, and what case it is in.

The indefinite article is formed as follows:

Case	Masculine	Feminine	Neuter
Nominative	**ein**	**eine**	**ein**
Accusative	**einen**	**eine**	**ein**
Genitive	**eines**	**einer**	**eines**
Dative	**einem**	**einer**	**einem**

In German, you use a separate negative form of the indefinite article, which is formed exactly like **ein** in the singular, and also has plural forms. It means *no/not a/not one/not any*.

Case	Masculine Singular	Feminine Singular	Neuter Singular	All Genders Plural
Nominative	**kein**	**keine**	**kein**	**keine**
Accusative	**keinen**	**keine**	**kein**	**keine**
Genitive	**keines**	**keiner**	**keines**	**keiner**
Dative	**keinem**	**keiner**	**keinem**	**keinen**

The possessive adjectives – **mein**, **dein**, **sein**, **ihr**, **unser**, **euer**, **ihr**, **Ihr** – follow the same pattern as the indefinite articles **ein** and **kein**.

2 Nouns

2.1 Gender of nouns

Whenever you are using a noun, you need to know whether it is masculine, feminine or neuter as this affects the form of other words used with it, such as:

- adjectives that describe it
- articles (such as **der** or **ein**) that go before it
- pronouns (such as **er** or **sie**) that replace it

Note that German nouns are always written with a capital letter.

Nouns with the following endings are masculine:

Masculine Ending	Example	Meaning
-ich	**der Teppich**	*carpet*
-ig	**der Essig**	*vinegar*
-ling	**der Frühling**	*spring*

Most nouns ending in **-e** are feminine.

die Falte *crease, wrinkle*
die Brücke *bridge*

Nouns with the following endings are feminine:

Feminine Ending	Example	Meaning
-heit	**die Schönheit**	*beauty*
-keit	**die Sehenswürdigkeit**	*sight*
-schaft	**die Gewerkschaft**	*trade union*
-ung	**die Zeitung**	*newspaper*
-ei	**die Bäckerei**	*bakery*

Many masculine German nouns can be made feminine by adding **-in** in the singular and **-innen** in the plural.

der Lehrer *(male) teacher*
die Lehrerin *(female) teacher*
Lehrer und Lehrerinnen *(male and female) teachers*

Most nouns beginning with **Ge-** are neuter.

das Geschirr *crockery, dishes*
das Geschöpf *creature*

Nouns ending in **-lein** or **-chen** are also neuter. These are called the diminutive form and refer to small persons or objects.

das Tischlein	*little table*
das Häuschen	*little house*

Infinitives (the "to" form of verbs) used as nouns are neuter.

das Schwimmen	*swimming*
das Radfahren	*cycling*

Nouns with the endings **-nis** and **-tum** are neuter.

das Ereignis	*event*
das Eigentum	*property*

Some nouns have two genders and the meaning of the word changes depending on which gender it has.

der See	*lake*
die See	*sea*
der Leiter	*leader, manager*
die Leiter	*ladder*

2.2 Compound nouns

Compound nouns are made up of two or more words. In German, these words nearly always take their gender from the last noun of the compound word.

die Armbanduhr (**Armband** + **die Uhr**)	*wristwatch*
der Tomatensalat (**Tomaten** + **der Salat**)	*tomato salad*

2.3 The cases

In German, there are four grammatical cases – nominative, accusative, genitive and dative. The case you should use depends on the grammatical function of the noun in the sentence.

Nominative case

The nominative case is the basic form of the noun and is the one you find in the dictionary. It is used for the subject of the sentence, that is, the person, animal or thing 'doing' the action:

Das Mädchen singt.	*The girl is singing.*

Accusative case

The article for feminine and neuter nouns in the accusative case has the same form as in the nominative. **Der** for masculine nouns changes to **den** and **ein** to **einen**.

The accusative case is used:

- to show the direct object of a verb. This is the person, animal or thing affected by the action of the verb.

Ich sehe den Hund.	*I see the dog.*

- after certain prepositions which are always used with the accusative.

Es ist für seine Freundin.	*It's for his girlfriend.*

Genitive case

Der for masculine nouns and **das** for neuter nouns change to **des** in the genitive case. **Ein** changes to **eines.** The endings of masculine and neuter singular nouns also change in the genitive case.

-s is added to masculine and neuter nouns ending in **-en**, **-el**, **-er**.

> **der Wagen** *(car)* → **des Wagens**
> **der Computer** *(computer)* → **des Computers**

-es is added to most masculine and neuter nouns of one syllable ending in a consonant.

> **der Freund** *(friend)* → **des Freundes**

Die changes to **der** and **eine** to **einer** in the genitive case. The endings of feminine singular nouns in the genitive case are the same as in the nominative.

> **die Ärztin** *(female) doctor* → **der Ärztin**

The genitive case is used:

- to show that something belongs to someone
  Das Auto der Frau war rot. *The woman's car was red.*
- after certain prepositions which always take the genitive
  Wegen des schlechten Wetters müssen wir nach Hause gehen.
  We'll have to go home because of the bad weather.

Dative case

Die changes to **der** and **eine** to **einer** in the dative case. Singular nouns in the dative have the same form as in the nominative.

The dative case is used:

- to show the indirect object of a verb – an indirect object answers the question *who to/for?* or *to/for what?*
  Er gab dem Mann das Buch. *He gave the book to the man.*
- after certain verbs
  Er hilft seiner Mutter im Haushalt.
  He helps his mother with the housework.
- after certain prepositions which always take the dative
  Er kam mit einer Freundin. *He came with a friend.*

2.4 Forming plurals

Most German feminine nouns form their plural by adding **-n**, **-en** or **-nen** to their singular form.

> **die Frau** *(woman)* → **die Frauen**

Many nouns have no plural ending – these are mostly masculine or neuter nouns ending in **-en**, **-er** or **-el**.

> **der Kuchen** *(cake)* → **die Kuchen**

Some of these nouns also have an umlaut added to the first vowel **a**, **o** or **u** in the plural.

> **der Apfel** *(apple)* → **die Äpfel**

Some masculine nouns add an umlaut above the first vowel **a**, **o** or **u** and an **-e** ending to form the plural.

die Angst *(fear)* ➜ **die Ängste**

Masculine or neuter nouns often add **-e** or **-er** to form the plural.

das Geschenk *(present)* ➜ **die Geschenke**

Some masculine and neuter nouns add an umlaut above the first vowel **a**, **o** or **u** and an **-er** ending in the plural.

der Mann *(man)* ➜ **die Männer**

Some nouns are always plural in English, but singular in German.

eine Brille	*glasses, spectacles*
eine Schere	*scissors*

2.5 Weak nouns

Weak masculine nouns follow the pattern shown:

Case	Singular	Plural
Nominative	der Junge	die Jungen
Accusative	den Jungen	die Jungen
Genitive	des Jungen	der Jungen
Dative	dem Jungen	den Jungen

2.6 Proper nouns

In German, names of people and places only change in the genitive singular when they add **-s**, unless they are preceded by the definite article or a demonstrative adjective.

Annas Buch	*Anna's book*
Klaras Mantel	*Klara's coat*

3 Adjectives

3.1 Making adjectives agree

To make an adjective agree with the noun or pronoun it describes, you simply add one of three sets of different endings:

The weak declension

The endings used after the definite articles **der**, **die** and **das** and other words declined like them are shown below:

Case	Masculine Singular	Feminine Singular	Neuter Singular	All Genders Plural
Nominative	-e	-e	-e	-en
Accusative	-en	-e	-e	-en
Genitive	-en	-en	-en	-en
Dative	-en	-en	-en	-en

The mixed declension

The endings used after **ein**, **kein**, **irgendein** and the possessive adjectives are shown below:

Case	Masculine Singular	Feminine Singular	Neuter Singular	All Genders Plural
Nominative	**-er**	**-e**	**-es**	**-en**
Accusative	**-en**	**-e**	**-es**	**-en**
Genitive	**-en**	**-en**	**-en**	**-en**
Dative	**-en**	**-en**	**-en**	**-en**

The strong declension

The endings used when there is no article before the noun are shown below:

Case	Masculine Singular	Feminine Singular	Neuter Singular	All Genders Plural
Nominative	**-er**	**-e**	**-es**	**-e**
Accusative	**-en**	**-e**	**-es**	**-e**
Genitive	**-en**	**-er**	**-en**	**-er**
Dative	**-em**	**-er**	**-em**	**-en**

3.2 Comparatives of adjectives

In German, to say that something is *easier*, *more expensive* and so on, you add **-er** to the simple form of most adjectives.

einfach (*simple*) → **einfacher**

Note that adjectives whose simple form ends in **-en** or **-er** may drop the final **-e** to form the comparative, as in **teurer**.

teuer (*expensive*) → **teurer**

3.3 Superlatives of adjectives

In German, to say that something or someone is *easiest*, *youngest*, *most expensive* and so on, you add **-st** to the simple form of the adjective.

einfach (*simple*) → **einfachsten**

Adjectives ending in **-t**, **-tz**, **-z**, **-sch**, **-ss** or **-ß** form the superlative by adding **-est** instead of **-st**.

der/die/das schlechteste *the worst*

German also has a few irregular forms for comparatives and superlatives:

Adjective	Meaning	Comparative	Meaning	Comparative	Meaning
gut	*good*	**besser**	*better*	**der beste**	*the best*
hoch	*high*	**höher**	*higher*	**der höchste**	*the highest*
viel	*much/a lot*	**mehr**	*more*	**der meiste**	*the most*
nah	*near*	**näher**	*nearer*	**der nächste**	*the nearest*

4 Pronouns

4.1 Personal pronouns

Here are the German personal pronouns in all cases:

Nominative		Accusative		Dative	
ich	*I*	**mich**	*me*	**mir**	*to/for me*
du	*you*	**dich**	*you*	**dir**	*to/for you*
er	*he/it*	**ihn**	*him/it*	**ihm**	*to/for him/it*
sie	*she/it*	**sie**	*her/it*	**ihr**	*to/for her/it*
es	*it/he/she*	**es**	*it/him/her*	**ihm**	*to/for it/him/her*
wir	*we*	**uns**	*us*	**uns**	*to/for us*
ihr	*you (familiar plural)*	**euch**	*you*	**euch**	*to/for you*
sie	*they*	**sie**	*them*	**ihnen**	*to/for them*
Sie	*you (polite)*	**Sie**	*you*	**Ihnen**	*to/for you*
man	*one*	**einen**	*one*	**einem**	*to/for one*

In German, there are three words for saying *you*: **du**, **ihr** and **Sie**:

- Use the familiar **du** if talking to one person you know well, such as a friend, someone younger than you or a relative

  Kommst du mit ins Kino? *Are you coming to the cinema?*

- Use the formal or polite **Sie** if talking to one person you do not know so well, such as your teacher, your boss or a stranger.

  Was haben Sie gesagt? *What did you say?*

- Use the familiar **ihr** if talking to more than one person you know well or relatives.

  Was wollt ihr heute Abend essen?
  What do you want to eat tonight?

- Use **Sie** if talking to more than one person you do not know so well.

  Wo fahren Sie hin? *Where are you going to?*

Use **er** for masculine nouns, **sie** for feminine nouns and **es** for neuter nouns.

Der Tisch ist groß. → **Er ist groß.**
Die Jacke ist blau. → **Sie ist blau.**
Das Kind stand auf. → **Es stand auf.**

Man is often used in German in the same way as we use *you* in English to mean people in general.

Wie schreibt man das? *How do you spell that?*

4.2 Possessive pronouns

Here is the German possessive pronoun **meiner**, meaning *mine*, in all its forms:

Case	Masculine Singular	Feminine Singular	Neuter Singular	All Genders Plural
Nominative	**meiner**	**meine**	**mein(e)s**	**meine**
Accusative	**meinen**	**meine**	**mein(e)s**	**meine**
Genitive	**meines**	**meiner**	**meines**	**meiner**
Dative	**meinem**	**meiner**	**meinem**	**meinen**

Note that **deiner**, **seiner**, **ihrer**, **Ihrer**, **unserer**, and **euerer** have the same endings as **meiner**.

4.3 Reflexive pronouns

German reflexive pronouns have two forms: accusative (for the direct object pronoun) and dative (for the indirect object pronoun), as follows:

Accusative Form	Dative Form	Meaning
mich	**mir**	*myself*
dich	**dir**	*yourself (familiar)*
sich	**sich**	*himself/herself/itself*
uns	**uns**	*ourselves*
euch	**euch**	*yourselves (plural)*
sich	**sich**	*themselves*
sich	**sich**	*yourself/yourselves (polite)*

The reflexive pronoun usually follows the first verb in the sentence.

Sie wird sich darüber freuen. *She'll be pleased about that.*

4.4 Interrogative pronouns

Wer and **was** only have a singular form.

Case	Persons	Things
Nominative	**wer?**	**was?**
Accusative	**wen?**	**was?**
Genitive	**wessen?**	–
Dative	**wem?**	–

Wer hat es gemacht? *Who did it?*
Mit wem bist du gekommen? *Who did you come with?*

5 Verbs

German verbs can be:

- weak; their forms follow a set pattern.
- strong and irregular; their forms change according to different patterns.
- mixed; their forms follow a mixture of the patterns for weak and strong verbs.

5.1 Present tense

Weak verbs

Nearly all weak verbs in German end in **-en** in their infinitive form. This is the form of the verb you find in the dictionary, for example, **spielen**, **machen**, **holen**. Weak verbs are regular and their changes follow a set pattern or conjugation.

To know which form of the verb to use in German, you need to work out what the stem of the verb is and then add the correct ending. The stem of most verbs in the present tense is formed by chopping the **-en** off the infinitive.

Here are the present tense endings for weak verbs ending in **-en**:

Pronoun	Ending	Add to Stem, e.g. spiel-	Meanings
ich	**-e**	**ich spiele**	*I play* *I am playing*
du	**-st**	**du spielst**	*you play* *you are playing*
er **sie** **es**	**-t**	**er spielt** **sie spielt** **es spielt**	*he/she/it plays* *he/she/it is playing*
wir	**-en**	**wir spielen**	*we play* *we are playing*
ihr	**-t**	**ihr spielt**	*you (plural) play* *you are playing*
sie	**-en**	**sie spielen**	*they play* *they are playing*
Sie		**Sie spielen**	*you (polite) play* *you are playing*

Sometimes an extra **-e** is added before the usual endings in the **du**, **er**, **sie**, **es** and **ihr** parts of the verb to make pronunciation easier.

Sie arbeitet übers Wochenende. *She's working over the weekend.*

Strong verbs

The present tense of most strong verbs is formed with the same endings that are used for weak verbs.

Pronoun	Ending	Add to Stem, e.g. sing-	Meanings
ich	**-e**	**ich singe**	*I sing* *I am singing*
du	**-st**	**du singst**	*you sing* *you are singing*
er **sie** **es**	**-t**	**er singt** **sie singt** **es singt**	*he/she/it sings* *he/she/it is singing*
wir	**-en**	**wir singen**	*we sing* *we are singing*
ihr	**-t**	**ihr singt**	*you (plural) sing* *you are singing*
sie	**-en**	**sie singen**	*they sing* *they are singing*
Sie		**Sie singen**	*you (polite) sing* *you are singing*

However, the vowels in stems of most strong verbs change for the **du** and **er/sie/es** forms.

Siehst du fern? *Are you watching TV?*
Heute hilft er beim Kochen. *He's helping with the cooking today.*

Mixed verbs

The nine mixed verbs are:

Mixed Verb	Meaning	Mixed Verb	Meaning	Mixed Verb	Meaning
brennen	*to burn*	**kennen**	*to know*	**senden**	*to send*
bringen	*to bring*	**nennen**	*to name*	**wenden**	*to turn*
denken	*to think*	**rennen**	*to run*	**wissen**	*to know*

The present tense of mixed verbs has the same endings as weak verbs and has no vowel or consonant changes in the stem:

Sie bringt mich nach Hause. *She's bringing me home.*

Reflexive verbs

Reflexive verbs consist of two parts: the reflexive pronoun **sich** and the infinitive of the verb.

The present tense forms of a reflexive verb work in just the same way as an ordinary verb, except that the reflexive pronoun is used as well.

The reflexive pronouns are:

Accusative Form	Dative Form	Meaning
mich	**mir**	*myself*
dich	**dir**	*yourself (familiar)*
sich	**sich**	*himself/herself/itself*
uns	**uns**	*ourselves*
euch	**euch**	*yourselves (plural)*
sich	**sich**	*themselves*
sich	**sich**	*yourself/yourselves (polite)*

Some of the most common German reflexive verbs are:

sich anziehen *to get dressed*
sich beeilen *to hurry*
sich erinnern an *to remember*
sich freuen auf *to look forward to*
sich setzen *or* **hinsetzen** *to sit down*

Verb prefixes

Many verbs in German begin with a prefix. Often the addition of the prefix changes the meaning of the basic verb. Prefixes can be found in strong, weak and mixed verbs. Some prefixes are always joined to the verb and never separated from it – these are called inseparable prefixes. However, the majority are separated from the verb in certain tenses and forms, and come at the end of the sentence. They are called separable prefixes.

There are eight inseparable prefixes in German:

Inseparable Verb	Meaning	Inseparable Verb	Meaning
beschreiben	*to describe*	**gehören**	*to belong*
empfangen	*to receive*	**misstrauen**	*to mistrust*
enttäuschen	*to disappoint*	**verlieren**	*to lose*
erhalten	*to preserve*	**zerlegen**	*to dismantle*

There are many separable prefixes in German, for example:

abfahren	*to leave*
ankommen	*to arrive*
aufstehen	*to get up*
einsteigen	*to get on*
mitmachen	*to join in*
vorziehen	*to prefer*

In tenses consisting of one verb part only, for example the present and the imperfect, the separable prefix is placed at the end of the main clause.

Der Bus kam immer spät an. *The bus was always late.*

In infinitive phrases using **zu**, the **zu** is inserted between the verb and its prefix to form one word.

Um rechtzeitig aufzustehen, muss ich den Wecker stellen.
In order to get up on time I'll have to set the alarm.

5.2 Perfect tense

Unlike the present and imperfect tenses, the perfect tense has two parts to it:

- the present tense of the irregular weak verb **haben** (meaning *to have*) or the irregular strong verb **sein** (meaning *to be*).
- a part of the main verb called the *past participle*.

The verbs **haben** and **sein** have irregular forms:

Pronoun	Ending	Present Tense: haben	Meanings
ich	-e	ich habe	*I have*
du	-st	du hast	*you have*
er sie es	-t	er hat sie hat es hat	*he/she/it has*
wir	-en	wir haben	*we have*
ihr	-t	ihr habt	*you (plural) have*
sie	-en	sie haben	*they have*
Sie		Sie haben	*you (polite) have*

Pronoun	Ending	Present Tense: sein	Meanings
ich	–	ich bin	*I am*
du	–	du bist	*you are*
er sie es	–	er ist sie ist es ist	*he/she/it is*
wir	–	wir sind	*we are*
ihr	–	ihr seid	*you (plural) are*
sie	–	sie sind	*they are*
Sie	–	Sie sind	*you (polite) are*

To form the past participle of weak verbs, you add **ge-** to the beginning of the verb stem and **-t** to the end.

Infinitive	Take off -en	Add ge- and -t
holen (*to fetch*)	**hol-**	**geholt**
machen (*to do*)	**mach-**	**gemacht**

To form the past participle of strong verbs, you add **ge-** to the beginning of the verb stem and **-en** to the end. The vowel in the stem may also change.

Infinitive	Take off -en	Add ge- and -en
laufen (*to run*)	**lauf-**	**gelaufen**
singen (*to sing*)	**sing-**	**gesungen**

To form the past participle of mixed verbs, you add **ge-** to the beginning of the verb stem and, like weak verbs, **-t** to the end. As with many strong verbs, the stem vowel may also change.

Infinitive	Take off -en	Add ge- and -t
bringen (*to run*)	**bring-**	**gebracht**
denken (*to think*)	**denk-**	**gedacht**

The perfect tense of separable verbs is also formed in the above way, except that the separable prefix is joined on to the front of the **ge-**: **aufgemacht**.

With inseparable verbs, the only difference is that past participles are formed without the **ge-**: **bestellt**.

Most verbs form their perfect tense with **haben.**

Ich habe das schon gemacht. *I've already done that.*
Wo haben Sie früher gearbeitet? *Where did you work before?*

With reflexive verbs the reflexive pronoun comes immediately after **haben**.

Sie hat sich nicht daran erinnert. *She didn't remember.*

There are two main groups of verbs which form their perfect tense with **sein** instead of **haben**, and most of them are strong verbs:

- verbs which take no direct object and are used mainly to talk about movement or a change of some kind, such as:

gehen	*to go*
kommen	*to come*
ankommen	*to arrive*
abfahren	*to leave*
aussteigen	*to get off*
einsteigen	*to get on*
sterben	*to die*
sein	*to be*
werden	*to become*
bleiben	*to remain*
aufstehen	*to get up*
fallen	*to fall*

- two verbs which mean *to happen*.

Was ist geschehen/passiert? *What happened?*

5.3 Imperfect tense

Weak verbs

To form the imperfect tense of weak verbs, you use the same stem of the verb as for the present tense. As with the present tense, some weak verbs change their spellings slightly when they are used in the imperfect tense.

Pronoun	Ending	Add to Stem, e.g. spiel-	Meanings
ich	-te	ich spiele	*I played* *I was playing*
du	-test	du spieltest	*you played* *you were playing*
er sie es	-te	er spielte sie spielte es spielte	*he/she/it played* *he/she/it was playing*
wir	-ten	wir spielten	*we played* *we were playing*
ihr	-tet	ihr spieltet	*you (plural) played* *you were playing*
sie	-ten	sie spielten	*they played* *they were playing*
Sie		Sie spielten	*you (polite) played* *you were playing*

Strong verbs

The main difference between strong verbs and weak verbs in the imperfect is that strong verbs have a vowel change and take a different set of endings.

To form the imperfect tense of strong verbs you add the following endings to the stem, which undergoes a vowel change.

Pronoun	Ending	Add to Stem, e.g. rief- (*from* **rufen**)	Meanings
ich	–	ich rief	*I shouted* *I was shouting*
du	-st	du riefst	*you shouted* *you were shouting*
er sie es	–	er rief sie rief es rief	*he/she/it shouted* *he/she/it was shouting*
wir	-en	wir riefen	*we shouted* *we were shouting*
ihr	-t	ihr rieft	*you (plural) shouted* *you were shouting*
sie	-en	sie riefen	*they shouted* *they were shouting*
Sie		Sie riefen	*you (polite) shouted* *you were shouting*

Mixed verbs

The imperfect tense of mixed verbs is formed by adding the weak verb endings to a stem whose vowel has been changed as for a strong verb.

Pronoun	Ending	Add to Stem, e.g. kann- (*from* **können**)	Meanings
ich	**-te**	**ich kannte**	*I knew*
du	**-test**	**du kanntest**	*you knew*
er **sie** **es**	**-te**	**er kannte** **sie kannte** **es kannte**	*he/she/it knew*
wir	**-ten**	**wir kannten**	*we knew*
ihr	**-tet**	**ihr kanntet**	*you (plural) knew*
sie	**-ten**	**sie kannten**	*they knew*
Sie		**Sie kannten**	*you (polite) knew*

5.4 Future tense

The future tense has two parts to it and is formed in the same way for all verbs, whether they are weak, strong or mixed:

- the present tense of the strong verb **werden** (meaning *to become*). **Werden** has irregular forms in the present tense.
- the infinitive of the main verb, which normally goes at the end of the clause or sentence.

Wir werden draußen warten. *We'll wait outside.*

Pronoun	Ending	Present Tense: werden	Meanings
ich	**-e**	**ich werde**	*I become*
du	**-st**	**du wirst**	*you become*
er **sie** **es**	–	**er wird** **sie wird** **es wird**	*he/she/it becomes*
wir	**-en**	**wir werden**	*we become*
ihr	**-t**	**ihr werdet**	*you (plural) become*
sie	**-en**	**sie werden**	*they become*
Sie	**-en**	**Sie werden**	*you (polite) become*

Note that in reflexive verbs, the reflexive pronoun comes after the present tense of **werden**.

5.5 Modal verbs

In German, the modal verbs are **dürfen**, **können**, **mögen**, **müssen**, **sollen** and **wollen**. Modal verbs have unusual present tenses:

dürfen	können	mögen
ich darf	**ich kann**	**ich mag**
du darfst	**du kannst**	**du magst**
er/sie/es/man darf	**er/sie/es/man kann**	**er/sie/es/man mag**
wir dürfen	**wir können**	**wir mögen**
ihr dürft	**ihr könnt**	**ihr mögt**
sie/Sie dürfen	**sie/Sie können**	**sie/Sie mögen**

müssen	sollen	wollen
ich muss	ich soll	ich will
du musst	du sollst	du willst
er/sie/es/man muss	er/sie/es/man soll	er/sie/es/man will
wir müssen	wir sollen	wir wollen
ihr müsst	ihr sollt	ihr wollt
sie/Sie müssen	sie/Sie sollen	sie/Sie wollen

6 Prepositions

In German, the noun following a preposition must be put into the accusative, genitive or dative case:

- Some of the most common prepositions taking the dative case are: **aus**, **außer**, **bei**, **gegenüber**, **mit**, **nach**, **seit**, **von**, **zu**

  Er trinkt aus der Flasche. *He is drinking out of the bottle.*

- The most common prepositions taking the accusative case are: **durch**, **entlang**, **für**, **gegen**, **ohne**, **um**, **wider**

  Ich habe es für dich getan. *I did it for you.*

- There are a number of prepositions which can be followed by the accusative or the dative case. The most common prepositions in this category are: **an**, **auf**, **hinter**, **in**, **neben**, **über**, **unter**, **vor**, **zwischen**.

  You use:

  - the accusative case when there is some movement towards a different place

    Sie ging ins Zimmer. *She entered the room.*

  - the dative case when a location is described rather than movement, or when there is movement within the same place

    Im Zimmer waren viele Leute. *A lot of people were in the room.*

- The following are some of the more common prepositions which take the genitive case: **außerhalb**, **infolge**, **innerhalb**, **statt**, **trotz**, **um ... willen**, **während**, **wegen**

  Sie kam statt ihres Bruders. *She came instead of her brother.*

7 Conjunctions

aber, **denn**, **oder**, **sondern** and **und** are the most important co-ordinating conjunctions.

Wir wollten ins Kino, aber wir hatten kein Geld.
We wanted to go to the cinema, but we had no money.

als, **da**, **damit**, **dass**, **ob**, **obwohl**, **während**, **wenn**, **weil**, **um ... zu**, and **ohne ... zu** are some of the most important subordinating conjunctions. Note that the verb almost always comes at the end of the subordinate clause.

Ich weiß, dass du besser in Mathe bist als ich.
I know (that) you're better at maths than me.

Morgen komme ich nicht, weil ich keine Zeit habe.
I'm not coming tomorrow because I don't have the time.

Englische Grammatik

1 Die Verben

1.1 Die einfache Gegenwart (simple present)

Die einfache Gegenwart wird verwendet:

- für allgemeine Aussagen.

  February is the shortest month.
  Februar ist der kürzeste Monat.

- wenn man von der Gegenwart allgemein spricht, von etwas Üblichem, das regelmäßig passiert.

  I take the bus every morning.
  Ich nehme jeden Morgen den Bus.
  George lives in Birmingham.
  George wohnt in Birmingham.

Bejahungen	Verneinungen	Fragen
I work	I don't work	Do I work?
you work	you don't work	Do you work?
he/she/it works	he/she/it doesn't work	Does he/she/it work?
we work	we don't work	Do we work?
you work	you don't work	Do you work
they work	they don't work	Do they work?

Anmerkungen:

- Das Verb besteht in allen Personen aus dem Wortstamm, außer in der 3. Person Singular (**he/she/it**), der ein **-s** angehängt wird.
- Endet der Wortstamm mit **-o/-os/-ch/-sh/-ss/-x**, wird in der 3. Person Singular **-es** angehängt:

  watch → watches
  go → goes

- Endet der Wortstamm mit einem auf einen Konsonanten folgenden **-y**, wird dieses in der 3. Person Singular zu **-ies** à:

  study → studies
  cry → cries

- Aus **have** wird in der 3. Person Singular **has**.

  She has a computer in her room.
  Sie hat einen Computer in ihrem Zimmer.

- Für Fragen und Verneinungen wird das Hilfsverb **do** (**does** in der 3. Person Singular) gebraucht. Bei einer Verneinung wird die Langform (**do not/does not**) meistens durch die Kurzform (**don't/doesn't**) ersetzt.

  Do you know Peter? No, I don't know him.
  Kennst du Peter? Nein, ich kenne ihn nicht.

  Does she go to university?
  Geht sie zur Universität?

  He doesn't eat meat.
  Er isst kein Fleisch.

Das Verb *be*

Be entspricht dem Verb *sein*. In der einfachen Gegenwart wird es folgendermaßen konjugiert:

Bejahungen			
In positiven Aussagen		Deutsch	Fragen
Langform	**Kurzform**		
I am alone.	**I'm** alone.	**Ich bin** allein.	**Am I** alone?
You are next.	**You're** next.	**Du bist** (oder **Sie sind**) der Nächste.	**Are you** next?
He is blond.	**He's** blond.	**Er ist** blond.	**Is he** blond?
She is at home.	**She's** at home.	**Sie ist** zu Hause.	**Is she** at home?
It is on the table.	**It's** on the table.	**Er/Sie/Es** (Objekt) **ist** auf dem Tisch.	**Is it** on the table?
We are British.	**We're** British.	**Wir sind** Briten.	**Are we** British?
You are here.	**You're** here.	**Ihr seid** hier.	**Are you** here?
They are happy.	**They're** happy.	**Sie sind** glücklich.	**Are they** happy?

Verneinungen			
In negativen Aussagen		Deutsch	Fragen
Langform	**Kurzform**		
I am not alone.	**I'm not** alone.	**Ich bin nicht** ...	Aren't I alone?
You are not next.	**You're not/ aren't** next.	**Du bist** (oder **Sie sind**) **nicht** ...	Aren't you next?
He is not blond.	**He's not/isn't** blond.	**Er ist nicht** ...	Isn't he blond?
She is not at home.	**She's not/isn't** at home.	**Sie ist nicht** ...	Isn't she at home?
It is not on the table.	**It's not/isn't** on the table.	**Er/Sie/Es** (Objekt) **ist nicht** ...	Isn't it on the table?
We are not British.	**We're not/ aren't** British.	**Wir sind nicht** ...	Aren't we British?
You are not here.	**You're not/ aren't** here.	**Ihr seid nicht** ...	Aren't you here?
They are not happy.	**They're not/ aren't** happy.	**Sie sind nicht** ...	Aren't they happy?

1.2 Die Verlaufsform der Gegenwart (Present Progressive)

Der *present progressive* wird in folgenden Fällen verwendet:

- für Handlungen, die im Moment des Sprechens geschehen („*gerade dabei sein, etwas zu tun*").

  They're talking to the teacher.
  Sie sprechen gerade mit dem Lehrer.

- für vorübergehende Handlungen.

  I'm living with my friends at the moment.
  Ich wohne im Moment mit Freunden zusammen.

Der *present progressive* wird folgendermaßen zusammengestellt:

BE im Präsens + Verb **-ing**

Bejahung	Verneinung	Fragen
I am playing	**I'm not playing**	**Am I playing?**
You are playing	**You're not playing**	**Are you playing?**
He/She/It is playing	**He/She/It's not playing**	**Is he/she/it playing?**
We are playing	**We're not playing**	**Are we playing?**
You are playing	**You're not playing**	**Are you playing?**
They are playing	**They're not playing**	**Are they playing?**

Anmerkung:

- In der Verneinung wird eher die Kurzform (**I'm not ...**) als die Langform (**I am not ...**) verwendet.

1.3 Die vollendete Gegenwart (Present Perfect)

Der *present perfect* wird folgendermaßen verwendet:

- um das Ergebnis einer Handlung oder eines Ereignisses zu schildern.

  I'm afraid I have forgotten my book.
  Es tut mir leid, ich habe mein Buch vergessen.

- für eine Handlung, die gerade abgeschlossen wurde (mit **just**).

  Karen has just finished her homework.
  Karen hat gerade ihre Hausaufgaben erledigt.

- für Ereignisse, die in der Vergangenheit begannen und bis in die Gegenwar dauern.

  I've lived in London for three years.
  Ich wohne seit drei Jahren in London.

- für vergangene Erlebnisse oder Erfahrungen.

  Have you ever been to the US?
  Warst du schon mal in den Vereinigten Staaten?

Der *present perfect* wird folgendermaßen zusammengestellt:

Have im Präsens + Partizip Perfekt

Für das Partizip Perfekt wird **-ed** an das Ende des Verbes gehängt, bis auf die unregelmäßigen Verben. Die Liste der unregelmäßigen Verben befindet sich Seite xvii des Wörterbuchs.

Bejahungen	Verneinungen	Fragen
I have visited	**I haven't visited**	**Have I visited?**
You have visited	**You haven't visited**	**Have you visited?**
He/She/It has visited	**He/She/It hasn't visited**	**Has he/she/it visited?**
We have eaten	**We haven't eaten**	**Have we eaten?**
You have eaten	**You haven't eaten**	**Have you eaten?**
They have eaten	**They haven't eaten**	**Have they eaten?**

Anmerkungen:

- In einer Verneinung wird eher die Kurzform (**haven't/hasn't**) als die Langform (**have not/has not**) verwendet. Umgangssprachlich kann man die Kurzform auch in einer Bejahung verwenden, indem man **have** durch **'ve** und **has** durch **'s** ersetzt.
- Der *present perfect* wird ohne Angabe eines bestimmten Zeitpunktes verwendet.

  I've read that book (before). I read it last week.
  Ich habe das Buch (schon einmal) gelesen. Ich habe es letzte Woche gelesen.
- Der *present perfect* wird in Deutsch nicht unbedingt mit dem Perfekt übersetzt.

  They've known each other for ten years.
  Sie kennen sich seit zehn Jahren.

  I've been to Canada twice.
  Ich war zwei Mal in Kanada.

.4 Die einfache Vergangenheit oder Imperfekt (Simple Past)

Der *simple past* wird verwendet, um eine Handlung oder einen Vorgang zu schildern, der in der Vergangenheit endete.

He went home last night.
Er ging gestern Abend nach Hause.

I often watched TV when I was a child.
Als Kind sah ich oft fern.

Für den Imperfekt wird **-ed** an das Ende des Verbes gehängt, bis auf die unregelmäßigen Verben. Die Liste der unregelmäßigen Verben befindet sich Seite xiv des Wörterbuchs.

Bejahungen	Verneinungen	Fragen
I walked	**I didn't walk**	**Did I walk?**
You walked	**You didn't walk**	**Did you walk?**
He/She/It walked	**He/She/It didn't walk**	**Did he/she/it walk?**
We left	**We didn't leave**	**Did we leave?**
You left	**You didn't leave**	**Did you leave?**
They left	**They didn't leave**	**Did they leave?**

Anmerkungen:

- Das Verb ist in jeder Person gleich, außer für **be** (**was** in der 1. und 3. Person Singular, **were** in allen anderen Formen).
- Für Fragen und Verneinungen wird das Hilfsverb **do** im Imperfekt (**did**) verwendet. In einer Verneinung wird eher die Kurzform (**didn't**) als die Langform (**did not**) verwendet.
- Der *simple past* wird in Deutsch nicht unbedingt mit dem Imperfekt übersetzt.

  I was so tired yesterday.
  Ich war gestern so müde.

  Did you go by train last night?
  Bist du gestern mit dem Zug gefahren?

1.5 Die Zukunftsformen

Englisch besitzt keine bestimmte Zeitform für das Futur. Dieses wird auf unterschiedliche Weise ausgedrückt:

- mit dem Modalverb **will**
- mit **be going to**
- in den Zeitformen der Gegenwart

Will

Das Modalverb **will** wird folgendermaßen verwendet:

- für Vorhersagen der Zukunft.

  The weather tomorrow will be warm and sunny.
  Morgen wird es warm und sonnig sein.

- für ein Versprechen oder Angebot.

  I'll come next week.
  Ich komme nächste Woche.

- wenn man von einer weit entfernten Zukunft spricht.

  In ten years' time, we'll be retired.
  In zehn Jahren werden wir im Ruhestand sein.

Der Satzbau mit **will** ist wie folgt:

Will + Verb

Bejahungen	Verneinungen	Fragen
I will come	**I won't come**	**Will I come?**
You will come	**You won't come**	**Will you come?**
He/She/It will come	**He/She/It won't come**	**Will he/she/it come?**
We will come	**We won't come**	**Will we come?**
You will come	**You won't come**	**Will you come?**
They will come	**They won't come**	**Will they come?**

Anmerkung: die Kurzform von **will** ist **'ll**, die von **will not** ist **won't**.

Be going to

Be going to wird folgendermaßen verwendet:

- um eine nahe Zukunft auszudrücken.

  They're going to sleep.

  Sie gehen schlafen.

- für Vorhersagen.

  I think he's going to leave.

  Ich denke, er wird gehen.

- wenn bestimmt Faktoren der Gegenwart eine zukünftige Handlung vorhersehen lassen.

  It's cloudy today: it's going to rain.

  Es ist heute bewölkt: Es wird regnen.

Der Satzbau mit **be going to** ist wie folgt:

Be im Präsens + **going to** + Verb

Bejahungen	Verneinungen	Fragen
I am going to stay	**I am not going to stay**	**Am I going to stay?**
You are going to stay	**You are not going to stay**	**Are you going to stay?**
He/She/It is going to stay	**He/She/It is not going to stay**	**Is he/she/it going to stay?**
We are going to stay	**We are not going to stay**	**Are we going to stay?**
You are going to stay	**You are not going to stay**	**Are you going to stay?**
They are going to stay	**They are not going to stay**	**Are they going to stay?**

Anmerkungen:

- Die Kurzform des Verbs **be** kann verwendet werden.

  You aren't going to stay. / You're not going to stay.
  Du wirst nicht oder Sie werden nicht bleiben.

Die Gegenwartsform

Das Futur kann auch mit dem *simple present* oder dem *present progressive* ausgedrückt werden:

- für ein geplantes oder vorhersehbares Ereignis.

  The train arrives at 9:00 am.
  Der Zug kommt um 9 Uhr an.

  We're having a party next week.
  Wir geben nächste Woche eine Party.

- wenn es um die nahe Zukunft geht.

  What are you doing on Sunday?
  Was machst du am Sonntag?

1.6 *There is / There are*

Für **there + be** wird manchmal das Verb *sein* mit „da" oder „dort" verwendet, ansonsten ein anderes, passendes Verb. Auf **there** kann **be** in der Gegenwart, in der Vergangenheit oder im Futur (mit **will**) folgen.

There is a spider in my room.
Da ist eine Spinne in meinem Zimmer.

There were many people at this party.
Es oder *da waren viele Leute auf der Party.*

There will be a meeting tomorrow.
Morgen ist eine Sitzung geplant.

In einer Frage steht **there** hinter **be**.

Is there anyone at home?
Ist jemand zu Hause?

1.7 Die *phrasal verbs*

Die *phrasal verbs* bestehen aus Verben und darauffolgenden Adverbpartikeln oder Präpositionen (**in/on/out/up/off/...**). Der übliche Sinn eines Verbs kann sich durch die Partikel oder Präposition radikal ändern.

Turn right at the next corner.
Bieg an der nächsten Kreuzung rechts ab.

She turned off the radio.
Sie hat das Radio ausgemacht.

Es gibt verschiedene Wortstellungen:

- Verb + Partikel

  We grew up in Dublin.
  Wir sind in Dublin aufgewachsen.

She works out twice a week.
Sie trainiert zweimal die Woche.

- Verb + Partikel + Objekt

Can you look after the children?
Kannst du dich um die Kinder kümmern?

Please fill out this form.
Bitte füllen Sie das Formular aus.

- Verb + Objekt + Partikel

She'll call me back later.
Sie ruft mich später noch mal an.

He turned the job down.
Er hat die Stelle abgelehnt.

Bei manchen dieser *phrasal verbs* kann sich das Objekt in gleicher Weise vor oder hinter der Partikel befinden.

He took his coat off. / He took off his coat.
Er hat seinen Mantel ausgezogen.

I brought the book back. / I brought back the book.
Ich habe das Buch zurückgebracht.

Wenn es sich aber beim Objekt um ein Pronomen handelt, steht es unbedingt vor der Partikel.

He took it off.
Er hat ihn ausgezogen.

I brought it back.
Ich habe es zurückgebracht.

1.8 Die Modalverben

Die Modalverben haben eine einzige Form und stehen vor dem Verb im Infinitiv (ohne **to**). Es ist nicht möglich, zwei Modalverben oder ein Modalverb und ein Hilfsverb miteinander zu kombinieren.

Can (Gegenwart) und **could** (Vergangenheit und Konditional) drücken die Fähigkeit, die Möglichkeit oder eine Erlaubnis aus. Sie werden meistens mit „kennen" oder „dürfen" übersetzt. **Can't** ist die Kurzform der Verneinung **can not** und **couldn't** die Kurzform von **could not**.

She can run very fast.
Sie kann sehr schnell rennen.

He could be at his grandma's house.
Er könnte bei seiner Großmutter sein.

Can I go out tonight? No, you can't.
Darf ich heute abend ausgehen? Nein, das darfst du nicht.

May (Gegenwart) und **might** (Vergangenheit oder Konditional) drücken eine Wahrscheinlichkeit aus. In einem gehobenen Stil kann mit **may** auch eine Erlaubnis erbeten oder erteilt werden. **Might** wird verwendet, wenn die Wahrscheinlichkeit eines Ereignisses eher gering ist.

Diese beiden Modalverben haben in der Verneinung keine Kurzform.

He might come.
Vielleicht kommt er.

I may go to London next month.
Vielleicht fahre ich nächsten Monat nach London.

May I open the window? No, you may not.
Kann ich das Fenster öffnen? Nein, das kannst du nicht.

Mit dem Modalverb **must** wird ein Zwang, eine Verpflichtung ausgedrückt. Die häufigste Übersetzung ist „müssen". **Mustn't** ist die Kurzform der Verneinung **must not**.

I must see her.
Ich muss sie sehen.

They mustn't leave now.
Sie dürfen jetzt nicht gehen.

Should wird für einen Ratschlag oder eine Verpflichtung verwendet und entspricht „sollen". **Shouldn't** ist die Kurzform der Verneinung **should not**.

We should send her a postcard.
Wir sollten ihr eine Postkarte schicken.

You shouldn't drink and drive.
Du solltest nicht fahren, wenn du getrunken hast.

Would entspricht dem Konditional. **Wouldn't** ist die Kurzform der Verneinung **would not**.

I would like to come with you.
Ich würde gern mit dir kommen.

Anmerkung: Das Modalverb **will** wird Seite 23 behandelt.

2 Die Substantive

2.1 Zählbare Substantive

Manche Dinge sind Elemente, die einzeln gezählt werden können. Sie werden als **zählbare Substantive** bezeichnet und besitzen eine Singularform sowie einen Plural mit der Endung **-s**.

book → books
holiday → holidays

Zur Pluralformung der Substantive, die mit **-ss/ -s/ -ch/ -sh/ -x/ -o** enden, hängt man **-es** ans Wortende:

boss → bosses
ditch → ditches
domino → dominoes

Endet das Substantiv mit einem auf einen Konsonanten folgenden **-y**, wird dieses im Plural zu **-ies**:

baby → babies

Einige Substantive haben einen unregelmäßigen Plural:

Singular	Plural	Deutsch
child	**children**	*Kind(er)*
foot	**feet**	*Fuß, Füße*
mouse	**mice**	*Maus, Mäuse*
fish	**fish**	*Fisch(e)*
man	**men**	*Mann, Männer*
woman	**women**	*Frau(en)*
person	**people**	*Person(en)*
tooth	**teeth**	*Zahn, Zähne*

2.2 Singular- und Plural-Substantive, Sammelbezeichnungen

Manche Substantive werden nur im Singular verwendet. Es kann sein, dass das Substantiv etwas Einziges bezeichnet (**the air** *die Luft*, **the sun** *die Sonne*, **the past** *die Vergangenheit*); oft wird diese Art Substantiv mit dem Artikel **the** verwendet.

Manche Substantive haben keine Singularform (**your clothes** *deine Kleidung*). Sie werden mit **the** oder einem Possessivpronomen verwendet, und das Verb steht im Plural. Manche Sachen, die aus zwei gleichen Teilen bestehen, sind auch Plural-Substantive (**jeans** *die Jeans*, **glasses** *eine Brille*, **pyjamas** *ein Schlafanzug*, **scissors** *eine Schere*).

Sammelbezeichnungen sind Oberbegriffe, die eine Gruppe von Menschen oder Dingen bezeichnen (**family** *Familie*, **team** *Team, Mannschaft*, **army** *Armee*).

Die Verwendung des Verbs im Singular oder im Plural hängt davon ab, ob die Gruppe als einzelnes Element oder als Reihe mehrerer Personen betrachtet wird.

My family is in Brazil.
Meine Familie ist in Brasilien.

His family are all strange.
Seine ganze Familie ist seltsam.

2.3 Unzählbare Substantive

Manche Dinge können nicht gezählt werden und werden als unzählbare Substantive bezeichnet. Es handelt sich öfters um Substanzen, menschliche Eigenschaften, Gefühle, Aktivitäten oder abstrakte Begriffe.

Achtung! In manchen Fällen ist das englische Wort unzählbar, das deutsche aber zählbar: **advice** (*Ratschlag*), **progress** (*Fortschritt*), **furniture** (*Möbel*).

She has made a lot of progress in German.
Sie hat in Deutsch große Fortschritte gemacht.

Please forward all necessary information to us.
Bitte leiten Sie alle nötigen Informationen an uns weiter.

Unzählbare Substantive haben keine Pluralform und werden mit einem Verb im Singular verwendet. Man kann sie nicht mit den Artikeln **a/an**, aber mit **the/this/that**, einem Possessivpronomen und Wörtern oder Ausdrücken wie **some**, **much**, **any**, **a piece of**, usw. verbinden.

We sold this old piece of furniture.
Wir haben dieses alte Möbel verkauft.

This deal caused him a lot of harm.
Dieses Geschäft hat ihm sehr geschadet.

3 Die Determinative

3.1 Der unbestimmte und der bestimmte Artikel

A/an entsprechen den deutschen unbestimmten Artikeln „ein, eine" (**a week** *eine Woche*, **a book** *ein Buch*, **a person** *eine Person*). **An** steht vor Substantiven, die mit einem Vokal anfangen (**an elephant** *ein Elefant*, **an aunt** *eine Tante*, **an apple** *ein Apfel*).

Wenn man im Englischen von einer Art Sache, Tier oder Person im Allgemeinen spricht, wird der Plural des Substantivs ohne Artikel verwendet.

Adults often don't listen to children.
Oft hören Erwachsene den Kindern nicht zu.

The entspricht den deutschen bestimmten Artikeln „der, die, das, die" (**the person** *die Person*, **the people** *die Leute*; **the chair** *der Stuhl*, **the chairs** *die Stühle*).

3.2 Die Possessivbegleiter

Englisch	Deutsch
my	*mein/meine/meine*
your	*dein/deine/deine od. Ihr/Ihre/Ihre* (Höflichkeitsform)
his	*sein/seine/seine*
her	*ihr/ihre/ihre*
its	*sein/seine/seine*
our	*unser/unsere/unsere*
your	*euer/eure/eure*
their	*ihr/ihre/ihre*

Wie im Deutschen wird der Possessivbegleiter dem Besitzer und nicht dem Besessenen angeglichen.

She's eating her sandwich.
Sie isst ihr Sandwich.

He's meeting his girlfriend.
Er trifft sich mit seiner Freundin.

Um Besitz auszudrücken, wird auch der folgende Satzbau verwendet:

Besitzer + **'s** + Besessenes

Mark is Jane's brother.
Mark ist Janes Bruder.

Next week I am looking after my uncle's dog.
Nächste Woche hüte ich den Hund von meinem Onkel.

Steht der Besitzer im Plural und endet auf **-s**, wird nur ein Apostroph hinzugefügt.

My parents' new car is great.
Das neue Auto meiner Eltern ist super.

Her friends' house is in Burgundy.
Das Haus ihrer Freunde ist in Burgund.

3.3 Die Demonstrativpronomen

This bedeutet „dieser, diese, dieses" und wird im Deutschen auch mit „der, die, das" übersetzt; **these** ist die Pluralform („diese", „die"). **That** hat dieselbe Bedeutung und wird in manchen Fällen anstatt **this** verwendet, wenn man eine gewisse Vorstellung der Entfernung geben will (wie *jener, jene, jenes* im Deutschen, aber nicht gehoben). **Those** ist die Pluralform.

This book is a present from my mother.
Dieses Buch ist ein Geschenk von meiner Mutter.

When did you buy that hat?
Wann hast du diesen Hut gekauft?

Die Demonstrativpronomen werden auch substantivisch verwendet und werden dann meistens mit „der/die/das/die" übersetzt:

This is a list of rules.
Das ist die Liste der Vorschriften.

Those are mine.
Die gehören mir.

4 Die Pronomen

4.1 Personalpronomen (Subjekt und Objekt) und Possessivpronomen

Pronomen – Subjekt	Pronomen – Objekt	Possessivpronomen
I	me	mine
you	you	yours
he	him	his
she	her	hers
it	it	its
we	us	ours
you	you	yours
they	them	theirs

Anmerkungen:

- Es gibt auch das Possessivpronomen **its** aber es wird sehr selten verwendet.
- Die englischen Pronomen werden wie im Deutschen verwendet.

Have you seen him?
Hast du ihn gesehen?

Is that coffee yours or mine?
Ist das dein Kaffee oder meiner?

Can you help us?
Können Sie uns helfen?

Whose house is this? This is ours.
Wem gehört dieses Haus? Das ist unseres.

4.2 Die Fragewörter (Interrogativpronomen)

Die englischen Fragewörter sind: **what** (*was*), **when** (*wann*), **where** (*wo*), **why** (*warum*), **who** (*wer*), **how** (*wie*), **how many/how much** (*wie viel(e)*) und **which** (*welcher/welche/welches*). Sie dienen dazu, offene Fragen zu stellen, auf die man anders als mit Ja oder Nein antworten kann. Wie in allen Fragen verschiebt sich auch hier die Stellung von Subjekt und Hilfsverb.

Which do you like best?
Welche(n/s) magst du lieber?

Where do you live?
Wo wohnst du?

When did she arrive?
Wann ist sie angekommen?

Why did you do it?
Warum hast du das gemacht?

What have you done with my book?
Was hast du mit meinem Buch gemacht?

How did he get here?
Wie ist er hierher gekommen?

How many cats does she have?
Wie viele Katzen hat sie?

Zu dieser Regel gibt es eine Ausnahme: Wenn das Subjekt der Frage auch Subjekt des Verbs ist, ändert sich die Wortstellung nicht und man verwendet ein einfaches Verb (ohne Hilfsverb).

Who is this person?
Wer ist diese Person?

What happened?
Was ist passiert?

Where are they?
Wo sind sie?

How could you do this?
Wie konntest du das tun?

Englisch – Deutsch

English – German

KEYWORD

a [ə] (*before vowel and silent h*: **an**) *indef art* **1** ein; (*before feminine noun*) eine; **a book** ein Buch; **a lamp** eine Lampe; **she's a doctor** sie ist Ärztin; **a hundred/thousand** *etc* **pounds** einhundert/eintausend *etc* Pfund
2 (*in expressing ratios, prices etc*) pro; **3 a day/week** 3 pro Tag/Woche, 3 am Tag/in der Woche; **10 km an hour** 10 km pro Stunde

AA *n abbr* (Brit: = *Automobile Association*) *Autofahrerorganisation*, ≈ ADAC *m*
aback [əˈbæk] *adv*: **to be taken ~** verblüfft sein
abandon [əˈbændən] *vt* verlassen; (*give up*) aufgeben
abbey [ˈæbɪ] *n* Abtei *f*
abbreviate [əˈbriːvɪeɪt] *vt* abkürzen
abbreviation [əbriːvɪˈeɪʃən] *n* Abkürzung *f*
ABC *n* Abc *nt*
abdicate [ˈæbdɪkeɪt] *vi* (*monarch*) abdanken
abdication [æbdɪˈkeɪʃən] *n* Abdankung *f*
abdomen [ˈæbdəmɛn] *n* Unterleib *m*
ability [əˈbɪlɪtɪ] *n* Fähigkeit *f*
able [ˈeɪbl] *adj* fähig; **to be ~ to do sth** etw tun können
abnormal [æbˈnɔːməl] *adj* abnorm; (*child*) anormal
aboard [əˈbɔːd] *adv* (*Naut, Aviat*) an Bord ▸ *prep* an Bord +*gen*
abolish [əˈbɔlɪʃ] *vt* abschaffen
Aborigine [æbəˈrɪdʒɪnɪ] *n* Ureinwohner(in) *m(f)* Australiens
abort [əˈbɔːt] *vt* abtreiben; (*Comput*) abbrechen
abortion [əˈbɔːʃən] *n* Abtreibung *f*

KEYWORD

about [əˈbaut] *adv* **1** (*approximately*) etwa, ungefähr; **about a hundred/thousand** *etc* etwa hundert/tausend *etc*; **at about two o'clock** etwa um zwei Uhr; **I've just about finished** ich bin gerade fertig
2 (*referring to place*) herum; **to run/walk** *etc* **about** herumlaufen/-gehen *etc*
3: **to be about to do sth** im Begriff sein, etw zu tun; **she was about to leave/wash the dishes** sie wollte gerade gehen/das Geschirr spülen
▸ *prep* **1** (*relating to*) über +*acc*; **what is it about?** worum geht es?; (*book etc*) wovon handelt es?; **we talked about it** wir haben darüber geredet; **what** *or* **how about going to the cinema?** wollen wir ins Kino gehen?
2 (*referring to place*) um ... herum; **to walk about the town** durch die Stadt gehen; **her clothes were scattered about the room** ihre Kleider waren über das ganze Zimmer verstreut

above [əˈbʌv] *adv* oben ▸ *prep* über +*dat*; **~ all** vor allem
abroad [əˈbrɔːd] *adv* (*be*) im Ausland; (*go*) ins Ausland
abrupt [əˈbrʌpt] *adj* abrupt
abscess [ˈæbsɪs] *n* Abszess *m*
absence [ˈæbsəns] *n* Abwesenheit *f*
absent [ˈæbsənt] *adj* abwesend; **to be ~** fehlen
absent-minded [ˈæbsəntˈmaɪndɪd] *adj* zerstreut
absolute [ˈæbsəluːt] *adj* absolut; (*power*) uneingeschränkt
absolutely [æbsəˈluːtlɪ] *adv* absolut; (*agree*) vollkommen; **~!** genau!
absorb [əbˈzɔːb] *vt* (*light, heat*) absorbieren; **to be absorbed in a book** in ein Buch vertieft sein
absorbent [əbˈzɔːbənt] *adj* saugfähig
absorbent cotton (US) *n* Watte *f*
absorbing [əbˈzɔːbɪŋ] *adj* saugfähig; (*book, film, work etc*) fesselnd

abstain [əb'steɪn] *vi* (*voting*) sich (der Stimme) enthalten
abstract ['æbstrækt] *adj* abstrakt
absurd [əb'sə:d] *adj* absurd
abundance [ə'bʌndəns] *n* Reichtum *m*
abuse *n* [ə'bju:s] (*insults*) Beschimpfungen *pl*; (*misuse*) Missbrauch *m* ▶ *vt* [ə'bju:z] beschimpfen; missbrauchen
abusive [ə'bju:sɪv] *adj* beleidigend
AC *abbr* = **alternating current**
a/c *abbr* (*Banking etc*) = **account**
academic [ækə'dɛmɪk] *adj* akademisch (*also pej*); (*work*) wissenschaftlich ▶ *n* Akademiker(in) *m(f)*
accelerate [æk'sɛləreɪt] *vt* beschleunigen ▶ *vi* (*Aut*) Gas geben
acceleration [æksɛlə'reɪʃən] *n* Beschleunigung *f*
accelerator [æk'sɛləreɪtə^r] *n* Gaspedal *nt*
accent ['æksɛnt] *n* Akzent *m*
accept [ək'sɛpt] *vt* annehmen; (*risk*) in Kauf nehmen; (*responsibility*) übernehmen
acceptable [ək'sɛptəbl] *adj* annehmbar
access ['æksɛs] *n* Zugang *m*
accessible [æk'sɛsəbl] *adj* erreichbar
accessory [æk'sɛsərɪ] *n* Zubehörteil *nt*
access road *n* Zufahrt(sstraße) *f*
accident ['æksɪdənt] *n* (*mishap, disaster*) Unfall *m*; **by ~** zufällig
accidental [æksɪ'dɛntl] *adj* zufällig; (*death, damage*) Unfall-
accident-prone ['æksɪdənt'prəun] *adj* vom Pech verfolgt
acclimatize [ə'klaɪmətaɪz], (*US*) **acclimate** [ə'klaɪmət] *vt*: **to become acclimatized to** sich gewöhnen an *+acc*
accommodate [ə'kɔmədeɪt] *vt* unterbringen
accommodation [əkɔmə'deɪʃən] *n* Unterkunft *f* ■ **accommodations** *npl* (*US*) Unterkunft *f*
accompany [ə'kʌmpənɪ] *vt* begleiten
accomplish [ə'kʌmplɪʃ] *vt* vollenden; (*achieve*) erreichen
accord [ə'kɔ:d] *n*: **of his own ~** freiwillig
according [ə'kɔ:dɪŋ] *prep*: **~ to** zufolge *+dat*
account [ə'kaunt] *n* (*in bank, department store*) Konto *nt*; (*report*) Bericht *m*; **on no ~** auf keinen Fall; **on ~ of** wegen *+gen*; **to take into ~, take ~ of** berücksichtigen
▶ **account for** *vt fus* erklären; (*expenditure*) Rechenschaft ablegen für
accountant [ə'kauntənt] *n* Buchhalter(in) *m(f)*
account number *n* Kontonummer *f*
accumulate [ə'kju:mjuleɪt] *vt* ansammeln ▶ *vi* sich ansammeln
accuracy ['ækjurəsɪ] *n* Genauigkeit *f*
accurate ['ækjurɪt] *adj* genau
accusation [ækju'zeɪʃən] *n* (*instance*) Beschuldigung *f*; (*Law*) Anklage *f*
accusative [ə'kju:zətɪv] *n* Akkusativ *m*
accuse [ə'kju:z] *vt*: **to ~ sb (of sth)** jdn (einer Sache *gen*) beschuldigen; (*Law*) jdn (wegen etw *dat*) anklagen
accused [ə'kju:zd] *n* (*Law*): **the ~** der/die Angeklagte
accustom [ə'kʌstəm] *vt* gewöhnen; **to ~ o.s. to sth** sich an etw *acc* gewöhnen
accustomed [ə'kʌstəmd] *adj* gewohnt; **~ to** gewohnt an *+acc*
ace [eɪs] *n* Ass *nt*
ache [eɪk] *n* Schmerz *m* ▶ *vi* wehtun; **my head aches** mir tut der Kopf weh
achieve [ə'tʃi:v] *vt* (*aim, result*) erreichen
achievement [ə'tʃi:vmənt] *n* (*success, feat*) Leistung *f*
acid ['æsɪd] *adj* sauer ▶ *n* (*Chem*) Säure *f*
acid rain *n* saurer Regen *m*
acknowledge [ək'nɔlɪdʒ] *vt* (*also*: **~ receipt of**) den Empfang *+gen* bestätigen; (*fact*) zugeben; (*situation*) zur Kenntnis nehmen
acknowledgement [ək'nɔlɪdʒmənt] *n* Empfangsbestätigung *f*
acne ['æknɪ] *n* Akne *f*
acorn ['eɪkɔ:n] *n* Eichel *f*
acoustic [ə'ku:stɪk] *adj* akustisch
acoustics [ə'ku:stɪks] *n* Akustik *f*
acquaintance [ə'kweɪntəns] *n* Bekannte(r) *f(m)*
acquire [ə'kwaɪə^r] *vt* erwerben
acquisition [ækwɪ'zɪʃən] *n* (*of skills*) Erwerb *m*; (*object*) Anschaffung *f*
acrobat ['ækrəbæt] *n* Akrobat(in) *m(f)*
across [ə'krɔs] *prep* über *+acc*; (*on the other side of*) auf der anderen Seite *+gen* ▶ *adv* (*direction*) hinüber, herüber; (*measurement*) breit
act [ækt] *n* Tat *f*; (*of play*) Akt *m*; (*Law*) Gesetz *nt* ▶ *vi* handeln; (*behave*) sich

verhalten; (*Theat*) spielen ▶ *vt* spielen; **it's only an ~** es ist nur Schau; **to be in the ~ of doing sth** dabei sein, etw zu tun; **to ~ as** fungieren als

action [ˈækʃən] *n* Tat *f*; (*motion*) Bewegung *f*; (*Mil*) Kampf *m*; **out of ~** (*person*) nicht einsatzfähig; (*thing*) außer Betrieb; **to take ~** etwas unternehmen; **to put a plan into ~** einen Plan in die Tat umsetzen

action replay *n* (*TV*) Wiederholung *f*

activate [ˈæktɪveɪt] *vt* in Betrieb setzen; (*Chem, Phys*) aktivieren

active [ˈæktɪv] *adj* aktiv; (*volcano*) tätig

activity [ækˈtɪvɪtɪ] *n* Aktivität *f*; (*pastime, pursuit*) Betätigung *f*

actor [ˈæktəʳ] *n* Schauspieler *m*

actress [ˈæktrɪs] *n* Schauspielerin *f*

actual [ˈæktjuəl] *adj* wirklich

actually [ˈæktjuəlɪ] *adv* wirklich; (*in fact*) tatsächlich

acupuncture [ˈækjupʌŋktʃəʳ] *n* Akupunktur *f*

acute [əˈkjuːt] *adj* akut; (*mind*) scharf; (*Math*: *angle*) spitz

AD *adv abbr* (= *Anno Domini*) n. Chr.

ad [æd] (*inf*) *n* = **advertisement**

adapt [əˈdæpt] *vt* anpassen; (*novel etc*) bearbeiten ▶ *vi*: **to ~ (to)** sich anpassen (an +*acc*)

adaptable [əˈdæptəbl] *adj* anpassungsfähig

adaptation [ædæpˈteɪʃən] *n* (*of novel etc*) Bearbeitung *f*

adapter [əˈdæptəʳ] *n* (*Elec*) Adapter *m*

add [æd] *vt* hinzufügen; (*figures*: *also*: **~ up**) zusammenzählen
▶ **add up** *vt* (*figures*) zusammenzählen
▶ *vi*: **it doesn't ~ up** (*fig*) es ergibt keinen Sinn

addict [ˈædɪkt] *n* Süchtige(r) *f*(*m*)

addicted [əˈdɪktɪd] *adj*: **to be ~ to drugs/drink** drogensüchtig/ alkoholsüchtig sein

addition [əˈdɪʃən] *n* (*adding up*) Zusammenzählen *nt*; (*thing added*) Zusatz *m*; (: *to payment, bill*) Zuschlag *m*; **in ~ (to)** zusätzlich (zu)

additional [əˈdɪʃənl] *adj* zusätzlich

additive [ˈædɪtɪv] *n* Zusatz *m*

address [əˈdrɛs] *n* Adresse *f* ▶ *vt* adressieren; (*speak to*: *person*) ansprechen

adequate [ˈædɪkwɪt] *adj* ausreichend, adäquat; (*satisfactory*) angemessen

adhesive [ədˈhiːzɪv] *n* Klebstoff *m*

adhesive tape *n* (BRIT) Klebstreifen *m*

adjacent [əˈdʒeɪsənt] *adj*: **~ to** neben +*dat*

adjective [ˈædʒɛktɪv] *n* Adjektiv *nt*

adjoining [əˈdʒɔɪnɪŋ] *adj* benachbart, Neben-

adjust [əˈdʒʌst] *vt* anpassen; (*clothing*) zurechtrücken; (*machine etc*) einstellen ▶ *vi*: **to ~ (to)** sich anpassen (an +*acc*)

adjustable [əˈdʒʌstəbl] *adj* verstellbar

admin [ˈædmɪn] (*inf*) *n* = **administration**

administration [ədmɪnɪsˈtreɪʃən] *n* (*management*) Verwaltung *f*; (*government*) Regierung *f*

admirable [ˈædmərəbl] *adj* bewundernswert

admiration [ædməˈreɪʃən] *n* Bewunderung *f*

admire [ədˈmaɪəʳ] *vt* bewundern

admission [ədˈmɪʃən] *n* (*admittance*) Zutritt *m*; (*entry fee*) Eintritt(spreis) *m*; (*confession*) Geständnis *nt*

admission charge, admission fee *n* Eintrittspreis *m*

admit [ədˈmɪt] *vt* (*confess*) gestehen; (*permit to enter*) einlassen; (*to club, hospital*) aufnehmen

adolescent [ædəuˈlɛsnt] *n* Jugendliche(r) *f*(*m*)

adopt [əˈdɔpt] *vt* adoptieren; (*policy, attitude, accent*) annehmen

adoption [əˈdɔpʃən] *n* Adoption *f*; Annahme *f*

adorable [əˈdɔːrəbl] *adj* entzückend

adore [əˈdɔːʳ] *vt* (*person*) verehren

ADSL *abbr* (= *asymmetric digital subscriber line*) ADSL *nt*

adult [ˈædʌlt] *n* Erwachsene(r) *f*(*m*) ▶ *adj* erwachsen; (*literature etc*) für Erwachsene

adultery [əˈdʌltərɪ] *n* Ehebruch *m*

advance [ədˈvɑːns] *n* (*progress*) Fortschritt *m*; (*money*) Vorschuss *m* ▶ *vt* (*money*) vorschießen ▶ *vi* (*move forward*) vorrücken ▶ *adj*: **~ booking** Vorverkauf *m*; **~ payment** Vorauszahlung *f*; **in ~** im Voraus

advanced [ədˈvɑːnst] *adj* (*Scol*: *studies*) für Fortgeschrittene; (*ideas*) fortschrittlich

advantage [ədˈvɑːntɪdʒ] *n* Vorteil *m*; **to take ~ of** ausnutzen; (*opportunity*) nutzen; **it's to our ~ (to)** es ist für uns von Vorteil(, wenn wir)

adventure [əd'vɛntʃə^r] *n* Abenteuer *nt*

adventure holiday *n* Abenteuerurlaub *m*

adventure playground *n* Abenteuerspielplatz *m*

adventurous [əd'vɛntʃərəs] *adj* abenteuerlustig

adverb ['ædvəːb] *n* Adverb *nt*

adverse ['ædvəːs] *adj* ungünstig

advert ['ædvəːt] (BRIT) *n* = **advertisement**

advertise ['ædvətaɪz] *vi* (*Comm*) werben; (*in newspaper*) annoncieren, inserieren ▶ *vt* (*product, event*) werben für; (*job*) ausschreiben; **to ~ for** (*staff, accommodation etc*) (per Anzeige) suchen

advertisement [əd'vəːtɪsmənt] *n* (*Comm*) Werbung *f*; (*in classified ads*) Anzeige *f*

advertising ['ædvətaɪzɪŋ] *n* Werbung *f*

advice [əd'vaɪs] *n* Rat *m*; **a piece of ~** ein Rat(schlag)

advisable [əd'vaɪzəbl] *adj* ratsam

advise [əd'vaɪz] *vt* (*person*) raten +*dat*; **to ~ sb of sth** jdn von etw in Kenntnis setzen; **to ~ against sth** von etw abraten; **to ~ against doing sth** davon abraten, etw zu tun

Aegean [iː'dʒiːən] *n*: **the ~ (Sea)** (*Geog*) die Ägäis, das Ägäische Meer

aerial ['ɛərɪəl] *n* Antenne *f* ▶ *adj* (*view, bombardment etc*) Luft-

aerobatics ['ɛərəu'bætɪks] *npl* fliegerische Kunststücke *pl*

aerobics [ɛə'rəubɪks] *n* Aerobic *nt*

aeroplane ['ɛərəpleɪn] (BRIT) *n* Flugzeug *nt*

afaik *abbr* (*SMS: = as far as I know*) ≈ soweit ich weiß

affair [ə'fɛə^r] *n* Angelegenheit *f*; (*romance: also:* **love ~**) Verhältnis *nt*

affect [ə'fɛkt] *vt* (*influence*) sich auswirken auf +*acc*; (*subj: disease*) befallen; (*move deeply*) bewegen; (*concern*) betreffen

affection [ə'fɛkʃən] *n* Zuneigung *f*

affectionate [ə'fɛkʃənɪt] *adj* liebevoll

affluent ['æfluənt] *adj* wohlhabend

afford [ə'fɔːd] *vt* sich *dat* leisten; **can we ~ a car?** können wir uns ein Auto leisten?

affordable [ə'fɔːdəbl] *adj* erschwinglich

Afghanistan [æf'gænɪstæn] *n* Afghanistan *nt*

aforementioned [ə'fɔːmɛnʃənd] *adj* oben erwähnt

afraid [ə'freɪd] *adj* ängstlich; **to be ~ of** Angst haben vor +*dat*; **I am ~ that …** leider …

Africa ['æfrɪkə] *n* Afrika *nt*

African ['æfrɪkən] *adj* afrikanisch ▶ *n* Afrikaner(in) *m(f)*

African American, Afro-American ['æfrəuə'mɛrɪkən] *n* Afroamerikaner(in) *m(f)*

after ['ɑːftə^r] *prep* nach +*dat*; (*of place*) hinter +*dat* ▶ *adv* danach ▶ *conj* nachdem; **what are you ~?** was willst du?; **the police are ~ him** die Polizei ist hinter ihm her; **it's twenty ~ eight** (*US*) es ist zwanzig nach acht; **~ all** schließlich

aftercare ['ɑːftəkɛə^r] (BRIT) *n* Nachbehandlung *f*

aftereffects ['ɑːftərɪfɛkts] *npl* Nachwirkungen *pl*

afternoon ['ɑːftə'nuːn] *n* Nachmittag *m*

afternoon tea *n siehe Info-Artikel*

AFTERNOON TEA

Der **afternoon tea** ist eine ziemlich gehaltvolle Zwischenmahlzeit, die am Nachmittag eingenommen wird. Sie wurde im 19. Jahrhundert von der englischen Oberschicht eingeführt, deren Mitglieder sich bei dem einen oder anderen zum Tee versammelten. Der *afternoon tea* ist auch heute noch geläufig, obwohl man sich eher im Freundeskreis in einem Hotel oder Café trifft, meistens zu besonderen Anlässen. Ein typischer *afternoon tea* besteht aus Toastbrot-Sandwiches, *scones* mit Rahm und Marmelade, einer Auswahl an Feingebäck und Tee oder Kaffee.

afterparty ['ɑːftəpɑːtɪ] *n* anschließende Feier *f*

afters ['ɑːftəz] (BRIT *inf*) *n* Nachtisch *m*

after-sales service [ɑːftə'seɪlz-] (BRIT) *n* Kundendienst *m*

aftershave, aftershave lotion *n* Rasierwasser *nt*

aftersun ['ɑːftəsʌn] *n* After-Sun-Lotion *f*

afterwards [ˈɑːftəwədz], (*US*) **afterward** [ˈɑːftəwəd] *adv* danach
again [əˈgɛn] *adv* (*once more*) noch einmal; (*repeatedly*) wieder; **not him ~!** nicht schon wieder er!; **~ and ~** immer wieder
against [əˈgɛnst] *prep* gegen *+acc*
age [eɪdʒ] *n* Alter *nt*; (*period*) Zeitalter *nt* ▶ *vi* altern, alt werden; **what ~ is he?** wie alt ist er?; **under ~** minderjährig; **to come of ~** mündig werden
aged[1] [eɪdʒd] *adj*: **~ ten** zehn Jahre alt, zehnjährig
aged[2] [ˈeɪdʒɪd] *npl*: **the ~** die Alten *pl*
age group *n* Altersgruppe *f*
ageism [ˈeɪdʒɪzəm] *n* Diskriminierung *f* aufgrund des Alters
age limit *n* Altersgrenze *f*
agency [ˈeɪdʒənsɪ] *n* Agentur *f*
agenda [əˈdʒɛndə] *n* Tagesordnung *f*
agent [ˈeɪdʒənt] *n* (*Comm*) Vertreter(in) *m*(*f*); (*representative, spy*) Agent(in) *m*(*f*)
aggression [əˈgrɛʃən] *n* Aggression *f*
aggressive [əˈgrɛsɪv] *adj* aggressiv
agitated [ˈædʒɪteɪtɪd] *adj* aufgeregt
AGM *n abbr* (= *annual general meeting*) JHV *f*
ago [əˈgəu] *adv*: **two days ~** vor zwei Tagen; **not long ~** vor Kurzem
agonize [ˈægənaɪz] *vi*: **to ~ over sth** sich *dat* den Kopf über etw *acc* zermartern
agonizing [ˈægənaɪzɪŋ] *adj* qualvoll
agony [ˈægənɪ] *n* (*pain*) Schmerz *m*
agree [əˈgriː] *vt* (*price, date*) vereinbaren ▶ *vi* übereinstimmen; (*consent*) zustimmen; **to ~ to sth** einer Sache *dat* zustimmen; **to ~ to do sth** sich bereit erklären, etw zu tun; **to ~ that** (*admit*) zugeben, dass
agreement [əˈgriːmənt] *n* (*concurrence*) Übereinstimmung *f*; (*contract*) Vertrag *m*
agricultural [ægrɪˈkʌltʃərəl] *adj* landwirtschaftlich; (*show*) Landwirtschafts-
agriculture [ˈægrɪkʌltʃəʳ] *n* Landwirtschaft *f*
ahead [əˈhɛd] *adv* vor uns/ihnen *etc*; **~ of** (*in advance of*) vor *+dat*; **to be ~ of sb** (*in progress, ranking*) vor jdm liegen
aid [eɪd] *n* Hilfe *f* ▶ *vt* (*help*) helfen, unterstützen; **with the ~ of** mithilfe von; **in ~ of** zugunsten *+gen*; **to ~ and abet** Beihilfe leisten; *see also* **hearing aid**
AIDS [eɪdz] *n abbr* (= *acquired immune deficiency syndrome*) AIDS *nt*
aim [eɪm] *vt*: **to ~ at** (*gun, missile, camera*) richten auf *+acc* ▶ *vi* (*also:* **take ~**) zielen ▶ *n* (*objective*) Ziel *nt*; **to ~ at** zielen auf *+acc*; (*objective*) anstreben *+acc*; **to ~ to do sth** vorhaben, etw zu tun
air [ɛəʳ] *n* Luft *f* ▶ *vt* lüften; **to be on the ~** (*Radio, TV: programme*) gesendet werden; (*: station*) senden
airbag [ˈɛəbæg] *n* (*Aut*) Airbag *m*
air-conditioned [ˈɛəkənˈdɪʃənd] *adj* klimatisiert
air conditioning *n* Klimaanlage *f*
aircraft [ˈɛəkrɑːft] *n inv* Flugzeug *nt*
airfield [ˈɛəfiːld] *n* Flugplatz *m*
Air Force *n* Luftwaffe *f*
air gun *n* Luftgewehr *nt*
airline [ˈɛəlaɪn] *n* Fluggesellschaft *f*
air mail *n*: **by ~** per *or* mit Luftpost
airplane [ˈɛəpleɪn] (*US*) *n* Flugzeug *nt*
airport [ˈɛəpɔːt] *n* Flughafen *m*
airsick [ˈɛəsɪk] *adj* luftkrank
airtight [ˈɛətaɪt] *adj* luftdicht
air-traffic controller [ˈɛətræfɪk-] *n* Fluglotse *m*
airy [ˈɛərɪ] *adj* luftig; (*casual*) lässig
aisle [aɪl] *n* Gang *m*; (*section of church*) Seitenschiff *nt*
aisle seat *n* Sitz *m* am Gang
ajar [əˈdʒɑːʳ] *adj* angelehnt
alarm [əˈlɑːm] *n* (*anxiety*) Besorgnis *f*; (*in shop, bank*) Alarmanlage *f* ▶ *vt* (*worry*) beunruhigen
alarm clock *n* Wecker *m*
alarmed [əˈlɑːmd] *adj* beunruhigt
alarming [əˈlɑːmɪŋ] *adj* (*worrying*) beunruhigend
Albania [ælˈbeɪnɪə] *n* Albanien *nt*
Albanian [ælˈbeɪnɪən] *adj* albanisch ▶ *n* (*Ling*) Albanisch *nt*
album [ˈælbəm] *n* Album *nt*
alcohol [ˈælkəhɔl] *n* Alkohol *m*
alcohol-free [ˈælkəhɔlfriː] *adj* alkoholfrei
alcoholic [ælkəˈhɔlɪk] *adj* alkoholisch ▶ *n* Alkoholiker(in) *m*(*f*)
alcoholism [ˈælkəhɔlɪzəm] *n* Alkoholismus *m*
ale [eɪl] *n* Ale *nt*
alert [əˈləːt] *adj* aufmerksam ▶ *n* Alarm *m* ▶ *vt*: **to ~ sb (to sth)** jdn (vor etw *dat*) warnen

A level (BRIT) *n Abschluss der britischen Sekundarstufe II*, ≈ Abitur *nt*

A LEVEL

Die **A levels** (*Advanced levels*) sind in England, Wales und Nordirland die Prüfungen zum höchsten Schulabschluss. Sie werden über zwei Jahre vorbereitet, wobei das erste Jahr selbst mit einer Reihe von Prüfungen (*AS levels*) abgeschlossen wird. Die *A2*-Prüfungen finden am Ende des Jahres statt. Die Ergebnisse der *AS levels* und *A2* bestimmen die *A levels*. Ähnlich dem Abitur erfolgen die Prüfungen in drei bis fünf Fächern. Die Hochschulreife und die eventuelle Aufnahme in eine der gewünschten Universitäten sind von den Noten abhängig.

algebra [ˈældʒɪbrə] *n* Algebra *f*
Algeria [ælˈdʒɪərɪə] *n* Algerien *nt*
alibi [ˈælɪbaɪ] *n* Alibi *nt*
alien [ˈeɪlɪən] *n* Ausländer(in) *m(f)*; (*extraterrestrial*) außerirdisches Wesen *nt*
align [əˈlaɪn] *vt* ausrichten
alike [əˈlaɪk] *adj* ähnlich ▸ *adv* (*similarly*) ähnlich; (*equally*) gleich
alive [əˈlaɪv] *adj* (*lively*) lebendig

 **KEYWORD**

all [ɔːl] *adj* alle(r, s); **all day/night** den ganzen Tag/die ganze Nacht (über); **all men are equal** alle Menschen sind gleich; **all five came** alle fünf kamen; **all the books** die ganzen Bücher, alle Bücher; **all the time** die ganze Zeit (über); **all his life** sein ganzes Leben (lang)
▸ *pron* **1** alles; **I ate it all, I ate all of it** ich habe alles gegessen; **all of us/the boys went** wir alle/alle Jungen gingen; **we all sat down** wir setzten uns alle
2 (*in phrases*): **above all** vor allem; **after all** schließlich; **all in all** alles in allem; **not at all** (*in answer to question*) überhaupt nicht; (*in answer to thanks*) gern geschehen; **I'm not at all tired** ich bin überhaupt nicht müde; **anything at all will do** es ist egal, welche(r, s)
▸ *adv* ganz; **all alone** ganz allein; **it's not as hard as all that** so schwer ist es nun auch wieder nicht; **all the more/the better** um so mehr/besser; **the score is 2 all** der Spielstand ist 2 zu 2

allegation [ælɪˈgeɪʃən] *n* Behauptung *f*
alleged [əˈlɛdʒd] *adj* angeblich
allergic [əˈləːdʒɪk] *adj* (*rash, reaction*) allergisch; **~ to** (*person*) allergisch gegen
allergy [ˈælədʒɪ] *n* Allergie *f*
alleviate [əˈliːvɪeɪt] *vt* lindern
alley [ˈælɪ] *n* Gasse *f*
alliance [əˈlaɪəns] *n* Bündnis *nt*
alligator [ˈælɪgeɪtə^r] *n* Alligator *m*
all-night [ˈɔːlˈnaɪt] *adj* (*café, cinema*) die ganze Nacht geöffnet
allocate [ˈæləkeɪt] *vt* zuteilen
allotment [əˈlɔtmənt] *n* (*garden*) Schrebergarten *m*
allow [əˈlau] *vt* erlauben; (*sum, time*) einplanen; (*claim, goal*) anerkennen
▸ **allow for** *vt fus* einplanen, berücksichtigen
allowance [əˈlauəns] *n* (*welfare payment*) Beihilfe *f*; (*pocket money*) Taschengeld *nt*
all right *adv* (*well*) gut; (*correctly*) richtig; (*as answer*) okay, in Ordnung
all-time [ˈɔːlˈtaɪm] *adj* aller Zeiten
allusion [əˈluːʒən] *n* Anspielung *f*
ally [ˈælaɪ] *n* Verbündete(r) *f(m)*; (*during wars*) Alliierte(r) *f(m)*
almond [ˈɑːmənd] *n* Mandel *f*
almost [ˈɔːlməust] *adv* fast
alone [əˈləun] *adj, adv* allein
along [əˈlɔŋ] *prep* entlang *+acc* ▸ *adv*: **is he coming ~ with us?** kommt er mit?; **~ with** (*together with*) zusammen mit; **all ~** (*all the time*) die ganze Zeit
alongside [əˈlɔŋˈsaɪd] *prep* neben *+dat* ▸ *adv* (*come*) nebendran
aloud [əˈlaud] *adv* laut
alphabet [ˈælfəbɛt] *n* Alphabet *nt*
alpine [ˈælpaɪn] *adj* alpin
Alps [ælps] *npl*: **the ~** die Alpen
already [ɔːlˈrɛdɪ] *adv* schon
Alsace [ˈælsæs] *n* Elsass *nt*
Alsatian [ælˈseɪʃən] (BRIT) *n* (*dog*) Schäferhund *m*
also [ˈɔːlsəu] *adv* (*too*) auch
altar [ˈɔltə^r] *n* Altar *m*
alter [ˈɔltə^r] *vt* ändern
alteration [ɔltəˈreɪʃən] *n* Änderung *f*
■ **alterations** *npl* (*Archit*) Umbau *m*

alternate *adj* [ɔlˈtəːnɪt] abwechselnd ▶ *vi* [ˈɔltəneɪt]: **to ~ (with)** sich abwechseln (mit)
alternating current [ˈɔltəːneɪtɪŋ-] *n* Wechselstrom *m*
alternative [ɔlˈtəːnətɪv] *adj* alternativ; (*solution etc*) Alternativ- ▶ *n* Alternative *f*
although [ɔːlˈðəu] *conj* obwohl
altitude [ˈæltɪtjuːd] *n* Höhe *f*
altogether [ɔːltəˈgɛðəʳ] *adv* ganz; (*on the whole, in all*) insgesamt
aluminium [ælјuˈmɪnɪəm], (*US*) **aluminum** [əˈluːmɪnəm] *n* Aluminium *nt*
always [ˈɔːlweɪz] *adv* immer
am [æm] *vb see* **be**
a.m. *adv abbr* (= *ante meridiem*) vormittags
amateur [ˈæmətəʳ] *n* Amateur *m* ▶ *adj* (*Sport*) Amateur-; **~ dramatics** Laientheater *nt*
amaze [əˈmeɪz] *vt* erstaunen; **to be amazed (at)** erstaunt sein (über +*acc*)
amazing [əˈmeɪzɪŋ] *adj* erstaunlich
Amazon [ˈæməzən] *n* (*river*) Amazonas *m*
ambassador [æmˈbæsədəʳ] *n* Botschafter(in) *m(f)*
amber [ˈæmbəʳ] *n* Bernstein *m*
ambiguity [æmbɪˈgjuɪtɪ] *n* Zweideutigkeit *f*
ambiguous [æmˈbɪgjuəs] *adj* zweideutig
ambition [æmˈbɪʃən] *n* Ehrgeiz *m*; (*desire*) Ambition *f*
ambitious [æmˈbɪʃəs] *adj* ehrgeizig
ambulance [ˈæmbjuləns] *n* Krankenwagen *m*
amend [əˈmɛnd] *vt* ändern
America [əˈmɛrɪkə] *n* Amerika *nt*
American [əˈmɛrɪkən] *adj* amerikanisch ▶ *n* Amerikaner(in) *m(f)*
amiable [ˈeɪmɪəbl] *adj* liebenswürdig
amicable [ˈæmɪkəbl] *adj* freundschaftlich; (*settlement*) gütlich
amnesia [æmˈniːzɪə] *n* Gedächtnisschwund *m*
among [əˈmʌŋ], **amongst** [əˈmʌŋst] *prep* unter +*dat*
amount [əˈmaunt] *n* (*quantity*) Menge *f*; (*sum of money*) Betrag *m*; (*of bill etc*) Höhe *f* ▶ *vi*: **to ~ to** (*total*) sich belaufen auf +*acc*
amp [æmp], **ampère** [ˈæmpɛəʳ] *n* Ampere *nt*
amplifier [ˈæmplɪfaɪəʳ] *n* Verstärker *m*
amputate [ˈæmpjuteɪt] *vt* amputieren
amuse [əˈmjuːz] *vt* (*entertain*) unterhalten; (*make smile*) amüsieren; **he was not amused** er fand das gar nicht komisch *or* zum Lachen
amusement [əˈmjuːzmənt] *n* (*mirth*) Vergnügen *nt*; (*pleasure*) Unterhaltung *f*
amusement arcade *n* Spielhalle *f*
amusement park *n* Vergnügungspark *m*
amusing [əˈmjuːzɪŋ] *adj* amüsant
an [æn, ən] *indef art see* **a**
anaemic, (*US*) **anemic** [əˈniːmɪk] *adj* blutarm
anaesthetic, (*US*) **anesthetic** [ænɪsˈθɛtɪk] *n* Betäubungsmittel *nt*
analyse, (*US*) **analyze** [ˈænəlaɪz] *vt* analysieren
analysis [əˈnæləsɪs] (*pl* **analyses**) *n* Analyse *f*
analyze [ˈænəlaɪz] (*US*) *vt* = **analyse**
anatomy [əˈnætəmɪ] *n* Anatomie *f*; (*body*) Körper *m*
ancestor [ˈænsɪstəʳ] *n* Vorfahr(in) *m(f)*
anchor [ˈæŋkəʳ] *n* Anker *m* ▶ *vt* (*fig*) verankern
anchorage [ˈæŋkərɪdʒ] *n* Ankerplatz *m*
anchovy [ˈæntʃəvɪ] *n* Sardelle *f*
ancient [ˈeɪnʃənt] *adj* alt; (*person, car*) uralt
and [ænd] *conj* und
Andorra [ænˈdɔːrə] *n* Andorra *nt*
anesthetic *etc* [ænɪsˈθɛtɪk] (*US*) = **anaesthetic** *etc*
angel [ˈeɪndʒəl] *n* Engel *m*
anger [ˈæŋgəʳ] *n* Zorn *m* ▶ *vt* ärgern
angina [ænˈdʒaɪnə] *n* Angina pectoris *f*
angle [ˈæŋgl] *n* Winkel *m*; (*viewpoint*): **from their ~** von ihrem Standpunkt aus
angler [ˈæŋgləʳ] *n* Angler(in) *m(f)*
angling [ˈæŋglɪŋ] *n* Angeln *nt*
angry [ˈæŋgrɪ] *adj* verärgert; **to be ~ with sb** auf jdn böse sein
angular [ˈæŋgjuləʳ] *adj* eckig; (*features*) kantig
animal [ˈænɪməl] *n* Tier *nt*
animated [ˈænɪmeɪtɪd] *adj* lebhaft; (*film*) Zeichentrick-
aniseed [ˈænɪsiːd] *n* Anis *m*
ankle [ˈæŋkl] *n* Knöchel *m*
annex [ˈænɛks] *n* (*extension*) Anbau *m*
anniversary [ænɪˈvəːsərɪ] *n* Jahrestag *m*

announce [əˈnauns] *vt* ankündigen; (*birth, death etc*) anzeigen
announcement [əˈnaunsmənt] *n* Ankündigung *f*; (*official*) Bekanntmachung *f*
announcer [əˈnaunsəʳ] *n* Ansager(in) *m(f)*
annoy [əˈnɔɪ] *vt* ärgern; **to be annoyed (at sth/with sb)** sich (über etw/jdn) ärgern
annoyance [əˈnɔɪəns] *n* Ärger *m*
annoying [əˈnɔɪɪŋ] *adj* ärgerlich; (*person, habit*) lästig
annual [ˈænjuəl] *adj* jährlich ▸ *n* (*book*) Jahresband *m*
anonymous [əˈnɔnɪməs] *adj* anonym
anorak [ˈænəræk] *n* Anorak *m*
anorexia [ænəˈrɛksɪə] *n* Magersucht *f*
anorexic [ænəˈrɛksɪk] *adj* magersüchtig
another [əˈnʌðəʳ] *pron* (*different*) ein anderer, eine andere, ein anderes ▸ *adj*: **~ book** (*one more*) noch ein Buch
answer [ˈɑːnsəʳ] *n* Antwort *f*; (*to problem*) Lösung *f* ▸ *vi* antworten ▸ *vt* (*reply to: person*) antworten *+dat*; (*: letter, question*) beantworten; **to ~ the phone** ans Telefon gehen; **to ~ the bell** *or* **the door** die Tür aufmachen
▸ **answer back** *vi* widersprechen
answering machine [ˈɑːnsərɪŋ-] *n* Anrufbeantworter *m*
ant [ænt] *n* Ameise *f*
Antarctic [æntˈɑːktɪk] *n*: **the ~** die Antarktis
Antarctic Circle *n*: **the ~** der südliche Polarkreis
antelope [ˈæntɪləup] *n* Antilope *f*
antenna [ænˈtɛnə] (*pl* **antennae**) *n* (*of insect*) Fühler *m*; (*Radio, TV*) Antenne *f*
anti... [ˈæntɪ] *pref* Anti-, anti-
antibiotic [ˈæntɪbaɪˈɔtɪk] *n* Antibiotikum *nt*
anticipate [ænˈtɪsɪpeɪt] *vt* erwarten
anticipation [æntɪsɪˈpeɪʃən] *n* Erwartung *f*
anticlimax [ˈæntɪˈklaɪmæks] *n* Enttäuschung *f*
anticlockwise [ˈæntɪˈklɔkwaɪz] (Brit) *adv* gegen den Uhrzeigersinn
antidote [ˈæntɪdəut] *n* Gegenmittel *nt*
antifreeze [ˈæntɪfriːz] *n* Frostschutzmittel *nt*
Antipodes [ænˈtɪpədiːz] *npl*: **the ~** Australien und Neuseeland *nt*
antiquarian [æntɪˈkwɛərɪən] *adj*: **~ bookshop** Antiquariat *nt*
antique [ænˈtiːk] *n* Antiquität *f* ▸ *adj* antik
antique shop *n* Antiquitätenladen *m*
anti-Semitism [ˈæntɪˈsɛmɪtɪzəm] *n* Antisemitismus *m*
antiseptic [æntɪˈsɛptɪk] *n* Antiseptikum *nt*
antisocial *adj* unsozial; (*person*) ungesellig
antivirus *adj* (*Comput*) Antiviren-
antivirus software *n* Antivirensoftware *f*
antlers [ˈæntləz] *npl* Geweih *nt*
anxiety [æŋˈzaɪətɪ] *n* (*worry*) Sorge *f*
anxious [ˈæŋkʃəs] *adj* (*worried*) besorgt

KEYWORD

any [ˈɛnɪ] *adj* **1** (*in questions etc*): **have you any butter/children?** haben Sie Butter/Kinder?; **if there are any tickets left** falls noch Karten da sind
2 (*with negative*) kein(e); **I haven't any money/books** ich habe kein Geld/keine Bücher
3 (*no matter which*) irgendein(e); **choose any book you like** nehmen Sie irgendein Buch *or* ein beliebiges Buch
4 (*in phrases*): **in any case** in jedem Fall; **any day now** jeden Tag; **at any moment** jeden Moment; **at any rate** auf jeden Fall
▸ *pron* **1** (*in questions etc*): **have you got any?** haben Sie welche?; **can any of you sing?** kann (irgend)einer von euch singen?
2 (*with negative*): **I haven't any (of them)** ich habe keine (davon)
3 (*no matter which one(s)*) egal welche; **take any of those books (you like)** nehmen Sie irgendwelche von diesen Büchern
▸ *adv* **1** (*in questions etc*): **do you want any more soup/sandwiches?** möchtest du noch Suppe/Butterbrote?; **are you feeling any better?** geht es Ihnen etwas besser?
2 (*with negative*): **I can't hear him any more** ich kann ihn nicht mehr hören

anybody [ˈɛnɪbɔdɪ] *pron* = **anyone**

KEYWORD

anyhow [ˈɛnɪhau] *adv* (*at any rate*) sowieso, ohnehin; **I shall go anyhow** ich gehe auf jeden Fall

KEYWORD

anyone [ˈɛnɪwʌn] *pron* **1** (*in questions etc*) (irgend)jemand; **can you see anyone?** siehst du jemanden?
2 (*with negative*) keine(r); **I can't see anyone** ich kann keinen *or* n iemanden sehen
3 (*no matter who*) jede(r); **anyone could do it** das kann jeder

anyplace [ˈɛnɪpleɪs] (*US*) *adv* = **anywhere**

KEYWORD

anything [ˈɛnɪθɪŋ] *pron* **1** (*in questions etc*) (irgend)etwas; **can you see anything?** kannst du etwas sehen?
2 (*with negative*): **I can't see anything** ich kann nichts sehen
3 (*no matter what*): **you can say anything you like** du kannst sagen, was du willst; **anything between 15 and 20 pounds** (ungefähr) zwischen 15 und 20 Pfund; **he'll eat anything** er isst alles

anytime *adv* jederzeit

KEYWORD

anyway [ˈɛnɪweɪ] *adv* **1** (*at any rate*) sowieso, ohnehin
2 (*besides*): **anyway, I can't come** jedenfalls kann ich nicht kommen; **why are you phoning, anyway?** warum rufst du überhaupt *or* eigentlich an?

KEYWORD

anywhere [ˈɛnɪwɛəʳ] *adv* **1** (*in questions etc*) irgendwo
2 (*no matter where*) irgendwo; **put the books down anywhere** legen Sie die Bücher irgendwohin

apart [əˈpɑːt] *adv* (*move*) auseinander; **they are living ~** sie leben getrennt; **~ from** (*excepting*) abgesehen von

apartment [əˈpɑːtmənt] *n* (*US: flat*) Wohnung *f*

apartment block, (*US*) **apartment building** *n* Wohnblock *m*

ape [eɪp] *n* (Menschen)affe *m*

apéritif *n* Aperitif *m*

apologize [əˈpɔlədʒaɪz] *vi*: **to ~ (for sth to sb)** sich (für etw bei jdm) entschuldigen

apology [əˈpɔlədʒɪ] *n* Entschuldigung *f*

apostrophe [əˈpɔstrəfɪ] *n* Apostroph *m*

app [æp] *n abbr* (*inf: Comput:* = *application*) App *f*

appal [əˈpɔːl] *vt* entsetzen; **to be appalled by** entsetzt sein über +*acc*

appalling *adj* entsetzlich

apparatus [æpəˈreɪtəs] *n* Gerät *nt*; (*of organization*) Apparat *m*

apparent [əˈpærənt] *adj* (*seeming*) scheinbar; (*obvious*) offensichtlich

apparently [əˈpærəntlɪ] *adv* anscheinend

appeal [əˈpiːl] *vi* (*Law*) Berufung einlegen ▶ *n* (*Law*) Berufung *f*; (*plea*) Aufruf *m*; (*charm*) Reiz *m*; **to ~ to** (*be attractive to*) gefallen +*dat*

appealing [əˈpiːlɪŋ] *adj* ansprechend

appear [əˈpɪəʳ] *vi* erscheinen; (*seem*) scheinen

appearance [əˈpɪərəns] *n* Erscheinen *nt*; (*look*) Aussehen *nt*; (*in public, on TV*) Auftritt *m*

appendicitis [əpɛndɪˈsaɪtɪs] *n* Blinddarmentzündung *f*

appendix [əˈpɛndɪks] (*pl* **appendices**) *n* (*Anat*) Blinddarm *m*; (*to publication*) Anhang *m*

appetite [ˈæpɪtaɪt] *n* Appetit *m*; (*fig*) Lust *f*

appetizing [ˈæpɪtaɪzɪŋ] *adj* appetitanregend

applause [əˈplɔːz] *n* Applaus *m*, Beifall *m*

apple [ˈæpl] *n* Apfel *m*

apple crumble *n mit Streuseln bestreutes Apfeldessert*

apple juice *n* Apfelsaft *m*

apple pie *n* gedeckter Apfelkuchen *m*

apple puree, apple sauce *n* Apfelmus *nt*

apple tart *n* Apfelkuchen *m*

apple tree *n* Apfelbaum *m*
appliance [əˈplaɪəns] *n* Gerät *nt*
applicable [əˈplɪkəbl] *adj*: **~ (to)** anwendbar (auf +*acc*); (*on official forms*) zutreffend (auf +*acc*)
applicant [ˈæplɪkənt] *n* Bewerber(in) *m(f)*
application [æplɪˈkeɪʃən] *n* (*for job*) Bewerbung *f*; (*for grant etc*) Antrag *m*
application form *n* (*for grant etc*) Antragsformular *nt*
apply [əˈplaɪ] *vt* anwenden; (*paint etc*) auftragen ▸ *vi*: **to ~ (to)** (*be applicable*) gelten (für); **to ~ the brakes** die Bremse betätigen, bremsen; **to ~ for** (*permit, grant*) beantragen
appoint [əˈpɔɪnt] *vt* ernennen
appointment [əˈpɔɪntmənt] *n* Ernennung *f*; (*arranged meeting*) Termin *m*; **by ~** nach Anmeldung, mit Voranmeldung
appreciate [əˈpriːʃɪeɪt] *vt* (*be grateful for*) zu schätzen wissen; (*understand*) verstehen ▸ *vi* (*Comm*: *currency, shares*) im Wert steigen; **I ~ your help** ich weiß Ihre Hilfe zu schätzen
appreciation [əpriːʃɪˈeɪʃən] *n* (*enjoyment*) Wertschätzung *f*; (*understanding*) Verständnis *nt*; (*gratitude*) Dankbarkeit *f*
apprehensive [æprɪˈhɛnsɪv] *adj* ängstlich
apprentice [əˈprɛntɪs] *n* Lehrling *m*
approach [əˈprəutʃ] *vi* sich nähern ▸ *vt* (*come to*) sich nähern +*dat*; (*ask, apply to*: *person*) herantreten an +*acc*; (*situation, problem*) angehen
appropriate [əˈprəuprɪɪt] *adj* (*apt*) angebracht; (*relevant*) entsprechend
appropriately [əˈprəuprɪɪtlɪ] *adv* entsprechend
approval [əˈpruːvəl] *n* (*approbation*) Zustimmung *f*; (*permission*) Einverständnis *f*
approve [əˈpruːv] *vt* billigen
▸ **approve of** *vt fus* etwas halten von; **I don't ~ of it/him** ich halte nichts davon/von ihm
approx. *abbr* = **approximately**
approximate [əˈprɔksɪmɪt] *adj* ungefähr
approximately *adv* ungefähr
apricot [ˈeɪprɪkɔt] *n* Aprikose *f*
April [ˈeɪprəl] *n* April *m*; *see also* **July**
April Fools' Day *n siehe Info-Artikel*

APRIL FOOLS' DAY

April Fools' Day, der 1. April, bietet die Gelegenheit zu Streichen aller Art, deren Opfer die *April fools* sind. Traditionsgemäß nach sollen solche Streiche nur bis Mittag gespielt werden.

apron [ˈeɪprən] *n* Schürze *f*
aptitude [ˈæptɪtjuːd] *n* Begabung *f*
aquarium [əˈkwɛərɪəm] *n* Aquarium *nt*
Aquarius [əˈkwɛərɪəs] *n* Wassermann *m*
Arab [ˈærəb] *n* Araber(in) *m(f)*
Arabian [əˈreɪbɪən] *adj* arabisch
Arabic [ˈærəbɪk] *adj* arabisch ▸ *n* (*Ling*) Arabisch *nt*
arbitrary [ˈɑːbɪtrərɪ] *adj* willkürlich
arcade [ɑːˈkeɪd] *n* Arkade *f*; (*shopping mall*) Passage *f*
arch [ɑːtʃ] *n* Bogen *m*
archaeologist, (*US*) **archeologist** [ɑːkɪˈɔlədʒɪst] *n* Archäologe *m*, Archäologin *f*
archaeology, (*US*) **archeology** [ɑːkɪˈɔlədʒɪ] *n* Archäologie *f*
archaic [ɑːˈkeɪɪk] *adj* altertümlich; (*language*) veraltet, archaisch
archbishop [ɑːtʃˈbɪʃəp] *n* Erzbischof *m*
archeology *etc* [ɑːkɪˈɔlədʒɪ] (*US*) = **archaeology** *etc*
archery [ˈɑːtʃərɪ] *n* Bogenschießen *nt*
architect [ˈɑːkɪtɛkt] *n* Architekt(in) *m(f)*
architecture [ˈɑːkɪtɛktʃəʳ] *n* Architektur *f*
archives [ˈɑːkaɪvz] *npl* Archiv *nt*
archway [ˈɑːtʃweɪ] *n* Torbogen *m*
Arctic [ˈɑːktɪk] *n*: **the ~** die Arktis
Arctic Circle *n*: **the ~** der nördliche Polarkreis
are [ɑːʳ] *vb see* **be**
area [ˈɛərɪə] *n* Gebiet *nt*; (*dining area etc*) Bereich *m*; **in the London ~** im Raum London
area code (*US*) *n* Vorwahl(nummer) *f*
aren't [ɑːnt] = **are not**
Argentina [ɑːdʒənˈtiːnə] *n* Argentinien *nt*
argue [ˈɑːgjuː] *vi* (*quarrel*) sich streiten; **to ~ that ...** den Standpunkt vertreten, dass ...; **to ~ for/against sth** sich für/gegen etw aussprechen
argument [ˈɑːgjumənt] *n* (*reasons*) Argument *nt*; (*quarrel*) Streit *m*,

Auseinandersetzung *f*; **to have an ~** sich streiten
Aries [ˈɛərɪz] *n* Widder *m*
arise [əˈraɪz] (*pt* **arose**, *pp* **arisen**) *vi* (*difficulty etc*) sich ergeben; (*question*) sich stellen
aristocracy [ærɪsˈtɔkrəsɪ] *n* Adel *m*
aristocrat [ˈærɪstəkræt] *n* Ad(e)lige(r) *f*(*m*)
aristocratic [ærɪstəˈkrætɪk] *adj* aristokratisch, ad(e)lig
arm [ɑːm] *n* Arm *m*; (*of clothing*) Ärmel *m*; (*of chair*) Armlehne *f* ▸ *vt* bewaffnen ▪ **arms** *npl* (*weapons*) Waffen *pl*
armchair [ˈɑːmtʃɛəʳ] *n* Lehnstuhl *m*
armed [ɑːmd] *adj* bewaffnet
armpit [ˈɑːmpɪt] *n* Achselhöhle *f*
army [ˈɑːmɪ] *n* Armee *f*, Heer *nt*
aroma [əˈrəumə] *n* Aroma *nt*, Duft *m*
aromatherapy [ərəuməˈθɛrəpɪ] *n* Aromatherapie *f*
arose [əˈrəuz] *pt of* **arise**
around [əˈraund] *adv* (*about*) herum; (*in the area*) in der Nähe ▸ *prep* (*encircling*) um ... herum; (*near*) in der Nähe von; (*fig: time*) gegen
arr. *abbr* (= *arrival*; *arrives*) Ank.
arrange [əˈreɪndʒ] *vt* (*meeting etc*) vereinbaren; (*tour etc*) planen; (*books etc*) anordnen; (*flowers*) arrangieren; **it was arranged that ...** es wurde vereinbart, dass ...; **to ~ to do sth** vereinbaren *or* ausmachen, etw zu tun
arrangement [əˈreɪndʒmənt] *n* (*agreement*) Vereinbarung *f*; (*layout*) Anordnung *f* ▪ **arrangements** *npl* Pläne *pl*; (*preparations*) Vorbereitungen *pl*
arrest [əˈrɛst] *vt* (*person*) verhaften ▸ *n* Verhaftung *f*; **under ~** verhaftet
arrival [əˈraɪvl] *n* Ankunft *f*; **new ~** (*person*) Neuankömmling *m*
arrivals *n* (*airport*) Ankunftshalle *f*
arrive [əˈraɪv] *vi* ankommen
▸ **arrive at** *vt fus* (*fig: conclusion*) kommen zu
arrogant [ˈærəgənt] *adj* arrogant
arrow [ˈærəu] *n* Pfeil *m*
arse [ɑːs] (Brit *!*) *n* Arsch *m* (*!*)
art [ɑːt] *n* Kunst *f* ▪ **Arts** *npl* (*Scol*) Geisteswissenschaften *pl*
artery [ˈɑːtərɪ] *n* Arterie *f*, Schlagader *f*
art gallery *n* Kunstgalerie *f*
arthritis [ɑːˈθraɪtɪs] *n* Arthritis *f*
artichoke [ˈɑːtɪtʃəuk] *n* (*also:* **globe ~**) Artischocke *f*
article [ˈɑːtɪkl] *n* Artikel *m*; (*object, item*) Gegenstand *m*
artificial [ɑːtɪˈfɪʃəl] *adj* künstlich; (*manner*) gekünstelt
artist [ˈɑːtɪst] *n* Künstler(in) *m*(*f*)
artistic [ɑːˈtɪstɪk] *adj* künstlerisch

 **KEYWORD**

as [æz] *conj* **1** (*referring to time*) als; **as the years went by** mit den Jahren; **he came in as I was leaving** als er hereinkam, ging ich gerade; **as from tomorrow** ab morgen
2 (*in comparisons*): **as big as** so groß wie; **twice as big as** zweimal so groß wie; **as much/many as** so viel/so viele wie; **as soon as** sobald
3 (*since, because*) da, weil; **he left early as he had to be home by 10** er ging früher, da er um 10 zu Hause sein musste
4 (*referring to manner, way*) wie; **do as you wish** mach, was du willst; **as she said** wie sie sagte; **he gave it to me as a present** er gab es mir als Geschenk
5 (*in the capacity of*) als; **he works as a driver** er arbeitet als Fahrer
6 (*concerning*): **as for** *or* **to that** was das betrifft *or* angeht
7: **as if** *or* **though** als ob
see also **long**; **such**; **well**

a.s.a.p. *adv abbr* (= *as soon as possible*) baldmöglichst
ash [æʃ] *n* Asche *f*; (*wood, tree*) Esche *f*
ashamed [əˈʃeɪmd] *adj* beschämt; **to be ~ of** sich schämen für
ashore [əˈʃɔːʳ] *adv* an Land
ashtray [ˈæʃtreɪ] *n* Aschenbecher *m*
Asia [ˈeɪʃə] *n* Asien *nt*
Asian [ˈeɪʃən] *adj* asiatisch ▸ *n* Asiat(in) *m*(*f*)
aside [əˈsaɪd] *adv* zur Seite; (*take*) beiseite
ask [ɑːsk] *vt* fragen; (*invite*) einladen; **to ~ sb to do sth** jdn bitten, etw zu tun; **to ~ (sb) sth** (jdn) etw fragen; **to ~ sb a question** jdm eine Frage stellen
▸ **ask for** *vt fus* bitten um
asleep [əˈsliːp] *adj*: **to be ~** schlafen; **to fall ~** einschlafen
AS level *n abbr* (= *Advanced Subsidiary level*) erstes Jahr der britischen Sekundarstufe II
asparagus [əsˈpærəgəs] *n* Spargel *m*

aspect [ˈæspɛkt] *n* (*of subject*) Aspekt *m*
aspirin [ˈæsprɪn] *n* Aspirin® *nt*
ass [æs] *n* (*also fig*) Esel *m*; (*US inf*) Arsch *m* (!)
assassinate [əˈsæsɪneɪt] *vt* ermorden
assassination [əsæsɪˈneɪʃən] *n* Ermordung *f*
assault [əˈsɔːlt] *n* Angriff *m* ▶ *vt* angreifen
assemble [əˈsɛmbl] *vt* versammeln; (*car, machine*) montieren ▶ *vi* sich versammeln
assembly [əˈsɛmblɪ] *n* Versammlung *f*; (*of car, machine*) Montage *f*
assembly hall *n* Aula *f*
assert [əˈsəːt] *vt* behaupten
assertion [əˈsəːʃən] *n* Behauptung *f*
assess [əˈsɛs] *vt* (*situation*) einschätzen
assessment [əˈsɛsmənt] *n* Einschätzung *f*
asset [ˈæsɛt] *n* Vorteil *m*; (*person*) Stütze *f* ■ **assets** *npl* (*property, funds*) Vermögen *nt*
assign [əˈsaɪn] *vt*: **to ~ (to)** (*date*) zuweisen (+*dat*)
assignment [əˈsaɪnmənt] *n* Aufgabe *f*
assist [əˈsɪst] *vt* helfen
assistance [əˈsɪstəns] *n* Hilfe *f*
assistant [əˈsɪstənt] *n* Assistent(in) *m(f)*; (Brit: *also*: **shop ~**) Verkäufer(in) *m(f)*
assistant referee *n* (*Sport*) Schiedsrichterassistent(in) *m(f)*
associate [əˈsəuʃɪeɪt] *vt* in Verbindung bringen
association [əsəusɪˈeɪʃən] *n* (*group*) Verband *m*; (*involvement*) Verbindung *f*; **in ~ with** in Zusammenarbeit mit
assorted [əˈsɔːtɪd] *adj* gemischt
assortment [əˈsɔːtmənt] *n* Mischung *f*; (*of books, people etc*) Ansammlung *f*
assume [əˈsjuːm] *vt* annehmen; (*responsibilities etc*) übernehmen
assumption [əˈsʌmpʃən] *n* Annahme *f*
assurance [əˈʃuərəns] *n* Versicherung *f*; (*confidence*) Zuversicht *f*
assure [əˈʃuəʳ] *vt* versichern; (*guarantee*) sichern
assured [əˈʃuəd] *adj* sicher
asterisk [ˈæstərɪsk] *n* Sternchen *nt*
asthma [ˈæsmə] *n* Asthma *nt*
astonish [əˈstɔnɪʃ] *vt* erstaunen
astonished [əˈstɔnɪʃt] *adj* erstaunt (*at* über)
astonishing [əˈstɔnɪʃɪŋ] *adj* erstaunlich
astonishment [əˈstɔnɪʃmənt] *n* Erstaunen *nt*
astound [əˈstaund] *vt* sehr erstaunen
astounding [əˈstaundɪŋ] *adj* erstaunlich
astray [əˈstreɪ] *adv*: **to go ~** (*letter*) verloren gehen; **to lead ~** auf Abwege bringen
astrology [əsˈtrɔlədʒɪ] *n* Astrologie *f*
astronaut [ˈæstrənɔːt] *n* Astronaut(in) *m(f)*
astronomy [əsˈtrɔnəmɪ] *n* Astronomie *f*
asylum [əˈsaɪləm] *n* Asyl *nt*; (*mental hospital*) psychiatrische Klinik *f*
asylum seeker *n* Asylbewerber(in) *m(f)*

 KEYWORD

at [æt] *prep* **1** (*referring to position, direction*) an +*dat*, in +*dat*; **at the top** an der Spitze; **at home** zu Hause; **at school** in der Schule; **at the baker's** beim Bäcker; **to look at sth** auf etw *acc* blicken
2 (*referring to time*): **at four o'clock** um vier Uhr; **at night/dawn** bei Nacht/Tagesanbruch; **at Christmas** zu Weihnachten; **at times** zuweilen
3 (*referring to rates, speed etc*): **at £2 a kilo** zu £2 pro Kilo; **two at a time** zwei auf einmal; **at 50 km/h** mit 50 km/h
4 (*referring to activity*): **to be at work** (*in office etc*) auf der Arbeit sein; **to play at cowboys** Cowboy spielen; **to be good at sth** gut in etw *dat* sein
5 (*referring to cause*): **shocked/surprised/annoyed at sth** schockiert/überrascht/verärgert über etw *acc*; **I went at his suggestion** ich ging auf seinen Vorschlag hin
6: **not at all** (*in answer to question*) überhaupt nicht, ganz und gar nicht; (*in answer to thanks*) nichts zu danken, keine Ursache; **I'm not at all tired** ich bin überhaupt nicht müde; **anything at all** irgendetwas
7 (*@ symbol*) At-Zeichen *nt*

ate [eɪt] *pt of* **eat**
athlete [ˈæθliːt] *n* Athlet(in) *m(f)*
athletic [æθˈlɛtɪk] *adj* sportlich; (*muscular*) athletisch

athletics [æθˈlɛtɪks] *n* Leichtathletik *f*
Atlantic [ətˈlæntɪk] *n*: **the ~ (Ocean)** der Atlantik
atlas [ˈætləs] *n* Atlas *m*
ATM *abbr (= automated teller machine)* Geldautomat *m*
atmosphere [ˈætməsfɪəʳ] *n* Atmosphäre *f*
atom [ˈætəm] *n* Atom *nt*
atom bomb, atomic bomb *n* Atombombe *f*
atomic [əˈtɔmɪk] *adj* atomar; (*energy, weapons*) Atom-
A to Z® [ˈeɪtəˈzed] *n* Stadtplan *m*
atrocious [əˈtrəuʃəs] *adj* grauenhaft
atrocity [əˈtrɔsɪtɪ] *n* Gräueltat *f*
attach [əˈtætʃ] *vt* befestigen; (*document, letter*) anheften, beiheften; (*importance etc*) beimessen; **to be attached to sb/sth** (*like*) an jdm/etw hängen; **to ~ a file to an email** eine Datei an eine E-Mail anhängen
attachment [əˈtætʃmənt] *n* (*to email*) Attachment *nt*, Anhang *m*; (*love*): **~ (to sb)** Zuneigung *f* (zu jdm)
attack [əˈtæk] *vt* angreifen ▸ *n* (*also fig*) Angriff *m*; (*of illness*) Anfall *m*
attempt [əˈtɛmpt] *n* Versuch *m* ▸ *vt* versuchen
attend [əˈtɛnd] *vt* besuchen
▸ **attend to** *vt fus* sich kümmern um; (*customer*) bedienen
attendance [əˈtɛndəns] *n* Anwesenheit *f*; (*people present*) Besucherzahl *f*
attendant [əˈtɛndənt] *n* (*helper*) Begleiter(in) *m(f)*; (*in museum*) Aufseher(in) *m(f)*
attention [əˈtɛnʃən] *n* Aufmerksamkeit *f* ▸ *excl* (*Mil*) Achtung!; **for the ~ of ...** zu Händen von ...
attentive [əˈtɛntɪv] *adj* aufmerksam
attic [ˈætɪk] *n* Dachboden *m*
attitude [ˈætɪtjuːd] *n* (*posture, manner*) Haltung *f*; (*mental*): **~ to** *or* **towards** Einstellung *f* zu
attorney [əˈtəːnɪ] *n* (*US: lawyer*) (Rechts)anwalt *m*, (Rechts)anwältin *f*
attract [əˈtrækt] *vt* (*draw*) anziehen; (*interest*) auf sich *acc* lenken; (*attention*) erregen
attraction [əˈtrækʃən] *n* Anziehungskraft *f*; (*gen pl: amusements*) Attraktion *f*
attractive [əˈtræktɪv] *adj* attraktiv; (*price, idea, offer*) reizvoll
aubergine [ˈəubəʒiːn] *n* Aubergine *f*
auction [ˈɔːkʃən] *n* (*also:* **sale by ~**) Versteigerung *f*, Auktion *f* ▸ *vt* versteigern
audible [ˈɔːdɪbl] *adj* hörbar
audience [ˈɔːdɪəns] *n* Publikum *nt*; (*Radio*) Zuhörer *pl*; (*TV*) Zuschauer *pl*
audition [ɔːˈdɪʃən] *n* Vorsprechprobe *f* ▸ *vi*: **to ~ (for)** vorsprechen (für)
auditorium [ɔːdɪˈtɔːrɪəm] *n* (*audience area*) Zuschauerraum *m*
Aug. *abbr* = **August**
August [ˈɔːgəst] *n* August *m*; *see also* **July**
aunt [ɑːnt] *n* Tante *f*
au pair [ˈəuˈpɛəʳ] *n* (*also:* **au pair girl**) Aupair(mädchen) *nt*, Au-pair(-Mädchen) *nt*
Australia [ɔsˈtreɪlɪə] *n* Australien *nt*
Australian [ɔsˈtreɪlɪən] *adj* australisch ▸ *n* Australier(in) *m(f)*
Austria [ˈɔstrɪə] *n* Österreich *nt*
Austrian [ˈɔstrɪən] *adj* österreichisch ▸ *n* Österreicher(in) *m(f)*
authentic [ɔːˈθɛntɪk] *adj* authentisch
authenticity [ɔːθɛnˈtɪsɪtɪ] *n* Echtheit *f*
author [ˈɔːθəʳ] *n* (*of text*) Verfasser(in) *m(f)*; (*profession*) Autor(in) *m(f)*
authority [ɔːˈθɔrɪtɪ] *n* Autorität *f*; (*government body*) Behörde *f*, Amt *nt*; (*official permission*) Genehmigung *f*
■ **the authorities** *npl* (*ruling body*) die Behörden *pl*
authorize [ˈɔːθəraɪz] *vt* genehmigen; **to ~ sb to do sth** jdn ermächtigen, etw zu tun
auto [ˈɔːtəu] (*US*) *n* Auto *nt*
autobiography [ɔːtəbaɪˈɔgrəfɪ] *n* Autobiografie *f*
autograph [ˈɔːtəgrɑːf] *n* Autogramm *nt*
automatic [ɔːtəˈmætɪk] *adj* automatisch ▸ *n* (*car*) Automatikwagen *m*
automobile [ˈɔːtəməbiːl] (*US*) *n* Auto(mobil) *nt*
autumn [ˈɔːtəm] *n* Herbst *m*
auxiliary [ɔːgˈzɪlɪərɪ] *adj* (*tool, verb*) Hilfs- ▸ *n* (*assistant*) Hilfskraft *f*
availability [əveɪləˈbɪlɪtɪ] *n* Erhältlichkeit *f*; (*of staff*) Vorhandensein *nt*
available [əˈveɪləbl] *adj* erhältlich; (*person: unoccupied*) frei, abkömmlich;

(: *unattached*) zu haben; (*time*) frei, verfügbar
avalanche [ˈævəlɑːnʃ] *n* (*also fig*) Lawine *f*
avatar [ˈævətɑːʳ] *n* (*Comput*) Avatar *m*
Ave *abbr* = **avenue**
avenue [ˈævənjuː] *n* Straße *f*
average [ˈævərɪdʒ] *n* Durchschnitt *m* ▶ *adj* durchschnittlich, Durchschnitts-; **on ~** im Durchschnitt, durchschnittlich
avian flu [ˈeɪvɪən-] *n* Vogelgrippe *f*
aviation [eɪvɪˈeɪʃən] *n* Luftfahrt *f*
avocado [ævəˈkɑːdəu] (BRIT) *n* (*also*: **~ pear**) Avocado *f*
avoid [əˈvɔɪd] *vt* (*person, obstacle*) ausweichen *+dat*; (*trouble*) vermeiden
avoidable [əˈvɔɪdəbl] *adj* vermeidbar
awake [əˈweɪk] (*pt* **awoke**, *pp* **awoken** *or* **awaked**) *adj* wach ▶ *vi* aufwachen
award [əˈwɔːd] *n* Preis *m*; (*for bravery*) Auszeichnung *f* ▶ *vt* (*prize*) verleihen; (*damages*) zusprechen
aware [əˈwɛəʳ] *adj*: **~ (of)** bewusst (*+gen*); **to become ~ of** sich *dat* bewusst werden *+gen*; **I am fully ~ that** es ist mir völlig klar *or* bewusst, dass
away [əˈweɪ] *adv* weg; (*position*) entfernt; **two kilometres ~** zwei Kilometer entfernt; **he's ~ for a week** er ist eine Woche nicht da
away game *n* Auswärtsspiel *nt*
awful [ˈɔːfəl] *adj* furchtbar, schrecklich
awfully [ˈɔːfəlɪ] *adv* furchtbar
awkward [ˈɔːkwəd] *adj* (*clumsy*) unbeholfen; (*inconvenient, difficult*) ungünstig; (*embarrassing*) peinlich
awning [ˈɔːnɪŋ] *n* (*of shop etc*) Markise *f*
awoke [əˈwəuk] *pt of* **awake**
awoken [əˈwəukən] *pp of* **awake**
axe, (*US*) **ax** [æks] *n* Axt *f*
axle [ˈæksl] *n* Achse *f*

b

BA *n abbr* (= *Bachelor of Arts*) *see* **bachelor**
babe [beɪb] *n* (*liter*) Kindlein *nt*; (*esp US*: *address*) Schätzchen *nt*
baby [ˈbeɪbɪ] *n* Baby *nt*; (*US inf*: *darling*) Schatz *m*, Schätzchen *nt*
baby carriage (*US*) *n* Kinderwagen *m*
baby food *n* Babynahrung *f*
babyish [ˈbeɪbɪɪʃ] *adj* kindlich
baby-sit [ˈbeɪbɪsɪt] *vi* babysitten
baby-sitter [ˈbeɪbɪsɪtəʳ] *n* Babysitter(in) *m(f)*
bachelor [ˈbætʃələʳ] *n* Junggeselle *m*; **B~ of Arts/Science (degree)** ≈ Magister *m* der philosophischen Fakultät/der Naturwissenschaften
bachelor party (*US*) *n* Junggesellenparty *f*
back [bæk] *n* Rücken *m*; (*of house, page*) Rückseite *f*; (*of chair*) (Rücken)lehne *f*; (*of train*) Ende *nt*; (*Football*) Verteidiger *m* ▶ *vt* (*support*) unterstützen; (*car*) rückwärtsfahren ▶ *vi* (*person*) rückwärtsgehen ▶ *adv* hinten; **in the ~ (of the car)** hinten (im Auto); **at the ~ of the book/crowd/audience** hinten im Buch/in der Menge/im Publikum; **~ to front** verkehrt herum; **~ room** Hinterzimmer *nt*; **~ wheels** Hinterräder *pl*; **he's ~** er ist zurück *or* wieder da
▶ **back away** *vi* sich zurückziehen
▶ **back down** *vi* nachgeben
▶ **back up** *vt* (*support*) unterstützen; (*Comput*) sichern; (*car*) zurückfahren ▶ *vi* (*car etc*) zurücksetzen
backache [ˈbækeɪk] *n* Rückenschmerzen *pl*

backbone [ˈbækbəun] *n* (*also fig*) Rückgrat *nt*
backdate [bækˈdeɪt] *vt* (zu) rückdatieren
back door *n* Hintertür *f*
backfire [bækˈfaɪəʳ] *vi* (*Aut*) Fehlzündungen haben; (*plans*) ins Auge gehen
background [ˈbækgraund] *n* Hintergrund *m*
backhand [ˈbækhænd] *n* (*Tennis: also:* **~ stroke**) Rückhand *f*
backlog [ˈbæklɔg] *n*: **to have a ~ of work** mit der Arbeit im Rückstand sein
backpack [ˈbækpæk] *n* Rucksack *m*
backpacker [ˈbækpækəʳ] *n* Rucksacktourist(in) *m(f)*
backpacking [ˈbækpækɪŋ] *n* Rucksacktourismus *m*
back seat *n* Rücksitz *m*
backside [ˈbæksaɪd] (*inf*) *n* Hintern *m*
backstreet [ˈbækstri:t] *n* Seitenstraße *f*
backstroke [ˈbækstrəuk] *n* Rückenschwimmen *nt*
backup *n* (*support*) Unterstützung *f*; (*Comput*) Sicherungskopie *f*
backward [ˈbækwəd] *adj* (*movement*) Rückwärts-; (*person*) zurückgeblieben; (*country*) rückständig; **~ and forward movement** Vor- und Zurückbewegung *f*
backwards [ˈbækwədz] *adv* rückwärts
back yard *n* Hinterhof *m*
bacon [ˈbeɪkən] *n* (Frühstücks)speck *m*
bacteria [bækˈtɪərɪə] *npl* Bakterien *pl*
bad [bæd] *adj* schlecht; **his ~ leg** sein schlimmes Bein; **to go ~** verderben, schlecht werden
badge [bædʒ] *n* Plakette *f*
badger [ˈbædʒəʳ] *n* Dachs *m*
badly [ˈbædlɪ] *adv* schlecht; **~ wounded** schwer verletzt; **he needs it ~** er braucht es dringend
bad-tempered [ˈbædˈtɛmpəd] *adj* schlecht gelaunt
bag [bæg] *n* Tasche *f*; (*made of paper, plastic*) Tüte *f*; (*handbag*) (Hand)tasche *f*; **to pack one's bags** die Koffer packen
baggage [ˈbægɪdʒ] *n* Gepäck *nt*
baggage allowance *n* Freigepäck *nt*
baggage (re)claim *n* Gepäckausgabe *f*
baggy [ˈbægɪ] *adj* weit; (*out of shape*) ausgebeult
bag lady (*inf*) *n* Stadtstreicherin *f*
bagpipes [ˈbægpaɪps] *npl* Dudelsack *m*
Bahamas [bəˈhɑ:məz] *npl*: **the ~** die Bahamas *pl*, die Bahamainseln *pl*
bail [beɪl] *n* (*Law: payment*) Kaution *f*
bait [beɪt] *n* Köder *m*
bake [beɪk] *vt* backen ▸ *vi* backen
baked beans [beɪkt-] *npl* gebackene Bohnen *pl* (in Tomatensoße)
baked potato [beɪkt-] *n* in der Schale gebackene Kartoffel *f*
baker [ˈbeɪkəʳ] *n* Bäcker(in) *m(f)*
bakery [ˈbeɪkərɪ] *n* Bäckerei *f*
baking powder *n* Backpulver *nt*
balance [ˈbæləns] *n* (*equilibrium*) Gleichgewicht *nt* ▸ *vt* ausgleichen
balanced [ˈbælənst] *adj* ausgeglichen
balance sheet *n* Bilanz *f*
balcony [ˈbælkənɪ] *n* Balkon *m*
bald [bɔ:ld] *adj* kahl
Balkan [ˈbɔ:lkən] *n*: **the Balkans** der Balkan, die Balkanländer *pl*
ball [bɔ:l] *n* Ball *m*
ballet [ˈbæleɪ] *n* Ballett *nt*
ballet dancer *n* Balletttänzer(in) *m(f)*
balloon [bəˈlu:n] *n* (Luft)ballon *m*
ballot [ˈbælət] *n* (geheime) Abstimmung *f*
ballot box *n* Wahlurne *f*
ballot paper *n* Stimmzettel *m*
ballpoint [ˈbɔ:lpɔɪnt], **ballpoint pen** *n* Kugelschreiber *m*
ballroom [ˈbɔ:lrum] *n* Tanzsaal *m*
Baltic [ˈbɔ:ltɪk] *n*: **the ~ (Sea)** die Ostsee
bamboo [bæmˈbu:] *n* Bambus *m*
ban [bæn] *n* Verbot *nt* ▸ *vt* verbieten
banana [bəˈnɑ:nə] *n* Banane *f*
band [bænd] *n* (*group*) Gruppe *f*; (*Mus: jazz, rock etc*) Band *f*; (*: military etc*) (Musik)kapelle *f*
bandage [ˈbændɪdʒ] *n* Verband *m* ▸ *vt* verbinden
B & B *n abbr* = **bed and breakfast**
bang [bæŋ] *n* (*of gun, exhaust*) Knall *m*; (*blow*) Schlag *m* ▸ *vt* (*door*) zuschlagen, zuknallen ▸ *vi* knallen
banger [ˈbæŋəʳ] (Brit *inf*) *n* (*car: also:* **old ~**) Klapperkiste *f*; (*sausage*) Würstchen *nt*; (*firework*) Knallkörper *m*
bangs [bæŋz] (*US*) *npl* (*fringe*) Pony *m*
banish [ˈbænɪʃ] *vt* verbannen
banister [ˈbænɪstəʳ] *n*, **banisters** [ˈbænɪstəz] *npl* Geländer *nt*
bank [bæŋk] *n* Bank *f*; (*of river, lake*) Ufer *nt*

bank account *n* Bankkonto *nt*
bank balance *n* Kontostand *m*
bank card *n* Scheckkarte *f*
bank holiday (BRIT) *n* (öffentlicher) Feiertag *m*

BANK HOLIDAY

Als **bank holiday** wird in Großbritannien ein gesetzlicher Feiertag bezeichnet, an dem die Banken geschlossen sind. Die meisten dieser Feiertage, abgesehen von Weihnachten und Ostern, fallen auf Montage im Mai und August. An diesen langen Wochenenden (*bank holiday weekends*) fahren viele Briten in Urlaub, sodass dann auf den Straßen, Flughäfen und bei der Bahn sehr viel Betrieb ist.

bank manager *n* Filialleiter(in) *m(f)* (einer Bank)
banknote [ˈbæŋknəut] *n* Banknote *f*
bankrupt [ˈbæŋkrʌpt] *adj* bankrott; **to go ~** Bankrott machen
bank statement *n* Kontoauszug *m*
baptism [ˈbæptɪzəm] *n* Taufe *f*
baptize [bæpˈtaɪz] *vt* taufen
bar [bɑːʳ] *n* (*for drinking*) Lokal *nt*; (*counter*) Theke *f*; (*rod*) Stange *f*; (*slab*: *of chocolate*) Tafel *f*; **~ of soap** Stück *nt* Seife; **~ none** ohne Ausnahme
barbecue [ˈbɑːbɪkjuː] *n* Grill *m*; (*meal, party*) Barbecue *nt*
barbed wire [ˈbɑːbd-] *n* Stacheldraht *m*
barber [ˈbɑːbəʳ] *n* (Herren)friseur *m*
bar code *n* Strichcode *m*
bare [bɛəʳ] *adj* nackt; (*trees, countryside*) kahl
barefoot [ˈbɛəfut] *adj* barfüßig ▶ *adv* barfuß
bareheaded [bɛəˈhɛdɪd] *adj* barhäuptig ▶ *adv* ohne Kopfbedeckung
barely [ˈbɛəlɪ] *adv* kaum
bargain [ˈbɑːgɪn] *n* (*deal*) Geschäft *nt*; (*transaction*) Handel *m*; (*good offer*) Sonderangebot *nt* ▶ *vi*: **to ~ (with sb)** (mit jdm) verhandeln
barge [bɑːdʒ] *n* Lastkahn *m*
bark [bɑːk] *n* (*of tree*) Rinde *f*; (*of dog*) Bellen *nt* ▶ *vi* bellen
barley [ˈbɑːlɪ] *n* Gerste *f*
barmaid [ˈbɑːmeɪd] *n* Bardame *f*
barman [ˈbɑːmən] *n* (*irreg*) Barmann *m*
barn [bɑːn] *n* Scheune *f*
barometer [bəˈrɔmɪtəʳ] *n* Barometer *nt*
barracks [ˈbærəks] *npl* Kaserne *f*
barrel [ˈbærəl] *n* Fass *nt*
barrel organ *n* Drehorgel *f*
barricade [bærɪˈkeɪd] *n* Barrikade *f*
barrier [ˈbærɪəʳ] *n* (*at frontier, entrance*) Schranke *f*; (*fig*) Barriere *f*
barrow [ˈbærəu] *n* Schubkarren *m*
bartender [ˈbɑːtɛndəʳ] (*US*) *n* Barmann *m*
base [beɪs] *n* (*of tree etc*) Fuß *m*; (*centre*) Stützpunkt *m*, Standort *m* ▶ *vt*: **to ~ sth on** etw gründen *or* basieren auf +*acc*
baseball [ˈbeɪsbɔːl] *n* Baseball *m*
basement [ˈbeɪsmənt] *n* Keller *m*
bash [bæʃ] (*inf*) *vt* hauen ▶ *n*: **I'll have a ~ (at it)** (BRIT) ich probier's mal
basic [ˈbeɪsɪk] *adj* (*method, needs etc*) Grund-; (*principles*) grundlegend; (*problem*) grundsätzlich; (*facilities*) primitiv
basically [ˈbeɪsɪklɪ] *adv* im Grunde
basics [ˈbeɪsɪks] *npl*: **the ~** das Wesentliche
basil [ˈbæzl] *n* Basilikum *nt*
basin [ˈbeɪsn] *n* Gefäß *nt*; (*also*: **wash ~**) (Wasch)becken *nt*
basis [ˈbeɪsɪs] (*pl* **bases**) *n* Basis *f*; **on a part-time ~** stundenweise; **on the ~ of what you've said** aufgrund dessen, was Sie gesagt haben
basket [ˈbɑːskɪt] *n* Korb *m*
basketball [ˈbɑːskɪtbɔːl] *n* Basketball *m*
Basque [bæsk] *adj* baskisch ▶ *n* Baske *m*, Baskin *f*
bass [beɪs] *n* Bass *m*
bastard [ˈbɑːstəd] *n* (!) Arschloch *nt* (!)
bat [bæt] *n* (*Zool*) Fledermaus *f*; (*for cricket, baseball etc*) Schlagholz *nt*; (BRIT: *for table tennis*) Schläger *m*
batch [bætʃ] *n* (*of bread*) Schub *m*; (*of letters, papers*) Stoß *m*
bath [bɑːθ] *n* Bad *nt*; (*bathtub*) (Bade)wanne *f* ▶ *vt* baden; **to have a ~** baden, ein Bad nehmen
bathe [beɪð] *vi, vt* (*also fig*) baden
bathing cap *n* Badekappe *f*
bathing costume, (*US*) **bathing suit** *n* Badeanzug *m*
bath mat *n* Badematte *f*, Badevorleger *m*
bathrobe [ˈbɑːθrəub] *n* Bademantel *m*

bathroom ['bɑːθrum] *n* Bad(ezimmer) *nt*
baths [bɑːðz] *npl* (*also:* **swimming ~**) (Schwimm)bad *nt*
bath towel *n* Badetuch *nt*
bathtub ['bɑːθtʌb] *n* (Bade)wanne *f*
baton ['bætən] *n* (*Mus*) Taktstock *m*; (*policeman's*) Schlagstock *m*
batter ['bætəʳ] *vt* schlagen ▸ *n* (*Culin*) Teig *m*
battered ['bætəd] *adj* (*hat, pan*) verbeult; **~ wife** misshandelte Ehefrau; **~ child** misshandeltes Kind
battery ['bætərɪ] *n* Batterie *f*
battery charger *n* (Batterie) ladegerät *nt*
battle ['bætl] *n* (*Mil*) Schlacht *f*; (*fig*) Kampf *m*
battlefield ['bætlfiːld] *n* Schlachtfeld *nt*
battlements ['bætlmənts] *npl* Zinnen *pl*
Bavaria [bə'vɛərɪə] *n* Bayern *nt*
Bavarian [bə'vɛərɪən] *adj* bay(e)risch ▸ *n* Bayer(in) *m(f)*
bay [beɪ] *n* Bucht *f*; **to hold sb at ~** jdn in Schach halten
bay leaf *n* Lorbeerblatt *nt*
bay window *n* Erkerfenster *nt*
BBC *n abbr* BBC *f*
BC *adv abbr* (= *before Christ*) v. Chr.

KEYWORD

be [biː] (*pt* **was**, **were**, *pp* **been**) *aux vb*
1 (*with present participle: forming continuous tenses*): **what are you doing?** was machst du?; **it is raining** es regnet
2 (*with pp: forming passives*): **to be killed** getötet werden; **the box had been opened** die Kiste war geöffnet worden
3 (*in tag questions*): **he's good-looking, isn't he?** er sieht gut aus, nicht (wahr)?
4 (+ *to* + *infinitive*): **the house is to be sold** das Haus soll verkauft werden; **he's not to open it** er darf es nicht öffnen
▸ *vb + complement* **1** sein; **I'm tired/English** ich bin müde/Engländer(in); **I'm hot/cold** mir ist heiß/kalt; **he's a doctor** er ist Arzt; **2 and 2 are 4** 2 und 2 ist *or* macht 4; **she's tall/pretty** sie ist groß/hübsch; **be careful/quiet** sei vorsichtig/ruhig
2 (*of health*): **how are you?** wie geht es Ihnen?; **he's very ill** er ist sehr krank; **I'm fine now** jetzt geht es mir gut
3 (*of age*): **how old are you?** wie alt bist du?; **I'm sixteen (years old)** ich bin sechzehn (Jahre alt)
4 (*cost*) kosten; **how much was the meal?** was hat das Essen gekostet?; **that'll be 5 pounds please** das macht 5 Pfund, bitte
▸ *vi* **1** (*exist, occur etc*) sein; **is there a God?** gibt es einen Gott?; **be that as it may** wie dem auch sei; **so be it** gut (und schön)
2 (*referring to place*) sein, liegen; **I won't be here tomorrow** morgen bin ich nicht da
3 (*referring to movement*) sein; **where have you been?** wo warst du?
▸ *impers vb* **1** (*referring to time, distance, weather*) sein; **it's 5 o'clock** es ist 5 Uhr; **it's 10 km to the village** es sind 10 km bis zum Dorf; **it's too hot/cold** es ist zu heiß/kalt
2 (*emphatic*): **it's only me** ich bins nur; **it's only the postman** es ist nur der Briefträger

beach [biːtʃ] *n* Strand *m*
beachwear ['biːtʃwɛəʳ] *n* Strandkleidung *f*
bead [biːd] *n* Perle *f*
beak [biːk] *n* Schnabel *m*
beam [biːm] *n* (*Archit*) Balken *m*; (*of light*) Strahl *m* ▸ *vi* (*smile*) strahlen
bean [biːn] *n* Bohne *f*
bear [bɛəʳ] (*pt* **bore**, *pp* **borne**) *n* Bär *m* ▸ *vt* tragen; (*tolerate, endure*) ertragen
bearable ['bɛərəbl] *adj* erträglich
beard [bɪəd] *n* Bart *m*
beast [biːst] *n* (*animal*) Tier *nt*; (*inf: person*) Biest *nt*
beat [biːt] (*pt* **~**, *pp* **beaten**) *n* (*of heart*) Schlag *m*; (*Mus*) Takt *m* ▸ *vt* schlagen; (*record*) brechen; **off the beaten track** abgelegen
▸ **beat up** *vt* (*person*) zusammenschlagen
beautiful ['bjuːtɪful] *adj* schön
beauty ['bjuːtɪ] *n* Schönheit *f*
beauty spot (BRIT) *n* besonders schöner Ort *m*
beaver ['biːvəʳ] *n* Biber *m*
became [bɪ'keɪm] *pt of* **become**
because [bɪ'kɔz] *conj* weil; **~ of** wegen +*gen or* (*inf*) +*dat*

become [bɪˈkʌm] *vi* (*irreg: like* **come**) werden; **it became known that** es wurde bekannt, dass
bed [bɛd] *n* Bett *nt*; (*of flowers*) Beet *nt*
bed and breakfast *n* (*terms*) Übernachtung *f* mit Frühstück
bedclothes [ˈbɛdkləuðz] *npl* Bettzeug *nt*
bedding [ˈbɛdɪŋ] *n* Bettzeug *nt*
bed linen *n* Bettwäsche *f*
bedroom [ˈbɛdrum] *n* Schlafzimmer *nt*
bedsit, bedsitter *n* (Brit) möbliertes Zimmer *nt*
bedspread [ˈbɛdsprɛd] *n* Tagesdecke *f*
bedtime [ˈbɛdtaɪm] *n* Schlafenszeit *f*
bee [biː] *n* Biene *f*
beech [biːtʃ] *n* Buche *f*
beef [biːf] *n* Rind(fleisch) *nt*
beefburger [ˈbiːfbəːgəʳ] *n* Hamburger *m*
beehive [ˈbiːhaɪv] *n* Bienenstock *m*
been [biːn] *pp of* **be**
beer [bɪəʳ] *n* Bier *nt*
beetle [ˈbiːtl] *n* Käfer *m*
beetroot [ˈbiːtruːt] (Brit) *n* Rote Bete *f*
before [bɪˈfɔːʳ] *prep* vor *+dat* ▸ *conj* bevor ▸ *adv* (*time*) vorher; **the week ~** die Woche davor; **I've never seen it ~** ich habe es noch nie gesehen
beforehand [bɪˈfɔːhænd] *adv* vorher
beg [bɛg] *vi* betteln ▸ *vt*: **to ~ sb to do sth** jdn bitten, etw zu tun
began [bɪˈgæn] *pt of* **begin**
beggar [ˈbɛgəʳ] *n* Bettler(in) *m(f)*
begin [bɪˈgɪn] (*pt* **began**, *pp* **begun**) *vt, vi* beginnen, anfangen; **to ~ doing** *or* **to do sth** anfangen, etw zu tun
beginner [bɪˈgɪnəʳ] *n* Anfänger(in) *m(f)*
beginning [bɪˈgɪnɪŋ] *n* Anfang *m*
begun [bɪˈgʌn] *pp of* **begin**
behalf [bɪˈhɑːf] *n*: **on ~ of**, (*US*) **in ~ of** (*as representative of*) im Namen von; **on my/his ~** in meinem/seinem Namen
behave [bɪˈheɪv] *vi* (*also*: **~ o.s.**) sich benehmen
behaviour, (*US*) **behavior** [bɪˈheɪvjəʳ] *n* Benehmen *nt*
behind [bɪˈhaɪnd] *prep* hinter ▸ *adv* (*at/towards the back*) hinten ▸ *n* (*buttocks*) Hintern *m*, Hinterteil *nt*; **to be ~** (*schedule*) im Rückstand *or* Verzug sein
beige [beɪʒ] *adj* beige
being [ˈbiːɪŋ] *n* (*creature*) (Lebe)wesen *nt*; (*existence*) (Da)sein *nt*
Belarus [bɛləˈrus] *n* Weißrussland *nt*
belch [bɛltʃ] *vi* rülpsen
belfry [ˈbɛlfrɪ] *n* Glockenstube *f*
Belgian [ˈbɛldʒən] *adj* belgisch ▸ *n* Belgier(in) *m(f)*
Belgium [ˈbɛldʒəm] *n* Belgien *nt*
belief [bɪˈliːf] *n* Glaube *m*; (*opinion*) Überzeugung *f*
believe [bɪˈliːv] *vt* glauben; **to ~ in** (*God, ghosts*) glauben an *+acc*
believer [bɪˈliːvəʳ] *n* (*Rel*) Gläubige(r) *f(m)*
bell [bɛl] *n* Glocke *f*; (*on door*) Klingel *f*
bellboy [ˈbɛlbɔɪ] (Brit) *n* Page *m*
bellows [ˈbɛləuz] *npl* Blasebalg *m*
belly [ˈbɛlɪ] *n* Bauch *m*
bellyache [ˈbɛlɪeɪk] (*inf*) *n* Bauchschmerzen *pl* ▸ *vi* murren
bellybutton [ˈbɛlɪbʌtn] *n* Bauchnabel *m*
belong [bɪˈlɔŋ] *vi*: **to ~ to** (*person*) gehören *+dat*; (*club etc*) angehören *+dat*
belongings [bɪˈlɔŋɪŋz] *npl* Sachen *pl*, Habe *f*
below [bɪˈləu] *prep* (*beneath*) unterhalb *+gen*; (*less than*) unter *+dat* ▸ *adv* (*beneath*) unten; **see ~** siehe unten
belt [bɛlt] *n* Gürtel *m* ▸ *vi* (Brit *inf*): **to ~ along** rasen
beltway [ˈbɛltweɪ] (*US*) *n* Umgehungsstraße *f*
bench [bɛntʃ] *n* Bank *f*
bend [bɛnd] (*pt, pp* **bent**) *vt* (*leg, arm*) beugen; (*pipe*) biegen ▸ *vi* (*person*) sich beugen ▸ *n* (Brit: *in road*) Kurve *f*; (*in pipe, river*) Biegung *f*
▸ **bend down** *vi* sich bücken
beneath [bɪˈniːθ] *prep* unter *+dat* ▸ *adv* darunter
beneficial [bɛnɪˈfɪʃəl] *adj* (*effect*) nützlich; **~ (to)** gut (für)
benefit [ˈbɛnɪfɪt] *n* (*advantage*) Vorteil *m*; (*money*) Beihilfe *f* ▸ *vt* nützen *+dat* ▸ *vi*: **he'll ~ from it** er wird davon profitieren
benign [bɪˈnaɪn] *adj* gütig; (*Med*) gutartig
Benin [bɛˈniːn] *n* Benin *nt*
bent [bɛnt] *pt, pp of* **bend** ▸ *adj* (*wire, pipe*) gebogen; (*inf: dishonest*) korrupt
beret [ˈbɛreɪ] *n* Baskenmütze *f*
Bermuda [bəːˈmjuːdə] *n* Bermuda *nt*, die Bermudinseln *pl*
Bermuda shorts *npl* Bermudashorts *pl*
berry [ˈbɛrɪ] *n* Beere *f*

berth [bə:θ] *n* (*bed*) Bett *nt*; (*on ship*) Koje *f*; (*on train*) Schlafwagenbett *nt*; (*for ship*) Liegeplatz *m* ▶ *vi* anlegen
beside [bɪ'saɪd] *prep* neben *+dat*
besides [bɪ'saɪdz] *adv* außerdem ▶ *prep* außer *+dat*
besiege [bɪ'si:dʒ] *vt* belagern
best [bɛst] *adj* beste(r, s) ▶ *adv* am besten ▶ *n*: **at ~** bestenfalls; **to make the ~ of sth** das Beste aus etw machen; **to the ~ of my ability** so gut ich kann
best-before date *n* Mindesthaltbarkeitsdatum *nt*
best man *n* (*irreg*) Trauzeuge *m* (*des Bräutigams*)
best seller *n* Bestseller *m*
bet [bɛt] (*pt, pp* **~**) *n* Wette *f* ▶ *vi* wetten ▶ *vt*: **to ~ sb sth** mit jdm um etw wetten; **to ~ money on sth** Geld auf etw *acc* setzen
betray [bɪ'treɪ] *vt* verraten
betrayal [bɪ'treɪəl] *n* Verrat *m*
better ['bɛtə^r] *adj, adv* besser; **you had ~ do it** tun Sie es lieber; **to get ~** gesund werden; **that's ~!** so ist es besser!; **a change for the ~** eine Wendung zum Guten
betting ['bɛtɪŋ] *n* Wetten *nt*
betting shop (Brit) *n* Wettbüro *nt*
between [bɪ'twi:n] *prep* zwischen *+dat*; (*amongst*) unter *+acc or dat* ▶ *adv* dazwischen
beverage ['bɛvərɪdʒ] *n* Getränk *nt*
beware [bɪ'wɛə^r] *vi*: **to ~ (of)** sich in Acht nehmen (vor *+dat*); **"~ of the dog"** „Vorsicht, bissiger Hund"
bewildered [bɪ'wɪldəd] *adj* verwirrt
beyond [bɪ'jɔnd] *prep* (*in space*) jenseits *+gen*; (*exceeding*) über *+acc* ... hinaus; (*above*) über *+dat* ▶ *adv* (*in space*) dahinter; (*in time*) darüber hinaus; **it's ~ me** das geht über meinen Verstand
Bhutan [bu:'tɑ:n] *n* (Königreich *nt*) Bhutan *nt*
bias ['baɪəs] *n* (*prejudice*) Vorurteil *nt*
biased, biassed *adj* voreingenommen
bib [bɪb] *n* Latz *m*
Bible ['baɪbl] *n* Bibel *f*
bicycle ['baɪsɪkl] *n* Fahrrad *nt*
bid [bɪd] (*pt* **bade** *or* **~**, *pp* **bidden** *or* **~**) *n* (*at auction*) Gebot *nt*; (*attempt*) Versuch *m* ▶ *vt* bieten
big [bɪg] *adj* groß
Big Apple *n siehe Info-Artikel*

BIG APPLE

Apple ist in Wirklichkeit Jargon für eine Großstadt. Auch wenn man schon weiß, dass mit **The Big Apple** die Stadt von New York gemeint ist, kennt man die Spitznamen anderer amerikanischen Großstädte weniger. So wird Chicago *Windy City* genannt, vielleicht wegen der heftige Windböen, die vom Michigansee her blasen; New Orleans verdankt den Namen *Big Easy* ihrem entspannten Lebensstil; die Automobilindustrie hat Detroit zu *Motown* gemacht.

bigheaded *adj* eingebildet
bike [baɪk] *n* (Fahr)rad *nt*
bikini [bɪ'ki:nɪ] *n* Bikini *m*
bilingual [baɪ'lɪŋgwəl] *adj* zweisprachig
bill [bɪl] *n* Rechnung *f*; (*Pol*) (Gesetz)entwurf *m*; (*US: banknote*) Banknote *f*; (*of bird*) Schnabel *m*
billfold ['bɪlfəuld] (*US*) *n* Brieftasche *f*
billiards ['bɪljədz] *n* Billard *nt*
billion ['bɪljən] *n* (Brit) Billion *f*; (*US*) Milliarde *f*
bin [bɪn] *n* (Brit) Mülleimer *m*; (*container*) Behälter *m*
bind [baɪnd] (*pt, pp* **bound**) *vt* binden; (*tie together: hands and feet*) fesseln
binge [bɪndʒ] (*inf*) *n*: **to go on a ~** auf eine Sauftour gehen
bingo ['bɪŋgəu] *n* Bingo *nt*
binoculars [bɪ'nɔkjuləz] *npl* Fernglas *nt*
biodegradable ['baɪəudɪ'greɪdəbl] *adj* biologisch abbaubar
biodiesel ['baɪəudi:zl] *n* Biodiesel *m*
biofuel ['baɪəu'fjuəl] *n* Biokraftstoff *m*
biography [baɪ'ɔgrəfɪ] *n* Biografie *f*
biological [baɪə'lɔdʒɪkl] *adj* biologisch
biology [baɪ'ɔlədʒɪ] *n* Biologie *f*
biosecurity ['baɪəusɪ'kjuərɪtɪ] *n* Vorkehrungen *pl* gegen Biogefährdung
bipolar [baɪ'pəulə^r] *adj* bipolar
birch [bə:tʃ] *n* Birke *f*
bird [bə:d] *n* Vogel *m*; (Brit *inf*: *girl*) Biene *f*
bird-watcher *n* Vogelbeobachter(in) *m(f)*
birth [bə:θ] *n* Geburt *f*

birth certificate *n* Geburtsurkunde *f*
birth control *n* Geburtenkontrolle *f*
birthday [ˈbəːθdeɪ] *n* Geburtstag *m* ▸ *cpd* Geburtstags-; *see also* **happy**
birthplace [ˈbəːθpleɪs] *n* Geburtsort *m*
biscuit [ˈbɪskɪt] *n* (BRIT) Keks *m or nt*
bisexual [ˈbaɪˈsɛksjuəl] *adj* bisexuell
bishop [ˈbɪʃəp] *n* (*Rel*) Bischof *m*; (*Chess*) Läufer *m*
bit [bɪt] *pt of* **bite** ▸ *n* (*piece*) Stück *nt*; (*Comput*) Bit *nt*; **a ~ of** ein bisschen; **a ~ dangerous** etwas gefährlich; **~ by ~** nach und nach
bitch [bɪtʃ] *n* (*dog*) Hündin *f*; (*!: woman*) Miststück *nt*
bitcoin [ˈbɪtkɔɪn] *n* (*Comput: unit*) Bitcoin *f or m*; (*: system*) Bitcoin®
bite [baɪt] (*pt* **bit**, *pp* **bitten**) *vt*, *vi* beißen ▸ *n* (*insect bite*) Stich *m*; (*mouthful*) Bissen *m*; **let's have a ~ (to eat)** (*inf*) lasst uns eine Kleinigkeit essen
bitten [ˈbɪtn] *pp of* **bite**
bitter [ˈbɪtəʳ] *adj* bitter; (*criticism*) scharf ▸ *n* (BRIT: *beer*) *halbdunkles obergäriges Bier*
bizarre [bɪˈzɑːʳ] *adj* bizarr
black [blæk] *adj* schwarz; **to give sb a ~ eye** jdm ein blaues Auge schlagen
blackberry [ˈblækbərɪ] *n* Brombeere *f*
blackbird [ˈblækbəːd] *n* Amsel *f*
blackboard [ˈblækbɔːd] *n* Tafel *f*
black box *n* (*Aviat*) Flugschreiber *m*
blackcurrant [ˈblækkʌrənt] *n* Johannisbeere *f*
Black Forest *n*: **the ~** der Schwarzwald
blackmail [ˈblækmeɪl] *n* Erpressung *f* ▸ *vt* erpressen
black market *n* Schwarzmarkt *m*
blackout [ˈblækaut] *n* (*faint*) Ohnmachtsanfall *m*
Black Sea *n*: **the ~** das Schwarze Meer
blacksmith [ˈblæksmɪθ] *n* Schmied *m*
bladder [ˈblædəʳ] *n* Blase *f*
blade [bleɪd] *n* (*of knife etc*) Klinge *f*; (*of oar, propeller*) Blatt *nt*; **a ~ of grass** ein Grashalm *m*
blame [bleɪm] *n* Schuld *f* ▸ *vt*: **to ~ sb for sth** jdm die Schuld an etw *dat* geben; **to be to ~** Schuld daran haben, schuld sein
bland [blænd] *adj* (*taste, food*) fade
blank [blæŋk] *adj* (*paper*) leer, unbeschrieben; (*look*) ausdruckslos
blank cheque *n* Blankoscheck *m*
blanket [ˈblæŋkɪt] *n* Decke *f*
blast [blɑːst] *n* (*of wind*) Windstoß *m*; (*of whistle*) Trillern *nt*; (*shock wave*) Druckwelle *f* ▸ *vt* (*blow up*) sprengen ▸ *excl* (BRIT *inf*) verdammt!, so ein Mist!
blatant [ˈbleɪtənt] *adj* offensichtlich
blaze [bleɪz] *n* (*fire*) Feuer *nt*, Brand *m*; (*fig: of colour*) Farbenpracht *f* ▸ *vi* (*fire*) lodern
blazer [ˈbleɪzəʳ] *n* Blazer *m*
bleach [bliːtʃ] *n* ≈ Reinigungsmittel *nt* ▸ *vt* bleichen
bleak [bliːk] *adj* (*countryside*) öde; (*weather, situation*) trostlos
bleary-eyed [ˈblɪərɪˈaɪd] *adj* triefäugig
bleed [bliːd] (*pt, pp* **bled**) *vi* bluten
blend [blɛnd] *n* Mischung *f* ▸ *vt* (*Culin*) mischen ▸ *vi* (*colours etc: also:* **~ in**) harmonieren
blender [ˈblɛndəʳ] *n* (*Culin*) Mixer *m*
bless [blɛs] (*pt, pp* **blessed** *or* **blest**) *vt* segnen; **~ you!** (*after sneeze*) Gesundheit!
blessing [ˈblɛsɪŋ] *n* (*Rel, fig*) Segen *m*
blew [bluː] *pt of* **blow**
blind [blaɪnd] *adj* blind ▸ *n* (*for window*) Rollo *nt* ▸ *vt* blind machen; (*dazzle*) blenden; **to turn a ~ eye (on** *or* **to)** ein Auge zudrücken (bei)
blind alley *n* (*fig*) Sackgasse *f*
blind spot *n* (*Aut*) toter Winkel *m*; (*fig: weak spot*) schwacher Punkt *m*
blink [blɪŋk] *vi* blinzeln; (*light*) blinken
bliss [blɪs] *n* Glück *nt*, Seligkeit *f*
blister [ˈblɪstəʳ] *n* Blase *f*
blizzard [ˈblɪzəd] *n* Schneesturm *m*
bloated [ˈbləutɪd] *adj* aufgedunsen
block [blɔk] *n* Block *m*; (*toy*) Bauklotz *m* ▸ *vt* blockieren; **~ of flats** (BRIT) Wohnblock *m*
blockage [ˈblɔkɪdʒ] *n* Verstopfung *f*
blockbuster [ˈblɔkbʌstəʳ] *n* Knüller *m*
block letters *npl* Blockschrift *f*
blog [blɔg] *n* (*Comput*) Blog *m*, Weblog *m* ▸ *vi* bloggen
blogger *n* Blogger(in) *m(f)*
blogosphere [ˈblɔgəsfɪəʳ] *n* Blogosphäre *f*
blogpost [ˈblɔgpəust] *n* Blogpost *m*
bloke [bləuk] (BRIT *inf*) *n* Typ *m*
blond, blonde [blɔnd] *adj* blond ▸ *n* (*person*) Blondine *f*, Blonder Typ *m*
blood [blʌd] *n* Blut *nt*
blood count *n* Blutbild *nt*

blood donor *n* Blutspender(in) *m(f)*
blood group *n* Blutgruppe *f*
blood poisoning *n* Blutvergiftung *f*
blood pressure *n* Blutdruck *m*
blood sport *n* Jagdsport *m* (*und andere Sportarten, bei denen Tiere getötet werden*)
bloodthirsty ['blʌdθəːstɪ] *adj* blutrünstig
bloody ['blʌdɪ] *adj* blutig; (Brit *!*): **this ~ ...** diese(r, s) verdammte ...
bloom [bluːm] *n* Blüte *f* ▶ *vi* blühen
blossom ['blɔsəm] *n* Blüte *f* ▶ *vi* blühen
blot [blɔt] *n* Klecks *m*; (*fig: on name etc*) Makel *m*
blouse [blauz] *n* Bluse *f*
blow [bləu] (*pt* **blew**, *pp* **blown**) *n* (*also fig*) Schlag *m* ▶ *vi* (*wind*) wehen; (*person*) blasen ▶ *vt* (*subj: wind*) wehen; (*instrument, whistle*) blasen; **to ~ one's nose** sich *dat* die Nase putzen
▶ **blow out** *vi* ausgehen
▶ **blow up** *vi* ausbrechen ▶ *vt* (*bridge*) in die Luft jagen; (*tyre*) aufblasen; (*Phot*) vergrößern
blow-dry ['bləudraɪ] *vt* föhnen
blown [bləun] *pp of* **blow**
blowout ['bləuaut] *n* Reifenpanne *f*
blue [bluː] *adj* blau; (*depressed*) deprimiert, niedergeschlagen ▶ *n*
■ **blues** *npl* (*Mus*): **the blues** der Blues; **to have the blues** deprimiert *or* niedergeschlagen sein
bluebell ['bluːbɛl] *n* Glockenblume *f*
blueberry ['bluːbərɪ] *n* Blaubeere *f*
blue cheese *n* Blauschimmelkäse *m*
blunder ['blʌndə^r] *n* (dummer) Fehler *m*
blunt [blʌnt] *adj* stumpf; (*talk*) unverblümt
bluntly ['blʌntlɪ] *adv* (*speak*) unverblümt
blurred [bləːd] *adj* (*photograph, TV picture etc*) verschwommen
blush [blʌʃ] *vi* erröten
board [bɔːd] *n* Brett *nt*; (*committee*) Ausschuss *m*; (*in firm*) Vorstand *m* ▶ *vt* (*ship*) an Bord +*gen* gehen; (*train*) einsteigen in +*acc*; **on ~** (*Naut, Aviat*) an Bord; **~ and lodging** Unterkunft und Verpflegung *f*
boarder ['bɔːdə^r] *n* Internatsschüler(in) *m(f)*
board game *n* Brettspiel *nt*
boarding card ['bɔːdɪŋ-] *n* (*Aviat, Naut*) = **boarding pass**
boarding pass ['bɔːdɪŋ-] *n* Bordkarte *f*
boarding school ['bɔːdɪŋ-] *n* Internat *nt*
board meeting *n* Vorstandssitzung *f*
boardroom ['bɔːdruːm] *n* Sitzungssaal *m*
boast [bəust] *vi* prahlen
boat [bəut] *n* Boot *nt*; (*ship*) Schiff *nt*
bobsleigh ['bɔbsleɪ] *n* Bob *m*
bodily ['bɔdɪlɪ] *adj* körperlich ▶ *adv* (*lift, carry*) mit aller Kraft
body ['bɔdɪ] *n* Körper *m*; (*corpse*) Leiche *f*; (*of car*) Karosserie *f*
body building *n* Bodybuilding *nt*
bodyguard ['bɔdɪgɑːd] *n* (*group*) Leibwache *f*; (*one person*) Leibwächter *m*
bodywork ['bɔdɪwəːk] *n* Karosserie *f*
boil [bɔɪl] *vt, vi* kochen ▶ *n* (*Med*) Furunkel *m or nt*
boiler ['bɔɪlə^r] *n* Boiler *m*
boiling ['bɔɪlɪŋ] *adj*: **I'm ~ (hot)** (*inf*) mir ist fürchterlich heiß
boiling point *n* Siedepunkt *m*
bold [bəuld] *adj* (*brave*) mutig; (*pattern, colours*) kräftig
Bolivia [bə'lɪvɪə] *n* Bolivien *nt*
bolt [bəult] *n* Riegel *m*; (*with nut*) Schraube *f* ▶ *vt* (*door*) verriegeln
bomb [bɔm] *n* Bombe *f* ▶ *vt* bombardieren
bond [bɔnd] *n* Bindung *f*; (*Fin*) festverzinsliches Wertpapier *nt*
bone [bəun] *n* Knochen *m*; (*of fish*) Gräte *f*
boner ['bəunə^r] (US) *n* Schnitzer *m*
bonfire ['bɔnfaɪə^r] *n* Feuer *nt*
bonnet ['bɔnɪt] *n* Haube *f*; (*for baby*) Häubchen *nt*; (Brit: *of car*) Motorhaube *f*
bonny ['bɔnɪ] (Scot, Northern English) *adj* schön, hübsch
bonus ['bəunəs] *n* Prämie *f*
boo [buː] *vt* auspfeifen, ausbuhen
book [buk] *n* Buch *nt*; (*of stamps, tickets*) Heftchen *nt* ▶ *vt* bestellen; (*seat, room*) buchen
▶ **book in** (Brit) *vi* sich eintragen
bookcase ['bukkeɪs] *n* Bücherregal *nt*
booking ['bukɪŋ] (Brit) *n* Bestellung *f*; (*of seat, room*) Buchung *f*
booking office (Brit) *n* (*Rail*) Fahrkartenschalter *m*; (*Theat*) Vorverkaufsstelle *f*
book-keeping ['buk'kiːpɪŋ] *n* Buchhaltung *f*

booklet [ˈbuklɪt] *n* Broschüre *f*
bookmark [ˈbukmɑːk] *n* Lesezeichen *nt*; (*Comput*) Bookmark *nt*
bookshelf [ˈbukʃɛlf] *n* Bücherbord *nt* ■ **bookshelves** *npl* Bücherregal *nt*
bookshop [ˈbukʃɔp] *n* Buchhandlung *f*
boom [buːm] *n* Donnern *nt*, Dröhnen *nt* ▶ *vi* (*voice*) dröhnen; (*business*) florieren
boomerang [ˈbuːməræŋ] *n* Bumerang *m*
boost [buːst] *n* Auftrieb *m* ▶ *vt* (*confidence*) stärken; (*sales, economy etc*) ankurbeln
booster *n* (*Med*) Wiederholungsimpfung *f*
boot [buːt] *n* Stiefel *m*; (Brit: *of car*) Kofferraum *m* ▶ *vt* (*Comput*) laden
booth [buːð] *n* (*at fair*) Bude *f*, Stand *m*
booze [buːz] (*inf*) *n* Alkohol *m*
border [ˈbɔːdəʳ] *n* Grenze *f*; (*on cloth etc*) Bordüre *f*
borderline [ˈbɔːdəlaɪn] *n* (*fig*): **on the ~** an der Grenze
bore [bɔːʳ] *pt of* **bear** ▶ *vt* bohren; (*person*) langweilen ▶ *n* Langweiler *m*; (*of gun*) Kaliber *nt*; **to be bored** sich langweilen
boredom [ˈbɔːdəm] *n* Langeweile *f*
boring [ˈbɔːrɪŋ] *adj* langweilig
born [bɔːn] *adj*: **I was ~ in 1960** ich bin *or* wurde 1960 geboren
borne [bɔːn] *pp of* **bear**
borough [ˈbʌrə] *n* Bezirk *m*
borrow [ˈbɔrəu] *vt*: **to ~ sth** etw borgen, sich *dat* etw leihen
Bosnia and Herzegovina [-hɛrtsəˈgəuviːnə] *n* Bosnien und Herzegowina *nt*
Bosnian [ˈbɔznɪən] *adj* bosnisch ▶ *n* Bosnier(in) *m(f)*
boss [bɔs] *n* Chef(in) *m(f)*; (*leader*) Boss *m* ▶ *vt* (*also:* **~ around, ~ about**) herumkommandieren
bossy [ˈbɔsɪ] *adj* herrisch
botanical [bəˈtænɪkl] *adj* botanisch
both [bəuθ] *adj* beide ▶ *pron* beide; (*two different things*) beides ▶ *adv*: **~ A and B** sowohl A als auch B; **~ (of them)** (alle) beide; **~ of us went, we ~ went** wir gingen beide
bother [ˈbɔðəʳ] *vt* Sorgen machen +*dat* ▶ *vi* (*also:* **~ o.s.**) sich *dat* Sorgen *or* Gedanken machen ▶ *n* (*trouble*) Mühe *f*; (*nuisance*) Plage *f*; **don't ~ phoning** du brauchst nicht anzurufen; **I'm sorry to ~ you** es tut mir leid, dass ich Sie belästigen muss; **I can't be bothered** ich habe keine Lust
bottle [ˈbɔtl] *n* Flasche *f* ▶ *vt* in Flaschen abfüllen
▶ **bottle out** *vi* (*inf*) den Mut verlieren, aufgeben
bottle bank *n* Altglascontainer *m*
bottleneck [ˈbɔtlnɛk] *n* (*also fig*) Engpass *m*
bottle-opener *n* Flaschenöffner *m*
bottom [ˈbɔtəm] *n* Boden *m*; (*buttocks*) Hintern *m*; (*of page, list*) Ende *nt* ▶ *adj* (*lower*) untere(r, s); (*last*) unterste(r, s); **at the ~ of** unten an/in +*dat*; **at the ~ of the page/list** unten auf der Seite/Liste; **to be at the ~ of the class** der/die Letzte in der Klasse sein
bought [bɔːt] *pt, pp of* **buy**
bounce [bauns] *vi* (auf)springen; (*cheque*) platzen
bouncy castle [ˈbaunsɪ-] *n* Hüpfburg *f*
bound [baund] *pt, pp of* **bind** ▶ *adj*: **to be ~ to do sth** (*obliged*) verpflichtet sein, etw zu tun; (*very likely*) etw bestimmt tun; **he's ~ to fail** es kann ihm ja gar nicht gelingen; **~ for** nach
boundary [ˈbaundrɪ] *n* Grenze *f*
bouquet [ˈbukeɪ] *n* (Blumen)strauß *m*; (*of wine*) Bukett *nt*
boutique [buːˈtiːk] *n* Boutique *f*
bow¹ [bəu] *n* Schleife *f*; (*weapon, Mus*) Bogen *m*
bow² [bau] *n* Verbeugung *f*; (*Naut: also:* **bows**) Bug *m* ▶ *vi* sich verbeugen
bowels [ˈbauəlz] *npl* Darm *m*
bowl [bəul] *n* Schüssel *f*; (*shallower*) Schale *f*; (*ball*) Kugel *f* ▶ *vi* werfen
bowler [ˈbəuləʳ] *n* Werfer(in) *m(f)*; (Brit: *also:* **~ hat**) Melone *f*
bowling [ˈbəulɪŋ] *n* Kegeln *nt*
bowling alley *n* Kegelbahn *f*
bowling green *n* Bowlingrasen *m*
bowls [bəulz] *n* Bowling *nt*
bow tie [bəu-] *n* Fliege *f*
box [bɔks] *n* Schachtel *f*; (*cardboard box*) Karton *m*; (*Theat*) Loge *f*; (*on form*) Feld *nt*
boxer [ˈbɔksəʳ] *n* (*person, dog*) Boxer *m*
boxers, boxer shorts *npl* Boxershorts *pl*
boxing [ˈbɔksɪŋ] *n* Boxen *nt*

Boxing Day (*BRIT*) *n* zweiter Weihnachts(feier)tag *m*

BOXING DAY

Boxing Day ist ein Feiertag in Großbritannien. Wenn Weihnachten auf ein Wochenende fällt, wird der Feiertag am nächsten darauffolgenden Wochentag nachgeholt. Der Name geht auf einen alten Brauch zurück; früher erhielten Händler und Lieferanten an diesem Tag ein Geschenk, die sogenannte *Christmas Box*.

boxing gloves *npl* Boxhandschuhe *pl*
boxing ring *n* Boxring *m*
box number *n* Chiffre *f*
box office *n* Kasse *f*
boy [bɔɪ] *n* Junge *m*
boycott [ˈbɔɪkɔt] *n* Boykott *m* ▸ *vt* boykottieren
boyfriend [ˈbɔɪfrɛnd] *n* Freund *m*
boy scout *n* Pfadfinder *m*
bra [brɑː] *n* BH *m*
brace [breɪs] *n* (*on teeth*) (Zahn)spange *f* ■ **braces** *npl* (*BRIT*) Hosenträger *pl*
bracelet [ˈbreɪslɪt] *n* Armband *nt*
bracket [ˈbrækɪt] *n* Träger *m*; (*also*: **round ~**) (runde) Klammer *f* ▸ *vt* (*word, phrase*) einklammern
brag [bræg] *vi* prahlen
Braille [breɪl] *n* Blindenschrift *f*
brain [breɪn] *n* Gehirn *nt* ■ **brains** *npl* (*intelligence*) Intelligenz *f*
brainstorm [ˈbreɪnstɔːm] *n* (*fig*) Anfall *m* geistiger Umnachtung; (*US*: *brain wave*) Geistesblitz *m*
brain wave *n* Geistesblitz *m*
brainy [ˈbreɪnɪ] *adj* intelligent
braise [breɪz] *vt* schmoren
brake [breɪk] *n* Bremse *f* ▸ *vi* bremsen
brake fluid *n* Bremsflüssigkeit *f*
brake light *n* Bremslicht *nt*
brake pedal *n* Bremspedal *nt*
branch [brɑːntʃ] *n* Ast *m*; (*Comm*) Filiale *f*, Zweigstelle *f*
brand [brænd] *n* (*also*: **~ name**) Marke *f*
brand-new [ˈbrændˈnjuː] *adj* nagelneu
brandy [ˈbrændɪ] *n* Weinbrand *m*
brass [brɑːs] *n* Messing *nt*; **the ~** (*Mus*) die Blechbläser *pl*
brass band *n* Blaskapelle *f*
brat [bræt] (*pej*) *n* Gör *nt*
brave [breɪv] *adj* mutig; (*attempt, smile*) tapfer
bravery [ˈbreɪvərɪ] *n* Mut *m*; Tapferkeit *f*
brawl [brɔːl] *n* Schlägerei *f*
brawn [brɔːn] *n* Muskeln *pl*; (*meat*) Schweinskopfsülze *f*
brawny [ˈbrɔːnɪ] *adj* muskulös
Brazil [brəˈzɪl] *n* Brasilien *nt*
Brazilian [brəˈzɪljən] *adj* brasilianisch ▸ *n* Brasilianer(in) *m(f)*
Brazil nut *n* Paranuss *f*
bread [brɛd] *n* Brot *nt*
bread bin (*BRIT*) *n* Brotkasten *m*
bread box (*US*) *n* Brotkasten *m*
breadcrumbs [ˈbrɛdkrʌmz] *npl* Brotkrumen *pl*; (*Culin*) Paniermehl *nt*
breaded [ˈbrɛdɪd] *adj* paniert
breadth [brɛtθ] *n* (*also fig*) Breite *f*
break [breɪk] (*pt* **broke**, *pp* **broken**) *vt* zerbrechen; (*leg, arm*) sich *dat* brechen; (*promise, record*) brechen; (*law*) verstoßen gegen ▸ *vi* zerbrechen, kaputtgehen; (*dawn*) anbrechen; (*story, news*) bekannt werden ▸ *n* Pause *f*; (*fracture*) Bruch *m*; (*chance*) Chance *f*, Gelegenheit *f*; (*holiday*) Urlaub *m*; **to ~ the news to sb** es jdm sagen; **to ~ free** *or* **loose** sich losreißen
▸ **break down** *vi* (*car*) eine Panne haben; (*machine*) kaputtgehen; (*person, resistance*) zusammenbrechen
▸ **break in** *vt* (*horse*) zureiten ▸ *vi* einbrechen
▸ **break into** *vt fus* einbrechen in +*acc*
▸ **break off** *vi* abbrechen ▸ *vt* (*talks*) abbrechen
▸ **break out** *vi* ausbrechen; **to ~ out in spots/a rash** Pickel/einen Ausschlag bekommen
▸ **break up** *vi* (*ship*) zerbersten; (*crowd, meeting, partnership*) sich auflösen; (*marriage*) scheitern; (*friends*) sich trennen; (*Scol*) in die Ferien gehen ▸ *vt* zerbrechen; (*meeting*) auflösen; (*marriage*) zerstören
breakable [ˈbreɪkəbl] *adj* zerbrechlich
breakage [ˈbreɪkɪdʒ] *n* Bruch *m*
breakdown [ˈbreɪkdaun] *n* (*Aut*) Panne *f*; (*in communications*) Zusammenbruch *m*; (*also*: **nervous ~**) (Nerven)zusammenbruch *m*
breakdown service (*BRIT*) *n* Pannendienst *m*
breakdown van (*BRIT*) *n* Abschleppwagen *m*

breakfast [ˈbrɛkfəst] *n* Frühstück *nt* ▸ *vi* frühstücken
breakfast cereal *n* Getreideflocken *pl*
break-in [ˈbreɪkɪn] *n* Einbruch *m*
break-up [ˈbreɪkʌp] *n* (*of partnership*) Auflösung *f*; (*of marriage*) Scheitern *nt*
breast [brɛst] *n* Brust *f*
breast-feed [ˈbrɛstfiːd] *vt, vi* stillen
breaststroke [ˈbrɛststrəuk] *n* Brustschwimmen *nt*
breath [brɛθ] *n* Atem *m*; **out of ~** außer Atem, atemlos
breathalyse [ˈbrɛθəlaɪz] *vt* blasen lassen (*inf*)
Breathalyser® *n* Promillemesser *m*
breathe [briːð] *vt, vi* atmen
▸ **breathe in** *vt, vi* einatmen
▸ **breathe out** *vt, vi* ausatmen
breathless [ˈbrɛθlɪs] *adj* atemlos
breathtaking [ˈbrɛθteɪkɪŋ] *adj* atemberaubend
bred [brɛd] *pt, pp of* **breed**
breed [briːd] (*pt, pp* **bred**) *vt* züchten ▸ *vi* Junge *pl* haben ▸ *n* Rasse *f*
breeder [ˈbriːdəʳ] *n* Züchter(in) *m(f)*
breeding [ˈbriːdɪŋ] *n* Erziehung *f*
breeze [briːz] *n* Brise *f*
brevity [ˈbrɛvɪtɪ] *n* Kürze *f*
brew [bruː] *vt* (*tea*) aufbrühen, kochen; (*beer*) brauen
brewery [ˈbruːərɪ] *n* Brauerei *f*
bribe [braɪb] *n* Bestechungsgeld *nt* ▸ *vt* bestechen
bribery [ˈbraɪbərɪ] *n* Bestechung *f*
brick [brɪk] *n* Backstein *m*
bricklayer [ˈbrɪkleɪəʳ] *n* Maurer(in) *m(f)*
bride [braɪd] *n* Braut *f*
bridegroom [ˈbraɪdgruːm] *n* Bräutigam *m*
bridesmaid [ˈbraɪdzmeɪd] *n* Brautjungfer *f*
bridge [brɪdʒ] *n* Brücke *f*; (*Cards*) Bridge *nt*
brief [briːf] *adj* kurz ▸ *n* (*task*) Aufgabe *f* ▸ *vt* instruieren ■ **briefs** *npl* Slip *m*
briefcase [ˈbriːfkeɪs] *n* Aktentasche *f*
bright [braɪt] *adj* (*light, room*) hell; (*clever*) intelligent; (*lively*) heiter, fröhlich; (*colour*) leuchtend; (*outlook, future*) glänzend
brighten *vt* (*also:* **~ up**) aufheitern ▸ *vi* (*weather, face: also:* **~ up**) sich aufheitern; (*person*) fröhlicher werden
brilliant [ˈbrɪljənt] *adj* strahlend; (*person, idea*) genial, brillant; (*career*) großartig; (*inf: holiday etc*) fantastisch
brim [brɪm] *n* Rand *m*
bring [brɪŋ] (*pt, pp* **brought**) *vt* bringen; (*with you*) mitbringen
▸ **bring about** *vt* herbeiführen
▸ **bring back** *vt* (*restore*) wiedereinführen; (*return*) zurückbringen
▸ **bring down** *vt* (*government*) zu Fall bringen; (*price*) senken
▸ **bring in** *vt* (*money*) (ein)bringen; (*legislation*) einbringen
▸ **bring out** *vt* herausholen; (*meaning, book, album*) herausbringen
▸ **bring round** *vt* (*after faint*) wieder zu Bewusstsein bringen
▸ **bring up** *vt* heraufbringen; (*question, subject*) zur Sprache bringen
brisk [brɪsk] *adj* (*pace*) flott; (*trade*) lebhaft
bristle [ˈbrɪsl] *n* Borste *f*
Brit [brɪt] (*inf*) *n* (= *British person*) Brite *m*, Britin *f*
Britain [ˈbrɪtən] *n* (*also:* **Great ~**) Großbritannien *nt*
British [ˈbrɪtɪʃ] *adj* britisch ▸ *npl*: **the ~** die Briten *pl*
British Isles *npl*: **the ~** die Britischen Inseln
Brittany [ˈbrɪtənɪ] *n* die Bretagne
brittle [ˈbrɪtl] *adj* spröde
broad [brɔːd] *adj* breit; (*accent*) stark; **in ~ daylight** am helllichten Tag
broadcast [ˈbrɔːdkɑːst] (*pt, pp* **~**) *n* Sendung *f* ▸ *vt, vi* senden
broaden [ˈbrɔːdn] *vt* erweitern; **to ~ one's mind** seinen Horizont erweitern
broad-minded [ˈbrɔːdˈmaɪndɪd] *adj* tolerant
broccoli [ˈbrɔkəlɪ] *n* Brokkoli *pl*
brochure [ˈbrəuʃjuəʳ] *n* Broschüre *f*
broke [brəuk] *pt of* **break** ▸ *adj* (*inf*) pleite
broken [ˈbrəukn] *pp of* **break**
brokenhearted *adj* untröstlich
broker [ˈbrəukəʳ] *n* Makler(in) *m(f)*
brolly [ˈbrɔlɪ] (Brit *inf*) *n* (Regen)schirm *m*
bromance [ˈbrəumæns] *n* (*inf*) *enge Freundschaft zwischen zwei heterosexuellen Männern*

bronchitis [brɔŋˈkaɪtɪs] *n* Bronchitis *f*
bronze [brɔnz] *n* Bronze *f*
brooch [brəutʃ] *n* Brosche *f*
broom [brum] *n* Besen *m*
bros., Bros. *abbr (Comm: = brothers)* Gebr.
broth [brɔθ] *n* Fleischbrühe *f*
brothel [ˈbrɔθl] *n* Bordell *nt*
brother [ˈbrʌðəʳ] *n* Bruder *m*
brother-in-law [ˈbrʌðərɪnˈlɔː] *n* Schwager *m*
brought [brɔːt] *pt, pp of* **bring**
brow [brau] *n* Stirn *f*; *(eyebrow)* (Augen)braue *f*
brown [braun] *adj* braun
brown bread *n* Graubrot *nt*, Mischbrot *nt*
Brownie [ˈbraunɪ] *n* Wichtel *m*
brownie [ˈbraunɪ] *(US) n kleiner Schokoladenkuchen*
brown paper *n* Packpapier *nt*
brown rice *n* Naturreis *m*
brown sugar *n* brauner Zucker *m*
browse [brauz] *vi (in shop)* sich umsehen; **to ~ through a book** in einem Buch schmökern
browser [ˈbrauzəʳ] *n (Comput)* Browser *m*
bruise [bruːz] *n* blauer Fleck *m* ▶ *vt (arm, leg etc)* sich *dat* stoßen
Brunei [bruːˈnaɪ, ˈbruːnaɪ] *n* Brunei *nt*
brunette [bruːˈnɛt] *n* Brünette *f*
brush [brʌʃ] *n* Bürste *f*; *(for painting, shaving etc)* Pinsel *m* ▶ *vt* fegen; *(groom)* bürsten; *(teeth)* putzen
▶ **brush up** *vt* auffrischen
Brussels sprouts *npl* Rosenkohl *m*
brutal [ˈbruːtl] *adj* brutal
brutality [bruːˈtælɪtɪ] *n* Brutalität *f*
BSc *abbr (= Bachelor of Science) akademischer Grad für Naturwissenschaftler*
BSE *n abbr (= bovine spongiform encephalopathy)* BSE *f*
bubble [ˈbʌbl] *n* Blase *f*
bubble bath *n* Schaumbad *nt*
bubbly [ˈbʌblɪ] *adj (person)* lebendig; *(liquid)* sprudelnd ▶ *n (inf: champagne)* Schampus *m*
buck [bʌk] *n (deer)* Bock *m*; *(US inf)* Dollar *m*
bucket [ˈbʌkɪt] *n* Eimer *m*
bucket list *n Liste von Dingen, die man vor seinem Tod gerne gemacht haben würde*
Buckingham Palace *n siehe Info-Artikel*

BUCKINGHAM PALACE

Buckingham Palace ist die offizielle Londoner Residenz der britischen Monarchen und liegt am St James Park. Der Palast wurde 1703 für den Herzog von Buckingham erbaut, 1762 von Georg III. gekauft, zwischen 1821 und 1836 von John Nash umgebaut und Anfang des 20. Jahrhunderts teilweise neu gestaltet. Teile des Buckingham Palace sind heute der Öffentlichkeit zugänglich.

buckle [ˈbʌkl] *n* Schnalle *f* ▶ *vt* zuschnallen ▶ *vi* sich verbiegen
bud [bʌd] *n* Knospe *f*
Buddhism [ˈbudɪzəm] *n* Buddhismus *m*
Buddhist [ˈbudɪst] *adj* buddhistisch ▶ *n* Buddhist(in) *m(f)*
buddy [ˈbʌdɪ] *(US) n* Kumpel *m*
budget [ˈbʌdʒɪt] *n* Budget *nt*
budget airline *n* Billigflieger *m*
budgie [ˈbʌdʒɪ] *n* = **budgerigar**
buff [bʌf] *n (inf)* Fan *m*
buffalo [ˈbʌfələu] *(pl ~ or* **buffaloes**) *n (BRIT)* Büffel *m*
buffer [ˈbʌfəʳ] *n* Puffer *m*; *(Comput)* Zwischenspeicher *m*, Pufferspeicher *m*
buffet [ˈbufeɪ] *(BRIT) n* Büfett *nt*
bug [bʌg] *n (esp US)* Insekt *nt*; *(Comput: of program)* Programmfehler *m*; *(fig: germ)* Bazillus *m*; *(hidden microphone)* Wanze *f* ▶ *vt (inf)* nerven
bugger [ˈbʌgəʳ] *(!) n* Scheißkerl *m (!)* ▶ *vb*: **~ off!** hau ab!; **~ (it)!** Scheiße! *(!)*
buggy [ˈbʌgɪ] *n (for baby)* Sportwagen *m*
build [bɪld] *(pt, pp* **built**) *vt* bauen
▶ **build up** *vt* aufbauen
builder [ˈbɪldəʳ] *n* Bauunternehmer *m*
building [ˈbɪldɪŋ] *n (structure)* Gebäude *nt*
building site *n* Baustelle *f*
building society *(BRIT) n* Bausparkasse *f*
built [bɪlt] *pt, pp of* **build** ▶ *adj*: **built-in** eingebaut, Einbau-
bulb [bʌlb] *n* (Blumen)zwiebel *f*; *(Elec)* (Glüh)birne *f*
Bulgaria [bʌlˈgɛərɪə] *n* Bulgarien *nt*

Bulgarian [bʌl'gɛərɪən] *adj* bulgarisch ▸ *n* Bulgare *m*, Bulgarin *f*; (*Ling*) Bulgarisch *nt*
bulimia [bə'lɪmɪə] *n* Bulimie *f*
bulk [bʌlk] *n* (*of thing*) massige Form *f*; (*of person*) massige Gestalt *f*; **in ~** im Großen, en gros; **the ~ of** der Großteil *+gen*
bulky ['bʌlkɪ] *adj* sperrig
bull [bul] *n* Stier *m*
bulldog ['buldɔg] *n* Bulldogge *f*
bulldoze ['buldəuz] *vt* mit Bulldozern wegräumen
bulldozer ['buldəuzə^r] *n* Planierraupe *f*
bullet ['bulɪt] *n* Kugel *f*
bulletin ['bulɪtɪn] *n* (*TV etc*) Kurznachrichten *pl*; (*journal*) Bulletin *nt*
bulletin board *n* (*Comput*) Schwarzes Brett *nt*
bullfight ['bulfaɪt] *n* Stierkampf *m*
bullshit ['bulʃɪt] (*!*) *n* Scheiß *m* (*!*)
bully ['bulɪ] *n* Tyrann *m*
bum [bʌm] (*inf*) *n* Hintern *m*; (*esp US: good-for-nothing*) Rumtreiber *m*; (*tramp*) Penner *m*
▸ **bum around** (*inf*) *vi* herumgammeln
bumblebee ['bʌmblbi:] *n* Hummel *f*
bumf [bʌmf] (*inf*) *n* Papierkram *m*
bump [bʌmp] *n* Zusammenstoß *m*; (*swelling*) Beule *f*; (*on road*) Unebenheit *f* ▸ *vt* stoßen
▸ **bump into** *vt fus* (*obstacle*) stoßen gegen; (*inf: person*) treffen
bumper ['bʌmpə^r] *n* Stoßstange *f* ▸ *adj*: **~ crop, ~ harvest** Rekordernte *f*
bumpy ['bʌmpɪ] *adj* holperig
bun [bʌn] *n* Brötchen *nt*
bunch [bʌntʃ] *n* Strauß *m*; (*of keys*) Bund *m*; (*of people*) Haufen *m*; **~ of grapes** Weintraube *f*
bundle ['bʌndl] *n* Bündel *nt*
bungalow ['bʌŋgələu] *n* Bungalow *m*
bungee jumping ['bʌndʒi:'dʒʌmpɪŋ] *n* Bungeespringen *nt*
bunk [bʌŋk] *n* Koje *f*
bunk beds *npl* Etagenbett *nt*
bunker ['bʌŋkə^r] *n* (*Mil, Golf*) Bunker *m*
bunny ['bʌnɪ] *n* Häschen *nt*
buoy [bɔɪ] *n* Boje *f*
buoyant ['bɔɪənt] *adj* (*ship, object*) schwimmfähig
burden ['bə:dn] *n* Belastung *f*; (*load*) Last *f*
bureau ['bjuərəu] (*pl* **bureaux**) *n* (*office*) Büro *nt*
bureaucracy [bjuə'rɔkrəsɪ] *n* Bürokratie *f*
bureaucratic [bjuərə'krætɪk] *adj* bürokratisch
burger ['bə:gə^r] (*inf*) *n* Hamburger *m*
burglar ['bə:glə^r] *n* Einbrecher(in) *m(f)*
burglar alarm *n* Alarmanlage *f*
burglarize ['bə:gləraɪz] (*US*) *vt* einbrechen in *+acc*
burglary ['bə:glərɪ] *n* Einbruch *m*
burgle ['bə:gl] *vt* einbrechen in *+acc*
burial ['bɛrɪəl] *n* Beerdigung *f*
burkha ['bə:kə] *n* Burka *f*
Burkina Faso [bə:'ki:nə'fæsəu] *n* Burkina Faso *nt*
burn [bə:n] (*pt, pp* **burned** *or* **burnt**) *vt* verbrennen; (*food*) anbrennen lassen; (*house etc*) niederbrennen ▸ *vi* brennen ▸ *n* Verbrennung *f*; **I've burnt myself!** ich habe mich verbrannt!
▸ **burn down** *vt* abbrennen
burp [bə:p] (*inf*) *vt* (*baby*) aufstoßen lassen ▸ *vi* rülpsen
bursary ['bə:sərɪ] (*Brit*) *n* Stipendium *nt*
burst [bə:st] (*pt, pp* **~**) *vt* platzen lassen ▸ *vi* platzen; **to ~ into tears** in Tränen ausbrechen
Burundi [bə'rundɪ] *n* Burundi *nt*
bury ['bɛrɪ] *vt* begraben; (*at funeral*) beerdigen; **to ~ one's face in one's hands** das Gesicht in den Händen vergraben
bus [bʌs] *n* (Auto)bus *m*
bush [buʃ] *n* Busch *m*
business ['bɪznɪs] *n* (*matter*) Angelegenheit *f*; (*trading*) Geschäft *nt*; (*occupation*) Beruf *m*; **I'm here on ~** ich bin geschäftlich hier; **it's none of my ~** es geht mich nichts an
business card *n* (Visiten)karte *f*
business class *n* (*Aviat*) Businessclass *f*
businessman ['bɪznɪsmən] *n* (*irreg*) Geschäftsmann *m*
business studies *npl* Betriebswirtschaftslehre *f*
businesswoman ['bɪznɪswumən] *n* (*irreg*) Geschäftsfrau *f*
bus service *n* Busverbindung *f*
bus shelter *n* Wartehäuschen *nt*
bus station *n* Busbahnhof *m*
bus stop *n* Bushaltestelle *f*
bust [bʌst] *n* Busen *m*; (*sculpture*) Büste *f* ▸ *adj* (*inf*) kaputt; **to go ~** pleitegehen
bust-up ['bʌstʌp] (*Brit inf*) *n* Krach *m*

busy [ˈbɪzɪ] *adj* (*person*) beschäftigt; (*shop, street*) belebt; (*Tel: esp US*) besetzt

KEYWORD

but [bʌt] *conj* **1** (*yet*) aber; **not blue but red** nicht blau, sondern rot
2 (*however*): **I'd love to come, but I'm busy** ich würde gern kommen, bin aber beschäftigt
3 (*showing disagreement, surprise etc*): **but that's fantastic!** das ist doch toll!
▸ *prep* (*apart from, except*) außer +*dat*; **nothing but trouble** nichts als Ärger; **no-one but him can do it** keiner außer ihm kann es machen; **but for you** wenn Sie nicht gewesen wären; **but for your help** ohne Ihre Hilfe; **I'll do anything but that** ich mache alles, nur nicht das
▸ *adv* (*just, only*) nur; **she's but a child** sie ist doch noch ein Kind; **I can but try** ich kann es ja versuchen

butcher [ˈbutʃəʳ] *n* Fleischer *m*, Metzger *m*
butler [ˈbʌtləʳ] *n* Butler *m*
butt [bʌt] *n* (*US!*) Arsch *m* (*!*)
butter [ˈbʌtəʳ] *n* Butter *f* ▸ *vt* buttern
buttercup [ˈbʌtəkʌp] *n* Butterblume *f*
butterfly [ˈbʌtəflaɪ] *n* Schmetterling *m*
buttocks [ˈbʌtəks] *npl* Gesäß *nt*
button [ˈbʌtn] *n* Knopf *m*; (*US: badge*) Plakette *f* ▸ *vt* (*also:* **~ up**) zuknöpfen
buttonhole [ˈbʌtnhəul] *n* Knopfloch *nt*
buy [baɪ] (*pt, pp* **bought**) *vt* kaufen ▸ *n* Kauf *m*; **to ~ sb sth** jdm etw kaufen
buyer [ˈbaɪəʳ] *n* Käufer(in) *m*(*f*)
buzz [bʌz] *vi* summen ▸ *n* Summen *nt*; (*inf*): **to give sb a ~** jdn anrufen
buzzer [ˈbʌzəʳ] *n* Summer *m*
buzz word (*inf*) *n* Modewort *nt*

KEYWORD

by [baɪ] *prep* **1** (*referring to cause, agent*) von +*dat*, durch +*acc*; **killed by lightning** vom Blitz *or* durch einen Blitz getötet; **a painting by Picasso** ein Bild von Picasso
2 (*referring to method, manner, means*): **by bus/car/train** mit dem Bus/Auto/Zug; **to pay by cheque** mit *or* per Scheck bezahlen; **by saving hard, he was able to ...** indem er eisern sparte, konnte er ...
3 (*via, through*) über +*acc*; **we came by Dover** wir sind über Dover gekommen; **he came in by the back door** er kam durch die Hintertür herein
4 (*close to*) bei +*dat*, an +*dat*; **the house by the river** das Haus am Fluss
5 (*past*) an ... *dat* vorbei; **she rushed by me** sie eilte an mir vorbei
6 (*not later than*) bis +*acc*; **by 4 o'clock** bis 4 Uhr; **by this time tomorrow** morgen um diese Zeit
7 (*amount*): **by the kilo/metre** kilo-/meterweise; **to be paid by the hour** stundenweise bezahlt werden
8 (*Math, measure*): **to divide by 3** durch 3 teilen; **to multiply by 3** mit 3 malnehmen; **it missed me by inches** es hat mich um Zentimeter verfehlt; **a room 3 metres by 4** ein Zimmer 3 mal 4 Meter; **it's broader by a metre** es ist (um) einem Meter breiter
9 (*according to*): **to play by the rules** sich an die Regeln halten; **it's all right by me** von mir aus ist es in Ordnung
10: **(all) by myself/himself** *etc* (ganz) allein
11: **by the way** übrigens
▸ *adv* **1** *see* **go**; **pass**
2: **by and by** irgendwann
3: **by and large** im Großen und Ganzen

bye [baɪ], **bye-bye** [ˈbaɪˈbaɪ] *excl* (auf) Wiedersehen, tschüss (*inf*)
by-election (Brit) *n* Nachwahl *f*
bypass [ˈbaɪpɑːs] *n* Umgehungsstraße *f*; (*Med*) Bypassoperation *f*
by-product *n* Nebenprodukt *nt*
bystander [ˈbaɪstændəʳ] *n* Zuschauer(in) *m*(*f*)
byte [baɪt] *n* (*Comput*) Byte *nt*

C

c *abbr* = **century**; (= *circa*) ca.; (*US etc*: = *cent(s)*) Cent *m*
cab [kæb] *n* Taxi *nt*
cabbage [ˈkæbɪdʒ] *n* Kohl *m*
cabin [ˈkæbɪn] *n* Kabine *f*; (*house*) Hütte *f*
cabin cruiser *n* Kajütboot *nt*
cabinet [ˈkæbɪnɪt] *n* kleiner Schrank *m*; (*also*: **display ~**) Vitrine *f*; (*Pol*) Kabinett *nt*
cable [ˈkeɪbl] *n* Kabel *nt*
cable car *n* (Draht)seilbahn *f*
cable railway *n* Seilbahn *f*
cable television *n* Kabelfernsehen *nt*
cactus [ˈkæktəs] (*pl* **cacti**) *n* Kaktus *m*
CAD *n abbr* (= *computer-aided design*) CAD *nt*
Caesarean [siːˈzɛərɪən] *n*: **~ (section)** Kaiserschnitt *m*
café [ˈkæfeɪ] *n* Café *nt*
cafeteria [kæfɪˈtɪərɪə] *n* Cafeteria *f*
caffeine, caffein [ˈkæfiːn] *n* Koffein *nt*
cage [keɪdʒ] *n* Käfig *m*
Cairo [ˈkaɪərəu] *n* Kairo *nt*
cake [keɪk] *n* Kuchen *m*
cake shop *n* Konditorei *f*
calamity [kəˈlæmɪtɪ] *n* Katastrophe *f*
calculate [ˈkælkjuleɪt] *vt* (*work out*) berechnen; (*estimate*) abschätzen
calculating [ˈkælkjuleɪtɪŋ] *adj* (*scheming*) berechnend
calculation [kælkjuˈleɪʃən] *n* Berechnung *f*; Abschätzung *f*
calculator [ˈkælkjuleɪtəʳ] *n* Rechner *m*
calendar [ˈkæləndəʳ] *n* Kalender *m*
calf [kɑːf] (*pl* **calves**) *n* Kalb *nt*; (*Anat*) Wade *f*
California [kælɪˈfɔːnɪə] *n* Kalifornien *nt*
call [kɔːl] *vt* (*name, consider*) nennen; (*shout out, summon*) rufen; (*Tel*) anrufen; (*witness, flight*) aufrufen ▸ *vi* rufen; (*Tel*) anrufen; (*visit*) vorbeigehen, vorbeikommen ▸ *n* Ruf *m*; (*Tel*) Anruf *m*; (*for flight etc*) Aufruf *m*; **to be called** (*named*) heißen; **please give me a ~ at 7** rufen Sie mich bitte um 7 an; **to make a ~** ein (Telefon) gespräch führen; **to be on ~** einsatzbereit sein
▸ **call at** *vt fus* (*subj*: *train*) halten in +*dat*
▸ **call back** *vt* (*Tel*) zurückrufen
▸ **call for** *vt fus* (*demand*) fordern; (*fetch*) abholen
▸ **call off** *vt* absagen
call centre *n* Callcenter *nt*
caller [ˈkɔːləʳ] *n* Besucher(in) *m(f)*; (*Tel*) Anrufer(in) *m(f)*
calm [kɑːm] *adj* ruhig; (*unworried*) gelassen ▸ *n* Ruhe *f* ▸ *vt* beruhigen
▸ **calm down** *vi* sich beruhigen
calorie [ˈkælərɪ] *n* Kalorie *f*
calves [kɑːvz] *npl of* **calf**
Cambodia [kæmˈbəudɪə] *n* Kambodscha *nt*
camcorder [ˈkæmkɔːdəʳ] *n* Camcorder *m*
came [keɪm] *pt of* **come**
camel [ˈkæməl] *n* Kamel *nt*
camera [ˈkæmərə] *n* (*Cine, Phot*) Kamera *f*
camera phone *n* Fotohandy *nt*
camomile [ˈkæməumaɪl] *n* Kamille *f*
camouflage [ˈkæməflɑːʒ] *n* Tarnung *f*
camp [kæmp] *n* Lager *nt* ▸ *vi* zelten ▸ *adj* (*effeminate*) tuntenhaft (*inf*)
campaign [kæmˈpeɪn] *n* (*Mil*) Feldzug *m*; (*Pol etc*) Kampagne *f* ▸ *vi*: **to ~ for/against** sich einsetzen für/gegen
camp bed (BRIT) *n* Campingliege *f*
camper [ˈkæmpəʳ] *n* (*person*) Camper *m*; (*vehicle*) Wohnmobil *nt*
camping [ˈkæmpɪŋ] *n* Camping *nt*
camping site, camp site *n* Campingplatz *m*
campus [ˈkæmpəs] *n* (*Univ*) Universitätsgelände *nt*, Campus *m*
can¹ [kæn] *n* Büchse *f*, Dose *f*

KEYWORD

can² (*negative* **cannot**, **can't**, *conditional*, *pt* **could**) *aux vb* **1** (*be able*

to, know how to) können; **I can't see you** ich kann dich nicht sehen; **I can swim/drive** ich kann schwimmen/ Auto fahren; **can you speak English?** sprechen Sie Englisch?
2 (*may*) können, dürfen; **could I have a word with you?** könnte ich Sie mal sprechen?

Canada [ˈkænədə] *n* Kanada *nt*
Canadian [kəˈneɪdɪən] *adj* kanadisch ▸ *n* Kanadier(in) *m(f)*
canal [kəˈnæl] *n* (*also Anat*) Kanal *m*
canary [kəˈnɛərɪ] *n* Kanarienvogel *m*
cancel [ˈkænsəl] *vt* absagen; (*reservation*) abbestellen; (*train, flight*) ausfallen lassen; (*contract*) annullieren; (*order*) stornieren
cancellation [kænsəˈleɪʃən] *n* Absage *f*; (*of reservation*) Abbestellung *f*; (*of train, flight*) Ausfall *m*
cancer [ˈkænsəʳ] *n* Krebs *m*; **C~** (*Astrol*) Krebs *m*
candid [ˈkændɪd] *adj* offen
candidate [ˈkændɪdeɪt] *n* Kandidat(in) *m(f)*; (*for job*) Bewerber(in) *m(f)*
candle [ˈkændl] *n* Kerze *f*
candlelight [ˈkændllaɪt] *n*: **by ~** bei Kerzenlicht
candlestick [ˈkændlstɪk] *n* Kerzenhalter *m*
candy [ˈkændɪ] *n* (*US*) Bonbon *m or nt*
candyfloss (BRIT) *n* Zuckerwatte *f*
cane [keɪn] *n* Rohr *nt*; (*stick*) Stock *m*
cannabis [ˈkænəbɪs] *n* Cannabis *m*
canned [kænd] *adj* Dosen-
cannot [ˈkænɔt] = **can not**
canny [ˈkænɪ] *adj* schlau
canoe [kəˈnuː] *n* Kanu *nt*
canoeing [kəˈnuːɪŋ] *n* Kanusport *m*
can-opener [ˈkænəupnəʳ] *n* Dosenöffner *m*
canopy [ˈkænəpɪ] *n* (*also fig*) Baldachin *m*
can't [kænt] = **can not**
canteen [kænˈtiːn] *n* (*in school, workplace*) Kantine *f*
canvas [ˈkænvəs] *n* Leinwand *f*; (*Naut*) Segeltuch *nt*; **under ~** im Zelt
canvass [ˈkænvəs] *vi*: **to ~ for ...** (*Pol*) um Stimmen für ... werben
canyon [ˈkænjən] *n* Cañon *m*
cap [kæp] *n* Mütze *f*; (*of bottle*) Verschluss *m*, Deckel *m*
capability [keɪpəˈbɪlɪtɪ] *n* Fähigkeit *f*
capable [ˈkeɪpəbl] *adj* fähig; **to be ~ of doing sth** etw tun können, fähig sein, etw zu tun
capacity [kəˈpæsɪtɪ] *n* Fassungsvermögen *nt*; (*capability*) Fähigkeit *f*; (*of factory*) Kapazität *f*; **in his ~ as ...** in seiner Eigenschaft als ...
cape [keɪp] *n* Kap *nt*; (*cloak*) Cape *nt*, Umhang *m*
caper [ˈkeɪpəʳ] *n* (*Culin: usu pl*) Kaper *f*
capital [ˈkæpɪtl] *n* (*also:* **~ city**) Hauptstadt *f*; (*money*) Kapital *nt*; (*also:* **~ letter**) Großbuchstabe *m*
capitalism [ˈkæpɪtəlɪzəm] *n* Kapitalismus *m*
capital punishment *n* Todesstrafe *f*
Capricorn [ˈkæprɪkɔːn] *n* Steinbock *m*
capsize [kæpˈsaɪz] *vi* kentern
capsule [ˈkæpsjuːl] *n* Kapsel *f*
captain [ˈkæptɪn] *n* Kapitän *m*; (*in army*) Hauptmann *m*
caption [ˈkæpʃən] *n* Bildunterschrift *f*
captive [ˈkæptɪv] *n* Gefangene(r) *f(m)*
capture [ˈkæptʃəʳ] *vt* (*person*) gefangen nehmen; (*town, country, share of market*) erobern; (*Comput*) erfassen ▸ *n* (*of person*) Gefangennahme *f*; (*Comput*) Erfassung *f*
car [kɑːʳ] *n* Auto *nt*; (*Rail*) Wagen *m*
carafe [kəˈræf] *n* Karaffe *f*
caramel [ˈkærəməl] *n* Karamelle *f*
caravan [ˈkærəvæn] *n* (BRIT) Wohnwagen *m*
caravan site (BRIT) *n* Campingplatz *m* für Wohnwagen
caraway seed *n* Kümmel *m*
carb [kɑːb] *n abbr* (*inf:* = *carbohydrate*) Kohle(n)hydrat *nt*
carbohydrate [kɑːbəuˈhaɪdreɪt] *n* Kohle(n)hydrat *nt*
car bomb *n* Autobombe *f*
carbon [ˈkɑːbən] *n* Kohlenstoff *m*
carbon footprint *n* ökologischer Fußabdruck
carbon-neutral [ˈkɑːbənˈnjuːtrəl] *adj* CO^2-neutral
carbon offset *n* Klimakompensation *f*
car-boot sale [ˈkɑːbuːt-] *n auf einem Parkplatz stattfindender Flohmarkt mit dem Kofferraum als Auslage*
carburettor, (*US*) **carburetor** [kɑːbjuˈrɛtəʳ] *n* Vergaser *m*
card [kɑːd] *n* Karte *f*; (*material*) (dünne) Pappe *f*

cardboard [ˈkɑːdbɔːd] *n* Pappe *f*
cardboard box *n* (Papp)karton *m*
card game *n* Kartenspiel *nt*
cardigan [ˈkɑːdɪgən] *n* Strickjacke *f*
card index *n* Kartei *f*
cardphone [ˈkɑːdfəun] *n* Kartentelefon *nt*
care [kɛəʳ] *n* (*attention*) Versorgung *f*; (*worry*) Sorge *f*; (*charge*) Obhut *f*, Fürsorge *f* ▸ *vi*: **to ~ about** sich kümmern um; **~ of** bei; **"handle with ~"** „Vorsicht, zerbrechlich"; **to take ~** aufpassen; **to take ~ of** sich kümmern um; **I don't ~** es ist mir egal *or* gleichgültig
▸ **care for** *vt fus* (*look after*) sich kümmern um; (*like*) mögen
career [kəˈrɪəʳ] *n* Karriere *f*; (*life*) Laufbahn *f*
careers officer [kəˈrɪəz-], **careers adviser** *n* Berufsberater(in) *m(f)*
career woman *n* (*irreg*) Karrierefrau *f*
carefree [ˈkɛəfriː] *adj* sorglos
careful [ˈkɛəful] *adj* vorsichtig; (*thorough*) sorgfältig
carefully *adv* vorsichtig; (*methodically*) sorgfältig
careless [ˈkɛəlɪs] *adj* leichtsinnig; (*negligent*) nachlässig; (*remark*) gedankenlos
carelessly *adv* leichtsinnig; nachlässig; gedankenlos
carer [ˈkɛərəʳ] *n* Betreuer(in) *m(f)*, Pfleger(in) *m(f)*
caretaker [ˈkɛəteɪkəʳ] *n* Hausmeister(in) *m(f)*
car ferry *n* Autofähre *f*
cargo [ˈkɑːgəu] (*pl* **cargoes**) *n* Ladung *f*
car hire (Brit) *n* Autovermietung *f*
Caribbean [kærɪˈbiːən] *adj* karibisch ▸ *n*: **the ~ (Sea)** die Karibik, das Karibische Meer
caring [ˈkɛərɪŋ] *adj* liebevoll; (*society, organization*) sozial; (*behaviour*) fürsorglich
car insurance *n* Kraftfahrzeug-versicherung *f*
carnation [kɑːˈneɪʃən] *n* Nelke *f*
carnival [ˈkɑːnɪvl] *n* Karneval *m*; (*US: funfair*) Kirmes *f*
carol [ˈkærəl] *n*: **(Christmas) ~** Weihnachtslied *nt*
carp [kɑːp] *n* Karpfen *m*
car park *n* Parkplatz *m*; (*building*) Parkhaus *nt*
carpenter [ˈkɑːpɪntəʳ] *n* Zimmermann *m*
carpet [ˈkɑːpɪt] *n* (*also fig*) Teppich *m*
car phone *n* (*Tel*) Autotelefon *nt*
car rental *n* Autovermietung *f*
carriage [ˈkærɪdʒ] *n* (*Rail, of typewriter*) Wagen *m*; (*horse-drawn vehicle*) Kutsche *f*; (*of goods*) Beförderung *f*
carriageway [ˈkærɪdʒweɪ] (Brit) *n* Fahrbahn *f*
carrier [ˈkærɪəʳ] *n* Spediteur *m*
carrier bag (Brit) *n* Tragetasche *f*
carrot [ˈkærət] *n* Karotte *f*
carry [ˈkærɪ] *vt* tragen; (*transport*) transportieren; (*responsibilities etc*) mit sich bringen
▸ **carry on** *vi* weitermachen; (*inf: make a fuss*) (ein) Theater machen ▸ *vt* fortführen; **to ~ on singing/eating** weitersingen/-essen
▸ **carry out** *vt* (*orders*) ausführen; (*investigation*) durchführen
carrycot [ˈkærɪkɔt] (Brit) *n* Babytragetasche *f*
cart [kɑːt] *n* Wagen *m*, Karren *m*
carton [ˈkɑːtən] *n* (Papp)karton *m*; (*of cigarettes*) Stange *f*
cartoon [kɑːˈtuːn] *n* (*drawing*) Karikatur *f*; (Brit: *comic strip*) Cartoon *m*; (*Cine*) Zeichentrickfilm *m*
cartridge [ˈkɑːtrɪdʒ] *n* (*for gun, pen*) Patrone *f*; (*music tape, for camera*) Kassette *f*
carve [kɑːv] *vt* (*meat*) (ab)schneiden; (*wood*) schnitzen; (*stone*) meißeln
carving [ˈkɑːvɪŋ] *n* Skulptur *f*; (*in wood etc*) Schnitzerei *f*
car wash *n* Autowaschanlage *f*
case [keɪs] *n* Fall *m*; (*for spectacles etc*) Etui *nt*; (Brit: *also*: **suitcase**) Koffer *m*; (*of wine, whisky etc*) Kiste *f*; **in ~ ...** falls ...; **in ~ of fire** bei Feuer; **in ~ of emergency** im Notfall
cash [kæʃ] *n* (Bar)geld *nt* ▸ *vt* (*cheque etc*) einlösen; **to pay (in) ~** bar bezahlen; **~ on delivery** per Nachnahme
cash desk (Brit) *n* Kasse *f*
cash dispenser (Brit) *n* Geldautomat *m*
cashier [kæˈʃɪəʳ] *n* Kassierer(in) *m(f)*
cashless [ˈkæʃlɪs] *adj* bargeldlos
cash machine *n* (Brit) Geldautomat *m*
cashmere [ˈkæʃmɪəʳ] *n* Kaschmir *m*

cash point *n* Geldautomat *m*

casing ['keɪsɪŋ] *n* Gehäuse *nt*

casino [kə'siːnəu] *n* Kasino *nt*

cask [kɑːsk] *n* Fass *nt*

casserole ['kæsərəul] *n* Auflauf *m*; (*pot, container*) Kasserolle *f*

cassette [kæ'sɛt] *n* Kassette *f*

cassette recorder *n* Kassettenrekorder *m*

cast [kɑːst] (*pt, pp* **~**) *vt* werfen ▶ *n* (*Theat*) Besetzung *f*; (*also:* **plaster ~**) Gipsverband *m*; **to ~ sb as Hamlet** (*Theat*) die Rolle des Hamlet mit jdm besetzen

▶ **cast off** *vi* (*Naut*) losmachen

caster sugar ['kɑːstə-] (Brit) *n* Streuzucker *m*

castle ['kɑːsl] *n* (*fortified*) Burg *f*

cast-off *n* abgelegtes Kleidungsstück *nt*

castrate [kæs'treɪt] *vt* kastrieren

casual ['kæʒjul] *adj* (*by chance*) zufällig; (*work etc*) Gelegenheits-; (*unconcerned*) lässig, gleichgültig; (*clothes*) leger; **~ wear** Freizeitkleidung *f*

casually ['kæʒjulɪ] *adv* (*glance*) beiläufig; (*dress*) leger; (*by chance*) zufällig

casualty ['kæʒjultɪ] *n* (*someone injured*) Verletzte(r) *f(m)*; (*someone killed*) Tote(r) *f(m)*; (*Med*) Unfallstation *f*

cat [kæt] *n* Katze *f*

catalogue, (*US*) **catalog** ['kætəlɔg] *n* Katalog *m* ▶ *vt* katalogisieren

cataract ['kætərækt] *n* (*Med*) grauer Star *m*

catarrh [kə'tɑː^{r}] *n* Katarrh *m*

catastrophe [kə'tæstrəfɪ] *n* Katastrophe *f*

catch [kætʃ] (*pt, pp* **caught**) *vt* fangen; (*take: bus, train etc*) nehmen; (*arrest*) festnehmen; (*surprise*) erwischen, ertappen; (*illness*) sich *dat* zuziehen *or* holen ▶ *n* Fang *m*; **to ~ fire** Feuer fangen

▶ **catch on** *vi* (*grow popular*) sich durchsetzen

▶ **catch up** *vi* (*fig: on work*) aufholen ▶ *vt*: **to ~ sb up, to ~ up with sb** jdn einholen

catching ['kætʃɪŋ] *adj* ansteckend

category ['kætɪgərɪ] *n* Kategorie *f*

cater ['keɪtə^{r}] *vi*: **to ~ (for)** die Speisen und Getränke liefern (für)

▶ **cater for** (Brit) *vt fus* (*readers, consumers*) eingestellt *or* ausgerichtet sein auf *+acc*

catering ['keɪtərɪŋ] *n* Gastronomie *f*

caterpillar ['kætəpɪlə^{r}] *n* Raupe *f*

cathedral [kə'θiːdrəl] *n* Kathedrale *f*, Dom *m*

Catholic ['kæθəlɪk] *adj* katholisch ▶ *n* Katholik(in) *m(f)*

Catseye® ['kæts'aɪ] (Brit) *n* (*Aut*) Katzenauge *nt*

catsup ['kætsəp] (*US*) *n* Ket(s)chup *m or nt*

cattle ['kætl] *npl* Vieh *nt*

caught [kɔːt] *pt, pp of* **catch**

cauliflower ['kɔlɪflauə^{r}] *n* Blumenkohl *m*; **~ cheese** Blumenkohl in Käsesoße

cause [kɔːz] *n* Ursache *f*; (*reason*) Grund *m*; (*aim*) Sache *f* ▶ *vt* verursachen; **there is no ~ for concern** es besteht kein Grund zur Sorge

causeway ['kɔːzweɪ] *n* Damm *m*

caution ['kɔːʃən] *n* Vorsicht *f*; (*Law*) Verwarnung *f* ▶ *vt* warnen; (*Law*) verwarnen

cautious ['kɔːʃəs] *adj* vorsichtig

cave [keɪv] *n* Höhle *f*

▶ **cave in** *vi* einstürzen

cavity ['kævɪtɪ] *n* Hohlraum *m*; (*in tooth*) Loch *nt*

cayenne [keɪ'ɛn] *n* (*also:* **~ pepper**) Cayennepfeffer *m*

CCTV *n abbr* = **closed-circuit television**

CCTV camera *n* Überwachungskamera *f*

CD *n abbr* (*= compact disc*) CD *f*

CD player *n* CD-Spieler *m*

CD-ROM ['siːdiː'rɔm] *n abbr* (*= compact disc read-only memory*) CD-ROM *f*

cease [siːs] *vt* beenden ▶ *vi* aufhören

ceasefire *n* Waffenruhe *f*

ceiling ['siːlɪŋ] *n* Decke *f*

celebrate ['sɛlɪbreɪt] *vt* feiern ▶ *vi* feiern

celebrated ['sɛlɪbreɪtɪd] *adj* gefeiert

celebration [sɛlɪ'breɪʃən] *n* Feier *f*

celebrity [sɪ'lɛbrɪtɪ] *n* berühmte Persönlichkeit *f*

celeriac [sə'lɛrɪæk] *n* (Knollen)sellerie *f*

celery ['sɛlərɪ] *n* (Stangen)sellerie *f*

cell [sɛl] *n* Zelle *f*

cellar ['sɛlə^{r}] *n* Keller *m*

cello ['tʃɛləu] *n* Cello *nt*

cell phone *n* Handy *nt*, Mobiltelefon *nt*
cell tower *n* (*US Tel*) Mobilfunkmast *m*
Celt [kɛlt] *n* Kelte *m*, Keltin *f*
Celtic [ˈkɛltɪk] *adj* keltisch
cement [səˈmɛnt] *n* Zement *m*
cemetery [ˈsɛmɪtrɪ] *n* Friedhof *m*
censorship [ˈsɛnsəʃɪp] *n* Zensur *f*
cent [sɛnt] *n* Cent *m*; *see also* **per cent**
center *etc* [ˈsɛntəʳ] (*US*) = **centre** *etc*
centilitre, (*US*) **centiliter** [ˈsɛntɪli:təʳ] *n* Zentiliter *m or nt*
centimetre, (*US*) **centimeter** [ˈsɛntɪmi:təʳ] *n* Zentimeter *m or nt*
central [ˈsɛntrəl] *adj* zentral
Central America *n* Mittelamerika *nt*
central heating *n* Zentralheizung *f*
centralize [ˈsɛntrəlaɪz] *vt* zentralisieren
central reservation (Brit) *n* Mittelstreifen *m*
centre, (*US*) **center** [ˈsɛntəʳ] *n* Mitte *f*; (*health centre etc, town centre*) Zentrum *nt* ▶ *vt* zentrieren
centre forward *n* Mittelstürmer(in) *m(f)*
century [ˈsɛntjurɪ] *n* Jahrhundert *nt*
ceramic [sɪˈræmɪk] *adj* keramisch
cereal [ˈsi:rɪəl] *n* Getreide *nt*; (*food*) Getreideflocken *pl* (*Cornflakes etc*)
ceremony [ˈsɛrɪmənɪ] *n* Zeremonie *f*
certain [ˈsə:tən] *adj* sicher; **~ days/ places** bestimmte Tage/Orte; **for ~** ganz sicher, ganz genau
certainly [ˈsə:tənlɪ] *adv* bestimmt; (*of course*) sicherlich; **~!** (aber) sicher!
certificate [səˈtɪfɪkɪt] *n* Urkunde *f*; (*diploma*) Zeugnis *nt*
certify [ˈsə:tɪfaɪ] *vt* bescheinigen ▶ *vi*: **to ~ to** sich verbürgen für
cervical [ˈsə:vɪkl] *adj*: **~ smear** Abstrich *m*
CFC *n abbr* (= *chlorofluorocarbon*) FCKW *m*
chain [tʃeɪn] *n* Kette *f* ▶ *vt* (*also*: **~ up**: *prisoner*) anketten
chain reaction *n* Kettenreaktion *f*
chain store *n* Kettenladen *m*
chair [tʃɛəʳ] *n* Stuhl *m*; (*armchair*) Sessel *m*; (*of university*) Lehrstuhl *m*; (*of meeting, committee*) Vorsitz *m*
chair lift *n* Sessellift *m*
chairman [ˈtʃɛəmən] *n* (*irreg*) Vorsitzende(r) *f(m)*; (Brit: *of company*) Präsident *m*
chairperson [ˈtʃɛəpə:sn] *n* Vorsitzende(r) *f(m)*
chairwoman [ˈtʃɛəwumən] *n* (*irreg*) Vorsitzende *f*
chalet [ˈʃæleɪ] *n* Chalet *nt*
chalk [tʃɔ:k] *n* Kreide *f*
challenge [ˈtʃælɪndʒ] *n* (*dare*) Herausforderung *f* ▶ *vt* herausfordern; (*authority, right, idea etc*) infrage stellen
chambermaid [ˈtʃeɪmbəmeɪd] *n* Zimmermädchen *nt*
chamois leather [ˈʃæmɪ-] *n* Fensterleder *nt*
champagne [ʃæmˈpeɪn] *n* Champagner *m*
champion [ˈtʃæmpɪən] *n* Meister(in) *m(f)*
championship [ˈtʃæmpɪənʃɪp] *n* Meisterschaft *f*
chance [tʃɑ:ns] *n* (*hope*) Aussicht *f*; (*likelihood, possibility*) Möglichkeit *f*; (*opportunity*) Gelegenheit *f*; (*risk*) Risiko *nt*; **by ~** durch Zufall, zufällig
chancellor [ˈtʃɑ:nsələʳ] *n* Kanzler *m*
chandelier [ʃændəˈlɪəʳ] *n* Kronleuchter *m*
change [tʃeɪndʒ] *vt* ändern; (*wheel, job, money, baby's nappy*) wechseln; (*bulb*) auswechseln; (*baby*) wickeln ▶ *vi* sich verändern; (*traffic lights*) umspringen ▶ *n* Veränderung *f*; (*difference*) Abwechslung *f*; (*coins*) Kleingeld *nt*; (*money returned*) Wechselgeld *nt*; **to ~ sb into** jdn verwandeln in +*acc*; **to ~ gear** (*Aut*) schalten; **to ~ one's mind** seine Meinung ändern, es sich *dat* anders überlegen; **to give sb ~ for** *or* **of £10** jdm £10 wechseln; **for a ~** zur Abwechslung
changeable *adj* (*weather*) wechselhaft, veränderlich
change machine *n* (Geld) wechselautomat *m*
changing room (Brit) *n* (Umkleide) kabine *f*
channel [ˈtʃænl] *n* (*TV*) Kanal *m*; **the (English) C~** der Ärmelkanal; **the C~ Islands** die Kanalinseln *pl*
channel-hopping [ˈtʃænlhɔpɪŋ] *n* (*TV*) ständiges Umschalten
Channel Tunnel *n*: **the ~** der Kanaltunnel
chaos [ˈkeɪɔs] *n* Chaos *nt*
chaotic [keɪˈɔtɪk] *adj* chaotisch
chap [tʃæp] (Brit *inf*) *n* Kerl *m*, Typ *m*
chapel [ˈtʃæpl] *n* Kapelle *f*

chapped [tʃæpt] *adj* aufgesprungen
chapter [ˈtʃæptəʳ] *n* Kapitel *nt*
character [ˈkærɪktəʳ] *n* Charakter *m*; (*personality*) Persönlichkeit *f*; (*in novel, film*) Figur *f*, Gestalt *f*; (*letter, also Comput*) Zeichen *nt*
characteristic [kærɪktəˈrɪstɪk] *n* Merkmal *nt*
charcoal [ˈtʃɑːkəul] *n* Holzkohle *f*
charge [tʃɑːdʒ] *n* (*fee*) Gebühr *f*; (*accusation*) Anklage *f* ▸ *vt* (*battery*) (auf)laden; **to be in ~ of** die Verantwortung haben für; **how much do you ~?** was verlangen Sie?; **to ~ sb (with)** (*Law*) jdn anklagen (wegen)
charge card *n* Kundenkreditkarte *f*
charity [ˈtʃærɪtɪ] *n* (*organization*) karitative Organisation *f*
charm [tʃɑːm] *n* Charme *m* ▸ *vt* bezaubern
charming [ˈtʃɑːmɪŋ] *adj* reizend, charmant
chart [tʃɑːt] *n* Diagramm *nt*; (*map*) Karte *f* ■ **charts** *npl* (*hit parade*) Hitliste *f*
charter [ˈtʃɑːtəʳ] *vt* chartern ▸ *n* (*of university, company*) Gründungsurkunde *f*
charter flight *n* Charterflug *m*
chase [tʃeɪs] *vt* jagen, verfolgen ▸ *n* Verfolgungsjagd *f*
chassis [ˈʃæsɪ] *n* Fahrgestell *nt*
chat [tʃæt] *vi* plaudern; (*Comput*) chatten ▸ *n* Plauderei *f*; (*Comput*) Chat *m*
▸ **chat up** (Brit *inf*) *vt* anmachen
chatroom [ˈtʃætruːm] *n* (*Comput*) Chatroom *m*
chat show (Brit) *n* Talkshow *f*
chatty [ˈtʃætɪ] *adj* geschwätzig
chauffeur [ˈʃəufəʳ] *n* Chauffeur *m*, Fahrer *m*
cheap [tʃiːp] *adj* billig; (*poor quality*) minderwertig
cheat [tʃiːt] *vi* mogeln (*inf*) ▸ *vt*: **to ~ sb (out of sth)** jdn (um etw) betrügen
cheat sheet *n* (*US*: *in exam*) Spickzettel *m*
Chechen [ˈtʃɛtʃɛn] *adj* tschetschenisch ▸ *n* Tschetschene *m*, Tschetschenin *f*
Chechnya [ˈtʃɛtʃnɪə] *n* Tschetschenien *nt*
check [tʃɛk] *vt* überprüfen; (*passport, ticket*) kontrollieren ▸ *n* Kontrolle *f*; (*US*) = **cheque**; (*: bill*) Rechnung *f*; (*pattern*: *gen pl*) Karo(muster) *nt*; **to ~ o.s.** sich beherrschen
▸ **check in** *vi* (*at hotel*) sich anmelden; (*at airport*) einchecken ▸ *vt* (*luggage*) abfertigen lassen
▸ **check out** *vi* (*of hotel*) abreisen
▸ **check up** *vi*: **to ~ up on sth** etw überprüfen; **to ~ up on sb** Nachforschungen über jdn anstellen
checkers [ˈtʃɛkəz] (*US*) *npl* Damespiel *nt*
check-in [ˈtʃɛkɪn], **check-in desk** *n* (*at airport*) Abfertigung *f*, Abfertigungsschalter *m*
checking account [ˈtʃɛkɪŋ-] (*US*) *n* Girokonto *nt*
check list *n* Prüfliste *f*, Checkliste *f*
checkout [ˈtʃɛkaut] *n* Kasse *f*
checkpoint [ˈtʃɛkpɔɪnt] *n* Kontrollpunkt *m*
checkroom [ˈtʃɛkrum] (*US*) *n* (*left-luggage office*) Gepäckaufbewahrung *f*
checkup [ˈtʃɛkʌp] *n* Untersuchung *f*
cheddar [ˈtʃedəʳ] *n* Cheddarkäse *m*
cheek [tʃiːk] *n* Backe *f*; (*impudence*) Frechheit *f*
cheekbone [ˈtʃiːkbəun] *n* Backenknochen *m*
cheeky [ˈtʃiːkɪ] *adj* frech
cheer [tʃɪəʳ] *vt* zujubeln +*dat* ▸ *vi* jubeln ▸ *n* (*gen pl*) Beifallsruf *m*
■ **cheers** *npl* Hurrageschrei *nt*, Jubel *m*; **cheers!** prost!
▸ **cheer up** *vi* vergnügter *or* fröhlicher werden ▸ *vt* aufmuntern
cheerful [ˈtʃɪəful] *adj* fröhlich
cheese [tʃiːz] *n* Käse *m*
cheeseboard [ˈtʃiːzbɔːd] *n* Käsebrett *nt*; (*with cheese on it*) Käseplatte *f*
cheesecake [ˈtʃiːzkeɪk] *n* Käsekuchen *m*
chef [ʃɛf] *n* Küchenchef(in) *m(f)*
chemical [ˈkɛmɪkl] *adj* chemisch ▸ *n* Chemikalie *f*
chemist [ˈkɛmɪst] *n* (Brit: *pharmacist*) Apotheker(in) *m(f)*; (*scientist*) Chemiker(in) *m(f)*
chemistry [ˈkɛmɪstrɪ] *n* Chemie *f*
chemist's [ˈkɛmɪsts], **chemist's shop** (Brit) *n* Apotheke *f*
cheque [tʃɛk] (Brit) *n* Scheck *m*
chequebook [ˈtʃɛkbuk] *n* Scheckbuch *nt*
cheque card (Brit) *n* Scheckkarte *f*

chequered [ˈtʃɛkəd] *adj* (*fig*) bewegt
cherish [ˈtʃɛrɪʃ] *vt* (*person*) liebevoll sorgen für; (*memory*) in Ehren halten; (*hope*) hegen
cherry [ˈtʃɛrɪ] *n* Kirsche *f*
chess [tʃɛs] *n* Schach(spiel) *nt*
chessboard [ˈtʃɛsbɔːd] *n* Schachbrett *nt*
chest [tʃɛst] *n* Brust *f*; (*box*) Kiste *f*
chestnut [ˈtʃɛsnʌt] *n* Kastanie *f*
chest of drawers *n* Kommode *f*
chew [tʃuː] *vt* kauen
chewing gum [ˈtʃuːɪŋ-] *n* Kaugummi *m*
chick [tʃɪk] *n* Küken *nt*
chicken [ˈtʃɪkɪn] *n* Huhn *nt*; (*meat*) Hähnchen *nt*; (*inf*: *coward*) Feigling *m*
chickenpox [ˈtʃɪkɪnpɔks] *n* Windpocken *pl*
chickpea [ˈtʃɪkpiː] *n* Kichererbse *f*
chicory [ˈtʃɪkərɪ] *n* (*salad vegetable*) Chicorée *m or f*
chief [tʃiːf] *n* Häuptling *m*; (*of organization, department*) Leiter(in) *m(f)*, Chef(in) *m(f)* ▶ *adj* Haupt-
chiefly [ˈtʃiːflɪ] *adv* hauptsächlich
child [tʃaɪld] (*pl* **children**) *n* Kind *nt*
childbirth [ˈtʃaɪldbəːθ] *n* Geburt *f*, Entbindung *f*
childcare [ˈtʃaɪldkɛə[r]] *n* Kinderbetreuung *f*
childhood [ˈtʃaɪldhud] *n* Kindheit *f*
childish [ˈtʃaɪldɪʃ] *adj* kindisch
children [ˈtʃɪldrən] *npl of* **child**
Chile [ˈtʃɪlɪ] *n* Chile *nt*
chill [tʃɪl] *n* Kühle *f*; (*illness*) Erkältung *f* ▶ *vt* kühlen
▶ **chill out** (*inf*) *vi* sich entspannen, relaxen
chilli, (*US*) **chili** [ˈtʃɪlɪ] *n* Peperoni *pl*
chilly [ˈtʃɪlɪ] *adj* kühl; frostig
chimney [ˈtʃɪmnɪ] *n* Schornstein *m*
chimney sweep *n* Schornsteinfeger(in) *m(f)*
chimpanzee [tʃɪmpænˈziː] *n* Schimpanse *m*
chin [tʃɪn] *n* Kinn *nt*
China [ˈtʃaɪnə] *n* China *nt*
china [ˈtʃaɪnə] *n* Porzellan *nt*
Chinese [tʃaɪˈniːz] *adj* chinesisch ▶ *n inv* Chinese *m*, Chinesin *f*; (*Ling*) Chinesisch *nt*
chip [tʃɪp] *n* (*gen pl*) Pommes frites *pl*; (*US*: *also*: **potato ~**) Chip *m*; (*of wood*) Span *m*; (*in glass, cup etc*) abgestoßene Stelle *f*; (*Comput*: *also*: **microchip**) Chip *m* ▶ *vt* (*cup, plate*) anschlagen
▶ **chip in** (*inf*) *vi* (*contribute*) etwas beisteuern; (*interrupt*) sich einschalten
chiropodist [kɪˈrɔpədɪst] (Brit) *n* Fußpfleger(in) *m(f)*
chirp [tʃəːp] *vi* (*bird*) zwitschern
chisel [ˈtʃɪzl] *n* (*for stone*) Meißel *m*
chitchat [ˈtʃɪttʃæt] *n* Plauderei *f*
chives [tʃaɪvz] *npl* Schnittlauch *m*
chlorine [ˈklɔːriːn] *n* Chlor *nt*
chocolate [ˈtʃɔklɪt] *n* Schokolade *f*; (*sweet*) Praline *f* ▶ *cpd* Schokoladen-
chocolate cake *n* Schokoladenkuchen *m*
choice [tʃɔɪs] *n* Auswahl *f*; (*preference*) Wahl *f* ▶ *adj* Qualitäts-, erstklassig
choir [ˈkwaɪə[r]] *n* Chor *m*
choke [tʃəuk] *vi* ersticken ▶ *vt* erdrosseln ▶ *n* (*Aut*) Choke *m*
cholera [ˈkɔlərə] *n* Cholera *f*
cholesterol [kəˈlɛstərɔl] *n* Cholesterin *nt*
chook [tʃuk] *n* (Aust, *NZ inf*) Huhn *nt*
choose [tʃuːz] (*pt* **chose**, *pp* **chosen**) *vt* (aus)wählen; (*profession, friend*) sich *dat* aussuchen ▶ *vi*: **to ~ from** wählen aus *or* unter +*dat*; **to ~ to do sth** beschließen, etw zu tun
chop [tʃɔp] *vt* (*wood*) hacken; (*vegetables, fruit, meat*) klein schneiden ▶ *n* Kotelett *nt*; **to get the ~** (Brit *inf*: *be sacked*) rausgeschmissen werden
chopper [ˈtʃɔpə[r]] (*inf*) *n* Hubschrauber *m*
chopsticks [ˈtʃɔpstɪks] *npl* Stäbchen *pl*
chorus [ˈkɔːrəs] *n* Chor *m*; (*refrain*) Refrain *m*
chose [tʃəuz] *pt of* **choose**
chosen [ˈtʃəuzn] *pp of* **choose**
chowder [ˈtʃaudə[r]] *n* (sämige) Fischsuppe *f*
christen [ˈkrɪsn] *vt* taufen
christening [ˈkrɪsnɪŋ] *n* Taufe *f*
Christian [ˈkrɪstɪən] *adj* christlich ▶ *n* Christ(in) *m(f)*
Christian name *n* Vorname *m*
Christmas [ˈkrɪsməs] *n* Weihnachten *nt*
Christmas card *n* Weihnachtskarte *f*
Christmas Day *n* der erste Weihnachtstag
Christmas Eve *n* Heiligabend *m*
Christmas pudding *n* Plumpudding *m*
Christmas tree *n* Weihnachtsbaum *m*
chronic [ˈkrɔnɪk] *adj* (*also fig*) chronisch; (*severe*) schlimm
chrysanthemum [krɪˈsænθəməm] *n* Chrysantheme *f*

chubby ['tʃʌbɪ] *adj* pummelig
chuck [tʃʌk] (*inf*) *vt* schmeißen
▸ **chuck out** *vt* (*person*) rausschmeißen
▸ **chuck up** *vi* (*inf*) kotzen
chugger ['tʃʌgəʳ] *n* (*inf*) *für gemeinnützige Organisationen arbeitender Spendensammler, der bei Fussgängern um regelmäßige Spenden ansucht*
chunk [tʃʌŋk] *n* großes Stück *nt*
chunky ['tʃʌŋkɪ] *adj* (*person*) stämmig
church [tʃə:tʃ] *n* Kirche *f*
churchyard ['tʃə:tʃjɑ:d] *n* Friedhof *m*
chute [ʃu:t] *n* (Brit) Rutsche *f*
chutney ['tʃʌtnɪ] *n* Chutney *nt*
CIA (*US*) *n abbr* (= *Central Intelligence Agency*) CIA *m or f*
CID (Brit) *n abbr* = **Criminal Investigation Department**
cider ['saɪdəʳ] *n* Apfelwein *m*
cigar [sɪ'gɑ:ʳ] *n* Zigarre *f*
cigarette [sɪgə'rɛt] *n* Zigarette *f*
cinema ['sɪnəmə] *n* Kino *nt*
cinnamon ['sɪnəmən] *n* Zimt *m*
circle ['sə:kl] *n* Kreis *m* ▸ *vi* kreisen
circuit ['sə:kɪt] *n* Runde *f*; (*Elec*) Stromkreis *m*; (*track*) Rennbahn *f*
circular ['sə:kjuləʳ] *adj* rund ▸ *n* (*letter*) Rundschreiben *nt*
circulation [sə:kju'leɪʃən] *n* (*of newspaper*) Auflage *f*; (*Med: of blood*) Kreislauf *m*
circumstances ['sə:kəmstənsɪz] *npl* Umstände *pl*; (*financial condition*) (finanzielle) Verhältnisse *pl*; **in the ~** unter diesen Umständen; **under no ~** unter (gar) keinen Umständen, auf keinen Fall
circus ['sə:kəs] *n* Zirkus *m*
cistern ['sɪstən] *n* Zisterne *f*; (*of toilet*) Spülkasten *m*
citizen ['sɪtɪzn] *n* Staatsbürger(in) *m(f)*; (*of town*) Bürger(in) *m(f)*
citizenship ['sɪtɪznʃɪp] *n* Staatsbürgerschaft *f*
city ['sɪtɪ] *n* (Groß)stadt *f*; **the C~** (*Fin*) die City, das Londoner Banken- und Börsenviertel
city centre *n* Stadtzentrum *nt*, Innenstadt *f*
civil ['sɪvɪl] *adj* (*disturbances, rights*) Bürger-; (*liberties, law*) bürgerlich
civil ceremony *n* standesamtliche Hochzeit
civil engineering *n* Hoch- und Tiefbau *m*
civilian [sɪ'vɪlɪən] *n* Zivilist *m*
civilization [sɪvɪlaɪ'zeɪʃən] *n* Zivilisation *f*; (*a society*) Kultur *f*
civilized ['sɪvɪlaɪzd] *adj* zivilisiert; (*person*) kultiviert
civil partnership *n* eingetragene Partnerschaft
civil rights *npl* Bürgerrechte *pl*
civil servant *n* (Staats)beamter *m*, (Staats)beamtin *f*
Civil Service *n* Beamtenschaft *f*
civil war *n* Bürgerkrieg *m*
cl *abbr* (= *centilitre*) cl
claim [kleɪm] *vt* (*assert*) behaupten; (*responsibility*) übernehmen; (*rights, inheritance*) Anspruch erheben auf +*acc*; (*expenses*) sich *dat* zurückerstatten lassen ▸ *n* (*assertion*) Behauptung *f*; (*for pension, wage rise, compensation*) Forderung *f*; (*right: to inheritance, land*) Anspruch *m*; **(insurance) ~** (Versicherungs)anspruch *m*; **to put in a ~ for** beantragen
claimant ['kleɪmənt] *n* Antragsteller(in) *m(f)*
clam [klæm] *n* Venusmuschel *f*
clap [klæp] *vi* (Beifall) klatschen
claret ['klærət] *n* roter Bordeaux(wein) *m*
clarify ['klærɪfaɪ] *vt* klären
clarinet [klærɪ'nɛt] *n* Klarinette *f*
clarity ['klærɪtɪ] *n* Klarheit *f*
clash [klæʃ] *n* (*fight*) Zusammenstoß *m*; (*disagreement*) Auseinandersetzung *f* ▸ *vi* (*fight*) zusammenstoßen; (*disagree*) eine Auseinandersetzung haben; (*colours*) sich beißen
clasp [klɑ:sp] *n* (*of necklace, bag*) Verschluss *m*
class [klɑ:s] *n* Klasse *f* ▸ *vt* einordnen, einstufen
classic ['klæsɪk] *adj* klassisch ▸ *n* Klassiker *m*
classical ['klæsɪkl] *adj* klassisch
classification [klæsɪfɪ'keɪʃən] *n* Klassifikation *f*
classify ['klæsɪfaɪ] *vt* klassifizieren
classroom ['klɑ:srum] *n* Klassenzimmer *nt*
classy ['klɑ:sɪ] (*inf*) *adj* nobel, exklusiv
clatter ['klætəʳ] *vi* klappern
clause [klɔ:z] *n* (*Law*) Klausel *f*; (*Ling*) Satz *m*

claw [klɔː] *n* Kralle *f*
clay [kleɪ] *n* Ton *m*; (*soil*) Lehm *m*
clean [kliːn] *adj* sauber ▶ *vt* sauber machen; (*car, hands, face etc*) waschen; **to have a ~ driving licence**, **to have a ~ driving record** (*US*) keine Strafpunkte haben
▶ **clean out** *vt* gründlich sauber machen
▶ **clean up** *vt* (*child*) sauber machen ▶ *vi* aufräumen
cleaner [ˈkliːnəʳ] *n* Raumpfleger(in) *m(f)*; (*woman*) Putzfrau *f*; (*substance*) Reinigungsmittel *nt*, Putzmittel *nt*
cleanse [klɛnz] *vt* (*purify*) läutern; (*face, cut*) reinigen
cleanser [ˈklɛnzəʳ] *n* (*for face*) Reinigungscreme *f*
clean technology *n* umweltfreundliche Technologie *f*
clear [klɪəʳ] *adj* klar; (*footprint*) deutlich; (*road, way, floor etc*) frei; (*conscience, skin*) rein ▶ *vt* (*room*) ausräumen; (*slums etc, stock*) räumen; (*Law*) freisprechen ▶ *vi* (*weather, sky*) aufklaren; (*fog, smoke*) sich auflösen ▶ *adv*: **to be ~ of the ground** den Boden nicht berühren; **to make o.s. ~** sich klar ausdrücken; **to ~ the table** den Tisch abräumen
▶ **clear off** (*inf*) *vi* abhauen
▶ **clear up** *vt* aufräumen; (*problem*) lösen ▶ *vi* (*bad weather*) sich aufklären
clearing *n* Lichtung *f*
clearly [ˈklɪəlɪ] *adv* klar; (*obviously*) eindeutig
clearway [ˈklɪəweɪ] (Brit) *n* Straße *f* mit Halteverbot
clench [klɛntʃ] *vt* (*fist*) ballen; (*teeth*) zusammenbeißen
clergyman [ˈkləːdʒɪmən] *n* (*irreg*) Geistliche(r) *m*
clerk [klɑːk, (*US*) kləːrk] *n* (Brit) Büroangestellte(r) *f(m)*; (*US: sales person*) Verkäufer(in) *m(f)*
clever [ˈklɛvəʳ] *adj* klug; (*deft, crafty*) schlau, clever (*inf*)
cliché [ˈkliːʃeɪ] *n* Klischee *nt*
click [klɪk] *n* Klicken *nt*; (*Comput*) Mausklick *m* ▶ *vi* klicken
client [ˈklaɪənt] *n* Kunde *m*, Kundin *f*; (*of bank, lawyer*) Klient(in) *m(f)*
cliff [klɪf] *n* Kliff *nt*
climate [ˈklaɪmɪt] *n* Klima *nt*
climate change *n* Klimawandel *m*
climax [ˈklaɪmæks] *n* Höhepunkt *m*
climb [klaɪm] *vi* klettern; (*plane, sun, prices, shares*) steigen ▶ *vt* (*tree*) klettern auf +*acc*; (*hill*) steigen auf +*acc* ▶ *n* Aufstieg *m*
climber [ˈklaɪməʳ] *n* Bergsteiger(in) *m(f)*
climbing [ˈklaɪmɪŋ] *n* Bergsteigen *nt*
cling [klɪŋ] (*pt, pp* **clung**) *vi*: **to ~ to** (*mother, support*) sich festklammern an +*dat*
clingfilm *n* Frischhaltefolie *f*
clinic [ˈklɪnɪk] *n* Klinik *f*
clinical [ˈklɪnɪkl] *adj* klinisch
clip [klɪp] *n* (Brit) Klammer *f* ▶ *vt* festklemmen; (*cut*) schneiden
clippers [ˈklɪpəz] *npl* (*for gardening*) Schere *f*; (*also:* **nail ~**) Nagelzange *f*
cloak [kləuk] *n* Umhang *m*
cloakroom [ˈkləukrum] *n* Garderobe *f*
clock [klɔk] *n* Uhr *f*; **round the ~** rund um die Uhr; **30,000 on the ~** (Brit *Aut*) ein Tachostand von 30.000
clockwise [ˈklɔkwaɪz] *adv* im Uhrzeigersinn
clog [klɔg] *n* (*wooden*) Holzschuh *m* ▶ *vt* verstopfen
cloister [ˈklɔɪstəʳ] *n* Kreuzgang *m*
clone [kləun] *n* Klon *m*
close¹ [kləus] *adj* (*writing, friend, contact*) eng; (*examination*) genau, gründlich; (*contest*) knapp ▶ *adv* nahe; **~ (to)** nahe (+*gen*); **~ to** in der Nähe +*gen*; **~ by, ~ at hand** in der Nähe; **a ~ friend** ein guter *or* enger Freund
close² [kləuz] *vt* schließen; (*sale, deal, case*) abschließen ▶ *vi* schließen ▶ *n* Ende *nt*
▶ **close down** *vi* (*factory*) stillgelegt werden
closed [kləuzd] *adj* geschlossen; (*road*) gesperrt
closed-circuit television [ˈkləuzdˈsəːkɪt-] *n* Fernsehüberwachungsanlage *f*
closely [ˈkləuslɪ] *adv* (*examine, watch*) genau; (*connected*) eng; (*related*) nah(e)
closet [ˈklɔzɪt] *n* Wandschrank *m*
close-up [ˈkləusʌp] *n* Nahaufnahme *f*
closing [ˈkləuzɪŋ] *adj* (*stages*) Schluss-; (*remarks*) abschließend
closure [ˈkləuʒəʳ] *n* (*of factory*) Stilllegung *f*; (*of border*) Schließung *f*
clot [klɔt] *n* (*blood clot*) (Blut)gerinnsel *nt*; (*inf: idiot*) Trottel *m* ▶ *vi* gerinnen

cloth [klɔθ] *n* (*material*) Tuch *nt*; (*rag*) Lappen *m*
clothe [kləuð] *vt* kleiden
clothes [kləuðz] *npl* Kleidung *f*, Kleider *pl*
clothesline [ˈkləuðzlaɪn] *n* Wäscheleine *f*
clothes peg, (*US*) **clothes pin** *n* Wäscheklammer *f*
clothing [ˈkləuðɪŋ] *n* = **clothes**
clotted cream [ˈklɔtɪd-] (Brit) *n Sahne aus erhitzter Milch*
cloud [klaud] *n* Wolke *f*
cloud computing *n* Cloud Computing *nt*
cloudy [ˈklaudɪ] *adj* bewölkt; (*liquid*) trüb
clove [kləuv] *n* Gewürznelke *f*; **~ of garlic** Knoblauchzehe *f*
clover [ˈkləuvəʳ] *n* Klee *m*
cloverleaf [ˈkləuvəliːf] *n* Kleeblatt *nt*
clown [klaun] *n* Clown *m*
club [klʌb] *n* Klub *m*, Verein *m*; (*weapon*) Knüppel *m*; (*object: also:* **golf ~**) Golfschläger *m* ▪ **clubs** *npl* (*Cards*) Kreuz *nt*
club class *n* Businessklasse *f*
clue [kluː] *n* Hinweis *m*, Anhaltspunkt *m*; **I haven't a ~** ich habe keine Ahnung
clumsy [ˈklʌmzɪ] *adj* ungeschickt
clung [klʌŋ] *pt, pp of* **cling**
clutch [klʌtʃ] *n* (*Aut*) Kupplung *f* ▶ *vt* (*purse, hand*) umklammern; (*stick*) sich festklammern an *+dat*
cm *abbr* (= *centimetre*) cm
Co. *abbr* = **company**
c/o *abbr* (= *care of*) bei, c/o
coach [kəutʃ] *n* (Reise)bus *m*; (*of train*) Wagen *m*; (*Sport*) Trainer *m* ▶ *vt* trainieren; (*student*) Nachhilfeunterricht geben *+dat*
coach trip *n* Busfahrt *f*
coal [kəul] *n* Kohle *f*
coalition [kəuəˈlɪʃən] *n* (*Pol*) Koalition *f*
coal mine *n* Kohlenbergwerk *nt*
coal miner *n* Bergmann *m*
coast [kəust] *n* Küste *f*
coastguard [ˈkəustgɑːd] *n* (*officer*) Küstenwächter *m*
coastline [ˈkəustlaɪn] *n* Küste *f*
coat [kəut] *n* Mantel *m*; (*of animal*) Fell *nt*; (*layer*) Schicht *f*; (: *of paint*) Anstrich *m*
coat hanger *n* Kleiderbügel *m*
coating [ˈkəutɪŋ] *n* (*of chocolate etc*) Überzug *m*; (*of dust etc*) Schicht *f*
coat of arms *n* Wappen *nt*
cobbles [ˈkɔblz] *npl* Kopfsteinpflaster *nt*
cobblestones [ˈkɔblstəunz] *npl* = **cobbles**
cobweb [ˈkɔbwɛb] *n* Spinnennetz *nt*
cocaine [kəˈkeɪn] *n* Kokain *nt*
cock [kɔk] *n* Hahn *m*
cockerel [ˈkɔkərl] *n* junger Hahn *m*
cockle [ˈkɔkl] *n* Herzmuschel *f*
cockpit [ˈkɔkpɪt] *n* Cockpit *nt*
cockroach [ˈkɔkrəutʃ] *n* Kakerlak *m*
cocktail [ˈkɔkteɪl] *n* Cocktail *m*
cock-up [ˈkɔkʌp] (*!*) *n* Schlamassel *m*
cocky [ˈkɔkɪ] *adj* großspurig
cocoa [ˈkəukəu] *n* Kakao *m*
coconut [ˈkəukənʌt] *n* Kokosnuss *f*
COD *abbr* (Brit) = **cash on delivery**
cod [kɔd] *n* Kabeljau *m*
code [kəud] *n* (*cipher*) Chiffre *f*
coeducational [ˈkəuɛdjuˈkeɪʃənl] *adj* (*school*) gemischt
coffee [ˈkɔfɪ] *n* Kaffee *m*
coffee bar (Brit) *n* Café *nt*
coffee break *n* Kaffeepause *f*
coffeepot *n* Kaffeekanne *f*
coffee table *n* Couchtisch *m*
coffin [ˈkɔfɪn] *n* Sarg *m*
coil [kɔɪl] *n* Rolle *f*; (*Aut, Elec*) Spule *f*; (*contraceptive*) Spirale *f*
coin [kɔɪn] *n* Münze *f*
coincide [kəuɪnˈsaɪd] *vi* (*events*) zusammenfallen
coincidence [kəuˈɪnsɪdəns] *n* Zufall *m*
Coke® [kəuk] *n* Coca-Cola® *f or nt*, Coke® *nt*
coke [kəuk] *n* Koks *m*
cold [kəuld] *adj* kalt; (*unemotional*) kalt, kühl ▶ *n* Kälte *f*; (*Med*) Erkältung *f*; **to be/feel ~** (*person*) frieren; **to catch ~, to catch a ~** sich erkälten
cold sore *n* Bläschenausschlag *m*
cold turkey *n* (*inf*): **to go ~** Totalentzug machen
coleslaw [ˈkəulslɔː] *n* Krautsalat *m*
collaborate [kəˈlæbəreɪt] *vi* zusammenarbeiten
collaboration [kəlæbəˈreɪʃən] *n* Zusammenarbeit *f*; Kollaboration *f*
collapse [kəˈlæps] *vi* zusammenbrechen; (*building*) einstürzen ▶ *n* Zusammenbruch *m*; Einsturz *m*

collapsible [kəˈlæpsəbl] *adj* Klapp-, zusammenklappbar
collar [ˈkɔləʳ] *n* Kragen *m*; (*of dog, cat*) Halsband *nt*
collarbone [ˈkɔləbəun] *n* Schlüsselbein *nt*
colleague [ˈkɔli:g] *n* Kollege *m*, Kollegin *f*
collect [kəˈlɛkt] *vt* sammeln; (*mail*: BRIT: *fetch*) abholen ▶ *vi* sich ansammeln
collected [kəˈlɛktɪd] *adj*: **~ works** gesammelte Werke *pl*
collection [kəˈlɛkʃən] *n* Sammlung *f*; (*from place, person, of mail*) Abholung *f*; (*in church*) Kollekte *f*
collector [kəˈlɛktəʳ] *n* Sammler(in) *m(f)*; (*of taxes etc*) Einnehmer(in) *m(f)*
college [ˈkɔlɪdʒ] *n* College *nt*; (*of agriculture, technology*) Fachhochschule *f*; **to go to ~** studieren
collide [kəˈlaɪd] *vi*: **to ~ (with)** zusammenstoßen (mit)
collision [kəˈlɪʒən] *n* Zusammenstoß *m*
colloquial [kəˈləukwɪəl] *adj* umgangssprachlich
Cologne [kəˈləun] *n* Köln *nt*
colon [ˈkəulən] *n* Doppelpunkt *m*
colonial [kəˈləunɪəl] *adj* Kolonial-
colonize [ˈkɔlənaɪz] *vt* kolonisieren
colony [ˈkɔlənɪ] *n* Kolonie *f*
color *etc* (*US*) = **colour** *etc*
colour, (*US*) **color** [ˈkʌləʳ] *n* Farbe *f*; (*skin colour*) Hautfarbe *f* ▶ *vt* bemalen; (*dye*) färben
colour-blind [ˈkʌləblaɪnd] *adj* farbenblind
coloured [ˈkʌləd] *adj* (*person, race*: *offensive*) farbig
colour film *n* Farbfilm *m*
colourful [ˈkʌləful] *adj* bunt; (*account, story*) farbig
colouring [ˈkʌlərɪŋ] *n* Gesichtsfarbe *f*; (*in food*) Farbstoff *m*
colour television *n* Farbfernsehen *nt*
column [ˈkɔləm] *n* Säule *f*; (*of print*) Spalte *f*
comb [kəum] *n* Kamm *m* ▶ *vt* kämmen
combination [kɔmbɪˈneɪʃən] *n* Kombination *f*
combine [kəmˈbaɪn] *vt* verbinden

KEYWORD

come [kʌm] (*pt* **came**, *pp* **come**) *vi*
1 (*movement towards*) kommen; **coming!** ich komme!
2 (*arrive*) kommen; **to come home** nach Hause kommen
3 (*reach*): **to come to** kommen an *+acc*; **to come to a decision** zu einer Entscheidung kommen
4 (*occur*): **an idea came to me** mir kam eine Idee
5 (*be, become*) werden; **I've come to like him** mittlerweile mag ich ihn; **if it comes to it** wenn es darauf ankommt
▶ **come across** *vt fus* (*find*: *person, thing*) stoßen auf *+acc*
▶ **come back** *vi* zurückkommen
▶ **come down** *vi* (*price*) sinken, fallen; (*building*: *be demolished*) abgerissen werden; (*tree*: *during storm*) umstürzen
▶ **come from** *vt fus* kommen von, stammen aus; (*person*) kommen aus; **where do you come from?** wo kommen Sie her?; **I come from London** ich komme aus London
▶ **come in** *vi* (*enter*) hereinkommen; **come in!** herein!
▶ **come off** *vi* (*become detached*: *button, handle*) sich lösen; (*succeed*: *attempt, plan*) klappen ▶ *vt fus* (*inf*): **come off it!** mach mal halblang!
▶ **come on** *vi* (*pupil, work, project*) vorankommen; **come on!** (*hurry up*) mach schon!; (*giving encouragement*) los!
▶ **come out** *vi* herauskommen
▶ **come round** *vi* (*after faint, operation*) wieder zu sich kommen; (*visit*) vorbeikommen
▶ **come to** *vi* (*regain consciousness*) wieder zu sich kommen ▶ *vt fus* (*add up to*): **how much does it come to?** was macht das zusammen?
▶ **come up** *vi* (*approach*) herankommen; (*sun*) aufgehen; (*in conversation*) genannt werden
▶ **come up against** *vt fus* (*resistance, difficulties*) stoßen auf *+acc*
▶ **come upon** *vt fus* (*find*) stoßen auf *+acc*
▶ **come up to** *vt fus*: **the film didn't come up to our expectations** der Film entsprach nicht unseren Erwartungen; **it's coming up to 10 o'clock** es ist gleich 10 Uhr
▶ **come up with** *vt fus* (*idea*) aufwarten mit; (*solution, answer*) kommen auf *+acc*; **to come up with a suggestion** einen Vorschlag machen

comedian [kəˈmiːdɪən] *n* Komiker(in) *m(f)*
comedown [ˈkʌmdaun] (*inf*) *n* (*professional*) Abstieg *m*
comedy [ˈkɔmɪdɪ] *n* Komödie *f*; (*humour*) Witz *m*
comfort [ˈkʌmfət] *n* (*material*) Komfort *m*; (*solace, relief*) Trost *m* ▸ *vt* trösten
comfortable [ˈkʌmfətəbl] *adj* bequem; (*income*) ausreichend
comic [ˈkɔmɪk] *adj* (*also*: **comical**) komisch ▸ *n* Komiker(in) *m(f)*; (Brit: *magazine*) Comicheft *nt*
coming [ˈkʌmɪŋ] *adj* kommend
comma [ˈkɔmə] *n* Komma *nt*
command [kəˈmɑːnd] *n* (*also Comput*) Befehl *m*; (*control, charge*) Führung *f*; (*Mil: authority*) Kommando *nt* ▸ *vt*: **to ~ sb to do sth** jdm befehlen, etw zu tun
commemorate [kəˈmɛməreɪt] *vt* gedenken *+gen*
commemoration [kəmɛməˈreɪʃən] *n* Gedenken *nt*
comment [ˈkɔmɛnt] *n* Bemerkung *f*; (*on situation etc*) Kommentar *m* ▸ *vi*: **to ~ (on)** sich äußern (über *+acc or* zu)
commentary [ˈkɔməntərɪ] *n* Kommentar *m*; (*Sport*) Reportage *f*
commentator [ˈkɔmənteɪtə^r] *n* Kommentator(in) *m(f)*; (*Sport*) Reporter(in) *m(f)*
commerce [ˈkɔməːs] *n* Handel *m*
commercial [kəˈməːʃəl] *adj* kommerziell; (*organization*) Wirtschafts- ▸ *n* Werbespot *m*
commission [kəˈmɪʃən] *n* (*order for work*) Auftrag *m*; (*Comm*) Provision *f*; (*committee*) Kommission *f* ▸ *vt* (*work of art*) in Auftrag geben
commit [kəˈmɪt] *vt* (*crime*) begehen; **to ~ o.s. to do sth** sich (dazu) verpflichten, etw zu tun
commitment [kəˈmɪtmənt] *n* Verpflichtung *f*; (*to ideology, system*) Engagement *nt*
committee [kəˈmɪtɪ] *n* Ausschuss *m*, Komitee *nt*
commodity [kəˈmɔdɪtɪ] *n* Ware *f*
common [ˈkɔmən] *adj* (*shared by all*) gemeinsam; (*usual, ordinary*) häufig; (*vulgar*) gewöhnlich ▸ *n* Gemeindeland *nt*; **in ~ use** allgemein gebräuchlich; **to have sth in ~ (with sb)** etw (mit jdm) gemein haben
commonly [ˈkɔmənlɪ] *adv* häufig
commonplace [ˈkɔmənpleɪs] *adj* alltäglich
common room *n* Aufenthaltsraum *m*
common sense *n* gesunder Menschenverstand *m*
Commonwealth [ˈkɔmənwɛlθ] (Brit) *n*: **the ~** das Commonwealth
communal [ˈkɔmjuːnl] *adj* gemeinsam, Gemeinschafts-
communicate [kəˈmjuːnɪkeɪt] *vi*: **to ~ (with)** (*by speech, gesture*) sich verständigen (mit)
communication [kəmjuːnɪˈkeɪʃən] *n* Kommunikation *f*
communications satellite [kəmjuːnɪˈkeɪʃənz-] *n* Nachrichtensatellit *m*
communicative [kəˈmjuːnɪkətɪv] *adj* gesprächig
communion [kəˈmjuːnɪən] *n*: **(Holy) C~** Heiliges Abendmahl nt; (*Catholic*) Kommunion *f*
communism [ˈkɔmjunɪzəm] *n* Kommunismus *m*
communist [ˈkɔmjunɪst] *adj* kommunistisch ▸ *n* Kommunist(in) *m(f)*
community [kəˈmjuːnɪtɪ] *n* Gemeinschaft *f*
community centre *n* Gemeindezentrum *nt*
community service *n* Sozialdienst *m*
commutation ticket [kɔmjuˈteɪʃən-] (*US*) *n* Zeitkarte *f*
commute [kəˈmjuːt] *vi* pendeln
commuter [kəˈmjuːtə^r] *n* Pendler(in) *m(f)*
compact *adj* [kəmˈpækt] kompakt ▸ *n* [ˈkɔmpækt] (*also*: **powder ~**) Puderdose *f*
compact disc *n* Compact Disc *f*, CD *f*
companion [kəmˈpænjən] *n* Begleiter(in) *m(f)*
company [ˈkʌmpənɪ] *n* Firma *f*; (*companionship*) Gesellschaft *f*; **to keep sb ~** jdm Gesellschaft leisten
company car *n* Firmenwagen *m*
comparable [ˈkɔmpərəbl] *adj* vergleichbar
comparative [kəmˈpærətɪv] *adj* relativ; (*Ling*) komparativ
comparatively [kəmˈpærətɪvlɪ] *adv* relativ

compare [kəmˈpɛəʳ] *vt*: **to ~ (with** *or* **to)** vergleichen (mit); **compared with** *or* **to** im Vergleich zu, verglichen mit
comparison [kəmˈpærɪsn] *n* Vergleich *m*; **in ~ (with)** im Vergleich (zu)
compartment [kəmˈpɑːtmənt] *n* (*Rail*) Abteil *nt*; (*section*) Fach *nt*
compass [ˈkʌmpəs] *n* Kompass *m* ▪ **compasses** *npl* Zirkel *m*
compassion [kəmˈpæʃən] *n* Mitgefühl *nt*
compatible [kəmˈpætɪbl] *adj* (*ideas etc*) vereinbar; (*people*) zueinanderpassend; (*Comput*) kompatibel
compensate [ˈkɔmpənseɪt] *vt* entschädigen ▸ *vi*: **to ~ for** (*loss*) ersetzen; (*disappointment, change etc*) (wieder) ausgleichen
compensation [kɔmpənˈseɪʃən] *n* Entschädigung *f*; (*money*) Schaden(s) ersatz *m*
compete [kəmˈpiːt] *vi* (*in contest, game*) teilnehmen; **to ~ (with)** (*companies, rivals*) konkurrieren (mit)
competence [ˈkɔmpɪtəns] *n* Fähigkeit *f*
competent [ˈkɔmpɪtənt] *adj* fähig
competition [kɔmpɪˈtɪʃən] *n* Konkurrenz *f*; (*contest*) Wettbewerb *m*
competitive [kəmˈpɛtɪtɪv] *adj* (*price, product*) konkurrenzfähig
competitor [kəmˈpɛtɪtəʳ] *n* Konkurrent(in) *m(f)*; (*participant*) Teilnehmer(in) *m(f)*
complain [kəmˈpleɪn] *vi* (*protest*) sich beschweren
complaint [kəmˈpleɪnt] *n* Klage *f*; (*in shop etc*) Beschwerde *f*; (*illness*) Beschwerden *pl*
complement [ˈkɔmplɪmɛnt] *vt* ergänzen
complete [kəmˈpliːt] *adj* (*total*: *silence*) vollkommen; (*set*) vollständig; (*finished*) fertig ▸ *vt* fertigstellen; (*task*) beenden; (*fill in*) ausfüllen; **it's a ~ disaster** es ist eine totale Katastrophe
completely [kəmˈpliːtlɪ] *adv* völlig
complex [ˈkɔmplɛks] *adj* kompliziert ▸ *n* Komplex *m*
complexion [kəmˈplɛkʃən] *n* Teint *m*, Gesichtsfarbe *f*
complicated [ˈkɔmplɪkeɪtɪd] *adj* kompliziert
complication [kɔmplɪˈkeɪʃən] *n* Komplikation *f*
compliment *n* [ˈkɔmplɪmənt] Kompliment *nt* ▸ *vt* [ˈkɔmplɪmɛnt] ein Kompliment/Komplimente machen ▪ **compliments** *npl* (*regards*) Grüße *pl*; **to pay sb a ~** jdm ein Kompliment machen
complimentary [kɔmplɪˈmɛntərɪ] *adj* schmeichelhaft; (*ticket, copy of book etc*) Frei-
comply [kəmˈplaɪ] *vi*: **to ~ with** (*law*) einhalten +*acc*
component [kəmˈpəunənt] *n* Bestandteil *m*
compose [kəmˈpəuz] *vt* (*music*) komponieren; **to ~ o.s.** sich sammeln
composed [kəmˈpəuzd] *adj* ruhig, gelassen
composer [kəmˈpəuzəʳ] *n* Komponist(in) *m(f)*
composition [kɔmpəˈzɪʃən] *n* Zusammensetzung *f*; (*Mus*) Komposition *f*
comprehend [kɔmprɪˈhɛnd] *vt* verstehen
comprehension [kɔmprɪˈhɛnʃən] *n* Verständnis *nt*
comprehensive [kɔmprɪˈhɛnsɪv] *adj* umfassend ▸ *n* = **comprehensive school**
comprehensive school (Brit) *n* Gesamtschule *f*
compress [kəmˈprɛs] *vt* (*air*) komprimieren
comprise [kəmˈpraɪz] *vt* (*also*: **be comprised of**) bestehen aus
compromise [ˈkɔmprəmaɪz] *n* Kompromiss *m* ▸ *vi* Kompromisse schließen
compulsory [kəmˈpʌlsərɪ] *adj* obligatorisch
computer [kəmˈpjuːtəʳ] *n* Computer *m*
computer game *n* Computerspiel *nt*
computer literate *adj*: **to be ~** Computerkenntnisse haben
computer scientist *n* Informatiker(in) *m(f)*
computing [kəmˈpjuːtɪŋ] *n* Informatik *f*
con [kɔn] *vt* betrügen ▸ *n* Schwindel *m*
conceal [kənˈsiːl] *vt* verbergen
conceivable [kənˈsiːvəbl] *adj* denkbar, vorstellbar

conceive [kən'si:v] *vt* (*child*) empfangen; **to ~ of sth** sich *dat* etw vorstellen
concentrate ['kɔnsəntreɪt] *vi* sich konzentrieren
concentration [kɔnsən'treɪʃən] *n* Konzentration *f*
concept ['kɔnsɛpt] *n* (*principle*) Begriff *m*
concern [kən'sə:n] *n* Angelegenheit *f*; (*anxiety, worry*) Sorge *f*; (*Comm*) Konzern *m* ▸ *vt* Sorgen machen *+dat*; (*involve*) angehen; (*relate to*) betreffen; **to be concerned (about)** sich *dat* Sorgen machen (um); **as far as I am concerned** was mich betrifft
concerning [kən'sə:nɪŋ] *prep* bezüglich *+gen*, hinsichtlich *+gen*
concert ['kɔnsət] *n* Konzert *nt*
concert hall *n* Konzertsaal *m*
concession [kən'sɛʃən] *n* Zugeständnis *nt*
concise [kən'saɪs] *adj* kurz gefasst, prägnant
conclude [kən'klu:d] *vt* beenden, schließen; (*treaty, deal etc*) abschließen; (*decide*) schließen, folgern ▸ *vi* schließen; **I ~ that ...** ich komme zu dem Schluss, dass ...
conclusion [kən'klu:ʒən] *n* Ende *nt*; Schluss *m*; Abschluss *m*; Folgerung *f*
concrete ['kɔŋkri:t] *n* Beton *m* ▸ *adj* (*proposal, idea*) konkret
concussion [kən'kʌʃən] *n* Gehirnerschütterung *f*
condemn [kən'dɛm] *vt* verurteilen; (*building*) für abbruchreif erklären
condensed milk *n* Kondensmilch *f*, Büchsenmilch *f*
condition [kən'dɪʃən] *n* Zustand *m*; (*requirement*) Bedingung *f*
■ **conditions** *npl* (*circumstances*) Verhältnisse *pl*; **on ~ that ...** unter der Bedingung, dass ...
conditional [kən'dɪʃənl] *adj* bedingt
conditioner [kən'dɪʃənəʳ] *n* (*for hair*) Pflegespülung *f*; (*for fabrics*) Weichspüler *m*
condo ['kɔndəu] (*US inf*) *n abbr* = **condominium**
condolences [kən'dəulənsɪz] *npl* Beileid *nt*
condom ['kɔndəm] *n* Kondom *m or nt*
condominium [kɔndə'mɪnɪəm] (*US*) *n* (*rooms*) Eigentumswohnung *f*
conduct *n* ['kɔndʌkt] Verhalten *nt* ▸ *vt* [kən'dʌkt] (*manage*) führen; (*orchestra, choir etc*) dirigieren
conductor [kən'dʌktəʳ] *n* (*of orchestra*) Dirigent(in) *m(f)*; (*on bus*) Schaffner *m*; (*US: on train*) Zugführer(in) *m(f)*
cone [kəun] *n* Kegel *m*; (*Bot*) Zapfen *m*; (*ice cream cornet*) (Eis)tüte *f*
conference ['kɔnfərəns] *n* Konferenz *f*
confess [kən'fɛs] *vt* (*crime*) gestehen ▸ *vi* (*admit*) gestehen
confession [kən'fɛʃən] *n* Geständnis *nt*; (*Rel*) Beichte *f*
confetti [kən'fɛtɪ] *n* Konfetti *nt*
confidence ['kɔnfɪdns] *n* Vertrauen *nt*; (*self-assurance*) Selbstvertrauen *nt*
confident ['kɔnfɪdənt] *adj* (selbst) sicher; (*positive*) zuversichtlich
confidential [kɔnfɪ'dɛnʃəl] *adj* vertraulich
confine [kən'faɪn] *vt*: **to ~ (to)** beschränken (auf *+acc*)
confirm [kən'fə:m] *vt* bestätigen
confirmation [kɔnfə'meɪʃən] *n* Bestätigung *f*; (*Rel*) Konfirmation *f*
confirmed [kən'fə:md] *adj* (*bachelor*) eingefleischt; (*teetotaller*) überzeugt
confiscate ['kɔnfɪskeɪt] *vt* beschlagnahmen, konfiszieren
conflict ['kɔnflɪkt] *n* Konflikt *m*
confuse [kən'fju:z] *vt* verwirren; (*mix up*) verwechseln; (*complicate*) durcheinanderbringen
confused [kən'fju:zd] *adj* (*person*) verwirrt; (*situation*) verworren, konfus
confusing [kən'fju:zɪŋ] *adj* verwirrend
confusion [kən'fju:ʒən] *n* (*mix-up*) Verwechslung *f*; (*perplexity*) Verwirrung *f*; (*disorder*) Durcheinander *nt*
congested [kən'dʒɛstɪd] *adj* (*road*) verstopft; (*area*) überfüllt
congestion [kən'dʒɛstʃən] *n* (*in traffic*) Stau *m*
congratulate [kən'grætjuleɪt] *vt* gratulieren; **to ~ sb (on sth)** jdm (zu etw) gratulieren
congratulations [kəngrætju'leɪʃənz] *npl* Glückwünsche *pl*; **~!** herzlichen Glückwunsch!
congregation [kɔŋgrɪ'geɪʃən] *n* Gemeinde *f*
congress ['kɔŋgrɛs] *n* Kongress *m*; (*US*): **C~** der Kongress
congressman ['kɔŋgrɛsmən] (*US*) *n* (*irreg*) Kongressabgeordnete(r) *m*

congresswoman [ˈkɔŋgrɛswumən] (*US*) *n* (*irreg*) Kongressabgeordnete *f*
conifer [ˈkɔnɪfəʳ] *n* Nadelbaum *m*
conjunction [kənˈdʒʌŋkʃən] *n* Konjunktion *f*; **in ~ with** zusammen mit, in Verbindung mit
conk out [kɔŋk-] (*inf*) *vi* den Geist aufgeben
connect [kəˈnɛkt] *vt* verbinden; (*Elec*) anschließen; (*Tel*: *caller*) verbinden ▶ *vi*: **to ~ with** (*train, plane etc*) Anschluss haben an +*acc*
connection [kəˈnɛkʃən] *n* Verbindung *f*; (*Elec*) Kontakt *m*; (*train, plane etc, Tel*: *subscriber*) Anschluss *m*; (*fig*: *association*) Zusammenhang *m*; **in ~ with** in Zusammenhang mit
conscience [ˈkɔnʃəns] *n* Gewissen *nt*
conscientious [kɔnʃɪˈɛnʃəs] *adj* gewissenhaft
conscious [ˈkɔnʃəs] *adj* bewusst; (*awake*) bei Bewusstsein
consciousness [ˈkɔnʃəsnɪs] *n* Bewusstsein *nt*
consecutive [kənˈsɛkjutɪv] *adj* aufeinanderfolgend
consent [kənˈsɛnt] *n* Zustimmung *f* ▶ *vi*: **to ~ to** zustimmen +*dat*
consequence [ˈkɔnsɪkwəns] *n* Folge *f*
consequently [ˈkɔnsɪkwəntlɪ] *adv* folglich
conservation [kɔnsəˈveɪʃən] *n* Erhaltung *f*; (*also*: **nature ~**) Umweltschutz *m*
conservative [kənˈsəːvətɪv] *adj* konservativ; (*Brit Pol*): **C~** konservativ
conservatory [kənˈsəːvətrɪ] *n* Wintergarten *m*
consider [kənˈsɪdəʳ] *vt* (*study*) sich *dat* überlegen; (*take into account*) in Betracht ziehen; **to ~ sb/sth as …** jdn/etw für … halten; **they ~ themselves to be superior** sie halten sich für etwas Besseres
considerable [kənˈsɪdərəbl] *adj* beträchtlich
considerate [kənˈsɪdərɪt] *adj* rücksichtsvoll
consideration [kənsɪdəˈreɪʃən] *n* Überlegung *f*; (*thoughtfulness*) Rücksicht *f*
considering [kənˈsɪdərɪŋ] *prep* in Anbetracht +*gen*; **~ (that)** wenn man bedenkt(, dass)
consist [kənˈsɪst] *vi*: **to ~ of** bestehen aus
consistent [kənˈsɪstənt] *adj* konsequent; (*argument, idea*) folgerichtig
consolation [kɔnsəˈleɪʃən] *n* Trost *m*
console [kənˈsəul] *vt* trösten
consolidate [kənˈsɔlɪdeɪt] *vt* festigen
consonant [ˈkɔnsənənt] *n* Konsonant *m*
conspicuous [kənˈspɪkjuəs] *adj* auffallend
conspiracy [kənˈspɪrəsɪ] *n* Komplott *nt*
conspire [kənˈspaɪəʳ] *vi* sich verschwören
constable [ˈkʌnstəbl] (*Brit*) *n* Polizist *m*
constant [ˈkɔnstənt] *adj* dauernd, ständig; (*fixed*) gleichbleibend
constantly [ˈkɔnstəntlɪ] *adv* (an) dauernd
consternation [kɔnstəˈneɪʃən] *n* Bestürzung *f*
constituency [kənˈstɪtjuənsɪ] *n* (*Pol*) Wahlkreis *m*
constitution [kɔnstɪˈtjuːʃən] *n* (*Pol*) Verfassung *f*; (*health*) Konstitution *f*
construct [kənˈstrʌkt] *vt* bauen
construction [kənˈstrʌkʃən] *n* Bau *m*; (*structure*) Konstruktion *f*; **under ~** in *or* im Bau
consulate [ˈkɔnsjulɪt] *n* Konsulat *nt*
consult [kənˈsʌlt] *vt* (*doctor, lawyer*) konsultieren; (*reference book*) nachschlagen in +*dat*
consultant [kənˈsʌltənt] *n* (*Med*) Facharzt *m*, Fachärztin *f*
consultation [kɔnsəlˈteɪʃən] *n* (*Med, Law*) Konsultation *f*; (*discussion*) Beratung *f*
consulting room (*Brit*) *n* Sprechzimmer *nt*
consume [kənˈsjuːm] *vt* (*food, drink*) konsumieren; (*fuel, energy*) verbrauchen
consumer [kənˈsjuːməʳ] *n* Verbraucher(in) *m*(*f*)
contact [ˈkɔntækt] *n* Kontakt *m*; (*touch*) Berührung *f*; (*person*) Kontaktperson *f* ▶ *vt* sich in Verbindung setzen mit; **to be in ~ with sb/sth** mit jdm/etw in Verbindung *or* Kontakt stehen
contact lenses *npl* Kontaktlinsen *pl*
contactless [ˈkɔntæktlɪs] *adj* kontaktlos

contagious [kən'teɪdʒəs] *adj* ansteckend
contain [kən'teɪn] *vt* enthalten
container [kən'teɪnə^r] *n* Behälter *m*; (*for shipping etc*) Container *m*
contaminate [kən'tæmɪneɪt] *vt* (*water, food*) verunreinigen; (*soil etc*) verseuchen
contamination [kəntæmɪ'neɪʃən] *n* Verunreinigung *f*; Verseuchung *f*
contemporary [kən'tɛmpərərɪ] *adj* zeitgenössisch
contempt [kən'tɛmpt] *n* Verachtung *f*
contemptuous [kən'tɛmptjuəs] *adj* verächtlich, geringschätzig
content *adj* [kən'tɛnt] zufrieden ▶ *vt* [kən'tɛnt] zufriedenstellen ▶ *n* ['kɔntɛnt] Inhalt *m* ■ **contents** *npl* Inhalt
contest *n* ['kɔntɛst] (*competition*) Wettkampf *m*; (*for control, power etc*) Kampf *m* ▶ *vt* [kən'tɛst] (*compete for*) kämpfen um; (*statement*) bestreiten
contestant [kən'tɛstənt] *n* (*in competition*) Teilnehmer(in) *m(f)*
context ['kɔntɛkst] *n* Zusammenhang *m*; **out of ~** aus dem Zusammenhang gerissen
continent ['kɔntɪnənt] *n* Kontinent *m*, Erdteil *m*; **the C~** (Brit) (Kontinental) europa *nt*
continental [kɔntɪ'nɛntl] *adj* kontinental
continental breakfast *n* kleines Frühstück *nt*
continual [kən'tɪnjuəl] *adj* ständig; (*process*) ununterbrochen
continually [kən'tɪnjuəlɪ] *adv* ständig; ununterbrochen
continuation [kəntɪnju'eɪʃən] *n* Fortsetzung *f*
continue [kən'tɪnju:] *vi* weitermachen; (*performance, road*) weitergehen; (*person: talking*) fortfahren ▶ *vt* fortsetzen; **"to be continued"** „Fortsetzung folgt"
continuous [kən'tɪnjuəs] *adj* ununterbrochen; (*growth etc*) kontinuierlich
contraceptive [kɔntrə'sɛptɪv] *n* Verhütungsmittel *nt*
contract *n* ['kɔntrækt] Vertrag *m* ▶ *cpd* ['kɔntrækt] (*work*) Auftrags- ▶ *vi* [kən'trækt] schrumpfen ▶ *vt* [kən'trækt] (*illness*) erkranken an +*dat*
contradict [kɔntrə'dɪkt] *vt* widersprechen +*dat*
contradiction [kɔntrə'dɪkʃən] *n* Widerspruch *m*
contrary ['kɔntrərɪ] *adj* entgegengesetzt ▶ *n* Gegenteil *nt*; **~ to what we thought** im Gegensatz zu dem, was wir dachten; **on the ~** im Gegenteil
contrast *n* ['kɔntrɑ:st] Gegensatz *m*, Kontrast *m* ▶ *vt* [kən'trɑ:st] vergleichen, gegenüberstellen; **in ~ to** *or* **with** im Gegensatz zu
contribute [kən'trɪbju:t] *vi* beitragen ▶ *vt*: **to ~ to** (*charity*) spenden für
contribution [kɔntrɪ'bju:ʃən] *n* Beitrag *m*
control [kən'trəul] *vt* (*machinery, process*) steuern; (*temper*) zügeln; (*disease, fire*) unter Kontrolle bringen ▶ *n* (*of country*) Kontrolle *f*; (*of oneself, emotions*) Beherrschung *f* ■ **controls** *npl* (*of vehicle*) Steuerung *f*; (*on radio, television etc*) Bedienungsfeld *nt*; **to ~ o.s.** sich beherrschen; **out of/under ~** außer/unter Kontrolle
control panel *n* Schalttafel *f*; (*on television*) Bedienungsfeld *nt*
controversial [kɔntrə'və:ʃl] *adj* umstritten
convalesce [kɔnvə'lɛs] *vi* genesen
convalescence [kɔnvə'lɛsns] *n* Genesungszeit *f*
convenience [kən'vi:nɪəns] *n* Annehmlichkeit *f*; **at your ~** wann es Ihnen passt; **with all modern conveniences**, **with all mod cons** (Brit) mit allem modernen Komfort; *see also* **public convenience**
convenience foods *npl* Fertiggerichte *pl*
convenient [kən'vi:nɪənt] *adj* günstig
convent ['kɔnvənt] *n* Kloster *nt*
convention [kən'vɛnʃən] *n* Konvention *f*; (*conference*) Konferenz *f*
conventional [kən'vɛnʃənl] *adj* konventionell
conversation [kɔnvə'seɪʃən] *n* Gespräch *nt*, Unterhaltung *f*
conversion [kən'və:ʃən] *n* Umwandlung *f*; (*of weights etc*) Umrechnung *f*; (Brit: *of house*) Umbau *m*
conversion table *n* Umrechnungstabelle *f*

convert *vt* [kən'vəːt] umwandeln; (*person*) bekehren; (*Comm*) konvertieren ▶ *n* ['kɔnvəːt] Bekehrte(r) *f*(*m*)
convertible [kən'vəːtəbl] *adj* (*currency*) konvertierbar ▶ *n* (*Aut*) Kabriolett *nt*
convey [kən'veɪ] *vt* (*information etc*) vermitteln; (*cargo, traveller*) befördern
conveyor belt *n* Fließband *nt*
convict *vt* [kən'vɪkt] verurteilen ▶ *n* ['kɔnvɪkt] Sträfling *m*
conviction [kən'vɪkʃən] *n* Überzeugung *f*; (*Law*) Verurteilung *f*
convince [kən'vɪns] *vt* überzeugen
convincing [kən'vɪnsɪŋ] *adj* überzeugend
cook [kuk] *vt* kochen ▶ *n* Koch *m*, Köchin *f*
cookbook ['kukbuk] *n* Kochbuch *nt*
cooker ['kukəʳ] *n* Herd *m*
cookery ['kukərɪ] *n* Kochkunst *f*
cookery book (Brit) *n* = **cookbook**
cookie ['kukɪ] *n* (*US*) Keks *m or nt*
cooking ['kukɪŋ] *n* Kochen *nt*
cool [kuːl] *adj* kühl; (*person: calm*) besonnen ▶ *vt* kühlen ▶ *vi* abkühlen; **it's ~** es ist kühl; **to keep one's ~** die Ruhe bewahren
▶ **cool down** *vi* abkühlen; (*fig*) sich beruhigen
cooperate [kəu'ɔpəreɪt] *vi* zusammenarbeiten; (*assist*) kooperieren
cooperation [kəuɔpə'reɪʃən] *n* Zusammenarbeit *f*; Mitarbeit *f*, Kooperation *f*
cooperative [kəu'ɔpərətɪv] *adj* (*helpful*) hilfsbereit ▶ *n* Genossenschaft *f*
coordinate [kəu'ɔːdɪneɪt] *vt* koordinieren
cop [kɔp] (*inf*) *n* Bulle *m* (*pej*)
co-parent *vt Elternteil einer Co-Parenting-Beziehung*
co-parenting *n* Co-Parenting *nt*
cope [kəup] *vi* zurechtkommen; **to ~ with** fertig werden mit
Copenhagen ['kəupn'heɪgən] *n* Kopenhagen *nt*
copier ['kɔpɪəʳ] *n* Kopierer *m*
copper ['kɔpəʳ] *n* Kupfer *nt*; (Brit *inf*) Bulle *m* (*pej*) ■ **coppers** *npl* (*small change, coins*) Kleingeld *nt*
copy ['kɔpɪ] *n* Kopie *f*; (*of book, record, newspaper*) Exemplar *nt* ▶ *vt* (*person*) nachahmen; (*idea etc*) nachmachen
copyright ['kɔpɪraɪt] *n* Urheberrecht *nt*
coral ['kɔrəl] *n* Koralle *f*
cord [kɔːd] *n* Schnur *f*; (*fabric*) Cord(samt) *m*
cordless ['kɔːdlɪs] *adj* schnurlos
core [kɔːʳ] *n* Kern *m*; (*of fruit*) Kerngehäuse *nt*
core (business) activity *n* (*Econ*) Kerngeschäft *nt*
cork [kɔːk] *n* (*stopper*) Korken *m*; (*substance*) Kork *m*
corkscrew ['kɔːkskruː] *n* Korkenzieher *m*
corn [kɔːn] *n* (Brit) Getreide *nt*, Korn *nt*; (*US*) Mais *m*; (*on foot*) Hühnerauge *nt*; **~ on the cob** Maiskolben *m*
corned beef ['kɔːnd-] *n* Corned Beef *nt*
corner ['kɔːnəʳ] *n* Ecke *f*; (*bend*) Kurve *f* ▶ *vt* in die Enge treiben
cornflakes ['kɔːnfleɪks] *npl* Cornflakes *pl*
Cornish ['kɔːnɪʃ] *adj* kornisch, aus Cornwall
Cornwall ['kɔːnwəl] *n* Cornwall *nt*
coronation [kɔrə'neɪʃən] *n* Krönung *f*
corporation [kɔːpə'reɪʃən] *n* (*Comm*) Körperschaft *f*
corpse [kɔːps] *n* Leiche *f*
correct [kə'rɛkt] *adj* richtig; (*proper*) korrekt ▶ *vt* korrigieren; (*mistake*) verbessern
correction [kə'rɛkʃən] *n* Korrektur *f*
correspond [kɔrɪs'pɔnd] *vi*: **to ~ (with)** (*write*) korrespondieren (mit); (*be in accordance*) übereinstimmen (mit); **to ~ to** (*be equivalent*) entsprechen *+dat*
corresponding [kɔrɪs'pɔndɪŋ] *adj* entsprechend
corridor ['kɔrɪdɔːʳ] *n* Korridor *m*; (*in train*) Gang *m*
corrupt [kə'rʌpt] *adj* korrupt
cosmetic [kɔz'mɛtɪk] *adj* kosmetisch; **~ surgery** (*Med*) kosmetische Chirurgie *f*
cosmopolitan [kɔzmə'pɔlɪtn] *adj* kosmopolitisch
cost [kɔst] (*pt, pp* **~**) *n* Kosten *pl* ▶ *vt* kosten; **the ~ of living** die Lebenshaltungskosten *pl*; **at all costs** um jeden Preis
costly ['kɔstlɪ] *adj* kostspielig

costume [ˈkɔstjuːm] *n* Kostüm *nt*
cosy [ˈkəuzɪ] *adj* gemütlich
cot [kɔt] *n* (Brit) Kinderbett *nt*; (*US*: *campbed*) Feldbett *nt*
cottage [ˈkɔtɪdʒ] *n* Cottage *nt*, Häuschen *nt*
cottage cheese *n* Hüttenkäse *m*
cottage pie *n Hackfleisch mit Kartoffelbrei überbacken*
cotton [ˈkɔtn] *n* (*fabric*) Baumwollstoff *m*
cotton candy (US) *n* Zuckerwatte *f*
cotton wool (Brit) *n* Watte *f*
couch [kautʃ] *n* Couch *f*
couchette [kuːˈʃɛt] *n* Liegewagen(platz) *m*
couchsurfing [ˈkautʃsəːfɪŋ] *n* Couchsurfing *nt*, *kostenlose zeitweilige Unterkunft bei einer Privatperson*
cough [kɔf] *vi* husten ▸ *n* Husten *m*
cough drop *n* Hustenpastille *f*
cough mixture *n* Hustensaft *m*
could [kud] *pt of* **can²**
couldn't [ˈkudnt] = **could not**
council [ˈkaunsl] *n* Rat *m*; **city/town ~** Stadtrat *m*
council estate (Brit) *n* Siedlung *f* mit Sozialwohnungen
council house (Brit) *n* Sozialwohnung *f*
councillor [ˈkaunsləʳ] *n* Stadtrat *m*, Stadträtin *f*
council tax (Brit) *n* Gemeindesteuer *f*
count [kaunt] *vt* zählen; (*include*) mitrechnen ▸ *vi* zählen ▸ *n* Zählung *f*; (*nobleman*) Graf *m*
▸ **count on** *vt fus* rechnen mit; (*depend on*) sich verlassen auf *+acc*
counter [ˈkauntəʳ] *n* (*in shop*) Ladentisch *m*; (*in café*) Theke *f*; (*in bank, post office*) Schalter *m*
counterattack [ˈkauntərəˈtæk] *n* Gegenangriff *m* ▸ *vi* einen Gegenangriff starten
counterclockwise *adv* gegen den Uhrzeigersinn
counterpart [ˈkauntəpɑːt] *n* (*of document etc*) Gegenstück *nt*
counterterrorism [kauntəˈtɛrərɪzəm] *n* Terrorismusbekämpfung *f*
countess [ˈkauntɪs] *n* Gräfin *f*
countless [ˈkauntlɪs] *adj* unzählig, zahllos
country [ˈkʌntrɪ] *n* Land *nt*; **in the ~** auf dem Land
country dancing (Brit) *n* Volkstanz *m*
country house *n* Landhaus *nt*
countryman [ˈkʌntrɪmən] *n* (*irreg*) (*compatriot*) Landsmann *m*
countryside [ˈkʌntrɪsaɪd] *n* Land *nt*; (*scenery*) Landschaft *f*, Gegend *f*
county [ˈkauntɪ] *n* (Brit) Grafschaft *f*; (*US*) (Verwaltungs)bezirk *m*
county town (Brit) *n Hauptstadt einer Grafschaft*
couple [ˈkʌpl] *n* Paar *nt*; **a ~ of** (*two*) zwei; (*a few*) ein paar
coupon [ˈkuːpɔn] *n* Gutschein *m*
courage [ˈkʌrɪdʒ] *n* Mut *m*
courageous [kəˈreɪdʒəs] *adj* mutig
courgette [kuəˈʒɛt] (Brit) *n* Zucchino *m*
courier [ˈkurɪəʳ] *n* (*messenger*) Kurier(in) *m(f)*; (*for tourists*) Reiseleiter(in) *m(f)*
course [kɔːs] *n* (*Scol*) Kurs(us) *m*; (*of ship*) Kurs *m*; (*of life, events, time etc, of river*) Lauf *m*; (*part of meal*) Gang *m*; **of ~** natürlich; **in the ~ of the next few days** während *or* im Laufe der nächsten paar Tage; **~ of lectures** Vorlesungsreihe *f*
court [kɔːt] *n* (*Law*) Gericht *nt*; (*for tennis, badminton etc*) Platz *m*
courteous [ˈkəːtɪəs] *adj* höflich
courtesy [ˈkəːtəsɪ] *n* Höflichkeit *f*
courtesy bus, courtesy coach *n* gebührenfreier Bus *m*
courthouse [ˈkɔːthaus] (*US*) *n* Gerichtsgebäude *nt*
court order *n* Gerichtsbeschluss *m*
courtroom [ˈkɔːtrum] *n* Gerichtssaal *m*
courtyard [ˈkɔːtjɑːd] *n* Hof *m*
cousin [ˈkʌzn] *n* (*male*) Cousin *m*; (*female*) Cousine *f*
cover [ˈkʌvəʳ] *vt* bedecken; (*distance*) zurücklegen ▸ *n* (*for furniture*) Bezug *m*; (*of book, magazine*) Umschlag *m*; (*Insurance*) Versicherung *f*; **to be covered in** *or* **with** bedeckt sein mit
▸ **cover up** *vt* zudecken; (*fig*: *mistakes*) vertuschen
coverage [ˈkʌvərɪdʒ] *n* Berichterstattung *f*
cover charge *n* Kosten *pl* für ein Gedeck
covering [ˈkʌvərɪŋ] *n* (*of snow, dust etc*) Decke *f*
covering letter, (*US*) **cover letter** *n* Begleitbrief *m*

cow [kau] *n* (*animal, inf!: woman*) Kuh *f*
coward [ˈkauəd] *n* Feigling *m*
cowardly [ˈkauədlɪ] *adj* feige
cowboy [ˈkaubɔɪ] *n* (*in US*) Cowboy *m*
coy [kɔɪ] *adj* verschämt
cozy [ˈkəuzɪ] (*US*) *adj* = **cosy**
CPU *n abbr* (*Comput*) = **central processing unit**
crab [kræb] *n* Krabbe *f*
crack [kræk] *n* (*in bone, dish, glass*) Sprung *m*; (*in wall*) Riss *m*; (*Drugs*) Crack *nt* ▸ *vt* (*bone*) anbrechen; (*nut, code*) knacken; **to get cracking** (*inf*) loslegen
cracker [ˈkrækəʳ] *n* (*biscuit*) Cracker *m*; (*also:* **Christmas ~**) Knallbonbon *nt*; **he's crackers** (*Brit inf*) er ist übergeschnappt
crackle [ˈkrækl] *vi* (*fire*) knistern; (*twig*) knacken
crackling [ˈkræklɪŋ] *n* (*of pork*) Kruste *f* (*des Schweinebratens*)
cradle [ˈkreɪdl] *n* Wiege *f*
craft [krɑːft] *n* (*art*) Kunsthandwerk *nt*; (*trade*) Handwerk *nt*; (*pl inv: boat*) Boot *nt*
craftsman [ˈkrɑːftsmən] *n* (*irreg*) Handwerker *m*
craftsmanship [ˈkrɑːftsmənʃɪp] *n* handwerkliche Ausführung *f*
crafty [ˈkrɑːftɪ] *adj* schlau, clever
cram [kræm] *vt* vollstopfen ▸ *vi* pauken (*inf*); **to ~ with** vollstopfen mit; **to ~ sth into** etw hineinstopfen in *+acc*
cramp [kræmp] *n* Krampf *m*
cranberry [ˈkrænbərɪ] *n* Preiselbeere *f*
crane [kreɪn] *n* Kran *m*; (*bird*) Kranich *m*
crap [kræp] (*!*) *n* Scheiße *f* (*!*)
crash [kræʃ] *n* (*noise*) Krachen *nt*; (*of car*) Unfall *m*; (*of plane etc*) Unglück *nt*; (*collision*) Zusammenstoß *m* ▸ *vt* (*car*) einen Unfall haben mit ▸ *vi* (*plane*) abstürzen; (*car*) einen Unfall haben; (*two cars*) zusammenstoßen; (*market*) zusammenbrechen
crash barrier (*Brit*) *n* Leitplanke *f*
crash course *n* Intensivkurs *m*
crash helmet *n* Sturzhelm *m*
crash-landing *n* Bruchlandung *f*
crate [kreɪt] *n* (*also inf*) Kiste *f*; (*for bottles*) Kasten *m*
crater [ˈkreɪtəʳ] *n* Krater *m*
craving [ˈkreɪvɪŋ] *n*: **~ (for)** Verlangen *nt* (nach)
crawl [krɔːl] *vi* kriechen; (*child*) krabbeln ▸ *n* (*Swimming*) Kraul(en) *nt*
crawler lane [ˈkrɔːlə-] (*Brit*) *n* (*Aut*) Kriechspur *f*
crayfish [ˈkreɪfɪʃ] *n inv* (*saltwater*) Languste *f*
crayon [ˈkreɪən] *n* Buntstift *m*
crazy [ˈkreɪzɪ] *adj* verrückt; **~ about sb/sth** (*inf*) verrückt *or* wild auf jdn/etw
cream [kriːm] *n* Sahne *f*, Rahm *m* (*Südd*); (*artificial cream, cosmetic*) Creme *f* ▸ *adj* cremefarben
cream cake *n* Sahnetorte *f*; (*small*) Sahnetörtchen *nt*
cream cheese *n* (Doppelrahm)-frischkäse *m*
creamy [ˈkriːmɪ] *adj* (*taste*) sahnig
crease [kriːs] *n* Falte *f* ▸ *vt* zerknittern
create [kriːˈeɪt] *vt* schaffen; (*problems*) verursachen
creative [kriːˈeɪtɪv] *adj* kreativ, schöpferisch
creature [ˈkriːtʃəʳ] *n* Geschöpf *nt*
crèche [krɛʃ] *n* (Kinder)krippe *f*
credibility [krɛdɪˈbɪlɪtɪ] *n* Glaubwürdigkeit *f*
credible [ˈkrɛdɪbl] *adj* glaubwürdig
credit [ˈkrɛdɪt] *n* (*loan*) Kredit *m*; (*recognition*) Anerkennung *f* ■ **credits** *npl* (*Cine, TV: at beginning*) Vorspann *m*; (*: at end*) Nachspann *m*
credit card *n* Kreditkarte *f*
credit crunch *n* Kreditklemme *f*
credit rating *n* Rating *nt*, Bonitätsindex *m*
creep [kriːp] (*pt, pp* **crept**) *vi* schleichen; **it gives me the creeps** davon kriege ich das kalte Grausen
creepy [ˈkriːpɪ] *adj* gruselig
crept [krɛpt] *pt, pp of* **creep**
cress [krɛs] *n* Kresse *f*
crest [krɛst] *n* (*of hill*) Kamm *m*; (*coat of arms*) Wappen *nt*
crew [kruː] *n* Besatzung *f*
crib [krɪb] *n* Kinderbett *nt*
crib sheet *n* (*Brit: in exam*) Spickzettel *m*
cricket [ˈkrɪkɪt] *n* Kricket *nt*; (*insect*) Grille *f*
crime [kraɪm] *n* (*no pl: illegal activities*) Verbrechen *pl*
criminal [ˈkrɪmɪnl] *n* Verbrecher(in) *m(f)* ▸ *adj* kriminell
cripple [ˈkrɪpl] *n* (*offensive*) Krüppel *m* ▸ *vt* zum Krüppel machen; (*production, exports*) lähmen

crisis [ˈkraɪsɪs] (*pl* **crises**) *n* Krise *f*
crisp [krɪsp] *adj* (*bacon etc*) knusprig
crisps [krɪsps] (BRIT) *npl* Chips *pl*
criterion [kraɪˈtɪərɪən] (*pl* **criteria**) *n* Kriterium *nt*
critic [ˈkrɪtɪk] *n* Kritiker(in) *m(f)*
critical [ˈkrɪtɪkl] *adj* kritisch
critically [ˈkrɪtɪklɪ] *adv* kritisch; (*ill*) schwer
criticism [ˈkrɪtɪsɪzəm] *n* Kritik *f*
criticize [ˈkrɪtɪsaɪz] *vt* kritisieren
Croat *n* Kroate *m*, Kroatin *f*
Croatia [krəuˈeɪʃə] *n* Kroatien *nt*
Croatian [krəuˈeɪʃən] *adj* kroatisch
crockery [ˈkrɔkərɪ] *n* Geschirr *nt*
crocodile [ˈkrɔkədaɪl] *n* Krokodil *nt*
crocus [ˈkrəukəs] *n* Krokus *m*
crop [krɔp] *n* (*amount produced*) Ernte *f* ▶ **crop up** *vi* aufkommen
croquette [krəˈkɛt] *n* Krokette *f*
cross [krɔs] *n* Kreuz *nt* ▶ *vt* (*street*) überqueren; (*legs*) übereinanderschlagen ▶ *adj* ärgerlich, böse
▶ **cross out** *vt* streichen
crossbar [ˈkrɔsbɑːʳ] *n* (*Sport*) Querlatte *f*; (*of bicycle*) Stange *f*
cross-country [ˈkrɔsˈkʌntrɪ], **cross-country race** *n* Querfeldeinrennen *nt*
cross-examination [ˈkrɔsɪgzæmɪˈneɪʃən] *n* Kreuzverhör *nt*
cross-eyed [ˈkrɔsaɪd] *adj*: **to be ~** schielen
crossing [ˈkrɔsɪŋ] *n* Überfahrt *f*; (*also*: **pedestrian ~**) Fußgängerüberweg *m*
crossroads [ˈkrɔsrəudz] *n* Kreuzung *f*
cross section *n* Querschnitt *m*
crosswalk [ˈkrɔswɔːk] (*US*) *n* Fußgängerüberweg *m*
crossword *n* (*also*: **~ puzzle**) Kreuzworträtsel *nt*
crouch [krautʃ] *vi* kauern
crouton [ˈkruːtɔn] *n* Crouton *m*
crow [krəu] *n* (*bird*) Krähe *f*
crowbar [ˈkrəubɑːʳ] *n* Brechstange *f*
crowd [kraud] *n* (Menschen)menge *f* ▶ *vi*: **to ~ round** sich herumdrängen; **to ~ in** sich hineindrängen
crowded [ˈkraudɪd] *adj* überfüllt; (*densely populated*) dicht besiedelt
crowdsource [ˈkraudsɔːs] *vt* *Arbeitsprozesse auf freiwillige Nutzer auslagern*
crowdsourcing [ˈkraudsɔːsɪŋ] *n* Auslagerung *f* (*von Arbeitsprozessen auf freiwillige Nutzer*), Crowdsourcing *nt*
crown [kraun] *n* (*also of tooth*) Krone *f* ▶ *vt* krönen; **and to ~ it all ...** (*fig*) und zur Krönung des Ganzen ...
crucial [ˈkruːʃl] *adj* (*vote*) entscheidend
crude [kruːd] *adj* (*fig*: *basic*) primitiv; (: *vulgar*) ordinär ▶ *n* = **crude oil**
crude oil *n* Rohöl *nt*
cruel [ˈkruəl] *adj* grausam
cruelty [ˈkruəltɪ] *n* Grausamkeit *f*
cruise [kruːz] *n* Kreuzfahrt *f* ▶ *vi* (*ship*) kreuzen; (*car*) (mit Dauergeschwindigkeit) fahren
cruise missile *n* Marschflugkörper *m*
cruising speed [ˈkruːzɪŋ-] *n* Reisegeschwindigkeit *f*
crumb [krʌm] *n* Krümel *m*
crumble [ˈkrʌmbl] *vt* (*bread*) zerbröckeln ▶ *vi* (*building, earth etc*) zerbröckeln
crumpet [ˈkrʌmpɪt] *n* Teekuchen *m* (*zum Toasten*)
crumple [ˈkrʌmpl] *vt* zerknittern
crunchy [ˈkrʌntʃɪ] *adj* knusprig
crusade [kruːˈseɪd] *n* Feldzug *m*
crush [krʌʃ] *vt* quetschen; (*paper, clothes*) zerknittern; (*garlic, ice*) (zer)stoßen; **to have a ~ on sb** (*love*) für jdn schwärmen
crushing [ˈkrʌʃɪŋ] *adj* vernichtend
crust [krʌst] *n* Kruste *f*
crusty [ˈkrʌstɪ] *adj* knusprig
crutch [krʌtʃ] *n* Krücke *f*
cry [kraɪ] *vi* weinen; (*also*: **~ out**) aufschreien ▶ *n* Schrei *m*; (*shout*) Ruf *m*
crypt [krɪpt] *n* Krypta *f*
crystal [ˈkrɪstl] *n* Kristall *m*
cu [ˈsiːjuː] *abbr* (*in text messages*: = *see you*) bis dann
Cuba [ˈkjuːbə] *n* Kuba *nt*
cube [kjuːb] *n* Würfel *m*
cubic [ˈkjuːbɪk] *adj* (*volume*) Kubik-
cubicle [ˈkjuːbɪkl] *n* Kabine *f*
cuckoo [ˈkukuː] *n* Kuckuck *m*
cucumber [ˈkjuːkʌmbəʳ] *n* Gurke *f*
cuddle [ˈkʌdl] *vt* in den Arm nehmen, drücken ▶ *vi* schmusen
cuddly [ˈkʌdlɪ] *adj* (*person*) knuddelig (*Inf*); **~ toy** Plüschtier *nt*
cuff [kʌf] *n* (*of sleeve*) Manschette *f*; (*US*: *of trousers*) Aufschlag *m*; **off the ~** aus dem Stegreif
cuff links *npl* Manschettenknöpfe *pl*

cuisine [kwɪˈziːn] *n* Küche *f*
cul-de-sac [ˈkʌldəsæk] *n* Sackgasse *f*
culprit [ˈkʌlprɪt] *n* Täter(in) *m(f)*
cult [kʌlt] *n* Kult *m*
cultivate [ˈkʌltɪveɪt] *vt* (*land*) bebauen; (*crop*) anbauen
cultural [ˈkʌltʃərəl] *adj* kulturell
culture [ˈkʌltʃəʳ] *n* Kultur *f*
cultured [ˈkʌltʃəd] *adj* kultiviert
cumbersome [ˈkʌmbəsəm] *adj* (*suitcase etc*) unhandlich
cumin [ˈkʌmɪn] *n* Kreuzkümmel *m*
cunning [ˈkʌnɪŋ] *adj* gerissen; (*device, idea*) schlau
cup [kʌp] *n* Tasse *f*; (*as prize*) Pokal *m*
cupboard [ˈkʌbəd] *n* Schrank *m*
cup final (Brit) *n* Pokalendspiel *nt*
cupola [ˈkjuːpələ] *n* Kuppel *f*
cup tie (Brit) *n* Pokalspiel *nt*
curable [ˈkjuərəbl] *adj* heilbar
curb [kəːb] *n* (*US: kerb*) Bordstein *m*
curd cheese *n* Weißkäse *m*
cure [kjuəʳ] *vt* heilen; (*Culin: salt*) pökeln; (*: smoke*) räuchern ▸ *n* (*remedy*) (Heil)mittel *nt*; (*treatment*) Heilverfahren *nt*
curious [ˈkjuərɪəs] *adj* (*nosy*) neugierig; (*strange, unusual*) sonderbar
curl [kəːl] *n* Locke *f* ▸ *vi* sich kräuseln
▸ **curl up** *vi* sich zusammenrollen
curly [ˈkəːlɪ] *adj* lockig
currant [ˈkʌrnt] *n* Korinthe *f*; (*blackcurrant, redcurrant*) Johannisbeere *f*
currency [ˈkʌrnsɪ] *n* (*system*) Währung *f*; **foreign ~** Devisen *pl*
current [ˈkʌrnt] *n* Strömung *f*; (*Elec*) Strom *m* ▸ *adj* gegenwärtig; (*expression*) gebräuchlich
current account (Brit) *n* Girokonto *nt*
currently [ˈkʌrntlɪ] *adv* zurzeit
curriculum [kəˈrɪkjuləm] (*pl* **curriculums** *or* **curricula**) *n* Lehrplan *m*
curriculum vitae [-ˈviːtaɪ] *n* Lebenslauf *m*
curry [ˈkʌrɪ] *n* (*dish*) Currygericht *nt*
curry powder *n* Curry *m or nt*, Currypulver *nt*
curse [kəːs] *vi* fluchen ▸ *n* Fluch *m*
cursor [ˈkəːsəʳ] *n* (*Comput*) Cursor *m*
curt [kəːt] *adj* knapp, kurz angebunden
curtain [ˈkəːtn] *n* Vorhang *m*
curve [kəːv] *n* (*in the road*) Kurve *f* ▸ *vi* einen Bogen machen
curved [kəːvd] *adj* gebogen
cushion [ˈkuʃən] *n* Kissen *nt*
custard [ˈkʌstəd] *n* (*for pouring*) Vanillesoße *f*
custom [ˈkʌstəm] *n* Brauch *m*; (*habit*) (An)gewohnheit *f*
customary [ˈkʌstəmərɪ] *adj* (*conventional*) üblich
custom-built [ˈkʌstəmˈbɪlt] *adj* speziell angefertigt
customer [ˈkʌstəməʳ] *n* Kunde *m*, Kundin *f*
customize [ˈkʌstəmaɪz] *vt* individuell anpassen
customs [ˈkʌstəmz] *npl* Zoll *m*; **to go through ~** durch den Zoll gehen
customs officer *n* Zollbeamte(r) *m*, Zollbeamtin *f*
cut [kʌt] (*pt, pp* **~**) *vt* schneiden; (*text, programme, spending*) kürzen ▸ *n* Schnitt *m*; (*in skin*) Schnittwunde *f*; (*in salary, spending etc*) Kürzung *f*; (*of meat*) Stück *nt*; **to ~ one's finger/hand/knee** sich in den Finger/in die Hand/am Knie schneiden
▸ **cut back** *vt* (*production*) zurückschrauben
▸ **cut down** *vt* (*tree*) fällen
▸ **cut down on** *vt fus* einschränken
▸ **cut in** *vi* (*Aut*) sich direkt vor ein anderes Auto setzen; **to ~ in (on)** (*conversation*) sich einschalten (in *+acc*)
▸ **cut off** *vt* abschneiden; (*supply*) sperren; (*Tel*) unterbrechen; **we've been ~ off** (*Tel*) wir sind unterbrochen worden
cutback *n* Kürzung *f*
cute [kjuːt] *adj* süß, niedlich; (*clever*) schlau
cutlery [ˈkʌtlərɪ] *n* Besteck *nt*
cutlet [ˈkʌtlɪt] *n* Schnitzel *nt*
cut-price *adj* (*goods*) heruntergesetzt
cutting [ˈkʌtɪŋ] *adj* (*edge, remark*) scharf ▸ *n* (Brit: *from newspaper*) Ausschnitt *m*; (*from plant*) Ableger *m*
cutting-edge [kʌtɪŋˈɛdʒ] *adj* wegbereitend, innovativ
CV *n abbr* = **curriculum vitae**
cwt *abbr* = **hundredweight**
cyberattack [ˈsaɪbərətæk] *n* Cyberangriff *m*
cyberbully *n* Cybermobber(in) *m(f)*
cyberbullying [ˈsaɪbəbulɪɪŋ] *n* Cybermobbing *nt*
cybercafé [ˈsaɪbəkæfeɪ] *n* Internetcafé *nt*

cybersecurity [saɪbəsɪˈkjuərɪtɪ] *n* Internetsicherheit *f*
cyberspace [ˈsaɪbəspeɪs] *n* Cyberspace *m*
cycle [ˈsaɪkl] *n* (*bicycle*) (Fahr)rad *nt* ▶ *vi* Rad fahren
cycle lane, cycle path *n* (Fahr) radweg *m*
cycling [ˈsaɪklɪŋ] *n* Radfahren *nt*
cyclist [ˈsaɪklɪst] *n* (Fahr)radfahrer(in) *m(f)*
cylinder [ˈsɪlɪndəʳ] *n* Zylinder *m*
cynical [ˈsɪnɪkl] *adj* zynisch
cypress [ˈsaɪprɪs] *n* Zypresse *f*
Cypriot [ˈsɪprɪət] *adj* zypriotisch, zyprisch ▶ *n* Zypriot(in) *m(f)*
Cyprus [ˈsaɪprəs] *n* Zypern *nt*
czar [zɑːʳ] *n* = **tsar**
Czech [tʃɛk] *adj* tschechisch ▶ *n* Tscheche *m*, Tschechin *f*; (*language*) Tschechisch *nt*; **the ~ Republic** die Tschechische Republik *f*
Czechia [ˈtʃɛkɪə] *n* (*Czech Republic*) Tschechien *nt*, Tschechische Republik *f*

d

dab [dæb] *vt* betupfen
dachshund [ˈdækshund] *n* Dackel *m*
dad [dæd] (*inf*) *n* Papa *m*, Vati *m*
daddy [ˈdædɪ] (*inf*) *n* = **dad**
daddy-longlegs [dædɪˈlɔŋlɛgz] (*inf*) *n* Schnake *f*
daffodil [ˈdæfədɪl] *n* Osterglocke *f*
daft [dɑːft] (*inf*) *adj* doof (*inf*), blöd (*inf*)
dahlia [ˈdeɪljə] *n* Dahlie *f*
daily [ˈdeɪlɪ] *adj* täglich ▶ *n* (*paper*) Tageszeitung *f* ▶ *adv* täglich
dairy [ˈdɛərɪ] *n* (*on farm*) Milchkammer *f*
dairy products *npl* Milchprodukte *pl*
daisy [ˈdeɪzɪ] *n* Gänseblümchen *nt*
dam [dæm] *n* (Stau)damm *m* ▶ *vt* stauen
damage [ˈdæmɪdʒ] *n* Schaden *m* ▶ *vt* schaden +*dat*; (*spoil, break*) beschädigen ■ **damages** *npl* (*Law*) Schaden(s)ersatz *m*
damn [dæm] *vt* verfluchen; (*condemn*) verurteilen ▶ *adj* (*inf*: *also*: **damned**) verdammt ▶ *n* (*inf*): **I don't give a ~** das ist mir scheißegal (*!*); **~ (it)!** verdammt (noch mal)!
damp [dæmp] *adj* feucht ▶ *n* Feuchtigkeit *f* ▶ *vt* (*also*: **dampen**) befeuchten
dance [dɑːns] *n* Tanz *m*; (*social event*) Tanz(abend) *m* ▶ *vi* tanzen
dancer [ˈdɑːnsəʳ] *n* Tänzer(in) *m(f)*
dancing [ˈdɑːnsɪŋ] *n* Tanzen *nt*
dandelion [ˈdændɪlaɪən] *n* Löwenzahn *m*
dandruff [ˈdændrəf] *n* Schuppen *pl*
Dane [deɪn] *n* Däne *m*, Dänin *f*

danger [ˈdeɪndʒəʳ] *n* Gefahr *f*; **there is a ~ of sth happening** es besteht die Gefahr, dass etw geschieht; **"~!"** „Achtung!"; **in ~** in Gefahr
dangerous [ˈdeɪndʒrəs] *adj* gefährlich
Danish [ˈdeɪnɪʃ] *adj* dänisch ▶ *n* (*Ling*) Dänisch *nt*
Danish pastry *n* Plundergebäck *nt*
Danube [ˈdænju:b] *n*: **the ~** die Donau
dare [dɛəʳ] *vi*: **to ~ (to) do sth** es wagen, etw zu tun; **I daren't tell him** (Brit) ich wage nicht, es ihm zu sagen
daring [ˈdɛərɪŋ] *adj* kühn; (*bold*) gewagt
dark [dɑ:k] *adj* dunkel; (*look*) finster ▶ *n*: **in the ~** im Dunkeln; **it is/is getting ~** es ist/wird dunkel; **~ chocolate** Zartbitterschokolade *f*
dark glasses *npl* Sonnenbrille *f*
darkness [ˈdɑ:knɪs] *n* Dunkelheit *f*
darling [ˈdɑ:lɪŋ] *n* Liebling *m*; **she is a ~** sie ist ein Schatz
darts [dɑ:ts] *n* Darts *nt*
dash [dæʃ] *n* (*sign*) Gedankenstrich *m* ▶ *vt* (*hopes*) zunichtemachen ▶ *vi*: **to ~ towards** zustürzen auf +*acc*
dashboard [ˈdæʃbɔ:d] *n* Armaturenbrett *nt*
data [ˈdeɪtə] *npl* Daten *pl*
data capture *n* Datenerfassung *f*
data processing *n* Datenverarbeitung *f*
date [deɪt] *n* Datum *nt*; (*with friend*) Verabredung *f*; (*fruit*) Dattel *f* ▶ *vt* datieren; (*person*) ausgehen mit; **what's the ~ today?** der Wievielte ist heute?; **~ of birth** Geburtsdatum *nt*; **out of ~** altmodisch; (*expired*) abgelaufen; **up to ~** auf dem neuesten Stand
dated [ˈdeɪtɪd] *adj* altmodisch
dative [ˈdeɪtɪv] *n* Dativ *m*
daughter [ˈdɔ:təʳ] *n* Tochter *f*
daughter-in-law [ˈdɔ:tərɪnlɔ:] *n* Schwiegertochter *f*
dawn [dɔ:n] *n* Tagesanbruch *m* ▶ *vi* dämmern; (*fig*): **it dawned on him that ...** es dämmerte ihm, dass ...
day [deɪ] *n* Tag *m*; **the ~ before/after** am Tag zuvor/danach; **the ~ after tomorrow** übermorgen; **the ~ before yesterday** vorgestern; **~ by ~** jeden Tag, täglich; **by ~** tagsüber; **these days, in the present ~** heute, heutzutage
daybreak [ˈdeɪbreɪk] *n* Tagesanbruch *m*
day-care centre *n* (*for children*) (Kinder)tagesstätte *f*
daydream [ˈdeɪdri:m] *vi* (mit offenen Augen) träumen ▶ *n* Tagtraum *m*
daylight [ˈdeɪlaɪt] *n* Tageslicht *nt*
day return (Brit) *n* Tagesrückfahrkarte *f*
daytime [ˈdeɪtaɪm] *n*: **in the ~** tagsüber, bei Tage
day trip *n* Tagesausflug *m*
dazed [deɪzd] *adj* benommen
dazzle [ˈdæzl] *vt* blenden
dazzling [ˈdæzlɪŋ] *adj* (*light*) blendend; (*career, achievements*) glänzend
dead [dɛd] *adj* tot; (*numb*) abgestorben ▶ *adv* total, völlig; (*directly, exactly*) genau; **~ tired** todmüde
dead end *n* Sackgasse *f*
deadline [ˈdɛdlaɪn] *n* (letzter) Termin *m*
deadly [ˈdɛdlɪ] *adj* tödlich ▶ *adv*: **~ dull** todlangweilig
deaf [dɛf] *adj* taub
deafen [ˈdɛfn] *vt* taub machen
deafening [ˈdɛfnɪŋ] *adj* ohrenbetäubend
deal [di:l] (*pt, pp* **dealt**) *n* Geschäft *nt* ▶ *vt* (*card*) geben, austeilen; **it's a ~!** (*inf*) abgemacht!; **a good ~** (*a lot*) ziemlich viel; **a great ~ (of)** ziemlich viel
▶ **deal in** *vt fus* handeln mit
▶ **deal with** *vt fus* (*person*) sich kümmern um; (*problem*) sich befassen mit; (*successfully*) fertig werden mit; (*subject*) behandeln
dealbreaker [ˈdi:lbreɪkəʳ] *n*: **it was a ~** es hat das Geschäft gekippt
dealer [ˈdi:ləʳ] *n* Händler(in) *m*(*f*); (*in drugs*) Dealer *m*
dealings [ˈdi:lɪŋz] *npl* Geschäfte *pl*
dealt [dɛlt] *pt, pp of* **deal**
dear [dɪəʳ] *adj* lieb; (*expensive*) teuer ▶ *n*: **(my) ~** (mein) Liebling *m* ▶ *excl*: **~ me!** (ach) du liebe Zeit!; **D~ Sir/Madam** Sehr geehrte Damen und Herren
dearly [ˈdɪəlɪ] *adv* (*love*) von ganzem Herzen; (*pay*) teuer
death [dɛθ] *n* Tod *m*; (*fatality*) Todesfall *m*
death certificate *n* Sterbeurkunde *f*, Totenschein *m*

death penalty *n* Todesstrafe *f*
death toll *n* Zahl *f* der Todesopfer *or* Toten
deathtrap [ˈdɛθtræp] *n* Todesfalle *f*
debatable [dɪˈbeɪtəbl] *adj* fraglich
debate [dɪˈbeɪt] *n* Debatte *f* ▶ *vt* debattieren über *+acc*
debit [ˈdɛbɪt] *n* Schuldposten *m* ▶ *vt*: **to ~ a sum to sb/sb's account** jdn/jds Konto mit einer Summe belasten; *see also* **direct debit**
debit card *n* Geldkarte *f*
debris [ˈdɛbriː] *n* Trümmer *pl*
debt [dɛt] *n* Schuld *f*; **to be in ~** Schulden haben, verschuldet sein
debug [ˈdiːˈbʌg] *vt* (*Comput*) Fehler beseitigen in *+dat*
decade [ˈdɛkeɪd] *n* Jahrzehnt *nt*
decadent [ˈdɛkədənt] *adj* dekadent
decaf [ˈdiːkæf] *n* koffeinfreier Kaffee *m*
decaffeinated [dɪˈkæfɪneɪtɪd] *adj* koffeinfrei
decanter [dɪˈkæntəʳ] *n* Karaffe *f*
decay [dɪˈkeɪ] *n* Verfall *m*; (*of tooth*) Fäule *f* ▶ *vi* (*body*) verwesen; (*teeth*) faulen; (*leaves*) verrotten; (*fig*: *society etc*) verfallen
deceased [dɪˈsiːst] *n*: **the ~** der/die Tote *or* Verstorbene
deceit [dɪˈsiːt] *n* Betrug *m*
deceive [dɪˈsiːv] *vt* täuschen
December [dɪˈsɛmbəʳ] *n* Dezember *m*; *see also* **July**
decent [ˈdiːsənt] *adj* anständig
deception [dɪˈsɛpʃən] *n* Betrug *m*
deceptive [dɪˈsɛptɪv] *adj* irreführend, täuschend
decide [dɪˈsaɪd] *vt* entscheiden ▶ *vi* sich entscheiden; **to ~ to do sth/that** beschließen, etw zu tun/dass; **to ~ on sth** sich für etw entscheiden
decided [dɪˈsaɪdɪd] *adj* entschieden; (*difference*) deutlich
decidedly [dɪˈsaɪdɪdlɪ] *adv* entschieden
decimal [ˈdɛsɪməl] *adj* (*system, number*) Dezimal-
decipher [dɪˈsaɪfəʳ] *vt* entziffern
decision [dɪˈsɪʒən] *n* Entscheidung *f*; **to make a ~** eine Entscheidung treffen
decisive [dɪˈsaɪsɪv] *adj* (*action etc*) entscheidend; (*person*) entschlussfreudig
deck [dɛk] *n* Deck *nt*; (*of cards*) Spiel *nt*
deck chair *n* Liegestuhl *m*
declaration [dɛkləˈreɪʃən] *n* Erklärung *f*
declare [dɪˈklɛəʳ] *vt* erklären; (*result*) bekannt geben; (*goods at customs*) verzollen
decline [dɪˈklaɪn] *n* Rückgang *m*; (*decay*) Verfall *m* ▶ *vt* ablehnen ▶ *vi* (*strength*) nachlassen; (*business*) zurückgehen
declutter *vt* entrümpeln, aufräumen
decode [diːˈkəud] *vt* entschlüsseln
decompose [diːkəmˈpəuz] *vi* (*organic matter*) sich zersetzen
decontaminate [diːkənˈtæmɪneɪt] *vt* entgiften
decorate [ˈdɛkəreɪt] *vt* (*room, house*: *from bare walls*) anstreichen und tapezieren
decoration [dɛkəˈreɪʃən] *n* (*on tree, building*) Schmuck *m*; (*act*) Verzieren *nt*; Schmücken *nt*; (An)streichen *nt*; Tapezieren *nt*
decorator [ˈdɛkəreɪtəʳ] *n* Maler(in) *m(f)*
decrease *vi* [dɪˈkriːs] abnehmen ▶ *n* [ˈdiːkriːs]: **~ (in)** Abnahme *f* (*+gen*)
dedicate [ˈdɛdɪkeɪt] *vt*: **to ~ to** widmen *+dat*
dedicated [ˈdɛdɪkeɪtɪd] *adj* engagiert
dedication [dɛdɪˈkeɪʃən] *n* Hingabe *f*; (*in book, on radio*) Widmung *f*
deduce [dɪˈdjuːs] *vt*: **to ~ (that)** schließen(, dass), folgern(, dass)
deduct [dɪˈdʌkt] *vt* abziehen
deduction [dɪˈdʌkʃən] *n* (*act of deducting*) Abzug *m*; (*act of deducing*) Folgerung *f*
deed [diːd] *n* Tat *f*
deep [diːp] *adj* tief
deepen [ˈdiːpn] *vt* vertiefen
deepfreeze *n* Tiefkühltruhe *f*
deep-fry [ˈdiːpˈfraɪ] *vt* frittieren
deer [dɪəʳ] *n inv* Reh *nt*; (*male*) Hirsch *m*
defeat [dɪˈfiːt] *vt* besiegen ▶ *n* (*failure*) Niederlage *f*
defect *n* [ˈdiːfɛkt] Fehler *m* ▶ *vi* [dɪˈfɛkt]: **to ~ to the enemy** zum Feind überlaufen
defective [dɪˈfɛktɪv] *adj* fehlerhaft
defence, (*US*) **defense** [dɪˈfɛns] *n* Verteidigung *f*
defend [dɪˈfɛnd] *vt* verteidigen
defendant [dɪˈfɛndənt] *n* Angeklagte(r) *f(m)*

defender [dɪˈfɛndəʳ] *n* Verteidiger(in) *m(f)*
defensive [dɪˈfɛnsɪv] *adj* defensiv
deficiency [dɪˈfɪʃənsɪ] *n* Mangel *m*
deficient [dɪˈfɪʃənt] *adj*: **sb/sth is ~ in sth** jdm/etw fehlt es an etw *dat*
deficit [ˈdɛfɪsɪt] *n* Defizit *nt*
define [dɪˈfaɪn] *vt* (*limits, boundaries*) bestimmen; (*word*) definieren
definite [ˈdɛfɪnɪt] *adj* (*clear, obvious*) klar, eindeutig; (*certain*) bestimmt; **he was ~ about it** er war sich *dat* sehr sicher
definitely [ˈdɛfɪnɪtlɪ] *adv* bestimmt
definition [dɛfɪˈnɪʃən] *n* (*of word*) Definition *f*; (*of photograph etc*) Schärfe *f*
defriend [di:ˈfrɛnd] *vt* (*on social network*) entfreunden
defrost [di:ˈfrɔst] *vt* (*fridge*) abtauen; (*food*) auftauen
degrading [dɪˈgreɪdɪŋ] *adj* erniedrigend
degree [dɪˈgri:] *n* Grad *m*; (*Scol*) akademischer Grad *m*; **a considerable ~ of risk** ein gewisses Risiko; **a ~ in maths** ein Hochschulabschluss *m* in Mathematik; **to some ~, to a certain ~** einigermaßen, in gewissem Maße
dehydrated [di:haɪˈdreɪtɪd] *adj* ausgetrocknet, dehydriert
de-ice [ˈdi:ˈaɪs] *vt* enteisen
delay [dɪˈleɪ] *vt* (*decision, ceremony*) verschieben, aufschieben; (*person, plane, train*) aufhalten ▸ *vi* zögern ▸ *n* Verzögerung *f*; **to be delayed** (*person*) sich verspäten; (*departure etc*) verspätet sein; (*flight etc*) Verspätung haben; **without ~** unverzüglich
delegate *n* [ˈdɛlɪgɪt] Delegierte(r) *f(m)* ▸ *vt* [ˈdɛlɪgeɪt] delegieren
delegation [dɛlɪˈgeɪʃən] *n* (*group*) Abordnung *f*, Delegation *f*
delete [dɪˈli:t] *vt* streichen; (*Comput*) löschen
deli [ˈdɛlɪ] *n* Feinkostgeschäft *nt*
deliberate *adj* [dɪˈlɪbərɪt] absichtlich ▸ *vi* [dɪˈlɪbəreɪt] überlegen
deliberately [dɪˈlɪbərɪtlɪ] *adv* absichtlich, bewusst
delicate [ˈdɛlɪkɪt] *adj* fein; (*colour, health*) zart; (*problem*) delikat, heikel
delicatessen [dɛlɪkəˈtɛsn] *n* Feinkostgeschäft *nt*
delicious [dɪˈlɪʃəs] *adj* köstlich
delight [dɪˈlaɪt] *n* Freude *f* ▸ *vt* erfreuen
delighted [dɪˈlaɪtɪd] *adj*: **~ (at** *or* **with)** erfreut (über +*acc*), entzückt (über +*acc*)
delightful [dɪˈlaɪtful] *adj* reizend, wunderbar
deliver [dɪˈlɪvəʳ] *vt* liefern; (*letters, papers*) zustellen; (*speech*) halten; (*Med: baby*) zur Welt bringen
delivery [dɪˈlɪvərɪ] *n* Lieferung *f*; (*of letters, papers*) Zustellung *f*; (*Med*) Entbindung *f*
delivery van, (*US*) **delivery truck** *n* Lieferwagen *m*
delude [dɪˈlu:d] *vt* täuschen; **to ~ o.s.** sich *dat* etwas vormachen
delusion [dɪˈlu:ʒən] *n* Irrglaube *m*
de luxe [dəˈlʌks] *adj* (*hotel, model*) Luxus-
demand [dɪˈmɑ:nd] *vt* verlangen; (*rights*) fordern ▸ *n* Verlangen *nt*; (*claim*) Forderung *f*; (*Econ*) Nachfrage *f*; **to be in ~** gefragt sein; **on ~** (*available*) auf Verlangen
demanding [dɪˈmɑ:ndɪŋ] *adj* anspruchsvoll
demented [dɪˈmɛntɪd] *adj* wahnsinnig
demister (Brit) *n* (*Aut*) Gebläse *nt*
demo [ˈdɛməu] (*inf*) *n abbr* = **demonstration**
democracy [dɪˈmɔkrəsɪ] *n* Demokratie *f*
democrat [ˈdɛməkræt] *n* Demokrat(in) *m(f)*
democratic [dɛməˈkrætɪk] *adj* demokratisch
demolish [dɪˈmɔlɪʃ] *vt* abreißen; (*fig: argument*) widerlegen
demolition [dɛməˈlɪʃən] *n* Abbruch *m*
demonstrate [ˈdɛmənstreɪt] *vt* (*theory*) demonstrieren; (*skill*) zeigen, beweisen ▸ *vi*: **to ~ (for/against)** demonstrieren (für/gegen)
demonstration [dɛmənˈstreɪʃən] *n* Demonstration *f*
demoralize [dɪˈmɔrəlaɪz] *vt* entmutigen
denial [dɪˈnaɪəl] *n* Leugnen *nt*
denim [ˈdɛnɪm] *n* Jeansstoff *m* ■ **denims** *npl* (Blue) Jeans *pl*
denim jacket *n* Jeansjacke *f*
Denmark [ˈdɛnmɑ:k] *n* Dänemark *nt*
denomination [dɪnɔmɪˈneɪʃən] *n* (*of money*) Nennwert *m*; (*Rel*) Konfession *f*

dense [dɛns] *adj* dicht; (*inf: person*) beschränkt
density [ˈdɛnsɪtɪ] *n* Dichte *f*
dent [dɛnt] *n* Beule *f* ▶ *vt* (*also*: **make a ~ in**) einbeulen
dental [ˈdɛntl] *adj* (*filling, hygiene etc*) Zahn-
dentist [ˈdɛntɪst] *n* Zahnarzt *m*, Zahnärztin *f*
dentures [ˈdɛntʃəz] *npl* Zahnprothese *f*; (*full*) Gebiss *nt*
deny [dɪˈnaɪ] *vt* leugnen; (*permission, chance*) verweigern
deodorant [diːˈəudərənt] *n* Deodorant *nt*
depart [dɪˈpɑːt] *vi* (*visitor*) abreisen; (*bus, train*) abfahren; (*plane*) abfliegen
department [dɪˈpɑːtmənt] *n* Abteilung *f*; (*Scol*) Fachbereich *m*; (*Pol*) Ministerium *nt*
department store *n* Warenhaus *nt*
departure [dɪˈpɑːtʃəʳ] *n* (*on foot, of employee etc*) Weggang *m*; (*of bus, train*) Abfahrt *f*; (*of plane*) Abflug *m*
departure lounge *n* Abflughalle *f*
depend [dɪˈpɛnd] *vi*: **to ~ on** abhängen von; (*rely on, trust*) sich verlassen auf *+acc*; (*financially*) abhängig sein von, angewiesen sein auf *+acc*; **it depends** es kommt darauf an
dependable [dɪˈpɛndəbl] *adj* zuverlässig
dependence [dɪˈpɛndəns] *n* Abhängigkeit *f*
dependent [dɪˈpɛndənt] *adj*: **to be ~ on** (*person*) abhängig sein von
deport [dɪˈpɔːt] *vt* (*illegal immigrant*) abschieben
deportation [diːpɔːˈteɪʃən] *n* Abschiebung *f*
deposit [dɪˈpɔzɪt] *n* (*in account*) Guthaben *nt*; (*down payment*) Anzahlung *f*; (*for hired goods etc*) Kaution *f*; (*on bottle etc*) Pfand *nt*; (*Chem*) Ablagerung *f* ▶ *vt* deponieren; **to put down a ~ of £50** eine Anzahlung von £50 machen
deposit account *n* Sparkonto *nt*
depot [ˈdɛpəu] *n* (*for vehicles*) Depot *nt*
depreciate [dɪˈpriːʃɪeɪt] *vi* an Wert verlieren
depress [dɪˈprɛs] *vt* deprimieren
depressed [dɪˈprɛst] *adj* deprimiert, niedergeschlagen; (*area*) Notstands-
depressing [dɪˈprɛsɪŋ] *adj* deprimierend
depression [dɪˈprɛʃən] *n* (*Psych*) Depressionen *pl*; (*Met*) Tief(druckgebiet) *nt*
deprive [dɪˈpraɪv] *vt*: **to ~ sb of sth** jdm etw entziehen
deprived [dɪˈpraɪvd] *adj* benachteiligt
dept *abbr* = **department**
depth [dɛpθ] *n* Tiefe *f*
deputy [ˈdɛpjutɪ] *cpd* stellvertretend ▶ *n* (Stell)vertreter(in) *m(f)*; (*Pol*) Abgeordnete(r) *f(m)*
derail [dɪˈreɪl] *vt*: **to be derailed** entgleisen
deranged [dɪˈreɪndʒd] *adj*: **to be mentally ~** (*pej*) geistesgestört sein
derivation [dɛrɪˈveɪʃən] *n* Ableitung *f*
derive [dɪˈraɪv] *vt*: **to ~ (from)** gewinnen (aus); (*benefit*) ziehen (aus)
dermatitis [dəːməˈtaɪtɪs] *n* Hautentzündung *f*
derogatory [dɪˈrɔgətərɪ] *adj* abfällig
descend [dɪˈsɛnd] *vt* hinuntergehen, hinuntersteigen ▶ *vi* hinuntergehen; **to ~ from** abstammen von
descendant [dɪˈsɛndənt] *n* Nachkomme *m*
descent [dɪˈsɛnt] *n* Abstieg *m*; (*origin*) Abstammung *f*
describe [dɪsˈkraɪb] *vt* beschreiben
description [dɪsˈkrɪpʃən] *n* Beschreibung *f*
desert *n* [ˈdɛzət] Wüste *f* ▶ *vt* [dɪˈzəːt] verlassen
deserve [dɪˈzəːv] *vt* verdienen
design [dɪˈzaɪn] *n* Design *nt*; (*process*) Entwurf *m*, Gestaltung *f*; (*sketch*) Entwurf *m*; (*of car*) Konstruktion *f* ▶ *vt* entwerfen
designate *vt* [ˈdɛzɪgneɪt] bestimmen, ernennen ▶ *adj* [ˈdɛzɪgnɪt] designiert
designer [dɪˈzaɪnəʳ] *n* Designer(in) *m(f)*; (*Tech*) Konstrukteur(in) *m(f)*
desirable [dɪˈzaɪərəbl] *adj* (*proper*) wünschenswert
desire [dɪˈzaɪəʳ] *n* Wunsch *m*; (*sexual*) Begehren *nt* ▶ *vt* wünschen; (*lust after*) begehren
desk [dɛsk] *n* Schreibtisch *m*; (*in hotel*) Empfang *m*; (*at airport*) Schalter *m*
desktop [ˈdɛsktɔp] *n* (*Comput*) Desktop *m*
desktop publishing *n* Desktop-Publishing *nt*

desolate [ˈdɛsəlɪt] *adj* trostlos
despair [dɪsˈpɛəʳ] *n* Verzweiflung *f* ▶ *vi*: **to be in ~** verzweifelt sein
despatch [dɪsˈpætʃ] *n, vt* = **dispatch**
desperate [ˈdɛspərɪt] *adj* verzweifelt; (*shortage*) akut; **to be ~ for sth/to do sth** etw dringend brauchen/ unbedingt tun wollen
desperation [dɛspəˈreɪʃən] *n* Verzweiflung *f*
despicable [dɪsˈpɪkəbl] *adj* (*action*) verabscheuungswürdig
despise [dɪsˈpaɪz] *vt* verachten
despite [dɪsˈpaɪt] *prep* trotz +*gen*
dessert [dɪˈzəːt] *n* Nachtisch *m*
dessertspoon [dɪˈzəːtspuːn] *n* Dessertlöffel *m*
destination [dɛstɪˈneɪʃən] *n* (Reise) ziel *nt*; (*of mail*) Bestimmungsort *m*
destiny [ˈdɛstɪnɪ] *n* Schicksal *nt*
destroy [dɪsˈtrɔɪ] *vt* zerstören; (*animal*) töten
destruction [dɪsˈtrʌkʃən] *n* Zerstörung *f*
destructive [dɪsˈtrʌktɪv] *adj* zerstörerisch; (*child, criticism etc*) destruktiv
detach [dɪˈtætʃ] *vt* (*remove*) entfernen; (*unclip*) abnehmen; (*unstick*) ablösen
detachable [dɪˈtætʃəbl] *adj* abnehmbar
detached [dɪˈtætʃt] *adj* distanziert; (*house*) frei stehend, Einzel-
detail [ˈdiːteɪl] *n* Einzelheit *f*; (*no pl: in picture, one's work etc*) Detail *nt*; **in ~** in Einzelheiten; **to go into details** auf Einzelheiten eingehen, ins Detail gehen
detailed [ˈdiːteɪld] *adj* detailliert, genau
detain [dɪˈteɪn] *vt* aufhalten; (*in captivity*) in Haft halten
detect [dɪˈtɛkt] *vt* wahrnehmen; (*Med, Tech*) feststellen
detective [dɪˈtɛktɪv] *n* Kriminalbeamte(r) *m*
detective story *n* Kriminalgeschichte *f*
detention [dɪˈtɛnʃən] *n* (*captivity*) Haft *f*; (*Scol*) Nachsitzen *nt*
deter [dɪˈtəːʳ] *vt* (*discourage*) abschrecken
detergent [dɪˈtəːdʒənt] *n* Reinigungsmittel *nt*; (*for clothes*) Waschmittel *nt*
deteriorate [dɪˈtɪərɪəreɪt] *vi* sich verschlechtern
determination [dɪtəːmɪˈneɪʃən] *n* Entschlossenheit *f*
determine [dɪˈtəːmɪn] *vt* (*facts*) feststellen
determined [dɪˈtəːmɪnd] *adj* entschlossen
deterrent [dɪˈtɛrənt] *n* Abschreckungsmittel *nt*
detest [dɪˈtɛst] *vt* verabscheuen
detestable [dɪˈtɛstəbl] *adj* abscheulich, widerwärtig
detour [ˈdiːtuəʳ] *n* Umweg *m*; (*US Aut*) Umleitung *f*
detox [ˈdiːtɔks] (*inf*) *n* Entzug *m*
detoxification [diːtɔksɪfɪˈkeɪʃən] *n* (*from drugs*) Drogenentzug *m*; (*from alcohol etc*) Entgiftung *f*
detoxify [diːˈtɔksɪfaɪ] *vi* (*from drugs*) entziehen, Entzug machen; (*from alcohol etc*) entgiften
deuce [djuːs] *n* (*Tennis*) Einstand *m*
devalue [ˈdiːˈvæljuː] *vt* abwerten
devastate [ˈdɛvəsteɪt] *vt* verwüsten
devastating [ˈdɛvəsteɪtɪŋ] *adj* verheerend
develop [dɪˈvɛləp] *vt* entwickeln; (*disease*) bekommen ▶ *vi* sich entwickeln
developing country [dɪˈvɛləpɪŋ-] *n* Entwicklungsland *nt*
development [dɪˈvɛləpmənt] *n* Entwicklung *f*; (*of land*) Erschließung *f*
device [dɪˈvaɪs] *n* Gerät *nt*
devil [ˈdɛvl] *n* Teufel *m*
devilish [ˈdɛvlɪʃ] *adj* teuflisch
devote [dɪˈvəut] *vt*: **to ~ sth/o.s. to** etw/sich widmen +*dat*
devoted [dɪˈvəutɪd] *adj* treu; (*admirer*) eifrig
devotion [dɪˈvəuʃən] *n* (*affection*) Ergebenheit *f*; (*dedication*) Hingabe *f*; (*Rel*) Andacht *f*
devour [dɪˈvauəʳ] *vt* verschlingen
dew [djuː] *n* Tau *m*
diabetes [daɪəˈbiːtiːz] *n* Zuckerkrankheit *f*
diabetic [daɪəˈbɛtɪk] *adj* zuckerkrank; (*chocolate, jam*) Diabetiker- ▶ *n* Diabetiker(in) *m(f)*
diagnosis [daɪəgˈnəusɪs] (*pl* **diagnoses**) *n* Diagnose *f*
diagonal [daɪˈægənl] *adj* diagonal
diagram [ˈdaɪəgræm] *n* Diagramm *nt*

dial [ˈdaɪəl] *n* Zifferblatt *nt*; (*on radio set*) Einstellskala *f* ▶ *vt* wählen

dial code (*US*) *n* = **dialling code**

dialect [ˈdaɪəlɛkt] *n* Dialekt *m*

dialling code, (*US*) **dial code** *n* Vorwahl *f*

dialling tone [ˈdaɪəlɪŋ-], (*US*) **dial tone** *n* Amtszeichen *nt*

dialogue, (*US*) **dialog** [ˈdaɪəlɔg] *n* Dialog *m*

dial tone (*US*) *n* = **dialling tone**

dialysis [daɪˈælɪsɪs] *n* Dialyse *f*

diameter [daɪˈæmɪtəʳ] *n* Durchmesser *m*

diamond [ˈdaɪəmənd] *n* Diamant *m*
■ **diamonds** *npl* (*Cards*) Karo *nt*

diaper [ˈdaɪəpəʳ] (*US*) *n* Windel *f*

diarrhoea, (*US*) **diarrhea** [daɪəˈriːə] *n* Durchfall *m*

diary [ˈdaɪərɪ] *n* (Termin)kalender *m*; (*daily account*) Tagebuch *nt*

dice [daɪs] *n inv* Würfel *m* ▶ *vt* in Würfel schneiden

diced [daɪst] *adj* in Würfel geschnitten

dictate *vt* [dɪkˈteɪt] diktieren

dictation [dɪkˈteɪʃən] *n* Diktat *nt*

dictator [dɪkˈteɪtəʳ] *n* Diktator *m*

dictatorship [dɪkˈteɪtəʃɪp] *n* Diktatur *f*

dictionary [ˈdɪkʃənrɪ] *n* Wörterbuch *nt*

did [dɪd] *pt of* **do**

didn't [ˈdɪdnt] = **did not**

die [daɪ] *vi* sterben; (*plant*) eingehen; (*engine*) stehen bleiben; **to be dying for sth** etw unbedingt brauchen; **to be dying to do sth** darauf brennen, etw zu tun
▶ **die away** *vi* (*sound*) schwächer werden
▶ **die down** *vi* (*excitement, noise*) nachlassen
▶ **die out** *vi* aussterben

diesel [ˈdiːzl] *n* (*vehicle*) Diesel *m*

diesel engine *n* Dieselmotor *m*

diet [ˈdaɪət] *n* Ernährung *f*; (*Med*) Diät *f* ▶ *vi* (*also:* **be on a ~**) eine Schlankheitskur machen

differ [ˈdɪfəʳ] *vi* (*be different*): **to ~ (from)** sich unterscheiden (von); (*disagree*): **to ~ (about)** anderer Meinung sein (über +*acc*)

difference [ˈdɪfrəns] *n* Unterschied *m*; **it makes no ~ to me** das ist mir egal *or* einerlei

different [ˈdɪfrənt] *adj* (*various people, things*) verschieden, unterschiedlich; **to be ~ (from)** anders sein (als)

differentiate [dɪfəˈrɛnʃɪeɪt] *vi*: **to ~ (between)** unterscheiden (zwischen) ▶ *vt*: **to ~ A from B** A von B unterscheiden

differently [ˈdɪfrəntlɪ] *adv* anders; (*shaped, designed*) unterschiedlich

difficult [ˈdɪfɪkəlt] *adj* schwierig; (*task, problem*) schwer, schwierig

difficulty [ˈdɪfɪkəltɪ] *n* Schwierigkeit *f*; **to be in/get into difficulties** in Schwierigkeiten sein/geraten

dig [dɪg] (*pt, pp* **dug**) *vt* graben
▶ **dig in** *vi* (*inf: eat*) reinhauen
▶ **dig up** *vt* ausgraben

digest [daɪˈdʒɛst] *vt* verdauen

digestible [dɪˈdʒɛstəbl] *adj* verdaulich

digestion [dɪˈdʒɛstʃən] *n* Verdauung *f*

digestive [dɪˈdʒɛstɪv] *adj* (*system, upsets*) Verdauungs- ▶ *n Keks aus Vollkornmehl*

digit [ˈdɪdʒɪt] *n* (*number*) Ziffer *f*

digital [ˈdɪdʒɪtl] *adj* (*watch, display etc*) Digital-

digital camera *n* Digitalkamera *f*

digital computer *n* Digitalrechner *m*

digital television, digital TV *n* Digitalfernsehen *nt*

dignified [ˈdɪgnɪfaɪd] *adj* würdevoll

dignity [ˈdɪgnɪtɪ] *n* Würde *f*

dilapidated [dɪˈlæpɪdeɪtɪd] *adj* verfallen

dilemma [daɪˈlɛmə] *n* Dilemma *nt*

dill [dɪl] *n* Dill *m*

dilute [daɪˈluːt] *vt* verdünnen

dim [dɪm] *adj* schwach; (*outline, figure*) undeutlich; (*inf: person*) schwer von Begriff ▶ *vt* (*light*) dämpfen; (*US Aut*) abblenden

dime [daɪm] (*US*) *n* Zehncentstück *nt*

dimension [daɪˈmɛnʃən] *n* (*aspect*) Dimension *f*; (*measurement*) Abmessung *f*, Maß *nt*

diminish [dɪˈmɪnɪʃ] *vi* sich verringern ▶ *vt* verringern

dimple [ˈdɪmpl] *n* Grübchen *nt*

dine [daɪn] *vi* speisen

diner [ˈdaɪnəʳ] *n* Gast *m*; (*US: restaurant*) Esslokal *nt*

dinghy [ˈdɪŋgɪ] *n* (*also:* **rubber ~**) Schlauchboot *nt*; (*also:* **sailing ~**) Dingi *nt*

dingy [ˈdɪndʒɪ] *adj* schäbig; (*clothes, curtains etc*) schmuddelig

dining car [ˈdaɪnɪŋ-] (Brit) *n* Speisewagen *m*

dining room [ˈdaɪnɪŋ-] *n* Esszimmer *nt*; (*in hotel*) Speiseraum *m*
dinner [ˈdɪnəʳ] *n* (*evening meal*) Abendessen *nt*; (*lunch*) Mittagessen *nt*; (*banquet*) (Fest)essen *nt*
dinner jacket *n* Smokingjackett *nt*
dinner party *n* Abendgesellschaft *f* (mit Essen)
dinner time *n* Essenszeit *f*
dinosaur [ˈdaɪnəsɔːʳ] *n* Dinosaurier *m*
dip [dɪp] *n* Senke *f*; (*Culin*) Dip *m* ▶ *vt* eintauchen; (Brit *Aut*) abblenden
diploma [dɪˈpləumə] *n* Diplom *nt*
diplomat [ˈdɪpləmæt] *n* Diplomat(in) *m(f)*
diplomatic [dɪpləˈmætɪk] *adj* diplomatisch
dipstick [ˈdɪpstɪk] (Brit) *n* Ölmessstab *m*
direct [daɪˈrɛkt] *adj*, *adv* direkt ▶ *vt* richten; (*play*, *film*) Regie führen bei; **can you ~ me to ...?** können Sie mir den Weg nach ... sagen?
direct current *n* Gleichstrom *m*
direct debit (Brit) *n* Einzugsauftrag *m*; (*transaction*) automatische Abbuchung *f*
direction [dɪˈrɛkʃən] *n* Richtung *f*; (*Cine*) Regie *f* ■ **directions** *npl* (*instructions*) Anweisungen *pl*; **in the ~ of** in Richtung
directly [dɪˈrɛktlɪ] *adv* direkt; (*at once*) sofort
director [dɪˈrɛktəʳ] *n* Direktor(in) *m(f)*; (*of project*, *TV*, *Radio*) Leiter(in) *m(f)*; (*Cine*) Regisseur(in) *m(f)*
directory [dɪˈrɛktərɪ] *n* (*also*: **telephone ~**) Telefonbuch *nt*
directory enquiries, (*US*) **directory assistance** *n* (Fernsprech)auskunft *f*
dirt [dəːt] *n* Schmutz *m*; (*earth*) Erde *f*
dirt-cheap *adj* spottbillig
dirt road *n* unbefestigte Straße *f*
dirty [ˈdəːtɪ] *adj* schmutzig
disability [dɪsəˈbɪlɪtɪ] *n* Behinderung *f*
disabled [dɪsˈeɪbld] *adj* behindert; **~ people** Behinderte *pl*
disadvantage [dɪsədˈvɑːntɪdʒ] *n* Nachteil *m*; **to be at a ~** benachteiligt *or* im Nachteil sein
disagree [dɪsəˈgriː] *vi* nicht übereinstimmen; (*to be against*, *think differently*): **to ~ (with)** nicht einverstanden sein (mit)
disagreeable [dɪsəˈgriːəbl] *adj* unangenehm; (*person*) unsympathisch
disagreement [dɪsəˈgriːmənt] *n* (*argument*) Meinungsverschiedenheit
disappear [dɪsəˈpɪəʳ] *vi* verschwinden
disappearance [dɪsəˈpɪərəns] *n* Verschwinden *nt*
disappoint [dɪsəˈpɔɪnt] *vt* enttäuschen
disappointing [dɪsəˈpɔɪntɪŋ] *adj* enttäuschend
disappointment [dɪsəˈpɔɪntmənt] *n* Enttäuschung *f*
disapproval [dɪsəˈpruːvəl] *n* Missbilligung *f*
disapprove [dɪsəˈpruːv] *vi*: **to ~ of** missbilligen *+acc*
disarm [dɪsˈɑːm] *vt* entwaffnen ▶ *vi* abrüsten
disarmament [dɪsˈɑːməmənt] *n* Abrüstung *f*
disarming [dɪsˈɑːmɪŋ] *adj* entwaffnend
disaster [dɪˈzɑːstəʳ] *n* Katastrophe *f*
disastrous [dɪˈzɑːstrəs] *adj* katastrophal
disbelief [dɪsbəˈliːf] *n* Ungläubigkeit *f*
disc [dɪsk] *n* (*Anat*) Bandscheibe *f*; (*Comput*) = **disk**
disc brake *n* Scheibenbremse *f*
discharge [dɪsˈtʃɑːdʒ] *vt* (*waste*) ablassen; (*Med*) ausscheiden; (*patient*, *employee*, *soldier*) entlassen ▶ *n* (*Med*) Ausfluss *m*
discipline [ˈdɪsɪplɪn] *n* Disziplin *f*
disc jockey *n* Discjockey *m*
disclose [dɪsˈkləuz] *vt* enthüllen, bekannt geben
disco [ˈdɪskəu] *n* = **discotheque**
discomfort [dɪsˈkʌmfət] *n* (*unease*) Unbehagen *nt*; (*physical*) Beschwerden *pl*
disconnect [dɪskəˈnɛkt] *vt* abtrennen; (*Elec*, *Radio*) abstellen; **I've been disconnected** (*Tel*) das Gespräch ist unterbrochen worden; (*supply*, *connection*) man hat mir das Telefon/den Strom/das Gas *etc* abgestellt
discontent [dɪskənˈtɛnt] *n* Unzufriedenheit *f*
discontented [dɪskənˈtɛntɪd] *adj* unzufrieden
discontinue [dɪskənˈtɪnjuː] *vt* einstellen; **"discontinued"** (*Comm*) „ausgelaufene Serie"
discount *n* [ˈdɪskaunt] Rabatt *m* ▶ *vt* [dɪsˈkaunt] nachlassen

discover [dɪsˈkʌvəʳ] *vt* entdecken

discovery [dɪsˈkʌvərɪ] *n* Entdeckung *f*

discredit [dɪsˈkrɛdɪt] *vt* in Misskredit bringen ▶ *n*: **to sb's ~** zu jds Schande

discreet [dɪsˈkriːt] *adj* diskret

discrepancy [dɪsˈkrɛpənsɪ] *n* Diskrepanz *f*

discriminate [dɪsˈkrɪmɪneɪt] *vi*: **to ~ between** unterscheiden zwischen *+dat*; **to ~ against** diskriminieren *+acc*

discrimination [dɪskrɪmɪˈneɪʃən] *n* Diskriminierung *f*

discus [ˈdɪskəs] *n* Diskus *m*

discuss [dɪsˈkʌs] *vt* besprechen; (*debate*) diskutieren

discussion [dɪsˈkʌʃən] *n* (*debate*) Diskussion *f*

disease [dɪˈziːz] *n* Krankheit *f*

disembark [dɪsɪmˈbɑːk] *vi* (*passengers*) von Bord gehen

disentangle [dɪsɪnˈtæŋgl] *vt* (*wool, wire*) entwirren

disgrace [dɪsˈgreɪs] *n* Schande *f* ▶ *vt* Schande bringen über *+acc*

disgraceful [dɪsˈgreɪsful] *adj* skandalös

disguise [dɪsˈgaɪz] *n* Verkleidung *f* ▶ *vt*: **to ~ (as)** (*person*) verkleiden (als); (*object*) tarnen (als); **in ~** (*person*) verkleidet

disgust [dɪsˈgʌst] *n* Abscheu *m* ▶ *vt* anwidern

disgusting [dɪsˈgʌstɪŋ] *adj* widerlich

dish [dɪʃ] *n* Schüssel *f*; (*recipe, food*) Gericht *nt*; **to do** *or* **wash the dishes** Geschirr spülen, abwaschen

dishcloth [ˈdɪʃklɔθ] *n* Spültuch *nt*, Spüllappen *m*

dishearten [dɪsˈhɑːtn] *vt* entmutigen

dishonest [dɪsˈɔnɪst] *adj* unehrlich

dishonour [dɪsˈɔnəʳ] *n* Schande *f*

dishtowel (*US*) *n* Geschirrtuch *nt*

dishwasher *n* (*machine*) (Geschirr) spülmaschine *f*

dishy [ˈdɪʃɪ] (BRIT *inf*) *adj* attraktiv

disillusion [dɪsɪˈluːʒən] *vt* desillusionieren; **to become disillusioned (with)** seine Illusionen (über *+acc*) verlieren

disinfect [dɪsɪnˈfɛkt] *vt* desinfizieren

disinfectant [dɪsɪnˈfɛktənt] *n* Desinfektionsmittel *nt*

disintegrate [dɪsˈɪntɪgreɪt] *vi* zerfallen; (*organization*) sich auflösen

disjointed [dɪsˈdʒɔɪntɪd] *adj* unzusammenhängend

disk [dɪsk] *n* Diskette *f*

disk drive *n* Diskettenlaufwerk *nt*

diskette [dɪsˈkɛt] (*US*) *n* = **disk**

dislike [dɪsˈlaɪk] *n* Abneigung *f* ▶ *vt* nicht mögen

dislocate [ˈdɪsləkeɪt] *vt* verrenken, ausrenken

dismal [ˈdɪzml] *adj* trostlos

dismantle [dɪsˈmæntl] *vt* (*machine*) demontieren

dismay [dɪsˈmeɪ] *n* Bestürzung *f*

dismiss [dɪsˈmɪs] *vt* entlassen

dismissal [dɪsˈmɪsl] *n* Entlassung *f*

disobedience [dɪsəˈbiːdɪəns] *n* Ungehorsam *m*

disobedient [dɪsəˈbiːdɪənt] *adj* ungehorsam

disobey [dɪsəˈbeɪ] *vt* nicht gehorchen *+dat*

disorder [dɪsˈɔːdəʳ] *n* Unordnung *f*; (*rioting*) Unruhen *pl*; (*Med*) (Funktions) störung *f*; **civil ~** öffentliche Unruhen *pl*

disorganized [dɪsˈɔːgənaɪzd] *adj* chaotisch

disparaging [dɪsˈpærɪdʒɪŋ] *adj* (*remarks*) geringschätzig

dispatch [dɪsˈpætʃ] *vt* senden, schicken

dispensable [dɪsˈpensəbl] *adj* entbehrlich

dispense [dɪsˈpɛns] *vt* (*medicines*) abgeben
▶ **dispense with** *vt fus* verzichten auf *+acc*

dispenser [dɪsˈpɛnsəʳ] *n* (*machine*) Automat *m*

disperse [dɪsˈpəːs] *vi* (*crowd*) sich auflösen *or* zerstreuen

display [dɪsˈpleɪ] *n* (*in shop*) Auslage *f*; (*exhibition*) Ausstellung *f*; (*of feeling*) Zeigen *nt*; (*Comput, Tech*) Anzeige *f* ▶ *vt* zeigen; (*ostentatiously*) zur Schau stellen

disposable [dɪsˈpəuzəbl] *adj* (*lighter*) Wegwerf-

disposable nappy (BRIT) *n* Wegwerfwindel *f*

disposal [dɪsˈpəuzl] *n* (*of goods for sale*) Loswerden *nt*; (*of rubbish*) Beseitigung *f*; **at one's ~** zur Verfügung; **to put sth at sb's ~** jdm etw zur Verfügung stellen

dispose [dɪsˈpəuz]: **to ~ of** *vt fus* (*body*) aus dem Weg schaffen; (*unwanted goods*) loswerden
dispute [dɪsˈpjuːt] *n* Streit *m*; (*also*: **industrial ~**) Auseinandersetzung *f* zwischen Arbeitgebern und Arbeitnehmern ▶ *vt* bestreiten
disqualification [dɪskwɔlɪfɪˈkeɪʃən] *n*
disqualify [dɪsˈkwɔlɪfaɪ] *vt* disqualifizieren
disregard [dɪsrɪˈgɑːd] *vt* nicht beachten
disreputable [dɪsˈrɛpjutəbl] *adj* (*person*) unehrenhaft
disrupt [dɪsˈrʌpt] *vt* (*plans*) durcheinanderbringen; (*conversation, proceedings*) unterbrechen
disruption [dɪsˈrʌpʃən] *n* Unterbrechung *f*; (*disturbance*) Störung *f*
dissatisfied [dɪsˈsætɪsfaɪd] *adj*: **~ (with)** unzufrieden (mit)
dissent [dɪˈsɛnt] *n* abweichende Meinungen *pl*
dissolve [dɪˈzɔlv] *vt* auflösen ▶ *vi* sich auflösen
dissuade [dɪˈsweɪd] *vt*: **to ~ sb (from sth)** jdn (von etw) abbringen
distance [ˈdɪstns] *n* Entfernung *f*; **in the ~** in der Ferne
distant [ˈdɪstnt] *adj* (*place*) weit entfernt, fern; (*time*) weit zurückliegend; (*relative*) entfernt; (*manner*) distanziert
distaste [dɪsˈteɪst] *n* Widerwille *m*
distil, (US) **distill** [dɪsˈtɪl] *vt* destillieren
distillery [dɪsˈtɪlərɪ] *n* Brennerei *f*
distinct [dɪsˈtɪŋkt] *adj* deutlich, klar; (*different*) verschieden
distinction [dɪsˈtɪŋkʃən] *n* Unterschied *m*; (*in exam*) Auszeichnung *f*
distinctive [dɪsˈtɪŋktɪv] *adj* unverwechselbar
distinctly [dɪsˈtɪŋktlɪ] *adv* deutlich
distinguish [dɪsˈtɪŋgwɪʃ] *vt* unterscheiden
distort [dɪsˈtɔːt] *vt* verzerren; (*argument*) verdrehen
distract [dɪsˈtrækt] *vt* ablenken
distraction [dɪsˈtrækʃən] *n* (*sth which distracts*) Ablenkung *f*; (*amusement*) Zerstreuung *f*
distress [dɪsˈtrɛs] *n* Verzweiflung *f* ▶ *vt* Kummer machen +*dat*; **distressed area** (BRIT) Notstandsgebiet *nt*
distress signal *n* Notsignal *nt*
distribute [dɪsˈtrɪbjuːt] *vt* verteilen; (*profits*) aufteilen
distribution [dɪstrɪˈbjuːʃən] *n* Vertrieb *m*; (*of profits*) Aufteilung *f*
distributor [dɪsˈtrɪbjutə^r] *n* (*Comm*) Vertreiber(in) *m(f)*; (*Aut, Tech*) Verteiler *m*
district [ˈdɪstrɪkt] *n* Gebiet *nt*; (*Admin*) (Verwaltungs)bezirk *m*
district attorney (US) *n* Bezirksstaatsanwalt *m*, Bezirksstaatsanwältin *f*
distrust [dɪsˈtrʌst] *n* Misstrauen *nt* ▶ *vt* misstrauen +*dat*
disturb [dɪsˈtəːb] *vt* stören; (*upset*) beunruhigen
disturbance [dɪsˈtəːbəns] *n* Störung *f*
disturbing [dɪsˈtəːbɪŋ] *adj* beunruhigend
ditch [dɪtʃ] *n* Graben *m* ▶ *vt* (*inf*: *partner*) sitzen lassen; (: *plan*) sausen lassen
ditto [ˈdɪtəu] *adv* dito, ebenfalls
dive [daɪv] *n* Sprung *m*; (*underwater*) Tauchen *nt*; (*pej*: *place*) Spelunke *f* (*inf*) ▶ *vi* (*under water*) tauchen
diver [ˈdaɪvə^r] *n* Taucher(in) *m(f)*
diverse [daɪˈvəːs] *adj* verschiedenartig
diversion [daɪˈvəːʃən] *n* (BRIT *Aut*) Umleitung *f*; (*distraction*) Ablenkung *f*
divert [daɪˈvəːt] *vt* (*sb's attention*) ablenken; (*re-route*) umleiten
divide [dɪˈvaɪd] *vt* trennen; (*share out*) verteilen ▶ *vi* sich teilen
dividend [ˈdɪvɪdɛnd] *n* Dividende *f*
divine [dɪˈvaɪn] *adj* göttlich
diving [ˈdaɪvɪŋ] *n* Tauchen *nt*; (*Sport*) Kunstspringen *nt*
diving board *n* Sprungbrett *nt*
division [dɪˈvɪʒən] *n* Teilung *f*; (*Math*) Division *f*; (*Comm*) Abteilung *f*; (*esp Football*) Liga *f*
divorce [dɪˈvɔːs] *n* Scheidung *f* ▶ *vt* sich scheiden lassen von
divorced [dɪˈvɔːst] *adj* geschieden
divorcee [dɪvɔːˈsiː] *n* Geschiedene(r) *f(m)*
DIY (BRIT) *n abbr* = **do-it-yourself**
dizzy [ˈdɪzɪ] *adj* schwind(e)lig
DJ *n abbr* = **disc jockey**
DNA *n abbr* (= *deoxyribonucleic acid*) DNS *f*

KEYWORD

do [du:] (*pt* **did**, *pp* **done**) *aux vb* **1** (*in negative constructions*): **I don't understand** ich verstehe nicht
2 (*to form questions*): **didn't you know?** wusstest du das nicht?; **what do you think?** was meinst du?
3 (*for emphasis*): **she does seem rather upset** sie scheint wirklich recht aufgeregt zu sein; **do sit down/help yourself** bitte nehmen Sie Platz/ bedienen Sie sich
4 (*to avoid repeating vb*): **she swims better than I do** sie schwimmt besser als ich; **she lives in Glasgow — so do I** sie wohnt in Glasgow — ich auch
5 (*in question tags*): **you like him, don't you?** du magst ihn, nicht wahr?
▸ *vt* **1** (*carry out, perform*) tun, machen; **what are you doing tonight?** was machen Sie heute Abend?; **to do one's teeth** sich *dat* die Zähne putzen; **to do one's hair/nails** sich die Haare/ Nägel machen; **I've got nothing to do** ich habe nichts zu tun
2 (*Aut etc*) fahren
▸ *vi* **1** (*act, behave*): **do as I do** mach es wie ich
2 (*get on, fare*): **he's doing well/badly at school** er ist gut/schlecht in der Schule; **how do you do?** guten Tag/ Morgen/Abend!
3 (*suit, be sufficient*) reichen; **to make do with** auskommen mit
▸ *n* (*inf: party etc*) Party *f*, Fete *f*
▸ **do away with** *vt fus* (*get rid of*) abschaffen
▸ **do up** *vt fus* (*laces, dress, buttons*) zumachen; (*renovate: room, house*) renovieren
▸ **do with** *vt fus* (*need*) brauchen; (*be connected with*): **it has to do with money** es hat mit Geld zu tun
▸ **do without** *vt fus* auskommen ohne

dock [dɔk] *n* Dock *nt*; (*Law*) Anklagebank *f*
docker [ˈdɔkəʳ] *n* Hafenarbeiter *m*
dockyard [ˈdɔkjɑːd] *n* Werft *f*
doctor [ˈdɔktəʳ] *n* Arzt *m*, Ärztin *f*; (*PhD etc*) Doktor *m*
document [ˈdɔkjumənt] *n* Dokument *nt*
documentary [dɔkjuˈmɛntərɪ] *n* Dokumentarfilm *m*
documentation [dɔkjumənˈteɪʃən] *n* Dokumentation *f*
doddering [ˈdɔdərɪŋ] *adj* (*shaky, unsteady*) zittrig
doddery [ˈdɔdərɪ] *adj* = **doddering**
Dodgems® [ˈdɔdʒəmz] (Brit) *npl* Autoskooter *pl*
dodgy [ˈdɔdʒɪ] (*inf*) *adj* (*person*) zweifelhaft; (*plan etc*) gewagt
dog [dɔg] *n* Hund *m*
dog food *n* Hundefutter *nt*
doggy bag [ˈdɔgɪ-] *n* *Tüte für Essensreste, die man nach Hause mitnehmen möchte*
do-it-yourself [ˈduːɪtjɔːˈsɛlf] *n* Heimwerken *nt*, Do-it-yourself *nt*
doll [dɔl] *n* (*toy, also US inf: woman*) Puppe *f*
dollar [ˈdɔləʳ] (*US etc*) *n* Dollar *m*
dolphin [ˈdɔlfɪn] *n* Delfin *m*
domain *n* Bereich *m*; (*empire*) Reich *nt*
dome [dəum] *n* Kuppel *f*
domestic [dəˈmɛstɪk] *adj* (*trade*) Innen-; (*duty, happiness*) häuslich
domesticated [dəˈmɛstɪkeɪtɪd] *adj* (*animal*) zahm; (*person*) häuslich
domestic flight *n* Inlandsflug *m*
domicile [ˈdɔmɪsaɪl] *n* Wohnsitz *m*
dominant [ˈdɔmɪnənt] *adj* dominierend
dominate [ˈdɔmɪneɪt] *vt* beherrschen
dominoes [ˈdɔmɪnəuz] *n* (*game*) Domino(spiel) *nt*
donate [dəˈneɪt] *vt*: **to ~ (to)** (*organization, cause*) spenden (für)
donation [dəˈneɪʃən] *n* (*contribution*) Spende *f*
done [dʌn] *pp of* **do**
doner (kebab) [ˈdɔnə-] *n* Döner (Kebab) *m*
dongle [ˈdɔŋgl] *n* (*Comput*) Dongle *m*
donkey [ˈdɔŋkɪ] *n* Esel *m*
donor [ˈdəunəʳ] *n* Spender(in) *m(f)*
don't [dəunt] = **do not**
doom [duːm] *n* Unheil *nt*
door [dɔːʳ] *n* Tür *f*
door bell *n* Türklingel *f*
door handle *n* Türklinke *f*
doormat [ˈdɔːmæt] *n* Fußmatte *f*
doorstep [ˈdɔːstɛp] *n* Türstufe *f*; **on the ~** vor der Haustür
dope [dəup] *n* (*inf*) Stoff *m*, Drogen *pl*
▸ *vt* dopen

dormitory [ˈdɔːmɪtrɪ] *n* Schlafsaal *m*; (*US*: *building*) Wohnheim *nt*
dosage [ˈdəusɪdʒ] *n* (*on label*) Dosierung *f*
dose [dəus] *n* Dosis *f*
dot [dɔt] *n* Punkt *m*; **on the ~** (auf die Minute) pünktlich
dote [dəut]: **~ on** *vt fus* abgöttisch lieben
dotted line [ˈdɔtɪd-] *n* punktierte Linie *f*
double [ˈdʌbl] *adj* doppelt ▶ *adv* (*cost*) doppelt so viel ▶ *n* Doppelgänger(in) *m*(*f*) ▶ *vt* verdoppeln
double bass *n* Kontrabass *m*
double bed *n* Doppelbett *nt*
double-click [ˈdʌblˈklɪk] *vt* (*Comput*) doppelklicken
double cream (Brit) *n* Sahne *f* mit hohem Fettgehalt
double-decker *n* Doppeldecker *m*
double glazing [-ˈgleɪzɪŋ] (Brit) *n* Doppelverglasung *f*
double-parking *n* Parken *nt* in der zweiten Reihe
double room *n* Doppelzimmer *nt*
doubles [ˈdʌblz] *n* (*Tennis*) Doppel *nt*
doubt [daut] *n* Zweifel *m* ▶ *vt* bezweifeln; **without (a) ~** ohne Zweifel; **I ~ it (very much)** das bezweifle ich (sehr), das möchte ich (stark) bezweifeln
doubtful [ˈdautful] *adj* zweifelhaft; **to be ~ about sth** an etw *dat* zweifeln
doubtless [ˈdautlɪs] *adv* ohne Zweifel, sicherlich
dough [dəu] *n* Teig *m*
doughnut, (*US*) **donut** [ˈdəunʌt] *n* ≈ Berliner (Pfannkuchen) *m*
dove [dʌv] *n* Taube *f*
down [daun] *n* Daunen *pl* ▶ *adv* hinunter, herunter; (*on the ground*) unten ▶ *prep* hinunter, herunter; (*movement along*) entlang ▶ *vt* (*inf*: *drink*) runterkippen; **~ there/here** da/hier unten
down-and-out *n* Penner(in) *m*(*f*) (*inf*)
downcast [ˈdaunkɑːst] *adj* niedergeschlagen
downfall [ˈdaunfɔːl] *n* (*of dictator etc*) Sturz *m*
downhearted [daunˈhɑːtɪd] *adj* entmutigt
downhill [ˈdaunˈhɪl] *adv* bergab; **to go ~** (*road*) bergab führen; (*fig*) auf dem absteigenden Ast sein
Downing Street *n siehe Info-Artikel*

Downing Street

Downing Street ist die Straße in London, die von *Whitehall* zum *St James's Park* führt und in der sich der offizielle Wohnsitz des Premierministers (Nr. 10) und des Finanzministers (Nr. 11) befindet. Im weiteren Sinne bezieht sich der Begriff *Downing Street* auf die britische Regierung.

download [ˈdaunləud] *vt* (*Comput*) herunterladen, downloaden
downloadable [daunˈləudəbl] *adj* (*Comput*) herunterladbar
down-market *adj* (*product*) für den Massenmarkt
down payment *n* Anzahlung *f*
downpour [ˈdaunpɔːʳ] *n* Wolkenbruch *m*
Downs (Brit) *npl*: **the ~** die Downs *pl*, *Hügellandschaft in Südengland*
downsize [ˈdaunsaɪz] *vi* (*Econ*: *company*) sich verkleinern
Down's syndrome *n* (*Med*) Downsyndrom *nt*
downstairs [ˈdaunˈstɛəz] *adv* unten; (*downwards*) nach unten
downstream [ˈdaunstriːm] *adv* flussabwärts
downtime [ˈdauntaɪm] *n* Ausfallzeit *f*
downtown [ˈdaunˈtaun] (*esp US*) *adv* im Zentrum, in der (Innen)stadt; (*go*) ins Zentrum, in die (Innen)stadt ▶ *adj*: **~ Chicago** das Zentrum von Chicago
down under *adv* (*be*) in Australien/Neuseeland; (*go*) nach Australien/Neuseeland
downward *adj*, *adv* nach unten; **a ~ trend** ein Abwärtstrend *m*
downwards [ˈdaunwədz] *adv* = **downward**
doze [dəuz] *vi* ein Nickerchen *nt* machen
dozen [ˈdʌzn] *n* Dutzend *nt*; **a ~ books** ein Dutzend Bücher; **dozens of** Dutzende von
drab [dræb] *adj* trist
draft [drɑːft] *n* Entwurf *m*; (*US*: *call-up*) Einberufung *f*

rag [dræg] *vt* schleppen ▶ *n* (*inf*): **to be a ~** (*boring*) langweilig sein; (*a nuisance*) lästig sein
▶ **drag on** *vi* sich hinziehen
ragon [ˈdrægn] *n* Drache *m*
ragonfly [ˈdrægənflaɪ] *n* Libelle *f*
rain [dreɪn] *n* (*in street*) Gully *m* ▶ *vt* entwässern; (*vegetables*) abgießen; (*glass, cup*) leeren ▶ *vi* ablaufen
rainpipe [ˈdreɪnpaɪp] *n* Abflussrohr *nt*
rama [ˈdrɑːmə] *n* Drama *nt*
ramatic [drəˈmætɪk] *adj* dramatisch
rank [dræŋk] *pt of* **drink**
rapes [dreɪps] (*US*) *npl* Vorhänge *pl*
rastic [ˈdræstɪk] *adj* drastisch
raught, (*US*) **draft** [drɑːft] *n* (Luft) zug *m*; **on ~** vom Fass
raughts [drɑːfts] (Brit) *n* Damespiel *nt*
raughty *adj* zugig
raw [drɔː] (*pt* **drew**, *pp* **drawn**) *vt* zeichnen; (*cart, gun, tooth, conclusion*) ziehen; (*admiration, attention*) erregen ▶ *vi* (*Sport*) unentschieden spielen ▶ *n* (*Sport*) Unentschieden *nt*; (*lottery*) Lotterie *f*
▶ **draw out** *vt* (*money*) abheben
▶ **draw up** *vi* (an)halten ▶ *vt* (*chair etc*) heranziehen; (*document*) aufsetzen
rawback [ˈdrɔːbæk] *n* Nachteil *m*
rawbridge [ˈdrɔːbrɪdʒ] *n* Zugbrücke *f*
rawer [drɔːʳ] *n* Schublade *f*
rawing [ˈdrɔːɪŋ] *n* Zeichnung *f*
rawing pin (Brit) *n* Reißzwecke *f*
rawn [drɔːn] *pp of* **draw**
read [drɛd] *n* Angst *f*, Furcht *f* ▶ *vt* große Angst haben vor +*dat*
readful [ˈdrɛdful] *adj* furchtbar
ream [driːm] (*pt, pp* **dreamed** *or* **dreamt**) *n* Traum *m* ▶ *vt, vi* träumen
reamt [drɛmt] *pt, pp of* **dream**
reary [ˈdrɪərɪ] *adj* langweilig; (*weather*) trüb
rench [drɛntʃ] *vt* durchnässen
ress [drɛs] *n* Kleid *nt*; (*no pl*: *clothing*) Kleidung *f* ▶ *vt* anziehen; (*wound*) verbinden; **to get dressed** sich anziehen
▶ **dress up** *vi* sich fein machen; (*in fancy dress*) sich verkleiden
ress circle (Brit) *n* (*Theat*) erster Rang *m*
resser [ˈdrɛsəʳ] *n* (Brit) Anrichte *f*; (*US*) Kommode *f*
dressing [ˈdrɛsɪŋ] *n* Verband *m*; (*Culin*) (Salat)soße *f*
dressing gown (Brit) *n* Morgenrock *m*
dressing room *n* (*Theat*) (Künstler) garderobe *f*
dressing table *n* Frisierkommode *f*
dress rehearsal *n* Generalprobe *f*
drew [druː] *pt of* **draw**
dried [draɪd] *adj* (*fruit*) getrocknet, Dörr-; **~ egg** Trockenei *nt*, Eipulver *nt*; **~ milk** Trockenmilch *f*, Milchpulver *nt*
drier [ˈdraɪəʳ] *n* = **dryer**
drift [drɪft] *n* (*of snow*) Schneewehe *f*; (*of questions*) Richtung *f* ▶ *vi* treiben; **I get** *or* **catch your ~** ich verstehe, worauf Sie hinauswollen
drill [drɪl] *n* Bohrer *m* ▶ *vt* bohren ▶ *vi*: **to ~ (for)** bohren (nach)
drink [drɪŋk] (*pt* **drank**, *pp* **drunk**) *n* Getränk *nt*; (*alcoholic*) Drink *m* ▶ *vt, vi* trinken
drink-driving [ˈdrɪŋkˈdraɪvɪŋ] *n* Trunkenheit *f* am Steuer
drinking water [ˈdrɪŋkɪŋ-] *n* Trinkwasser *nt*
drip [drɪp] *n* Tropfen *nt* ▶ *vi* tropfen
drip-dry [ˈdrɪpˈdraɪ] *adj* bügelfrei
dripping [ˈdrɪpɪŋ] *n* Bratenfett *nt* ▶ *adj*: **~ wet** triefnass
drive [draɪv] (*pt* **drove**, *pp* **driven**) *n* Fahrt *f*; (*also*: **driveway**) Einfahrt *f*; (: *longer*) Auffahrt *f*; (*Comput*: *also*: **disk ~**) Laufwerk *nt* ▶ *vt* fahren; (*Tech*) antreiben ▶ *vi* fahren; **to go for a ~** ein bisschen (raus)fahren
▶ **drive away, drive off** *vt* vertreiben
drive-in [ˈdraɪvɪn] *adj, n*: **~ (cinema)** Autokino *nt*
driven [ˈdrɪvn] *pp of* **drive**
driver [ˈdraɪvəʳ] *n* Fahrer(in) *m(f)*; (*Rail*) Führer(in) *m(f)*
driver's license (*US*) *n* Führerschein *m*
driving [ˈdraɪvɪŋ] *n* Fahren *nt*
driving lesson *n* Fahrstunde *f*
driving licence (Brit) *n* Führerschein *m*
driving school *n* Fahrschule *f*
driving test *n* Fahrprüfung *f*
drizzle [ˈdrɪzl] *n* Nieselregen *m*
drop [drɔp] *n* Tropfen *m*; (*lessening*) Rückgang *m* ▶ *vt* fallen lassen ▶ *vi* (herunter)fallen
▶ **drop by, drop in** (*inf*) *vi* vorbeikommen
▶ **drop off** *vi* einschlafen

▸ **drop out** *vi* (*withdraw*) ausscheiden; (*student*) sein Studium abbrechen
dropout [ˈdrɔpaut] *n* Aussteiger(in) *m(f)*
drought [draut] *n* Dürre *f*
drove [drəuv] *pt of* **drive**
drown [draun] *vt* ertränken ▸ *vi* ertrinken
drowsy [ˈdrauzɪ] *adj* schläfrig
drug [drʌg] *n* Medikament *nt*, Arzneimittel *nt*; (*narcotic*) Droge *f*, Rauschgift *nt* ▸ *vt* betäuben; **to be on drugs** drogensüchtig sein
drug addict *n* Rauschgiftsüchtige(r) *f(m)*
drug dealer *n* Drogenhändler(in) *m(f)*
drug-driving [drʌgˈdraɪvɪŋ] *n* Fahren *nt* unter Drogeneinfluss
druggist [ˈdrʌgɪst] (*US*) *n* Drogist(in) *m(f)*
drugstore [ˈdrʌgstɔːʳ] (*US*) *n* Drogerie *f*
drum [drʌm] *n* Trommel *f* ▪ **drums** *npl* (*kit*) Schlagzeug *nt*
drummer [ˈdrʌməʳ] *n* (*in band, pop group*) Schlagzeuger(in) *m(f)*
drunk [drʌŋk] *pp of* **drink** ▸ *adj* betrunken ▸ *n* (*also:* **drunkard**) Trinker(in) *m(f)*; **to get ~** sich betrinken
drunken [ˈdrʌŋkən] *adj* betrunken
dry [draɪ] *adj* trocken ▸ *vt, vi* trocknen; **to ~ the dishes** (das Geschirr) abtrocknen
▸ **dry up** *vi* austrocknen
dry-clean [ˈdraɪˈkliːn] *vt* chemisch reinigen
dry-cleaning [ˈdraɪˈkliːnɪŋ] *n* (*process*) chemische Reinigung *f*
dryer [ˈdraɪəʳ] *n* Wäschetrockner *m*; (*US: spin-dryer*) Wäscheschleuder *f*
DTP *n abbr* (= *desktop publishing*) DTP *nt*
dual [ˈdjuəl] *adj* doppelt
dual carriageway (Brit) *n* ≈ Schnellstraße *f*
dual nationality *n* doppelte Staatsangehörigkeit *f*
dubbed [dʌbd] *adj* synchronisiert
dubious [ˈdjuːbɪəs] *adj* zweifelhaft
duchess [ˈdʌtʃɪs] *n* Herzogin *f*
duck [dʌk] *n* Ente *f*
due [djuː] *adj* fällig; (*attention etc*) gebührend ▸ *adv*: **~ north** direkt nach Norden; **in ~ course** zu gegebener Zeit; **~ to** (*owing to*) wegen +*gen*, aufgrund +*gen*
dug [dʌg] *pt, pp of* **dig**
duke [djuːk] *n* Herzog *m*
dull [dʌl] *adj* trüb; (*event*) langweilig
duly [ˈdjuːlɪ] *adv* (*properly*) gebührend (*on time*) pünktlich
dumb [dʌm] *adj* (*pej: stupid*) dumm, doof (*inf*)
dumbbell [ˈdʌmbɛl] *n* Hantel *f*
dummy [ˈdʌmɪ] *n* (Schneider)puppe *f* (*mock-up*) Attrappe *f*; (Brit: *for baby*) Schnuller *m* ▸ *adj* (*firm*) fiktiv
dummy run *n* Probe *f*
dump [dʌmp] *n* (*also:* **rubbish ~**) Abfallhaufen *m*; (*inf: place*) Müllkippe ▸ *vt* (*get rid of*) abladen
dumpling [ˈdʌmplɪŋ] *n* Kloß *m*, Knödel *m*
dune [djuːn] *n* Düne *f*
dung [dʌŋ] *n* (*Agr*) Mist *m*; (*Zool*) Dung *m*
dungarees [dʌŋgəˈriːz] *npl* Latzhose
dungeon [ˈdʌndʒən] *n* Kerker *m*
duplex [ˈdjuːplɛks] (*US*) *n* Zweifamilienhaus *nt*; (*apartment*) zweistöckige Wohnung *f*
duplicate *n* [ˈdjuːplɪkət] (*also:* **~ copy**) Duplikat *nt* ▸ *adj* [ˈdjuːplɪkət] doppelt ▸ *vt* [ˈdjuːplɪkeɪt] kopieren; (*repeat*) wiederholen
durable [ˈdjuərəbl] *adj* haltbar
duration [djuəˈreɪʃən] *n* Dauer *f*
during [ˈdjuərɪŋ] *prep* während +*gen*
dusk [dʌsk] *n* (Abend)dämmerung *f*
dust [dʌst] *n* Staub *m* ▸ *vt* abstauben
dustbin [ˈdʌstbɪn] (Brit) *n* Mülltonne
duster [ˈdʌstəʳ] *n* Staubtuch *nt*
dust jacket *n* (Schutz)umschlag *m*
dustpan [ˈdʌstpæn] *n* Kehrschaufel *f*
dusty [ˈdʌstɪ] *adj* staubig
Dutch [dʌtʃ] *adj* holländisch ▸ *n* Holländisch *nt* ▪ **the Dutch** *npl* die Holländer *pl*
Dutchman [ˈdʌtʃmən] *n* (*irreg*) Holländer *m*
Dutchwoman [ˈdʌtʃwumən] *n* (*irreg*) Holländerin *f*
duty [ˈdjuːtɪ] *n* Pflicht *f*; (*tax*) Zoll *m*; **on/off ~** im/nicht im Dienst
duty-free [ˈdjuːtɪˈfriː] *adj* zollfrei; **~ shop** Dutyfreeshop *m*
duvet [ˈduːveɪ] (Brit) *n* Federbett *nt*
DVD *n abbr* (= *digital versatile or video disc*) DVD *f*
DVD player *n* DVD-Player *m*
DVD recorder *n* DVD-Rekorder *m*
dwelling [ˈdwɛlɪŋ] *n* Wohnhaus *nt*

windle [ˈdwɪndl] *vi* (*interest*) schwinden
ye [daɪ] *n* Farbstoff *m* ▶ *vt* färben
ynamic [daɪˈnæmɪk] *adj* dynamisch
ynamo [ˈdaɪnəməu] *n* Dynamo *m*
yslexia [dɪsˈlɛksɪə] *n* Legasthenie *f*
yslexic [dɪsˈlɛksɪk] *adj* legasthenisch
yspraxia [dɪsˈpræksɪə] *n* Dyspraxie *f*

E [iː] *abbr* (= *east*) O ▶ *n abbr* (*drug*: = *Ecstasy*) Ecstasy *nt*
each [iːtʃ] *adj, pron* jede(r, s); **~ other** sich, einander; **they have 2 books ~** sie haben je 2 Bücher; **they cost £5 ~** sie kosten 5 Pfund das Stück
eager [ˈiːgəʳ] *adj* eifrig; **to be ~ to do sth** etw unbedingt tun wollen
eagle [ˈiːgl] *n* Adler *m*
ear [ɪəʳ] *n* Ohr *nt*
earache [ˈɪəreɪk] *n* Ohrenschmerzen *pl*
eardrum [ˈɪədrʌm] *n* Trommelfell *nt*
earl [əːl] (Brit) *n* Graf *m*
early [ˈəːlɪ] *adv* früh; (*ahead of time*) zu früh ▶ *adj* früh; **in the ~** *or* **~ in the spring/19th century** Anfang des Frühjahrs/des 19. Jahrhunderts; **at your earliest convenience** so bald wie möglich
early retirement *n*: **to take ~** vorzeitig in den Ruhestand gehen
early warning system *n* Frühwarnsystem *nt*
earn [əːn] *vt* verdienen
earnest [ˈəːnɪst] *adj* ernsthaft; **to be in ~** es ernst meinen
earnings [ˈəːnɪŋz] *npl* Verdienst *m*; (*of company etc*) Ertrag *m*
earplugs *npl* Ohropax® *nt*
earring [ˈɪərɪŋ] *n* Ohrring *m*
earth [əːθ] *n* Erde *f* ▶ *vt* (Brit *Elec*) erden
earthenware [ˈəːθnwɛəʳ] *n* Tongeschirr *nt*
earthquake [ˈəːθkweɪk] *n* Erdbeben *nt*
earwig [ˈɪəwɪg] *n* Ohrwurm *m*
ease [iːz] *n* Leichtigkeit *f* ▶ *vt* (*problem*) vereinfachen; (*pain*) lindern

easily [ˈiːzɪlɪ] *adv* leicht; ungezwungen; bequem
east [iːst] *n* Osten *m* ▸ *adj* (*coast, Asia etc*) Ost- ▸ *adv* ostwärts, nach Osten; **the E~** der Osten
Easter [ˈiːstəʳ] *n* Ostern *nt*
Easter egg *n* Osterei *nt*
eastern [ˈiːstən] *adj* östlich; **E~ Europe** Osteuropa *nt*
Easter Sunday *n* Ostersonntag *m*
East Germany *n* (*formerly*) die DDR *f*
eastward [ˈiːstwəd], **eastwards** [ˈiːstwədz] *adv* nach Osten
easy [ˈiːzɪ] *adj* leicht; (*relaxed*) ungezwungen; (*comfortable*) bequem
easy-going [ˈiːzɪˈgəuɪŋ] *adj* gelassen
eat [iːt] (*pt* **ate**, *pp* **eaten**) *vt*, *vi* essen; (*animal*) fressen
▸ **eat away at** *vt fus* (*metal*) anfressen; (*savings*) angreifen
▸ **eat into** *vt fus* = **eat away at**
▸ **eat out** *vi* essen gehen
▸ **eat up** *vt* aufessen
eavesdrop [ˈiːvzdrɔp] *vi* lauschen; **to ~ on** belauschen *+acc*
e-bike [ˈiːbaɪk] *n* E-Bike *nt*, Elektrofahrrad *nt*
e-book [ˈiːbuk] *n* E-Book *nt*
eccentric [ɪkˈsɛntrɪk] *adj* exzentrisch
echo [ˈɛkəu] (*pl* **echoes**) *n* Echo *nt* ▸ *vi* widerhallen
e-cigarette [ˈiːsɪgərɛt] *n* E-Zigarette *f*
ecological [iːkəˈlɔdʒɪkəl] *adj* ökologisch; (*damage, disaster*) Umwelt-
ecology [ɪˈkɔlədʒɪ] *n* Ökologie *f*
economic [iːkəˈnɔmɪk] *adj* (*system, policy etc*) Wirtschafts-; (*profitable*) wirtschaftlich
economical [iːkəˈnɔmɪkl] *adj* wirtschaftlich; (*person*) sparsam
economics [iːkəˈnɔmɪks] *n* Wirtschaftswissenschaften *pl* ▸ *npl* Wirtschaftlichkeit *f*
economist [ɪˈkɔnəmɪst] *n* Wirtschaftswissenschaftler(in) *m(f)*
economize [ɪˈkɔnəmaɪz] *vi* sparen
economy [ɪˈkɔnəmɪ] *n* Wirtschaft *f*; (*financial prudence*) Sparsamkeit *f*
economy class *n* Touristenklasse *f*
ecstasy [ˈɛkstəsɪ] *n* Ekstase *f*; (*drug*) Ecstasy *nt*
eczema [ˈɛksɪmə] *n* Ekzem *nt*
edge [ɛdʒ] *n* Rand *m*; (*of knife etc*) Schneide *f*; **on ~** (*fig*) = **edgy**
edgy [ˈɛdʒɪ] *adj* nervös
edible [ˈɛdɪbl] *adj* essbar
Edinburgh [ˈɛdɪnbərə] *n* Edinburg(h) *nt*

EDINBURGH FESTIVAL

Das **Edinburgh Festival** findet jedes Jahr während drei Wochen im August statt und gehört zu den bedeutenden kulturellen Festivals Europas. Es ist nicht nur für sein offizielles Programm berühmt, sondern auch für das „inoffizielle", *The Fringe*, das eine große Auswahl an traditionellen wie auch entschieden avantgardistischen Theaterstücken, Konzerten, Komödien- und Tanzvorführungen bietet. Während des Festivals wird ebenfalls eine große Show von Militärmusik, das *Military Tattoo*, vorgeführt.

edit [ˈɛdɪt] *vt* (*text*) redigieren; (*film, broadcast*) schneiden; (*newspaper, magazine*) herausgeben; (*Comput*) editieren
edition [ɪˈdɪʃən] *n* Ausgabe *f*
editor [ˈɛdɪtəʳ] *n* Redakteur(in) *m(f)*; (*of newspaper, magazine*) Herausgeber(in) *m(f)*
editorial [ɛdɪˈtɔːrɪəl] *adj* (*staff*) Redaktions- ▸ *n* Leitartikel *m*
educate [ˈɛdjukeɪt] *vt* erziehen
educated [ˈɛdjukeɪtɪd] *adj* gebildet
education [ɛdjuˈkeɪʃən] *n* Erziehung *f*; (*schooling*) Ausbildung *f*; (*knowledge, culture*) Bildung *f*
educational [ɛdjuˈkeɪʃənl] *adj* pädagogisch; (*experience*) lehrreich
eel [iːl] *n* Aal *m*
eerie [ˈɪərɪ] *adj* unheimlich
effect [ɪˈfɛkt] *n* Wirkung *f*; **to put into ~** in Kraft setzen
effective [ɪˈfɛktɪv] *adj* effektiv, wirksam
effeminate [ɪˈfɛmɪnɪt] *adj* feminin, effeminiert
efficiency [ɪˈfɪʃənsɪ] *n* Fähigkeit *f*, Tüchtigkeit *f*; Rationalität *f*; Leistungsfähigkeit *f*
efficient [ɪˈfɪʃənt] *adj* fähig, tüchtig; (*organization*) rationell; (*machine*) leistungsfähig

effort [ˈɛfət] *n* Anstrengung *f*; (*attempt*) Versuch *m*; **to make an ~ to do sth** sich bemühen, etw zu tun

effortless [ˈɛfətlɪs] *adj* mühelos

e.g. *adv abbr* (= *exempli gratia*) z. B.

egg [ɛg] *n* Ei *nt*

egg cup *n* Eierbecher *m*

eggplant [ˈɛgplɑːnt] *n* (*esp US*) Aubergine *f*

eggshell [ˈɛgʃɛl] *n* Eierschale *f*

ego [ˈiːgəu] *n* (*self-esteem*) Selbstbewusstsein *nt*

egoist [ˈɛgəuɪst] *n* Egoist(in) *m(f)*

egotist [ˈɛgəutɪst] *n* Egotist(in) *m(f)*

Egypt [ˈiːdʒɪpt] *n* Ägypten *nt*

Egyptian [ɪˈdʒɪpʃən] *adj* ägyptisch ▸ *n* Ägypter(in) *m(f)*

eiderdown [ˈaɪdədaun] *n* Daunendecke *f*

eight [eɪt] *num* acht

eighteen [eɪˈtiːn] *num* achtzehn

eighteenth [eɪˈtiːnθ] *num* achtzehnte(r, s)

eighth [eɪtθ] *num* achte(r, s) ▸ *n* Achtel *nt*

eightieth [ˈeɪtɪəθ] *adj* achtzigste(r, s)

eighty [ˈeɪtɪ] *num* achtzig

Eire [ˈɛərə] *n* (Republik *f*) Irland *nt*

either [ˈaɪðəʳ] *adj* (*both, each*) beide *pl* ▸ *pron*: **~ (of them)** eine(r, s) (davon) ▸ *adv* auch nicht ▸ *conj*: **~ yes or no** entweder ja oder nein; **on ~ side** (*on both sides*) auf beiden Seiten; **no, I don't ~** nein, ich auch nicht

eject [ɪˈdʒɛkt] *vt* ausstoßen; (*tenant, gatecrasher*) hinauswerfen

elaborate *adj* [ɪˈlæbərɪt] kompliziert; (*plan*) ausgefeilt ▸ *vi* [ɪˈlæbəreɪt]; **to ~ on** näher ausführen

elastic [ɪˈlæstɪk] *adj* elastisch

elastic band (Brit) *n* Gummiband *nt*

elbow [ˈɛlbəu] *n* Ell(en)bogen *m*

elder [ˈɛldəʳ] *adj* älter ▸ *n* (*Bot*) Holunder *m*; (*older person*: *gen pl*) Ältere(r) *f(m)*

elderly [ˈɛldəlɪ] *adj* ältere(r, s); **~ people** ältere Leute *pl*

eldest [ˈɛldɪst] *adj* älteste(r, s)

elect [ɪˈlɛkt] *vt* wählen

election [ɪˈlɛkʃən] *n* Wahl *f*

election campaign *n* Wahlkampf *m*

electioneering [ɪlɛkʃəˈnɪərɪŋ] *n* Wahlkampf *m*

electorate [ɪˈlɛktərɪt] *n* Wähler *pl*

electric [ɪˈlɛktrɪk] *adj* elektrisch

electrical [ɪˈlɛktrɪkl] *adj* elektrisch; (*appliance*) Elektro-

electric blanket *n* Heizdecke *f*

electric cooker *n* Elektroherd *m*

electric current *n* elektrischer Strom *m*

electrician [ɪlɛkˈtrɪʃən] *n* Elektriker(in) *m(f)*

electricity [ɪlɛkˈtrɪsɪtɪ] *n* Elektrizität *f*

electric shock *n* Stromschlag *m*

electrocute [ɪˈlɛktrəkjuːt] *vt* durch einen Stromschlag töten

electronic [ɪlɛkˈtrɔnɪk] *adj* elektronisch

elegance [ˈɛlɪgəns] *n* Eleganz *f*

elegant [ˈɛlɪgənt] *adj* elegant

element [ˈɛlɪmənt] *n* Element *nt*

elementary [ɛlɪˈmɛntərɪ] *adj* grundlegend; **~ school** (*US*) Grundschule *f*; **~ education** Elementarunterricht *m*; **~ maths/French** Grundbegriffe *pl* der Mathematik/des Französischen

elephant [ˈɛlɪfənt] *n* Elefant *m*

elevator [ˈɛlɪveɪtəʳ] *n* (*US*) Fahrstuhl *m*

eleven [ɪˈlɛvn] *num* elf

eleventh [ɪˈlɛvnθ] *num* elfte(r, s)

eligible [ˈɛlɪdʒəbl] *adj* (*marriage partner*) begehrt; **to be ~ for sth** für etw infrage kommen; **to be ~ for a pension** pensionsberechtigt sein

eliminate [ɪˈlɪmɪneɪt] *vt* beseitigen; (*candidate etc*) ausschließen

elimination [ɪlɪmɪˈneɪʃən] *n* Beseitigung *f*; Ausschluss *m*; Ausscheiden *nt*

elm [ɛlm] *n* Ulme *f*

elope [ɪˈləup] *vi* weglaufen

eloquent [ˈɛləkwənt] *adj* wortgewandt

El Salvador [ɛlˈsælvədɔːʳ] *n* El Salvador *nt*

else [ɛls] *adv*: **something ~** etwas anderes; **somewhere ~** woanders, anderswo; **is there anything ~ I can do?** kann ich sonst noch etwas tun?; **everyone ~** alle anderen; **nobody ~ spoke** niemand anders sagte etwas, sonst sagte niemand etwas

elsewhere [ɛlsˈwɛəʳ] *adv* woanders, anderswo; (*go*) woandershin, anderswohin

ELT *n abbr* (*Scol*: = *English Language Teaching*) *Englisch als Unterrichtsfach*

email [ˈiːmeɪl] *n abbr* (= *electronic mail*) E-Mail *f* ▸ *vt*: **to ~ sb (sth)** jdm (etw) mailen

email address *n* E-Mail-Adresse *f*
embankment [ɪmˈbæŋkmənt] *n* Böschung *f*; (*of railway*) Bahndamm *m*
embargo [ɪmˈbɑːgəu] (*pl* **embargoes**) *n* Embargo *nt*
embark [ɪmˈbɑːk] *vi*: **to ~ (on)** sich einschiffen (auf)
embarrass [ɪmˈbærəs] *vt* in Verlegenheit bringen
embarrassed [ɪmˈbærəst] *adj* verlegen
embarrassing [ɪmˈbærəsɪŋ] *adj* peinlich
embassy [ˈɛmbəsɪ] *n* Botschaft *f*
embrace [ɪmˈbreɪs] *vt* umarmen ▶ *n* Umarmung *f*
embroider [ɪmˈbrɔɪdəʳ] *vt* (*cloth*) besticken
embroidery [ɪmˈbrɔɪdərɪ] *n* Stickerei *f*
embryo [ˈɛmbrɪəu] *n* Embryo *m*
emerald [ˈɛmərəld] *n* Smaragd *m*
emerge [ɪˈməːdʒ] *vi*: **to ~ (from)** auftauchen (aus); **it emerges that** (BRIT) es stellt sich heraus, dass
emergency [ɪˈməːdʒənsɪ] *n* Notfall *m* ▶ *cpd* Not-
emergency exit *n* Notausgang *m*
emergency landing *n* Notlandung *f*
emergency services *npl*: **the ~** der Notdienst
emergency stop (BRIT) *n* Vollbremsung *f*
emigrate [ˈɛmɪgreɪt] *vi* auswandern
emit [ɪˈmɪt] *vt* abgeben; (*light, heat*) ausstrahlen
emoji [ɪˈməudʒɪ] *n* Emoji *nt*
emoticon [ɪˈməutɪkən] *n* (*Comput*) Emoticon *nt*
emotion [ɪˈməuʃən] *n* Gefühl *nt*
emotional [ɪˈməuʃənl] *adj* emotional; (*scene*) ergreifend
emperor [ˈɛmpərəʳ] *n* Kaiser *m*
emphasis [ˈɛmfəsɪs] (*pl* **emphases**) *n* Betonung *f*
emphasize [ˈɛmfəsaɪz] *vt* betonen
emphatic [ɛmˈfætɪk] *adj* nachdrücklich
empire [ˈɛmpaɪəʳ] *n* Reich *nt*
employ [ɪmˈplɔɪ] *vt* beschäftigen; (*tool, weapon*) verwenden; **he's employed in a bank** er ist bei einer Bank angestellt
employee [ɪmplɔɪˈiː] *n* Angestellte(r) *f(m)*
employer [ɪmˈplɔɪəʳ] *n* Arbeitgeber(in) *m(f)*
employment [ɪmˈplɔɪmənt] *n* Arbeit *f*; **to find ~** Arbeit *or* eine (An)stellung finden
employment agency *n* Stellenvermittlung *f*
empress [ˈɛmprɪs] *n* Kaiserin *f*
empty [ˈɛmptɪ] *adj* leer ▶ *vt* leeren; (*place, house etc*) räumen
enable [ɪˈneɪbl] *vt*: **to ~ sb to do sth** (*permit*) es jdm erlauben, etw zu tun; (*make possible*) es jdm ermöglichen, etw zu tun
enamel [ɪˈnæməl] *n* Email *nt*; (*of tooth*) Zahnschmelz *m*
enchanting [ɪnˈtʃɑːntɪŋ] *adj* bezaubernd
enclose [ɪnˈkləuz] *vt* umgeben; (*letter etc*): **to ~ (with)** beilegen (*+dat*)
enclosure [ɪnˈkləuʒəʳ] *n* eingefriedeter Bereich *m*
encore [ɔŋˈkɔːʳ] *n* Zugabe *f*
encounter [ɪnˈkauntəʳ] *n* Begegnung ▶ *vt* begegnen *+dat*; (*problem*) stoßen auf *+acc*
encourage [ɪnˈkʌrɪdʒ] *vt* (*activity, attitude*) unterstützen
encouragement [ɪnˈkʌrɪdʒmənt] *n* Ermutigung *f*
encyclopaedia, encyclopedia [ɛnsaɪkləuˈpiːdɪə] *n* Lexikon *nt*, Enzyklopädie *f*
end [ɛnd] *n* Ende *nt*; (*of film, book*) Schluss *m*, Ende *nt*; (*aim*) Zweck *m* ▶ *vt* (*also*: **bring to an ~, put an ~ to**) beenden ▶ *vi* enden; **to come to an ~** zu Ende gehen; **in the ~** schließlich ▶ **end up** *vi*: **to ~ up in** (*place*) landen in *+dat*
endanger [ɪnˈdeɪndʒəʳ] *vt* gefährden; **an endangered species** eine vom Aussterben bedrohte Art
endeavour, (*US*) **endeavor** [ɪnˈdɛvəʳ] *n* Bemühung *f* ▶ *vi*: **to ~ to do sth** (*attempt*) sich anstrengen *or* bemühen etw zu tun
ending [ˈɛndɪŋ] *n* Ende *nt*, Schluss *m*; (*Ling*) Endung *f*
endless [ˈɛndlɪs] *adj* endlos; (*patience, resources, possibilities*) unbegrenzt
endurance [ɪnˈdjuərəns] *n* Durchhaltevermögen *nt*
endure [ɪnˈdjuəʳ] *vt* ertragen ▶ *vi* Bestand haben

enemy [ˈɛnəmɪ] *adj* feindlich ▸ *n* Feind(in) *m(f)*
energetic [ɛnəˈdʒɛtɪk] *adj* aktiv
energy [ˈɛnədʒɪ] *n* Energie *f*
energy drink *n* Energiegetränk *nt*, Energydrink *m*
enforce [ɪnˈfɔːs] *vt* (*law, rule, decision*) Geltung verschaffen *+dat*
engage [ɪnˈgeɪdʒ] *vt* in Anspruch nehmen; (*employ*) einstellen
engaged [ɪnˈgeɪdʒd] *adj* verlobt; (BRIT: *busy, in use*) besetzt; **to get ~** sich verloben
engaged tone (BRIT) *n* Besetztzeichen *nt*
engagement [ɪnˈgeɪdʒmənt] *n* (*to marry*) Verlobung *f*
engagement ring *n* Verlobungsring *m*
engaging [ɪnˈgeɪdʒɪŋ] *adj* einnehmend
engine [ˈɛndʒɪn] *n* Motor *m*; (*Rail*) Lok(omotive) *f*
engineer [ɛndʒɪˈnɪəʳ] *n* Ingenieur(in) *m(f)*; (*US Rail*) Lok(omotiv)führer(in) *m(f)*
engineering [ɛndʒɪˈnɪərɪŋ] *n* Technik *f*; (*design, construction*) Konstruktion *f*
engine failure *n* (*Aut*) Motorschaden *m*
engine trouble *n* Maschinenschaden *m*
England [ˈɪŋglənd] *n* England *nt*
English [ˈɪŋglɪʃ] *adj* englisch ▸ *n* Englisch *nt* ▪ **the English** *npl* die Engländer *pl*
English Channel *n*: **the ~** der Ärmelkanal
Englishman [ˈɪŋglɪʃmən] *n* (*irreg*) Engländer *m*
Englishwoman [ˈɪŋglɪʃwumən] *n* (*irreg*) Engländerin *f*
engrave [ɪnˈgreɪv] *vt* (*name etc*) eingravieren
engraving [ɪnˈgreɪvɪŋ] *n* Stich *m*
engrossed [ɪnˈgrəust] *adj*: **~ in** vertieft in *+acc*
enigma [ɪˈnɪgmə] *n* Rätsel *nt*
enjoy [ɪnˈdʒɔɪ] *vt* genießen; **to ~ o.s.** sich amüsieren; **I ~ dancing** ich tanze gerne
enjoyable [ɪnˈdʒɔɪəbl] *adj* nett, angenehm
enjoyment [ɪnˈdʒɔɪmənt] *n* Vergnügen *nt*; (*activity*) Freude *f*
enlarge [ɪnˈlɑːdʒ] *vt* vergrößern; (*scope*) erweitern
enlargement [ɪnˈlɑːdʒmənt] *n* Vergrößerung *f*
enormous [ɪˈnɔːməs] *adj* ungeheuer; (*pleasure, success etc*) riesig
enough [ɪˈnʌf] *adj* genug, genügend ▸ *adv*: **big ~** groß genug; **~ to eat** genug zu essen; **I've had ~!** jetzt reichts mir aber!; **~!** es reicht!; **that's ~, thanks** danke, das reicht *or* ist genug
enquire [ɪnˈkwaɪəʳ] *vt, vi* = **inquire**
enquiry [ɪnˈkwaɪərɪ] = **inquiry**
enrol, (*US*) **enroll** [ɪnˈrəul] *vt* anmelden; (*at university*) einschreiben, immatrikulieren ▸ *vi* sich anmelden; sich einschreiben, sich immatrikulieren
enrolment, (*US*) **enrollment** [ɪnˈrəulmənt] *n* Anmeldung *f*; Einschreibung *f*
en suite [ɔnˈswiːt] *adj*, *n*: **room with ~ bathroom** Zimmer *nt* mit eigenem Bad
ensure [ɪnˈʃuəʳ] *vt*: **to ~ that** sicherstellen, dass
enter [ˈɛntəʳ] *vt* betreten; (*race, contest*) sich beteiligen an *+dat*; (*write down*) eintragen; (*Comput*: *data*) eingeben ▸ *vi* (*come in*) hereinkommen; (*go in*) hineingehen
enterprise [ˈɛntəpraɪz] *n* Unternehmen *nt*
entertain [ɛntəˈteɪn] *vt* unterhalten; (*invite*) einladen
entertaining [ɛntəˈteɪnɪŋ] *adj* amüsant
entertainment [ɛntəˈteɪnmənt] *n* Unterhaltung *f*
enthusiasm [ɪnˈθuːzɪæzəm] *n* Begeisterung *f*
enthusiastic [ɪnθuːzɪˈæstɪk] *adj* begeistert
entice [ɪnˈtaɪs] *vt* locken; (*tempt*) verleiten
entire [ɪnˈtaɪəʳ] *adj* ganz
entitle [ɪnˈtaɪtl] *vt*: **to ~ sb to sth** jdn zu etw berechtigen
entitled [ɪnˈtaɪtld] *adj*: **a book/film** *etc* **~ ...** ein Buch/Film *etc* mit dem Titel ...
entrance *n* [ˈɛntrns] Eingang *m*; (*arrival*) Ankunft *f*; (*on stage*) Auftritt *m* ▸ *vt* [ɪnˈtrɑːns] bezaubern
entrance examination *n* Aufnahmeprüfung *f*
entrance fee *n* Eintrittsgeld *nt*

entrust [ɪnˈtrʌst] *vt*: **to ~ sb with sth** (*task*) jdn mit etw betrauen
entry [ˈɛntrɪ] *n* Eingang *m*; (*in register, account book, reference book*) Eintrag *m*; (*arrival*) Eintritt *m*; (*to country*) Einreise *f*; **"no ~"** „Zutritt verboten"; (*Aut*) „Einfahrt verboten"
entry phone (BRIT) *n* Türsprechanlage *f*
E-number *n* (*food additive*) E-Nummer *f*
envelope [ˈɛnvələup] *n* Umschlag *m*
enviable [ˈɛnvɪəbl] *adj* beneidenswert
envious [ˈɛnvɪəs] *adj* neidisch
environment [ɪnˈvaɪərnmənt] *n* Umwelt *f*
environmental [ɪnvaɪərnˈmɛntl] *adj* (*problems, pollution etc*) Umwelt-
environmentalist [ɪnvaɪərnˈmɛntlɪst] *n* Umweltschützer(in) *m(f)*
envy [ˈɛnvɪ] *n* Neid *m* ▶ *vt* beneiden
epic [ˈɛpɪk] *n* Epos *nt*
epidemic [ɛpɪˈdɛmɪk] *n* Epidemie *f*
epilepsy [ˈɛpɪlɛpsɪ] *n* Epilepsie *f*
epileptic [ɛpɪˈlɛptɪk] *adj* epileptisch
episode [ˈɛpɪsəud] *n* Episode *f*; (*TV, Radio*) Folge *f*
epoch [ˈiːpɔk] *n* Epoche *f*
equal [ˈiːkwl] *adj* gleich ▶ *n* Gleichgestellte(r) *f(m)* ▶ *vt* gleichkommen *+dat*; (*number*) gleich sein *+dat*; **two times two equals four** zwei mal zwei ist (gleich) vier
equality [iːˈkwɔlɪtɪ] *n* Gleichheit *f*
equalize [ˈiːkwəlaɪz] *vi* (*Sport*) ausgleichen
equalizer [ˈiːkwəlaɪzəʳ] *n* (*Sport*) Ausgleichstreffer *m*
equally [ˈiːkwəlɪ] *adv* gleichmäßig; (*good, bad etc*) gleich
equation [ɪˈkweɪʒən] *n* Gleichung *f*
equator [ɪˈkweɪtəʳ] *n* Äquator *m*
equilibrium [iːkwɪˈlɪbrɪəm] *n* Gleichgewicht *nt*
equip [ɪˈkwɪp] *vt*: **to ~ (with)** (*person, army*) ausrüsten (mit); (*room, car etc*) ausstatten (mit)
equipment [ɪˈkwɪpmənt] *n* Ausrüstung *f*
equivalent [ɪˈkwɪvələnt] *adj* gleich, gleichwertig ▶ *n* Gegenstück *nt*
era [ˈɪərə] *n* Ära *f*, Epoche *f*
erase [ɪˈreɪz] *vt* (*tape, Comput*) löschen; (*writing*) ausradieren
eraser [ɪˈreɪzəʳ] *n* Radiergummi *m*
e-reader [ˈiːˈriːdəʳ] *n* E-Book-Lesegerät *nt*
erect [ɪˈrɛkt] *adj* aufrecht ▶ *vt* bauen; (*assemble*) aufstellen
erection [ɪˈrɛkʃən] *n* (*of statue*) Errichten *nt*; (*Physiol*) Erektion *f*
erode [ɪˈrəud] *vt* erodieren, auswaschen; (*confidence, power*) untergraben
erosion [ɪˈrəuʒən] *n* Erosion *f*, Auswaschen *nt*; Untergraben *nt*
erotic [ɪˈrɔtɪk] *adj* erotisch
errand [ˈɛrənd] *n* Besorgung *f*
erratic [ɪˈrætɪk] *adj* unberechenbar; (*bus link etc*) unregelmäßig; (*performance*) unbeständig
error [ˈɛrəʳ] *n* Fehler *m*; **in ~** irrtümlicherweise
error message *n* Fehlermeldung *f*
erupt [ɪˈrʌpt] *vi* ausbrechen
escalator [ˈɛskəleɪtəʳ] *n* Rolltreppe *f*
escape [ɪsˈkeɪp] *n* Flucht *f* ▶ *vi* entkommen; (*from prison*) ausbrechen; (*liquid*) ausfließen; (*gas*) ausströmen ▶ *vt* (*pursuers etc*) entkommen *+dat*; (*punishment etc*) entgehen *+dat*; **to ~ from** flüchten aus; (*prison*) ausbrechen aus; (*person*) entkommen *+dat*
escort *n* [ˈɛskɔːt] Eskorte *f*; (*companion*) Begleiter(in) *m(f)* ▶ *vt* [ɪsˈkɔːt] begleiten
especially [ɪsˈpɛʃlɪ] *adv* besonders
espionage [ˈɛspɪənɑːʒ] *n* Spionage *f*
Esquire [ɪsˈkwaɪəʳ] *n* (*abbr Esq.*): **J. Brown, ~** Herrn J. Brown
essay [ˈɛseɪ] *n* Aufsatz *m*; (*Liter*) Essay *m or nt*
essential [ɪˈsɛnʃl] *adj* notwendig; (*basic*) wesentlich ▶ *n* Notwendigste(s) *nt*; Wesentliche(s) *nt*
essentially [ɪˈsɛnʃəlɪ] *adv* im Grunde genommen
establish [ɪsˈtæblɪʃ] *vt* gründen; (*facts*) feststellen; (*proof*) erstellen; (*relations, contact*) aufnehmen; (*reputation*) sich *dat* verschaffen
establishment [ɪsˈtæblɪʃmənt] *n* Gründung *f*; Feststellung *f*; Erstellung *f*; Aufnahme *f*; (*of reputation*) Begründung *f*; (*shop etc*) Unternehmen *nt*
estate [ɪsˈteɪt] *n* Gut *nt*; (BRIT: *also*: **housing ~**) Siedlung *f*; (*Law*) Nachlass *m*

estate agent (BRIT) *n* Immobilienmakler(in) *m(f)*
estate car (BRIT) *n* Kombiwagen *m*
estimate *n* [ˈɛstɪmət] Schätzung *f*; (*Comm*) (Kosten)voranschlag *m* ▶ *vt* [ˈɛstɪmeɪt] schätzen
Estonia [ɛsˈtəunɪə] *n* Estland *nt*
Estonian [ɛsˈtəunɪən] *adj* estnisch ▶ *n* Este *m*, Estin *f*; (*Ling*) Estnisch *nt*
estuary [ˈɛstjuərɪ] *n* Mündung *f*
eternal [ɪˈtəːnl] *adj* ewig
eternity [ɪˈtəːnɪtɪ] *n* Ewigkeit *f*
ethical [ˈɛθɪkl] *adj* ethisch
ethics [ˈɛθɪks] *n* Ethik *f*
Ethiopia [iːθɪˈəupɪə] *n* Äthiopien *nt*
ethnic [ˈɛθnɪk] *adj* ethnisch; (*music*) folkloristisch
ethnic minority *n* ethnische Minderheit *f*
e-ticket [ˈiːtɪkɪt] *n abbr* (= *electronic ticket*) E-Ticket *nt*
EU *n abbr* (= *European Union*) EU *f*
euphemism [ˈjuːfəmɪzəm] *n* Euphemismus *m*
euro [ˈjuərəu] *n* (*Fin*) Euro *m*
Europe [ˈjuərəp] *n* Europa *nt*
European [juərəˈpiːən] *adj* europäisch ▶ *n* Europäer(in) *m(f)*
Euro-sceptic [ˈjuərəuskɛptɪk] *n* Euroskeptiker(in) *m(f)*
evacuate [ɪˈvækjueɪt] *vt* evakuieren; (*place*) räumen
evade [ɪˈveɪd] *vt* (*person, question*) ausweichen +*dat*; (*duty, responsibility*) sich entziehen +*dat*
evaluate [ɪˈvæljueɪt] *vt* bewerten
evaporate [ɪˈvæpəreɪt] *vi* verdampfen; (*feeling, attitude*) dahinschwinden
evaporated milk [ɪˈvæpəreɪtɪd-] *n* Kondensmilch *f*
even [ˈiːvn] *adj* (*level*) eben; (*smooth*) glatt; (*equal*) gleich; (*number*) gerade ▶ *adv* sogar, selbst; **~ if, ~ though** selbst wenn; **not ~** nicht einmal; **~ he was there** sogar er war da ▶ **even out** *vi* sich ausgleichen
evening [ˈiːvnɪŋ] *n* Abend *m*; **in the ~** abends, am Abend; **this ~** heute Abend
evening class *n* Abendkurs *m*
evening dress *n* (*no pl*) Abendkleidung *f*; (*woman's*) Abendkleid *nt*
evenly [ˈiːvnlɪ] *adv* gleichmäßig
event [ɪˈvɛnt] *n* Ereignis *nt*; (*Sport*) Wettkampf *m*; **in the ~ of** im Falle +*gen*
eventful [ɪˈvɛntful] *adj* ereignisreich
eventual [ɪˈvɛntʃuəl] *adj* (*goal*) letztlich
eventually [ɪˈvɛntʃuəlɪ] *adv* endlich; (*in time*) schließlich
ever [ˈɛvəʳ] *adv* immer; (*at any time*) je(mals); **the best ~** der/die/das Allerbeste; **have you ~ seen it?** haben Sie es schon einmal gesehen?; **for ~** für immer; **~ so pretty** unheimlich hübsch (*inf*); **thank you ~ so much** ganz herzlichen Dank
every [ˈɛvrɪ] *adj* jede(r, s); **every day** jeden Tag; **every other/third day** alle zwei/drei Tage
everybody [ˈɛvrɪbɔdɪ] *pron* jeder, alle *pl*
everyday [ˈɛvrɪdeɪ] *adj* (*usual, common*) alltäglich; (*life, language*) Alltags-
everyone [ˈɛvrɪwʌn] *pron* = **everybody**
everything [ˈɛvrɪθɪŋ] *pron* alles
everywhere [ˈɛvrɪwɛəʳ] *adv* überall; (*wherever*) wo auch *or* immer
evidence [ˈɛvɪdns] *n* Beweis *m*; (*of witness*) Aussage *f*; (*sign, indication*) Spur *f*
evident [ˈɛvɪdnt] *adj* offensichtlich
evil [ˈiːvl] *adj* böse ▶ *n* Böse(s) *nt*; (*unpleasant situation or activity*) Übel *nt*
evolution [iːvəˈluːʃən] *n* Evolution *f*; (*development*) Entwicklung *f*
evolve [ɪˈvɔlv] *vi* sich entwickeln
ex- [ɛks] *pref* Ex-, frühere(r, s)
exact [ɪgˈzækt] *adj* genau
exactly [ɪgˈzæktlɪ] *adv* genau; **not ~** (*hardly*) nicht gerade
exaggerate [ɪgˈzædʒəreɪt] *vt, vi* übertreiben
exaggerated [ɪgˈzædʒəreɪtɪd] *adj* übertrieben
exaggeration [ɪgzædʒəˈreɪʃən] *n* Übertreibung *f*
exam [ɪgˈzæm] *n abbr* = **examination**
examination [ɪgzæmɪˈneɪʃən] *n* Untersuchung *f*; Prüfung *f*
examine [ɪgˈzæmɪn] *vt* untersuchen; (*accounts, candidate*) prüfen
examiner [ɪgˈzæmɪnəʳ] *n* Prüfer(in) *m(f)*
example [ɪgˈzɑːmpl] *n* Beispiel *nt*; **for ~** zum Beispiel

excavation [ɛkskəˈveɪʃən] *n* Ausgrabung *f*
exceed [ɪkˈsi:d] *vt* (*hopes*) übertreffen; (*limit, budget, powers*) überschreiten
exceedingly [ɪkˈsi:dɪŋlɪ] *adv* äußerst
excel [ɪkˈsɛl] *vt* übertreffen ▸ *vi*: **to ~ (in** *or* **at)** sich auszeichnen (in +*dat*); **to ~ o.s.** (BRIT) sich selbst übertreffen
excellent [ˈɛksələnt] *adj* ausgezeichnet
except [ɪkˈsɛpt] *prep* (*also*: **~ for**) außer +*dat* ▸ *vt*: **to ~ sb (from)** jdn ausnehmen (bei)
exception [ɪkˈsɛpʃən] *n* Ausnahme *f*
exceptional [ɪkˈsɛpʃənl] *adj* außergewöhnlich
excess [ɪkˈsɛs] *n* Übermaß *nt* ▪ **excesses** *npl* Exzesse *pl*
excess baggage *n* Übergepäck *nt*
excessive [ɪkˈsɛsɪv] *adj* übermäßig
exchange [ɪksˈtʃeɪndʒ] *n* Austausch *m*; (*also*: **telephone ~**) Fernsprechamt *nt* ▸ *vt*: **to ~ (for)** tauschen (gegen); (*in shop*) umtauschen (gegen); **foreign ~** Devisenhandel *m*
exchange rate *n* Wechselkurs *m*
excite [ɪkˈsaɪt] *vt* (*arouse*) erregen; **to get excited** sich aufregen
exciting [ɪkˈsaɪtɪŋ] *adj* aufregend
exclamation [ɛkskləˈmeɪʃən] *n* Ausruf *m*
exclamation mark *n* Ausrufezeichen *nt*
exclude [ɪksˈklu:d] *vt* ausschließen
exclusion [ɪksˈklu:ʒən] *n* Ausschluss *m*
exclusive [ɪksˈklu:sɪv] *adj* exklusiv; (*use*) ausschließlich
exclusively [ɪksˈklu:sɪvlɪ] *adv* ausschließlich
excrement [ˈɛkskrəmənt] *n* Kot *m*, Exkremente *pl*
excruciating [ɪksˈkru:ʃɪeɪtɪŋ] *adj* grässlich, fürchterlich
excursion [ɪksˈkə:ʃən] *n* Ausflug *m*
excusable [ɪksˈkju:zəbl] *adj* verzeihlich, entschuldbar
excuse *n* [ɪksˈkju:s] Entschuldigung *f* ▸ *vt* [ɪksˈkju:z] entschuldigen; (*forgive*) verzeihen; **to ~ sb from sth** jdm etw erlassen; **to ~ sb from doing sth** jdn davon befreien, etw zu tun; **~ me!** entschuldigen Sie!, Entschuldigung!; **that's no ~!** das ist keine Ausrede!
ex-directory [ˈɛksdɪˈrɛktərɪ] (BRIT) *adj* (*number*) geheim; **she's ~** sie steht nicht im Telefonbuch
executable [ˈɛksɪkju:təbl] *adj* (*Comput*) ausführbar
execute [ˈɛksɪkju:t] *vt* ausführen; (*person*) hinrichten
execution [ɛksɪˈkju:ʃən] *n* Ausführung *f*; Hinrichtung *f*
executive [ɪgˈzɛkjutɪv] *n* leitende(r) Angestellte(r) *f*(*m*)
exemplary [ɪgˈzɛmplərɪ] *adj* beispielhaft
exempt [ɪgˈzɛmpt] *adj*: **~ from** befreit von ▸ *vt*: **to ~ sb from** jdn befreien von
exercise [ˈɛksəsaɪz] *n* Übung *f*; (*no pl*: *keep-fit*) Gymnastik *f*; (: *energetic movement*) Bewegung *f*
exercise bike *n* Heimtrainer *m*
exercise book *n* (Schul)heft *nt*
exert [ɪgˈzə:t] *vt* (*influence*) ausüben
exhaust [ɪgˈzɔ:st] *n* (*also*: **~ pipe**) Auspuff *m*; (*fumes*) Auspuffgase *pl*
exhausted [ɪgˈzɔ:stɪd] *adj* erschöpft
exhausting [ɪgˈzɔ:stɪŋ] *adj* anstrengend
exhibit [ɪgˈzɪbɪt] *n* Ausstellungsstück *nt*
exhibition [ɛksɪˈbɪʃən] *n* Ausstellung *f*
exhibitionist [ɛksɪˈbɪʃənɪst] *n* Exhibitionist(in) *m*(*f*)
exhibitor [ɪgˈzɪbɪtə[r]] *n* Aussteller(in) *m*(*f*)
exhilarating [ɪgˈzɪləreɪtɪŋ] *adj* erregend, berauschend
exile [ˈɛksaɪl] *n* Exil *nt*; (*person*) Verbannte(r) *f*(*m*) ▸ *vt* verbannen
exist [ɪgˈzɪst] *vi* existieren
existence [ɪgˈzɪstəns] *n* Existenz *f*
existing [ɪgˈzɪstɪŋ] *adj* bestehend
exit [ˈɛksɪt] *n* Ausgang *m*; (*from motorway*) Ausfahrt *f*
exit poll *n bei Wählern unmittelbar nach Verlassen der Wahllokale durchgeführte Umfrage*
exorbitant [ɪgˈzɔ:bɪtnt] *adj* (*prices, rents*) astronomisch
exotic [ɪgˈzɔtɪk] *adj* exotisch
expand [ɪksˈpænd] *vt* erweitern; (*influence*) ausdehnen ▸ *vi* (*gas, metal*) sich ausdehnen
expansion [ɪksˈpænʃən] *n* Expansion *f*
expect [ɪksˈpɛkt] *vt* erwarten; (*suppose*) denken, glauben ▸ *vi*: **to be**

expecting ein Kind erwarten; **to ~ sb to do sth** erwarten, dass jd etw tut; **I ~ so** ich glaube schon
expedition [ɛkspəˈdɪʃən] *n* Expedition *f*
expenditure [ɪksˈpɛndɪtʃəʳ] *n* Ausgaben *pl*
expense [ɪksˈpɛns] *n* Kosten *pl*; (*expenditure*) Ausgabe *f* ▪ **expenses** *npl* Spesen *pl*; **at the ~ of** auf Kosten *+gen*
expensive [ɪksˈpɛnsɪv] *adj* teuer
experience [ɪksˈpɪərɪəns] *n* Erfahrung *f*; (*event, activity*) Erlebnis *nt* ▶ *vt* erleben; **by** *or* **from ~** aus Erfahrung
experienced [ɪksˈpɪərɪənst] *adj* erfahren
experiment [ɪksˈpɛrɪmənt] *n* Experiment *nt*, Versuch *m* ▶ *vi*: **to ~ (with/on)** experimentieren (mit/an *+dat*)
expert [ˈɛkspəːt] *adj* (*opinion, help etc*) eines Fachmanns ▶ *n* Fachmann *m*, Fachfrau *f*, Experte *m*, Expertin *f*; **~ witness** (*Law*) sachverständiger Zeuge *m*
expertise [ɛkspəːˈtiːz] *n* Sachkenntnis *f*
expire [ɪksˈpaɪəʳ] *vi* ablaufen
expiry date *n* (*of voucher, special offer etc*) Verfallsdatum *nt*
explain [ɪksˈpleɪn] *vt* erklären
explanation [ɛkspləˈneɪʃən] *n* Erklärung *f*
explicit [ɪksˈplɪsɪt] *adj* ausdrücklich
explode [ɪksˈpləud] *vi* explodieren
exploit [ɪksˈplɔɪt] *vt* (*workers etc*) ausbeuten
explore [ɪksˈplɔːʳ] *vt* erforschen
explosion [ɪksˈpləuʒən] *n* Explosion *f*
explosive [ɪksˈpləusɪv] *adj* explosiv ▶ *n* Sprengstoff *m*
export *vt* [ɛksˈpɔːt] exportieren ▶ *n* [ˈɛkspɔːt] Export *m* ▶ *cpd* [ˈɛkspɔːt] Export-
expose [ɪksˈpəuz] *vt* freilegen; (*to heat, radiation*) aussetzen; (*unmask*) entlarven
exposed [ɪksˈpəuzd] *adj* ungeschützt
exposure [ɪksˈpəuʒəʳ] *n* (*Phot*) Belichtung *f*; (*: shot*) Aufnahme *f*; **to be suffering from ~** an Unterkühlung leiden
express [ɪksˈprɛs] *adj* (Brit: *letter etc*) Express-, Eil- ▶ *n* (*train*) Schnellzug *m* ▶ *vt* ausdrücken; **to ~ o.s.** sich ausdrücken
expression [ɪksˈprɛʃən] *n* Ausdruck *m*; (*on face*) (Gesichts)ausdruck *m*
expressive [ɪksˈprɛsɪv] *adj* ausdrucksvoll
expressway [ɪksˈprɛsweɪ] (*US*) *n* Schnellstraße *f*
extend [ɪksˈtɛnd] *vt* verlängern; (*building*) anbauen an *+acc*; (*offer, invitation*) aussprechen; (*arm, hand*) ausstrecken
extension [ɪksˈtɛnʃən] *n* Verlängerung *f*; (*of building*) Anbau *m*; (*of campaign, rights*) Erweiterung *f*; (*Tel*) (Neben) anschluss *m*
extensive [ɪksˈtɛnsɪv] *adj* (*inquiries*) umfangreich; (*use*) häufig
extent [ɪksˈtɛnt] *n* Ausdehnung *f*; (*of problem, damage, loss etc*) Ausmaß *nt*; **to a certain ~** in gewissem Maße; **to a large ~** in hohem Maße
exterior [ɛksˈtɪərɪəʳ] *n* (*appearance*) Äußere(s) *nt*
external [ɛksˈtəːnl] *adj* (*wall etc*) Außen-
externally [ɛksˈtəːnəlɪ] *adv* äußerlich
extinct [ɪksˈtɪŋkt] *adj* ausgestorben
extinguish [ɪksˈtɪŋgwɪʃ] *vt* löschen
extinguisher [ɪksˈtɪŋgwɪʃəʳ] *n* (*also:* **fire ~**) Feuerlöscher *m*
extra [ˈɛkstrə] *adj* zusätzlich ▶ *adv* extra ▶ *n* Extra *nt*; (*surcharge*) zusätzliche Kosten *pl*
extract *vt* [ɪksˈtrækt] (*tooth*) ziehen ▶ *n* [ˈekstrækt] Auszug *m*; **to ~ (from)** (*object*) herausziehen (aus)
extraordinary [ɪksˈtrɔːdnrɪ] *adj* ungewöhnlich; (*special*) außerordentlich
extreme [ɪksˈtriːm] *adj* extrem; (*point, edge, poverty*) äußerste(r, s) ▶ *n* Extrem *nt*
extremely [ɪksˈtriːmlɪ] *adv* äußerst, extrem
extremist [ɪksˈtriːmɪst] *n* Extremist(in) *m(f)* ▶ *adj* extremistisch
extricate [ˈɛkstrɪkeɪt] *vt*: **to ~ sb/sth (from)** jdn/etw befreien (aus)
extrovert [ˈɛkstrəvəːt] *n* extravertierter Mensch *m*
exuberance [ɪgˈzjuːbərns] *n* Überschwänglichkeit *f*
exuberant [ɪgˈzjuːbərnt] *adj* überschwänglich
exultation [ɛgzʌlˈteɪʃən] *n* Jubel *m*
eye [aɪ] *n* Auge *nt* ▶ *vt* betrachten; **to keep an ~ on** aufpassen auf *+acc*

eyebrow [ˈaɪbrau] *n* Augenbraue *f*
eyelash [ˈaɪlæʃ] *n* Augenwimper *f*
eyelid [ˈaɪlɪd] *n* Augenlid *nt*
eyeliner [ˈaɪlaɪnəʳ] *n* Eyeliner *m*
eye-opener [ˈaɪəupnəʳ] *n* Überraschung *f*
eye shadow *n* Lidschatten *m*
eyesight [ˈaɪsaɪt] *n* Sehvermögen *nt*
eyesore [ˈaɪsɔːʳ] *n* Schandfleck *m*
eyewitness [ˈaɪwɪtnɪs] *n* Augenzeuge *m*, Augenzeugin *f*

fabric [ˈfæbrɪk] *n* Stoff *m*
fabulous [ˈfæbjuləs] *adj* (*extraordinary*) sagenhaft
façade [fəˈsɑːd] *n* Fassade *f*
face [feɪs] *n* Gesicht *nt*; (*of clock*) Zifferblatt *nt*; (*of mountain, cliff*) (Steil)wand *f* ▸ *vt* (*subj*: *person*) gegenübersitzen/-stehen +*dat etc*; (: *building, street etc*) liegen zu; (*north, south etc*) liegen nach; (*unpleasant situation*) sich gegenübersehen +*dat*; **in the ~ of** trotz +*gen*; **to come ~ to ~ with sb** jdn treffen; **to come ~ to ~ with a problem** einem Problem gegenüberstehen
▸ **face up to** *vt fus* (*danger, fact*) ins Auge sehen +*dat*
Facebook® [ˈfeɪsbuk] *n* Facebook® *nt*
facebook [ˈfeɪsbuk] *vi* eine Facebook-Nachricht schicken
face-lift [ˈfeɪslɪft] *n* Facelifting *nt*; (*of building etc*) Verschönerung *f*
face powder *n* Gesichtspuder *m*
facet [ˈfæsɪt] *n* Seite *f*, Aspekt *m*
face value *n* Nennwert *m*
facial [ˈfeɪʃl] *adj* (*expression, massage etc*) Gesichts- ▸ *n* kosmetische Gesichtsbehandlung *f*
facilitate [fəˈsɪlɪteɪt] *vt* erleichtern
facilities [fəˈsɪlɪtɪz] *npl* Einrichtungen *pl*; **cooking ~** Kochgelegenheit *f*
facility [fəˈsɪlɪtɪ] *n* Einrichtung *f*
fact [fækt] *n* Tatsache *f*; **in ~** eigentlich
factor [ˈfæktəʳ] *n* Faktor *m*
factory [ˈfæktərɪ] *n* Fabrik *f*
factual [ˈfæktjuəl] *adj* sachlich

faculty [ˈfækəltɪ] *n* (*ability*) Talent *nt*; (*of university*) Fakultät *f*; (*US: teaching staff*) Lehrkörper *m*
fade [feɪd] *vi* verblassen
fag [fæg] *n* (BRIT *inf: cigarette*) Glimmstängel *m*; (*US: offensive*) Schwule(r) *m*
fail [feɪl] *vt* (*exam*) nicht bestehen ▶ *vi* (*candidate*) durchfallen; (*attempt*) fehlschlagen; (*brakes*) versagen; (*eyesight, light*) nachlassen
failing [ˈfeɪlɪŋ] *n* Schwäche *f*
failure [ˈfeɪljəʳ] *n* Misserfolg *m*; (*person*) Versager(in) *m(f)*; (*of brakes, heart*) Versagen *nt*; (*of engine, power*) Ausfall *m*
faint [feɪnt] *adj* schwach; (*breeze, trace*) leicht ▶ *vi* ohnmächtig werden
faintest *adj, n*: **I haven't the ~ (idea)** ich habe keinen blassen Schimmer
fair [fɛəʳ] *adj* gerecht, fair; (*size, number*) ansehnlich; (*chance, guess*) recht gut; (*hair*) blond; (*skin, complexion*) hell; (*weather*) schön ▶ *adv*: **to play ~** fair spielen ▶ *n* (*also*: **trade ~**) Messe *f*; (BRIT: *funfair*) Jahrmarkt *m*; **a ~ amount of** ziemlich viel
fair-haired [fɛəˈhɛəd] *adj* blond
fairly [ˈfɛəlɪ] *adv* gerecht; (*quite*) ziemlich
fair trade *n* Fairer Handel *m*
fairy [ˈfɛərɪ] *n* Fee *f*
fairy tale *n* Märchen *nt*
faith [feɪθ] *n* Glaube *m*; (*trust*) Vertrauen *nt*
faithful [ˈfeɪθful] *adj* (*account*) genau; **~ (to)** (*person*) treu +*dat*
faithfully *adv* genau; treu
fake [feɪk] *n* Fälschung *f* ▶ *adj* gefälscht ▶ *vt* fälschen
falcon [ˈfɔːlkən] *n* Falke *m*
fall [fɔːl] (*pt* **fell**, *pp* **fallen**) *n* Fall *m*; (*of price, temperature*) Sinken *nt*; (*: sudden*) Sturz *m*; (*US: autumn*) Herbst *m* ▶ *vi* fallen; **to ~ in love (with sb/sth)** sich (in jdn/etw) verlieben
▶ **fall apart** *vi* auseinanderfallen
▶ **fall back** *vi* zurückweichen
▶ **fall back on** *vi* zurückgreifen auf +*acc*
▶ **fall behind** *vi* zurückbleiben; (*fig: with payment*) in Rückstand geraten
▶ **fall down** *vi* hinfallen
▶ **fall for** *vt fus* (*trick, story*) hereinfallen auf +*acc*; (*person*) sich verlieben in +*acc*
▶ **fall in** *vi* einstürzen; (*Mil*) antreten
▶ **fall off** *vi* herunterfallen; (*takings, attendance*) zurückgehen
▶ **fall out** *vi* (*hair, teeth*) ausfallen; **to ~ out with sb** sich mit jdm zerstreiten
▶ **fall over** *vi* hinfallen
▶ **fall through** *vi* (*plan, project*) ins Wasser fallen
fallen [ˈfɔːlən] *pp of* **fall**
fallout [ˈfɔːlaut] *n* radioaktiver Niederschlag *m*
false [fɔːls] *adj* falsch; (*imprisonment*) widerrechtlich
false alarm *n* falscher *or* blinder Alarm *m*
false teeth (BRIT) *npl* Gebiss *nt*
fame [feɪm] *n* Ruhm *m*
familiar [fəˈmɪlɪəʳ] *adj* vertraut; **to be ~ with** vertraut sein mit
familiarity [fəmɪlɪˈærɪtɪ] *n* Vertrautheit *f*
family [ˈfæmɪlɪ] *n* Familie *f*; (*relations*) Verwandtschaft *f*
family man *n* (*irreg*) Familienvater *m*
famine [ˈfæmɪn] *n* Hungersnot *f*
famished [ˈfæmɪʃt] (*inf*) *adj* ausgehungert
famous [ˈfeɪməs] *adj* berühmt
fan [fæn] *n* (*person*) Fan *m*; (*object: folding*) Fächer *m*; (*: Elec*) Ventilator *m*
fanatic [fəˈnætɪk] *n* Fanatiker(in) *m(f)*
fancy [ˈfænsɪ] *adj* (*hotel*) fein, vornehm; (*food*) ausgefallen ▶ *vt* mögen; **to ~ that ...** meinen, dass ...; **~ that!** (nein) so was!; **he fancies her** (*inf*) sie gefällt ihm
fancy dress *n* Verkleidung *f*, (Masken) kostüm *nt*
fan heater (BRIT) *n* Heizlüfter *m*
fanlight [ˈfænlaɪt] *n* Oberlicht *nt*
fantasize *vi* fantasieren
fantastic [fænˈtæstɪk] *adj* fantastisch
fantasy [ˈfæntəsɪ] *n* Fantasie *f*
far [fɑːʳ] *adj*: **at the ~ side** auf der anderen Seite ▶ *adv* weit; **by ~** bei Weitem; **go as ~ as the church** gehen/fahren Sie bis zur Kirche; **as ~ as I know** soweit ich weiß
faraway [ˈfɑːrəweɪ] *adj* weit entfernt; (*look, voice*) abwesend
fare [fɛəʳ] *n* Fahrpreis *m*; (*money*) Fahrgeld *nt*
Far East *n*: **the ~** der Ferne Osten
farm [fɑːm] *n* Bauernhof *m*

farmer [ˈfɑːməʳ] *n* Bauer *m*, Bäu(e)rin *f*, Landwirt(in) *m(f)*
farmhouse [ˈfɑːmhaus] *n* Bauernhaus *nt*
farming [ˈfɑːmɪŋ] *n* Landwirtschaft *f*
farmland [ˈfɑːmlænd] *n* Ackerland *nt*
farmyard [ˈfɑːmjɑːd] *n* Hof *m*
far-reaching [ˈfɑːˈriːtʃɪŋ] *adj* weitreichend
far-sighted [ˈfɑːˈsaɪtɪd] *adj* weitsichtig; (*fig*) weitblickend
fart [fɑːt] (*inf*) *vi* furzen (!) ▶ *n* Furz *m* (!)
farther [ˈfɑːðəʳ] *adj comp of* **far**
farthest [ˈfɑːðɪst] *superl of* **far**
fascinating [ˈfæsɪneɪtɪŋ] *adj* faszinierend
fascination [fæsɪˈneɪʃən] *n* Faszination *f*
fascism [ˈfæʃɪzəm] *n* Faschismus *m*
fascist [ˈfæʃɪst] *adj* faschistisch ▶ *n* Faschist(in) *m(f)*
fashion [ˈfæʃən] *n* Mode *f*; (*manner*) Art *f*; **in ~** modern; **out of ~** unmodern
fashionable [ˈfæʃnəbl] *adj* modisch; (*club, writer*) in Mode
fast [fɑːst] *adj* schnell ▶ *adv* schnell; (*stuck, held*) fest ▶ *n* Fasten *nt* ▶ *vi* fasten; **my watch is (5 minutes) ~** meine Uhr geht (5 Minuten) vor; **to be ~ asleep** tief *or* fest schlafen
fasten [ˈfɑːsn] *vt* festmachen; (*coat, belt etc*) zumachen
fastener [ˈfɑːsnəʳ] *n* Verschluss *m*
fast food *n* Fast Food *nt*
fast lane *n* (*Aut*): **the ~** die Überholspur
fat [fæt] *adj* dick; (*person*) dick, fett (*pej*); (*animal*) fett ▶ *n* Fett *nt*
fatal [ˈfeɪtl] *adj* tödlich
fate [feɪt] *n* Schicksal *nt*
fat-free *adj* fettfrei
father [ˈfɑːðəʳ] *n* Vater *m*
Father Christmas *n* der Weihnachtsmann
father-in-law [ˈfɑːðərɪnlɔː] *n* Schwiegervater *m*
fatigue [fəˈtiːg] *n* Erschöpfung *f*
fatten [ˈfætn] *vi* (*person*) dick werden; **chocolate is fattening** Schokolade macht dick
fatty [ˈfætɪ] *adj* fett
faucet [ˈfɔːsɪt] (*US*) *n* (Wasser)hahn *m*
fault [fɔːlt] *n* Fehler *m*; (*blame*) Schuld *f*; (*in machine*) Defekt *m*; **it's my ~** es ist meine Schuld
faulty [ˈfɔːltɪ] *adj* defekt
favor *etc* [ˈfeɪvəʳ] (*US*) = **favour** *etc*
favour, (*US*) **favor** [ˈfeɪvəʳ] *n* (*approval*) Wohlwollen *nt*; (*help*) Gefallen *m* ▶ *vt* bevorzugen; **to do sb a ~** jdm einen Gefallen tun; **to be in ~ of doing sth** dafür sein, etw zu tun
favourable [ˈfeɪvrəbl] *adj* günstig
favourite [ˈfeɪvrɪt] *adj* Lieblings- ▶ *n* Liebling *m*; (*in race*) Favorit(in) *m(f)*
fax [fæks] *n* Fax *nt* ▶ *vt* faxen
fax number *n* Faxnummer *f*
faze [feɪz] *vt* (*inf*) aus der Fassung bringen
FBI (*US*) *n abbr* (= *Federal Bureau of Investigation*) FBI *nt*
fear [fɪəʳ] *n* Angst *f* ▶ *vt* (*be worried about*) befürchten
fearful [ˈfɪəful] *adj* (*frightening*) furchtbar, schrecklich; (*apprehensive*) ängstlich
fearless [ˈfɪəlɪs] *adj* furchtlos
feasible [ˈfiːzəbl] *adj* machbar
feast [fiːst] *n* Festmahl *nt*
feather [ˈfɛðəʳ] *n* Feder *f*
feature [ˈfiːtʃəʳ] *n* Merkmal *nt*; (*Press, TV*) Feature *nt* ▶ *vt*: **the film features Marlon Brando** Marlon Brando spielt in dem Film mit ■ **features** *npl* (*of face*) (Gesichts)züge *pl*
feature film *n* Spielfilm *m*
February [ˈfɛbruərɪ] *n* Februar *m*; *see also* **July**
fed [fɛd] *pt, pp of* **feed**
federal [ˈfɛdərəl] *adj* föderalistisch
fed up *adj*: **to be ~ with** die Nase vollhaben von
fee [fiː] *n* Gebühr *f*; (*of doctor, lawyer*) Honorar *nt*
feeble [ˈfiːbl] *adj* schwach
feed [fiːd] (*pt, pp* **fed**) *n* Mahlzeit *f*; (*of animal*) Fütterung *f*; (*on printer*) Papiervorschub *m* ▶ *vt* füttern; (*family etc*) ernähren
feedback [ˈfiːdbæk] *n* Feedback *nt*
feel [fiːl] (*pt, pp* **felt**) *vt* (*object*) fühlen; (*desire, anger, grief*) empfinden; (*think, believe*): **I ~ that you ought to do it** ich meine *or* ich bin der Meinung, dass Sie es tun sollten; **I ~ cold** mir ist kalt; **it feels soft** es fühlt sich weich an; **to ~ like** (*desire*) Lust haben auf *+acc*
feeling [ˈfiːlɪŋ] *n* Gefühl *nt*
feet [fiːt] *npl of* **foot**
fell [fɛl] *pt of* **fall** ▶ *vt* fällen

fellow [ˈfɛləu] *n* Mann *m*, Typ *m* (*inf*); **his ~ workers** seine Kollegen (und Kolleginnen)
fellow citizen *n* Mitbürger(in) *m(f)*
fellow countryman *n* (*irreg*) Landsmann *m*, Landsmännin *f*
felt [fɛlt] *pt*, *pp of* **feel** ▸ *n* Filz *m*
felt-tip pen *n* Filzstift *m*
female [ˈfiːmeɪl] *n* Weibchen *nt* ▸ *adj* weiblich; **male and ~ students** Studenten und Studentinnen
feminine [ˈfɛmɪnɪn] *adj* weiblich
feminist [ˈfɛmɪnɪst] *n* Feminist(in) *m(f)*
fence [fɛns] *n* Zaun *m*
fencing *n* (*Sport*) Fechten *nt*
fender [ˈfɛndə^r] *n* (*US*: *of car*) Kotflügel *m*
fennel [ˈfɛnl] *n* Fenchel *m*
fern [fəːn] *n* Farn *m*
ferocious [fəˈrəuʃəs] *adj* wild
ferry [ˈfɛrɪ] *n* (*also*: **ferryboat**) Fähre *f* ▸ *vt*: **to ~ sth/sb across** *or* **over** jdn/etw übersetzen
fertile [ˈfəːtaɪl] *adj* fruchtbar
fertility [fəˈtɪlɪtɪ] *n* Fruchtbarkeit *f*
fertilize [ˈfəːtɪlaɪz] *vt* düngen; (*Biol*) befruchten
fertilizer [ˈfəːtɪlaɪzə^r] *n* Dünger *m*
festival [ˈfɛstɪvəl] *n* Fest *nt*; (*Art*, *Mus*) Festival *nt*, Festspiele *pl*
festive [ˈfɛstɪv] *adj* festlich
festivities [fɛsˈtɪvɪtɪz] *npl* Feierlichkeiten *pl*
fetch [fɛtʃ] *vt* holen; (*sell for*) (ein)bringen
fetching [ˈfɛtʃɪŋ] *adj* reizend
fetish [ˈfɛtɪʃ] *n* Fetisch *m*
fetus [ˈfiːtəs] (*US*) *n* = **foetus**
fever [ˈfiːvə^r] *n* Fieber *nt*
feverish [ˈfiːvərɪʃ] *adj* fiebrig; (*activity*, *emotion*) fieberhaft
few [fjuː] *adj* wenige; **a ~** (*adj*) ein paar; (*pron*) ein paar
fewer [ˈfjuːə^r] *adj* weniger
fewest [ˈfjuːɪst] *adj* die wenigsten
fiancé [fɪˈɑ̃ːŋseɪ] *n* Verlobte(r) *m*
fiancée [fɪˈɑ̃ːŋseɪ] *n* Verlobte *f*
fiasco [fɪˈæskəu] *n* Fiasko *nt*
fibre, (*US*) **fiber** [ˈfaɪbə^r] *n* Faser *f*; (*cloth*) (Faser)stoff *m*
fickle [ˈfɪkl] *adj* unbeständig; (*weather*) wechselhaft
fiction [ˈfɪkʃən] *n* (*Liter*) Prosaliteratur *f*
fictional [ˈfɪkʃənl] *adj* erfunden
fictitious [fɪkˈtɪʃəs] *adj* (*invented*) frei erfunden
fiddle [ˈfɪdl] *n* Geige *f*; (*fraud*, *swindle*) Schwindelei *f* ▸ *vt* (BRIT: *accounts*) frisieren (*inf*)
▸ **fiddle with** *vt fus* herumspielen mit
fiddly [ˈfɪdlɪ] *adj* knifflig (*inf*)
fidelity [fɪˈdɛlɪtɪ] *n* Treue *f*
fidget [ˈfɪdʒɪt] *vi* zappeln
fidgety [ˈfɪdʒɪtɪ] *adj* zappelig
field [fiːld] *n* Feld *nt*; (*subject*, *area of interest*) Gebiet *nt*
fierce [fɪəs] *adj* wild; (*fighting*, *wind*) heftig; (*loyalty*) leidenschaftlich
fifteen [fɪfˈtiːn] *num* fünfzehn
fifteenth [fɪfˈtiːnθ] *num* fünfzehnte(r, s)
fifth [fɪfθ] *num* fünfte(r, s) ▸ *n* Fünftel *nt*
fiftieth [ˈfɪftɪɪθ] *num* fünfzigste(r, s)
fifty [ˈfɪftɪ] *num* fünfzig
fig [fɪg] *n* Feige *f*
fight [faɪt] (*pt*, *pp* **fought**) *n* Kampf *m*; (*quarrel*) Streit *m*; (*punch-up*) Schlägerei *f* ▸ *vt* kämpfen mit *or* gegen; (*prejudice etc*) bekämpfen ▸ *vi* kämpfen
▸ **fight back** *vi* zurückschlagen
▸ **fight off** *vt* abwehren
fighter [ˈfaɪtə^r] *n* Kämpfer(in) *m(f)*
figurative [ˈfɪgjurətɪv] *adj* übertragen
figure [ˈfɪgə^r] *n* Figur *f*; (*number*, *statistic*, *cipher*) Zahl *f*; (*person*) Gestalt *f* ▸ *vt* (*esp US*) glauben ▸ *vi* eine Rolle spielen
▸ **figure out** *vt* ausrechnen
figure skating *n* Eiskunstlaufen *nt*
file [faɪl] *n* Akte *f*; (*folder*) (Akten)ordner *m*; (*Comput*) Datei *f*; (*tool*) Feile *f* ▸ *vt* ablegen; (*wood*, *metal*, *fingernails*) feilen ▸ *vi*: **to ~ in/out** nacheinander hereinkommen/hinausgehen
file sharing [-ʃɛərɪŋ] *n* Filesharing *nt*
filing cabinet *n* Aktenschrank *m*
fill [fɪl] *vt* füllen; (*tooth*) plombieren; (*need*) erfüllen; **we've already filled that vacancy** wir haben diese Stelle schon besetzt
▸ **fill in** *vt* füllen; (*form*) ausfüllen
▸ **fill out** *vt* ausfüllen
▸ **fill up** *vi* (*Aut*) tanken
fillet [ˈfɪlɪt] *n* Filet *nt*
filling [ˈfɪlɪŋ] *n* Füllung *f*; (*for tooth*) Plombe *f*
filling station *n* Tankstelle *f*
film [fɪlm] *n* Film *m* ▸ *vt*, *vi* filmen
film star *n* Filmstar *m*
film studio *n* Filmstudio *nt*
filter [ˈfɪltə^r] *n* Filter *m* ▸ *vt* filtern
filter lane (BRIT) *n* Abbiegespur *f*

filth [fɪlθ] *n* Dreck *m*
filthy [ˈfɪlθɪ] *adj* dreckig
fin [fɪn] *n* Flosse *f*
final [ˈfaɪnl] *adj* letzte(r, s); (*definitive*) endgültig ▶ *n* Finale *nt*, Endspiel *nt* ■ **finals** *npl* (*Univ*) Abschlussprüfung *f*
finalize [ˈfaɪnəlaɪz] *vt* endgültig festlegen
finally [ˈfaɪnəlɪ] *adv* endlich, schließlich; (*lastly*) schließlich
finance [faɪˈnæns] *n* (*money management*) Finanzwesen *nt* ▶ *vt* finanzieren ■ **finances** *npl* (*personal*) Finanzen *pl*
financial [faɪˈnænʃəl] *adj* finanziell
find [faɪnd] (*pt, pp* **found**) *vt* finden; **to ~ (some) difficulty in doing sth** (einige) Schwierigkeiten haben, etw zu tun
▶ **find out** *vt* herausfinden
findings [ˈfaɪndɪŋz] *npl* (*Law*) Urteil *nt*; (*of report*) Ergebnis *nt*
fine [faɪn] *adj* fein; (*excellent*) gut; (*thin*) dünn ▶ *adv* gut ▶ *n* Geldstrafe *f* ▶ *vt* mit einer Geldstrafe belegen; **he's ~** es geht ihm gut; **the weather is ~** das Wetter ist schön
fine arts *npl* schöne Künste *pl*
finely [ˈfaɪnlɪ] *adv* (*slice*) dünn; (*adjust*) fein
finger [ˈfɪŋgəʳ] *n* Finger *m* ▶ *vt* befühlen
fingernail [ˈfɪŋgəneɪl] *n* Fingernagel *m*
fingerprint [ˈfɪŋgəprɪnt] *n* Fingerabdruck *m*
fingertip [ˈfɪŋgətɪp] *n* Fingerspitze *f*
finicky [ˈfɪnɪkɪ] *adj* pingelig
finish [ˈfɪnɪʃ] *n* Ende *nt*; (*Sport*) Finish *nt*; (*polish etc*) Verarbeitung *f* ▶ *vt* fertig sein mit; (*work*) erledigen; (*book*) auslesen ▶ *vi* enden; (*person*) fertig sein; **to ~ third** als Dritter durchs Ziel gehen; **to have finished with sth** mit etw fertig sein
▶ **finish up** *vt* (*food*) aufessen; (*drink*) austrinken
finishing line [ˈfɪnɪʃɪŋ-] *n* Ziellinie *f*
Finland [ˈfɪnlənd] *n* Finnland *nt*
Finn [fɪn] *n* Finne *m*, Finnin *f*
Finnish [ˈfɪnɪʃ] *adj* finnisch ▶ *n* (*Ling*) Finnisch *nt*
fir [fəːʳ] *n* Tanne *f*
fire [ˈfaɪəʳ] *n* Feuer *nt*; (*accidental fire*) Brand *m* ▶ *vt* (*enthusiasm*) befeuern; (*inf: dismiss*) feuern ▶ *vi* feuern, schießen; **to ~ a gun** ein Gewehr abschießen; **to be on ~** brennen; **to set ~ to sth, set sth on ~** etw anzünden
fire alarm *n* Feuermelder *m*
fire brigade *n* Feuerwehr *f*
fire engine *n* Feuerwehrauto *nt*
fire escape *n* Feuertreppe *f*
fire exit *n* Notausgang *m*
fire extinguisher *n* Feuerlöscher *m*
firefighter [ˈfaɪəfaɪtəʳ] *n* Feuerwehrmann *m*, Feuerwehrfrau *f*
fireman [ˈfaɪəmən] *n* (*irreg*) Feuerwehrmann *m*
fireplace [ˈfaɪəpleɪs] *n* Kamin *m*
fireproof [ˈfaɪəpruːf] *adj* feuerfest
fire station *n* Feuerwache *f*
firewood [ˈfaɪəwud] *n* Brennholz *nt*
fireworks [ˈfaɪəwəːks] *npl* (*display*) Feuerwerk *nt*
firm [fəːm] *adj* fest; (*measures*) durchgreifend ▶ *n* Firma *f*
first [fəːst] *adj* erste(r, s) ▶ *adv* als Erste(r, s); (*before other things*) zuerst; (*when listing reasons etc*) erstens; (*for the first time*) zum ersten Mal ▶ *n* Erste(r, s); (*Aut: also:* **~ gear**) der erste Gang; (BRIT *Scol*) ≈ Eins *f*; **at ~** zuerst, zunächst; **~ of all** vor allem
first aid *n* erste Hilfe *f*
first-class [ˈfəːstˈklɑːs] *adj* erstklassig; (*carriage, ticket*) Erste(r)-Klasse-; (*post*) bevorzugt befördert ▶ *adv* (*travel, send*) erster Klasse
first lady (*US*) *n* First Lady *f*
firstly [ˈfəːstlɪ] *adv* erstens
first name *n* Vorname *m*
first night *n* Premiere *f*
first-rate [ˈfəːstˈreɪt] *adj* erstklassig
fir tree *n* Tannenbaum *m*
fish [fɪʃ] *n inv* Fisch *m* ▶ *vi* fischen; (*as sport, hobby*) angeln; **to go fishing** fischen/angeln gehen
fish bone *n* (Fisch)gräte *f*
fish cake *n* Fischfrikadelle *f*
fish farm *n* Fischzucht(anlage) *f*
fish fingers (BRIT) *npl* Fischstäbchen *pl*
fishing [ˈfɪʃɪŋ] *n* Fischen *nt*; (*with rod*) Angeln *nt*; (*as industry*) Fischerei *f*
fishing boat *n* Fischerboot *nt*
fishing line *n* Angelschnur *f*
fishing rod *n* Angelrute *f*
fishmonger [ˈfɪʃmʌŋgəʳ] (*esp* BRIT) *n* Fischhändler(in) *m(f)*

fish sticks (*US*) *npl* = **fish fingers**
fish tank *n* Aquarium *nt*
fishy [ˈfɪʃɪ] (*inf*) *adj* verdächtig, faul
fist [fɪst] *n* Faust *f*
fit [fɪt] *adj* geeignet; (*healthy*) gesund; (*Sport*) fit ▶ *vt* passen +*dat*; (*put in*) einbauen; (*attach*) anbringen ▶ *vi* passen; (*in space, gap*) hineinpassen ▶ *n* (*Med*) Anfall *m*; **to keep ~** sich fit halten; **this dress is a good ~** dieses Kleid sitzt *or* passt gut
▶ **fit in** *vi* (*person*) sich einfügen; (*object*) hineinpassen ▶ *vt* (*fig: appointment*) unterbringen, einschieben; **to ~ in with sb's plans** sich mit jds Plänen vereinbaren lassen
fitness [ˈfɪtnɪs] *n* Gesundheit *f*; (*Sport*) Fitness *f*
fitness instructor *n* Fitnesstrainer(in) *m(f)*
fitted carpet [ˈfɪtɪd-] *n* Teppichboden *m*
fitted kitchen [ˈfɪtɪd-] (*BRIT*) *n* Einbauküche *f*
fitting [ˈfɪtɪŋ] *adj* passend ▶ *n* (*of dress*) Anprobe *f* ■ **fittings** *npl* Ausstattung *f*
five [faɪv] *num* fünf
fiver [ˈfaɪvəʳ] (*inf*) *n* (*BRIT*) Fünfpfundschein *m*
fix [fɪks] *vt* (*attach*) befestigen; (*arrange*) festsetzen, festlegen; (*mend*) reparieren; (*meal, drink*) machen
fixture [ˈfɪkstʃəʳ] *n* Ausstattungsgegenstand *m*; (*Football etc*) Spiel *nt*; (*Athletics etc*) Veranstaltung *f*
fizzy [ˈfɪzɪ] *adj* sprudelnd
flabbergasted [ˈflæbəgɑːstɪd] *adj* verblüfft
flabby [ˈflæbɪ] *adj* schwammig, wabbelig (*inf*)
flag [flæg] *n* Fahne *f*
flagstone [ˈflægstəun] *n* (Stein)platte *f*
flake [fleɪk] *n* (*of snow, soap powder*) Flocke *f* ▶ *vi* (*also:* **~ off**) abblättern
flamboyant [flæmˈbɔɪənt] *adj* extravagant
flame [fleɪm] *n* Flamme *f*; **an old ~** (*inf*) eine alte Flamme
flan [flæn] *n* Kuchen *m*
flannel [ˈflænl] *n* Flanell *m*; (*BRIT: also:* **face ~**) Waschlappen *m*; (*inf*) Geschwafel *nt* ■ **flannels** *npl* (*trousers*) Flanellhose *f*
flap [flæp] *n* Klappe *f* ▶ *vt* schlagen mit ▶ *vi* flattern; (*inf: also:* **be in a ~**) in heller Aufregung sein
flared [flɛəd] *adj* (*trousers*) mit Schlag
flash [flæʃ] *n* Aufblinken *nt*; (*also:* **newsflash**) Eilmeldung *f*; (*Phot*) Blitz *m*, Blitzlicht *nt* ▶ *vt* aufleuchten lassen ▶ *vi* aufblinken; (*eyes*) blitzen; **in a ~** im Nu
flashback [ˈflæʃbæk] *n* Rückblende *f*
flash drive *n* USB-Stick *m*
flashlight [ˈflæʃlaɪt] *n* Blitzlicht *nt*
flashy [ˈflæʃɪ] (*pej*) *adj* auffällig, protzig
flat [flæt] *adj* flach; (*surface*) eben; (*tyre*) platt; (*battery*) leer; (*beer*) schal; (*refusal, denial*) glatt ▶ *n* (*BRIT: apartment*) Wohnung *f*; (*Aut*) (Reifen)panne *f*
flat screen *n* Flachbildschirm *m*
flatten [ˈflætn] *vt* (*also:* **~ out**) (ein) ebnen
flatter [ˈflætəʳ] *vt* schmeicheln +*dat*
flattering [ˈflætərɪŋ] *adj* schmeichelhaft
flavour, (*US*) **flavor** [ˈfleɪvəʳ] *n* Geschmack *m* ▶ *vt* Geschmack verleihen +*dat*
flavouring, (*US*) **flavoring** [ˈfleɪvərɪŋ] *n* Aroma *nt*
flaw [flɔː] *n* Fehler *m*
flawless [ˈflɔːlɪs] *adj* (*performance*) fehlerlos; (*complexion*) makellos
flea [fliː] *n* Floh *m*
fled [flɛd] *pt, pp of* **flee**
flee [fliː] (*pt, pp* **fled**) *vi* fliehen
fleece [fliːs] *n* Schafwolle *f*; (*sheep's coat*) Vlies *nt*
fleet [fliːt] *n* Flotte *f*
Flemish [ˈflɛmɪʃ] *adj* flämisch ▶ *n* (*Ling*) Flämisch *nt*
flesh [flɛʃ] *n* Fleisch *nt*
flew [fluː] *pt of* **fly**
flex [flɛks] *n* Kabel *nt*
flexibility [flɛksɪˈbɪlɪtɪ] *n* Flexibilität *f*; Biegsamkeit *f*
flexible [ˈflɛksəbl] *adj* flexibel; (*material*) biegsam
flexitarian [flɛksɪˈtɛərɪən] *adj* flexitarisch ▶ *n* Flexitarier(in) *m(f)*
flexitime [ˈflɛksɪtaɪm] *n* gleitende Arbeitszeit *f*, Gleitzeit *f*
flicker [ˈflɪkəʳ] *vi* flackern
flight [flaɪt] *n* Flug *m*; (*escape*) Flucht *f*; (*also:* **~ of steps**) Treppe *f*
flight attendant (*US*) *n* Flugbegleiter(in) *m(f)*
flight recorder *n* Flugschreiber *m*

flimsy [ˈflɪmzɪ] *adj* leicht, dünn; (*building*) leicht gebaut; (*excuse*) fadenscheinig
fling [flɪŋ] (*pt, pp* **flung**) *vt* schleudern ▸ *n* (flüchtige) Affäre *f*
flip [flɪp] *vt* (*switch*) knipsen; (*coin*) werfen
▸ **flip through** *vt fus* durchblättern
flipchart [ˈflɪptʃɑːt] *n* Flipchart *nt*
flipper [ˈflɪpəʳ] *n* Flosse *f*
flirt [fləːt] *vi* flirten
float [fləut] *n* (*for fishing*) Schwimmer *m*; (*lorry*) Festwagen *m*; (*money*) Wechselgeld *nt* ▸ *vi* schwimmen; (*through air*) schweben
flock [flɔk] *n* Herde *f*; (*of birds*) Schwarm *m*
flog [flɔg] *vt* auspeitschen; (*inf: sell*) verscherbeln
flood [flʌd] *n* Überschwemmung *f*; (*of letters, imports etc*) Flut *f* ▸ *vt* überschwemmen
floodlight [ˈflʌdlaɪt] *n* Flutlicht *nt*
floodlit [ˈflʌdlɪt] *adj* (*building*) angestrahlt
floor [flɔːʳ] *n* (Fuß)boden *m*; (*storey*) Stock *nt*; **ground ~** (BRIT), **first ~** (*US*) Erdgeschoss *nt*, Erdgeschoß *nt* (ÖSTERR); **first ~** (BRIT), **second ~** (*US*) erster Stock *m*
floorboard [ˈflɔːbɔːd] *n* Diele *f*
flop [flɔp] *n* Reinfall *m* ▸ *vi* (*play, book*) durchfallen
floppy disk *n* Diskette *f*, Floppy Disk *f*
Florence [ˈflɔrəns] *n* Florenz *nt*
florist [ˈflɔrɪst] *n* Blumenhändler(in) *m(f)*
florist's [ˈflɔrɪsts], **florist's shop** *n* Blumengeschäft *nt*
flounder [ˈflaundəʳ] *n* Flunder *f*
flour [ˈflauəʳ] *n* Mehl *nt*
flourish [ˈflʌrɪʃ] *vi* gedeihen; (*business*) blühen, florieren
flourishing [ˈflʌrɪʃɪŋ] *adj* gut gehend
flow [fləu] *n* Fluss *m* ▸ *vi* fließen
flower [ˈflauəʳ] *n* Blume *f* ▸ *vi* blühen
flowerbed *n* Blumenbeet *nt*
flowerpot [ˈflauəpɔt] *n* Blumentopf *m*
flown [fləun] *pp of* **fly**
flu [fluː] *n* Grippe *f*
fluent *adj*: **he speaks ~ German, he's ~ in German** er spricht fließend Deutsch
fluid [ˈfluːɪd] *adj* fließend ▸ *n* Flüssigkeit *f*
flung [flʌŋ] *pt, pp of* **fling**
fluorescent [fluəˈrɛsnt] *adj* fluoreszierend; (*paint*) Leucht-
flush [flʌʃ] *n* Röte *f* ▸ *vt* (durch)spülen, (aus)spülen
flute [fluːt] *n* Querflöte *f*
fly [flaɪ] (*pt* **flew**, *pp* **flown**) *n* Fliege *f*; (*on trousers: also:* **flies**) (Hosen)schlitz *m* ▸ *vt* fliegen ▸ *vi* fliegen
▸ **fly away** *vi* wegfliegen
fly-drive [ˈflaɪdraɪv] *n* Urlaub *m* mit Flug und Mietwagen
flyover [ˈflaɪəuvəʳ] *n* (BRIT) Überführung *f*
flysheet [ˈflaɪʃiːt] *n* (*for tent*) Überzelt *nt*
FM *abbr* (*Radio: = frequency modulation*) FM, ≈ UKW
FO (BRIT) *n abbr* = **Foreign Office**
foal [fəul] *n* Fohlen *nt*
foam [fəum] *n* Schaum *m* ▸ *vi* schäumen
fob [fɔb] *vt*: **to ~ sb off** jdn abspeisen
focus [ˈfəukəs] (*pl* **focuses**) *n* Brennpunkt *m* ▸ *vt* einstellen ▸ *vi*: **to ~ (on)** (*with camera*) klar *or* scharf einstellen +*acc*; (*person*) sich konzentrieren (auf +*acc*); **in/out of ~** (*camera etc*) scharf/unscharf eingestellt; (*photograph*) scharf/unscharf
foetus, (*US*) **fetus** [ˈfiːtəs] *n* Fötus *m*
fog [fɔg] *n* Nebel *m*
foggy [ˈfɔgɪ] *adj* neb(e)lig
fog lamp, (*US*) **fog light** *n* (*Aut*) Nebelscheinwerfer *m*
foil [fɔɪl] *vt* vereiteln ▸ *n* Folie *f*
fold [fəuld] *n* Falte *f* ▸ *vt* (zusammen)falten ▸ *vi* (*business*) eingehen (*inf*)
▸ **fold up** *vi* (*business*) eingehen (*inf*) ▸ *vt* zusammenfalten
folder [ˈfəuldəʳ] *n* Aktenmappe *f*; (*binder*) Hefter *m*; (*brochure*) Informationsblatt *nt*
folding [ˈfəuldɪŋ] *adj* (*chair, bed*) Klapp-
folk [fəuk] *npl* Leute *pl* ▸ *cpd* Volks-; **my folks** (*parents*) meine alten Herrschaften
follow [ˈfɔləu] *vt* folgen +*dat*; (*advice, instructions*) befolgen ▸ *vi* (*also on Twitter*) folgen; **I don't quite ~ you** ich kann Ihnen nicht ganz folgen
▸ **follow up** *vt* nachgehen +*dat*; (*case*) weiterverfolgen
follower [ˈfɔləuəʳ] *n* Anhänger(in) *m(f)*
following [ˈfɔləuɪŋ] *adj* folgend

follow-up *n* Weiterführung *f*
fond [fɔnd] *adj*: **to be ~ of** mögen
fondly [ˈfɔndlɪ] *adv* liebevoll
fondness [ˈfɔndnɪs] *n* (*for things*) Vorliebe *f*; (*for people*) Zuneigung *f*
font [fɔnt] *n* Taufbecken *nt*; (*Typ*) Schrift *f*
food [fuːd] *n* Essen *nt*; (*for animals*) Futter *nt*; (*groceries*) Lebensmittel *pl*
food poisoning *n* Lebensmittelvergiftung *f*
food processor *n* Küchenmaschine *f*
foodstuffs *npl* Lebensmittel *pl*
fool [fuːl] *n* Dummkopf *m* ▶ *vt* hereinlegen ▶ *vi* herumalbern; **to make a ~ of o.s.** sich blamieren
▶ **fool about** (*pej*) *vi* herumtrödeln
▶ **fool around** *vi* = **fool about**
foolish [ˈfuːlɪʃ] *adj* dumm
foolproof [ˈfuːlpruːf] *adj* idiotensicher
foot [fut] (*pl* **feet**) *n* Fuß *m* ▶ *vt* (*bill*) bezahlen; **on ~** zu Fuß
foot-and-mouth, foot-and-mouth disease *n* Maul- und Klauenseuche *f*
football [ˈfutbɔːl] *n* Fußball *m*; (*US*) Football *m*, amerikanischer Fußball *m*
footballer [ˈfutbɔːləʳ] (BRIT) *n* Fußballspieler(in) *m(f)*
footbridge [ˈfutbrɪdʒ] *n* Fußgängerbrücke *f*
footfall [ˈfutfɔːl] *n* (*footstep*) Schritt *m*; (*Comm*) Kundenfrequenz *f*
footing [ˈfutɪŋ] *n*: **to lose one's ~** den Halt verlieren
footlights [ˈfutlaɪts] *npl* Rampenlicht *nt*
footnote [ˈfutnəut] *n* Fußnote *f*
footpath [ˈfutpɑːθ] *n* Fußweg *m*
footprint [ˈfutprɪnt] *n* Fußabdruck *m*
footwear [ˈfutwɛəʳ] *n* Schuhwerk *nt*

KEYWORD

for [fɔːʳ] *prep* **1** für +*acc*; **is this for me?** ist das für mich?; **the train for London** der Zug nach London; **he went for the paper** er ging die Zeitung holen; **give it to me — what for?** gib es mir — warum?
2 (*because of*): **for this reason** aus diesem Grund
3 (*referring to distance*): **there are roadworks for 5 km** die Straßenbauarbeiten erstrecken sich über 5 km; **we walked for miles** wir sind meilenweit gelaufen
4 (*referring to time*): **he was away for 2 years** er war 2 Jahre lang weg
5 (*with infinitive clause*): **it is not for me to decide** es liegt nicht an mir, das zu entscheiden; **for this to be possible ...** um dies möglich zu machen, ...
6 (*in spite of*) trotz +*gen or dat*; **for all his complaints, he is very fond of her** trotz seiner vielen Klagen mag er sie sehr
▶ *conj* (*formal*: *since, as*) denn

forbad, forbade [fəˈbæd] *pt of* **forbid**
forbid [fəˈbɪd] (*pt* **forbade**, *pp* **forbidden**) *vt* verbieten
force [fɔːs] *n* Kraft *f*; (*violence*) Gewalt *f* ▶ *vt* zwingen ■ **the Forces** *npl* (BRIT) die Streitkräfte *pl*; **to come into ~** in Kraft treten
forced [fɔːst] *adj* gezwungen; **~ landing** Notlandung *f*
forceful [ˈfɔːsful] *adj* energisch
forceps [ˈfɔːsɛps] *npl* Zange *f*
forearm [ˈfɔːrɑːm] *n* Unterarm *m*
forecast [ˈfɔːkɑːst] *n* (*of weather*) (Wetter)vorhersage *f* ▶ *vt* (*irreg: like* **cast**) voraussagen
forefinger [ˈfɔːfɪŋgəʳ] *n* Zeigefinger *m*
foreground [ˈfɔːgraund] *n* Vordergrund *m*
forehand [ˈfɔːhænd] *n* (*Tennis*) Vorhand *f*
forehead [ˈfɔrɪd] *n* Stirn *f*
foreign [ˈfɔrɪn] *adj* ausländisch; (*trade, policy*) Außen-
foreigner [ˈfɔrɪnəʳ] *n* Ausländer(in) *m(f)*
foreign exchange *n* Devisenhandel *m*
foreign language *n* Fremdsprache *f*
foreign minister *n* Außenminister(in) *m(f)*
Foreign Office (BRIT) *n* Außenministerium *nt*
foreign policy *n* Außenpolitik *f*
Foreign Secretary (BRIT) *n* Außenminister(in) *m(f)*
foremost [ˈfɔːməust] *adj* führend
forerunner [ˈfɔːrʌnəʳ] *n* Vorläufer *m*
foresee [fɔːˈsiː] *vt* (*irreg: like* **see**) vorhersehen
foreseeable [fɔːˈsiːəbl] *adj*: **in the ~ future** in absehbarer Zeit
forest [ˈfɔrɪst] *n* Wald *m*
forestry [ˈfɔrɪstrɪ] *n* Forstwirtschaft *f*

forever [fəˈrɛvəʳ] *adv* für immer
forgave [fəˈgeɪv] *pt of* **forgive**
forge [fɔːdʒ] *n* Schmiede *f* ▸ *vt* fälschen; (*wrought iron*) schmieden
forger [ˈfɔːdʒəʳ] *n* Fälscher(in) *m(f)*
forgery [ˈfɔːdʒərɪ] *n* Fälschung *f*
forget [fəˈgɛt] (*pt* **forgot**, *pp* **forgotten**) *vt* vergessen ▸ *vi* es vergessen
forgetful [fəˈgɛtful] *adj* vergesslich
forgetfulness [fəˈgɛtfulnɪs] *n* Vergesslichkeit *f*
forget-me-not [fəˈgɛtmɪnɔt] *n* Vergissmeinnicht *nt*
forgive [fəˈgɪv] (*pt* **forgave**, *pp* **forgiven**) *vt* verzeihen *+dat*; **to ~ sb for sth** jdm etw verzeihen *or* vergeben
forgot [fəˈgɔt] *pt of* **forget**
forgotten [fəˈgɔtn] *pp of* **forget**
fork [fɔːk] *n* Gabel *f*; (*in road, river, railway*) Gabelung *f* ▸ *vi* (*road*) sich gabeln
form [fɔːm] *n* Form *f*; (*Scol*) Klasse *f*; (*questionnaire*) Formular *nt* ▸ *vt* (*queue, organization, group*) bilden; **to be in good ~** gut in Form sein
formal [ˈfɔːməl] *adj* (*person, behaviour*) förmlich, formell
formality [fɔːˈmælɪtɪ] *n* Förmlichkeit *f*
format [ˈfɔːmæt] *n* Format *nt* ▸ *vt* (*Comput*) formatieren
formatting *n* (*Comput*) Formatierung *f*
former [ˈfɔːməʳ] *adj* früher; **the ~ ... the latter ...** Erstere(r, s, r) ... Letztere(s)
formerly [ˈfɔːməlɪ] *adv* früher
formidable [ˈfɔːmɪdəbl] *adj* (*task*) gewaltig, enorm; (*opponent*) furchterregend
formula [ˈfɔːmjulə] (*pl* **formulae** *or* **formulas**) *n* Formel *f*
formulate [ˈfɔːmjuleɪt] *vt* formulieren
forth [fɔːθ] *adv*: **and so ~** und so weiter
forthcoming [fɔːθˈkʌmɪŋ] *adj* (*event*) bevorstehend
fortieth [ˈfɔːtɪɪθ] *num* vierzigste(r, s)
fortnight [ˈfɔːtnaɪt] (Brit) *n* vierzehn Tage *pl*
fortress [ˈfɔːtrɪs] *n* Festung *f*
fortunate [ˈfɔːtʃənɪt] *adj* glücklich; **to be ~** Glück haben
fortunately [ˈfɔːtʃənɪtlɪ] *adv* zum Glück
fortune [ˈfɔːtʃən] *n* Glück *nt*; (*wealth*) Vermögen *nt*
fortune-teller [ˈfɔːtʃəntɛləʳ] *n* Wahrsager(in) *m(f)*
forty [ˈfɔːtɪ] *num* vierzig
forward [ˈfɔːwəd] *adv* (*movement*) vorwärts ▸ *n* (*Sport*) Stürmer *m* ▸ *vt* (*letter etc*) nachsenden
forwards [ˈfɔːwədz] *adv* (*movement*) vorwärts
fossick [ˈfɔsɪk] *vi* (Aust, NZ *inf*) suchen (for nach); **to ~ around** herumstöbern (*inf*); **to ~ for gold** nach Gold graben
foster child *n* (*irreg*) Pflegekind *nt*
foster mother *n* Pflegemutter *f*
foster sister *n* Ziehschwester *f*
fought [fɔːt] *pt, pp of* **fight**
foul [faul] *adj* (*taste, smell, temper*) übel; (*air*) schlecht ▸ *n* (*Sport*) Foul *nt*
found [faund] *pt, pp of* **find** ▸ *vt* gründen
foundation [faunˈdeɪʃən] *n* Gründung *f* ▪ **foundations** *npl* (*of building*) Fundament *nt*
fountain [ˈfauntɪn] *n* Brunnen *m*
fountain pen *n* Füller *m*
four [fɔːʳ] *num* vier
four-by-four [fɔːbaɪˈfɔːʳ] *n* Geländewagen *m*, Fahrzeug *nt* mit Vierradantrieb
fourteen [ˈfɔːˈtiːn] *num* vierzehn
fourteenth [ˈfɔːˈtiːnθ] *num* vierzehnte(r, s)
fourth [fɔːθ] *num* vierte(r, s)
four-wheel drive *n* (*Aut*): **with ~** mit Vierradantrieb *m*
fowl [faul] *n* Vogel *m* (*besonders Huhn, Gans, Ente etc*)
fox [fɔks] *n* Fuchs *m*
fracking [ˈfrækɪŋ] *n* Fracking *nt*
fraction [ˈfrækʃən] *n* Bruchteil *m*; (*Math*) Bruch *m*
fracture [ˈfræktʃəʳ] *n* Bruch *m* ▸ *vt* brechen
fragile [ˈfrædʒaɪl] *adj* zerbrechlich
fragment *n* [ˈfrægmənt] Stück *nt* ▸ *vt* [frægˈmɛnt] aufsplittern
fragrance [ˈfreɪgrəns] *n* Duft *m*
frail [freɪl] *adj* schwach, gebrechlich
frame [freɪm] *n* Rahmen *m*; (*of spectacles*) Gestell *nt* ▸ *vt* (*picture*) rahmen; **~ of mind** Stimmung *f*; **to ~ sb** (*inf*) jdm etwas anhängen
framework [ˈfreɪmwəːk] *n* Rahmen *m*
France [frɑːns] *n* Frankreich *nt*
frank [fræŋk] *adj* offen

frankfurter [ˈfræŋkfəːtəʳ] *n* (Frankfurter) Würstchen *nt*
frankly [ˈfræŋklɪ] *adv* ehrlich gesagt; (*candidly*) offen
frankness [ˈfræŋknɪs] *n* Offenheit *f*
frantic [ˈfræntɪk] *adj* verzweifelt; (*hectic*) hektisch; (*desperate*) übersteigert
fraud [frɔːd] *n* Betrug *m*; (*person*) Betrüger(in) *m(f)*
freak [friːk] *n* Irre(r) *f(m)*; (*in appearance*) Missgeburt *f*; (*event, accident*) außergewöhnlicher Zufall *m*
▸ **freak out** (*inf*) *vi* (*on drugs*) ausflippen
freckle [ˈfrɛkl] *n* Sommersprosse *f*
free [friː] *adj* frei; (*costing nothing*) kostenlos, gratis ▸ *vt* freilassen; **~ (of charge), for ~** umsonst, gratis
freebie [ˈfriːbɪ] (*inf*) *n* (*promotional gift*) Werbegeschenk *nt*
freedom [ˈfriːdəm] *n* Freiheit *f*
Freefone® [ˈfriːfəun] *n*: **call ~ 0800** rufen Sie gebührenfrei 0800 an
free kick *n* Freistoß *m*
freelance [ˈfriːlɑːns] *adj* (*journalist etc*) frei(schaffend), freiberuflich tätig
free-range [ˈfriːˈreɪndʒ] *adj* (*eggs*) von frei laufenden Hühnern
Freeview® [ˈfriːvjuː] *n* (Brit) terrestrisches Digitalfernsehen *nt*
freeway [ˈfriːweɪ] (*US*) *n* Autobahn *f*
freeze [friːz] (*pt* **froze**, *pp* **frozen**) *vi* frieren; (*liquid*) gefrieren ▸ *vt* einfrieren
▸ **freeze over** *vi* (*river*) überfrieren
freezer [ˈfriːzəʳ] *n* Tiefkühltruhe *f*; (*in fridge*: *also*: **~ compartment**) Gefrierfach *nt*
freezing [ˈfriːzɪŋ] *adj*: **~ (cold)** eiskalt; **I'm ~** mir ist eiskalt
freezing point *n* Gefrierpunkt *m*
freight [freɪt] *n* Fracht *f*; (*money charged*) Frachtkosten *pl*
freight car (*US*) *n* Güterwagen *m*
freight train (*US*) *n* Güterzug *m*
French [frɛntʃ] *adj* französisch ▸ *n* (*Ling*) Französisch *nt* ■ **the French** *npl* die Franzosen *pl*
French bean (Brit) *n* grüne Bohne *f*
French bread *n* Baguette *f*
French dressing *n* Vinaigrette *f*
French fried potatoes *npl* Pommes frites *pl*
French fries [-fraɪz] (*US*) *npl* = **French fried potatoes**
Frenchman [ˈfrɛntʃmən] *n* (*irreg*) Franzose *m*
French window *n* Verandatür *f*
Frenchwoman [ˈfrɛntʃwumən] *n* (*irreg*) Französin *f*
frequency [ˈfriːkwənsɪ] *n* Häufigkeit *f*; (*Radio*) Frequenz *f*
frequent *adj* [ˈfriːkwənt] häufig ▸ *vt* [frɪˈkwɛnt] (*pub, restaurant*) oft *or* häufig besuchen
frequently [ˈfriːkwəntlɪ] *adv* oft, häufig
fresco [ˈfrɛskəu] *n* Fresko *nt*
fresh [frɛʃ] *adj* frisch; (*instructions, approach, start*) neu
freshen [ˈfrɛʃən] *vi* (*wind*) auffrischen
▸ **freshen up** *vi* sich frisch machen
fresher [ˈfrɛʃəʳ] (Brit *inf*) *n* Erstsemester(in) *m(f)*
freshman [ˈfrɛʃmən] (*US*) *n* (*irreg*) = **fresher**
freshwater [ˈfrɛʃwɔːtəʳ] *adj* (*fish etc*) Süßwasser-
Fri. *abbr* (= *Friday*) Fr.
friction [ˈfrɪkʃən] *n* Reibung *f*
Friday [ˈfraɪdɪ] *n* Freitag *m*; *see also* **Tuesday**
fridge [frɪdʒ] (Brit) *n* Kühlschrank *m*
fried [fraɪd] *pt, pp of* **fry** ▸ *adj* gebraten; **~ egg** Spiegelei *nt*
friend [frɛnd] *n* Freund(in) *m(f)*; (*less intimate*) Bekannte(r) *f(m)*; **to make friends with** sich anfreunden mit
friendly [ˈfrɛndlɪ] *adj* freundlich; (*government*) befreundet ▸ *n* (*also*: **~ match**) Freundschaftsspiel *nt*; **to be ~ with** befreundet sein mit
friendship [ˈfrɛndʃɪp] *n* Freundschaft *f*
fright [fraɪt] *n* Schreck(en) *m*
frighten [ˈfraɪtn] *vt* erschrecken
frightening [ˈfraɪtnɪŋ] *adj* furchterregend
frill [frɪl] *n* Rüsche *f*; **without frills** (*fig*) schlicht
fringe [frɪndʒ] *n* (Brit: *of hair*) Pony *m*; (*decoration*) Fransen *pl*; (*edge, also fig*) Rand *m*
frivolous [ˈfrɪvələs] *adj* frivol; (*activity*) leichtfertig
frizzy [ˈfrɪzɪ] *adj* kraus
frog [frɔg] *n* Frosch *m*

 **KEYWORD**

from [frɔm] *prep* **1** (*indicating starting place, origin*) von +*dat*; **where do you come from?** woher kommen Sie?; **a**

letter/telephone call from my sister ein Brief/Anruf von meiner Schwester; **to drink from the bottle** aus der Flasche trinken
2 (*indicating time*) von (... an); **from one o'clock to** *or* **until** *or* **till now** von ein Uhr bis jetzt; **from January (on)** von Januar an, ab Januar
3 (*indicating distance*) von ... entfernt
4 (*indicating price, number etc*): **trousers from £20** Hosen ab £20; **prices range from £10 to £50** die Preise liegen zwischen £10 und £50
5 (*indicating difference*): **he can't tell red from green** er kann Rot und Grün nicht unterscheiden; **to be different from sb/sth** anders sein als jd/etw
6 (*because of, on the basis of*): **from what he says** nach dem, was er sagt; **weak from hunger** schwach vor Hunger

front [frʌnt] *n* Vorderseite *f*; (*promenade*: *also*: **sea ~**) Strandpromenade *f*; (*Mil, Met*) Front *f*; (*fig*: *appearances*) Fassade *f* ▸ *adj* vorderste(r, s); (*wheel, tooth, view*) Vorder-; **in ~** vorne; **in ~ of** vor; **at the ~ of the coach/train/car** vorne im Bus/Zug/Auto
front door *n* Haustür *f*
frontier [ˈfrʌntɪəʳ] *n* Grenze *f*
front page *n* Titelseite *f*
front-wheel drive *n* (*Aut*) Vorderradantrieb *m*
frost [frɔst] *n* Frost *m*; (*also*: **hoarfrost**) Raureif *m*
frosting [ˈfrɔstɪŋ] (*esp US*) *n* Zuckerguss *m*
frosty [ˈfrɔstɪ] *adj* frostig
froth [frɔθ] *n* Schaum *m*
frothy [ˈfrɔθɪ] *adj* schäumend
frown [fraun] *vi* die Stirn runzeln
froze [frəuz] *pt of* **freeze**
frozen [ˈfrəuzn] *pp of* **freeze** ▸ *adj* tiefgekühlt; (*food*) Tiefkühl-
fruit [fru:t] *n inv* Frucht *f*; (*collectively*) Obst *nt*
fruit machine (Brit) *n* Spielautomat *m*
fruit salad *n* Obstsalat *m*
frustrated [frʌsˈtreɪtɪd] *adj* frustriert
frustration *n* Frustration *f*
fry [fraɪ] (*pt, pp* **fried**) *vt* braten; *see also* **small fry**
frying pan [ˈfraɪɪŋ-] *n* Bratpfanne *f*
fuchsia [ˈfju:ʃə] *n* Fuchsie *f*
fuck [fʌk] (!) *vt, vi* ficken (!); **~ off!** verpiss dich! (!)
fudge [fʌdʒ] *n* Fondant *m*
fuel [ˈfjuəl] *n* Brennstoff *m*; (*for vehicle*) Kraftstoff *m*
fuel consumption *n* Kraftstoffverbrauch *m*
fuel gauge *n* Benzinuhr *f*
fuel oil *n* Gasöl *nt*
fuel tank *n* Öltank *m*; (*in vehicle*) (Benzin)tank *m*
fugitive [ˈfju:dʒɪtɪv] *n* Flüchtling *m*
fulfil [fulˈfɪl] *vt* erfüllen
full [ful] *adj* voll; (*complete*) vollständig
full beam *n* (*Aut*) Fernlicht *nt*
full employment *n* Vollbeschäftigung *f*
full moon *n* Vollmond *m*
full stop *n* Punkt *m*
full-time [ˈfulˈtaɪm] *adj* (*work*) Ganztags-
fully [ˈfulɪ] *adv* völlig
fumble [ˈfʌmbl] *vi*: **to ~ with** herumfummeln an *+dat*
fumes [fju:mz] *npl* (*of fuel*) Dämpfe *pl*; (*of car*) Abgase *pl*
fun [fʌn] *n* Spaß *m*; **for ~** aus *or* zum Spaß; **to make ~ of, to poke ~ at** sich lustig machen über *+acc*
function [ˈfʌŋkʃən] *n* Funktion *f*; (*social occasion*) Feier *f* ▸ *vi* funktionieren
function key *n* (*Comput*) Funktionstaste *f*
fund [fʌnd] *n* (*of money*) Fonds *m*
▪ **funds** *npl* (*money*) Mittel *pl*
fundamental [fʌndəˈmɛntl] *adj* grundlegend
fundamentally [fʌndəˈmɛntəlɪ] *adv* im Grunde
funding [ˈfʌndɪŋ] *n* Finanzierung *f*
funeral [ˈfju:nərəl] *n* Beerdigung *f*
funfair [ˈfʌnfɛəʳ] (Brit) *n* Jahrmarkt *m*
fungus [ˈfʌŋgəs] (*pl* **fungi**) *n* Pilz *m*
funicular [fju:ˈnɪkjuləʳ] *n* (*also*: **~ railway**) Seilbahn *f*
funnel [ˈfʌnl] *n* Trichter *m*; (*of ship*) Schornstein *m*
funny [ˈfʌnɪ] *adj* komisch; (*strange*) seltsam, komisch
fur [fə:ʳ] *n* Fell *nt*, Pelz *m*
furious [ˈfjuərɪəs] *adj* wütend; **to be ~ with sb** wütend auf jdn sein

furnish [ˈfəːnɪʃ] *vt* einrichten; **furnished flat** (BRIT), **furnished apartment** (*US*) möblierte Wohnung *f*
furniture [ˈfəːnɪtʃəʳ] *n* Möbel *pl*; **piece of ~** Möbelstück *nt*
further [ˈfəːðəʳ] *adj comp of* **far**; weitere(r, s) ▶ *adv* weiter; **until ~ notice** bis auf Weiteres
further education (BRIT) *n* Weiterbildung *f*
furthest [ˈfəːðɪst] *superl of* **far**
fury [ˈfjuərɪ] *n* Wut *f*
fuse, (*US*) **fuze** [fjuːz] *n* (*Elec*) Sicherung *f* ▶ *vt* (*pieces of metal*) verschmelzen ▶ *vi*: **to ~ the lights** (BRIT) die Sicherung durchbrennen lassen
fuse box *n* Sicherungskasten *m*
fuss [fʌs] *n* Theater *nt* (*inf*); **to make a ~** Krach schlagen (*inf*)
fussy [ˈfʌsɪ] *adj* kleinlich, pingelig (*inf*)
future [ˈfjuːtʃəʳ] *adj* zukünftig ▶ *n* Zukunft *f*
fuze [fjuːz] (*US*) *n, vt, vi* = **fuse**
fuzzy [ˈfʌzɪ] *adj* verschwommen; (*hair*) kraus

g

gable [ˈgeɪbl] *n* Giebel *m*
gadget [ˈgædʒɪt] *n* Gerät *nt*
Gaelic [ˈgeɪlɪk] *adj* gälisch ▶ *n* (*Ling*) Gälisch *nt*
gage [geɪdʒ] (*US*) *n* = **gauge**
gain [geɪn] *n* Gewinn *m* ▶ *vt* gewinnen ▶ *vi* (*clock, watch*) vorgehen; **to ~ weight** zunehmen; **to ~ (in) confidence** sicherer werden
gale [geɪl] *n* Sturm *m*
gall bladder *n* Gallenblase *f*
gallery [ˈgælərɪ] *n* (*also*: **art ~**) Galerie *f*, Museum *nt*
gallon [ˈgæln] *n* Gallone *f* (*BRIT* = 4,5 *l*, *US* = 3,8 *l*)
gallop [ˈgæləp] *n* Galopp *m* ▶ *vi* galoppieren
gallstone [ˈgɔːlstəun] *n* Gallenstein *m*
Gambia [ˈgæmbɪə] *n* Gambia *nt*
gamble [ˈgæmbl] *n* Risiko *nt* ▶ *vi* ein Risiko eingehen; **to ~ on sth** (*horses, race*) auf etw *acc* wetten
gambling [ˈgæmblɪŋ] *n* Spielen *nt*
game [geɪm] *n* Spiel *nt*; (*Culin, Hunting*) Wild *nt* ■ **games** *npl* (*Scol*) Sport *m*; **to play a ~ of football/ tennis** Fußball/(eine Partie) Tennis spielen
games console *n* Spielkonsole *f*
game show *n* (*TV*) Spielshow *f*
gammon [ˈgæmən] *n* Schinken *m*
gang [gæŋ] *n* Bande *f*
▶ **gang up** *vi*: **to ~ up on sb** sich gegen jdn zusammentun
gangster [ˈgæŋstəʳ] *n* Gangster *m*
gangway [ˈgæŋweɪ] *n* Gangway *f*; (*in cinema, bus, plane etc*) Gang *m*

gap [gæp] *n* Lücke *f*; (*in time*) Pause *f*; (*difference*): **~ (between)** Kluft *f* (zwischen +*dat*)
gape [geɪp] *vi* starren
gap year *n Jahr zwischen Schulabschluss und Studium, das oft zu Auslandsaufenthalten genutzt wird*
garage [ˈgærɑːʒ] *n* Garage *f*; (*for car repairs*) (Reparatur)werkstatt *f*; (*petrol station*) Tankstelle *f*
garbage [ˈgɑːbɪdʒ] *n* (*US*: *rubbish*) Müll *m*; (*inf*: *nonsense*) Quatsch *m*
garbage can (*US*) *n* Mülleimer *m*, Abfalleimer *m*
garbage truck (*US*) *n* Müllwagen *m*
garden [ˈgɑːdn] *n* Garten *m* ■ **gardens** *npl* (*public park*) Park *m*
garden centre *n* Gartencenter *nt*
gardener [ˈgɑːdnəʳ] *n* Gärtner(in) *m(f)*
gardening [ˈgɑːdnɪŋ] *n* Gartenarbeit *f*
gargle [ˈgɑːgl] *vi* gurgeln
gargoyle [ˈgɑːgɔɪl] *n* Wasserspeier *m*
garlic [ˈgɑːlɪk] *n* Knoblauch *m*
garlic bread *n* Knoblauchbrot *nt*
gas [gæs] *n* Gas *nt*; (*US*: *gasoline*) Benzin *nt*
gas cooker (Brit) *n* Gasherd *m*
gas cylinder *n* Gasflasche *f*
gas fire (Brit) *n* Gasofen *m*
gasket [ˈgæskɪt] *n* Dichtung *f*
gas mask *n* Gasmaske *f*
gas meter *n* Gaszähler *m*
gasoline [ˈgæsəliːn] (*US*) *n* Benzin *nt*
gasp [gɑːsp] *vi* keuchen; (*in surprise*) nach Luft schnappen
gas station (*US*) *n* Tankstelle *f*
gas tank *n* Benzintank *m*
gastric [ˈgæstrɪk] *adj* (*upset, ulcer etc*) Magen-
gastric band *n* Magenband *nt*
gasworks [ˈgæswəːks] *n* Gaswerk *nt*
gate [geɪt] *n* (*of building*) Tor *nt*; (*at airport*) Flugsteig *m*; (*of level crossing*) Schranke *f*
gateau [ˈgætəu] (*pl* **gateaux**) *n* Torte *f*
gateway *n* (*also fig*) Tor *nt*
gather [ˈgæðəʳ] *vt* sammeln ▶ *vi* (*assemble*) sich versammeln; **to ~ (from)** schließen (aus); **to ~ speed** schneller werden
gathering [ˈgæðərɪŋ] *n* Versammlung *f*
gauge, (*US*) **gage** [geɪdʒ] *n* Messgerät *nt*
gauze [gɔːz] *n* Gaze *f*
gave [geɪv] *pt of* **give**
gay [geɪ] *adj* schwul
gay marriage *n* Homoehe *f* (*inf*)
gaze [geɪz] *n* Blick *m* ▶ *vi*: **to ~ at sth** etw anstarren
GCSE (Brit) *n abbr* (= *General Certificate of Secondary Education*) *Schulabschlusszeugnis*, ≈ mittlere Reife *f*

GCSE

Das **GCSE** (*General Certificate of Secondary Education*) sind die Prüfungen in mehreren Fächern, die junge Engländer, Waliser und Nordiren um die 16 Jahre ablegen müssen. Ihr erfolgreiches Absolvieren ist eine der Voraussetzungen für die Weiterführung der Oberstufenbildung bis zu den *A levels* (siehe auch *A level*). Die GCSE-Ergebnisse sind ebenso wichtig für die Schüler, die in diesem Stadium die Schule verlassen, um einen Arbeitsplatz zu finden. Die Anzahl der geprüften Fächer liegt zwischen 8 und 11. Gewisse sind obligatorisch, wie z.B. Englisch, Mathe und Naturwissenschaften.

gear [gɪəʳ] *n* (*equipment*) Ausrüstung *f*; (*belongings*) Sachen *pl*; (*Aut*) Gang *m*; **to put a car into ~** einen Gang einlegen
gearbox [ˈgɪəbɔks] *n* Getriebe *nt*
gear lever, (*US*) **gear shift** *n* Schalthebel *m*
geese [giːs] *npl of* **goose**
gel [dʒɛl] *n* Gel *nt*
gem [dʒɛm] *n* Edelstein *m*; **she/the house is a ~** (*fig*) sie/das Haus ist ein Juwel
Gemini [ˈdʒɛmɪnaɪ] *n* Zwillinge *pl*
gender [ˈdʒɛndəʳ] *n* Geschlecht *nt*
gene [dʒiːn] *n* Gen *nt*
general [ˈdʒɛnərl] *adj* allgemein
general election *n* Parlamentswahlen *pl*
generalize [ˈdʒɛnrəlaɪz] *vi* verallgemeinern
generally [ˈdʒɛnrəlɪ] *adv* im Allgemeinen
general practitioner *n* praktischer Arzt *m*, praktische Ärztin *f*
generation [dʒɛnəˈreɪʃən] *n* Generation *f*

generator [ˈdʒɛnəreɪtəʳ] *n* Generator *m*
generosity [dʒɛnəˈrɔsɪtɪ] *n* Großzügigkeit *f*
generous [ˈdʒɛnərəs] *adj* großzügig; (*measure, remuneration*) reichlich
genetic [dʒɪˈnɛtɪk] *adj* genetisch
genetically *adv* genetisch; **~ modified** genmanipuliert
Geneva [dʒɪˈniːvə] *n* Genf *nt*
genitals [ˈdʒɛnɪtlz] *npl* Geschlechtsteile *pl*
genitive [ˈdʒɛnɪtɪv] *n* Genitiv *m*
genius [ˈdʒiːnɪəs] *n* (*person*) Genie *nt*
genome [ˈdʒiːnəum] *n* Genom *nt*
gentle [ˈdʒɛntl] *adj* sanft; (*movement, breeze*) leicht
gentleman [ˈdʒɛntlmən] *n* (*irreg*) Herr *m*; (*referring to social position or good manners*) Gentleman *m*
gents [dʒɛnts] *n*: **the ~** die Herrentoilette
genuine [ˈdʒɛnjuɪn] *adj* echt
geographic [dʒɪəˈgræfɪk], **geographical** [dʒɪəˈgræfɪkl] *adj* geografisch
geography [dʒɪˈɔgrəfɪ] *n* Geografie *f*; (*Scol*) Erdkunde *f*
geological [dʒɪəˈlɔdʒɪkl] *adj* geologisch
geology [dʒɪˈɔlədʒɪ] *n* Geologie *f*
geometry [dʒɪˈɔmətrɪ] *n* Geometrie *f*
geranium [dʒɪˈreɪnɪəm] *n* Geranie *f*
gerbil [ˈdʒəːbɪl] *n* (*Zool*) Wüstenrennmaus *f*
germ [dʒəːm] *n* Bazillus *m*; (*Biol, fig*) Keim *m*
German [ˈdʒəːmən] *adj* deutsch ▸ *n* Deutsche(r) *f*(*m*); (*Ling*) Deutsch *nt*
German measles (Brit) *n* Röteln *pl*
Germany [ˈdʒəːmənɪ] *n* Deutschland *nt*
gesture [ˈdʒɛstjəʳ] *n* Geste *f*

 **KEYWORD**

get [gɛt] (*pt, pp* **got**, *US pp* **gotten**) *vi*
1 (*become, be*) werden; **to get old/tired/cold** alt/müde/kalt werden; **to get married** heiraten
2 (*go*): **to get (from ...) to ...** (von ...) nach ... kommen
3 (*begin*): **to get to know sb** jdn kennenlernen; **let's get going** *or* **started** fangen wir an!
▸ *modal aux vb*: **you've got to do it** du musst es tun
▸ *vt* **1**: **to get sth done** (*do oneself*) etw gemacht bekommen; (*have done*) etw machen lassen; **to get the car going** *or* **to go** das Auto in Gang bringen; **to get sb to do sth** etw von jdm machen lassen
2 (*obtain: money, permission, results*) erhalten
3 (*fetch: person, doctor, object*) holen
4 (*find: job, flat*) finden; **to get sth for sb** jdm etw besorgen
5 (*receive, acquire: present, prize*) bekommen
6 (*catch*) bekommen, kriegen (*inf*)
7 (*hit: target etc*) treffen
8 (*take, move*) bringen; **to get sth to sb** jdm etw zukommen lassen
9 (*plane, bus etc: take*) nehmen
10 (*understand: joke etc*) verstehen; **I get it** ich verstehe
11 (*have, possess*): **to have got** haben; **how many have you got?** wie viele hast du?
▸ **get about** *vi* (*person*) herumkommen; (*news, rumour*) sich verbreiten
▸ **get across** *vt* (*message, meaning*) klarmachen
▸ **get along** *vi* (*be friends*) (miteinander) auskommen; (*depart*) sich auf den Weg machen
▸ **get at** *vt fus* (*attack, criticize*) angreifen; (*reach*) herankommen an *+acc*; **what are you getting at?** worauf willst du hinaus?
▸ **get away** *vi* (*leave*) wegkommen; (*escape*) entkommen
▸ **get away with** *vt fus* (*stolen goods*) entkommen mit
▸ **get back** *vi* (*return*) zurückkommen ▸ *vt* (*regain*) zurückbekommen
▸ **get by** *vi* (*pass*) vorbeikommen; (*manage*) zurechtkommen
▸ **get down** *vi* (*from tree, ladder etc*) heruntersteigen ▸ *vt* (*depress: person*) fertigmachen; (*write*) aufschreiben
▸ **get down to** *vt fus*: **to get down to sth** (*work*) etw in Angriff nehmen; (*find time*) zu etw kommen
▸ **get in** *vi* (*arrive*) ankommen
▸ **get into** *vt fus* (*conversation, argument, fight*) geraten in *+acc*; (*vehicle*) einsteigen in *+acc*; (*clothes*) hineinkommen in *+acc*; **to get into trouble** in Schwierigkeiten kommen

▸ **get off** *vi* (*from train etc*) aussteigen ▸ *vt* (*remove*: *clothes*) ausziehen; (: *stain*) herausbekommen ▸ *vt fus* (*leave*: *train, bus*) aussteigen aus
▸ **get on** *vi* (*be friends*) (miteinander) auskommen ▸ *vt fus* (*bus, train*) einsteigen in +*acc*; **how are you getting on?** wie kommst du zurecht?
▸ **get out** *vi* (*leave*: *on foot*) hinausgehen; (*of vehicle*) aussteigen ▸ *vt* (*take out*: *book etc*) herausholen; (*remove*: *stain*) herausbekommen
▸ **get out of** *vt fus* (*avoid*: *duty etc*) herumkommen um
▸ **get over** *vt fus* (*overcome*) überwinden; (: *illness*) sich erholen von
▸ **get round** *vt fus* (*person*) herumkriegen
▸ **get through** *vi* (*Tel*) durchkommen
▸ **get through to** *vt fus* (*Tel*) durchkommen zu
▸ **get together** *vi* (*people*) zusammenkommen
▸ **get up** *vi* (*rise*) aufstehen ▸ *vt*: **to get up enthusiasm for sth** Begeisterung für etw aufbringen
▸ **get up to** *vt fus* (*prank etc*) anstellen

getaway *n*: **to make a/one's ~** sich davonmachen
get-together [ˈgɛttəgɛðəʳ] *n* Treffen *nt*
Ghana [ˈgɑːnə] *n* Ghana *nt*
gherkin [ˈgəːkɪn] *n* Gewürzgurke *f*
ghetto [ˈgɛtəu] *n* G(h)etto *nt*
ghost [gəust] *n* Geist *m*, Gespenst *nt*
giant [ˈdʒaɪənt] *n* (*also fig*) Riese *m* ▸ *adj* riesig, riesenhaft
Gibraltar [dʒɪˈbrɔːltəʳ] *n* Gibraltar *nt*
giddy [ˈgɪdɪ] *adj*: **I am/feel ~** mir ist schwind(e)lig
gift [gɪft] *n* Geschenk *nt*; (*ability*) Gabe *f*
gifted [ˈgɪftɪd] *adj* begabt
gig [gɪg] *n* (*inf*: *performance*) Gig *m*
gigantic [dʒaɪˈgæntɪk] *adj* riesig, riesengroß
giggle [ˈgɪgl] *vi* kichern ▸ *n* Spaß *m*
gills [gɪlz] *npl* Kiemen *pl*
gimmick [ˈgɪmɪk] *n* Gag *m*; **sales ~** Verkaufsmasche *f*
gin [dʒɪn] *n* Gin *m*
ginger [ˈdʒɪndʒəʳ] *n* Ingwer *m* ▸ *adj* (*hair*) rötlich
ginger ale *n* Gingerale *nt*
ginger beer *n* Ingwerbier *nt*
gingerbread [ˈdʒɪndʒəbrɛd] *n* (*cake*) Ingwerkuchen *m*
gingerly [ˈdʒɪndʒəlɪ] *adv* vorsichtig
gipsy [ˈdʒɪpsɪ] *n* Zigeuner(in) *m(f)*
giraffe [dʒɪˈrɑːf] *n* Giraffe *f*
girl [gəːl] *n* Mädchen *nt*
girlfriend [ˈgəːlfrɛnd] *n* Freundin *f*
Girl Guide *n* Pfadfinderin *f*
gist [dʒɪst] *n* Wesentliche(s) *nt*

 KEYWORD

give [gɪv] (*pt* **gave**, *pp* **given**) *vt*
1 (*hand over*): **to give sb sth, give sth to sb** jdm etw geben
2 (*used with noun to replace a verb*): **to give a sigh/cry/laugh** *etc* seufzen/schreien/lachen *etc*; **to give a speech/a lecture** eine Rede/einen Vortrag halten
3 (*tell, deliver*: *news, message etc*) mitteilen; (: *advice, answer*) geben
4 (*supply, provide*: *opportunity, job etc*) geben
5 (*bestow*: *title, honour, right*) geben, verleihen
6 (*devote*: *time, one's life*) geben; (: *attention*) schenken
7 (*organize*: *party, dinner etc*) geben
▸ *vi* (*break, collapse*: *also*: **~ way**) nachgeben
▸ **give away** *vt* (*money, opportunity*) verschenken; (*secret, information*) verraten
▸ **give back** *vt* (*money, book etc*) zurückgeben
▸ **give in** *vi* (*yield*) nachgeben
▸ **give up** *vt, vi* aufgeben
▸ **give way** *vi* (*yield, collapse*) nachgeben; (BRIT *Aut*) die Vorfahrt achten

given [ˈgɪvn] *pp of* **give** ▸ *adj* (*time, amount*) bestimmt ▸ *conj*: **~ the circumstances ...** unter den Umständen ...; **~ that ...** angesichts der Tatsache, dass ...
glacier [ˈglæsɪəʳ] *n* Gletscher *m*
glad [glæd] *adj* froh; **to be ~ that** sich freuen, dass
gladly [ˈglædlɪ] *adv* gern(e)
glance [glɑːns] *n* Blick *m* ▸ *vi*: **to ~ at** einen Blick werfen auf +*acc*
gland [glænd] *n* Drüse *f*
glandular fever [ˈglændjulə-] (BRIT) *n* Drüsenfieber *nt*

glare [glɛəʳ] *n* wütender Blick *m*; (*of publicity*) grelles Licht *nt* ▸ *vi*: **to ~ at** (wütend) anstarren
glaring [ˈglɛərɪŋ] *adj* eklatant
glass [glɑːs] *n* Glas *nt* ▪ **glasses** *npl* (*spectacles*) Brille *f*
glen [glɛn] *n* Tal *nt*
glide [glaɪd] *vi* gleiten
glider [ˈglaɪdəʳ] *n* Segelflugzeug *nt*
gliding [ˈglaɪdɪŋ] *n* Segelfliegen *nt*
glimmer [ˈglɪməʳ] *n* Schimmer *m*
glimpse [glɪmps] *n* Blick *m*
glitter [ˈglɪtəʳ] *vi* glitzern; (*eyes*) funkeln
glitzy [ˈglɪtsɪ] *adj* (*inf*) glanzvoll, Schickimicki-
global [ˈgləubl] *adj* global
global warming [-ˈwɔːmɪŋ] *n* Erwärmung *f* der Erdatmosphäre
globe [gləub] *n* Erdball *m*; (*model*) Globus *m*; (*shape*) Kugel *f*
gloomily [ˈgluːmɪlɪ] *adv* düster
glorious [ˈglɔːrɪəs] *adj* herrlich; (*victory*) ruhmreich
glory [ˈglɔːrɪ] *n* (*splendour*) Herrlichkeit *f*
gloss [glɔs] *n* Glanz *m*
glossary [ˈglɔsərɪ] *n* Glossar *nt*
glossy [ˈglɔsɪ] *adj* glänzend ▸ *n* (*also*: **~ magazine**) (Hochglanz)magazin *nt*
glove [glʌv] *n* Handschuh *m*
glove compartment *n* Handschuhfach *nt*
glow [gləu] *vi* glühen
glucose [ˈgluːkəus] *n* Traubenzucker *m*
glue [gluː] *n* Klebstoff *m* ▸ *vt*: **to ~ sth onto sth** etw an etw *acc* kleben
glute [gluːt] *n* (*inf*) Gesäßmuskel *m*
glutton [ˈglʌtn] *n* Vielfraß *m*; **a ~ for punishment** ein Masochist *m*
GM *abbr* = **genetically modified**
GM crop *n abbr* GV-Pflanze *f*
GM foods *n* GV-Lebensmittel *pl*
GMT *abbr* (= *Greenwich Mean Time*) WEZ *f*

KEYWORD

go [gəu] (*pt* **went**, *pp* **gone**) *vi* **1** gehen; (*travel*) fahren
2 (*depart*) gehen; **she has gone to Sheffield/Australia** (*permanently*) sie ist nach Sheffield/Australien gegangen
3 (*attend, take part in activity*) gehen; **she went to university in Oxford** sie ist in Oxford zur Universität gegangen; **to go for a walk** spazieren gehen; **to go dancing** tanzen gehen
4 (*work*) funktionieren
5 (*become*): **to go pale/mouldy** blass/schimmelig werden
6 (*be sold*): **to go for £100** für £100 weggehen *or* verkauft werden
7 (*be about to, intend to*): **we're going to stop in an hour** wir hören in einer Stunde auf; **are you going to come?** kommst du?, wirst du kommen?
8 (*time*) vergehen
9 (*event, activity*) ablaufen; **how did it go?** wie wars?
10 (*be given*): **the job is to go to someone else** die Stelle geht an jemand anders
11 (*break etc*) kaputtgehen
12 (*be placed*) hingehören; **the milk goes in the fridge** die Milch kommt in den Kühlschrank
▸ *n* **1** (*try*): **to have a go at sth** etw versuchen; **I'll have a go at mending it** ich will versuchen, es zu reparieren; **to have a go** es versuchen
2 (*turn*): **whose go is it?** wer ist dran *or* an der Reihe?
▸ **go after** *vt fus* (*pursue: person*) nachgehen +*dat*
▸ **go ahead** *vi* (*proceed*) weitergehen; **to go ahead with** weitermachen mit
▸ **go away** *vi* (*leave*) weggehen
▸ **go back** *vi* zurückgehen
▸ **go by** *vi* (*years, time*) vergehen ▸ *vt fus* (*rule etc*) sich richten nach
▸ **go down** *vi* (*descend*) hinuntergehen; (*ship, sun*) untergehen; (*price, level*) sinken ▸ *vt fus* (*stairs, ladder*) hinuntergehen; **his speech went down well** seine Rede kam gut an
▸ **go in** *vi* (*enter*) hineingehen
▸ **go into** *vt fus* (*enter*) hineingehen in +*acc*; (*investigate*) sich befassen mit; (*career*) gehen in +*acc*
▸ **go off** *vi* (*leave*) weggehen; (*food*) schlecht werden; (*bomb, gun*) losgehen; (*event*) verlaufen; (*lights etc*) ausgehen ▸ *vt fus* (*inf*): **I've gone off it/him** ich mache mir nichts mehr daraus/aus ihm
▸ **go on** *vi* (*continue*) weitergehen; (*lights*) angehen; **to go on doing sth** mit etw weitermachen

▶ **go out** *vt fus* (*leave*) hinausgehen ▶ *vi* (*for entertainment*) ausgehen; (*fire, light*) ausgehen
▶ **go up** *vi* (*ascend*) hinaufgehen; (*price, level*) steigen
▶ **go without** *vt fus* (*food, treats*) verzichten auf +*acc*

go-ahead [ˈgəuəhɛd] *adj* (*firm*) fortschrittlich ▶ *n* grünes Licht *nt*
goal [gəul] *n* Tor *nt*; (*aim*) Ziel *nt*
goalie [ˈgəulɪ] (*inf*) *n* Tormann *m*
goalkeeper [ˈgəulkiːpəʳ] *n* Torwart *m*
goal post *n* Torpfosten *m*
goat [gəut] *n* Ziege *f*
gob [gɔb] *n* (BRIT *inf*) Maul *nt* ▶ *vi* spucken; **shut your ~** halt's Maul!
gobsmacked [ˈgɔbsmækt] *adj* (*inf: surprised*) platt
go-cart [ˈgəukɑːt] *n* Gokart *m*
god [gɔd] *n* Gott *m*
godchild [ˈgɔdtʃaɪld] *n* (*irreg*) Patenkind *nt*
goddaughter [ˈgɔddɔːtəʳ] *n* Patentochter *f*
goddess [ˈgɔdɪs] *n* Göttin *f*
godfather [ˈgɔdfɑːðəʳ] *n* Pate *m*
godmother [ˈgɔdmʌðəʳ] *n* Patin *f*
godson [ˈgɔdsʌn] *n* Patensohn *m*
goggles *npl* Schutzbrille *f*
going [ˈgəuɪŋ] *adj*: **the ~ rate** der gängige Preis
goings-on [ˈgəuɪŋzˈɔn] (*inf*) *npl* Vorgänge *pl*
go-kart [ˈgəukɑːt] *n* = **go-cart**
gold [gəuld] *n* Gold *nt*
golden [ˈgəuldən] *adj* (*also fig*) golden
goldfish [ˈgəuldfɪʃ] *n* Goldfisch *m*
gold-plated [ˈgəuldˈpleɪtɪd] *adj* vergoldet
golf [gɔlf] *n* Golf *nt*
golf ball *n* (*for game*) Golfball *m*
golf club *n* Golfklub *m*; (*stick*) Golfschläger *m*
golf course *n* Golfplatz *m*
golfer [ˈgɔlfəʳ] *n* Golfspieler(in) *m(f)*, Golfer(in) *m(f)*
gone [gɔn] *pp of* **go** ▶ *adj* weg
good [gud] *adj* gut; (*well-behaved*) brav, lieb ▶ *n* (*virtue, morality*) Gute(s) *nt*; (*benefit*) Wohl *nt* ■ **goods** *npl* (*Comm*) Güter *pl*; **to have a ~ time** sich (gut) amüsieren; **to be ~ at sth** (*swimming, talking etc*) etw gut können; (*science, sports etc*) gut in etw *dat* sein; **it's ~ for you** das tut dir gut; **a ~ deal (of)** ziemlich viel; **a ~ many** ziemlich viele; **a ~ while ago** vor einiger Zeit; **it's no ~ complaining** es ist sinnlos *or* es nützt nichts, sich zu beklagen; **~ morning/afternoon/evening!** guten Morgen/Tag/Abend!; **~ night!** gute Nacht!; **for the common ~** zum Wohle aller; **for ~** für immer
goodbye [gudˈbaɪ] *excl* auf Wiedersehen!
Good Friday *n* Karfreitag *m*
good-looking *adj* gut aussehend
goods train (BRIT) *n* Güterzug *m*
goodwill [gudˈwɪl] *n* Wohlwollen *nt*
Google® [ˈguːgl] *n* Google® *nt* ▶ *vt*: **to google** googeln
goose [guːs] (*pl* **geese**) *n* Gans *f*
gooseberry [ˈguzbərɪ] *n* Stachelbeere *f*
goose bumps *n* = **goose pimples**
goose pimples *npl* Gänsehaut *f*
gorge [gɔːdʒ] *n* Schlucht *f*
gorgeous [ˈgɔːdʒəs] *adj* herrlich; (*person*) hinreißend
gorilla [gəˈrɪlə] *n* Gorilla *m*
gossip [ˈgɔsɪp] *n* (*rumours*) Klatsch *m*; (*person*) Klatschbase *f* ▶ *vi* schwatzen
got [gɔt] *pt, pp of* **get**
gotten [ˈgɔtn] (*US*) *pp of* **get**
govern [ˈgʌvən] *vt* (*also Ling*) regieren; (*event, conduct*) bestimmen
government [ˈgʌvnmənt] *n* Regierung *f*
governor [ˈgʌvənəʳ] *n* Gouverneur(in) *m(f)*
Govt *abbr* = **government**
gown [gaun] *n* (Abend)kleid *nt*; (*of teacher, Brit: of judge*) Robe *f*
GP *n abbr* = **general practitioner**
GPS *abbr* (= *global positioning system*) GPS *nt*
grab [græb] *vt* packen; (*chance, opportunity*) (beim Schopf) ergreifen
grace [greɪs] *n* (*gracefulness*) Anmut *f*; **5 days' ~** 5 Tage Aufschub; **to say ~** das Tischgebet sprechen
graceful [ˈgreɪsful] *adj* anmutig
grade [greɪd] *n* (*Comm*) (Güte)klasse *f*; (*in hierarchy*) Rang *m*; (*Scol: mark*) Note *f*; (*US: school class*) Klasse *f*; **to make the ~** (*fig*) es schaffen
grade crossing (*US*) *n* Bahnübergang *m*
grade school (*US*) *n* Grundschule *f*
gradient [ˈgreɪdɪənt] *n* (*upward*) Steigung *f*; (*downward*) Gefälle *nt*

gradual [ˈgrædjuəl] *adj* allmählich
graduate *n* [ˈgrædjuɪt] (*of university*) Hochschulabsolvent(in) *m*(*f*) ▶ *vi* [ˈgrædjueɪt] (*from university*) graduieren
grain [greɪn] *n* Korn *nt*; (*no pl*: *cereals*) Getreide *nt*; (*of wood*) Maserung *f*
gram [græm] *n* Gramm *nt*
grammar [ˈgræmə^r] *n* Grammatik *f*
grammar school (BRIT) *n* ≈ Gymnasium *nt*
gran [græn] (*inf*) *n* Oma *f*
grand [grænd] *adj* großartig; (*inf*: *wonderful*) fantastisch ▶ *n* (*inf*) ≈ Riese *m* (*1000 Pfund/Dollar*)
grandad *n* (*inf*) = **granddad**
granddad (*inf*) *n* Opa *m*
granddaughter [ˈgrændɔːtə^r] *n* Enkelin *f*
grandfather [ˈgrændfɑːðə^r] *n* Großvater *m*
grandma [ˈgrænmɑː] (*inf*) *n* Oma *f*
grandmother [ˈgrænmʌðə^r] *n* Großmutter *f*
grandpa [ˈgrænpɑː] (*inf*) *n* Opa *m*
grandparents [ˈgrændpɛərənts] *npl* Großeltern *pl*
grandson [ˈgrænsʌn] *n* Enkel *m*
grandstand *n* Haupttribüne *f*
granny [ˈgrænɪ] (*inf*) *n* Oma *f*
grant [grɑːnt] *vt* (*request etc*) gewähren ▶ *n* Stipendium *nt*; (*subsidy*) Subvention *f*; **to take sth for granted** etw für selbstverständlich halten; **to take sb for granted** jdn als selbstverständlich hinnehmen
granular *adj* körnig, granulär; (*detailed*) detailliert
grape [greɪp] *n* (Wein)traube *f*
grapefruit [ˈgreɪpfruːt] (*pl* ~ *or* **grapefruits**) *n* Grapefruit *f*
graph [grɑːf] *n* (*diagram*) grafische Darstellung *f*
graphic [ˈgræfɪk] *adj* plastisch, anschaulich
grasp [grɑːsp] *vt* (*seize*) ergreifen; (*understand*) begreifen
grass [grɑːs] *n* Gras *nt*; (*lawn*) Rasen *m*
grasshopper [ˈgrɑːshɔpə^r] *n* Heuschrecke *f*
grate [greɪt] *n* (Feuer)rost *m* ▶ *vt* reiben ▶ *vi*: **to ~ (on)** kratzen (auf +*dat*)
grateful [ˈgreɪtful] *adj* dankbar
gratefully [ˈgreɪtfəlɪ] *adv* dankbar
grater [ˈgreɪtə^r] *n* Reibe *f*
gratify [ˈgrætɪfaɪ] *vt* (*please*) erfreuen
gratifying [ˈgrætɪfaɪɪŋ] *adj* erfreulich
gratitude [ˈgrætɪtjuːd] *n* Dankbarkeit *f*
grave [greɪv] *n* Grab *nt* ▶ *adj* (*decision, mistake*) schwer (wiegend)
gravel [ˈgrævl] *n* Kies *m*
graveyard [ˈgreɪvjɑːd] *n* Friedhof *m*
gravity [ˈgrævɪtɪ] *n* Schwerkraft *f*; (*seriousness*) Ernst *m*
gravy [ˈgreɪvɪ] *n* (*sauce*) (Braten)soße *f*
gray [greɪ] (US) *adj* = **grey**
graze [greɪz] *vi* grasen ▶ *vt* streifen; (*scrape*) aufschürfen ▶ *n* (*Med*) Abschürfung *f*
grease [griːs] *n* (*lubricant*) Schmiere *f*; (*fat*) Fett *nt* ▶ *vt* schmieren; fetten
greasy [ˈgriːsɪ] *adj* fettig; (*food*: *containing grease*) fett; (*tools*) schmierig
great [greɪt] *adj* groß; (*inf*: *terrific*) prima, toll
Great Britain *n* Großbritannien *nt*

GREAT BRITAIN

Auch wenn man meistens unterschiedslos von **Great Britain** (Großbritannien) oder vom *United Kingdom* (das Vereinigte Königreich) spricht, stehen doch diese Begriffe für verschiedene Sachlagen. England, Wales und Schottland bilden *Great Britain*, während das Vereinigte Königreich aus Großbritannien und Nordirland besteht.

great-grandfather [greɪtˈgrænfɑːðə^r] *n* Urgroßvater *m*
great-grandmother [greɪtˈgrænmʌðə^r] *n* Urgroßmutter *f*
greatly [ˈgreɪtlɪ] *adv* sehr; (*influenced*) stark
Greece [griːs] *n* Griechenland *nt*
greed [griːd] *n* (*also*: **greediness**): **~ for** Gier *f* nach
greedy [ˈgriːdɪ] *adj* gierig
Greek [griːk] *adj* griechisch ▶ *n* Grieche *m*, Griechin *f*; (*Ling*) Griechisch *nt*
green [griːn] *adj* (*also ecological*) grün ▶ *n* (*also Golf*) Grün *nt*; (*also*: **village ~**) Dorfwiese *f* ■ **greens** *npl* (*vegetables*) Grüngemüse *nt*; **the Greens** (*Pol*) die Grünen *pl*

green card *n* (*Aut*) grüne (Versicherungs)karte *f*; (*US*) ≈ Aufenthaltserlaubnis *f*
greengage [ˈgri:ngeɪdʒ] *n* Reneklode *f*
greengrocer [ˈgri:ngrəusəʳ] (Brit) *n* Obst- und Gemüsehändler(in) *m*(*f*)
greenhouse [ˈgri:nhaus] *n* Gewächshaus *nt*; **~ effect** Treibhauseffekt *m*
Greenland [ˈgri:nlənd] *n* Grönland *nt*
green pepper *n* grüne Paprikaschote *f*
green tax *n* Ökosteuer *f*
Greenwich Mean Time [ˈgrɛnɪdʒ-] *n* westeuropäische Zeit
greet [gri:t] *vt* begrüßen
greeting [ˈgri:tɪŋ] *n* Gruß *m*
Grenada [grɛˈneɪdə] *n* Grenada *nt*
grew [gru:] *pt of* **grow**
grey, (*US*) **gray** [greɪ] *adj* grau
grey-haired [greɪˈhɛəd] *adj* grauhaarig
greyhound [ˈgreɪhaund] *n* Windhund *m*
grid [grɪd] *n* Gitter *nt*
gridlock [ˈgrɪdlɔk] *n* (*esp US: on road*) totaler Stau *m* ▶ *vt*: **to be gridlocked** (*roads*) total verstopft sein; (*talks etc*) festgefahren sein
grief [gri:f] *n* Kummer *m*, Trauer *f*
grievance [ˈgri:vəns] *n* Beschwerde *f*
grieve [gri:v] *vi* trauern
grill [grɪl] *n* Grill *m* ▶ *vt* (Brit) grillen
grim [grɪm] *adj* trostlos; (*serious, stern*) grimmig
grin [grɪn] *n* Grinsen *nt*
grind [graɪnd] (*pt, pp* **ground**) *vt* (*coffee, pepper etc*) mahlen; (*US: meat*) hacken, durch den Fleischwolf drehen; (*knife*) schleifen
grip [grɪp] *n* Griff *m* ▶ *vt* packen; **to come to grips with sth** etw in den Griff bekommen
gripping [ˈgrɪpɪŋ] *adj* fesselnd
groan [grəun] *vi* stöhnen
grocer [ˈgrəusəʳ] *n* Lebensmittelhändler(in) *m*(*f*)
groceries [ˈgrəusərɪz] *npl* Lebensmittel *pl*
groin [grɔɪn] *n* Leistengegend *f*
groom [gru:m] *n* (*also:* **bridegroom**) Bräutigam *m* ▶ *vt*: **well-groomed** gepflegt
grope [grəup] *vi*: **to ~ for** tasten nach
gross [grəus] *adj* (*neglect*) grob; (*injustice*) krass; (*behaviour, speech*) grob, derb; (*Comm: income, weight*) Brutto-
gross national product *n* Bruttosozialprodukt *nt*
grotty [ˈgrɔtɪ] (*inf*) *adj* mies
ground [graund] *pt, pp of* **grind** ▶ *n* Boden *m*, Erde *f*; (*Sport*) Platz *m*, Feld *nt*; (*reason: gen pl*) Grund *m* ■ **grounds** *npl* (*of coffee etc*) Satz *m*; (*gardens etc*) Anlagen *pl*; **on the grounds that** mit der Begründung, dass
ground floor *n* Erdgeschoss *nt*, Erdgeschoß *nt* (Österr)
group [gru:p] *n* Gruppe *f* ▶ *vt* (*also:* **~ together**: *in one group*) zusammentun
grouse [graus] *n inv* schottisches Moorhuhn *nt*
grow [grəu] (*pt* **grew**, *pp* **grown**) *vi* wachsen; (*increase*) zunehmen; (*become*) werden ▶ *vt* (*vegetables*) anbauen, ziehen; (*beard*) sich *dat* wachsen lassen
▶ **grow up** *vi* aufwachsen; (*mature*) erwachsen werden
growing [ˈgrəuɪŋ] *adj* wachsend; (*number*) zunehmend
growl [graul] *vi* knurren
grown [grəun] *pp of* **grow**
grown-up [ˈgrəunʌp] *n* Erwachsene(r) *f*(*m*)
growth [grəuθ] *n* Wachstum *nt*; (*Med*) Wucherung *f*
grubby [ˈgrʌbɪ] *adj* (*dirty*) schmuddelig
grudge [grʌdʒ] *n* Groll *m* ▶ *vt*: **to ~ sb sth** jdm etw nicht gönnen
gruelling, (*US*) **grueling** [ˈgruəlɪŋ] *adj* (*encounter*) aufreibend; (*trip, journey*) äußerst strapaziös
gruesome [ˈgru:səm] *adj* grauenhaft
grumble [ˈgrʌmbl] *vi* murren
grumpy [ˈgrʌmpɪ] *adj* mürrisch, brummig
grunt [grʌnt] *vi* grunzen
G-string [ˈdʒi:strɪŋ] *n* Minislip *m*, Tangaslip *m*
guarantee [gærənˈti:] *n* Garantie *f* ▶ *vt* garantieren
guard [gɑ:d] *n* Wache *f*; (Brit *Rail*) Schaffner(in) *m*(*f*) ▶ *vt* (*prisoner*) bewachen; (*secret*) hüten (vor +*dat*)
guardian [ˈgɑ:dɪən] *n* Vormund *m*
guess [gɛs] *vt* schätzen; (*answer*) (er)raten ▶ *vi* schätzen; raten ▶ *n* Vermutung *f*; **I ~ you're right** da

haben Sie wohl recht; **to take** *or* **have a ~** raten; (*estimate*) schätzen
guest [gɛst] *n* Gast *m*; **be my ~** (*inf*) nur zu!
guesthouse *n* Pension *f*
guest room *n* Gästezimmer *nt*
guidance [ˈgaɪdəns] *n* Rat *m*, Beratung *f*
guide [gaɪd] *n* (*person*) Führer(in) *m*(*f*); (*book*) Führer *m*; (BRIT: *also*: **girl ~**) Pfadfinderin *f* ▶ *vt* führen
guidebook [ˈgaɪdbuk] *n* Führer *m*
guide dog *n* Blindenhund *m*
guidelines [ˈgaɪdlaɪnz] *npl* Richtlinien *pl*
guilt [gɪlt] *n* Schuld *f*
guilty [ˈgɪltɪ] *adj* schuldig; (*expression*) schuldbewusst
guinea pig *n* Meerschweinchen *nt*; (*fig*: *person*) Versuchskaninchen *nt*
guitar [gɪˈtɑːʳ] *n* Gitarre *f*
gulf [gʌlf] *n* Golf *m*; (*fig*: *difference*) Kluft *f*
Gulf States *npl*: **the ~** die Golfstaaten *pl*
gull [gʌl] *n* Möwe *f*
gullible [ˈgʌlɪbl] *adj* leichtgläubig
gulp [gʌlp] *vi* schlucken ▶ *n*: **at one ~** mit einem Schluck
gum [gʌm] *n* (*Anat*) Zahnfleisch *nt*; (*also*: **chewing-gum**) Kaugummi *m*
gun [gʌn] *n* (*small*) Pistole *f*; (*medium-sized*) Gewehr *nt*; (*large*) Kanone *f*
gunfire [ˈgʌnfaɪəʳ] *n* Geschützfeuer *nt*
gunpowder [ˈgʌnpaudəʳ] *n* Schießpulver *nt*
gunshot [ˈgʌnʃɔt] *n* Schuss *m*
gush [gʌʃ] *vi* hervorströmen
gut [gʌt] *n* (*Anat*) Darm *m* ▪ **guts** *npl* (*Anat*) Eingeweide *pl*; (*inf*: *courage*) Mumm *m*
gutter [ˈgʌtəʳ] *n* (*in street*) Gosse *f*, Rinnstein *m*; (*of roof*) Dachrinne *f*
gutter press *n* Boulevardpresse *f*
guy [gaɪ] *n* (*inf*: *man*) Typ *m*, Kerl *m*
gym [dʒɪm] *n* (*also*: **gymnasium**) Turnhalle *f*
gymnasium [dʒɪmˈneɪzɪəm] *n* Turnhalle *f*
gymnastics [dʒɪmˈnæstɪks] *n* Turnen *nt*
gynaecologist, (*US*) **gynecologist** [gaɪnɪˈkɔlədʒɪst] *n* Gynäkologe *m*, Gynäkologin *f*, Frauenarzt *m*, Frauenärztin *f*
gynaecology, (*US*) **gynecology** [gaɪnɪˈkɔlədʒɪ] *n* Gynäkologie *f*, Frauenheilkunde *f*
gypsy [ˈdʒɪpsɪ] *n* = **gipsy**

habit [ˈhæbɪt] *n* Gewohnheit *f*
habitual [həˈbɪtjuəl] *adj* (*action*) gewohnt; (*drinker*) Gewohnheits-; (*liar*) gewohnheitsmäßig
hack [hæk] *vt, vi* (*also Comput*) hacken
hacker [ˈhækəʳ] *n* (*Comput*) Hacker *m*
had [hæd] *pt, pp of* **have**
haddock [ˈhædək] (*pl* ~) *n* Schellfisch *m*
hadn't [ˈhædnt] = **had not**
haemorrhage, (*US*) **hemorrhage** [ˈhɛmərɪdʒ] *n* Blutung *f*
haemorrhoids, (*US*) **hemorrhoids** [ˈhɛmərɔɪdz] *npl* Hämorr(ho)iden *pl*
haggis [ˈhægɪs] (SCOT) *n Gericht aus gehackten Schafsinnereien und Haferschrot, im Schafsmagen gekocht*
Hague [heɪg] *n*: **The ~** Den Haag *m*
hail [heɪl] *n* Hagel *m* ▸ *vt* (*person*) zurufen +*dat* ▸ *vi* hageln
hailstone [ˈheɪlstəun] *n* Hagelkorn *nt*
hair [hɛəʳ] *n* (*of person*) Haar *nt*, Haare *pl*; **to do one's ~** sich frisieren
hairbrush [ˈhɛəbrʌʃ] *n* Haarbürste *f*
haircut [ˈhɛəkʌt] *n* Haarschnitt *m*
hairdo [ˈhɛədu:] *n* Frisur *f*
hairdresser [ˈhɛədrɛsəʳ] *n* Friseur *m*, Friseuse *f*
hair dryer *n* Haartrockner *m*, Fön® *m*
hair gel *n* Haargel *nt*
hairpin [ˈhɛəpɪn] *n* Haarnadel *f*
hair remover *n* Enthaarungscreme *f*
hair spray *n* Haarspray *nt*
hair straighteners *npl* Haarglätter *m*
hairstyle [ˈhɛəstaɪl] *n* Frisur *f*
hairy [ˈhɛərɪ] *adj* behaart; (*inf: situation*) brenzlig
hake [heɪk] (*pl* ~) *n* Seehecht *m*
half [hɑ:f] (*pl* **halves**) *n* Hälfte *f* ▸ *adj, adv* halb; **two and a ~** zweieinhalb; **half-an-hour** eine halbe Stunde; **a week and a ~** eineinhalb *or* anderthalb Wochen; **~ past three** halb vier; **~ empty** halb leer
half board *n* Halbpension *f*
half-hearted [ˈhɑ:fˈhɑ:tɪd] *adj* halbherzig
half-hour [hɑ:fˈauəʳ] *n* halbe Stunde *f*
half-price [ˈhɑ:fˈpraɪs] *adj, adv* zum halben Preis
half term (BRIT) *n* kleine Ferien *pl* (*in der Mitte des Trimesters*)
half-time [hɑ:fˈtaɪm] *n* (*Sport*) Halbzeit *f*
halfway [ˈhɑ:fˈweɪ] *adv*: **~ to** auf halbem Wege nach
halibut [ˈhælɪbət] *n inv* Heilbutt *m*
hall [hɔ:l] *n* Diele *f*, (Haus)flur *m*; (*for concerts etc*) Halle *f*
hallmark [ˈhɔ:lmɑ:k] *n* (*on gold, silver*) (Feingehalts)stempel *m*; (*of writer, artist etc*) Kennzeichen *nt*
hallo [həˈləu] *excl* = **hello**
hall of residence (*pl* **halls of residence**) (BRIT) *n* Studentenwohnheim *nt*
Hallowe'en [ˈhæləuˈi:n] *n* der Tag vor Allerheiligen

HALLOWE'EN

Hallowe'en ist der 31. Oktober, der Vorabend von Allerheiligen und nach altem Glauben der Abend, an dem man Geister und Hexen sehen kann. In Großbritannien und vor allem in den USA feiern die Kinder *Hallowe'en*, indem sie sich verkleiden und mit selbst gemachten Laternen aus Kürbissen von Tür zu Tür ziehen.

halo [ˈheɪləu] *n* Heiligenschein *m*
halt [hɔ:lt] *vt* anhalten ▸ *vi* anhalten ▸ *n*: **to come to a ~** zum Stillstand kommen
halve [hɑ:v] *vt* halbieren
ham [hæm] *n* Schinken *m*
hamburger [ˈhæmbə:gəʳ] *n* Hamburger *m*
hammer [ˈhæməʳ] *n* Hammer *m* ▸ *vt* hämmern ▸ *vi* hämmern
hammock [ˈhæmək] *n* Hängematte *f*
hamper [ˈhæmpəʳ] *vt* behindern ▸ *n* Korb *m*

hamster [ˈhæmstəʳ] *n* Hamster *m*
hand [hænd] *n* Hand *f*; (*of clock*) Zeiger *m*; (*of cards*) Blatt *nt* ▶ *vt* geben, reichen; **to give** *or* **lend sb a ~** jdm helfen; **by ~** von Hand; **out of ~** *adj* außer Kontrolle; **on the one ~ ..., on the other ~ ...** einerseits ... andererseits ...; **to have in one's ~** (*also fig*) in der Hand halten; **"hands off!"** „Hände weg!"
▶ **hand down** *vt* (*knowledge*) weitergeben; (*possessions*) vererben
▶ **hand in** *vt* abgeben, einreichen
▶ **hand out** *vt* verteilen
▶ **hand over** *vt* übergeben
handbag *n* Handtasche *f*
handbook [ˈhændbuk] *n* Handbuch *nt*
handbrake [ˈhændbreɪk] *n* Handbremse *f*
handcuffs [ˈhændkʌfs] *npl* Handschellen *pl*
handful [ˈhændful] *n* Handvoll *f*
hand-held [ˈhændˈhɛld] *adj* (*camera*) Hand-
handicap [ˈhændɪkæp] *n* Behinderung *f*; (*Sport*) Handicap *nt* ▶ *vt* benachteiligen
handicraft [ˈhændɪkrɑːft] *n* Kunsthandwerk *nt*
handkerchief [ˈhæŋkətʃɪf] *n* Taschentuch *nt*
handle [ˈhændl] *n* Griff *m*; (*of door*) Klinke *f*; (*of cup*) Henkel *m*; (*for winding*) Kurbel *f* ▶ *vt* anfassen, berühren; (*problem etc*) sich befassen mit; (*: successfully*) fertig werden mit; (*people*) umgehen mit
handlebar *n*, **handlebars** *npl* Lenkstange *f*
hand luggage *n* Handgepäck *nt*
handmade [ˈhændˈmeɪd] *adj* handgearbeitet
hand-out [ˈhændaut] *n* (*publicity leaflet*) Flugblatt *nt*; (*summary*) Informationsblatt *nt*
handset [ˈhændsɛt] *n* (*Tel*) Hörer *m*
hands-free [ˈhændzfriː] *adj* (*telephone, microphone*) Freisprech-
handshake [ˈhændʃeɪk] *n* Händedruck *m*
handsome [ˈhænsəm] *adj* gut aussehend
hands-on [ˈhændzˈɔn] *adj* (*training*) praktisch; **~ experience** praktische Erfahrung
handwriting [ˈhændraɪtɪŋ] *n* Handschrift *f*
handy [ˈhændɪ] *adj* praktisch
hang [hæŋ] (*pt, pp* **hung**) *vt* aufhängen; (*pt, pp* **hanged**: *criminal*) hängen ▶ *vi* hängen ▶ *n*: **to get the ~ of sth** (*inf*) den richtigen Dreh (bei etw) herauskriegen
▶ **hang about** *vi* herumlungern
▶ **hang on** *vi* warten ▶ *vt fus*: **to ~ on to** festhalten *+dat*; (*for protection, support*) sich festhalten an *+dat*
▶ **hang up** *vt* aufhängen ▶ *vi* (*Tel*): **to ~ up (on sb)** einfach auflegen
hangar [ˈhæŋəʳ] *n* Hangar *m*, Flugzeughalle *f*
hanger [ˈhæŋəʳ] *n* Bügel *m*
hang-glider [ˈhæŋglaɪdəʳ] *n* (Flug)drachen *m*
hang-gliding [ˈhæŋglaɪdɪŋ] *n* Drachenfliegen *nt*
hangover [ˈhæŋəuvəʳ] *n* Kater *m*; (*from past*) Überbleibsel *nt*
hankie, hanky [ˈhæŋkɪ] *n* = **handkerchief**
happen [ˈhæpən] *vi* geschehen; **to ~ to do sth** zufällig(erweise) etw tun; **as it happens** zufälligerweise; **she happened to be free** sie hatte zufällig(erweise) gerade Zeit; **if anything happened to him** wenn ihm etwas zustoßen *or* passieren sollte
happening [ˈhæpnɪŋ] *n* Ereignis *nt*, Vorfall *m*
happily [ˈhæpɪlɪ] *adv* (*luckily*) glücklicherweise; (*cheerfully*) fröhlich
happiness [ˈhæpɪnɪs] *n* Glück *nt*
happy [ˈhæpɪ] *adj* glücklich; (*cheerful*) fröhlich; **to be ~ (with)** zufrieden sein (mit); **to be ~ to do sth** etw gerne tun; **~ birthday!** herzlichen Glückwunsch zum Geburtstag!
happy hour *n Zeit, in der Bars, Pubs usw Getränke zu ermäßigten Preisen anbieten*
harass [ˈhærəs] *vt* schikanieren
harassment [ˈhærəsmənt] *n* Schikanierung *f*
harbour, (*US*) **harbor** [ˈhɑːbəʳ] *n* Hafen *m*
hard [hɑːd] *adj* hart; (*question, problem*) schwierig; (*evidence*) gesichert ▶ *adv* (*work*) hart, schwer; (*try*) sehr; **no ~ feelings!** ich nehme es dir nicht übel; **I find it ~ to believe that ...** ich kann es kaum glauben, dass ...

hardback [ˈhɑːdbæk] *n* gebundene Ausgabe *f*
hard-boiled egg [ˈhɑːdˈbɔɪld-] *n* hart gekochtes Ei *nt*
hard copy *n* (*Comput*) Ausdruck *m*
hard disk *n* (*Comput*) Festplatte *f*
harden [ˈhɑːdn] *vt* härten ▸ *vi* hart werden, sich verhärten
hardened [ˈhɑːdnd] *adj*: **to be ~ to sth** gegen etw abgehärtet sein
hardhearted *adj* hartherzig
hardliner [hɑːdˈlaɪnəʳ] *n* Vertreter(in) *m(f)* der harten Linie
hardly [ˈhɑːdlɪ] *adv* kaum
hardship [ˈhɑːdʃɪp] *n* Not *f*
hard shoulder (Brit) *n* (*Aut*) Seitenstreifen *m*
hardware [ˈhɑːdwɛəʳ] *n* Eisenwaren *pl*; (*household goods*) Haushaltswaren *pl*; (*Comput*) Hardware *f*
hard-working [hɑːdˈwəːkɪŋ] *adj* fleißig
hare [hɛəʳ] *n* Hase *m*
harm [hɑːm] *n* Schaden *m*; (*injury*) Verletzung *f* ▸ *vt* schaden *+dat*; (*person: physically*) verletzen; **there's no ~ in trying** es kann nicht schaden, es zu versuchen
harmful [ˈhɑːmful] *adj* schädlich
harmless [ˈhɑːmlɪs] *adj* harmlos
harp [hɑːp] *n* Harfe *f*
harsh [hɑːʃ] *adj* (*sound, light*) grell; (*judge, winter*) streng; (*criticism, life*) hart
harvest [ˈhɑːvɪst] *n* Ernte *f* ▸ *vt* ernten
has [hæz] *vb see* **have**
hash [hæʃ] *n* (*Culin*) Haschee *nt*; (*fig*): **to make a ~ of sth** etw verpfuschen (*inf*) ▸ *n abbr* (*inf*: = *hashish*) Hasch *nt*
hash tag *n* (*esp on Twitter*) Hashtag *nt*
hasn't [ˈhæznt] = **has not**
hassle [ˈhæsl] (*inf*) *n* (*bother*) Theater *nt* ▸ *vt* schikanieren
haste [heɪst] *n* (*speed*) Eile *f*
hastily [ˈheɪstɪlɪ] *adv* hastig, eilig; vorschnell
hat [hæt] *n* Hut *m*
hatch [hætʃ] *n* (*Naut: also:* **hatchway**) Luke *f*; (*also:* **serving ~**) Durchreiche *f*
hatchback [ˈhætʃbæk] *n* (*Aut: car*) Heckklappenmodell *nt*
hate [heɪt] *vt* hassen ▸ *n* Hass *m*; **to ~ to do/doing sth** es hassen, etw zu tun
haul [hɔːl] *vt* ziehen ▸ *n* Beute *f*
haulage [ˈhɔːlɪdʒ] *n* (*cost*) Transportkosten *pl*; (*business*) Transport *m*
haunted [ˈhɔːntɪd] *adj*: **this building/room is ~** in diesem Gebäude/Zimmer spukt es

KEYWORD

have [hæv] (*pt, pp* **had**) *aux vb* **1** haben; (*with verbs of motion*) sein; **to have arrived/gone** angekommen/gegangen sein; **to have eaten/slept** gegessen/geschlafen haben; **having eaten** *or* **when he had eaten, he left** nachdem er gegessen hatte, ging er
2 (*in tag questions*): **you've done it, haven't you?** du hast es gemacht, nicht wahr?; **he hasn't done it, has he?** er hat es nicht gemacht, oder?
3 (*in short answers and questions*): **you've made a mistake — no I haven't/so I have** du hast einen Fehler gemacht — nein(, das habe ich nicht)/ja, stimmt; **we haven't paid — yes we have!** wir haben nicht bezahlt — doch!; **I've been there before — have you?** ich war schon einmal da — wirklich *or* tatsächlich?
▸ *modal aux vb* (*be obliged*): **to have (got) to do sth** etw tun müssen
▸ *vt* **1** (*possess*) haben; **she has (got) blue eyes/dark hair** sie hat blaue Augen/dunkle Haare; **I have (got) an idea** ich habe eine Idee
2 (*referring to meals etc*): **to have breakfast** frühstücken
3 (*receive, obtain etc*) haben; **may I have your address?** kann ich Ihre Adresse haben *or* bekommen?; **to have a baby** ein Kind bekommen
4 (*allow*): **I won't have this nonsense** dieser Unsinn kommt nicht infrage!; **we can't have that** das kommt nicht infrage
5: **to have sth done** etw machen lassen; **to have one's hair cut** sich *dat* die Haare schneiden lassen; **to have sb do sth** (*order*) jdn etw tun lassen; **he soon had them all laughing/working** bald hatte er alle zum Lachen/Arbeiten gebracht
6 (*experience, suffer*): **to have a cold/flu** eine Erkältung/die Grippe haben;

she had her bag stolen ihr *dat* wurde die Tasche gestohlen
7 (+ *noun*: *take, hold etc*): **to have a swim** schwimmen gehen; **to have a walk** spazieren gehen; **to have a rest** sich ausruhen; **to have a meeting** eine Besprechung haben; **to have a party** eine Party geben
▶ **have on** *vt* (*wear*) anhaben; (Brit *inf*: *tease*) auf den Arm nehmen; **do you have** *or* **have you anything on tomorrow?** haben Sie morgen etwas vor?
▶ **have out** *vt*: **to have it out with sb** (*settle a problem etc*) ein Wort mit jdm reden

Hawaii [həˈwaɪiː] *n* Hawaii *nt*
hawk [hɔːk] *n* Habicht *m*
hay [heɪ] *n* Heu *nt*
hay fever *n* Heuschnupfen *m*
hazard [ˈhæzəd] *n* Gefahr *f*
hazard lights, hazard warning lights *npl* (*Aut*) Warnblinkanlage *f*
hazardous [ˈhæzədəs] *adj* gefährlich
haze [heɪz] *n* Dunst *m*
hazelnut [ˈheɪzlnʌt] *n* Haselnuss *f*
hazy [ˈheɪzɪ] *adj* dunstig; (*idea, memory*) verschwommen
he [hiː] *pron* er
head [hɛd] *n* Kopf *m*; (*of company, organization*) Leiter(in) *m(f)*; (*of school*) Schulleiter(in) *m(f)* ▶ *vt* anführen, an der Spitze stehen von; (*group, company*) leiten; **heads (or tails)** Kopf (oder Zahl); **at the ~ of the list** oben auf der Liste
▶ **head for** *vt fus* (*on foot*) zusteuern auf *+acc*; **you are heading for trouble** du wirst Ärger bekommen
headache [ˈhɛdeɪk] *n* Kopfschmerzen *pl*, Kopfweh *nt*
header [ˈhɛdəʳ] (Brit *inf*) *n* (*Football*) Kopfball *m*
headfirst [ˈhɛdˈfəːst] *adv* (*lit*) kopfüber; (*fig*) Hals über Kopf
head-hunt *vt* abwerben
heading [ˈhɛdɪŋ] *n* Überschrift *f*
headlamp [ˈhɛdlæmp] (Brit) *n* = **headlight**
headline [ˈhɛdlaɪn] *n* Schlagzeile *f*
headmaster [hɛdˈmɑːstəʳ] *n* Schulleiter *m*
headmistress [hɛdˈmɪstrɪs] *n* Schulleiterin *f*
head of state (*pl* **heads of state**) *n* Staatsoberhaupt *nt*
head-on *adj* (*collision*) frontal
headphones [ˈhɛdfəunz] *npl* Kopfhörer *pl*
headquarters [ˈhɛdkwɔːtəz] *npl* Zentrale *f*
headrest [ˈhɛdrɛst] *n* (*Aut*) Kopfstütze *f*
headscarf [ˈhɛdskɑːf] *n* Kopftuch *nt*
head teacher *n* Schulleiter(in) *m(f)*
heal [hiːl] *vt, vi* heilen
health [hɛlθ] *n* Gesundheit *f*
health centre (Brit) *n* Ärztezentrum *nt*
health club *n* Fitnesscenter *nt*
health food *n* Reformkost *f*, Naturkost *f*
health insurance *n* Krankenversicherung *f*
health service (Brit) *n*: **the Health Service** das Gesundheitswesen
healthy [ˈhɛlθɪ] *adj* gesund
heap [hiːp] *n* Haufen *m* ▶ *vt*: **to ~ (up)** (auf)häufen; **heaps of** (*inf*) jede Menge
hear [hɪəʳ] (*pt, pp* **heard**) *vt* hören; **to ~ about** hören von; **I've never heard of that book** von dem Buch habe ich noch nie etwas gehört
hearing [ˈhɪərɪŋ] *n* Gehör *nt*; (*of a case*) Verhandlung *f*
hearing aid *n* Hörgerät *nt*
hearsay [ˈhɪəseɪ] *n*: **by ~** vom Hörensagen
heart [hɑːt] *n* Herz *nt* ■ **hearts** *npl* (*Cards*) Herz *nt*; **to lose ~** den Mut verlieren; **to take ~** Mut fassen; **by ~** auswendig
heart attack *n* Herzanfall *m*
heartbeat [ˈhɑːtbiːt] *n* Herzschlag *m*
heartbreaking [ˈhɑːtbreɪkɪŋ] *adj* herzzerreißend
heartbroken [ˈhɑːtbrəukən] *adj*: **to be ~** todunglücklich sein
heartburn [ˈhɑːtbəːn] *n* Sodbrennen *nt*
heart failure *n* Herzversagen *nt*
heartfelt [ˈhɑːtfɛlt] *adj* tief empfunden
heartless [ˈhɑːtlɪs] *adj* herzlos
heart-throb [ˈhɑːtθrɔb] (*inf*) *n* Schwarm *m*
heart-to-heart [ˈhɑːttəˈhɑːt] *adj, adv* ganz im Vertrauen
hearty [ˈhɑːtɪ] *adj* (*laugh, appetite*) herzhaft; (*welcome*) herzlich

heat [hiːt] *n* Hitze *f*; (*warmth*) Wärme *f*; (*temperature*) Temperatur *f*; (*Sport*: *also*: **qualifying ~**) Vorrunde *f* ▸ *vt* (*room, house*) heizen
▸ **heat up** *vi* warm werden ▸ *vt* aufwärmen
heated [ˈhiːtɪd] *adj* geheizt; (*argument*) hitzig
heater [ˈhiːtəʳ] *n* (Heiz)ofen *m*; (*in car*) Heizung *f*
heath [hiːθ] (Brit) *n* Heide *f*
heather [ˈhɛðəʳ] *n* Heidekraut *nt*
heating [ˈhiːtɪŋ] *n* Heizung *f*
heat-resistant [ˈhiːtrɪzɪstənt] *adj* hitzebeständig
heat wave *n* Hitzewelle *f*
heaven [ˈhɛvn] *n* Himmel *m*
heavenly [ˈhɛvnlɪ] *adj* himmlisch
heavily [ˈhɛvɪlɪ] *adv* schwer; (*drink, smoke, depend, rely*) stark
heavy [ˈhɛvɪ] *adj* schwer; (*rain, snow, drinker, smoker*) stark
heavy goods vehicle *n* Lastkraftwagen *m*
Hebrew [ˈhiːbruː] *adj* hebräisch ▸ *n* (*Ling*) Hebräisch *nt*
hectic [ˈhɛktɪk] *adj* hektisch
he'd [hiːd] = **he would**; **he had**
hedge [hɛdʒ] *n* Hecke *f*
hedgehog [ˈhɛdʒhɔg] *n* Igel *m*
heel [hiːl] *n* Ferse *f*; (*of shoe*) Absatz *m*
hefty [ˈhɛftɪ] *adj* kräftig; (*parcel etc*) schwer; (*profit*) ansehnlich
height [haɪt] *n* Höhe *f*; (*of person*) Größe *f*
heir [ɛəʳ] *n* Erbe *m*
heiress [ˈɛərɛs] *n* Erbin *f*
held [hɛld] *pt, pp of* **hold**
helicopter [ˈhɛlɪkɔptəʳ] *n* Hubschrauber *m*
heliport [ˈhɛlɪpɔːt] *n* Hubschrauberflugplatz *m*, Heliport *m*
hell [hɛl] *n* Hölle *f*; **~!** (*inf*) verdammt! (*!*); **a ~ of a lot** (*inf*) verdammt viel (*inf*)
he'll [hiːl] = **he will**; **he shall**
hello [həˈləu] *excl* hallo
helmet [ˈhɛlmɪt] *n* Helm *m*
help [hɛlp] *n* Hilfe *f* ▸ *vt* helfen +*dat*; **to be of ~ to sb** jdm behilflich sein, jdm helfen; **can I ~ you?** (*in shop*) womit kann ich Ihnen dienen?; **~ yourself** bedienen Sie sich; **he can't ~ it** er kann nichts dafür; **I can't ~ thinking that ...** ich kann mir nicht helfen, ich glaube, dass ...
help desk *n* (*esp Comput*) Benutzerunterstützung *f*, Helpdesk *nt, m*
helpful [ˈhɛlpful] *adj* hilfsbereit; (*advice, suggestion*) nützlich
helping [ˈhɛlpɪŋ] *n* Portion *f*
helpless [ˈhɛlplɪs] *adj* hilflos
hem [hɛm] *n* Saum *m*
hemorrhage [ˈhɛmərɪdʒ] (*US*) *n* = **haemorrhage**
hemorrhoids [ˈhɛmərɔɪdz] (*US*) *npl* = **haemorrhoids**
hen [hɛn] *n* Henne *f*
hence [hɛns] *adv* daher; **2 years ~** in zwei Jahren
hen night, hen party (*inf*) *n* Damenkränzchen *nt*
henpecked [ˈhɛnpɛkt] *adj*: **to be ~** unter dem Pantoffel stehen
hepatitis [hɛpəˈtaɪtɪs] *n* Hepatitis *f*
her [həːʳ] *pron* sie; (*indirect*) ihr ▸ *adj* ihr; **I see ~** ich sehe sie; **give ~ a book** gib ihr ein Buch; **after ~** nach ihr; *see also* **me**; **my**
herb [həːb] *n* Kraut *nt*
herbal [ˈhəːbl] *adj* (*tea, medicine*) Kräuter-
herd [həːd] *n* Herde *f*
here [hɪəʳ] *adv* hier; **~ she is!** da ist sie ja!; **come ~!** komm hierher *or* hierhin!; **~ and there** hier und da
hereditary [hɪˈrɛdɪtrɪ] *adj* erblich
heritage [ˈhɛrɪtɪdʒ] *n* Erbe *nt*
hernia [ˈhəːnɪə] *n* Bruch *m*
hero [ˈhɪərəu] (*pl* **heroes**) *n* Held *m*
heroin [ˈhɛrəuɪn] *n* Heroin *nt*
heroine [ˈhɛrəuɪn] *n* Heldin *f*
heroism [ˈhɛrəuɪzəm] *n* Heldentum *nt*
herring [ˈhɛrɪŋ] *n* Hering *m*
hers [həːz] *pron* ihre(r, s); **a friend of ~** ein Freund von ihr; **this is ~** das gehört ihr; *see also* **mine²**
herself [həːˈsɛlf] *pron* sich; (*emphatic*) (sie) selbst
he's [hiːz] = **he is**; **he has**
hesitant [ˈhɛzɪtənt] *adj* zögernd
hesitate [ˈhɛzɪteɪt] *vi* zögern; (*be unwilling*) Bedenken haben; **don't ~ to see a doctor if you are worried** gehen Sie ruhig zum Arzt, wenn Sie sich Sorgen machen
hesitation [hɛzɪˈteɪʃən] *n* Zögern *nt*; **to have no ~ in saying sth** etw ohne Weiteres sagen können
heterosexual [ˈhɛtərəuˈsɛksjuəl] *adj* heterosexuell

HGV (BRIT) *n abbr* (= *heavy goods vehicle*) Lkw *m*
hi [haɪ] *excl* hallo
hiccough [ˈhɪkʌp] *vi* hicksen
hiccoughs [ˈhɪkʌps] *npl* Schluckauf *m*; **to have (the) ~** den Schluckauf haben
hiccup [ˈhɪkʌp] *vi* = **hiccough**
hiccups [ˈhɪkʌps] *npl* = **hiccoughs**
hid [hɪd] *pt of* **hide**
hidden [ˈhɪdn] *pp of* **hide**
hide [haɪd] (*pt* **hid**, *pp* **hidden**) *vt* verstecken; (*feeling, information*) verbergen; (*obscure*) verdecken ▸ *vi*: **to ~ (from sb)** sich (vor jdm) verstecken
hideous [ˈhɪdɪəs] *adj* scheußlich
hiding [ˈhaɪdɪŋ] *n*: **to be in ~** (*concealed*) sich versteckt halten
hiding place *n* Versteck *nt*
hi-fi [ˈhaɪfaɪ] *n abbr* (= *high fidelity*) Hi-Fi *nt* ▸ *adj* (*equipment etc*) Hi-Fi-
high [haɪ] *adj* hoch; (*wind*) stark; (*risk*) groß; (*inf: on drugs*) high ▸ *adv* hoch
highchair [ˈhaɪtʃɛəʳ] *n* Hochstuhl *m*
higher [ˈhaɪəʳ] *adj* (*form of study, life etc*) höher (entwickelt)
higher education *n* Hochschulbildung *f*
high-flier, high-flyer [haɪˈflaɪəʳ] *n* Senkrechtstarter(in) *m(f)*
high heels *npl* hochhackige Schuhe *pl*
high jump *n* Hochsprung *m*
Highlands [ˈhaɪləndz] *npl*: **the ~** das Hochland
highlight [ˈhaɪlaɪt] *n* (*of event*) Höhepunkt *m*; (*in hair*) Strähnchen *nt* ▸ *vt* (*problem, need*) ein Schlaglicht werfen auf *+acc*
highlighter [ˈhaɪlaɪtəʳ] *n* Textmarker *m*
highly [ˈhaɪlɪ] *adv* hoch-; **to think ~ of** eine hohe Meinung haben von
high school *n* ≈ Oberschule *f*
high-speed [ˈhaɪspiːd] *adj* Schnell-; **~ train** Hochgeschwindigkeitszug *m*
high street (BRIT) *n* Hauptstraße *f*
high tide *n* Flut *f*
highway [ˈhaɪweɪ] (US) *n* Straße *f*; (*between towns, states*) Landstraße *f*
hijack [ˈhaɪdʒæk] *vt* entführen
hijacker [ˈhaɪdʒækəʳ] *n* Entführer(in) *m(f)*
hike [haɪk] *vi* wandern ▸ *n* Wanderung *f*
hiker [ˈhaɪkəʳ] *n* Wanderer *m*, Wanderin *f*
hiking [ˈhaɪkɪŋ] *n* Wandern *nt*
hilarious [hɪˈlɛərɪəs] *adj* urkomisch
hill [hɪl] *n* Hügel *m*; (*fairly high*) Berg *m*
hilly [ˈhɪlɪ] *adj* hügelig
him [hɪm] *pron* ihn; (*indirect*) ihm; *see also* **me**
himself [hɪmˈsɛlf] *pron* sich; (*emphatic*) (er) selbst
hinder [ˈhɪndəʳ] *vt* behindern
hindrance [ˈhɪndrəns] *n* Behinderung *f*
Hindu [ˈhɪnduː] *adj* hinduistisch, Hindu-
hinge [hɪndʒ] *n* (*on door*) Angel *f*
hint [hɪnt] *n* Andeutung *f*; (*sign, glimmer*) Spur *f* ▸ *vi*: **to ~ at** andeuten
hip [hɪp] *n* Hüfte *f*
hippopotamus [hɪpəˈpɔtəməs] (*pl* **hippopotamuses** *or* **hippopotami**) *n* Nilpferd *nt*
hipster [ˈhɪpstəʳ] *n* (*inf: fashionable person*) Hipster *m*
hire [ˈhaɪəʳ] *vt* (BRIT) mieten; (*worker*) einstellen ▸ *n* (BRIT) Mieten *nt*; **for ~** (*taxi*) frei
hire car, (BRIT) **hired car** *n* Mietwagen *m*
hire-purchase (BRIT) *n* Ratenkauf *m*
his [hɪz] *pron* seine(r, s) ▸ *adj* sein; *see also* **my**; **mine²**
historic [hɪˈstɔrɪk] *adj* historisch
historical [hɪˈstɔrɪkl] *adj* historisch
history [ˈhɪstərɪ] *n* Geschichte *f*
hit [hɪt] (*pt, pp* **~**) *vt* schlagen; (*reach, affect*) treffen; (*wall, tree*) fahren gegen ▸ *n* Schlag *m*; (*success*) Erfolg *m*; (*song*) Hit *m*
▸ **hit (up)on** *vt fus* stoßen auf *+acc*, finden
hit-and-run driver *n* unfallflüchtiger Fahrer *m*, unfallflüchtige Fahrerin *f*
hitch [hɪtʃ] *vt* (*trousers, skirt: also:* **~ up**) hochziehen ▸ *n* Schwierigkeit *f*, Problem *nt*
hitchhike *vi* trampen
hitchhiker [ˈhɪtʃhaɪkəʳ] *n* Tramper(in) *m(f)*
hitchhiking [ˈhɪtʃhaɪkɪŋ] *n* Trampen *nt*
HIV *n abbr* (= *human immunodeficiency virus*) HIV; **HIV-negative** HIV-negativ; **HIV-positive** HIV-positiv
hive [haɪv] *n* Bienenkorb *m*
HM *abbr* (= *His/Her Majesty*) S./I.M.
HMS (BRIT) *abbr* (= *His* (*or Her*) *Majesty's Ship*) *Namensteil von Schiffen der Kriegsmarine*
hoarse [hɔːs] *adj* heiser

hoax [həuks] *n* (*false alarm*) blinder Alarm *m*
hob [hɔb] *n* Kochmulde *f*
hobble [ˈhɔbl] *vi* humpeln
hobby [ˈhɔbɪ] *n* Hobby *nt*
hobo [ˈhəubəu] (*US*) *n* Penner *m* (*inf*)
hockey [ˈhɔkɪ] *n* Hockey *nt*
hold [həuld] (*pt, pp* **held**) *vt* halten; (*contain*) enthalten; (*meeting*) abhalten; (*conversation*) führen; (*prisoner, hostage*) festhalten ▶ *vi* halten; (*weather*) sich halten ▶ *n* (*grasp*) Griff *m*; (*of ship, plane*) Laderaum *m*; **~ the line!** (*Tel*) bleiben Sie am Apparat!
▶ **hold back** *vt* zurückhalten; (*secret*) verbergen
▶ **hold on** *vi* sich festhalten; (*wait*) warten
▶ **hold on to** *vt fus* sich festhalten an *+dat*
▶ **hold out** *vt* (*hand*) ausstrecken; (*prospect*) bieten ▶ *vi* nicht nachgeben
▶ **hold up** *vt* hochheben; (*support*) stützen; (*delay*) aufhalten
holdall [ˈhəuldɔːl] (Brit) *n* (*for clothes*) Reisetasche *f*
holder [ˈhəuldəʳ] *n* (*of ticket, record, office, title etc*) Inhaber(in) *m(f)*
hold-up [ˈhəuldʌp] *n* bewaffneter Raubüberfall *m*; (Brit: *in traffic*) Stockung *f*
hole [həul] *n* Loch *nt*
holiday [ˈhɔlɪdeɪ] *n* (Brit) Urlaub *m*; (*Scol*) Ferien *pl*; (*day off*) freier Tag *m*; (*also*: **public ~**) Feiertag *m*; **on ~** im Urlaub, in den Ferien
holiday camp (Brit) *n* (*also*: **holiday centre**) Feriendorf *nt*
holiday home *n* Ferienhaus *nt*
holiday-maker [ˈhɔlɪdɪmeɪkəʳ] (Brit) *n* Urlauber(in) *m(f)*
holiday resort *n* Ferienort *m*
Holland [ˈhɔlənd] *n* Holland *nt*
hollow [ˈhɔləu] *adj* hohl; (*fig*) leer ▶ *n* Vertiefung *f*
holly [ˈhɔlɪ] *n* Stechpalme *f*
holy [ˈhəulɪ] *adj* heilig
home [həum] *n* Heim *nt*; (*house, flat*) Zuhause *nt*; (*area, country*) Heimat *f* ▶ *adv* (*go etc*) nach Hause; **at ~** zu Hause; **make yourself at ~** machen Sie es sich *dat* gemütlich *or* bequem
home address *n* Heimatanschrift *f*
homeless [ˈhəumlɪs] *adj* obdachlos
homely [ˈhəumlɪ] *adj* einfach; (*US*: *plain*) unscheinbar
home-made [həumˈmeɪd] *adj* selbst gemacht
Home Office (Brit) *n* Innenministerium *nt*
home page *n* (*Comput*) Homepage *f*
Home Secretary (Brit) *n* Innenminister(in) *m(f)*
homesick [ˈhəumsɪk] *adj*: **to be ~** Heimweh haben
home town *n* Heimatstadt *f*
homework [ˈhəumwəːk] *n* Hausaufgaben *pl*
homicide [ˈhɔmɪsaɪd] (*US*) *n* Mord *m*
homosexual [hɔməuˈsɛksjuəl] *adj* homosexuell ▶ *n* Homosexuelle(r) *f(m)*
Honduras [hɔnˈdjuərəs] *n* Honduras *nt*
honest [ˈɔnɪst] *adj* ehrlich
honesty [ˈɔnɪstɪ] *n* Ehrlichkeit *f*
honey *n* Honig *m*
honeycomb [ˈhʌnɪkəum] *n* Bienenwabe *f*
honeymoon [ˈhʌnɪmuːn] *n* Flitterwochen *pl*
Hong Kong [ˈhɔŋˈkɔŋ] *n* Hongkong *nt*
honor *etc* [ˈɔnəʳ] (*US*) = **honour** *etc*
honorary [ˈɔnərərɪ] *adj* ehrenamtlich; (*title, degree*) Ehren-
honour, (*US*) **honor** [ˈɔnəʳ] *vt* ehren; (*commitment, promise*) stehen zu ▶ *n* Ehre *f*
honourable [ˈɔnərəbl] *adj* (*person*) ehrenwert
honours degree [ˈɔnəz-] *n* *akademischer Grad mit Prüfung im Spezialfach*
hood [hud] *n* (*of coat etc*) Kapuze *f*; (*Aut*: Brit: *folding roof*) Verdeck *nt*; (: *US*: *bonnet*) (Motor)haube *f*
hoof [huːf] (*pl* **hooves**) *n* Huf *m*
hook [huk] *n* Haken *m*
hooligan [ˈhuːlɪgən] *n* Rowdy *m*
hoot [huːt] *vi* hupen
Hoover® [ˈhuːvəʳ] (Brit) *n* Staubsauger *m* ▶ *vt*: **to hoover** (*carpet*) saugen
hop [hɔp] *vi* hüpfen ▶ *n* Hüpfer *m*
hope [həup] *vi* hoffen ▶ *n* Hoffnung *f* ▶ *vt*: **to ~ that** hoffen, dass; **I ~ so** ich hoffe es, hoffentlich; **I ~ not** ich hoffe nicht, hoffentlich nicht; **to have no ~ of sth/doing sth** keine Hoffnung auf etw *+acc* haben/darauf haben, etw zu tun

hopeful [ˈhəupful] *adj* hoffnungsvoll
hopefully [ˈhəupfulɪ] *adv* hoffnungsvoll
hopeless [ˈhəuplɪs] *adj* hoffnungslos
horizon [həˈraɪzn] *n* Horizont *m*
horizontal [hɔrɪˈzɔntl] *adj* horizontal
hormone [ˈhɔːməun] *n* Hormon *nt*
horn [hɔːn] *n* Horn *nt*; (*Aut*) Hupe *f*
hornet [ˈhɔːnɪt] *n* Hornisse *f*
horny [ˈhɔːnɪ] (*inf*) *adj* (*aroused*) geil
horoscope [ˈhɔrəskəup] *n* Horoskop *nt*
horrible [ˈhɔrɪbl] *adj* schrecklich
horrid [ˈhɔrɪd] *adj* entsetzlich
horrify [ˈhɔrɪfaɪ] *vt* entsetzen
horror [ˈhɔrəʳ] *n* Entsetzen *nt*; **the horrors of war** die Schrecken *pl* des Krieges
hors d'œuvre [ɔːˈdəːvrə] *n* Vorspeise *f*
horse [hɔːs] *n* Pferd *nt*
horse chestnut *n* Rosskastanie *f*
horsepower [ˈhɔːspauəʳ] *n* Pferdestärke *f*
horse racing *n* Pferderennen *nt*
horseradish [ˈhɔːsrædɪʃ] *n* Meerrettich *m*
horse riding *n* Reiten *nt*
horseshoe [ˈhɔːsʃuː] *n* Hufeisen *nt*
horticulture [ˈhɔːtɪkʌltʃəʳ] *n* Gartenbau *m*
hose [həuz] *n* (*also*: **~ pipe**) Schlauch *m*
hospitable [ˈhɔspɪtəbl] *adj* gastfreundlich
hospital [ˈhɔspɪtl] *n* Krankenhaus *nt*
hospitality [hɔspɪˈtælɪtɪ] *n* Gastfreundschaft *f*
host [həust] *n* Gastgeber *m*; (*Rel*) Hostie *f* ▸ *vt* Gastgeber sein bei
hostage [ˈhɔstɪdʒ] *n* Geisel *f*
hostel [ˈhɔstl] *n* (Wohn)heim *nt*; (*also*: **youth ~**) Jugendherberge *f*
hostess [ˈhəustɪs] *n* Gastgeberin *f*
hostile [ˈhɔstaɪl] *adj* (*person*): **~ (to** *or* **towards)** feindselig (gegenüber *+dat*)
hostility [hɔˈstɪlɪtɪ] *n* Feindseligkeit *f*
hot [hɔt] *adj* heiß; (*moderately hot*) warm; (*spicy*) scharf; **I am** *or* **feel ~** mir ist heiß
hot dog *n* Hotdog *m or nt*
hotel [həuˈtɛl] *n* Hotel *nt*
hotel room *n* Hotelzimmer *nt*
hothouse *n* Treibhaus *nt*
hot line *n* (*Pol*) heißer Draht *m*
hotplate [ˈhɔtpleɪt] *n* Kochplatte *f*
hotpot [ˈhɔtpɔt] (*Brit*) *n* Fleischeintopf *m*
hotspot [ˈhɔtspɔt] *n* (*Comput*) Hotspot *m*
hot-water bottle [hɔtˈwɔːtəʳ-] *n* Wärmflasche *f*
hour [ˈauəʳ] *n* Stunde *f*
hourly [ˈauəlɪ] *adj* stündlich
house [haus] *n* Haus *nt* ▸ *vt* unterbringen; **at my ~** bei mir (zu Hause); **to my ~** zu mir (nach Hause); **on the ~** (*fig*) auf Kosten des Hauses; **the H~ (of Commons)** (*Brit*) das Unterhaus; **the H~ (of Lords)** (*Brit*) das Oberhaus
houseboat [ˈhausbəut] *n* Hausboot *nt*
household [ˈaushəuld] *n* Haushalt *m*
housekeeping [ˈhauskiːpɪŋ] *n* Hauswirtschaft *f*; (*money*) Haushaltsgeld *nt*
house-trained [ˈhaustreɪnd] (*Brit*) *adj* (*animal*) stubenrein
house-warming, house-warming party *n* Einzugsparty *f*
housewife [ˈhauswaɪf] *n* (*irreg*) Hausfrau *f*
house wine *n* Hauswein *m*
housework [ˈhauswəːk] *n* Hausarbeit *f*
housing [ˈhauzɪŋ] *n* Wohnungen *pl*; (*provision*) Wohnungsbeschaffung *f*
housing benefit *n* ≈ Wohngeld *nt*
housing development *n* (Wohn)siedlung *f*
housing estate *n* (Wohn)siedlung *f*
hover [ˈhɔvəʳ] *vi* schweben
hovercraft [ˈhɔvəkrɑːft] *n* Luftkissenfahrzeug *nt*

 **KEYWORD**

how [hau] *adv* **1** (*in what way*) wie; **how is school?** was macht die Schule?; **how are you?** wie geht es Ihnen?; **how about ...?** wie wäre es mit ...?
2 (*to what degree*): **how much milk?** wie viel Milch?; **how many people?** wie viele Leute?; **how old are you?** wie alt bist du?

however [hauˈɛvəʳ] *conj* jedoch, aber ▸ *adv* wie ... auch
howl [haul] *vi* heulen
howler [ˈhauləʳ] (*inf*) *n* (*mistake*) Schnitzer *m*
HP (*Brit*) *n abbr* = **hire-purchase**

h.p. *abbr* (*Aut*: = *horsepower*) PS
HQ *abbr* = **headquarters**
HTML *abbr* (*Comput*: = *hypertext markup language*) HTML *f*
hubcap [ˈhʌbkæp] *n* Radkappe *f*
hug [hʌg] *vt* umarmen ▶ *n* Umarmung *f*
huge [hjuːdʒ] *adj* riesig
hum [hʌm] *vt* summen ▶ *vi* summen
human [ˈhjuːmən] *adj* menschlich ▶ *n* (*also:* **~ being**) Mensch *m*
humanitarian [hjuːmænɪˈtɛərɪən] *adj* humanitär
humanity [hjuːˈmænɪtɪ] *n* Menschlichkeit *f*; (*mankind*) Menschheit *f* ■ **humanities** *npl* (*Scol*): **the humanities** die Geisteswissenschaften *pl*
humble [ˈhʌmbl] *adj* bescheiden
humid [ˈhjuːmɪd] *adj* feucht
humidity [hjuːˈmɪdɪtɪ] *n* Feuchtigkeit *f*
humiliate [hjuːˈmɪlɪeɪt] *vt* demütigen
humiliation [hjuːmɪlɪˈeɪʃən] *n* Demütigung *f*
humor (*US*) = **humour**
humorous [ˈhjuːmərəs] *adj* (*remark*) witzig; (*book*) lustig; (*person*) humorvoll
humour, (*US*) **humor** [ˈhjuːmə^r] *n* Humor *m*; **sense of ~** (Sinn *m* für) Humor
hump [hʌmp] *n* (*deformity*) Buckel *m*
hunch [hʌntʃ] *n* Gefühl *nt*, Ahnung *f*
hunchback [ˈhʌntʃbæk] *n* Bucklige(r) *f*(*m*)
hundred [ˈhʌndrəd] *num* hundert; **a** *or* **one ~ books/people/dollars** (ein) hundert Bücher/Personen/Dollar
hundredth [ˈhʌndrədθ] *num* hundertste(r, s)
hundredweight [ˈhʌndrɪdweɪt] *n* *Gewichtseinheit* (*BRIT* = *50,8 kg*; *US* = *45,3 kg*), ≈ Zentner *m*
hung [hʌŋ] *pt, pp of* **hang**
Hungarian [hʌŋˈgɛərɪən] *adj* ungarisch ▶ *n* Ungar(in) *m*(*f*); (*Ling*) Ungarisch *nt*
Hungary [ˈhʌŋgərɪ] *n* Ungarn *nt*
hunger [ˈhʌŋgə[r]] *n* Hunger *m*
hungry [ˈhʌŋgrɪ] *adj* hungrig; **to be ~** Hunger haben
hunk [hʌŋk] *n* (*inf*: *man*) (großer, gut aussehender) Mann *m*
hunt [hʌnt] *vt* jagen ▶ *vi* (*Sport*) jagen ▶ *n* Jagd *f*; (*search*) Suche *f*; **to ~ for** (*search*) suchen (nach)
hunting [ˈhʌntɪŋ] *n* Jagd *f*, Jagen *nt*
hurdle [ˈhəːdl] *n* Hürde *f*
hurl [həːl] *vt* schleudern
hurricane [ˈhʌrɪkən] *n* Orkan *m*
hurried [ˈhʌrɪd] *adj* eilig
hurry [ˈhʌrɪ] *n* Eile *f* ▶ *vi* eilen; (*to do sth*) sich beeilen ▶ *vt* (zur Eile) antreiben; **there's no ~** es eilt nicht; **they hurried to help him** sie eilten ihm zu Hilfe
▶ **hurry up** *vt* (zur Eile) antreiben ▶ *vi* sich beeilen
hurt [həːt] (*pt, pp* **~**) *vt* wehtun +*dat*; (*injure, fig*) verletzen ▶ *vi* wehtun; **I've ~ my arm** ich habe mir am Arm wehgetan; **where does it ~?** wo tut es weh?
husband [ˈhʌzbənd] *n* (Ehe)mann *m*
husky [ˈhʌskɪ] *adj* (*voice*) rau ▶ *n* Schlittenhund *m*
hut [hʌt] *n* Hütte *f*
hyacinth [ˈhaɪəsɪnθ] *n* Hyazinthe *f*
hybrid [ˈhaɪbrɪd] *n* (*plant, animal*) Kreuzung *f*; **~ car** Hybridauto *nt*
hydroelectric [ˈhaɪdrəuɪˈlɛktrɪk] *adj* hydroelektrisch
hydrofoil [ˈhaɪdrəfɔɪl] *n* Tragflächenboot *nt*
hydrogen [ˈhaɪdrədʒən] *n* Wasserstoff *m*
hygiene [ˈhaɪdʒiːn] *n* Hygiene *f*
hygienic [haɪˈdʒiːnɪk] *adj* hygienisch
hymn [hɪm] *n* Kirchenlied *nt*
hyperconnectivity [ˈhaɪpəkɔnɛkˈtɪvəti] *n* Hypervernetzung *f*
hyperlink [ˈhaɪpəlɪŋk] *n* Hyperlink *m*
hypermarket [ˈhaɪpəmɑːkɪt] (BRIT) *n* Verbrauchermarkt *m*
hyperventilation [haɪpəventɪˈleɪʃən] *n* Hyperventilation *f*
hyphen [ˈhaɪfn] *n* Bindestrich *m*
hypnosis [hɪpˈnəusɪs] *n* Hypnose *f*
hypnotize [ˈhɪpnətaɪz] *vt* hypnotisieren
hypochondriac [haɪpəˈkɔndrɪæk] *n* Hypochonder *m*
hypocrisy [hɪˈpɔkrɪsɪ] *n* Heuchelei *f*
hypocrite [ˈhɪpəkrɪt] *n* Heuchler(in) *m*(*f*)
hypodermic [haɪpəˈdəːmɪk] *adj* (*injection*) subkutan ▶ *n* (Injektions)spritze *f*

hypothetical [haɪpəu'θɛtɪkl] *adj* hypothetisch
hysteria [hɪ'stɪərɪə] *n* Hysterie *f*
hysterical [hɪ'stɛrɪkl] *adj* hysterisch; (*situation*) wahnsinnig komisch

I

I [aɪ] *pron* ich
ice [aɪs] *n* Eis *nt* ▸ *vt* (*cake*) glasieren
iceberg ['aɪsbəːg] *n* Eisberg *m*
icebox ['aɪsbɔks] *n* (*US*: *fridge*) Kühlschrank *m*
ice-cold *adj* eiskalt
ice cream *n* Eis *nt*
ice cube *n* Eiswürfel *m*
iced [aɪst] *adj* (*cake*) mit Zuckerguss überzogen, glasiert; (*tea, coffee*) Eis-
ice hockey *n* Eishockey *nt*
Iceland ['aɪslənd] *n* Island *nt*
Icelander ['aɪsləndəʳ] *n* Isländer(in) *m(f)*
Icelandic [aɪs'lændɪk] *adj* isländisch ▸ *n* (*Ling*) Isländisch *nt*
ice lolly (Brit) *n* Eis *nt* am Stiel
ice rink *n* (Kunst)eisbahn *f*
ice-skating *n* Schlittschuhlaufen *nt*
icing ['aɪsɪŋ] *n* (*Culin*) Zuckerguss *m*
icon ['aɪkɔn] *n* Ikone *f*; (*Comput*) Ikon *nt*
icy ['aɪsɪ] *adj* eisig; (*road*) vereist
ID *n abbr* (= *identification (document)*) Ausweis *m*
I'd [aɪd] = **I would**; **I had**
Ida. (*US*) *abbr* (*Post*) = **Idaho**
ID card *n* = **identity card**
idea [aɪ'dɪə] *n* Idee *f*; **I haven't the least ~** ich habe nicht die leiseste Ahnung
ideal [aɪ'dɪəl] *n* Ideal *nt* ▸ *adj* ideal
ideally [aɪ'dɪəlɪ] *adv* ideal; **~ the book should …** idealerweise *or* im Idealfall sollte das Buch …
identical [aɪ'dɛntɪkl] *adj* identisch; (*twins*) eineiig
identify [aɪ'dɛntɪfaɪ] *vt* (*distinguish*) identifizieren
identity [aɪ'dɛntɪtɪ] *n* Identität *f*

identity card *n* (Personal)ausweis *m*
identity theft *n* Identitätsdiebstahl *m*
idiom [ˈɪdɪəm] *n* (*phrase*) Redewendung *f*
idiomatic [ɪdɪəˈmætɪk] *adj* idiomatisch
idiot [ˈɪdɪət] *n* Idiot(in) *m(f)*, Dummkopf *m*
idle [ˈaɪdl] *adj* untätig; (*lazy*) faul; (*unemployed*) unbeschäftigt; (*machinery, factory*) stillstehend; (*conversation, pleasure*) leer
idol [ˈaɪdl] *n* Idol *nt*
idolize [ˈaɪdəlaɪz] *vt* vergöttern
idyllic [ɪˈdɪlɪk] *adj* idyllisch
i.e. *abbr* (= *id est*) d. h.
IED *abbr* (= *improvised explosive device*) USBV *f* (= *unbekannte Spreng- und Brandvorrichtung*)

 **KEYWORD**

if [ɪf] *conj* **1** (*given that, providing that etc*) wenn, falls; **if I were you** wenn ich Sie wäre, an Ihrer Stelle
2 (*whenever*) wenn
3 (*although*): **(even) if** auch *or* selbst wenn
4 (*whether*) ob
5: **if so/not** falls ja/nein; **if only** wenn nur; **if only I could** wenn ich doch nur könnte; *see also* **as**

ignition [ɪgˈnɪʃən] *n* (*Aut*) Zündung *f*
ignition key *n* (*Aut*) Zündschlüssel *m*
ignorance [ˈɪgnərəns] *n* Unwissenheit *f*
ignorant [ˈɪgnərənt] *adj* unwissend
ignore [ɪgˈnɔːʳ] *vt* ignorieren
ill [ɪl] *adj* krank
I'll [aɪl] = **I will**; **I shall**
ill at ease *adj* unbehaglich
illegal [ɪˈliːgl] *adj* illegal
illegitimate [ɪlɪˈdʒɪtɪmət] *adj* (*child*) unehelich
illiterate [ɪˈlɪtərət] *adj* (*person*) des Lesens und Schreibens unkundig
illness [ˈɪlnɪs] *n* Krankheit *f*
illuminate [ɪˈluːmɪneɪt] *vt* beleuchten
illuminating [ɪˈluːmɪneɪtɪŋ] *adj* aufschlussreich
illusion [ɪˈluːʒən] *n* Illusion *f*; **to be under the ~ that ...** sich *dat* einbilden, dass ...
illustrate [ˈɪləstreɪt] *vt* (*book*) illustrieren
illustration [ɪləˈstreɪʃən] *n* Illustration *f*; (*example*) Veranschaulichung *f*
I'm [aɪm] = **I am**
image [ˈɪmɪdʒ] *n* Bild *nt*; (*public face*) Image *nt*
imaginable [ɪˈmædʒɪnəbl] *adj* denkbar
imaginary [ɪˈmædʒɪnərɪ] *adj* erfunden; (*danger*) eingebildet
imagination [ɪmædʒɪˈneɪʃən] *n* Fantasie *f*; (*illusion*) Einbildung *f*
imaginative [ɪˈmædʒɪnətɪv] *adj* fantasievoll
imagine [ɪˈmædʒɪn] *vt* sich *dat* vorstellen; (*suppose*) vermuten
imam [ɪˈmɑːm] *n* Imam *m*
imbecile [ˈɪmbəsiːl] *n* Schwachkopf *m*
imitate [ˈɪmɪteɪt] *vt* imitieren; (*mimic*) nachahmen
imitation [ɪmɪˈteɪʃən] *n* Nachahmung *f*
immaculate [ɪˈmækjulət] *adj* makellos; (*appearance, piece of work*) tadellos
immature [ɪməˈtjuəʳ] *adj* unreif
immediate [ɪˈmiːdɪət] *adj* sofortig; (*need*) dringend
immediately [ɪˈmiːdɪətlɪ] *adv* sofort
immense [ɪˈmɛns] *adj* riesig, enorm
immersion heater [ɪˈməːʃən-] (Brit) *n* elektrischer Heißwasserboiler *m*
immigrant [ˈɪmɪgrənt] *n* Einwanderer *m*, Einwanderin *f*
immigration [ɪmɪˈgreɪʃən] *n* Einwanderung *f*; (*at airport etc*) Einwanderungsstelle *f*
immobilize [ɪˈməubɪlaɪz] *vt* (*person*) handlungsunfähig machen; (*machine*) zum Stillstand bringen
immobilizer [ɪˈməubɪlaɪzəʳ] *n* (*Aut*) Wegfahrsperre *f*
immoral [ɪˈmɔrl] *adj* unmoralisch
immortal [ɪˈmɔːtl] *adj* unsterblich
immune [ɪˈmjuːn] *adj*: **~ (to)** (*disease*) immun (gegen)
immune system *n* Immunsystem *nt*
impact [ˈɪmpækt] *n* Aufprall *m*; (*of law, measure*) (Aus)wirkung *f*
impatience [ɪmˈpeɪʃəns] *n* Ungeduld *f*
impatient [ɪmˈpeɪʃənt] *adj* ungeduldig
impeccable [ɪmˈpɛkəbl] *adj* (*manners*) tadellos
impede [ɪmˈpiːd] *vt* behindern
imperative [ɪmˈpɛrətɪv] *adj* dringend ▸ *n* (*Ling*) Imperativ *m*

mperfect [ɪmˈpəːfɪkt] *adj* mangelhaft; (*goods*) fehlerhaft ▶ *n* (*Ling*: *also*: **~ tense**) Imperfekt *nt*
mperfection [ɪmpəˈfɛkʃən] *n* Fehler *m*
mperial [ɪmˈpɪərɪəl] *adj* kaiserlich
mperialism [ɪmˈpɪərɪəlɪzəm] *n* Imperialismus *m*
mpertinence [ɪmˈpəːtɪnəns] *n* Unverschämtheit *f*, Zumutung *f*
mpertinent [ɪmˈpəːtɪnənt] *adj* unverschämt
mplant [ɪmˈplɑːnt] *vt* (*Med*) einpflanzen
mplausible [ɪmˈplɔːzɪbl] *adj* unglaubwürdig
mplement *n* [ˈɪmplɪmənt] Gerät *nt*, Werkzeug *nt* ▶ *vt* [ˈɪmplɪmɛnt] durchführen
mplication [ɪmplɪˈkeɪʃən] *n* Auswirkung *f*; (*involvement*) Verwicklung *f*
mplicit [ɪmˈplɪsɪt] *adj* (*inferred*) implizit, unausgesprochen
mply [ɪmˈplaɪ] *vt* andeuten; (*mean*) bedeuten
impolite [ɪmpəˈlaɪt] *adj* unhöflich
import *vt* [ɪmˈpɔːt] importieren, einführen ▶ *n* [ˈɪmpɔːt] Import *m*, Einfuhr *f*
importance [ɪmˈpɔːtns] *n* Wichtigkeit *f*; Bedeutung *f*; **to be of little/great ~** nicht besonders wichtig/sehr wichtig sein
important [ɪmˈpɔːtənt] *adj* wichtig; (*influential*) bedeutend; **it's not ~** es ist unwichtig
impose [ɪmˈpəuz] *vt* auferlegen; (*sanctions*) verhängen
imposing [ɪmˈpəuzɪŋ] *adj* eindrucksvoll
impossible [ɪmˈpɔsɪbl] *adj* unmöglich
impotence [ˈɪmpətns] *n* Machtlosigkeit *f*; Impotenz *f*
impotent [ˈɪmpətnt] *adj* machtlos; (*Med*) impotent
impractical [ɪmˈpræktɪkl] *adj* (*plan*) undurchführbar; (*person*) unpraktisch
impress [ɪmˈprɛs] *vt* beeindrucken
impression [ɪmˈprɛʃən] *n* Eindruck *m*
impressive [ɪmˈprɛsɪv] *adj* beeindruckend
imprison [ɪmˈprɪzn] *vt* inhaftieren, einsperren
imprisonment [ɪmˈprɪznmənt] *n* Gefangenschaft *f*
improbable [ɪmˈprɔbəbl] *adj* unwahrscheinlich
improper [ɪmˈprɔpəʳ] *adj* ungehörig; (*dishonest*) unlauter
improve [ɪmˈpruːv] *vt* verbessern ▶ *vi* sich bessern; **the patient is improving** dem Patienten geht es besser
improvement [ɪmˈpruːvmənt] *n*: **~ (in)** Verbesserung *f* (+*gen*)
improvise [ˈɪmprəvaɪz] *vt*, *vi* improvisieren
impulse [ˈɪmpʌls] *n* Impuls *m*
impulsive [ɪmˈpʌlsɪv] *adj* impulsiv

KEYWORD

in [ɪn] *prep* **1** (*indicating place, position*) in +*dat*; (: *with motion*) in +*acc*; **in here** hierin; **in there** darin
2 (*with place names*: *of town, region, country*) in +*dat*; **in London/Bavaria** in London/Bayern
3 (*indicating time*) in +*dat*; **in spring/summer/May** im Frühling/Sommer/Mai; **in 1994** 1994; **in the afternoon** am Nachmittag; **at 4 o'clock in the afternoon** um 4 Uhr nachmittags
4 (*indicating manner, circumstances, state*) in +*dat*; **in a loud/soft voice** mit lauter/weicher Stimme; **in English/German** auf Englisch/Deutsch; **in the sun** in der Sonne; **in the rain** im Regen
5 (*with ratios, numbers*): **1 in 10** eine(r, s) von 10; **20 pence in the pound** 20 Pence pro Pfund; **they lined up in twos** sie stellten sich in Zweierreihen auf
6 (*referring to people, works*): **the disease is common in children** die Krankheit ist bei Kindern verbreitet; **in (the works of) Dickens** bei Dickens; **they have a good leader in him** in ihm haben sie einen guten Führer
7 (*indicating profession etc*): **to be in teaching/the army** Lehrer(in)/beim Militär sein
8 (*with present participle*): **in saying this, I ...** wenn ich das sage, ...
▶ *adv*: **to be in** (*person*: *at home, work*) da sein; (*train, ship, plane*) angekommen sein; (*in fashion*) in sein; **to ask sb in** jdn hereinbitten; **to run/limp** *etc* **in** hereinlaufen/-humpeln *etc*
▶ *n*: **the ins and outs** (*of proposal, situation etc*) die Einzelheiten *pl*

inability [ɪnəˈbɪlɪtɪ] *n* Unfähigkeit *f*
inaccessible [ɪnəkˈsɛsɪbl] *adj* unzugänglich
inaccurate [ɪnˈækjurət] *adj* ungenau
inadequate [ɪnˈædɪkwət] *adj* unzulänglich
inapplicable [ɪnˈæplɪkəbl] *adj* unzutreffend
inappropriate [ɪnəˈprəuprɪət] *adj* unpassend; (*word, expression*) unangebracht
inborn [ɪnˈbɔːn] *adj* angeboren
inbox [ˈɪnbɔks] *n* (*Comput*) Posteingang *m*; (*US: in-tray*) Ablage *f* für Eingänge
incapable [ɪnˈkeɪpəbl] *adj*: **to be ~ of sth** unfähig zu etw sein; **to be ~ of doing sth** unfähig sein, etw zu tun
incense *n* [ˈɪnsɛns] Weihrauch *m* ▶ *vt* [ɪnˈsɛns] wütend machen
incentive [ɪnˈsɛntɪv] *n* Anreiz *m*
incessant [ɪnˈsɛsnt] *adj* unablässig
incessantly [ɪnˈsɛsntlɪ] *adv* unablässig
incest [ˈɪnsɛst] *n* Inzest *m*
inch [ɪntʃ] *n* Zoll *m*
incident [ˈɪnsɪdnt] *n* Vorfall *m*; (*diplomatic etc*) Zwischenfall *m*
incidentally [ɪnsɪˈdɛntəlɪ] *adv* übrigens
inclination [ɪnklɪˈneɪʃən] *n* Neigung *f*
incline *n* [ˈɪnklaɪn] Abhang *m* ▶ *vi* [ɪnˈklaɪn] sich neigen; **to be inclined to** neigen zu
include [ɪnˈkluːd] *vt* einbeziehen; (*in price*) einschließen
including [ɪnˈkluːdɪŋ] *prep* einschließlich
inclusive [ɪnˈkluːsɪv] *adj* (*price*) Pauschal-; **~ of** einschließlich *+gen*
incoherent [ɪnkəuˈhɪərənt] *adj* zusammenhanglos
income [ˈɪnkʌm] *n* Einkommen *nt*; (*from property, investment, pension*) Einkünfte *pl*
income tax *n* Einkommenssteuer *f*
incoming [ˈɪnkʌmɪŋ] *adj* (*passenger*) ankommend; (*call, mail*) eingehend
incompatible [ɪnkəmˈpætɪbl] *adj* unvereinbar
incompetent [ɪnˈkɔmpɪtnt] *adj* unfähig; (*job*) unzulänglich
incomplete [ɪnkəmˈpliːt] *adj* (*partial*) unvollständig
incomprehensible [ɪnkɔmprɪˈhɛnsɪbl] *adj* unverständlich
inconceivable [ɪnkənˈsiːvəbl] *adj*: **it is ~ (that ...)** es ist unvorstellbar *or* undenkbar(, dass ...)
inconsiderate [ɪnkənˈsɪdərət] *adj* rücksichtslos
inconsistency [ɪnkənˈsɪstənsɪ] *n* Widersprüchlichkeit *f*; Inkonsequenz *f*; Unbeständigkeit *f*
inconsistent [ɪnkənˈsɪstnt] *adj* widersprüchlich; (*person*) inkonsequent; (*work*) unbeständig
inconvenience [ɪnkənˈviːnjəns] *n* Unannehmlichkeit *f*; (*trouble*) Umstände *pl*
inconvenient [ɪnkənˈviːnjənt] *adj* (*time, place*) ungünstig; (*house*) unbequem; (*visitor*) ungelegen
incorporate [ɪnˈkɔːpəreɪt] *vt* aufnehmen; (*contain*) enthalten
incorrect [ɪnkəˈrɛkt] *adj* falsch
increase *vi* [ɪnˈkriːs] (*level etc*) zunehmen; (*price*) steigen; (*in size*) sich vergrößern; (*in number, quantity*) sich vermehren ▶ *vt* [ɪnˈkriːs] vergrößern; (*price*) erhöhen ▶ *n* [ˈɪnkriːs]: **~ (in)** Zunahme *f +gen*; (*in wages, spending etc*) Erhöhung *f +gen*
increasingly [ɪnˈkriːsɪŋlɪ] *adv* zunehmend
incredible [ɪnˈkrɛdɪbl] *adj* unglaublich
incredulous [ɪnˈkrɛdjuləs] *adj* ungläubig
incriminate [ɪnˈkrɪmɪneɪt] *vt* belasten
incubator [ˈɪnkjubeɪtə[r]] *n* (*for babies*) Brutkasten *m*
incurable [ɪnˈkjuərəbl] *adj* unheilbar
indecent [ɪnˈdiːsnt] *adj* unanständig, anstößig
indecisive [ɪndɪˈsaɪsɪv] *adj* unentschlossen
indeed [ɪnˈdiːd] *adv* (*in fact*) tatsächlich; **yes ~!** oh ja!, das kann man wohl sagen!
indefinite [ɪnˈdɛfɪnɪt] *adj* (*period, number*) unbestimmt
indefinitely [ɪnˈdɛfɪnɪtlɪ] *adv* (*continue*) endlos; (*postpone*) auf unbestimmte Zeit
independence [ɪndɪˈpɛndns] *n* Unabhängigkeit *f*

ndependence Day *n siehe Info-Artikel*

INDEPENDENCE DAY

Independence Day (der 4. Juli) ist in den USA ein gesetzlicher Feiertag zum Gedenken an die Unabhängigkeitserklärung vom 4. Juli 1776, mit der die 13 amerikanischen Kolonien ihre Freiheit und Unabhängigkeit von Großbritannien erklärten.

ndependent [ɪndɪˈpɛndnt] *adj* unabhängig
ndescribable [ɪndɪsˈkraɪbəbl] *adj* unbeschreiblich
ndex [ˈɪndɛks] *n* (*in book*) Register *nt*
ndex finger *n* Zeigefinger *m*
ndia [ˈɪndɪə] *n* Indien *nt*
ndian [ˈɪndɪən] *adj* indisch; (*American Indian*) indianisch ▶ *n* Inder(in) *m(f)*; **American ~** Indianer(in) *m(f)*
ndian Ocean *n*: **the ~** der Indische Ozean
ndian summer *n* Altweibersommer *m*
ndicate [ˈɪndɪkeɪt] *vt* (an)zeigen; (*point to*) deuten auf +*acc* ▶ *vi* (BRIT *Aut*): **to ~ left/right** links/rechts blinken
ndication [ɪndɪˈkeɪʃən] *n* (An)zeichen *nt*
ndicator [ˈɪndɪkeɪtəʳ] *n* (*Aut*) Blinker *m*
ndifferent [ɪnˈdɪfrənt] *adj* gleichgültig; (*mediocre*) mittelmäßig
ndigestible [ɪndɪˈdʒɛstɪbl] *adj* unverdaulich
indigestion [ɪndɪˈdʒɛstʃən] *n* Magenverstimmung *f*
indignity [ɪnˈdɪgnɪtɪ] *n* Demütigung *f*
indirect [ɪndɪˈrɛkt] *adj* indirekt
indirectly [ɪndɪˈrɛktlɪ] *adv* indirekt
ndiscreet [ɪndɪsˈkriːt] *adj* indiskret
ndispensable [ɪndɪsˈpɛnsəbl] *adj* unentbehrlich
indisposed [ɪndɪsˈpəuzd] *adj* unpässlich
indisputable [ɪndɪsˈpjuːtəbl] *adj* unbestreitbar
individual [ɪndɪˈvɪdjuəl] *n* Einzelne(r) *f(m)* ▶ *adj* eigen; (*single*) einzeln; (*case, portion*) Einzel-; (*particular*) individuell
ndividually [ɪndɪˈvɪdjuəlɪ] *adv* einzeln
ndonesia [ɪndəˈniːzɪə] *n* Indonesien *nt*
indoor [ˈɪndɔːʳ] *adj* (*plant, aerial*) Zimmer-; (*clothes, shoes*) Haus-; (*swimming pool, sport*) Hallen-
indoors [ɪnˈdɔːz] *adv* drinnen
indulge [ɪnˈdʌldʒ] *vi*: **to ~ in** sich hingeben +*dat*
indulgence [ɪnˈdʌldʒəns] *n* (*pleasure*) Luxus *m*; (*leniency*) Nachgiebigkeit *f*
indulgent [ɪnˈdʌldʒənt] *adj* nachsichtig
industrial [ɪnˈdʌstrɪəl] *adj* industriell; (*city*) Industrie-
industrial estate (BRIT) *n* Industriegebiet *nt*
industry [ˈɪndəstrɪ] *n* Industrie *f*
inedible [ɪnˈɛdɪbl] *adj* ungenießbar
ineffective [ɪnɪˈfɛktɪv] *adj* wirkungslos
inefficient [ɪnɪˈfɪʃənt] *adj* ineffizient; (*machine*) leistungsunfähig
ineligible [ɪnˈɛlɪdʒɪbl] *adj*: **to be ~ for sth** zu etw nicht berechtigt sein
inequality [ɪnɪˈkwɔlɪtɪ] *n* Ungleichheit *f*
inevitable [ɪnˈɛvɪtəbl] *adj* unvermeidlich
inevitably [ɪnˈɛvɪtəblɪ] *adv* zwangsläufig
inexcusable [ɪnɪksˈkjuːzəbl] *adj* unverzeihlich
inexpensive [ɪnɪkˈspɛnsɪv] *adj* preisgünstig
inexperience [ɪnɪkˈspɪərɪəns] *n* Unerfahrenheit *f*
inexperienced [ɪnɪkˈspɪərɪənst] *adj* unerfahren
inexplicable [ɪnɪkˈsplɪkəbl] *adj* unerklärlich
infallible [ɪnˈfælɪbl] *adj* unfehlbar
infamous [ˈɪnfəməs] *adj* niederträchtig
infancy [ˈɪnfənsɪ] *n* frühe Kindheit *f*
infant [ˈɪnfənt] *n* Säugling *m*; (*young child*) Kleinkind *nt*
infant school (BRIT) *n* Grundschule *f* (*für die ersten beiden Jahrgänge*)
infatuated [ɪnˈfætjueɪtɪd] *adj*: **~ with** vernarrt in +*acc*
infect [ɪnˈfɛkt] *vt* anstecken (*also fig*), infizieren
infection [ɪnˈfɛkʃən] *n* Infektion *f*
infectious [ɪnˈfɛkʃəs] *adj* ansteckend
inferior [ɪnˈfɪərɪəʳ] *adj* (*in rank*) untergeordnet; (*in quality*) minderwertig

inferiority [ɪnfɪərɪ'ɔrətɪ] *n* untergeordnete Stellung *f*; Minderwertigkeit *f*
inferiority complex *n* Minderwertigkeitskomplex *m*
infertile [ɪn'fə:taɪl] *adj* unfruchtbar
infidelity [ɪnfɪ'dɛlɪtɪ] *n* Untreue *f*
infinite ['ɪnfɪnɪt] *adj* unendlich
infinitive [ɪn'fɪnɪtɪv] *n* (*Ling*) Infinitiv *m*
infinity [ɪn'fɪnɪtɪ] *n* Unendlichkeit *f*
infirmary [ɪn'fə:mərɪ] *n* Krankenhaus *nt*
inflame [ɪn'fleɪm] *vt* aufbringen
inflammation [ɪnflə'meɪʃən] *n* Entzündung *f*
inflatable [ɪn'fleɪtəbl] *adj* aufblasbar; (*dinghy*) Schlauch-
inflate [ɪn'fleɪt] *vt* aufpumpen; (*balloon*) aufblasen; (*price*) hochtreiben
inflation [ɪn'fleɪʃən] *n* Inflation *f*
inflexible [ɪn'flɛksɪbl] *adj* inflexibel
inflict [ɪn'flɪkt] *vt*: **to ~ sth on sb** (*damage, suffering, wound*) jdm etw zufügen; (*punishment*) jdm etw auferlegen
in-flight ['ɪnflaɪt] *adj* während des Fluges
influence ['ɪnfluəns] *n* Einfluss *m* ▶ *vt* beeinflussen
influential [ɪnflu'ɛnʃl] *adj* einflussreich
influenza [ɪnflu'ɛnzə] *n* (*Med*) Grippe *f*
inform [ɪn'fɔ:m] *vt*: **to ~ sb of sth** jdn von etw unterrichten, jdn über etw *acc* informieren
informal [ɪn'fɔ:ml] *adj* ungezwungen
information [ɪnfə'meɪʃən] *n* Informationen *pl*, Auskunft *f*; (*knowledge*) Wissen *nt*; **a piece of ~** eine Auskunft *or* Information; **for your ~** zu Ihrer Information
information desk *n* Auskunftsschalter *m*
information technology *n* Informationstechnik *f*
informative [ɪn'fɔ:mətɪv] *adj* aufschlussreich
infrared [ɪnfrə'rɛd] *adj* infrarot
infrastructure *n* Infrastruktur *f*
infuriate [ɪn'fjuərɪeɪt] *vt* wütend machen
infuriating [ɪn'fjuərɪeɪtɪŋ] *adj* äußerst ärgerlich
infusion [ɪn'fju:ʒən] *n* (*tea etc*) Aufguss *m*
ingenious [ɪn'dʒi:njəs] *adj* genial
ingredient [ɪn'gri:dɪənt] *n* (*of cake etc*) Zutat *f*
inhabit [ɪn'hæbɪt] *vt* bewohnen, wohnen in *+dat*
inhabitant [ɪn'hæbɪtnt] *n* Einwohner(in) *m(f)*
inhale [ɪn'heɪl] *vt* einatmen ▶ *vi* (*when smoking*) inhalieren
inhaler [ɪn'heɪlə^r] *n* Inhalationsapparat *m*
inherit [ɪn'hɛrɪt] *vt* erben
inheritance [ɪn'hɛrɪtəns] *n* Erbe *nt*
inhibited [ɪn'hɪbɪtɪd] *adj* gehemmt
inhibition [ɪnhɪ'bɪʃən] *n* Hemmung *f*
in-house ['ɪn'haus] *adj*, *adv* hausintern
inhuman [ɪn'hju:mən] *adj* (*behaviour*) unmenschlich
initial [ɪ'nɪʃl] *adj* anfänglich; (*stage*) Anfangs- ▶ *vt* (*document*) abzeichnen
■ **initials** *npl* Initialen *pl*
initially [ɪ'nɪʃəlɪ] *adv* zu Anfang
initiative [ɪ'nɪʃətɪv] *n* Initiative *f*
inject [ɪn'dʒɛkt] *vt* (ein)spritzen; **to ~ sb with sth** jdm etw spritzen *or* injizieren
injection [ɪn'dʒɛkʃən] *n* Spritze *f*, Injektion *f*
injure ['ɪndʒə^r] *vt* verletzen; **to ~ o.s.** sich verletzen
injury ['ɪndʒərɪ] *n* Verletzung *f*
injustice [ɪn'dʒʌstɪs] *n* Ungerechtigkeit *f*
ink [ɪŋk] *n* Tinte *f*
ink-jet printer ['ɪŋkdʒɛt-] *n* Tintenstrahldrucker *m*
inland ['ɪnlənd] *adj* (*port, sea, waterway*) Binnen- ▶ *adv* (*travel*) landeinwärts
Inland Revenue (Brit) *n* ≈ Finanzamt *nt*
in-laws ['ɪnlɔ:z] *npl* (*parents-in-law*) Schwiegereltern *pl*
inmate ['ɪnmeɪt] *n* Insasse *m*
inn [ɪn] *n* Gasthaus *nt*
innate [ɪ'neɪt] *adj* angeboren
inner ['ɪnə^r] *adj* innere(r, s); (*courtyard*) Innen-
innocence ['ɪnəsns] *n* Unschuld *f*
innocent ['ɪnəsnt] *adj* unschuldig
innovation [ɪnəu'veɪʃən] *n* Neuerung *f*
innumerable [ɪ'nju:mrəbl] *adj* unzählig
inoculate [ɪ'nɔkjuleɪt] *vt*: **to ~ sb against sth** jdn gegen etw impfen
inoculation [ɪnɔkju'leɪʃən] *n* Impfung *f*

npatient [ˈɪnpeɪʃənt] *n* stationär behandelter Patient *m*, stationär behandelte Patientin *f*

nput [ˈɪnput] *n* (*of capital, manpower*) Investition *f*; (*Comput*) Eingabe *f*, Input *m or nt*

nquest [ˈɪnkwɛst] *n* gerichtliche Untersuchung *f* der Todesursache

nquire [ɪnˈkwaɪəʳ] *vi*: **to ~ about** sich erkundigen nach, fragen nach

nquiry [ɪnˈkwaɪərɪ] *n* Untersuchung *f*; (*question*) Anfrage *f*

nsane [ɪnˈseɪn] *adj* wahnsinnig; (*Med*) geisteskrank

nsanity [ɪnˈsænɪtɪ] *n* Wahnsinn *m*

nsatiable [ɪnˈseɪʃəbl] *adj* unersättlich

nscription [ɪnˈskrɪpʃən] *n* Inschrift *f*

nsect [ˈɪnsɛkt] *n* Insekt *nt*

nsecticide [ɪnˈsɛktɪsaɪd] *n* Insektizid *nt*, Insektengift *nt*

nsect repellent *n* Insektenbekämpfungsmittel *nt*

nsecure [ɪnsɪˈkjuəʳ] *adj* unsicher

nsensitive [ɪnˈsɛnsɪtɪv] *adj* gefühllos

nsensitivity [ɪnsɛnsɪˈtɪvɪtɪ] *n* Gefühllosigkeit *f*

nseparable [ɪnˈsɛprəbl] *adj* (*friends*) unzertrennlich

nsert *vt* [ɪnˈsəːt] einfügen; (*into sth*) hineinstecken ▶ *n* [ˈɪnsəːt] (*in newspaper etc*) Beilage *f*

nsertion [ɪnˈsəːʃən] *n* (*of comment*) Einfügen *nt*

nside [ˈɪnˈsaɪd] *n* Innere(s) *nt*, Innenseite *f* ▶ *adj* innere(r, s); (*pocket, cabin, light*) Innen- ▶ *adv* (*go*) nach innen, hinein ▶ *prep* (*location*) in +*dat*; (*motion*) in +*acc*; **~ 10 minutes** innerhalb von 10 Minuten

nside out *adv* (*piece of clothing*: *be*) links *or* verkehrt herum; (: *turn*) nach links; (*know*) in- und auswendig

nsider [ɪnˈsaɪdəʳ] *n* Insider *m*, Eingeweihte(r) *f*(*m*)

nsight [ˈɪnsaɪt] *n*: **to gain (an) ~ into** einen Einblick gewinnen in +*acc*

nsignificant [ɪnsɪgˈnɪfɪknt] *adj* belanglos

nsincere [ɪnsɪnˈsɪəʳ] *adj* unaufrichtig, falsch

nsinuate [ɪnˈsɪnjueɪt] *vt* anspielen auf +*acc*

nsinuation [ɪnsɪnjuˈeɪʃən] *n* Anspielung *f*

insist [ɪnˈsɪst] *vi* bestehen; **to ~ on** bestehen auf +*dat*

insistent [ɪnˈsɪstənt] *adj* (*determined*) hartnäckig

insoluble [ɪnˈsɔljubl] *adj* unlösbar

insomnia [ɪnˈsɔmnɪə] *n* Schlaflosigkeit *f*

inspect [ɪnˈspɛkt] *vt* kontrollieren; (*examine*) prüfen

inspection [ɪnˈspɛkʃən] *n* Kontrolle *f*; Prüfung *f*

inspector [ɪnˈspɛktəʳ] *n* Inspektor(in) *m*(*f*); (Brit: *on buses, trains*) Kontrolleur(in) *m*(*f*); (: *Police*) Kommissar(in) *m*(*f*)

inspiration [ɪnspəˈreɪʃən] *n* Inspiration *f*

inspire [ɪnˈspaɪəʳ] *vt* inspirieren; (*confidence, hope etc*) (er)wecken

install [ɪnˈstɔːl] *vt* installieren

installment plan (*US*) *n* Ratenzahlung *f*

instalment, (*US*) **installment** [ɪnˈstɔːlmənt] *n* Rate *f*; (*of story*) Fortsetzung *f*; **in instalments** in Raten

instance [ˈɪnstəns] *n* Beispiel *nt*; **for ~** zum Beispiel; **in that ~** in diesem Fall

instant [ˈɪnstənt] *n* Augenblick *m* ▶ *adj* (*success*) sofortig; **~ coffee** Instantkaffee *m*

instantly [ˈɪnstəntlɪ] *adv* sofort

instant message *n* Sofortnachricht *f*

instead [ɪnˈstɛd] *adv* stattdessen; **~ of** statt +*gen*; **~ of sb** an jds Stelle *dat*; **~ of doing sth** anstatt *or* anstelle etw zu tun

instinct [ˈɪnstɪŋkt] *n* Instinkt *m*

instinctive [ɪnˈstɪŋktɪv] *adj* instinktiv

instinctively [ɪnˈstɪŋktɪvlɪ] *adv* instinktiv

institute [ˈɪnstɪtjuːt] *n* Institut *nt*

institution [ɪnstɪˈtjuːʃən] *n* (*organization*) Institution *f*, Einrichtung *f*; (*hospital, mental home*) Anstalt *f*

instruct [ɪnˈstrʌkt] *vt*: **to ~ sb to do sth** jdn anweisen, etw zu tun

instruction [ɪnˈstrʌkʃən] *n* Unterricht *m* ■ **instructions** *npl* (*orders*) Anweisungen *pl*; **instructions (for use)** Gebrauchsanweisung *f*

instructor [ɪnˈstrʌktəʳ] *n* Lehrer(in) *m*(*f*)

instrument [ˈɪnstrumənt] *n* Instrument *nt*

instrument panel *n* Armaturenbrett *nt*
insufficient [ɪnsəˈfɪʃənt] *adj* unzureichend
insulate [ˈɪnsjuleɪt] *vt* isolieren
insulating tape [ˈɪnsjuleɪtɪŋ-] *n* Isolierband *nt*
insulation [ɪnsjuˈleɪʃən] *n* Isolierung *f*
insulin [ˈɪnsjulɪn] *n* Insulin *nt*
insult *n* [ˈɪnsʌlt] Beleidigung *f* ▶ *vt* [ɪnˈsʌlt] beleidigen
insulting [ɪnˈsʌltɪŋ] *adj* beleidigend
insurance [ɪnˈʃuərəns] *n* Versicherung *f*
insurance policy *n* Versicherungspolice *f*
insure [ɪnˈʃuəʳ] *vt* versichern
intact [ɪnˈtækt] *adj* intakt
intake [ˈɪnteɪk] *n* (*of food*) Aufnahme *f*
integrate [ˈɪntɪgreɪt] *vt* integrieren
integration [ɪntɪˈgreɪʃən] *n* Integration *f*
integrity [ɪnˈtɛgrɪtɪ] *n* Integrität *f*
intellect [ˈɪntəlɛkt] *n* Intellekt *m*
intellectual [ɪntəˈlɛktjuəl] *adj* intellektuell, geistig
intelligence [ɪnˈtɛlɪdʒəns] *n* Intelligenz *f*
intelligent [ɪnˈtɛlɪdʒənt] *adj* intelligent
intend [ɪnˈtɛnd] *vt*: **to be intended for sb** für jdn gedacht sein; **to ~ to do sth** beabsichtigen, etw zu tun
intense [ɪnˈtɛns] *adj* intensiv; (*anger, joy*) äußerst groß; (*person*) ernsthaft
intensity [ɪnˈtɛnsɪtɪ] *n* Intensität *f*
intensive [ɪnˈtɛnsɪv] *adj* intensiv
intensive care unit *n* Intensivstation *f*
intent [ɪnˈtɛnt] *adj*: **to be ~ on doing sth** entschlossen sein, etw zu tun
intention [ɪnˈtɛnʃən] *n* Absicht *f*
intentional [ɪnˈtɛnʃənl] *adj* absichtlich
interact [ɪntərˈækt] *vi* (*things*) aufeinander einwirken
interaction [ɪntərˈækʃən] *n* Interaktion *f*
interactive [ɪntərˈæktɪv] *adj* (*also Comput*) interaktiv
interchange [ˈɪntətʃeɪndʒ] *n* (*on motorway*) (Autobahn)kreuz *nt*
interchangeable [ɪntəˈtʃeɪndʒəbl] *adj* austauschbar
intercity [ɪntəˈsɪtɪ] *adj*: **~ train** Intercityzug *m*
intercom [ˈɪntəkɔm] *n* (Gegen)sprechanlage *f*
intercourse [ˈɪntəkɔːs] *n* (*sexual*) (Geschlechts)verkehr *m*
interest [ˈɪntrɪst] *n* Interesse *nt*; (*Comm: in company*) Anteil *m*; (*: sum of money*) Zinsen *pl* ▶ *vt* interessieren
interested [ˈɪntrɪstɪd] *adj* interessiert; **to be ~ in sth** sich für etw interessieren; **to be ~ in doing sth** daran interessiert sein, etw zu tun
interest-free [ˈɪntrɪstˈfriː] *adj, adv* zinslos
interesting [ˈɪntrɪstɪŋ] *adj* interessant
interest rate *n* Zinssatz *m*
interface [ˈɪntəfeɪs] *n* (*Comput*) Schnittstelle *f*
interfere [ɪntəˈfɪəʳ] *vi*: **to ~ in** sich einmischen in *+acc*; **to ~ with** (*object*) sich zu schaffen machen an *+dat*
interference [ɪntəˈfɪərəns] *n* Einmischung *f*; (*Radio, TV*) Störung *f*
interior [ɪnˈtɪərɪəʳ] *n* Innere(s) *nt*; (*decor etc*) Innenausstattung *f* ▶ *adj* Innen-
intermediate [ɪntəˈmiːdɪət] *adj* (*stage*) Zwischen-
intermission [ɪntəˈmɪʃən] *n* Pause *f*
intern *vt* [ɪnˈtəːn] internieren ▶ *n* [ˈɪntəːn] (*esp US*) Assistenzarzt *m*, Assistenzärztin *f*
internal [ɪnˈtəːnl] *adj* innere(r, s)
internally [ɪnˈtəːnəlɪ] *adv*: **"not to be taken ~"** „nicht zum Einnehmen"
Internal Revenue Service (*US*) *n* ≈ Finanzamt *nt*
international [ɪntəˈnæʃənl] *adj* international ▶ *n* (*BRIT Sport*) Länderspiel *nt*
internet [ˈɪntənɛt] *n* Internet *nt*
internet access *n* Internetzugang *m*
internet auction *n* Internetauktion *f*
internet banking *n* Onlinebanking *nt*
internet café *n* Internetcafé *nt*
internet connection *n* Internetanschluss *m*
internet provider *n* Internetprovider *m*
interpret [ɪnˈtəːprɪt] *vt* interpretieren; (*translate*) dolmetschen ▶ *vi* dolmetschen
interpretation [ɪntəːprɪˈteɪʃən] *n* Interpretation *f*
interpreter [ɪnˈtəːprɪtəʳ] *n* Dolmetscher(in) *m(f)*
interrogate [ɪnˈtɛrəugeɪt] *vt* verhören
interrogation [ɪntɛrəuˈgeɪʃən] *n* Verhör *nt*

terrupt [ɪntəˈrʌpt] *vt, vi* unterbrechen
terruption [ɪntəˈrʌpʃən] *n* Unterbrechung *f*
tersection [ɪntəˈsɛkʃən] *n* Kreuzung *f*
terval [ˈɪntəvl] *n* Pause *f*; **at intervals** in Abständen
tervene [ɪntəˈviːn] *vi* eingreifen
tervention [ɪntəˈvɛnʃən] *n* Eingreifen *nt*
terview [ˈɪntəvjuː] *n* (*for job*) Vorstellungsgespräch *nt*; (*for place at college etc*) Auswahlgespräch *nt*; (*Radio, TV etc*) Interview *nt* ▸ *vt* ein Vorstellungsgespräch/ Auswahlgespräch führen mit; interviewen
terviewer [ˈɪntəvjuəʳ] *n* (*Radio, TV etc*) Interviewer(in) *m(f)*
testine [ɪnˈtɛstɪn] *n* Darm *m*
timate *adj* [ˈɪntɪmət] eng; (*sexual, also restaurant, dinner, atmosphere*) intim ▸ *vt* [ˈɪntɪmeɪt] andeuten
timidate [ɪnˈtɪmɪdeɪt] *vt* einschüchtern
timidation [ɪntɪmɪˈdeɪʃən] *n* Einschüchterung *f*

KEYWORD

to [ˈɪntu] *prep* **1** (*indicating motion or direction*) in *+acc*; **to go into town** in die Stadt gehen; **the car bumped into the wall** der Wagen fuhr gegen die Mauer
2 (*indicating change of condition, result*): **it broke into pieces** es zerbrach in Stücke; **she translated into English** sie übersetzte ins Englische; **to change into sth** (*turn into*) zu etw werden; (*put on*) sich etw anziehen
3 (*inf*): **to be into sth** (*like*) auf etw *+acc* stehen

tolerable [ɪnˈtɔlərəbl] *adj* unerträglich
tolerant [ɪnˈtɔlərnt] *adj*: **~ (of)** intolerant (gegenüber)
toxicated [ɪnˈtɔksɪkeɪtɪd] *adj* betrunken; (*fig*) berauscht
tricate [ˈɪntrɪkət] *adj* kompliziert
trigue [ɪnˈtriːg] *vt* faszinieren
triguing [ɪnˈtriːgɪŋ] *adj* faszinierend
troduce [ɪntrəˈdjuːs] *vt* (*sth new*) einführen; **to ~ sb (to sb)** jdn (jdm) vorstellen
introduction [ɪntrəˈdʌkʃən] *n* Einführung *f*; (*of person*) Vorstellung *f*; (*to book*) Einleitung *f*
introvert [ˈɪntrəuvəːt] *n* Introvertierte(r) *f(m)*
intuition [ɪntjuːˈɪʃən] *n* Intuition *f*
invade [ɪnˈveɪd] *vt* einfallen in *+acc*
invalid *n* [ˈɪnvəlɪd] Kranke(r) *f(m)*; (*disabled*) Invalide *m* ▸ *adj* [ɪnˈvælɪd] ungültig
invaluable [ɪnˈvæljuəbl] *adj* unschätzbar
invariably [ɪnˈvɛərɪəblɪ] *adv* ständig; **she is ~ late** sie kommt immer zu spät
invasion [ɪnˈveɪʒən] *n* Invasion *f*; **an ~ of privacy** ein Eingriff *m* in die Privatsphäre
invent [ɪnˈvɛnt] *vt* erfinden
invention [ɪnˈvɛnʃən] *n* Erfindung *f*
inventor [ɪnˈvɛntəʳ] *n* Erfinder(in) *m(f)*
inverted commas [ɪnˈvəːtɪd-] (Brit) *npl* Anführungszeichen *pl*
invest [ɪnˈvɛst] *vt* investieren ▸ *vi*: **to ~ in** investieren in *+acc*
investigate [ɪnˈvɛstɪgeɪt] *vt* untersuchen
investigation [ɪnvɛstɪˈgeɪʃən] *n* Untersuchung *f*
investment [ɪnˈvɛstmənt] *n* Investition *f*
invigorating [ɪnˈvɪgəreɪtɪŋ] *adj* belebend; (*experience etc*) anregend
invisible [ɪnˈvɪzɪbl] *adj* unsichtbar
invitation [ɪnvɪˈteɪʃən] *n* Einladung *f*
invite [ɪnˈvaɪt] *vt* einladen
invoice [ˈɪnvɔɪs] *n* Rechnung *f*
involuntary [ɪnˈvɔləntrɪ] *adj* unbeabsichtigt
involve [ɪnˈvɔlv] *vt* (*person*) beteiligen; (*thing*) verbunden sein mit; (*concern, affect*) betreffen; **to ~ sb in sth** jdn in etw *acc* verwickeln
inward [ˈɪnwəd] *adj* innerste(r, s)
inwardly [ˈɪnwədlɪ] *adv* innerlich
inwards [ˈɪnwədz] *adv* nach innen
iodine [ˈaɪəudiːn] *n* Jod *nt*
IOU *n abbr* (= *I owe you*) Schuldschein *m*
iPad® [ˈaɪpæd] *n* iPad® *nt*, I-Pad *nt*
iPhone® [ˈaɪfəun] *n* iPhone® *nt*, I-Phone *nt*
iPlayer® [ˈaɪpleɪəʳ] *n* *Online-Mediathek der BBC*
iPod® [ˈaɪpɔd] *n* iPod® *m*

IQ *n abbr* (= *intelligence quotient*) IQ *m*
Iran [ɪˈrɑːn] *n* (der) Iran
Iraq [ɪˈrɑːk] *n* (der) Irak
Ireland [ˈaɪələnd] *n* Irland *nt*
iris [ˈaɪrɪs] (*pl* **irises**) *n* (*Anat*) Iris *f*; (*Bot*) Schwertlilie *f*
Irish [ˈaɪrɪʃ] *adj* irisch ▶ *npl*: **the ~** die Iren *pl*, die Irländer *pl*
Irishman [ˈaɪrɪʃmən] *n* (*irreg*) Ire *m*
Irish Sea *n*: **the ~** die Irische See
Irishwoman [ˈaɪrɪʃwumən] *n* (*irreg*) Irin *f*
iron [ˈaɪən] *n* Eisen *nt*; (*for clothes*) Bügeleisen *nt* ▶ *cpd* Eisen- ▶ *vt* bügeln
ironic [aɪˈrɔnɪk], **ironical** [aɪˈrɔnɪkl] *adj* ironisch
ironing board *n* Bügelbrett *nt*
irony [ˈaɪrənɪ] *n* Ironie *f*
irrational [ɪˈræʃənl] *adj* irrational
irregular [ɪˈrɛgjuləʳ] *adj* unregelmäßig; (*surface*) uneben
irrelevant [ɪˈrɛləvənt] *adj* unwesentlich, irrelevant
irreplaceable [ɪrɪˈpleɪsəbl] *adj* unersetzlich
irresistible [ɪrɪˈzɪstɪbl] *adj* unwiderstehlich
irrespective [ɪrɪˈspɛktɪv]: **~ of** *prep* ungeachtet +*gen*
irresponsible [ɪrɪˈspɔnsɪbl] *adj* verantwortungslos
irretrievable [ɪrɪˈtriːvəbl] *adj* (*object*) nicht mehr wiederzubekommen; (*loss*) unersetzlich
irritable [ˈɪrɪtəbl] *adj* reizbar
irritate [ˈɪrɪteɪt] *vt* ärgern; (*Med*) reizen
irritation [ɪrɪˈteɪʃən] *n* Ärger *m*; (*Med*) Reizung *f*
IRS (*US*) *n abbr* (= *Internal Revenue Service*) *Steuereinzugsbehörde*
is [ɪz] *vb see* **be**
Islam [ˈɪzlɑːm] *n* der Islam
Islamic [ɪzˈlæmɪk] *adj* islamisch
island [ˈaɪlənd] *n* Insel *f*
isle [aɪl] *n* Insel *f*; (*in names*): **the I~ of Man** die Insel Man; **the I~ of Wight** die Insel Wight; **the British Isles** die Britischen Inseln
isn't [ˈɪznt] = **is not**
isolate [ˈaɪsəleɪt] *vt* isolieren
isolated [ˈaɪsəleɪtɪd] *adj* isoliert; (*place*) abgelegen; **~ incident** Einzelfall *m*
isolation [aɪsəˈleɪʃən] *n* Isolierung *f*
Israel [ˈɪzreɪl] *n* Israel *nt*
Israeli [ɪzˈreɪlɪ] *adj* israelisch ▶ *n* Israeli *mf*
issue [ˈɪʃuː] *n* Frage *f*; (*subject*) Thema *nt*; (*problem*) Problem *nt*; (*of book, stamps etc*) Ausgabe *f* ▶ *vt* ausgeben; (*statement*) herausgeben; (*documents*) ausstellen; **the point at ~** der Punkt, um den es geht
IT *n abbr* (= *information technology*) IT *f*

 **KEYWORD**

it [ɪt] *pron* **1** (*specific*: *subject*) er/sie/es; (: *direct object*) ihn/sie/es; (: *indirect object*) ihm/ihr/ihm; **about it** darüber; **from it** davon; **in it** darin; **of it** davon
2 (*impersonal*) es; **it's raining** es regnet; **it's Friday tomorrow** morgen ist Freitag; **who is it? — it's me** wer ist da? — ich bins

Italian [ɪˈtæljən] *adj* italienisch ▶ *n* Italiener(in) *m(f)*; (*Ling*) Italienisch *nt*
italics [ɪˈtælɪks] *npl* Kursivschrift *f*
Italy [ˈɪtəlɪ] *n* Italien *nt*
itch [ɪtʃ] *n* Juckreiz *m* ▶ *vi* jucken; **I am itching all over** mich juckt es überall; **to ~ to do sth** darauf brennen, etw zu tun
itchy [ˈɪtʃɪ] *adj* juckend
it'd [ˈɪtd] = **it would**; **it had**
item [ˈaɪtəm] *n* Punkt *m*; (*of collection*) Stück *nt*; (*also*: **news ~**) Meldung *f*; (: *newspaper*) Zeitungsnotiz *f*; **items of clothing** Kleidungsstücke *pl*
itinerary [aɪˈtɪnərərɪ] *n* Reiseroute *f*
it'll [ˈɪtl] = **it will**; **it shall**
its [ɪts] *adj* sein(e), ihr(e); *see also* **my**
it's [ɪts] = **it is**; **it has**
itself [ɪtˈsɛlf] *pron* sich; (*emphatic*) selbst
I've [aɪv] = **I have**
ivory [ˈaɪvərɪ] *n* Elfenbein *nt*
ivy [ˈaɪvɪ] *n* Efeu *m*

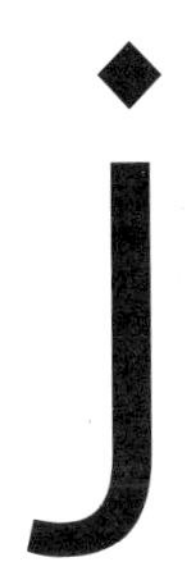

ab [dʒæb] *vt* (*with finger, needle*) stechen ▶ *n* (*inf*) Spritze *f*; **to ~ sth into sth** etw in etw *acc* stoßen/ stechen

ack [dʒæk] *n* (*Aut*) Wagenheber *m*; (*Cards*) Bube *m*
▶ **jack in** (*inf*) *vt* aufgeben

acket [ˈdʒækɪt] *n* Jackett *nt*; (*of book*) Schutzumschlag *m*; **potatoes in their jackets, ~ potatoes** in der Schale gebackene Kartoffeln *pl*

ack-knife [ˈdʒæknaɪf] *n* Klappmesser *nt* ▶ *vi*: **the lorry jack-knifed** der Anhänger (des Lastwagens) hat sich quer gestellt

ackpot [ˈdʒækpɔt] *n* Hauptgewinn *m*

acuzzi® [dʒəˈkuːzɪ] *n* Whirlpool *m*

ail [dʒeɪl] *n* Gefängnis *nt* ▶ *vt* einsperren

am [dʒæm] *n* Marmelade *f*, Konfitüre *f*; (*also*: **traffic ~**) Stau *m* ▶ *vt* blockieren; (*mechanism, drawer etc*) verklemmen; (*Radio*) stören; **the telephone lines are jammed** die Leitungen sind belegt

amaica [dʒəˈmeɪkə] *n* Jamaika *nt*

am-packed *adj*: **~ (with)** vollgestopft (mit)

an. *abbr* (= *January*) Jan.

anitor [ˈdʒænɪtəʳ] *n* Hausmeister(in) *m(f)*

anuary [ˈdʒænjuərɪ] *n* Januar *m*; *see also* **July**

apan [dʒəˈpæn] *n* Japan *nt*

apanese [dʒæpəˈniːz] *adj* japanisch ▶ *n inv* Japaner(in) *m(f)*; (*Ling*) Japanisch *nt*

ar [dʒɑːʳ] *n* (*glass*) Glas *nt*

jaundice [ˈdʒɔːndɪs] *n* Gelbsucht *f*

javelin [ˈdʒævlɪn] *n* Speer *m*

jaw [dʒɔː] *n* Kiefer *m*

jazz [dʒæz] *n* Jazz *m*

jealous [ˈdʒɛləs] *adj* eifersüchtig; (*envious*) neidisch

jealousy [ˈdʒɛləsɪ] *n* Eifersucht *f*

jeans [dʒiːnz] *npl* Jeans *pl*

Jeep® [dʒiːp] *n* Jeep® *m*

jeggings [ˈdʒɛgɪŋz] *npl* Jeggings *pl*

jelly [ˈdʒɛlɪ] *n* Götterspeise *f*; (*jam*) Gelee *m or nt*

jelly baby (*Brit*) *n* Gummibärchen *nt*

jellyfish [ˈdʒɛlɪfɪʃ] *n* Qualle *f*

jeopardize [ˈdʒɛpədaɪz] *vt* gefährden

jerk [dʒəːk] *n* Ruck *m*; (*pej: idiot*) Trottel *m* ▶ *vt* reißen ▶ *vi* (*vehicle*) ruckeln

Jerusalem [dʒəˈruːsləm] *n* Jerusalem *nt*

jet [dʒɛt] *n* Strahl *m*; (*Aviat*) Düsenflugzeug *nt*

jet lag *n* Jetlag *nt*

Jew [dʒuː] *n* Jude *m*, Jüdin *f*

jewel [ˈdʒuːəl] *n* Edelstein *m*, Juwel *nt* (*also fig*)

jeweller, (*US*) **jeweler** [ˈdʒuːələʳ] *n* Juwelier *m*

jewellery, (*US*) **jewelry** [ˈdʒuːəlrɪ] *n* Schmuck *m*

Jewish [ˈdʒuːɪʃ] *adj* jüdisch

jigsaw [ˈdʒɪgsɔː] *n* (*also*: **~ puzzle**) Puzzle(spiel) *nt*

jilbab [ˈdʒɪlbæb] *n* Dschilbab *m or nt*

jilt [dʒɪlt] *vt* sitzen lassen

jingle [ˈdʒɪŋgl] *n* (*tune*) Jingle *m*

jitters [ˈdʒɪtəz] (*inf*) *npl*: **to get the ~** das große Zittern bekommen

jittery [ˈdʒɪtərɪ] (*inf*) *adj* nervös

job [dʒɔb] *n* Arbeit *f*; (*post, employment*) Stelle *f*, Job *m*; **it's not my ~** es ist nicht meine Aufgabe; **it's a good ~ that …** nur gut, dass …

job centre (*Brit*) *n* Arbeitsamt *nt*

job-hunting *n*: **to go ~** auf Arbeitssuche gehen

jobless [ˈdʒɔblɪs] *adj* arbeitslos

jobseeker's allowance *n* Arbeitslosengeld *nt*

job sharing *n* Arbeitsplatzteilung *f*

jockey [ˈdʒɔkɪ] *n* Jockey *m*

jog [dʒɔg] *vt* (an)stoßen ▶ *vi* joggen

jogging [ˈdʒɔgɪŋ] *n* Jogging *nt*

john [dʒɔn] (*US inf*) *n* (*toilet*) Klo *nt*

join [dʒɔɪn] *vt* (*club, party*) beitreten +*dat*; (*things, places*) verbinden; (*group of people*) sich anschließen +*dat* ▸ *vi* (*roads*) sich treffen; (*rivers*) zusammenfließen ▸ *n* Verbindungsstelle *f*
▸ **join in** *vi* mitmachen
joint [dʒɔɪnt] *n* (*in pipe etc*) Verbindungsstelle *f*; (*Anat*) Gelenk *nt*; (Brit *Culin*) Braten *m*; (*inf: of cannabis*) Joint *m* ▸ *adj* gemeinsam
joint account *n* gemeinsames Konto *nt*
jointly [ˈdʒɔɪntlɪ] *adv* gemeinsam
joke [dʒəuk] *n* Witz *m*; (*also*: **practical ~**) Streich *m* ▸ *vi* Witze machen; **to play a ~ on sb** jdm einen Streich spielen
jolly [ˈdʒɔlɪ] *adj* fröhlich; (*enjoyable*) lustig
Jordan [ˈdʒɔːdən] *n* Jordanien *nt*; (*river*) Jordan *m*
jot [dʒɔt] *n*: **not one ~** kein bisschen
▸ **jot down** *vt* notieren
jotter [ˈdʒɔtəʳ] (Brit) *n* Notizbuch *nt*
journal [ˈdʒəːnl] *n* Zeitschrift *f*; (*diary*) Tagebuch *nt*
journalism [ˈdʒəːnəlɪzəm] *n* Journalismus *m*
journalist [ˈdʒəːnəlɪst] *n* Journalist(in) *m(f)*
journey [ˈdʒəːnɪ] *n* Reise *f*; **a 5-hour ~** eine Fahrt von 5 Stunden
joy [dʒɔɪ] *n* Freude *f*
joystick [ˈdʒɔɪstɪk] *n* (*Aviat*) Steuerknüppel *m*; (*Comput*) Joystick *m*
judge [dʒʌdʒ] *n* Richter(in) *m(f)*; (*in competition*) Preisrichter(in) *m(f)* ▸ *vt* (*Law: person*) die Verhandlung führen über +*acc* ▸ *vi*: **judging by** *or* **to ~ by his expression** seinem Gesichtsausdruck nach zu urteilen; **as far as I can ~** soweit ich es beurteilen kann
judgment, judgement [ˈdʒʌdʒmənt] *n* Urteil *nt*; (*view, opinion*) Meinung *f*
judo [ˈdʒuːdəu] *n* Judo *nt*
jug [dʒʌg] *n* Krug *m*
juggle [ˈdʒʌgl] *vi* jonglieren
juice [dʒuːs] *n* Saft *m*
juicy [ˈdʒuːsɪ] *adj* saftig
July [dʒuːˈlaɪ] *n* Juli *m*; **on the eleventh of ~** am elften Juli; **in the month of ~** im (Monat) Juli; **at the beginning/end of ~** Anfang/Ende Juli; **in the middle of ~** Mitte Juli; **in ~ of next year** im Juli nächsten Jahres
jumble [ˈdʒʌmbl] *n* Durcheinander *nt* ▸ *vt* (*also*: **~ up**) durcheinanderbringen
jumbo, jumbo jet *n* Jumbo(jet) *m*
jumbo-size [ˈdʒʌmbəusaɪz] *adj* (*packet etc*) Riesen-
jump [dʒʌmp] *vi* springen; (*with fear, surprise*) zusammenzucken ▸ *vt* springen über +*acc* ▸ *n* Sprung *m*; **to ~ the queue** (Brit) sich vordrängeln
jumper [ˈdʒʌmpəʳ] *n* (Brit) Pullover *m*; (*US: dress*) Trägerkleid *nt*; (*Sport*) Springer(in) *m(f)*
jumper cables (*US*) *npl* = **jump leads**
jump leads (Brit) *npl* Starthilfekabel *nt*
junction [ˈdʒʌŋkʃən] (Brit) *n* Kreuzung *f*; (*Rail*) Gleisanschluss *m*
June [dʒuːn] *n* Juni *m*; *see also* **July**
jungle [ˈdʒʌŋgl] *n* Dschungel *m* (*also fig*)
junior [ˈdʒuːnɪəʳ] *adj* jünger; (*subordinate*) untergeordnet; **he's ~ to me (by 2 years), he's my ~ (by 2 years)** (*younger*) er ist (2 Jahre) jünger als ich
junior high school (*US*) *n* ≈ Mittelschule *f*
junior school (Brit) *n* ≈ Grundschule
junk [dʒʌŋk] *n* (*rubbish*) Gerümpel *nt*
junk food *n* ungesundes Essen *nt*
junkie [ˈdʒʌŋkɪ] (*inf*) *n* Fixer(in) *m(f)*
junk mail *n* (Post)wurfsendungen *pl*
junk shop *n* Trödelladen *m*
jury [ˈdʒuərɪ] *n*: **the ~** die Schöffen *pl*; (*for capital crimes*) die Geschworenen *pl*; (*for competition*) die Jury
just [dʒʌst] *adj* gerecht ▸ *adv* (*exactly*) genau; (*only*) nur; **he's ~ done it/left** er hat es gerade getan/ist gerade gegangen; **~ as I expected** genau wie ich erwartet habe; **~ right** genau richtig; **she's ~ as clever as you** sie ist genauso klug wie du; **it's ~ as well (that) …** nur gut, dass …; **~ as he was leaving** gerade als er gehen wollte; **~ before** gerade noch; **~ enough** gerade genug; **~ here** genau hier, genau an dieser Stelle; **he ~ missed** er hat genau danebengetroffen; **it's ~ me** ich bins nur; **~ a minute!, ~ one moment!** einen Moment, bitte!
justice [ˈdʒʌstɪs] *n* (*fairness*) Gerechtigkeit *f*
justifiable [dʒʌstɪˈfaɪəbl] *adj* berechtig

ustifiably [dʒʌstɪˈfaɪəblɪ] *adv* zu Recht
ustify [ˈdʒʌstɪfaɪ] *vt* rechtfertigen
ut [dʒʌt] *vi* (*also:* **~ out**) vorstehen
uvenile [ˈdʒuːvənaɪl] *adj* (*crime, offenders*) Jugend- ▸ *n* Jugendliche(r) *f*(*m*)

K [keɪ] *abbr* (= *one thousand*) K; (*Comput:* = *kilobyte*) KB
kangaroo [kæŋgəˈruː] *n* Känguru *nt*
karaoke [kɑːrəˈəukɪ] *n* Karaoke *nt*
karate [kəˈrɑːtɪ] *n* Karate *nt*
kart [kəːt] *n* Gokart *m*
kayak [ˈkaɪæk] *n* Kajak *m or nt*
Kazakhstan [kæzækˈstɑːn] *n* Kasachstan *nt*
kebab [kəˈbæb] *n* Kebab *m*
keel [kiːl] *n* Kiel *m*
▸ **keel over** *vi* kentern; (*person*) umkippen
keen [kiːn] *adj* begeistert, eifrig; (*interest*) groß; (*eye, intelligence, competition, edge*) scharf; **to be ~ to do** *or* **on doing sth** scharf darauf sein, etw zu tun (*inf*); **to be ~ on sth** an etw *dat* sehr interessiert sein; **to be ~ on sb** von jdm sehr angetan sein
keep [kiːp] (*pt, pp* **kept**) *vt* behalten; (*preserve, store*) aufbewahren; (*house, shop, accounts, diary*) führen; (*chickens, bees, promise*) halten; (*family etc*) versorgen, unterhalten ▸ *vi* (*remain*) bleiben; (*food*) sich halten ▸ *n* (*food etc*) Unterhalt *m*; **to ~ doing sth** etw immer wieder tun; **to ~ sb happy** jdn zufriedenstellen; **to ~ a room tidy** ein Zimmer in Ordnung halten; **to ~ sb waiting** jdn warten lassen; **to ~ sth to o.s.** etw für sich behalten; **to ~ sth (back) from sb** etw vor jdm geheim halten; **to ~ sb from doing sth** jdn davon abhalten, etw zu tun
▸ **keep back** *vt* zurückhalten; (*money*) einbehalten ▸ *vi* zurückbleiben

▸**keep off** *vt* fernhalten; **"~ off the grass"** „Betreten des Rasens verboten"
▸**keep on** *vi*: **to ~ on doing sth** (*continue*) etw weiter tun
▸**keep out** *vt* fernhalten; **"~ out"** „Zutritt verboten"
▸**keep up** *vt* (*payments*) weiterbezahlen; (*standards etc*) aufrechterhalten ▸*vi*: **to ~ up (with)** mithalten können (mit)

keeper [ˈkiːpəʳ] *n* Wärter(in) *m(f)*
keep fit *n* Fitnesstraining *nt*
kennel [ˈkɛnl] *n* Hundehütte *f*
kennels [ˈkɛnlz] *n* Hundeheim *nt*
Kenya [ˈkɛnjə] *n* Kenia *nt*
kept [kɛpt] *pt, pp of* **keep**
kerb [kəːb] (Brit) *n* Bordstein *m*
kerbside *n* Straßenrand *m*, Bordsteinkante *f*
kerosene [ˈkɛrəsiːn] *n* Kerosin *nt*
ketchup [ˈkɛtʃəp] *n* Ket(s)chup *m or nt*
kettle [ˈkɛtl] *n* Kessel *m*
kettling [ˈkɛtəlɪŋ] *n* (*by police*) Einkesselung *f*
key [kiː] *n* Schlüssel *m*; (*Mus*) Tonart *f*; (*of piano, computer, typewriter*) Taste *f* ▸*cpd* (*issue etc*) Schlüssel- ▸*vt* (*also*: **~ in**) eingeben
keyboard [ˈkiːbɔːd] *n* Tastatur *f*
keyhole [ˈkiːhəul] *n* Schlüsselloch *nt*
keypad [ˈkiːpæd] *n* Tastenfeld *nt*
key ring *n* Schlüsselring *m*
kick [kɪk] *vt* treten ▸*vi* (*horse*) ausschlagen ▸*n* Tritt *m*; (*to ball*) Schuss *m*; (*thrill*): **he does it for kicks** er macht es zum Spaß
▸**kick out** (*inf*) *vt* rausschmeißen (*of* aus)

kick-off *n* (*Sport*) Anstoß *m*
kid [kɪd] (*inf*) *n* (*child*) Kind *nt* ▸*vi* Witze machen
kidnap [ˈkɪdnæp] *vt* entführen
kidnapper [ˈkɪdnæpəʳ] *n* Entführer(in) *m(f)*
kidnapping [ˈkɪdnæpɪŋ] *n* Entführung *f*
kidney [ˈkɪdnɪ] *n* Niere *f*
kidney machine *n* (*Med*) künstliche Niere *f*
kill [kɪl] *vt* töten; (*murder*) umbringen; (*plant*) eingehen lassen
killer [ˈkɪləʳ] *n* Mörder(in) *m(f)*
kilo [ˈkiːləu] *n* Kilo *nt*
kilobyte [ˈkɪːləubaɪt] *n* Kilobyte *nt*
kilogram, kilogramme [ˈkɪləugræm] *n* Kilogramm *nt*
kilometre, (US) **kilometer** [ˈkɪləmiːtəʳ] *n* Kilometer *m*
kilowatt [ˈkɪləuwɔt] *n* Kilowatt *nt*
kilt [kɪlt] *n* Schottenrock *m*
kind [kaɪnd] *adj* freundlich ▸*n* Art *f*; (*sort*) Sorte *f*
kindergarten [ˈkɪndəgɑːtn] *n* Kindergarten *m*
Kindle® [ˈkɪndl] *n* Kindle® *m*
kindly [ˈkaɪndlɪ] *adj, adv* freundlich, nett
kindness [ˈkaɪndnɪs] *n* Freundlichkeit
king [kɪŋ] *n* (*also fig*) König *m*
kingdom [ˈkɪŋdəm] *n* Königreich *nt*
kingfisher [ˈkɪŋfɪʃəʳ] *n* Eisvogel *m*
king-size [ˈkɪŋsaɪz], **king-sized** [ˈkɪŋsaɪzd] *adj* extragroß
kipper [ˈkɪpəʳ] *n* Räucherhering *m*
kiss [kɪs] *n* Kuß *m* ▸*vt* küssen
kiss of life (Brit) *n*: **the ~** Mund-zu-Mund-Beatmung *f*
kit [kɪt] *n* Sachen *pl*; (*equipment, also Mil*) Ausrüstung *f*; (*for assembly*) Bausatz *m*
kitchen [ˈkɪtʃɪn] *n* Küche *f*
kitchen unit (Brit) *n* Küchenschrank *m*
kitchenware [ˈkɪtʃɪnwɛəʳ] *n* Küchengeräte *pl*
kite [kaɪt] *n* Drachen *m*
kitten [ˈkɪtn] *n* Kätzchen *nt*
kiwi [ˈkiːwiː] *n* Kiwi(frucht) *f*
km *abbr* (= *kilometre*) km
knack [næk] *n*: **to have the ~ of doing sth** es heraushaben, wie man etw macht; **there's a ~ to doing this** da ist ein Trick *or* Kniff dabei
knackered [ˈnækəd] (Brit *inf*) *adj* kaputt
knee [niː] *n* Knie *nt*
kneecap [ˈniːkæp] *n* Kniescheibe *f*
kneejerk reaction [ˈniːdʒəːk-] *n* (*fig*) instinktive Reaktion *f*
kneel [niːl] (*pt, pp* **knelt**) *vi* knien; (*also*: **~ down**) niederknien
knelt [nɛlt] *pt, pp of* **kneel**
knew [njuː] *pt of* **know**
knickers [ˈnɪkəz] (Brit) *npl* Schlüpfer *m*
knife [naɪf] (*pl* **knives**) *n* Messer *nt*
knight [naɪt] *n* (Brit) Ritter *m*; (*Chess*) Springer *m*, Pferd *nt*
knit [nɪt] *vt* stricken ▸*vi* stricken
knitting [ˈnɪtɪŋ] *n* Stricken *nt*; (*garment being made*) Strickzeug *nt*
knitting needle *n* Stricknadel *f*
knitwear [ˈnɪtwɛəʳ] *n* Strickwaren *pl*

knob [nɔb] *n* (*of stick*) Knauf *m*; (*on radio, TV etc*) Knopf *m*
knock [nɔk] *vt* schlagen; (*bump into*) stoßen gegen *+acc* ▶ *n* Schlag *m*; (*on door*) Klopfen *nt*; **he knocked at the door** er klopfte an, er klopfte an die Tür
▶ **knock down** *vt* anfahren; (*building etc*) abreißen
▶ **knock out** *vt* bewusstlos schlagen; (*Boxing*) k. o. schlagen
▶ **knock over** *vt* umstoßen; (*with car*) anfahren
knocker [ˈnɔkə^r] *n* Türklopfer *m*
knockout [ˈnɔkaut] *n* (*Boxing*) K.-o.-Schlag *m*
knot [nɔt] *n* Knoten *m*
know [nəu] (*pt* **knew**, *pp* **known**) *vt* kennen; (*facts*) wissen; (*language*) können ▶ *vi*: **to ~ about** *or* **of sth/sb** von etw/jdm gehört haben; **to get to ~ sth** etw erfahren; (*place*) etw kennenlernen
▶ **know about** *vt* Bescheid wissen über *+acc*; (*subject*) sich auskennen in *+dat*; (*cars, horses etc*) sich auskennen mit
know-all [ˈnəuɔːl] (Brit *pej*) *n* Alleswisser *m*
know-how [ˈnəuhau] *n* Know-how *nt*, Sachkenntnis *f*
knowing [ˈnəuɪŋ] *adj* wissend
knowledge [ˈnɔlɪdʒ] *n* Wissen *nt*; (*learning, things learnt*) Kenntnisse *pl*; **not to my ~** nicht, dass ich wüsste
known [nəun] *pp of* **know**
knuckle [ˈnʌkl] *n* (Finger)knöchel *m*
▶ **knuckle down** (*inf*) *vi*: **to ~ down to work** sich an die Arbeit machen
Koran [kɔˈrɑːn] *n*: **the ~** der Koran
Korea [kəˈrɪə] *n* Korea *nt*
Kosovo [ˈkɔsɔvəu] *n* der Kosovo
Kremlin [ˈkrɛmlɪn] *n*: **the ~** der Kreml
Kurd [kəːd] *n* Kurde *m*, Kurdin *f*
Kuwait [kuˈweɪt] *n* Kuwait *nt*

l

L [ɛl] *abbr* (Brit *Aut*: = *learner*) *am Auto angebrachtes Kennzeichen für Fahrschüler*
LA (*US*) *n abbr* = **Los Angeles**
lab [læb] *n abbr* = **laboratory**
label [ˈleɪbl] *n* Etikett *nt*; (*of record*) Label *nt* ▶ *vt* etikettieren; (*fig: person*) abstempeln
labor *etc* [ˈleɪbə^r] (*US*) *n* = **labour** *etc*
laboratory [ləˈbɔrətərɪ] *n* Labor *nt*
Labor Day *n siehe Info-Artikel*

Labor Day

Labor Day ist in den USA und Kanada der Name für den Tag der Arbeit. Er wird dort als gesetzlicher Feiertag am ersten Montag im September begangen.

laborious [ləˈbɔːrɪəs] *adj* mühsam
labor union (*US*) *n* Gewerkschaft *f*
labour, (*US*) **labor** [ˈleɪbə^r] *n* Arbeit *f*; (*Med*): **to be in ~** in den Wehen liegen; **L~, the L~ Party** (Brit) die Labour Party
labourer [ˈleɪbərə^r] *n* Arbeiter(in) *m(f)*
lace [leɪs] *n* (*fabric*) Spitze *f*; (*of shoe etc*) Schnürsenkel *m* ▶ *vt* (*also*: **~ up**) (zu)schnüren
lace-up [ˈleɪsʌp] *adj* (*shoes etc*) Schnür-
lack [læk] *n* Mangel *m* ▶ *vt*, *vi*: **sb lacks sth, sb is lacking in sth** jdm fehlt es an etw *dat*; **through** *or* **for ~ of** aus Mangel an *+dat*; **to be lacking** fehlen
lacquer [ˈlækə^r] *n* Lack *m*; (*also*: **hair ~**) Haarspray *nt*
lad [læd] *n* Junge *m*

ladder [ˈlædəʳ] *n (also fig)* Leiter *f*; (*BRIT: in tights*) Laufmasche *f*
laden [ˈleɪdn] *adj*: **~ (with)** beladen (mit)
lad mag *n* Männerzeitschrift *f*
lady [ˈleɪdɪ] *n (dignified, graceful etc)* Dame *f*; (*BRIT: title*) Lady *f*; **the ladies' (room)** die Damentoilette
ladybird [ˈleɪdɪbəːd], (*US*) **ladybug** [ˈleɪdɪbʌg] *n* Marienkäfer *m*
lag [læg] *vi* (*also:* **~ behind**) zurückbleiben ▸ *vt (pipes etc)* isolieren
lager [ˈlɑːgəʳ] *n* helles Bier *nt*
lager lout (*BRIT inf*) *n* betrunkener Rowdy *m*
lagging [ˈlægɪŋ] *n* Isoliermaterial *nt*
laid [leɪd] *pt, pp of* **lay**
laid-back [leɪdˈbæk] (*inf*) *adj* locker
lain [leɪn] *pp of* **lie²**
lake [leɪk] *n* See *m*
Lake District *n*: **the ~** der Lake Distrikt, *Seengebiet im NW Englands*
lamb [læm] *n* Lamm *nt*; (*meat*) Lammfleisch *nt*
lamb chop *n* Lammkotelett *nt*
lame [leɪm] *adj* lahm; (*argument, answer*) schwach
lament [ləˈmɛnt] *n* Klage *f* ▸ *vt* beklagen
laminated [ˈlæmɪneɪtɪd] *adj* laminiert
lamp [læmp] *n* Lampe *f*
lamppost [ˈlæmppəust] (*BRIT*) *n* Laternenpfahl *m*
lampshade [ˈlæmpʃeɪd] *n* Lampenschirm *m*
land [lænd] *n* Land *nt* ▸ *vi (Aviat, fig)* landen; (*from ship*) an Land gehen ▸ *vt* (*passengers*) absetzen; (*goods*) an Land bringen
landing [ˈlændɪŋ] *n (on stairs)* Treppenabsatz *m*; (*Aviat*) Landung *f*
landing stage *n* Landesteg *m*
landing strip *n* Landebahn *f*
landlady *n* Vermieterin *f*; (*of pub*) Wirtin *f*
landline *n* Festnetz *nt*
landlord [ˈlændlɔːd] *n* Vermieter *m*; (*of pub*) Wirt *m*
landmark [ˈlændmɑːk] *n (famous building)* Wahrzeichen *nt*; (*fig*) Meilenstein *m*
landowner [ˈlændəunəʳ] *n* Grundbesitzer(in) *m(f)*
landscape [ˈlændskeɪp] *n* Landschaft *f*
landslide [ˈlændslaɪd] *n* Erdrutsch *m*
lane [leɪn] *n (in country)* Weg *m*; (*in town*) Gasse *f*; (*of carriageway*) Spur *f*; (*of race course, swimming pool*) Bahn *f*
language [ˈlæŋgwɪdʒ] *n* Sprache *f*
lantern [ˈlæntən] *n* Laterne *f*
lap [læp] *n* Schoß *m*; (*in race*) Runde *f*
lapse [læps] *n (bad behaviour)* Fehltritt *m*; (*of memory etc*) Schwäche *f* ▸ *vi* ablaufen
laptop [ˈlæptɔp] (*Comput*) *n* Laptop *m*
large [lɑːdʒ] *adj* groß; **by and ~** im Großen und Ganzen
largely [ˈlɑːdʒlɪ] *adv (mostly)* zum größten Teil
large-scale [ˈlɑːdʒˈskeɪl] *adj* im großen Rahmen
lark [lɑːk] *n (bird)* Lerche *f*
laryngitis [lærɪnˈdʒaɪtɪs] *n* Kehlkopfentzündung *f*
larynx [ˈlærɪŋks] *n* Kehlkopf *m*
laser [ˈleɪzəʳ] *n* Laser *m*
laser printer *n* Laserdrucker *m*
lash [læʃ] *vt* peitschen
▸ **lash out** *vi* um sich schlagen
lass [læs] (*BRIT*) *n* Mädchen *nt*
last [lɑːst] *adj* letzte(r, s) ▸ *adv (most recently)* zuletzt, das letzte Mal; (*finally*) als Letztes ▸ *vi (continue)* dauern; (*: in good condition*) sich halten; (*money, commodity*) reichen; **~ night** gestern Abend; **~ but one** vorletzte(r, s); **at ~** endlich
lasting [ˈlɑːstɪŋ] *adj* dauerhaft
lastly [ˈlɑːstlɪ] *adv (finally)* schließlich
last-minute [ˈlɑːstmɪnɪt] *adj* in letzter Minute
late [leɪt] *adj* spät; (*not on time*) verspätet ▸ *adv* spät; (*behind time*) zu spät; **the ~ Mr X** (*deceased*) der verstorbene Herr X; **to be (10 minutes) ~** (10 Minuten) zu spät kommen
lately [ˈleɪtlɪ] *adv* in letzter Zeit
late opening *n* verlängerte Öffnungszeiten *pl*
later [ˈleɪtəʳ] *adj, adv* später; **~ on** nachher
latest [ˈleɪtɪst] *adj* neueste(r, s) ▸ *n*: **at the ~** spätestens
Latin [ˈlætɪn] *n* Latein *nt* ▸ *adj* lateinisch
Latin America *n* Lateinamerika *nt*
Latin American *adj* lateinamerikanisch ▸ *n* Lateinamerikaner(in) *m(f)*

atter [ˈlætəʳ] *adj* (*of two*) letztere(r, s); (*recent*) letzte(r, s)
atvia [ˈlætvɪə] *n* Lettland *nt*
atvian [ˈlætvɪən] *adj* lettisch ▸ *n* Lette *m*, Lettin *f*; (*Ling*) Lettisch *nt*
augh [lɑːf] *n* Lachen *nt* ▸ *vi* lachen; **(to do sth) for a ~** (etw) aus Spaß (tun)
▸ **laugh at** *vt fus* lachen über *+acc*
aughter [ˈlɑːftəʳ] *n* Gelächter *nt*
aunch [lɔːntʃ] *n* (*of rocket, missile*) Abschuss *m*; (*Comm: of product*) Einführung *f*; (*: with publicity*) Lancierung *f* ▸ *vt* (*ship*) vom Stapel lassen; (*rocket, missile*) abschießen; (*Comm*) auf den Markt bringen; (*: with publicity*) lancieren
aunder [ˈlɔːndəʳ] *vt* waschen und bügeln; (*pej: money*) waschen
aunderette® [lɔːnˈdrɛt] (Brit) *n* Waschsalon *m*
aundry [ˈlɔːndrɪ] *n* Wäsche *f*; (*business*) Wäscherei *f*
avatory [ˈlævətərɪ] *n* Toilette *f*
avender [ˈlævəndəʳ] *n* Lavendel *m*
avish [ˈlævɪʃ] *adj* großzügig; (*meal*) üppig; (*wasteful*) verschwenderisch
aw [lɔː] *n* Recht *nt*; (*a rule: also of nature, science*) Gesetz *nt*; (*Scol*) Jura *no art*; **against the ~** rechtswidrig
aw-abiding [ˈlɔːəbaɪdɪŋ] *adj* gesetzestreu
law court *n* Gerichtshof *m*
lawful [ˈlɔːful] *adj* rechtmäßig
lawn [lɔːn] *n* Rasen *m*
lawn mower *n* Rasenmäher *m*
lawsuit [ˈlɔːsuːt] *n* Prozess *m*
lawyer [ˈlɔːjəʳ] *n* (Rechts)anwalt *m*, (Rechts)anwältin *f*
laxative [ˈlæksətɪv] *n* Abführmittel *nt*
lay [leɪ] (*pt, pp* **laid**) *pt of* **lie²** ▸ *adj* (*Rel: preacher etc*) Laien- ▸ *vt* legen; (*table*) decken; **to get laid** (*!*) bumsen (*!*)
▸ **lay down** *vt* hinlegen
▸ **lay off** *vt* (*workers*) entlassen
▸ **lay on** *vt* (*meal*) auftischen; (*entertainment etc*) sorgen für
layabout [ˈleɪəbaut] (*inf, pej*) *n* Faulenzer *m*
lay-by [ˈleɪbaɪ] (Brit) *n* Parkbucht *f*
layer [ˈleɪəʳ] *n* Schicht *f*
layman [ˈleɪmən] *n* (*irreg*) Laie *m*
layout [ˈleɪaut] *n* (*of building*) Aufteilung *f*; (*Typ*) Layout *nt*
laze [leɪz] *vi* (*also:* **~ about**) (herum) faulenzen
laziness [ˈleɪzɪnɪs] *n* Faulheit *f*
lazy [ˈleɪzɪ] *adj* faul
lb *abbr* (*= pound (weight)*) *britisches Pfund (0,45 kg)*, ≈ Pfd.
lead¹ [liːd] (*pt, pp* **led**) *n* (*Sport, fig*) Führung *f*; (*clue*) Spur *f*; (*in play, film*) Hauptrolle *f*; (*for dog*) Leine *f*; (*Elec*) Kabel *nt* ▸ *vt* (*guide*) führen; (*organization, orchestra*) leiten ▸ *vi* führen; **to be in the ~** (*Sport, fig*) in Führung liegen; **to ~ the way** vorangehen; **to ~ sb astray** jdn vom rechten Weg abführen
▸ **lead away** *vt* wegführen
▸ **lead back** *vt* zurückführen
▸ **lead on** *vt* (*tease*) aufziehen
▸ **lead to** *vt fus* führen zu
▸ **lead up to** *vt fus* (*events*) vorangehen *+dat*
lead² [lɛd] *n* Blei *nt*
leaded [ˈlɛdɪd] *adj* (*petrol*) verbleit
leader [ˈliːdəʳ] *n* Führer(in) *m(f)*; (*Sport*) Erste(r) *f(m)*
leadership [ˈliːdəʃɪp] *n* Führung *f*
lead-free [ˈlɛdfriː] (*old*) *adj* bleifrei
leading [ˈliːdɪŋ] *adj* führend
leaf [liːf] (*pl* **leaves**) *n* Blatt *nt*
leaflet [ˈliːflɪt] *n* Informationsblatt *nt*
leafleting *n* (*for company*) Verteilen *nt* von Flyern; (*for political party*) Flugblattaktion *f*
league [liːg] *n* (*of countries*) Bund *m*; (*Football*) Liga *f*
leak [liːk] *n* Leck *nt*; (*in roof, pipe etc*) undichte Stelle *f* ▸ *vi* (*shoes, roof, pipe*) undicht sein; (*liquid*) auslaufen
leaky [ˈliːkɪ] *adj* (*roof, container*) undicht
lean [liːn] (*pt, pp* **leaned** *or* **leant**) *adj* (*person*) schlank; (*meat, time*) mager ▸ *vt*: **to ~ sth on sth** etw an etw *acc* lehnen ▸ *vi* (*slope*) sich neigen; **to ~ against** sich lehnen gegen; **to ~ on** sich stützen auf *+acc*; **to ~ forward/back** sich vorbeugen/zurücklehnen; **to ~ towards** tendieren zu
▸ **lean out** *vi* sich hinauslehnen
▸ **lean over** *vi* sich vorbeugen
leant [lɛnt] *pt, pp of* **lean**
leap [liːp] (*pt, pp* **leaped** *or* **leapt**) *n* Sprung *m* ▸ *vi* springen
leapt [lɛpt] *pt, pp of* **leap**
leap year *n* Schaltjahr *nt*
learn [ləːn] (*pt, pp* **learned** *or* **learnt**) *vt* lernen; (*facts*) erfahren ▸ *vi* lernen; **to ~ to do sth** etw lernen

learned [ˈlə:nɪd] *adj* gelehrt
learner [ˈlə:nəʳ] (BRIT) *n* (*also:* **~ driver**) Fahrschüler(in) *m(f)*
learnt [lə:nt] *pt, pp of* **learn**
lease [li:s] *n* Pachtvertrag *m* ▸ *vt*: **to ~ sth (to sb)** etw (an jdn) verpachten; **to ~ sth (from sb)** etw (von jdm) pachten
▸ **lease out** *vt* vermieten
least [li:st] *adv* am wenigsten ▸ *adj*: **the ~** (+ *noun*) der/die/das wenigste; (*slightest*) der/die/das geringste; **the ~ expensive car** das billigste Auto; **at ~** mindestens; (*still, rather*) wenigstens; **you could at ~ have written** du hättest wenigstens schreiben können; **not in the ~** nicht im Geringsten; **it was the ~ I could do** das war das wenigste, was ich tun konnte
leather [ˈlɛðəʳ] *n* Leder *nt*
leave [li:v] (*pt, pp* **left**) *vt* verlassen; (*leave behind*) zurücklassen; (*mark, stain*) hinterlassen; (*object: accidentally*) liegen lassen, stehen lassen; (*food*) übrig lassen ▸ *vi* (*go away*) (weg)gehen; (*bus, train*) abfahren ▸ *n* Urlaub *m*; **to ~ sth to sb** (*money etc*) jdm etw hinterlassen; **to be left** übrig sein; **to be left over** (*remain*) übrig (geblieben) sein; **to ~ for** gehen/fahren nach; **to take one's ~ of sb** sich von jdm verabschieden; **on ~** auf Urlaub
▸ **leave behind** *vt* zurücklassen; (*object: accidentally*) liegen lassen, stehen lassen
▸ **leave out** *vt* auslassen
leaver [ˈli:vəʳ] *n* (BRIT: *from EU*) *Befürworter des Austritts aus der Europäischen Union*
leaves [li:vz] *npl of* **leaf**
leaving do [ˈli:vɪŋdu:] (*inf*) *n* Abschiedsfeier *f*
Lebanon [ˈlɛbənən] *n* Libanon *m*
lecture [ˈlɛktʃəʳ] *n* Vortrag *m*; (*Univ*) Vorlesung *f*; **to give a ~ on** einen Vortrag/eine Vorlesung halten über +*acc*
lecturer [ˈlɛktʃərəʳ] (BRIT) *n* Dozent(in) *m(f)*
lecture theatre *n* Hörsaal *m*
LED *n abbr* (*Elec*: = *light-emitting diode*) LED *f*
led [lɛd] *pt, pp of* **lead²**
ledge [lɛdʒ] *n* (*of window*) Fensterbrett *nt*; (*on wall*) Leiste *f*
leek [li:k] *n* Lauch *m*
left [lɛft] *pt, pp of* **leave** ▸ *adj* (*of position*) links; (*of direction*) nach links ▸ *n* linke Seite *f* ▸ *adv* links; nach links; **on the ~, to the ~** links; **the L~** (*Pol*) die Linke
left-hand drive [ˈlɛfthænd-] *adj* mit Linkssteuerung
left-handed [lɛftˈhændɪd] *adj* linkshändig
left-hand side [ˈlɛfthænd-] *n* linke Seite *f*
left-luggage, left-luggage office (BRIT) *n* Gepäckaufbewahrung *f*
left-luggage locker *n* Gepäckschließfach *nt*
leftovers [ˈlɛftəuvəz] *npl* Reste *pl*
left wing *n* (*Pol, Sport*) linker Flügel *m*
left-wing [ˈlɛftˈwɪŋ] *adj* (*Pol*) linke(r, s)
leg [lɛg] *n* Bein *nt*; (*Culin*) Keule *f*
legacy [ˈlɛgəsɪ] *n* Erbschaft *f*; (*fig*) Erbe *nt*
legal [ˈli:gl] *adj* (*requirement*) rechtlich, gesetzlich; (*system*) Rechts-; (*allowed by law*) legal
legalize [ˈli:gəlaɪz] *vt* legalisieren
legally [ˈli:gəlɪ] *adv* rechtlich
legend [ˈlɛdʒənd] *n* Legende *f*
legible [ˈlɛdʒəbl] *adj* leserlich
legislation [lɛdʒɪsˈleɪʃən] *n* (*laws*) Gesetze *pl*
legitimate [lɪˈdʒɪtɪmət] *adj* (*legal*) rechtmäßig
legroom [ˈlɛgru:m] *n* Beinfreiheit *f*
leisure [ˈlɛʒəʳ] *n* Freizeit *f*
leisurely [ˈlɛʒəlɪ] *adj* geruhsam
lemon [ˈlɛmən] *n* Zitrone *f*
lemonade [lɛməˈneɪd] *n* Limonade *f*
lemon curd *n zähflüssiger Brotaufstrich mit Zitronengeschmack*
lemon juice *n* Zitronensaft *m*
lemon sole *n* Seezunge *f*
lend [lɛnd] (*pt, pp* **lent**) *vt*: **to ~ sth to sb** jdm etw leihen; **to ~ sb a hand (with sth)** jdm (bei etw) helfen
lending library [ˈlɛndɪŋ-] *n* Leihbücherei *f*
length [lɛŋθ] *n* Länge *f*; **2 metres in ~** 2 Meter lang; **at ~** (*at last*) schließlich
lengthen [ˈlɛŋθn] *vt* verlängern
lengthy [ˈlɛŋθɪ] *adj* lang
lenient [ˈli:nɪənt] *adj* nachsichtig

ens [lɛnz] *n* (*of camera*) Objektiv *nt*; (*of telescope*) Linse *f*
.ent [lɛnt] *n* Fastenzeit *f*
ent [lɛnt] *pt, pp of* **lend**
entil [ˈlɛntɪl] *n* Linse *f*
.eo [ˈliːəu] *n* Löwe *m*
eopard [ˈlɛpəd] *n* Leopard *m*
esbian [ˈlɛzbɪən] *adj* lesbisch ▶ *n* Lesbe *f*
ess [lɛs] *adj, pron, adv* weniger; **~ and ~** immer weniger
essen [ˈlɛsn] *vi* nachlassen, abnehmen ▶ *vt* verringern
esser [ˈlɛsəʳ] *adj* geringer; **to a ~ extent** in geringerem Maße
esson [ˈlɛsn] *n* (*class*) Stunde *f*; (*example, warning*) Lehre *f*
et [lɛt] (*pt, pp* **~**) *vt* (*allow*) lassen; (BRIT: *lease*) vermieten; **to ~ sb do sth** jdn etw tun lassen, jdm erlauben, etw zu tun; **~'s go** gehen wir!
▶ **let down** *vt* (*tyre etc*) die Luft herauslassen aus; (*person*) im Stich lassen
▶ **let go** *vi* loslassen; **to ~ go of** loslassen
▶ **let in** *vt* hereinlassen
▶ **let off** *vt* (*culprit*) laufen lassen; (*firework, bomb*) hochgehen lassen
▶ **let out** *vt* herauslassen; (*sound*) ausstoßen
▶ **let up** *vi* (*cease*) aufhören; (*diminish*) nachlassen
ethal [ˈliːθl] *adj* tödlich
etter [ˈlɛtəʳ] *n* Brief *m*; (*of alphabet*) Buchstabe *m*
etter bomb *n* Briefbombe *f*
etter box (BRIT) *n* Briefkasten *m*
ettuce [ˈlɛtɪs] *n* Kopfsalat *m*
eukaemia, (*US*) **leukemia** [luːˈkiːmɪə] *n* Leukämie *f*
evel [ˈlɛvl] *adj* eben ▶ *n* (*on scale, of liquid*) Stand *m*; (*height*) Höhe *f*; (*fig: standard*) Niveau *nt* ▶ *vt* (*forest etc*) einebnen ▶ *vi*: **to ~ with sb** (*inf*) ehrlich mit jdm sein ▶ *adv*: **to draw ~ with** einholen; **to be ~ with** auf gleicher Höhe sein mit
evel crossing (BRIT) *n* (beschrankter) Bahnübergang *m*
evel-headed [lɛvlˈhɛdɪd] *adj* (*calm*) ausgeglichen
ever [ˈliːvəʳ] *n* Hebel *m*; (*fig*) Druckmittel *nt* ▶ *vt*: **to ~ up** hochhieven
LGBT *abbr* (= *lesbian, gay, bisexual and transgender*) LGBT, LSBT (*Sammelbegriff für Lesben, Schwule, Bisexuelle und Transsexuelle*)
liability [laɪəˈbɪlətɪ] *n* Belastung *f*; (*Law*) Haftung *f* ▪ **liabilities** *npl* (*Comm*) Verbindlichkeiten *pl*
liable [ˈlaɪəbl] *adj*: **~ for** (*responsible*) haftbar für
liar [ˈlaɪəʳ] *n* Lügner(in) *m(f)*
Lib Dem [lɪbˈdem] *abbr* = **Liberal Democrat**
liberal [ˈlɪbərl] *adj* (*Pol*) liberal; (*generous: offer*) großzügig
Liberal Democrat *n* Liberaldemokrat(in) *m(f)*
liberate [ˈlɪbəreɪt] *vt* befreien
liberation [lɪbəˈreɪʃən] *n* Befreiung *f*
Liberia [laɪˈbɪərɪə] *n* Liberia *nt*
liberty [ˈlɪbətɪ] *n* Freiheit *f*
Libra [ˈliːbrə] *n* Waage *f*
library [ˈlaɪbrərɪ] *n* Bibliothek *f*; (*institution*) Bücherei *f*
Libya [ˈlɪbɪə] *n* Libyen *nt*
lice [laɪs] *npl of* **louse**
licence, (*US*) **license** [ˈlaɪsns] *n* (*document*) Genehmigung *f*; (*also*: **driving ~**) Führerschein *m*; (*Comm*) Lizenz *f*
license [ˈlaɪsns] *n* (*US*) = **licence** ▶ *vt* (*person, organization*) eine Lizenz vergeben an *+acc*
licensed [ˈlaɪsnst] *adj*: **~ hotel/ restaurant** Hotel/Restaurant mit Schankerlaubnis
license plate (*US*) *n* Nummernschild *nt*
licensing hours [ˈlaɪsnsɪŋ-] (BRIT) *npl* Ausschankzeiten *pl*
lick [lɪk] *vt* lecken ▶ *n* Lecken *nt*
licorice [ˈlɪkərɪs] (*US*) *n* = **liquorice**
lid [lɪd] *n* Deckel *m*; (*eyelid*) Lid *nt*
lie¹ [laɪ] (*pt, pp* **lied**) *vi* lügen ▶ *n* Lüge *f*
lie² [laɪ] (*pt* **lay**, *pp* **lain**) *vi* (*lit, fig*) liegen
▶ **lie about** *vi* herumliegen
▶ **lie down** *vi* sich hinlegen
Liechtenstein [ˈlɪktənstaɪn] *n* Liechtenstein *nt*
lie-in [ˈlaɪɪn] (BRIT) *n*: **to have a ~** (sich) ausschlafen
life [laɪf] (*pl* **lives**) *n* Leben *nt*; **to be sent to prison for ~** zu einer lebenslänglichen Freiheitsstrafe verurteilt werden; **to come to ~** (*fig: person*) munter werden

life assurance (BRIT) *n* = **life insurance**
life belt (BRIT) *n* Rettungsgürtel *m*
lifeboat [ˈlaɪfbəut] *n* Rettungsboot *nt*
lifeguard [ˈlaɪfgɑːd] *n* (*at beach*) Rettungsschwimmer(in) *m(f)*; (*at swimming pool*) Bademeister(in) *m(f)*
life insurance *n* Lebensversicherung *f*
life jacket *n* Schwimmweste *f*
lifeless [ˈlaɪflɪs] *adj* leblos
lifelong [ˈlaɪflɔŋ] *adj* lebenslang
life preserver (US) *n* = **life belt**; **life jacket**
life-saving *adj* lebensrettend
life-size [ˈlaɪfsaɪz], **life-sized** [ˈlaɪfsaɪzd] *adj* in Lebensgröße
life span *n* Lebensdauer *f*
lifestyle [ˈlaɪfstaɪl] *n* Lebensstil *m*
lifetime [ˈlaɪftaɪm] *n* Lebenszeit *f*
lift [lɪft] *vt* (*raise*) heben; (*end: ban etc*) aufheben ▶ *n* (BRIT) Aufzug *m*; **to give sb a ~** (BRIT) jdn (im Auto) mitnehmen ▶ **lift up** *vt* hochheben
liftoff [ˈlɪftɔf] *n* Abheben *nt*
ligament [ˈlɪgəmənt] *n* (*Anat*) Band *nt*
light [laɪt] (*pt, pp* **lit**) *n* Licht *nt* ▶ *vt* (*candle, cigarette, fire*) anzünden; (*room*) beleuchten ▶ *adj* leicht; (*pale, bright*) hell ■ **lights** *npl* (*Aut: of car*) Beleuchtung *f*; (: *also:* **traffic lights**) Ampel *f*; **have you got a ~?** haben Sie Feuer?; **in the ~ of** angesichts *+gen*; **~ blue/green** *etc* hellblau/-grün *etc* ▶ **light up** *vi* (*face*) sich erhellen ▶ *vt* (*illuminate*) beleuchten
light bulb *n* Glühbirne *f*
lighten [ˈlaɪtn] *vt* (*make less heavy*) leichter machen ▶ *vi* (*become less dark*) sich aufhellen
lighter [ˈlaɪtəʳ] *n* (*also:* **cigarette ~**) Feuerzeug *nt*
light-hearted *adj* unbeschwert
lighthouse [ˈlaɪthaus] *n* Leuchtturm *m*
lighting [ˈlaɪtɪŋ] *n* Beleuchtung *f*
lightly [ˈlaɪtlɪ] *adv* leicht
light meter *n* Belichtungsmesser *m*
lightning [ˈlaɪtnɪŋ] *n* Blitz *m*
lightweight *adj* leicht
like [laɪk] *vt* mögen ▶ *prep* wie ▶ *n*: **I would ~, I'd ~** ich hätte *or* möchte gern; **would you ~ a coffee?** möchten Sie einen Kaffee?; **to be/look ~ sb/sth** jdm/etw ähnlich sein/sehen; **what does it look/taste/sound ~?** wie sieht es aus/schmeckt es/hört es sich an?; **what's he/the weather ~?** wie ist er/das Wetter?; **do it ~ this** mach es so
likeable [ˈlaɪkəbl] *adj* sympathisch
likelihood [ˈlaɪklɪhud] *n* Wahrscheinlichkeit *f*
likely [ˈlaɪklɪ] *adj* wahrscheinlich; **to be ~ to do sth** wahrscheinlich etw tun
like-minded [ˈlaɪkˈmaɪndɪd] *adj* gleich gesinnt
likewise [ˈlaɪkwaɪz] *adv* ebenso; **to do ~** das Gleiche tun
liking [ˈlaɪkɪŋ] *n*: **~ (for)** (*person*) Zuneigung *f* (zu); (*thing*) Vorliebe *f* (für)
lilac [ˈlaɪlək] *n* (*Bot*) Flieder *m* ▶ *adj* fliederfarben
lily [ˈlɪlɪ] *n* Lilie *f*
limb [lɪm] *n* Glied *nt*
limbo [ˈlɪmbəu] *n*: **to be in ~** (*fig: plans etc*) in der Schwebe sein
lime [laɪm] *n* (*fruit*) Limone *f*; (*tree*) Linde *f*; (*also:* **~ juice**) Limonensaft *m*; (*for soil*) Kalk *m*
limelight [ˈlaɪmlaɪt] *n*: **to be in the ~** im Rampenlicht stehen
limerick [ˈlɪmərɪk] *n* Limerick *m*
limestone [ˈlaɪmstəun] *n* Kalkstein *m*
limit [ˈlɪmɪt] *n* Grenze *f*; (*restriction*) Beschränkung *f* ▶ *vt* begrenzen, einschränken
limitation [lɪmɪˈteɪʃən] *n* Einschränkung *f*
limited [ˈlɪmɪtɪd] *adj* begrenzt, beschränkt
limited company, limited liability company (BRIT) *n* ≈ Gesellschaft *f* mit beschränkter Haftung
limousine [ˈlɪməziːn] *n* Limousine *f*
limp [lɪmp] *adj* schlaff ▶ *vi* hinken
line [laɪn] *n* Linie *f*; (*written, printed*) Zeile *f*; (*wrinkle*) Falte *f*; (*row: of people*) Schlange *f*; (: *of things*) Reihe *f*; (*for fishing, washing*) Leine *f*; (*wire, Tel*) Leitung *f*; (*railway track*) Gleise *pl* ▶ *vt* (*road*) säumen; (*clothing*) füttern; **hold the ~ please!** (*Tel*) bleiben Sie am Apparat!; **in ~** in einer Reihe; **in ~ with** im Einklang mit, in Übereinstimmung mit ▶ **line up** *vi* sich aufstellen
lined [laɪnd] *adj* (*face*) faltig; (*paper*) liniert
linen [ˈlɪnɪn] *n* (*cloth*) Leinen *nt*; (*tablecloths, sheets etc*) Wäsche *f*
liner [ˈlaɪnəʳ] *n* (*ship*) Passagierschiff *nt*; (*also:* **bin ~**) Müllbeutel *m*

linger ['lɪŋgə^r] *vi* (*smell*) sich halten; (*person*) sich aufhalten
lingerie ['lænʒəri:] *n* (Damen) unterwäsche *f*
lining ['laɪnɪŋ] *n* (*cloth*) Futter *nt*; (*of brakes*) (Brems)belag *m*
link [lɪŋk] *n* Verbindung *f*, Beziehung *f*; (*of a chain*) Glied *nt* ▸ *vt* (*join*) verbinden
lion ['laɪən] *n* Löwe *m*
lioness ['laɪənɪs] *n* Löwin *f*
lip [lɪp] *n* (*Anat*) Lippe *f*
lipstick ['lɪpstɪk] *n* Lippenstift *m*
liqueur [lɪ'kjuə^r] *n* Likör *m*
liquid ['lɪkwɪd] *adj* flüssig ▸ *n* Flüssigkeit *f*
liquidate ['lɪkwɪdeɪt] *vt* liquidieren
liquidizer ['lɪkwɪdaɪzə^r] *n* Mixer *m*
liquor ['lɪkə^r] (*US*) *n* Spirituosen *pl*
liquorice ['lɪkərɪs] (Brit) *n* Lakritze *f*
Lisbon ['lɪzbən] *n* Lissabon *nt*
lisp [lɪsp] *vi* lispeln
list [lɪst] *n* Liste *f* ▸ *vt* aufführen; (*Comput*) auflisten ▸ *vi* (*ship*) Schlagseite haben
listed building (Brit) *n* unter Denkmalschutz stehendes Gebäude *nt*
listen ['lɪsn] *vi* hören; **to ~ (out) for** horchen auf *+acc*; **to ~ to sb** jdm zuhören; **to ~ to sth** etw hören
listener ['lɪsnə^r] *n* Zuhörer(in) *m(f)*; (*Radio*) Hörer(in) *m(f)*
lit [lɪt] *pt, pp of* **light**
liter ['li:tə^r] (*US*) *n* = **litre**
literacy ['lɪtərəsɪ] *n* die Fähigkeit, lesen und schreiben zu können
literal ['lɪtərəl] *adj* wörtlich; (*translation*) (wort)wörtlich
literally ['lɪtrəlɪ] *adv* buchstäblich
literary ['lɪtərərɪ] *adj* literarisch
literature ['lɪtrɪtʃə^r] *n* Literatur *f*; (*printed information*) Informationsmaterial *nt*
Lithuania [lɪθju'eɪnɪə] *n* Litauen *nt*
Lithuanian [lɪθju'eɪnɪən] *adj* litauisch ▸ *n* Litauer(in) *m(f)*; (*Ling*) Litauisch *nt*
litre, (*US*) **liter** ['li:tə^r] *n* Liter *m or nt*
litter ['lɪtə^r] *n* (*rubbish*) Abfall *m*; (*young animals*) Wurf *m*
litter bin (Brit) *n* Abfalleimer *m*
little ['lɪtl] *adj* klein; (*short*) kurz ▸ *adv* wenig; **a ~** ein wenig, ein bisschen; **a ~ bit** ein kleines bisschen; **to have ~ time/money** wenig Zeit/Geld haben; **~ by ~** nach und nach
little finger *n* kleiner Finger *m*
live *vi* [lɪv] leben; (*in house, town*) wohnen ▸ *adj* [laɪv] lebend; (*TV, Radio*) live; (*performance, pictures etc*) Live-; (*Elec*) Strom führend
▸ **live down** *vt* hinwegkommen über *+acc*
▸ **live on** *vt fus* leben von
▸ **live together** *vi* zusammenleben
▸ **live up to** *vt fus* erfüllen, entsprechen *+dat*
▸ **live with** *vt* (*parents etc*) wohnen bei; (*partner*) zusammenleben mit; **you'll just have to ~ with it** du musst dich/Sie müssen sich eben damit abfinden
liveblog ['laɪvblɔg] *n* Live-Blog *m* ▸ *vt, vi* live bloggen
liveliness ['laɪvlɪnɪs] *n* Lebhaftigkeit *f*
lively ['laɪvlɪ] *adj* lebhaft
liver ['lɪvə^r] *n* (*Anat, Culin*) Leber *f*
lives [laɪvz] *npl of* **life**
livestock ['laɪvstɔk] *n* Vieh *nt*
livestream ['laɪvstri:m] *n* Livestream *m* ▸ *vt* livestreamen
living ['lɪvɪŋ] *adj* lebend ▸ *n*: **to earn** *or* **make a ~** sich *dat* seinen Lebensunterhalt verdienen
living room *n* Wohnzimmer *nt*
living will *n* Patientenverfügung *f*
lizard ['lɪzəd] *n* Eidechse *f*
llama ['lɑ:mə] *n* Lama *nt*
load [ləud] *n* Last *f*; (*of vehicle*) Ladung *f*; (*weight, Elec*) Belastung *f* ▸ *vt* (*also:* **~ up**) beladen; (*gun, program, data*) laden; **that's a ~ of rubbish** (*inf*) das ist alles Blödsinn; **loads of, a ~ of** (*fig*) jede Menge; **to ~ a camera** einen Film einlegen
loaf [ləuf] (*pl* **loaves**) *n* Brot *nt*, Laib *m*
loan [ləun] *n* Darlehen *nt* ▸ *vt*: **to ~ sth to sb** jdm etw leihen; **on ~** geliehen
loathe [ləuð] *vt* verabscheuen
loaves [ləuvz] *npl of* **loaf**
lobby ['lɔbɪ] *n* (*of building*) Eingangshalle *f*; (*Pol: pressure group*) Interessenverband *m*
lobster ['lɔbstə^r] *n* Hummer *m*
local ['ləukl] *adj* örtlich; (*council*) Stadt-, Gemeinde-; (*paper*) Lokal- ▸ *n* (*pub*) Stammkneipe *f* ■ **the locals** *npl* (*local inhabitants*) die Einheimischen *pl*
local anaesthetic *n* örtliche Betäubung *f*
local call *n* Ortsgespräch *nt*

local government *n* Kommunalverwaltung *f*
locally [ˈləukəlɪ] *adv* am Ort
locate [ləuˈkeɪt] *vt* (*find*) ausfindig machen; **to be located in** sich befinden in *+dat*
location [ləuˈkeɪʃən] *n* (*position*) Lage *f*; (*Cine*) Drehort *m*
loch [lɔx] (*Scot*) *n* See *m*
lock [lɔk] *n* (*of door etc*) Schloss *nt*; (*on canal*) Schleuse *f*; (*also*: **~ of hair**) Locke *f* ▸ *vt* (*door etc*) abschließen ▸ *vi* (*door etc*) sich abschließen lassen; (*wheels, mechanism etc*) blockieren
▸ **lock in** *vt* einschließen
▸ **lock out** *vt* aussperren
▸ **lock up** *vt* (*criminal etc*) einsperren; (*house*) abschließen
locker [ˈlɔkəʳ] *n* Schließfach *nt*
locker room *n* Umkleideraum *m*
locksmith [ˈlɔksmɪθ] *n* Schlosser *m*
locust [ˈləukəst] *n* Heuschrecke *f*
lodge [lɔdʒ] *n* Pförtnerhaus *nt*; (*also*: **hunting ~**) Hütte *f* ▸ *vi* (*bullet*) stecken bleiben; (*person*): **to ~ (with)** zur Untermiete wohnen (bei)
lodger [ˈlɔdʒəʳ] *n* Untermieter(in) *m(f)*
lodging [ˈlɔdʒɪŋ] *n* Unterkunft *f*
loft [lɔft] *n* Boden *m*
log [lɔg] *n* (*of wood*) Holzblock *m*, Holzklotz *m*; (*written account*) Log *nt*
▸ **log in** *vi* (*Comput*) sich anmelden
▸ **log off** *vi* (*Comput*) sich abmelden
▸ **log on** *vi* (*Comput*) = **log in**
▸ **log out** *vi* (*Comput*) = **log off**
logic [ˈlɔdʒɪk] *n* Logik *f*
logical [ˈlɔdʒɪkl] *adj* logisch
login [ˈlɔgɪn] *n* (*Comput*) Log-in *nt*, Anmeldung *f*
logo [ˈləugəu] *n* Logo *nt*
loin [lɔɪn] *n* Lende *f*
loiter [ˈlɔɪtəʳ] *vi* sich aufhalten
lollipop [ˈlɔlɪpɔp] *n* Lutscher *m*
lollipop lady (*Brit*) *n* ≈ Schülerlotsin *f*
lollipop man (*Brit*) *n* ≈ Schülerlotse *m*
lolly [ˈlɔlɪ] (*inf*) *n* (*lollipop*) Lutscher *m*; (*money*) Mäuse *pl*
London [ˈlʌndən] *n* London *nt*
Londoner [ˈlʌndənəʳ] *n* Londoner(in) *m(f)*
loneliness [ˈləunlɪnɪs] *n* Einsamkeit *f*
lonely [ˈləunlɪ] *adj* einsam
long [lɔŋ] *adj* lang ▸ *adv* lang(e) ▸ *vi*: **to ~ for sth** sich nach etw sehnen; **in the ~ run** auf die Dauer; **how ~ is the lesson?** wie lange dauert die Stunde?; **6 metres/months ~** 6 Meter/Monate lang; **so** *or* **as ~ as** (*on condition that*) solange; **don't be ~!** bleib nicht so lange!; **all night ~** die ganze Nacht; **he no longer comes** er kommt nicht mehr; **~ ago** vor langer Zeit; **before ~** bald
long-distance [lɔŋˈdɪstəns] *adj* (*travel, phone call*) Fern-
longing [ˈlɔŋɪŋ] *n* Sehnsucht *f*
longingly [ˈlɔŋɪŋlɪ] *adv* sehnsüchtig
longitude [ˈlɔŋgɪtjuːd] *n* Länge *f*
long jump *n* Weitsprung *m*
long-life [ˈlɔŋlaɪf] *adj*: **~ milk** H-Milch *f*
long-range [ˈlɔŋˈreɪndʒ] *adj* (*plan, forecast*) langfristig; (*missile, plane etc*) Langstrecken-
long-sighted [ˈlɔŋˈsaɪtɪd] *adj* weitsichtig
long-standing [ˈlɔŋˈstændɪŋ] *adj* langjährig
long-term [ˈlɔŋtəːm] *adj* langfristig
long wave *n* Langwelle *f*
loo [luː] (*Brit inf*) *n* Klo *nt*
look [luk] *vi* sehen, schauen, gucken (*inf*); (*seem, appear*) aussehen ▸ *n* (*glance*) Blick *m* ■ **looks** *npl* (*good looks*) (gutes) Aussehen; **to ~ like sb/sth** wie jd/etw aussehen; **to have a ~ at sth** sich *dat* etw ansehen; **let me have a ~** lass mich mal sehen
▸ **look after** *vt fus* sich kümmern um
▸ **look at** *vt fus* ansehen
▸ **look back** *vi*: **to ~ back (on)** zurückblicken (auf *+acc*)
▸ **look down on** *vt fus* (*fig*) herabsehen auf *+acc*
▸ **look for** *vt fus* suchen
▸ **look forward to** *vt fus* sich freuen auf *+acc*
▸ **look into** *vt fus* (*investigate*) untersuchen
▸ **look out** *vi* (*beware*) aufpassen
▸ **look out for** *vt fus* Ausschau halten nach
▸ **look up** *vi* aufsehen ▸ *vt* (*word etc*) nachschlagen
▸ **look up to** *vt fus* aufsehen zu
loony [ˈluːnɪ] (*pej*) *adj* verrückt
loop [luːp] *n* (*Comput*) Schleife *f*
loose [luːs] *adj* lose, locker
loosen [ˈluːsn] *vt* lösen; (*clothing, belt etc*) lockern
loot [luːt] *n* (*inf*) Beute *f*

lopsided ['lɔp'saɪdɪd] *adj* schief
lord [lɔ:d] *n* (BRIT) Lord *m*; **the L~** (*Rel*) der Herr; **the (House of) Lords** (BRIT) das Oberhaus
lorry ['lɔrɪ] (BRIT) *n* Lastwagen *m*
lose [lu:z] (*pt, pp* **lost**) *vt* verlieren; (*opportunity*) verpassen ▶ *vi* verlieren; **to ~ (time)** (*clock*) nachgehen; **to ~ weight** abnehmen; **to ~ 5 pounds** 5 Pfund abnehmen
loser ['lu:zə^r] *n* Verlierer(in) *m(f)*
loss [lɔs] *n* Verlust *m*
lost [lɔst] *pt, pp of* **lose** ▶ *adj* (*object*) verloren; **to be ~** sich verlaufen/verfahren haben
lost and found (*US*) *n* = **lost property**
lost property (BRIT) *n* (*also:* **lost property office**) Fundbüro *nt*
lot [lɔt] *n* (*group*) Gruppe *f*; **the ~** alles; **a ~ (of)** (*a large number (of)*) viele; (*a great deal (of)*) viel; **lots of** viele; **I read a ~** ich lese viel; **this happens a ~** das kommt oft vor
lotion ['ləuʃən] *n* Lotion *f*
lottery ['lɔtərɪ] *n* Lotterie *f*
loud [laud] *adj* laut; (*clothes*) schreiend
loudspeaker [laud'spi:kə^r] *n* Lautsprecher *m*
lounge [laundʒ] *n* (*in house*) Wohnzimmer *nt*; (*in hotel*) Lounge *f*; (*at airport, station*) Wartehalle *f* ▶ *vi* faulenzen
louse [laus] (*pl* **lice**) *n* Laus *f*
lousy ['lauzɪ] (*inf*) *adj* (*bad quality*) lausig
lout [laut] *n* Lümmel *m*
lovable ['lʌvəbl] *adj* liebenswert
love [lʌv] *n* Liebe *f* ▶ *vt* lieben; (*thing, activity etc*) gern mögen; **"~ (from) Anne"** (*on letter*) „mit herzlichen Grüßen, Anne"; **to be in ~ with** verliebt sein in *+acc*; **to fall in ~ with** sich verlieben in *+acc*; **to make ~** sich lieben; **to send one's ~ to sb** jdn grüßen lassen; **"fifteen ~"** (*Tennis*) „fünfzehn null"; **to ~ doing sth** etw gern tun; **I'd ~ to come** ich würde sehr gerne kommen
love affair *n* Verhältnis *nt*, Liebschaft *f*
love letter *n* Liebesbrief *m*
love life *n* Liebesleben *nt*
lovely ['lʌvlɪ] *adj* (*beautiful*) schön; (*delightful*) herrlich; (*person*) sehr nett
lover ['lʌvə^r] *n* Geliebte(r) *f(m)*
loving ['lʌvɪŋ] *adj* (*actions*) liebevoll
low [ləu] *adj* niedrig; (*bow, curtsey*) tief; (*quality*) schlecht; (*sound: deep*) tief; (*: quiet*) leise; (*depressed*) niedergeschlagen ▶ *n* (*Met*) Tief *nt*; **to be/run ~** knapp sein/werden; **sb is running ~ on sth** jdm wird etw knapp
low-calorie ['ləu'kælərɪ] *adj* kalorienarm
low-cut ['ləukʌt] *adj* (*dress*) tief ausgeschnitten
low-emission *adj* schadstoffarm
lower ['ləuə^r] *adj* untere(r, s) ▶ *vt* senken
low-fat ['ləu'fæt] *adj* fettarm
low tide [ləu'taɪd] *n* Ebbe *f*
loyal ['lɔɪəl] *adj* treu
loyalty ['lɔɪəltɪ] *n* Treue *f*
lozenge ['lɔzɪndʒ] *n* Pastille *f*
Ltd *abbr* (*Comm: = limited (liability)*) ≈ GmbH *f*
lubricant ['lu:brɪkənt] *n* Schmiermittel *nt*
luck [lʌk] *n* (*esp good luck*) Glück *nt*; **bad ~** Unglück *nt*; **bad** *or* **hard** *or* **tough ~!** so ein Pech!
luckily ['lʌkɪlɪ] *adv* glücklicherweise
lucky ['lʌkɪ] *adj* (*situation, event*) glücklich; (*object*) Glück bringend; (*person*): **to be ~** Glück haben; **~ charm** Glücksbringer *m*
ludicrous ['lu:dɪkrəs] *adj* grotesk
luggage ['lʌgɪdʒ] *n* Gepäck *nt*
luggage compartment *n* Gepäckraum *m*
luggage rack *n* Gepäckträger *m*
lukewarm ['lu:kwɔ:m] *adj* lauwarm
lullaby ['lʌləbaɪ] *n* Schlaflied *nt*
lumbago [lʌm'beɪgəu] *n* Hexenschuss *m*
luminous ['lu:mɪnəs] *adj* leuchtend, Leucht-
lump [lʌmp] *n* Klumpen *m*; (*on body*) Beule *f*; (*in breast*) Knoten *m*; (*also:* **sugar ~**) Stück *nt* (Zucker); **a ~ sum** eine Pauschalsumme
lumpy ['lʌmpɪ] *adj* klumpig
lunacy ['lu:nəsɪ] *n* Wahnsinn *m*
lunatic ['lu:nətɪk] *adj* wahnsinnig ▶ *n* Wahnsinnige(r) *f(m)*
lunch [lʌntʃ] *n* Mittagessen *nt*
lunch break *n* Mittagspause *f*
luncheon ['lʌntʃən] *n* Mittagessen *nt*
lunch time *n* Mittagszeit *f*
lung [lʌŋ] *n* Lunge *f*

lurch [lə:tʃ] *n*: **to leave sb in the ~** jdn im Stich lassen
lurid ['luərɪd] *adj* (*story etc*) reißerisch; (*pej: brightly coloured*) grell
lurk [lə:k] *vi* (*also fig*) lauern
lust [lʌst] (*pej*) *n* (*sexual*) (sinnliche) Begierde *f*
Luxembourg ['lʌksəmbə:g] *n* Luxemburg *nt*
luxurious [lʌg'zjuərɪəs] *adj* luxuriös
luxury ['lʌkʃərɪ] *n* Luxus *m* (*no pl*) ▶ *cpd* (*hotel, car etc*) Luxus-
lynx [lɪŋks] *n* Luchs *m*
lyrics ['lɪrɪks] *npl* (*of song*) Text *m*

M [ɛm] *n abbr* (Brit) = **motorway**; **the M8** ≈ die A8 ▶ *abbr* = **medium**
m *abbr* (= *metre*) m; = **mile**; (= *million*) Mio.
MA *n abbr* (= *Master of Arts*) *akademischer Grad für Geisteswissenschaftler*
mac [mæk] (*Brit*) *n* Regenmantel *m*
macaroon [mækə'ru:n] *n* Makrone *f*
Macedonia [mæsɪ'dəunɪə] *n* Makedonien *nt*
machine [mə'ʃi:n] *n* Maschine *f*
machine gun *n* Maschinengewehr *nt*
machinery [mə'ʃi:nərɪ] *n* Maschinen *pl*; (*fig: of government*) Apparat *m*
machine washable *adj* waschmaschinenfest
mackerel ['mækrl] *n inv* Makrele *f*
macro... ['mækrəu] *pref* Makro-, makro-
mad [mæd] *adj* wahnsinnig, verrückt; (*angry*) böse, sauer (*inf*); **to be ~ about** verrückt sein auf +*acc*; **to be ~ at sb** böse *or* sauer auf jdn sein
madam ['mædəm] *n* gnädige Frau *f*
mad cow disease *n* Rinderwahn *m*
maddening ['mædnɪŋ] *adj* unerträglich
made [meɪd] *pt, pp of* **make**
made-to-measure ['meɪdtə'mɛʒə^r] (*Brit*) *adj* maßgeschneidert
madly ['mædlɪ] *adv* wie verrückt
madman ['mædmən] *n* (*irreg*) Verrückte(r) *m*
madness ['mædnɪs] *n* Wahnsinn *m*
magazine [mægə'zi:n] *n* Zeitschrift *f*
maggot ['mægət] *n* Made *f*

magic [ˈmædʒɪk] *n* Magie *f*; (*conjuring*) Zauberei *f* ▶ *adj* magisch; (*formula*) Zauber-
magician [məˈdʒɪʃən] *n* (*conjurer*) Zauberer *m*
magnet [ˈmæɡnɪt] *n* Magnet *m*
magnetic [mæɡˈnɛtɪk] *adj* magnetisch
magnetism [ˈmæɡnɪtɪzəm] *n* (*of person*) Anziehungskraft *f*
magnificent [mæɡˈnɪfɪsnt] *adj* großartig
magnify [ˈmæɡnɪfaɪ] *vt* vergrößern
magnifying glass [ˈmæɡnɪfaɪɪŋ-] *n* Vergrößerungsglas *nt*, Lupe *f*
magpie [ˈmæɡpaɪ] *n* Elster *f*
maid [meɪd] *n* Dienstmädchen *nt*
maiden name *n* Mädchenname *m*
mail [meɪl] *n* Post *f* ▶ *vt* aufgeben
mailbox [ˈmeɪlbɔks] *n* (*US*) Briefkasten *m*; (*Comput*) Mailbox *f*, elektronischer Briefkasten *m*
mailing list [ˈmeɪlɪŋ-] *n* Anschriftenliste *f*
mailman [ˈmeɪlmæn] (*US*) *n* (*irreg*) Briefträger *m*
mail order *n* (*system*) Versand *m* ▶ *cpd*: **mail-order firm** *or* **business** Versandhaus *nt*; **by ~** durch Bestellung per Post
mailshot [ˈmeɪlʃɔt] (Brit) *n* Werbebrief *m*
main [meɪn] *adj* Haupt-, wichtigste(r, s); (*door, entrance, meal*) Haupt- ▶ *n* Hauptleitung *f*
main course *n* (*Culin*) Hauptgericht *nt*
mainframe [ˈmeɪnfreɪm] *n* (*Comput*) Großrechner *m*
mainland [ˈmeɪnlənd] *n* Festland *nt*
mainly [ˈmeɪnlɪ] *adv* hauptsächlich
main road *n* Hauptstraße *f*
main street *n* (*US*) Hauptstraße *f*
maintain [meɪnˈteɪn] *vt* (*preserve*) aufrechterhalten; (*keep up*) beibehalten; (*look after: building*) instand halten; (*: equipment*) warten; **to ~ that …** behaupten, dass …
maintenance [ˈmeɪntənəns] *n* (*of building*) Instandhaltung *f*; (*of equipment*) Wartung *f*
maize [meɪz] *n* Mais *m*
majestic [məˈdʒɛstɪk] *adj* erhaben
majesty [ˈmædʒɪstɪ] *n* (*title*): **Your M~** Eure Majestät
major [ˈmeɪdʒəʳ] *adj* bedeutend; (*Mus*) Dur ▶ *vi* (*US*): **to ~ in French** Französisch als Hauptfach belegen; **a ~ operation** eine größere Operation
Majorca [məˈjɔːkə] *n* Mallorca *nt*
majority [məˈdʒɔrɪtɪ] *n* Mehrheit *f*
make [meɪk] (*pt, pp* **made**) *vt* machen; (*clothes*) nähen; (*cake*) backen; (*speech*) halten; (*manufacture*) herstellen; (*earn*) verdienen; (*cause to be*): **to ~ sb sad** jdn traurig machen; (*force*): **to ~ sb do sth** jdn zwingen, etw zu tun; (*cause*) jdn dazu bringen, etw zu tun ▶ *n* Marke *f*; **to ~ it** (*arrive*) es schaffen; (*succeed*) Erfolg haben; **what time do you ~ it?** wie spät hast du?
▶ **make for** *vt fus* (*place*) zuhalten auf *+acc*
▶ **make off** *vi* sich davonmachen
▶ **make out** *vt* (*decipher*) entziffern; (*understand*) verstehen; (*see*) ausmachen; (*write: cheque*) ausstellen; (*claim, imply*) behaupten
▶ **make up** *vt* (*constitute*) bilden; (*invent*) erfinden ▶ *vi* (*after quarrel*) sich versöhnen; **to ~ up one's mind** sich entscheiden
▶ **make up for** *vt fus* (*loss*) ersetzen; (*disappointment etc*) ausgleichen
make-believe *n* Fantasie *f*
makeover [ˈmeɪkəuvəʳ] *n grundlegende Veränderung des Aussehens*
maker [ˈmeɪkəʳ] *n* Hersteller *m*
makeshift [ˈmeɪkʃɪft] *adj* behelfsmäßig
make-up [ˈmeɪkʌp] *n* Make-up *nt*, Schminke *f*
making [ˈmeɪkɪŋ] *n* (*fig*): **in the ~** im Entstehen
maladjusted [mæləˈdʒʌstɪd] *adj* verhaltensgestört
malaria [məˈlɛərɪə] *n* Malaria *f*
Malaysia [məˈleɪzɪə] *n* Malaysia *nt*
male [meɪl] *n* (*animal*) Männchen *nt*; (*man*) Mann *m* ▶ *adj* männlich
male chauvinist *n* Chauvinist *m*
male nurse *n* Krankenpfleger *m*
malfunction [mælˈfʌŋkʃən] *n* (*of machine*) Defekt *m* ▶ *vi* (*computer*) eine Funktionsstörung haben
malice [ˈmælɪs] *n* Bosheit *f*
malicious [məˈlɪʃəs] *adj* boshaft; (*Law*) böswillig
malignant [məˈlɪɡnənt] *adj* bösartig

mall [mɔːl] *n* (*also:* **shopping ~**) Einkaufszentrum *nt*
malnutrition [mælnjuːˈtrɪʃən] *n* Unterernährung *f*
malt [mɔːlt] *n* Malz *nt*
Malta [ˈmɔːltə] *n* Malta *nt*
Maltese [mɔːlˈtiːz] *adj* maltesisch ▸ *n inv* Malteser(in) *m(f)*; (*Ling*) Maltesisch *nt*
maltreat [mælˈtriːt] *vt* schlecht behandeln; (*violently*) misshandeln
malware [ˈmælwɛəʳ] *n* (*Comput*) Schadprogramm *nt*, Malware *f*
mammal [ˈmæml] *n* Säugetier *nt*
mammoth [ˈmæməθ] *adj* (*task*) Mammut-
man [mæn] (*pl* **men**) *n* Mann *m*; (*mankind*) der Mensch, die Menschen *pl*; (*Chess*) Figur *f* ▸ *vt* (*post*) besetzen
manage [ˈmænɪdʒ] *vi*: **to ~ to do sth** es schaffen, etw zu tun; (*get by financially*) zurechtkommen ▸ *vt* (*business, organization*) leiten; (*control*) zurechtkommen mit
manageable [ˈmænɪdʒəbl] *adj* (*task*) zu bewältigen
management [ˈmænɪdʒmənt] *n* Leitung *f*; (*persons*) Unternehmensleitung *f*
management consultant *n* Unternehmensberater(in) *m(f)*
manager [ˈmænɪdʒəʳ] *n* (*of business*) Geschäftsführer(in) *m(f)*; (*of department*) Leiter(in) *m(f)*; (*of pop star*) Manager(in) *m(f)*; (*Sport*) Trainer(in) *m(f)*
managing director [ˈmænɪdʒɪŋ-] *n* Geschäftsführer(in) *m(f)*
mane [meɪn] *n* Mähne *f*
maneuver *etc* [məˈnuːvəʳ] (*US*) = **manoeuvre** *etc*
mango [ˈmæŋgəu] (*pl* **mangoes**) *n* Mango *f*
man-hour *n* Arbeitsstunde *f*
manhunt *n* Fahndung *f*
mania [ˈmeɪnɪə] *n* Manie *f*
maniac [ˈmeɪnɪæk] *n* Wahnsinnige(r) *f(m)*; (*fig*) Fanatiker(in) *m(f)*
manicure [ˈmænɪkjuəʳ] *n* Maniküre *f*
manipulate [məˈnɪpjuleɪt] *vt* manipulieren
mankind [mænˈkaɪnd] *n* Menschheit *f*
manly [ˈmænlɪ] *adj* männlich
man-made [ˈmænˈmeɪd] *adj* künstlich
manner [ˈmænəʳ] *n* (*way*) Art *f* ■ **manners** *npl* (*conduct*) Manieren *pl*
manoeuvre, (*US*) **maneuver** [məˈnuːvəʳ] *vt* manövrieren ▸ *vi* manövrieren ▸ *n* (*skilful move*) Manöver *nt*
manor [ˈmænəʳ] *n* (*also:* **~ house**) Herrenhaus *nt*
manpower [ˈmænpauəʳ] *n* Arbeitskräfte *pl*
mansion [ˈmænʃən] *n* Villa *f*
manslaughter [ˈmænslɔːtəʳ] *n* Totschlag *m*
mantelpiece [ˈmæntlpiːs] *n* Kaminsims *m or nt*
manual [ˈmænjuəl] *adj* manuell, Hand- ▸ *n* Handbuch *nt*
manufacture [mænjuˈfæktʃəʳ] *vt* herstellen ▸ *n* Herstellung *f*
manufacturer [mænjuˈfæktʃərəʳ] *n* Hersteller *m*
manure [məˈnjuəʳ] *n* Dung *m*
many [ˈmɛnɪ] *adj, pron* viele; **how ~?** wie viele?; **too ~ difficulties** zu viele Schwierigkeiten; **twice as ~** doppelt so viele; **~ a time** so manches Mal
map [mæp] *n* (Land)karte *f*; (*of town*) Stadtplan *m*
maple [ˈmeɪpl] *n* (*tree, wood*) Ahorn *m*
marathon [ˈmærəθən] *n* Marathon *m*
marble [ˈmɑːbl] *n* Marmor *m*; (*toy*) Murmel *f*
March [mɑːtʃ] *n* März *m*; *see also* **July**
march [mɑːtʃ] *vi* marschieren ▸ *n* Marsch *m*; (*demonstration*) Demonstration *f*
mare [mɛəʳ] *n* Stute *f*
margarine [mɑːdʒəˈriːn] *n* Margarine *f*
margin [ˈmɑːdʒɪn] *n* Rand *m*; (*for safety, error etc*) Spielraum *m*; (*Comm*) Gewinnspanne *f*
marginal [ˈmɑːdʒɪnl] *adj* geringfügig
marijuana [mærɪˈwɑːnə] *n* Marihuana *nt*
marine [məˈriːn] *adj* (*plant, biology*) Meeres-
marital [ˈmærɪtl] *adj* ehelich; **~ status** Familienstand *m*
maritime [ˈmærɪtaɪm] *adj* (*nation*) Seefahrer-; (*law*) See-
marjoram [ˈmɑːdʒərəm] *n* Majoran *m*
mark [mɑːk] *n* Zeichen *nt*; (*stain*) Fleck *m*; (*BRIT Scol*) Note *f* ▸ *vt* (*stain*) Flecken

machen auf *+dat*; (*indicate*) markieren; (*BRIT Scol*) korrigieren (und benoten)
markedly [ˈmɑːkɪdlɪ] *adv* deutlich
marker [ˈmɑːkəʳ] *n* Markierung *f*; (*bookmark*) Lesezeichen *nt*
market [ˈmɑːkɪt] *n* Markt *m* ▶ *vt* (*sell*) vertreiben; (*new product*) auf den Markt bringen; **to play the ~** (*Stock Exchange*) an der Börse spekulieren
marketing [ˈmɑːkɪtɪŋ] *n* Marketing *nt*
market leader *n* Marktführer *m*
marketplace [ˈmɑːkɪtpleɪs] *n* Marktplatz *m*
market research *n* Marktforschung *f*
marmalade [ˈmɑːməleɪd] *n* Orangenmarmelade *f*
maroon [məˈruːn] *adj* kastanienbraun
marquee [mɑːˈkiː] *n* Festzelt *nt*
marriage [ˈmærɪdʒ] *n* Ehe *f*; (*wedding*) Hochzeit *f*
married [ˈmærɪd] *adj* verheiratet
marrow [ˈmærəu] *n* (*vegetable*) Kürbis *m*; (*also:* **bone ~**) (Knochen)mark *nt*
marry [ˈmærɪ] *vt* heiraten; (*priest*) trauen ▶ *vi* heiraten
marsh [mɑːʃ] *n* Sumpf *m*; (*also:* **salt ~**) Salzsumpf *m*
marshal [ˈmɑːʃl] *n* (*official*) Ordner *m*; (*US: of police*) Bezirkspolizeichef *m*
martial arts *npl* Kampfsport *m*
martyr [ˈmɑːtəʳ] *n* Märtyrer(in) *m(f)*
marvel [ˈmɑːvl] *n* Wunder *nt* ▶ *vi*: **to ~ (at)** staunen (über *+acc*)
marvellous, (*US*) **marvelous** [ˈmɑːvləs] *adj* wunderbar
marzipan [ˈmɑːzɪpæn] *n* Marzipan *nt*
mascara [mæsˈkɑːrə] *n* Wimperntusche *f*
mascot [ˈmæskət] *n* Maskottchen *nt*
masculine [ˈmæskjulɪn] *adj* männlich
mashed potatoes [mæʃt-] *npl* Kartoffelpüree *nt*, Kartoffelbrei *m*
mask [mɑːsk] *n* Maske *f* ▶ *vt* (*hide*) verbergen
masochist [ˈmæsəukɪst] *n* Masochist(in) *m(f)*
mason [ˈmeɪsn] *n* (*also:* **stone ~**) Steinmetz *m*
masonry [ˈmeɪsnrɪ] *n* Mauerwerk *nt*
mass [mæs] *n* Masse *f*; (*of people*) Menge *f*; (*Rel*): **M~** Messe *f*; **masses of** (*inf*) massenhaft
massacre [ˈmæsəkəʳ] *n* Massaker *nt*
massage [ˈmæsɑːʒ] *n* Massage *f* ▶ *vt* massieren
massive [ˈmæsɪv] *adj* (*furniture, person*) wuchtig; (*support*) massiv
mass media *npl* Massenmedien *pl*
mass-produce [ˈmæsprəˈdjuːs] *vt* in Massenproduktion herstellen
mass-production *n* Massenproduktion *f*
master [ˈmɑːstəʳ] *n* Herr *m*; (*teacher*) Lehrer *m*; (*Art, Mus, of craft etc*) Meister *m* ▶ *vt* meistern; (*skill, language*) beherrschen
masterly [ˈmɑːstəlɪ] *adj* meisterhaft
masterpiece [ˈmɑːstəpiːs] *n* Meisterwerk *nt*
masturbate [ˈmæstəbeɪt] *vi* masturbieren
mat [mæt] *n* Matte *f*; (*also:* **table ~**) Untersetzer *m*
match [mætʃ] *n* Wettkampf *m*; (*team game*) Spiel *nt*; (*Tennis*) Match *nt*; (*for lighting fire etc*) Streichholz *nt* ▶ *vt* (*go well with*) passen zu; (*equal*) gleichkommen *+dat* ▶ *vi* zusammenpassen
matchbox [ˈmætʃbɔks] *n* Streichholzschachtel *f*
matching [ˈmætʃɪŋ] *adj* (dazu) passend
mate [meɪt] *n* (*inf: friend*) Kumpel *m*; (*animal*) Männchen *nt*, Weibchen *nt* ▶ *vi* (*animals*) sich paaren
material [məˈtɪərɪəl] *n* Material *nt*; (*cloth*) Stoff *m*
materialistic [mətɪərɪəˈlɪstɪk] *adj* materialistisch
materialize [məˈtɪərɪəlaɪz] *vi* (*event*) zustande kommen; (*hope*) sich verwirklichen
maternal [məˈtəːnl] *adj* mütterlich
maternity [məˈtəːnɪtɪ] *n* Mutterschaft *f* ▶ *cpd* (*ward etc*) Entbindungs-
maternity dress *n* Umstandskleid *nt*
maternity leave *n* Mutterschaftsurlaub *m*
math [mæθ] (*US*) *n* = **maths**
mathematical [mæθəˈmætɪkl] *adj* mathematisch
mathematics [mæθəˈmætɪks] *n* Mathematik *f*
maths [mæθs], (*US*) **math** [mæθ] *n* Mathe *f*
matinée [ˈmætɪneɪ] *n* Nachmittagsvorstellung *f*
matter [ˈmætəʳ] *n* (*event, situation*) Sache *f*, Angelegenheit *f*; (*Phys*)

Materie *f* ▶ *vi* (*be important*) wichtig sein; **what's the ~?** was ist los?; **no ~ what** egal was (passiert); **as a ~ of fact** eigentlich; **it doesn't ~** es macht nichts

matter-of-fact [ˈmætərəvˈfækt] *adj* sachlich

mattress [ˈmætrɪs] *n* Matratze *f*

mature [məˈtjuəʳ] *adj* reif; (*wine*) ausgereift ▶ *vi* reifen

maturity [məˈtjuərɪtɪ] *n* Reife *f*

maximum [ˈmæksɪməm] (*pl* **maxima** *or* **maximums**) *adj* (*amount, speed etc*) Höchst- ▶ *n* Maximum *nt*

May [meɪ] *n* Mai *m*; *see also* **July**

may [meɪ] (*conditional* **might**) *vi* (*be possible*) können; (*have permission*) dürfen; **he ~ come** vielleicht kommt er; **~ I smoke?** darf ich rauchen?; **he might be there** er könnte da sein; **you ~ as well go** Sie können ruhig gehen

maybe [ˈmeɪbiː] *adv* vielleicht

May Day *n* der 1. Mai

mayor [mɛəʳ] *n* Bürgermeister *m*

maze [meɪz] *n* Irrgarten *m*

MB *abbr* (*Comput*: = *megabyte*) MB

KEYWORD

me [miː] *pron* **1** (*direct*) mich; **it's me** ich bins

2 (*indirect*) mir; **he gave me the money, he gave the money to me** er gab mir das Geld

3 (*after prep*): **it's for me** es ist für mich; **with me** mit mir; **without me** ohne mich

meadow [ˈmɛdəu] *n* Wiese *f*

meal [miːl] *n* Mahlzeit *f*; (*food*) Essen *nt*; **to go out for a ~** essen gehen

mealtime [ˈmiːltaɪm] *n* Essenszeit *f*

mean [miːn] (*pt, pp* **meant**) *adj* (*with money*) geizig; (*unkind*) gemein ▶ *vt* (*signify*) bedeuten; (*refer to*) meinen; (*intend*) beabsichtigen ▪ **means** *npl* (*money*) Mittel *pl*; **by means of** durch; **by all means!** aber natürlich *or* selbstverständlich!; **do you ~ it?** meinst du das ernst?; **what do you ~?** was willst du damit sagen?; **to be meant for sb/sth** für jdn/etw bestimmt sein; **to ~ to do sth** etw tun wollen

meaning [ˈmiːnɪŋ] *n* Sinn *m*; (*of word, gesture*) Bedeutung *f*

meaningful [ˈmiːnɪŋful] *adj* sinnvoll

meaningless [ˈmiːnɪŋlɪs] *adj* sinnlos

meant [mɛnt] *pt, pp of* **mean**

meantime [ˈmiːntaɪm] *adv* (*also*: **in the ~**) inzwischen

meanwhile [ˈmiːnwaɪl] *adv* = **meantime**

measles [ˈmiːzlz] *n* Masern *pl*

measure [ˈmɛʒəʳ] *vt, vi* messen ▶ *n* (*amount*) Menge *f*; (*of achievement*) Maßstab *m*; **to take measures to do sth** Maßnahmen ergreifen, um etw zu tun

measurement [ˈmɛʒəmənt] *n* (*measure*) Maß *nt*

meat [miːt] *n* Fleisch *nt*

meatball [ˈmiːtbɔːl] *n* Fleischkloß *m*

mechanic [mɪˈkænɪk] *n* Mechaniker(in) *m(f)*

mechanical [mɪˈkænɪkl] *adj* mechanisch

mechanics [mɪˈkænɪks] *n* (*Phys*) Mechanik *f*

mechanism [ˈmɛkənɪzəm] *n* Mechanismus *m*

medal [ˈmɛdl] *n* Medaille *f*; (*decoration*) Orden *m*

medallist, (*US*) **medalist** [ˈmɛdlɪst] *n* Medaillengewinner(in) *m(f)*

media [ˈmiːdɪə] *npl* Medien *pl*

median [ˈmiːdɪən] (*US*) *n* (*also*: **~ strip**) Mittelstreifen *m*

mediate [ˈmiːdɪeɪt] *vi* vermitteln

medical [ˈmɛdɪkl] *adj* (*care*) medizinisch; (*treatment*) ärztlich ▶ *n* (ärztliche) Untersuchung *f*

medicalize [ˈmɛdɪkəlaɪz] *vt* medikalisieren

Medicare [ˈmɛdɪkɛəʳ] (*US*) *n staatliche Krankenversicherung und Gesundheitsfürsorge für ältere Bürger*

medication [mɛdɪˈkeɪʃən] *n* Medikamente *pl*

medicinal [mɛˈdɪsɪnl] *adj* (*substance*) Heil-

medicine [ˈmɛdsɪn] *n* Medizin *f*; (*drug*) Arznei *f*

medieval [mɛdɪˈiːvl] *adj* mittelalterlich

mediocre [miːdɪˈəukəʳ] *adj* mittelmäßig

meditate [ˈmɛdɪteɪt] *vi* nachdenken; (*Rel*) meditieren

Mediterranean [mɛdɪtəˈreɪnɪən] *adj* (*country, climate etc*) Mittelmeer-; **the ~ (Sea)** das Mittelmeer
medium [ˈmiːdɪəm] (*pl* **media** *or* **mediums**) *adj* mittlere(r, s) ▶ *n* (*means*) Mittel *nt*; (*substance, material*) Medium *nt*; **of ~ height** mittelgroß
meet [miːt] (*pt, pp* **met**) *vt* (*encounter*) treffen; (*by arrangement*) sich treffen mit; (*for the first time*) kennenlernen; (*go and fetch*) abholen; (*condition, standard*) erfüllen; (*problem*) stoßen auf *+acc*; (*challenge*) begegnen *+dat* ▶ *vi* (*by arrangement*) sich treffen; (*for the first time*) sich kennenlernen
▶ **meet up** *vi*: **to ~ up with sb** sich mit jdm treffen
▶ **meet with** *vt fus* (*difficulty, success*) haben
meeting [ˈmiːtɪŋ] *n* (*assembly, people assembling*) Versammlung *f*; (*Comm, of committee etc*) Sitzung *f*; (*also:* **business ~**) Besprechung *f*; (*arranged*) Treffen *nt*
meeting place *n* Treffpunkt *m*
megabyte [ˈmɛgəbaɪt] *n* (*Comput*) Megabyte *nt*
megastore [ˈmɛgəstɔːʳ] *n* Megastore *m*
melody [ˈmɛlədɪ] *n* Melodie *f*
melon [ˈmɛlən] *n* Melone *f*
melt [mɛlt] *vi* (*lit, fig*) schmelzen
member [ˈmɛmbəʳ] *n* Mitglied *nt*; **M~ of Parliament** (Brit) Abgeordnete(r) *f*(*m*) (des Unterhauses)
membership [ˈmɛmbəʃɪp] *n* Mitgliedschaft *f*
membership card *n* Mitgliedsausweis *m*
meme [miːm] *n* (*Internet*) Mem(e) *nt*
memento [məˈmɛntəu] *n* Andenken *nt*
memo [ˈmɛməu] *n* Memo *nt*, Mitteilung *f*
memo pad *n* Notizblock *m*
memorable [ˈmɛmərəbl] *adj* (*unforgettable*) unvergesslich
memorial [mɪˈmɔːrɪəl] *n* Denkmal *nt*
memorize [ˈmɛməraɪz] *vt* sich *dat* einprägen
memory [ˈmɛmərɪ] *n* Gedächtnis *nt*; (*sth remembered*) Erinnerung *f*; (*Comput*) Speicher *m*; **in ~ of** zur Erinnerung an *+acc*
memory card *n* Speicherkarte *f*
memory stick *n* (*Comput*) Memorystick® *nt*
men [mɛn] *npl of* **man**
menace [ˈmɛnɪs] *n* Bedrohung *f* ▶ *vt* bedrohen; **a public ~** eine Gefahr für die Öffentlichkeit
mend [mɛnd] *vt* reparieren; (*darn*) flicken ▶ *n*: **to be on the ~** auf dem Wege der Besserung sein
meningitis [mɛnɪnˈdʒaɪtɪs] *n* Hirnhautentzündung *f*
menopause [ˈmɛnəupɔːz] *n*: **the ~** die Wechseljahre *pl*
mental [ˈmɛntl] *adj* geistig
mentality [mɛnˈtælɪtɪ] *n* Mentalität *f*
mentally [ˈmɛntlɪ] *adv*: **~ ill** geisteskrank
mention [ˈmɛnʃən] *n* Erwähnung *f* ▶ *vt* erwähnen; **don't ~ it!** (bitte,) gern geschehen!
menu [ˈmɛnjuː] *n* Menü *nt*; (*printed*) Speisekarte *f*
merchandise [ˈməːtʃəndaɪz] *n* Ware *f*
merchant [ˈməːtʃənt] *n* Kaufmann *m*
merchant bank (Brit) *n* Handelsbank *f*
merciful [ˈməːsɪful] *adj* gnädig
mercifully [ˈməːsɪflɪ] *adv* glücklicherweise
mercury [ˈməːkjurɪ] *n* Quecksilber *nt*
mercy [ˈməːsɪ] *n* Gnade *f*
mere [mɪəʳ] *adj* bloß
merely [ˈmɪəlɪ] *adv* lediglich, bloß
merge [məːdʒ] *vi* (*Comm*) fusionieren; (*colours, sounds, shapes*) ineinander übergehen; (*roads*) zusammenlaufen
merger [ˈməːdʒəʳ] *n* (*Comm*) Fusion *f*
meringue [məˈræŋ] *n* Baiser *nt*
merit [ˈmɛrɪt] *n* (*advantage*) Vorzug *m*; (*achievement*) Verdienst *nt*
merry [ˈmɛrɪ] *adj* vergnügt; (*music*) fröhlich; **M~ Christmas!** fröhliche *or* frohe Weihnachten!
merry-go-round [ˈmɛrɪgəuraund] *n* Karussell *nt*
mess [mɛs] *n* Durcheinander *nt*; (*dirt*) Dreck *m*; **to be in a ~** (*untidy*) unordentlich sein; (*in difficulty*) in Schwierigkeiten stecken; **to be a ~** (*fig: life*) verkorkst sein; **to get o.s. in a ~** in Schwierigkeiten geraten
▶ **mess about** (*inf*) *vi* (*fool around*) herumalbern

▶ **mess about with** (*inf*) *vt fus* (*play around with*) herumfummeln an +*dat* ▶ **mess up** *vt* durcheinanderbringen; (*dirty*) verdrecken
message ['mɛsɪdʒ] *n* Mitteilung *f*, Nachricht *f*; (*meaning*) Aussage *f* ▶ *vt* eine Nachricht senden +*dat*; **she messaged me on Facebook** sie schickte mir eine Facebook-Nachricht; **to get the ~** (*inf*: *fig*) kapieren
message board *n* (*Internet*) Internetforum *nt*
messenger ['mɛsɪndʒəʳ] *n* Bote *m*
messy ['mɛsɪ] *adj* (*dirty*) dreckig; (*untidy*) unordentlich
met [mɛt] *pt*, *pp of* **meet**
metal ['mɛtl] *n* Metall *nt*
metallic [mɪ'tælɪk] *adj* metallisch
meteorology [mi:tɪə'rɔlədʒɪ] *n* Meteorologie *f*
meter ['mi:təʳ] *n* Zähler *m*; (*also*: **parking ~**) Parkuhr *f*; (*US*: *unit*) = **metre**
method ['mɛθəd] *n* Methode *f*
methodical [mɪ'θɔdɪkl] *adj* methodisch
meticulous [mɪ'tɪkjuləs] *adj* (*detail*) genau
metre, (*US*) **meter** ['mi:təʳ] *n* Meter *m or nt*
metric ['mɛtrɪk] *adj* metrisch
metric system *n* metrisches Maßsystem *nt*
Mexico ['mɛksɪkəu] *n* Mexiko *nt*
mice [maɪs] *npl of* **mouse**
microblog ['maɪkrəublɔg] *n* Mikroblog *nt*
microchip ['maɪkrəutʃɪp] *n* Mikrochip *m*
microphone ['maɪkrəfəun] *n* Mikrofon *nt*
microscope ['maɪkrəskəup] *n* Mikroskop *nt*
microwave ['maɪkrəuweɪv] *n* Mikrowelle *f*; (*also*: **~ oven**) Mikrowellenherd *m*
mid- [mɪd] *adj*: **in mid-May** Mitte Mai; **he's in his mid-thirties** er ist Mitte dreißig
midday [mɪd'deɪ] *n* Mittag *m*
middle ['mɪdl] *n* Mitte *f* ▶ *adj* mittlere(r, s); **in the ~ of the night** mitten in der Nacht; **a ~ course** ein Mittelweg *m*
middle-aged [mɪdl'eɪdʒd] *adj* mittleren Alters
Middle Ages *npl* Mittelalter *nt*
middle class *n*, **middle classes** *npl* Mittelstand *m*
middle-class [mɪdl'klɑ:s] *adj* mittelständisch
Middle East *n* Naher Osten *m*
middle name *n* zweiter Vorname *m*
Midlands ['mɪdləndz] (*Brit*) *npl*: **the ~** Mittelengland *nt*
midnight ['mɪdnaɪt] *n* Mitternacht *f*
midst [mɪdst] *n*: **in the ~ of** mitten in +*dat*
midsummer [mɪd'sʌməʳ] *n* Hochsommer *m*; **M~('s) Day** Sommersonnenwende *f*
midway [mɪd'weɪ] *adj*: **we have reached the ~ point** wir haben die Hälfte hinter uns *dat* ▶ *adv* auf halbem Weg
midweek [mɪd'wi:k] *adv* mitten in der Woche ▶ *adj* Mitte der Woche
midwife ['mɪdwaɪf] *n* (*irreg*) Hebamme *f*
midwinter [mɪd'wɪntəʳ] *n*: **in ~** im tiefsten Winter
might [maɪt] *vb see* **may** ▶ *n* Macht *f*; **with all one's ~** mit aller Kraft
mighty ['maɪtɪ] *adj* mächtig
migraine ['mi:greɪn] *n* Migräne *f*
migrant ['maɪgrənt] *n* (*bird*) Zugvogel *m*; (*worker*) Wanderarbeiter(in) *m(f)*
migrate [maɪ'greɪt] *vi* (*bird*) ziehen; (*person*) abwandern
mike [maɪk] *n* = **microphone**
Milan [mɪ'læn] *n* Mailand *nt*
mild [maɪld] *adj* mild; (*gentle*) sanft
mildly ['maɪldlɪ] *adv*: **to put it ~** gelinde gesagt
mildness ['maɪldnɪs] *n* Milde *f*
mile [maɪl] *n* Meile *f*
mileage ['maɪlɪdʒ] *n* Meilenzahl *f*
mileometer [maɪ'lɔmɪtəʳ] *n* ≈ Kilometerzähler *m*
milestone ['maɪlstəun] *n* (*lit*, *fig*) Meilenstein *m*
militant ['mɪlɪtnt] *adj* militant
military ['mɪlɪtərɪ] *adj* (*history*, *leader etc*) Militär-
milk [mɪlk] *n* Milch *f* ▶ *vt* (*lit*, *fig*) melken
milk chocolate *n* Vollmilchschokolade *f*
milkman ['mɪlkmən] *n* (*irreg*) Milchmann *m*

milk shake *n* Milchmixgetränk *nt*
mill [mɪl] *n* Mühle *f*; (*factory*) Fabrik *f*
millennium [mɪˈlɛnɪəm] (*pl* **millenniums** *or* **millennia**) *n* Jahrtausend *nt*
milligram, milligramme [ˈmɪlɪgræm] *n* Milligramm *nt*
millilitre, (*US*) **milliliter** [ˈmɪlɪliːtəʳ] *n* Milliliter *m or nt*
millimetre, (*US*) **millimeter** [ˈmɪlɪmiːtəʳ] *n* Millimeter *m or nt*
million [ˈmɪljən] *n* Million *f*; **a ~ times** (*fig*) tausend Mal, x-mal
millionaire [mɪljəˈnɛəʳ] *n* Millionär *m*
mime [maɪm] *n* Pantomime *f* ▸ *vt* pantomimisch darstellen
mimic [ˈmɪmɪk] *n* Imitator *m* ▸ *vt* (*for amusement*) parodieren; (*animal, person*) nachahmen
mimicry [ˈmɪmɪkrɪ] *n* Nachahmung *f*
mince [mɪns] *vt* (*meat*) durch den Fleischwolf drehen ▸ *n* (Brit: *meat*) Hackfleisch *nt*
mincemeat [ˈmɪnsmiːt] *n süße Gebäckfüllung aus Dörrobst und Sirup*
mince pie *n mit Mincemeat gefülltes Gebäck*
mind [maɪnd] *n* Geist *m*, Verstand *m*; (*thoughts*) Gedanken *pl*; (*memory*) Gedächtnis *nt* ▸ *vt* aufpassen auf *+acc*; (*object to*) etwas haben gegen; **to be out of one's ~** verrückt sein; **it is on my ~** es beschäftigt mich; **to keep** *or* **bear sth in ~** etw nicht vergessen, an etw denken; **to make up one's ~** sich entscheiden; **to change one's ~** es sich *dat* anders überlegen; **"~ the step"** „Vorsicht Stufe"; **do you ~ if ...?** macht es Ihnen etwas aus, wenn ...?; **I don't ~** es ist mir egal; **~ you, ...** allerdings ...; **never ~!** (*it makes no odds*) ist doch egal!; (*don't worry*) macht nichts!
mindfulness [ˈmaɪndfulnəs] *n* Achtsamkeit *f*
mine¹ [maɪn] *n* (*also:* **coal ~, gold ~**) Bergwerk *nt*; (*bomb*) Mine *f*
mine² [maɪn] *pron* meine(r, s); **that book is ~** das Buch ist mein(e)s, das Buch gehört mir; **this is ~** das ist meins; **a friend of ~** ein Freund/eine Freundin von mir
miner [ˈmaɪnəʳ] *n* Bergarbeiter *m*
mineral [ˈmɪnərəl] *n* Mineral *nt*
mineral water *n* Mineralwasser *nt*
mingle [ˈmɪŋgl] *vi*: **to ~ (with)** sich vermischen (mit)
miniature [ˈmɪnətʃəʳ] *adj* (*version etc*) Miniatur-
minibus [ˈmɪnɪbʌs] *n* Kleinbus *m*
minicab [ˈmɪnɪkæb] *n* Kleintaxi *nt*
minimal [ˈmɪnɪml] *adj* minimal
minimize [ˈmɪnɪmaɪz] *vt* auf ein Minimum reduzieren
minimum [ˈmɪnɪməm] (*pl* **minima**) *n* Minimum *nt* ▸ *adj* (*income, speed*) Mindest-
mining [ˈmaɪnɪŋ] *n* Bergbau *m*
miniskirt *n* Minirock *m*
minister [ˈmɪnɪstəʳ] (Brit) *n* (*Pol*) Minister(in) *m*(*f*); (*Rel*) Pfarrer *m*
ministry [ˈmɪnɪstrɪ] (Brit) *n* (*Pol*) Ministerium *nt*
minor [ˈmaɪnəʳ] *adj* kleinere(r, s); (*poet*) unbedeutend; (*planet*) klein; (*Mus*) Moll ▸ *n* Minderjährige(r) *f*(*m*)
minority [maɪˈnɔrɪtɪ] *n* Minderheit *f*
mint [mɪnt] *n* Minze *f*; (*sweet*) Pfefferminz(bonbon) *nt*
mint sauce *n* Minzsoße *f*
minus [ˈmaɪnəs] *prep* minus, weniger; **~ 24°C** 24 Grad unter null
minute¹ [maɪˈnjuːt] *adj* winzig; (*detail*) kleinste(r, s); **in ~ detail** in allen Einzelheiten
minute² [ˈmɪnɪt] *n* Minute *f*; (*fig*) Augenblick *m* ■ **minutes** *npl* (*of meeting*) Protokoll *nt*; **wait a ~!** einen Augenblick *or* Moment!
miracle [ˈmɪrəkl] *n* (*Rel, fig*) Wunder *nt*
miraculous [mɪˈrækjuləs] *adj* (*success, change*) unglaublich
mirage [ˈmɪrɑːʒ] *n* Fata Morgana *f*
mirror [ˈmɪrəʳ] *n* Spiegel *m*
misbehave [mɪsbɪˈheɪv] *vi* sich schlecht benehmen
miscalculation [ˈmɪskælkjuˈleɪʃən] *n* Rechenfehler *m*; (*misjudgement*) Fehleinschätzung *f*
miscarriage [ˈmɪskærɪdʒ] *n* (*Med*) Fehlgeburt *f*
miscellaneous [mɪsɪˈleɪnɪəs] *adj* verschieden
mischief [ˈmɪstʃɪf] *n* (*bad behaviour*) Unfug *m*
mischievous [ˈmɪstʃɪvəs] *adj* (*naughty*) ungezogen; (*playful*) verschmitzt
misconception [ˈmɪskənˈsɛpʃən] *n* fälschliche Annahme *f*

misconduct [mɪsˈkɔndʌkt] *n* Fehlverhalten *nt*
miser [ˈmaɪzəʳ] *n* Geizhals *m*
miserable [ˈmɪzərəbl] *adj* (*unhappy*) unglücklich; (*wretched*) erbärmlich, elend; (*unpleasant: weather*) trostlos; (*: person*) gemein
miserly [ˈmaɪzəlɪ] *adj* geizig
misery [ˈmɪzərɪ] *n* (*unhappiness*) Kummer *m*; (*wretchedness*) Elend *nt*
misfit [ˈmɪsfɪt] *n* Außenseiter(in) *m(f)*
misfortune [mɪsˈfɔːtʃən] *n* Pech *nt*
misguided [mɪsˈgaɪdɪd] *adj* (*opinion, view*) irrig; (*misplaced*) unangebracht
misinform [mɪsɪnˈfɔːm] *vt* falsch informieren
misinterpret [mɪsɪnˈtəːprɪt] *vt* (*gesture, situation*) falsch auslegen
misjudge [mɪsˈdʒʌdʒ] *vt* falsch einschätzen
mislay [mɪsˈleɪ] *vt* (*irreg: like* **lay**) verlegen
mislead [mɪsˈliːd] *vt* (*irreg: like* **lead¹**) irreführen
misleading [mɪsˈliːdɪŋ] *adj* irreführend
misprint [ˈmɪsprɪnt] *n* Druckfehler *m*
mispronounce [mɪsprəˈnauns] *vt* falsch aussprechen
Miss [mɪs] *n* Fräulein *nt*
miss [mɪs] *vt* (*train etc, chance, opportunity*) verpassen; (*target*) verfehlen; (*notice loss of, regret absence of*) vermissen; (*class, meeting*) fehlen bei ▸ *vi* danebentreffen; (*missile, object*) danebengehen
▸ **miss out** (Brit) *vt* auslassen
▸ **miss out on** *vt fus* (*party*) verpassen
missile [ˈmɪsaɪl] *n* (*Mil*) Rakete *f*; (*object thrown*) (Wurf)geschoss *nt*
missing [ˈmɪsɪŋ] *adj* (*lost: person*) vermisst; (*absent, removed*) fehlend; **to go ~** verschwinden
mission [ˈmɪʃən] *n* (*task*) Mission *f*, Auftrag *m*
missionary [ˈmɪʃənrɪ] *n* Missionar(in) *m(f)*
mist [mɪst] *n* Nebel *m*; (*light*) Dunst *m* ▸ *vi* (Brit: *windows: also:* **~ over, ~ up**) beschlagen
mistake [mɪsˈteɪk] *n* Fehler *m* ▸ *vt* (*irreg: like* **take**) (*intentions*) falsch verstehen; **by ~** aus Versehen; **to ~ A for B** A mit B verwechseln
mistaken [mɪsˈteɪkən] *pp of* **mistake** ▸ *adj* falsch; **to be ~** sich irren
mistletoe [ˈmɪsltəu] *n* Mistel *f*
mistreat [mɪsˈtriːt] *vt* schlecht behandeln
mistress [ˈmɪstrɪs] *n* (*lover*) Geliebte *f*
mistrust [mɪsˈtrʌst] *vt* misstrauen *+dat* ▸ *n*: **~ (of)** Misstrauen *nt* (gegenüber)
misty [ˈmɪstɪ] *adj* (*day etc*) neblig; (*glasses, windows*) beschlagen
misunderstand [mɪsʌndəˈstænd] *vt* (*irreg: like* **understand**) falsch verstehen ▸ *vi* es falsch verstehen
misunderstanding [ˈmɪsʌndəˈstændɪŋ] *n* Missverständnis *nt*; (*disagreement*) Meinungsverschiedenheit *f*
mitt [mɪt], **mitten** [ˈmɪtn] *n* Fausthandschuh *m*
mix [mɪks] *vt* mischen; (*drink*) mixen; (*sauce, cake*) zubereiten ▸ *vi*: **to ~ (with)** verkehren (mit) ▸ *n* Mischung *f*; **to ~ sth with sth** etw mit etw vermischen
▸ **mix up** *vt* (*people*) verwechseln; (*things*) durcheinanderbringen
mixed [mɪkst] *adj* gemischt
mixed grill (Brit) *n* Grillteller *m*
mixer [ˈmɪksəʳ] *n* (*for food*) Mixer *m*
mixture [ˈmɪkstʃəʳ] *n* Mischung *f*; (*Med*) Mixtur *f*
mix-up [ˈmɪksʌp] *n* Durcheinander *nt*
ml *abbr* (*= millilitre*) ml
mm *abbr* (*= millimetre*) mm
moan [məun] *n* Stöhnen *nt* ▸ *vi* stöhnen; (*inf: complain*): **to ~ (about)** meckern (über *+acc*)
mobbing [ˈmɔbɪŋ] *n* Mobbing *nt*
mobile [ˈməubaɪl] *adj* beweglich ▸ *n* (*decoration*) Mobile *nt*; (*also:* **~ phone**) Handy *nt*
mobile phone *n* Funktelefon *nt*, Handy *nt*
mobile-phone mast *n* Handymast *m*
mobility [məuˈbɪlɪtɪ] *n* Beweglichkeit *f*
mock [mɔk] *vt* sich lustig machen über *+acc* ▸ *adj* (*battle*) Schein-
mockery [ˈmɔkərɪ] *n* Spott *m*
mod cons [ˈmɔdˈkɔnz] (Brit) *npl* (*= modern conveniences*) Komfort *m*
mode [məud] *n* Form *f*; (*Comput, Tech*) Betriebsart *f*
model [ˈmɔdl] *n* Modell *nt*; (*also:* **fashion ~**) Mannequin *nt*; (*example*)

Muster *nt* ▶ *adj* (*excellent*) vorbildlich; (*small scale: railway etc*) Modell- ▶ *vt* (*with clay etc*) formen ▶ *vi* (*for designer, photographer etc*) als Modell arbeiten
modem [ˈməudɛm] *n* Modem *nt*
moderate *adj* [ˈmɔdərət] gemäßigt; (*amount*) nicht allzu groß ▶ *vt* [ˈmɔdəreɪt] (*tone, demands*) mäßigen
moderation [mɔdəˈreɪʃən] *n* Mäßigung *f*; **in ~** in *or* mit Maßen
modern [ˈmɔdən] *adj* modern
modernize [ˈmɔdənaɪz] *vt* modernisieren
modest [ˈmɔdɪst] *adj* bescheiden
modesty [ˈmɔdɪstɪ] *n* Bescheidenheit *f*
modification [mɔdɪfɪˈkeɪʃən] *n* Änderung *f*
modify [ˈmɔdɪfaɪ] *vt* (ver)ändern
moist [mɔɪst] *adj* feucht
moisten [ˈmɔɪsn] *vt* anfeuchten
moisture [ˈmɔɪstʃəʳ] *n* Feuchtigkeit *f*
moisturizer [ˈmɔɪstʃəraɪzəʳ] *n* Feuchtigkeitscreme *f*
molar [ˈməuləʳ] *n* Backenzahn *m*
mold *etc* [məuld] (*US*) *n*, *vt* = **mould** *etc*
mole [məul] *n* (*on skin*) Leberfleck *m*; (*Zool*) Maulwurf *m*
molecule [ˈmɔlɪkju:l] *n* Molekül *nt*
molest [məˈlɛst] *vt* (*harass*) belästigen
molt (*US*) *vi* = **moult**
molten [ˈməultən] *adj* geschmolzen
mom [mɔm] (*US*) *n* = **mum**
moment [ˈməumənt] *n* Moment *m*, Augenblick *m*; **for a ~** (für) einen Moment *or* Augenblick; **at the ~** momentan; **in a ~** gleich
momentous [məuˈmɛntəs] *adj* (*occasion*) bedeutsam
Monaco [ˈmɔnəkəu] *n* Monaco *nt*
monarchy [ˈmɔnəkɪ] *n* Monarchie *f*
monastery [ˈmɔnəstərɪ] *n* Kloster *nt*
Monday [ˈmʌndɪ] *n* Montag *m*; *see also* **Tuesday**
monetary [ˈmʌnɪtərɪ] *adj* (*system, union*) Währungs-
money [ˈmʌnɪ] *n* Geld *nt*
money order *n* Zahlungsanweisung *f*
mongrel [ˈmʌŋgrəl] *n* Promenadenmischung *f*
monitor [ˈmɔnɪtəʳ] *n* Monitor *m* ▶ *vt* überwachen; (*broadcasts*) mithören
monk [mʌŋk] *n* Mönch *m*
monkey [ˈmʌŋkɪ] *n* Affe *m*
monkey business (*inf*) *n* faule Sachen *pl*
monopolize [məˈnɔpəlaɪz] *vt* beherrschen; (*person*) mit Beschlag belegen
monopoly [məˈnɔpəlɪ] *n* Monopol *nt*
monotonous [məˈnɔtənəs] *adj* monoton, eintönig
monsoon [mɔnˈsu:n] *n* Monsun *m*
monster [ˈmɔnstəʳ] *n* Monstrum *nt*
monstrosity [mɔnˈstrɔsɪtɪ] *n* Ungetüm *nt*, Monstrum *nt*
Montenegro [mɔntɪˈni:grəu] *n* Montenegro *nt*
month [mʌnθ] *n* Monat *m*
monthly [ˈmʌnθlɪ] *adj* monatlich; (*ticket, magazine*) Monats- ▶ *adv* monatlich
monument [ˈmɔnjumənt] *n* Denkmal *nt*
monumental [mɔnjuˈmɛntl] *adj* (*building, statue*) gewaltig
mood [mu:d] *n* Stimmung *f*; (*of person*) Laune *f*, Stimmung *f*; **to be in a good/bad ~** gut/schlecht gelaunt sein; **to be in the ~ for** aufgelegt sein zu
moody [ˈmu:dɪ] *adj* launisch
moon [mu:n] *n* Mond *m*
moonlight [ˈmu:nlaɪt] *n* Mondschein *m*
moonlit [ˈmu:nlɪt] *adj* (*night*) mondhell
moor [muəʳ] *n* (Hoch)moor *nt* ▶ *vt* vertäuen ▶ *vi* anlegen
mooring [ˈmuərɪŋ] *n* Anlegeplatz *m* ▪ **moorings** *npl* (*chains*) Verankerung *f*
moorland [ˈmuələnd] *n* Moorlandschaft *f*, Heidelandschaft *f*
moose [mu:s] *n inv* Elch *m*
mop [mɔp] *n* (*for floor*) Mop *m* ▶ **mop up** *vt* aufwischen
mope [məup] *vi* Trübsal blasen
moped [ˈməupɛd] *n* Moped *nt*
moral [ˈmɔrl] *adj* moralisch; (*welfare, values*) sittlich ▶ *n* Moral *f* ▪ **morals** *npl* (*principles, values*) Moralvorstellungen *pl*
morale [mɔˈrɑ:l] *n* Moral *f*
morality [məˈrælɪtɪ] *n* (*system of morals*) Moral *f*, Ethik *f*
morbid [ˈmɔ:bɪd] *adj* (*imagination*) krankhaft

KEYWORD

more [mɔ:ʳ] *adj* **1** (*greater in number etc*) mehr; **I have more wine/money than you** ich habe mehr Wein/Geld als du

2 (*additional*): **do you want (some) more tea?** möchten Sie noch mehr Tee?; **I have no more money, I don't have any more money** ich habe kein Geld mehr
▶ *pron* **1** (*greater amount*) mehr; **it cost more than we expected** es kostete mehr, als wir erwarteten
2 (*further or additional amount*): **is there any more?** gibt es noch mehr?; **there's no more** es ist nichts mehr da
▶ *adv* mehr; **more dangerous/ difficult/easily** *etc* **(than)** gefährlicher/schwerer/leichter *etc* (als); **more and more** mehr und mehr, immer mehr; **more and more excited/expensive** immer aufgeregter/teurer; **more or less** mehr oder weniger; **more than ever** mehr denn je, mehr als jemals zuvor; **more beautiful than ever** schöner denn je

moreover [mɔːˈrəuvəʳ] *adv* außerdem
morgue [mɔːg] *n* Leichenschauhaus *nt*
morning [ˈmɔːnɪŋ] *n* Morgen *m* ▶ *cpd* Morgen-; **in the ~** morgens; vormittags; (*tomorrow*) morgen früh; **this ~** heute Morgen
morning-after pill *n* Pille *f* danach
morning sickness *n* (Schwangerschafts)übelkeit *f*
Morocco [məˈrɔkəu] *n* Marokko *nt*
moron [ˈmɔːrɔn] (*!*) *n* Schwachkopf *m*
morphine [ˈmɔːfiːn] *n* Morphium *nt*
morsel [ˈmɔːsl] *n* Stückchen *nt*
mortal [ˈmɔːtl] *adj* sterblich; (*wound, combat*) tödlich ▶ *n* (*human being*) Sterbliche(r) *f(m)*
mortality [mɔːˈtælɪtɪ] *n* (*number of deaths*) Todesfälle *pl*
mortality rate *n* Sterblichkeitsziffer *f*
mortally *adv* tödlich
mortgage [ˈmɔːgɪdʒ] *n* Hypothek *f* ▶ *vt* mit einer Hypothek belasten
mortified [ˈmɔːtɪfaɪd] *adj*: **he was ~** er empfand das als beschämend; (*embarrassed*) es war ihm schrecklich peinlich
mortuary [ˈmɔːtjuərɪ] *n* Leichenhalle *f*
mosaic [məuˈzeɪɪk] *n* Mosaik *nt*
Moscow [ˈmɔskəu] *n* Moskau *nt*
Moslem [ˈmɔzləm] *adj*, *n* = **Muslim**
mosque [mɔsk] *n* Moschee *f*
mosquito [mɔsˈkiːtəu] (*pl* **mosquitoes**) *n* Stechmücke *f*; (*in tropics*) Moskito *m*
mosquito net *n* Moskitonetz *nt*
moss [mɔs] *n* Moos *nt*

 KEYWORD

most [məust] *adj* **1** (*almost all*: *people, things etc*) meiste(r, s); **most people** die meisten Leute
2 (*largest, greatest*: *interest, money etc*) meiste(r, s); **who has (the) most money?** wer hat das meiste Geld?
▶ *pron* (*greatest quantity, number*) der/die/das meiste; **most of them** die meisten von ihnen; **most of the time/work** die meiste Zeit/Arbeit; **to make the most of sth** das Beste aus etw machen; **for the most part** zum größten Teil; **at the (very) most** (aller)höchstens
▶ *adv* **1** (+ *vb*: *spend, eat, work etc*) am meisten; **he ate (the) most** er hat am meisten gegessen
2 (+ *adv*: *carefully, easily etc*) äußerst
3 (+ *adj*): **the most intelligent/ expensive** *etc* der/die/das intelligenteste/teuerste ... *etc*
4 (*very*: *polite, interesting etc*) höchst; **a most interesting book** ein höchst interessantes Buch

mostly [ˈməustlɪ] *adv* (*chiefly*) hauptsächlich; (*usually*) meistens
MOT (Brit) *n abbr* (= *Ministry of Transport*): **~ (test)** ≈ TÜV *m*
motel [məuˈtɛl] *n* Motel *nt*
moth [mɔθ] *n* Nachtfalter *m*; (*also*: **clothes ~**) Motte *f*
mothball [ˈmɔθbɔːl] *n* Mottenkugel *f*
mother [ˈmʌðəʳ] *n* Mutter *f* ▶ *vt* (*pamper, protect*) bemuttern
mother-in-law [ˈmʌðərɪnlɔː] *n* Schwiegermutter *f*
mother-to-be [ˈmʌðətəˈbiː] *n* werdende Mutter *f*
motif [məuˈtiːf] *n* Motiv *nt*
motion [ˈməuʃən] *n* Bewegung *f*; (*proposal*) Antrag *m*
motionless [ˈməuʃənlɪs] *adj* reg(ungs)los
motivate [ˈməutɪveɪt] *vt* motivieren
motive [ˈməutɪv] *n* Motiv *nt*
motor [ˈməutəʳ] *n* Motor *m*; (Brit *inf*: *car*) Auto *nt* ▶ *cpd* (*industry, trade*) Auto(mobil)-

motorbike [ˈməutəbaɪk] *n* Motorrad *nt*
motorboat [ˈməutəbəut] *n* Motorboot *nt*
motorcycle [ˈməutəsaɪkl] *n* Motorrad *nt*
motoring [ˈməutərɪŋ] (BRIT) *n* Autofahren *nt*
motorist [ˈməutərɪst] *n* Autofahrer(in) *m(f)*
motor oil *n* Motorenöl *nt*
motor racing (BRIT) *n* Autorennen *nt*
motor scooter *n* Motorroller *m*
motor show *n* Automobilausstellung *f*
motor vehicle *n* Kraftfahrzeug *nt*
motorway [ˈməutəweɪ] (BRIT) *n* Autobahn *f*
motto [ˈmɔtəu] (*pl* **mottoes**) *n* Motto *nt*
mould, (*US*) **mold** [məuld] *n* (*cast*) Form *f*; (*mildew*) Schimmel *m* ▸ *vt* (*lit, fig*) formen
mouldy [ˈməuldɪ] *adj* schimmelig
moult, (*US*) **molt** [məult] *vi* (*animal*) sich haaren; (*bird*) sich mausern
mount [maunt] *n* (*horse*) Pferd *nt*; (*for picture*) Passepartout *nt* ▸ *vt* (*horse*) besteigen; (*exhibition etc*) vorbereiten; (*picture*) mit einem Passepartout versehen ▸ *vi* (*increase*) steigen
▸ **mount up** *vi* (*costs, savings*) sich summieren
mountain [ˈmauntɪn] *n* Berg *m*
mountain bike *n* Mountainbike *nt*
mountaineer [mauntɪˈnɪəʳ] *n* Bergsteiger(in) *m(f)*
mountaineering [mauntɪˈnɪərɪŋ] *n* Bergsteigen *nt*
mountainous [ˈmauntɪnəs] *adj* gebirgig
mountainside [ˈmauntɪnsaɪd] *n* (Berg)hang *m*
mourn [mɔːn] *vt* betrauern ▸ *vi*: **to ~ (for)** trauern (um)
mourner [ˈmɔːnəʳ] *n* Trauernde(r) *f(m)*
mournful [ˈmɔːnful] *adj* traurig
mourning [ˈmɔːnɪŋ] *n* Trauer *f*; **to be in ~** trauern
mouse [maus] (*pl* **mice**) *n* (*Zool, Comput*) Maus *f*
mouse mat, (*US*) **mouse pad** *n* Mauspad *nt*
mousetrap [ˈmaustræp] *n* Mausefalle *f*
mousse [muːs] *n* (*Culin*) Mousse *f*; (*cosmetic*) Schaumfestiger *m*
moustache, (*US*) **mustache** [məsˈtɑːʃ] *n* Schnurrbart *m*
mouth [mauθ] *n* Mund *m*; (*of cave, hole, bottle*) Öffnung *f*; (*of river*) Mündung *f*
mouthful [ˈmauθful] *n* (*of food*) Bissen *m*; (*of drink*) Schluck *m*
mouth organ *n* Mundharmonika *f*
mouthwash [ˈmauθwɔʃ] *n* Mundwasser *nt*
mouth-watering [ˈmauθwɔːtərɪŋ] *adj* appetitlich
move [muːv] *n* (*movement*) Bewegung *f*; (*in game*) Zug *m*; (*change: of house*) Umzug *m* ▸ *vt* bewegen; (*furniture*) (ver)rücken; (*car*) umstellen; (*emotionally*) bewegen, ergreifen ▸ *vi* sich bewegen; (*traffic*) vorankommen; (*in game*) ziehen; (*also*: **~ house**) umziehen; **it's my ~** ich bin am Zug; **to get a ~ on** sich beeilen
▸ **move about** *vi* sich (hin- und her) bewegen; (*travel*) unterwegs sein
▸ **move away** *vi* (*from town, area*) wegziehen
▸ **move in** *vi* (*to house*) einziehen
▸ **move off** *vi* (*car*) abfahren
▸ **move on** *vi* (*leave*) weitergehen; (*travel*) weiterfahren
▸ **move out** *vi* (*of house*) ausziehen
▸ **move up** *vi* (*deputy*) aufrücken
movement [ˈmuːvmənt] *n* (*action, group*) Bewegung *f*
movie [ˈmuːvɪ] *n* Film *m*; **to go to the movies** ins Kino gehen
moving [ˈmuːvɪŋ] *adj* beweglich; (*emotional*) ergreifend
mow [məu] (*pt* **mowed**, *pp* **mowed** *or* **mown**) *vt* mähen
mower [ˈməuəʳ] *n* (*also*: **lawnmower**) Rasenmäher *m*
mown [məun] *pp of* **mow**
Mozambique [məuzəmˈbiːk] *n* Mosambik *nt*
MP *n abbr* (= *Member of Parliament*) ≈ MdB
MP3 player *n* (*Comput*) MP3-Spieler *m*
mph *abbr* (= *miles per hour*) Meilen pro Stunde
Mr [ˈmɪstəʳ] *n*: **Mr Smith** Herr Smith
Mrs [ˈmɪsɪz] *n*: **~ Smith** Frau Smith
MS *n abbr* (= *multiple sclerosis*) MS *f*

Ms [mɪz] *n* (= *Miss or Mrs*): **Ms Smith** Frau Smith

Ms

Der Titel **Ms** ersetzt *Mrs* (Frau) oder *Miss* (Fräulein), um die herkömmliche Unterscheidung zwischen verheirateten und ledigen Frauen zu vermeiden.

Mt *abbr* (*Geog*) = **mount**

KEYWORD

much [mʌtʃ] *adj* (*time, money, effort*) viel; **how much money/time do you need?** wie viel Geld/Zeit brauchen Sie?; **as much as** so viel wie
▶ *pron* viel; **how much is it?** was kostet es?
▶ *adv* **1** (*greatly, a great deal*) sehr; **thank you very much** vielen Dank, danke sehr; **I read as much as I can** ich lese so viel wie ich kann
2 (*by far*) viel; **I'm much better now** mir geht es jetzt viel besser
3 (*almost*) fast; **how are you feeling? — much the same** wie fühlst du dich? — fast genauso

muck [mʌk] *n* (*dirt*) Dreck *m*
▶ **muck about** (*inf*) *vi* (*fool about*) herumalbern
▶ **muck up** (*inf*) *vt* (*exam etc*) verpfuschen

mucky [ˈmʌkɪ] *adj* (*dirty*) dreckig

mucus [ˈmjuːkəs] *n* Schleim *m*

mud [mʌd] *n* Schlamm *m*

muddle [ˈmʌdl] *n* (*mess*) Durcheinander *nt* ▶ *vt* (*also*: **~ up**) durcheinanderbringen; **to be in a ~** völlig durcheinander sein

muddled *adj* konfus

muddy [ˈmʌdɪ] *adj* (*floor*) schmutzig; (*field*) schlammig

mudguard [ˈmʌdgɑːd] (Brit) *n* Schutzblech *nt*

muesli [ˈmjuːzlɪ] *n* Müsli *nt*

muffin [ˈmʌfɪn] *n kleiner runder Rührkuchen*; (Brit) *weiches, flaches Milchbrötchen, meist warm gegessen*

muffle [ˈmʌfl] *vt* (*sound*) dämpfen

muffler [ˈmʌfləʳ] *n* (*US Aut*) Auspufftopf *m*

mug [mʌg] *n* (*cup*) Becher *m*; (*inf*: *fool*) Trottel *m* ▶ *vt* (auf der Straße) überfallen

mugging [ˈmʌgɪŋ] *n* Straßenraub *m*

muggy [ˈmʌgɪ] *adj* (*weather, day*) schwül

mule [mjuːl] *n* Maultier *nt*

mulled [mʌld] *adj*: **~ wine** Glühwein *m*

mull over [mʌl-] *vt* sich *dat* durch den Kopf gehen lassen

multicoloured, (*US*) **multicolored** [ˈmʌltɪkʌləd] *adj* mehrfarbig

multicultural *adj* multikulturell

multigrain [ˈmʌltɪgreɪn] *adj* Mehrkorn-

multilingual *adj* mehrsprachig

multinational [mʌltɪˈnæʃənl] *n* Multi *m* (*inf*)

multiple [ˈmʌltɪpl] *adj* (*injuries*) mehrfach; (*interests, causes*) vielfältig ▶ *n* Vielfache(s) *nt*

multiple-choice [ˈmʌltɪpltʃɔɪs] *adj* (*question etc*) Multiple-Choice-

multiple sclerosis *n* multiple Sklerose *f*

multiplex [ˈmʌltɪplɛks] *n*: **~ (cinema)** Multiplexkino *nt* ▶ *adj* (*Tech*) Mehrfach-

multiplication [mʌltɪplɪˈkeɪʃən] *n* Multiplikation *f*

multiply [ˈmʌltɪplaɪ] *vt* multiplizieren ▶ *vi* (*breed*) sich vermehren

multi-purpose [ˈmʌltɪˈpəːpəs] *adj* Mehrzweck-

multistorey (Brit) *adj* (*building, car park*) mehrstöckig

mum [mʌm] (Brit *inf*) *n* Mutti *f*, Mama *f*

mumble [ˈmʌmbl] *vt, vi* (*quietly*) murmeln

mummy [ˈmʌmɪ] *n* (Brit: *mother*) Mami *f*; (*embalmed body*) Mumie *f*

mumps [mʌmps] *n* Mumps *m or f*

munch [mʌntʃ] *vt, vi* mampfen

Munich [ˈmjuːnɪk] *n* München *nt*

municipal [mjuːˈnɪsɪpl] *adj* städtisch

mural [ˈmjuərl] *n* Wandgemälde *nt*

murder [ˈməːdəʳ] *n* Mord *m* ▶ *vt* ermorden

murderer [ˈməːdərəʳ] *n* Mörder *m*

murky [ˈməːkɪ] *adj* düster; (*water*) trübe

murmur [ˈməːməʳ] *vt, vi* murmeln

muscle [ˈmʌsl] *n* Muskel *m*

muscular [ˈmʌskjuləʳ] *adj* (*pain, dystrophy*) Muskel-; (*person, build*) muskulös
museum [mjuːˈzɪəm] *n* Museum *nt*
mushroom [ˈmʌʃrum] *n* (*edible*) (essbarer) Pilz *m*; (*button mushroom*) Champignon *m* ▶ *vi* (*fig: buildings etc*) aus dem Boden schießen
mushy [ˈmʌʃɪ] *adj* (*consistency*) breiig; **~ peas** Erbsenbrei *m*
music [ˈmjuːzɪk] *n* Musik *f*; (*written music, score*) Noten *pl*
musical [ˈmjuːzɪkl] *adj* musikalisch; (*sound, tune*) melodisch ▶ *n* Musical *nt*
musically *adv* musikalisch
musician [mjuːˈzɪʃən] *n* Musiker(in) *m(f)*
Muslim [ˈmʌzlɪm] *adj* moslemisch ▶ *n* Moslem *m*, Moslime *f*
mussel [ˈmʌsl] *n* (Mies)muschel *f*
must [mʌst] *aux vb* müssen; (*in negative*) dürfen ▶ *n* Muss *nt*; **I ~ do it** ich muss es tun; **you ~ not do that** das darfst du nicht tun; **he ~ be there by now** jetzt müsste er schon dort sein; **you ~ come and see me soon** Sie müssen mich bald besuchen; **I ~ have made a mistake** ich muss mich geirrt haben; **the film is a ~** den Film muss man unbedingt gesehen haben
mustache [ˈmʌstæʃ] (*US*) *n* = **moustache**
mustard [ˈmʌstəd] *n* Senf *m*
mustn't [ˈmʌsnt] = **must not**
mutter [ˈmʌtəʳ] *vt, vi* murmeln
mutton [ˈmʌtn] *n* Hammelfleisch *nt*
mutual [ˈmjuːtʃuəl] *adj* (*feeling, attraction*) gegenseitig

KEYWORD

my [maɪ] *adj* mein(e); **I've washed my hair/cut my finger** ich habe mir die Haare gewaschen/mir *or* mich in den Finger geschnitten

Myanmar [ˈmaɪænmɑːʳ] *n* Myanmar *nt*
myself [maɪˈsɛlf] *pron* (*acc*) mich; (*dat*) mir; (*emphatic*) selbst
mysterious [mɪsˈtɪərɪəs] *adj* geheimnisvoll, mysteriös
mystery [ˈmɪstərɪ] *n* (*puzzle*) Rätsel *nt*; (*strangeness*) Rätselhaftigkeit *f*
mystify [ˈmɪstɪfaɪ] *vt* vor ein Rätsel stellen
myth [mɪθ] *n* Mythos *m*; (*fallacy*) Märchen *nt*
mythical [ˈmɪθɪkl] *adj* mythisch; (*jobs, opportunities etc*) fiktiv
mythology [mɪˈθɔlədʒɪ] *n* Mythologie *f*

N [ɛn] *abbr* (= *north*) N
nag [næg] *vt* herumnörgeln an +*dat* ▶ *vi* nörgeln
nagging [ˈnægɪŋ] *adj* (*doubt, suspicion*) quälend
nail [neɪl] *n* Nagel *m* ▶ *vt*: **to ~ sth to sth** etw an etw *acc* nageln; **to ~ sb down (to sth)** jdn (auf etw *acc*) festnageln
nailbrush [ˈneɪlbrʌʃ] *n* Nagelbürste *f*
nail clippers *npl* Nagelknipser *m*
nailfile [ˈneɪlfaɪl] *n* Nagelfeile *f*
nail polish *n* Nagellack *m*
nail polish remover *n* Nagellackentferner *m*
nail scissors *npl* Nagelschere *f*
nail varnish (Brit) *n* = **nail polish**
naive [nɑːˈiːv] *adj* naiv
naked [ˈneɪkɪd] *adj* nackt
name [neɪm] *n* Name *m* ▶ *vt* nennen; (*identify*) (beim Namen) nennen; **what's your ~?** wie heißen Sie?; **my ~ is Peter** ich heiße Peter; **to give sb a bad ~** jdn in Verruf bringen
namely [ˈneɪmlɪ] *adv* nämlich
nameplate [ˈneɪmpleɪt] *n* Namensschild *nt*
Namibia [nɑːˈmɪbɪə] *n* Namibia *nt*
nan bread [nɑːn-] *n* Nan-Brot *nt*, *fladenförmiges Weißbrot als Beilage zu indischen Gerichten*
nanny [ˈnænɪ] *n* Kindermädchen *nt*
nap [næp] *n* Schläfchen *nt*; **to have a ~** ein Schläfchen *or* ein Nickerchen (*inf*) machen
napkin [ˈnæpkɪn] *n* (*also*: **table ~**) Serviette *f*
Naples [ˈneɪplz] *n* Neapel *nt*
nappy [ˈnæpɪ] (Brit) *n* Windel *f*
narcotic [nɑːˈkɔtɪk] *n* Narkotikum *nt*; **~ drug** Rauschgift *nt*
narrate [nəˈreɪt] *vt* erzählen
narration [nəˈreɪʃən] *n* Kommentar *m*
narrator [nəˈreɪtəʳ] *n* Erzähler(in) *m(f)*
narrow [ˈnærəu] *adj* eng; (*ledge etc*) schmal; (*majority, advantage, victory, defeat*) knapp ▶ *vi* sich verengen; **to have a ~ escape** mit knapper Not davonkommen; **to ~ sth down (to sth)** etw (auf etw *acc*) beschränken
narrow-minded [nærəuˈmaɪndɪd] *adj* engstirnig
nasty [ˈnɑːstɪ] *adj* (*remark*) gehässig; (*person*) gemein; (*taste, smell*) ekelhaft; (*wound, disease, accident, shock*) schlimm
nation [ˈneɪʃən] *n* Nation *f*
national [ˈnæʃənl] *adj* (*character, flag*) National-; (*interests*) Staats- ▶ *n* Staatsbürger(in) *m(f)*
national anthem *n* Nationalhymne *f*
National Health Service (Brit) *n* Staatlicher Gesundheitsdienst *m*

National Health Service

Seit seiner Gründung 1948 ist es das Ziel des **National Health Service** (oder *NHS*), allen im Vereinigten Königreiches wohnhaften Personen medizinische Versorgung zu bieten. Es handelt sich um das größte staatliche Gesundheitssystem weltweit und wird aus Steuergeldern finanziert. Das Grundprinzip des *NHS* ist die kostenlose medizinische Behandlung für alle, unabhängig ihres Einkommens. Bis auf gewisse Ausnahmen (vor allem Zahnbehandlung und Medikamente in England, Wales und Nordirland) sind alle Leistungen kostenlos, einschließlich der Sprechstunden und des Krankenhausaufenthalts. Die vier Länder des Vereinigten Königreichs besitzen alle ihr eigenes Gesundheitssystem, das unabhängig finanziert und verwaltet wird. Das *NHS* ist aufgrund der langen Wartezeit für Operationen und der Unterbesetzung in den

Krankenhäusern häufig der Kritik ausgesetzt, und diese Lage soll regelmäßig anhand Reformen verbessert werden.

National Insurance (BRIT) *n* Sozialversicherung *f*

NATIONAL INSURANCE

Die **National Insurance** ist ein System von Pflichtbeiträgen der Arbeitnehmer (als Quellensteuer) und Arbeitgeber Großbritanniens und Nordirlands, die einen Anteil der Kosten verschiedener Sozialleistungen tragen: Rente, Mutterschaftsurlaub, Arbeitslosengeld, Erwerbsunfähigkeitsrente. Sie wurde 1911 als Versicherungssystem für Gesundheit und Arbeitslosigkeit gegründet und seitdem erheblich erweitert.

nationality [næʃəˈnælɪtɪ] *n* Staatsangehörigkeit *f*, Nationalität *f*
nationalize [ˈnæʃnəlaɪz] *vt* verstaatlichen
national park *n* Nationalpark *m*
national service *n* Wehrdienst *m*
National Trust (BRIT) *siehe Info-Artikel*

NATIONAL TRUST

Der **National Trust** ist ein 1895 gegründeter Natur- und Denkmalschutzverband in Großbritannien, der Gebäude und Gelände von besonderem historischem oder ästhetischem Interesse erhält und der Öffentlichkeit zugänglich macht. Viele Gebäude im Besitz des *National Trust* sind (z. T. gegen ein Eintrittsgeld) zu besichtigen.

nationwide [ˈneɪʃənwaɪd] *adj, adv* landesweit
native [ˈneɪtɪv] *n* Einheimische(r) *f(m)* ▶ *adj* einheimisch; (*country*) Heimat-; (*language*) Mutter-; (*innate*) angeboren; **a ~ of Germany, a ~ German** ein gebürtiger Deutscher, eine gebürtige Deutsche
Native American *n* Ureinwohner(in) *m(f)* Amerikas
native speaker *n* Muttersprachler(in) *m(f)*
nativity play [nəˈtɪvɪtɪ-] *n* Krippenspiel *nt*
NATO [ˈneɪtəu] *n abbr* (= *North Atlantic Treaty Organization*) NATO *f*
natural [ˈnætʃrəl] *adj* natürlich; (*disaster*) Natur-; (*innate*) angeboren
natural gas *n* Erdgas *nt*
naturally [ˈnætʃrəlɪ] *adv* natürlich; (*occur, cheerful, talented, blonde*) von Natur aus
natural resources *npl* Naturschätze *pl*
nature [ˈneɪtʃə^r] *n* (*also*: **N~**) Natur *f*; (*kind, sort*) Art *f*; **by ~** von Natur aus
nature reserve (BRIT) *n* Naturschutzgebiet *nt*
naughty [ˈnɔːtɪ] *adj* (*child*) ungezogen
nausea [ˈnɔːsɪə] *n* Übelkeit *f*
nautical [ˈnɔːtɪkl] *adj* (*chart*) See-
nautical mile *n* Seemeile *f*
nave [neɪv] *n* Hauptschiff *nt*
navel [ˈneɪvl] *n* Nabel *m*
navigate [ˈnævɪgeɪt] *vi* navigieren; (*Aut*) den Fahrer dirigieren
navigation [nævɪˈgeɪʃən] *n* Navigation *f*
navy [ˈneɪvɪ] *n* (Kriegs)marine *f* ▶ *adj* marineblau
Nazi [ˈnɑːtsɪ] *n* Nazi *m*
NB *abbr* (= *nota bene*) NB
NE *abbr* = **north-east**
near [nɪə^r] *adj* nahe ▶ *adv* nahe; (*almost*) fast, beinahe ▶ *prep* (*also*: **~ to**: *in space*) nahe an +*dat*; (: *in time*) um *acc* ... herum; (: *in situation, in intimacy*) nahe +*dat*; **in the ~ future** in naher Zukunft, bald; **a ~ tragedy** beinahe eine Tragödie; **~ here/there** hier/dort in der Nähe
nearby [nɪəˈbaɪ] *adj* nahe gelegen ▶ *adv* in der Nähe
nearly [ˈnɪəlɪ] *adv* fast
near miss *n* Beinahezusammenstoß *m*; **that was a ~** (*shot*) das war knapp daneben
nearside [ˈnɪəsaɪd] (*Aut*) *n*: **the ~** (*when driving on left*) die linke Seite; (*when driving on right*) die rechte Seite
near-sighted [nɪəˈsaɪtɪd] *adj* kurzsichtig
neat [niːt] *adj* ordentlich; (*handwriting*) sauber; (*spirits*) pur

necessarily [ˈnɛsɪsərɪlɪ] *adv* notwendigerweise; **not ~** nicht unbedingt
necessary [ˈnɛsɪsrɪ] *adj* notwendig, nötig; **it is ~ to …** man muss …
necessity [nɪˈsɛsɪtɪ] *n* Notwendigkeit *f*; **the necessities (of life)** das Notwendigste (zum Leben)
neck [nɛk] *n* Hals *m*
necklace [ˈnɛklɪs] *n* (Hals)kette *f*
necktie [ˈnɛktaɪ] (*esp US*) *n* Krawatte *f*
nectarine [ˈnɛktərɪn] *n* Nektarine *f*
née [neɪ] *prep*: **~ Scott** geborene Scott
need [ni:d] *n* (*necessity*) Notwendigkeit *f*; (*requirement*) Bedürfnis *nt*; (*poverty*) Not *f* ▶ *vt* brauchen; **to be in ~ of sth** etw nötig haben; **there's no ~ to get so worked up about it** du brauchst dich darüber nicht so aufzuregen; **he had no ~ to work** er hatte es nicht nötig zu arbeiten; **I ~ to do it** ich muss es tun; **you don't ~ to go, you needn't go** du brauchst nicht zu gehen
needle [ˈni:dl] *n* Nadel *f*
needless [ˈni:dlɪs] *adj* unnötig; **~ to say** natürlich
needlessly [ˈni:dlɪslɪ] *adv* unnötig
needy [ˈni:dɪ] *adj* bedürftig
negative [ˈnɛgətɪv] *adj* negativ; (*answer*) abschlägig ▶ *n* (*Phot*) Negativ *nt*; (*Ling*) Verneinungswort *nt*
neglect [nɪˈglɛkt] *vt* vernachlässigen ▶ *n* Vernachlässigung *f*
negligence [ˈnɛglɪdʒəns] *n* Nachlässigkeit *f*
negligent [ˈnɛglɪdʒənt] *adj* nachlässig
negligible [ˈnɛglɪdʒɪbl] *adj* geringfügig
negotiate [nɪˈgəuʃɪeɪt] *vi* verhandeln
negotiation [nɪgəuʃɪˈeɪʃən] *n* Verhandlung *f*
neigh [neɪ] *vi* wiehern
neighbour, (*US*) **neighbor** [ˈneɪbə^r] *n* Nachbar(in) *m(f)*
neighbourhood [ˈneɪbəhud] *n* (*people*) Nachbarschaft *f*
neighbouring [ˈneɪbərɪŋ] *adj* benachbart
neither [ˈnaɪðə^r] *conj*: **I didn't move and ~ did John** ich bewegte mich nicht und John auch nicht ▶ *pron* keine(r, s) (von beiden) ▶ *adv*: **~ … nor …** weder … noch …
neon [ˈni:ɔn] *n* Neon *nt*
neon sign *n* Neonreklame *f*
nephew [ˈnɛvju:] *n* Neffe *m*
nerd [nə:d] (*pej*) *n* Schwachkopf *m*
nerve [nə:v] *n* (*Anat*) Nerv *m*; **he gets on my nerves** er geht mir auf die Nerven; **to lose one's ~** die Nerven verlieren
nerve-racking [ˈnə:vrækɪŋ] *adj* nervenaufreibend
nervous [ˈnə:vəs] *adj* (*anxious*) nervös; **to be ~ of/about** Angst haben vor *+dat*
nervous breakdown *n* Nervenzusammenbruch *m*
nest [nɛst] *n* Nest *nt* ▶ *vi* nisten
net [nɛt] *n* Netz *nt* ▶ *adj* (*Comm*) Netto-
netball [ˈnɛtbɔ:l] *n* Netzball *m*
Netherlands [ˈnɛðələndz] *npl*: **the ~** die Niederlande *pl*
nettle [ˈnɛtl] *n* Nessel *f*
network [ˈnɛtwə:k] *n* Netz *nt*; (*TV, Radio*) Sendenetz *nt*
neurotic [njuəˈrɔtɪk] *adj* neurotisch
neuter [ˈnju:tə^r] *adj* (*Ling*) sächlich
neutral [ˈnju:trəl] *adj* neutral ▶ *n* (*Aut*) Leerlauf *m*
never [ˈnɛvə^r] *adv* nie; (*not*) nicht; **~ in my life** noch nie; *see also* **mind**
never-ending [nɛvərˈɛndɪŋ] *adj* endlos
nevertheless [nɛvəðəˈlɛs] *adv* trotzdem
new [nju:] *adj* neu; **to be ~ to sb** jdm neu sein
newcomer [ˈnju:kʌmə^r] *n* Neuankömmling *m*; (*in job*) Neuling *m*
Newfoundland [ˈnju:fənlənd] *n* Neufundland *nt*
newly [ˈnju:lɪ] *adv* neu
newly-weds [ˈnju:lɪwɛdz] *npl* Frischvermählte *pl*
new moon *n* Neumond *m*
news [nju:z] *n* Nachricht *f*; **a piece of ~** eine Neuigkeit; **the ~** (*Radio, TV*) die Nachrichten *pl*
newsagent [ˈnju:zeɪdʒənt] (*Brit*) *n* Zeitungshändler(in) *m(f)*
news bulletin *n* Bulletin *nt*
newsdealer [ˈnju:zdi:lə^r] (*US*) *n* = **newsagent**
newsflash [ˈnju:zflæʃ] *n* Kurzmeldung *f*
newsgroup [ˈnju:zgru:p] *n* (*Comput*) Diskussionsforum *nt*, Newsgroup *f*
newsletter [ˈnju:zlɛtə^r] *n* Mitteilungsblatt *nt*
newspaper [ˈnju:zpeɪpə^r] *n* Zeitung *f*

New Year *n* neues Jahr *nt*; (*New Year's Day*) Neujahr *nt*; **Happy ~!** (ein) glückliches *or* frohes neues Jahr!
New Year's Day *n* Neujahr *nt*, Neujahrstag *m*
New Year's Eve *n* Silvester *nt*
New York [-ˈjɔːk] *n* New York *nt*
New Zealand [-ˈziːlənd] *n* Neuseeland *nt* ▶ *adj* neuseeländisch
New Zealander [-ˈziːləndəʳ] *n* Neuseeländer(in) *m(f)*
next [nɛkst] *adj* nächste(r, s); (*room*) Neben- ▶ *adv* dann; (*do, happen*) als Nächstes; **~ time** das nächste Mal; **who's ~?** wer ist der Nächste?; **the week after ~** übernächste Woche; **~ to** neben *+dat*; **~ to nothing** so gut wie nichts; **the ~ best** der/die/das Nächstbeste
next door *adv* nebenan
NHS (Brit) *n abbr* = **National Health Service**
Niagara Falls [naɪˈægərə-] *npl* Niagarafälle *pl*
nibble [ˈnɪbl] *vt* knabbern; (*bite*) knabbern an *+dat*
Nicaragua [nɪkəˈrægjuə] *n* Nicaragua *nt*
nice [naɪs] *adj* nett; (*holiday, weather, picture etc*) schön; (*taste*) gut; (*person, clothes etc*) hübsch
nicely [ˈnaɪslɪ] *adv* (*attractively*) hübsch; (*satisfactorily*) gut
nick [nɪk] *vt* (Brit *inf*: *steal*) klauen
nickel [ˈnɪkl] *n* Nickel *nt*; (*US*) Fünfcentstück *nt*
nickname [ˈnɪkneɪm] *n* Spitzname *m*
nicotine [ˈnɪkətiːn] *n* Nikotin *nt*
nicotine patch *n* Nikotinpflaster *nt*
niece [niːs] *n* Nichte *f*
Nigeria [naɪˈdʒɪərɪə] *n* Nigeria *nt*
night [naɪt] *n* Nacht *f*; (*evening*) Abend *m*; **at ~, by ~** nachts, abends
nightcap [ˈnaɪtkæp] *n* Schlaftrunk *m*
nightclub [ˈnaɪtklʌb] *n* Nachtlokal *nt*
nightdress [ˈnaɪtdrɛs] *n* Nachthemd *nt*
nightie [ˈnaɪtɪ] *n* = **nightdress**
nightingale [ˈnaɪtɪŋgeɪl] *n* Nachtigall *f*
nightlife [ˈnaɪtlaɪf] *n* Nachtleben *nt*
nightly [ˈnaɪtlɪ] *adv* jede Nacht; (*every evening*) jeden Abend
nightmare [ˈnaɪtmɛəʳ] *n* Albtraum *m*
night-time [ˈnaɪttaɪm] *n* Nacht *f*
nil [nɪl] *n* (Brit *Sport*) Null *f*
Nile [naɪl] *n*: **the ~** der Nil
nine [naɪn] *num* neun
nineteen [ˈnaɪnˈtiːn] *num* neunzehn
nineteenth [naɪnˈtiːnθ] *num* neunzehnte(r, s)
ninetieth [ˈnaɪntɪɪəθ] *adj* neunzigste(r, s)
ninety [ˈnaɪntɪ] *num* neunzig
ninth [naɪnθ] *num* neunte(r, s) ▶ *n* Neuntel *nt*
nipple [ˈnɪpl] *n* (*Anat*) Brustwarze *f*
nitrogen [ˈnaɪtrədʒən] *n* Stickstoff *m*

 **KEYWORD**

no [nəu] (*pl* **noes**) *adv* (*opposite of "yes"*) nein; **no thank you** nein danke
▶ *adj* (*not any*) kein(e); **I have no money/time/books** ich habe kein Geld/keine Zeit/keine Bücher; **"no smoking"** „Rauchen verboten"
▶ *n* Nein *nt*; **there were 20 noes and one abstention** es gab 20 Neinstimmen und eine Enthaltung

nobility [nəuˈbɪlɪtɪ] *n* Adel *m*
noble [ˈnəubl] *adj* edel; (*aristocratic*) ad(e)lig
nobody [ˈnəubədɪ] *pron* niemand, keiner ▶ *n*: **he's a ~** er ist ein Niemand *m*
no-claims bonus [nəuˈkleɪmz-] *n* Schadenfreiheitsrabatt *m*
nod [nɔd] *vi* nicken ▶ *vt*: **to ~ one's head** mit dem Kopf nicken
▶ **nod off** *vi* einnicken
noise [nɔɪz] *n* Geräusch *nt*; (*din*) Lärm *m*
noisy [ˈnɔɪzɪ] *adj* laut
nominate [ˈnɔmɪneɪt] *vt* nominieren; (*appoint*) ernennen
nominee [nɔmɪˈniː] *n* Kandidat(in) *m(f)*
non- [nɔn] *pref* nicht-, Nicht-
non-alcoholic [nɔnælkəˈhɔlɪk] *adj* alkoholfrei
none [nʌn] *pron* (*not one*) kein(e, er, es); (*not any*) nichts; **~ of us** keiner von uns; **I've ~ left** (*not any*) ich habe nichts übrig; (*not one*) ich habe kein(e, en, es) übrig; **I was ~ the wiser** ich war auch nicht klüger
nonentity [nɔˈnɛntɪtɪ] *n* (*person*) Nichts *nt*
nonetheless [ˈnʌnðəˈlɛs] *adv* nichtsdestoweniger, trotzdem
non-event [nɔnɪˈvɛnt] *n* Reinfall *m*
non-existent [nɔnɪgˈzɪstənt] *adj* nicht vorhanden

non-fiction [nɔn'fɪkʃən] *n* Sachbücher *pl*
non-returnable [nɔnrə'tə:nəbl] *adj*: **~ bottle** Einwegflasche *f*
nonsense ['nɔnsəns] *n* Unsinn *m*
non-smoker ['nɔn'sməukəʳ] *n* Nichtraucher(in) *m(f)*
non-stop ['nɔn'stɔp] *adj* ununterbrochen; (*flight*) Nonstop- ▶ *adv* ununterbrochen; (*fly*) nonstop
noodles ['nu:dlz] *npl* Nudeln *pl*
noon [nu:n] *n* Mittag *m*
no-one ['nəuwʌn] *pron* = **nobody**
nor [nɔ:ʳ] *conj, adv* = **neither**
norm [nɔ:m] *n* Norm *f*
normal ['nɔ:məl] *adj* normal ▶ *n*: **to return to ~** sich wieder normalisieren
normally ['nɔ:məlɪ] *adv* normalerweise
north [nɔ:θ] *n* Norden *m* ▶ *adj* nördlich, Nord- ▶ *adv* nach Norden; **~ of** nördlich von
North America *n* Nordamerika *nt*
northbound ['nɔ:θbaund] *adj* in Richtung Norden
north-east [nɔ:θ'i:st] *n* Nordosten *m* ▶ *adj* Nordost- ▶ *adv* nach Nordosten; **~ of** nordöstlich von
northern ['nɔ:ðən] *adj* nördlich, Nord-
Northern Ireland *n* Nordirland *nt*

NORTHERN IRELAND

Nordirland (**Northern Ireland**) liegt im Nordosten der irischen Insel. Es ist ein Teil des Vereinigten Königreichs und besteht aus sechs historischen Grafschaften (*Counties*), ist verwaltungsmäßig aber in 11 Distrikte unterteilt. Es entstand 1921 durch die Teilung in einen irischen Freistaat (der danach zur unabhängigen Republik führte) und Nordirland. Letzteres bestand mehrheitlich aus protestantischen Unionisten, aber mit einer großen Minderheit an Republikanern, meistens Katholiken und Befürworter einer vereinigten Republik. Von Ende der 60er Jahre bis Ende der 90er war Nordirland der Schauplatz eines gewaltsamen Machtkampfes, *The Troubles* (der Nordirlandkonflikt), dem Tausende von Menschen zum Opfer fielen. Das 1998 verhandelte *Good Friday Agreement* (Karfreitagsabkommen) stellt eine wichtige Etappe auf dem Weg zum Frieden dar, auch wenn weiterhin religiöse Spaltung und Diskrimination zu Problemen führt.

North Pole *n*: **the ~** der Nordpol
North Sea *n*: **the ~** die Nordsee *f*
northward ['nɔ:θwəd], **northwards** ['nɔ:θwədz] *adv* nach Norden
north-west [nɔ:θ'wɛst] *n* Nordwesten *m* ▶ *adj* Nordwest- ▶ *adv* nach Nordwesten; **~ of** nordwestlich von
Norway ['nɔ:weɪ] *n* Norwegen *nt*
Norwegian [nɔ:'wi:dʒən] *adj* norwegisch ▶ *n* Norweger(in) *m(f)*; (*Ling*) Norwegisch *nt*
nos. *abbr* (= *numbers*) Nrn.
nose [nəuz] *n* Nase *f*
▶ **nose about** *vi* herumschnüffeln
▶ **nose around** *vi* = **nose about**
nosebleed ['nəuzbli:d] *n* Nasenbluten *nt*
nose-dive ['nəuzdaɪv] *n* (*of plane*) Sturzflug *m*
nosey ['nəuzɪ] (*inf*) *adj* = **nosy**
nostalgia [nɔs'tældʒɪə] *n* Nostalgie *f*
nostalgic [nɔs'tældʒɪk] *adj* nostalgisch
nostril ['nɔstrɪl] *n* Nasenloch *nt*
nosy ['nəuzɪ] (*inf*) *adj* neugierig

KEYWORD

not [nɔt] *adv* nicht; **he is not** *or* **isn't here** er ist nicht hier; **you must not** *or* **you mustn't do that** das darfst du nicht tun; **not that I don't like him** nicht, dass ich ihn nicht mag; **not yet** noch nicht; **not now** nicht jetzt
see also **all**; **only**

notable ['nəutəbl] *adj* bemerkenswert
note [nəut] *n* Notiz *f*; (*of student etc*) Aufzeichnung *f*; (*in book etc*) Anmerkung *f*; (*letter*) ein paar Zeilen *pl*; (*banknote*) Note *f*, Schein *m*; (*Mus: sound*) Ton *m*; (*: symbol*) Note *f*; (*tone*) Ton *m* ▶ *vt* (*point out*) anmerken; (*also:* **~ down**) notieren; **to make a ~ of sth** sich *dat* etw notieren; **to take notes** Notizen machen, mitschreiben
notebook ['nəutbuk] *n* Notizbuch *nt*
notepad ['nəutpæd] *n* Notizblock *m*

notepaper [ˈnəutpeɪpəʳ] *n* Briefpapier *nt*
nothing [ˈnʌθɪŋ] *n* nichts; **~ much** nicht viel; **for ~** umsonst; **~ at all** überhaupt nichts
notice [ˈnəutɪs] *n* Bekanntmachung *f*; (*sign*) Schild *nt*; (*warning*) Ankündigung *f*; (*dismissal*) Kündigung *f* ▶ *vt* bemerken; **to take no ~ of** ignorieren, nicht beachten; **to give sb ~ of sth** jdm von etw Bescheid geben; **at short/a moment's ~** kurzfristig/innerhalb kürzester Zeit; **until further ~** bis auf Weiteres; **to hand in one's ~** kündigen
noticeable [ˈnəutɪsəbl] *adj* deutlich
noticeboard [ˈnəutɪsbɔ:d] (Brit) *n* Anschlagbrett *nt*
notification [nəutɪfɪˈkeɪʃən] *n* Benachrichtigung *f*
notify [ˈnəutɪfaɪ] *vt*: **to ~ sb (of sth)** jdn (von etw) benachrichtigen
notion [ˈnəuʃən] *n* Vorstellung *f*
notorious [nəuˈtɔ:rɪəs] *adj* berüchtigt
nought [nɔ:t] *n* Null *f*
noun [naun] *n* Substantiv *nt*
nourish [ˈnʌrɪʃ] *vt* nähren
nourishing [ˈnʌrɪʃɪŋ] *adj* nahrhaft
nourishment [ˈnʌrɪʃmənt] *n* Nahrung *f*
novel [ˈnɔvl] *n* Roman *m* ▶ *adj* neu(artig)
novelist [ˈnɔvəlɪst] *n* Romanschriftsteller(in) *m(f)*
novelty [ˈnɔvəltɪ] *n* Neuheit *f*
November [nəuˈvɛmbəʳ] *n* November *m*; *see also* **July**
novice [ˈnɔvɪs] *n* Neuling *m*
now [nau] *adv* jetzt; **right ~** gleich, sofort; **by ~** inzwischen, mittlerweile; **I saw her just ~** ich habe sie gerade gesehen; **(every) ~ and then, (every) ~ and again** ab und zu, gelegentlich; **from ~ on** von nun an
nowadays [ˈnauədeɪz] *adv* heute, heutzutage
nowhere [ˈnəuwɛəʳ] *adv* (*be*) nirgends
nozzle [ˈnɔzl] *n* Düse *f*
nuclear [ˈnju:klɪəʳ] *adj* (*bomb, industry etc*) Atom-; **~ physics** Kernphysik *f*
nuclear waste *n* Atommüll *m*
nude [nju:d] *adj* nackt ▶ *n* (*Art*) Akt *m*
nudge [nʌdʒ] *vt* anstoßen
nudist [ˈnju:dɪst] *n* Nudist(in) *m(f)*
nuisance [ˈnju:sns] *n*: **to be a ~** lästig sein; (*situation*) ärgerlich sein; **what a ~!** wie ärgerlich/lästig!
numb [nʌm] *adj* taub, gefühllos ▶ *vt* (*pain, mind*) betäuben
number [ˈnʌmbəʳ] *n* Zahl *f*; (*quantity*) (An)zahl *f*; (*of house, bank account, bus etc*) Nummer *f* ▶ *vt* (*pages etc*) nummerieren; (*amount to*) zählen; **a ~ of** einige; **to be numbered among** zählen zu
number plate (Brit) *n* (*Aut*) Nummernschild *nt*
numeral [ˈnju:mərəl] *n* Ziffer *f*
numerical [nju:ˈmɛrɪkl] *adj* numerisch
numerous [ˈnju:mərəs] *adj* zahlreich
nun [nʌn] *n* Nonne *f*
nurse [nə:s] *n* Krankenschwester *f* ▶ *vt* pflegen; (*baby*) stillen
nursery [ˈnə:sərɪ] *n* Kindergarten *m*; (*room*) Kinderzimmer *nt*; (*for plants*) Gärtnerei *f*
nursery rhyme *n* Kinderreim *m*
nursery school *n* Kindergarten *m*
nursing [ˈnə:sɪŋ] *n* Krankenpflege *f*
nursing home *n* Pflegeheim *nt*
nut [nʌt] *n* (*Tech*) (Schrauben)mutter *f*; (*Bot*) Nuss *f*
nutcase [ˈnʌtkeɪs] (*inf*) *n* Spinner(in) *m(f)*
nutcrackers [ˈnʌtkrækəz] *npl* Nussknacker *m*
nutmeg [ˈnʌtmɛg] *n* Muskat *m*, Muskatnuss *f*
nutrient [ˈnju:trɪənt] *n* Nährstoff *m*
nutrition [nju:ˈtrɪʃən] *n* Ernährung *f*
nutritious [nju:ˈtrɪʃəs] *adj* nahrhaft
nuts [nʌts] (*inf*) *adj* verrückt
nutshell [ˈnʌtʃɛl] *n* Nussschale *f*; **in a ~** (*fig*) kurz gesagt
nutty [ˈnʌtɪ] *adj* (*inf: idea etc*) bekloppt
NW *abbr* = **north-west**
nylon [ˈnaɪlɔn] *n* Nylon *nt* ▶ *adj* Nylon-

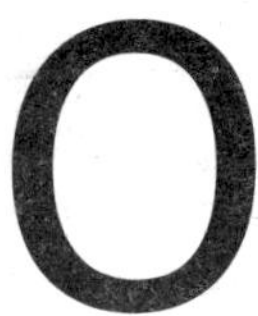

O, o [əu] *n* (*Tel etc*) Null *f*
oak [əuk] *n* (*tree, wood*) Eiche *f* ▶ *adj* (*furniture, door*) Eichen-
OAP (Brit) *n abbr* = **old age pensioner**
oar [ɔːʳ] *n* Ruder *nt*
oasis [əuˈeɪsɪs] (*pl* **oases**) *n* (*lit, fig*) Oase *f*
oath [əuθ] *n* (*promise*) Eid *m*
oats [əuts] *npl* Hafer *m*
obedience [əˈbiːdɪəns] *n* Gehorsam *m*
obedient [əˈbiːdɪənt] *adj* gehorsam
obey [əˈbeɪ] *vt* (*person*) gehorchen +*dat* ▶ *vi* gehorchen
object *n* [ˈɔbdʒɪkt] (*also Ling*) Objekt *nt*; (*aim, purpose*) Ziel *nt* ▶ *vi* [əbˈdʒɛkt] dagegen sein; **he objected that …** er wandte ein, dass …; **do you ~ to my smoking?** haben Sie etwas dagegen, wenn ich rauche?
objection [əbˈdʒɛkʃən] *n* (*argument*) Einwand *m*
objective [əbˈdʒɛktɪv] *adj* objektiv ▶ *n* Ziel *nt*
objectivity [ɔbdʒɪkˈtɪvɪtɪ] *n* Objektivität *f*
obligation [ɔblɪˈgeɪʃən] *n* Pflicht *f*; **to be under an ~ to do sth** verpflichtet sein, etw zu tun; **"no ~ to buy"** (*Comm*) „kein Kaufzwang"
obligatory [əˈblɪgətərɪ] *adj* obligatorisch
oblige [əˈblaɪdʒ] *vt* (*compel*) zwingen; (*do a favour for*) einen Gefallen tun +*dat*; **I felt obliged to invite him in** ich fühlte mich verpflichtet, ihn hereinzubitten
oblique [əˈbliːk] *adj* (*line, angle*) schief
oboe [ˈəubəu] *n* Oboe *f*
obscene [əbˈsiːn] *adj* obszön
obscure [əbˈskjuəʳ] *adj* (*little known*) unbekannt; (*difficult to understand*) unklar
observant [əbˈzəːvənt] *adj* aufmerksam
observation [ɔbzəˈveɪʃən] *n* (*remark*) Bemerkung *f*; (*act of observing, Med*) Beobachtung *f*
observe [əbˈzəːv] *vt* (*watch*) beobachten; (*notice, comment*) bemerken; (*abide by: rule etc*) einhalten
obsess [əbˈsɛs] *vt* verfolgen; **to be obsessed by** *or* **with sb/sth** von jdm/etw besessen sein
obsession [əbˈsɛʃən] *n* Besessenheit *f*
obsolete [ˈɔbsəliːt] *adj* veraltet
obstacle [ˈɔbstəkl] *n* (*lit, fig*) Hindernis *nt*
obstinate [ˈɔbstɪnɪt] *adj* (*refusal, cough etc*) hartnäckig
obstruct [əbˈstrʌkt] *vt* (*road, path*) blockieren; (*traffic, fig*) behindern
obstruction [əbˈstrʌkʃən] *n* (*object*) Hindernis *nt*; (*of plan, law*) Behinderung *f*
obtain [əbˈteɪn] *vt* erhalten
obtainable [əbˈteɪnəbl] *adj* erhältlich
obvious [ˈɔbvɪəs] *adj* offensichtlich
obviously [ˈɔbvɪəslɪ] *adv* (*clearly*) offensichtlich
occasion [əˈkeɪʒən] *n* Gelegenheit *f*; (*celebration etc*) Ereignis *nt*; **on that ~** bei der Gelegenheit
occasional [əˈkeɪʒənl] *adj* gelegentlich
occupant [ˈɔkjupənt] *n* (*of house etc*) Bewohner(in) *m(f)*; (*temporary: of car*) Insasse *m*, Insassin *f*
occupation [ɔkjuˈpeɪʃən] *n* (*job*) Beruf *m*; (*pastime*) Beschäftigung *f*; (*of building, country etc*) Besetzung *f*
occupied [ˈɔkjupaɪd] *adj* (*country, seat, toilet*) besetzt; (*person*) beschäftigt; **to keep sb/oneself ~** jdn/sich beschäftigen
occupy [ˈɔkjupaɪ] *vt* (*building, country etc*) besetzen; (*time, attention*) beanspruchen; **to ~ o.s. (in** *or* **with sth)** sich (mit etw) beschäftigen; **to ~ o.s. in** *or* **with doing sth** sich damit beschäftigen, etw zu tun
occur [əˈkəːʳ] *vi* (*take place*) geschehen; **to ~ to sb** jdm einfallen
occurrence [əˈkʌrəns] *n* (*event*) Ereignis *nt*; (*incidence*) Auftreten *nt*

OCD *n abbr* (= *obsessive compulsive disorder*) Zwangsstörung *f*
ocean [ˈəuʃən] *n* Ozean *m*, Meer *nt*
o'clock [əˈklɔk] *adv*: **it is 5 o'clock** es ist 5 Uhr
October [ɔkˈtəubəʳ] *n* Oktober *m*; *see also* **July**
octopus [ˈɔktəpəs] *n* Tintenfisch *m*
odd [ɔd] *adj* (*person*) sonderbar; (*behaviour, shape*) seltsam; (*number*) ungerade; (*sock, shoe etc*) einzeln; (*occasional*) gelegentlich; **at ~ times** ab und zu; **to be the ~ one out** der Außenseiter/die Außenseiterin sein
odds [ɔdz] *npl* (*fig*) Chancen *pl*; **to succeed against all the ~** allen Erwartungen zum Trotz erfolgreich sein; **it makes no ~** es spielt keine Rolle; **to be at ~ (with)** (*in disagreement*) uneinig sein (mit); (*at variance*) sich nicht vertragen (mit)
odds and ends *npl* Kleinigkeiten *pl*
odometer [ɔˈdɔmɪtəʳ] (*US*) *n* Tacho(meter) *m*
odor (*US*) = **odour**
odour, (*US*) **odor** [ˈəudəʳ] *n* Geruch *m*

KEYWORD

of [ɔv] *prep* **1** von; **the history of Germany** die Geschichte Deutschlands; **a friend of ours** ein Freund von uns; **a boy of ten** ein Junge von zehn Jahren, ein zehnjähriger Junge; **that was kind of you** das war nett von Ihnen
2 (*expressing quantity, amount, dates etc*): **a kilo of flour** ein Kilo Mehl; **how much of this do you need?** wie viel brauchen Sie davon?; **3 of them** (*people*) 3 von ihnen; (*objects*) 3 davon; **a cup of tea** eine Tasse Tee; **a vase of flowers** eine Vase mit Blumen; **the 5th of July** der 5. Juli
3 (*from, out of*) aus; **made of wood** aus Holz (gemacht)

KEYWORD

off [ɔf] *adv* **1** (*referring to distance, time*): **it's a long way off** es ist sehr weit weg
2 (*departure*): **to go off to Paris/Italy** nach Paris/Italien fahren; **I must be off** ich muss gehen
3 (*removal*): **to take off one's coat/clothes** seinen Mantel/sich ausziehen; **10 % off** (*Comm*) 10% Nachlass
4: **to be off** (*on holiday*) im Urlaub sein; (*due to sickness*) krank sein; **I'm off on Fridays** freitags habe ich frei; **to have a day off** (*from work*) einen Tag freihaben
▶ *adj* **1** (*not turned on: machine, light, engine etc*) aus
2: **to be off** (*meeting, match*) ausfallen
3 (Brit: *not fresh*) verdorben, schlecht
▶ *prep* **1** (*indicating motion, removal etc*) von +*dat*; **to fall off a cliff** von einer Klippe fallen; **to take a picture off the wall** ein Bild von der Wand nehmen
2 (*distant from*): **5 km off the main road** 5 km von der Hauptstraße entfernt

offence, (*US*) **offense** [əˈfɛns] *n* (*crime*) Vergehen *nt*; **to take ~ (at)** Anstoß nehmen (an +*dat*)
offend [əˈfɛnd] *vt* (*upset*) kränken
offender [əˈfɛndəʳ] *n* Straftäter(in) *m(f)*
offense [əˈfɛns] (*US*) *n* = **offence**
offensive [əˈfɛnsɪv] *adj* (*remark, behaviour*) verletzend; (*smell etc*) übel; (*weapon*) Angriffs- ▶ *n* (*Mil*) Offensive *f*
offer [ˈɔfəʳ] *n* Angebot *nt* ▶ *vt* anbieten; (*money, opportunity, service*) bieten; **on ~** (*Comm: available*) erhältlich; (*: cheaper*) im Angebot
off-grid [ɔfˈgrɪd] *adj* netzunabhängig
off-hand [ɔfˈhænd] *adj* (*casual*) lässig ▶ *adv* auf Anhieb
office [ˈɔfɪs] *n* Büro *nt*; (*position*) Amt *nt*; **doctor's ~** (*US*) Praxis *f*
office block, (*US*) **office building** *n* Bürogebäude *nt*
office hours *npl* (*Comm*) Bürostunden *pl*; (*US Med*) Sprechstunde *f*
officer [ˈɔfɪsəʳ] *n* (*Mil etc*) Offizier *m*; (*also:* **police ~**) Polizeibeamte(r) *m*, Polizeibeamtin *f*
office worker *n* Büroangestellte(r) *f(m)*
official [əˈfɪʃl] *adj* offiziell ▶ *n* (*in government*) Beamte(r) *m*, Beamtin *f*; (*in trade union etc*) Funktionär *m*
off-licence [ˈɔflaɪsns] (Brit) *n* ≈ Wein- und Spirituosenhandlung *f*
off-line [ɔfˈlaɪn] (*Comput*) *adj* Offline-
off-peak [ˈɔfˈpiːk] *adj* (*train*) außerhalb der Stoßzeit; **~ ticket** Fahrkarte *f* zur Fahrt außerhalb der Stoßzeit

off-putting [ˈɔfputɪŋ] (BRIT) *adj* (*remark, behaviour*) abstoßend
off-season [ˈɔfˈsi:zn] *adj, adv* außerhalb der Saison
offshore [ɔfˈʃɔ:ʳ] *adj* (*oil rig, fishing*) küstennah
offside [ˈɔfˈsaɪd] *adj* (*Sport*) im Abseits ▶ *n*: **the ~** (*Aut*: *when driving on left*) die rechte Seite; (: *when driving on right*) die linke Seite
often [ˈɔfn] *adv* oft; **every so ~** ab und zu
oil [ɔɪl] *n* Öl *nt* ▶ *vt* ölen
oil painting *n* Ölgemälde *nt*
oil rig *n* (*at sea*) Bohrinsel *f*
oil slick *n* Ölteppich *m*
oil tanker *n* (*ship*) (Öl)tanker *m*; (*truck*) Tankwagen *m*
oily [ˈɔɪlɪ] *adj* (*substance*) ölig; (*food*) fettig
ointment [ˈɔɪntmənt] *n* Salbe *f*
OK [ˈəuˈkeɪ] (*inf*) *adj* (*acceptable*) in Ordnung; **it's OK with** *or* **by me** mir ist es recht
okay [ˈəuˈkeɪ] *excl* = **OK**
old [əuld] *adj* alt
old age *n* Alter *nt*
old age pension *n* Rente *f*
old age pensioner *n* (BRIT) Rentner(in) *m(f)*
old-fashioned [ˈəuldˈfæʃnd] *adj* altmodisch
old people's home *n* Altersheim *nt*
oligarch [ˈɔlɪgɑ:k] *n* Oligarch(in) *m(f)*
olive [ˈɔlɪv] *n* Olive *f*
olive oil *n* Olivenöl *nt*
Olympic® [əuˈlɪmpɪk] *adj* olympisch; **the ~ Games**®, **the Olympics**® die Olympischen Spiele *pl*
omelette, (*US*) **omelet** [ˈɔmlɪt] *n* Omelett *nt*
OMG (*inf*) *abbr* (= *oh my God*) Oh Gott , Mein Gott
omission [əuˈmɪʃən] *n* (*thing omitted*) Auslassung *f*
omit [əuˈmɪt] *vt* (*by mistake*) auslassen

KEYWORD

on [ɔn] *prep* **1** (*indicating position*) auf +*dat*; (*with vb of motion*) auf +*acc*; **it's on the table** es ist auf dem Tisch; **she put the book on the table** sie legte das Buch auf den Tisch; **on the left** links
2 (*indicating means, method, condition etc*): **on foot** (*go, be*) zu Fuß; **to be on the train/plane** im Zug/Flugzeug sein; **to go on the train/plane** mit dem Zug/Flugzeug reisen; **on the radio/television** im Radio/Fernsehen; **to be on drugs** Drogen nehmen; **to be on holiday** im Urlaub sein; **I'm here on business** ich bin geschäftlich hier
3 (*referring to time*): **on Friday** am Freitag; **on Fridays** freitags; **on June 20th** am 20. Juni; **a week on Friday** Freitag in einer Woche; **on (his) arrival he went straight to his hotel** bei seiner Ankunft ging er direkt in sein Hotel
4 (*about, concerning*) über +*acc*
▶ *adv* **1** (*referring to dress*): **to have one's coat on** seinen Mantel anhaben
2 (*referring to covering*): **screw the lid on tightly** dreh den Deckel fest zu
3 (*further, continuously*): **to walk/drive/read on** weitergehen/-fahren/-lesen
▶ *adj* **1** (*functioning, in operation*: *machine, radio, TV, light*) an; (: *tap*) auf; (: *handbrake*) angezogen; **there's a good film on at the cinema** im Kino läuft ein guter Film
2: **that's not on!** (*inf*: *of behaviour*) das ist nicht drin!

once [wʌns] *adv* (*on one occasion*) einmal ▶ *conj* (*as soon as*) sobald; **at ~** (*immediately*) sofort; (*simultaneously*) gleichzeitig; **~ more** *or* **again** noch einmal; **~ in a while** ab und zu; **for ~** ausnahmsweise (einmal)
oncoming [ˈɔnkʌmɪŋ] *adj* (*traffic etc*) entgegenkommend

KEYWORD

one [wʌn] *num* ein(e); (*counting*) eins; **one hundred and fifty** (ein) hundert(und)fünfzig; **one by one** einzeln
▶ *adj* **1** (*sole*) einzige(r, s); **the one book which ...** das einzige Buch, das ...
2 (*same*): **they came in the one car** sie kamen in demselben Wagen
▶ *pron* **1**: **this one** diese(r, s); **that one** der/die/das (da); **which one?** welcher/welche/welches?; **he is one of us** er ist einer von uns; **I've already**

got one/a red one ich habe schon eins/ein rotes
2: **one another** einander; **do you two ever see one another?** seht ihr zwei euch jemals?
3 (*impersonal*) man; **one never knows** man weiß nie; **to cut one's finger** sich *dat* in den Finger schneiden

one-off [wʌnˈɔf] (Brit *inf*) *n* einmaliges Ereignis *nt*
one-parent family [ˈwʌnpɛərənt-] *n* Familie *f* mit nur einem Elternteil
one-piece [ˈwʌnpiːs] *adj*: **~ swimsuit** einteiliger Badeanzug *m*
oneself [wʌnˈsɛlf] *pron* (*reflexive*: *after prep*) sich
onesie [ˈwʌnzɪ] *n* Strampler *m*, Einteiler *m*
one-way [ˈwʌnweɪ] *adj* (*street, traffic*) Einbahn-; (*ticket*) Einzel-
onion [ˈʌnjən] *n* Zwiebel *f*
online, on-line (*Comput*) *adj* [ˈɔnlaɪn] online ▸ *adv* [ɔnˈlaɪn]: **to go ~** online gehen
only [ˈəunlɪ] *adv* nur ▸ *adj* einzige(r, s); **I saw her ~ yesterday** ich habe sie erst gestern gesehen; **not ~ … but (also) …** nicht nur …, sondern auch …; **an ~ child** ein Einzelkind *nt*
ono (Brit) *abbr* (*in classified ads*: = *or near(est) offer*): **£250 ono** £250 oder das nächstbeste Angebot
onto [ˈɔntu] *prep* = **on to**
onward [ˈɔnwəd], **onwards** [ˈɔnwədz] *adv* weiter; **from that time ~(s)** von der Zeit an
open [ˈəupn] *adj* offen; (*packet, shop, museum*) geöffnet ▸ *vt* öffnen, aufmachen; (*account*) eröffnen; (*blocked road*) frei machen ▸ *vi* (*door, eyes, mouth*) sich öffnen; (*shop, bank etc*) aufmachen; (*commence*) beginnen; **in the ~ (air)** im Freien; **to be ~ to the public** für die Öffentlichkeit zugänglich sein
▸ **open on to** *vt fus* (*room, door*) führen auf +*acc*
▸ **open up** *vi* (*unlock*) aufmachen; (*confide*) sich äußern
open-air [əupnˈɛəʳ] *adj* (*concert*) im Freien
open day *n* Tag *m* der offenen Tür
opening [ˈəupnɪŋ] *n* (*gap, hole*) Öffnung *f*; (*of play etc*) Anfang *m*; (*of new building etc*) Eröffnung *f*; (*opportunity*) Gelegenheit *f*
opening hours *npl* Öffnungszeiten *pl*
openly [ˈəupnlɪ] *adv* offen
open-minded [əupnˈmaɪndɪd] *adj* aufgeschlossen
open-plan [ˈəupnˈplæn] *adj* (*office*) Großraum-
opera [ˈɔpərə] *n* Oper *f*
opera glasses *npl* Opernglas *nt*
opera house *n* Opernhaus *nt*
opera singer *n* Opernsänger(in) *m(f)*
operate [ˈɔpəreɪt] *vt* (*machine etc*) bedienen ▸ *vi* (*machine etc*) funktionieren; (*company*) arbeiten; **to ~ on sb** jdn operieren
operating theatre [ˈɔpəreɪtɪŋ-] *n* (*Med*) Operationssaal *m*
operation [ɔpəˈreɪʃən] *n* (*of machine etc*) Betrieb *m*; (*Mil, Med*) Operation *f*; **to have an ~** (*Med*) operiert werden
operator [ˈɔpəreɪtəʳ] *n* (*Tel*) Vermittlung *f*
opinion [əˈpɪnjən] *n* Meinung *f*; **in my ~** meiner Meinung nach
opponent [əˈpəunənt] *n* Gegner(in) *m(f)*
opportunity [ɔpəˈtjuːnɪtɪ] *n* Gelegenheit *f*
oppose [əˈpəuz] *vt* (*opinion, plan*) ablehnen; **to be opposed to sth** gegen etw sein; **as opposed to** im Gegensatz zu
opposing [əˈpəuzɪŋ] *adj* (*side, team*) gegnerisch; (*ideas, tendencies*) entgegengesetzt
opposite [ˈɔpəzɪt] *adj* (*house, door*) gegenüberliegend; (*end, direction*) entgegengesetzt ▸ *adv* gegenüber ▸ *prep* (*in front of*) gegenüber ▸ *n*: **the ~** das Gegenteil; **the ~ sex** das andere Geschlecht
opposition [ɔpəˈzɪʃən] *n* (*resistance*) Widerstand *m*; **the O~** (*Pol*) die Opposition
oppress [əˈprɛs] *vt* unterdrücken
oppressive [əˈprɛsɪv] *adj* (*weather, heat*) bedrückend
opt [ɔpt] *vi*: **to ~ for** sich entscheiden für; **to ~ to do sth** sich entscheiden, etw zu tun
optician [ɔpˈtɪʃən] *n* Optiker(in) *m(f)*
optimist [ˈɔptɪmɪst] *n* Optimist(in) *m(f)*
optimistic [ɔptɪˈmɪstɪk] *adj* optimistisch

option [ˈɔpʃən] *n* (*choice*) Möglichkeit *f*; (*Comm*) Option *f*; **to have no ~** keine (andere) Wahl haben
optional [ˈɔpʃənl] *adj* freiwillig; **~ extras** (*Comm*) Extras *pl*
or [ɔːʳ] *conj* oder; **he hasn't seen or heard anything** er hat weder etwas gesehen noch gehört; **or else** (*otherwise*) sonst
oral [ˈɔːrəl] *adj* (*test, report*) mündlich ▸ *n* (*exam*) mündliche Prüfung *f*
orange [ˈɔrɪndʒ] *n* Orange *f* ▸ *adj* (*colour*) orange
orange juice *n* Orangensaft *m*
orbit [ˈɔːbɪt] *n* (*of planet etc*) Umlaufbahn *f* ▸ *vt* umkreisen
orchard [ˈɔːtʃəd] *n* Obstgarten *m*
orchestra [ˈɔːkɪstrə] *n* Orchester *nt*; (*US: stalls*) Parkett *nt*
orchid [ˈɔːkɪd] *n* Orchidee *f*
ordeal [ɔːˈdiːl] *n* Qual *f*
order [ˈɔːdəʳ] *n* (*command*) Befehl *m*; (*Comm, in restaurant*) Bestellung *f*; (*sequence*) Reihenfolge *f*; (*discipline, organization*) Ordnung *f* ▸ *vt* (*command*) befehlen; (*Comm, in restaurant*) bestellen; (*also:* **put in ~**) ordnen; **in ~** (*permitted*) in Ordnung; **in ~ to do sth** um etw zu tun; **out of ~** (*not working*) außer Betrieb; (*motion, proposal*) nicht zulässig; **to ~ sb to do sth** jdn anweisen, etw zu tun
order form *n* Bestellschein *m*
ordinary [ˈɔːdnrɪ] *adj* (*everyday*) gewöhnlich, normal; (*pej: mediocre*) mittelmäßig
ore [ɔːʳ] *n* Erz *nt*
organ [ˈɔːgən] *n* (*Anat*) Organ *nt*; (*Mus*) Orgel *f*
organic [ɔːˈgænɪk] *adj* organisch; (*farming, vegetables*) Bio-, Öko-; **~ food** Biokost *f*
organization [ɔːgənaɪˈzeɪʃən] *n* Organisation *f*
organize [ˈɔːgənaɪz] *vt* organisieren
organizer [ˈɔːgənaɪzəʳ] *n* (*of conference etc*) Organisator *m*
orgasm [ˈɔːgæzəm] *n* Orgasmus *m*
orgy [ˈɔːdʒɪ] *n* Orgie *f*
oriental [ɔːrɪˈɛntl] *adj* orientalisch
origin [ˈɔrɪdʒɪn] *n* Ursprung *m*; (*of person*) Herkunft *f*
original [əˈrɪdʒɪnl] *adj* (*first*) ursprünglich; (*genuine*) original; (*imaginative*) originell ▸ *n* Original *nt*
originality [ərɪdʒɪˈnælɪtɪ] *n* Originalität *f*
originally [əˈrɪdʒɪnəlɪ] *adv* (*at first*) ursprünglich
Orkneys [ˈɔːknɪz] *npl*: **the ~** (*also:* **the Orkney Islands**) die Orkneyinseln *pl*
ornament [ˈɔːnəmənt] *n* (*object*) Ziergegenstand *m*
ornamental [ɔːnəˈmɛntl] *adj* (*garden, pond*) Zier-
orphan [ˈɔːfn] *n* Waise *f*, Waisenkind *nt*
orphanage [ˈɔːfənɪdʒ] *n* Waisenhaus *nt*
orthodox [ˈɔːθədɔks] *adj* orthodox
orthopaedic, (*US*) **orthopedic** [ɔːθəˈpiːdɪk] *adj* orthopädisch
ostentatious [ɔstɛnˈteɪʃəs] *adj* (*person*) protzig
ostrich [ˈɔstrɪtʃ] *n* Strauß *m*
other [ˈʌðəʳ] *adj* andere(r, s) ▸ *pron*: **the ~ (one)** der/die/das andere; **others** andere *pl*; **the others** die anderen *pl*; **~ than** (*apart from*) außer; **the ~ day** (*recently*) neulich; **somebody or ~** irgendjemand
otherwise [ˈʌðəwaɪz] *adv* (*differently*) anders; (*apart from that, if not*) sonst
OTT (*inf*) *abbr* (= *over the top*) *see* **top**
otter [ˈɔtəʳ] *n* Otter *m*
ought [ɔːt] (*pt* **~**) *aux vb*: **I ~ to do it** ich sollte es tun; **this ~ to have been corrected** das hätte korrigiert werden müssen; **he ~ to win** (*he probably will win*) er dürfte wohl gewinnen
ounce [auns] *n* Unze *f*
our [ˈauəʳ] *adj* unsere(r, s); *see also* **my**
ours [auəz] *pron* unsere(r, s); *see also* **mine²**
ourselves [auəˈsɛlvz] *pl pron* uns (selbst); (*emphatic*) selbst

 **KEYWORD**

out¹ [aut] *adv* **1** (*not in*) draußen; **out in the rain/snow** draußen im Regen/Schnee; **out here** hier; **out there** dort; **to go/come** *etc* **out** hinausgehen/-kommen *etc*; **to speak out loud** laut sprechen
2 (*not at home, absent*) nicht da
3 (*indicating distance*): **the boat was 10 km out** das Schiff war 10 km weit draußen
4 (*Sport*) aus; **the ball is out/has gone out** der Ball ist aus

▸ *adj* **1**: **to be out** (*person*: *unconscious*) bewusstlos sein; (: *out of game*) ausgeschieden sein; (*out of fashion*: *style, singer*) out sein
2 (*have appeared*: *flowers*) da; (: *news, secret*) heraus
3 (*extinguished, finished*: *fire, light, gas*) aus
4: **to be out to do sth** (*intend*) etw tun wollen
5 (*wrong*): **to be out in one's calculations** sich in seinen Berechnungen irren

out² [aut] *vt* (*inf*: *expose as gay*) outen
outback [ˈautbæk] *n* (*in Australia*): **the ~** das Hinterland
outboard [ˈautbɔːd] *n* (*also*: **~ motor**) Außenbordmotor *m*
outbox [ˈautbɔks] *n* (*Comput*) Postausgang *m*; (*US*: *out-tray*) Ablage *f* für Ausgänge
outbreak [ˈautbreɪk] *n* (*of war, disease etc*) Ausbruch *m*
outburst [ˈautbəːst] *n* (*of anger etc*) Gefühlsausbruch *m*
outcome [ˈautkʌm] *n* Ergebnis *nt*
outcry [ˈautkraɪ] *n* Aufschrei *m*
outdo [autˈduː] *vt* (*irreg*: *like* **do**) übertreffen
outdoor [autˈdɔːʳ] *adj* (*activities*) im Freien; **~ swimming pool** Freibad *nt*
outdoors [autˈdɔːz] *adv* (*play, sleep*) draußen, im Freien
outer [ˈautəʳ] *adj* äußere(r, s)
outer space *n* der Weltraum
outfit [ˈautfɪt] *n* (*clothes*) Kleidung *f*
outgoing [ˈautgəuɪŋ] *adj* (*extrovert*) kontaktfreudig
outgrow [autˈgrəu] *vt* (*irreg*: *like* **grow**) (*clothes*) herauswachsen aus
outing [ˈautɪŋ] *n* Ausflug *m*
outlet [ˈautlɛt] *n* (*hole, pipe*) Abfluss *m*; (*US Elec*) Steckdose *f*; (*Comm*: *also*: **retail ~**) Verkaufsstelle *f*
outline [ˈautlaɪn] *n* (*shape*) Umriss *m*; (*brief explanation*) Abriss *m*
outlive [autˈlɪv] *vt* (*survive*) überleben
outlook [ˈautluk] *n* (*attitude*) Einstellung *f*; (*prospects*) Aussichten *pl*
outnumber [autˈnʌmbəʳ] *vt* zahlenmäßig überlegen sein +*dat*; **to be outnumbered (by) 5 to 1** im Verhältnis 5 zu 1 in der Minderheit sein

KEYWORD

out of *prep* **1** (*outside, beyond*: *position*) nicht in +*dat*; (: *motion*) aus +*dat*; **to be out of danger** außer Gefahr sein
2 (*cause, origin*) aus +*dat*; **out of curiosity/fear/greed** aus Neugier/Angst/Habgier
3 (*from among*) von +*dat*
4 (*without*): **to be out of sugar/milk/petrol** *etc* keinen Zucker/keine Milch/kein Benzin *etc* mehr haben

out-of-date [autəvˈdeɪt] *adj* (*clothes, idea*) veraltet
out-of-the-way [ˈautəvðəˈweɪ] *adj* (*place*) entlegen
outpatient [ˈautpeɪʃənt] *n* ambulanter Patient *m*, ambulante Patientin *f*
output [ˈautput] *n* (*production*: *of factory, writer etc*) Produktion *f*; (*Comput*) Ausgabe *f*
outrage [ˈautreɪdʒ] *n* (*scandal*) Skandal *m*; (*atrocity*) Verbrechen *nt*; (*anger*) Empörung *f*
outrageous [autˈreɪdʒəs] *adj* (*remark etc*) empörend; (*clothes*) unmöglich
outright [autˈraɪt] *adv* (*kill*) auf der Stelle ▸ *adj* (*winner, victory*) unbestritten; (*refusal, hostility*) total
outside [autˈsaɪd] *n* (*of building etc*) Außenseite *f* ▸ *adj* (*wall, lavatory*) Außen- ▸ *adv* (*be, wait*) draußen; (*go*) nach draußen ▸ *prep* außerhalb +*gen*
outsider [autˈsaɪdəʳ] *n* (*odd one out, in race etc*) Außenseiter(in) *m*(*f*)
outskirts [ˈautskəːts] *npl* (*of town*) Stadtrand *m*
outstanding [autˈstændɪŋ] *adj* (*exceptional*) hervorragend; (*remaining*) ausstehend
outward [ˈautwəd] *adj* (*sign, appearances*) äußere(r, s); **~ journey** Hinreise *f*
outwardly [ˈautwədlɪ] *adv* (*on the surface*) äußerlich
outwards [ˈautwədz] *adv* (*move, face*) nach außen
oval [ˈəuvl] *adj* oval
ovary [ˈəuvərɪ] *n* (*Anat, Med*) Eierstock *m*
ovation [əuˈveɪʃən] *n* Ovation *f*
oven [ˈʌvn] *n* (*Culin*) Backofen *m*
ovenproof [ˈʌvnpruːf] *adj* (*dish etc*) feuerfest
oven-ready [ˈʌvnrɛdɪ] *adj* backfertig

KEYWORD

over [ˈəuvəʳ] *adv* **1** (*across*: *walk, jump, fly etc*) hinüber; **over here** hier; **over there** dort (drüben)
2 (*indicating movement*): **to fall over** (*person*) hinfallen
3 (*finished*): **to be over** (*game, life, relationship etc*) vorbei sein, zu Ende sein
4 (*excessively*: *clever, rich, fat etc*) übermäßig
5 (*remaining*: *money, food etc*) übrig
6: **all over** (*everywhere*) überall
7 (*repeatedly*): **over and over (again)** immer (und immer) wieder
▶ *prep* **1** (*on top of, above*) über +*dat*; (*with vb of motion*) über +*acc*
2 (*on the other side of*): **the pub over the road** die Kneipe gegenüber
3 (*more than*) über +*acc*; **over 200 people** über 200 Leute; **over and above my normal duties** über meine normalen Pflichten hinaus; **over and above that** darüber hinaus
4 (*during*) während; **let's discuss it over dinner** wir sollten es beim Abendessen besprechen

overall [ˈəuvərɔːl] *adj* (*length, cost etc*) Gesamt-; (*impression, view*) allgemein ▶ *adv* (*measure, cost*) insgesamt; (*generally*) im Allgemeinen ▶ *n* (Brit) Kittel *m* ▪ **overalls** *npl* Overall *m*
overboard [ˈəuvəbɔːd] *adv* (*Naut*) über Bord
overbook [əuvəˈbuk] *vt* überbuchen
overcharge [əuvəˈtʃɑːdʒ] *vt* zu viel berechnen +*dat*
overcoat [ˈəuvəkəut] *n* Mantel *m*
overcome [əuvəˈkʌm] *vt* (*irreg: like* **come**) (*problem, fear*) überwinden ▶ *adj* überwältigt; **she was ~ with grief** der Schmerz übermannte sie
overcooked [əuvəˈkukt] *adj* verkocht; (*meat*) zu lange gebraten
overcrowded [əuvəˈkraudɪd] *adj* überfüllt
overdo [əuvəˈduː] *vt* (*irreg: like* **do**) übertreiben
overdone [əuvəˈdʌn] *adj* übertrieben; (*food*) zu lange gekocht; (*meat*) zu lange gebraten
overdose [ˈəuvədəus] *n* Überdosis *f*
overdraft [ˈəuvədrɑːft] *n* Kontoüberziehung *f*
overdrawn [əuvəˈdrɔːn] *adj* (*account*) überzogen
overdue [əuvəˈdjuː] *adj* überfällig
overestimate [əuvərˈɛstɪmeɪt] *vt* überschätzen
overexpose [əuvərɪkˈspəuz] *vt* (*Phot*) überbelichten
overflow [əuvəˈfləu] *vi* (*bath, jar etc*) überlaufen
overhead [əuvəˈhɛd] *adv* (*above*) oben ▶ *adj* (*lighting*) Decken-; (*cables, wires*) Überland- ▶ *n* (*US*) = **overheads** ▪ **overheads** *npl* allgemeine Unkosten *pl*
overhear [əuvəˈhɪəʳ] *vt* (*irreg: like* **hear**) (zufällig) mit anhören
overheat [əuvəˈhiːt] *vi* (*engine*) heißlaufen
overjoyed [əuvəˈdʒɔɪd] *adj* überglücklich
overland [ˈəuvəlænd] *adj* (*journey*) Überland- ▶ *adv* (*travel*) über Land
overlap [əuvəˈlæp] *vi* (*figures, ideas etc*) sich überschneiden
overload [əuvəˈləud] *vt* (*vehicle*) überladen
overlook [əuvəˈluk] *vt* (*have view over*) überblicken; (*fail to notice*) übersehen; (*excuse, forgive*) hinwegsehen über +*acc*
overnight [əuvəˈnaɪt] *adv* über Nacht ▶ *adj* (*bag, clothes*) Reise-; (*accommodation, stop*) für die Nacht; **to stay ~** über Nacht bleiben
overpass [ˈəuvəpɑːs] (*esp US*) *n* Überführung *f*
overpay [əuvəˈpeɪ] *vt* (*irreg: like* **pay**): **to ~ sb by £50** jdm £50 zu viel bezahlen
overrule [əuvəˈruːl] *vt* (*claim, person*) zurückweisen; (*decision*) aufheben
overseas [əuvəˈsiːz] *adv* (*live, work*) im Ausland; (*travel*) ins Ausland ▶ *adj* (*market, trade*) Übersee-; (*student, visitor*) aus dem Ausland
oversee [əuvəˈsiː] *vt* (*irreg: like* **see**) (*supervise*) beaufsichtigen
overshadow [əuvəˈʃædəu] *vt* (*place, building etc*) überschatten
overshoot [əuvəˈʃuːt] *vt* (*irreg: like* **shoot**) (*target, runway*) hinausschießen über +*acc*
oversight [ˈəuvəsaɪt] *n* Versehen *nt*
oversimplify [əuvəˈsɪmplɪfaɪ] *vt* zu stark vereinfachen
oversleep [əuvəˈsliːp] *vi* (*irreg: like* **sleep**) verschlafen

vertake [əuvəˈteɪk] *vt* (*irreg: like* **take**) (*Aut*) überholen ▸ *vi* (*Aut*) überholen
vertime [ˈəuvətaɪm] *n* Überstunden *pl*
verturn [əuvəˈtəːn] *vt* (*car, chair*) umkippen ▸ *vi* (*train etc*) umkippen
verweight [əuvəˈweɪt] *adj* (*person*) übergewichtig
verwhelm [əuvəˈwɛlm] *vt* überwältigen
verwhelming [əuvəˈwɛlmɪŋ] *adj* überwältigend
verwork [əuvəˈwəːk] *n* Überarbeitung *f* ▸ *vi* sich überarbeiten
verworked [əuvəˈwəːkt] *adj* überarbeitet
we [əu] *vt*: **to ~ sb sth, to ~ sth to sb** (*lit, fig*) jdm etw schulden; (*life, talent, good looks etc*) jdm etw verdanken
wing to [ˈəuɪŋ-] *prep* (*because of*) wegen +*gen*
wl [aul] *n* Eule *f*
wn [əun] *vt* (*possess*) besitzen ▸ *adj* eigen; **a room of my ~** mein eigenes Zimmer; **on one's ~** allein
▸ **own up** *vi* gestehen, es zugeben
wner [ˈəunəʳ] *n* Besitzer(in) *m(f)*
wnership [ˈəunəʃɪp] *n* Besitz *m*; **under new ~** (*shop etc*) unter neuer Leitung
x [ɔks] (*pl* **oxen**) *n* Ochse *m*
xtail [ˈɔksteɪl] *n*: **~ soup** Ochsenschwanzsuppe *f*
xygen [ˈɔksɪdʒən] *n* Sauerstoff *m*
yster [ˈɔɪstəʳ] *n* Auster *f*
z [ɔz] *n* (*inf*) Australien *nt*
z *abbr* = **ounce**
zone [ˈəuzəun] *n* Ozon *nt*
zone layer *n*: **the ~** die Ozonschicht

p

p (Brit) *abbr* = **penny**; **pence**
p.a. *abbr* (= *per annum*) p.a.
pace [peɪs] *n* (*step*) Schritt *m*; (*speed*) Tempo *nt*
pacemaker [ˈpeɪsmeɪkəʳ] *n* (*Med*) (Herz)schrittmacher *m*
Pacific [pəˈsɪfɪk] *n* (*Geog*): **the ~ (Ocean)** der Pazifik, der Pazifische Ozean
pacifier [ˈpæsɪfaɪəʳ] (*US*) *n* (*dummy*) Schnuller *m*
pack [pæk] *n* (*US: of cigarettes*) Schachtel *f*; (*of people, hounds*) Meute *f*; (*also:* **back ~**) Rucksack *m*; (*of cards*) (Karten)spiel *nt* ▸ *vt* (*clothes etc*) einpacken; (*suitcase etc, Comput*) packen ▸ *vi* packen
▸ **pack in** (Brit *inf*) *vt* (*job*) hinschmeißen
package [ˈpækɪdʒ] *n* (*parcel, Comput*) Paket *nt*; (*also:* **~ deal**) Pauschalangebot *nt*
package holiday, (*US*) **package tour** *n* Pauschalreise *f*
packaging [ˈpækɪdʒɪŋ] *n* Verpackung *f*
packed lunch [pækt-] (Brit) *n* Lunchpaket *nt*
packet [ˈpækɪt] *n* Packung *f*; (*of cigarettes*) Schachtel *m*
pad [pæd] *n* (*paper*) Block *m*; (*to prevent damage*) Polster *nt*
padded envelope [ˈpædɪd-] *n* wattierter Umschlag
padding [ˈpædɪŋ] *n* (*material*) Polsterung *f*
paddle [ˈpædl] *n* (*oar*) Paddel *nt* ▸ *vi* (*at seaside*) plan(t)schen
paddling pool [ˈpædlɪŋ-] (Brit) *n* Plan(t)schbecken *nt*

padlock [ˈpædlɔk] *n* Vorhängeschloss *nt*
page [peɪdʒ] *n* (*of book etc*) Seite *f*
pager [ˈpeɪdʒəʳ] *n* Piepser *m* (*inf*)
paid [peɪd] *pt, pp of* **pay** ▶ *adj* bezahlt
pain [peɪn] *n* Schmerz *m*; **to be in ~** Schmerzen haben; **he is/it is a right ~ (in the neck)** (*inf*) er/das geht einem auf den Wecker
painful [ˈpeɪnful] *adj* (*back, injury etc*) schmerzhaft; (*embarrassing*) peinlich
painkiller [ˈpeɪnkɪləʳ] *n* schmerzstillendes Mittel *nt*
painstaking [ˈpeɪnzteɪkɪŋ] *adj* (*work, person*) gewissenhaft
paint [peɪnt] *n* Farbe *f* ▶ *vt* (*door, house etc*) anstreichen; (*person, picture*) malen
paintbrush [ˈpeɪntbrʌʃ] *n* Pinsel *m*
painter [ˈpeɪntəʳ] *n* (*artist*) Maler(in) *m*(*f*)
painting [ˈpeɪntɪŋ] *n* (*picture*) Bild *nt*, Gemälde *nt*
pair [pɛəʳ] *n* Paar *nt*; **a ~ of scissors** eine Schere; **a ~ of trousers** eine Hose
pajamas [pəˈdʒɑːməz] (*US*) *npl* Schlafanzug *m*
Pakistan [pɑːkɪˈstɑːn] *n* Pakistan *nt*
pal [pæl] (*inf*) *n* (*friend*) Kumpel *m*
palace [ˈpæləs] *n* Palast *m*
pale [peɪl] *adj* blass; (*light*) fahl
palm [pɑːm] *n* (*also:* **~ tree**) Palme *f*; (*of hand*) Handteller *m*
pamper [ˈpæmpəʳ] *vt* verwöhnen
pan [pæn] *n* (*also:* **saucepan**) Topf *m*; (*also:* **frying ~**) Pfanne *f*
pancake [ˈpænkeɪk] *n* Pfannkuchen *m*
Pancake Day (Brit) *n* Fastnachtsdienstag *m*
panda [ˈpændə] *n* Panda *m*
pandemic [pænˈdɛmɪk] *n* Pandemie *f*
p&p (Brit) *abbr* (= *postage and packing*) Porto und Verpackung
panel [ˈpænl] *n* (*wood, metal, glass etc*) Tafel *f*; (*group of experts etc*) Diskussionsrunde *f*; **~ of judges** Jury *f*
panic [ˈpænɪk] *n* Panik *f* ▶ *vi* in Panik geraten
panicky [ˈpænɪkɪ] *adj* (*feeling*) Angst-
panini [pæˈniːnɪ] *n* Panini *nt*
pansy [ˈpænzɪ] *n* (*Bot*) Stiefmütterchen *nt*
panties [ˈpæntɪz] *npl* Höschen *nt*
pants [pænts] *npl* (Brit: *man's*) Unterhose *f*; (*US: trousers*) Hose *f*
panty hose [ˈpæntɪ-] (*US*) *npl* Strumpfhose *f*
paper [ˈpeɪpəʳ] *n* Papier *nt*; (*also:* **newspaper**) Zeitung *f*; (*exam*) Arbeit *f* (*academic essay*) Referat *nt*; (*document*) Dokument *nt*, Papier ▶ *vt* (*room*) tapezieren ■ **papers** *npl* (*also:* **identity papers**) Papiere *pl*
paperback [ˈpeɪpəbæk] *n* Taschenbuch *nt*
paperclip [ˈpeɪpəklɪp] *n* Büroklammer
paper round *n*: **to do a ~** Zeitungen austragen
paperwork [ˈpeɪpəwəːk] *n* Schreibarbeit *f*
paracetamol [pærəˈsiːtəmɔl] *n* (*tablet*) Paracetamoltablette *f*
parachute [ˈpærəʃuːt] *n* Fallschirm *m*
parade [pəˈreɪd] *n* (*procession*) Parade *f*; (*ceremony*) Zeremonie *f* ▶ *vi* (*Mil*) aufmarschieren
paradise [ˈpærədaɪs] *n* (*also fig*) Paradies *nt*
paragraph [ˈpærəgrɑːf] *n* Absatz *m*
parallel [ˈpærəlɛl] *adj* (*also Comput*) parallel ▶ *n* Parallele *f*
paralyse [ˈpærəlaɪz] (Brit) *vt* (*also fig*) lähmen
paralyze [ˈpærəlaɪz] (*US*) *vt* = **paralyse**
paranoid [ˈpærənɔɪd] *adj* paranoid
paraphrase [ˈpærəfreɪz] *vt* umschreiben
parasol [ˈpærəsɔl] *n* Sonnenschirm *m*
parcel [ˈpɑːsl] *n* Paket *nt*
pardon [ˈpɑːdn] *n* (*Law*) Begnadigung *f*; **~ me!, I beg your ~!** (*I'm sorry!*) verzeihen Sie bitte!; **(I beg your) ~?**, **~ me?** (*US*) (*what did you say?*) bitte?
parent [ˈpɛərənt] *n* (*mother*) Mutter *f*; (*father*) Vater *m* ■ **parents** *npl* (*mother and father*) Eltern *pl*
parental [pəˈrɛntl] *adj* (*love, control etc*) elterlich
parish [ˈpærɪʃ] *n* Gemeinde *f*
park [pɑːk] *n* Park *m* ▶ *vt, vi* (*Aut*) parken
park and ride *n* Park-and-Ride(-System) *nt*, Parken und Reisen *nt*
parking [ˈpɑːkɪŋ] *n* Parken *nt*; **"no ~"** „Parken verboten"
parking lights *npl* Parklicht *nt*
parking lot (*US*) *n* Parkplatz *m*
parking meter *n* Parkuhr *f*
parking place *n* Parkplatz *m*
parking ticket *n* Strafzettel *m*
parkour [pɑːˈkuəʳ] *n* Parkour *m or nt*

arliament [ˈpɑːləmənt] *n* Parlament *nt*
arrot [ˈpærət] *n* Papagei *m*
arsley [ˈpɑːslɪ] *n* Petersilie *f*
arsnip [ˈpɑːsnɪp] *n* Pastinake *f*
art [pɑːt] *n* Teil *m*; (*Tech*) Teil *nt*; (*Theat*, *Cine etc*: *role*) Rolle *f*; (*US*: *in hair*) Scheitel *m* ▶ *adv* = **partly** ▶ *vt* (*separate*) trennen; (*hair*) scheiteln ▶ *vi* (*roads*, *people*) sich trennen; **to take ~ in** teilnehmen an +*dat*; **for the most ~** (*generally*) zumeist
artial [ˈpɑːʃl] *adj* (*victory*, *solution*) Teil-; **to be ~ to** (*person*, *drink etc*) eine Vorliebe haben für
articipant [pɑːˈtɪsɪpənt] *n* Teilnehmer(in) *m(f)*
articipate [pɑːˈtɪsɪpeɪt] *vi*: **to ~ in** teilnehmen an +*dat*
articular [pəˈtɪkjuləʳ] *adj* (*distinct*: *person*, *time*, *place etc*) bestimmt, speziell; (*special*) speziell, besondere(r, s) ▶ *n*: **in ~** im Besonderen, besonders ▪ **particulars** *npl* Einzelheiten *pl*; (*name*, *address etc*) Personalien *pl*; **to be very ~ about sth** (*fussy*) in Bezug auf etw *acc* sehr eigen sein
articularly [pəˈtɪkjuləlɪ] *adv* besonders
arting [ˈpɑːtɪŋ] *n* (*farewell*) Abschied *m*; (Brit: *in hair*) Scheitel *m*
artly [ˈpɑːtlɪ] *adv* teilweise, zum Teil
artner [ˈpɑːtnəʳ] *n* Partner(in) *m(f)*
artnership [ˈpɑːtnəʃɪp] *n* (*Pol etc*) Partnerschaft *f*
artridge [ˈpɑːtrɪdʒ] *n* Rebhuhn *nt*
art-time [ˈpɑːtˈtaɪm] *adj* (*work*, *staff*) Teilzeit- ▶ *adv*: **to work ~** Teilzeit arbeiten
arty [ˈpɑːtɪ] *n* (*Pol*, *Law*) Partei *f*; (*celebration*, *social event*) Party *f*; (*group of people*) Gruppe *f*
ass [pɑːs] *vt* (*spend*: *time*) verbringen; (*hand over*) reichen, geben; (*go past*) vorbeikommen an +*dat*; (: *in car*) vorbeifahren an +*dat*; (*overtake*) überholen; (*exam*) bestehen; (*law*, *proposal*) genehmigen ▶ *vi* (*go past*) vorbeigehen; (: *in car*) vorbeifahren; (*in exam*) bestehen ▶ *n* (*permit*) Ausweis *m*; (*in mountains*, *Sport*) Pass *m*
▶ **pass away** *vi* (*die*) dahinscheiden
▶ **pass by** *vi* (*go past*) vorbeigehen; (: *in car*) vorbeifahren ▶ *vt* (*ignore*) vorbeigehen an +*dat*
▶ **pass on** *vt*: **to ~ on (to)** weitergeben (an +*acc*)
▶ **pass out** *vi* (*faint*) ohnmächtig werden
passage [ˈpæsɪdʒ] *n* Gang *m*; (*in book*) Passage *f*
passageway [ˈpæsɪdʒweɪ] *n* Gang *m*
passenger [ˈpæsɪndʒəʳ] *n* (*in boat*, *plane*) Passagier *m*; (*in car*) Fahrgast *m*
passer-by [pɑːsəˈbaɪ] (*pl* **passers-by**) *n* Passant(in) *m(f)*
passion [ˈpæʃən] *n* Leidenschaft *f*
passionate [ˈpæʃənɪt] *adj* leidenschaftlich
passion fruit *n* Passionsfrucht *f*
passive [ˈpæsɪv] *adj* passiv; (*Ling*) Passiv- ▶ *n* (*Ling*) Passiv *nt*
passport [ˈpɑːspɔːt] *n* Pass *m*
passport control *n* Passkontrolle *f*
password [ˈpɑːswəːd] *n* (*Comput*) Passwort *nt*
past [pɑːst] *prep* (*in front of*) vorbei an +*dat*; (*beyond*) hinter +*dat*; (*later than*) nach ▶ *adj* (*government etc*) ehemalig; (*week*, *month etc*) vergangen ▶ *n* Vergangenheit *f* ▶ *adv*: **to run ~** vorbeilaufen; **ten/quarter ~ eight** zehn/Viertel nach acht; **for the ~ few/3 days** während der letzten Tage/3 Tage
pasta [ˈpæstə] *n* Nudeln *pl*
paste [peɪst] *n* (*glue*) Kleister *m* ▶ *vt* (*stick*) kleben
pastime [ˈpɑːstaɪm] *n* Zeitvertreib *m*
pastry [ˈpeɪstrɪ] *n* (*dough*) Teig *m*; (*cake*) Gebäckstück *nt*
pasty *n* [ˈpæstɪ] (*pie*) Pastete *f* ▶ *adj* [ˈpeɪstɪ] (*complexion*) blässlich
patch [pætʃ] *n* (*piece of material*) Flicken *m*; (*damp*, *bald etc*) Fleck *m* ▶ *vt* (*clothes*) flicken
patchy [ˈpætʃɪ] *adj* (*colour*) ungleichmäßig
pâté [ˈpæteɪ] *n* Pastete *f*
paternal [pəˈtəːnl] *adj* väterlich; **my ~ grandmother** meine Großmutter väterlicherseits
paternity leave [pəˈtəːnɪtɪ-] *n* Vaterschaftsurlaub *m*
path [pɑːθ] *n* (*also fig*) Weg *m*; (*trail*, *track*) Pfad *m*
pathetic [pəˈθɛtɪk] *adj* (*pitiful*) mitleiderregend; (*very bad*) erbärmlich
patience [ˈpeɪʃns] *n* Geduld *f*; (Brit *Cards*) Patience *f*

patient [ˈpeɪʃnt] *n* Patient(in) *m(f)* ▸ *adj* geduldig
patio [ˈpætɪəu] *n* Terrasse *f*
patriotic [pætrɪˈɔtɪk] *adj* patriotisch
patrol car [pəˈtrəul-] *n* Streifenwagen *m*
patrolman [pəˈtrəulmən] (*US*) *n* (*irreg*) (*Police*) (Streifen)polizist *m*
patron [ˈpeɪtrən] *n* (*customer*) Kunde *m*, Kundin *f*; (*benefactor*) Förderer *m*
patronize [ˈpætrənaɪz] *vt* (*pej: look down on*) von oben herab behandeln
patronizing [ˈpætrənaɪzɪŋ] *adj* herablassend
pattern [ˈpætən] *n* Muster *nt*
pause [pɔːz] *n* Pause *f* ▸ *vi* (*hesitate*) innehalten
pavement [ˈpeɪvmənt] *n* (Brit) Bürgersteig *m*
pay [peɪ] (*pt, pp* **paid**) *n* (*wage*) Lohn *m*; (*salary*) Gehalt *nt* ▸ *vt* (*bill, person*) bezahlen ▸ *vi* (*be profitable*) sich bezahlt machen; (*fig*) sich lohnen; **how much did you ~ for it?** wie viel hast du dafür bezahlt?; **to ~ attention (to)** achtgeben (auf *+acc*); **to ~ sb a visit** jdn besuchen
▸ **pay back** *vt* zurückzahlen
▸ **pay for** *vt fus* (*also fig*) (be)zahlen für
▸ **pay in** *vt* einzahlen
payable [ˈpeɪəbl] *adj* zahlbar
payday [ˈpeɪdeɪ] *n* Zahltag *m*
payee [peɪˈiː] *n* Zahlungsempfänger(in) *m(f)*
payment [ˈpeɪmənt] *n* (*act*) Bezahlung *f*; (*sum of money*) Zahlung *f*
pay TV *n* Pay-TV *nt*
paywall [ˈpeɪwɔːl] *n* (*Comput*) Bezahlschranke *f*
PC *n abbr* (= *personal computer*) PC *m* ▸ *adj abbr* = **politically correct**
PDA *abbr* (*Comput*: = *personal digital assistant*) PDA *m*
PE *n abbr* (*Scol*) = **physical education**
pea [piː] *n* Erbse *f*
peace [piːs] *n* Frieden *m*
peaceful [ˈpiːsful] *adj* friedlich
peach [piːtʃ] *n* Pfirsich *m*
peacock [ˈpiːkɔk] *n* Pfau *m*
peak [piːk] *n* (*of mountain*) Gipfel *m*; (*fig*) Höhepunkt *m*
peak period *n* Spitzenzeit *f*, Stoßzeit *f*
peanut [ˈpiːnʌt] *n* Erdnuss *f*
peanut butter *n* Erdnussbutter *f*
pear [pɛəʳ] *n* Birne *f*
pearl [pəːl] *n* Perle *f*
pebble [ˈpɛbl] *n* Kieselstein *m*
pecan [pɪˈkæn] *n* Pekannuss
peck [pɛk] *vt* (*bird*) picken; (*also*: **~ at**) picken an *+dat*
peckish [ˈpɛkɪʃ] (Brit *inf*) *adj* (*hungry*) leicht hungrig
peculiar [pɪˈkjuːlɪəʳ] *adj* (*strange*) seltsam; **~ to** (*exclusive to*) charakteristisch für
peculiarity [pɪkjuːlɪˈærɪtɪ] *n* (*strange habit*) Eigenart *f*; (*distinctive feature*) Besonderheit *f*
pedal [ˈpɛdl] *n* Pedal *nt*
pedestrian [pɪˈdɛstrɪən] *n* Fußgänger(in) *m(f)*
pedestrian crossing (Brit) *n* Fußgängerüberweg *m*
pee [piː] (*inf*) *vi* pinkeln
peel [piːl] *n* Schale *f* ▸ *vt* schälen ▸ *vi* (*paint*) abblättern; (*skin, back etc*) sich schälen
peer [pɪəʳ] *n* (*equal*) Gleichrangige(r) *f(m)* ▸ *vi*: **to ~ at** starren auf *+acc*
peg [pɛg] *n* (*hook, knob*) Haken *m*; (Brit: *also*: **clothes ~**) Wäscheklamme[r] *f*; (*also*: **tent ~**) Hering *m*
pelvis [ˈpɛlvɪs] *n* Becken *nt*
pen [pɛn] *n* (*also*: **fountain ~**) Füller *m*; (*also*: **ballpoint ~**) Kugelschreiber *m*
penalize [ˈpiːnəlaɪz] *vt* (*punish*) bestrafen
penalty [ˈpɛnltɪ] *n* Strafe *f*; (*Sport: Football*) Elfmeter *m*
pence [pɛns] *npl of* **penny**
pencil [ˈpɛnsl] *n* Bleistift *m*
pencil sharpener *n* Bleistiftspitzer *m*
penetrate [ˈpɛnɪtreɪt] *vt* (*person, territory etc*) durchdringen; (*light, water, sound*) eindringen in *+acc*
pen friend (Brit) *n* Brieffreund(in) *m(f)*
penguin [ˈpɛŋgwɪn] *n* Pinguin *m*
penicillin [pɛnɪˈsɪlɪn] *n* Penizillin *nt*
peninsula [pəˈnɪnsjulə] *n* Halbinsel *f*
penis [ˈpiːnɪs] *n* Penis *m*
penknife [ˈpɛnnaɪf] *n* Taschenmesser *nt*
penny [ˈpɛnɪ] (*pl* **pennies** *or* Brit **pence**) *n* Penny *m*; (*US*) Cent *m*
pension [ˈpɛnʃən] *n* Rente *f*
pensioner [ˈpɛnʃənəʳ] (Brit) *n* Rentner(in) *m(f)*
pension scheme, pension plan *n* Rentenversicherung *f*
penultimate [pɛˈnʌltɪmət] *adj* vorletzte(r, s)

eople [ˈpiːpl] *npl* (*persons*) Leute *pl*; (*inhabitants*) Bevölkerung *f* ▶ *n* (*nation, race*) Volk *nt*
epper [ˈpɛpəʳ] *n* (*spice*) Pfeffer *m*; (*vegetable*) Paprika *m*
eppermint [ˈpɛpəmɪnt] *n* (*sweet*) Pfefferminz *nt*
er [pəːʳ] *prep* (*for each*) pro; **~ day/person/kilo** pro Tag/Person/Kilo; **~ annum** pro Jahr
er cent *n* Prozent *nt*
ercentage [pəˈsɛntɪdʒ] *n* Prozentsatz *m*
erceptible [pəˈsɛptɪbl] *adj* (*difference, change*) wahrnehmbar
ercolator [ˈpəːkəleɪtəʳ] *n* (*also:* **coffee ~**) Kaffeemaschine *f*
ercussion [pəˈkʌʃən] *n* (*Mus*) Schlagzeug *nt*
erfect *adj* [ˈpəːfɪkt] perfekt; (*nonsense, idiot etc*) ausgemacht ▶ *vt* [pəˈfɛkt] (*technique*) perfektionieren
erfectly [ˈpəːfɪktlɪ] *adv* vollkommen; (*faultlessly*) perfekt
erform [pəˈfɔːm] *vt* (*operation, ceremony etc*) durchführen; (*task*) erfüllen; (*piece of music, play etc*) aufführen ▶ *vi* auftreten
erformance [pəˈfɔːməns] *n* Leistung *f*; (*of play, show*) Vorstellung *f*
erfume [ˈpəːfjuːm] *n* Parfüm *nt*; (*fragrance*) Duft *m*
erhaps [pəˈhæps] *adv* vielleicht
eriod [ˈpɪərɪəd] *n* (*length of time*) Zeitraum *m*, Periode *f*; (*era*) Zeitalter *nt*; (*Scol*) Stunde *f*; (*esp US: full stop*) Punkt *m*; (*Med: also:* **menstrual ~**) Periode; **for a ~ of 3 weeks** für eine Dauer *or* einen Zeitraum von 3 Wochen
eriodical [pɪərɪˈɔdɪkl] *n* Zeitschrift *f*
eripheral [pəˈrɪfərəl] *n* (*Comput*) Peripheriegerät *nt*
erjury [ˈpəːdʒərɪ] *n* (*in court*) Meineid *m*
erm [pəːm] *n* Dauerwelle *f*
ermanent [ˈpəːmənənt] *adj* dauerhaft; **~ address** ständiger Wohnsitz *m*
ermanently [ˈpəːmənəntlɪ] *adv* (*stay, live*) ständig
ermission [pəˈmɪʃən] *n* Erlaubnis *f*
ermit *n* [ˈpəːmɪt] Genehmigung *f* ▶ *vt* [pəˈmɪt] (*allow*) erlauben; **to ~ sb to do sth** jdm erlauben, etw zu tun
ersecute [ˈpəːsɪkjuːt] *vt* verfolgen
perseverance [pəːsɪˈvɪərns] *n* Ausdauer *f*
persist [pəˈsɪst] *vi*: **to ~ (with** *or* **in)** beharren (auf +*dat*), festhalten (an +*dat*)
persistent [pəˈsɪstənt] *adj* (*person, noise*) beharrlich
person [ˈpəːsn] *n* Person *f*, Mensch *m*; **in ~** persönlich
personal [ˈpəːsnl] *adj* persönlich; (*life*) Privat-
personality [pəːsəˈnælɪtɪ] *n* (*character, person*) Persönlichkeit *f*
personal organizer *n* Terminplaner *m*
personnel [pəːsəˈnɛl] *n* Personal *nt*
perspective [pəˈspɛktɪv] *n* (*also fig*) Perspektive *f*
persuade [pəˈsweɪd] *vt*: **to ~ sb to do sth** jdn dazu überreden, etw zu tun; **to ~ sb that** jdn davon überzeugen, dass
persuasive [pəˈsweɪsɪv] *adj* (*person, argument*) überzeugend
perverse [pəˈvəːs] *adj* (*person*) borniert; (*behaviour*) widernatürlich, pervers
pervert *n* [ˈpəːvəːt] (*sexual deviant*) perverser Mensch *m* ▶ *vt* [pəˈvəːt] (*person, mind*) verderben
perverted [pəˈvəːtɪd] *adj* pervers
pessimist [ˈpɛsɪmɪst] *n* Pessimist(in) *m(f)*
pessimistic [pɛsɪˈmɪstɪk] *adj* pessimistisch
pest [pɛst] *n* (*insect*) Schädling *m*; (*fig: nuisance*) Plage *f*
pester [ˈpɛstəʳ] *vt* belästigen
pesticide [ˈpɛstɪsaɪd] *n* Schädlingsbekämpfungsmittel *nt*, Pestizid *nt*
pet [pɛt] *n* (*animal*) Haustier *nt*; **a ~ rabbit/snake** *etc* ein Kaninchen/eine Schlange *etc* (als Haustier)
petal [ˈpɛtl] *n* Blütenblatt *nt*
petition [pəˈtɪʃən] *n* (*signed document*) Petition *f*
petrol [ˈpɛtrəl] (Brit) *n* Benzin *nt*
petrolhead [ˈpɛtrəlhɛd] *n* (*inf*) Autoliebhaber(in) *m(f)*, Autofreak *m* (*inf*)
petrol pump (Brit) *n* (*in garage*) Zapfsäule *f*
petrol station (Brit) *n* Tankstelle *f*
petrol tank (Brit) *n* Benzintank *m*
pharmacy [ˈfɑːməsɪ] *n* (*shop*) Apotheke *f*; (*science*) Pharmazie *f*

phase [feɪz] *n* Phase *f*
PhD *n abbr* (= *Doctor of Philosophy*) ≈ Dr. phil.
pheasant [ˈfɛznt] *n* Fasan *m*
phenomenon [fəˈnɔmɪnən] (*pl* **phenomena**) *n* Phänomen *nt*
Philippines [ˈfɪlɪpiːnz] *npl*: **the ~** die Philippinen *pl*
philosophical [fɪləˈsɔfɪkl] *adj* philosophisch; (*fig*: *calm, resigned*) gelassen
philosophy [fɪˈlɔsəfɪ] *n* Philosophie *f*
phone [fəun] *n* Telefon *nt* ▸ *vt* anrufen
phone book *n* Telefonbuch *nt*
phone call *n* Anruf *m*
phonecard [ˈfəunkɑːd] *n* Telefonkarte *f*
phone-in [ˈfəunɪn] (Brit) *n* (*Radio, TV*) *Radio-/Fernsehsendung mit Hörer-/ Zuschauerbeteiligung per Telefon*, Phone-in *nt*
photo [ˈfəutəu] *n* Foto *nt*
photobomb [ˈfəutəubɔm] *vt* (*inf*) fotobomben
photocopier [ˈfəutəukɔpɪəʳ] *n* Fotokopierer *m*
photocopy [ˈfəutəukɔpɪ] *n* Fotokopie *f* ▸ *vt* fotokopieren
photograph [ˈfəutəgræf] *n* Fotografie *f* ▸ *vt* fotografieren
photographer [fəˈtɔgrəfəʳ] *n* Fotograf(in) *m(f)*
photography [fəˈtɔgrəfɪ] *n* Fotografie *f*
Photoshop® [ˈfəutəuʃɔp] *n* Photoshop® *nt*
phrase [freɪz] *n* Satz *m*; (*Ling*) Redewendung *f*
phrase book *n* Sprachführer *m*
physical [ˈfɪzɪkl] *adj* (*bodily*) körperlich; **~ examination** ärztliche Untersuchung *f*
physical education *n* Sport-unterricht *m*
physically [ˈfɪzɪklɪ] *adv* (*fit, attractive*) körperlich
physics [ˈfɪzɪks] *n* Physik *f*
physiotherapy [fɪzɪəuˈθɛrəpɪ] *n* Physiotherapie *f*
physique [fɪˈziːk] *n* Körperbau *m*
piano [pɪˈænəu] *n* Klavier *nt*
pick [pɪk] *vt* (*select*) aussuchen; (*gather*: *fruit, mushrooms*) sammeln; (*: flowers*) pflücken
▸ **pick out** *vt* (*select*) aussuchen
▸ **pick up** *vi* (*health*) sich verbessern ▸ *vt* (*from floor etc*) aufheben; (*collect*: *person, parcel etc*) abholen; (*learn*: *skill etc*) mitbekommen
pickle [ˈpɪkl] *n* (*also*: **pickles**) Pickles *pl* ▸ *vt* einlegen
pickpocket [ˈpɪkpɔkɪt] *n* Taschendieb(in) *m(f)*
picnic [ˈpɪknɪk] *n* Picknick *nt*
picture [ˈpɪktʃəʳ] *n* Bild *nt* ▸ *vt* (*imagine*) sich *dat* vorstellen ■ **pictures** *npl* (*Mus*): **the pictures** (Brit *inf*: *the cinema*) das Kino
picture book *n* Bilderbuch *nt*
picturesque [pɪktʃəˈrɛsk] *adj* malerisch
pie [paɪ] *n* (*vegetable, meat*) Pastete *f*; (*fruit*) Torte *f*
piece [piːs] *n* Stück *nt*; (*Draughts etc*) Stein *m*; (*Chess*) Figur *f*; **a ~ of clothing/furniture/music** ein Kleidungs-/Möbel-/Musikstück *nt*; **to take sth to pieces** etw auseinandernehmen
pier [pɪəʳ] *n* Pier *m*
pierce [pɪəs] *vt* durchstechen
pierced [pɪəst] *adj* (*part of body*) gepierct
piercing [ˈpɪəsɪŋ] *adj* (*fig*: *cry, eyes, stare*) durchdringend
pig [pɪg] *n* (*also pej*) Schwein *nt*
pigeon [ˈpɪdʒən] *n* Taube *f*
pigeonhole [ˈpɪdʒənhəul] *n* (*for letters etc*) Fach *nt*
pig-headed [ˈpɪgˈhɛdɪd] (*pej*) *adj* dickköpfig
piglet [ˈpɪglɪt] *n* Ferkel *nt*
pigsty [ˈpɪgstaɪ] *n* (*also fig*) Schweinestall *m*
pigtail [ˈpɪgteɪl] *n* Zopf *m*
pile [paɪl] *n* (*heap*) Haufen *m*; (*stack*) Stapel *m*
▸ **pile up** *vi* sich stapeln
piles [paɪlz] *npl* (*Med*) Hämorr(ho)iden *pl*
pile-up [ˈpaɪlʌp] *n* (*Aut*) Massenkarambolage *f*
pilgrim [ˈpɪlgrɪm] *n* Pilger(in) *m(f)*

Pilgrim Fathers

Die **Pilgrim Fathers** (Pilgerväter) sind eine Gruppe Puritaner, die 1620 England verließen, um dort den religiösen Verfolgungen zu entkommen. Sie überquerten den

Atlantik an Bord der *Mayflower* und gründeten New Plymouth in Neuengland, im heutigen Massachusetts. Diese Pilgerväter werden als Gründer der Vereinigten Staaten betrachtet, und man gedenkt jedes Jahr zu *Thanksgiving* ihrer ersten erfolgreichen Ernte.

pill [pɪl] *n* Tablette *f*; **the ~** (*contraceptive*) die Pille; **to be on the ~** die Pille nehmen
pillar [ˈpɪləʳ] *n* Säule *f*
pillow [ˈpɪləu] *n* (Kopf)kissen *nt*
pillowcase [ˈpɪləukeɪs] *n* (Kopf) kissenbezug *m*
pilot [ˈpaɪlət] *n* (*Aviat*) Pilot(in) *m*(*f*)
pimple [ˈpɪmpl] *n* Pickel *m*
PIN *n abbr* (= *personal identification number*) PIN; **~ number** PIN-Nummer *f*
pin [pɪn] *n* (*metal: for clothes, papers*) Stecknadel *f*; (*Tech*) Stift *m* ▶ *vt* (*fasten with pin*) feststecken; **pins and needles** (*in arms, legs etc*) Kribbeln *nt*
pinch [pɪntʃ] *n* (*of salt etc*) Prise *f* ▶ *vt* (*with finger and thumb*) zwicken; (*inf: steal*) klauen ▶ *vi* (*shoe*) drücken
pine [paɪn] *n* (*also:* **~ tree**) Kiefer *f*
pineapple [ˈpaɪnæpl] *n* Ananas *f*
pink [pɪŋk] *adj* rosa *inv*
pinstripe [ˈpɪnstraɪp], **pinstriped** [ˈpɪnstraɪpt] *adj*: **~ suit** Nadelstreifenanzug *m*
pint [paɪnt] *n* (Bʀɪᴛ: = *568 cc*) (britisches) Pint *nt*; (*US:* = *473 cc*) (amerikanisches) Pint; **a ~** (Bʀɪᴛ *inf: of beer*) ≈ eine Halbe
pious [ˈpaɪəs] *adj* fromm
pip [pɪp] *n* (*of apple, orange*) Kern *m*
pipe [paɪp] *n* (*for water, gas*) Rohr *nt*; (*for smoking*) Pfeife *f*
pirate [ˈpaɪərət] *n* Pirat *m*
Pisces [ˈpaɪsiːz] *n* Fische *pl*; **to be ~** Fische *or* (ein) Fisch sein
piss [pɪs] (!) *vi* pissen (!) ▶ *n* Pisse *f* (!); **~ off!** verpiss dich!; **to take the ~ out of sb** (Bʀɪᴛ) jdn verarschen
pissed [pɪst] (!) *adj* (*drunk*) besoffen
pistachio [pɪˈstɑːʃɪəu] (*pl* **pistachios**) *n* Pistazie *f*
pistol [ˈpɪstl] *n* Pistole *f*
pit [pɪt] *n* Grube *f*; (*coal mine*) Zeche *f*
■ **the pits** *npl* (*Aut*) die Box
pitch [pɪtʃ] *n* (Bʀɪᴛ *Sport: field*) Spielfeld *nt*; (*Mus*) Tonhöhe *f* ▶ *vt* (*throw*) werfen; **to ~ a tent** ein Zelt aufschlagen
pitch-black [ˈpɪtʃˈblæk] *adj* pechschwarz
pitcher [ˈpɪtʃəʳ] *n* (*jug*) Krug *m*
pitiful [ˈpɪtɪful] *adj* (*excuse, attempt*) jämmerlich
pity [ˈpɪtɪ] *n* Mitleid *nt* ▶ *vt* bemitleiden, bedauern; **what a ~!** wie schade!; **to take ~ on sb** Mitleid mit jdm haben
pizza [ˈpiːtsə] *n* Pizza *f*
place [pleɪs] *n* Platz *m*; (*position*) Stelle *f*, Ort *m*; (*home*) Wohnung *f* ▶ *vt* (*put: object*) stellen, legen; **~ of birth** Geburtsort *m*; **to take ~** (*happen*) geschehen, passieren; **at/to his ~** (*home*) bei/zu ihm; **in sb's/sth's ~** anstelle von jdm/etw; **out of ~** (*inappropriate*) unangebracht; **in the first ~** (*first of all*) erstens; **to be placed** (*in race, exam*) platziert sein; **to be placed third** den dritten Platz belegen; **to ~ an order with sb (for sth)** eine Bestellung bei jdm (für etw) aufgeben
place mat *n* Set *m or nt*
plague [pleɪg] *n* (*Med*) Seuche *f*
plaice [pleɪs] *n inv* Scholle *f*
plain [pleɪn] *adj* (*simple*) einfach; (*clear, easily understood*) klar; (*not beautiful*) unattraktiv ▶ *adv* (*wrong, stupid etc*) einfach ▶ *n* (*area of land*) Ebene *f*
plainly [ˈpleɪnlɪ] *adv* (*obviously*) eindeutig; (*clearly*) deutlich, klar
plait [plæt] *n* (*of hair*) Zopf *m*
plan [plæn] *n* Plan *m* ▶ *vt* planen ▶ *vi* planen; **to ~ to do sth** planen *or* vorhaben, etw zu tun
plane [pleɪn] *n* (*Aviat*) Flugzeug *nt*; (*tool*) Hobel *m*
planet [ˈplænɪt] *n* Planet *m*
plank [plæŋk] *n* (*of wood*) Brett *nt*
plant [plɑːnt] *n* (*Bot*) Pflanze *f*; (*machinery*) Maschinen *pl*; (*factory*) Anlage *f* ▶ *vt* (*seed, plant, crops*) pflanzen
plantation [plænˈteɪʃən] *n* Plantage *f*
plaque [plæk] *n* (*on building etc*) Tafel *f*; (*on teeth*) Zahnbelag *m*
plaster [ˈplɑːstəʳ] *n* (*for walls*) Putz *m*; (*also:* **~ of Paris**) Gips *m*; (Bʀɪᴛ: *also: sticking* **~**) Pflaster *nt*; **in ~** (Bʀɪᴛ) in Gips
plastered [ˈplɑːstəd] (*inf*) *adj* (*drunk*) sturzbesoffen

plastic [ˈplæstɪk] *n* Plastik *nt* ▶ *adj* (*bucket, cup etc*) Plastik-
plastic bag *n* Plastiktüte *f*
plastic surgery *n* plastische Chirurgie *f*
plate [pleɪt] *n* Teller *m*; (*on door*) Schild *nt*
platform [ˈplætfɔːm] *n* (*stage*) Podium *nt*; (*Rail*) Bahnsteig *m*
platinum [ˈplætɪnəm] *n* Platin *nt*
play [pleɪ] *n* (*Theat*) (Theater)stück *nt*; (*activity*) Spiel *nt* ▶ *vt* spielen; (*team, opponent*) spielen gegen ▶ *vi* spielen; **to ~ a part** *or* **role in sth** (*fig*) eine Rolle bei etw spielen; **to ~ safe** auf Nummer sicher gehen
▶ **play at** *vt fus* (*do casually*) spielen mit; **what are you playing at?** was soll das?
▶ **play back** *vt* (*recording*) abspielen
▶ **play down** *vt* herunterspielen
player [ˈpleɪəʳ] *n* (*Sport, Mus*) Spieler(in) *m(f)*
playful [ˈpleɪful] *adj* (*person, gesture*) spielerisch; (*animal*) verspielt
playground [ˈpleɪgraund] *n* (*in park*) Spielplatz *m*; (*in school*) Schulhof *m*
playgroup [ˈpleɪgruːp] *n* Spielgruppe *f*
playing card [ˈpleɪɪŋ-] *n* Spielkarte *f*
playing field *n* Sportplatz *m*
playmate [ˈpleɪmeɪt] *n* Spielkamerad(in) *m(f)*
playwright [ˈpleɪraɪt] *n* Dramatiker(in) *m(f)*
plc (Brit) *n abbr* (*= public limited company*) ≈ AG *f*
plea [pliː] *n* (*request*) Bitte *f*
plead [pliːd] *vi* (*Law*) *vor Gericht eine Schuld-/Unschuldserklärung abgeben*; **to ~ with sb** (*beg*) jdn inständig bitten; **to ~ guilty/not guilty** sich schuldig/nicht schuldig bekennen
pleasant [ˈplɛznt] *adj* angenehm
pleasantly [ˈplɛzntlɪ] *adv* (*surprised*) angenehm
please [pliːz] *excl* bitte ▶ *vt* (*satisfy*) zufriedenstellen; **~ yourself!** (*inf*) wie du willst!
pleased [pliːzd] *adj* (*happy*) erfreut; (*satisfied*) zufrieden; **~ to meet you** freut mich(, Sie kennenzulernen)
pleasing [ˈpliːzɪŋ] *adj* (*remark, picture etc*) erfreulich
pleasure [ˈplɛʒəʳ] *n* (*happiness, satisfaction*) Freude *f*; (*fun, enjoyable experience*) Vergnügen *nt*; **it's a ~, my ~** gern geschehen
pledge [plɛdʒ] *n* (*promise*) Versprechen *nt* ▶ *vt* (*promise*) versprechen
plenty [ˈplɛntɪ] *n* (*lots*) eine Menge; (*sufficient*) reichlich; **~ of** eine Menge; **we've got ~ of time to get there** wir haben jede Menge Zeit, dorthin zu kommen
pliable [ˈplaɪəbl] *adj* (*material*) biegsam
pliers [ˈplaɪəz] *npl* Zange *f*
plimsolls [ˈplɪmsəlz] (Brit) *npl* Turnschuhe *pl*
plonk [plɔŋk] (*inf*) *n* (Brit: *wine*) (billiger) Wein *m* ▶ *vt*: **to ~ sth down** etw hinknallen
plot [plɔt] *n* (*secret plan*) Komplott *nt*; (*of story, play, film*) Handlung *f* ▶ *vi* (*conspire*) sich verschwören; **a ~ of land** ein Grundstück *nt*
plough, (US) **plow** [plau] *n* Pflug *m* ▶ *vt* pflügen
ploughman's lunch [ˈplaumənz-] (Brit) *n Imbiss aus Brot, Käse und Pickles*
plow [plau] (US) = **plough**
pluck [plʌk] *vt* (*musical instrument, eyebrows*) zupfen; (*bird*) rupfen; **to ~ up courage** allen Mut zusammennehmen
plug [plʌg] *n* (*Elec*) Stecker *m*; (*stopper*) Stöpsel *m*; (*Aut: also:* **spark(ing) ~**) Zündkerze *f* ▶ *vt* (*inf: advertise*) Reklame machen für
▶ **plug in** *vt* (*Elec*) anschließen
plug-in [ˈplʌgɪn] *n* (*Comput*) Zusatzprogramm *nt*, Plug-in *nt*
plum [plʌm] *n* (*fruit*) Pflaume *f* ▶ *adj* (*inf*): **a ~ job** ein Traumjob
plumber [ˈplʌməʳ] *n* Klempner *m*
plumbing [ˈplʌmɪŋ] *n* (*piping*) Rohrleitungen *pl*; (*trade*) Klempnerei *f*
plump [plʌmp] *adj* (*person*) füllig
plunge [plʌndʒ] *vt* (*hand, knife*) stoßen ▶ *vi* (*thing*) stürzen; (*bird, person*) sich stürzen; **the room was plunged into darkness** das Zimmer war in Dunkelheit getaucht
plural [ˈpluərl] *n* Plural *m*
plus [plʌs] *prep, adj* plus; **it's a ~** (*fig*) es ist ein Vorteil *or* ein Pluspunkt; **ten/twenty ~** (*more than*) über zehn/zwanzig
plus-one [ˈplʌsˈwʌn] *n* Begleitperson *f*; **he was my ~ for the party** er war meine Begleitperson auf der Party

plywood [ˈplaɪwud] *n* Sperrholz *nt*
p.m. *adv abbr* (= *post meridiem*) nachmittags; (*later*) abends
pneumonia [nju:ˈməunɪə] *n* Lungenentzündung *f*
poached [pəutʃt] *adj*: **~ eggs** verlorene Eier
PO Box *n abbr* (= *Post Office Box*) Postf.
pocket [ˈpɔkɪt] *n* Tasche *f* ▶ *vt* (*put in one's pocket, steal*) einstecken
pocketbook [ˈpɔkɪtbuk] *n* (*US: wallet*) Brieftasche *f*
pocket calculator *n* Taschenrechner *m*
pocket money *n* Taschengeld *nt*
poem [ˈpəuɪm] *n* Gedicht *nt*
poet [ˈpəuɪt] *n* Dichter(in) *m(f)*
poetic [pəuˈɛtɪk] *adj* poetisch
poetry [ˈpəuɪtrɪ] *n* (*poems*) Gedichte *pl*; (*writing*) Poesie *f*
point [pɔɪnt] *n* Punkt *m*; (*of needle, knife etc*) Spitze *f*; (*purpose*) Sinn *m*, Zweck *m*; (*moment*) Zeitpunkt *m*; (*also*: **decimal ~**) ≈ Komma *nt* ▶ *vt* (*show, mark*) deuten auf +*acc* ▶ *vi* (*with finger, stick etc*) zeigen ■ **points** *npl* (*Rail*) Weichen *pl*; **two ~ five** (= 2.5) zwei Komma fünf; **to be on the ~ of doing sth** im Begriff sein, etw zu tun; **to come** *or* **get to the ~** zur Sache kommen; **there's no ~ talking to you** es ist sinnlos, mit dir zu reden; **to ~ sth at sb** (*gun etc*) etw auf jdn richten; (*finger*) mit etw auf jdn *acc* zeigen; **to ~ at** zeigen auf +*acc*
▶ **point out** *vt* hinweisen auf +*acc*
pointed [ˈpɔɪntɪd] *adj* spitz; (*fig: remark*) spitz
pointer [ˈpɔɪntə^r] *n* (*on chart, machine*) Zeiger *m*; (*fig: piece of information or advice*) Hinweis *m*
pointless [ˈpɔɪntlɪs] *adj* sinnlos
poison [ˈpɔɪzn] *n* Gift *nt* ▶ *vt* vergiften
poisonous [ˈpɔɪznəs] *adj* (*fumes, chemicals etc*) giftig
poke [pəuk] *vt* (*with finger, stick etc*) stoßen; **to ~ sth in(to)** (*put*) etw stecken in +*acc*
Poland [ˈpəulənd] *n* Polen *nt*
polar [ˈpəulə^r] *adj* (*icecap*) polar; (*region*) Polar-
polar bear *n* Eisbär *m*
Pole [pəul] *n* Pole *m*, Polin *f*
pole [pəul] *n* (*post, stick*) Stange *f*; (*Geog, Elec*) Pol *m*
pole vault *n* Stabhochsprung *m*
police [pəˈli:s] *npl* (*organization*) Polizei *f*
police car *n* Polizeiauto *nt*
policeman [pəˈli:smən] *n* (*irreg*) Polizist *m*
police officer *n* Polizeibeamte(r) *m*, Polizeibeamtin *f*
police station *n* Polizeiwache *f*
policewoman [pəˈli:swumən] *n* (*irreg*) Polizistin *f*
policy [ˈpɔlɪsɪ] *n* (*Pol, Econ*) Politik *f*; (*also*: **insurance ~**) (Versicherungs) police *f*; (*of newspaper*) Grundsatz *m*
polio [ˈpəulɪəu] *n* Kinderlähmung *f*
Polish [ˈpəulɪʃ] *adj* polnisch ▶ *n* (*Ling*) Polnisch *nt*
polish [ˈpɔlɪʃ] *n* (*for shoes*) Creme *f*; (*for furniture*) Politur *f*; (*for floors*) Bohnerwachs *nt*; (*shine: on shoes, floor etc*) Glanz *m*; (*fig: refinement*) Schliff *m* ▶ *vt* (*shoes*) putzen; (*floor, furniture etc*) polieren
polite [pəˈlaɪt] *adj* höflich
politeness [pəˈlaɪtnɪs] *n* Höflichkeit *f*
political [pəˈlɪtɪkl] *adj* politisch
politically [pəˈlɪtɪklɪ] *adv* politisch; **~ correct** politisch korrekt
politician [pɔlɪˈtɪʃən] *n* Politiker(in) *m(f)*
politics [ˈpɔlɪtɪks] *n* Politik *f*
poll [pəul] *n* (*also*: **opinion ~**) (Meinungs)umfrage *f*; (*election*) Wahl *f*
pollen [ˈpɔlən] *n* Pollen *m*, Blütenstaub *m*
pollen count *n* Pollenkonzentration *f*
polling station [ˈpəulɪŋ-] (BRIT) *n* Wahllokal *nt*
pollute [pəˈlu:t] *vt* verschmutzen
pollution [pəˈlu:ʃən] *n* (*process*) Verschmutzung *f*
pompous [ˈpɔmpəs] (*pej*) *adj* (*person*) aufgeblasen; (*piece of writing*) geschwollen
pond [pɔnd] *n* Teich *m*
pony [ˈpəunɪ] *n* Pony *nt*
ponytail [ˈpəunɪteɪl] *n* Pferdeschwanz *m*
poodle [ˈpu:dl] *n* Pudel *m*
pool [pu:l] *n* (*also*: **swimming ~**) Schwimmbad *nt*; (*of blood*) Lache *f*; (*Sport*) Poolbillard *nt* ▶ *vt* (*money*) zusammenlegen
poor [puə^r] *adj* arm; (*bad*) schlecht ▶ *npl*: **the ~** die Armen *pl*
poorly [ˈpuəlɪ] *adj* (*ill*) krank ▶ *adv* (*badly: designed, paid*) schlecht
pop [pɔp] *n* (*Mus*) Pop *m*; (*sound*) Knall *m* ▶ *vi* (*balloon*) platzen; (*cork*) knallen ▶ *vt*: **to ~ sth into/onto sth**

etw schnell in etw *acc* stecken/auf etw *acc* legen
▶ **pop in** *vi* vorbeikommen
popcorn [ˈpɔpkɔːn] *n* Popcorn *nt*
pope [pəup] *n* Papst *m*
poppy [ˈpɔpɪ] *n* Mohn *m*
pop star *n* Popstar *m*
popular [ˈpɔpjuləʳ] *adj* (*well-liked, fashionable*) beliebt; (*idea*) weitverbreitet
population [pɔpjuˈleɪʃən] *n* Bevölkerung *f*
pop-up [ˈpɔpʌp] *adj* (*esp Comput*) Pop-up-, Popup- ▶ *n* (*also shop, restaurant*) Pop-up *nt*
porcelain [ˈpɔːslɪn] *n* Porzellan *nt*
porch [pɔːtʃ] *n* (*entrance*) Vorbau *m*; (*US*) Veranda *f*
porcupine [ˈpɔːkjupaɪn] *n* Stachelschwein *nt*
pork [pɔːk] *n* Schweinefleisch *nt*
pork chop *n* Schweinekotelett *nt*
porn [pɔːn] (*inf*) *n* Porno *m*
pornographic [pɔːnəˈgræfɪk] *adj* pornografisch
pornography [pɔːˈnɔgrəfɪ] *n* Pornografie *f*
porridge [ˈpɔrɪdʒ] *n* Haferbrei *m*
port [pɔːt] *n* (*harbour*) Hafen *m*; (*Naut: left side*) Backbord *nt*; (*wine*) Portwein *m*; (*Comput*) Port *m*
portable [ˈpɔːtəbl] *adj* (*television, typewriter etc*) tragbar
portal [ˈpɔːtl] *n* Portal *nt*
porter [ˈpɔːtəʳ] *n* (*for luggage*) Gepäckträger *m*; (*doorkeeper*) Pförtner *m*
porthole [ˈpɔːthəul] *n* Bullauge *nt*
portion [ˈpɔːʃən] *n* (*part*) Teil *m*; (*helping of food*) Portion *f*
portrait [ˈpɔːtreɪt] *n* Porträt *nt*
portray [pɔːˈtreɪ] *vt* darstellen
Portugal [ˈpɔːtjugl] *n* Portugal *nt*
Portuguese [pɔːtjuˈgiːz] *adj* portugiesisch ▶ *n inv* (*person*) Portugiese *m*, Portugiesin *f*; (*Ling*) Portugiesisch *nt*
pose [pəuz] *n* Pose *f* ▶ *vt* (*question, problem*) aufwerfen ▶ *vi*: **to ~ as** (*pretend*) sich ausgeben als
posh [pɔʃ] (*inf*) *adj* vornehm
position [pəˈzɪʃən] *n* (*place: of thing, person*) Position *f*, Lage *f*; (*of person's body*) Stellung *f*; (*job*) Stelle *f*; (*in race etc*) Platz *m* ▶ *vt* (*person, thing*) stellen
positive [ˈpɔzɪtɪv] *adj* positiv; (*certain*) sicher
possess [pəˈzɛs] *vt* besitzen
possession [pəˈzɛʃən] *n* Besitz *m*
▪ **possessions** *npl* (*belongings*) Besitz *m*
possessive [pəˈzɛsɪv] *adj* (*nature etc*) besitzergreifend
possibility [pɔsɪˈbɪlɪtɪ] *n* Möglichkeit *f*
possible [ˈpɔsɪbl] *adj* möglich; **as far as ~** so weit wie möglich; **if ~** falls *or* wenn möglich; **as soon as ~** so bald wie möglich
possibly [ˈpɔsɪblɪ] *adv* (*perhaps*) vielleicht; **if you ~ can** falls überhaupt möglich
post [pəust] *n* (Brit) Post *f*; (*pole, goal post*) Pfosten *m*; (*job*) Stelle *f* ▶ *vt* (Brit: *letter*) aufgeben; (*on website*) posten; **to keep sb posted** (*informed*) jdn auf dem Laufenden halten
postage [ˈpəustɪdʒ] *n* Porto *nt*
postal [ˈpəustl] *adj* (*charges, service*) Post-
postal order (Brit) *n* Postanweisung *f*
postbox [ˈpəustbɔks] *n* Briefkasten *m*
postcard [ˈpəustkɑːd] *n* Postkarte *f*
postcode [ˈpəustkəud] (Brit) *n* Postleitzahl *f*
poster [ˈpəustəʳ] *n* Poster *nt*, Plakat *nt*
postgraduate [ˈpəustˈgrædjuət] *n* Graduierte(r) *f*(*m*) (*im Weiterstudium*)
postman [ˈpəustmən] *n* (*irreg*) Briefträger *m*
postmark [ˈpəustmɑːk] *n* Poststempel *m*
postmortem [pəustˈmɔːtəm] *n* (*Med*) Obduktion *f*
post office *n* (*building*) Post *f*
postpone [pəusˈpəun] *vt* verschieben
posture [ˈpɔstʃəʳ] *n* (*also fig*) Haltung *f*
pot [pɔt] *n* Topf *m*; (*teapot, coffee pot, potful*) Kanne *f*; (*inf: marijuana*) Pot *nt* ▶ *vt* (*plant*) eintopfen
potato [pəˈteɪtəu] (*pl* **potatoes**) *n* Kartoffel *f*
potato chips (*US*) *npl* = **potato crisps**
potato crisps *npl* Kartoffelchips *pl*
potato peeler *n* Kartoffelschäler *m*
potent [ˈpəutnt] *adj* (*powerful*) stark
potential [pəˈtɛnʃl] *adj* potenziell ▶ *n* Potenzial *nt*
potentially [pəˈtɛnʃəlɪ] *adv* potenziell
pothole [ˈpɔthəul] *n* (*in road*) Schlagloch *nt*; (*cave*) Höhle *f*

potter [ˈpɔtəʳ] *n* Töpfer(in) *m(f)* ▸ *vi*: **to ~ around, ~ about** (BRIT) herumhantieren
pottery [ˈpɔtərɪ] *n* (*pots, dishes etc*) Töpferwaren *pl*
potty [ˈpɔtɪ] *adj* (*inf*: *mad*) verrückt ▸ *n* (*for child*) Töpfchen *nt*
poultry [ˈpəultrɪ] *n* Geflügel *nt*
pounce [pauns] *vi*: **to ~ on** (*also fig*) sich stürzen auf +*acc*
pound [paund] *n* (*unit of money*) Pfund *nt*; (*unit of weight*) (britisches) Pfund (=453,6*g*)
pour [pɔːʳ] *vt* (*tea, wine etc*) gießen; (*cereal etc*) schütten; **to ~ sb a glass of wine/a cup of tea** jdm ein Glas Wein/ eine Tasse Tee einschenken
pouring [ˈpɔːrɪŋ] *adj*: **~ rain** strömender Regen *m*
poverty [ˈpɔvətɪ] *n* Armut *f*
powder [ˈpaudəʳ] *n* Pulver *nt* ▸ *vt*: **to ~ one's face** sich *dat* das Gesicht pudern
powdered milk [ˈpaudəd-] *n* Milchpulver *nt*
powder room (*euph*) *n* Damentoilette *f*
power [ˈpauəʳ] *n* (*control, legal right*) Macht *f*; (*ability*) Fähigkeit *f*; (*electricity*) Strom *m*; **to be in ~** (*Pol etc*) an der Macht sein
power cut *n* Stromausfall *m*
powerful [ˈpauəful] *adj* (*person, organization*) mächtig; (*engine*) stark; (*argument, evidence*) massiv
powerless [ˈpauəlɪs] *adj* machtlos
power station *n* Kraftwerk *nt*
power steering *n* (*Aut*) Servolenkung *f*
PR *n abbr* = **public relations**; (*Pol*) = **proportional representation**
practical [ˈpræktɪkl] *adj* praktisch
practically [ˈpræktɪklɪ] *adv* praktisch
practice [ˈpræktɪs] *n* (*also Med, Law*) Praxis *f*; (*custom*) Brauch *m*; (*exercise*) Übung *f* ▸ *vt, vi* (*US*) = **practise**; **in ~** in der Praxis; **out of ~** aus der Übung; **to put sth into ~** etw in die Praxis umsetzen
practise, (*US*) **practice** [ˈpræktɪs] *vt* (*train at*) üben; (*carry out*: *custom*) pflegen; (: *activity etc*) ausüben ▸ *vi* (*lawyer, doctor etc*) praktizieren
Prague [prɑːg] *n* Prag *nt*
praise [preɪz] *n* Lob *nt* ▸ *vt* loben
pram [præm] (BRIT) *n* Kinderwagen *m*
prawn [prɔːn] *n* (*Culin, Zool*) Garnele *f*, Krabbe *f*

pray [preɪ] *vi* beten; **to ~ for sb/sth** (*Rel, fig*) für jdn/um etw beten
prayer [prɛəʳ] *n* Gebet *nt*
pre... [priː] *pref* prä-; **pre...-1970** vor 1970
preach [priːtʃ] *vi* (*Rel*) predigen
prearranged [priːəˈreɪndʒd] *adj* (vorher) vereinbart
precaution [prɪˈkɔːʃən] *n* Vorsichtsmaßnahme *f*
precede [prɪˈsiːd] *vt* (*event*) vorausgehen +*dat*
preceding [prɪˈsiːdɪŋ] *adj* vorhergehend
precinct [ˈpriːsɪŋkt] *n* (*US*: *part of city*) Bezirk *m*; **shopping ~** (BRIT) Einkaufsviertel *nt*
precious [ˈprɛʃəs] *adj* wertvoll, kostbar
precious stone *n* Edelstein *m*
précis [ˈpreɪsiː] *n inv* Zusammenfassung *f*
precise [prɪˈsaɪs] *adj* genau
precondition [ˈpriːkənˈdɪʃən] *n* Vorbedingung *f*
predecessor [ˈpriːdɪsɛsəʳ] *n* Vorgänger(in) *m(f)*
predicament [prɪˈdɪkəmənt] *n* Notlage *f*
predict [prɪˈdɪkt] *vt* vorhersagen
predictable [prɪˈdɪktəbl] *adj* vorhersagbar
predominant [prɪˈdɔmɪnənt] *adj* vorherrschend
predominantly [prɪˈdɔmɪnəntlɪ] *adv* überwiegend
preface [ˈprɛfəs] *n* Vorwort *nt*
prefer [prɪˈfəːʳ] *vt* (*like better*) vorziehen; **to ~ doing** *or* **to do sth** (es) vorziehen, etw zu tun
preferably [ˈprɛfrəblɪ] *adv* vorzugsweise, am besten
preference [ˈprɛfrəns] *n*: **to have a ~ for** (*liking*) eine Vorliebe haben für
preferential [prɛfəˈrɛnʃəl] *adj*: **~ treatment** bevorzugte Behandlung
prefix [ˈpriːfɪks] *n* (*Ling*) Präfix *nt*
pregnancy [ˈprɛgnənsɪ] *n* (*of woman*) Schwangerschaft *f*
pregnant [ˈprɛgnənt] *adj* (*woman*) schwanger; **3 months ~** im vierten Monat (schwanger)
prejudice [ˈprɛdʒudɪs] *n* (*bias against*) Vorurteil *nt*
prejudiced [ˈprɛdʒudɪst] *adj* (*person, view*) voreingenommen

preliminary [prɪˈlɪmɪnərɪ] *adj* (*step, arrangements*) vorbereitend; (*remarks*) einleitend
premature [ˈprɛmətʃuəʳ] *adj* (*earlier than expected*) vorzeitig; **you are being a little ~** Sie sind etwas voreilig
premiere [ˈprɛmɪɛəʳ] *n* Premiere *f*
premise [ˈprɛmɪs] *n* (*of argument*) Voraussetzung *f* ▪ **premises** *npl* (*of business etc*) Räumlichkeiten *pl*
preoccupied [pri:ˈɔkjupaɪd] *adj* (*with work, family*) beschäftigt
pre-owned [pri:ˈəund] *adj* gebraucht
prepaid [pri:ˈpeɪd] *adj* (*paid in advance*) im Voraus bezahlt; (*envelope*) frankiert
preparation [prɛpəˈreɪʃən] *n* Vorbereitung *f*
prepare [prɪˈpɛəʳ] *vt* vorbereiten; (*food, meal*) zubereiten ▶ *vi*: **to ~ for** sich vorbereiten auf *+acc*
prerequisite [pri:ˈrɛkwɪzɪt] *n* Grundvoraussetzung *f*
prescribe [prɪˈskraɪb] *vt* (*Med*) verschreiben; (*demand*) vorschreiben
prescription [prɪˈskrɪpʃən] *n* (*Med: slip of paper*) Rezept *nt*
presence [ˈprɛzns] *n* Gegenwart *f*
present *adj* [ˈprɛznt] (*current*) gegenwärtig; (*in attendance*) anwesend ▶ *n* (*gift*) Geschenk *nt*; (*Ling: also:* **~ tense**) Präsens *nt*, Gegenwart *f* ▶ *vt* [prɪˈzɛnt] (*plan, report*) vorlegen; (*cause, provide, portray*) darstellen; (*information, view*) darlegen; (*Radio, TV*) leiten; **at ~** gegenwärtig, im Augenblick; **to ~ sth to sb, ~ sb with sth** jdm etw übergeben *or* überreichen
present-day [ˈprɛzntdeɪ] *adj* heutig
presently [ˈprɛzntlɪ] *adv* (*soon*) bald; (*currently*) derzeit, gegenwärtig
preservative [prɪˈzə:vətɪv] *n* Konservierungsmittel *nt*
preserve [prɪˈzə:v] *vt* erhalten; (*food*) konservieren
president [ˈprɛzɪdənt] *n* (*Pol*) Präsident(in) *m(f)*
presidential [prɛzɪˈdɛnʃl] *adj* (*election, campaign etc*) Präsidentschafts-; (*adviser, representative etc*) des Präsidenten
press [prɛs] *n* (*also:* **printing ~**) Presse *f* ▶ *vt* drücken; (*button, sb's hand etc*) drücken ▶ *vi* (*squeeze*) drücken; **the P~** (*newspapers, journalists*) die Presse
pressing [ˈprɛsɪŋ] *adj* (*urgent*) dringend
press stud *n* (Brit) Druckknopf *m*
press-up [ˈprɛsʌp] (Brit) *n* Liegestütz *m*
pressure [ˈprɛʃəʳ] *n* (*also fig*) Druck *m* ▶ *vt*: **to ~ sb to do sth** jdn dazu drängen, etw zu tun; **to put ~ on sb (to do sth)** Druck auf jdn ausüben(, etw zu tun)
pressure cooker *n* Schnellkochtopf *m*
pressurize [ˈprɛʃəraɪz] *vt*: **to ~ sb (to do sth** *or* **into doing sth)** jdn unter Druck setzen(, etw zu tun)
presumably [prɪˈzju:məblɪ] *adv* vermutlich
presume [prɪˈzju:m] *vt*: **to ~ (that)** (*assume*) annehmen(, dass)
presumptuous [prɪˈzʌmpʃəs] *adj* anmaßend
presuppose [pri:səˈpəuz] *vt* voraussetzen
pretend [prɪˈtɛnd] *vt* (*feign*) vorgeben ▶ *vi* (*feign*) so tun, als ob; **I don't ~ to understand it** (*claim*) ich erhebe nicht den Anspruch, es zu verstehen
pretentious [prɪˈtɛnʃəs] *adj* anmaßend
pretty [ˈprɪtɪ] *adj* hübsch ▶ *adv*: **~ good** ganz gut
prevent [prɪˈvɛnt] *vt* verhindern; **to ~ sb from doing sth** jdn daran hindern, etw zu tun
preview [ˈpri:vju:] *n* (*of film*) Vorpremiere *f*; (*of exhibition*) Vernissage *f*
previous [ˈpri:vɪəs] *adj* (*earlier*) früher
previously [ˈpri:vɪəslɪ] *adv* (*formerly*) früher
prey [preɪ] *n* Beute *f*
price [praɪs] *n* (*also fig*) Preis *m* ▶ *vt*: **to be priced at £30** £30 kosten
priceless [ˈpraɪslɪs] *adj* (*inf: amusing*) unbezahlbar
price list *n* Preisliste *f*
price tag *n* Preisschild *nt*
prick [prɪk] *n* (*sting*) Stich *m*; (*offensive: penis*) Schwanz *m*; (*: idiot*) Arsch *m* (*!*) ▶ *vt* stechen
prickly [ˈprɪklɪ] *adj* (*plant*) stachelig
pride [praɪd] *n* Stolz *m*; (*pej: arrogance*) Hochmut *m* ▶ *vt*: **to take (a) ~ in** stolz sein auf *+acc*
priest [pri:st] *n* Priester *m*
priestess [ˈpri:stɪs] *n* Priesterin *f*

primarily [ˈpraɪmərɪlɪ] *adv* in erster Linie, hauptsächlich
primary [ˈpraɪmərɪ] *adj* (*principal*) Haupt-, hauptsächlich; (*education, teacher*) Grundschul-
primary school (BRIT) *n* Grundschule *f*
prime [praɪm] *adj* (*most important*) oberste(r, s); (*best quality*) erstklassig ▶ *n* (*of person's life*) die besten Jahre *pl*
Prime Minister *n* Premierminister(in) *m(f)*
prime time *n* (*Radio, TV*) Hauptsendezeit *f*
primitive [ˈprɪmɪtɪv] *adj* (*tribe, tool, conditions etc*) primitiv
primrose [ˈprɪmrəuz] *n* gelbe Schlüsselblume *f*
prince [prɪns] *n* Prinz *m*
princess [prɪnˈsɛs] *n* Prinzessin *f*
principal [ˈprɪnsɪpl] *adj* (*most important*) Haupt-, wichtigste(r, s) ▶ *n* (*of school, college*) Rektor(in) *m(f)*
principle [ˈprɪnsɪpl] *n* Prinzip *nt*; **in ~** im Prinzip, prinzipiell; **on ~** aus Prinzip
print [prɪnt] *n* (*Art*) Druck *m*; (*Phot*) Abzug *m* ▶ *vt* (*produce*) drucken; (*publish*) veröffentlichen; (*write in capitals*) in Druckschrift schreiben; **out of ~** vergriffen
▶ **print out** *vt* (*Comput*) ausdrucken
printed matter [ˈprɪntɪd-] *n* Drucksache *f*
printer [ˈprɪntə^r] *n* (*machine*) Drucker *m*; (*person*) Drucker(in) *m(f)*
print-out [ˈprɪntaut] (*Comput*) *n* Ausdruck *m*
prior [ˈpraɪə^r] *adj* (*previous: knowledge, warning*) vorherig; (*: engagement*) früher; **~ to** vor *+dat*
priority [praɪˈɔrɪtɪ] *n* vorrangige Angelegenheit *f* ▪ **priorities** *npl* Prioritäten *pl*
prison [ˈprɪzn] *n* Gefängnis *nt*
prisoner [ˈprɪznə^r] *n* Gefangene(r) *f(m)*
prisoner of war *n* Kriegsgefangene(r) *f(m)*
privacy [ˈprɪvəsɪ] *n* Privatsphäre *f*
private [ˈpraɪvɪt] *adj* privat ▶ *n* (*Mil*) Gefreite(r) *m*; **in ~** privat
privately [ˈpraɪvɪtlɪ] *adv* privat; (*secretly*) insgeheim
privatize [ˈpraɪvɪtaɪz] *vt* privatisieren
privilege [ˈprɪvɪlɪdʒ] *n* (*advantage*) Privileg *nt*
privileged [ˈprɪvɪlɪdʒd] *adj* privilegiert
prize [praɪz] *n* Preis *m*
prize money *n* Geldpreis *m*
prizewinner [ˈpraɪzwɪnə^r] *n* Preisträger(in) *m(f)*
prizewinning [ˈpraɪzwɪnɪŋ] *adj* preisgekrönt
pro [prəu] *n* (*Sport*) Profi *m*; **the pros and cons** das Für und Wider
pro- [prəu] *pref* (*in favour of*) pro-
probability [prɔbəˈbɪlɪtɪ] *n* Wahrscheinlichkeit *f*
probable [ˈprɔbəbl] *adj* wahrscheinlich
probably [ˈprɔbəblɪ] *adv* wahrscheinlich
probation [prəˈbeɪʃən] *n*: **on ~** (*lawbreaker*) auf Bewährung; (*employee*) auf Probe
probe [prəub] *n* (*Med, Space*) Sonde *f*; (*enquiry*) Untersuchung *f* ▶ *vt* (*investigate*) untersuchen; (*poke*) bohren in *+dat*
problem [ˈprɔbləm] *n* Problem *nt*; **no ~!** kein Problem!
procedure [prəˈsiːdʒə^r] *n* Verfahren *nt*
proceed [prəˈsiːd] *vi* (*carry on*) fortfahren; (*person: go*) sich bewegen; **to ~ to do sth** etw tun
proceedings [prəˈsiːdɪŋz] *npl* (*Law*) Verfahren *nt*
proceeds [ˈprəusiːdz] *npl* Erlös *m*
process [ˈprəusɛs] *n* (*series of actions*) Verfahren *nt*; (*Biol, Chem*) Prozess *m* ▶ *vt* (*raw materials, food, Comput: data*) verarbeiten; (*application*) bearbeiten; (*Phot*) entwickeln
procession [prəˈsɛʃən] *n* Umzug *m*
processor [ˈprəusesə^r] *n* (*Comput*) Prozessor *m*; (*Culin*) Küchenmaschine *f*
produce *n* [ˈprɔdjuːs] (*Agr*) (Boden) produkte *pl* ▶ *vt* [prəˈdjuːs] (*goods, commodity*) produzieren, herstellen; (*Biol, Chem*) erzeugen; (*fig: evidence etc*) liefern; (*: passport etc*) vorlegen; (*play, film, programme*) produzieren
producer [prəˈdjuːsə^r] *n* (*person*) Produzent(in) *m(f)*; (*country, company*) Produzent *m*, Hersteller *m*
product [ˈprɔdʌkt] *n* Produkt *nt*
production [prəˈdʌkʃən] *n* Produktion *f*; (*Theat*) Inszenierung *f*
productive [prəˈdʌktɪv] *adj* produktiv
profession [prəˈfɛʃən] *n* Beruf *m*
professional [prəˈfɛʃənl] *adj* (*organization, musician etc*) Berufs-;

(*misconduct, advice*) beruflich ▶ *n* (*Sport*) Profi *m*
professor [prəˈfɛsəʳ] *n* (Brit) Professor(in) *m(f)*; (*US*, Canada) Dozent(in) *m(f)*
proficient [prəˈfɪʃənt] *adj* fähig
profile [ˈprəufaɪl] *n* (*of person's face*) Profil *nt*; **to keep a low ~** (*fig*) sich zurückhalten
profit [ˈprɔfɪt] *n* (*Comm*) Gewinn *m* ▶ *vi*: **to ~ by** *or* **from** (*fig*) profitieren von
profitable [ˈprɔfɪtəbl] *adj* (*business, deal*) rentabel, einträglich
profound [prəˈfaund] *adj* (*shock*) schwer, tief; (*idea, book*) tief schürfend
program [ˈprəugræm] (*Comput*) *n* Programm *nt* ▶ *vt* programmieren
programme, (*US*) **program** [ˈprəugræm] *n* Programm *nt* ▶ *vt* (*machine, system*) programmieren
programmer [ˈprəugræməʳ] *n* Programmierer(in) *m(f)*
programming, (*US*) **programing** [ˈprəugræmɪŋ] *n* Programmierung *f*
programming language *n* Programmiersprache *f*
progress *n* [ˈprəugrɛs] Fortschritt *m* ▶ *vi* [prəˈgres] (*advance*) vorankommen; **to make ~** Fortschritte machen
progressive [prəˈgrɛsɪv] *adj* (*enlightened*) progressiv, fortschrittlich
progressively [prəˈgrɛsɪvlɪ] *adv* (*gradually*) zunehmend
prohibit [prəˈhɪbɪt] *vt* (*ban*) verbieten
project *n* [ˈprɔdʒɛkt] (*plan, scheme*) Projekt *nt* ▶ *vt* [prəˈdʒɛkt] (*plan*) planen ▶ *vi* (*stick out*) hervorragen
projector [prəˈdʒɛktəʳ] *n* Projektor *m*
prolong [prəˈlɔŋ] *vt* verlängern
prom [prɔm] *n abbr* = **promenade**; (*Mus*) = **promenade concert**; (*student ball*) Studentenball *m*
promenade [prɔməˈnɑːd] *n* Promenade *f*
promenade concert (Brit) *n* Promenadenkonzert *nt*
prominent [ˈprɔmɪnənt] *adj* (*person*) prominent; (*very noticeable*) herausragend
promiscuous [prəˈmɪskjuəs] *adj* promisk
promise [ˈprɔmɪs] *n* (*vow*) Versprechen *nt* ▶ *vi* versprechen ▶ *vt*: **to ~ sb sth, ~ sth to sb** jdm etw versprechen; **to ~ (sb) to do sth** (jdm) versprechen, etw zu tun
promising [ˈprɔmɪsɪŋ] *adj* vielversprechend
promote [prəˈməut] *vt* (*employee*) befördern; (*advertise*) werben für; (*encourage: peace etc*) fördern
promotion [prəˈməuʃən] *n* (*at work*) Beförderung *f*; (*of product, event*) Werbung *f*
prompt [prɔmpt] *adj* prompt, sofortig ▶ *adv* (*exactly*) pünktlich ▶ *vt* (*Theat*) soufflieren +*dat*; **at 8 o'clock ~** (um) Punkt 8 Uhr
prone [prəun] *adj*: **to be ~ to sth** zu etw neigen
pronounce [prəˈnauns] *vt* (*word*) aussprechen
pronounced [prəˈnaunst] *adj* (*noticeable*) ausgeprägt
pronunciation [prənʌnsɪˈeɪʃən] *n* Aussprache *f*
proof [pruːf] *n* (*evidence*) Beweis *m*; **to be 70 % ~** (*alcohol*) ≈ einen Alkoholgehalt von 40% haben
prop [prɔp] *n* (*support*) Stütze *f* ▶ *vt* (*lean*): **to ~ sth against sth** etw an etw *acc* lehnen
▶ **prop up** *vt sep* (*thing*) (ab)stützen; (*fig: government, industry*) unterstützen
proper [ˈprɔpəʳ] *adj* (*genuine, correct*) richtig; (*socially acceptable*) schicklich
property [ˈprɔpətɪ] *n* (*possessions*) Eigentum *nt*; (*building and its land*) Grundstück *nt*; (*quality*) Eigenschaft *f*
proportion [prəˈpɔːʃən] *n* (*part*) Teil *m*; (*ratio*) Verhältnis *nt*; **in ~ to** im Verhältnis zu
proportional [prəˈpɔːʃənl] *adj*: **~ to** proportional zu
proportional representation *n* Verhältniswahlrecht *nt*
proposal [prəˈpəuzl] *n* (*plan*) Vorschlag *m*; **~ (of marriage)** Heiratsantrag *m*
propose [prəˈpəuz] *vt* (*plan, idea*) vorschlagen ▶ *vi* (*offer marriage*) einen Heiratsantrag machen
proprietor [prəˈpraɪətəʳ] *n* (*of hotel, shop etc*) Inhaber(in) *m(f)*; (*of newspaper*) Besitzer(in) *m(f)*
prose [prəuz] *n* (*not poetry*) Prosa *f*
prosecute [ˈprɔsɪkjuːt] *vt* (*Law: person*) strafrechtlich verfolgen

prospect *n* [ˈprɔspɛkt] Aussicht *f* ▶ *vi* [prəˈspɛkt]: **to ~ (for)** suchen (nach)
prosperity [prɔˈspɛrɪtɪ] *n* Wohlstand *m*
prosperous [ˈprɔspərəs] *adj* (*person*) wohlhabend; (*business, city etc*) blühend
prostitute [ˈprɔstɪtjuːt] *n* (*female*) Prostituierte *f*
protect [prəˈtɛkt] *vt* schützen
protection [prəˈtɛkʃən] *n* Schutz *m*
protective [prəˈtɛktɪv] *adj* (*clothing, layer etc*) Schutz-
protein [ˈprəutiːn] *n* Protein *nt*, Eiweiß *nt*
protest *n* [ˈprəutɛst] Protest *m* ▶ *vi* [prəˈtɛst]: **to ~ about** *or* **against** *or* **at sth** gegen etw protestieren ▶ *vt*: **to ~ (that)** (*insist*) beteuern(, dass)
Protestant [ˈprɔtɪstənt] *adj* protestantisch ▶ *n* Protestant(in) *m(f)*
proud [praud] *adj* stolz
proudly [ˈpraudlɪ] *adv* stolz
prove [pruːv] *vt* beweisen ▶ *vi*: **to ~ (to be) correct** sich als richtig herausstellen *or* erweisen; **to ~ (o.s./itself) (to be) useful** sich als nützlich erweisen
proverb [ˈprɔvəːb] *n* Sprichwort *nt*
provide [prəˈvaɪd] *vt* (*food, money, shelter etc*) zur Verfügung stellen; (*answer, example etc*) liefern
▶ **provide for** *vt fus* (*person*) sorgen für
provided [prəˈvaɪdɪd] *conj*: **~ (that)** vorausgesetzt(, dass)
provision [prəˈvɪʒən] *n* (*stipulation, clause*) Bestimmung *f* ■ **provisions** *npl* (*food*) Proviant *m*
provisional [prəˈvɪʒənl] *adj* provisorisch
provisionally [prəˈvɪʒnəlɪ] *adv* vorläufig
provoke [prəˈvəuk] *vt* (*person*) provozieren; (*reaction etc*) hervorrufen
proximity [prɔkˈsɪmɪtɪ] *n* Nähe *f*
prudent [ˈpruːdnt] *adj* (*sensible*) klug
prudish [ˈpruːdɪʃ] *adj* prüde
prune [pruːn] *n* Backpflaume *f* ▶ *vt* (*plant*) stutzen, beschneiden
PS *abbr* (= *postscript*) PS
psalm [sɑːm] *n* Psalm *m*
pseudo- [ˈsjuːdəu] *pref* Pseudo-
pseudonym [ˈsjuːdənɪm] *n* Pseudonym *nt*
PST (US) *abbr* (= *Pacific Standard Time*) *pazifische Standardzeit*
psychiatric [saɪkɪˈætrɪk] *adj* psychiatrisch
psychiatrist [saɪˈkaɪətrɪst] *n* Psychiater(in) *m(f)*
psychiatry [saɪˈkaɪətrɪ] *n* Psychiatrie *f*
psychic [ˈsaɪkɪk] *adj* (*person*) übersinnlich begabt
psychoanalysis [saɪkəuəˈnælɪsɪs] *n* Psychoanalyse *f*
psychoanalyst [saɪkəuˈænəlɪst] *n* Psychoanalytiker(in) *m(f)*
psychological [saɪkəˈlɔdʒɪkl] *adj* psychologisch
psychology [saɪˈkɔlədʒɪ] *n* (*science*) Psychologie *f*
psychopath [ˈsaɪkəupæθ] *n* Psychopath(in) *m(f)*
pt *abbr* = **pint**; **point**
PTO *abbr* (= *please turn over*) b. w.
pub [pʌb] *n* = **public house**
puberty [ˈpjuːbətɪ] *n* Pubertät *f*
public [ˈpʌblɪk] *adj* öffentlich ▶ *n*: **the ~** (*in general*) die Öffentlichkeit
publication [pʌblɪˈkeɪʃən] *n* Veröffentlichung *f*
public convenience (Brit) *n* öffentliche Toilette *f*
public holiday *n* gesetzlicher Feiertag *m*
public house (Brit) *n* Gaststätte *f*
publicity [pʌbˈlɪsɪtɪ] *n* (*information*) Werbung *f*; (*attention*) Publicity *f*
public opinion *n* die öffentliche Meinung
public relations *n* Public Relations *pl*, Öffentlichkeitsarbeit *f*
public school *n* (Brit) Privatschule *f*
publish [ˈpʌblɪʃ] *vt* veröffentlichen
publisher [ˈpʌblɪʃəʳ] *n* (*person*) Verleger(in) *m(f)*; (*company*) Verlag *m*
publishing [ˈpʌblɪʃɪŋ] *n* (*profession*) das Verlagswesen
pub lunch *n in Pubs servierter Imbiss*
pudding [ˈpudɪŋ] *n* (Brit: *dessert*) Nachtisch *m*
puddle [ˈpʌdl] *n* (*of rain*) Pfütze *f*
puff [pʌf] *vi* (*gasp*) schnaufen
puffin [ˈpʌfɪn] *n* Papageientaucher *m*
puff pastry, (US) **puff paste** *n* Blätterteig *m*
pull [pul] *vt* (*rope, handle etc*) ziehen an +*dat*; (*cart etc*) ziehen; (*inf*: *attract*: *people*) anlocken; (: *sexual partner*) aufreißen ▶ *vi* ziehen ▶ *n* (*also fig*: *attraction*) Anziehungskraft *f*;

to ~ a muscle sich *dat* einen Muskel zerren; **to ~ sb's leg** (*fig*) jdn auf den Arm nehmen; **to give sth a ~** an etw *dat* ziehen
▶ **pull apart** *vt* (*separate*) trennen
▶ **pull down** *vt* (*building*) abreißen
▶ **pull in** *vi* (*Aut: at kerb*) anhalten; (*Rail*) einfahren
▶ **pull off** *vt* (*clothes etc*) ausziehen; (*fig: difficult thing*) schaffen, bringen (*inf*)
▶ **pull on** *vt* (*clothes*) anziehen
▶ **pull out** *vi* (*Aut: from kerb*) losfahren; (*: when overtaking*) ausscheren; (*Rail*) ausfahren; (*withdraw*) sich zurückziehen ▶ *vt* (*extract*) herausziehen
▶ **pull up** *vi* (*Aut, Rail: stop*) anhalten ▶ *vt* (*raise*) hochziehen; (*uproot*) herausreißen

pullover [ˈpuləuvəʳ] *n* Pullover *m*
pulp [pʌlp] *n* (*of fruit*) Fruchtfleisch *nt*; (*for paper*) (Papier)brei *m*
pulpit [ˈpulpɪt] *n* Kanzel *f*
pulse [pʌls] *n* (*Anat*) Puls *m*
pump [pʌmp] *n* Pumpe *f*; (*also:* **petrol ~**) Zapfsäule *f*
▶ **pump up** *vt* (*inflate*) aufpumpen
pumpkin [ˈpʌmpkɪn] *n* Kürbis *m*
pun [pʌn] *n* Wortspiel *nt*
punch [pʌntʃ] *n* (*blow*) Schlag *m*; (*tool*) Locher *m*; (*drink*) Bowle *f*, Punsch *m* ▶ *vt* (*hit*) schlagen; (*make a hole in*) lochen
punctual [ˈpʌŋktjuəl] *adj* pünktlich
punctually [ˈpʌŋktjuəlɪ] *adv* pünktlich
punctuation [pʌŋktjuˈeɪʃən] *n* Zeichensetzung *f*
punctuation mark *n* Satzzeichen *nt*
puncture [ˈpʌŋktʃəʳ] *n* (*Aut*) Reifenpanne *f*
punish [ˈpʌnɪʃ] *vt* bestrafen
punishment [ˈpʌnɪʃmənt] *n* (*act*) Bestrafung *f*; (*way of punishing*) Strafe *f*
pupil [ˈpjuːpl] *n* (*Scol*) Schüler(in) *m(f)*
puppet [ˈpʌpɪt] *n* (*with strings, fig: person*) Marionette *f*
puppy [ˈpʌpɪ] *n* (*young dog*) junger Hund *m*
purchase [ˈpəːtʃɪs] *n* Kauf *m* ▶ *vt* kaufen
pure [pjuəʳ] *adj* rein
purely [ˈpjuəlɪ] *adv* rein
purify [ˈpjuərɪfaɪ] *vt* reinigen
purity [ˈpjuərɪtɪ] *n* Reinheit *f*
purple [ˈpəːpl] *adj* violett
purpose [ˈpəːpəs] *n* (*reason*) Zweck *m*; (*aim*) Absicht *f*; **on ~** absichtlich
purr [pəːʳ] *vi* (*cat*) schnurren
purse [pəːs] *n* (Brit: *for money*) Geldbörse *f*; (*US: handbag*) Handtasche *f*
pursue [pəˈsjuː] *vt* (*person, vehicle, plan, aim*) verfolgen; (*fig: interest etc*) nachgehen *+dat*
pursuit [pəˈsjuːt] *n* (*chase*) Verfolgung *f*; (*pastime*) Beschäftigung *f*
pus [pʌs] *n* Eiter *m*
push [puʃ] *n* Stoß *m* ▶ *vt* (*press*) drücken; (*shove*) schieben; (*fig: put pressure on: person*) bedrängen; (*inf: sell: drugs*) pushen ▶ *vi* (*press*) drücken
▶ **push in** *vi* sich dazwischendrängeln
▶ **push off** (*inf*) *vi* abhauen
▶ **push on** *vi* (*continue*) weitermachen
▶ **push up** *vt* (*total, prices*) hochtreiben
pushchair [ˈpuʃtʃɛəʳ] (Brit) *n* Sportwagen *m*
pusher [ˈpuʃəʳ] *n* (*drug dealer*) Pusher *m*
push-up [ˈpuʃʌp] (*US*) *n* Liegestütz *m*
pushy [ˈpuʃɪ] (*pej*) *adj* aufdringlich
put [put] (*pt, pp* **~**) *vt* (*thing*) tun; (*: upright*) stellen; (*: flat*) legen; (*express: idea etc*) ausdrücken; (*write, type*) schreiben
▶ **put away** *vt* (*store*) wegräumen
▶ **put back** *vt* (*replace*) zurücktun; (*: upright*) zurückstellen
▶ **put down** *vt* (*in writing*) aufschreiben; (*riot, rebellion*) niederschlagen; (*kill*) töten
▶ **put forward** *vt* (*ideas etc*) vorbringen; (*watch, clock*) vorstellen
▶ **put in** *vt* (*application, complaint*) einreichen; (*gas, electricity etc*) installieren
▶ **put off** *vt* (*delay*) verschieben; (*distract*) ablenken; **to ~ sb off sth** (*discourage*) jdn von etw abbringen
▶ **put on** *vt* (*clothes, brake*) anziehen; (*glasses, kettle*) aufsetzen; (*make-up, ointment etc*) auftragen; (*light, TV*) anmachen; (*play etc*) aufführen; (*record, tape, video*) auflegen; **to ~ on weight** zunehmen
▶ **put out** *vt* (*fire, light*) ausmachen; (*one's hand*) ausstrecken
▶ **put up** *vt* (*fence, building*) errichten;

(*tent*) aufstellen; (*price, cost*) erhöhen; (*accommodate*) unterbringen
▸ **put up with** *vt fus* sich abfinden mit

putt [pʌt] *n* Putt *m*

puzzle [ˈpʌzl] *n* (*game, toy*) Puzzle(spiel) *nt*; (*mystery*) Rätsel *nt* ▸ *vt* verwirren ▸ *vi*: **to ~ over sth** sich *dat* über etw *acc* den Kopf zerbrechen; **to be puzzled as to why ...** vor einem Rätsel stehen, warum ...

puzzling [ˈpʌzlɪŋ] *adj* (*mysterious*) rätselhaft

pyjamas, (*US*) **pajamas** [pəˈdʒɑːməz] *npl* Schlafanzug *m*

pylon [ˈpaɪlən] *n* Mast *m*

pyramid [ˈpɪrəmɪd] *n* Pyramide *f*

quack [kwæk] *vi* schnattern, quaken

quaint [kweɪnt] *adj* (*house, village*) malerisch; (*ideas, customs*) kurios

qualification [kwɔlɪfɪˈkeɪʃən] *n* (*often pl: degree etc*) Qualifikation *f*

qualified [ˈkwɔlɪfaɪd] *adj* (*trained: doctor etc*) qualifiziert

qualify [ˈkwɔlɪfaɪ] *vt* (*entitle*) qualifizieren; (*modify: statement*) einschränken ▸ *vi*: **to ~ as an engineer** die Ausbildung zum Ingenieur abschließen

quality [ˈkwɔlɪtɪ] *n* Qualität *f*; (*characteristic*) Eigenschaft *f*

quantity [ˈkwɔntɪtɪ] *n* (*amount*) Menge *f*

quarantine [ˈkwɔrntiːn] *n* Quarantäne *f*

quarrel [ˈkwɔrl] *n* (*argument*) Streit *m* ▸ *vi* sich streiten

quarter [ˈkwɔːtəʳ] *n* Viertel *nt*; (*US: coin*) 25-Cent-Stück *nt*; (*of year*) Quartal *nt* ▸ *vt* (*divide*) vierteln ▪ **quarters** *npl* (*Mil*) Quartier *nt*; **a ~ of an hour** eine viertel Stunde; **it's a ~ to three, it's a ~ of three** (*US*) es ist Viertel vor drei; **it's a ~ past three, it's a ~ after three** (*US*) es ist Viertel nach drei

quarterfinal [ˈkwɔːtəˈfaɪnl] *n* Viertelfinale *nt*

quartet [kwɔːˈtɛt] *n* (*Mus*) Quartett *nt*

quay [kiː] *n* Kai *m*

queasy [ˈkwiːzɪ] *adj*: **I feel ~** mir ist übel *or* schlecht

queen [kwiːn] *n* (*also Zool*) Königin *f*; (*Cards, Chess*) Dame *f*

queer [kwɪəʳ] *adj* (*odd*) sonderbar, seltsam ▸ *n* (*!: male homosexual*) Schwule(r) *m*

quench [kwɛntʃ] *vt*: **to ~ one's thirst** seinen Durst stillen

query [ˈkwɪərɪ] *n* Anfrage *f* ▸ *vt* (*check*) nachfragen bezüglich *+gen*; (*express doubt about*) bezweifeln
question [ˈkwɛstʃən] *n* Frage *f* ▸ *vt* (*interrogate*) befragen; (*doubt*) bezweifeln; **to be out of the ~** nicht infrage kommen
questionable [ˈkwɛstʃənəbl] *adj* fraglich
question mark *n* Fragezeichen *nt*
questionnaire [kwɛstʃəˈnɛəʳ] *n* Fragebogen *m*
queue [kjuː] (BRIT) *n* Schlange *f* ▸ *vi* (*also:* **~ up**) Schlange stehen
quibble [ˈkwɪbl] *vi*: **to ~ about** *or* **over** sich streiten über *+acc*
quiche [kiːʃ] *n* Quiche *f*
quick [kwɪk] *adj* schnell; (*look, visit*) flüchtig; **be ~!** mach schnell!
quickly [ˈkwɪklɪ] *adv* schnell
quid [kwɪd] (BRIT *inf*) *n inv* Pfund *nt*
quiet [ˈkwaɪət] *adj* leise; (*place*) ruhig, still ▸ *n* (*peacefulness*) Stille *f*, Ruhe *f*; **keep** *or* **be ~!** sei still!
quieten [ˈkwaɪətn] (BRIT) *vi* (*also:* **~ down**) ruhiger werden ▸ *vt* (*person, animal: also:* **~ down**) beruhigen
quietly [ˈkwaɪətlɪ] *adv* leise; (*calmly*) ruhig
quilt [kwɪlt] *n* Decke *f*
quit [kwɪt] (*pt, pp* **~** *or* **quitted**) *vt* (*smoking*) aufgeben; (*job*) kündigen; (*premises*) verlassen ▸ *vi* (*give up*) aufgeben; (*resign*) kündigen
quite [kwaɪt] *adv* (*rather*) ziemlich; (*entirely*) ganz; **I don't ~ remember** ich erinnere mich nicht genau; **~ a few of them** eine ganze Reihe von Ihnen; **~ (so)!** ganz recht!
quits [kwɪts] *adj*: **we're ~** wir sind quitt
quiver [ˈkwɪvəʳ] *vi* zittern
quiz [kwɪz] *n* (*game*) Quiz *nt*
quota [ˈkwəutə] *n* (*allowance*) Quote *f*
quotation [kwəuˈteɪʃən] *n* (*from book etc*) Zitat *nt*; (*Comm*) Kostenvoranschlag *m*
quotation marks *npl* Anführungszeichen *pl*
quote [kwəut] *n* (*from book etc*) Zitat *nt*; (*estimate*) Kostenvoranschlag *m* ▸ *vt* zitieren; (*price*) nennen; **in quotes** in Anführungszeichen

r

rabbi [ˈræbaɪ] *n* Rabbi *m*
rabbit [ˈræbɪt] *n* Kaninchen *nt*
rabies [ˈreɪbiːz] *n* Tollwut *f*
raccoon, racoon [rəˈkuːn] *n* Waschbär *m*
race [reɪs] *n* (*species*) Rasse *f*; (*competition*) Rennen *nt* ▸ *vt* (*person*) um die Wette laufen mit ▸ *vi* (*hurry*) rennen
racecourse [ˈreɪskɔːs] *n* Rennbahn *f*
racehorse [ˈreɪshɔːs] *n* Rennpferd *nt*
racetrack [ˈreɪstræk] *n* Rennbahn *f*
racial [ˈreɪʃl] *adj* Rassen-
racing [ˈreɪsɪŋ] *n* (*also:* **horse ~**) Pferderennen *nt*; (*also:* **motor ~**) Rennsport *m*
racing car (BRIT) *n* Rennwagen *m*
racism [ˈreɪsɪzəm] *n* Rassismus *m*
racist [ˈreɪsɪst] *adj* rassistisch ▸ *n* (*pej*) Rassist(in) *m(f)*
rack [ræk] *n* (*for dresses etc*) Ständer *m*; (*for dishes*) Gestell *nt* ▸ *vt*: **to ~ one's brains** sich *dat* den Kopf zerbrechen
racket [ˈrækɪt] *n* (*for tennis etc*) Schläger *m*; (*noise*) Krach *m*
radar [ˈreɪdɑːʳ] *n* Radar *m or nt*
radar trap *n* Radarfalle *f*
radiation [reɪdɪˈeɪʃən] *n* (*from sun etc*) Strahlung *f*
radiator [ˈreɪdɪeɪtəʳ] *n* (*heater*) Heizkörper *m*; (*Aut*) Kühler *m*
radical [ˈrædɪkl] *adj* radikal
radio [ˈreɪdɪəu] *n* (*broadcasting*) Radio *nt*, Rundfunk *m*
radioactivity [ˈreɪdɪəuækˈtɪvɪtɪ] *n* Radioaktivität *f*
radio station *n* Radiosender *m*
radiotherapy [ˈreɪdɪəuˈθɛrəpɪ] *n* Strahlentherapie *f*

radish [ˈrædɪʃ] *n* Radieschen *nt*
radius [ˈreɪdɪəs] (*pl* **radii**) *n* Radius *m*; **within a ~ of 50 miles** in einem Umkreis von 50 Meilen
raffle [ˈræfl] *n* Tombola *f*; **~ ticket** Los *nt*
raft [rɑːft] *n* Floß *nt*
rag [ræg] *n* (*piece of cloth*) Lappen *m*
■ **rags** *npl* (*torn clothes*) Lumpen *pl*
rage [reɪdʒ] *n* (*fury*) Wut *f* ▸ *vi* toben, wüten; **it's all the ~** (*fashionable*) es ist der letzte Schrei
raid [reɪd] *n* (*Mil*) Überfall *m*; (*by police*) Razzia *f* ▸ *vt* (*Mil*) überfallen; (*police*) stürmen
rail [reɪl] *n* Geländer *nt*; (*on deck of ship*) Reling *f*
railcard [ˈreɪlkɑːd] (BRIT) *n* (*for young people*) ≈ Juniorenpass *m*; (*for pensioners*) ≈ Seniorenpass *m*
railing [ˈreɪlɪŋ] *n*, **railings** [ˈreɪlɪŋz] *npl* (*fence*) Zaun *m*
railroad [ˈreɪlrəud] (*US*) *n* = **railway**
railway [ˈreɪlweɪ] (BRIT) *n* Eisenbahn *f*
railway line (BRIT) *n* Bahnlinie *f*; (*track*) Gleis *nt*
railway station (BRIT) *n* Bahnhof *m*
rain [reɪn] *n* Regen *m* ▸ *vi* regnen; **it's raining** es regnet
rainbow [ˈreɪnbəu] *n* Regenbogen *m*
raincoat [ˈreɪnkəut] *n* Regenmantel *m*
rainfall [ˈreɪnfɔːl] *n* Niederschlag *m*
rainforest [ˈreɪnfɔrɪst] *n* Regenwald *m*
rainy [ˈreɪnɪ] *adj* (*day*) regnerisch
raise [reɪz] *n* (*pay rise*) Gehaltserhöhung *f* ▸ *vt* (*lift*: *hand*) hochheben; (*increase*) erhöhen; (*doubts etc*) vorbringen; (*child, cattle*) aufziehen; (*crop*) anbauen; (*funds*) aufbringen; **to ~ one's voice** die Stimme erheben
raisin [ˈreɪzn] *n* Rosine *f*
rally [ˈrælɪ] *n* (*Pol etc*) Kundgebung *f*; (*Aut*) Rallye *f*; (*Tennis etc*) Ballwechsel *m*
RAM [ræm] *n abbr* (*Comput*: = *random access memory*) RAM
ramble [ˈræmbl] *n* Wanderung *f* ▸ *vi* wandern; (*talk*: *also*: **~ on**) schwafeln
ramp [ræmp] *n* Rampe *f*
ran [ræn] *pt of* **run**
ranch [rɑːntʃ] *n* Ranch *f*
rancid [ˈrænsɪd] *adj* ranzig
random [ˈrændəm] *adj* (*arrangement*) willkürlich ▸ *n*: **at ~** aufs Geratewohl
rang [ræŋ] *pt of* **ring**
range [reɪndʒ] *n* (*of mountains*) Kette *f*; (*of missile*) Reichweite *f*; (*of products*) Auswahl *f*; (*Mil*: *also*: **rifle ~**) Schießstand *m* ▸ *vi*: **to ~ over** (*extend*) sich erstrecken über +*acc*; **do you have anything else in this price ~?** haben Sie noch etwas anderes in dieser Preisklasse?; **to ~ from ... to ...** sich zwischen ... und ... bewegen
rank [ræŋk] *n* (*Mil*) Rang *m*; (*social class*) Schicht *f* ▸ *vt*: **he is ranked third in the world** er steht weltweit an dritter Stelle
ransom [ˈrænsəm] *n* (*money*) Lösegeld *nt*
rap [ræp] *n* (*also*: **~ music**) Rap *m*
rape [reɪp] *n* Vergewaltigung *f* ▸ *vt* vergewaltigen
rapid [ˈræpɪd] *adj* schnell
rapidly [ˈræpɪdlɪ] *adv* schnell
rapist [ˈreɪpɪst] *n* Vergewaltiger *m*
rare [rɛəʳ] *adj* selten; (*steak*) nur angebraten, englisch (gebraten)
rarely [ˈrɛəlɪ] *adv* selten
rarity [ˈrɛərɪtɪ] *n* Seltenheit *f*
rash [ræʃ] *adj* (*person*) unbesonnen ▸ *n* (*Med*) Ausschlag *m*
rasher [ˈræʃəʳ] *n* (*of bacon*) Scheibe *f*
raspberry [ˈrɑːzbərɪ] *n* Himbeere *f*
rat [ræt] *n* Ratte *f*
rate [reɪt] *n* (*speed*: *of change etc*) Tempo *nt*; (*of inflation, unemployment etc*) Rate *f*; (*of interest, taxation*) Satz *m* ▸ *vt* einschätzen; **at any ~** auf jeden Fall
rather [ˈrɑːðəʳ] *adv* (*very*) ziemlich; **~ a lot** ziemlich *or* recht viel; **I would ~ go** ich würde lieber gehen; **or ~** (*more accurately*) oder vielmehr
ratio [ˈreɪʃɪəu] *n* Verhältnis *nt*
rational [ˈræʃənl] *adj* rational, vernünftig
rationalize [ˈræʃnəlaɪz] *vt* rationalisieren
rattle [ˈrætl] *n* (*toy*) Rassel *f* ▸ *vi* (*windows*) klappern; (*bottles*) klirren ▸ *vt* (*shake noisily*) rütteln an +*dat*; (*fig*: *unsettle*) nervös machen
rattlesnake [ˈrætlsneɪk] *n* Klapperschlange *f*
rave [reɪv] *vi* (*in anger*) toben ▸ *n* (BRIT *inf*: *party*) Rave *m*
▸ **rave about** *vt* schwärmen von
raven [ˈreɪvən] *n* Rabe *m*
raving [ˈreɪvɪŋ] *adj*: **a ~ lunatic** ein total verrückter Typ

ravishing [ˈrævɪʃɪŋ] *adj* hinreißend
raw [rɔː] *adj* roh; (*sore*) wund; (*weather, day*) rau
ray [reɪ] *n* Strahl *m*; **~ of hope** Hoffnungsschimmer *m*
razor [ˈreɪzəʳ] *n* Rasierapparat *m*
razor blade *n* Rasierklinge *f*
Rd *abbr* (= *road*) Str.
RE (Brit) *n abbr* (*Scol*) = **religious education**
re [riː] *prep* (*with regard to*) bezüglich *+gen*
reach [riːtʃ] *n* (*range*) Reichweite *f* ▶ *vt* erreichen; **within/out of ~** in/außer Reichweite; **within easy ~ of the supermarket/station** ganz in der Nähe des Supermarkts/Bahnhofs; **"keep out of the ~ of children"** „von Kindern fernhalten"
▶ **reach for** *vt* greifen nach
▶ **reach out** *vi* die Hand ausstrecken; **to ~ out for sth** nach etw greifen
react [riːˈækt] *vi*: **to ~ (to)** (*also Med*) reagieren (auf *+acc*)
reaction [riːˈækʃən] *n* Reaktion *f*
reactor [riːˈæktəʳ] *n* (*also*: **nuclear ~**) Kernreaktor *m*
read [riːd] (*pt, pp* **~** [rɛd]) *vi* lesen; (*piece of writing etc*) sich lesen ▶ *vt* lesen; (*meter, thermometer etc*) ablesen
▶ **read out** *vt* vorlesen
▶ **read over** *vt* durchlesen
▶ **read through** *vt* durchlesen
▶ **read up on** *vt fus* sich informieren über *+acc*
readable [ˈriːdəbl] *adj* (*legible*) lesbar; (*book, author etc*) lesenswert
reader [ˈriːdəʳ] *n* (*person*) Leser(in) *m(f)*
readership [ˈriːdəʃɪp] *n* (*of newspaper etc*) Leserschaft *f*
readily [ˈrɛdɪlɪ] *adv* (*without hesitation*) bereitwillig; (*easily*) ohne Weiteres
reading [ˈriːdɪŋ] *n* Lesen *nt*; (*on meter, thermometer etc*) Anzeige *f*
reading glasses *npl* Lesebrille *f*
reading lamp *n* Leselampe *f*
reading matter *n* Lesestoff *m*
readjust [riːəˈdʒʌst] *vt* (*position, knob, instrument etc*) neu einstellen ▶ *vi*: **to ~ (to)** sich anpassen (an *+acc*)
ready [ˈrɛdɪ] *adj* (*prepared*) bereit, fertig; (*willing*) bereit; **to be ~ to do sth** bereit sein, etw zu tun; **to get ~** sich fertig machen; **to get sth ~** etw bereitmachen
ready cash *n* Bargeld *nt*
ready-made [ˈrɛdɪˈmeɪd] *adj* (*clothes*) von der Stange, Konfektions-; **~ meal** Fertiggericht *nt*
real [rɪəl] *adj* (*reason, result etc*) wirklich; (*leather, gold etc*) echt; (*life, feeling*) wahr; **in ~ terms** effektiv
real ale *n* Real Ale *nt*
real estate *n* Immobilien *pl*
realistic [rɪəˈlɪstɪk] *adj* realistisch
reality [riːˈælɪtɪ] *n* Wirklichkeit *f*; **in ~** in Wirklichkeit
reality TV *n* Reality-TV *nt*
realization [rɪəlaɪˈzeɪʃən] *n* (*understanding*) Erkenntnis *f*
realize [ˈrɪəlaɪz] *vt* (*understand*) verstehen; (*fulfil*) realisieren
really [ˈrɪəlɪ] *adv* wirklich
Realtor® [ˈrɪəltɔːʳ] (*US*) *n* Immobilienmakler(in) *m(f)*
reappear [riːəˈpɪəʳ] *vi* wieder auftauchen
rear [rɪəʳ] *adj* hintere(r, s) ▶ *n* Rückseite *f*
rearm [riːˈɑːm] *vi* (*country*) wiederaufrüsten ▶ *vt* wiederbewaffnen
rearrange [riːəˈreɪndʒ] *vt* (*furniture*) umstellen; (*meeting*) den Termin ändern *+gen*
rear-view mirror [ˈrɪəvjuː-] *n* Rückspiegel *m*
reason [ˈriːzn] *n* (*cause*) Grund *m*; (*rationality*) Verstand *m*; (*common sense*) Vernunft *f* ▶ *vi*: **to ~ with sb** vernünftig mit jdm reden; **the ~ for/why** der Grund für/, warum
reasonable [ˈriːznəbl] *adj* vernünftig; (*number, amount*) angemessen
reasonably [ˈriːznəblɪ] *adv* (*fairly*) ziemlich; (*sensibly*) vernünftig
reassure [riːəˈʃuəʳ] *vt* beruhigen
rebel [ˈrɛbl] *n* Rebell(in) *m(f)* ▶ *vi* rebellieren
rebellion [rɪˈbɛljən] *n* Rebellion *f*
reboot [riːˈbuːt] *vt, vi* (*Comput*) rebooten
rebound [rɪˈbaund] *vi* (*ball*) zurückprallen
rebuild [riːˈbɪld] *vt* (*irreg: like* **build**) wiederaufbauen
recall [rɪˈkɔːl] *vt* (*remember*) sich erinnern an *+acc*; (*product*) zurückrufen
recap [ˈriːkæp] *vt, vi* zusammenfassen
receipt [rɪˈsiːt] *n* (*document*) Quittung *f*; (*act of receiving*) Erhalt *m* ■ **receipts** *npl* (*Comm*) Einnahmen *pl*

receive [rɪˈsiːv] *vt* erhalten, bekommen; (*treatment*) erhalten; (*visitor, guest*) empfangen
receiver [rɪˈsiːvəʳ] *n* (*Tel*) Hörer *m*; (*Radio, TV*) Empfänger *m*
recent [ˈriːsnt] *adj* (*event*) kürzlich; (*times*) letzte(r, s); **in ~ years** in den letzten Jahren
recently [ˈriːsntlɪ] *adv* (*not long ago*) kürzlich; (*lately*) in letzter Zeit
reception [rɪˈsɛpʃən] *n* (*party, Radio, TV*) Empfang *m*
receptionist [rɪˈsɛpʃənɪst] *n* (*in hotel*) Empfangschef *m*, Empfangsdame *f*; (*in doctor's surgery*) Sprechstundenhilfe *f*
recess [rɪˈsɛs] *n* (*in room*) Nische *f*; (*esp US Scol*) Pause *f*
recession [rɪˈsɛʃən] *n* (*Econ*) Rezession *f*
recharge [riːˈtʃɑːdʒ] *vt* (*battery*) aufladen
rechargeable [riːˈtʃɑːdʒəbl] *adj* (*battery*) aufladbar
recipe [ˈrɛsɪpɪ] *n* Rezept *nt*
recipient [rɪˈsɪpɪənt] *n* Empfänger(in) *m(f)*
reciprocal [rɪˈsɪprəkl] *adj* gegenseitig
recite [rɪˈsaɪt] *vt* (*poem*) vortragen; (*complaints etc*) aufzählen
reckless [ˈrɛkləs] *adj* (*driving, driver*) rücksichtslos; (*spending*) leichtsinnig
reckon [ˈrɛkən] *vt* (*consider*) halten für; (*calculate*) berechnen ▸ *vi*: **he is somebody to be reckoned with** mit ihm muss man rechnen; **I ~ that ...** (*think*) ich schätze, dass ...
▸ **reckon on** *vt fus* rechnen mit
reclaim [rɪˈkleɪm] *vt* (*luggage*) abholen; (*tax etc*) zurückfordern
recline [rɪˈklaɪn] *vi* (*sit or lie back*) zurückgelehnt sitzen
recognition [rɛkəgˈnɪʃən] *n* (*of achievement*) Anerkennung *f*; **in ~ of** in Anerkennung +*gen*
recognize [ˈrɛkəgnaɪz] *vt* (*sign, problem*) erkennen; (*qualifications, government, achievement*) anerkennen
recommend [rɛkəˈmɛnd] *vt* empfehlen
recommendation [rɛkəmɛnˈdeɪʃən] *n* Empfehlung *f*
reconfigure [riːkənˈfɪgəʳ] *vt* neu konfigurieren
reconsider [riːkənˈsɪdəʳ] *vt* (noch einmal) überdenken ▸ *vi* es sich *dat* noch einmal überlegen
reconstruct [riːkənˈstrʌkt] *vt* (*building*) wiederaufbauen; (*event, crime*) rekonstruieren
record *n* [ˈrɛkɔːd] (*Mus: disc*) Schallplatte *f*; (*Sport*) Rekord *m* ▸ *vt* [rɪˈkɔːd] aufzeichnen; (*song etc*) aufnehmen ▸ *adj* (*sales, profits*) Rekord-; **to keep a ~ of sth** etw schriftlich festhalten
recorded delivery [rɪˈkɔːdɪd-] (Brit) *n* (*Post*) Einschreiben *nt*; **to send sth (by) ~** etw per Einschreiben senden
recorder [rɪˈkɔːdəʳ] *n* (*Mus*) Blockflöte *f*
recording [rɪˈkɔːdɪŋ] *n* Aufnahme *f*
record player *n* Plattenspieler *m*
recover [rɪˈkʌvəʳ] *vt* (*get back*) zurückbekommen ▸ *vi* sich erholen
recreation [rɛkrɪˈeɪʃən] *n* (*leisure*) Erholung *f*
recreational [rɛkrɪˈeɪʃənl] *adj* (*facilities etc*) Freizeit-
recruit [rɪˈkruːt] *n* (*Mil*) Rekrut *m*; (*in company*) neuer Mitarbeiter *m*, neue Mitarbeiterin *f* ▸ *vt* (*Mil*) rekrutieren; (*staff, new members*) anwerben
recruitment agency [rɪˈkruːtmənt-] *n* Personalagentur *f*
rectangle [ˈrɛktæŋgl] *n* Rechteck *nt*
rectangular [rɛkˈtæŋgjuləʳ] *adj* (*shape*) rechteckig
rectify [ˈrɛktɪfaɪ] *vt* (*mistake etc*) korrigieren
recuperate [rɪˈkjuːpəreɪt] *vi* (*recover*) sich erholen
recyclable [riːˈsaɪkləbl] *adj* recycelbar, wiederverwertbar
recycle [riːˈsaɪkl] *vt* (*waste, paper etc*) recyceln, wiederverwerten
recycling [riːˈsaɪklɪŋ] *n* Recycling *nt*
red [rɛd] *adj* rot; **to be in the ~** (*business etc*) in den roten Zahlen sein
red cabbage *n* Rotkohl *m*
Red Cross *n* Rotes Kreuz *nt*
redcurrant [ˈrɛdkʌrənt] *n* Rote Johannisbeere *f*
redeem [rɪˈdiːm] *vt* (*voucher, sth in pawn*) einlösen
red-handed [rɛdˈhændɪd] *adj*: **to be caught ~** auf frischer Tat ertappt werden
redhead [ˈrɛdhɛd] *n* Rotschopf *m*

redirect [riːdaɪˈrɛkt] *vt* (*mail*) nachsenden; (*traffic*) umleiten
red light *n* (*Aut*): **to go through a ~** eine Ampel bei Rot überfahren
red meat *n Rind- und Lammfleisch*
redo [riːˈduː] *vt* (*irreg: like* **do**) noch einmal machen
reduce [rɪˈdjuːs] *vt* (*spending, numbers, risk etc*) reduzieren
reduction [rɪˈdʌkʃən] *n* (*in price etc*) Ermäßigung *f*, Reduzierung *f*
redundant [rɪˈdʌndnt] *adj* (Brit: *worker*) arbeitslos; (*word, object*) überflüssig; **to be made ~** (*worker*) den Arbeitsplatz verlieren
red wine [redˈwaɪn] *n* Rotwein *m*
reef [riːf] *n* (*at sea*) Riff *nt*
reel [riːl] *n* (*of thread etc, on fishing-rod*) Rolle *f*; (*of film, tape*) Spule *f*
▶ **reel off** *vt* (*say*) herunterrasseln
ref [rɛf] (*inf*) *n abbr* (*Sport*) = **referee**
refectory [rɪˈfɛktərɪ] *n* (*in university*) Mensa *f*
refer [rɪˈfəːʳ] *vt*: **to ~ sb to** (*book etc*) jdn verweisen auf *+acc*; (*doctor, hospital*) jdn überweisen zu
▶ **refer to** *vt fus* (*mention*) erwähnen; (*relate to*) sich beziehen auf *+acc*
referee [rɛfəˈriː] *n* (*Sport*) Schiedsrichter(in) *m*(*f*); (Brit: *for job application*) Referenz *f*
reference [ˈrɛfrəns] *n* (*mention*) Hinweis *m*; (*in book, article*) Quellenangabe *f*; (*for job application, person*) Referenz *f*; **with ~ to** mit Bezug auf *+acc*; **"please quote this ~"** (*Comm*) „bitte dieses Zeichen angeben"
reference book *n* Nachschlagewerk *nt*
referendum [rɛfəˈrɛndəm] (*pl* **referenda**) *n* Referendum *nt*
refill [riːˈfɪl] *vt* nachfüllen ▶ *n* (*for pen etc*) Nachfüllmine *f*
refine [rɪˈfaɪn] *vt* (*sugar, oil*) raffinieren; (*theory, idea*) verfeinern
refined [rɪˈfaɪnd] *adj* (*taste*) fein
reflect [rɪˈflɛkt] *vt* reflektieren; (*fig*) widerspiegeln ▶ *vi* (*think*) nachdenken
▶ **reflect on** *vt fus* (*discredit*) ein schlechtes Licht werfen auf *+acc*
reflection [rɪˈflɛkʃən] *n* (*image*) Spiegelbild *nt*; (*fig*) Widerspiegelung *f*; (: *thought*) Gedanke *m*; **on ~** nach genauerer Überlegung
reflex [ˈriːflɛks]: **reflexes** *npl* (*Physiol, Psych*) Reflexe *pl*
reform [rɪˈfɔːm] *n* Reform *f* ▶ *vt* reformieren ▶ *vi* (*criminal etc*) sich bessern
refrain [rɪˈfreɪn] *vi*: **to ~ from doing sth** etw unterlassen
refresh [rɪˈfrɛʃ] *vt* erfrischen
refresher course [rɪˈfrɛʃə-] *n* Auffrischungskurs *m*
refreshing [rɪˈfrɛʃɪŋ] *adj* erfrischend
refreshments [rɪˈfrɛʃmənts] *npl* (*food and drink*) Erfrischungen *pl*
refrigerator [rɪˈfrɪdʒəreɪtəʳ] *n* Kühlschrank *m*
refuel [riːˈfjuəl] *vt, vi* auftanken
refugee [rɛfjuˈdʒiː] *n* Flüchtling *m*
refund [ˈriːfʌnd] *n* Rückerstattung *f* ▶ *vt* (*money*) zurückerstatten
refusal [rɪˈfjuːzəl] *n*: **a ~ to do sth** eine Weigerung, etw zu tun
refuse¹ [rɪˈfjuːz] *vt* (*request, offer etc*) ablehnen; (*gift*) zurückweisen; (*permission*) verweigern ▶ *vi* ablehnen; (*horse*) verweigern; **to ~ to do sth** sich weigern, etw zu tun
refuse² [ˈrɛfjuːs] *n* (*rubbish*) Abfall *m*, Müll *m*
regain [rɪˈgeɪn] *vt* wiedererlangen
regard [rɪˈgɑːd] *n* (*esteem*) Achtung *f* ▶ *vt* (*consider*) ansehen, betrachten; (*view*) betrachten; **to give one's regards to sb** jdm Grüße bestellen; **"with kindest regards"** „mit freundlichen Grüßen"; **as regards, with ~ to** bezüglich *+gen*
regarding [rɪˈgɑːdɪŋ] *prep* bezüglich *+gen*
regardless [rɪˈgɑːdlɪs] *adv* trotzdem ▶ *adj*: **~ of** ohne Rücksicht auf *+acc*
regime [reɪˈʒiːm] *n* (*government*) Regime *nt*
region [ˈriːdʒən] *n* (*administrative division of country*) Region *f*; **in the ~ of** (*approximately*) im Bereich von
regional [ˈriːdʒənl] *adj* regional
register [ˈrɛdʒɪstəʳ] *n* (*list, Mus*) Register *nt*; (*Scol*) Klassenbuch *nt* ▶ *vt* registrieren; (*car*) anmelden ▶ *vi* (*person*) sich anmelden; (: *at doctor's*) sich (als Patient) eintragen
registered [ˈrɛdʒɪstəd] *adj* (*letter, parcel*) eingeschrieben
registration [rɛdʒɪsˈtreɪʃən] *n* Registrierung *f*; (*of students, unemployed etc*) Anmeldung *f*
registration number (Brit) *n* (*Aut*) polizeiliches Kennzeichen *nt*

registry office [ˈrɛdʒɪstrɪ-] (BRIT) *n* Standesamt *nt*
regret [rɪˈgrɛt] *n* Bedauern *nt* ▸ *vt* bedauern
regrettable [rɪˈgrɛtəbl] *adj* bedauerlich
regular [ˈrɛgjuləʳ] *adj* (*also Ling*) regelmäßig; (*Comm: size*) normal ▸ *n* (*client*) Stammkunde *m*, Stammkundin *f*
regularly [ˈrɛgjuləlɪ] *adv* regelmäßig
regulate [ˈrɛgjuleɪt] *vt* regulieren
regulation [rɛgjuˈleɪʃən] *n* (*rule*) Vorschrift *f*
rehabilitation [ˈriːəbɪlɪˈteɪʃən] *n* Wiedereingliederung *f* (in die Gesellschaft), Rehabilitation *f*
rehearsal [rɪˈhəːsəl] *n* (*Theat*) Probe *f*
rehearse [rɪˈhəːs] *vt* (*play, speech etc*) proben
reign [reɪn] *n* (*lit, fig*) Herrschaft *f* ▸ *vi* (*lit, fig*) herrschen
reimburse [riːɪmˈbəːs] *vt* die Kosten erstatten +*dat*
reindeer [ˈreɪndɪəʳ] *n inv* Ren(tier) *nt*
reinforce [riːɪnˈfɔːs] *vt* (*strengthen*) verstärken
reinstate [riːɪnˈsteɪt] *vt* (*employee*) wiedereinstellen; (*tax, law*) wiedereinführen; (*text*) wiedereinfügen
reject [ˈriːdʒɛkt] *n* (*Comm*) Ausschuss *m inv* ▸ *vt* ablehnen
rejection [rɪˈdʒɛkʃən] *n* Ablehnung *f*
relapse [rɪˈlæps] *n* (*Med*) Rückfall *m*
relate [rɪˈleɪt] *vt* (*tell*) berichten; (*connect*) in Verbindung bringen ▸ *vi*: **to ~ to** (*empathize with: person, subject*) eine Beziehung finden zu
related [rɪˈleɪtɪd] *adj*: **to be ~** (miteinander) verwandt sein
relation [rɪˈleɪʃən] *n* (*member of family*) Verwandte(r) *f(m)*; (*connection*) Beziehung *f* ■ **relations** *npl* (*contact*) Beziehungen *pl*
relationship [rɪˈleɪʃənʃɪp] *n* Beziehung *f*; (*affair*) Verhältnis *nt*
relative [ˈrɛlətɪv] *n* Verwandte(r) *f(m)* ▸ *adj* relativ
relatively [ˈrɛlətɪvlɪ] *adv* relativ
relax [rɪˈlæks] *vi* (*person, muscle*) sich entspannen ▸ *vt* (*one's grip*) lockern
relaxation [riːlækˈseɪʃən] *n* Entspannung *f*
relaxed [rɪˈlækst] *adj* (*person, atmosphere*) entspannt
relaxing [rɪˈlæksɪŋ] *adj* entspannend
release [rɪˈliːs] *n* (*from prison*) Entlassung *f*; (*record, film*) Veröffentlichung *f* ▸ *vt* (*from prison*) entlassen; (*Tech, Aut: catch, brake etc*) lösen; (*record, film*) herausbringen; (*news, figures*) bekannt geben
relent [rɪˈlɛnt] *vi* (*give in*) nachgeben
relentless [rɪˈlɛntlɪs] *adj* (*heat, noise*) erbarmungslos; (*enemy etc*) unerbittlich
relevance [ˈrɛləvəns] *n* Relevanz *f*
relevant [ˈrɛləvənt] *adj* relevant; **~ to** relevant für
reliable [rɪˈlaɪəbl] *adj* zuverlässig
reliably [rɪˈlaɪəblɪ] *adv*: **to be ~ informed that …** zuverlässige Informationen darüber haben, dass …
reliant [rɪˈlaɪənt] *adj*: **to be ~ on sth/sb** auf etw/jdn angewiesen sein
relic [ˈrɛlɪk] *n* (*of the past*) Relikt *nt*
relief [rɪˈliːf] *n* (*from pain etc*) Erleichterung *f*; (*aid*) Hilfe *f*
relieve [rɪˈliːv] *vt* (*pain*) lindern; (*take over from*) ablösen
relieved [rɪˈliːvd] *adj* erleichtert
religion [rɪˈlɪdʒən] *n* Religion *f*
religious [rɪˈlɪdʒəs] *adj* religiös
religious education *n* Religionsunterricht *m*
relish [ˈrɛlɪʃ] *n* (*Culin*) würzige Soße *f* ▸ *vt* (*enjoy*) genießen
reluctant [rɪˈlʌktənt] *adj* widerwillig; **I'm ~ to do that** es widerstrebt mir, das zu tun
reluctantly [rɪˈlʌktəntlɪ] *adv* widerwillig
rely on [rɪˈlaɪ-] *vt fus* (*be dependent on*) abhängen von; (*trust*) sich verlassen auf +*acc*
remain [rɪˈmeɪn] *vi* bleiben; (*survive*) übrig bleiben
remainder [rɪˈmeɪndəʳ] *n* Rest *m*
remainer [rɪˈmeɪnəʳ] *n* (BRIT: *in EU*) *Befürworter des Verbleibs in der Europäischen Union*
remaining [rɪˈmeɪnɪŋ] *adj* übrig
remains [rɪˈmeɪnz] *npl* (*of meal*) Überreste *pl*
remark [rɪˈmɑːk] *n* Bemerkung *f* ▸ *vt* bemerken ▸ *vi*: **to ~ on sth** Bemerkungen über etw *acc* machen
remarkable [rɪˈmɑːkəbl] *adj* bemerkenswert
remarry [riːˈmærɪ] *vi* wieder heiraten

remedy [ˈrɛmədɪ] *n* (*lit, fig*) (Heil)mittel *nt* ▶ *vt* (*mistake, situation*) abhelfen +*dat*
remember [rɪˈmɛmbəʳ] *vt* (*call back to mind*) sich erinnern an +*acc*; (*bear in mind*) denken an +*acc*
Remembrance Sunday [rɪˈmɛmbrəns-] (BRIT) *n* ≈ Volkstrauertag *m*

REMEMBRANCE SUNDAY

Remembrance Sunday oder *Remembrance Day* ist der britische Gedenktag für die Gefallenen der beiden Weltkriege und anderer Konflikte. Er fällt auf einen Sonntag vor oder nach dem 11. November (am 11. November 1918 endete der Erste Weltkrieg) und wird mit einer Schweigeminute, Kranzniederlegungen an Kriegerdenkmälern und dem Tragen von Anstecknadeln in Form einer Mohnblume begangen.

remind [rɪˈmaɪnd] *vt*: **to ~ sb to do sth** jdn daran erinnern, etw zu tun; **to ~ sb of sth** jdn an etw *acc* erinnern; **that reminds me!** dabei fällt mir etwas ein!
reminder [rɪˈmaɪndəʳ] *n* (*letter*) Mahnung *f*
reminisce [rɛmɪˈnɪs] *vi*: **to ~ (about)** sich in Erinnerungen ergehen (über +*acc*)
reminiscent [rɛmɪˈnɪsnt] *adj*: **to be ~ of sth** an etw *acc* erinnern
remittance [rɪˈmɪtns] *n* Überweisung *f*
remnant [ˈrɛmnənt] *n* (*Comm*: *of cloth*) Rest *m*
remortgage [riːˈmɔːgɪdʒ] *vt*: **to ~ one's house/home** die Hypothek seines Hauses neu festsetzen
remote [rɪˈməut] *adj* (*distant*: *place, time*) weit entfernt; (*slight*: *chance etc*) entfernt
remote control *n* Fernsteuerung *f*; (*TV etc*) Fernbedienung *f*
removal [rɪˈmuːvəl] *n* (*of object etc*) Entfernung *f*; (BRIT: *from house*) Umzug *m*
remove [rɪˈmuːv] *vt* entfernen; (*clothing*) ausziehen; (*bandage etc*) abnehmen; (*doubt, threat, obstacle*) beseitigen
rename [riːˈneɪm] *vt* umbenennen
renew [rɪˈnjuː] *vt* erneuern; (*loan, contract etc*) verlängern
renewable [rɪˈnjuːəbl] *adj* (*energy*) erneuerbar
renounce [rɪˈnauns] *vt* verzichten auf +*acc*; (*belief*) aufgeben
renovate [ˈrɛnəveɪt] *vt* (*building*) restaurieren; (*machine*) überholen
renowned [rɪˈnaund] *adj* berühmt
rent [rɛnt] *n* (*for house*) Miete *f* ▶ *vt* mieten; (*also*: **~ out**) vermieten
rental [ˈrɛntl] *n* (*for television, car*) Mietgebühr *f*
reoffend [riːəˈfɛnd] *vi* erneut straffällig werden
reorganize [riːˈɔːgənaɪz] *vt* umorganisieren
rep [rɛp] *n abbr* (*Comm*) = **representative**
repair [rɪˈpɛəʳ] *n* Reparatur *f* ▶ *vt* reparieren; (*clothes, road*) ausbessern
repair kit *n* (*for bicycle*) Flickzeug *nt*
repay [riːˈpeɪ] *vt* (*irreg*: *like* **pay**) zurückzahlen; **I'll ~ you next week** ich zahle es dir nächste Woche zurück
repeat [rɪˈpiːt] *n* (*Radio, TV*) Wiederholung *f* ▶ *vt, vi* wiederholen
repetition [rɛpɪˈtɪʃən] *n* (*repeat*) Wiederholung *f*
repetitive [rɪˈpɛtɪtɪv] *adj* eintönig, monoton
replace [rɪˈpleɪs] *vt* (*put back*: *upright*) zurückstellen; (: *flat*) zurücklegen
replacement [rɪˈpleɪsmənt] *n* Ersatz *m*
replacement part *n* Ersatzteil *nt*
replay [ˈriːpleɪ] *n* (*of match*) Wiederholungsspiel *nt* ▶ *vt* (*match*) wiederholen
replica [ˈrɛplɪkə] *n* (*of object*) Nachbildung *f*
reply [rɪˈplaɪ] *n* Antwort *f* ▶ *vi*: **to ~ (to sb/sth)** (jdm/auf etw *acc*) antworten
report [rɪˈpɔːt] *n* Bericht *m*; (BRIT: *also*: **school ~**) Zeugnis *nt* ▶ *vt* berichten; (*casualties, damage, theft etc*) melden; (*person*: *to police*) anzeigen ▶ *vi*: **to ~ to sb** (*present o.s. to*) sich bei jdm melden; **to ~ sick** sich krankmelden
report card (US, SCOT) *n* Zeugnis *nt*
reporter [rɪˈpɔːtəʳ] *n* Reporter(in) *m(f)*

represent [rɛprɪˈzɛnt] *vt* (*person, nation*) vertreten; (*show: view, opinion*) darstellen
representation [rɛprɪzɛnˈteɪʃən] *n* (*picture etc*) Darstellung *f*
representative [rɛprɪˈzɛntətɪv] *n* (*also Comm*) Vertreter(in) *m(f)*; (*US Pol*) Abgeordnete(r) *f(m)* des Repräsentantenhauses ▶ *adj* repräsentativ
reprimand [ˈrɛprɪmɑːnd] *n* Tadel *m* ▶ *vt* tadeln
reprint [ˈriːprɪnt] *n* Nachdruck *m*
reproduce [riːprəˈdjuːs] *vt* reproduzieren ▶ *vi* (*Biol*) sich vermehren
reproduction [riːprəˈdʌkʃən] *n* Reproduktion *f*; (*Biol*) Fortpflanzung *f*
reptile [ˈrɛptaɪl] *n* Reptil *nt*
republic [rɪˈpʌblɪk] *n* Republik *f*
republican [rɪˈpʌblɪkən] *adj* republikanisch ▶ *n* Republikaner(in) *m(f)*
repulsive [rɪˈpʌlsɪv] *adj* widerwärtig, abstoßend
reputable [ˈrɛpjutəbl] *adj* (*make, company etc*) angesehen
reputation [rɛpjuˈteɪʃən] *n* Ruf *m*; **to have a ~ for** einen Ruf haben für
request [rɪˈkwɛst] *n* (*polite*) Bitte *f* ▶ *vt* (*politely*) bitten um
require [rɪˈkwaɪəʳ] *vt* (*need*) benötigen; (*: situation*) erfordern; (*demand*) verlangen
required [rɪˈkwaɪəd] *adj* erforderlich
requirement [rɪˈkwaɪəmənt] *n* (*need*) Bedarf *m*; (*condition*) Anforderung *f*
rescue [ˈrɛskjuː] *n* Rettung *f* ▶ *vt* retten; **to come to sb's ~** jdm zu Hilfe kommen
rescue party *n* Rettungsmannschaft *f*
research [rɪˈsəːtʃ] *n* Forschung *f* ▶ *vt* erforschen ▶ *vi*: **to ~ into sth** etw erforschen
researcher [rɪˈsəːtʃəʳ] *n* Forscher(in) *m(f)*
resemblance [rɪˈzɛmbləns] *n* Ähnlichkeit *f*
resemble [rɪˈzɛmbl] *vt* ähneln *+dat*
resent [rɪˈzɛnt] *vt* (*attitude, treatment*) missbilligen
reservation [rɛzəˈveɪʃən] *n* (*booking*) Reservierung *f*; (*doubt*) Vorbehalt *m*; **to make a ~** (*in hotel etc*) eine Reservierung vornehmen
reserve [rɪˈzəːv] *n* Vorrat *m*; (*Sport*) Reservespieler(in) *m(f)*; (*also:* **nature ~**) Naturschutzgebiet *nt*; (*restraint*) Zurückhaltung *f* ▶ *vt* reservieren
reserved [rɪˈzəːvd] *adj* (*seat*) reserviert
reservoir [ˈrɛzəvwɑːʳ] *n* (*lit, fig*) Reservoir *nt*
reside [rɪˈzaɪd] *vi* (*live: person*) seinen/ihren Wohnsitz haben
residence [ˈrɛzɪdəns] *n* (*form: home*) Wohnsitz *m*; (*length of stay*) Aufenthalt *m*
residence permit (Brit) *n* Aufenthaltserlaubnis *f*
resident [ˈrɛzɪdənt] *n* (*of country, town*) Einwohner(in) *m(f)*; (*in hotel*) Gast *m*
resign [rɪˈzaɪn] *vt* (*one's post*) zurücktreten von ▶ *vi* (*from post*) zurücktreten
resignation [rɛzɪgˈneɪʃən] *n* (*from post*) Rücktritt *m*
resigned [rɪˈzaɪnd] *adj*: **to be ~ to sth** sich mit etw abgefunden haben
resist [rɪˈzɪst] *vt* (*urge etc*) widerstehen *+dat*
resistance [rɪˈzɪstəns] *n* (*also Elec*) Widerstand *m*
resit (Brit) *vt* [riːˈsɪt] (*irreg: like* **sit**) wiederholen ▶ *n* [ˈriːsɪt] Wiederholungsprüfung *f*
resolution [rɛzəˈluːʃən] *n* (*decision*) Beschluss *m*; (*determination*) Entschlossenheit *f*
resolve [rɪˈzɔlv] *vt* (*problem*) lösen
resort [rɪˈzɔːt] *n* (*town*) Urlaubsort *m* ▶ *vi*: **to ~ to** Zuflucht nehmen zu; **winter sports ~** Wintersportort *m*; **as a last ~** als letzter Ausweg
resource [rɪˈsɔːs] *n* (*raw material*) Bodenschatz *m* ■ **resources** *npl* (*coal, oil etc*) Energiequellen *pl*; (*money*) Mittel *pl*, Ressourcen *pl*
respect [rɪsˈpɛkt] *n* (*consideration, esteem*) Respekt *m* ▶ *vt* respektieren ■ **respects** *npl* (*greetings*) Grüße *pl*; **to have ~ for sb/sth** Respekt vor jdm/etw haben; **with ~ to, in ~ of** in Bezug auf *+acc*; **in this ~** in dieser Hinsicht
respectable [rɪsˈpɛktəbl] *adj* anständig; (*amount, income*) ansehnlich; (*standard, mark etc*) ordentlich
respected [rɪsˈpɛktɪd] *adj* angesehen
respective [rɪsˈpɛktɪv] *adj* jeweilig

respectively [rɪsˈpɛktɪvlɪ] *adv* beziehungsweise
respiratory [ˈrɛspərətərɪ] *adj* (*system, failure*) Atmungs-
respond [rɪsˈpɔnd] *vi* (*answer*) antworten; (*react*) reagieren
response [rɪsˈpɔns] *n* (*to question*) Antwort *f*; (*to event etc*) Reaktion *f*; **in ~ to** als Antwort/Reaktion auf *+acc*
responsibility [rɪspɔnsɪˈbɪlɪtɪ] *n* Verantwortung *f*
responsible [rɪsˈpɔnsɪbl] *adj* verantwortlich; (*reliable, important*) verantwortungsvoll; **to be ~ for sth** für etw verantwortlich sein
rest [rɛst] *n* (*relaxation*) Ruhe *f*; (*pause*) Ruhepause *f*; (*remainder*) Rest *m* ▸ *vi* (*relax*) sich ausruhen; **to ~ sth on/against sth** (*lean*) etw an *acc*/gegen etw lehnen
restaurant [ˈrɛstərɔŋ] *n* Restaurant *nt*
restaurant car (Brit) *n* (*Rail*) Speisewagen *m*
restful [ˈrɛstful] *adj* (*music*) ruhig
restless [ˈrɛstlɪs] *adj* (*audience*) unruhig
restore [rɪˈstɔːʳ] *vt* (*painting etc*) restaurieren; (*law and order, faith, health etc*) wiederherstellen; (*property*) zurückgeben
restrain [rɪsˈtreɪn] *vt* (*person*) zurückhalten; **to ~ o.s. from doing sth** sich beherrschen, etw nicht zu tun
restrict [rɪsˈtrɪkt] *vt* beschränken
restricted [rɪsˈtrɪktɪd] *adj* beschränkt
restriction [rɪsˈtrɪkʃən] *n* Beschränkung *f*
rest room (*US*) *n* Toilette *f*
result [rɪˈzʌlt] *n* Resultat *nt*; (*of match, election, exam etc*) Ergebnis *nt* ▸ *vi*: **to ~ in** führen zu; **as a ~ of the accident** als Folge des Unfalls; **to ~ from** resultieren *or* sich ergeben aus
resume [rɪˈzjuːm] *vt* (*work, journey*) wiederaufnehmen
résumé [ˈreɪzjuːmeɪ] *n* Zusammenfassung *f*; (*US*: *curriculum vitae*) Lebenslauf *m*
resuscitate [rɪˈsʌsɪteɪt] *vt* (*Med, fig*) wiederbeleben
retail [ˈriːteɪl] *adv* im Einzelhandel
retailer [ˈriːteɪləʳ] *n* Einzelhändler(in) *m(f)*
retain [rɪˈteɪn] *vt* (*keep*) behalten; (: *heat, moisture*) zurückhalten
rethink [ˈriːˈθɪŋk] *vt* noch einmal überdenken
retire [rɪˈtaɪəʳ] *vi* (*give up work*) in den Ruhestand treten; (*withdraw, go to bed*) sich zurückziehen
retired [rɪˈtaɪəd] *adj* (*person*) im Ruhestand
retirement [rɪˈtaɪəmənt] *n* (*state*) Ruhestand *m*
retirement age *n* Rentenalter *nt*
retrace [riːˈtreɪs] *vt*: **to ~ one's steps** (*lit, fig*) seine Schritte zurückverfolgen
retrain [riːˈtreɪn] *vi* umgeschult werden
retreat [rɪˈtriːt] *n* (*place*) Zufluchtsort *m*; (*withdrawal, also Mil*) Rückzug *m* ▸ *vi* sich zurückziehen
retrieve [rɪˈtriːv] *vt* (*object*) zurückholen; (*situation*) retten; (*Comput*) abrufen
retrospect [ˈrɛtrəspɛkt] *n*: **in ~** rückblickend, im Rückblick
retrospective [rɛtrəˈspɛktɪv] *adj* (*law, tax*) rückwirkend
return [rɪˈtəːn] *n* (*going or coming back*) Rückkehr *f*; (*of sth stolen etc*) Rückgabe *f*; (Brit: *also*: **~ ticket**) Rückfahrkarte *f*; (*Fin*: *from investment etc*) Ertrag *m* ▸ *cpd* (*journey*) Rück- ▸ *vi* (*person etc*: *come or go back*) zurückkehren; (*feelings, symptoms etc*) wiederkehren ▸ *vt* (*favour, greetings etc*) erwidern; (*sth stolen etc*) zurückgeben; **in ~ (for)** als Gegenleistung (für); **many happy returns (of the day)!** herzlichen Glückwunsch zum Geburtstag!
returnable [rɪˈtəːnəbl] *adj* (*bottle etc*) Mehrweg-
return key *n* (*Comput*) Return-Taste *f*
retweet [riːˈtwiːt] *vt* (*on Twitter*) weitertwittern , retweeten
reunification [riːjuːnɪfɪˈkeɪʃən] *n* Wiedervereinigung *f*
reunion [riːˈjuːnɪən] *n* Treffen *nt*
reunite [riːjuːˈnaɪt] *vt* wiedervereinigen
reusable [riːˈjuːzəbl] *adj* wiederverwendbar
reveal [rɪˈviːl] *vt* (*make known*) enthüllen; (*make visible*) zum Vorschein bringen
revealing [rɪˈviːlɪŋ] *adj* (*comment, action*) aufschlussreich; (*dress*) tief ausgeschnitten

revenge [rɪˈvɛndʒ] *n* (*for insult etc*) Rache *f*; **to get one's ~ (for sth)** seine Rache (für etw) bekommen
revenue [ˈrɛvənjuː] *n* (*of person, company*) Einnahmen *pl*
reverse [rɪˈvəːs] *n* (*opposite*) Gegenteil *nt*; (*back: of cloth*) linke Seite *f*; (*: of coin, paper*) Rückseite *f*; (*Aut: also:* **~ gear**) Rückwärtsgang *m* ▶ *adj* (*process*) umgekehrt ▶ *vt* (*position, trend etc*) umkehren; (*car*) zurücksetzen ▶ *vi* (*Brit Aut*) zurücksetzen; **in ~ order** in umgekehrter Reihenfolge; **to ~ direction** sich um 180 Grad drehen
review [rɪˈvjuː] *n* (*of book, film etc*) Kritik *f*, Rezension *f* ▶ *vt* (*book, film etc*) rezensieren; (*policy etc*) überprüfen; **to be/come under ~** überprüft werden
revise [rɪˈvaɪz] *vt* (*manuscript*) überarbeiten, revidieren ▶ *vi* (*study*) wiederholen
revision [rɪˈvɪʒən] *n* (*of manuscript, law etc*) Überarbeitung *f*; (*for exam*) Wiederholung *f*
revitalize [riːˈvaɪtəlaɪz] *vt* neu beleben
revive [rɪˈvaɪv] *vt* (*person*) wiederbeleben; (*custom*) wiederaufleben lassen ▶ *vi* (*person*) wieder zu sich kommen
revolt [rɪˈvəult] *n* Aufstand *m*
revolting [rɪˈvəultɪŋ] *adj* (*disgusting*) abscheulich, ekelhaft
revolution [rɛvəˈluːʃən] *n* (*Pol etc*) Revolution *f*; (*rotation*) Umdrehung *f*
revolutionary [rɛvəˈluːʃənrɪ] *adj* revolutionär ▶ *n* Revolutionär(in) *m(f)*
revolve [rɪˈvɔlv] *vi* sich drehen; **to ~ (a)round** sich drehen um
revolver [rɪˈvɔlvəʳ] *n* Revolver *m*
revolving door [rɪˈvɔlvɪŋ-] *n* Drehtür *f*
reward [rɪˈwɔːd] *n* Belohnung *f* ▶ *vt* belohnen
rewarding [rɪˈwɔːdɪŋ] *adj* lohnend
rewind [riːˈwaɪnd] *vt* (*irreg: like* **wind²**) (*tape etc*) zurückspulen
rewritable [riːˈraɪtəbl] *adj* (*CD, DVD*) wiederbeschreibbar
rewrite [riːˈraɪt] *vt* (*irreg: like* **write**) neu schreiben
rheumatism [ˈruːmətɪzəm] *n* Rheuma *nt*
Rhine [raɪn] *n*: **the ~** der Rhein
rhinoceros [raɪˈnɔsərəs] *n* Rhinozeros *nt*
Rhodes [rəudz] *n* Rhodos *nt*
rhubarb [ˈruːbɑːb] *n* Rhabarber *m*
rhyme [raɪm] *n* Reim *m* ▶ *vi*: **to ~ (with)** sich reimen (mit)
rhythm [ˈrɪðm] *n* Rhythmus *m*
rib [rɪb] *n* Rippe *f*
ribbon [ˈrɪbən] *n* (*for hair, decoration*) Band *nt*
rice [raɪs] *n* Reis *m*
rice pudding *n* Milchreis *m*
rich [rɪtʃ] *adj* reich; (*food*) schwer ▶ *npl*: **the ~** die Reichen
rickety [ˈrɪkɪtɪ] *adj* (*chair etc*) wackelig
rid [rɪd] (*pt, pp* **~**) *vt*: **to get ~ of** loswerden
ridden [ˈrɪdn] *pp of* **ride**
riddle [ˈrɪdl] *n* Rätsel *nt*
ride [raɪd] (*pt* **rode**, *pp* **ridden**) *n* (*in car, on bicycle*) Fahrt *f*; (*on horse*) Ritt *m* ▶ *vi* (*on horse*) reiten; (*on bicycle, bus etc*) fahren ▶ *vt* reiten; fahren; **to go for a ~** eine Fahrt/einen Ausritt machen; **to take sb for a ~** (*fig*) jdn hereinlegen
rider [ˈraɪdəʳ] *n* (*on horse*) Reiter(in) *m(f)*; (*on bicycle etc*) Fahrer(in) *m(f)*
ridiculous [rɪˈdɪkjuləs] *adj* lächerlich
riding [ˈraɪdɪŋ] *n* Reiten *nt*
rifle [ˈraɪfl] *n* (*gun*) Gewehr *nt*
rig [rɪg] *n* (*also:* **oil ~**: *at sea*) Bohrinsel *f* ▶ *vt* (*election, game etc*) manipulieren
right [raɪt] *adj* (*correct*) richtig; (*not left*) rechte(r, s) ▶ *n* Recht *nt* ▶ *adv* (*correctly, properly*) richtig; (*directly, exactly*) genau; (*not on the left*) rechts; **to be ~** (*person*) recht haben; (*clock*) genau gehen; **on/to the ~** rechts; **the R~** (*Pol*) die Rechte; **~ now** im Moment; **~ away** (*immediately*) sofort; **~ in the middle** genau in der Mitte
right angle *n* rechter Winkel *m*
right-hand drive [raɪtˈhænd-] *adj* (*vehicle*) mit Rechtssteuerung
right-handed [raɪtˈhændɪd] *adj* rechtshändig
right-hand side [raɪtˈhænd-] *n* rechte Seite *f*
rightly [ˈraɪtlɪ] *adv* (*with reason*) zu Recht
right of way *n* (*Aut*) Vorfahrt *f*
right wing *n* (*Pol, Sport*) rechter Flügel *m*
right-wing [raɪtˈwɪŋ] *adj* (*Pol*) rechtsgerichtet
rigid [ˈrɪdʒɪd] *adj* (*structure, views*) starr; (*principle, control etc*) streng

rigorous [ˈrɪgərəs] *adj* (*control etc*) streng
rigorously [ˈrɪgərəslɪ] *adv* (*test, assess etc*) streng
rim [rɪm] *n* (*of glass, spectacles*) Rand *m*; (*of wheel*) Felge *f*
rind [raɪnd] *n* (*of bacon*) Schwarte *f*; (*of lemon, melon*) Schale *f*; (*of cheese*) Rinde *f*
ring [rɪŋ] (*pt* **rang**, *pp* **rung**) *n* Ring *m*; (*of people, objects*) Kreis *m*; (*of circus*) Manege *f* ▶ *vi* (*Tel*: *person*) anrufen; (*bell*) läuten ▶ *vt* (BRIT *Tel*) anrufen; (*bell etc*) läuten; **to give sb a ~** (BRIT *Tel*) jdn anrufen
▶ **ring back** (BRIT) *vt, vi* (*Tel*) zurückrufen
▶ **ring up** (BRIT) *vt* (*Tel*) anrufen
ring binder *n* Ringbuch *nt*
ring-fence [rɪŋˈfɛns] *vt* (*money, tax*) zweckbinden
ringleader [ˈrɪŋliːdəʳ] *n* Rädelsführer(in) *m(f)*
ring road (BRIT) *n* Ringstraße *f*
ringtone [ˈrɪŋtəun] *n* (*of mobile phone*) Klingelton *m*
rink [rɪŋk] *n* (*also*: **ice ~**) Eisbahn *f*; (*also*: **roller skating ~**) Rollschuhbahn *f*
rinse [rɪns] *vt* spülen
riot [ˈraɪət] *n* (*disturbance*) Aufruhr *m*
rip [rɪp] *n* (*tear*) Riss *m* ▶ *vt* zerreißen ▶ *vi* reißen
▶ **rip off** *vt* (*inf*: *swindle*) übers Ohr hauen
▶ **rip up** *vt* zerreißen
ripe [raɪp] *adj* reif
ripen [ˈraɪpn] *vi* reifen
rip-off [ˈrɪpɔf] (*inf*) *n*: **it's a ~!** das ist Wucher!
rise [raɪz] (*pt* **rose**, *pp* **risen**) *n* (*incline*) Steigung *f*; (BRIT: *salary increase*) Gehaltserhöhung *f*; (*in prices, temperature etc*) Anstieg *m*; (*fig*: *to fame etc*) Aufstieg *m* ▶ *vi* (*prices, water*) steigen; (*sun, moon*) aufgehen; (*from bed, chair*) aufstehen; (*sound, voice*) ansteigen; (*tower, rebel*: *also*: **~ up**) sich erheben
risen [ˈrɪzn] *pp of* **rise**
risk [rɪsk] *n* (*deliberate*) Risiko *nt* ▶ *vt* riskieren; **to run the ~ of doing sth** Gefahr laufen, etw zu tun
risky [ˈrɪskɪ] *adj* riskant
ritual [ˈrɪtjuəl] *adj* (*dance*) rituell ▶ *n* Ritual *nt*
rival [ˈraɪvl] *n* Rivale *m*, Rivalin *f*
rivalry [ˈraɪvlrɪ] *n* Rivalität *f*
river [ˈrɪvəʳ] *n* Fluss *m*
river bank *n* Flussufer *nt*
riverside [ˈrɪvəsaɪd] *n* = **river bank**
road [rəud] *n* Straße *f*; (*fig*) Weg *m*; **to be on the ~** (*salesman etc*) unterwegs sein; **major/minor ~** Haupt-/Nebenstraße *f*
roadblock [ˈrəudblɔk] *n* Straßensperre *f*
road map *n* Straßenkarte *f*
road rage *n* Aggressivität *f* im Straßenverkehr
roadside [ˈrəudsaɪd] *n* Straßenrand *m*; **by the ~** am Straßenrand
road sign *n* Verkehrszeichen *nt*
road tax *n* Kraftfahrzeugssteuer *f*
road works *npl* Straßenbauarbeiten *pl*, Straßenbau *sing*
roadworthy [ˈrəudwəːðɪ] *adj* verkehrstüchtig
roar [rɔːʳ] *n* (*of animal, crowd*) Brüllen *nt*; (*of vehicle*) Getöse *nt* ▶ *vi* (*animal, person*) brüllen
roast [rəust] *n* Braten *m* ▶ *vt* (*meat, potatoes*) braten
roast beef *n* Roastbeef *nt*
rob [rɔb] *vt* (*person*) bestehlen; (*house, bank*) ausrauben
robber [ˈrɔbəʳ] *n* Räuber(in) *m(f)*
robbery [ˈrɔbərɪ] *n* Raub *m*
robe [rəub] *n* (*for ceremony etc*) Gewand *nt*; (*US*) Morgenrock *m*
robin [ˈrɔbɪn] *n* Rotkehlchen *nt*
robot [ˈrəubɔt] *n* Roboter *m*
robust [rəuˈbʌst] *adj* robust; (*appetite*) gesund
rock [rɔk] *n* (*substance*) Stein *m*; (*boulder*) Felsen *m*; (BRIT: *sweet*) ≈ Zuckerstange *f*; (*Mus*: *also*: **~ music**) Rock *m* ▶ *vt* (*swing gently*: *cradle*) schaukeln ▶ *vi* (*object*) schwanken; **on the rocks** (*drink*) mit Eis; (*marriage etc*) gescheitert
rock climbing *n* Felsenklettern *nt*
rocket [ˈrɔkɪt] *n* Rakete *f*
rocking chair [ˈrɔkɪŋ-] *n* Schaukelstuhl *m*
rocky [ˈrɔkɪ] *adj* (*path, ground*) felsig
rod [rɔd] *n* (*also Tech*) Stange *f*; (*also*: **fishing ~**) Angelrute *f*
rode [rəud] *pt of* **ride**
rogue [rəug] *n* Gauner *m*
role [rəul] *n* Rolle *f*

role model *n* Rollenmodell *nt*
roll [rəul] *n* (*of paper*) Rolle *f*; (*also:* **bread ~**) Brötchen *nt* ▸ *vt* rollen; (*cigarette*) drehen; (*pastry: also:* **~ out**) ausrollen ▸ *vi* rollen; (*ship*) schlingern; (*camera, printing press*) laufen
▸ **roll over** *vi* sich umdrehen
▸ **roll up** *vi* (*inf: arrive*) aufkreuzen ▸ *vt* (*carpet, umbrella etc*) aufrollen
roller [ˈrəuləʳ] *n* (*for hair*) Lockenwickler *m*
Rollerblades® [ˈrəuləbleɪdz] *npl* Rollerblades *pl*
rollerblading [ˈrəuləbleɪdɪŋ] *n* Inlineskaten *nt*
roller coaster *n* Achterbahn *f*
roller skates *npl* Rollschuhe *pl*
roller-skating [ˈrəuləskeɪtɪŋ] *n* Rollschuhlaufen *nt*
rolling pin [ˈrəulɪŋ-] *n* Nudelholz *nt*
ROM [rɔm] *n abbr* (*Comput:* = *read only memory*) ROM
Roman [ˈrəumən] *adj* römisch ▸ *n* (*person*) Römer(in) *m(f)*
Roman Catholic *adj* römisch-katholisch ▸ *n* Katholik(in) *m(f)*
romance [rəˈmæns] *n* (*love affair*) Romanze *f*; (*romanticism*) Romantik *f*
Romania [rəuˈmeɪnɪə] *n* Rumänien *nt*
Romanian [rəuˈmeɪnɪən] *adj* rumänisch ▸ *n* (*person*) Rumäne *m*, Rumänin *f*; (*Ling*) Rumänisch *nt*
romantic [rəˈmæntɪk] *adj* romantisch
roof [ru:f] (*pl* **roofs**) *n* Dach *nt*
roof rack *n* Dachgepäckträger *m*
rook [ruk] *n* (*Chess*) Turm *m*
room [ru:m] *n* (*in house, hotel*) Zimmer *nt*; (*space*) Raum *m*, Platz *m*; **to make ~ for sb** für jdn Platz machen
roommate [ˈru:mmeɪt] *n* Zimmergenosse *m*, Zimmergenossin *f*
room service *n* Zimmerservice *m*
roomy [ˈru:mɪ] *adj* (*building, car*) geräumig
root [ru:t] *n* (*also Math*) Wurzel *f*
▸ **root out** *vt* ausrotten
rope [rəup] *n* Seil *nt*; **to know the ropes** (*fig*) sich auskennen
rort [rɔ:t] *n* (Aust, *NZ inf*) Betrugsschema *nt*, Abzocke *f* (*inf*) ▸ *vt* austricksen (*inf*); (*money*) abschöpfen
rose [rəuz] *pt of* **rise** ▸ *n* (*flower*) Rose *f*
rosé [ˈrəuzeɪ] *n* (*wine*) Rosé *m*
rot [rɔt] *vi* (*teeth, wood, fruit etc*) verfaulen
rota [ˈrəutə] *n* Dienstplan *m*
rotate [rəuˈteɪt] *vt* (*spin*) rotieren lassen ▸ *vi* (*revolve*) rotieren
rotation [rəuˈteɪʃən] *n* (*of planet, drum etc*) Rotation *f*; **in ~** der Reihe nach
rotten [ˈrɔtn] *adj* (*decayed*) faul; (*inf: person, situation*) gemein; (*: film, weather, driver etc*) mies; **to feel ~** sich elend fühlen
rough [rʌf] *adj* rau; (*terrain, road*) uneben; (*person, plan, drawing, guess*) grob; (*life, conditions, journey*) hart; (*sea, crossing*) stürmisch ▸ *n* (*Golf*): **in the ~** im Rough ▸ *vt*: **to ~ it** primitiv *or* ohne Komfort leben; **the sea is ~ today** die See ist heute stürmisch; **can you give me a ~ idea of the cost?** können Sie mir eine ungefähre Vorstellung von den Kosten geben?; **to sleep ~** (Brit) im Freien übernachten
roughly [ˈrʌflɪ] *adv* grob; (*approximately*) ungefähr
round [raund] *adj* rund ▸ *n* Runde *f* ▸ *prep* um ▸ *adv*: **all ~** rundherum; **a ~ (of drinks)** eine Runde; **it's just ~ the corner** (*fig*) es steht vor der Tür; **~ the clock** rund um die Uhr; **to sail ~ the world** die Welt umsegeln; **~ about 300** (*approximately*) ungefähr 300; **the long way ~** auf Umwegen; **I'll be ~ at 6 o'clock** ich komme um 6 Uhr
▸ **round off** *vt* abrunden
▸ **round up** *vt* (*figure*) aufrunden
roundabout [ˈraundəbaut] (Brit) *n* (*Aut*) Kreisverkehr *m*; (*at fair*) Karussell *nt* ▸ *adj*: **in a ~ way** auf Umwegen
round trip *n* Rundreise *f*
round-trip ticket *n* (*US*) Rückfahrkarte *f*; (*for plane*) Rückflugticket *nt*
rouse [rauz] *vt* (*wake up*) aufwecken
route [ru:t] *n* Strecke *f*; (*of bus, train, shipping*) Linie *f*; (*of procession, fig*) Weg *m*
router [ˈru:təʳ] *n* (*Comput*) Router *m*
routine [ru:ˈti:n] *adj* (*work, check etc*) Routine- ▸ *n* (*habits*) Routine *f*
row¹ [rəu] *n* (*line*) Reihe *f* ▸ *vi* (*in boat*) rudern ▸ *vt* (*boat*) rudern; **three times in a ~** dreimal hintereinander
row² [rau] *n* (*din*) Krach *m*; (*dispute*) Streit *m*

rowboat [ˈrəubəut] (*US*) *n* = **rowing boat**
rowing [ˈrəuɪŋ] *n* (*sport*) Rudern *nt*
rowing boat (BRIT) *n* Ruderboot *nt*
royal [ˈrɔɪəl] *adj* königlich
royalty [ˈrɔɪəltɪ] *n* (*royal persons*) die königliche Familie ▪ **royalties** *npl* (*to author*) Tantiemen *pl*
RSPCA (BRIT) *n abbr* (= *Royal Society for the Prevention of Cruelty to Animals*) Tierschutzverein *m*
RSVP *abbr* (= *répondez s'il vous plaît*) u. A. w. g.
rub [rʌb] *vt* reiben
▸**rub in** *vt* (*ointment*) einreiben
▸**rub out** *vt* (*with eraser*) ausradieren
rubber [ˈrʌbəʳ] *n* (*also inf: condom*) Gummi *m or nt*; (BRIT: *eraser*) Radiergummi *m*
rubber band *n* Gummiband *nt*
rubber stamp *n* Stempel *m*
rubbish [ˈrʌbɪʃ] (BRIT) *n* (*waste*) Abfall *m*; (*fig: junk*) Schrott *m*; (: *pej: nonsense*) Quatsch *m*
rubbish bin (BRIT) *n* Abfalleimer *m*
rubbish dump (BRIT) *n* Müllabladeplatz *m*
rubble [ˈrʌbl] *n* (*Constr*) Schutt *m*
ruby [ˈruːbɪ] *n* (*gem*) Rubin *m*
rucksack [ˈrʌksæk] *n* Rucksack *m*
rude [ruːd] *adj* (*impolite*) unhöflich; (*naughty*) unanständig
rug [rʌg] *n* (*on floor*) Läufer *m*; (BRIT: *blanket*) Decke *f*
rugby [ˈrʌgbɪ] *n* (*also*: **~ football**) Rugby *nt*
rugged [ˈrʌgɪd] *adj* (*landscape*) rau; (*features, face*) markig
ruin [ˈruːɪn] *n* (*destruction, downfall*) Ruin *m*; (*remains*) Ruine *f* ▸ *vt* ruinieren
rule [ruːl] *n* (*norm*) Regel *f*; (*government*) Herrschaft *f* ▸ *vt* (*country, people*) herrschen über +*acc* ▸ *vi* (*monarch etc*) herrschen; **as a ~** in der Regel
ruler [ˈruːləʳ] *n* (*sovereign*) Herrscher(in) *m(f)*; (*for measuring*) Lineal *nt*
rum [rʌm] *n* Rum *m*
rumble [ˈrʌmbl] *vi* (*stomach*) knurren; (*traffic*) rumpeln
rummage [ˈrʌmɪdʒ] *vi* herumstöbern
rumour, (*US*) **rumor** [ˈruːməʳ] *n* Gerücht *nt*
run [rʌn] (*pt* **ran**, *pp* **~**) *n* (*as exercise, sport*) Lauf *m*; (*in car, train etc*) Fahrt *f*; (*series*) Serie *f*; (*Cricket, Baseball*) Run *m*; (*in tights etc*) Laufmasche *f* ▸ *vt* (*race, distance*) laufen, rennen; (*operate: business*) leiten; (: *hotel, shop*) führen; (*Comput: program*) laufen lassen; (*water, bath*) einlaufen lassen ▸ *vi* laufen, rennen; (*bus, train*) fahren; (*river, tears*) fließen; (*colours*) auslaufen; (*jumper*) färben; (*in election*) antreten; (*road, railway etc*) verlaufen; **to go for a ~** (*as exercise*) einen Dauerlauf machen; **there was a ~ on ...** (*meat, tickets*) es gab einen Ansturm auf +*acc*; **in the long ~** langfristig; **on the ~** (*fugitive*) auf der Flucht; **I'll ~ you to the station** ich fahre dich zum Bahnhof; **the baby's nose was running** dem Baby lief die Nase; **to ~ for president** für das Amt des Präsidenten kandidieren; **to ~ dry** (*well etc*) austrocknen; **blonde hair runs in the family** blonde Haare liegen in der Familie
▸**run about** *vi* herumlaufen
▸**run away** *vi* weglaufen
▸**run down** *vt* (*production*) verringern; (*Aut: person*) überfahren; (*criticize*) schlechtmachen
▸**run into** *vt fus* (*meet: person*) begegnen +*dat*; (: *trouble etc*) bekommen
▸**run off** *vi* weglaufen
▸**run out** *vi* (*time, passport*) ablaufen; (*money*) ausgehen
▸**run out of** *vt fus*: **we're running out of money/petrol** uns geht das Geld/das Benzin aus
▸**run over** *vt* (*Aut*) überfahren
▸**run up** *vt* (*debt*) anhäufen
rung [rʌŋ] *pp of* **ring**
runner [ˈrʌnəʳ] *n* Läufer(in) *m(f)*
runner bean (BRIT) *n* Stangenbohne *f*
running [ˈrʌnɪŋ] *n* (*sport*) Laufen *nt*; (*of business etc*) Leitung *f* ▸ *adj* (*water, stream*) laufend; **6 days ~** 6 Tage hintereinander
running costs *npl* (*of car, machine*) Unterhaltskosten *pl*
runny [ˈrʌnɪ] *adj* (*egg, butter*) dünnflüssig; (*nose, eyes*) triefend
runway [ˈrʌnweɪ] *n* (*Aviat*) Start- und Landebahn *f*
rural [ˈruərl] *adj* ländlich
rush [rʌʃ] *n* (*hurry*) Eile *f*; (*Comm: sudden demand*) starke Nachfrage *f* ▸ *vt* (*lunch,*

job etc) sich beeilen bei; (*person, supplies etc*) schnellstens bringen ▶ *vi* (*person*) sich beeilen; **I'm in a ~ (to do sth)** ich habe es eilig (, etw zu tun); **don't ~ me!** drängen Sie mich nicht!

rush hour *n* Hauptverkehrszeit *f*

rusk [rʌsk] *n* Zwieback *m*

Russia [ˈrʌʃə] *n* Russland *nt*

Russian [ˈrʌʃən] *adj* russisch ▶ *n* (*person*) Russe *m*, Russin *f*; (*Ling*) Russisch *nt*

rust [rʌst] *n* Rost *m* ▶ *vi* rosten

rustproof [ˈrʌstpru:f] *adj* nicht rostend

rusty [ˈrʌstɪ] *adj* (*car*) rostig; (*fig: skill etc*) eingerostet

ruthless [ˈru:θlɪs] *adj* rücksichtslos

rye [raɪ] *n* (*cereal*) Roggen *m*

rye bread *n* Roggenbrot *nt*

S

S [ɛs] *abbr* (= *south*) S

sabotage [ˈsæbətɑ:ʒ] *vt* (*plan, meeting*) sabotieren

sachet [ˈsæʃeɪ] *n* (*of shampoo*) Beutel *m*

sack [sæk] *n* Sack *m* ▶ *vt* (*dismiss*) entlassen; **to get the ~** rausfliegen (*inf*)

sacred [ˈseɪkrɪd] *adj* heilig

sacrifice [ˈsækrɪfaɪs] *n* Opfer *nt* ▶ *vt* opfern

sad [sæd] *adj* traurig

saddle [ˈsædl] *n* Sattel *m*

sadistic [səˈdɪstɪk] *adj* sadistisch

sadly [ˈsædlɪ] *adv* (*unfortunately*) leider

safari [səˈfɑ:rɪ] *n* Safari *f*

safe [seɪf] *adj* sicher; (*out of danger*) in Sicherheit ▶ *n* Safe *m or nt*; **~ journey!** gute Fahrt *or* Reise!

safeguard [ˈseɪfgɑ:d] *n* Schutz *m* ▶ *vt* schützen

safely [ˈseɪflɪ] *adv* sicher; (*arrive*) wohlbehalten

safety [ˈseɪftɪ] *n* Sicherheit *f*

safety belt *n* Sicherheitsgurt *m*

safety pin *n* Sicherheitsnadel *f*

Sagittarius [sædʒɪˈtɛərɪəs] *n* Schütze *m*

Sahara [səˈhɑ:rə] *n*: **the ~ (Desert)** die (Wüste) Sahara

said [sɛd] *pt, pp of* **say**

sail [seɪl] *n* Segel *nt* ▶ *vt* segeln ▶ *vi* fahren; (*Sport*) segeln; (*begin voyage: ship*) auslaufen; **to set ~** losfahren, abfahren

sailboat [ˈseɪlbəut] (*US*) *n* = **sailing boat**

sailing [ˈseɪlɪŋ] *n* (*Sport*) Segeln *nt*; **to go ~** segeln gehen

sailing boat *n* Segelboot *nt*

sailor [ˈseɪlə^r] *n* Seemann *m*, Matrose *m*

saint [seɪnt] *n* (*lit, fig*) Heilige(r) *f*(*m*)
sake [seɪk] *n*: **for the ~ of sb/sth, for sb's/sth's ~** um jds/einer Sache *gen* willen; (*out of consideration for*) jdm/etw zuliebe
salad [ˈsæləd] *n* Salat *m*
salad cream (BRIT) *n* ≈ Mayonnaise *f*
salad dressing *n* Salatsoße *f*
salary [ˈsælərɪ] *n* Gehalt *nt*
sale [seɪl] *n* Verkauf *m*; (*at reduced prices*) Ausverkauf *m*; **"for ~"** „zu verkaufen"; **closing-down ~, liquidation ~** (*US*) Räumungsverkauf *m*
sales assistant, (*US*) **sales clerk** *n* Verkäufer(in) *m*(*f*)
salesman [ˈseɪlzmən] *n* (*irreg*) Verkäufer *m*; (*representative*) Vertreter *m*
sales tax (*US*) *n* Verkaufssteuer *f*
saleswoman [ˈseɪlzwumən] *n* (*irreg*) Verkäuferin *f*; (*representative*) Vertreterin *f*
salmon [ˈsæmən] *n inv* Lachs *m*
saloon [səˈluːn] *n* (*US: bar*) Saloon *m*; (*ship's lounge*) Salon *m*
salt [sɔːlt] *n* Salz *nt* ▸ *vt* (*put salt on*) salzen; (*road*) mit Salz streuen
salt cellar *n* Salzstreuer *m*
salty [ˈsɔːltɪ] *adj* salzig
salvage [ˈsælvɪdʒ] *vt* bergen; (*fig*) retten
same [seɪm] *adj* (*similar*) gleiche(r, s); (*identical*) selbe(r, s) ▸ *pron*: **the ~** (*similar*) der/die/das Gleiche; (*identical*) derselbe/dieselbe/dasselbe; **they are exactly the ~** sie sind genau gleich; **on the ~ day** am gleichen *or* selben Tag; **at the ~ time** (*simultaneously*) gleichzeitig, zur gleichen Zeit; (*yet*) doch; **all** *or* **just the ~** trotzdem; **the ~ to you!** (danke) gleichfalls!; **it's all the ~ to me** es ist mir egal
Samoa [səˈməuə] *n* Samoa *nt*
sample [ˈsɑːmpl] *n* Probe *f*; (*of merchandise*) Muster *nt* ▸ *vt* probieren
sanction [ˈsæŋkʃən] *n* Zustimmung *f* ■ **sanctions** *npl* (*Pol*) Sanktionen *pl*
sanctuary [ˈsæŋktjuərɪ] *n* (*for birds/animals*) Schutzgebiet *nt*; (*place of refuge*) Zuflucht *f*
sand [sænd] *n* Sand *m*
sandal [ˈsændl] *n* Sandale *f*
sandpaper [ˈsændpeɪpə^r] *n* Schmirgelpapier *nt*
sandwich [ˈsændwɪtʃ] *n* Sandwich *nt*
sandy [ˈsændɪ] *adj* sandig; (*beach*) Sand-
sane [seɪn] *adj* geistig gesund; (*sensible*) vernünftig
sang [sæŋ] *pt of* **sing**
sanitary [ˈsænɪtərɪ] *adj* hygienisch
sanitary towel, (*US*) **sanitary napkin** *n* Damenbinde *f*
sank [sæŋk] *pt of* **sink**
Santa Claus [sæntəˈklɔːz] *n* ≈ der Weihnachtsmann
sarcastic [sɑːˈkæstɪk] *adj* sarkastisch
sardine [sɑːˈdiːn] *n* Sardine *f*
Sardinia [sɑːˈdɪnɪə] *n* Sardinien *nt*
sari [ˈsɑːrɪ] *n* Sari *m*
sat [sæt] *pt, pp of* **sit**
Sat. *abbr* (= *Saturday*) Sa.
satellite [ˈsætəlaɪt] *n* Satellit *m*
satellite dish *n* Satellitenantenne *f*
satellite television *n* Satellitenfernsehen *nt*
satin [ˈsætɪn] *n* Satin *m*
satisfaction [sætɪsˈfækʃən] *n* Befriedigung *f*; **has it been done to your ~?** sind Sie damit zufrieden?
satisfactory [sætɪsˈfæktərɪ] *adj* zufriedenstellend
satisfied [ˈsætɪsfaɪd] *adj* zufrieden
satisfy [ˈsætɪsfaɪ] *vt* zufriedenstellen; (*needs, demand*) befriedigen; (*requirements, conditions*) erfüllen; **to ~ sb/o.s. that …** jdn/sich davon überzeugen, dass …
satisfying [ˈsætɪsfaɪɪŋ] *adj* befriedigend
Saturday [ˈsætədɪ] *n* Samstag *m*
sauce [sɔːs] *n* Soße *f*
saucepan [ˈsɔːspən] *n* Kochtopf *m*
saucer [ˈsɔːsə^r] *n* Untertasse *f*
saucy [ˈsɔːsɪ] *adj* frech
Saudi Arabia [ˈsaudɪ-] *n* Saudi-Arabien *nt*
sauna [ˈsɔːnə] *n* Sauna *f*
sausage [ˈsɔsɪdʒ] *n* Wurst *f*
sausage roll *n* Wurst *f* im Schlafrock
savage [ˈsævɪdʒ] *adj* (*attack etc*) brutal; (*dog*) gefährlich
save [seɪv] *vt* (*rescue*) retten; (*money, time*) sparen; (*Comput: file*) abspeichern ▸ *vi* (*also:* **~ up**) sparen ▸ *n* (*Sport*) (Ball)abwehr *f*
saving [ˈseɪvɪŋ] *n* (*on price etc*) Ersparnis *f* ■ **savings** *npl* (*money*) Ersparnisse *pl*

savoury, (*US*) **savory** [ˈseɪvərɪ] *adj* pikant
saw [sɔː] (*pt* **sawed**, *pp* **sawed** *or* **sawn**) *vt* sägen ▶ *n* Säge *f* ▶ *pt of* **see**
sawdust [ˈsɔːdʌst] *n* Sägemehl *nt*
saxophone [ˈsæksəfəun] *n* Saxofon *nt*
say [seɪ] (*pt*, *pp* **said**) *vt* sagen ▶ *n*: **to have one's ~** seine Meinung äußern; **it says on the sign "No Smoking"** auf dem Schild steht „Rauchen verboten"; **that is to ~** das heißt; **~ (that) ...** angenommen, (dass) ...
saying [ˈseɪɪŋ] *n* Redensart *f*
scab [skæb] *n* (*on wound*) Schorf *m*
scaffolding [ˈskæfəldɪŋ] *n* Gerüst *nt*
scale [skeɪl] *n* Skala *f*; (*of fish*) Schuppe *f*; (*of map, model*) Maßstab *m* ▪ **(pair of) scales** *npl* (*for weighing*) Waage *f*; **pay ~** Lohnskala *f*; **to draw sth to ~** etw maßstabgetreu zeichnen; **on a large ~** im großen Rahmen
scalp [skælp] *n* Kopfhaut *f*
scan [skæn] *vt* (*horizon*) absuchen; (*newspaper etc*) überfliegen; (*TV*, *Radar*) abtasten ▶ *n* (*Med*) Scan *m*
▶ **scan in** *vt* (*Comput*) einscannen
scandal [ˈskændl] *n* Skandal *m*
scandalous [ˈskændələs] *adj* skandalös
Scandinavia [skændɪˈneɪvɪə] *n* Skandinavien *nt*
Scandinavian [skændɪˈneɪvɪən] *adj* skandinavisch ▶ *n* Skandinavier(in) *m(f)*
scanner [ˈskænəʳ] *n* (*Med*) Scanner *m*
scapegoat [ˈskeɪpgəut] *n* Sündenbock *m*
scar [skɑː] *n* Narbe *f*
scarce [skɛəs] *adj* knapp
scarcely [ˈskɛəslɪ] *adv* kaum
scare [skɛəʳ] *n* (*public fear*) Panik *f* ▶ *vt* (*frighten*) erschrecken; (*worry*) Angst machen *+dat*
scarf [skɑːf] (*pl* **scarfs** *or* **scarves**) *n* Schal *m*; (*headscarf*) Kopftuch *nt*
scarlet [ˈskɑːlɪt] *adj* (scharlach)rot
scarlet fever *n* Scharlach *m*
scary [ˈskɛərɪ] (*inf*) *adj* unheimlich; (*film*) gruselig
scatter [ˈskætəʳ] *vt* verstreuen; (*crowd*) zerstreuen
scene [siːn] *n* (*lit*, *fig*) Szene *f*; (*of accident*) Ort *m*; **to make a ~** (*inf*: *fuss*) eine Szene machen
scenery [ˈsiːnərɪ] *n* (*Theat*) Bühnenbild *nt*; (*landscape*) Landschaft *f*
scenic [ˈsiːnɪk] *adj* malerisch, landschaftlich schön
scent [sɛnt] *n* (*fragrance*) Duft *m*; (*liquid perfume*) Parfüm *nt*
sceptical, (*US*) **skeptical** [ˈskɛptɪkl] *adj* skeptisch
schedule [ˈʃɛdjuːl, (*US*) ˈskɛdjuːl] *n* (*of trains, buses*) Fahrplan *m*; (*of events*) Programm *nt*; (*of prices, details etc*) Liste *f* ▶ *vt* (*visit, meeting etc*) ansetzen; **on ~** wie geplant, pünktlich; **to be ahead of/behind ~** dem Zeitplan voraus sein/im Rückstand sein
scheduled [ˈʃɛdjuːld, (*US*) ˈskɛdjuːld] *adj* (*train, bus, stop*) planmäßig
scheduled flight *n* Linienflug *m*
scheme [skiːm] *n* (*personal plan*) Plan *m*; (*plot*) raffinierter Plan *m*; (*formal plan*) Programm *nt* ▶ *vi* Pläne schmieden, intrigieren
schizophrenic [skɪtsəˈfrɛnɪk] *adj* schizophren
scholar [ˈskɔləʳ] *n* Gelehrte(r) *f(m)*
scholarship [ˈskɔləʃɪp] *n* (*grant*) Stipendium *nt*
school [skuːl] *n* Schule *f*; (*US inf*: *university*) Universität *f*
school bag *n* Schultasche *f*
schoolbook [ˈskuːlbuk] *n* Schulbuch *nt*
schoolboy [ˈskuːlbɔɪ] *n* Schüler *m*
school bus *n* Schulbus *m*
schoolgirl [ˈskuːlgəːl] *n* Schülerin *f*
schoolteacher [ˈskuːltiːtʃəʳ] *n* Lehrer(in) *m(f)*
sciatica [saɪˈætɪkə] *n* Ischias *m or nt*
science [ˈsaɪəns] *n* Naturwissenschaft *f*; (*branch of knowledge*) Wissenschaft *f*
science fiction *n* Science-Fiction *f*
scientific [saɪənˈtɪfɪk] *adj* wissenschaftlich
scientist [ˈsaɪəntɪst] *n* Wissenschaftler(in) *m(f)*
scissors [ˈsɪzəz] *npl* Schere *f*
scone [skɔn] *n brötchenartiges Teegebäck*
scoop [skuːp] *n* (*amount*) Kugel *f*; (*Press*) Knüller *m*
▶ **scoop up** *vt* aufschaufeln
scooter [ˈskuːtəʳ] *n* (*also*: **motor ~**) Motorroller *m*; (*toy*) (Tret)roller *m*
scope [skəup] *n* (*opportunity*) Möglichkeiten *pl*; (*range*) Umfang *m*
score [skɔːʳ] *n* (*number of points*) (Punkte)stand *m*; (*of game*) Spielstand *m*; (*Mus*) Partitur *f* ▶ *vt* (*goal*) schießen;

(*point, success*) erzielen ▸ *vi* (*keep score*) (Punkte) zählen
scoreboard [ˈskɔ:bɔ:d] *n* Anzeigetafel *f*
scorn [skɔ:n] *n* Verachtung *f*
scornful [ˈskɔ:nful] *adj* verächtlich
Scorpio [ˈskɔ:pɪəu] *n* Skorpion *m*
scorpion [ˈskɔ:pɪən] *n* Skorpion *m*
Scot [skɔt] *n* Schotte *m*, Schottin *f*
Scotch [skɔtʃ] *n* Scotch *m*
Scotch tape® *n* ≈ Tesafilm® *m*
Scotland [ˈskɔtlənd] *n* Schottland *nt*
Scotsman [ˈskɔtsmən] *n* (*irreg*) Schotte *m*
Scotswoman [ˈskɔtswumən] *n* (*irreg*) Schottin *f*
Scottish [ˈskɔtɪʃ] *adj* schottisch

SCOTTISH PARLIAMENT

Nach drei Jahrhunderten politischen Zusammenschlusses zwischen England und Schottland hat sich Schottland mit einem Referendum für ein eigenständiges Parlament entschieden, das seinen Sitz in Edinburgh hat. 1999 wurden 129 Abgeordnete gewählt und mit gesetzgebender Gewalt versehen, besonders in den Bereichen Schulwesen, Umwelt, Gesundheitswesen, Rechtswesen, Steuerwesen und Kommunalverwaltung. Der Regierungsleiter ist der *First Minister*, aber das Staatsoberhaupt ist nach wie vor Königin Elizabeth II. Mit einer neuen Volksabstimmung haben sich die Schotten im September 2014 gegen die vollständige Unabhängigkeit vom Rest des Vereinigten Königreiches entschieden.

scout [skaut] *n* (*also*: **boy ~**) Pfadfinder *m*
scowl [skaul] *vi* ein böses Gesicht machen
scrambled eggs [ˈskræmbld-] *n* Rührei *nt*
scrap [skræp] *n* (*bit*) Stückchen *nt*; (*also*: **~ metal**) Schrott *m* ▸ *vt* (*machines etc*) verschrotten; (*fig*: *plans etc*) fallen lassen
scrapbook [ˈskræpbuk] *n* Sammelalbum *nt*
scrape [skreɪp] *vt* abkratzen; (*hand etc*) abschürfen; (*car*) verschrammen
▸ **scrape through** *vt* (*exam etc*) durchrutschen durch (*inf*)
scrap heap *n*: **to be on the ~** (*fig*) zum alten Eisen gehören
scrap metal *n* Schrott *m*
scrap paper *n* Schmierpapier *nt*
scratch [skrætʃ] *n* Kratzer *m* ▸ *vt* kratzen; (*one's nose etc*) sich kratzen an +*dat*; (*paint, car, record*) verkratzen ▸ *vi* sich kratzen; **to start from ~** ganz von vorne anfangen
scream [skri:m] *n* Schrei *m* ▸ *vi* schreien; **to ~ at sb (to do sth)** jdn anschreien(, etw zu tun)
screen [skri:n] *n* (*Cine*) Leinwand *f*; (*TV, Comput*) Bildschirm *m* ▸ *vt* (*protect*) abschirmen; (*conceal*) verdecken; (*film*) zeigen; (*candidates etc*) überprüfen
screenplay [ˈskri:npleɪ] *n* Drehbuch *nt*
screen saver *n* (*Comput*) Bildschirmschoner *m*
screenshot [ˈskri:nʃɔt] *n* (*Comput*) Screenshot *m*, Bildschirmfoto *nt*
screw [skru:] *n* Schraube *f* ▸ *vt* schrauben; (*!*) bumsen (*!*); **to ~ sth to the wall** etw an der Wand festschrauben
▸ **screw up** *vt* (*paper etc*) zusammenknüllen; (*inf*: *ruin*) vermasseln; **to ~ up one's eyes** die Augen zusammenkneifen
screwdriver [ˈskru:draɪvəʳ] *n* Schraubenzieher *m*
screw top *n* Schraubverschluss *m*
scribble [ˈskrɪbl] *vt*, *vi* kritzeln
script [skrɪpt] *n* (*Cine*) Drehbuch *nt*; (*of speech, play etc*) Text *m*; (*alphabet*) Schrift *f*
scroll [skrəul] *vi* (*Comput*) scrollen
▸ **scroll down** *vi* (*Comput*) runterscrollen
▸ **scroll up** *vi* (*Comput*) raufscrollen
scroll bar *n* (*Comput*) Bildaufleiste *f*
scrub [skrʌb] *vt* (*floor etc*) schrubben
scrubbing brush [ˈskrʌbɪŋ-] *n* Scheuerbürste *f*
scruffy [ˈskrʌfɪ] *adj* gammelig
scrupulous [ˈskru:pjuləs] *adj* gewissenhaft; (*honesty*) unbedingt
scrupulously [ˈskru:pjuləslɪ] *adv* gewissenhaft; (*clean*) peinlich

scuba diving [ˈsku:bə-] *n* Sporttauchen *nt*
sculptor [ˈskʌlptəʳ] *n* Bildhauer(in) *m(f)*
sculpture [ˈskʌlptʃəʳ] *n* (*art*) Bildhauerei *f*; (*object*) Skulptur *f*
sea [si:] *n* Meer *nt*, See *f*
seafood [ˈsi:fu:d] *n* Meeresfrüchte *pl*
seafront [ˈsi:frʌnt] *n* Strandpromenade *f*
seagull [ˈsi:gʌl] *n* Möwe *f*
seal [si:l] *n* (*animal*) Seehund *m*; (*official stamp*) Siegel *nt*; (*in machine etc*) Dichtung *f*; (*on bottle etc*) Verschluss *m* ▸ *vt* (*envelope*) zukleben; (*with seal*) versiegeln
seam [si:m] *n* Naht *f*
search [sə:tʃ] *n* Suche *f* ▸ *vt* durchsuchen ▸ *vi*: **to ~ for** suchen nach; **in ~ of** auf der Suche nach
search engine *n* (*Comput*) Suchmaschine *f*
seashell [ˈsi:ʃel] *n* Muschel *f*
seashore [ˈsi:ʃɔ:ʳ] *n* Strand *m*
seasick [ˈsi:sɪk] *adj* seekrank
seaside [ˈsi:saɪd] *n*: **to go to the ~** ans Meer *or* an die See fahren; **at the ~** am Meer, an der See
seaside resort *n* Badeort *m*
season [ˈsi:zn] *n* Jahreszeit *f*; (*Sport, of films etc*) Saison *f* ▸ *vt* (*food*) würzen
seasoning [ˈsi:znɪŋ] *n* Gewürz *nt*
season ticket *n* (*Rail*) Zeitkarte *f*; (*Sport*) Dauerkarte *f*; (*Theat*) Abonnement *nt*
seat [si:t] *n* (*chair, of government, Pol*) Sitz *m*; (*place*) Platz *m* ▸ *vt* setzen; (*have room for*) Sitzplätze bieten für; **to take one's ~** sich setzen; **please be seated** bitte nehmen Sie Platz; **to be seated** sitzen
seat belt *n* Sicherheitsgurt *m*
sea view [ˈsi:vju:] *n* Seeblick *m*
seaweed [ˈsi:wi:d] *n* Seetang *m*
secluded [sɪˈklu:dɪd] *adj* (*place*) abgelegen
second [ˈsɛkənd] *adj* zweite(r, s) ▸ *adv* (*come, be placed*) Zweite(r, s); (*when listing*) zweitens ▸ *n* (*time*) Sekunde *f*; (*Aut*: *also*: **~ gear**) der zweite Gang ▸ *vt* (*motion*) unterstützen; **just a ~!** einen Augenblick!
secondary [ˈsɛkəndərɪ] *adj* weniger wichtig
second-class [ˈsɛkəndˈklɑ:s] *adj* zweitklassig; (*Rail, Post*) Zweite-Klasse- ▸ *adv* (*Rail, Post*) zweiter Klasse
second-hand [ˈsɛkəndˈhænd] *adj* gebraucht ▸ *adv*: **to hear sth ~** etw aus zweiter Hand haben
secondly [ˈsɛkəndlɪ] *adv* zweitens
second-rate [ˈsɛkəndˈreɪt] *adj* zweitklassig
secret [ˈsi:krɪt] *adj* geheim; (*admirer*) heimlich ▸ *n* Geheimnis *nt*
secretary [ˈsɛkrətərɪ] *n* (*Comm*) Sekretär(in) *m(f)*; **S~ of State (for)** (Brit *Pol*) Minister(in) *m(f)* (für); **S~ of State** (*US Pol*) Außenminister(in) *m(f)*
secretive [ˈsi:krətɪv] *adj* verschlossen; (*pej*) geheimnistuerisch
secretly [ˈsi:krɪtlɪ] *adv* heimlich
sect [sɛkt] *n* Sekte *f*
section [ˈsɛkʃən] *n* (*part*) Teil *m*; (*department*) Abteilung *f*; (*of document*) Absatz *m*
secure [sɪˈkjuəʳ] *adj* sicher; (*firmly fixed*) fest ▸ *vt* (*fix*) festmachen; **to make sth ~** etw sichern
securely [sɪˈkjuəlɪ] *adv* (*firmly*) fest; (*safely*) sicher
security [sɪˈkjuərɪtɪ] *n* Sicherheit *f*
sedative [ˈsɛdɪtɪv] *n* (*Med*) Beruhigungsmittel *nt*
seduce [sɪˈdju:s] *vt* verführen
seductive [sɪˈdʌktɪv] *adj* verführerisch; (*fig*: *offer*) verlockend
see [si:] (*pt* **saw**, *pp* **seen**) *vt* sehen; (*look at*) sich *dat* ansehen; (*understand*) verstehen; (*doctor etc*) aufsuchen ▸ *vi* sehen; **to ~ sb to the door** jdn zur Tür bringen; **to ~ a doctor** zum Arzt gehen; **~ you!** tschüss! (*inf*); **~ you soon!** bis bald!; **let me ~** (*show me*) lass mich mal sehen
▸ **see about** *vt fus* sich kümmern um *+acc*
▸ **see off** *vt* verabschieden
▸ **see out** *vt* (*show out*) zur Tür bringen
▸ **see through** *vt fus* durchschauen ▸ *vt*: **to ~ sb through sth** jdm in etw *dat* beistehen
▸ **see to** *vt fus* sich kümmern um *+acc*
seed [si:d] *n* Samen *m*; (*of fruit*) Kern *m*
seedless [ˈsi:dlɪs] *adj* kernlos
seedy [ˈsi:dɪ] *adj* (*person, place*) zwielichtig
seek [si:k] (*pt, pp* **sought**) *vt* suchen; **to ~ advice from sb** jdn um Rat fragen

seem [siːm] *vi* scheinen; **there seems to be a mistake** da scheint ein Fehler zu sein; **it seems to me that ...** mir scheint, dass ...
seen [siːn] *pp of* **see**
seesaw [ˈsiːsɔː] *n* Wippe *f*
see-through [ˈsiːθruː] *adj* durchsichtig
segment [ˈsɛgmənt] *n* Teil *m*
seize [siːz] *vt* packen; (*fig: opportunity*) ergreifen; (*power, control*) an sich *acc* reißen
seldom [ˈsɛldəm] *adv* selten
select [sɪˈlɛkt] *adj* exklusiv ▸ *vt* (aus) wählen
selection [sɪˈlɛkʃən] *n* (*range*) Auswahl *f*
selective [sɪˈlɛktɪv] *adj* wählerisch
self [sɛlf] (*pl* **selves**) *n* Selbst *nt*, Ich *nt*; **she was her normal ~ again** sie war wieder ganz die Alte
self-adhesive [sɛlfədˈhiːzɪv] *adj* selbstklebend
self-assured [sɛlfəˈʃuəd] *adj* selbstsicher
self-catering [sɛlfˈkeɪtərɪŋ] (Brit) *adj* (*holiday, flat*) für Selbstversorger
self-centred, (*US*) **self-centered** [sɛlfˈsɛntəd] *adj* egozentrisch
self-confidence [sɛlfˈkɔnfɪdns] *n* Selbstbewusstsein *nt*
self-confident [sɛlfˈkɔnfɪdənt] *adj* selbstbewusst
self-conscious [sɛlfˈkɔnʃəs] *adj* befangen, gehemmt
self-contained [sɛlfkənˈteɪnd] (Brit) *adj* (*flat*) abgeschlossen
self-control [sɛlfkənˈtrəul] *n* Selbstbeherrschung *f*
self-defence, (*US*) **self-defense** [sɛlfdɪˈfɛns] *n* Selbstverteidigung *f*
self-employed [sɛlfɪmˈplɔɪd] *adj* selbstständig
self-evident [sɛlfˈɛvɪdnt] *adj* offensichtlich
self-harm [sɛlfˈhɑːm] *n* selbstverletzendes Verhalten *nt*
selfie [ˈselfɪ] *n* Selfie *nt*
selfish [ˈsɛlfɪʃ] *adj* egoistisch, selbstsüchtig
selfless [ˈsɛlflɪs] *adj* selbstlos
self-pity [sɛlfˈpɪtɪ] *n* Selbstmitleid *nt*
self-portrait [sɛlfˈpɔːtreɪt] *n* Selbstporträt *nt*
self-respect [sɛlfrɪsˈpɛkt] *n* Selbstachtung *f*
self-service [sɛlfˈsəːvɪs] *adj* (*shop, restaurant etc*) Selbstbedienungs-
sell [sɛl] (*pt, pp* **sold**) *vt* verkaufen; (*shop: goods*) haben (*inf*) ▸ *vi* sich verkaufen (lassen); **to ~ sb sth** jdm etw verkaufen
▸ **sell out** *vi*: **we/the tickets are sold out** wir/die Karten sind ausverkauft
sell-by date [ˈsɛlbaɪ-] *n* ≈ Haltbarkeitsdatum *nt*
Sellotape® [ˈsɛləuteɪp] (Brit) *n* ≈ Tesafilm® *m*
semester [sɪˈmɛstəʳ] (*esp US*) *n* Semester *nt*
semi [ˈsɛmɪ] *n* = **semidetached**
semicircle [ˈsɛmɪsəːkl] *n* Halbkreis *m*
semicolon [sɛmɪˈkəulən] *n* Semikolon *nt*
semidetached [sɛmɪdɪˈtætʃt], **semidetached house** (Brit) *n* Doppelhaushälfte *f*
semifinal [sɛmɪˈfaɪnl] *n* Halbfinale *nt*
seminar [ˈsɛmɪnɑːʳ] *n* Seminar *nt*
semi-skimmed [sɛmɪˈskɪmd] *adj* (*milk*) teilentrahmt, Halbfett-
senate [ˈsɛnɪt] *n* Senat *m*
senator [ˈsɛnɪtəʳ] *n* Senator(in) *m(f)*
send [sɛnd] (*pt, pp* **sent**) *vt* schicken; **she sends (you) her love** sie lässt dich grüßen
▸ **send away** *vt* wegschicken
▸ **send away for** *vt fus* (per Post) anfordern
▸ **send back** *vt* zurückschicken
▸ **send for** *vt fus* (per Post) anfordern; (*doctor, police*) rufen
▸ **send off** *vt* abschicken
▸ **send out** *vt* verschicken
sender [ˈsɛndəʳ] *n* Absender(in) *m(f)*
senior [ˈsiːnɪəʳ] *adj* (*staff, manager*) leitend; (*officer*) höher; **to be ~ to sb** jdm übergeordnet sein; **she is 15 years his ~** sie ist 15 Jahre älter als er
senior citizen *n* Senior(in) *m(f)*
sensation [sɛnˈseɪʃən] *n* (*feeling*) Gefühl *nt*; (*great success*) Sensation *f*
sensational [sɛnˈseɪʃənl] *adj* (*result*) sensationell
sense [sɛns] *n* Sinn *m*; (*feeling*) Gefühl *nt*; (*good sense*) Verstand *m* ▸ *vt* spüren; **~ of smell** Geruchssinn *m*; **it makes ~** (*can be understood*) es ergibt einen Sinn; (*is sensible*) es ist vernünftig *or* sinnvoll
senseless [ˈsɛnslɪs] *adj* (*pointless*) sinnlos

sensible [ˈsɛnsɪbl] *adj* vernünftig
sensitive [ˈsɛnsɪtɪv] *adj* empfindlich; (*touchy: person*) sensibel; (*: issue*) heikel
sensual [ˈsɛnsjuəl] *adj* sinnlich
sensuous [ˈsɛnsjuəs] *adj* sinnlich
sent [sɛnt] *pt, pp of* **send**
sentence [ˈsɛntns] *n* (*Ling*) Satz *m*; (*Law: judgement*) Urteil *nt*; (*: punishment*) Strafe *f* ▶ *vt*: **to ~ sb to death/to 5 years in prison** jdn zum Tode/zu 5 Jahren Haft verurteilen
sentiment [ˈsɛntɪmənt] *n* Sentimentalität *f*; (*also pl: opinion*) Ansicht *f*
sentimental [sɛntɪˈmɛntl] *adj* sentimental
separate [ˈsɛprɪt] *adj* getrennt; (*rooms*) separat ▶ *vt* trennen ▶ *vi* sich trennen
separately [ˈsɛprɪtlɪ] *adv* getrennt
September [sɛpˈtɛmbəʳ] *n* September *m*; *see also* **July**
septic [ˈsɛptɪk] *adj* vereitert
sequel [ˈsiːkwl] *n* (*of film, story*) Fortsetzung *f*
sequence [ˈsiːkwəns] *n* Folge *f*
Serbia [ˈsəːbɪə] *n* Serbien *nt*
sergeant [ˈsɑːdʒənt] *n* (*Mil etc*) Feldwebel *m*; (*Police*) Polizeimeister *m*
serial [ˈsɪərɪəl] *n* (*TV*) Serie *f*; (*in magazine*) Fortsetzungsroman *m* ▶ *adj* (*Comput*) seriell
series [ˈsɪərɪz] *n inv* (*of books*) Reihe *f*; (*TV*) Serie *f*
serious [ˈsɪərɪəs] *adj* ernst; (*important*) wichtig; (*: illness*) schwer; **are you ~ (about it)?** meinst du das ernst?
seriously [ˈsɪərɪəslɪ] *adv* ernst; (*talk, interested*) ernsthaft; (*ill, hurt, damaged*) schwer; (*not jokingly*) im Ernst; **to take sb/sth ~** jdn/etw ernst nehmen
sermon [ˈsəːmən] *n* Predigt *f*
servant [ˈsəːvənt] *n* (*lit, fig*) Diener(in) *m(f)*
serve [səːv] *vt* dienen +*dat*; (*in shop, with food/drink*) bedienen; (*food, meal*) servieren; (*prison term*) verbüßen ▶ *vi* (*at table*) auftragen, servieren; (*Tennis*) aufschlagen; (*be useful*): **to ~ as/for** dienen als ▶ *n* (*Tennis*) Aufschlag *m*; **are you being served?** werden Sie schon bedient?; **it serves him right** das geschieht ihm recht
server *n* (*Comput*) Server *m*
service [ˈsəːvɪs] *n* Dienst *m*; (*commercial*) Dienstleistung *f*; (*in hotel, restaurant*) Bedienung *f*; (*also*: **train ~**) Bahnverbindung *f*; (*Rel*) Gottesdienst *m*; (*Aut*) Inspektion *f*; (*plates etc*) Service *nt* ▶ *vt* (*car, machine*) warten
service area *n* (*on motorway*) Raststätte *f*
service charge (BRIT) *n* Bedienungsgeld *nt*
service provider *n* (*Comput*) Provider *m*
service station *n* Tankstelle *f*
session [ˈsɛʃən] *n* Sitzung *f*
set [sɛt] (*pt, pp* **~**) *n* (*of saucepans, books, keys etc*) Satz *m*; (*of cutlery*) Garnitur *f*; (*also*: **radio ~**) Radio(gerät) *nt*; (*also*: **TV ~**) Fernsehgerät *nt*; (*group of people*) Kreis *m*; (*Theat: stage*) Bühne *f*; (*: scenery*) Bühnenbild *nt*; (*Cine*) Drehort *m* ▶ *adj* (*fixed*) fest; (*ready*) bereit ▶ *vt* (*table*) decken; (*place*) auflegen; (*time, price, rules etc*) festsetzen; (*record*) aufstellen; (*alarm, watch, task*) stellen ▶ *vi* (*sun*) untergehen; (*jam, jelly, concrete*) fest werden; (*bone*) zusammenwachsen; **a novel ~ in Rome** ein Roman, der in Rom spielt; **to ~ free** freilassen
▶ **set aside** *vt* (*money etc*) beiseitelegen; (*time*) einplanen
▶ **set off** *vi* (*depart*) aufbrechen ▶ *vt* (*alarm, chain of events*) auslösen; (*show up well*) hervorheben
▶ **set out** *vi* (*depart*) aufbrechen ▶ *vt* (*chairs etc*) aufstellen; (*arguments*) darlegen; **to ~ out to do sth** sich *dat* vornehmen, etw zu tun
▶ **set up** *vt* (*organization*) gründen; (*monument*) errichten; **to ~ up shop** ein Geschäft eröffnen
setback [ˈsɛtbæk] *n* Rückschlag *m*
settee [sɛˈtiː] *n* Sofa *nt*
setting [ˈsɛtɪŋ] *n* (*background*) Rahmen *m*; (*position*) Einstellung *f*
settle [ˈsɛtl] *vt* (*matter*) regeln; (*argument*) beilegen; (*accounts*) begleichen ▶ *vi* (*also*: **~ down**) sich niederlassen; (*calm down*) sich beruhigen; **to ~ one's stomach** den Magen beruhigen
▶ **settle in** *vi* sich einleben; (*in job etc*) sich eingewöhnen
▶ **settle up** *vi*: **to ~ up with sb** mit jdm abrechnen

settlement [ˈsɛtlmənt] *n* (*payment*) Begleichung *f*; (*village etc*) Siedlung *f*
setup, set-up [ˈsɛtʌp] *n* (*organization*) Organisation *f*; (*system*) System *nt*
seven [ˈsɛvn] *num* sieben
seventeen [sɛvnˈtiːn] *num* siebzehn
seventeenth [sevnˈtiːnθ] *adj* siebzehnte(r, s); *see also* **eighth**
seventh [ˈsɛvnθ] *num* siebte(r, s)
seventieth [ˈsevntɪɪθ] *adj* siebzigste(r, s); *see also* **eighth**
seventy [ˈsɛvntɪ] *num* siebzig
several [ˈsɛvərl] *adj* mehrere ▶ *pron* einige
severe [sɪˈvɪəʳ] *adj* (*damage, shortage*) schwer; (*pain*) stark; (*person, expression, dress, winter*) streng; (*punishment*) hart
severely [sɪˈvɪəlɪ] *adv* (*punish*) hart; (*wounded, ill*) schwer
sew [səu] (*pt* **sewed**, *pp* **sewn**) *vt, vi* nähen
sewage [ˈsuːɪdʒ] *n* Abwasser *nt*
sewer [ˈsuːəʳ] *n* Abwasserkanal *m*
sewing [ˈsəuɪŋ] *n* Nähen *nt*
sewing machine *n* Nähmaschine *f*
sewn [səun] *pp of* **sew**
sex [sɛks] *n* (*gender*) Geschlecht *nt*; (*lovemaking*) Sex *m*; **to have ~ with sb** (Geschlechts)verkehr mit jdm haben
sexism [ˈsɛksɪzəm] *n* Sexismus *m*
sexist [ˈsɛksɪst] *adj* sexistisch
sex life *n* Sexualleben *nt*
sexual [ˈsɛksjuəl] *adj* sexuell
sexual harassment *n* sexuelle Belästigung *f*
sexual intercourse *n* Geschlechtsverkehr *m*
sexuality [seksjuˈælɪtɪ] *n* Sexualität *f*
sexually [ˈsɛksjuəlɪ] *adv* sexuell
sexy [ˈsɛksɪ] *adj* sexy
Seychelles [seɪˈʃɛl(z)] *npl*: **the ~** die Seychellen *pl*
shabby [ˈʃæbɪ] *adj* schäbig
shack [ʃæk] *n* Hütte *f*
shade [ʃeɪd] *n* Schatten *m*; (*for lamp*) (Lampen)schirm *m*; (*of colour*) (Farb) ton *m* ▶ *vt* beschatten; (*eyes*) abschirmen ■ **shades** *npl* (*inf*: *sunglasses*) Sonnenbrille *f*
shadow [ˈʃædəu] *n* Schatten *m*
shady [ˈʃeɪdɪ] *adj* schattig; (*fig*: *dishonest*) zwielichtig
shake [ʃeɪk] (*pt* **shook**, *pp* **shaken**) *vt* schütteln; (*weaken, upset, surprise*) erschüttern ▶ *vi* zittern; (*building, table*) wackeln; (*earth*) beben; **to ~ one's head** den Kopf schütteln; **to ~ hands with sb** jdm die Hand schütteln
▶ **shake off** *vt* (*lit, fig*) abschütteln
shaky [ˈʃeɪkɪ] *adj* (*hand, voice*) zittrig; (*knowledge, prospects, future, start*) unsicher
shall [ʃæl] *aux vb*: **I ~ go** ich werde gehen; **~ I open the door?** soll ich die Tür öffnen?; **I'll go, ~ I?** soll ich gehen?
shallow [ˈʃæləu] *adj* flach; (*fig*) oberflächlich
shame [ʃeɪm] *n* Scham *f*; (*disgrace*) Schande *f*; **it is a ~ that …** es ist eine Schande, dass …; **what a ~!** wie schade!
shampoo [ʃæmˈpuː] *n* Shampoo(n) *nt* ▶ *vt* waschen
shampoo and set *n* Waschen und Legen *nt*
shandy [ˈʃændɪ] *n* Bier *nt* mit Limonade, Radler *m*
shan't [ʃɑːnt] = **shall not**
shape [ʃeɪp] *n* Form *f* ▶ *vt* gestalten; (*form*) formen; **to take ~** Gestalt annehmen; **in the ~ of a heart** in Herzform; **to get (o.s.) into ~** in Form kommen
-shaped [ʃeɪpt] *suff*: **heart-shaped** herzförmig
shapeless [ˈʃeɪplɪs] *adj* formlos
share [ʃɛəʳ] *n* (*part*) Anteil *m*; (*Comm*) Aktie *f* ▶ *vt* teilen
shareholder [ˈʃɛəhəuldəʳ] *n* Aktionär(in) *m(f)*
shark [ʃɑːk] *n* Hai(fisch) *m*
sharp [ʃɑːp] *adj* scharf; (*point, nose, chin*) spitz; (*pain*) heftig; (*increase*) stark; (*person*: *quick-witted*) clever ▶ *adv*: **at 2 o'clock ~** um Punkt 2 Uhr; **C ~** (*Mus*) Cis *nt*
sharpen [ˈʃɑːpn] *vt* schärfen; (*pencil, stick etc*) (an)spitzen
sharpener [ˈʃɑːpnəʳ] *n* (*also*: **pencil ~**) (Bleistift)spitzer *m*
shatter [ˈʃætəʳ] *vt* zertrümmern; (*fig*: *hopes, dreams*) zunichtemachen; (: *confidence*) zerstören ▶ *vi* zerspringen
shattered [ˈʃætəd] *adj* erschüttert; (*inf*: *exhausted*) fertig, kaputt
shave [ʃeɪv] *vt* rasieren ▶ *vi* sich rasieren ▶ *n*: **to have a ~** sich rasieren

▸ **shave off** *vt*: **to ~ one's beard off** sich den Bart abrasieren
shaven [ˈʃeɪvn] *adj* (*head*) kahl geschoren
shaver [ˈʃeɪvəʳ] *n* (*also*: **electric ~**) Rasierapparat *m*
shaving brush [ˈʃeɪvɪŋ-] *n* Rasierpinsel *m*
shaving foam *n* Rasierschaum *m*
shawl [ʃɔːl] *n* (Woll)tuch *nt*
she [ʃiː] *pron* sie
shed [ʃɛd] (*pt, pp* **~**) *n* Schuppen *m* ▸ *vt* (*tears, blood*) vergießen; (*load*) verlieren
she'd [ʃiːd] = **she had**; **she would**
sheep [ʃiːp] *n inv* Schaf *nt*
sheepdog [ˈʃiːpdɔg] *n* Hütehund *m*
sheepskin [ˈʃiːpskɪn] *n* Schaffell *nt*
sheer [ʃɪəʳ] *adj* (*utter*) rein; (*steep*) steil; **by ~ chance** rein zufällig
sheet [ʃiːt] *n* (*on bed*) (Bett)laken *nt*; (*of paper*) Blatt *nt*; (*of glass, metal*) Platte *f*; (*of ice*) Fläche *f*
shelf [ʃɛlf] (*pl* **shelves**) *n* Brett *nt*, Bord *nt*; **set of shelves** Regal *nt*
shell [ʃɛl] *n* (*on beach*) Muschel *f*; (*of egg, nut etc*) Schale *f* ▸ *vt* (*peas*) enthülsen
she'll [ʃiːl] = **she will**; **she shall**
shellfish [ˈʃɛlfɪʃ] *n inv* Schalentier *nt*; (*as food*) Meeresfrüchte *pl*
shelter [ˈʃɛltəʳ] *n* (*building*) Unterstand *m*; (*refuge*) Schutz *m*; (*also*: **bus ~**) Wartehäuschen *nt* ▸ *vt* (*protect*) schützen ▸ *vi* sich unterstellen
sheltered [ˈʃɛltəd] *adj* (*life*) behütet; (*spot*) geschützt
shelve [ʃɛlv] *vt* (*fig*: *plan*) ad acta legen
shelves [ʃɛlvz] *npl of* **shelf**
shepherd [ˈʃɛpəd] *n* Schäfer *m*
shepherd's pie (Brit) *n Auflauf aus Hackfleisch und Kartoffelbrei*
sherry [ˈʃɛrɪ] *n* Sherry *m*
she's [ʃiːz] = **she is**; **she has**
shield [ʃiːld] *n* (*Mil*) Schild *m*; (*fig*: *protection*) Schutz *m* ▸ *vt*: **to ~ (from)** schützen (vor +*dat*)
shift [ʃɪft] *n* (*change*) Änderung *f*; (*work-period, workers*) Schicht *f* ▸ *vt* (*furniture*) (ver)rücken; (*stain*) herausbekommen ▸ *vi* (*move*) sich bewegen
shift key *n* Umschalttaste *f*
shin [ʃɪn] *n* Schienbein *nt*
shine [ʃaɪn] (*pt, pp* **shone**) *n* Glanz *m* ▸ *vi* (*sun, light*) scheinen; (*eyes*) leuchten; (*hair, fig*: *person*) glänzen ▸ *vt* (*pt, pp* **shined**) (*polish*) polieren
shingles [ˈʃɪŋglz] *npl* (*Med*) Gürtelrose *f*
shiny [ˈʃaɪnɪ] *adj* glänzend
ship [ʃɪp] *n* Schiff *nt* ▸ *vt* verschiffen; (*send*) versenden
shipment [ˈʃɪpmənt] *n* (*of goods*) Versand *m*; (*amount*) Sendung *f*
shipwreck [ˈʃɪprɛk] *n* Schiffbruch *m*
shipyard [ˈʃɪpjɑːd] *n* Werft *f*
shirt [ʃəːt] *n* (Ober)hemd *nt*
shit [ʃɪt] (!) *excl* Scheiße (!)
shitty [ˈʃɪtɪ] *adj* (*inf*) beschissen
shiver [ˈʃɪvəʳ] *vi* zittern
shock [ʃɔk] *n* Schock *m*; (*also*: **electric ~**) Schlag *m* ▸ *vt* (*offend*) schockieren; **to be in ~** unter Schock stehen
shock absorber *n* (*Aut*) Stoßdämpfer *m*
shocked [ʃɔkt] *adj* schockiert (by über +*acc*)
shocking [ˈʃɔkɪŋ] *adj* fürchterlich; (*outrageous*) schockierend
shoe [ʃuː] (*pt, pp* **shod**) *n* Schuh *m*
shoelace [ˈʃuːleɪs] *n* Schnürsenkel *m*
shoe polish *n* Schuhcreme *f*
shone [ʃɔn] *pt, pp of* **shine**
shonky [ˈʃɔŋkɪ] *adj* (Aust, NZ *inf*) schäbig; (*work*) stümperhaft
shook [ʃuk] *pt of* **shake**
shoot [ʃuːt] (*pt, pp* **shot**) *n* (*on branch*) Trieb *m* ▸ *vt* (*arrow, goal*) schießen; (*kill, execute*) erschießen; (*wound*) anschießen; (*film*) drehen ▸ *vi*: **to ~ (at)** schießen (auf +*acc*)
shooting [ˈʃuːtɪŋ] *n* (*attack*) Schießerei *f*; (*murder*) Erschießung *f*
shop [ʃɔp] *n* Geschäft *nt*, Laden *m* ▸ *vi* (*also*: **go shopping**) einkaufen (gehen)
shop assistant (Brit) *n* Verkäufer(in) *m(f)*
shopkeeper [ˈʃɔpkiːpəʳ] *n* Geschäftsinhaber(in) *m(f)*
shoplifting [ˈʃɔplɪftɪŋ] *n* Ladendiebstahl *m*
shopper [ˈʃɔpəʳ] *n* Käufer(in) *m(f)*
shopping [ˈʃɔpɪŋ] *n* (*goods*) Einkäufe *pl*
shopping bag *n* Einkaufstasche *f*
shopping cart *n* (US) Einkaufswagen *m*
shopping centre, (US) **shopping center** *n* Einkaufszentrum *nt*
shopping list *n* Einkaufszettel *m*
shopping trolley *n* (Brit) Einkaufswagen *m*

shop window *n* Schaufenster *nt*
shore [ʃɔːʳ] *n* Ufer *nt*; **on ~** an Land
short [ʃɔːt] *adj* kurz; (*person*) klein; **to be ~ of ...** zu wenig ... haben; **I'm 3 ~** ich habe 3 zu wenig, mir fehlen 3; **it is ~ for ...** es ist die Kurzform von ...; **to cut ~** abbrechen
shortage [ˈʃɔːtɪdʒ] *n*: **a ~ of** ein Mangel *m* an +*dat*
shortbread [ˈʃɔːtbrɛd] *n* Mürbegebäck *nt*
short circuit *n* Kurzschluss *m*
short cut *n* Abkürzung *f*
shorten [ˈʃɔːtn] *vt* verkürzen
shorthand [ˈʃɔːthænd] *n* Stenografie *f*
short list (BRIT) *n* Auswahlliste *f*; **to be on the ~** in der engeren Wahl sein
short-lived [ˈʃɔːtˈlɪvd] *adj* kurzlebig
shortly [ˈʃɔːtlɪ] *adv* bald
shorts [ʃɔːts] *npl*: **(a pair of) ~** Shorts *pl*
short-sighted [ʃɔːtˈsaɪtɪd] (BRIT) *adj* (*lit, fig*) kurzsichtig
short-sleeved [ʃɔːtˈsliːvd] *adj* kurzärmelig
short story *n* Kurzgeschichte *f*
short-term [ˈʃɔːttəːm] *adj* kurzfristig
short-wave [ˈʃɔːtweɪv] (*Radio*) *n* Kurzwelle *f*
shot [ʃɔt] *pt, pp of* **shoot** ▶ *n* Schuss *m*; (*injection*) Spritze *f*; (*Phot*) Aufnahme *f*
should [ʃud] *aux vb*: **I ~ go now** ich sollte jetzt gehen; **he ~ be there now** er müsste eigentlich schon da sein
shoulder [ˈʃəuldəʳ] *n* Schulter *f*
shouldn't [ˈʃudnt] = **should not**
should've [ˈʃudəv] = **should have**
shout [ʃaut] *n* Schrei *m*, Ruf *m* ▶ *vt* rufen ▶ *vi* (*also:* **~ out**) aufschreien
shove [ʃʌv] *vt* schieben; (*with one push*) stoßen, schubsen (*inf*)
shovel [ˈʃʌvl] *n* Schaufel *f* ▶ *vt* schaufeln
show [ʃəu] (*pt* **showed**, *pp* **shown**) *n* (*exhibition*) Ausstellung *f*; (*TV*) Show *f*; (*Cine*) Vorstellung *f* ▶ *vt* zeigen
▶ **show in** *vt* hereinführen
▶ **show off** (*pej*) *vi* angeben
▶ **show out** *vt* hinausbegleiten
▶ **show up** *vi* (*inf: turn up*) auftauchen
shower [ˈʃauəʳ] *n* (*of rain*) Schauer *m*; (*for bathing in*) Dusche *f* ▶ *vi* duschen; **to have** *or* **take a ~** duschen
shower gel *n* Duschgel *nt*
showing [ˈʃəuɪŋ] *n* (*of film*) Vorführung *f*
shown [ʃəun] *pp of* **show**
showroom [ˈʃəurum] *n* Ausstellungsraum *m*
shrank [ʃræŋk] *pt of* **shrink**
shred [ʃrɛd] *n* (*gen pl*) Fetzen *m* ▶ *vt* zerfetzen
shredder [ˈʃrɛdəʳ] *n* (*also:* **document ~**) Reißwolf *m*
shrimp [ʃrɪmp] *n* Garnele *f*
shrink [ʃrɪŋk] (*pt* **shrank**, *pp* **shrunk**) *vi* (*cloth*) einlaufen; (*profits, audiences*) schrumpfen
shrivel [ˈʃrɪvl], **shrivel up** *vi* austrocknen, verschrumpeln
Shrove Tuesday [ˈʃrəuv-] *n* Fastnachtsdienstag *m*
shrub [ʃrʌb] *n* Strauch *m*, Busch *m*
shrug [ʃrʌg] *vi, vt*: **to ~ (one's shoulders)** mit den Achseln zucken
shrunk [ʃrʌŋk] *pp of* **shrink**
shudder [ˈʃʌdəʳ] *vi* schaudern
shuffle [ˈʃʌfl] *vt* (*cards*) mischen
shut [ʃʌt] (*pt, pp* **~**) *vt* schließen, zumachen (*inf*) ▶ *vi* (*shop*) schließen, zumachen (*inf*)
▶ **shut down** *vt* (*factory etc*) schließen; (*machine*) abschalten ▶ *vi* schließen, zumachen (*inf*)
▶ **shut in** *vt* einschließen
▶ **shut out** *vt* (*person*) aussperren
▶ **shut up** *vi* (*inf: keep quiet*) den Mund halten ▶ *vt* (*silence*) zum Schweigen bringen
shutter [ˈʃʌtəʳ] *n* Fensterladen *m*
shutter speed *n* Belichtungszeit *f*
shuttlecock [ˈʃʌtlkɔk] *n* Federball *m*
shy [ʃaɪ] *adj* schüchtern; (*animal*) scheu
Siberia [saɪˈbɪərɪə] *n* Sibirien *nt*
Sicily [ˈsɪsɪlɪ] *n* Sizilien *nt*
sick [sɪk] *adj* krank; (*humour, joke*) makaber; **to be ~** (*vomit*) sich übergeben; **I feel ~** mir ist schlecht; **to be (off) ~** wegen Krankheit fehlen; **to be ~ of** (*fig*) satthaben +*acc*
sickbag [ˈsɪkbæg] *n* Spucktüte *f*
sick leave *n*: **to be on ~** krankgeschrieben sein
sickness [ˈsɪknɪs] *n* Krankheit *f*; (*vomiting*) Erbrechen *nt*
sickness benefit *n* Krankengeld *nt*
side [saɪd] *n* Seite *f*; (*team*) Mannschaft *f*; (*in conflict etc*) Partei *f*, Seite *f*; (*of hill*) Hang *m* ▶ *adj* (*door, entrance*) Seiten-; **by the ~ of** neben +*dat*; **~ by ~** Seite an Seite

sidebar [ˈsaɪdbɑːʳ] *n* (*on web page*) Seitenleiste *f*
sideboard [ˈsaɪdbɔːd] *n* Sideboard *nt*
sideburns [ˈsaɪdbəːnz] *npl* Koteletten *pl*
side dish *n* Beilage *f*
side effect *n* (*Med, fig*) Nebenwirkung *f*
sidelight [ˈsaɪdlaɪt] *n* (*Aut*) Begrenzungsleuchte *f*
side road *n* Nebenstraße *f*
side street *n* Seitenstraße *f*
sidewalk [ˈsaɪdwɔːk] (*US*) *n* Bürgersteig *m*
sideways [ˈsaɪdweɪz] *adv* seitwärts
sieve [sɪv] *n* Sieb *nt*
sift [sɪft] *vt* sieben
sigh [saɪ] *vi* seufzen
sight [saɪt] *n* (*faculty*) Sehvermögen *nt*; (*spectacle*) Anblick *m*; **out of ~** außer Sicht; **to lose ~ of sth** (*fig*) etw aus den Augen verlieren
sightseeing [ˈsaɪtsiːɪŋ] *n*: **to go ~** auf Besichtigungstour gehen
sign [saɪn] *n* Zeichen *nt*; (*notice*) Schild *nt* ▸ *vt* unterschreiben
▸ **sign in** *vi* sich eintragen
▸ **sign on** *vi* (Brit: *as unemployed*) sich arbeitslos melden
▸ **sign out** *vi* (*from hotel etc*) sich (aus dem Hotelgästebuch *etc*) austragen
▸ **sign up** *vi* (*Mil*) sich verpflichten; (*for course*) sich einschreiben
signal [ˈsɪgnl] *n* Zeichen *nt*; (*Rail*) Signal *nt* ▸ *vt*: **to ~ a right/left turn** (*Aut*) rechts/links blinken
signature [ˈsɪgnətʃəʳ] *n* Unterschrift *f*
significant [sɪgˈnɪfɪkənt] *adj* bedeutend, wichtig; (*look, smile*) bedeutsam
significantly [sɪgˈnɪfɪkəntlɪ] *adv* bedeutend
sign language *n* Zeichensprache *f*
signpost [ˈsaɪnpəust] *n* (*lit, fig*) Wegweiser *m*
silence [ˈsaɪləns] *n* Stille *f*; (*of person*) Schweigen *nt* ▸ *vt* zum Schweigen bringen
silent [ˈsaɪlənt] *adj* still; **to remain ~** still bleiben
silk [sɪlk] *n* Seide *f* ▸ *adj* (*dress etc*) Seiden-
silly [ˈsɪlɪ] *adj* (*person*) dumm; **to do something ~** etwas Dummes tun
silver [ˈsɪlvəʳ] *n* Silber *nt*; (*coins*) Silbergeld *nt* ▸ *adj* silbern
silver-plated [sɪlvəˈpleɪtɪd] *adj* versilbert
silver wedding, silver wedding anniversary *n* Silberhochzeit *f*
SIM card [ˈsɪmkɑːd] *n* (*Tel*: = *Subscriber Identity Module card*) SIM-Karte *f*
similar [ˈsɪmɪləʳ] *adj*: **~ (to)** ähnlich (wie *or* +*dat*)
similarity [sɪmɪˈlærɪtɪ] *n* Ähnlichkeit *f*
similarly [ˈsɪmɪləlɪ] *adv* ähnlich; (*likewise*) genauso
simple [ˈsɪmpl] *adj* einfach; (*dress*) schlicht
simplify [ˈsɪmplɪfaɪ] *vt* vereinfachen
simply [ˈsɪmplɪ] *adv* (*just, merely*) bloß; (*in a simple way*) einfach
simulate [ˈsɪmjuleɪt] *vt* (*illness*) simulieren
simultaneous [sɪməlˈteɪnɪəs] *adj* gleichzeitig
simultaneously [sɪməlˈteɪnɪəslɪ] *adv* gleichzeitig
sin [sɪn] *n* Sünde *f* ▸ *vi* sündigen
since [sɪns] *adv* inzwischen, seitdem ▸ *prep* seit ▸ *conj* (*time*) seit(dem); (*because*) da; **~ then, ever ~** seitdem
sincere [sɪnˈsɪəʳ] *adj* aufrichtig
sincerely [sɪnˈsɪəlɪ] *adv* aufrichtig; **yours ~** (*in letter*) mit freundlichen Grüßen
sing [sɪŋ] (*pt* **sang**, *pp* **sung**) *vt, vi* singen
Singapore [sɪŋgəˈpɔːʳ] *n* Singapur *nt*
singer [ˈsɪŋəʳ] *n* Sänger(in) *m(f)*
single [ˈsɪŋgl] *adj* (*solitary*) einzige(r, s); (*unmarried*) ledig; (*not double*) einfach ▸ *n* (Brit: *also*: **~ ticket**) Einzelfahrschein *m*; (*record*) Single *f*
▸ **single out** *vt* auswählen
single-handed [sɪŋglˈhændɪd] *adv* ganz allein
single parent *n* Alleinerziehende(r) *f(m)*
singular [ˈsɪŋgjuləʳ] *n* (*Ling*) Singular *m*
sinister [ˈsɪnɪstəʳ] *adj* unheimlich
sink [sɪŋk] (*pt* **sank**, *pp* **sunk**) *n* Spülbecken *nt* ▸ *vt* (*ship*) versenken ▸ *vi* (*ship*) sinken
sip [sɪp] *vt* nippen an +*dat*
sir [səʳ] *n*: **S~ John Smith** Sir John Smith; **yes, ~** ja(, Herr X)
sister [ˈsɪstəʳ] *n* Schwester *f*; (Brit: *nurse*) Oberschwester *f*
sister-in-law [ˈsɪstərɪnlɔː] *n* Schwägerin *f*

sit [sɪt] (*pt, pp* **sat**) *vi* (*sit down*) sich setzen; (*assembly*) tagen ▶ *vt* (*exam*) machen
▶ **sit down** *vi* sich (hin)setzen
▶ **sit up** *vi* sich aufsetzen
sitcom [ˈsɪtkɔm] *n abbr* (*TV*) = **situation comedy**
site [saɪt] *n* (*place*) Platz *m*; (*also:* **building ~**) Baustelle *f*; (*Comput*) Site *f*
sitting [ˈsɪtɪŋ] *n* Sitzung *f*
sitting room *n* Wohnzimmer *nt*
situated [ˈsɪtjueɪtɪd] *adj*: **to be ~** liegen
situation [sɪtjuˈeɪʃən] *n* Situation *f*, Lage *f*; (*job*) Stelle *f*; **"situations vacant** *or* **wanted"** „Stellenangebote"
situation comedy *n* (*TV*) Situationskomödie *f*
six [sɪks] *num* sechs
six-pack [ˈsɪkspæk] *n* Sechserpack *m*
sixteen [sɪksˈtiːn] *num* sechzehn
sixteenth [sɪksˈtiːnθ] *adj* sechzehnte(r, s); *see also* **eighth**
sixth [sɪksθ] *num* sechste(r, s); **the upper/lower ~** (Brit *Scol*) ≈ die Ober-/Unterprima
sixtieth [ˈsɪkstɪɪθ] *adj* sechzigste(r, s); *see also* **eighth**
sixty [ˈsɪkstɪ] *num* sechzig
size [saɪz] *n* Größe *f*; **I take ~ 14** ich habe Größe 14
sizzle [ˈsɪzl] *vi* brutzeln
skate [skeɪt] *n* (*also:* **ice ~**) Schlittschuh *m*; (*also:* **roller ~**) Rollschuh *m* ▶ *vi* Schlittschuh laufen
skateboard [ˈskeɪtbɔːd] *n* Skateboard *nt*
skatepark [ˈskeɪtpɑːk] *n* Skatepark *m*
skating [ˈskeɪtɪŋ] *n* Eislauf *m*
skating rink *n* Eisbahn *f*
skeleton [ˈskɛlɪtn] *n* Skelett *nt*
sketch [skɛtʃ] *n* Skizze *f*; (*Theat, TV*) Sketch *m* ▶ *vt* skizzieren
sketchbook [ˈskɛtʃbuk] *n* Skizzenbuch *nt*
ski [skiː] *n* Ski *m* ▶ *vi* Ski laufen *or* fahren
ski boot *n* Skistiefel *m*
skid [skɪd] *vi* rutschen; (*Aut*) schleudern
skier [ˈskiːə^r] *n* Skiläufer(in) *m(f)*
skiing [ˈskiːɪŋ] *n* Skilaufen *nt*; **to go ~** Ski laufen *or* Ski fahren gehen
ski instructor *n* Skilehrer(in) *m(f)*
skilful, (*US*) **skillful** [ˈskɪlful] *adj* geschickt
skilfully *adv* geschickt
ski lift *n* Skilift *m*
skill [skɪl] *n* (*ability*) Können *nt* ■ **skills** *npl* (*acquired abilities*) Fähigkeiten *pl*
skilled [skɪld] *adj* (*skilful*) geschickt; (*trained*) ausgebildet; (*work*) qualifiziert
skim [skɪm] *vt* (*cream, fat: also:* **~ off**) abschöpfen ▶ *vi*: **to ~ through** (*book etc*) überfliegen
skimmed milk [skɪmd-] *n* Magermilch *f*
skin [skɪn] *n* Haut *f*; (*fur*) Fell *nt*; (*of fruit*) Schale *f*
skin diving *n* Sporttauchen *nt*
skinny [ˈskɪnɪ] *adj* dünn
skip [skɪp] *vi* springen, hüpfen; (*with rope*) seilspringen ▶ *vt* überspringen; (*miss: lunch, lecture*) ausfallen lassen; **to ~ school** (*esp US*) die Schule schwänzen
ski pants *npl* Skihose *f*
ski pass *n* Skipass *m*
ski pole *n* Skistock *m*
ski resort *n* Wintersportort *m*
skirt [skəːt] *n* Rock *m*
ski run *n* Skipiste *f*
ski tow *n* Schlepplift *m*
skittle [ˈskɪtl] *n* Kegel *m*
skittles [ˈskɪtlz] *n* (*game*) Kegeln *nt*
skive [skaɪv] (Brit *inf*) *vi* blaumachen; (*from school*) schwänzen
skull [skʌl] *n* Schädel *m*
sky [skaɪ] *n* Himmel *m*
skydiving [ˈskaɪdaɪvɪŋ] *n* Fallschirmspringen *nt*
skylight [ˈskaɪlaɪt] *n* Dachfenster *nt*
skyscraper [ˈskaɪskreɪpə^r] *n* Wolkenkratzer *m*
slam [slæm] *vt* (*door*) zuschlagen; **to ~ on the brakes** (*Aut*) auf die Bremse steigen (*inf*)
slander [ˈslɑːndə^r] *n* (*Law*) Verleumdung *f* ▶ *vt* verleumden
slang [slæŋ] *n* Slang *m*
slap [slæp] *n* Klaps *m* ▶ *vt* schlagen
slash [slæʃ] *vt* aufschlitzen; (*fig: prices*) radikal senken
slate [sleɪt] *n* Schiefer *m*; (*piece*) Schieferplatte *f*
slaughter [ˈslɔːtə^r] *vt* (*animals*) schlachten; (*people*) abschlachten
Slav [slɑːv] *adj* slawisch ▶ *n* Slawe *m*, Slawin *f*
slave [sleɪv] *n* Sklave *m*, Sklavin *f* ▶ *vi* (*also:* **~ away**) schuften (*inf*)

slave-driver [ˈsleɪvdraɪvəʳ] *n* Sklaventreiber(in) *m(f)*
slavery [ˈsleɪvərɪ] *n* Sklaverei *f*
sleaze [sliːz] *n* (*corruption*) Korruption *f*
sleazy [ˈsliːzɪ] *adj* schäbig
sledge [slɛdʒ] *n* Schlitten *m*
sleep [sliːp] (*pt, pp* **slept**) *n* Schlaf *m* ▸ *vi* schlafen; **to go to ~** einschlafen; **to put to ~** (*euph: kill*) einschläfern; **to ~ with sb** (*euph: have sex*) mit jdm schlafen
▸ **sleep in** *vi* (*oversleep*) verschlafen
sleeper [ˈsliːpəʳ] *n* (*train*) Schlafwagenzug *m*; (*berth*) Platz *m* im Schlafwagen
sleeping bag *n* Schlafsack *m*
sleeping car *n* Schlafwagen *m*
sleeping pill *n* Schlaftablette *f*
sleepless [ˈsliːplɪs] *adj* (*night*) schlaflos
sleepover [ˈsliːpəuvəʳ] *n* Übernachtung *f* (*bei Freunden etc*)
sleepy [ˈsliːpɪ] *adj* schläfrig; (*fig: village etc*) verschlafen
sleet [sliːt] *n* Schneeregen *m*
sleeve [sliːv] *n* Ärmel *m*
sleeveless [ˈsliːvlɪs] *adj* (*garment*) ärmellos
sleigh [sleɪ] *n* (Pferde)schlitten *m*
slender [ˈslɛndəʳ] *adj* schlank; (*small*) knapp
slept [slɛpt] *pt, pp of* **sleep**
slice [slaɪs] *n* Scheibe *f* ▸ *vt* (in Scheiben) schneiden
slid [slɪd] *pt, pp of* **slide**
slide [slaɪd] (*pt, pp* **slid**) *n* (*in playground*) Rutschbahn *f*; (*Phot*) Dia *nt*; (Brit: *also:* **hair ~**) Spange *f* ▸ *vt* schieben ▸ *vi* (*slip*) rutschen; (*glide*) gleiten
slide show *n* Diavortrag *m*; (*Comput*) Bildschirmpräsentation *f*
slight [slaɪt] *adj* zierlich; (*small*) gering; (*error, accent, pain etc*) leicht ▸ *n*: **a ~ (on sb/sth)** ein Affront *m* (gegen jdn/etw); **not in the slightest** nicht im Geringsten
slightly [ˈslaɪtlɪ] *adv* etwas
slim [slɪm] *adj* schlank; (*chance*) gering ▸ *vi* eine Schlankheitskur machen, abnehmen
slime [slaɪm] *n* Schleim *m*
slimy [ˈslaɪmɪ] *adj* (*lit, fig*) schleimig
sling [slɪŋ] (*pt, pp* **slung**) *n* Schlinge *f* ▸ *vt* schleudern
slip [slɪp] *n* (*mistake*) Fehler *m*; (*also:* **~ of paper**) Zettel *m* ▸ *vt* (*slide*) stecken ▸ *vi* ausrutschen; **to ~ into/out of sth, to ~ sth on/off** in etw *acc*/aus etw schlüpfen
▸ **slip away** *vi* sich davonschleichen
slipper [ˈslɪpəʳ] *n* Hausschuh *m*
slippery [ˈslɪpərɪ] *adj* (*lit, fig*) glatt; (*fish etc*) schlüpfrig
slip road (Brit) *n* (*to motorway etc*) Auffahrt *f*; (*from motorway etc*) Ausfahrt *f*
slit [slɪt] (*pt, pp* **~**) *n* Schlitz *m* ▸ *vt* aufschlitzen
slope [sləup] *n* (*side of mountain*) Hang *m*; (*slant*) Neigung *f* ▸ *vi*: **to ~ down** abfallen; **to ~ up** ansteigen
sloping [ˈsləupɪŋ] *adj* (*roof, handwriting*) schräg
sloppy [ˈslɔpɪ] *adj* (*appearance*) schlampig
slot [slɔt] *n* Schlitz *m* ▸ *vt*: **to ~ sth in** etw hineinstecken
slot machine *n* (Brit) Münzautomat *m*; (*for gambling*) Spielautomat *m*
Slovak [ˈsləuvæk] *adj* slowakisch ▸ *n* Slowake *m*, Slowakin *f*; (*Ling*) Slowakisch *nt*
Slovakia [sləuˈvækɪə] *n* die Slowakei
Slovene [ˈsləuviːn] *n* Slowene *m*, Slowenin *f*; (*Ling*) Slowenisch *nt* ▸ *adj* slowenisch
Slovenia [sləuˈviːnɪə] *n* Slowenien *nt*
slow [sləu] *adj* langsam; (*not clever*) langsam, begriffsstutzig ▸ *vi* (*also:* **~ down, ~ up**) sich verlangsamen; **to be ~** (*watch, clock*) nachgehen
slowly [ˈsləulɪ] *adv* langsam
slow motion *n*: **in ~** in Zeitlupe
slug [slʌg] *n* Nacktschnecke *f*
slum [slʌm] *n* Slum *m*
slump [slʌmp] *n* Rezession *f* ▸ *vi* fallen; **~ in prices** Preissturz *m*
slung [slʌŋ] *pt, pp of* **sling**
slur [sləːʳ] *n* (*fig*): **~ (on)** Beleidigung *f* (für)
slurred [sləːd] *adj* (*speech, voice*) undeutlich
slush [slʌʃ] *n* (*melted snow*) Schneematsch *m*
slushy [ˈslʌʃɪ] *adj* matschig; (Brit *fig*) schmalzig
slut [slʌt] (*pej*) *n* Schlampe *f*
smack [smæk] *n* Klaps *m* ▸ *vt* (*hit*) schlagen; (*: child*) einen Klaps geben +*dat* ▸ *vi*: **to ~ of** riechen nach
small [smɔːl] *adj* klein

small ads (BRIT) *npl* Kleinanzeigen *pl*
small change *n* Kleingeld *nt*
small fry *npl* (*unimportant people*) kleine Fische *pl*
smallpox [ˈsmɔːlpɔks] *n* Pocken *pl*
small print *n*: **the ~** das Kleingedruckte
small-scale [ˈsmɔːlskeɪl] *adj* (*map, model*) in verkleinertem Maßstab
small talk *n* (oberflächliche) Konversation *f*
smart [smɑːt] *adj* (*fashionable*) chic *inv*, elegant; (*clever*) intelligent, clever (*inf*)
smart card *n* Chipkarte *f*
smartphone [ˈsmɑːtfəun] *n* (*Tel*) Smartphone *nt*
smartwatch [ˈsmɑːtwɔtʃ] *n* Smartwatch *f*
smash [smæʃ] *n* (*also*: **smash-up**) Unfall *m*; (*Tennis*) Schmetterball *m* ▸ *vt* (*break*) zerbrechen; (*Sport*: *record*) haushoch schlagen ▸ *vi* (*break*) zerbrechen; (*against wall, into sth etc*) krachen
smear [smɪəʳ] *n* (*trace*) verschmierter Fleck *m*; (*insult*) Verleumdung *f*; (*Med*) Abstrich *m* ▸ *vt* (*spread*) verschmieren; (*make dirty*) beschmieren
smell [smɛl] (*pt, pp* **smelt** *or* **smelled**) *n* Geruch *m* ▸ *vt* riechen ▸ *vi* riechen; (*pej*) stinken; **to ~ of** riechen nach
smelly [ˈsmɛlɪ] (*pej*) *adj* stinkend
smelt [smɛlt] *pt, pp of* **smell** ▸ *vt* schmelzen
smile [smaɪl] *n* Lächeln *nt* ▸ *vi* lächeln
smock [smɔk] *n* Kittel *m*; (*US*: *overall*) Overall *m*
smog [smɔg] *n* Smog *m*
smoke [sməuk] *n* Rauch *m* ▸ *vi, vt* rauchen
smoke alarm *n* Rauchmelder *m*
smoked [sməukt] *adj* geräuchert
smoker [ˈsməukəʳ] *n* Raucher(in) *m(f)*; (*Rail*) Raucherabteil *nt*
smoking [ˈsməukɪŋ] *n* Rauchen *nt*; **"no ~"** „Rauchen verboten"
smooth [smuːð] *adj* (*lit, fig*: *pej*) glatt; (*movement*) geschmeidig; (*flight*) ruhig
▸ **smooth out** *vt* glätten
smoothly [ˈsmuːðlɪ] *adv* reibungslos
smudge [smʌdʒ] *vt* verwischen
smug [smʌg] (*pej*) *adj* selbstgefällig
smuggle [ˈsmʌgl] *vt* schmuggeln; **to ~ in/out** einschmuggeln/ herausschmuggeln
smutty [ˈsmʌtɪ] *adj* (*fig*: *joke, book*) schmutzig
snack [snæk] *n* Kleinigkeit *f* (zu essen); **to have a ~** eine Kleinigkeit essen
snack bar *n* Imbissstube *f*
snail [sneɪl] *n* Schnecke *f*
snake [sneɪk] *n* Schlange *f*
snap [snæp] *n* (*photograph*) Schnappschuss *m* ▸ *adj* (*decision*) plötzlich ▸ *vt* (*break*) (zer)brechen ▸ *vi* (*break*) (zer)brechen; (*rope, thread etc*) reißen; **to ~ open/shut** auf-/ zuschnappen
▸ **snap at** *vt fus* (*dog*) schnappen nach
▸ **snap off** *vt* (*break*) abbrechen
snap fastener *n* Druckknopf *m*
snapshot [ˈsnæpʃɔt] *n* Schnappschuss *m*
snatch [snætʃ] *vt* (*grab*) greifen
sneak [sniːk] (*US pt* **snuck**) *vi*: **to ~ in/ out** sich einschleichen/sich hinausschleichen
sneakers [ˈsniːkəz] *npl* Freizeitschuhe *pl*
sneeze [sniːz] *vi* niesen
sniff [snɪf] *vi* schniefen ▸ *vt* schnuppern an +*dat*; (*glue*) schnüffeln
snob [snɔb] *n* Snob *m*
snobbish [ˈsnɔbɪʃ] *adj* versnobt (*inf*)
snog [snɔg] (BRIT *inf*) *vi* (rum) knutschen
snooker [ˈsnuːkəʳ] *n* Snooker *nt*
snoop [snuːp] *vi*: **to ~ about** herumschnüffeln
snooze [snuːz] *n* Schläfchen *nt* ▸ *vi* ein Schläfchen machen
snore [snɔːʳ] *vi* schnarchen
snorkel [ˈsnɔːkl] *n* Schnorchel *m*
snout [snaut] *n* Schnauze *f*
snow [snəu] *n* Schnee *m* ▸ *vi* schneien
snowball [ˈsnəubɔːl] *n* Schneeball *m*
snowboard [ˈsnəubɔːd] *n* Snowboard *nt*
snowboarding [ˈsnəubɔːdɪŋ] *n* Snowboarding *nt*
snowdrift [ˈsnəudrɪft] *n* Schneewehe *f*
snowdrop [ˈsnəudrɔp] *n* Schneeglöckchen *nt*
snowflake [ˈsnəufleɪk] *n* Schneeflocke *f*
snowman [ˈsnəumæn] *n* (*irreg*) Schneemann *m*
snowplough, (*US*) **snowplow** [ˈsnəuplau] *n* Schneepflug *m*

snowstorm ['snəustɔ:m] *n* Schneesturm *m*
snowy ['snəuɪ] *adj* schneeweiß; (*covered with snow*) verschneit
snug [snʌg] *adj* gemütlich
snuggle ['snʌgl] *vi*: **to ~ up to sb** sich an jdn kuscheln

KEYWORD

so [səu] *adv* **1** (*thus, likewise*) so; **so saying he walked away** mit diesen Worten ging er weg; **if so** falls ja; **I didn't do it — you did so!** ich hab es nicht getan — hast du wohl!; **so do I, so am I** *etc* ich auch; **it's 5 o'clock — so it is!** es ist 5 Uhr — tatsächlich!; **I hope/think so** ich hoffe/glaube ja; **so far** bis jetzt
2 (*in comparisons etc*: *to such a degree*) so; **so big/quickly (that)** so groß/schnell(, dass); **I'm so glad to see you** ich bin ja so froh, dich zu sehen
3 : **I've got so much work** ich habe so viel Arbeit; **I love you so much** ich liebe dich so sehr; **so many** so viele
4 (*phrases*): **10 or so** 10 oder so; **so long!** (*inf*: *goodbye*) tschüss!
▶ *conj* **1** (*expressing purpose*): **so as to do sth** um etw zu tun; **so (that)** damit
2 (*expressing result*) also; **so I was right after all** ich hatte also doch Recht; **so you see, I could have gone** wie Sie sehen, hätte ich gehen können

soak [səuk] *vt* (*drench*) durchnässen; (*steep*) einweichen
soaking ['səukɪŋ] *adj* (*also*: **~ wet**) patschnass
soap [səup] *n* Seife *f*
soap opera *n* (*TV*) Seifenoper *f* (*inf*)
soap powder *n* Seifenpulver *nt*
sob [sɔb] *vi* schluchzen
sober ['səubəʳ] *adj* nüchtern
▶ **sober up** *vi* nüchtern werden
so-called ['səu'kɔ:ld] *adj* sogenannt
soccer ['sɔkəʳ] *n* Fußball *m*
sociable ['səuʃəbl] *adj* gesellig
social ['səuʃl] *adj* sozial; (*person*) gesellig
socialist ['səuʃəlɪst] *adj* sozialistisch
▶ *n* Sozialist(in) *m(f)*
socialize ['səuʃəlaɪz] *vi* unter die Leute kommen
social media *n* Social Media *pl*, soziale Medien *fpl*
social networking [-'nɛtwə:kɪŋ] *n* Netzwerken *nt*
social networking site *n* soziales Netzwerk *nt*
social security (*BRIT*) *n* Sozialhilfe *f*
society [sə'saɪətɪ] *n* Gesellschaft *f*; (*club*) Verein *m*
sock [sɔk] *n* Socke *f*
socket ['sɔkɪt] *n* (*BRIT Elec*: *also*: **wall ~**) Steckdose *f*
soda ['səudə] *n* Soda *nt*; (*also*: **~ water**) Soda(wasser) *nt*; (*US*: *also*: **~ pop**) Brause *f*
sofa ['səufə] *n* Sofa *nt*
sofa bed *n* Schlafcouch *f*
soft [sɔft] *adj* weich; (*voice, music, light, colour*) gedämpft; (*lenient*) nachsichtig
softly ['sɔftlɪ] *adv* (*gently*) sanft; (*quietly*) leise
software ['sɔftwɛəʳ] *n* (*Comput*) Software *f*
soil [sɔɪl] *n* Erde *f*, Boden *m*
solar ['səuləʳ] *adj* (*eclipse, power station etc*) Sonnen-
solarium [sə'lɛərɪəm] (*pl* **solaria**) *n* Solarium *nt*
sold [səuld] *pt, pp of* **sell**
soldier ['səuldʒəʳ] *n* Soldat *m*
sole [səul] *n* Sohle *f*; (*fish*: *pl inv*) Seezunge *f* ▶ *adj* einzig, Allein-; (*exclusive*) alleinig; **the ~ reason** der einzige Grund
solely ['səullɪ] *adv* nur
solemn ['sɔləm] *adj* feierlich; (*person*) ernst
solicitor [sə'lɪsɪtəʳ] (*BRIT*) *n* Rechtsanwalt *m*, Rechtsanwältin *f*
solid ['sɔlɪd] *adj* (*not hollow, pure*) massiv; (*not liquid*) fest; (*reliable*) zuverlässig; (*strong*: *structure*) stabil; (: *foundations*) solide; **I read for 2 ~ hours** ich habe 2 Stunden ununterbrochen gelesen
solitary ['sɔlɪtərɪ] *adj* einsam; (*single*) einzeln
solitude ['sɔlɪtju:d] *n* Einsamkeit *f*
solo ['səuləu] *n* Solo *nt*
soluble ['sɔljubl] *adj* löslich
solution [sə'lu:ʃən] *n* (*answer, liquid*) Lösung *f*
solve [sɔlv] *vt* lösen
sombre, (*US*) **somber** ['sɔmbəʳ] *adj* (*dark*) düster

KEYWORD

some [sʌm] *adj* **1** (*a certain amount or number of*) einige; **some tea/water/money** etwas Tee/Wasser/Geld; **some biscuits** ein paar Plätzchen
2 (*certain: in contrasts*) manche(r, s); **some people say that ...** manche Leute sagen, dass ...
3 (*unspecified*) irgendein(e); **some woman was asking for you** eine Frau hat nach Ihnen gefragt; **some day** eines Tages; **some day next week** irgendwann nächste Woche
▶ *pron* **1** (*a certain number*) einige; **I've got some** (*books etc*) ich habe welche
2 (*a certain amount*) etwas; **I've read some of the book** ich habe das Buch teilweise gelesen
▶ *adv*: **some 10 people** etwa 10 Leute

somebody [ˈsʌmbədɪ] *pron* = **someone**
someday [ˈsʌmdeɪ] *adv* irgendwann
somehow [ˈsʌmhau] *adv* irgendwie
someone [ˈsʌmwʌn] *pron* (irgend) jemand; **there's ~ coming** es kommt jemand
someplace [ˈsʌmpleɪs] (*US*) *adv* = **somewhere**
something [ˈsʌmθɪŋ] *pron* etwas; **~ nice** etwas Schönes; **there's ~ wrong** da stimmt etwas nicht; **would you like ~ to eat/drink?** möchten Sie etwas zu essen/trinken?
sometime [ˈsʌmtaɪm] *adv* irgendwann
sometimes [ˈsʌmtaɪmz] *adv* manchmal
somewhat [ˈsʌmwɔt] *adv* ein wenig
somewhere [ˈsʌmwɛəʳ] *adv* (*be*) irgendwo; (*go*) irgendwohin; **~ else** (*be*) woanders
son [sʌn] *n* Sohn *m*
song [sɔŋ] *n* Lied *nt*
son-in-law [ˈsʌnɪnlɔː] *n* Schwiegersohn *m*
soon [suːn] *adv* bald; (*early*) früh; *see also* **as**
sooner [ˈsuːnəʳ] *adv* (*time*) früher; (*preference*) lieber
soot [sut] *n* Ruß *m*
soothe [suːð] *vt* beruhigen; (*pain*) lindern
sophisticated [səˈfɪstɪkeɪtɪd] *adj* (*woman, lifestyle*) kultiviert; (*machinery*) hoch entwickelt
sophomore [ˈsɔfəmɔːʳ] (*US*) *n* *Student(in) im 2. Studienjahr*
soppy [ˈsɔpɪ] (*inf*) *adj* (*person*) sentimental
soprano [səˈprɑːnəu] *n* Sopranist(in) *m(f)*
sore [sɔːʳ] *adj* wund ▶ *n* wunde Stelle *f*; **to have a ~ throat** Halsschmerzen haben
sorrow [ˈsɔrəu] *n* Trauer *f*
sorry [ˈsɔrɪ] *adj* traurig; **~!** Entschuldigung!, Verzeihung!; **~?** wie bitte?; **I feel ~ for him** er tut mir leid; **I'm ~ about ...** es tut mir leid wegen ...
sort [sɔːt] *n* Sorte *f* ▶ *vt* (*also*: **~ out**) sortieren; (: *problems*) ins Reine bringen; **all sorts of reasons** alle möglichen Gründe; **what ~ of car?** was für ein Auto?; **it's ~ of awkward** (*inf*) es ist irgendwie schwierig; **to ~ sth out** etw in Ordnung bringen
sought [sɔːt] *pt, pp of* **seek**
soul [səul] *n* Seele *f*; (*Mus*) Soul *m*
sound [saund] *adj* (*healthy*) gesund; (*safe, secure*) sicher; (*reliable*) solide; (*thorough*) gründlich; (*sensible, valid*) vernünftig ▶ *n* Geräusch *nt*; (*Mus*) Klang *m*; (*on TV etc*) Ton *m* ▶ *vt*: **to ~ the alarm** Alarm schlagen ▶ *vi* (*fig: seem*) klingen; **to ~ one's horn** (*Aut*) hupen
soundcard [ˈsaundkɑːd] *n* (*Comput*) Soundkarte *f*
sound effects *npl* Toneffekte *pl*
soundproof [ˈsaundpruːf] *adj* schalldicht
soundtrack [ˈsaundtræk] *n* Filmmusik *f*
soup [suːp] *n* Suppe *f*
sour [ˈsauəʳ] *adj* sauer; (*fig: bad-tempered*) säuerlich
source [sɔːs] *n* Quelle *f*; (*fig: of problem, anxiety*) Ursache *f*
south [sauθ] *n* Süden *m* ▶ *adj* Süd- ▶ *adv* nach Süden
South Africa *n* Südafrika *nt*
South African *adj* südafrikanisch ▶ *n* Südafrikaner(in) *m(f)*
South America *n* Südamerika *nt*
South American *adj* südamerikanisch ▶ *n* Südamerikaner(in) *m(f)*

southbound ['sauθbaund] *adj* in Richtung Süden
southern ['sʌðən] *adj* südlich, Süd-
Südsudan *m*
South Sudan *n* Südsudan *m*
southward ['sauθwəd], **southwards** ['sauθwədz] *adv* nach Süden
souvenir [su:və'nɪəʳ] *n* Andenken *nt*
sow¹ [sau] *n* Sau *f*
sow² [səu] (*pt* **sowed**, *pp* **sown**) *vt* (*lit, fig*) säen
soya ['sɔɪə], **soy** [sɔɪ] (*US*) *n*: **~ bean** Sojabohne *f*; **~ sauce** Sojasoße *f*
spa [spɑ:] *n* (*town*) Heilbad *nt*
space [speɪs] *n* Platz *m*, Raum *m*; (*gap*) Lücke *f*; (*beyond Earth*) der Weltraum
space bar *n* (*on keyboard*) Leertaste *f*
spacecraft ['speɪskrɑ:ft] *n* Raumfahrzeug *nt*
spaceship ['speɪsʃɪp] *n* Raumschiff *nt*
space shuttle *n* Raumtransporter *m*
spacing ['speɪsɪŋ] *n* Abstand *m*; **single/double ~** einfacher/doppelter Zeilenabstand
spacious ['speɪʃəs] *adj* geräumig
spade [speɪd] *n* Spaten *m* ▪ **spades** *npl* (*Cards*) Pik *nt*
spaghetti [spə'gɛtɪ] *n* Spag(h)etti *pl*
Spain [speɪn] *n* Spanien *nt*
spam [spæm] (*Comput*) *n* Spam *m*
spamming ['spæmɪŋ] *n* (*Comput*) Spammen *nt*, Spamming *nt*
Spaniard ['spænjəd] *n* Spanier(in) *m(f)*
Spanish ['spænɪʃ] *adj* spanisch ▸ *n* (*Ling*) Spanisch *nt*
spanner ['spænəʳ] (BRIT) *n* Schraubenschlüssel *m*
spare [spɛəʳ] *adj* (*free*) frei; (*extra: part, fuse etc*) Ersatz- ▸ *n* = **spare part** ▸ *vt* (*save: trouble etc*) (er)sparen; (*refrain from hurting*) verschonen
spare part *n* Ersatzteil *nt*
spare room *n* Gästezimmer *nt*
spare time *n* Freizeit *f*
spare tyre *n* Reservereifen *m*
spark [spɑ:k] *n* (*lit, fig*) Funke *m*
sparkle ['spɑ:kl] *vi* funkeln
sparkling ['spɑ:klɪŋ] *adj* (*water*) mit Kohlensäure; **~ wine** Schaumwein *m*
spark plug *n* Zündkerze *f*
sparrow ['spærəu] *n* Spatz *m*
sparse [spɑ:s] *adj* spärlich
spasm ['spæzəm] *n* (*Med*) Krampf *m*
spat [spæt] *pt, pp of* **spit**
speak [spi:k] (*pt* **spoke**, *pp* **spoken**) *vt* (*language*) sprechen ▸ *vi* sprechen, reden; (*make a speech*) sprechen; **to ~ one's mind** seine Meinung sagen; **to ~ to sb/of** *or* **about sth** mit jdm/über etw *acc* sprechen *or* reden; **~ up!** sprich lauter!; **so to ~** sozusagen
speaker ['spi:kəʳ] *n* (*in public*) Redner(in) *m(f)*; (*also:* **loudspeaker**) Lautsprecher *m*; (*Pol*): **the S~** (BRIT, *US*) der Sprecher, die Sprecherin
special ['spɛʃl] *adj* besondere(r, s) ▸ *n*: **today's ~** Tagesgericht *nt*
special delivery *n* (*Post*): **by ~** durch Eilzustellung
special effects *npl* Spezialeffekte *pl*
specialist ['spɛʃəlɪst] *n* Spezialist(in) *m(f)*; (*Med*) Facharzt *m*, Fachärztin *f*
speciality [spɛʃɪ'ælɪtɪ] *n* Spezialität *f*
specialize ['spɛʃəlaɪz] *vi*: **to ~ (in)** sich spezialisieren (auf +*acc*)
specially ['spɛʃlɪ] *adv* besonders, extra
special offer *n* Sonderangebot *nt*
specialty ['spɛʃəltɪ] (*esp US*) = **speciality**
species ['spi:ʃi:z] *n inv* Art *f*
specific [spə'sɪfɪk] *adj* (*fixed*) bestimmt; (*exact*) genau
specify ['spɛsɪfaɪ] *vt* angeben
specimen ['spɛsɪmən] *n* Exemplar *nt*; (*Med*) Probe *f*
specs [spɛks] (*inf*) *npl* Brille *f*
spectacle ['spɛktəkl] *n* (*scene*) Schauspiel *nt* ▪ **spectacles** *npl* (*glasses*) Brille *f*
spectacular [spɛk'tækjuləʳ] *adj* sensationell; (*success*) spektakulär
spectator [spɛk'teɪtəʳ] *n* Zuschauer(in) *m(f)*
sped [spɛd] *pt, pp of* **speed**
speech [spi:tʃ] *n* Sprache *f*; (*formal talk, Theat*) Rede *f*
speechless ['spi:tʃlɪs] *adj* sprachlos
speed [spi:d] (*pt, pp* **sped**) *n* Geschwindigkeit *f* ▸ *vi* (*exceed speed limit*) zu schnell fahren
▸ **speed up** (*pt, pp* **speeded up**) *vi* beschleunigen; (*fig*) sich beschleunigen ▸ *vt* beschleunigen
speedboat ['spi:dbəut] *n* Rennboot *nt*
speed bump *n* Bodenschwelle *f*
speed camera *n* Blitzgerät *nt*
speed limit *n* Geschwindigkeitsbegrenzung *f*
speedometer [spɪ'dɔmɪtəʳ] *n* Tachometer *m*

speed trap *n* Radarfalle *f*
speedy ['spi:dɪ] *adj* schnell
spell [spɛl] (*pt, pp* **spelt** *or* **spelled**) *n* (*also:* **magic ~**) Zauber *m*; (*period of time*) Weile *f* ▸ *vt* schreiben; (*aloud: also:* **~ out**) buchstabieren; **cold ~** Kältewelle *f*
spellchecker ['speltʃekəʳ] *n* (*Comput*) Rechtschreibprüfung *f*
spelling ['spɛlɪŋ] *n* Schreibweise *f*; (*ability*) Rechtschreibung *f*; **~ mistake** Rechtschreibfehler *m*
spelt [spɛlt] *pt, pp of* **spell**
spend [spɛnd] (*pt, pp* **spent**) *vt* (*money*) ausgeben; (*time, life*) verbringen
spending money ['spɛndɪŋ-] *n* Taschengeld *nt*
spent [spɛnt] *pt, pp of* **spend**
sperm [spə:m] *n* Samenzelle *f*, Spermium *nt*
sphere [sfɪəʳ] *n* Kugel *f*; (*area*) Gebiet *nt*
spice [spaɪs] *n* Gewürz *nt* ▸ *vt* würzen
spicy ['spaɪsɪ] *adj* stark gewürzt
spider ['spaɪdəʳ] *n* Spinne *f*
spike [spaɪk] *n* (*point*) Spitze *f*
spill [spɪl] (*pt, pp* **spilt** *or* **spilled**) *vt* verschütten
spin [spɪn] (*pt* **spun** *or* **span**, *pp* **spun**) *n* (*revolution*) Drehung *f* ▸ *vt* (*wheel*) drehen; (*ball, coin*) (hoch)werfen ▸ *vi* (*person*) sich drehen; **my head is spinning** mir dreht sich alles
spinach ['spɪnɪtʃ] *n* Spinat *m*
spin doctor *n* (*inf*) PR-Fachmann *m*, PR-Fachfrau *f*
spin-dry ['spɪn'draɪ] *vt* schleudern
spin-dryer [spɪn'draɪəʳ] (BRIT) *n* (Wäsche)schleuder *f*
spine [spaɪn] *n* (*Anat*) Rückgrat *nt*; (*thorn*) Stachel *m*
spiral ['spaɪərl] *n* Spirale *f*
spiral staircase *n* Wendeltreppe *f*
spire ['spaɪəʳ] *n* Turmspitze *f*
spirit ['spɪrɪt] *n* Geist *m*; (*energy*) Elan *m*; (*courage*) Mut *m*; (*frame of mind*) Stimmung *f* ■ **spirits** *npl* (*drink*) Spirituosen *pl*
spiritual ['spɪrɪtjuəl] *adj* geistig; (*religious*) geistlich
spit [spɪt] (*pt, pp* **spat**) *n* (*for roasting*) Spieß *m*; (*saliva*) Spucke *f* ▸ *vi* spucken
▸ **spit out** *vt* ausspucken
spite [spaɪt] *n* Boshaftigkeit *f*; **in ~ of** trotz +*gen*
spiteful ['spaɪtful] *adj* boshaft
spitting ['spɪtɪŋ] *adj*: **to be the ~ image of sb** jdm wie aus dem Gesicht geschnitten sein
splash [splæʃ] *vt* bespritzen ▸ *vi* (*also:* **~ about**) herumplan(t)schen; (*water, rain*) spritzen
splendid ['splɛndɪd] *adj* hervorragend
splinter ['splɪntəʳ] *n* Splitter *m*
split [splɪt] (*pt, pp* **~**) *n* (*tear*) Riss *m*; (*Pol*) Spaltung *f* ▸ *vt* (*party*) spalten; (*share equally*) teilen ▸ *vi* (*divide*) sich aufteilen
▸ **split up** *vi* sich trennen; (*meeting*) sich auflösen
splitting ['splɪtɪŋ] *adj*: **a ~ headache** rasende Kopfschmerzen *pl*
spoil [spɔɪl] (*pt, pp* **spoilt** *or* **spoiled**) *vt* verderben; (*child*) verwöhnen
spoilt [spɔɪlt] *pt, pp of* **spoil**
spoke [spəuk] *pt of* **speak** ▸ *n* Speiche *f*
spoken ['spəukn] *pp of* **speak**
spokesperson ['spəukspə:sn] *n* Sprecher(in) *m(f)*
sponge [spʌndʒ] *n* Schwamm *m*
sponge bag (BRIT) *n* Kulturbeutel *m*
sponge cake *n* Biskuitkuchen *m*
sponsor ['spɔnsəʳ] *n* Sponsor(in) *m(f)* ▸ *vt* sponsern; (*applicant*) unterstützen
spontaneous [spɔn'teɪnɪəs] *adj* spontan
spool [spu:l] *n* Spule *f*
spoon [spu:n] *n* Löffel *m*
sport [spɔ:t] *n* Sport *m*
sports car *n* Sportwagen *m*
sports centre *n* Sportzentrum *nt*
sports drink *n* Sportgetränk *nt*
sportsman ['spɔ:tsmən] *n* (*irreg*) Sportler *m*
sportswear ['spɔ:tswɛəʳ] *n* Sportkleidung *f*
sportswoman ['spɔ:tswumən] *n* (*irreg*) Sportlerin *f*
sporty ['spɔ:tɪ] *adj* sportlich
spot [spɔt] *n* (*mark*) Fleck *m*; (*dot*) Punkt *m*; (*on skin*) Pickel *m*; (*place*) Stelle *f* ▸ *vt* entdecken; **on the ~** (*in that place*) an Ort und Stelle; (*immediately*) auf der Stelle
spotless ['spɔtlɪs] *adj* makellos sauber
spotlight ['spɔtlaɪt] *n* Scheinwerfer *m*
spotty ['spɔtɪ] *adj* pickelig
spouse [spaus] *n* (*male*) Gatte *m*; (*female*) Gattin *f*
spout [spaut] *n* (*of jug, teapot*) Tülle *f*

sprain [spreɪn] *n* Verstauchung *f* ▶ *vt*: **to ~ one's ankle/wrist** sich *dat* den Knöchel/das Handgelenk verstauchen
sprang [spræŋ] *pt of* **spring**
spray [spreɪ] *n* (*small drops*) Sprühnebel *m*; (*container*) Sprühdose *f* ▶ *vt* sprühen, spritzen; (*crops*) spritzen; **~ can** Sprühdose *f*
spread [sprɛd] (*pt, pp* **~**) *n* (*distribution*) Verteilung *f*; (*for bread*) (Brot)aufstrich *m* ▶ *vt* ausbreiten; (*butter*) streichen; (*rumour, disease*) verbreiten ▶ *vi* (*disease, news*) sich verbreiten
spreadsheet [ˈsprɛdʃiːt] *n* (*Comput*) Tabellenkalkulation *f*
spring [sprɪŋ] (*pt* **sprang**, *pp* **sprung**) *n* (*coiled metal*) Sprungfeder *f*; (*season*) Frühling *m*; (*of water*) Quelle *f* ▶ *vi* (*leap*) springen
springboard [ˈsprɪŋbɔːd] *n* (*Sport, fig*) Sprungbrett *nt*
spring onion (Brit) *n* Frühlingszwiebel *f*
spring roll *n* Frühlingsrolle *f*
springy [ˈsprɪŋɪ] *adj* federnd; (*mattress*) weich gefedert
sprinkle [ˈsprɪŋkl] *vt* (*liquid*) sprenkeln; **to ~ water on, ~ with water** mit Wasser besprengen; **to ~ sugar** *etc* **on, ~ with sugar** *etc* mit Zucker *etc* bestreuen
sprinkler [ˈsprɪŋkləʳ] *n* (*for lawn*) Rasensprenger *m*; (*to put out fire*) Sprinkler *m*
sprint [sprɪnt] *vi* rennen; (*Sport*) sprinten
sprout [spraut] *vi* sprießen
sprouts [sprauts] *npl* (*also:* **Brussels ~**) Rosenkohl *m*
sprung [sprʌŋ] *pp of* **spring**
spun [spʌn] *pt, pp of* **spin**
spy [spaɪ] *n* Spion(in) *m(f)* ▶ *vi*: **to ~ on** nachspionieren *+dat* ▶ *vt* sehen
spycam [ˈspaɪkæm] *n* Überwachungskamera *f*
spyware [ˈspaɪwɛəʳ] *n* (*Comput*) Spyware *f*, Spionagesoftware *f*
squad [skwɔd] *n* (*Police*) Kommando *nt*; (*Sport*) Mannschaft *f*
square [skwɛəʳ] *n* Quadrat *nt*; (*in town*) Platz *m* ▶ *adj* quadratisch; **2 metres ~** 2 Meter im Quadrat; **2 ~ metres** 2 Quadratmeter
square root *n* Quadratwurzel *f*
squash [skwɔʃ] *n* (Brit): **lemon/orange ~** Zitronen-/Orangensaftgetränk *nt*; (*US: marrow etc*) Kürbis *m*; (*Sport*) Squash *nt* ▶ *vt* zerquetschen
squat [skwɔt] *vi* (*also:* **~ down**) sich (hin)hocken
squeak [skwiːk] *vi* quietschen; (*mouse etc*) piepsen
squeal [skwiːl] *vi* quietschen
squeeze [skwiːz] *vt* drücken; (*lemon etc*) auspressen ▶ *vi*: **to ~ under sth** sich unter etw *dat* durchzwängen
squid [skwɪd] *n* Tintenfisch *m*
squint [skwɪnt] *vi* (*in the sunlight*) blinzeln; **he has a ~** er schielt
squirrel [ˈskwɪrəl] *n* Eichhörnchen *nt*
squirt [skwəːt] *vi, vt* spritzen
Sri Lanka [srɪˈlæŋkə] *n* Sri Lanka *nt*
St *abbr* (= *saint*) St.; (= *street*) Str.
stab [stæb] *vt* (*body*) einstechen auf *+acc*; **to ~ sb to death** jdn erstechen
stabbing [ˈstæbɪŋ] *adj* (*pain*) stechend
stabilize [ˈsteɪbəlaɪz] *vt* stabilisieren ▶ *vi* sich stabilisieren
stable [ˈsteɪbl] *adj* stabil ▶ *n* Stall *m*
stack [stæk] *n* Stapel *m* ▶ *vt* (*also:* **~ up**) aufstapeln
stadium [ˈsteɪdɪəm] (*pl* **stadia** *or* **stadiums**) *n* Stadion *nt*
staff [stɑːf] *n* (*workforce, servants*) Personal *nt*; (Brit: *also:* **teaching ~**) (Lehrer)kollegium *nt*
stag [stæg] *n* Hirsch *m*
stage [steɪdʒ] *n* Bühne *f*; (*point, period*) Stadium *nt* ▶ *vt* (*play*) aufführen; (*demonstration*) organisieren
stagger [ˈstægəʳ] *vi* schwanken, taumeln ▶ *vt* (*amaze*) die Sprache verschlagen *+dat*
staggering [ˈstægərɪŋ] *adj* (*amazing*) atemberaubend
stagnate [stægˈneɪt] *vi* (*economy etc*) stagnieren
stag night, stag party *n* Herrenabend *m*
stain [steɪn] *n* Fleck *m*
stained glass window [steɪnd-] *n* buntes Glasfenster *nt*
stainless steel [ˈsteɪnlɪs-] *n* (rostfreier) Edelstahl *m*
stain remover *n* Fleckentferner *m*
stair [stɛəʳ] *n* (*step*) Stufe *f* ■ **stairs** *npl* (*flight of steps*) Treppe *f*
staircase [ˈstɛəkeɪs] *n* Treppe *f*

stake [steɪk] *n* (*post*) Pfahl *m*; (*Comm*) Anteil *m*; (*Betting*: *gen pl*) Einsatz *m*; **to be at ~** auf dem Spiel stehen
stale [steɪl] *adj* (*bread*) altbacken; (*beer*) schal
stalk [stɔːk] *n* Stiel *m* ▶ *vt* sich heranpirschen an *+acc*
stall [stɔːl] *n* (Brit: *in market etc*) Stand *m*; (*in stable*) Box *f* ▶ *vt* (*engine, car*) abwürgen ▶ *vi* (*engine*) absterben; (*car*) stehen bleiben ▪ **stalls** *npl* (Brit: *in cinema, theatre*) Parkett *nt*; **to ~ for time** versuchen, Zeit zu gewinnen
stamina [ˈstæmɪnə] *n* Ausdauer *f*
stammer [ˈstæməʳ] *vi* stottern
stamp [stæmp] *n* (*lit, fig*) Stempel *m*; (*also*: **postage ~**) Briefmarke *f* ▶ *vt* stempeln; (*with postage stamp*) frankieren; **stamped addressed envelope** frankierter Rückumschlag
stand [stænd] (*pt, pp* **stood**) *n* (*Comm*) Stand *m*; (*Sport*) Tribüne *f*; (*piece of furniture*) Ständer *m* ▶ *vi* stehen; (*in election etc*) kandidieren ▶ *vt* stellen; (*tolerate, withstand*) ertragen; **I can't ~ him** ich kann ihn nicht leiden *or* ausstehen
▶ **stand around** *vi* herumstehen
▶ **stand by** *vi* (*be ready*) sich bereithalten; (*fail to help*) (unbeteiligt) danebenstehen ▶ *vt fus* (*opinion, decision*) stehen zu; (*person*) halten zu
▶ **stand for** *vt fus* (*represent*) stehen für; (*tolerate*) sich *dat* gefallen lassen
▶ **stand in for** *vt fus* vertreten
▶ **stand out** *vi* hervorstechen
▶ **stand up** *vi* aufstehen
▶ **stand up for** *vt fus* eintreten für
▶ **stand up to** *vt fus* standhalten *+dat*; (*person*) sich behaupten gegenüber *+dat*
standard [ˈstændəd] *n* (*norm*) Norm *f* ▶ *adj* (*size, model, value etc*) Standard-
standardize [ˈstændədaɪz] *vt* vereinheitlichen
standby, stand-by [ˈstændbaɪ] *n* Reserve *f*; (*also*: **~ ticket**) Stand-by-Ticket *nt*; **to be on stand-by** (*crew, firemen etc*) in Bereitschaft sein
standby ticket *n* Stand-by-Ticket *nt*
standing order (Brit) *n* (*at bank*) Dauerauftrag *m*
standpoint [ˈstændpɔɪnt] *n* Standpunkt *m*
standstill [ˈstændstɪl] *n*: **to be at a ~** stillstehen; **to come to a ~** (*traffic*) zum Stillstand kommen
stank [stæŋk] *pt of* **stink**
staple [ˈsteɪpl] *n* (*for papers*) Heftklammer *f* ▶ *vt* heften
stapler [ˈsteɪpləʳ] *n* Hefter *m*
star [stɑːʳ] *n* Stern *m*; (*celebrity*) Star *m* ▶ *vi*: **to ~ in** die Hauptrolle haben in
starch [stɑːtʃ] *n* Stärke *f*
stare [stɛəʳ] *vi*: **to ~ at** anstarren
starfish [ˈstɑːfɪʃ] *n* Seestern *m*
star sign *n* Sternzeichen *nt*
start [stɑːt] *n* Beginn *m*, Anfang *m*; (*advantage*) Vorsprung *m* ▶ *vt* anfangen mit; (*found*) gründen; (*engine*) anlassen; (*car*) starten ▶ *vi* anfangen; (*with fright*) zusammenfahren; (*engine etc*) anspringen; **to ~ doing** *or* **to do sth** anfangen, etw zu tun
▶ **start off** *vi* (*begin*) anfangen; (*begin moving*) losgehen/-fahren
▶ **start up** *vt* (*business*) gründen; (*car*) starten
starter [ˈstɑːtəʳ] *n* (*Aut*) Anlasser *m*; (Brit *Culin*) Vorspeise *f*
starting point [ˈstɑːtɪŋ-] *n* (*lit, fig*) Ausgangspunkt *m*
startle [ˈstɑːtl] *vt* erschrecken
startling [ˈstɑːtlɪŋ] *adj* (*news etc*) überraschend
starve [stɑːv] *vi* hungern; (*to death*) verhungern; **I'm starving** ich sterbe vor Hunger
state [steɪt] *n* (*condition*) Zustand *m*; (*Pol*) Staat *m* ▶ *vt* (*say*) feststellen; (*declare*) erklären ▪ **the States** *npl* (*Geog*) die (Vereinigten) Staaten *pl*
stated [ˈsteɪtɪd] *adj* erklärt
statement [ˈsteɪtmənt] *n* (*declaration*) Erklärung *f*; **bank ~** Kontoauszug *m*
state of the art *n*: **the ~** der neueste Stand der Technik ▶ *adj*: **state-of-the-art** auf dem neuesten Stand der Technik
static [ˈstætɪk] *adj* (*not moving*) konstant
station [ˈsteɪʃən] *n* (*Rail*) Bahnhof *m*; (*also*: **police ~**) (Polizei)wache *f*; (*Radio*) Sender *m* ▶ *vt* (*soldiers etc*) stationieren
stationer's [ˈsteɪʃənəz], **stationer's shop** *n* Schreibwarenhandlung *f*
stationery [ˈsteɪʃnərɪ] *n* Schreibwaren *pl*

station wagon (*US*) *n* Kombi(wagen) *m*
statistics [stəˈtɪstɪks] *n* (*science*) Statistik *f*
statue [ˈstætjuː] *n* Statue *f*
status [ˈsteɪtəs] *n* Status *m*; (*position*) Stellung *f*
status bar, status line *n* (*Comput*) Statuszeile *f*
stay [steɪ] *n* Aufenthalt *m* ▸ *vi* bleiben; (*with sb, as guest*) wohnen; (*in hotel*) übernachten
▸ **stay away** *vi* wegbleiben; **to ~ away from sb** sich von jdm fernhalten
▸ **stay behind** *vi* zurückbleiben
▸ **stay in** *vi* (*at home*) zu Hause bleiben
▸ **stay out** *vi* (*of house*) wegbleiben
▸ **stay up** *vi* (*at night*) aufbleiben
steady [ˈstɛdɪ] *adj* (*job, boyfriend, girlfriend, look*) fest; (*income*) regelmäßig; (*speed*) gleichmäßig; (*rise*) stetig; (*person, character*) zuverlässig; (*voice, hand etc*) ruhig ▸ *vt* (*nerves*) beruhigen; **to ~ o.s. on sth** sich auf etw *acc* stützen
steak [steɪk] *n* Steak *nt*; (*fish*) Filet *nt*
steal [stiːl] (*pt* **stole**, *pp* **stolen**) *vt* stehlen
steam [stiːm] *n* Dampf *m* ▸ *vt* (*Culin*) dämpfen
steamer [ˈstiːməʳ] *n* Dampfer *m*; (*Culin*) Dämpfer *m*
steam iron *n* Dampfbügeleisen *nt*
steel [stiːl] *n* Stahl *m* ▸ *adj* (*girder, wool etc*) Stahl-
steep [stiːp] *adj* steil
steeple [ˈstiːpl] *n* Kirchturm *m*
steer [stɪəʳ] *vt* steuern; (*car etc*) lenken ▸ *vi* steuern
steering [ˈstɪərɪŋ] *n* (*Aut*) Lenkung *f*
steering wheel *n* (*Aut*) Lenkrad *nt*, Steuer *nt*
stem [stɛm] *n* Stiel *m*
step [stɛp] *n* (*lit, fig*) Schritt *m*; (*of stairs*) Stufe *f* ▸ *vi*: **to ~ forward/back** vor-/zurücktreten; **~ by ~** (*fig*) Schritt für Schritt
▸ **step down** *vi* (*fig: resign*) zurücktreten
▸ **step on** *vt fus* treten auf +*acc*
▸ **step up** *vt* (*efforts*) steigern; (*pace etc*) beschleunigen
stepbrother [ˈstɛpbrʌðəʳ] *n* Stiefbruder *m*
stepchild [ˈstɛptʃaɪld] *n* (*irreg*) Stiefkind *nt*
stepdad [ˈstepdæd] *n* Stiefvater *m*
stepfather [ˈstɛpfɑːðəʳ] *n* Stiefvater *m*
stepladder [ˈstɛplædəʳ] (*Brit*) *n* Trittleiter *f*
stepmother [ˈstɛpmʌðəʳ] *n* Stiefmutter *f*
stepmum [ˈstepmʌm] *n* Stiefmutter *f*
stepsister [ˈstɛpsɪstəʳ] *n* Stiefschwester *f*
stereo [ˈstɛrɪəu] *n* (*system*) Stereoanlage *f*
sterile [ˈstɛraɪl] *adj* steril
sterilize [ˈstɛrɪlaɪz] *vt* sterilisieren
sterling [ˈstəːlɪŋ] *n* (*Econ*) das Pfund Sterling
stew [stjuː] *n* Eintopf *m*
steward [ˈstjuːəd] *n* Steward *m*
stewardess [ˈstjuədɛs] *n* Stewardess *f*
stick [stɪk] (*pt, pp* **stuck**) *n* Zweig *m*; (*of dynamite, celery*) Stange *f*; (*of chalk etc*) Stück *nt*; (*as weapon*) Stock *m* ▸ *vt* (*with glue etc*) kleben; (*inf: put*) tun, stecken ▸ *vi*: **to ~ (to)** kleben (an +*dat*); (*door etc*) klemmen
▸ **stick out** *vi* (*ears etc*) abstehen
▸ **stick to** *vt fus* (*agreement, rules*) sich halten an +*acc*
sticker [ˈstɪkəʳ] *n* Aufkleber *m*
sticky [ˈstɪkɪ] *adj* klebrig; (*label, tape*) Klebe-; (*weather, day*) schwül
stiff [stɪf] *adj* steif
stifle [ˈstaɪfl] *vt* unterdrücken
stifling [ˈstaɪflɪŋ] *adj* (*heat*) drückend
still [stɪl] *adj* (*air, water*) still; (*Brit: drink*) ohne Kohlensäure ▸ *adv* (immer) noch; (*yet, even*) noch; **to stand ~** (*machine, motor*) stillstehen; (*motionless*) still stehen; **keep ~!** halte still!
still life *n* Stillleben *nt*
stimulate [ˈstɪmjuleɪt] *vt* anregen, stimulieren
stimulating [ˈstɪmjuleɪtɪŋ] *adj* anregend
sting [stɪŋ] (*pt, pp* **stung**) *n* Stich *m* ▸ *vt* stechen ▸ *vi* stechen; (*eyes, ointment, plant etc*) brennen
stingy [ˈstɪndʒɪ] (*pej*) *adj* geizig
stink [stɪŋk] (*pt* **stank**, *pp* **stunk**) *n* Gestank *m* ▸ *vi* stinken
stir [stəːʳ] *vt* umrühren
▸ **stir up** *vt*: **to ~ up trouble** Unruhe stiften; **to ~ things up** stänkern

stir-fry [ˈstəːˈfraɪ] *vt* unter Rühren kurz anbraten
stitch [stɪtʃ] *n* (*Sewing*) Stich *m*; (*Knitting*) Masche *f* ▸ *vt* nähen; **he had to have stitches** er musste genäht werden
stock [stɔk] *n* Vorrat *m*; (*Comm*) Bestand *m*; (*Culin*) Brühe *f* ▸ *vt* (*in shop*) führen; **in/out of ~** vorrätig/nicht vorrätig; **stocks and shares** (Aktien und) Wertpapiere *pl*; **to take ~ of** (*fig*) Bilanz ziehen über *+acc*
▸ **stock up** *vi*: **to ~ up (with)** sich eindecken (mit)
stockbroker [ˈstɔkbrəukəʳ] *n* Börsenmakler *m*
stock cube (Brit) *n* Brühwürfel *m*
stock exchange *n* Börse *f*
stocking [ˈstɔkɪŋ] *n* Strumpf *m*
stock market (Brit) *n* Börse *f*
stole [stəul] *pt of* **steal**
stolen [ˈstəuln] *pp of* **steal**
stomach [ˈstʌmək] *n* Magen *m*; (*belly*) Bauch *m*
stomach ache *n* Magenschmerzen *pl*
stone [stəun] *n* Stein *m*; (Brit: *weight*) *Gewichtseinheit* (= 6,35 kg) ▸ *adj* (*wall, jar etc*) Stein-
stonking [ˈstɔŋkɪŋ] (Brit *inf*) *adj, adv* irre, super; **a ~ good idea** eine geniale Idee
stony [ˈstəunɪ] *adj* steinig
stood [stud] *pt, pp of* **stand**
stool [stuːl] *n* Hocker *m*
stop [stɔp] *n* Halt *m*; (*bus stop etc*) Haltestelle *f* ▸ *vt* stoppen; (*car etc*) anhalten; (*block*) sperren; (*prevent*) verhindern ▸ *vi* (*car etc*) anhalten; (*pedestrian, watch, clock*) stehen bleiben; (*end*) aufhören; **to come to a ~** anhalten; **to ~ doing sth** aufhören, etw zu tun; **to ~ sb (from) doing sth** jdn davon abhalten, etw zu tun; **~ it!** lass das!, hör auf!
▸ **stop by** *vi* kurz vorbeikommen
▸ **stop off** *vi* kurz haltmachen, Zwischenstation machen
▸ **stop over** *vi* Halt machen; (*overnight*) übernachten
stopgap [ˈstɔpgæp] *n*: **~ measure** Überbrückungsmaßnahme *f*
stopover [ˈstɔpəuvəʳ] *n* Zwischenaufenthalt *m*
stopper [ˈstɔpəʳ] *n* Stöpsel *m*
stop sign *n* Stoppschild *nt*
stopwatch [ˈstɔpwɔtʃ] *n* Stoppuhr *f*
storage [ˈstɔːrɪdʒ] *n* Lagerung *f*
store [stɔːʳ] *n* Vorrat *m*; (*depot*) Lager *nt*; (Brit: *large shop*) Kaufhaus *nt*; (*US: shop*) Laden *m* ▸ *vt* lagern; (*information etc, Comput*) speichern
storeroom [ˈstɔːruːm] *n* Lagerraum *m*
storey, (*US*) **story** [ˈstɔːrɪ] *n* Stock *m*, Stockwerk *nt*
storm [stɔːm] *n* (*lit, fig*) Sturm *m*; (*also*: **electrical ~**) Gewitter *nt* ▸ *vt* (*attack*) stürmen
stormy [ˈstɔːmɪ] *adj* (*lit, fig*) stürmisch
story [ˈstɔːrɪ] *n* Geschichte *f*; (*US*) = **storey**
stout [staut] *adj* (*fat*) untersetzt
stove [stəuv] *n* Herd *m*; (*for heating*) (Heiz)ofen *m*
stow [stəu] *vt* (*also*: **~ away**) verstauen
stowaway [ˈstəuəweɪ] *n* blinder Passagier *m*
straight [streɪt] *adj* gerade; (*hair*) glatt; (*honest*) offen, direkt; (*inf: heterosexual*) hetero ▸ *adv* (*in time*) sofort; (*in direction*) direkt; (*drink*) pur; **to put** *or* **get sth ~** (*make clear*) etw klären; **~ away, ~ off** sofort, gleich
straightforward [streɪtˈfɔːwəd] *adj* (*simple*) einfach; (*honest*) offen
strain [streɪn] *n* Belastung *f* ▸ *vt* (*back etc*) überanstrengen; (*resources*) belasten; (*Culin*) abgießen
strained [streɪnd] *adj* (*muscle*) gezerrt; (*forced*) gezwungen; (*relations*) gespannt
strainer [ˈstreɪnəʳ] *n* Sieb *nt*
strand [strænd] *n* (*lit, fig*) Faden *m*; (*of hair*) Strähne *f*
stranded [ˈstrændɪd] *adj*: **to be ~** (*traveller*) festsitzen
strange [streɪndʒ] *adj* fremd; (*odd*) seltsam
strangely [ˈstreɪndʒlɪ] *adv* seltsam, merkwürdig
stranger [ˈstreɪndʒəʳ] *n* Fremde(r) *f(m)*; **I'm a ~ here** ich bin hier fremd
strangle [ˈstræŋgl] *vt* erdrosseln
strap [stræp] *n* Riemen *m*; (*of dress etc*) Träger *m* ▸ *vt* (*also*: **~ in**) anschnallen; (*also*: **~ on**) umschnallen
strapless [ˈstræplɪs] *adj* trägerlos
strategy [ˈstrætɪdʒɪ] *n* Strategie *f*
straw [strɔː] *n* Stroh *nt*; (*also*: **drinking ~**) Strohhalm *m*

strawberry *n* Erdbeere *f*
stray [streɪ] *adj* (*animal*) streunend ▶ *vi* (*animals*) streunen
streak [stri:k] *n* Streifen *m*; (*in hair*) Strähne *f*; (*fig: of madness etc*) Zug *m*
stream [stri:m] *n* (*small river*) Bach *m*; (*of people, vehicles*) Strom *m* ▶ *vi* strömen
streamer [ˈstri:mə^r] *n* Luftschlange *f*
street [stri:t] *n* Straße *f*
streetcar [ˈstri:tkɑ:^r] (*US*) *n* Straßenbahn *f*
street lamp *n* Straßenlaterne *f*
street map *n* Stadtplan *m*
strength [strɛŋθ] *n* (*lit, fig*) Stärke *f*; (*physical*) Kraft *f*
strengthen [ˈstrɛŋθn] *vt* (*lit, fig*) verstärken
strenuous [ˈstrɛnjuəs] *adj* anstrengend
stress [strɛs] *n* Druck *m*; (*mental*) Stress *m*; (*Ling*) Betonung *f* ▶ *vt* betonen; **to be under ~** unter Stress stehen, großen Belastungen ausgesetzt sein
stressed [strɛst] *adj*: **~ out** gestresst
stretch [strɛtʃ] *n* (*of sand, water etc*) Stück *nt* ▶ *vi* (*person, animal*) sich strecken; (*land, area*) sich erstrecken ▶ *vt* (*pull*) spannen; (*fig: job, task*) fordern; **to ~ one's legs** sich *dat* die Beine vertreten
▶ **stretch out** *vi* sich ausstrecken ▶ *vt* ausstrecken
stretcher [ˈstrɛtʃə^r] *n* (Trag)bahre *f*
strict [strɪkt] *adj* streng; (*precise*) genau
strictly [ˈstrɪktlɪ] *adv* streng; (*exactly*) genau; **~ speaking** genau genommen
strike [straɪk] (*pt, pp* **struck**) *n* Streik *m* ▶ *vt* (*hit*) schlagen; (*fig: idea, thought*) in den Sinn kommen +*dat*; (*oil etc*) finden ▶ *vi* streiken; (*illness, killer*) zuschlagen; (*clock*) schlagen; **to be on ~** streiken; **to ~ a match** ein Streichholz anzünden
▶ **strike down** *vt* niederschlagen
▶ **strike up** *vt* (*conversation*) anknüpfen; (*friendship*) schließen
striking [ˈstraɪkɪŋ] *adj* auffallend
string [strɪŋ] (*pt, pp* **strung**) *n* Schnur *f*; (*Mus*) Saite *f* ▪ **the strings** *npl* (*Mus*) die Streichinstrumente *pl*
strip [strɪp] *n* Streifen *m*; (*Sport*) Trikot *nt* ▶ *vi* (*undress*) sich ausziehen
stripe [straɪp] *n* Streifen *m*
striped [straɪpt] *adj* gestreift
stripper [ˈstrɪpə^r] *n* Stripper(in) *m(f)*
strip-search [ˈstrɪpsɛtʃ] *n* Leibesvisitation *f* (*bei der man sich ausziehen muss*)
striptease [ˈstrɪpti:z] *n* Striptease *m or nt*
stroke [strəuk] *n* Schlag *m*; (*of paintbrush*) Strich *m* ▶ *vt* (*caress*) streicheln
stroll [strəul] *n* Spaziergang *m* ▶ *vi* spazieren
stroller [ˈstrəulə^r] (*US*) *n* (*pushchair*) Sportwagen *m*
strong [strɔŋ] *adj* stark; (*healthy*) kräftig; (*object, material*) stabil
strongly [ˈstrɔŋlɪ] *adv* (*solidly*) stabil; (*deeply*) fest
struck [strʌk] *pt, pp of* **strike**
structural [ˈstrʌktʃrəl] *adj* strukturell
structurally [ˈstrʌktʃrəlɪ] *adv*: **~ sound** mit guter Bausubstanz
structure [ˈstrʌktʃə^r] *n* Struktur *f*, Aufbau *m*; (*building*) Gebäude *nt*
struggle [ˈstrʌgl] *n* Kampf *m* ▶ *vi* (*try hard*) sich abmühen; (*fight*) kämpfen; **to have a ~ to do sth** Mühe haben, etw zu tun
stub [stʌb] *n* (*of cheque, ticket etc*) Abschnitt *m*; (*of cigarette*) Kippe *f* ▶ *vt*: **to ~ one's toe** sich *dat* den Zeh stoßen
stubble [ˈstʌbl] *n* Stoppeln *pl*
stubborn [ˈstʌbən] *adj* hartnäckig
stuck [stʌk] *pt, pp of* **stick** ▶ *adj*: **to be ~** (*jammed*) klemmen; (*unable to answer*) nicht klarkommen; **to get ~** stecken bleiben
student [ˈstju:dənt] *n* Student(in) *m(f)*; (*at school*) Schüler(in) *m(f)*
studio [ˈstju:dɪəu] *n* Studio *nt*
studious [ˈstju:dɪəs] *adj* lernbegierig
study [ˈstʌdɪ] *n* Studium *nt*; (*room*) Arbeitszimmer *nt* ▶ *vt* studieren ▶ *vi* studieren
stuff [stʌf] *n* Zeug *nt* ▶ *vt* ausstopfen; (*Culin*) füllen; (*inf: push*) stopfen
stuffing [ˈstʌfɪŋ] *n* Füllung *f*
stuffy [ˈstʌfɪ] *adj* (*room*) stickig; (*person, ideas*) spießig
stumble [ˈstʌmbl] *vi* stolpern
stun [stʌn] *vt* betäuben; (*news*) fassungslos machen
stung [stʌŋ] *pt, pp of* **sting**
stunk [stʌŋk] *pp of* **stink**

stunning [ˈstʌnɪŋ] *adj* (*news, event*) sensationell; (*girl, dress*) hinreißend
stunt [stʌnt] *n* (*in film*) Stunt *m*
stupid [ˈstju:pɪd] *adj* dumm
stupidity [stju:ˈpɪdɪtɪ] *n* Dummheit *f*
sturdy [ˈstə:dɪ] *adj* (*person*) kräftig; (*thing*) stabil
stutter [ˈstʌtəʳ] *n* Stottern *nt* ▶ *vi* stottern
stye [staɪ] *n* Gerstenkorn *nt*
style [staɪl] *n* Stil *m*
stylish [ˈstaɪlɪʃ] *adj* elegant
subconscious [sʌbˈkɔnʃəs] *adj* unterbewusst
subdivide [sʌbdɪˈvaɪd] *vt* unterteilen
subject *n* [ˈsʌbdʒɪkt] (*matter*) Thema *nt*; (*Scol*) Fach *nt*; (*of country*) Staatsbürger(in) *m(f)*; (*Gram*) Subjekt *nt* ▶ *vt* [səbˈdʒɛkt]: **to ~ sb to sth** jdn einer Sache *dat* unterziehen; **to change the ~** das Thema wechseln; **to be ~ to** (*law, tax*) unterworfen sein *+dat*; (*heart attacks etc*) anfällig sein für
subjective [səbˈdʒɛktɪv] *adj* subjektiv
sublet [sʌbˈlɛt] *vt* (*irreg: like* **let**) untervermieten
submarine [sʌbməˈri:n] *n* U-Boot *nt*
submerge [səbˈmə:dʒ] *vt* untertauchen ▶ *vi* tauchen
submit [səbˈmɪt] *vt* (*application etc*) einreichen ▶ *vi*: **to ~ to sth** sich einer Sache *dat* unterwerfen
subordinate [səˈbɔ:dɪnət] *n* Untergebene(r) *f(m)* ▶ *adj* untergeordnet
subscribe [səbˈskraɪb] *vi* spenden; **to ~ to** (*magazine etc*) abonnieren
subscription [səbˈskrɪpʃən] *n* (*to magazine etc*) Abonnement *nt*; (*membership dues*) (Mitglieds)beitrag *m*
subsequent [ˈsʌbsɪkwənt] *adj* nachfolgend
subsequently [ˈsʌbsɪkwəntlɪ] *adv* später
subside [səbˈsaɪd] *vi* (*flood*) sinken; (*earth*) sich senken
substance [ˈsʌbstəns] *n* Substanz *f*
substantial [səbˈstænʃl] *adj* (*solid*) solide; (*considerable*) beträchtlich, größere(r, s); (*meal*) kräftig
substitute [ˈsʌbstɪtju:t] *n* Ersatz *m* ▶ *vt*: **to ~ A for B** B durch A ersetzen
subtitle [ˈsʌbtaɪtl] *n* Untertitel *m*
subtle [ˈsʌtl] *adj* fein; (*indirect*) raffiniert
subtotal [sʌbˈtəutl] *n* Zwischensumme *f*
subtract [səbˈtrækt] *vt* abziehen
suburb [ˈsʌbə:b] *n* Vorort *m*
suburban [səˈbə:bən] *adj* (*train etc*) Vorort-
subway [ˈsʌbweɪ] *n* (*US*) U-Bahn *f*; (*BRIT: underpass*) Unterführung *f*
succeed [səkˈsi:d] *vi* (*person*) erfolgreich sein, Erfolg haben ▶ *vt* (*in job*) Nachfolger werden *+gen*; **he succeeded in doing it** es gelang ihm(, es zu tun)
succeeding [səkˈsi:dɪŋ] *adj* folgend
success [səkˈsɛs] *n* Erfolg *m*
successful [səkˈsɛsful] *adj* erfolgreich
successive [səkˈsɛsɪv] *adj* aufeinanderfolgend
successor [səkˈsɛsəʳ] *n* Nachfolger(in) *m(f)*
succulent [ˈsʌkjulənt] *adj* saftig
succumb [səˈkʌm] *vi*: **to ~ to** (*temptation*) erliegen *+dat*
such [sʌtʃ] *adj* (*of that kind*): **~ a book** so ein Buch ▶ *adv* so; **~ a long trip** so eine lange Reise; **~ as** wie (zum Beispiel); **as ~** an sich
suck [sʌk] *vt* (*sweet etc*) lutschen; (*pump, machine*) saugen
Sudan [suˈdɑ:n] *n* der Sudan
sudden [ˈsʌdn] *adj* plötzlich; **all of a ~** ganz plötzlich
suddenly [ˈsʌdnlɪ] *adv* plötzlich
sudoku [suˈdəuku:] *n* Sudoku *nt*
sue [su:] *vt* verklagen
suede [sweɪd] *n* Wildleder *nt*
suffer [ˈsʌfəʳ] *vt* erleiden ▶ *vi* leiden; **to ~ from** leiden an *+dat*
sufficient [səˈfɪʃənt] *adj* ausreichend
sufficiently [səˈfɪʃəntlɪ] *adv* ausreichend
suffocate [ˈsʌfəkeɪt] *vi* (*lit, fig*) ersticken
sugar [ˈʃugəʳ] *n* Zucker *m* ▶ *vt* zuckern
sugar bowl *n* Zuckerdose *f*
sugary [ˈʃugərɪ] *adj* süß
suggest [səˈdʒɛst] *vt* vorschlagen; (*indicate*) andeuten; **what do you ~ I do?** was schlagen Sie vor?
suggestion [səˈdʒɛstʃən] *n* Vorschlag *m*
suggestive [səˈdʒɛstɪv] (*pej*) *adj* anzüglich
suicide [ˈsuɪsaɪd] *n* (*lit, fig*) Selbstmord *m*
suicide bomber *n* Selbstmordattentäter(in) *m(f)*

suit [suːt] *n* (*man's*) Anzug *m*; (*woman's*) Kostüm *nt*; (*Cards*) Farbe *f* ▶ *vt* passen *+dat*; (*colour, clothes*) stehen *+dat*
suitable [ˈsuːtəbl] *adj* (*appropriate*) geeignet
suitcase [ˈsuːtkeɪs] *n* Koffer *m*
suite [swiːt] *n* (*of rooms*) Suite *f*; **a three-piece ~** eine dreiteilige Polstergarnitur
sulk [sʌlk] *vi* schmollen
sulky [ˈsʌlkɪ] *adj* schmollend
sultana [sʌlˈtɑːnə] *n* Sultanine *f*
sum [sʌm] *n* (*calculation*) Rechenaufgabe *f*; (*amount*) Summe *f*, Betrag *m*
▶ **sum up** *vt* zusammenfassen
summarize [ˈsʌməraɪz] *vt* zusammenfassen
summary [ˈsʌmərɪ] *n* Zusammenfassung *f*
summer [ˈsʌməʳ] *n* Sommer *m*
summer camp (*US*) *n* Ferienlager *nt*
summer holidays *npl* Sommerferien *pl*
summertime [ˈsʌmətaɪm] *n* Sommer *m*
summit [ˈsʌmɪt] *n* Gipfel *m*
summon [ˈsʌmən] *vt* rufen; (*meeting*) einberufen
▶ **summon up** *vt* aufbringen
summons [ˈsʌmənz] *n* (*Law*) Vorladung *f*
sumptuous [ˈsʌmptjuəs] *adj* (*meal*) üppig; (*costume*) aufwendig
sun [sʌn] *n* Sonne *f*
Sun. *abbr* (= *Sunday*) So.
sunbathe [ˈsʌnbeɪð] *vi* sich sonnen
sunbed [ˈsʌnbɛd] *n* (*with sun lamp*) Sonnenbank *f*
sunblock [ˈsʌnblɔk] *n* Sonnenschutzcreme *f*
sunburn [ˈsʌnbəːn] *n* Sonnenbrand *m*
sunburnt [ˈsʌnbəːnt] *adj*: **to be ~** (*painfully*) einen Sonnenbrand haben
sundae [ˈsʌndeɪ] *n* Eisbecher *m*
Sunday [ˈsʌndɪ] *n* Sonntag *m*; *see also* **Tuesday**
sung [sʌŋ] *pp of* **sing**
sunglasses [ˈsʌnglɑːsɪz] *npl* Sonnenbrille *f*
sunk [sʌŋk] *pp of* **sink**
sunlamp [ˈsʌnlæmp] *n* Höhensonne *f*
sunlight [ˈsʌnlaɪt] *n* Sonnenlicht *nt*
sunny [ˈsʌnɪ] *adj* sonnig
sunrise [ˈsʌnraɪz] *n* Sonnenaufgang *m*
sun roof *n* (*Aut*) Schiebedach *nt*
sun screen *n* Sonnenschutzmittel *nt*
sunset [ˈsʌnsɛt] *n* Sonnenuntergang *m*
sunshade [ˈsʌnʃeɪd] *n* Sonnenschirm *m*
sunshine [ˈsʌnʃaɪn] *n* Sonnenschein *m*
sunstroke [ˈsʌnstrəuk] *n* Sonnenstich *m*
suntan [ˈsʌntæn] *n* (Sonnen)bräune *f*; **to get a ~** braun werden
suntan lotion *n* Sonnenmilch *f*
super [ˈsuːpəʳ] (*inf*) *adj* toll
superb [suːˈpəːb] *adj* ausgezeichnet
superficial [suːpəˈfɪʃəl] *adj* oberflächlich
superficially [suːpəˈfɪʃəlɪ] *adv* oberflächlich
superfluous [suˈpəːfluəs] *adj* überflüssig
superfood [ˈsuːpəfuːd] *n* Superfood *nt*
superglue [ˈsuːpəgluː] *n* Sekundenkleber *m*
superior [suˈpɪərɪəʳ] *adj* besser, überlegen *+dat*; (*more senior*) höhergestellt ▶ *n* Vorgesetzte(r) *f*(*m*)
supermarket [ˈsuːpəmɑːkɪt] *n* Supermarkt *m*
supersede [suːpəˈsiːd] *vt* ablösen
supersonic [ˈsuːpəˈsɔnɪk] *adj* (*aircraft etc*) Überschall-
superstition [suːpəˈstɪʃən] *n* Aberglaube *m*
superstitious [suːpəˈstɪʃəs] *adj* abergläubisch
superstore [ˈsuːpəstɔːʳ] (Brit) *n* Großmarkt *m*
supervise [ˈsuːpəvaɪz] *vt* beaufsichtigen
supervisor [ˈsuːpəvaɪzəʳ] *n* Aufseher(in) *m*(*f*); (*of students*) Tutor(in) *m*(*f*)
supper [ˈsʌpəʳ] *n* Abendessen *nt*
supplement [ˈsʌplɪmənt] *n* Zusatz *m*; (*of newspaper etc*) Beilage *f* ▶ *vt* ergänzen
supplementary [sʌplɪˈmɛntərɪ] *adj* zusätzlich
supplier [səˈplaɪəʳ] *n* Lieferant(in) *m*(*f*)
supply [səˈplaɪ] *vt* liefern; (*provide*) sorgen für ▶ *n* Vorrat *m*; **to ~ sth to sb** jdm etw liefern
support [səˈpɔːt] *n* Unterstützung *f*; (*Tech*) Stütze *f* ▶ *vt* unterstützen; (*financially: family etc*) unterhalten; (*: party etc*) finanziell unterstützen; **to ~ Arsenal** Arsenal-Fan sein
suppose [səˈpəuz] *vt* annehmen; **to be supposed to do sth** etw tun sollen; **I ~ so/not** ich glaube schon/nicht

supposedly [sə'pəuzɪdlɪ] *adv* angeblich
supposing [sə'pəuzɪŋ] *conj* angenommen
suppress [sə'prɛs] *vt* unterdrücken
surcharge ['sə:tʃɑ:dʒ] *n* Zuschlag *m*
sure [ʃuə^r] *adj* sicher; **to make ~ that** sich vergewissern, dass; **I'm not ~ how/why/when** ich bin mir nicht sicher *or* ich weiß nicht genau, wie/warum/wann; **~!** klar!; **~ enough** tatsächlich
surely ['ʃuəlɪ] *adv*: **~ you don't mean that!** das meinen Sie doch bestimmt *or* sicher nicht (so)!
surf [sə:f] *n* Brandung *f*
surface ['sə:fɪs] *n* Oberfläche *f* ▸ *vi* (*lit, fig*) auftauchen
surface mail *n* Post *f* auf dem Land-/Seeweg
surfboard ['sə:fbɔ:d] *n* Surfbrett *nt*
surfer ['sə:fə^r] *n* Surfer(in) *m(f)*
surfing ['sə:fɪŋ] *n* Surfen *nt*; **to go ~** surfen gehen
surgeon ['sə:dʒən] *n* Chirurg(in) *m(f)*
surgery ['sə:dʒərɪ] *n* Chirurgie *f*; (BRIT: *room*) Sprechzimmer *nt*; (: *building*) Praxis *f*; (*also*: **~ hours**) Sprechstunde *f*; **to have ~** operiert werden
surname ['sə:neɪm] *n* Nachname *m*
surpass [sə:'pɑ:s] *vt* übertreffen
surplus ['sə:pləs] *n* Überschuss *m*
surprise [sə'praɪz] *n* Überraschung *f* ▸ *vt* überraschen
surprising [sə'praɪzɪŋ] *adj* überraschend
surprisingly [sə'praɪzɪŋlɪ] *adv* (*quick*) überraschend, erstaunlich
surrender [sə'rɛndə^r] *vi* sich ergeben ▸ *vt* aufgeben
surround [sə'raund] *vt* umgeben; (*Mil, Police etc*) umstellen
surrounding [sə'raundɪŋ] *adj* umliegend; **the ~ area** die Umgebung
survey ['sə:veɪ] *n* (*of land*) Vermessung *f*; (*report*) Gutachten *nt*; (*comprehensive view*) Überblick *m* ▸ *vt* (*land*) vermessen; (*look at*) betrachten
survive [sə'vaɪv] *vi* überleben ▸ *vt* überleben
susceptible [sə'sɛptəbl] *adj*: **~ (to)** anfällig (für); (*influenced by*) empfänglich (für)
sushi ['su:ʃɪ] *n* Sushi *nt*
suspect *adj* ['sʌspɛkt] verdächtig ▸ *n* ['sʌspɛkt] Verdächtige(r) *f(m)* ▸ *vt* [sʌs'pɛkt]: **to ~ sb of** jdn verdächtigen *+gen*; (*think*) vermuten
suspend [səs'pɛnd] *vt* (*hang*) (auf)hängen; (*delay, stop*) einstellen; (*from employment*) suspendieren
suspenders *npl* (BRIT) Strumpfhalter *pl*; (*US*) Hosenträger *pl*
suspense [səs'pɛns] *n* Spannung *f*
suspicious [səs'pɪʃəs] *adj* (*suspecting*) misstrauisch; (*causing suspicion*) verdächtig
SUV *abbr* (= *sport utility vehicle*) SUV *m*, Geländewagen *m*
swallow ['swɔləu] *n* (*bird*) Schwalbe *f* ▸ *vt* (herunter)schlucken
swam [swæm] *pt of* **swim**
swamp [swɔmp] *n* Sumpf *m*
swan [swɔn] *n* Schwan *m*
swap [swɔp] *vt*: **to ~ (for)** (ein)tauschen (gegen)
sway [sweɪ] *vi* schwanken
swear [swɛə^r] (*pt* **swore**, *pp* **sworn**) *vi* (*curse*) fluchen ▸ *vt* (*promise*) schwören
swear by *vt* (*have faith in*) schwören auf *+acc*
swearword ['swɛəwə:d] *n* Fluch *m*
sweat [swɛt] *n* Schweiß *m* ▸ *vi* schwitzen
sweatband ['swɛtbænd] *n* Schweißband *nt*
sweater ['swɛtə^r] *n* Pullover *m*
sweatshirt ['swɛtʃə:t] *n* Sweatshirt *nt*
sweaty ['swɛtɪ] *adj* verschwitzt
Swede [swi:d] *n* Schwede *m*, Schwedin *f*
swede [swi:d] (BRIT) *n* Steckrübe *f*
Sweden ['swi:dn] *n* Schweden *nt*
Swedish ['swi:dɪʃ] *adj* schwedisch ▸ *n* Schwedisch *nt*
sweep [swi:p] (*pt, pp* **swept**) *vt* fegen, kehren ▸ *vi* (*wind*) fegen
▸ **sweep up** *vi* zusammenfegen, zusammenkehren
sweet [swi:t] *n* (*candy*) Bonbon *m or nt*; (BRIT *Culin*) Nachtisch *m* ▸ *adj* süß; (*kind*) lieb; **~ and sour** süß-sauer
sweetcorn ['swi:tkɔ:n] *n* Mais *m*
sweeten ['swi:tn] *vt* süßen
sweetener ['swi:tnə^r] *n* Süßstoff *m*
sweet potato *n* Süßkartoffel *f*
swell [swɛl] (*pt* **swelled**, *pp* **swollen** *or* **swelled**) *adj* (*US inf*) toll, prima ▸ *vi* (*also*: **~ up**) anschwellen

swelling [ˈswɛlɪŋ] *n* Schwellung *f*
sweltering [ˈswɛltərɪŋ] *adj* (*heat*) glühend
swept [swɛpt] *pt, pp of* **sweep**
swift [swɪft] *adj* schnell
swig [swɪg] (*inf*) *n* Schluck *m*
swim [swɪm] (*pt* **swam**, *pp* **swum**) *vi* schwimmen ▶ *n*: **to go for a ~** schwimmen gehen; **to go swimming** schwimmen gehen
swimmer [ˈswɪmə^{r}] *n* Schwimmer(in) *m(f)*
swimming [ˈswɪmɪŋ] *n* Schwimmen *nt*
swimming cap *n* Badekappe *f*
swimming costume (BRIT) *n* Badeanzug *m*
swimming pool *n* Schwimmbad *nt*
swimming trunks *npl* Badehose *f*
swimsuit [ˈswɪmsuːt] *n* Badeanzug *m*
swindle [ˈswɪndl] *vt*: **to ~ sb (out of sth)** jdn (um etw) betrügen *or* beschwindeln
swine [swaɪn] (*!*) *n* Schwein *nt*
swine flu *n* Schweinegrippe *f*
swing [swɪŋ] (*pt, pp* **swung**) *n* (*in playground*) Schaukel *f* ▶ *vt* (*arms, legs*) schwingen (mit)
swipe [swaɪp] *vt* (*inf: steal*) klauen
Swiss [swɪs] *adj* schweizerisch ▶ *n inv* Schweizer(in) *m(f)*
switch [swɪtʃ] *n* Schalter *m*
▶ **switch off** *vt* abschalten; (*light*) ausschalten
▶ **switch on** *vt* einschalten; (*radio*) anstellen
switchboard [ˈswɪtʃbɔːd] *n* Vermittlung *f*, Zentrale *f*
Switzerland [ˈswɪtsələnd] *n* die Schweiz *f*
swivel [ˈswɪvl] *vi* (*also:* **~ round**) sich (herum)drehen
swollen [ˈswəulən] *pp of* **swell** ▶ *adj* geschwollen
swop [swɔp] = **swap**
sword [sɔːd] *n* Schwert *nt*
swore [swɔː^{r}] *pt of* **swear**
sworn [swɔːn] *pp of* **swear**
swot [swɔt] *vi* pauken
swum [swʌm] *pp of* **swim**
swung [swʌŋ] *pt, pp of* **swing**
syllable [ˈsɪləbl] *n* Silbe *f*
syllabus [ˈsɪləbəs] *n* Lehrplan *m*
symbol [ˈsɪmbl] *n* Symbol *nt*
symbolic [sɪmˈbɔlɪk] *adj* symbolisch
symbolize [ˈsɪmbəlaɪz] *vt* symbolisieren
symmetrical [sɪˈmɛtrɪkl] *adj* symmetrisch
sympathetic [sɪmpəˈθɛtɪk] *adj* (*understanding*) verständnisvoll; (*showing pity*) mitfühlend
sympathize [ˈsɪmpəθaɪz] *vi*: **to ~ with** (*person*) Mitleid haben mit
sympathy [ˈsɪmpəθɪ] *n* Mitgefühl *nt*; **with our deepest ~** mit aufrichtigem *or* herzlichem Beileid
symphony [ˈsɪmfənɪ] *n* Sinfonie *f*
symptom [ˈsɪmptəm] *n* (*Med, fig*) Symptom *nt*
synagogue [ˈsɪnəgɔg] *n* Synagoge *f*
synonym [ˈsɪnənɪm] *n* Synonym *nt*
synonymous [sɪˈnɔnɪməs] *adj* (*fig*): **~ (with)** gleichbedeutend (mit)
synthetic [sɪnˈθɛtɪk] *adj* synthetisch
syphilis [ˈsɪfɪlɪs] *n* Syphilis *f*
Syria [ˈsɪrɪə] *n* Syrien *nt*
syringe [sɪˈrɪndʒ] *n* Spritze *f*
system [ˈsɪstəm] *n* System *nt*
systematic [sɪstəˈmætɪk] *adj* systematisch
system disk *n* (*Comput*) Systemdiskette *f*

tab [tæb] *n* (*on garment*) Etikett *nt*
table [ˈteɪbl] *n* Tisch *m*; (*Math, Chem etc*) Tabelle *f*
tablecloth [ˈteɪblklɔθ] *n* Tischdecke *f*
table lamp *n* Tischlampe *f*
tablemat [ˈteɪblmæt] *n* (*of cloth*) Set *m or nt*
table of contents *n* Inhaltsverzeichnis *nt*
tablespoon [ˈteɪblspuːn] *n* Esslöffel *m*; (*also*: **tablespoonful**) Esslöffel(voll) *m*
tablet [ˈtæblɪt] *n* (*Med*) Tablette *f*; (*Comput*) Tablet *nt*
table tennis *n* Tischtennis *nt*
table wine *n* Tafelwein *m*
tabloid [ˈtæblɔɪd] *n* (*newspaper*) Boulevardzeitung *f*
taboo [təˈbuː] *n* Tabu *nt* ▸ *adj* tabu
tacit [ˈtæsɪt] *adj* stillschweigend
tack [tæk] *n* (*nail*) Stift *m*
tackle [ˈtækl] *n* (*for fishing*) Ausrüstung *f*; (*Football, Rugby*) Angriff *m* ▸ *vt* (*deal with*: *difficulty*) in Angriff nehmen; (*challenge*: *person*) zur Rede stellen; (*physically, also Sport*) angreifen
tacky [ˈtækɪ] *adj* (*pej*: *cheap-looking*) schäbig
tact [tækt] *n* Takt *m*
tactful [ˈtæktful] *adj* taktvoll
tactics [ˈtæktɪks] *npl* Taktik *f*
tactless [ˈtæktlɪs] *adj* taktlos
tag [tæg] *n* (*label*) Anhänger *m*; **price/name ~** Preis-/Namensschild *nt*
▸ **tag along** *vi* sich anschließen
Tahiti [tɑːˈhiːtɪ] *n* Tahiti *nt*
tail [teɪl] *n* (*of animal*) Schwanz *m*
tailback [ˈteɪlbæk] (Brit) *n* (*Aut*) Stau *m*
taillight [ˈteɪllaɪt] *n* (*Aut*) Rücklicht *nt*
tailor [ˈteɪləʳ] *n* Schneider(in) *m(f)*
tainted [ˈteɪntɪd] *adj* (*food, water, air*) verdorben
Taiwan [ˈtaɪˈwɑːn] *n* Taiwan *nt*
take [teɪk] (*pt* **took**, *pp* **taken**) *vt* nehmen; (*photo, notes*) machen; (*decision*) fällen; (*tolerate*: *pain etc*) ertragen; (*hold*: *passengers etc*) fassen; (*accompany*: *person*) begleiten; (*carry, bring*) mitnehmen; (*exam, test*) machen; **I ~ it (that)** ich nehme an(, dass); **it won't ~ long** es dauert nicht lange; **I was quite taken with her/it** (*attracted to*) ich war von ihr/davon recht angetan
▸ **take after** *vt fus* (*resemble*) ähneln *+dat*, ähnlich sein *+dat*
▸ **take along** *vt* mitnehmen
▸ **take apart** *vt* auseinandernehmen
▸ **take away** *vt* wegnehmen; (*Math*) abziehen
▸ **take back** *vt* (*return*) zurückbringen; (*one's words*) zurücknehmen
▸ **take down** *vt* (*write down*) aufschreiben
▸ **take in** *vt* (*deceive*: *person*) hereinlegen, täuschen; (*understand*) begreifen; (*include*) einschließen; (*lodger*) aufnehmen
▸ **take off** *vi* (*Aviat*) starten ▸ *vt* (*clothes*) ausziehen; (*glasses*) abnehmen; (*imitate*: *person*) nachmachen
▸ **take on** *vt* (*work, responsibility*) übernehmen; (*employee*) einstellen; (*compete against*) antreten gegen
▸ **take out** *vt* (*invite*) ausgehen mit; (*remove*: *tooth*) herausnehmen; (*licence*) erwerben
▸ **take over** *vt* (*business*) übernehmen ▸ *vi* (*replace*): **to ~ over from sb** jdn ablösen
▸ **take to** *vt fus* (*person, thing*) mögen; (*form habit of*): **to ~ to doing sth** sich *dat* angewöhnen, etw zu tun
▸ **take up** *vt* (*hobby, sport*) anfangen mit; (*job*) antreten; (*idea etc*) annehmen; (*time, space*) beanspruchen
takeaway [ˈteɪkəweɪ] (Brit) *n* (*food*) Imbiss *m* (*zum Mitnehmen*)
taken [ˈteɪkən] *pp of* **take**
takeoff [ˈteɪkɔf] *n* (*Aviat*) Start *m*

takeout [ˈteɪkaut] (*US*) *n* = **takeaway**
takeover [ˈteɪkəuvəʳ] *n* (*Comm*) Übernahme *f*
takings [ˈteɪkɪŋz] *npl* Einnahmen *pl*
tale [teɪl] *n* Geschichte *f*
talent [ˈtælnt] *n* Talent *nt*
talented [ˈtæləntɪd] *adj* begabt
talk [tɔ:k] *n* (*speech*) Vortrag *m*; (*conversation, discussion*) Gespräch *nt*; (*gossip*) Gerede *nt* ▸ *vi* (*speak*) sprechen; (*chat*) reden; **to ~ about** (*discuss*) sprechen *or* reden über; **to ~ sb into doing sth** jdn zu etw überreden; **to ~ sb out of doing sth** jdm etw ausreden
▸ **talk over** *vt* (*problem etc*) besprechen
talkative [ˈtɔ:kətɪv] *adj* gesprächig
talk show *n* Talkshow *f*
tall [tɔ:l] *adj* (*person*) groß; (*glass, bookcase, tree, building*) hoch; **to be 6 feet ~** (*person*) ≈ 1,80m groß sein
tame [teɪm] *adj* (*animal, bird*) zahm; (*fig: story, party, performance*) lustlos
tampon [ˈtæmpɔn] *n* Tampon *m*
tan [tæn] *n* (*also:* **suntan**) (Sonnen)bräune *f* ▸ *vi* (*person, skin*) braun werden ▸ *adj* (*colour*) hellbraun; **to get a ~** braun werden
tangerine [tændʒəˈri:n] *n* (*fruit*) Mandarine *f*
tango [ˈtæŋgəu] *n* Tango *m*
tank [tæŋk] *n* Tank *m*; (*also:* **fish ~**) Aquarium *nt*; (*Mil*) Panzer *m*
tanker [ˈtæŋkəʳ] *n* (*ship*) Tanker *m*; (*truck*) Tankwagen *m*
tanned [tænd] *adj* (*person*) braun gebrannt
tantalizing [ˈtæntəlaɪzɪŋ] *adj* (*possibility*) verlockend
Tanzania [tænzəˈnɪə] *n* Tansania *nt*
tap [tæp] *n* (*on sink, gas tap*) Hahn *m* ▸ *vt* (*hit gently*) klopfen
tape [teɪp] *n* (*also:* **magnetic ~**) Tonband *nt*; (*cassette*) Kassette *f*; (*also:* **sticky ~**) Klebeband *nt* ▸ *vt* (*record, conversation*) aufnehmen
tape measure *n* Bandmaß *nt*
tape recorder *n* Tonband(gerät) *nt*
tapestry [ˈtæpɪstrɪ] *n* (*on wall*) Wandteppich *m*
tap water [ˈtæpwɔ:təʳ] *n* Leitungswasser *nt*
target [ˈtɑ:gɪt] *n* Ziel *nt*; (*fig: of joke, criticism etc*) Zielscheibe *f*
tariff [ˈtærɪf] *n* (*tax on goods*) Zoll *m*; (*BRIT: in hotels etc*) Preisliste *f*
tarmac® [ˈtɑ:mæk] *n* (*Aviat*): **on the ~** auf dem Rollfeld
tart [tɑ:t] *n* (*Culin*) Torte *f*; (*BRIT pej: prostitute*) Nutte *f*
tartan [ˈtɑ:tn] *n* Schottenstoff *m*
tartar sauce, tartare sauce [ˈtɑ:tə-] *n* Remouladensoße *f*
task [tɑ:sk] *n* Aufgabe *f*
taskbar [ˈtɑ:skbɑ:ʳ] *n* (*Comput*) Taskbar *f*
Tasmania [tæzˈmeɪnɪə] *n* Tasmanien *nt*
taste [teɪst] *n* Geschmack *m*; (*sample*) Kostprobe *f* ▸ *vt* (*get flavour of*) schmecken; (*test*) probieren ▸ *vi*: **to ~ of/like sth** nach/wie etw schmecken; **sense of ~** Geschmackssinn *m*
tasteful [ˈteɪstful] *adj* geschmackvoll
tasteless [ˈteɪstlɪs] *adj* geschmacklos
tasty [ˈteɪstɪ] *adj* schmackhaft
tattered [ˈtætəd] *adj* (*clothes, paper etc*) zerrissen; (*fig: hopes etc*) angeschlagen
tattoo [təˈtu:] *n* (*on skin*) Tätowierung *f*
taught [tɔ:t] *pt, pp of* **teach**
Taurus [ˈtɔ:rəs] *n* Stier *m*
tax [tæks] *n* Steuer *f* ▸ *vt* (*earnings, goods etc*) besteuern
taxable [ˈtæksəbl] *adj* steuerpflichtig
taxation [tækˈseɪʃən] *n* (*system*) Besteuerung *f*
tax disc (*BRIT*) *n* (*Aut*) Steuerplakette *f*
tax-free [ˈtæksfri:] *adj* steuerfrei
taxi [ˈtæksɪ] *n* Taxi *nt* ▸ *vi* (*Aviat: plane*) rollen
taxi driver *n* Taxifahrer(in) *m(f)*
taxi rank (*BRIT*) *n* Taxistand *m*
taxi stand *n* = **taxi rank**
tax return *n* Steuererklärung *f*
tea [ti:] *n* (*drink*) Tee *m*; (*BRIT: evening meal*) Abendessen *nt*; **afternoon ~** (*BRIT*) Nachmittagstee *m*
tea bag *n* Teebeutel *m*
tea break (*BRIT*) *n* Teepause *f*
teach [ti:tʃ] (*pt, pp* **taught**) *vt*: **to ~ sb sth, ~ sth to sb** (*instruct*) jdm etw beibringen; (*in school*) jdn in etw *dat* unterrichten ▸ *vi* unterrichten
teacher [ˈti:tʃəʳ] *n* Lehrer(in) *m(f)*
teaching [ˈti:tʃɪŋ] *n* (*work of teacher*) Unterricht *m*
teacup [ˈti:kʌp] *n* Teetasse *f*
team [ti:m] *n* (*Sport*) Mannschaft *f*, Team *nt*

teamwork [ˈtiːmwəːk] *n* Teamarbeit *f*
teapot [ˈtiːpɔt] *n* Teekanne *f*
tear¹ [tɛəʳ] (*pt* **tore**, *pp* **torn**) *n* (*hole*) Riss *m* ▸ *vt* (*rip*) zerreißen
▸ **tear up** *vt* (*sheet of paper etc*) zerreißen
tear² [tɪəʳ] *n* (*in eye*) Träne *f*
tearoom [ˈtiːruːm] *n* = **teashop**
tease [tiːz] *vt* necken
tea set *n* Teeservice *nt*
teashop [ˈtiːʃɔp] (Brit) *n* Teestube *f*
teaspoon [ˈtiːspuːn] *n* Teelöffel *m*
tea towel (Brit) *n* Geschirrtuch *nt*
technical [ˈtɛknɪkl] *adj* technisch; (*terms, language*) Fach-
technically [ˈtɛknɪklɪ] *adv* (*regarding technique*) technisch (gesehen)
technique [tɛkˈniːk] *n* Technik *f*
techno [ˈtɛknəu] *n* (*Mus*) Techno *nt*
technological [tɛknəˈlɔdʒɪkl] *adj* technologisch
technology [tɛkˈnɔlədʒɪ] *n* Technologie *f*
tedious [ˈtiːdɪəs] *adj* langweilig
teenage [ˈtiːneɪdʒ] *adj* (*fashions etc*) Jugend-
teenager [ˈtiːneɪdʒəʳ] *n* Teenager *m*
teens [tiːnz] *npl*: **to be in one's ~** im Teenageralter sein
teeth [tiːθ] *npl of* **tooth**
teetotal [ˈtiːˈtəutl] *adj* (*person*) abstinent
telegraph pole [ˈtɛlɪgrɑːf-] *n* Telegrafenmast *m*
telephone [ˈtɛlɪfəun] *n* Telefon *nt* ▸ *vt* (*person*) anrufen ▸ *vi* telefonieren
telephone box, (US) **telephone booth** *n* Telefonzelle *f*
telephone call *n* Anruf *m*
telephone directory *n* Telefonbuch *nt*
telephone number *n* Telefonnummer *f*
telephoto [ˈtɛlɪˈfəutəu] *adj*: **~ lens** Teleobjektiv *nt*
telescope [ˈtɛlɪskəup] *n* Teleskop *nt*
televise [ˈtɛlɪvaɪz] *vt* (im Fernsehen) übertragen
television [ˈtɛlɪvɪʒən] *n* Fernsehen *nt*
television programme *n* Fernsehprogramm *nt*
television set *n* Fernseher *m*
teleworking [ˈtɛlɪwəːkɪŋ] *n* Telearbeit *f*
tell [tɛl] (*pt, pp* **told**) *vt* (*say*) sagen; (*relate*: *story*) erzählen; (*distinguish*): **to ~ sth from** etw unterscheiden von; (*be sure*) wissen ▸ *vi* (*have an effect*) sich auswirken; **to ~ sb to do sth** jdm sagen, etw zu tun; **I can't ~ them apart** ich kann sie nicht unterscheiden
▸ **tell off** *vt*: **to ~ sb off** jdn ausschimpfen
telling [ˈtɛlɪŋ] *adj* (*remark etc*) verräterisch
telly [ˈtɛlɪ] (Brit *inf*) *n abbr* = **television**
temp [tɛmp] (Brit *inf*) *n abbr* (= *temporary office worker*) Zeitarbeitskraft *f* ▸ *vi* als Zeitarbeitskraft arbeiten
temper [ˈtɛmpəʳ] *n* (*mood*) Laune *f*; **a (fit of) ~** ein Wutanfall *m*; **to lose one's ~** die Beherrschung verlieren
temperamental [tɛmprəˈmɛntl] *adj* (*person, car*) launisch
temperature [ˈtɛmprətʃəʳ] *n* Temperatur *f*; **to have** *or* **run a ~** Fieber haben
temple [ˈtɛmpl] *n* (*building*) Tempel *m*; (*Anat*) Schläfe *f*
temporarily [ˈtɛmpərərɪlɪ] *adv* vorübergehend
temporary [ˈtɛmpərərɪ] *adj* (*arrangement*) provisorisch; (*worker, job*) Aushilfs-
tempt [tɛmpt] *vt* in Versuchung führen; **to be tempted to do sth** versucht sein, etw zu tun
temptation [tɛmpˈteɪʃən] *n* Versuchung *f*
tempting [ˈtɛmptɪŋ] *adj* (*offer*) verlockend
ten [tɛn] *num* zehn ▸ *n*: **tens of thousands** Zehntausende *pl*
tenant [ˈtɛnənt] *n* (*of room*) Mieter(in) *m(f)*; (*of land*) Pächter(in) *m(f)*
tend [tɛnd] *vi*: **to ~ to do sth** dazu neigen *or* tendieren, etw zu tun
tendency [ˈtɛndənsɪ] *n* (*of person*) Neigung *f*; (*of thing*) Tendenz *f*
tender [ˈtɛndəʳ] *adj* (*person, care*) zärtlich; (*sore*) empfindlich; (*meat, age*) zart
tendon [ˈtɛndən] *n* Sehne *f*
Tenerife [tɛnəˈriːf] *n* Teneriffa *nt*
tenner [ˈtɛnəʳ] (Brit *inf*) *n* Zehner *m*
tennis [ˈtɛnɪs] *n* Tennis *nt*
tennis ball *n* Tennisball *m*
tennis court *n* Tennisplatz *m*
tennis racket *n* Tennisschläger *m*
tenor [ˈtɛnəʳ] *n* (*Mus*) Tenor *m*

tenpin bowling [ˈtɛnpɪn-] (BRIT) *n* Bowling *nt*
tense [tɛns] *adj* (*person, muscle*) angespannt; (*period, situation*) gespannt
tension [ˈtɛnʃən] *n* (*nervousness*) Angespanntheit *f*; (*between ropes etc*) Spannung *f*
tent [tɛnt] *n* Zelt *nt*
tenth [tɛnθ] *num* zehnte(r, s) ▶ *n* Zehntel *nt*
tent peg *n* Hering *m*
tent pole *n* Zeltstange *f*
term [təːm] *n* (*word*) Ausdruck *m*; (*Scol: three per year*) Trimester *nt* ■ **terms** *npl* (*also Comm*) Bedingungen *pl*; **in the short/long ~** auf kurze/lange Sicht; **to be on good terms with sb** sich mit jdm gut verstehen; **to come to terms with** (*problem*) sich abfinden mit
terminal [ˈtəːmɪnl] *adj* (*disease, patient*) unheilbar ▶ *n* (*Aviat, Comm, Comput*) Terminal *nt*; (*Elec*) Anschluss *m*; (BRIT: *also*: **bus ~**) Endstation *f*
terminally [ˈtəːmɪnlɪ] *adv* (*ill*) unheilbar
terminate [ˈtəːmɪneɪt] *vt* beenden ▶ *vi*: **to ~ in** enden in +*dat*
terminology [təːmɪˈnɔlədʒɪ] *n* Terminologie *f*
terrace [ˈtɛrəs] *n* (BRIT: *row of houses*) Häuserreihe *f*; (*Agr, patio*) Terrasse *f*
terraced [ˈtɛrəst] *adj* (*garden*) terrassenförmig angelegt; (*house*) Reihen-
terrible [ˈtɛrɪbl] *adj* schrecklich
terrific [təˈrɪfɪk] *adj* (*time, party*) sagenhaft
terrify [ˈtɛrɪfaɪ] *vt* erschrecken
territory [ˈtɛrɪtərɪ] *n* (*also fig*) Gebiet *nt*
terror [ˈtɛrəʳ] *n* (*great fear*) panische Angst *f*
terrorism [ˈtɛrərɪzəm] *n* Terrorismus *m*
terrorist [ˈtɛrərɪst] *n* Terrorist(in) *m(f)*
test [tɛst] *n* Test *m*; (*Scol*) Prüfung *f*; (*also*: **driving ~**) Fahrprüfung *f* ▶ *vt* testen; (*check, Scol*) prüfen; **to put sth to the ~** etw auf die Probe stellen
testament [ˈtɛstəmənt] *n* Zeugnis *nt*; **the Old/New T~** das Alte/Neue Testament
testicle [ˈtɛstɪkl] *n* Hoden *m*
testify [ˈtɛstɪfaɪ] *vi* (*Law*) aussagen
test tube *n* Reagenzglas *nt*
tetanus [ˈtɛtənəs] *n* Tetanus *m*
text [tɛkst] *n* Text *m*; (*sent by mobile phone*) SMS *f* ▶ *vt* (*on mobile phone*): **to ~ sb** jdm eine SMS schicken
textbook [ˈtɛkstbuk] *n* Lehrbuch *nt*
texting [ˈtekstɪŋ] *n* SMS-Messaging *nt*
text message *n* (*Tel*) SMS *f*
text messaging *n* (*Tel*) Textnachrichten *pl*
texture [ˈtɛkstʃəʳ] *n* Beschaffenheit *f*
Thailand [ˈtaɪlænd] *n* Thailand *nt*
Thames [tɛmz] *n*: **the ~** die Themse
than [ðæn] *conj* (*in comparisons*) als; **she is older ~ you think** sie ist älter, als Sie denken
thank [θæŋk] *vt* danken +*dat*; **~ you** danke; **~ you very much** vielen Dank
thankful [ˈθæŋkful] *adj*: **~ (for/that)** dankbar (für/, dass)
thankfully [ˈθæŋkfəlɪ] *adv*: **~ there were few victims** zum Glück gab es nur wenige Opfer
thankless [ˈθæŋklɪs] *adj* undankbar
thanks [θæŋks] *npl* Dank *m* ▶ *excl* (*also*: **many ~, ~ a lot**) danke, vielen Dank; **~ to** dank +*gen*
Thanksgiving [ˈθæŋksgɪvɪŋ], (*US*) **Thanksgiving Day** *n siehe Info-Artikel*

THANKSGIVING (DAY)

Thanksgiving (Day) ist ein Feiertag in den USA, der auf den vierten Donnerstag im November fällt. Er soll daran erinnern, wie die Pilgerväter die gute Ernte im Jahre 1621 feierten. In Kanada gibt es einen ähnlichen Erntedanktag (der aber nichts mit den Pilgervätern zu tun hat) am zweiten Montag im Oktober.

 **KEYWORD**

that [ðæt, ðət] (*pl* **those**) *adj* (*demonstrative*) der/die/das; **that one** der/die/das da
▶ *pron* **1** (*demonstrative*) das; **who's/what's that?** wer/was ist das?; **is that you?** bist du das?; **that's what he said** das hat er gesagt; **what happened after that?** was geschah danach?; **that is (to say)** das heißt
2 (*relative: subject*) der/die/das; (: *pl*)

die; (: *direct object*) den/die/das; (: *pl*) die; (: *indirect object*) dem/der/dem; (: *pl*) denen; **all that I have** alles was ich habe
3 (*relative*: *of time*): **the day that he came** der Tag, an dem er kam; **the winter that he came to see us** der Winter, in dem er uns besuchte
▶ *conj* dass; **he thought that I was ill** er dachte, dass ich krank sei, er dachte, ich sei krank
▶ *adv* (*demonstrative*) so; **I can't work that much** ich kann nicht so viel arbeiten

thaw [θɔ:] *vi* (*ice*) tauen; (*food*) auftauen ▶ *vt* (*also*: **~ out**) auftauen

KEYWORD

the [ði:, ðə] *def art* **1** (*before masculine noun*) der; (*before feminine noun*) die; (*before neuter noun*) das; (*before plural noun*) die; **to play the piano/violin** Klavier/Geige spielen; **I'm going to the butcher's/the cinema** ich gehe zum Metzger/ins Kino
2 (*+ adj to form noun*): **the rich and the poor** die Reichen und die Armen
3 (*in titles*): **Elizabeth the First** Elisabeth die Erste
4 (*in comparisons*): **the more he works the more he earns** je mehr er arbeitet, desto mehr verdient er

theatre, (*US*) **theater** [ˈθɪətəʳ] *n* Theater *nt*; (*also*: **lecture ~**) Hörsaal *m*
theft [θɛft] *n* Diebstahl *m*
their [ðɛəʳ] *adj* ihr
theirs [ðɛəz] *pron* ihre(r, s); **a friend of ~** ein Freund/eine Freundin von ihnen; *see also* **my**; **mine²**
them [ðɛm] *pron* (*direct*) sie; (*indirect*) ihnen; **I see ~** ich sehe sie; **give ~ the book** gib ihnen das Buch; **give me a few of ~** geben Sie mir ein paar davon; **with ~** mit ihnen; **without ~** ohne sie; *see also* **me**
theme [θi:m] *n* (*also Mus*) Thema *nt*
theme park *n* Themenpark *m*
theme song *n* Titelmusik *f*
themselves [ðəmˈsɛlvz] *pl pron* (*reflexive, after prep*) sich; (*emphatic, alone*) selbst

then [ðɛn] *adv* (*at that time*) damals; (*next, later*) dann ▶ *conj* (*therefore*) also ▶ *adj*: **the ~ president** der damalige Präsident; **by ~** (*past*) bis dahin; **from ~ on** von da an
theoretical [θɪəˈrɛtɪkl] *adj* theoretisch
theory [ˈθɪərɪ] *n* Theorie *f*; **in ~** theoretisch
therapy [ˈθɛrəpɪ] *n* Therapie *f*

KEYWORD

there [ðɛəʳ] *adv* **1**: **there is/are** da ist/sind; (*there exist(s)*) es gibt; **there are 3 of them** es gibt 3 davon; **there has been an accident** da war ein Unfall
2 (*referring to place*) da, dort; **down/over there** da unten/drüben; **put it in/on there** leg es dorthinein/-hinauf
3: **there, there** (*esp to child*) ist ja gut

thereabouts [ˈðɛərəˈbauts] *adv*: **or ~** (*amount, time*) oder so
therefore [ˈðɛəfɔ:ʳ] *adv* daher, deshalb
thermometer [θəˈmɔmɪtəʳ] *n* Thermometer *nt*
Thermos® [ˈθə:məs] *n* (*also*: **~ flask**) Thermosflasche® *f*
these [ði:z] *pl adj, pl pron* diese
thesis [ˈθi:sɪs] (*pl* **theses**) *n* These *f*; (*for doctorate etc*) Doktorarbeit *f*
they [ðeɪ] *pl pron* sie; **~ say that ...** (*it is said that*) man sagt, dass ...
they'd [ðeɪd] = **they had**; **they would**
they'll [ðeɪl] = **they shall**; **they will**
they've [ðeɪv] = **they have**
thick [θɪk] *adj* dick; (*sauce etc*) dickflüssig; (*fog, forest, hair etc*) dicht; (*inf*: *stupid*) blöd
thicken [ˈθɪkn] *vi* (*fog etc*) sich verdichten ▶ *vt* (*sauce etc*) eindicken
thief [θi:f] (*pl* **thieves**) *n* Dieb(in) *m(f)*
thigh [θaɪ] *n* Oberschenkel *m*
thimble [ˈθɪmbl] *n* Fingerhut *m*
thin [θɪn] *adj* dünn
thing [θɪŋ] *n* Ding *nt*; (*matter*) Sache *f* ■ **things** *npl* (*belongings*) Sachen *pl*; **how are things?** wie gehts?
think [θɪŋk] (*pt, pp* **thought**) *vi* (*reason*) denken ▶ *vt* (*be of the opinion*) denken; (*believe*) glauben; **to ~ of** denken an *+acc*; (*recall*) sich erinnern an *+acc*; **what did you ~ of them?** was

hielten Sie von ihnen?; **I ~ so/not** ich glaube ja/nein
▸ **think over** *vt* (*offer, suggestion*) überdenken
▸ **think up** *vt* sich *dat* ausdenken

third [θəːd] *num* dritte(r, s) ▸ *n* (*fraction*) Drittel *nt*; (*Aut*: *also*: **~ gear**) dritter Gang *m*

thirdly [ˈθəːdlɪ] *adv* drittens

third party insurance (Brit) *n* ≈ Haftpflichtversicherung *f*

Third World *n*: **the ~** die Dritte Welt

thirst [θəːst] *n* Durst *m*

thirsty [ˈθəːstɪ] *adj*: **to be ~** Durst haben

thirteen [θəːˈtiːn] *num* dreizehn

thirteenth [ˈθəːˈtiːnθ] *num* dreizehnte(r, s)

thirtieth [ˈθəːtɪɪθ] *num* dreißigste(r, s)

thirty [ˈθəːtɪ] *num* dreißig

 **KEYWORD**

this [ðɪs] (*pl* **these**) *adj* (*demonstrative*) diese(r, s); **this one** diese(r, s) (hier)
▸ *pron* (*demonstrative*) dies, das; **who/what is this?** wer/was ist das?; **this is where I live** hier wohne ich; **this is what he said** das hat er gesagt; **this is Mr Brown** (*in introductions, photo*) das ist Herr Brown; (*on telephone*) hier ist Herr Brown
▸ *adv* (*demonstrative*): **this high/long** *etc* so hoch/lang *etc*

thistle [ˈθɪsl] *n* Distel *f*

thong [θɔŋ] *n* Riemen *m*

thorn [θɔːn] *n* Dorn *m*

thorough [ˈθʌrə] *adj* gründlich

thoroughly [ˈθʌrəlɪ] *adv* gründlich

those [ðəuz] *pl adj, pl pron* die (da); **~ (of you) who ...** diejenigen (von Ihnen), die ...

though [ðəu] *conj* obwohl ▸ *adv* aber; **even ~** obwohl

thought [θɔːt] *pt, pp of* **think** ▸ *n* Gedanke *m*; **after much ~** nach langer Überlegung

thoughtful [ˈθɔːtful] *adj* (*deep in thought*) nachdenklich; (*considerate*) aufmerksam

thoughtless [ˈθɔːtlɪs] *adj* gedankenlos

thousand [ˈθauzənd] *num* (ein) tausend; **two ~** zweitausend; **thousands of** Tausende von

thrash [θræʃ] *vt* (*beat*) verprügeln; (*defeat*) (vernichtend) schlagen

thread [θrɛd] *n* (*yarn*) Faden *m* ▸ *vt* (*needle*) einfädeln

threat [θrɛt] *n* Drohung *f*; (*fig*): **~ (to)** Gefahr *f* (für)

threaten [ˈθrɛtn] *vt*: **to ~ sb with sth** jdm mit etw drohen

threatening [ˈθrɛtnɪŋ] *adj* bedrohlich

three [θriː] *num* drei

three-dimensional [θriːdɪˈmɛnʃənl] *adj* dreidimensional

three-piece suit [ˈθriːpiːs-] *n* dreiteiliger Anzug *m*

three-quarters [θriːˈkwɔːtəz] *npl* drei Viertel *pl*

threshold [ˈθrɛʃhəuld] *n* Schwelle *f*

threw [θruː] *pt of* **throw**

thrifty [ˈθrɪftɪ] *adj* sparsam

thrill [θrɪl] *n* (*excitement*) Aufregung *f* ▸ *vt*: **to be thrilled** (*with gift etc*) sich riesig freuen

thriller [ˈθrɪlə^r] *n* Thriller *m*

thrilling [ˈθrɪlɪŋ] *adj* (*news*) aufregend

thrive [θraɪv] *vi* gedeihen

throat [θrəut] *n* Kehle *f*

throb [θrɔb] *n* (*of heart*) Klopfen *nt*; **my head is throbbing** ich habe rasende Kopfschmerzen

thrombosis [θrɔmˈbəusɪs] *n* Thrombose *f*

throne [θrəun] *n* Thron *m*

through [θruː] *prep* durch; (*time*) während ▸ *adj* (*ticket, train*) durchgehend ▸ *adv* durch; **to be ~** (*Tel*) verbunden sein; **to be ~ with sb/sth** mit jdm/etw fertig sein; **to put sb ~ to sb** (*Tel*) jdn mit jdm verbinden

throughout [θruːˈaut] *adv* (*everywhere*) überall; (*the whole time*) die ganze Zeit über ▸ *prep* (*place*) überall in +*dat*; (*time*): **~ the morning/afternoon** während des ganzen Morgens/Nachmittags; **~ her life** ihr ganzes Leben lang

throw [θrəu] (*pt* **threw**, *pp* **thrown**) *n* Wurf *m* ▸ *vt* werfen; (*rider*) abwerfen; (*fig*: *confuse*) aus der Fassung bringen; **to ~ a party** eine Party geben
▸ **throw away** *vt* wegwerfen
▸ **throw out** *vt* (*rubbish*) wegwerfen; (*person*) hinauswerfen
▸ **throw up** *vi* (*vomit*) sich übergeben

throw-in [ˈθrəuɪn] *n* (*Football*) Einwurf *m*

thrown [θrəun] *pp of* **throw**
thru [θru:] (*US*) *prep, adj, adv* = **through**
thrush [θrʌʃ] *n* (*bird*) Drossel *f*
thrust [θrʌst] (*pt, pp* **~**) *vt* stoßen
thumb [θʌm] *n* Daumen *m* ▸ *vt*: **to ~ a lift** per Anhalter fahren
thumbtack [ˈθʌmtæk] (*US*) *n* Heftzwecke *f*
thunder [ˈθʌndəʳ] *n* Donner *m* ▸ *vi* donnern
thunderstorm [ˈθʌndəstɔ:m] *n* Gewitter *nt*
Thur., Thurs. *abbr* (= *Thursday*) Do.
Thursday [ˈθə:zdɪ] *n* Donnerstag *m*
thus [ðʌs] *adv* (*in this way*) so; (*consequently*) somit
thyme [taɪm] *n* Thymian *m*
Tibet [tɪˈbɛt] *n* Tibet *nt*
tick [tɪk] *n* (*mark*) Häkchen *nt* ▸ *vi* (*clock, watch*) ticken ▸ *vt* (*item on list*) abhaken
ticket [ˈtɪkɪt] *n* (*for public transport*) Fahrkarte *f*; (*for theatre etc*) Eintrittskarte *f*; (*in shop: on goods*) Preisschild *nt*; (*for raffle*) Los *nt*; (*fine: also:* **parking ~**) Strafzettel *m*
ticket collector *n* (*Rail: at station*) Fahrkartenkontrolleur(in) *m*(*f*)
ticket machine *n* (*for public transport*) Fahrscheinautomat *m*; (*in car park*) Parkscheinautomat *m*
ticket office *n* (*Rail*) Fahrkartenschalter *m*; (*Theat*) Theaterkasse *f*
tickle [ˈtɪkl] *vt* kitzeln
ticklish [ˈtɪklɪʃ] *adj* (*person, situation*) kitzlig
tide [taɪd] *n* (*in sea*) Gezeiten *pl*; **the ~ is in/out** es ist Flut/Ebbe
tidy [ˈtaɪdɪ] *adj* (*room, desk*) ordentlich ▸ *vt* (*also:* **~ up**) aufräumen
tie [taɪ] *n* (Brit: *also:* **necktie**) Krawatte *f*; (*fig: link*) Verbindung *f*; (*Sport: match*) Spiel *nt*; (*: draw*) Unentschieden *nt* ▸ *vt* (*ribbon*) binden ▸ *vi* (*Sport etc*): **to ~ with sb for first place** sich mit jdm den ersten Platz teilen; **family ties** familiäre Bindungen; **to ~ sth in a bow** etw zu einer Schleife binden; **to ~ a knot in sth** einen Knoten in etw *acc* machen
▸ **tie down** *vt* (*fig: restrict*) binden; (*: to date, price etc*) festlegen
▸ **tie up** *vt* (*parcel*) verschnüren; (*dog*) anbinden; (*boat*) festmachen; **to be tied up** (*busy*) zu tun haben, beschäftigt sein
tiger [ˈtaɪgəʳ] *n* Tiger *m*
tight [taɪt] *adj* (*screw, knot, grip*) fest; (*shoes, clothes, bend*) eng; (*security*) streng; (*budget, money*) knapp; (*schedule*) gedrängt ▸ *adv* fest; **everybody hold ~!** alle festhalten!
tighten [ˈtaɪtn] *vt* (*rope, strap*) straffen; (*screw, bolt*) anziehen; (*security*) verschärfen
tights [taɪts] (Brit) *npl* Strumpfhose *f*
tile [taɪl] *n* (*on roof*) Ziegel *m*; (*on floor*) Fliese *f*
tiled [taɪld] *adj* (*floor*) mit Fliesen ausgelegt; (*wall*) gekachelt
till [tɪl] *n* (*in shop etc*) Kasse *f* ▸ *prep, conj* = **until**
tilt [tɪlt] *vt* neigen ▸ *vi* sich neigen
time [taɪm] *n* Zeit *f*; (*occasion*) Mal *nt*; (*Mus*) Takt *m* ▸ *vt* (*measure time of*) die Zeit messen bei; (*runner*) stoppen; **for the ~ being** vorläufig; **4 at a ~** 4 auf einmal; **at times** manchmal, zuweilen; **in ~** (*soon enough*) rechtzeitig; **on ~** rechtzeitig; **by the ~ he arrived** als er ankam; **5 times 5** 5 mal 5; **what ~ is it?** wie spät ist es?; **to have a good ~** sich amüsieren; **to ~ sth well/badly** den richtigen/falschen Zeitpunkt für etw wählen
time difference *n* Zeitunterschied *m*
time-lapse (photography) *n* Zeitraffer-Fotografie *f*
time limit *n* zeitliche Grenze *f*
timer [ˈtaɪməʳ] *n* (*time switch*) Schaltuhr *f*; (*on video*) Timer *m*
time-saving [ˈtaɪmseɪvɪŋ] *adj* zeitsparend
time switch *n* Zeitschalter *m*
timetable [ˈtaɪmteɪbl] *n* (*Rail etc*) Fahrplan *m*; (*Scol*) Stundenplan *m*
time zone *n* Zeitzone *f*
timid [ˈtɪmɪd] *adj* (*person*) schüchtern
timing [ˈtaɪmɪŋ] *n* (*Sport*) Timing *nt*; **the ~ of his resignation** der Zeitpunkt seines Rücktritts
tin [tɪn] *n* (*metal*) Blech *nt*; (Brit: *can*) Dose *f*
tinfoil [ˈtɪnfɔɪl] *n* Alufolie *f*
tinned [tɪnd] (Brit) *adj* (*food, peas*) Dosen-, in Dosen
tin-opener [ˈtɪnəupnəʳ] (Brit) *n* Dosenöffner *m*

tinsel [ˈtɪnsl] *n* Rauschgoldgirlanden *pl*
tint [tɪnt] *n* (*colour*) Ton *m*; (*for hair*) Tönung *f*
tinted [ˈtɪntɪd] *adj* getönt
tiny [ˈtaɪnɪ] *adj* winzig
tip [tɪp] *n* (*end*) Spitze *f*; (*gratuity*) Trinkgeld *nt*; (Brit: *for rubbish*) Müllkippe *f*; (*advice*) Tipp *m* ▶ *vt* (*waiter*) ein Trinkgeld geben +*dat*; (*overturn*: *also*: **~ over**) umkippen
tipsy [ˈtɪpsɪ] (*inf*) *adj* beschwipst
tiptoe [ˈtɪptəu] *n*: **on ~** auf Zehenspitzen
tire [ˈtaɪəʳ] *n* (*US*) = **tyre** ▶ *vt* müde machen ▶ *vi* (*become tired*) müde werden
tired [ˈtaɪəd] *adj* müde; **to be ~ of sth** etw satthaben; **to be ~ of doing sth** es satthaben, etw zu tun
tireless [ˈtaɪəlɪs] *adj* unermüdlich
tiresome [ˈtaɪəsəm] *adj* lästig
tiring [ˈtaɪərɪŋ] *adj* ermüdend
tissue [ˈtɪʃuː] *n* (*Anat, Biol*) Gewebe *nt*; (*paper handkerchief*) Papiertaschentuch *nt*
tissue paper *n* Seidenpapier *nt*
tit [tɪt] *n* (*bird*) Meise *f*; (*inf*: *breast*) Titte *f*
title [ˈtaɪtl] *n* Titel *m*
titter [ˈtɪtəʳ] *vi* kichern

KEYWORD

to [tuː] *prep* **1** (*direction*) nach +*dat*, zu +*dat*; **to go to France/London/school/the station** nach Frankreich/nach London/zur Schule/zum Bahnhof gehen; **to the left/right** nach links/rechts
2 (*as far as*) bis
3 (*with expressions of time*) vor +*dat*; **a quarter to 5** (Brit) Viertel vor 5
4 (*for, of*): **a letter to his wife** ein Brief an seine Frau
5 (*expressing indirect object*): **to give sth to sb** jdm etw geben; **to talk to sb** mit jdm sprechen; **I sold it to a friend** ich habe es an einen Freund verkauft
6 (*in relation to*) zu; **40 miles to the gallon** 40 Meilen pro Gallone
7 (*purpose, result*) zu; **to my surprise** zu meiner Überraschung
▶ *prep* (*with vb*) **1** (*simple infinitive*): **to go** gehen; **to eat** essen
2 (*following another vb*): **to want to do sth** etw tun wollen; **to try/start to do sth** versuchen/anfangen, etw zu tun
3 (*with vb omitted*): **I don't want to** ich will nicht
4 (*purpose, result*) (um ...) zu; **I did it to help you** ich habe es getan, um dir zu helfen
5 (*equivalent to relative clause*) zu; **he has a lot to lose** er hat viel zu verlieren
6 (*after adjective etc*): **ready to use** gebrauchsfertig; **too old/young to ...** zu alt/jung, um zu ...
▶ *adv*: **to push/pull the door to** die Tür zudrücken/zuziehen

toad [təud] *n* Kröte *f*
toadstool [ˈtəudstuːl] *n* Giftpilz *m*
toast [təust] *n* (*bread, drink*) Toast *m* ▶ *vt* (*bread etc*) toasten; (*drink to*) einen Toast *or* Trinkspruch ausbringen auf +*acc*; **a piece** *or* **slice of ~** eine Scheibe Toast
toaster [ˈtəustəʳ] *n* Toaster *m*
tobacco [təˈbækəu] *n* Tabak *m*
tobacconist's [təˈbækənɪsts], **tobacconist's shop** *n* Tabakwarenladen *m*
toboggan [təˈbɔgən] *n* Schlitten *m*
today [təˈdeɪ] *adv, n* heute; **~'s paper** die Zeitung von heute
toddler [ˈtɔdləʳ] *n* Kleinkind *nt*
toe [təu] *n* Zehe *f*, Zeh *m*
toenail [ˈtəuneɪl] *n* Zehennagel *m*
toffee [ˈtɔfɪ] *n* Toffee *m*
toffee apple (Brit) *n* ≈ kandierter Apfel *m*
tofu [ˈtəufuː] *n* Tofu *m*
together [təˈgɛðəʳ] *adv* zusammen
toilet [ˈtɔɪlət] *n* Toilette *f*; **to go to the ~** auf die Toilette gehen
toilet bag (Brit) *n* Kulturbeutel *m*
toilet paper *n* Toilettenpapier *nt*
toiletries [ˈtɔɪlətrɪz] *npl* Toilettenartikel *pl*
toilet roll *n* Rolle *f* Toilettenpapier
token [ˈtəukən] *n* (*sign, souvenir*) Zeichen *nt*; (*substitute coin*) Wertmarke *f*; **book/record/gift ~** (Brit) Bücher-/Platten-/Geschenkgutschein *m*
Tokyo [ˈtəukjəu] *n* Tokio *nt*
told [təuld] *pt, pp of* **tell**
tolerant [ˈtɔlərnt] *adj* tolerant; **to be ~ of sth** tolerant gegenüber etw sein
tolerate [ˈtɔləreɪt] *vt* (*pain, noise*) erdulden, ertragen; (*injustice*) tolerieren

toll [təul] *n* (*of casualties, deaths*) (Gesamt)zahl *f*; (*tax, charge*) Gebühr *f*
toll-free [ˈtəulfriː] (*US*) *adj* gebührenfrei
toll road *n* gebührenpflichtige Straße *f*
tomato [təˈmɑːtəu] (*pl* **tomatoes**) *n* Tomate *f*
tomato ketchup *n* Tomatenketchup *m or nt*
tomato sauce *n* Tomatensoße *f*; (BRIT: *ketchup*) Tomatenketchup *m or nt*
tomb [tuːm] *n* Grab *nt*
tombstone [ˈtuːmstəun] *n* Grabstein *m*
tomorrow [təˈmɔrəu] *adv* morgen ▸ *n* morgen; (*future*) Zukunft *f*; **the day after ~** übermorgen; **~ morning** morgen früh
ton [tʌn] *n* (BRIT) (britische) Tonne *f*; (*US: also:* **short ~**) (US-)Tonne *f* (*ca. 907 kg*); (*also:* **metric ~**) (metrische) Tonne *f*; **tons of** (*inf*) Unmengen von
tone [təun] *n* Ton *m*
▸ **tone down** *vt* (*also fig*) abschwächen
toner [ˈtəunəʳ] *n* (*for photocopier*) Toner *m*
toner cartridge *n* Tonerpatrone *f*
tongs [tɔŋz] *npl* Zange *f*; (*also:* **curling ~**) Lockenstab *m*
tongue [tʌŋ] *n* Zunge *f*
tonic [ˈtɔnɪk] *n* (*Med*) Tonikum *nt*; (*also:* **~ water**) Tonic *nt*
tonight [təˈnaɪt] *adv* (*this evening*) heute Abend; (*this night*) heute Nacht
tonsil [ˈtɔnsl] *n* Mandel *f*
tonsillitis [tɔnsɪˈlaɪtɪs] *n* Mandelentzündung *f*
too [tuː] *adv* (*excessively*) zu; (*also*) auch; **~ much** (*adj*) zu viel; (*adv*) zu sehr; **~ many** zu viele
took [tuk] *pt of* **take**
tool [tuːl] *n* (*also fig*) Werkzeug *nt*
toolbar [ˈtuːlbɑːʳ] *n* (*Comput*) Symbolleiste *f*
tool box *n* Werkzeugkasten *m*
tooth [tuːθ] (*pl* **teeth**) *n* (*also Tech*) Zahn *m*
toothache [ˈtuːθeɪk] *n* Zahnschmerzen *pl*
toothbrush [ˈtuːθbrʌʃ] *n* Zahnbürste *f*
toothpaste [ˈtuːθpeɪst] *n* Zahnpasta *f*
toothpick [ˈtuːθpɪk] *n* Zahnstocher *m*
top [tɔp] *n* (*of mountain, tree, ladder*) Spitze *f*; (*of cupboard, table, box*) Oberseite *f*; (*of street*) Ende *nt*; (*lid*) Verschluss *m*; (*Aut: also:* **~ gear**) höchster Gang *m*; (*blouse etc*) Oberteil *nt* ▸ *adj* höchste(r, s); (*highest in rank*) oberste(r, s) ▸ *vt* (*poll, vote, list*) anführen; (*estimate etc*) übersteigen; **at the ~ of the stairs/page** oben auf der Treppe/Seite; **on ~ of** (*above*) auf +*dat*; (*in addition to*) zusätzlich zu; **at the ~ of the list** oben auf der Liste; **over the ~** (*inf: behaviour etc*) übertrieben
▸ **top up**, (*US*) **top off** *vt* (*drink*) nachfüllen
topic [ˈtɔpɪk] *n* Thema *nt*
topical [ˈtɔpɪkl] *adj* (*issue etc*) aktuell
topless [ˈtɔplɪs] *adj* (*waitress*) Oben-ohne- ▸ *adv* oben ohne
topping [ˈtɔpɪŋ] *n* (*Culin*) Überzug *m*
top-secret [ˈtɔpˈsiːkrɪt] *adj* streng geheim
torch [tɔːtʃ] *n* Fackel *f*; (BRIT: *electric*) Taschenlampe *f*
tore [tɔːʳ] *pt of* **tear²**
torment *n* [ˈtɔːmɛnt] Qual *f* ▸ *vt* [tɔːˈmɛnt] quälen
torn [tɔːn] *pp of* **tear²**
tornado [tɔːˈneɪdəu] (*pl* **tornadoes**) *n* (*storm*) Tornado *m*
torrential [tɔˈrɛnʃl] *adj* (*rain*) wolkenbruchartig
tortoise [ˈtɔːtəs] *n* Schildkröte *f*
torture [ˈtɔːtʃəʳ] *n* Folter *f*; (*fig*) Qual *f* ▸ *vt* foltern
Tory [ˈtɔːrɪ] (BRIT *Pol*) *adj* konservativ ▸ *n* Tory *m*, Konservative(r) *f*(*m*)
toss [tɔs] *vt* (*throw*) werfen; (*salad*) anmachen; **to ~ a coin** eine Münze werfen
total [ˈtəutl] *adj* (*number etc*) gesamt ▸ *n* Gesamtzahl *f* ▸ *vt* (*add up to*) sich belaufen auf; **in ~** insgesamt
totally [ˈtəutəlɪ] *adv* völlig
touch [tʌtʃ] *n* (*sense of touch*) Gefühl *nt*; (*contact*) Berührung *f* ▸ *vt* berühren; (*emotionally*) rühren; **in ~ with** (*person, group*) in Verbindung mit; **to get in ~ with sb** mit jdm in Verbindung treten; **to lose ~** (*friends*) den Kontakt verlieren
▸ **touch on** *vt fus* (*topic*) berühren
touchdown [ˈtʌtʃdaun] *n* (*of rocket, plane*) Landung *f*; (*US Football*) Touchdown *m*
touching [ˈtʌtʃɪŋ] *adj* rührend

touch screen *n (Tech)* Berührungsbildschirm *m*, Touchscreen *m*
touchy [ˈtʌtʃɪ] *adj (person, subject)* empfindlich
tough [tʌf] *adj (strong, firm, difficult)* hart; *(meat, animal, person)* zäh
tour [ˈtuəʳ] *n (journey)* Tour *f*; *(of factory, museum etc)* Rundgang *m*; *(by pop group etc)* Tournee *f* ▸ *vt (country, factory etc: on foot)* ziehen durch; *(: in car)* fahren durch
tour guide *n* Reiseleiter(in) *m(f)*
tourism [ˈtuərɪzm] *n* Tourismus *m*
tourist [ˈtuərɪst] *n* Tourist(in) *m(f)*
tourist class *n* Touristenklasse *f*
tourist guide *n (book)* Reiseführer *m*; *(person)* Fremdenführer(in) *m(f)*
tourist office *n* Verkehrsamt *nt*
tournament [ˈtuənəmənt] *n* Turnier *nt*
tour operator (Brit) *n* Reiseveranstalter *m*
tow [təu] *vt (vehicle)* abschleppen; *(caravan, trailer)* ziehen
▸ **tow away** *vt (vehicle)* abschleppen
toward [təˈwɔːd], **towards** [təˈwɔːdz] *prep (direction)* zu; *(attitude)* gegenüber *+dat*; **to feel friendly ~(s) sb** jdm freundlich gesinnt sein
towel [ˈtauəl] *n* Handtuch *nt*
tower [ˈtauəʳ] *n* Turm *m*
tower block (Brit) *n* Hochhaus *nt*
town [taun] *n* Stadt *f*
town centre *n* Stadtzentrum *nt*
town hall *n* Rathaus *nt*
towrope [ˈtəurəup] *n* Abschleppseil *nt*
tow truck *(US) n* Abschleppwagen *m*
toxic [ˈtɔksɪk] *adj* giftig, toxisch
toy [tɔɪ] *n* Spielzeug *nt*
▸ **toy with** *vt fus (object, idea)* spielen mit
toyshop [ˈtɔɪʃɔp] *n* Spielzeugladen *m*
trace [treɪs] *n (sign, small amount)* Spur *f* ▸ *vt (locate)* aufspüren; **without ~** *(disappear)* spurlos
tracing paper [ˈtreɪsɪŋ-] *n* Pauspapier *nt*
track [træk] *n* Weg *m*; *(of suspect, animal)* Spur *f*; *(Rail)* Gleis *nt*; *(on tape, record)* Stück *nt* ▸ *vt (follow)* verfolgen; **to keep ~ of sb/sth** *(fig)* jdn/etw im Auge behalten
▸ **track down** *vt* aufspüren
tracksuit [ˈtræksuːt] *n* Trainingsanzug *m*
tractor [ˈtræktəʳ] *n* Traktor *m*
trade [treɪd] *n (activity)* Handel *m*; *(skill, job)* Handwerk *nt* ▸ *vi (do business)* handeln ▸ *vt*: **to ~ sth (for sth)** etw (gegen etw) eintauschen
trademark [ˈtreɪdmɑːk] *n* Warenzeichen *nt*
tradesman [ˈtreɪdzmən] *n (irreg) (shopkeeper)* Händler *m*
trade union *n* Gewerkschaft *f*
tradition [trəˈdɪʃən] *n* Tradition *f*
traditional [trəˈdɪʃənl] *adj* traditionell
traffic [ˈtræfɪk] *n* Verkehr *m*; *(in drugs etc)* Handel *m*
traffic circle *(US) n* Kreisverkehr *m*
traffic island *n* Verkehrsinsel *f*
traffic jam *n* Stau *m*
traffic lights *npl* Ampel *f*
traffic warden *n Verkehrspolizist für Parkvergehen*; *(woman)* ≈ Politesse *f*
tragedy [ˈtrædʒədɪ] *n* Tragödie *f*
tragic [ˈtrædʒɪk] *adj* tragisch
trail [treɪl] *n (path)* Weg *m*; *(track)* Spur *f* ▸ *vt (drag)* schleifen; *(follow)* folgen *+dat* ▸ *vi (hang loosely)* schleifen; *(in game, contest)* zurückliegen
▸ **trail behind** *vi* hinterhertrotten
trailer [ˈtreɪləʳ] *n (Aut)* Anhänger *m*; *(US: caravan)* Wohnwagen *m*; *(Cine, TV)* Trailer *m*
train [treɪn] *n (Rail)* Zug *m* ▸ *vt (apprentice etc)* ausbilden; *(athlete)* trainieren ▸ *vi (Sport)* trainieren; **to ~ sb to do sth** jdn dazu ausbilden, etw zu tun
trained [treɪnd] *adj (teacher)* ausgebildet
trainee [treɪˈniː] *n* Auszubildende(r) *f(m)*
traineeship [treɪˈniːʃɪp] *n* Praktikum *nt*
trainer [ˈtreɪnəʳ] *n (Sport: coach)* Trainer(in) *m(f)*; *(: shoe)* Trainingsschuh *m*
training [ˈtreɪnɪŋ] *n (for occupation)* Ausbildung *f*; *(Sport)* Training *nt*
train station *n* Bahnhof *m*
tram [træm] (Brit) *n (also:* **tramcar***)* Straßenbahn *f*
tramp [træmp] *n* Landstreicher *m* ▸ *vi* stapfen
tranquillizer, *(US)* **tranquilizer** [ˈtræŋkwɪlaɪzəʳ] *n* Beruhigungsmittel *nt*
transaction [trænˈzækʃən] *n* Geschäft *nt*
transatlantic [ˈtrænzətˈlæntɪk] *adj* transatlantisch; *(phone-call)* über den Atlantik

transfer [ˈtrænsfəʳ] *n* (*of money*) Überweisung *f* ▸ *vt* (*employees*) versetzen; (*money*) überweisen
transferable [trænsˈfəːrəbl] *adj* übertragbar
transform [trænsˈfɔːm] *vt* umwandeln
transformation [trænsfəˈmeɪʃən] *n* Umwandlung *f*
transfusion [trænsˈfjuːʒən] *n* (*also:* **blood ~**) Bluttransfusion *f*
transistor [trænˈzɪstəʳ] *n* (*Elec*) Transistor *m*; (*also:* **~ radio**) Transistorradio *nt*
transition [trænˈzɪʃən] *n* Übergang *m*
transit lounge [ˈtrænzɪt-] *n* Transithalle *f*
translate [trænzˈleɪt] *vt* übersetzen
translation [trænzˈleɪʃən] *n* Übersetzung *f*
translator [trænzˈleɪtəʳ] *n* Übersetzer(in) *m(f)*
transmission [trænzˈmɪʃən] *n* (*Aut*) Getriebe *nt*
transparent [trænsˈpærnt] *adj* durchsichtig; (*fig: obvious*) offensichtlich
transplant *vt* [trænsˈplɑːnt] (*organ, seedlings*) verpflanzen ▸ *n* [ˈtrɑːnsplɑːnt] (*Med*) Transplantation *f*
transport [ˈtrænspɔːt] *n* Beförderung *f* ▸ *vt* transportieren; **public ~** öffentliche Verkehrsmittel *pl*
transportation [ˈtrænspɔːˈteɪʃən] *n* Transport *m*, Beförderung *f*
trap [træp] *n* (*also fig*) Falle *f* ▸ *vt* (*animal*) (mit einer Falle) fangen
trash [træʃ] *n* (*rubbish*) Abfall *m*; (*pej: nonsense*) Schund *m*
trash can (*US*) *n* Mülleimer *m*
trashy [ˈtræʃɪ] *adj* (*goods*) minderwertig; (*novel etc*) Schund-
traumatic [trɔːˈmætɪk] *adj* traumatisch
travel [ˈtrævl] *n* (*travelling*) Reisen *nt* ▸ *vi* reisen ▸ *vt* (*distance*) zurücklegen
travel agency *n* Reisebüro *nt*
travel insurance *n* Reiseversicherung *f*
traveller, (*US*) **traveler** [ˈtrævləʳ] *n* Reisende(r) *f(m)*
traveller's cheque, (*US*) **traveler's check** *n* Reisescheck *m*
tray [treɪ] *n* (*for carrying*) Tablett *nt*; (*on desk: also:* **in-tray/out-tray**) Ablage *f* für Eingänge/Ausgänge
tread [trɛd] (*pt* **trod**, *pp* **trodden**) *n* (*of tyre*) Profil *nt*
▸ **tread on** *vt fus* treten auf +*acc*
treasure [ˈtrɛʒəʳ] *n* (*also fig*) Schatz *m* ▸ *vt* schätzen
treat [triːt] *n* (*present*) (besonderes) Vergnügen *nt* ▸ *vt* (*also Med, Tech*) behandeln; **to ~ sb to sth** jdm etw spendieren
treatment [ˈtriːtmənt] *n* Behandlung *f*
treaty [ˈtriːtɪ] *n* Vertrag *m*
tree [triː] *n* Baum *m*
tremble [ˈtrɛmbl] *vi* (*voice, body, trees*) zittern
tremendous [trɪˈmɛndəs] *adj* (*amount, success etc*) gewaltig; (*holiday, view etc*) fantastisch
trench [trɛntʃ] *n* Graben *m*
trend [trɛnd] *n* Tendenz *f*; (*fashion*) Trend *m*
trendy [ˈtrɛndɪ] *adj* modisch
trespass [ˈtrɛspəs] *vi*: **"no trespassing"** „Betreten verboten"
trial [ˈtraɪəl] *n* (*Law*) Prozess *m*; (*test, of machine, drug etc*) Versuch *m*; **by ~ and error** durch Ausprobieren
trial period *n* Probezeit *f*
triangle [ˈtraɪæŋgl] *n* Dreieck *nt*; (*Mus*) Triangel *f*
triangular [traɪˈæŋgjuləʳ] *adj* dreieckig
tribe [traɪb] *n* Stamm *m*
trick [trɪk] *n* Trick *m* ▸ *vt* hereinlegen; **to play a ~ on sb** jdm einen Streich spielen
tricky [ˈtrɪkɪ] *adj* (*job, problem*) schwierig
trifle [ˈtraɪfl] *n* (*detail*) Kleinigkeit *f*; (*Culin*) Trifle *nt*
trigger [ˈtrɪgəʳ] *n* Abzug *m*
▸ **trigger off** *vt fus* auslösen
trim [trɪm] *n* (*haircut etc*): **to have a ~** sich *dat* die Haare nachschneiden lassen ▸ *vt* (*hair, beard*) nachschneiden
trimmings [ˈtrɪmɪŋz] *npl* (*Culin*): **with all the ~** mit allem Drum und Dran
trip [trɪp] *n* (*journey*) Reise *f*; (*outing*) Ausflug *m* ▸ *vi* (*stumble*) stolpern
triple [ˈtrɪpl] *adj* dreifach ▸ *adv*: **~ the distance/speed** dreimal so weit/schnell
triplets [ˈtrɪplɪts] *npl* Drillinge *pl*
tripod [ˈtraɪpɔd] *n* (*Phot*) Stativ *nt*
trite [traɪt] (*pej*) *adj* (*comment, idea etc*) banal
triumph [ˈtraɪʌmf] *n* Triumph *m*

trivial [ˈtrɪvɪəl] *adj* trivial
trod [trɔd] *pt of* **tread**
trodden [ˈtrɔdn] *pp of* **tread**
troll [trɔl] *n* (*also Comput*) Troll *m*
trolley [ˈtrɔlɪ] *n* (*for luggage*) Kofferkuli *m*; (*for shopping*) Einkaufswagen *m*; (*table on wheels*) Teewagen *m*
trolling [ˈtrəulɪŋ] *n* (*Internet*) Trollen *nt*
trombone [trɔmˈbəun] *n* Posaune *f*
troop [tru:p] *n* (*of people, monkeys etc*) Gruppe *f* ▪ **troops** *npl* (*Mil*) Truppen *pl*
trophy [ˈtrəufɪ] *n* Trophäe *f*
tropical [ˈtrɔpɪkl] *adj* tropisch
trouble [ˈtrʌbl] *n* Schwierigkeiten *pl*; (*bother, effort*) Umstände *pl*; (*unrest*) Unruhen *pl* ▶ *vt* (*worry*) beunruhigen; (*disturb: person*) belästigen; **to be in ~** in Schwierigkeiten sein; **what's the ~?** wo fehlts?; **stomach** *etc* **~** Probleme mit dem Magen *etc*; **please don't ~ yourself** bitte bemühen Sie sich nicht
troubled [ˈtrʌbld] *adj* (*person*) besorgt
trouble-free [ˈtrʌblfri:] *adj* problemlos
troublemaker [ˈtrʌblmeɪkə^r] *n* Unruhestifter(in) *m(f)*
troublesome [ˈtrʌblsəm] *adj* (*cough etc*) lästig
trousers [ˈtrauzəz] *npl* Hose *f*
trout [traut] *n inv* Forelle *f*
truck [trʌk] *n* (*lorry*) Lastwagen *m*; (*Rail*) Güterwagen *m*
trucker [ˈtrʌkə^r] (*US*) *n* Lkw-Fahrer(in) *m(f)*
true [tru:] *adj* wahr; (*genuine*) echt; **to come ~** wahr werden
truly [ˈtru:lɪ] *adv* wirklich; **yours ~** (*in letter*) mit freundlichen Grüßen
trumpet [ˈtrʌmpɪt] *n* Trompete *f*
trunk [trʌŋk] *n* (*of tree*) Stamm *m*; (*of person*) Rumpf *m*; (*of elephant*) Rüssel *m*; (*case*) Schrankkoffer *m*; (*US Aut*) Kofferraum *m* ▪ **trunks** *npl* (*also:* **swimming trunks**) Badehose *f*
trust [trʌst] *n* Vertrauen *nt* ▶ *vt* vertrauen *+dat*
trusting [ˈtrʌstɪŋ] *adj* vertrauensvoll
trustworthy [ˈtrʌstwə:ðɪ] *adj* (*person*) vertrauenswürdig
truth [tru:θ] *n*: **the ~** die Wahrheit *f*
truthful [ˈtru:θful] *adj* (*person*) ehrlich; (*answer etc*) wahrheitsgemäß
try [traɪ] *n* (*also Rugby*) Versuch *m* ▶ *vt* (*attempt*) versuchen; (*test*) probieren; (*Law*) vor Gericht stellen; (*strain: patience*) auf die Probe stellen ▶ *vi* es versuchen
▶ **try on** *vt* (*clothes*) anprobieren
▶ **try out** *vt* ausprobieren
tsar [zɑ:^r] *n* Zar *m*
T-shirt [ˈti:ʃə:t] *n* T-Shirt *nt*
tub [tʌb] *n* (*container*) Kübel *m*
tube [tju:b] *n* (*pipe*) Rohr *nt*; (*container*) Tube *f*; (BRIT: *underground*) U-Bahn *f*
tube station (BRIT) *n* U-Bahn-Station *f*
tuck [tʌk] *vt* (*put*) stecken
▶ **tuck in** *vt* (*clothing*) feststecken; (*child*) zudecken ▶ *vi* (*eat*) zulangen
tucker [ˈtʌkə^r] *n* (AUST, *NZ inf*) Essen *nt*, Fressalien *pl* (*inf*)
Tue., Tues. *abbr* (= *Tuesday*) Di.
Tuesday [ˈtju:zdɪ] *n* Dienstag *m*; **on ~** am Dienstag; **on Tuesdays** dienstags; **every ~** jeden Dienstag; **last/next ~** letzten/nächsten Dienstag; **a week/ fortnight on ~** Dienstag in einer Woche/in vierzehn Tagen; **~ morning/lunchtime/afternoon/ evening** Dienstag Morgen/Mittag/ Nachmittag/Abend; **~ night** (*overnight*) Dienstag Nacht
tug [tʌg] *n* (*ship*) Schlepper *m* ▶ *vt* zerren
tuition [tju:ˈɪʃən] *n* (BRIT) Unterricht *m*; (*US: school fees*) Schulgeld *nt*
tulip [ˈtju:lɪp] *n* Tulpe *f*
tumble [ˈtʌmbl] *vi* (*fall*) stürzen
tumble dryer (BRIT) *n* Wäschetrockner *m*
tumbler [ˈtʌmblə^r] *n* (*glass*) Trinkglas *nt*
tummy [ˈtʌmɪ] (*inf*) *n* Bauch *m*
tumour, (*US*) **tumor** [ˈtju:mə^r] *n* (*Med*) Tumor *m*
tuna [ˈtju:nə] *n inv* (*also:* **~ fish**) T(h)unfisch *m*
tune [tju:n] *n* (*melody*) Melodie *f* ▶ *vt* (*Mus*) stimmen; (*Radio, TV, Aut*) einstellen; **to be in/out of ~** (*instrument*) richtig gestimmt/ verstimmt sein; (*singer*) richtig/falsch singen
tuner [ˈtju:nə^r] *n* (*radio set*) Tuner *m*
Tunisia [tju:ˈnɪzɪə] *n* Tunesien *nt*
tunnel [ˈtʌnl] *n* Tunnel *m*
turban [ˈtə:bən] *n* Turban *m*
turbulence [ˈtə:bjuləns] *n* (*Aviat*) Turbulenz *f*

turbulent [ˈtəːbjulənt] *adj* (*water, seas*) stürmisch
Turk [təːk] *n* Türke *m*, Türkin *f*
Turkey [ˈtəːkɪ] *n* die Türkei *f*
turkey [ˈtəːkɪ] *n* (*bird*) Truthahn *m*
Turkish [ˈtəːkɪʃ] *adj* türkisch ▶ *n* (*Ling*) Türkisch *nt*
turmoil [ˈtəːmɔɪl] *n* Aufruhr *m*
turn [təːn] *n* (*rotation*) Drehung *f*; (*performance*) Nummer *f* ▶ *vt* (*handle, key*) drehen; (*page*) umblättern ▶ *vi* (*object*) sich drehen; (*person*) sich umdrehen; (*change direction*) abbiegen; (*milk*) sauer werden; **"no left ~"** (*Aut*) „Linksabbiegen verboten"; **it's your ~** du bist dran; **in ~** der Reihe nach; **to take turns (at)** sich abwechseln (bei); **at the ~ of the century/year** zur Jahrhundertwende/Jahreswende; **to ~ nasty/forty/grey** unangenehm/vierzig/grau werden
▶ **turn away** *vt* (*applicants*) abweisen
▶ **turn back** *vi* umkehren ▶ *vt* (*person, vehicle*) zurückweisen
▶ **turn down** *vt* (*request*) ablehnen; (*heating*) kleiner stellen; (*radio etc*) leiser stellen
▶ **turn off** *vi* (*from road*) abbiegen ▶ *vt* (*light, radio etc*) ausmachen; (*tap*) zudrehen; (*engine*) abstellen
▶ **turn on** *vt* (*light, radio etc*) anmachen; (*tap*) aufdrehen; (*engine*) anstellen
▶ **turn out** *vt* (*light*) ausmachen ▶ *vi* (*appear, attend*) erscheinen; **to ~ out to be** (*prove to be*) sich erweisen als
▶ **turn over** *vi* (*person*) sich umdrehen ▶ *vt* (*object*) umdrehen; (*page*) umblättern
▶ **turn round** *vi* sich umdrehen
▶ **turn up** *vi* (*person*) erscheinen; (*lost object*) wieder auftauchen ▶ *vt* (*heater*) höher stellen; (*radio etc*) lauter stellen
turning [ˈtəːnɪŋ] *n* (*in road*) Abzweigung *f*
turning point *n* (*fig*) Wendepunkt *m*
turnip [ˈtəːnɪp] *n* Rübe *f*
turnover [ˈtəːnəuvəʳ] *n* (*Comm: amount of money*) Umsatz *m*
turnpike [ˈtəːnpaɪk] (*US*) *n* gebührenpflichtige Autobahn *f*
turntable [ˈtəːnteɪbl] *n* (*on record player*) Plattenteller *m*
turn-up [ˈtəːnʌp] (Brit) *n* (*on trousers*) Aufschlag *m*
turquoise [ˈtəːkwɔɪz] *adj* (*colour*) türkis
turtle [ˈtəːtl] *n* Schildkröte *f*
tutor [ˈtjuːtəʳ] *n* Tutor(in) *m(f)*; (*private tutor*) Privatlehrer(in) *m(f)*
tuxedo [tʌkˈsiːdəu], (*US*) **tux** *n* Smoking *m*
TV [tiːˈviː] *n abbr* (= *television*) TV *nt*
tweed [twiːd] *n* Tweed *m*
tweet [twiːt] *vi* (*on Twitter*) twittern
tweezers [ˈtwiːzəz] *npl* Pinzette *f*
twelfth [twɛlfθ] *num* zwölfte(r, s)
twelve [twɛlv] *num* zwölf
twentieth [ˈtwɛntɪɪθ] *num* zwanzigste(r, s)
twenty [ˈtwɛntɪ] *num* zwanzig
twice [twaɪs] *adv* zweimal; **~ as much** zweimal so viel
twig [twɪg] *n* Zweig *m*
twilight [ˈtwaɪlaɪt] *n* Dämmerung *f*
twin [twɪn] *adj* (*sister, brother*) Zwillings-; (*towers*) Doppel- ▶ *n* Zwilling *m* ▶ *vt* (*towns etc*): **to be twinned with ...** ... als Partnerstadt haben
twinge [twɪndʒ] *n* (*of pain*) Stechen *nt*
twinkle [ˈtwɪŋkl] *vi* funkeln
twin room [ˈtwɪnˈruːm] *n* Zweibettzimmer *nt*
twin town *n* Partnerstadt *f*
twist [twɪst] *vt* (*turn*) drehen; (*fig: meaning etc*) verdrehen
Twittersphere [ˈtwɪtəsfɪəʳ] *n* (*inf*): **the ~** die Twittersphäre *f*
two [tuː] *num* zwei
two-dimensional [tuːdɪˈmɛnʃənl] *adj* zweidimensional; (*fig*) oberflächlich
two-faced [tuːˈfeɪst] (*pej*) *adj* scheinheilig
two-piece [ˈtuːpiːs] *n* (*also:* **~ suit**) Zweiteiler *m*; (*also:* **~ swimsuit**) zweiteiliger Badeanzug *m*
two-way [ˈtuːweɪ] *adj*: **~ traffic** Verkehr *m* in beiden Richtungen
type [taɪp] *n* (*category, model, example*) Typ *m*; (*Typ*) Schrift *f* ▶ *vt* (*letter etc*) tippen, (mit der) Maschine schreiben; **a ~ of** eine Art von; **what ~ do you want?** welche Sorte möchten Sie?
typeface [ˈtaɪpfeɪs] *n* Schrift *f*, Schriftbild *nt*
typewriter [ˈtaɪpraɪtəʳ] *n* Schreibmaschine *f*
typhoid [ˈtaɪfɔɪd] *n* Typhus *m*
typhoon [taɪˈfuːn] *n* Taifun *m*

typical [ˈtɪpɪkl] *adj* typisch; **~ (of)** typisch (für)
typing error [ˈtaɪpɪŋ-] *n* Tippfehler *m*
tyre, (*US*) **tire** [ˈtaɪəʳ] *n* Reifen *m*
tyre pressure *n* Reifendruck *m*
Tyrol [tɪˈrəul] *n* Tirol *nt*

UFO [ˈju:fəu] *n abbr* (= *unidentified flying object*) UFO *nt*
Uganda [ju:ˈgændə] *n* Uganda *nt*
ugly [ˈʌglɪ] *adj* hässlich
UHF *abbr* (= *ultrahigh frequency*) UHF
UHT *abbr* (= *ultra heat treated*): **~ milk** H-Milch *f*
UK *n abbr* = **United Kingdom**
Ukraine [ju:ˈkreɪn] *n* Ukraine *f*
ulcer [ˈʌlsəʳ] *n* (*stomach ulcer etc*) Geschwür *nt*
ulterior [ʌlˈtɪərɪəʳ] *adj*: **~ motive** Hintergedanke *m*
ultimate [ˈʌltɪmət] *adj* (*final*) letztendlich; (*greatest*) größte(r, s); (: *authority*) höchste(r, s)
ultimately [ˈʌltɪmətlɪ] *adv* (*in the end*) schließlich, letzten Endes
ultimatum [ʌltɪˈmeɪtəm] *n* Ultimatum *nt*
ultrasound [ˈʌltrəsaund] *n* Ultraschall *m*
umbrella [ʌmˈbrɛlə] *n* (*for rain*) (Regen)schirm *m*
umpire [ˈʌmpaɪəʳ] *n* Schiedsrichter(in) *m*(*f*)
umpteen [ʌmpˈti:n] *adj* zig
UN *n abbr* (= *United Nations*) UNO *f*
unable [ʌnˈeɪbl] *adj*: **to be ~ to do sth** etw nicht tun können
unacceptable [ʌnəkˈsɛptəbl] *adj* unannehmbar
unaccountably [ʌnəˈkauntəblɪ] *adv* unerklärlich
unaccustomed [ʌnəˈkʌstəmd] *adj*: **to be ~ to** nicht gewöhnt sein an *+acc*
unanimous [ju:ˈnænɪməs] *adj* einstimmig

unanimously [juːˈnænɪməslɪ] *adv* einstimmig
unattached [ʌnəˈtætʃt] *adj* (*single: person*) ungebunden
unattended [ʌnəˈtɛndɪd] *adj* (*car, luggage, child*) unbeaufsichtigt
unauthorized [ʌnˈɔːθəraɪzd] *adj* (*visit, use*) unbefugt
unavailable [ʌnəˈveɪləbl] *adj* (*article, room*) nicht verfügbar; (*person*) nicht zu erreichen
unavoidable [ʌnəˈvɔɪdəbl] *adj* unvermeidlich
unaware [ʌnəˈwɛəʳ] *adj*: **he was ~ of it** er war sich *dat* dessen nicht bewusst
unbalanced [ʌnˈbælənst] *adj* (*report*) unausgewogen; **(mentally) ~** geistig gestört
unbearable [ʌnˈbɛərəbl] *adj* unerträglich
unbeatable [ʌnˈbiːtəbl] *adj* unschlagbar
unbelievable [ʌnbɪˈliːvəbl] *adj* unglaublich
unblock [ʌnˈblɔk] *vt* (*pipe*) frei machen
unbutton [ʌnˈbʌtn] *vt* aufknöpfen
uncertain [ʌnˈsəːtn] *adj* (*person*) unsicher
uncle [ˈʌŋkl] *n* Onkel *m*
uncomfortable [ʌnˈkʌmfətəbl] *adj* (*person, chair*) unbequem
unconditional [ʌnkənˈdɪʃənl] *adj* bedingungslos
unconscious [ʌnˈkɔnʃəs] *adj* (*in faint*) bewusstlos; (*unaware*): **~ of** nicht bewusst *+gen*
unconsciously [ʌnˈkɔnʃəslɪ] *adv* unbewusst
uncork [ʌnˈkɔːk] *vt* (*bottle*) entkorken
uncover [ʌnˈkʌvəʳ] *vt* aufdecken
undecided [ʌndɪˈsaɪdɪd] *adj* (*person*) unentschlossen
undeniable [ʌndɪˈnaɪəbl] *adj* unbestreitbar
under [ˈʌndəʳ] *prep* (*position*) unter *+dat*; (*motion*) unter *+acc* ▸ *adv* (*go, fly etc*) darunter; **~ there** darunter; **in ~ 2 hours** in weniger als 2 Stunden
underage [ʌndərˈeɪdʒ] *adj* (*person*) minderjährig
undercarriage [ˈʌndəkærɪdʒ] *n* (*Aviat*) Fahrgestell *nt*
underdog [ˈʌndədɔg] *n*: **the ~** der/die Benachteiligte
underdone [ʌndəˈdʌn] *adj* (*food*) nicht gar; (: *meat*) nicht durchgebraten
underestimate [ˈʌndərˈɛstɪmeɪt] *vt* unterschätzen
underexposed [ˈʌndərɪksˈpəuzd] *adj* (*Phot*) unterbelichtet
undergo [ʌndəˈgəu] *vt* (*irreg: like* **go**) (*change*) durchmachen; (*test, operation*) sich unterziehen
undergraduate [ʌndəˈgrædjuɪt] *n* Student(in) *m(f)*
underground [ˈʌndəgraund] *adj* unterirdisch ▸ *n*: **the ~** (BRIT) die U-Bahn
underground station *n* U-Bahn-Station *f*
underlie [ʌndəˈlaɪ] *vt* (*irreg: like* **lie²**) (*fig: be basis of*) zugrunde liegen *+dat*
underline [ʌndəˈlaɪn] *vt* unterstreichen
underlying [ʌndəˈlaɪɪŋ] *adj* zugrunde liegend
underneath [ʌndəˈniːθ] *adv* darunter ▸ *prep* (*position*) unter *+dat*; (*motion*) unter *+acc*
underpants [ˈʌndəpænts] *npl* Unterhose *f*
undershirt [ˈʌndəʃəːt] (*US*) *n* Unterhemd *nt*
undershorts [ˈʌndəʃɔːts] (*US*) *npl* Unterhose *f*
understand [ʌndəˈstænd] *vt, vi* (*irreg: like* **stand**) verstehen; **I ~ (that) you have …** (*believe*) soweit ich weiß, haben Sie …; **to make o.s. understood** sich verständlich machen
understandable [ʌndəˈstændəbl] *adj* verständlich
understanding [ʌndəˈstændɪŋ] *adj* verständnisvoll
undertake [ʌndəˈteɪk] *vt* (*irreg: like* **take**) (*task*) übernehmen ▸ *vi*: **to ~ to do sth** es übernehmen, etw zu tun
undertaker [ˈʌndəteɪkəʳ] *n* (Leichen)bestatter *m*
underwater [ˈʌndəˈwɔːtəʳ] *adv* (*swim etc*) unter Wasser ▸ *adj* (*exploration, camera etc*) Unterwasser-
underwear [ˈʌndəwɛəʳ] *n* Unterwäsche *f*
undesirable [ʌndɪˈzaɪərəbl] *adj* unerwünscht
undo [ʌnˈduː] *vt* (*irreg: like* **do**) (*unfasten*) aufmachen; (*spoil*) zunichtemachen

undoubtedly [ʌnˈdautɪdlɪ] *adv* zweifellos
undress [ʌnˈdrɛs] *vi* sich ausziehen
undue [ʌnˈdjuː] *adj* (*excessive*) übertrieben
unduly [ʌnˈdjuːlɪ] *adv* (*excessively*) übermäßig
unearth [ʌnˈəːθ] *vt* (*skeleton etc*) ausgraben; (*fig: secrets etc*) ausfindig machen
unease [ʌnˈiːz] *n* Unbehagen *nt*
uneasy [ʌnˈiːzɪ] *adj* (*person*) unruhig; (*feeling*) unbehaglich; **to feel ~ about doing sth** ein ungutes Gefühl dabei haben, etw zu tun
unemployed [ʌnɪmˈplɔɪd] *adj* arbeitslos ▶ *npl*: **the ~** die Arbeitslosen *pl*
unemployment [ʌnɪmˈplɔɪmənt] *n* Arbeitslosigkeit *f*
unemployment benefit (Brit) *n* Arbeitslosenunterstützung *f*
unequal [ʌnˈiːkwəl] *adj* ungleich
uneven [ʌnˈiːvn] *adj* (*teeth, road etc*) uneben; (*performance*) ungleichmäßig
unexpected [ʌnɪksˈpɛktɪd] *adj* unerwartet
unfair [ʌnˈfɛəʳ] *adj* unfair
unfamiliar [ʌnfəˈmɪlɪəʳ] *adj*: **to be ~ with sth** mit etw nicht vertraut sein
unfasten [ʌnˈfɑːsn] *vt* (*seat belt, strap*) lösen
unfit [ʌnˈfɪt] *adj* (*physically*) nicht fit; **~ for human consumption** zum Verzehr ungeeignet
unforeseen [ˈʌnfɔːˈsiːn] *adj* unvorhergesehen
unforgettable [ʌnfəˈgɛtəbl] *adj* unvergesslich
unforgivable [ʌnfəˈgɪvəbl] *adj* unverzeihlich
unfortunate [ʌnˈfɔːtʃənət] *adj* (*unlucky*) unglücklich
unfortunately [ʌnˈfɔːtʃənətlɪ] *adv* leider
unfounded [ʌnˈfaundɪd] *adj* (*allegations, fears*) unbegründet
unfriend [ʌnˈfrɛnd] *vt* (*on social network*) entfreunden
unhappy [ʌnˈhæpɪ] *adj* unglücklich; **~ about/with** (*dissatisfied*) unzufrieden über *+acc*/mit
unhealthy [ʌnˈhɛlθɪ] *adj* (*place*) ungesund
unheard-of [ʌnˈhəːdɔv] *adj* (*unknown*) unbekannt; (*outrageous*) unerhört
unhelpful [ʌnˈhɛlpful] *adj* (*person*) nicht hilfreich
unhurt [ʌnˈhəːt] *adj* unverletzt
uniform [ˈjuːnɪfɔːm] *n* Uniform *f* ▶ *adj* (*length, width etc*) einheitlich
unify [ˈjuːnɪfaɪ] *vt* vereinigen
unimportant [ʌnɪmˈpɔːtənt] *adj* unwichtig
uninhabited [ʌnɪnˈhæbɪtɪd] *adj* unbewohnt
uninstall [ʌnɪnˈstɔːl] *vt* (*Comput*) deinstallieren
unintentional [ʌnɪnˈtɛnʃənəl] *adj* unbeabsichtigt
union [ˈjuːnjən] *n* (*unification*) Vereinigung *f*; (*also*: **trade ~**) Gewerkschaft *f*
Union Jack *n* Union Jack *m*
unique [juːˈniːk] *adj* (*ability, skill*) einzigartig
unit [ˈjuːnɪt] *n* Einheit *f*; **kitchen ~** Küchen-Einbauelement *nt*
unite [juːˈnaɪt] *vt* vereinigen ▶ *vi* sich zusammenschließen
United Kingdom *n*: **the ~** das Vereinigte Königreich
United Nations *npl*: **the ~** die Vereinten Nationen *pl*
United States, United States of America *n*: **the ~ (of America)** die Vereinigten Staaten *pl* (von Amerika)
universe [ˈjuːnɪvəːs] *n* Universum *nt*
university [juːnɪˈvəːsɪtɪ] *n* Universität *f*
unkind [ʌnˈkaɪnd] *adj* (*person, comment etc*) unfreundlich
unknown [ʌnˈnəun] *adj* unbekannt
unleaded [ˈʌnˈlɛdɪd] *adj* (*petrol*) bleifrei
unless [ʌnˈlɛs] *conj* es sei denn; **~ he comes** wenn er nicht kommt; **~ I am mistaken** wenn ich mich nicht irre; **there will be a strike ~ …** es wird zum Streik kommen, es sei denn, …
unlicensed [ʌnˈlaɪsnst] (Brit) *adj* (*restaurant*) ohne Schankkonzession
unlike [ʌnˈlaɪk] *adj* (*not alike*) unähnlich; **~ me, she is very tidy** im Gegensatz zu mir ist sie sehr ordentlich
unlikely [ʌnˈlaɪklɪ] *adj* unwahrscheinlich
unload [ʌnˈləud] *vt* (*box etc*) ausladen

unlock [ʌnˈlɔk] *vt* aufschließen
unlucky [ʌnˈlʌkɪ] *adj* (*object*) Unglück bringend; **to be ~** (*person*) Pech haben
unmistakable, unmistakeable [ʌnmɪsˈteɪkəbl] *adj* unverkennbar
unnecessary [ʌnˈnɛsəsərɪ] *adj* unnötig
unobtainable [ʌnəbˈteɪnəbl] *adj* (*item*) nicht erhältlich
unoccupied [ʌnˈɔkjupaɪd] *adj* (*seat*) frei; (*house*) leer (stehend)
unpack [ʌnˈpæk] *vt, vi* auspacken
unpleasant [ʌnˈplɛznt] *adj* unangenehm
unplug [ʌnˈplʌg] *vt* (*iron, record player etc*) den Stecker herausziehen *+gen*
unprecedented [ʌnˈprɛsɪdɛntɪd] *adj* noch nie da gewesen
unpredictable [ʌnprɪˈdɪktəbl] *adj* (*person, weather*) unberechenbar
unreasonable [ʌnˈri:znəbl] *adj* (*person, attitude*) unvernünftig; (*demand, length of time*) unzumutbar
unreliable [ʌnrɪˈlaɪəbl] *adj* unzuverlässig
unsafe [ʌnˈseɪf] *adj* unsicher; (*machine, bridge, car etc*) gefährlich
unscrew [ʌnˈskru:] *vt* losschrauben
unsightly [ʌnˈsaɪtlɪ] *adj* unansehnlich
unskilled [ʌnˈskɪld] *adj* (*work, worker*) ungelernt
unsuccessful [ʌnsəkˈsɛsful] *adj* erfolglos
unsuitable [ʌnˈsu:təbl] *adj* (*clothes, person*) ungeeignet
until [ənˈtɪl] *prep* bis *+acc*; (*after negative*) vor *+dat* ▸ *conj* bis; (*after negative*) bevor; **not ~** erst; **~ then** bis dann
unusual [ʌnˈju:ʒuəl] *adj* ungewöhnlich
unusually [ʌnˈju:ʒuəlɪ] *adv* (*large, high etc*) ungewöhnlich
unwanted [ʌnˈwɔntɪd] *adj* unerwünscht
unwell [ʌnˈwɛl] *adj*: **to be ~, to feel ~** sich nicht wohlfühlen
unwilling [ʌnˈwɪlɪŋ] *adj*: **to be ~ to do sth** etw nicht tun wollen
unwind [ʌnˈwaɪnd] *vt* (*irreg: like* **wind²**) abwickeln ▸ *vi* (*relax*) sich entspannen
unwrap [ʌnˈræp] *vt* auspacken
unzip [ʌnˈzɪp] *vt* aufmachen

KEYWORD

up [ʌp] *prep*: **to be up sth** (oben) auf etw *dat* sein; **to go up sth** (auf) etw *acc* hinaufgehen; **go up that road and turn left** gehen Sie die Straße hinauf und biegen Sie links ab
▸ *adv* **1** (*upwards, higher*) oben; **put it a bit higher up** stelle es etwas höher; **up there** dort oben; **up above** hoch oben
2: **to be up** (*out of bed*) auf sein; (*prices, level*) gestiegen sein; (*building, tent*) stehen
3: **up to** (*as far as*) bis; **up to now** bis jetzt
4: **to be up to** (*depending on*) abhängen von; **it's up to you** das hängt von dir ab; **it's not up to me to decide** es liegt nicht bei mir, das zu entscheiden
5: **to be up to** (*equal to*) gewachsen sein *+dat*; **he's not up to it** (*job, task etc*) er ist dem nicht gewachsen; **his work is not up to the required standard** seine Arbeit entspricht nicht dem gewünschten Niveau
▸ *n*: **ups and downs** (*in life, career*) Höhen und Tiefen *pl*

upbringing [ˈʌpbrɪŋɪŋ] *n* Erziehung *f*
upcycle [ˈʌpsaɪkl] *vt* upcyceln
update [ʌpˈdeɪt] *vt* aktualisieren
upgrade [ʌpˈgreɪd] *vt* (*house*) Verbesserungen durchführen in *+dat*; (*Comput*) nachrüsten
upheaval [ʌpˈhi:vl] *n* Unruhe *f*
uphill [ˈʌpˈhɪl] *adv* (*go*) bergauf
upload [ʌpˈləud] *vt* hochladen
upon [əˈpɔn] *prep* (*position*) auf *+dat*; (*motion*) auf *+acc*
upper [ˈʌpəʳ] *adj* obere(r, s)
upright [ˈʌpraɪt] *adj* (*vertical*) vertikal ▸ *adv* (*sit, stand*) aufrecht
uprising [ˈʌpraɪzɪŋ] *n* Aufstand *m*
uproar [ˈʌprɔ:ʳ] *n* Aufruhr *m*
upset *vt* [ʌpˈsɛt] (*irreg: like* **set**) (*knock over*) umstoßen; (*person: offend, make unhappy*) verletzen; (*routine, plan*) durcheinanderbringen ▸ *adj* (*unhappy*) aufgebracht; (*stomach*) verstimmt ▸ *n* [ˈʌpsɛt]: **to have/get a stomach ~** (*BRIT*) eine Magenverstimmung haben/bekommen; **to get ~** sich aufregen

upside down [ˈʌpsaɪd-] *adv* verkehrt herum; **to turn a room ~** (*fig*) ein Zimmer auf den Kopf stellen
upstairs [ʌpˈstɛəz] *adv* (*be*) oben; (*go*) nach oben
up-to-date [ˈʌptəˈdeɪt] *adj* (*modern*) modern; (*person*) up to date
upwards [ˈʌpwədz] *adv* (*glance*) nach oben
urban [ˈəːbən] *adj* städtisch
urge [əːdʒ] *n* (*need, desire*) Verlangen *nt* ▶ *vt*: **to ~ sb to do sth** jdn eindringlich bitten, etw zu tun
urgent [ˈəːdʒənt] *adj* dringend
urine [ˈjuərɪn] *n* Urin *m*
URL *abbr* = **uniform resource locator**; (*Comput*) URL-Adresse *f*
US *n abbr* (= *United States*) USA *pl*
us [ʌs] *pl pron* uns; (*emphatic*) wir; *see also* **me**
USA *n abbr* (= *United States of America*) USA *f*
USB stick *n* USB-Stick *m*
use *n* [juːs] (*using*) Gebrauch *m*, Verwendung *f*; (*usefulness, purpose*) Nutzen *m* ▶ *vt* [juːz] benutzen, gebrauchen; (*phrase*) verwenden; **in ~** in Gebrauch; **out of ~** außer Gebrauch; **to make ~ of sth** Gebrauch von etw machen; **it's no ~** es hat keinen Zweck; **to be used to sth** etw gewohnt sein; **to get used to sth** sich an etw *acc* gewöhnen; **she used to do it** sie hat es früher gemacht
▶ **use up** *vt* (*food, leftovers*) aufbrauchen
used [juːzd] *adj* gebraucht
useful [ˈjuːsful] *adj* nützlich
useless [ˈjuːslɪs] *adj* nutzlos; (*person: hopeless*) hoffnungslos
user [ˈjuːzəʳ] *n* Benutzer(in) *m(f)*
user-friendly [ˈjuːzəˈfrɛndlɪ] *adj* benutzerfreundlich
username [ˈjuːzəneɪm] *n* Benutzername *m*
usual [ˈjuːʒuəl] *adj* üblich, gewöhnlich; **as ~** wie gewöhnlich
usually [ˈjuːʒuəlɪ] *adv* gewöhnlich
ute [juːt] *n* (Aust, *NZ inf*) Kleintransporter *m*
utensil [juːˈtɛnsl] *n* Gerät *nt*
uterus [ˈjuːtərəs] *n* Gebärmutter *f*
utilize [ˈjuːtɪlaɪz] *vt* verwenden
utmost [ˈʌtməust] *adj* äußerste(r, s) ▶ *n*: **to do one's ~** sein Möglichstes tun
utter [ˈʌtəʳ] *adj* (*amazement*) äußerste(r, s); (*rubbish, fool*) total ▶ *vt* (*sounds, words*) äußern
utterly [ˈʌtəlɪ] *adv* (*totally*) vollkommen
U-turn [ˈjuːˈtəːn] *n* (*also fig*) Kehrtwendung *f*

V

vacancy [ˈveɪkənsɪ] *n* (BRIT: *job*) freie Stelle *f*; (*room in hotel etc*) freies Zimmer *nt*
vacant [ˈveɪkənt] *adj* (*room, seat, job*) frei
vacate [vəˈkeɪt] *vt* (*house*) räumen; (*one's seat*) frei machen
vacation [vəˈkeɪʃən] (*esp US*) *n* (*holiday*) Urlaub *m*; (*Scol*) Ferien *pl*; **to take a ~** Urlaub machen; **on ~** im Urlaub
vacation course *n* Ferienkurs *m*
vaccinate [ˈvæksɪneɪt] *vt*: **to ~ sb (against sth)** jdn (gegen etw) impfen
vaccination [væksɪˈneɪʃən] *n* Impfung *f*
vacuum [ˈvækjum] *n* (*empty space*) Vakuum *nt*
vacuum cleaner *n* Staubsauger *m*
vagina [vəˈdʒaɪnə] *n* Scheide *f*
vague [veɪg] *adj* (*memory*) vage; (*outline*) undeutlich
vaguely [ˈveɪglɪ] *adv* (*slightly*) in etwa
vain [veɪn] *adj* (*person*) eitel; (*attempt, action*) vergeblich; **in ~** vergebens
vainly [ˈveɪnlɪ] *adv* vergebens
valentine [ˈvæləntaɪn] *n* (*also*: **~ card**) Valentinsgruß *m*
Valentine's Day *n* Valentinstag *m*
valid [ˈvælɪd] *adj* (*ticket, document*) gültig; (*argument, reason*) stichhaltig
valley [ˈvælɪ] *n* Tal *nt*
valuable [ˈvæljuəbl] *adj* wertvoll; (*time*) kostbar
valuables [ˈvæljuəblz] *npl* Wertsachen *pl*
value [ˈvælju:] *n* Wert *m* ▶ *vt* schätzen
value-added tax [vælju:ˈædɪd-] (BRIT) *n* Mehrwertsteuer *f*
valve [vælv] *n* Ventil *nt*
van [væn] *n* (*Aut*) Lieferwagen *m*
vanilla [vəˈnɪlə] *n* Vanille *f*
vanish [ˈvænɪʃ] *vi* verschwinden
vanity [ˈvænɪtɪ] *n* (*of person*) Eitelkeit *f*
vanity case *n* Kosmetikkoffer *m*
vaping [ˈveɪpɪŋ] *n* Dampfen *nt*
vapour, (US) **vapor** [ˈveɪpəʳ] *n* (*gas, steam*) Dampf *m*; (*mist*) Dunst *m*
variable [ˈvɛərɪəbl] *adj* (*likely to change: mood, quality, weather*) veränderlich, wechselhaft; (*able to be changed: temperature, height, speed*) variabel
varied [ˈvɛərɪd] *adj* (*diverse*) unterschiedlich; (*full of changes*) abwechslungsreich
variety [vəˈraɪətɪ] *n* (*diversity*) Vielfalt *f*; (*varied collection*) Auswahl *f*; (*type*) Sorte *f*; **a wide ~ of ...** eine Vielfalt an +*acc* ...
various [ˈvɛərɪəs] *adj* (*reasons, people*) verschiedene
varnish [ˈvɑ:nɪʃ] *n* Lack *m* ▶ *vt* (*wood, one's nails*) lackieren
vary [ˈvɛərɪ] *vt* verändern ▶ *vi* (*be different*) variieren; **to ~ with** (*weather, season etc*) sich ändern mit
vase [vɑ:z] *n* Vase *f*
vast [vɑ:st] *adj* (*knowledge*) enorm; (*expense, area*) riesig
VAT [væt] (BRIT) *n abbr* (= *value-added tax*) MwSt *f*
Vatican [ˈvætɪkən] *n*: **the ~** der Vatikan
VDU *n abbr* (*Comput*) = **visual display unit**
veal [vi:l] *n* Kalbfleisch *nt*
vegan [ˈvi:gən] *n* Veganer(in) *m(f)*
vegeburger [ˈvɛdʒɪbə:gəʳ] *n* vegetarischer Hamburger *m*
vegetable [ˈvɛdʒtəbl] *n* (*plant*) Gemüse *nt*
vegetarian [vɛdʒɪˈtɛərɪən] *n* Vegetarier(in) *m(f)* ▶ *adj* vegetarisch
veggieburger [ˈvɛdʒɪbə:gəʳ] *n* = **vegeburger**
vehicle [ˈvi:ɪkl] *n* (*machine*) Fahrzeug *nt*
veil [veɪl] *n* Schleier *m*
vein [veɪn] *n* Ader *f*
Velcro® [ˈvɛlkrəu] *n* (*also*: **~ fastener** *or* **fastening**) Klettverschluss *m*
velvet [ˈvɛlvɪt] *n* Samt *m*
vending machine [ˈvɛndɪŋ-] *n* Automat *m*

Venetian blind [vɪˈni:ʃən-] *n* Jalousie *f*
Venezuela [vɛnɛˈzweɪlə] *n* Venezuela *nt*
Venice [ˈvɛnɪs] *n* Venedig *nt*
venison [ˈvɛnɪsn] *n* Rehfleisch *nt*
vent [vɛnt] *n* (*also:* **air ~**) Abzug *m*
ventilate [ˈvɛntɪleɪt] *vt* (*room*) lüften
ventilation [vɛntɪˈleɪʃən] *n* Belüftung *f*
ventilator [ˈvɛntɪleɪtəʳ] *n* (*Tech*) Ventilator *m*; (*Med*) Beatmungsgerät *nt*
venture [ˈvɛntʃəʳ] *n* Unternehmung *f* ▶ *vi* (*dare to go*) sich wagen
venue [ˈvɛnju:] *n* (*for meeting*) Treffpunkt *m*; (*for big events*) Austragungsort *m*
verb [və:b] *n* Verb *nt*
verbal [ˈvə:bl] *adj* verbal; (*skills*) sprachlich
verbally [ˈvə:bəlɪ] *adv* (*communicate etc*) mündlich
verdict [ˈvə:dɪkt] *n* (*Law, fig*) Urteil *nt*
verge [və:dʒ] (Brit) *n* (*of road*) Rand *m* ▶ **verge on** *vt fus* grenzen an *+acc*
verification [vɛrɪfɪˈkeɪʃən] *n* Bestätigung *f*; Überprüfung *f*
verify [ˈvɛrɪfaɪ] *vt* (*confirm*) bestätigen; (*check*) überprüfen
vermin [ˈvə:mɪn] *npl* Ungeziefer *nt*
verruca [veˈru:kə] *n* Warze *f*
versatile [ˈvə:sətaɪl] *adj* vielseitig
verse [və:s] *n* (*poetry*) Poesie *f*; (*stanza*) Strophe *f*
version [ˈvə:ʃən] *n* Version *f*
versus [ˈvə:səs] *prep* gegen
vertical [ˈvə:tɪkl] *adj* vertikal, senkrecht
very [ˈvɛrɪ] *adv* sehr ▶ *adj*: **the ~ book which ...** genau das Buch, das ...; **the ~ last** der/die/das Allerletzte; **the ~ thought (of it) alarms me** der bloße Gedanke (daran) beunruhigt mich; **at the ~ end** ganz am Ende
vest [vɛst] *n* (Brit: *underwear*) Unterhemd *nt*; (*US: waistcoat*) Weste *f*
vet [vɛt] (Brit) *n* = **veterinary surgeon**
veterinary surgeon [ˈvɛtrɪnərɪ-] (Brit) *n* Tierarzt *m*, Tierärztin *f*
veto [ˈvi:təu] (*pl* **vetoes**) *n* Veto *nt* ▶ *vt* ein Veto einlegen gegen
VHF *abbr* (*Radio: = very high frequency*) VHF
via [ˈvaɪə] *prep* über *+acc*
viable [ˈvaɪəbl] *adj* (*project*) durchführbar; (*company*) rentabel
vibrate [vaɪˈbreɪt] *vi* (*machine, sound etc*) vibrieren
vibration [vaɪˈbreɪʃən] *n* (*instance*) Vibration *f*
vicar [ˈvɪkəʳ] *n* Pfarrer(in) *m(f)*
vice [vaɪs] *n* (*moral fault*) Laster *nt*; (*Tech*) Schraubstock *m*
vice-chairman [vaɪsˈtʃɛəmən] *n* (*irreg*) stellvertretender Vorsitzender *m*
vice president *n* Vizepräsident(in) *m(f)*
vice versa [ˈvaɪsɪˈvə:sə] *adv* umgekehrt
vicinity [vɪˈsɪnɪtɪ] *n*: **in the ~ (of)** in der Nähe *or* Umgebung (*+gen*)
vicious [ˈvɪʃəs] *adj* (*attack, blow*) brutal; (*words, look*) gemein
vicious circle *n* Teufelskreis *m*
victim [ˈvɪktɪm] *n* Opfer *nt*
Victorian [vɪkˈtɔ:rɪən] *adj* viktorianisch
victory [ˈvɪktərɪ] *n* Sieg *m*
video [ˈvɪdɪəu] *n* (*film, cassette, recorder*) Video *nt* ▶ *vt* auf Video aufnehmen ▶ *cpd* Video-
videocam [ˈvɪdɪəukæm] *n* Videokamera *f*
video camera *n* Videokamera *f*
video game *n* Videospiel *nt*, Telespiel *nt*
videophone [ˈvɪdɪəufəun] *n* Bildtelefon *nt*
video recorder *n* Videorekorder *m*
video tape *n* Videoband *nt*
Vienna [vɪˈɛnə] *n* Wien *nt*
Vietnam [ˈvjɛtˈnæm] *n* Vietnam *nt*
view [vju:] *n* (*from window etc*) Aussicht *f*; (*sight*) Blick *m*; (*opinion*) Ansicht *f* ▶ *vt* betrachten; (*house*) besichtigen; **in full ~ of** vor den Augen *+gen*
viewer [ˈvju:əʳ] *n* (*person*) Zuschauer(in) *m(f)*
viewpoint [ˈvju:pɔɪnt] *n* (*attitude*) Standpunkt *m*
vigilant [ˈvɪdʒɪlənt] *adj* wachsam
vile [vaɪl] *adj* abscheulich
village [ˈvɪlɪdʒ] *n* Dorf *nt*
villager [ˈvɪlɪdʒəʳ] *n* Dorfbewohner(in) *m(f)*
villain [ˈvɪlən] *n* (*scoundrel*) Schurke *m*; (*in novel etc*) Bösewicht *m*
vine [vaɪn] *n* (*Bot: producing grapes*) Weinrebe *f*
vinegar [ˈvɪnɪgəʳ] *n* Essig *m*
vineyard [ˈvɪnjɑ:d] *n* Weinberg *m*
vintage [ˈvɪntɪdʒ] *n* (*of wine*) Jahrgang *m*

vintage wine *n* erlesener Wein *m*
vinyl [ˈvaɪnl] *n* Vinyl *nt*
viola [vɪˈəulə] *n* Bratsche *f*
violate [ˈvaɪəleɪt] *vt* (*agreement*) verletzen; (*peace*) stören
violence [ˈvaɪələns] *n* Gewalt *f*; (*strength*) Heftigkeit *f*
violent [ˈvaɪələnt] *adj* (*behaviour*) gewalttätig; (*death*) gewaltsam
violet [ˈvaɪələt] *n* (*plant*) Veilchen *nt*
violin [vaɪəˈlɪn] *n* Geige *f*, Violine *f*
VIP *n abbr* (= *very important person*) VIP *m*
virgin [ˈvəːdʒɪn] *n* Jungfrau *f*
Virgo [ˈvəːgəu] *n* (*sign*) Jungfrau *f*
virile [ˈvɪraɪl] *adj* (*person*) männlich
virtual [ˈvəːtjuəl] *adj* (*Comput*, *Phys*) virtuell
virtually [ˈvəːtjuəlɪ] *adv* praktisch
virtual reality *n* virtuelle Realität *f*
virtue [ˈvəːtjuː] *n* Tugend *f*; **by ~ of** aufgrund +*gen*
virtuous [ˈvəːtjuəs] *adj* tugendhaft
virus [ˈvaɪərəs] *n* (*Med*, *Comput*) Virus *m or nt*
visa [ˈviːzə] *n* Visum *nt*
visibility [vɪzɪˈbɪlɪtɪ] *n* (*range of vision*) Sicht(weite) *f*
visible [ˈvɪzəbl] *adj* sichtbar
visibly [ˈvɪzəblɪ] *adv* sichtlich
vision [ˈvɪʒən] *n* (*sight*) Sicht *f*; (*foresight*) Weitblick *m*; (*in dream*) Vision *f*
visit [ˈvɪzɪt] *n* Besuch *m* ▸ *vt* besuchen
visiting hours *npl* Besuchszeiten *pl*
visitor [ˈvɪzɪtəʳ] *n* Besucher(in) *m*(*f*)
visitor centre *n* Informationszentrum *nt*
visitors' book [ˈvɪzɪtəz-] *n* Gästebuch *nt*
visor [ˈvaɪzəʳ] *n* (*of helmet etc*) Visier *nt*
visual [ˈvɪzjuəl] *adj* (*image etc*) visuell
visual aid *n* Anschauungsmaterial *nt*
visual display unit *n* (Daten) sichtgerät *nt*
visualize [ˈvɪzjuəlaɪz] *vt* sich *dat* vorstellen
visually [ˈvɪzjuəlɪ] *adv* visuell; **~ handicapped** sehbehindert
vital [ˈvaɪtl] *adj* (*essential*) unerlässlich; **of ~ importance (to sb/sth)** von größter Wichtigkeit (für jdn/etw)
vitality [vaɪˈtælɪtɪ] *n* (*liveliness*) Vitalität *f*
vitally [ˈvaɪtəlɪ] *adv*: **~ important** äußerst wichtig
vitamin [ˈvɪtəmɪn] *n* Vitamin *nt*
vivacious [vɪˈveɪʃəs] *adj* lebhaft
vivid [ˈvɪvɪd] *adj* (*description*) lebendig; (*memory*, *imagination*) lebhaft; (*colour*) leuchtend
vlog [vlɔg] *n* Vlog *m*
vlogger [ˈvlɔgəʳ] *n* Vlogger(in) *m*(*f*)
V-neck [ˈviːnɛk] *n* (*also*: **~ jumper** *or* **pullover**) Pullover *m* mit V-Ausschnitt
vocabulary [vəuˈkæbjulərɪ] *n* (*words known*) Vokabular *nt*, Wortschatz *m*
vocal [ˈvəukl] *adj* (*of the voice*) stimmlich; (*articulate*) lautstark
vocation [vəuˈkeɪʃən] *n* (*calling*) Berufung *f*
vocational [vəuˈkeɪʃənl] *adj* (*training*, *guidance etc*) Berufs-
vodka [ˈvɔdkə] *n* Wodka *m*
voice [vɔɪs] *n* (*also fig*) Stimme *f* ▸ *vt* (*opinion*) zum Ausdruck bringen
voice mail *n* (*Comput*) Voicemail *f*
void [vɔɪd] *n* (*fig*: *emptiness*) Leere *f* ▸ *adj* (*invalid*) ungültig; **~ of** (*empty*) ohne
volcano [vɔlˈkeɪnəu] (*pl* **volcanoes**) *n* Vulkan *m*
volley [ˈvɔlɪ] *n* (*Tennis etc*) Volley *m*
volleyball [ˈvɔlɪbɔːl] *n* Volleyball *m*
volt [vəult] *n* Volt *nt*
voltage [ˈvəultɪdʒ] *n* Spannung *f*
volume [ˈvɔljuːm] *n* (*space*) Volumen *nt*; (*amount*) Umfang *m*; (*book*) Band *m*; (*sound level*) Lautstärke *f*
volume control *n* (*Radio*, *TV*) Lautstärkeregler *m*
voluntarily [ˈvɔləntrɪlɪ] *adv* freiwillig
voluntary [ˈvɔləntərɪ] *adj* freiwillig
volunteer [vɔlənˈtɪəʳ] *n* Freiwillige(r) *f*(*m*) ▸ *vi* (*for army etc*) sich freiwillig melden; **to ~ to do sth** sich anbieten, etw zu tun
voluptuous [vəˈlʌptjuəs] *adj* sinnlich
vomit [ˈvɔmɪt] *vi* sich übergeben
vote [vəut] *n* Stimme *f*; (*votes cast*) Stimmen *pl*; (*right to vote*) Wahlrecht *nt*; (*ballot*) Abstimmung *f* ▸ *vt* (*elect*): **to be voted chairman** *etc* zum Vorsitzenden *etc* gewählt werden ▸ *vi* (*in election etc*) wählen; **to ~ for** *or* **in favour of sth/against sth** für/gegen etw stimmen
voter [ˈvəutəʳ] *n* Wähler(in) *m*(*f*)
voucher [ˈvautʃəʳ] *n* Gutschein *m*
vow [vau] *n* Versprechen *nt* ▸ *vt*: **to ~ to do sth/that** geloben, etw zu tun/dass

vowel [ˈvauəl] *n* Vokal *m*
voyage [ˈvɔɪɪdʒ] *n* Reise *f*
vulgar [ˈvʌlgəʳ] *adj (remarks, gestures)* vulgär
vulnerable [ˈvʌlnərəbl] *adj (person, position)* verletzlich
vulture [ˈvʌltʃəʳ] *n (also fig)* Geier *m*

W[1], w [ˈdʌblju:] *n (letter)* W *nt*, w *nt*; **W for William** ≈ W wie Wilhelm
W[2] [ˈdʌblju:] *abbr (= west)* W
wade [weɪd] *vi*: **to ~ across** *(a river, stream)* waten durch
wafer [ˈweɪfəʳ] *n (biscuit)* Waffel *f*
wafer-thin [ˈweɪfəˈθɪn] *adj* hauchdünn
waffle [ˈwɔfl] *n (Culin)* Waffel *f*; *(inf: empty talk)* Geschwafel *nt* ▸ *vi (in speech etc)* schwafeln
wag [wæg] *vt (tail)* wedeln mit
wage [weɪdʒ] *n* Lohn *m*
wagon, waggon [ˈwægən] *n (horse-drawn)* Fuhrwerk *nt*; (BRIT *Rail*) Wa(g)gon *m*
waist [weɪst] *n (Anat, of clothing)* Taille *f*
waistcoat [ˈweɪstkəut] (BRIT) *n* Weste *f*
waistline [ˈweɪstlaɪn] *n* Taille *f*
wait [weɪt] *n* Wartezeit *f* ▸ *vi* warten; **~ a minute!** Moment mal!
▸ **wait up** *vi* aufbleiben
waiter *n* Kellner *m*
waiting [ˈweɪtɪŋ] *n*: **"no ~"** (BRIT *Aut*) „Halten verboten"
waiting list *n* Warteliste *f*
waiting room *n (in surgery)* Wartezimmer *nt*; *(in railway station)* Wartesaal *m*
waitress [ˈweɪtrɪs] *n* Kellnerin *f*
wake [weɪk] (*pt* **woke** *or* **waked**, *pp* **woken** *or* **waked**) *vt (also:* **~ up***)* wecken ▸ *vi (also:* **~ up***)* aufwachen
wakeboard [ˈweɪkbɔ:d] *n* Wakeboard *nt* ▸ *vi* wakeboarden
wake-up call [ˈweɪkʌp-] *n (Tel)* Weckruf *m*

Wales [weɪlz] *n* Wales *nt*

> **NATIONAL ASSEMBLY FOR WALES**
>
> Die **National Assembly for Wales** wurde 1998 gegründet, nachdem sich die walisischen Wähler mehrheitlich bei einer im Vorjahr gehaltenen Volksabstimmung für die Dezentralisierung entschieden. Sie unterscheidet sich vom schottischen Parlament, welches in den Bereichen, die unter seiner Verantwortung stehen, sowie im Finanzwesen gesetzgebende Gewalt besitzt. Die walisiche National-versammlung dagegen darf diese Gewalt nur beschränkt ausüben und hat keine Autorität, Steuern zu erheben. Sie besteht aus 60 Abgeordneten, die *AMs* (*Assembly Members*), die für vier Jahre gewählt werden, und wird von einem *Presiding Officer* geleitet. Sie steht unter der Kontrolle des *First Minister*.

walk [wɔːk] *n* (*hike*) Wanderung *f*; (*shorter*) Spaziergang *m*; (*path*) Weg *m* ▸ *vi* gehen; (*for pleasure, exercise*) spazieren gehen ▸ *vt* (*dog*) ausführen; **it's 10 minutes' ~ from here** es ist 10 Minuten zu Fuß von hier; **to go for a ~** spazieren gehen

walking [ˈwɔːkɪŋ] *n* Wandern *nt*

walking shoes *npl* Wanderschuhe *pl*

walking stick *n* Spazierstock *m*

wall [wɔːl] *n* Wand *f*; (*exterior, city wall etc*) Mauer *f*

wallet [ˈwɔlɪt] *n* Brieftasche *f*

wallpaper [ˈwɔːlpeɪpəʳ] *n* Tapete *f* ▸ *vt* tapezieren

walnut [ˈwɔːlnʌt] *n* (*nut*) Walnuss *f*

waltz [wɔːlts] *n* Walzer *m*

wander [ˈwɔndəʳ] *vi* (*person*) herumlaufen

want [wɔnt] *vt* (*wish for*) wollen; (*need*) brauchen ▸ *n* (*lack*): **for ~ of** aus Mangel an +*dat*; **to ~ to do sth** etw tun wollen

war [wɔːʳ] *n* Krieg *m*

ward [wɔːd] *n* (*in hospital*) Station *f*; (*Law: also:* **~ of court**) Mündel *nt* unter Amtsvormundschaft

warden [ˈwɔːdn] *n* (*of park etc*) Aufseher(in) *m(f)*; (BRIT: *of youth hostel*) Herbergsvater *m*, Herbergsmutter *f*

wardrobe [ˈwɔːdrəub] *n* (*for clothes*) Kleiderschrank *m*

warehouse [ˈwɛəhaus] *n* Lager *nt*

warfare [ˈwɔːfɛəʳ] *n* Krieg *m*

warm [wɔːm] *adj* warm; (*thanks, applause, welcome, person*) herzlich; **I'm ~** mir ist warm

▸ **warm up** *vi* warm werden; (*athlete*) sich aufwärmen ▸ *vt* aufwärmen

warmly [ˈwɔːmlɪ] *adv* (*applaud, welcome*) herzlich; (*dress*) warm

warmth [wɔːmθ] *n* Wärme *f*; (*friendliness*) Herzlichkeit *f*

warn [wɔːn] *vt*: **to ~ sb of sth** jdn vor etw *dat* warnen; **to ~ sb not to do sth** *or* **against doing sth** jdn davor warnen, etw zu tun

warning [ˈwɔːnɪŋ] *n* Warnung *f*

warning light *n* Warnlicht *nt*

warning triangle *n* (*Aut*) Warndreieck *nt*

warranty [ˈwɔrəntɪ] *n* Garantie *f*

wart [wɔːt] *n* Warze *f*

wary [ˈwɛərɪ] *adj* (*person*) vorsichtig

was [wɔz] *pt of* **be**

wash [wɔʃ] *vt* waschen; (*dishes*) abwaschen ▸ *vi* (*person*) sich waschen ▸ *n* (*clothes etc*) Wäsche *f*; **to have a ~** sich waschen

▸ **wash off** *vt* abwaschen

▸ **wash up** *vi* (BRIT: *wash dishes*) spülen, abwaschen; (*US: have a wash*) sich waschen

washable [ˈwɔʃəbl] *adj* (*fabric*) waschbar

washbasin [ˈwɔʃbeɪsn] *n* Waschbecken *nt*

washcloth [ˈwɔʃklɔθ] (*US*) *n* Waschlappen *m*

washer [ˈwɔʃəʳ] *n* (*on tap etc*) Dichtungsring *m*

washing [ˈwɔʃɪŋ] *n* Wäsche *f*

washing machine *n* Waschmaschine *f*

washing powder (BRIT) *n* Waschpulver *nt*

washing-up [wɔʃɪŋˈʌp] *n* Abwasch *m*; **to do the ~** spülen, abwaschen

washing-up liquid (BRIT) *n* (Geschirr) spülmittel *nt*

washroom [ˈwɔʃrum] (*US*) *n* Waschraum *m*

wasn't [ˈwɔznt] = **was not**
wasp [wɔsp] *n* Wespe *f*
waste [weɪst] *n* Verschwendung *f*; (*rubbish*) Abfall *m* ▶ *adj* (*left over: paper etc*) ungenutzt ▶ *vt* verschwenden; (*opportunity*) vertun
wastepaper basket [ˈweɪstpeɪpə-] (BRIT) *n* Papierkorb *m*
watch [wɔtʃ] *n* (*also:* **wristwatch**) (Armband)uhr *f* ▶ *vt* (*look at*) betrachten; (: *match, programme*) sich *dat* ansehen; (*spy on, guard*) beobachten; (*be careful of*) aufpassen auf +*acc* ▶ *vi* (*look*) zusehen; **to ~ TV** fernsehen
▶ **watch out** *vi* aufpassen; **~ out!** Vorsicht!
watchdog [ˈwɔtʃdɔg] *n* (*dog*) Wachhund *m*; (*fig*) Aufpasser(in) *m*(*f*)
watchful [ˈwɔtʃful] *adj* wachsam
water [ˈwɔːtəʳ] *n* Wasser *nt* ▶ *vt* (*plant*) gießen ▶ *vi* (*eyes*) tränen; **my mouth is watering** mir läuft das Wasser im Mund zusammen
▶ **water down** *vt* (*also fig*) verwässern
waterboarding [ˈwɔːtəbɔːdɪŋ] *n* Waterboarding *nt*, *Foltermethode durch simuliertes Ertränken*
watercolour, (*US*) **watercolor** [ˈwɔːtəkʌləʳ] *n* (*picture*) Aquarell *nt*
watercress [ˈwɔːtəkrɛs] *n* Brunnenkresse *f*
waterfall [ˈwɔːtəfɔːl] *n* Wasserfall *m*
watering can [ˈwɔːtərɪŋ-] *n* Gießkanne *f*
water level *n* Wasserstand *m*
watermelon [ˈwɔːtəmɛlən] *n* Wassermelone *f*
waterproof [ˈwɔːtəpruːf] *adj* (*trousers, jacket etc*) wasserdicht
water-skiing [ˈwɔːtəskiːɪŋ] *n* Wasserski *nt*
water sports *npl* Wassersport *m*
watertight [ˈwɔːtətaɪt] *adj* wasserdicht
watery [ˈwɔːtərɪ] *adj* (*coffee, soup etc*) wässrig
wave [weɪv] *n* (*also fig*) Welle *f* ▶ *vi* (*signal*) winken; (*flag*) wehen ▶ *vt* (*hand, flag etc*) winken mit; (*gun, stick*) schwenken
wavelength [ˈweɪvlɛŋθ] *n* (*Radio*) Wellenlänge *f*; **on the same ~** (*fig*) auf derselben Wellenlänge
wavy [ˈweɪvɪ] *adj* (*hair*) wellig
wax [wæks] *n* Wachs *nt*; (*in ear*) Ohrenschmalz *nt*
way [weɪ] *n* Weg *m*; (*direction*) Richtung *f*; (*manner*) Art *f*; **which ~ to ...?** wo geht es zu ...?; **to be on one's ~** auf dem Weg sein; **to go out of one's ~ to do sth** sich sehr bemühen, etw zu tun; **to be in the ~** im Weg sein; **to lose one's ~** sich verirren; **under ~** (*project etc*) im Gang; **to make ~ (for sb/sth)** (für jdn/etw) Platz machen; **to get one's own ~** seinen Willen bekommen; **in a ~** in gewisser Weise; **in some ways** in mancher Hinsicht; **no ~!** (*inf*) kommt nicht infrage!; **by the ~ ...** übrigens ...; **"~ in"** (BRIT) „Eingang"; **"~ out"** (BRIT) „Ausgang"; **"give ~"** (BRIT *Aut*) „Vorfahrt beachten"; **~ of life** Lebensstil *m*
we [wiː] *pl pron* wir
weak [wiːk] *adj* schwach
weaken [ˈwiːkn] *vi* (*resolve, person*) schwächer werden ▶ *vt* schwächen
wealth [wɛlθ] *n* Reichtum *m*
wealthy [ˈwɛlθɪ] *adj* reich
weapon [ˈwɛpən] *n* Waffe *f*
wear [wɛəʳ] (*pt* **wore**, *pp* **worn**) *vt* (*clothes, shoes, beard*) tragen; (*put on*) anziehen ▶ *vi* (*become old: carpet, jeans*) sich abnutzen ▶ *n* (*damage*) Verschleiß *m*
▶ **wear off** *vi* (*pain etc*) nachlassen
▶ **wear out** *vt* (*shoes, clothing*) verschleißen; (*person, strength*) erschöpfen
weather [ˈwɛðəʳ] *n* Wetter *nt*; **under the ~** (*fig: ill*) angeschlagen
weather forecast *n* Wettervorhersage *f*
weave [wiːv] (*pt* **wove**, *pp* **woven**) *vt* (*cloth*) weben; (*basket*) flechten
web [wɛb] *n* (*also fig*) Netz *nt*; (Comput): **the W~** das Web, das Internet
webcam [ˈwebkæm] *n* Webcam *f*
webinar [ˈwɛbɪnɑːʳ] *n* (*Comput*) Webinar *nt*, Web-Seminar *nt*
webmail [ˈwɛbmeɪl] *n* (*Comput*) Webmail *nt*
web page *n* Webseite *f*
website [ˈwɛbsaɪt] *n* (*Comput*) Website *f*
Wed. *abbr* (= *Wednesday*) Mi.
we'd [wiːd] = **we had**; **we would**
wedding [ˈwɛdɪŋ] *n* Hochzeit *f*

wedding dress *n* Hochzeitskleid *nt*
wedding ring *n* Trauring *m*
wedge [wɛdʒ] *n* Keil *m*; (*of cake*) Stück *nt*
Wednesday [ˈwɛdnzdɪ] *n* Mittwoch *m*; *see also* **Tuesday**
wee [wiː] (Scot) *adj* klein
weed [wiːd] *n* (*Bot*) Unkraut *nt* ▸ *vt* (*garden*) jäten
week [wiːk] *n* Woche *f*; **once/twice a ~** einmal/zweimal die Woche; **in two weeks' time** in zwei Wochen; **a ~ today/on Friday** heute/Freitag in einer Woche
weekday [ˈwiːkdeɪ] *n* Wochentag *m*
weekend [wiːkˈɛnd] *n* Wochenende *nt*
weekly [ˈwiːklɪ] *adv* wöchentlich ▸ *adj* (*newspaper*) Wochen-
weep [wiːp] (*pt, pp* **wept**) *vi* (*person*) weinen
weigh [weɪ] *vt* wiegen ▸ *vi* wiegen
▸ **weigh up** *vt* (*person, offer, risk*) abschätzen
weight [weɪt] *n* Gewicht *nt*; **to lose ~** abnehmen; **to put on ~** zunehmen
weightlifting [ˈweɪtlɪftɪŋ] *n* Gewichtheben *nt*
weight training *n* Krafttraining *nt*
weighty [ˈweɪtɪ] *adj* (*fig: important*) gewichtig
weird [wɪəd] *adj* (*person*) seltsam
weirdo [ˈwɪədəu] (*inf*) *n* verrückter Typ *m*
welcome [ˈwɛlkəm] *adj* willkommen ▸ *n* Willkommen *nt* ▸ *vt* begrüßen, willkommen heißen; **~ to London!** willkommen in London!
welcoming [ˈwɛlkəmɪŋ] *adj* (*person*) freundlich
welfare [ˈwɛlfɛəʳ] *n* (*well-being*) Wohl *nt*; (*social aid*) Sozialhilfe *f*
welfare state *n* Wohlfahrtsstaat *m*
well [wɛl] *n* (*for water*) Brunnen *m* ▸ *adv* gut ▸ *adj*: **to be ~** (*person*) gesund sein ▸ *excl* nun!, na!; **as ~** (*in addition*) ebenfalls; **~ done!** gut gemacht!; **~ over 40** weit über 40; **I don't feel ~** ich fühle mich nicht gut *or* wohl; **get ~ soon!** gute Besserung!
we'll [wiːl] = **we will**; **we shall**
well-behaved [ˈwɛlbɪˈheɪvd] *adj* wohlerzogen
well-being [ˈwɛlˈbiːɪŋ] *n* Wohl(ergehen) *nt*
well-built [ˈwɛlˈbɪlt] *adj* gut gebaut
well-done [ˈwelˈdʌn] *adj* (*steak*) durchgebraten
well-earned [ˈwɛlˈəːnd] *adj* (*rest*) wohlverdient
wellingtons [ˈwɛlɪŋtənz] *npl* (*also:* **wellington boots**) Gummistiefel *pl*
well-known [ˈwɛlˈnəun] *adj* wohlbekannt
well-off [ˈwɛlˈɔf] *adj* (*rich*) begütert
well-paid [ˈwelˈpeɪd] *adj* gut bezahlt
Welsh [wɛlʃ] *adj* walisisch ▸ *n* (*Ling*) Walisisch *nt* ■ **the Welsh** *npl* die Waliser *pl*
Welshman [ˈwɛlʃmən] *n* (*irreg*) Waliser *m*
Welshwoman [ˈwɛlʃwumən] *n* (*irreg*) Waliserin *f*
went [wɛnt] *pt of* **go**
wept [wɛpt] *pt, pp of* **weep**
were [wəːʳ] *pt of* **be**
we're [wɪəʳ] = **we are**
weren't [wəːnt] = **were not**
west [wɛst] *n* Westen *m* ▸ *adj* (*wind, side, coast*) West- ▸ *adv* (*to or towards the west*) westwärts; **the W~** (*Pol*) der Westen
westbound [ˈwɛstbaund] *adj* (*traffic, carriageway*) in Richtung Westen
western [ˈwɛstən] *adj* westlich ▸ *n* (*Cine*) Western *m*
West Germany *n* (*formerly*) Bundesrepublik *f* Deutschland
westward [ˈwɛstwəd], **westwards** [ˈwɛstwədz] *adv* westwärts
wet [wɛt] *adj* nass; **"~ paint"** „frisch gestrichen"; **to ~ one's pants/o.s.** sich *dat* in die Hosen machen
wet suit *n* Taucheranzug *m*
we've [wiːv] = **we have**
whale [weɪl] *n* Wal *m*
wharf [wɔːf] (*pl* **wharves**) *n* Kai *m*

KEYWORD

what [wɔt] *adj* **1** (*in direct/indirect questions*) welche(r, s); **what colour/shape is it?** welche Farbe/Form hat es?
2 (*in exclamations*) was für ein(e); **what a mess!** was für ein Durcheinander!
▸ *pron* (*interrogative, relative*) was; **what are you doing?** was machst du?; **what are you talking about?** wovon redest du?; **what is it called?** wie

heißt das?; **what about me?** und ich?; **I saw what you did/what was on the table** ich habe gesehen, was du getan hast/was auf dem Tisch war
▶ *excl* (*disbelieving*) was, wie; **what, no coffee!** was *or* wie, kein Kaffee?

whatever [wɔt'ɛvəʳ] *pron*: **do ~ is necessary/you want** tun Sie, was nötig ist/was immer Sie wollen; **~ happens** was auch passiert
wheat [wi:t] *n* Weizen *m*
wheel [wi:l] *n* Rad *nt*; (*also*: **steering ~**) Lenkrad *nt* ▶ *vt* (*pram etc*) schieben
wheelbarrow ['wi:lbærəu] *n* Schubkarre *f*
wheelchair ['wi:ltʃɛəʳ] *n* Rollstuhl *m*
wheel clamp *n* Parkkralle *f*

KEYWORD

when [wɛn] *adv* wann
▶ *conj* **1** (*at, during, after the time that*) wenn; **she was reading when I came in** als ich hereinkam, las sie gerade; **be careful when you cross the road** sei vorsichtig, wenn du die Straße überquerst
2 (*on, at which*) als; **on the day when I met him** am Tag, als ich ihn traf
3 (*whereas*) wo ... doch

whenever [wɛn'ɛvəʳ] *adv, conj* (*any time that*) wann immer; **I go ~ I can** ich gehe, wann immer ich kann
where [wɛəʳ] *adv, conj* wo; **this is ~ ...** hier ...; **~ are you from?** woher kommen Sie?
whereabouts [wɛərə'bauts] *adv* wo ▶ *n*: **nobody knows his ~** keiner weiß, wo er ist
whereas [wɛər'æz] *conj* während
whereby [wɛə'baɪ] (*form*) *adv* wonach
wherever [wɛər'ɛvəʳ] *conj* (*position*) wo (auch) immer; (*motion*) wohin (auch) immer ▶ *adv* (*surprise*) wo (um alles in der Welt)
whether ['wɛðəʳ] *conj* ob

KEYWORD

which [wɪtʃ] *adj* **1** (*interrogative*: *direct, indirect*) welche(r, s)
2: **in which case** in diesem Fall; **by which time** zu dieser Zeit
▶ *pron* **1** (*interrogative*) welche(r, s); **which of you are coming?** wer von Ihnen kommt?
2 (*relative*) der/die/das; **the apple which you ate/which is on the table** der Apfel, den du gegessen hast/der auf dem Tisch liegt; **he said he saw her, which is true** er sagte, er habe sie gesehen, was auch stimmt

whichever [wɪtʃ'ɛvəʳ] *adj*: **~ book you take** welches Buch Sie auch nehmen
while [waɪl] *n* Weile *f* ▶ *conj* während; **for a ~** eine Weile (lang); **in a ~** gleich
whine [waɪn] *vi* (*person*) jammern
whip [wɪp] *n* Peitsche *f* ▶ *vt* (*person, animal*) peitschen
whipped cream [wɪpt-] *n* Schlagsahne *f*
whirl [wə:l] *vt* (*arms, sword etc*) herumwirbeln ▶ *vi* wirbeln
whirlpool ['wə:lpu:l] *n* (*lit*) Strudel *m*
whisk [wɪsk] *n* (*Culin*) Schneebesen *m* ▶ *vt* (*cream, eggs*) schlagen
whiskers ['wɪskəz] *npl* (*of animal*) Barthaare *pl*; (*of man*) Backenbart *m*
whisky, (*US*, IRISH) **whiskey** ['wɪskɪ] *n* Whisky *m*
whisper ['wɪspəʳ] *vt, vi* flüstern; **to ~ sth to sb** jdm etw zuflüstern
whistle ['wɪsl] *n* (*sound*) Pfiff *m*; (*object*) Pfeife *f* ▶ *vi* pfeifen
whistleblower ['wɪslbləuəʳ] *n* Whistleblower(in) *m*(*f*), Enthüller(in) *m*(*f*)
white [waɪt] *adj* weiß ▶ *n* (*of egg, eye*) Weiße(s) *nt*; **to turn** *or* **go ~** (*person*: *with fear*) weiß *or* bleich werden
white lie *n* Notlüge *f*
white water *n*: **white-water rafting** Wildwasserflößen *nt*
white wine *n* Weißwein *m*
Whitsun ['wɪtsn] *n* Pfingsten *nt*

KEYWORD

who [hu:] *pron* **1** (*interrogative*) wer; (: *acc*) wen; (: *dat*) wem; **who is it?, who's there?** wer ist da?
2 (*relative*) der/die/das; **the man/woman who spoke to me** der Mann, der/die Frau, die mit mir gesprochen hat

whoever [huːˈɛvəʳ] *pron*: **~ finds it** wer (auch immer) es findet; **~ he marries** ganz gleich *or* egal, wen er heiratet
whole [həul] *adj* (*entire*) ganz ▸ *n* Ganze(s) *nt*; **the ~ of** der/die/das ganze; **on the ~** im Ganzen (gesehen)
wholefood [ˈhəulfuːd] *n*, **wholefoods** [ˈhəulfuːdz] *npl* Vollwertkost *f*
wholeheartedly [həulˈhɑːtɪdlɪ] *adv* (*agree etc*) rückhaltlos
wholemeal [ˈhəulmiːl] (Brit) *adj* (*bread, flour*) Vollkorn-
wholesale [ˈhəulseɪl] *adv* (*buy, sell*) im Großhandel
wholesome [ˈhəulsəm] *adj* (*food*) gesund
wholewheat [ˈhəulwiːt] *adj* = **wholemeal**
wholly [ˈhəulɪ] *adv* ganz und gar

KEYWORD

whom [huːm] *pron* **1** (*interrogative*: *acc*) wen; (: *dat*) wem; **whom did you see?** wen hast du gesehen?; **to whom did you give it?** wem hast du es gegeben?
2 (*relative*: *acc*) den/die/das; (: *dat*) dem/der/dem; **the man whom I saw/to whom I spoke** der Mann, den ich gesehen habe/mit dem ich gesprochen habe

whooping cough [ˈhuːpɪŋ-] *n* Keuchhusten *m*

KEYWORD

whose [huːz] *adj*
1 (*possessive*: *interrogative*) wessen; **whose book is this?, whose is this book?** wessen Buch ist das?, wem gehört das Buch?
2 (*possessive*: *relative*) dessen/deren/dessen
▸ *pron*: **whose is this?** wem gehört das?

KEYWORD

why [waɪ] *adv* warum
▸ *conj* warum; **I wonder why he said that** ich frage mich, warum er das gesagt hat; **that's not why I'm here** ich bin nicht deswegen hier; **the reason why** der Grund, warum *or* weshalb
▸ *excl* (*expressing surprise, shock*) na so was; **why, yes (of course)** aber ja doch; **why, it's you!** na so was, du bists!

wicked [ˈwɪkɪd] *adj* (*crime, person*) böse; (*smile, wit*) frech
wide [waɪd] *adj* breit; (*area*) weit ▸ *adv*: **to open sth ~** etw weit öffnen
wide-angle lens [ˈwaɪdæŋgl-] *n* Weitwinkelobjektiv *nt*
wide-awake [waɪdəˈweɪk] *adj* hellwach
widely [ˈwaɪdlɪ] *adv* (*spaced*) weit; **to be ~ read** (*reader*) sehr belesen sein
widen [ˈwaɪdn] *vt* (*road, river*) verbreitern; (*one's experience*) erweitern
wide open *adj* (*window, eyes, mouth*) weit geöffnet
widescreen TV [ˈwaɪdskriːn-] *n* Breitbildfernseher *m*
widespread [ˈwaɪdsprɛd] *adj* weitverbreitet
widow [ˈwɪdəu] *n* Witwe *f*
widowed [ˈwɪdəud] *adj* verwitwet
widower [ˈwɪdəuəʳ] *n* Witwer *m*
width [wɪdθ] *n* Breite *f*
wife [waɪf] (*pl* **wives**) *n* Frau *f*
Wi-Fi [ˈwaɪfaɪ] *n* Wi-Fi *nt*
wig [wɪg] *n* Perücke *f*
wiggle [ˈwɪgl] *vt* wackeln mit
wiki [ˈwɪkɪ] *n* (*Internet*) Wiki *nt*
wild [waɪld] *adj* wild; (*person, behaviour*) ungestüm; (*idea*) weit hergeholt ▸ *n*: **the ~** (*natural surroundings*) die freie Natur *f*
wildlife [ˈwaɪldlaɪf] *n* (*animals*) die Tierwelt *f*
wildly [ˈwaɪldlɪ] *adv* wild; (*very*: *romantic*) wild-; (: *inefficient*) furchtbar

KEYWORD

will [wɪl] *aux vb* **1** (*forming future tense*): **I will finish it tomorrow** ich werde es morgen fertig machen, ich mache es morgen fertig
2 (*in conjectures, predictions*): **that will be the postman** das ist bestimmt der Briefträger
3 (*in commands, requests, offers*): **will**

you sit down (*politely*) bitte nehmen Sie Platz; (*angrily*) nun setz dich doch; **will you be quiet!** seid jetzt still!; **will you help me?** hilfst du mir?; **will you have a cup of tea?** möchten Sie eine Tasse Tee?; **I won't put up with it!** das lasse ich mir nicht gefallen!
▸ *vt* (*pt, pp* **willed**): **to will sb to do sth** jdn durch Willenskraft dazu bewegen, etw zu tun
▸ *n* **1** (*volition*) Wille *m*
2 (*testament*) Testament *nt*

willing [ˈwɪlɪŋ] *adj* (*enthusiastic*) bereitwillig; **he's ~ to do it** er ist bereit, es zu tun
willingly [ˈwɪlɪŋlɪ] *adv* bereitwillig
willow [ˈwɪləu] *n* (*tree*) Weide *f*
willpower [ˈwɪlˈpauəʳ] *n* Willenskraft *f*
wimp [wɪmp] (*inf, pej*) *n* Waschlappen *m*
win [wɪn] (*pt, pp* **won**) *n* Sieg *m* ▸ *vt* gewinnen ▸ *vi* siegen, gewinnen
▸ **win over** *vt* (*persuade*) gewinnen
wind[1] [wɪnd] *n* (*air*) Wind *m*; (*Med*) Blähungen *pl*
wind[2] [waɪnd] (*pt, pp* **wound**) *vt* (*thread, rope, bandage*) wickeln
▸ **wind down** *vt* (*car window*) herunterdrehen
▸ **wind up** *vt* (*clock, toy*) aufziehen; (*debate*) abschließen
wind farm [ˈwɪnd-] *n* Windpark *m*
wind instrument [ˈwɪnd-] *n* Blasinstrument *nt*
windmill [ˈwɪndmɪl] *n* Windmühle *f*
window [ˈwɪndəu] *n* (*also Comput*) Fenster *nt*; (*in shop*) Schaufenster *nt*
window box *n* Blumenkasten *m*
window pane *n* Fensterscheibe *f*
window-shopping [ˈwɪndəuʃɔpɪŋ] *n* Schaufensterbummel *m*; **to go ~** einen Schaufensterbummel machen
windowsill [ˈwɪndəusɪl] *n* Fensterbank *f*
windpipe [ˈwɪndpaɪp] *n* Luftröhre *f*
windscreen [ˈwɪndskriːn] *n* Windschutzscheibe *f*
windscreen wiper [-waɪpəʳ] *n* Scheibenwischer *m*
windshield [ˈwɪndʃiːld] (*US*) *n* = **windscreen**
windsurfing [ˈwɪndsəːfɪŋ] *n* Windsurfen *nt*
wind turbine *n* Windturbine *f*
windy [ˈwɪndɪ] *adj* windig
wine [waɪn] *n* Wein *m*
wine bar *n* Weinlokal *nt*
wine glass *n* Weinglas *nt*
wine list *n* Weinkarte *f*
wine tasting [-teɪstɪŋ] *n* Weinprobe *f*
wing [wɪŋ] *n* (*of bird, insect, plane*) Flügel *m*; (*of building*) Trakt *m*; (*of car*) Kotflügel *m* ■ **the wings** *npl* (*Theat*) die Kulissen *pl*
wink [wɪŋk] *vi* (*with eye*) zwinkern
winner [ˈwɪnəʳ] *n* (*of race, competition*) Sieger(in) *m(f)*; (*of prize*) Gewinner(in) *m(f)*
winning [ˈwɪnɪŋ] *adj* (*team, entry*) siegreich; (*shot, goal*) entscheidend; *see also* **winnings**
winnings [ˈwɪnɪŋz] *npl* Gewinn *m*
winter [ˈwɪntəʳ] *n* Winter *m*
winter sports *npl* Wintersport *m*
wintry [ˈwɪntrɪ] *adj* (*weather, day*) winterlich
wipe [waɪp] *vt* wischen; (*clean*) abwischen; **to ~ one's nose** sich *dat* die Nase putzen
▸ **wipe off** *vt* abwischen
▸ **wipe out** *vt* (*destroy: city etc*) auslöschen
wire [ˈwaɪəʳ] *n* Draht *m*; (*US: telegram*) Telegramm *nt* ▸ *vt* (*US*): **to ~ sb** jdm telegrafieren; (*electrical fitting: also:* **~ up**) anschließen
wireless [ˈwaɪəlɪs] (Brit: *old*) *n* Funk *m*
wisdom [ˈwɪzdəm] *n* (*of person*) Weisheit *f*
wisdom tooth *n* Weisheitszahn *m*
wise [waɪz] *adj* (*person*) weise
wisely [ˈwaɪzlɪ] *adv* klug, weise
wish [wɪʃ] *n* Wunsch *m* ▸ *vt* wünschen; **with best wishes** (*in letter*) mit den besten Wünschen *or* Grüßen; **he wished me well** er wünschte mir alles Gute
witch [wɪtʃ] *n* Hexe *f*

 **KEYWORD**

with [wɪð] *prep* **1** (*accompanying, in the company of*) mit; **we stayed with friends** wir wohnten bei Freunden; **I'll be with you in a minute** einen Augenblick, ich bin sofort da; **I'm with you** (*I understand*) ich verstehe; **to be with it** (*inf: up-to-date*) auf dem Laufenden sein; (*: alert*) da sein

2 (*descriptive, indicating manner*) mit; **the man with the grey hat/blue eyes** der Mann mit dem grauen Hut/ den blauen Augen; **red with anger** rot vor Wut

withdraw [wɪθˈdrɔː] *vt* (*irreg: like* **draw**) (*object, offer*) zurückziehen; (*remark*) zurücknehmen ▸ *vi* (*person*) sich zurückziehen
wither [ˈwɪðəʳ] *vi* (*plant*) verwelken
withhold [wɪθˈhəuld] *vt* (*irreg: like* **hold**) vorenthalten
within [wɪðˈɪn] *prep* (*place*) innerhalb *+gen*; **~ reach** in Reichweite
without [wɪðˈaut] *prep* ohne; **~ speaking** ohne zu sprechen
withstand [wɪθˈstænd] *vt* (*irreg: like* **stand**) widerstehen *+dat*
witness [ˈwɪtnɪs] *n* Zeuge *m*, Zeugin *f* ▸ *vt* (*event*) Zeuge/Zeugin sein *+gen*
witness box *n* Zeugenstand *m*
witness stand (*US*) *n* = **witness box**
witty [ˈwɪtɪ] *adj* geistreich
wives [waɪvz] *npl of* **wife**
wobble [ˈwɔbl] *vi* wackeln; (*legs*) zittern
wobbly [ˈwɔblɪ] *adj* (*table, chair*) wack(e)lig
wok [wɔk] *n* Wok *m*
woke [wəuk] *pt of* **wake**
woken [ˈwəukn] *pp of* **wake**
wolf [wulf] (*pl* **wolves**) *n* Wolf *m*
woman [ˈwumən] (*pl* **women**) *n* Frau *f*
womb [wuːm] *n* (*Med*) Gebärmutter *f*
women [ˈwɪmɪn] *npl of* **woman**
won [wʌn] *pt, pp of* **win**
wonder [ˈwʌndəʳ] *n* (*miracle*) Wunder *nt*; (*awe*) Verwunderung *f* ▸ *vi*: **to ~ whether/why** *etc* sich fragen, ob/ warum *etc*
wonderful [ˈwʌndəful] *adj* wunderbar
won't [wəunt] = **will not**
wood [wud] *n* (*timber*) Holz *nt*; (*forest*) Wald *m*
wooden [ˈwudn] *adj* (*also fig*) hölzern
woodpecker [ˈwudpɛkəʳ] *n* Specht *m*
woodwork [ˈwudwəːk] *n* (*skill*) Holzarbeiten *pl*
wool [wul] *n* Wolle *f*
woollen, (*US*) **woolen** [ˈwulən] *adj* (*hat*) Woll-, wollen
word [wəːd] *n* Wort *nt* ▸ *vt* (*letter, message*) formulieren; **in other words** mit anderen Worten; **to break/keep one's ~** sein Wort brechen/halten; **to have a ~ with sb** mit jdm sprechen
wording [ˈwəːdɪŋ] *n* (*of message, contract etc*) Wortlaut *m*, Formulierung *f*
word processing *n* Textverarbeitung *f*
word processor [-prəusɛsəʳ] *n* Textverarbeitungssystem *nt*
wore [wɔːʳ] *pt of* **wear**
work [wəːk] *n* Arbeit *f*; (*Art, Liter*) Werk *nt* ▸ *vi* arbeiten; (*mechanism*) funktionieren; (*be successful: medicine etc*) wirken ▸ *vt* (*machine*) bedienen; **to be at ~ (on sth)** (an etw *dat*) arbeiten; **to be out of ~** arbeitslos sein
▸ **work out** *vi* (*plans etc*) klappen; (*Sport*) trainieren ▸ *vt* (*problem*) lösen; (*plan*) ausarbeiten; **it works out at 100 pounds** es ergibt 100 Pfund
▸ **work up** *vt*: **to get worked up** sich aufregen
workaholic [wəːkəˈhɔlɪk] *n* Arbeitstier *nt*
worker [ˈwəːkəʳ] *n* Arbeiter(in) *m(f)*
working class [ˈwəːkɪŋ-] *n* Arbeiterklasse *f*
workman [ˈwəːkmən] *n* (*irreg*) Arbeiter *m*
workout [ˈwəːkaut] *n* Fitnesstraining *nt*
work permit *n* Arbeitserlaubnis *f*
workshop [ˈwəːkʃɔp] *n* (*building*) Werkstatt *f*; (*practical session*) Workshop *nt*
work station *n* (*Comput*) Workstation *f*
world [wəːld] *n* Welt *f*
World War *n*: **~ I/II, the First/Second ~** der Erste/Zweite Weltkrieg
worldwide [ˈwəːldˈwaɪd] *adj, adv* weltweit
World Wide Web *n* World Wide Web *nt*
worm [wəːm] *n* Wurm *m*
worn [wɔːn] *pp of* **wear** ▸ *adj* (*carpet*) abgenutzt; (*shoe*) abgetragen
worn-out [ˈwɔːnaut] *adj* (*object*) abgenutzt; (*person*) erschöpft
worried [ˈwʌrɪd] *adj* besorgt; **to be ~ about sth** sich wegen etw Sorgen machen
worry [ˈwʌrɪ] *n* Sorge *f* ▸ *vi* sich *dat*

Sorgen machen; **to ~ about** *or* **over sth/sb** sich um etw/jdn Sorgen machen

worrying [ˈwʌrɪɪŋ] *adj* beunruhigend

worse [wəːs] *adj* schlechter, schlimmer ▸ *adv* schlechter

worsen [ˈwəːsn] *vt* verschlimmern ▸ *vi* sich verschlechtern

worship [ˈwəːʃɪp] *vt* (*god*) anbeten

worst [wəːst] *adj* schlechteste(r, s), schlimmste(r, s) ▸ *adv* am schlimmsten ▸ *n* Schlimmste(s) *nt*; **at ~** schlimmstenfalls

worth [wəːθ] *n* Wert *m* ▸ *adj*: **to be ~** wert sein; **£2 ~ of apples** Äpfel für £ 2; **how much is it ~?** was *or* wie viel ist es wert?; **it's ~ it** (*effort, time*) es lohnt sich

worthless [ˈwəːθlɪs] *adj* wertlos

worthwhile [ˈwəːθˈwaɪl] *adj* lohnend

worthy [ˈwəːðɪ] *adj* (*person*) würdig; **~ of** wert +*gen*

KEYWORD

would [wud] *aux vb* **1** (*conditional tense*): **if you asked him he would do it** wenn du ihn fragtest, würde er es tun; **if you had asked him he would have done it** wenn du ihn gefragt hättest, hätte er es getan

2 (*in offers, invitations, requests*): **would you like a biscuit?** möchten Sie ein Plätzchen?; **would you ask him to come in?** würden Sie ihn bitten hereinzukommen?

3 (*in indirect speech*): **I said I would do it** ich sagte, ich würde es tun

4 (*emphatic*): **it WOULD have to snow today!** ausgerechnet heute musste es schneien!

5 (*insistence*): **she wouldn't behave** sie wollte sich partout nicht benehmen

6 (*conjecture*): **it would have been midnight** es mochte etwa Mitternacht gewesen sein; **it would seem so** so scheint es wohl

7 (*indicating habit*): **he would go there on Mondays** er ging montags immer dorthin

wouldn't [ˈwudnt] = **would not**

wound¹ [waund] *pt, pp of* **wind²**

wound² [wuːnd] *n* Wunde *f* ▸ *vt* verwunden; **wounded in the leg** am Bein verletzt

wove [wəuv] *pt of* **weave**

woven [ˈwəuvn] *pp of* **weave**

wrap [ræp] *vt* einwickeln; (*pack: also:* **~ up**) einpacken

wrapper [ˈræpəʳ] *n* (*on chocolate*) Papier *nt*

wrapping paper [ˈræpɪŋ-] *n* (*brown*) Packpapier *nt*; (*fancy*) Geschenkpapier *nt*

wreath [riːθ] (*pl* **wreaths**) *n* Kranz *m*

wreck [rɛk] *n* Wrack *nt* ▸ *vt* (*car*) zu Schrott fahren; (*chances*) zerstören

wreckage [ˈrɛkɪdʒ] *n* (*of car, plane, building*) Trümmer *pl*

wrench [rɛntʃ] *n* (*Tech*) Schraubenschlüssel *m*

wrestling [ˈrɛslɪŋ] *n* Ringen *nt*

wring [rɪŋ] (*pt, pp* **wrung**) *vt* (*wet clothes*) auswringen

wrinkle [ˈrɪŋkl] *n* Falte *f* ▸ *vt* (*nose, forehead etc*) runzeln ▸ *vi* (*skin, paint etc*) sich runzeln

wrist [rɪst] *n* Handgelenk *nt*

wristwatch [ˈrɪstwɔtʃ] *n* Armbanduhr *f*

write [raɪt] (*pt* **wrote**, *pp* **written**) *vt* schreiben; (*cheque*) ausstellen ▸ *vi* schreiben; **to ~ to sb** jdm schreiben

▸ **write away** *vi*: **to ~ away for sth** etw anfordern

▸ **write down** *vt* aufschreiben

▸ **write off** *vt* (*debt, project*) abschreiben

▸ **write out** *vt* (*put in writing*) schreiben; (*cheque, receipt etc*) ausstellen

write-protected [ˈraɪtprəˈtɛktɪd] *adj* (*Comput*) schreibgeschützt

writer [ˈraɪtəʳ] *n* (*author*) Schriftsteller(in) *m(f)*; (*of report, document etc*) Verfasser(in) *m(f)*

writing [ˈraɪtɪŋ] *n* Schrift *f*; (*activity*) Schreiben *nt*; **in ~** schriftlich

writing paper *n* Schreibpapier *nt*

written [ˈrɪtn] *pp of* **write**

wrong [rɔŋ] *adj* falsch; (*morally bad*) unrecht; **to be ~** (*answer*) falsch sein; (*in doing, saying sth*) unrecht haben; **what's ~?** wo fehlts?; **to go ~** (*person*) einen Fehler machen; (*plan*) schiefgehen; **to be in the ~** im Unrecht sein

wrongly [ˈrɔŋlɪ] *adv* falsch; (*unjustly*) zu Unrecht

wrong number *n* (*Tel*): **you've got the ~** Sie sind falsch verbunden
wrote [rəut] *pt of* **write**
WWW *n abbr* (= *World Wide Web*) WWW *nt*

xenophobia [zenəˈfəubɪə] *n* Ausländerfeindlichkeit *f*
XL *abbr* (= *extra large*) XL
Xmas [ˈɛksməs] *n abbr* = **Christmas**
X-ray [ˈɛksreɪ] *n* (*photo*) Röntgenbild *nt* ▶ *vt* röntgen
xylophone [ˈzaɪləfəun] *n* Xylofon *nt*

yacht [jɔt] *n* Jacht *f*
yachting [ˈjɔtɪŋ] *n* Segeln *nt*
yam [jæm] *n* Jamswurzel *f*, Yamswurzel *f*
yard [jɑːd] *n* (*of house etc*) Hof *m*; (*US: garden*) Garten *m*; (*measure*) Yard *nt* (= 0,91 *m*)
yawn [jɔːn] *vi* gähnen
yd *abbr* = **yard**
year [jɪəʳ] *n* Jahr *nt*; **this ~** dieses Jahr; **to be 8 years old** 8 Jahre alt sein; **an eight-year-old child** ein achtjähriges Kind
yearly [ˈjɪəlɪ] *adj, adv* (*once a year*) jährlich
yearn [jəːn] *vi*: **to ~ for sth** sich nach etwas sehnen; **to ~ to do sth** sich danach sehnen, etw zu tun
yeast [jiːst] *n* Hefe *f*
yell [jɛl] *n* Schrei *m* ▶ *vi* schreien
yellow [ˈjɛləu] *adj* gelb
yellow fever *n* Gelbfieber *nt*
Yellow Pages® *npl*: **the ~** die gelben Seiten *pl*, das Branchenverzeichnis
yes [jɛs] *adv* ja; (*in reply to negative*) doch ▶ *n* Ja *nt*; **to say ~** Ja sagen
yesterday [ˈjɛstədɪ] *adv* gestern ▶ *n* Gestern *nt*; **~ morning/evening** gestern Morgen/Abend; **~'s paper** die Zeitung von gestern; **the day before ~** vorgestern; **all day ~** gestern den ganzen Tag (lang)
yet [jɛt] *adv* noch ▶ *conj* jedoch; **it is not finished ~** es ist noch nicht fertig; **the best ~** der/die/das bisher Beste; **as ~** bisher; **not for a few days ~** nicht in den nächsten paar Tagen; **~ again** wiederum

yield [jiːld] *n* (*Agr*) Ertrag *m* ▶ *vt* (*produce: results, profit*) hervorbringen ▶ *vi* (*surrender, give way*) nachgeben; (*US Aut*) die Vorfahrt achten
yikes [ˈjaiks] *excl* (*inf: esp hum*) ich glaub's nicht!, Wahnsinn!
yoga [ˈjəugə] *n* Yoga *m or nt*
yoghurt, yogurt [ˈjəugət] *n* Joghurt *m or nt*
yolk [jəuk] *n* (*of egg*) Eigelb *nt*

 **KEYWORD**

you [juː] *pron*
1 (*subject: familiar: singular*) du; (*: plural*) ihr; (*: polite*) Sie; **you Germans enjoy your food** ihr Deutschen esst gern gut
2 (*object: direct: familiar: singular*) dich; (*: plural*) euch; (*: polite*) Sie; (*: indirect: familiar: singular*) dir; (*: plural*) euch; (*: polite*) Ihnen; **I know you** ich kenne dich/euch/Sie; **I gave it to you** ich habe es dir/euch/Ihnen gegeben
3 (*after prep, in comparisons*): **it's for you** es ist für dich/euch/Sie
4 (*impersonal: one*) man

you'd [juːd] = **you had**; **you would**
you'll [juːl] = **you will**; **you shall**
young [jʌŋ] *adj* jung ■ **the young** *npl* (*of animal*) die Jungen *pl*; (*people*) die jungen Leute *pl*
youngster [ˈjʌŋstəʳ] *n* Kind *nt*
your [jɔːʳ] *adj* (*familiar: sing*) dein/deine/dein; (*: pl*) euer/eure/euer; (*polite*) Ihr/Ihre/Ihr; *see also* **my**
you're [juəʳ] = **you are**
yours [jɔːz] *pron* (*familiar: sing*) deiner/deine/dein(e)s; (*: pl*) eurer/eure/eures; (*polite*) Ihrer/Ihre/Ihres; **a friend of ~** ein Freund von dir/Ihnen; **is it ~?** gehört es dir/Ihnen?; **~ sincerely/faithfully** mit freundlichen Grüßen; *see also* **mine²**
yourself [jɔːˈsɛlf] *pron* (*reflexive: familiar: sing: acc*) dich; (*: dat*) dir; (*: pl*) euch; (*: polite*) sich; (*emphatic*) selbst
yourselves [jɔːˈsɛlvz] *pl pron* (*reflexive: familiar*) euch; (*: polite*) sich; (*emphatic*) selbst
youth [juːθ] *n* Jugend *f*; (*young man: pl youths*) Jugendliche(r) *m*
youth hostel *n* Jugendherberge *f*

you've [ju:v] = **you have**
yucky ['jʌkɪ] *adj* (*inf*) eklig
yummy ['jʌmɪ] *adj* (*inf*) lecker
yuppie ['jʌpɪ] (*inf*) *n* Yuppie *m*

Z

zap [zæp] *vt* (*Comput*: *delete*) löschen
zapping ['zæpɪŋ] *n* (*TV*) ständiges Umschalten, Zapping *nt*
zebra ['zi:brə] *n* Zebra *nt*
zebra crossing (BRIT) *n* Zebrastreifen *m*
zero ['zɪərəu] *n* (*number*) Null *f*; **5 degrees below ~** 5 Grad unter null
zest [zɛst] *n* (*for life*) Begeisterung *f*
zigzag ['zɪgzæg] *n* Zickzack *m* ▶ *vi* sich im Zickzack bewegen
zinc [zɪŋk] *n* Zink *nt*
zip [zɪp] *n* (*also*: **~ fastener**) Reißverschluss *m* ▶ *vt* (*dress etc*: *also*: **~ up**) den Reißverschluss zumachen an +*dat*
zip code (*US*) *n* Postleitzahl *f*
Zip file® *n* (*Comput*) ZIP-Datei® *f*
zipper ['zɪpər] (*US*) *n* = **zip**
zit [zɪt] *n* (*inf*) Pickel *m*
zodiac ['zəudɪæk] *n* Tierkreis *m*
zone [zəun] *n* (*also Mil*) Zone *f*, Gebiet *nt*; (*in town*) Bezirk *m*
zoo [zu:] *n* Zoo *m*
zoom [zu:m] *vi*: **to ~ past** vorbeisausen; **to ~ in (on sth/sb)** (*Phot*, *Cine*) (etw/jdn) näher heranholen
zoom lens *n* Zoomobjektiv *nt*
zucchini [zu:'ki:nɪ] (*US*) *n* Zucchini *pl*
Zumba® ['zumbə] *n* Zumba *nt*